# The Law of
# INTELLECTUAL
# PROPERTY

# The Law of
# INTELLECTUAL PROPERTY

**Craig Allen Nard**

*Tom J.E. and Bette Lou Walker Professor of Law*
*Case School of Law*
*Case Western Reserve University*

**David W. Barnes**

*Distinguished Research Professor of Law*
*Seton Hall University School of Law*

**Michael J. Madison**

*Associate Professor of Law*
*University of Pittsburgh School of Law*

**PUBLISHERS**

76 Ninth Avenue, New York, NY 10011
http://lawschool.aspenpublishers.com

ISBN 0-7355-5379-3

**Library of congress Cataloging-in-Publication Data**

Nard, Craig Allen.
    The law of intellectual property / Craig Allen Nard, David W.
Barnes, Michael J. Madison.

        p. cm.
    ISBN 0-7355-5379-3
    1. Intellectual property — United States.
    I. Barnes, David W. II. Madison, Michael J., 1961-
    III. Title.

    KF2979.N36 2006
    346.7304'8 — dc22

                                                2006007498

# About Aspen Publishers

Aspen Publishers, headquartered in New York City, is a leading information provider for attorneys, business professionals, and law students. Written by preeminent authorities, our products consist of analytical and practical information covering both U.S. and international topics. We publish in the full range of formats, including updated manuals, books, periodicals, CDs, and online products.

Our proprietary content is complemented by 2,500 legal databases, containing over 11 million documents, available through our Loislaw division. Aspen Publishers also offers a wide range of topical legal and business databases linked to Loislaw's primary material. Our mission is to provide accurate, timely, and authoritative content in easily accessible formats, supported by unmatched customer care.

To order any Aspen Publishers title, go to *http://lawschool.aspenpublishers.com* or call 1-800-638-8437.

To reinstate your manual update service, call 1-800-638-8437.

For more information on Loislaw products, go to *www.loislaw.com* or call 1-800-364-2512.

For Customer Care issues, e-mail *CustomerCare@aspenpublishers.com*; call 1-800-234-1660; or fax 1-800-901-9075.

**Aspen Publishers**
**a Wolters Kluwer business**

*For Patricia, Victor, and Gabriel*
                    *CAN*

*For Melissa and Ray*
                    *DWB*

*For Susan, Kate, and David*
                    *MJM*

# SUMMARY OF CONTENTS

# CONTENTS

## CHAPTER 7
# Enforcing Copyrights                                                   445

## CHAPTER 8
# Defenses to Copyright Infringement     531

## CHAPTER 9
# Remedies for Copyright Infringement     595

## Copyright Statutes 637

CHAPTER **10**
## Acquiring Patent Rights 651

CHAPTER **11**
# Enforcing Patent Rights                                          765

## CHAPTER 12
## Defenses to Patent Infringement                                815

## CHAPTER 13
## Remedies for Patent Infringement                             853

# PREFACE

Traditionally, intellectual property law has primarily comprised three substantive areas: trademarks, copyrights, and patents, while also including various state law doctrines such as trade secrets, rights of publicity, and rights in ideas. Although these individual areas of the law have always been important to our legal and commercial systems, recent economic and technological developments have increased the relevance, breadth, and complexity of these IP regimes. With these developments in mind, this book is designed to expose students to the intricacies of IP's specialized applications and theoretical perspectives in the context of fundamental principles. Accordingly, *The Law of Intellectual Property* concentrates on the traditional areas of IP and presents them in a doctrinally straightforward and accessible way. We do not mean to suggest that there is no room in our book for intellectual property theory, policy, cutting edge technologies, and substantive issues related to cyberlaw and international aspects of IP. All are present, but they are integrated into principal cases, comments, and problems that focus on the fundamentals.

We believe, first, that preparation for advanced courses begins with a foundation that integrates an introduction of the novel applications into the traditional analytic structure and, second, that detailed analysis of those applications belongs in a specialized course. Thus, our book is designed for a survey course and for those who wish to acquire a broad-based understanding of the fundamentals of intellectual property. This structure also allows students with particular occupational or intellectual interests to use the foundation as a springboard to specialized courses in, for instance, patents, copyrights, or trademarks.

Our integrated approach also is illustrated by our incorporation of statutory material into the text. Each case or set of cases in our book is preceded by reference to applicable statutory provisions, tailored to the specific issues raised in the cases. Each set of substantive law chapters is followed by the relevant statutes, eliminating the need for students to buy a separate statutory supplement and increasing the likelihood that students will read the relevant statutes. Each case is also preceded with a description of the issues to be discussed in the case. As a result of these two design characteristics, students know what rules apply and what they need to know to understand the cases. This structure allows the statutes and cases to work together to great pedagogic advantage.

Three other design elements promote learning of the broad foundations of intellectual property law. The first is a series of perspective notes. These are short explorations of intriguing (1) policy perspectives that highlight the goals of the law and help the student understand why the law is the way it is; (2) comparative perspectives that illustrate alternative approaches taken by different countries to suggest different ways in which the balance between exclusive rights and public access may be struck; (3) historical perspectives that place a particular IP doctrine in historical context; and (4) counseling perspectives relating to items an IP attorney may want to consider in counseling clients on a particular issue. The second design element consists of comments following each case that discuss the issues raised in the case, place those issues in the larger context of intellectual property law, and elaborate on how the rules are applied in other contexts. Third, the book is replete with problems based on actual cases to which citation is provided. These problems are intended to test the application of rules to the issues presented in the principal cases. These elements are combined with cases selected and edited so as to be as accessible to students as possible. We have chosen cases with facts students can relate to and, we hope, will find interesting. While this has been a constant focus in our selection of cases in all substantive areas, nowhere is it more important than in the patent law chapters, where we carefully considered the ability of students to understand the innovations discussed in the cases.

The result is a book that is comprehensive and accessible to both students and teachers. It will be appealing to teachers and students who prefer a theory-based approach, a straightforward case method approach, a problem-based approach, or a combination thereof.

*Craig Allen Nard*
*David W. Barnes*
*Michael J. Madison*

April 2006

# ACKNOWLEDGMENTS

---

We are grateful to several individuals for their assistance in preparing this book. We would like to thank Alison Lee and Ingrid Pelzer for their capable research assistance and for their input regarding the selection of particularly interesting cases. We would also like to thank the students at Case School of Law and Seton Hall University School of Law, particularly Eric Mercurio, Jill Kelly, Richard Chang, and Amy Varghese, who contributed valuable suggestions relating to case selection.

*The Law of*
# INTELLECTUAL
# PROPERTY

# CHAPTER

# 1

# Introduction

Intellectual property (or IP as it is commonly known) has rapidly assumed center stage in the global marketplace and information economy, presenting some of the most exciting, important, and complex issues facing not only our legal system, but also the business, entertainment, and technology communities. Indeed, in the last 20 years IP has "moved from an arcane area of legal analysis and a policy backwater to the forefront of global economic policymaking."[1] Advances in software and digital technology have tested the limits of copyright and trademark law; patent law is frequently at issue as our understanding of genomics and the life sciences evolves and new discoveries are made. And more traditional industries regularly turn to trade secrets for protection of their valuable information, with some industries preferring it to patent protection.

All of these exciting developments add to the important role of IP in more conventional creations and commercial practices. Authors and publishers still copyright books and music, established trademark owners such as Coca-Cola continue to renew their marks and protect their valuable formulae as trade secrets, and inventors still apply for patents on can openers and pizza boxes. Thus, regardless of the technology at issue, it remains essential that the student of IP obtain a solid understanding of the fundamentals of IP doctrine and policy. Only after one acquires an appreciation of IP foundations and goals can one begin to fully understand the workings of an IP regime in a given technologic or commercial context. Moreover, the law of intellectual property is much broader than the American experience, reaching into every industrialized country and, increasingly, developing nations, thus making necessary a greater understanding of how IP is treated around the world.

This book explores intellectual property's foundational principles, its nuanced policies, and its role in innovation, creative expression, commercial behavior, competition, and consumer welfare. In addition, throughout the book, various comparative perspectives are explored to enrich students' understanding of IP's global scope.

---

1. Keith E. Maskus, INTELLECTUAL PROPERTY RIGHTS IN THE GLOBAL ECONOMY 1 (2000).

## A. INTELLECTUAL PROPERTY REGIMES

Intellectual property is an umbrella term that includes a number of federal and state legal regimes, including trademarks, copyrights, patents, and trade secrets. The discussion below is devoted to an overview of these four areas of law because of their prominence within intellectual property and their rich underlying policy frameworks. The IP spectrum also includes rights of publicity, rights in ideas, and unfair competition. These state law schemes, which are introduced in subsequent chapters, are also important to intellectual property practitioners and laden with interesting policy issues.

### 1. Trademark Law

Trademark law protects the symbols firms use to indicate the source, quality, and characteristics of their products and services. These symbols can include words, logos, pictures, slogans, colors, smells, symbols, and product packaging and designs. For example, the name of a restaurant can be protected as well as the trade dress or "look and feel" of the restaurant design. There are three principal policies underlying trademark law. First, exclusive rights to trademarks prevent consumer confusion and reduce consumer search costs. Trademarks serve as signals, allowing consumers to make qualitative judgments about a product and identify otherwise unobservable characteristics. Second, these consumer expectations encourage trademark owners to invest in and maintain a consistent level of quality. Thus, it is important that trademark law protects the good will a trademark owner has in a given mark, which may be worth millions of dollars. Lastly, would-be competitors cannot free ride on the good will of the trademark owner. A soft drink upstart, for instance, cannot use COCA-COLA as its own mark. Parallel state and federal trademark laws encourage competitors to develop trademarks of their own so that consumers will associate their marks with their products' qualities and characteristics.

Trademark law has also been extended into areas where confusion is absent or irrelevant. The dilution doctrine in both state and federal law protects trademark owners from use of their marks in a disparaging way ("tarnishment") and from overuse by others ("blurring"). An example of a use that puts the KODAK mark in a bad light is "KODAK XXX Adult Movie Theatre." Examples of uses that diminish the firmness of the connection between KOKAK and the original seller of camera film would be another's use of KODAK in connection with the sale of watches, tires, or shoes. The idea is that through these types of uses, the power and signaling effect of the KODAK mark as used for photographic-related products would be weakened or diluted. Dilution law protects trademarks' signaling power from tarnishing and blurring uses even by suppliers who do not compete with the mark owner.

Trademark rights last in perpetuity as long as the mark is continuously being used in a source-identifying manner in connection with the same products. Trademark protection does not extend either to functional aspects of the product or to generic words that are the customary name of the product or service being sold. Functional features (e.g., how a camera's shutter speed mechanism works) are the domain of patent law and generic words (e.g., the word "camera" for, well, cameras) should be free for all to use in customary language.

Congress derives its power to enact trademark legislation from the Commerce Clause of the Constitution. Trademark law is a mix of federal and state statutory and common law. The federal statutory scheme is set forth in Title 15 of the United States Code and is frequently referred to as the Lanham Act. The Lanham Act was enacted in 1947 and has been amended several times. Because federal trademark law is based on the Commerce Clause, federal rights in a mark exist only when the mark is used in interstate commerce. State trademark law, which is nearly identical to federal law, applies to intrastate commerce. One does not have to register a mark federally with the Patent and Trademark Office (PTO) to obtain federal trademark protection, although there are several advantages to registration. These advantages are explored in Chapters 2 through 5.

Closely related to trademark law are misappropriation law and the right to publicity. These legal theories are recognized in some states, but are not specifically recognized in federal law. They both are designed to protect a person's investments in business ventures and in their own celebrity. The classic misappropriation case involved one news-gathering organization free riding on the investigative work of a competitor. A typical right to publicity case involves a person who, for promotion purposes, uses the name or likeness of a famous sports figure or entertainer without permission. Because their conceptual roots are similar to those of trademark law, they are discussed in the trademark portion of this book.

Trademarks are often powerful signals, allowing consumers to identify prestigious "high end" luxury goods when the goods are being sold or being worn or used by others. Consider the following excerpt from the *New York Times* and the *Omega* case, and ask yourself if you would likely be confused when shopping on Canal Street. If not, what is the harm to the consumer? How is the trademark owner harmed?

## MICHAEL WILSON, CHINATOWN STORES RAIDED IN COUNTERFEIT-GOODS SWEEP

**New York Times, Wednesday, December 3, 2003, p. B2 cols. 1 and 2**

Not only was a raid in Chinatown yesterday timed to grab the attention of tourists and holiday shoppers, but it also involved enough fake Louis Vuitton clutch bags, bogus Kate Spade calfskin totes and faux Fendis to keep hundreds of low-rent supermodels happy through all 12 days of Christmas.

The raid on what the police called a counterfeit purse warehouse took place just after 1 p.m. at 415 Broadway, at Canal Street. The stylish shops were suddenly awash in blue vinyl windbreakers of four different law enforcement agencies. Several men and women scrambled from two stores, each one pursued and overtaken by a detective and led back to the corner. Tourists gaped.

Investigators said they seized more than $2 million worth of counterfeit goods, although that was an almost arbitrary number, based on the prices of the counterfeits, a number that can greatly vary from one back room or one customer to the next.

"We wanted to send a message" to sellers and buyers alike, said Capt. Kevin McGowan of the police division of the Waterfront Commission of New York Harbor, his teeth chattering in the cold wind. "It looks like this was the distribution center. We've got nine rooms; they were all secreted under there. We've got a lot of stuff to bring out." The items were to be loaded onto a tractor-trailer.

The counterfeit industry is a perennial target of law enforcement and Fortune 500 corporations alike. Private detectives on the Louis Vuitton payroll, for example, comb the bodegas and gift shops of Chinatown. The sellers use "watchers" with walkie-talkies to scan for undercover experts posing as customers, and alert the shops to close the metal gates. The shops at 415 Broadway seemed to be caught unaware yesterday, but others across the street quickly closed their gates.

"Yep," an officer said. "They're bagging up."

Last year, the International Chamber of Commerce said that counterfeiting accounted for an estimated 5 to 7 percent of global trade, and that it continues to grow. A 1994 study by the city estimated the cost of unpaid taxes on counterfeit goods to be $350 million. . . .

Stairs beneath the two small showrooms led to twisting hallways and cramped rooms stacked with handbags wrapped in white tissue, from the large leatheresque bags marked with Gucci labels to the tubular Burberry Hobo purses in trademark plaid. Officers bagged enough Montblanc pens for a large school's graduation, and stacks of Gucci belts curled in coils, complete with their own signature boxes.

"Anything that has a trademark on it is bad," Kevin Dougherty, a private counterfeit expert and founder of Counter-Tech Investigations, said to several officers conducting an inventory. "The only thing you have to worry about is anything that doesn't have a name on it." Some of the items arrive in the country as generic, their labels stamped or sewn on later, he said. . . .

---

## OMEGA, S.A. v. S & N JEWELRY INC.

### No. 92 Civ. 3656 (PKL), 1992 WL 142746 (S.D.N.Y. June 8, 1992)

LEISURE, District Judge.

This is an action for trademark infringement. . . . Plaintiffs have moved for a preliminary injunction prohibiting certain defendants in this action from pursuing infringing activities. For the reasons stated below, plaintiffs' motion for a preliminary injunction is granted.

Plaintiffs claim that the defendants in this action, who consist largely of retail establishments located in the Chinatown area of Manhattan, have been selling watches bearing counterfeit OMEGA trademarks and a trade dress substantially identical to watches sold by plaintiffs. Plaintiffs have asserted claims in this action for trademark infringement under §32 of the Lanham Act....

Section 32(1) of the Lanham Act applies to claims for the infringement of registered trademarks and provides in part that:

> Any person who shall, without the consent of the registrant—(a) use in commerce any reproduction, counterfeit, copy, or colorable imitation of a registered mark in connection with the sale, offering for sale, distribution, or advertising of any goods or services on or in connection with which such use is likely to cause confusion, or to cause mistake, or to deceive;...shall be liable in a civil action by the registrant for the remedies hereinafter provided.

In order to prevail on their claims for trademark infringement under §32, plaintiffs ultimately will have to prove (1) ownership of a valid registered trademark and (2) that defendants' use of the trademark creates a likelihood of confusion as to the source of the goods.

Plaintiffs have produced uncontroverted evidence of ownership of valid registered trademarks.... Under §7(b) of the Lanham Act, a certificate of registration of a trademark upon the principal register is *prima facie* evidence of the validity and registration of the registered mark, of the registrant's ownership of the mark, and of the registrant's exclusive right to use the registered mark in commerce on or in connection with the goods or services specified in the certificate.

In determining whether plaintiffs have demonstrated a likelihood of confusion, the Court adheres to the eight-factor test articulated by Judge Friendly in *Polaroid Corp. v. Polarad Electronics Corp.*, 287 F.2d 492 (2d Cir. 1961). The *Polaroid* test looks to the following factors: the strength of the prior owner's mark, the similarity between the two marks, the competitive proximity of the products, the likelihood that the prior user will bridge the gap, actual confusion, the defendant's good faith, the quality of defendant's product, and the sophistication of the buyers. "In applying this test, the list of factors does not exhaust the possibilities, and no single *Polaroid* factor is determinative." *Lang v. Retirement Living Publishing Co.*, 949 F.2d 576, 580 (2d Cir. 1991). Based on an analysis of the relevant *Polaroid* factors, the Court concludes that plaintiffs have demonstrated a likelihood of confusion.

*Strength of Plaintiffs' Marks:* This inquiry "focuses on 'the distinctiveness of the mark, or more precisely, its tendency to identify the goods' as coming from a particular source." *Lang*, 949 F.2d at 581. Two factors are used to measure the relative strength of a mark: the level of protection of the mark and the recognition value of the mark in the marketplace as identifying the source of the goods or services. With respect to the first factor, it is well settled that there are four levels of trademark protection, which, progressing from least to most protected, are (1) generic, (2) descriptive, (3) suggestive, and (4) fanciful or arbitrary. *Lois Sportswear U.S.A., Inc. v. Levi Strauss & Co.*, 799 F.2d 867, 871 (2d Cir. 1986). "Superimposed on this framework is the rule that registered trademarks are presumed to be distinctive and should be afforded the utmost protection." *Id.* As noted above, plaintiffs have produced evidence of Omega, S.A.'s ownership of the OMEGA registered trademarks; as such, the OMEGA marks should be afforded a high level of trademark protection. Plaintiffs have also produced evidence of the high degree to which watches bearing an OMEGA mark are readily identified in the marketplace and are associated with plaintiffs. The strength of plaintiffs' registered marks therefore weighs heavily in plaintiffs' favor.

*Similarity of the Marks:* The registered OMEGA marks and the counterfeit OMEGA marks are substantially identical in terms of spelling, appearance, size, and placement of the marks on the watch faces. Indeed, it is exceedingly difficult, if not impossible, to distinguish the registered OMEGA marks from the counterfeit OMEGA marks, even in a side-by-side comparison. The substantial identity of the marks weighs most heavily in plaintiffs' favor.

*Proximity of the Products:* In analyzing the proximity of the products marketed by plaintiffs and defendants, which the Second Circuit has referred to as "competitive proximity," "[t]he concern is whether it is likely that customers mistakenly will assume either that the junior user's goods somehow are associated with the senior user or are made by the senior user." *Centaur Communications, Ltd. v. A/S/M Communications, Inc.,* 830 F.2d 1217, 1226 (2d Cir. 1987). In the instant action, the competitive proximity of plaintiffs' and defendants' products is readily apparent, because both plaintiffs and defendants are marketing watches with a substantially similar appearance bearing an OMEGA mark. The proximity of the products therefore weighs heavily in plaintiffs' favor.

*Bridging the Gap:* "The fourth factor looks to whether the senior user of the mark is likely to enter the market in which the junior user is operating, that is, bridge the gap." *Id.* at 1227. [This factor is relevant where the parties do not compete directly to protect the senior user's right to expand his line of products and to protect consumers who believe the senior user has done so.] Where, as here, the parties are selling substantially identical products—watches—there is no gap to bridge. This factor therefore weighs heavily in plaintiffs' favor.

*Actual Confusion:* Although plaintiffs have not presented the Court with evidence of actual confusion, "[i]t is black letter law that actual confusion need not be shown to prevail under the Lanham Act, since actual confusion is very difficult to prove and the Act requires only a likelihood of confusion as to source." *Lois Sportswear,* 799 F.2d at 875. Moreover, plaintiffs have instituted this action to protect their rights under the Lanham Act in order to avoid consumer confusion in the marketplace. Because "[i]t would be unfair to penalize [plaintiffs] for acting to protect [their] trademark rights before serious damage has occurred," the lack of evidence of actual confusion does not weaken plaintiffs' position.

*Defendant's Good Faith:* There is absolutely no evidence of good faith on the part of the defendants in this action. To the contrary, the watches sold by defendants appear to be intentionally designed to imitate plaintiffs' watches, which raises a presumption of likelihood of consumer confusion. The lack of evidence of good faith on the part of the defendants in this action therefore weighs heavily in plaintiffs' favor.

*Quality of Defendants' Products:* Although plaintiffs' watches and defendants' watches have a substantially identical appearance, the Court's examination of each of the watches' features leads the Court to the conclusion that defendants' watches are of a markedly inferior quality to plaintiffs' watches. In particular, the Court observed substantial differences in the quality of the watches' time pieces, mechanical features, and fastening devices. Under certain circumstances, a difference in quality might weigh against a finding of likelihood of confusion, because while the lack of a difference in quality supports an inference that the goods emanate from the same source, the existence of such a difference supports an inference to the contrary. However, courts have recognized that the existence of inferior infringing goods strengthens a plaintiff's interest in protecting its reputation from debasement, which is one of the major goals of the trademark laws.

*Sophistication of Buyers:* The final factor considers the sophistication of consumers in the relevant market. There is no reason to believe that consumers who purchase watches in the $10 to $15 price range from the retail establishments run by defendants are, in general, sophisticated purchasers. It is true that at least some of these consumers undoubtedly recognize that a watch bearing an OMEGA mark but selling for only $10 to $15 must be a counterfeit watch, since genuine OMEGA watches sell for many times that amount in jewelry stores and department stores' jewelry departments; nonetheless, the Court must also take into account the effects of infringing watches in the post-sale context, because individuals who receive or observe defendants' watches after the initial purchase may well be confused as to the source of the watches. Therefore, the eighth *Polaroid* factor does not undermine plaintiffs' position, and may even support it.

On the basis of the foregoing, the Court concludes that plaintiffs have established a likelihood of success on the merits with respect to their §32 trademark infringement claim. Moreover, the Court finds that the continuing sale by the defendants of watches bearing counterfeit OMEGA marks will cause a loss of good will and reputation to plaintiffs that cannot be compensated adequately by money damages. There is a substantial risk that defendants' watches will cause consumer alienation and dissatisfaction, particularly because their appearance is substantially identical to that of plaintiffs' watches while their quality is substantially inferior to that of plaintiffs' watches. Plaintiffs have therefore demonstrated that they will suffer irreparable harm if a preliminary injunction does not issue with respect to plaintiffs' registered trademarks. . . .

## 2. Copyright Law

Copyright law protects authors' creative expressions of their ideas (not the ideas themselves) in whatever tangible form the expression might take, such as sculpture, painting, drawing, writing, or music. Thus, like trademark law, one does not need to register with a government body to acquire protection, but there are important advantages to registration, which will be explored in subsequent chapters. An owner of a copyright enjoys several exclusive rights, including the right to make copies of the copyrighted work, to prepare derivative works, to distribute copies of the copyrighted work, and to perform and display the copyrighted work publicly. The term of copyright for a work is life of the author plus 70 years, or, if the copyright is owned by a corporate entity (or the like) 120 years from creation of the work or 95 years from publication, whichever expires first. There are also important limitations to these exclusive rights. For instance, others may make a "fair use" of the copyrighted material (e.g., uses related to parody or scholarship). And unlike patent law, independent creation is a defense for copyright infringement. (There is no "fair use" or independent creation defense in patent law.) Copyright law is exclusively federal and is set forth in Title 17.

Because the threshold of "creativity" that is required to obtain copyright protection is quite low, copyright applies extremely broadly. Economic sectors that have long depended on copyright protection include book and music publishing, the motion picture industry, television broadcasting, and, more recently, the computer software industry. Copyrightable "creativity" is also found, however, in academic scholarship; in personal diaries, journals, and letters; in journalists' news reports and photographs; in maps; and even in day-to-day communications such as electronic mail. In the first place, then, the operation of copyright law should be assessed in the context of particular industry practices. Copyright law provides the legal foundation for international, multi-billion dollar enterprises. In addition, however, because copyright protection extends beyond the boundaries of for-profit industries, and because it restricts unauthorized reproduction and distribution of copyrighted works by individuals as well as by competitors, the effects of copyright also must be understood in relation to other important social values, most importantly interests in free speech guaranteed by the First Amendment to the U.S. Constitution.

Copyright law represents not only a delicate, evolving balance between the interests of those who create and publish creative works, and those who would compete with them, but also a balance between those who create those works and those who consume and use them. Finally, it is important to remember that those balances must be drawn in a myriad of technological contexts, from the most fixed and traditional — books — to the most fleeting and dynamic — the Internet. The existence of these competing perspectives creates enormous difficulties in calibrating copyright doctrines. Consider these balances as you read the following excerpt on music file sharing.

### TOM ZELLER, LINK BY LINK; THE IMPS OF FILE SHARING MAY LOSE IN COURT, BUT THEY ARE WINNING IN THE MARKETPLACE

New York Times, Monday, July 4, 2005, Sec. 3, p. 3, col. 3

Not more than an hour after the Supreme Court ruled last week against a pair of file-sharing software companies, Hilary Rosen, the former head of the Recording Industry Association of America, had this to say on her Web log at The Huffington Post:

"Wow. We won big. Unanimous. That doesn't happen very often," she wrote. "I was right. Winning is a big psychological lift."

And yet, she was not sanguine about the future. "Knowing we were right legally really still isn't the same thing as being right in the real world," she wrote.

Having arrived at the helm of the R.I.A.A. at precisely the moment in 1998 when revolutionary terms like MP3, Napster, and peer-to-peer were entering the popular lexicon, Ms. Rosen steered the recording industry's antipiracy battle tank.

By the time she stepped down in 2003, Napster had been sued into oblivion, its successors, Grokster and StreamCast, appeared similarly fated, and lawsuits against individual file sharers were in the offing.

Despite the music industry's legal victories against file sharing, Ms. Rosen wrote, the strategy has not earned the industry any more control over a marketplace forever changed by digital technology — "no matter how many times it was hoped it would." . . .

Even the most ardent supporters of Big Entertainment concede that, in the long run, copyright holders are no match for the ability of file-sharing technology to adapt, mutate, evolve and expand. In fairness to Ms. Rosen, it is a stark reality she noted early on.

"As a practical matter going forward," she told Salon.com in early 2000, "lawsuits get a lot of headlines and they raise a lot of passion — I understand that. But ultimately the future of music on the Internet is not going to be about legalities and litigation, it's going to be about how are we bringing music to fans."

Or, perhaps more accurately, it's about how fans are demanding that music be brought to them.

"I have always thought that people were just putting their finger in the dam with litigation and other kinds of enforcement," Ms. Rosen said in a phone call last week.

Indeed, almost from the moment in the late 1980s when researchers at the Fraunhofer Institute in Germany developed an audio compression technology that would become known as MP3, disruption of the music industry's equilibrium became inevitable. In the digital age, the music industry faces two basic choices — either make it too risky to upload and download copyrighted files (or to even create software that allows people to do so), or completely rethink the business.

So far, the industry has relied on the former strategy. But each new court victory arrives years behind the next digital innovation, born in some college dorm where an abiding geekiness is the motivator and earning profits means little. However valid the industry's desire to protect its products, trying to stop file sharing has become a Sisyphean exercise. . . .

[E]ven the file-sharing company Mashboxx, which announced last week that it had entered a deal with Sony BMG to become "the first P2P authorized by a major label," might prove, at 99 cents per download, just a pit stop on the road to a day when music and film content flows freely over the Internet, as it does now in radio and television broadcasts over the airwaves.

[T]hat might mean charging all users a flat media fee, paid through their Internet service providers, which in turn would pay the studios. In return, copyrighted media files would be unleashed for unrestricted swapping, sharing, sampling and saving—which is, after all, what millions of people all over the world are already doing.

The problem, Mr. Garland said, is that even law-abiding citizens now expect to be able to exchange content freely on the Internet. "It really may one day have to become a utility," he said, "like water from a tap."

So where does that leave the entertainment industry's victory in the Supreme Court last week? "While I think it has legal value," Ms. Rosen said, "it will be meaningless."

## 3. Patent Law

Patent law protects inventors' technologic creations, which may include software, pharmaceuticals, processes, compositions of matter, or electronic and mechanical devices. Unlike trademark, copyright, and trade secret protection, one must file a patent application with the Patent and Trademark Office to obtain patent protection and, of course, not all applications result in issued patents. To be patentable, an invention must be useful, novel, and non-obvious; and several disclosure requirements also must be satisfied. A patent's term is typically 20 years from date of filing, and provides its owner with a right to exclude others from making, using, and selling the claimed invention. A patent does *not* give its owner the right to make, use, and sell the claimed invention. (See the Introduction in Chapter 10 for a discussion of this doctrine.) Neither independent creation nor third-party experimental use, other than for amusement or philosophical reasons, are recognized as defenses. Patent law is exclusively federal and is set forth in Title 35.

Patent law, like copyright law, also seeks to strike a balance. On one hand, patent law strives to promote technologic innovations through proprietary rights, and, on the other hand, to provide legal space for access to those innovations. Interestingly, recent scholarship has shown that the patent system's role in inducing technologic innovation is more important to some industries (e.g., drugs and medical equipment) than to others, which may rely more on trade secrecy (e.g., chemical processes and petroleum) or lead time into the market (e.g., software).[2] And some industries seek patent protection with an eye toward commercialization and generating revenue, while others obtain patents to block competitors from developing competing products or to enhance their bargaining position during cross-licensing negotiations, particularly when a "complex" technology (i.e., a product or process that comprises several patented components) is involved.[3] Indeed, patent law is not a one-size-fits-all regime.

2. *See* Wesley M. Cohen et al., *Protecting Their Intellectual Assets: Appropriability Conditions and Why U.S. Manufacturing Firms Patent (or Not)*, 24 (Nat'l Bureau of Econ. Research, Working Paper No. 7552, 2000) ("We find that the key appropriability mechanisms in most industries are secrecy, lead time and complementary capabilities").
3. *Id.*

The excerpt below reveals that a patent can provide a powerful property right with important economic implications. As you read through the article, and indeed through the patent law chapters, ask yourself what are the costs and benefits of a patent system to inventors, corporations, and society.

## ADAM LIPTAK, SAVING SEEDS SUBJECTS FARMERS TO SUITS OVER PATENT

**New York Times, Sunday, Nov. 2, 2003, Sec. 1, p. 18, col. 3**

TUPELO, Miss., Oct. 30 — Homan McFarling has been farming here all his life, growing mostly soybeans along with a little corn. After each harvest, he puts some seed aside. "Every farmer that ever farmed has saved some of his seed to plant again," he said. In 1998, Mr. McFarling bought 1,000 bags of genetically altered soybean seeds, and he did what he had always done. But the seeds, called Roundup Ready, are patented. When Monsanto, which holds the patent, learned what Mr. McFarling had sown, it sued him in federal court in St. Louis for patent infringement and was awarded $780,000.

The company calls the planting of saved seed piracy, and it says it has won millions of dollars from farmers in lawsuits and settlements in such cases. Mr. McFarling's is the first to reach a federal appeals court, which will consider how the law should reconcile patented food with a practice as old as farming itself.

If the appeals court rules against him, said Mr. McFarling, 61, he will be forced into bankruptcy and early retirement. "It doesn't look right for them to have a patent on something that you can grow yourself," he said. Janice Armstrong, a Monsanto spokeswoman, said the company invested hundreds of millions of dollars to develop the seed. "We need to protect our intellectual property so that we can continue to develop the next wave of products," she said.

Were farmers allowed to replant the seed, the company said in its appeals court brief, "Monsanto would effectively, and rapidly, lose control of its rights."

That is because one bag of the patented seed can produce about 36 bags of seed for use in the next growing season. The number grows exponentially. By the third season, the single bag of seed could generate almost 50,000 bags.

Ms. Armstrong said that there are about 300,000 soybean farmers in the United States, and that Monsanto has disputes with only about 100 of them a year. Most disputes are resolved quickly and informally, she said.

Farmers here said the company's efforts to investigate the replanting of saved seeds have been intrusive, divisive and heavy-handed.

"They hired the whole city of Tupelo's night police force," said Mitchell Scruggs, 54, who is a defendant in another saved-seed lawsuit. "They bought a lot across the street from me for surveillance. They're spending all this money on airplanes, helicopters, detectives, lawyers."

"They told a federal judge that it wasn't a monetary issue," Mr. Scruggs said over the roar of three cotton gins at his farm here. "They wanted to make an example of me. They want to destroy me to show others what could happen to them."

In this respect, the seed lawsuits resemble the record industry's actions against people who share music files on the Internet. There, too, the goal is not primarily to recover money from particular defendants but to educate the public, and perhaps to scare other potential offenders.

Ms. Armstrong acknowledges that Monsanto must walk a fine line.

"These people are our customers," she said, "and we do value them. But we also have to protect our intellectual property rights." . . .

Mr. Scruggs said the courts should find a way to weigh traditions almost as old as humanity against fostering high-technology innovations.

"It's a God-given right that farmers were given when they were born to save these seeds," he said. "All we are is farmers trying to scrape a living out of this dirt."

---

Would failing to enforce Monsanto's legal monopoly lead to an underproduction of genetically modified seeds? In Monsanto's suit against Mr. McFarling, discussed in the *New York Times* article, Mr. McFarling complained that the price charged for ROUNDUP READY seeds was higher than for other soybean seeds, and that it was cheaper for him to produce his own ROUNDUP READY seeds from his previous year's crop. The appellate court was unsympathetic and enjoined his use of the seeds from his own crop, stating "[w]e need not repeat that in a market economy a purveyor may charge the price the product can sustain; there is no requirement that a patentee must lower his price to that of the less desired products he replaces." *Monsanto Co. v. McFarling*, 302 F.3d 1291, 1299 (Fed. Cir. 2002).

Giving Monsanto a right to exclude others from making, using, and selling ROUNDUP READY is quite likely to lead to higher prices. If Monsanto has no competition for genetically modified seeds and its unique seeds are valuable enough, it can charge enough to cover all of its costs and more, earning a profit for the duration of its patent. The most obvious results are that farmers pay more for seeds than they would if any seed seller could copy Monsanto's invention. But if everyone could compete in selling the genetically modified seeds, the market price would reflect the cost of producing the seeds they sell. Only Monsanto would have to charge enough to cover its research and development costs, so they would lose customers to other sellers or to farmers who saved seeds from the previous year. Thus, a balance must be struck, as discussed in Section 4 below, between encouraging innovation through property rights in the form of a patent and access to the patented product. In determining this balance, it is important to keep in mind that patents rarely provide an economic monopoly as there are usually viable substitutes available that compete with the patented product.[4]

4. The term "monopoly" is used throughout this book to refer to *legal* monopoly, not economic monopoly. A legal monopoly means an exclusive right. An economic monopoly

## 4. Copyright and Patent Law's Common Foundation

Copyright law and patent law have the same broad goals and constitutional foundation. Of course, they achieve these goals through different legal means and focus on different subject matter and creative segments of society. But the two regimes have much in common. For instance, both are expressly grounded in Article I, Section 8, Clause 8 of the Constitution, which states that Congress shall have the power:

> To promote the Progress of Science and useful Arts, by securing for limited Times to Authors and Inventors the exclusive Right to their respective Writings and Discoveries.[5]

This clause implies that the foremost goal of copyright and patent law is to benefit society — a utilitarian, result-oriented focus. As the Supreme Court noted in *Mazer v. Stein*, 347 U.S. 201, 219 (1954), the "economic policy behind the clause empowering Congress to grant patents and copyrights is the conviction that it is the best way to advance public welfare through the talents of authors and inventors in 'Science and useful Arts.'" Copyrights and patents are something tolerated for the greater societal good. Thus, our copyright and patent laws are generally seen to operate as part of an interdependent mix of incentives and restraints that bestow benefits and impose costs on society and individuals alike. Viewed this way, copyright and patent law strive to strike a balance between the promotion of creative and technologic expression and the dissemination of and access to its fruits. It does this by offering a potential financial reward as an inducement to create, invent, disclose, or invest in commercialization — bringing the product to market.

Think about a world without patents and copyrights. To do so, one must appreciate that intellectual property has characteristics that distinguish it from tangible property. Unlike real or personal property (a house or a car), some intellectual property is what economists call a public good, meaning that it is both non-rivalrous and non-excludable. For example, many people can benefit from information without interfering in the pleasure others get from the same information — non-rivalrous. One person's use of the creative ideas embodied in a word processing program do not interfere with another's use of those ideas. One person's enjoyment of the creative expression in a poem does not generally diminish another's enjoyment of

---

means market power to obtain higher than normal profits. Thus, "legal monopoly" does not mean that substitute goods are unavailable and, indeed, many patents confer little or no market power despite their legal monopoly status. Similarly, an economic monopoly is not necessarily legal.

5. The framers, employing colonial syntax as one would expect, were respectively referring to works of authors and inventors when they used the terms "Science" and "useful Arts." In the eighteenth century, the term "Science," from the Latin, *scire*, "to know," meant learning or knowledge in general and had no particular connection to the physical or biological sciences like it does today. Thus, the operational relationships are between "authors," "science," and "writings" for copyright on the one hand and "inventors," "useful Arts," and "discoveries" for patents on the other. *See* Giles S. Rich, *Principles of Patentability*, in NONOBVIOUSNESS — THE ULTIMATE CONDITION OF PATENTABILITY (John Witherspoon ed. 1980); Karl B. Lutz, *Patents and Science: A Clarification of the Patent Clause of the U.S. Constitution*, 18 GEO. WASH. L. REV. 50 (1949).

those words. Because many can simultaneously benefit from an idea, it makes sense to make it as widely available as possible. As Thomas Jefferson wrote in a letter to Isaac McPherson, "He who receives an idea from me, receives instruction himself without lessening mine; as he who lights his taper at mine, receives light without darkening me."[6]

While inventions and creative expressions neatly fit the model of public goods, trademarks do not. While consumers may freely use the mark to refer to a product's source, rival sellers cannot freely use the same mark to indicate that they are the source. Thus, while users of creative expressions and inventions are non-rivalrous, only some uses of trademarks are non-rivalrous.

Because they are non-rivalrous, public goods, should, in theory, be made widely available. But creators often need compensation to spur their efforts. It is especially difficult physically to exclude people from using others' intangible ideas, and sometimes even the physical embodiment of those ideas and to arrange necessary compensation for creators. Music companies struggle to keep people from downloading their recordings. Companies work hard to keep their secret formulas secure. Inventors often need to disclose their ideas to secure venture capital or manufacturing capabilities, but absent a patent right will likely be reticent for fear of inducing competition or free riding. Trademark owners will be reluctant to invest in the information-signaling power of the mark if other sellers can simultaneously use the same mark. There is an inherent conflict between the desire to make intangible ideas widely available and the need to limit access to those who pay the IP creator. This problem is commonly referred to as Arrow's Information Paradox, named after the economist, Kenneth Arrow.[7]

The two distinctive features of public goods — non-rivalous and non-excludable — suggest that public goods will tend to be underproduced, if produced at all, by the market — a type of market failure. Indeed, public goods present a special type of problem called the free-rider problem. Patent law and copyright law are the government's response to this free-rider/public goods problem for creative expressions and inventions. Of course, there are other responses such as direct government funding of R&D and arts organizations, or the use of prominent rewards as a means of incentivizing innovation and creation. Ask yourself, as you study the various IP systems set forth in this book, if any of these alternatives are preferable.

The policy issue underlying patent law is whether it is worthwhile suffering the wealth transfer effect and the deadweight loss (i.e., the social costs) for a limited period of time in order to encourage people to invent, disclose, and commercialize new and useful information and products. The same issue arises in copyright law. Thus, owners of patented inventions (e.g., drugs) and copyrighted creations (e.g., music) may be able to charge higher prices and make greater profits than if anyone could reproduce them, but fewer people may have access to those products. (Now you can appreciate, even if you do not sympathize, the music industry's (and con-

---

6. Letter to Isaac McPherson (Aug. 13, 1813), reprinted in Jefferson Writings 1291-92 (M. Peterson ed. 1984).

7. *See* Kenneth Arrow, *Economic Welfare and the Allocation of Resources for Invention*, in Rate and Direction of Inventive Activity 609 (NBER ed. 1962).

tent industry generally) uproar over peer-to-peer file sharing software.) These two IP regimes have social costs, and thus, as you explore the materials, it is important that you always consider whether the benefits are worth the costs.

## 5. Trade Secret Law

Trade secret law provides an important form of protection for valuable commercial information. Information eligible for trade secret protection may or may not be eligible for patent protection. If information is eligible for both, recent empirical studies have shown that many industries prefer trade secrecy as a form of protection, particularly for process-related inventions.[8] This preference is particularly true when the secret is not easy for others to discover (i.e., reverse engineer) once the owner makes use of it. Some secrets, such as the invention of the paper clip, disclose themselves when the product is put on the market. Other secrets, such as the process for manufacture of a particular type of crystal, are not revealed by selling the product. The Coca-Cola Company's formula for COKE is often cited as a famous example of the best-kept trade secret.

Types of information eligible for trade secret protection are much broader than that which is patentable. Trade secrets include not only technologic information, but also formulae, customer lists, business plans, and marketing strategies. Trade secret law considers the forms of information that are subject to trade secret protection to be socially valuable and encourages its production. Trade secret protection can last in perpetuity as long as the information remains secret and maintains its value whereas a patent expires 20 years from its filing date.

Trade secret law is grounded in both property and tort law. Under the property theory, trade secret law has a utilitarian justification, encouraging the production of valuable commercial information — much like patent law. The tort theory of trade secrets, first expressed in the 1939 Restatement of Torts, is more concerned with deterring unethical commercial behavior (e.g., theft). Thus, while trade secret law is considered a form of intellectual property law because it creates a protectible interest in valuable information, it is also concerned with ethical duties and behavior among commercial entities. As such, a cause of action for trade secret misappropriation will arise only if the trade secret is acquired by "improper means" or through a breach of a confidential relationship, which is usually in the form of an express or implied contract. Indeed, independent creation and reverse engineering are defenses to a trade secret misappropriation claim because trade secret law does not consider them "unethical" practices. In fact, these practices are encouraged because they enhance competition and force innovators to think twice before forgoing patent protection. (Recall, independent creation and reverse engineering are unavailable to an alleged patent infringer.)

Note that trade secret law possesses its own social benefits and costs, although different from those of patent law. Trade secret law has the social

---

8. *See* Cohen et al., *Protecting Their Intellectual Assets, supra,* page 10, note 2.

advantage of not giving a right to exclude over secrets other firms discover independently or through reverse engineering, thus avoiding the social costs associated with patents. On the other hand, trade secret law does not encourage disclosure to the extent patent law (and copyright law) does, thereby failing to provide some of the social benefits of those systems.

Trade secret law is also concerned with protecting employers' secrets from being disclosed to competitors by departing employees. On the one hand, if the secret were disclosed, the employer's competitive advantage would diminish, along with the incentives necessary to encourage research on improved methods of doing business. On the other hand, restraining employees' economic mobility and personal freedom to pursue alternative employment is also undesirable. An employee would become fettered to her present employment if unable to use the increased expertise that came with experience in the industry. Should an employer be able to prevent a former employee from disclosing the employer's trade secrets? Prevent an erstwhile employee from working for a competitor?

With the exception of the Economic Espionage Act, trade secret protection is a creature of state law and is recognized in one form or another by every jurisdiction. While trade secrets have their origin in state common law, over 40 states have adopted the Uniform Trade Secrets Act (UTSA) in its original form or a version thereof. The UTSA and other aspects of trade secret law are discussed in detail in Chapter 14.

## B. THE STRUCTURE OF THIS BOOK

Each area of intellectual property has its own statutes and its own common law development. Each strikes a different balance between exclusive rights and public access. Each offers important societal benefits and distinct costs. That makes understanding the foundations of intellectual property law quite challenging. This book is designed to meet that challenge by presenting IP law in an accessible manner without sacrificing the law's nuances and rich policies.

The first design element of the book is that the sections on each of the three federal statutory schemes are presented in the same way. The purpose of this parallel approach is to emphasize the similar structure of each intellectual property regime. By understanding the basic similarities, the differences among these regimes are easier to appreciate. So, for instance, the first chapter of each of the trademark, patent, and copyright sections discusses how people obtain rights. Understanding how rights are acquired is the first step in appreciating the structure of the law.

The second chapter of each of these sections discusses the extent and enforcement of IP rights. IP law defines what rights the owner has and how to tell when another has interfered with those rights. In each area, the primary legal theory is infringement. If a seller of watches puts another's trademark on its watches, consumers may be confused about which company is the source of the watch. That might be the basis for a trademark infringement action. If a songwriter borrows lyrics or a musical phrase from another songwriter that might be the basis for a copyright infringement action. If a farmer produces seeds patented by another that might be the basis for a patent infringement action. Because of its close connection to state law, the trademark section includes discussion of additional legal theories such as dilution, passing off, misappropriation, and publicity.

The third chapter explores defenses available to a defendant who has been sued for allegedly infringing the plaintiff's IP rights. The balancing between an IP owner's exclusive rights in his creation and access to that creation by the public or a competitor is of fundamental importance.

The fourth chapter discusses the remedies available to IP owners in infringement actions. While there are overarching goals of making injured plaintiffs whole and discouraging infringers, there are a variety of ways of accomplishing that result. In all areas, injunctions aimed at stopping the infringing activity are common. Injunctions must carefully reflect the respective rights of the IP holder and the public. Damages are also available in all three areas for at least lost sales suffered by the IP owner.

The second design element is the inclusion of cases with interesting or appealing facts. The cases in each of the chapters are followed by comments that discuss important aspects in the cases, guiding readers to the issues raised in the cases. The book includes trademark cases that involve products and services people use every day, such as bread and search engines; and copyright cases that involve products common in popular culture, such as music and art. The patent cases pertain to inventions that are technologically simple, such as baseballs, pizza boxes, and corset springs.

The third design element is the frequent inclusion of problems coming from real cases, with case citations included. The book minimizes the number of rhetorical and imponderable questions, relying primarily on explanations. When questions are asked in problems, readers can discover the answer by looking at the citations for the cases. The book minimizes the use of hypotheticals in favor of factual issues that have arisen in actual cases to which readers have access.

The fourth design element is inclusion of relevant statutory materials at the end of each substantive area. The location is helpful because a reader need not refer to or obtain a separate statutory supplement. The statute is handy to the cases. Moreover, only relevant parts of the statute are included. The bulk of intellectual property statutes is far beyond the scope of a survey course in IP.

The final design element is a series of perspective notes. These are short explorations of intriguing (1) policy perspectives that highlight the goals of the law, which help the reader understand why the law is the way it is; (2) comparative perspectives that illustrate alternative approaches taken by different countries to suggest different ways in which the balance between exclusive rights and public access may be struck; (3) historical perspectives that place a particular IP doctrine in historical context; and (4) counseling perspectives relating to items an IP attorney may want to consider in counseling clients on a particular issue.

These design elements are also carried through the final chapters of the book on trade secrets and idea law. While any of the sections or either of these final chapters may be approached in any order, the book offers trade secrets and idea law last. After reading about the complexities of getting a patent under federal law, the option of getting state law protection of a discovery just by keeping it secret may seem very appealing. Of course, keeping a secret may not be all that easy and, being law, there are always the questions of whether something really is a secret, whether a person tried hard enough to keep it a secret, and whether the person who discovered the secret did so improperly.

After all of the intellectual property regimes have been explored, it is natural to wonder how one can profit by coming up with and selling an idea — for a marketing method that might involve trademark law, a TV show or movie that might involve copyright law, or a better mousetrap that might involve patent law. Idea law is concerned with how to approach and contract with prospective buyers of your intellectual creations. Cases in this chapter include ideas for developing a tourist attraction in Alaska and Bill Cosby's TV show. It is no surprise that contract law principles are involved, but the intangible nature of intellectual property and the twin goals of encouraging invention and protecting access introduce new elements to familiar common law principles.

# CHAPTER
# 2

# Acquiring Trademark Rights

Trademark law is concerned with preventing confusion among consumers and protecting people's investments in their source-indicating marks. Honest sellers spend millions to create brand identity and do not want buyers to confuse their products with others' products. Nor do they want other sellers to use similar marks that dilute their name recognition. Prudent buyers do not want to be confused about which producer is the source of a product and rely on a mark to indicate what characteristics and quality the product has. A seller may use a distinctive word (such as Exxon Mobil Corporation's EXXON) or a symbol (Nike's ✔ "swoosh") to avoid confusion by creating an association in consumers' minds between itself as the source of the good or service it supplies and to distinguish its products from the products of its competitors. Buyers would be confused if other sellers of gas used EXXON. Nike's investment in the "swoosh" would be less valuable if other sellers could freely use it, even if those other sellers did not sell sporting goods and clothing.

Sellers use trademarks to signal consumers about the qualities and characteristics of their products. The JEEP mark (used in connection with automotive vehicles) creates different signals than the marks HUMMER and MERCEDES. Consumers relying on these signals and the information they convey with regard to quality, price, and luxury save money and time searching for goods that fit their needs and budgets. Protecting trademarks encourages sellers to create consistent signals that distinguish their products and services from those provided by others. Protecting trademarks promotes competition by enabling producers to satisfy demands of different kinds of consumers. It also forces competitors to develop their own reputation for consistent quality because they cannot simply free ride on the mark owner's goodwill.

Marks may take many forms, including words, symbols, colors, even scents and sounds. The federal statute protecting marks is the Lanham Act, 15 USC §§1051 *et seq.* Consistent with the purposes of trademark law, the only marks that are protectible are those capable of identifying and distinguishing the user's goods or services from the goods manufactured or sold by others. To obtain protection, the seller must use the mark in commerce to distinguish its goods and services from those of others. Trademarks and service marks are governed by the same rules and most people generally use the word "trademark" to cover both types of marks.

*STATUTE:* **Trademark and Service Mark Defined**
15 U.S.C. §1127 (Lanham Act §45)

The more distinctive a mark is, the more likely it will create a strong association between a product and its source. The terms BIG MAC used by McDonald's Corporation to sell hamburgers and CORVETTE used by General Motors to sell cars readily call to mind the suppliers of those products. Consumers recognize that EXCEDRIN pain reliever and ALTOID mints are supplied by a specific source, even if consumers don't know the sources (Bristol-Myers Squibb Corporation and Smith Kendon Limited, respectively). These are all distinctive marks because of the clear source identification, unlike "Raisin Bran" cereal, which simply describes the product, or "cellophane" food wrap, which merely names the type of product. These latter examples do not suggest to consumers that the products come from a particular source, whether known or not. To protect the source-identifying power of marks, trademark law gives strong protection to highly distinctive marks and little or no protection to descriptive marks and marks that merely name the product.

This chapter discusses what kind of signaling devices are considered acceptable marks and how people acquire rights to marks. Only marks that are distinctive, capable of signaling that a product or service comes from a particular source, are protectible. Signaling devices vary in their distinctiveness. As Section A below reveals, marks are classified by their distinctiveness and more protection is given to more distinctive marks.

Until a person exposes consumers to a mark by using it in commerce, the mark cannot establish a connection between the product and the origin of the product in the minds of consumers. Section B describes the requirement that a mark be used in connection with a particular product or service before it can be protected and the types of uses that do not qualify. It also introduces the use requirements for two additional types of marks, certification and collective marks. Unlike trademarks and service marks, which indicate source, certification and collective marks are used to indicate that, whatever their source, the goods or services have particular characteristics, such as being certified safe by a testing agency or having been produced by members of an organization such as the International Ladies Garment Workers Union.

Section C focuses on statutorily enumerated prohibitions on registering certain types of marks, such as those that are deceptive, confusing, scandalous, merely descriptive, or functional. After we describe in this chapter when marks can be protected, we follow with Chapter 3 discussing the scope of that protection.

## A. DISTINCTIVENESS OF MARKS

The broad definition of protectible source-indicating devices in the Lanham Act allows for familiar types of marks, such as words and pictures, and more exotic devices, such as smells, colors, and sounds. It is not surprising that IPOD is a trademarked word used in connection with handheld digital electronic devices for recording, organizing, transmitting, manipulating, and reviewing audio files. It is stranger to think that the shape of a bottle (the indented sides of a PINCH scotch bottle) or the design of a box (the triangular shape of a TOBLERONE chocolate bar container) may serve as a source-indicating device.

This part of the chapter is divided into two sections. The first considers the traditional classifications of marks by their "strength," that is, their ability to signal to consumers that the goods to which they are affixed come from a particular source. The second considers nontraditional marks such as trade dress (packaging) and product design.

## 1. Classification of Marks by Strength

Lanham Act §45 requires that marks be capable of identifying and distinguishing the user's goods and services from those manufactured or sold or provided by others and to indicate the source of the goods, even if that source is unknown. Some symbols are obviously source indicators while others might just be terms describing the goods. What could the term "infinity" mean, when used in the context of selling an automobile? The INFINITI mark used in connection with cars is *inherently distinctive* because consumers are likely to recognize it as a term one manufacturer has chosen to distinguish its cars from other manufacturers' cars. Used in connection with cars, this mark is likely to be a source indicator because it is just not another generic name for "automobile" and it does not describe any characteristic of any automobile. Aside from its source-indicating power, the term "infinity" has nothing to do with automobiles at all. It does not matter whether consumers know that an INFINITI is manufactured by Nissan, only that they know the mark indicates a source. By contrast, when consumers see or hear the term "speedy" used by a restaurant selling burritos, they might sensibly conclude that the burrito will be ready to eat quickly. A restaurant can call itself SPEEDY BURRITO, but consumers might still react to the term by thinking it is merely descriptive.

Some devices used as marks are inherently distinctive because they have no obvious connection with the product or service. Other devices, including some descriptive terms, are *capable of becoming distinctive*. With sufficient advertising effort, a supplier might establish consumer recognition of a descriptive mark as indicating a particular source. Combining the words with graphics also may make the mark more distinctive, that is, a better indicator of source. When the efforts of the user of the mark have created sufficient consumer recognition of the term as a source indicator that the source-indicating meaning dominates the merely descriptive meaning, the mark is said to have acquired *secondary meaning*. Inherently distinctive marks, such as INFINITI used in connection with cars, EXXON used in

*[handwritten margin note: "if no relation to product + no descriptive terms ⇒ stronger mark"]*

connection with gasoline, are considered stronger marks than descriptive marks that have acquired secondary meaning and generally receive greater legal protection.

The cases in the first part of this chapter explore the classification of marks by strength and the degree of protection given to marks of different strength. Recall that the definition of *mark* is broad: "any word, name, symbol, or device or combination thereof." The cases in Section A.1 involve words or letters used as marks. The cases in Section A.2 involve product packaging and product designs that users want consumers to associate with them as the source.

There is a traditional classification scheme for the strength of word and letter marks discussed in Section A.1. As *Horizon Mills Corp. v. QVC, Inc.* indicates, there are five classifications, increasing in strength from generic marks to fanciful marks. Generic marks receive no protection. Merely descriptive marks receive protection only if they have acquired secondary meaning. Suggestive, arbitrary, and fanciful marks are protected without secondary meaning. Because of these rules, the first big issue for classification is whether the mark is protectible at all. *Horizon Mills* discusses the distinction between generic marks, which are not protectible, and descriptive marks, which are protectible with proof of secondary meaning. The second big issue is whether proof of secondary meaning is required for a particular mark. *Bristol-Myers Squibb Co. v. McNeil-P.P.C., Inc.* discusses the distinctions between descriptive marks, which require secondary meaning, and suggestive marks, which are protected without such proof. These issues are presented next.

*[handwritten margin note: "Stronger terms"]*

## HORIZON MILLS CORP. v. QVC, INC.

### 161 F. Supp. 2d 208 (S.D.N.Y. 2001)

SCHWARTZ, District Judge.

This action, filed on March 24, 2000, arises out of defendant's use of the term "Slinky" to advertise women's apparel for home shopping customers. Plaintiff, the owner of the trademark in SLINKY for "fabrics used in clothing and household products," alleges claims for trademark infringement and unfair competition under the Lanham Act. . . . Defendant moves for summary judgment as to each of plaintiff's claims on the ground that plaintiff's mark is generic. For the reasons set forth below, the motion is denied.

Plaintiff Horizon Mills Corp. ("Horizon") is a corporation organized and existing under the laws of New York, with its principal place of business in New York, New York. It is a textile converter, involved primarily in developing and marketing both knit and woven textiles for the "womanswear" trade. Defendant QVC, Inc. ("QVC") is a corporation organized and existing under the laws of Pennsylvania with its principal place of business in West Chester, Pennsylvania. According to QVC, it has been engaged since 1986 in the business of providing home-shopping retail services. In addition to its cable television network, it also operates an online retail service called "iQVC," and markets goods through mail-order catalogs and retail outlets in Pennsylvania and Delaware. Through these commercial channels, QVC markets, *inter alia*, women's apparel made from acetate and spandex and man-made fibers, under certain private labels and other brand name designers.

Horizon alleges that its first use of the term "slinky" as a mark in connection with fabrics, specifically a combination of acetate and spandex, occurred on July 16, 1991. On September 16, 1993, Horizon filed an intent to use application for registration of the mark SLINKY in the United States Patent and Trademark Office ("PTO"). On November 7, 1995, the mark was registered on the Principal Register covering the use of said mark on "fabrics used in the manufacture of clothing and household products."

Since Horizon's first use in 1991, certain members of the media, trade, and consuming public have come to employ the term "slinky" to describe a stretchy, fluid or sinuous-looking fabric normally consisting of acetate or spandex, and used in dresses and women's sportswear. QVC states that it uses the terms "slinky," "slinky knit," and "slinky fabric" to describe such fabric and the apparel made therefrom. Plaintiff filed this action to enjoin such use on the ground it is infringing, and to recover damages. Prior to discovery, QVC moved for summary judgment on the ground that the generic nature of the terms in question bar Horizon's claims. QVC's argument is twofold. First, it contends that the term "slinky" was generic to the relevant category of products prior to Horizon's use and registration. Second, it contends that the public has appropriated the term "slinky" for the stretchy, fluid, and sinuous fabric and women's apparel made from acetate, spandex and other man-made fibers, therefore precluding exclusive use of the term by any manufacturer. Horizon contends that the references to "slinky" fabrics or garments in the media and trade are not generic references, but rather references to its trademarked fabric. . . .

Terms are classified in four categories for the purposes of trademark protection. In increasing degrees of distinctiveness, and protectibility, the categories are: (i) generic, (ii) descriptive,[3] (iii) suggestive, and (iv) arbitrary or fanciful.

A term is generic when it refers to the genus or class of product, rather than a particular product; a generic term is one which is commonly used as the name for a type of goods. *Murphy Door Bed Co. v. Interior Sleep Sys., Inc.*, 874 F.2d 95, 100 (2d Cir. 1989); *Miller Brewing Co. v. G. Heileman Brewing Co.*, 561 F.2d 75, 79 (7th Cir. 1977). The generic name of a product can never function as a trademark to indicate the origin of that product. Moreover, as Judge Friendly observed, to permit exclusive trademark rights in a generic name "would grant the owner of a mark a monopoly, since a competitor could not describe his goods as what they are." *CES Publ'g Corp. v. St. Regis Publications*, 531 F.2d 11, 13 (2d Cir. 1975). The trademark laws are primarily consumer protection laws, designed to prevent confusion among the public resulting from fraud and deception in the marketing and sales of products. With generic terms, such protection is unnecessary, because consumers understand exactly what they are buying by knowing the name; the source of the goods is immaterial. *See Bayer v. United Drug Co.*, 272 F. 505, 509-10 (S.D.N.Y. 1921).

---

3. Descriptive terms are often referred to as "merely descriptive," while generic terms are also referred to as "common descriptive" names. *See, e.g., Abercrombie & Fitch Co. v. Hunting World, Inc.*, 537 F.2d 4, 10 (2d Cir. 1976).

Descriptive terms are those that describe a thing, or "how it is," rather than name that thing, or "what it is."[4] McCarthy's §12-19 at 12-52. As one court of this district has stated, "The distinction between descriptive and generic terms is one of degree. A generic name conveys information with respect to the nature or class of an article, whereas a descriptive term supplies the characteristics and qualities of the article, its color, order, function, dimensions." *Gear Inc. v. L.A. Gear California, Inc.*, 670 F. Supp. 508, 514. This Court recognizes the difficulty involved in precisely defining the generic and descriptive categories; "[t]he lines of demarcation...are not always bright." *Abercrombie & Fitch Co.*, 537 F.2d at 9. Nevertheless, the distinction is critical because "if determined to be generic, [a] term can never function as a mark or be given trademark protection; but if determined to be descriptive, the term can be given trademark protection upon proof of secondary meaning," referring to consumers' recognition of the term and association with a source.

The test for genericness is based upon a term's "primary significance" to the buying public. As Judge Learned Hand stated: "The single question...in all these cases, is merely one of fact: What do buyers understand by the word for whose use the parties are contending?" *Bayer*, 272 F. at 509; McCarthy §12:9 at 12-19 ("It is the use and understanding of the term in the context of purchasing decisions...that determines the primary significance of a designation.") A term is generic when the majority of the buying public associates the term with a product, rather than the source of the product, whether the source is known or unknown. *See King-Seeley Thermos Co. v. Aladdin Indus., Inc.*, 321 F.2d 577, 579-81 (2d Cir. 1963). In general, the buying class refers to consumers, rather than professionals in the trade. *Something Old, Something New, Inc. v. QVC*, 53 U.S.P.Q.2d 1715, 1720 (S.D.N.Y. 1999).

Courts have determined terms to be generic and hence unprotectible, under two principal circumstances. The first case is where a seller appropriates an existing generic term and claims exclusive rights in it as a "trademark" of that term. In such a case, because the term was generic before the seller used it, the seller never had trademark rights in the term. An individual challenging the mark need only establish that the term is generic through an examination of the term itself. Notable examples include "flor-tile" as a mark for wooden flooring, "The Computer Store" for computer sales services, "cola" for a type of soft drink, "fontina" for a type of cheese, "baby oil" for mineral oil, and "hog" for large motorcycles.

Generic terms need not only be nouns that directly name a product, but also may be adjectives that designate a distinctive characteristic of a genus of products. One well-known example is the Seventh Circuit's decision finding "Light Beer" and "Lite Beer" to be generic names for a type of beer light in body or taste and low in alcoholic and caloric content. *See Miller Brewing Co.*, 561 F.2d at 79-81. Other notable examples of adjectives held to be generic are "matchbox" for a type of toy car, "warehouse" in the

---

4. A suggestive term suggests rather than describes an ingredient or characteristic of the goods and "requires imagination, thought and perception to reach a conclusion as to the nature of the goods." *Abercrombie & Fitch*, 537 F.2d at 11 (citation omitted). An arbitrary term is a common term applied in an unfamiliar way, and a fanciful term normally refers to words invented or coined solely for their use as trademarks.

context of its use as a shoe store, "safari" as applied to the specific types of clothing one would wear on a safari, and "super glue" for certain strong, rapid-setting adhesives.

The second case in which courts have determined a mark to be generic involves matters where a seller establishes trademark rights in a term which a majority of the relevant public then appropriates as the name of a product. In such a case, the mark is said to be a victim of "genericide" and trademark rights may cease. The public's appropriation is set in motion by two, often concurrent processes, namely, (i) the trademark owner's failure to police the mark, resulting in widespread usage by competitors, and (ii) the public's inability to call the product by any other name than the trademarked term. Notable examples include "aspirin" for acetyl salicylic acid, "cellophane" for transparent cellulose sheets and films, "escalator" for a moving stairway, "Murphy Bed" for a bed that folds into a closet; and "Thermos" for vacuum-insulated bottles.

The evidence used to show a term's common usage and understanding by the relevant public is varied. Courts have relied upon evidence such as: (i) proof of widespread use by competitors that has not been contested by the seller; (ii) generic use by the seller himself; (iii) dictionary definitions; (iv) media usage, such as newspaper or magazine articles; and (v) consumer surveys. While none of such evidentiary sources are required for a finding of genericness, it is unlikely that any of them, standing alone, will constitute conclusive proof that the contested mark has been appropriated by the public. . . .

If a plaintiff has a federal trademark registration, it constitutes a strong presumption that the term is not generic, or, if merely descriptive, is accorded secondary meaning by the relevant public.[8] *Liquid Controls Corp. v. Liquid Control Corp.*, 802 F.2d 934, 936 (7th Cir. 1986). However, the presumption is rebuttable; defendant bears the burden of overcoming the presumption. The Seventh Circuit has held that while a contestable federal registration is prima facie evidence that the term is not generic, such presumption "bursts" when the defendant presents sufficient evidence of genericness, e.g., in the evidentiary forms outlined *supra*. In the face of such evidence, the plaintiff may not simply rely upon the registration as sufficient evidence to preclude summary judgment. *Id.* at 938. The Second Circuit has stated that the "presumption of non-genericness" in the case of a product name for which there are allegations of public appropriation is justified by the "commercial protection a developer of innovations deserves." *Murphy Door Bed*, 874 F.2d at 101.

On this summary judgment motion, QVC argues that Horizon's SLINKY mark is invalid because it is generic. The Court must presume the SLINKY mark to be valid because it has been federally registered since 1995. Such registration constitutes prima facie evidence of Horizon's exclusive right to use the term "Slinky" to refer to certain clothing and household products made of acetate and spandex. The burden of production therefore shifts to QVC to provide evidence that the mark is generic. Here, the Court finds, QVC has not adequately met its burden of showing either that

8. If the term is not federally registered, courts have found that once defendant raises the defense of genericness, the plaintiff bears the burden of proving trademark status.

(i) Horizon appropriated a previously generic term for use as a trademark, or that (ii) the term's principal significance among the buying public is a type of material rather than an indication of the source of such material.

Contrary to QVC's contention, neither the current record nor generally accepted English usage enable the Court to conclude that "slinky" was a generic term when associated with women's apparel before Horizon's first use in 1991. Rather, the adjective "slinky" was, and still is, a descriptive term capable of trademark protection upon a showing of sufficient secondary meaning.

The Court agrees with QVC's analysis that "slinky" is a "common *descriptive* name," and that "the term 'slinky' has long been used in connection with fabric to *describe* lush, fluid, and clinging fabrics that have a close fit on the figure." (Memorandum of Law in Support of Motion for Summary Judgment (Def. Mem.) at 2-3.) Evidence from dictionary sources supports this point. In particular, the unabridged *Random House Dictionary of the English Language* 1341 (1983), defined "slinky" especially in relation to women's clothing as "made of soft, often clinging material and fitting the figure closely so as to enhance or flatter one's appearance and movements." The unabridged *Webster's Third New International Dictionary* 2143 (1981) defined "slinky" as used in women's clothing to mean "following the lines of the figure in a graceful flowing manner." ... Further, evidence of media usage prior to Horizon's first use in 1991 also shows that "slinky" described fluid, clinging, and sinuous fabrics. *See, e.g.,* Judy Jeannin, "Donna Karan," *The Record (NJ)*, Nov. 14, 1985, at U08 ("If there is a quibble with the Karan collection it is that few women have the perfectly toned bodies required to wear most of the clothes, and that slinky fabrics allow the outline of the body suits to show through the skirts."); Diane Reischel, "L.A. Designers Go Their Own Ways in Spring '86 Collections, *Los Angeles Times*, Nov. 22, 1985, at 1 (describing the "L.A. look" to include "slinky dress fabrics with a knack for revealing or most kindly disguising the body"); (*see* Declaration of Salvatore Guerriero dated July 13, 2000 ("Guerriero Decl."), Exs. 9-13.)

However, the Court disagrees with QVC that such sources reflect that "slinky" was generic as to certain women's apparel before Horizon first used the term, as opposed to merely descriptive. As the above references demonstrate, the adjective "slinky" describes the characteristics or qualities of several classes of garments which have a sinuous, sleek texture that hugs the body, rather than identifying a specific material or garment. The term does not identify *what* a product is, but rather *how* several products are. The critical distinction may be observed by comparing this case to the Seventh Circuit cases considering the protectibility of the adjectival terms in "light beer" and "tasty salad dressing." In the former case, *Miller Brewing Co.,* 561 F.2d at 80-81, the court found that the term "light," when applied to "beer," had long referred to a class of beer with a light color, flavor, body, alcoholic content, or a combination of these elements. The court therefore found that the plaintiff's proposed trademark, "Light Beer" or "Lite Beer," was generic because such terms clearly identified a particularly genus of alcohol.[10] The court stated that it could no more

_____

10. The court also rejected the defendant's argument that "light beer" was protectible because "light" had not theretofore been used to refer to a "less filling" or "low calorie"

grant the plaintiff an exclusive right to identify its beer as "light" than it could grant an individual such right to call his wine "rose," his whisky "blended," or his bread "white." *Id*. at 81. Such adjectives define what the product is, rather than certain qualities or characteristics of the product. In contrast, the same court determined that the adjective "tasty" was descriptive in reference to salad dressing. The Court stated that unlike "light beer," "tasty salad dressing" is "not a kind, sort, genus, or subcategory of salad dressing.... It is not an adjective which in any way serves to *classify* the noun to which it is attached." *Henri's Food Prods. Co. v. Tasty Snacks, Inc.*, 817 F.2d 1303, 1306 (7th Cir. 1987). Thus, the court found that "tasty" and its phonetic equivalent "tastee" could be protected upon proof of secondary meaning. Similarly, the Court of Customs and Patent Appeals found that the term "custom blended" was descriptive in relation to gasoline, and the Trademark Trial and Appeal Board found "softsoap" to be descriptive of certain forms of soap, *cf. Expoconsul Int'l Inc. v. A/E Sys.*, 755 F. Supp. 1237, 1243 (S.D.N.Y. 1991) (assuming application of tools for carpentry, comparing "carpentry tools," which would be generic, with "durable tools," which would be descriptive).

Like "tasty," "custom blended," or "softsoap," the term "slinky," as it existed before Horizon's use and registration, did not classify the garments to which it was attached, e.g. "slinky evening gown" or "slinky dress," but rather described the visual or textual characteristics of such garments. Horizon adopted the descriptive term in developing its new material consisting of acetate and spandex most likely because its material had similar qualities to garments that had historically been described as slinky. Horizon itself described its product as "a knit fabric using bright acetate and spandex ... [which] allows the fabric, and hence, garments to drape in a very natural manner which is highly flattering to the wearer." (Declaration of Joel Schecter dated Aug. 29, 2000 (Schechter Decl.) ¶ 4.) Accordingly, the Court finds that Horizon's mark is not an historically generic term, but a descriptive one, and that with sufficient secondary meaning,[11] could be protectible as a trademark.

Even if the term "slinky" were not generic prior to Horizon's first use, it would still be generic if the *current* public perception of the term supported such finding. While QVC has presented approximately 60 examples of the term's media usage from 1991 to the present—in magazine and newspaper articles, trade publications, and Internet advertisements—the Court declines to find, on this evidence alone, that the primary significance of "slinky" to the buying public is merely a product, without association with Horizon as the source.

The media sources that QVC cites are frequently ambiguous as to the public perception of the products at issue. First, more than one half of the periodical articles originate from a trade publication, *Women's Wear Daily*. The opinion of trade professionals or fashion experts is not the focus of a test of genericness for a mass consumed product such as the

beer, on the ground that "less filling" meant "light in body" and "low calorie" depends primarily on alcoholic content.

11. The issue of secondary meaning with reference to this case is addressed in note 18, *infra*.

"slinky" garments at issue; rather, the test is the "common usage or understanding by the general public." *Something Old, Something New*, 53 U.S.P.Q.2d at 1720. It is clear from the content of such articles that they are written for a community of individuals that is familiar with the women's apparel industry, not the general buying public. While such public *may* include certain wholesale or retail buyers, these individuals, by themselves, cannot be considered representative of the public perception.

Second, there is significant ambiguity in many of the sources as to the object of the "slinky" designation. In those articles which use "slinky" as an adjective, it is not clear whether the word is used to refer to apparel consisting of acetate and spandex, or merely to describe the sinuous, close-fitting, and flattering nature of such products. (*See* Ex. 16 to Declaration of Salvatore Guerriero dated July 13, 2000 ("Guerriero Decl.") ("slinky fabric of acetate and Lycra")); *Id*. Ex. 30 ("the slinky retro tops, typically made of lycra or spandex, that fit close to the body"); *Id*. Ex. 33 ("The fabric is 'slinky' and gives the garment nice drape."). Further, although they do not refer directly to Horizon, several references to "slinky" are either in quotations or capitalized, which may indicate a reference to the trademarked product as opposed to a commonly descriptive usage. Several of the periodical references also demonstrate this ambiguity. (*See id*. Ex. 18 (the "acetate and Lycra rib with a distressed look the firm calls Slinky")); *Id*. Ex. 41 ("a luxurious acetate spandex material aptly called "slinky fabric"); *Id*. Ex. 43 ("develop a line of large-size fashions featuring, for example 'slinky', a stretch fabric"). Similar ambiguity pervades most of QVC's Internet references and the company's own use of the "Slinky" on its iQVC retail site. (*See, e.g., id*. Ex. 67) ("Slinky is an incredible fabric that looks great on all sizes and body types... Dresses and sportswear made of Slinky are perfect for work, casual, or dressy occasions; *Id*. ("Detailed Index of Nylon Acetate 'Slinky' Lycra")).

Third, contrary to QVC's suggestion, the absence of mention of the trademark holder and the absence of a trademark designation (e.g. ® or TM) in the media is not significant evidence of the generic nature of a mark. The two articles that do mention Horizon by name recognize it as the trademark holder and, apparently in deference to Horizon's rights, capitalize the term "Slinky." While the authors' recognition that "slinky" is "commonly used to describe similar fabrics by other manufacturers" indicates that there may be substantial infringing activity, the acknowledgment of the trademark holder's rights reflects that the buying public is aware of such rights and suggests that "genericide" has not occurred.

Fourth, the characterization of the "slinky" fabric as "new" by sources published over the last five years also indicates that the public perception may not be uniform, and it is too early to tell whether the term has been so adopted by the public as to become generic. (*Id*. Ex. 27 (stating in Nov. 1998 article, What in the world is this new fabric called slinky knit?)); *Id*. Ex. 64 (describing in Mar. 2000 article "a new fabric simply known as 'slinky' fabric").

Fifth, the media sources that QVC provides are the only evidence it presents to show that SLINKY has become generic. QVC's other source of evidence, dictionary definitions, do not indicate that the public associates the term "slinky" with a particular product; as noted *supra*, such definitions merely describe the characteristics of slinky garments, i.e. sinuous, graceful, and close-fitting. Although consumer surveys are not required, they "have become almost de rigueur in litigation over genericness." McCarthy's §12:14 at 12-31; *Schering Corp. v. Pfizer Inc.*, 189 F.3d 218, 225 (2d Cir. 1999) (noting that consumer surveys are "routinely employed" in testing the genericness of a mark); *cf. Am. Thermos Prods. Co.*, 207 F. Supp. 9 (addressing the "Thermos Survey" which asks participants how they would identify a particular product given that it performs certain functions, in an effort to identify if the name of the product is generic); *E.I. DuPont de Nemours and Co. v. Yoshida Int'l, Inc.*, 393 F. Supp. 502 (E.D.N.Y. 1975) (addressing a "Teflon Survey" in which participants are given a series of names and asked whether those names are brand names or common names, in an effort to discern how the public perceives each name). In a case such as the instant one, where the term at issue is not a household name, the Court finds that, on summary judgment, a consumer survey would be particularly helpful in divining what the principal significance of "slinky" is to the consuming public.

The record reflects that Horizon's "Slinky" fabric has become a commercial success, both to Horizon and to other fabric manufacturers. Several other mills are currently manufacturing similar fabrics and selling them on the market under the "slinky" designation. It also appears, from the evidence submitted by QVC, that Horizon's mark has been adopted by an undefined percentage of the buying public as a generic term for fabrics or women's apparel consisting of acetate and spandex, or like materials. Horizon itself concedes that its fabric has been "copied in some instances, along with its brand name," and the record reflects that Horizon has only managed to defend its mark against misuse with respect to a small number of offenders. There are clear policy considerations militating in favor of granting summary judgment, namely, preventing Horizon from gaining an effective monopoly by preventing use of the "slinky" term by its competitors, who must be able to describe the genus of their fabrics. However, this remedy can be harsh on a business, because "it places a penalty on the manufacturer who has made skillful use of advertising and has popularized his product." *King-Seeley*, 321 F.2d at 581. As discussed *supra*, the test for classifying a term as generic is the primary significance of that term to the buying public. Given the fact that the SLINKY mark is registered, QVC's failure to produce evidence sufficient to demonstrate how the public truly perceives the term "slinky" leaves genuine issues of material fact as to each of Horizon's claims. Accordingly, because the Court finds that a genuine issue of material fact exists as to whether "slinky" has become generic, and therefore, whether it is still entitled to protection as a trademark upon a showing of secondary meaning,[18] QVC's motion for summary judgment must be denied.

For the foregoing reasons, QVC's motion for summary judgment is denied.

18. There are issues of fact which preclude the Court from making a finding as to secondary meaning on this summary judgment motion. The record is sparse on evidence relating to the existence of secondary meaning in SLINKY. QVC did not address the issue in its motion papers, and Horizon, which ultimately has the burden of proving secondary meaning, only makes conclusory statements thereto in its papers.

# Comments

*1. Use of a "Distinctive" Mark: The Primary Significance Test.* The classification of a trademark relies on the primary significance test. To be protectible, the primary significance of a term in the minds of the consuming public must be the producer rather than the product. A term may have a dual function, with some significance as an indication of the category of goods or services into which a product or service falls, but it is generic only if the principal significance of the word is the category. The primary significance of "shredded wheat" and "thermos" is the category of goods, despite the fact that, for a time, there was only one producer of shredded wheat cereal and of thermoses. The "category of goods" approach is sometimes described as the "genus-species test," where the category of goods (shredded wheat cereals) is the genus, while the product of a particular manufacturer (Nabisco) is the species. If Kellogg Company also sells these cereal biscuits, its mark (MINI WHEATS) is also the species of the genus "shredded wheat."

A mark is descriptive if the primary significance of the term is the characteristic or quality of the product or service. The primary significance of RICH N CHIPS used in association with chocolate chip cookies and 5 MINUTE used in association with glue may be descriptive. Consumers are likely to believe that the descriptive term is simply giving information about the product rather than the source.

The primary significance test applies to terms that were generic before a supplier's adoption of the term, such as HOAGIE used in association with a sandwich alternatively named a "grinder" or "submarine" sandwich, or became generic as a result of the producer's (often the inventor's) extensive and exclusive use, such as ELEVATOR, ESCALATOR, SHREADED WHEAT, and THERMOS, which were once marks. It is easy to observe modern examples of producers striving to prevent "genericide," having their marks become generic, as in the case of Daimler/Chrysler's JEEP mark and Xerox Corporation's efforts to encourage people to use the verb "to photocopy" rather than "to Xerox." To determine whether JEEP and XEROX have suffered from genericide, consider the tests and types of evidence used in *Horizon Mills*. A recent *New York Times* article reported that the website operated by the provider of the TiVo digital recording device and service instructs that "trademarks are always proper adjectives" and "always singular." The website states that it is incorrect to say "I want two TiVos." It is correct to say "I want two TiVo DVRs." Despite their instructions, TiVo.com also states "TiVo automatically finds and digitally records up to 140 hours of programming you want — your favorite show, every Coppola movie, home improvement programs, Dora cartoons, whatever you choose — all while you're out living life." Is TiVo's own use leading to genericide?

*2. Generic Nouns and Adjectives.* To acquire trademark rights, a supplier must choose a distinctive mark as its source indicator. Some marks, however, are inherently incapable of being distinctive. Generic nouns, such as "Bed" or "Beer," name the product and customers looking at such a mark naturally think of the category of products to which that product belongs rather than thinking that the mark indicates a particular supplier. Similarly, generic adjectives, such as those used in the terms "*Twin* Bed" or "*Light* Beer," name subcategories of products and indicate the genus of the product while two members of the species of light beer are "BUD LIGHT" and "MILLER LITE." Generic nouns and adjectives are inherently incapable of being distinctive and cannot obtain trademark protection. While "light" or "lite" may be unprotectible as marks, BUD LIGHT and MILLER LITE are protectible because of the addition of the source-indicating words.

**3. *Advantages of Registration: Burdens of Proof.*** A registered mark, such as SLINKY, has a strong presumption that it is not generic and, if merely descriptive, has secondary meaning. A defendant in an infringement action has the burden of overcoming this presumption with prima facie evidence to the contrary. Sufficient evidence bursts the presumption and compels the mark owner to respond with contrary evidence or lose the registration. Given these procedural rules, what evidence supported the court's denial of the defendant's motion for summary judgment?

If Horizon had not registered SLINKY, Horizon would have had the burden of showing it was not generic. In *Horizon Mills*, the defendant, who had the burden of proof on the "generic" issue, moved for summary judgment on the ground that the mark was generic. Imagine that the situation was reversed because Horizon had not registered the mark. Given the evidence in *Horizon Mills*, should a motion by Horizon for summary judgment on the ground that SLINKY was not generic as a matter of law be granted? *[handwritten: if not registered burden on p]*

**4. *Commercial Impression and the Importance of Context.*** For the purpose of determining whether a term is generic or descriptive, consumers' understanding of terms is based on the commercial impression made by the term. Context and surrounding circumstances are critical to determining the commercial impression. A term may be generic in some contexts, but not in others. IVORY would be generic when used to describe elephant tusks but not soap. BEERMAN may be a generic name for beer vendors at ball games, but arbitrary when used in connection with sales of clothing. Consumers are likely to take the same impression from a misspelled word, such as SWIM SKOOL (used in association with devices to aid those learning to swim) as if "school" were properly spelled.

Similarly, the commercial impression of foreign words is their English translation if a substantial portion of consumers would be familiar with the translation. This rule is referred to as the doctrine of foreign equivalents. *Enrique Bernat F., S.A. v. Guadalajara, Inc.*, 210 F.3d 439 (5th Cir. 2000), involved an infringement claim brought by the manufacturer of ice-cream flavored lollipops bearing the CHUPA CHUPS trademark against a competitor using the CHUPA GURTS trademark for frozen yogurt-flavored cones. The court observed that "chupa" is a generic (idiomatic) Spanish word for lollipop in Mexico—literally "to lick" but understood as lollipop when used as a noun. Because a substantial portion of consumers would understand that meaning, the plaintiff manufacturer could make no claim to the word "chupa" alone and the infringement analysis must consider the commercial impression of the entire mark when classifying it. Context and commercial impression are more important, however, than simple rules of translation. In the case of In re Bruckner Enterprises Corp., 6 U.S.P.Q.2d 1316 (Trademark Tr. and App. Bd. 1987), the Trademark Trial and Appeals Board distinguished DOVE and PALOMA used in connection with furnaces and gas heaters on the grounds that "paloma" in Spanish means "dove" but also "pigeon" and the terms were different in sight and sound, thereby leaving a different commercial impression. More recently, the Court of Appeals for the Federal Circuit faulted the Trademark Trial and Appeals Board for ruling that consumers would translate "Veuve" as "widow," the French translation. Veuve Clicquot, user of the VEUVE CLICQUOT and THE WIDOW marks, opposed registration by Palm Bay Imports of the VEUVE ROYALE mark. While affirming that confusion was likely with the VEUVE CLICQUOT mark, the court held that it was unlikely that the ordinary American purchaser would stop and translate "veuve" into its English equivalent so confusion with THE WIDOW was unlikely. See Palm Bay Imports Inc. v. Veuve Clicquot Ponsardin Maison Fondee en 1772, 396 F.3d 1369 (Fed. Cir. 2005).

## Problem

**2-1.** The court in *Horizon Mills* referred to "softsoap" as a term that is descriptive rather than generic, in its use in connection with liquid hand soap in a pump-type dispenser. The examining attorney handling the application for registration of the mark considered conflicting evidence. On one hand, instead of being a soft solid, the product is liquid and the term "softsoap" has the additional positive connotation of gentleness, which is desirable for soap. Competitors of the applicant all referred to their products as "liquid soap." On the other hand, the examiner cited a dozen references where the term "soft soap" is a recognized term in the soap industry referring to an industrial type of soap used in the manufacturing of shampoos and shaving cream, and for cleaning floors, automobiles, and textiles. Applying the primary significance test to this term, is "softsoap" generic or descriptive? See In re Minnetonka Inc., 3 U.S.P.Q.2d 1711 (TTAB 1987).

## BRISTOL-MYERS SQUIBB CO. v. McNEIL-P.P.C., INC.

### 973 F.2d 1033 (2d Cir. 1992)

MESKILL, Chief Judge.

This is an appeal from a preliminary injunction entered in the United States District Court for the Eastern District of New York, Spatt, J., in an action brought under section 43(a) of the Lanham Act. [Omitted from this opinion is an appeal by McNeil from a preliminary injunction preventing McNeil from marketing its product in packaging, "trade dress" resembling that of Bristol-Myers.] [B]efore us is a cross-appeal by Bristol-Myers Squibb Company (Bristol) from the denial of preliminary injunctive relief preventing McNeil from using the term "PM" in connection with a combination analgesic/sleep aid....

Bristol is a major pharmaceutical company that produces and markets "Excedrin," a nationally known over-the-counter analgesic pain reliever. Since 1968 Bristol has manufactured and distributed "Excedrin PM," a product that combines an analgesic with a sleep aid. . . .

McNeil is also a major pharmaceutical company. Among McNeil's products is "Tylenol," which, like "Excedrin," is a nationally famous over-the-counter analgesic. In 1991 McNeil introduced "Tylenol PM," which, like "Excedrin PM," is a combination analgesic/sleep aid. Although there are slight differences in the composition of the two products, it is undisputed that those differences are not material and that the two products are functionally interchangeable. Like "Excedrin PM," "Tylenol PM" comes in two forms: tablet and caplet. . . .

Neither the "PM" designator nor the "Excedrin PM" trade dress is a registered trademark. Bristol, therefore, relies on that part of the Lanham Act that addresses unregistered marks. Section 43(a) of the Lanham Act prohibits any person from using

> in connection with any goods . . . or any container for goods, . . . any word, term, name, symbol, or device, or any combination thereof . . . which . . . is likely to cause confusion, or to cause mistake, or to deceive . . . as to the origin, sponsorship, or approval of his or her goods . . . by another person.

15 U.S.C. §1125(a). "[I]t is common ground that §43(a) protects qualifying unregistered trademarks and that the general principles qualifying a mark for registration under §2 of the Lanham Act are for the most part applicable in determining whether an unregistered mark is entitled to protection under §43(a)." *Two Pesos, Inc. v. Taco Cabana, Inc.*, 505 U.S. 763, ___, 112 S. Ct. 2753, 2757 (1992). As the words of the statute indicate, the central inquiry is whether the use of a marking is likely to cause consumer confusion.

. . . Bristol claims that the use by McNeil of the term "PM" in connection with its combination analgesic/sleep aid is likely to cause confusion as to the source, sponsorship or approval of "Tylenol PM." . . .

Before we will address whether an allegedly infringing mark is likely to cause consumer confusion, the plaintiff must show that its trademark or trade dress is of the type that deserves protection under section 43(a). . . .

In making the preliminary inquiry into whether a particular mark is eligible for protection under section 43(a), we have established several categories into which we classify various marks. "Arrayed in an ascending order which roughly reflects their eligibility to trademark status and the degree of protection accorded, these classes are (1) generic, (2) descriptive, (3) suggestive, and (4) arbitrary or fanciful." *Abercrombie & Fitch Co. v. Hunting World*, 537 F.2d 4, 9 (2d Cir. 1976). Suggestive, arbitrary and fanciful marks, "because their intrinsic nature serves to identify a particular source of a product, are deemed inherently distinctive and are entitled to protection." *Two Pesos*, 505 U.S. 763, 112 S. Ct. at 2757. Generic marks are never entitled to protection, while a descriptive mark is eligible for protection "if it 'has become distinctive of the [producer's] goods in commerce.' This acquired distinctiveness is generally called 'secondary meaning.'" *Id.* 505 U.S. at ___, 112 S. Ct. at 2757 (citations omitted). . . .

The district court classified the "PM" mark as descriptive. Bristol argues that the mark is suggestive. Neither party claims that the mark is generic, arbitrary or fanciful. The question in this case, therefore, is whether "PM," when affixed to an analgesic trade name, is descriptive or suggestive of the product, a combination analgesic/sleep aid.

A descriptive mark is one that "'forthwith conveys an immediate idea of the ingredients, qualities or characteristics of the goods.'" *Abercrombie & Fitch*, 537 F.2d at 11 (citation omitted). "[A] term can be descriptive in two ways. It can literally describe the product, or it can describe the purpose or utility of the product." *20th Century Wear v. Sanmark-Stardust*, 747 F.2d 81, 88 (2d Cir.1984), *cert. denied*, 470 U.S. 1052, 105 S.Ct. 1755, 84 L. Ed. 2d 818 (1985). A term is suggestive "'if it requires imagination, thought and perception to reach a conclusion as to the nature of goods.'" *Abercrombie & Fitch*, 537 F.2d at 11 (citation omitted).

Although the line between descriptive and suggestive may be difficult to discern, the consequence of the classification is important. A descriptive term is subject to protection under section 43(a) only if the proponent of protection demonstrates that, in addition to the ordinary common meaning of the word or words, the term has acquired a secondary meaning in its particular market—that the consuming public primarily associates the term with a particular source. The public presumably will not be confused by a descriptive term, but if the proponent of protection can show that the descriptive term is primarily associated with a single producer, a sufficient question is raised to justify further inquiry into the likelihood of confusion. In contrast, if its mark is suggestive a plaintiff need not prove such secondary meaning in order to qualify for trademark protection.

In this case, the "PM" acts as a modifier to the analgesic brand name. Both "Tylenol" and "Excedrin" are well known brand names for analgesics; the "PM" modifies each to show that they are a particular type of analgesic. "PM," usually abbreviated "p.m." or "P.M." (for "post meridiem"), is a common term that refers to the period of time between noon and midnight. It is often associated with the time when most people go to sleep.

As used here, "PM" does not literally describe the presence of a sleep aid in the product. The "PM" refers to the purpose or utility of the product— it is an analgesic that should be used at night. The issue, therefore, is whether the connection between "PM" and a nighttime sleep aid is direct enough that the term may be categorized as descriptive or whether the connection is more indirect, requiring categorization as suggestive.

Bristol argues that "PM" is suggestive because a consumer must engage in a multi-step analysis before coming to the conclusion that it denotes the presence of a sleep aid in the analgesic. Bristol asserts that the consumer first must eliminate possible alternate meanings for "PM"—*e.g.*, "Pre-Menstrual" or "Pain Medication"—before arriving at "Post Meridiem." Next, Bristol argues, the consumer must make a leap from all the post meridiem hours to those at night, and a further intellectual leap from nighttime to sleeping.

The magistrate judge found that several other over-the-counter products are designated as nighttime products by the use of some close variant of "PM." The magistrate judge held in that context that "[t]he direct connotation of 'PM' is nighttime. There is *no* 'multi-stage reasoning process' that a consumer must indulge in to associate the term 'PM' with a nighttime product."

We cannot say that the district court's adoption of this finding was clearly erroneous. The focus in categorizing a mark is on how the words are used in context rather than their meaning in the abstract. One of the leading commentators has offered the following example to demonstrate the context-dependent nature of the classification: "[T]he word 'apple' would be arbitrary when used on personal computers, suggestive when used in 'Apple-A-Day' on vitamin tablets, descriptive when used in 'Tomapple' for combination tomato-apple juice and generic when used on apples." 1 J.T. McCarthy, Trademarks and Unfair Competition §11:22, at 498-99 (2d ed. 1984). There was sufficient evidence before the magistrate judge to support the finding that several nighttime products were sold using some variant of "PM." Given that context, the conclusion that "PM" describes rather than suggests a nighttime product was not clearly erroneous. Once the consumer arrives at an awareness that the product is useful at nighttime, the "purpose or utility" of the product has been conveyed, even though the consumer is not aware of why the product is useful at night. Therefore, the consumer need not conclude that the analgesic contains a sleep aid.

Given the deferential standard of review, and the fact that this matter is before us at the preliminary injunction stage, we will not disturb the district court's finding that "PM" is descriptive.

Because "PM" is a descriptive term it is not entitled to trademark protection unless Bristol demonstrates secondary meaning. The district court found that Bristol had not established that the "PM" designator had acquired secondary meaning. We agree with the district court.

"To establish secondary meaning, a manufacturer must show that, in the minds of the public, the primary significance of a product feature or term is to identify the source of the product rather than the product itself." *Inwood Laboratories v. Ives Laboratories*, 456 U.S. 844, 851 n. 11 (1982). Secondary meaning is an essentially factual determination, proof of which "'entails vigorous evidentiary requirements.'" *Thompson Medical Co. v. Pfizer, Inc.*, 753 F.2d 208, 217 (2d Cir. 1985). We will reverse the district court's determination that a term has not acquired secondary meaning only if that determination is clearly erroneous.

Among the factors that we have found relevant to this inquiry in the past are advertising expenditures, consumer studies, sales success, unsolicited media coverage, attempts to plagiarize and length and exclusivity of use. There are undoubtedly other types of evidence that would also be relevant to a claim of secondary meaning. The fundamental question, however, is whether "'the *primary* significance of the term in the minds of the consuming public is not the product but the producer.'" *Centaur Communications, Ltd. v. A/S/M Communications*, 830 F.2d 1217, 1221 (2d Cir. 1987).

"The existence of secondary meaning is a question of fact with the burden of proof on the party claiming exclusive rights in the designation." *PaperCutter, Inc. v. Fay's Drug Co.*, 900 F.2d 558, 564 (2d Cir. 1990). The district court found that Bristol had not presented sufficient evidence that consumers recognized the source of "Excedrin PM" by the "PM" designator and that there was no evidence that Bristol had ever marketed the product as "PM."

Bristol suggests two grounds in support of its contention that the district court's finding that the "PM" mark had not acquired secondary meaning was clearly erroneous. First, Bristol argues that McNeil's intentional copying of its mark is indicative of secondary meaning. Although imitative intent can help support a finding of secondary meaning, it does not necessarily mandate one. Therefore, we believe that, even assuming McNeil's imitative intent, the district court was not bound to find that the "PM" designator had acquired secondary meaning.

Second, Bristol argues that the fact that each "Excedrin PM" tablet is imprinted with "PM" shows that the consuming public must associate "PM" with Bristol. However, "[a]lthough the mark owner strives to create a secondary meaning for its product, it is the consuming public which, in effect, determines whether that effort has succeeded." *Centaur Communications*, 830 F.2d at 1221. The mere fact that Bristol places the name "PM" on its tablets does not persuade us that the consuming public associates that term with Bristol. Moreover, on the larger caplet version of the product, Bristol placed the entire "Excedrin PM" mark.

The district court was not clearly erroneous in classifying "PM" as a descriptive term in these circumstances. Because "PM" had not become primarily associated with a single producer in these circumstances, "PM" as used by Bristol is not by itself subject to protection under the Lanham Act. The district court therefore properly declined to enjoin McNeil from using the "PM" designator in connection with its combination analgesic/sleep aid. . . .

## Comments

1. *The Descriptive/Suggestive Distinction*. The opinion in *Bristol-Myers* identifies several approaches to determining whether a mark is descriptive or suggestive: How much imagination is required to infer what the product is or is like, keeping in mind that buyers do not spend much time thinking; does the mark directly convey an unequivocal idea about characteristic, function, quality, or ingredient of the product or service to a reasonably informed buyer? Or is some reflection or multistage reasoning required? Even if the mark tells something about the good or service, is it equally likely to conjure up some other, purely arbitrary connotation? Applying these tests, a court found the mark SUGAR & SPICE used in connection with baked goods suggestive even though the terms "sugar" and "spice" were descriptive. What would account for that classification? See *In re Colonial Stores, Inc.*, 394 F.2d 549 (C.C.P.A. 1969).

2. *Implication of the Descriptive/Suggestive Decision: Secondary Meaning*. A term that is descriptive is registrable only if the applicant can prove secondary meaning. The primary significance test used for the generic/descriptive distinction also applies here. The applicant has the burden of proving that the primary significance of the term is source-indicating rather than descriptive. Secondary meaning may be shown by

amount and manner of advertising, consumer studies, direct consumer testimony, sales success, unsolicited media coverage, established place in the market, attempts to plagiarize, and length and exclusivity of use. It is *success* in establishing the source-indicating power of a term rather than simply expenditures, so consumer surveys are particularly helpful. Once a mark is registered as a trademark, it is presumed to be valid and a person challenging the validity of the mark has the burden of proving that it is generic or descriptive.

3. *Fanciful and Arbitrary Marks*. The court in *Bristol-Myers* identified APPLE as an arbitrary mark when used in connection with computers. Apple is a real word that in other contexts might be suggestive, descriptive, or generic. EXXON, when used in connection with petroleum products, is a fanciful name. It is a made-up word and has no independent meaning in any context. Another example of a fanciful mark is the graphic mark for Kellogg's Froot Loops cereal, Toucan Sam. *See Kellogg Co. v. Toucan Golf, Inc.*, 337 F.3d 616 (6th Cir. 2003).

4. *Classification and Strength*. The classification of a term as generic, descriptive, suggestive, fanciful, or arbitrary is sufficient for the purpose of registration, but does not end the inquiry in an infringement case. Suggestive marks, while registerable without secondary meaning, do not get as much protection as arbitrary or fanciful marks. The classifications give a general indication of how much protection a mark deserves, but a mark may be only weakly suggestive or have barely enough evidence of secondary meaning. The weaker the mark, the more evidence courts require to prove that an alleged infringer's mark causes confusion. A court might require proof that confusion actually occurred for a descriptive mark, but might accept evidence that confusion was likely to occur for a fanciful mark.

There is also more to the strength of a mark than simply its classification. In *Taj Mahal Enterprises, Ltd. v. Trump*, 745 F. Supp. 240 (D.N.J. 1990), the owner of the TAJ MAHAL, a small Indian restaurant in the DuPont Circle area of Washington, D.C. sued Donald Trump and the TRUMP TAJ MAHAL CASINO AND RESORT in Atlantic City, New Jersey for service mark infringement. The court found that the plaintiff's registered TAJ MAHAL mark in connection with an Indian restaurant was suggestive because it takes some imagination to link those services to the name of a palatial crypt located in India, and the term brings to mind grandeur and opulence and is evocative of an exotic, Eastern flavor. The court held that the mark was weak, however, because there are few terms that "engender the same images with the same panache." Moreover, the term TAJ MAHAL had been used by 70 other restaurants in the United States and there were currently at least 24 restaurants by that name including two in New Jersey.

The frequency of use by others was also a factor in determining the strength of a mark in *Echo Drain v. Newsted*, 68 U.S.P.Q. 1203 (D. Cal. 2003). A Texas progressive funk and groove bank with elements of heavy metal called itself ECHO DRAIN. It sued Jason Newsted, former Metallica member, and other members of a pop rock band calling itself ECHOBRAIN. The court held that the mark was descriptive or suggestive at best, in part because a member of the Echo Drain band testified that the name was intended to convey the "image of swirling sounds, of echoing the various styles of music we create, and maybe a drain that kind of pulls it all together as those echoed sounds [sic, "sounds echoed"?] our influences, and draining it into water, and as a band, as a whole, that we represent — that those sounds represent the defining theme, or the Echo Drain name defines that particular art that we create." As a term, the mark was considered weak because it was undisputed that more than 500 other music groups used the term "echo" in their names, album titles, and song titles. Thirteen bands in Texas alone had "echo" in their names, and Echo Drain even performed live with another band named "Echojar."

As the previous examples illustrate, the key is the ability of a mark to distinguish its source. In 1994, Kendall-Jackson Winery, maker of high-quality, mid-priced varietal wines produced the best-selling chardonnay in the United States. Its label featured a downward-pointing, stylized grapple leaf design. Gallo, the largest wine producer in the world, had a reputation for producing lower-priced, nonpremium wines, decided to produce a premium wine to compete with Kendall-Jackson and began marketing a wine in a bottle featuring a label with a prominent downward-pointing, stylized grape leaf design. Kendall-Jackson sued for infringement of its trade dress, which is packaging that indicates a source. The court held that the grape leaf design would ordinarily be suggestive because one has to go through two or three steps to associate the leaf with the product — a grape leaf comes from a grape vine, which has grapes from which wine is produced. In this case, however, wine bottlers have long used grape leaves to decorate their labels so the emblem has become generic; it has lost its power to differentiate brands. While a stylized version of a grape leaf may be protected if it is distinctive, there was no copying of the distinctive features of Kendall-Jackson's leaf. Thus Gallo was entitled to summary judgment as a matter of law. The opinion does not mention that liquor stores frequently

displayed Gallo's TURNING LEAF chardonnay next to the Kendall-Jackson product and that Gallo's TURNING LEAF became the second best-selling chardonnay in the United States. *See Kendall-Jackson Winery, LTD v. E&J Gallo Winery*, 150 F.3d 1042 (1998).

# Problems

**2-2**. The plaintiff owns a federally registered trademark for the domain name 555-1212.com for use in connection with the service of "providing databases featuring telephone and directory information accessible via electronic communication networks." The defendant has reserved the domain name 5551212.com for Internet directory assistance services through one of the companies that is licensed by ICANN, a private, non-profit, public-benefit corporation established by the U.S. government to administer the Internet domain name system. The plaintiff sued for infringement. Both parties seek summary judgment. Defendant claims the mark is either generic or descriptive. There is no evidence of secondary meaning. Should either party be granted summary judgment? *See 555-1212.COM, Inc. v. Communication House International, Inc.*, 157 F. Supp. 2d 1084 (D. Cal. 2001). *No*

**2-3**. Applying the tests developed in this section, classify the following trademarks in the context of the product listed:

King Size — clothing for men
Arrow — liquor
Skinvisible — transparent
    medical tape
Playboy — men's magazine
Holiday Inn — motel
Coppertone — suntan lotion
Ice Cream — chewing gum

Chap Stick — lip balm in stick form
Yellow Pages — telephone directory
Camel — cigarettes
Polaroid — photographic equip-
    ment
Kodak — film
Jujubes — gummy candy
Chicken of the Sea — canned tuna

**2-4**. In *Professional Sound Service, Inc. v. Guzzi*, 349 F. Supp. 2d 722 (S.D.N.Y. 2004), PSS, a company engaged in supply and repair of on-location sound recording equipment, claimed that it used the capital letter "S" as a trademark to identify itself as the source of its products. It placed the "S" on invoices, documents accompanying shipments, and on the outsides of packages it sells in a leading position in front of catalog numbers for parts. For instance, a product manufactured by a company called Lectrosonics, with a catalog number of 0211, is resold by PSS with the code "SLE0211." The letter "S" is either typed in the same basic font as the rest of the invoice or handwritten by whichever employee wrote up the order form. What classification of mark is the "S"? Is it distinctive?

### THEORETICAL PERSPECTIVE
## Justifications For Varying Degrees of Protection of Marks

Judge Leval, justifying strong protection of the VIRGIN mark used in connection with retail services in VIRGIN MEGASTORES, which included music recordings, computer games, books, and luggage, offered the following justification for awarding different degrees of protection to different kinds of marks:

> [T]he law accords broad, muscular protection to marks that are arbitrary or fanciful in relation to the products on which they are used, and lesser protection, or no protection at all, to marks consisting of words that identify or describe the goods or their attributes. The reasons for the distinction arise from two aspects of market efficiency. The paramount objective of the trademark law is to avoid confusion in the marketplace. The purpose for which the trademark law accords merchants the exclusive right to the use of a name or symbol in their area or commerce is *identification*, so that the merchants can establish goodwill for their goods based on past satisfactory performance, and the consuming public can rely on a mark as a guarantee that the goods or services so marked come from the merchant who has been found to be satisfactory in the past. At the same time, efficiency and the public interest require that every merchant trading in a class of goods be permitted to refer to the goods by their name, and to make claims about their quality. Thus, a merchant who sells pencils under the trademark *Pencil* or *Clear Mark*, for example, and seeks to exclude other sellers of pencils from using those words in their trade, is seeking an advantage the trademark law does not intend to offer. To grant such exclusivity would deprive the consuming public of the useful market information it receives where every seller of pencils is free to call them pencils. The trademark right does not protect the exclusive right to an advertising message — only the exclusive right to an identifier, to protect against confusion in the marketplace. Thus, as a matter of policy, the trademark law accords broader protection to marks that serve exclusively as identifiers and lesser protection where a grant of exclusiveness would tend to diminish the access of others to the full range of discourse relating to their goods.

*Virgin Enterprises Ltd. v. NAWAB*, 335 F.3d 141 (2d Cir. 2003).

## 2. Trade Dress and Product Design

Instead of words, names, or symbols, some providers of goods and services package or design their products in ways that attract consumers' attention and indicate to consumers that the product comes from a unique source. Gateway Computers uses packaging with the pattern of a Holstein cow as its trade dress and people associate that pattern, when used in connection with computers, as an indication that Gateway is the source of the computer. United Parcel Service uses a particular shade of brown on its trucks and uniforms, hoping that consumers will associate that brown with its services. Like trademarks and service marks, trade dress is potentially protectible. The first case in this section, *Two Pesos, Inc. v. Taco Cabana, Inc.*, involves the "packaging" of a restaurant, including the colors and themes used in its presentation to the public. The second case, *Wal-Mart Stores, Inc. v. Samara Brothers, Inc.*, relates to product design, which is also potentially protectible. The example of product design the plaintiff is trying to protect in *Wal-Mart Stores* is a seersucker outfit for children decorated with cute appliques. This section explores how the distinctiveness of trade dress and product design is analyzed.

## TWO PESOS, INC. v. TACO CABANA, INC.
### 505 U.S. 763 (1992)

Justice WHITE.

The issue in this case is whether the trade dress of a restaurant may be protected under §43(a) of the Trademark Act of 1946 (Lanham Act), based on a finding of inherent distinctiveness, without proof that the trade dress has secondary meaning.

Respondent Taco Cabana, Inc., operates a chain of fast-food restaurants in Texas. The restaurants serve Mexican food. The first Taco Cabana restaurant was opened in San Antonio in September 1978, and five more restaurants had been opened in San Antonio by 1985. Taco Cabana describes its Mexican trade dress as

> a festive eating atmosphere having interior dining and patio areas decorated with artifacts, bright colors, paintings and murals. The patio includes interior and exterior areas with the interior patio capable of being sealed off from the outside patio by overhead garage doors. The stepped exterior of the building is a festive and vivid color scheme using top border paint and neon stripes. Bright awnings and umbrellas continue the theme. 932 F.2d 1113, 1117 (CA5 1991).

In December 1985, a Two Pesos, Inc., restaurant was opened in Houston. Two Pesos adopted a motif very similar to the foregoing description of Taco Cabana's trade dress. Two Pesos restaurants expanded rapidly in Houston and other markets, but did not enter San Antonio. In 1986, Taco Cabana entered the Houston and Austin markets and expanded into other Texas cities, including Dallas and El Paso where Two Pesos was also doing business.

In 1987, Taco Cabana sued Two Pesos in the United States District Court for the Southern District of Texas for trade dress infringement under §43(a) of the Lanham Act, 15 U.S.C. §1125(a) (1982 ed.), and for theft of trade secrets under Texas common law. The case was tried to a jury, which was instructed to return its verdict in the form of answers to five questions propounded by the trial judge. The jury's answers were: Taco Cabana has a trade dress; taken as a whole, the trade dress is nonfunctional; the trade dress is inherently distinctive; the trade dress has not acquired a secondary meaning in the Texas market; and the alleged infringement creates a likelihood of confusion on the part of ordinary customers as to the source or association of the restaurant's goods or services. Because, as the jury was told, Taco Cabana's trade dress was protected if it either was inherently distinctive or had acquired a secondary meaning, judgment was entered awarding damages to Taco Cabana. In the course of calculating damages, the trial court held that Two Pesos had intentionally and deliberately infringed Taco Cabana's trade dress.

The Court of Appeals ruled that the instructions adequately stated the applicable law and that the evidence supported the jury's findings. In particular, the Court of Appeals rejected petitioner's argument that a finding of no secondary meaning contradicted a finding of inherent distinctiveness. . . .

The Lanham Act was intended to make "actionable the deceptive and misleading use of marks" and "to protect persons engaged in . . . commerce against unfair competition." §45, 15 U.S.C. §1127. Section 43(a) "prohibits a broader range of practices than does §32," which applies to registered marks, *Inwood Laboratories, Inc. v. Ives Laboratories, Inc.*, 456 U.S. 844, 858 (1982), but it is common ground that §43(a) protects qualifying unregistered trademarks and that the general principles qualifying a mark for registration under §2 of the Lanham Act are for the most part applicable in determining whether an unregistered mark is entitled to protection under §43(a).

A trademark is defined in 15 U.S.C. §1127 as including "any word, name, symbol, or device or any combination thereof" used by any person "to identify and distinguish his or her goods, including a unique product, from those manufactured or sold by others and to indicate the source of the goods, even if that source is unknown." In order to be registered, a mark must be capable of distinguishing the applicant's goods from those of others. §1052. Marks are often classified in categories of generally increasing distinctiveness; following the classic formulation set out by Judge Friendly, they may be (1) generic; (2) descriptive; (3) suggestive; (4) arbitrary; or (5) fanciful. See *Abercrombie & Fitch Co. v. Hunting World, Inc.*, 537 F.2d 4, 9 (CA2 1976). The Court of Appeals followed this classification and petitioner accepts it. Brief for Petitioner 11-15. The latter three categories of marks, because their intrinsic nature serves to identify a particular source of a product, are deemed inherently distinctive and are entitled to protection. In contrast, generic marks — those that "refe[r] to the genus of which the particular product is a species," *Park 'N Fly, Inc. v. Dollar Park & Fly, Inc.*, 469 U.S. 189, 194 (1985), citing *Abercrombie & Fitch, supra*, at 9 — are not registrable as trademarks. . . .

The general rule regarding distinctiveness is clear: An identifying mark is distinctive and capable of being protected if it *either* (1) is inherently distinctive *or* (2) has acquired distinctiveness through secondary meaning. It is also clear that eligibility for protection under §43(a) depends on non-functionality. It is, of course, also undisputed that liability under §43(a) requires proof of the likelihood of confusion. . . .

Petitioner argues that the jury's finding that the trade dress has not acquired a secondary meaning shows conclusively that the trade dress is not inherently distinctive. The Court of Appeals' disposition of this issue was sound:

Two Pesos' argument—that the jury finding of inherent distinctiveness contradicts its finding of no secondary meaning in the Texas market—ignores the law in this circuit. While the necessarily imperfect (and often prohibitively difficult) methods for assessing secondary meaning address the empirical question of current consumer association, the legal recognition of an inherently distinctive trademark or trade dress acknowledges the owner's legitimate proprietary interest in its unique and valuable informational device, regardless of whether substantial consumer association yet bestows the additional empirical protection of secondary meaning. 932 F.2d, at 1120, n. 7.

Although petitioner makes the above argument, it appears to concede elsewhere in its brief that it is possible for a trade dress, even a restaurant trade dress, to be inherently distinctive and thus eligible for protection under §43(a). Recognizing that a general requirement of secondary meaning imposes "an unfair prospect of theft [or] financial loss" on the developer of fanciful or arbitrary trade dress at the outset of its use, petitioner suggests that such trade dress should receive limited protection without proof of secondary meaning. Petitioner argues that such protection should be only temporary and subject to defeasance when over time the dress has failed to acquire a secondary meaning. This approach is also vulnerable for the reasons given by the Court of Appeals. If temporary protection is available from the earliest use of the trade dress, it must be because it is neither functional nor descriptive, but an inherently distinctive dress that is capable of identifying a particular source of the product. Such a trade dress, or mark, is not subject to copying by concerns that have an equal opportunity to choose their own inherently distinctive trade dress. To terminate protection for failure to gain secondary meaning over some unspecified time could not be based on the failure of the dress to retain its fanciful, arbitrary, or suggestive nature, but on the failure of the user of the dress to be successful enough in the marketplace. This is not a valid basis to find a dress or mark ineligible for protection. The user of such a trade dress should be able to maintain what competitive position it has and continue to seek wider identification among potential customers.

This brings us to the line of decisions by the Court of Appeals for the Second Circuit that would find protection for trade dress unavailable absent proof of secondary meaning, a position that petitioner concedes would have to be modified if the temporary protection that it suggests is to be recognized. In *Vibrant Sales, Inc. v. New Body Boutique, Inc.*, 652 F.2d 299 (1981), the plaintiff claimed protection under §43(a) for a product whose features the defendant had allegedly copied. The Court of Appeals held that unregistered marks did not enjoy the "presumptive source association" enjoyed by registered marks and hence could not qualify for protection under §43(a) without proof of secondary meaning. The court's rationale seemingly denied protection for unregistered, but inherently distinctive, marks of all kinds, whether the claimed mark used distinctive words or symbols or distinctive product design. The court thus did not accept the arguments that an unregistered mark was capable of identifying a source and that copying such a mark could be making any kind of a false statement or representation under §43(a).

This holding is in considerable tension with the provisions of the Lanham Act. If a verbal or symbolic mark or the features of a product design may be registered under §2, it necessarily is a mark "by which the goods of the applicant may be distinguished from the goods of others," and must be registered unless otherwise disqualified. Since §2 requires secondary meaning only as a condition to registering descriptive marks, there are plainly marks that are registrable without showing secondary meaning. These same marks, even if not registered, remain inherently capable of distinguishing the goods of the users of these marks. Furthermore, the copier of such a mark may be seen as falsely claiming that his products may for some reason be thought of as originating from the plaintiff....

The Fifth Circuit was quite right in *Chevron*, and in this case, to follow the *Abercrombie* classifications consistently and to inquire whether trade dress for which protection is claimed under §43(a) is inherently distinctive. If it is, it is capable of identifying products or services as coming from a specific source and secondary meaning is not required. This is the rule generally applicable to trademarks, and the protection of trademarks and trade dress under §43(a) serves the same statutory purpose of preventing deception and unfair competition. There is no persuasive reason to apply different analysis to the two....

It would be a different matter if there were textual basis in §43(a) for treating inherently distinctive verbal or symbolic trademarks differently from inherently distinctive trade dress. But there is none. The section does not mention trademarks or trade dress, whether they be called generic, descriptive, suggestive, arbitrary, fanciful, or functional. Nor does the concept of secondary meaning appear in the text of §43(a). Where secondary meaning does appear in the statute, it is a requirement that applies only to merely descriptive marks and not to inherently distinctive ones. We see no basis for requiring secondary meaning for inherently distinctive trade dress protection under §43(a) but not for other distinctive words, symbols, or devices capable of identifying a producer's product.

Engrafting onto §43(a) a requirement of secondary meaning for inherently distinctive trade dress also would undermine the purposes of the Lanham Act. Protection of trade dress, no less than of trademarks, serves the Act's purpose to "secure to the owner of the mark the goodwill of his business and to protect the ability of consumers to distinguish among competing producers. National protection of trademarks is desirable, Congress concluded, because trademarks foster competition and the maintenance of quality by securing to the producer the benefits of good reputation." *Park 'N Fly*, 469 U.S., at 198. By making more difficult the identification of a producer with its product, a secondary meaning requirement for a nondescriptive trade dress would hinder improving or maintaining the producer's competitive position.

Suggestions that under the Fifth Circuit's law, the initial user of any shape or design would cut off competition from products of like design and shape are not persuasive. Only nonfunctional, distinctive trade dress is protected under §43(a). The Fifth Circuit holds that a design is legally functional, and thus unprotectible, if it is one of a limited number of equally efficient options available to competitors and free competition would be unduly hindered by according the design trademark protection. This serves to assure that competition will not be stifled by the exhaustion of a limited number of trade dresses.

On the other hand, adding a secondary meaning requirement could have anticompetitive effects, creating particular burdens on the startup of small companies. It would present special difficulties for a business, such as respondent, that seeks to start a new product in a limited area and then expand into new markets. Denying protection for inherently distinctive nonfunctional trade dress until after secondary meaning has been established would allow a competitor, which has not adopted a distinctive trade dress of its own, to appropriate the originator's dress in other markets and to deter the originator from expanding into and competing in these areas.

As noted above, petitioner concedes that protecting an inherently distinctive trade dress from its inception may be critical to new entrants to the market and that withholding protection until secondary meaning has been established would be contrary to the goals of the Lanham Act. Petitioner specifically suggests, however, that the solution is to dispense with the requirement of secondary meaning for a reasonable, but brief, period at the outset of the use of a trade dress. If §43(a) does not require secondary meaning at the outset of a business' adoption of trade dress, there is no basis in the statute to support the suggestion that such a requirement comes into being after some unspecified time.

We agree with the Court of Appeals that proof of secondary meaning is not required to prevail on a claim under §43(a) of the Lanham Act where the trade dress at issue is inherently distinctive, and accordingly the judgment of that court is affirmed. It is so ordered.

## WAL-MART STORES, INC. v. SAMARA BROTHERS, INC.
### 529 U.S. 205 (2000)

Justice SCALIA.

In this case, we decide under what circumstances a product's design is distinctive, and therefore protectible, in an action for infringement of unregistered trade dress under §43(a) of the Trademark Act of 1946 (Lanham Act).

Respondent Samara Brothers, Inc., designs and manufactures children's clothing. Its primary product is a line of spring/summer one-piece seersucker outfits decorated with appliqués of hearts, flowers, fruits, and the like. A number of chain stores, including JC Penney, sell this line of clothing under contract with Samara.

Petitioner Wal-Mart Stores, Inc., is one of the Nation's best known retailers, selling among other things children's clothing. In 1995, Wal-Mart contracted with one of its suppliers, Judy-Philippine, Inc., to manufacture a line of children's outfits for sale in the 1996 spring/summer season. Wal-Mart sent Judy-Philippine photographs of a number of garments from Samara's line, on which Judy-Philippine's garments were to be based; Judy-Philippine duly copied, with only minor modifications, 16 of

Samara's garments, many of which contained copyrighted elements. In 1996, Wal-Mart briskly sold the so-called knockoffs, generating more than $1.15 million in gross profits.

In June 1996, a buyer for JC Penney called a representative at Samara to complain that she had seen Samara garments on sale at Wal-Mart for a lower price than JC Penney was allowed to charge under its contract with Samara. The Samara representative told the buyer that Samara did not supply its clothing to Wal-Mart. Their suspicions aroused, however, Samara officials launched an investigation, which disclosed that Wal-Mart and several other major retailers—Kmart, Caldor, Hills, and Goody's—were selling the knockoffs of Samara's outfits produced by Judy-Philippine.

After sending cease-and-desist letters, Samara brought this action in the United States District Court for the Southern District of New York against Wal-Mart, Judy-Philippine, Kmart, Caldor, Hills, and Goody's for copyright infringement under federal law, consumer fraud and unfair competition under New York law, and—most relevant for our purposes—infringement of unregistered trade dress under §43(a) of the Lanham Act, 15 U.S.C. §1125(a). All of the defendants except Wal-Mart settled before trial.

After a weeklong trial, the jury found in favor of Samara on all of its claims. Wal-Mart then renewed a motion for judgment as a matter of law, claiming, *inter alia*, that there was insufficient evidence to support a conclusion that Samara's clothing designs could be legally protected as distinctive trade dress for purposes of §43(a). The District Court denied the motion, 969 F. Supp. 895 (S.D.N.Y. 1997), and awarded Samara damages, interest, costs, and fees totaling almost $1.6 million, together with injunctive relief, see App. To Pet. For Cert. 56-58. The Second Circuit affirmed the denial of the motion for judgment as a matter of law, 165 F.3d 120 (1998), and we granted certiorari.

The Lanham Act provides for the registration of trademarks, which it defines in §45 to include "any word, name, symbol, or device, or any combination thereof [used or intended to be used] to identify and distinguish [a producer's] goods . . . from those manufactured or sold by others and to indicate the source of the goods. . . ." 15 U.S.C. §1127. . . .

The text of §43(a) provides little guidance as to the circumstances under which unregistered trade dress may be protected. It does require that a producer show that the allegedly infringing feature is not "functional," and is likely to cause confusion with the product for which protection is sought. Nothing in §43(a) explicitly requires a producer to show that its trade dress is distinctive, but courts have universally imposed that requirement, since without distinctiveness the trade dress would not "cause confusion as to the origin, sponsorship, or approval of [the] goods," as the section requires. Distinctiveness is, moreover, an explicit prerequisite for registration of trade dress under §2, and "the general principles qualifying a mark for registration under §2 of the Lanham Act are for the most part applicable in determining whether an unregistered mark is entitled to protection under §43(a)." *Two Pesos, Inc. v. Taco Cabana, Inc.*, 505 U.S. 763 (1992).

In evaluating the distinctiveness of a mark under §2 (and therefore, by analogy, under §43(a)), courts have held that a mark can be distinctive in one of two ways. First, a mark is inherently distinctive if "[its] intrinsic nature serves to identify a particular source." *Id.*...Second, a mark has acquired distinctiveness, even if it is not inherently distinctive, if it has developed secondary meaning, which occurs when, "in the minds of the public, the primary significance of a [mark] is to identify the source of the product rather than the product itself." *Inwood Laboratories, Inc. v. Ives Laboratories, Inc.*, 456 U.S. 844, 851, n. 11 (1982).

The judicial differentiation between marks that are inherently distinctive and those that have developed secondary meaning has solid foundation in the statute itself. Section 2 requires that registration be granted to any trademark "by which the goods of the applicant may be distinguished from the goods of others" — subject to various limited exceptions. It also provides, again with limited exceptions, that "nothing in this chapter shall prevent the registration of a mark used by the applicant which has become distinctive of the applicant's goods in commerce" — that is, which is not inherently distinctive but has become so only through secondary meaning. §2(f). Nothing in §2, however, demands the conclusion that every category of mark necessarily includes some marks "by which the goods of the applicant may be distinguished from the goods of others" *without* secondary meaning — that in every category some marks are inherently distinctive.

Indeed, with respect to at least one category of mark — colors — we have held that no mark can ever be inherently distinctive. See *Qualitex Co. v. Jacobson Products Co.*, 514 U.S. 159, 162-63 (1995). In *Qualitex*, petitioner manufactured and sold green-gold dry-cleaning press pads. After respondent began selling pads of a similar color, petitioner brought suit under §43(a), then added a claim under §32 after obtaining registration for the color of its pads. We held that a color could be protected as a trademark, but only upon a showing of secondary meaning. Reasoning by analogy to the *Abercrombie & Fitch* test developed for word marks, we noted that a product's color is unlike a "fanciful," "arbitrary," or "suggestive" mark, since it does not "almost *automatically* tell a customer that [it] refer[s] to a brand," 514 U.S., at 162-163, and does not "immediately...signal a brand or a product 'source,'" *id.*, at 163. However, we noted that, "over time, customers may come to treat a particular color on a product or its packaging...as signifying a brand." *Ibid.* Because a color, like a "descriptive" word mark, could eventually "come to indicate a product's origin," we concluded that it could be protected *upon a showing of secondary meaning*. *Ibid.*

It seems to us that design, like color, is not inherently distinctive. The attribution of inherent distinctiveness to certain categories of word marks and product packaging derives from the fact that the very purpose of attaching a particular word to a product, or encasing it in a distinctive packaging, is most often to identify the source of the product. Although the words and packaging can serve subsidiary functions — a suggestive word mark (such as "Tide" for laundry detergent), for instance, may invoke positive connotations in the consumer's mind, and a garish form of packaging (such as Tide's squat, brightly decorated plastic bottles for its liquid laundry detergent) may attract an otherwise indifferent consumer's attention on a crowded store shelf — their predominant function remains source identification. Consumers are therefore predisposed to regard those symbols as indication of the producer, which is why such symbols "almost *automatically* tell a customer that they refer to a brand," *id.*, at 162-163, and "immediately...signal a brand or a product 'source,'" *id.*, at 163. And where it is not reasonable to assume consumer predisposition to take an affixed word or packaging as indication of source—where, for example, the affixed word is descriptive of the product ("Tasty" bread) or of a geographic origin ("Georgia" peaches)—inherent distinctiveness will not be found. That is why the statute generally excludes, from those word marks that can be registered as inherently distinctive, words that are "merely descriptive" of the goods, or "primarily geographically descriptive of them." In the case of product design, as in the case of color, we think consumer predisposition to equate the feature with the source does not exist. Consumers are aware of the reality that, almost invariably, even the most unusual of product designs—such as a cocktail shaker shaped like a penguin—is intended not to identify the source, but to render the product itself more useful or more appealing.

The fact that product design almost invariably serves purposes other than source identification not only renders inherent distinctiveness problematic; it also renders application of an inherent-distinctiveness principle more harmful to other consumer interests. Consumers should not be deprived of the benefits of competition with regard to the utilitarian and esthetic purposes that product design ordinarily serves by a rule of law that facilitates plausible threats of suit against new entrants based upon alleged inherent distinctiveness. How easy it is to mount a plausible suit depends, of course, upon the clarity of the test for inherent distinctiveness, and where product design is concerned we have little confidence that a reasonably clear test can be devised. Respondent and the United States as *amicus curiae* urge us to adopt for product design relevant portions of the test formulated by the Court of Customs and Patent Appeals for product packaging in *Seabrook Foods, Inc. v. Bar-Well Foods, Ltd.*, 568 F.2d 1342 (1977). That opinion, in determining the inherent distinctiveness of a product's packaging, considered, among other things, "whether it was a 'common' basic shape or design, whether it was unique or unusual in a particular field, [and] whether it was a mere refinement of a commonly-adopted and well-known form of ornamentation for a particular class of goods viewed by the public as a dress or ornamentation for the goods." *Id.*, at 1344 (footnotes omitted). Such a test would rarely provide the basis for summary disposition of an anticompetitive strike suit. Indeed, at oral argument, counsel for the United States quite understandably would not give a definitive answer as to whether the test was met in this very case, saying only that "[t]his is a very difficult case for that purpose." Tr. of Oral Arg. 19....

Respondent contends that our decision in *Two Pesos* forecloses a conclusion that product-design trade dress can never be inherently distinctive. In that case, we held that the trade dress of a chain of Mexican restaurants, which the plaintiff described as "a festive eating atmosphere having interior dining and patio areas decorated with artifacts, bright colors, paintings and murals," 505 U.S., at 765, could be protected under §43(a) without a showing of secondary meaning. *Two Pesos* unquestionably establishes the legal principle that trade dress can be inherently distinctive, but it does not

*[handwritten margin note: product design trade dress is not inherently distinctive]*

establish that *product-design* trade dress can be. *Two Pesos* is inapposite to our holding here because the trade dress at issue, the décor of a restaurant, seems to us not to constitute product *design*. It was either product packaging—which, as we have discussed, normally *is* taken by the consumer to indicate origin—or else some *tertium quid* that is akin to product packaging and has no bearing on the present case.

Respondent replies that this manner of distinguishing *Two Pesos* will force courts to draw difficult lines between product-design and product-packaging trade dress. There will indeed be some hard cases at the margin: a classic glass Coca-Cola bottle, for instance, may constitute packaging for those consumers who drink the Coke and then discard the bottle, but may constitute the product itself for those consumers who are bottle collectors, or part of the product itself for those consumers who buy Coke in the classic glass bottle, rather than a can, because they think it more stylish to drink from the former. We believe, however, that the frequency and the difficulty of having to distinguish between product design and product packaging will be much less than the frequency and the difficulty of having to decide when a product design is inherently distinctive. To the extent there are close cases, we believe that courts should err on the side of caution and classify ambiguous trade dress as product design, thereby requiring secondary meaning. The very closeness will suggest the existence of relatively small utility in adopting an inherent-distinctiveness principle, and relatively great consumer benefit in requiring a demonstration of secondary meaning.

We hold that, in an action for infringement of unregistered trade dress under §43(a) of the Lanham Act, a product's design is distinctive, and therefore protectible, only upon a showing of secondary meaning. The judgment of the Second Circuit is reversed, and the case is remanded for further proceedings consistent with this opinion.

*It is so ordered.*

## Comments

1. *Trade Dress Protection.* Suppliers of goods and services use trade dress to distinguish their products from the products of others. Trade dress refers to how a product or service looks, its total image, or its overall appearance. Features of trade dress include a product's composition and its design characteristics, such as size, shape, color, texture and graphics. Fiberglass insulation made by Owens-Corning Fiberglas Corp. is pink, which is its trade dress. It serves no practical purpose and only serves to distinguish that supplier from others. Distinctive trade dress is entitled to the same protections as trademarks and service marks. The distinctiveness of trade dress is evaluated by the same standards as other devices and is based on the appearance of the article as a whole, not a single aspect of the design.

While the five categories of distinctiveness apply to nonword marks, courts often simply consider whether trade dress is inherently distinctive, capable of becoming distinctive with secondary meaning, or inherently incapable of becoming distinctive. The Federal Circuit adopted a three-part test to gauge the inherent distinctiveness of a trade dress, which has been adopted by many of the federal circuits. Under this test, from *Seabrook Foods, Inc. v. Barr-Well Foods, Ltd.*, 568 F.2d 1342, 1344 (CCPA 1977), one asks whether (1) the design or shape is a common basic shape or design; (2) the design is unique or unusual in a particular field; and (3) the design is a mere refinement of a commonly adopted and well-known form of ornamentation for a particular class of goods that consumers view as mere ornamentation. This test boils down to whether the design or shape is so uncommon, unique, and unusual that consumers will perceive it as a source designator. A maker of private label cosmetics products argued that the shape and black color of its compacts were protectible trade dress. The court concluded that, because the compacts' size and shape were common features of the entire genre of makeup compacts and that black was as common a color for a makeup case as brown is for a paper bag, the trade dress was not inherently distinctive. *See Mana Products, Inc. v. Columbia Cosmetics Mfg., Inc.*, 65 F.3d 1063 (2d Cir. 1995).

If trade dress is not inherently distinctive, it might become distinctive of a supplier's goods through acquisition of secondary meaning. Adidas applied to register a mark for its athletic shoes consisting of "three parallel bands on each side of the shoe in contrasting color of the body of the shoe." The TTAB found that the trade dress had acquired distinctiveness based on evidence that the shoes had consistently been marketed as "3-stripes" and had been used widely in the Olympic Games and countless other track and field events and on affidavits from distributors and track coaches stating that the 3-stripe shoe makes the shoes readily identifiable as Adidas products. *See In re Dassler*, 134 U.S.P.Q. 265 (Trademark Tr. & App. Bd. 1962).

2. ***Product Design Protection***. After *Two Pesos*, trade dress may either be inherently distinctive or have acquired distinctiveness. Product design cannot, after *Wal-Mart Stores, Inc. v. Samara Brothers, Inc.*, be considered inherently distinctive because its "intrinsic nature" does not serve to identify a particular source: "[W]here it is not reasonable to assume consumer predisposition to take an affixed word or packaging as indication of source...inherent distinctiveness will not be found." As applied to the seersucker children's clothing in *Wal-Mart*, the design of the fabric (appliquéd with hearts, flowers, fruits, and the like) is not obviously source indicating. Is the Court accurate in concluding that color, such as the pink color of one company's insulation, can never be inherently distinctive?

3. ***Trade Dress or Product Design?*** The Court recognizes the difficulty of distinguishing between product packaging (trade dress) and product design. Their COKE bottle illustration in the penultimate paragraph illustrates the problem. Reconsider all of the examples mentioned in this and the previous case: COKE bottles, fiberglass insulation,

children's clothing, restaurant décor, dry-cleaning dress pads, TIDE laundry detergent bottles, wine bottle labels, running shoes, PINCH bottles, black makeup cases. Which are clearly trade dress and which are product designs? The Supreme Court's solution to the difficulty puts questionable cases into the "product design" category where secondary meaning must be proved.

*INTERNATIONAL PERSPECTIVE*
**International Protection of Nontraditional Marks**

To a greater extent than other areas of intellectual property, trademark law has been harmonized by treaties among the major trading partners of the United States. Some differences remain, however, offering fascinating opportunities for countries to learn from each other's experience. Comparative protection of nontraditional marks is one such difference.

Nontraditional marks consisting of a sound, a color, or a scent abound. Familiar sound marks include NBC's three note chimes, the Pillsbury Dough Boy's giggle, and MGM/UA Entertainment Company's lion's roar. Registered color marks include pink used in association with Owens-Corning's insulation materials and brown used in association with United Parcel Service's transportation and delivery services. Registration was granted for the smell of plumeria flower blossoms used in connection with knitting yarn and another company applies the scent of newly mown grass to its tennis balls. As long as they are distinctive and nonfunctional, such marks are potentially registrable in the United States under the provisions of the Lanham Act discussed in this chapter.

The European Union instituted a graphic representation requirement for registration of marks, which creates obstacles to protection of nontraditional marks. This requirement is designed to ensure that marks can be precisely identified so that competitors know exactly what marks have been used by others and consumers may rely on the consistent representation of the mark in the marketplace. The experience of the EU reveals a variety of ways to represent nontraditional marks. Sounds may be represented by detailed musical notation on a stave (with bars, notes, clefs, rests, etc.) for musical sounds and sonograms (which depict pitch, volume, and progression of sound over time) for ordinary sounds like animal noises and giggles. Colors may be designated by reference to an internationally recognized identification code such as the RGB or RAL Color Codes. When considering registrations of scents, the EU has rejected the use of chemical formulas (because few people would recognize the scent from the formula), descriptions (because users would not perceive the description uniformly), and samples (because they are not graphic or stable over time). *See Melissa Roth, Something Old, Something New, Something Borrowed, Something Blue: A New Tradition in Nontraditional Trademark Registration*, 27 CARDOZO L. REV. 457 (2005). Roth argues that the Lanham Act requirement that applications include descriptions and deposits of specimens for nontraditional marks allows for too much subjectivity in consumer interpretation of the marks, so there is no consistent commercial impression. Roth argues that the Act requirement creates too much difficulty for competitors to determine what marks have previously been used by others. She recommends increasing the precision of marks to aid consumers including downloadable color pictures, sound recordings, and digitized scents from the PTO's Trademark Electronic Search System website to aid competitors. *Id.*

### *THEORETICAL PERSPECTIVE*
### Trademarks and Public Goods Theory

Chapter 1 described intellectual property as having the non-rivalry characteristic of public goods. Simultaneous use of the property by others does not interfere with the benefits one person obtains. Some resources have a mixed character, with some potential uses that are non-rivalrous and some that are rivalrous. Many people can simultaneously picnic in Central Park or breathe the air without interfering with each other's use of those resources. But if many ranchers graze their cattle in Central Park or multiple factories discharge pollutants into the air, they interfere with benefits other ranchers or breathers obtain. Some uses are non-rivalrous, others interfere. These types of resources, the air and common land, are called mixed public goods or "congestible" public goods.

A device used as a trademark has both public and private characteristics, both non-rivalrous and rivalrous uses. First consider the two non-rivalrous uses, customary uses and referential uses. A word like "apple" has a customary use in language, to refer to fruit. If adopted as a trademark, APPLE also has a referential use; people can use it to refer to a particular source of computers. These are non-rivalrous uses because everyone can simultaneously use "apple" in its customary linguistic sense and APPLE to refer to one source of computers.

Non-rivalrous customary and referential uses contrast with rivalrous source-indicating use by sellers. If a single seller is strongly associated with a mark, that reinforces the referential utility of the mark. APPLE is strongly associated with a computer supplier, which enhances the utility of the mark both to the seller and to consumers. If multiple computer manufacturers use APPLE to indicate that they are the source of a line of computers, they interfere with each other's source-indicating use and with consumers' referential use by causing confusion. Simultaneous source-indicating use diminishes the incentive each has to invest in the signaling characteristics of its mark. This results in the underproduction of information just as overgrazing of a commons results in too little feed for cattle and overpollution results in unhealthy breathers.

The rule prohibiting adoption of a generic term as a trademark reflects the public goods character of customary language. No person may have an exclusive right to use the customary name for a product as the source-indicating mark for that product. No beer manufacturer may, for instance, have exclusive right to use the mark BEER in connection with its product. That source-indicating use would deprive others from the customary use and inhibit competition. If Budweiser had the exclusive right to use the word "beer" in connection with its beverage, what would Guinness call its product? Trademark law protects the customary use of a term.

Trademark law, however, also protects referential use of terms. It protects the information content of terms used as marks. The term BUD, used in connection with beer, tells consumers something about the product's characteristics. They can use the term BUD to refer to Budweiser's product when ordering beer or discussing beer with their friends. When consumers use a mark to refer to the source of a product, that use has the characteristics of a public good because many can use a term referentially without diminishing (and perhaps enhancing) the utility of that mark as a signaling device.

As a matter of policy, the interest in promoting competition outweighs the interest in using a generic term referentially. The competitive interest is great because competitors need to use the customary generic name for their products to promote their products. The referential interest is weak because a generic term is a poor source indicator.

The five familiar categories of marks from generic to fanciful reflect the extent to which there is a customary publicness component to the mark that would be diminished by granting exclusive rights to using the device. From generic marks with a critical publicness component as the name of a category of goods to fanciful marks with no prior customary meaning, the law recognizes increasing protection as the degree of public customary use decreases and the source-indicating potential increases. Descriptive marks have customary uses to describe the goods in connection with which the term is used. Granting exclusive rights would impede competition somewhat (though not as much as with generic marks), but would be acceptable if the primary significance became the source-indicating meaning, that is, if the term acquired secondary meaning. The other classifications of marks do not have the customary uses in relation to the goods being sold, so no proof of secondary meaning is required.

# B. OBTAINING RIGHTS BY USING A MARK

Federal intellectual property rights derives from different constitutional sources. Power to award patent and copyright protection comes from Article 1, Section 8, Clause 8, granting Congress the right "to promote the progress of science and useful arts, by securing for limited times, to authors and inventors, the exclusive right to their respective writings and discoveries." At one time, many thought that the power to regulate trademarks came from that power as well. In the 1879 Trademark Cases, the United States Supreme Court held that the power of Congress to regulate trademarks comes from the third clause of that article, granting Congress power to regulate commerce with foreign nations, and among the several states, and with the Indian tribes. Accordingly, Congress conditions any exclusive rights to a trademark on use of the mark in commerce.

There is logic behind the use requirement. Consumers cannot benefit from a source-indicating device until familiarity with the mark reduces their search costs. Widespread use in commerce creates this benefit. This section of the chapter deals with the Lanham Act requirement that a mark be used in commerce before rights attach.

A producer of a good or service must use a mark in commerce regardless of whether the mark is registered or unregistered or how distinctive the mark is. Trademark rights depend on priority. The person who first uses a mark for a particular product (or service) in a particular geographic market is called the "senior" user and gets the right to use the mark. Someone who begins using that mark in the same market later is called a "junior" user. A junior user may not use any mark similar enough to the senior user's mark that it is likely to cause confusion about who is the source of the goods or services. The senior user's prior rights continue for as long as it does not abandon the mark. Registration is not required in the United States to obtain trademark protection and the rights of junior users are limited by the rights of senior users, even if the junior user registers first, as the principal case in this section, *Allard Enterprises, Inc. v. Advanced Programming Resources, Inc.*, illustrates. *Allard* focuses on the important issues of how much and what kind of use is necessary to obtain rights to a mark.

*STATUTE:* **Application for Registration Based on Use**
15 U.S.C. §1051(a) (Lanham Act §1(a))

*STATUTE:* **Use in Commerce Defined**
15 U.S.C. §1127 (Lanham Act §45)

## ALLARD ENTERPRISES, INC. v. ADVANCED PROGRAMMING RESOURCES, INC.

### 146 F.3d 350 (6th Cir. 1998)

KENNEDY, Circuit Judge.

Plaintiff Allard Enterprises, Inc. ("Allard Enterprises") sued Advanced Programming Resources, Inc., and its sole shareholder, Barry Heagren, (collectively "defendants") in the United States District Court for the Southern District of Ohio, alleging federal [and state] claims of trademark infringement. . . . Their dispute arises from plaintiff's use of the mark "APR OF OHIO" in connection with the placement of employees with computer and data processing skills and defendants' use of the mark "APR" in association with similar services. The parties stipulated that their service marks were confusingly similar and consented to trial before a United States magistrate judge, who determined that defendants first used the mark in commerce and permanently enjoined plaintiff from continuing to use its service mark. Plaintiff now appeals. For the following reasons, we affirm the trial court's priority determination. . . .

[In the 1980s, a company called Advanced Programming Resolutions, Inc. ("Old APR") used the APR mark in connection with its personnel placement services. In 1986, Old APR was taken over by AGS Information Systems ("AGS"), a company that found positions for contract employees. Barry Heagren, who had been a co-owner of Old APR, and Charles Allard both worked for AGS. AGS abandoned the APR mark in 1988. On January 31, 1989, while still working for AGS, Heagren started his own business, Advanced Programming Resources, Inc. ("New APR"), placing permanent employees in the computer and data processing fields.

On December 1, 1993, Allard left AGS to start his own business referring employees in the same field to potential employers. In 1994 and 1996, respectively, Allard obtained federal and state registrations on the mark APR OF OHIO, claiming to have first used the mark in commerce "at least as early as April 30, 1994."

Heagren claims that his use of the APR mark prior to that date without registering it. Based on that claim, Heagren argues that Allard has no right to enjoin Heagren use of the mark. The trial court concluded that Heagren use of the APR mark was sufficient to establish rights to the mark.]

The trial court . . . identified several instances that showed Heagren used the APR mark when he solicited business for New APR from employers who might be interested in hiring permanent employees. The earliest of these came in 1991, when Heagren told Vincent Carter, who worked for AT & T, that he was doing permanent placements through New APR. This contact, however, did not lead to any business. In 1993 and 1994, Robert Sheehan, who had known Heagren since the 1970s, gave Heagren his resume and asked Heagren to help find him a job. In 1994, the Ohio Department of Liquor received Sheehan's resume from either New APR or Heagren, and eventually hired Sheehan.

Tom Norman testified that he contacted Heagren in 1993 seeking assistance in finding a new job. Heagren and Norman met at least twice and had approximately one dozen conversations regarding Norman's job search. The court found that Heagren contacted Riverside Methodist Hospital, WEC Engineering, and Blue Cross of Central Ohio on behalf of Norman, and arranged interviews for him at the first two of these potential employers. The trial court credited Norman's testimony that "when interviewed by WEC Engineering, . . . the interviewer's copy of his resume bore the name 'APR.'"

According to the trial court's findings, Heagren also arranged interviews for Mike Greely, who previously worked for Old APR and AGS. Greely testified that he "saw [Heagren] in 1993, early fall of '93, while I was employed at the State, and we chatted briefly. And [Heagren] told me that he was doing permanent placement under APR, and I had asked him to help me find a permanent position at that time." Although Greely interviewed with Nationwide Insurance and a company called Highlights for Children, APR's efforts did not lead to a job offer. In 1993, Heagren also represented Richard Behrens, another employee of Old APR, in his search for a permanent job. Behrens produced a copy of his own resume with a header bearing the APR logo for Heagren to use in his job search.

Heagren talked to a number of companies on behalf of Behrens, and Behrens testified that this resulted in two interviews. The trial court determined, however, that there was no evidence that Behrens' resume bearing the APR logo was ever distributed to a potential employer.

The court also noted that, in 1993, Heagren talked to Dwight Smith, who owned a small business named Sophisticated Systems, Inc. ("SSI"), which Smith could market to the State of Ohio as a minority-owned company. With this opportunity in mind, Smith and Heagren discussed the possibility that SSI could operate as a subcontractor to New APR in the permanent employee placement business. According to Smith's testimony, Heagren and Smith also discussed the opportunity for a similar subcontracting relationship for the placement of temporary employees between SSI and AGS. Smith testified, however, that it "was very clear" that New APR handled permanent employee placement and AGS handled contract employee placement. Heagren provided Smith with the resume of at least one potential employee.

Finally, the trial court pointed to Heagren's dealings with a company named Lane Bryant. It found that "sometime in 1993 Heagren talked to Steve Stuthard, an executive with Lane Bryant, about Heagren's desire to place people in permanent positions at companies like Lane Bryant." Stuthard referred Heagren to the executive in charge of hiring, one Al Shutz, and the trial court found that "Heagren sent Shutz a fax on March 6, 1994 which referred to resumes which the two had discussed. The fax is on letterhead of Advanced Programming Resources, Inc., which uses the 'APR' logo in a distinctive fashion which had been designed by Heagren for use with old APR."

Although the court found no evidence that Heagren used the APR mark in any effort to recruit potential employees to satisfy employers, it concluded that "there is no question that he used the name APR in connection with his effort to find employers who had permanent vacancies to fill, and that he did so not only when he was presenting a resume of one of the people who called for assistance, but independently of those efforts. His contact with Steve Stuthard [at Lane Bryant] is a direct example of this type of business activity. To a lesser extent, his contacts with Dwight Smith [at SSI] and Vincent Carter [at AT & T] fall also into this category." After finding that Allard and Heagren each adopted the APR marks to capitalize on any remaining name recognition of Old APR, the court concluded that defendants' uses of the APR mark in connection with their permanent employee placement services were commercial and sufficiently continuous to establish his ownership rights in the mark prior to March 30, 1994. On that basis, the court concluded that defendants were entitled to permanent injunctive relief, and final judgment was entered on March 10, 1997. . . .

One of the bedrock principles of trademark law is that trademark or "service mark ownership is not acquired by federal or state registration. Rather, ownership rights flow only from prior appropriation and actual use in the market." *Homeowners Group, Inc.*, 931 F.2d at 1105. Allard Enterprises' federal registration of the APR OF OHIO service mark, however, serves as prima facie evidence of ownership and places on defendants the burden of showing their prior appropriation and continued use of their

APR mark. Thus, we must determine whether defendants carried their burden of showing that their uses of the APR mark before March 30, 1994 were legally sufficient to establish prior ownership. Our analysis focuses on the meaning of the phrase "use in commerce."

In 1988, Congress passed the Trademark Law Revision Act of 1988 ("TLRA"), Pub. L. No. 100-667, 102 Stat. 3935 (1988), which amended the Lanham Act and redefined the term "use in commerce" as "the bona fide use of a mark in the ordinary course of trade, and not made merely to reserve a mark." 15 U.S.C. §1127. This section of the Lanham Act further provides that "a mark shall be deemed to be in use in commerce . . . on services when it is used or displayed in the sale or advertising of services and the services are rendered in commerce." *Id.* The Trademark Trial and Appeal Board ("TTAB") has explained that the purpose of this revision "was to eliminate 'token use' as a basis for registration, and that the stricter standard contemplates instead commercial use of the type common to the particular industry in question." *Paramount Pictures Corp. v. White*, 31 U.S.P.Q.2d 1768, 1774, 1994 WL 484936 (Trademark Tr. & App. Bd. 1994), *aff'd*, 108 F.3d 1392 (Fed. Cir. 1997) (Table). One commentator described the TLRA's revisions to the process of trademark registration as follows:

> Prior to 1989, in order to qualify for federal registration, the extent of actual use of the mark was irrelevant so long as it amounted to more than a mere sham attempt to conform with statutory requirements. However, effective November 16, 1989, Congress changed the statutory definition of "use" so as to require a greater degree of activity.

2 J. Thomas McCarthy, MCCARTHY ON TRADEMARKS AND UNFAIR COMPETITION §16:8 (4th ed. 1997) (footnote omitted). . . .

For example, in *Blue Bell, Inc. v. Farah Manufacturing Co., Inc.*, 508 F.2d 1260 (5th Cir. 1975), the Fifth Circuit considered which one of two competing manufacturers first used the trademark "TIME OUT" in connection with men's clothing. Farah Manufacturing sold and shipped one pair of slacks bearing the mark to each of its regional sales managers on July 3, but did not ship clothing bearing the mark to customers until September. In an attempt to gain priority, Blue Bell attached the TIME OUT mark to clothes that were designed for, and were identified by, a different label. Blue Bell shipped the clothing bearing the two marks on July 5, but did not ship the line of clothing designed for the TIME OUT mark until October. In its oft-cited opinion, the Fifth Circuit noted that common-law "ownership of a trademark accrues when goods bearing the mark are placed on the market," *id.* at 1265, and held that Farah's sale of clothes to its sales managers "was insufficiently public to secure trademark ownership," because "[s]ecret, undisclosed internal shipments are generally inadequate to support the denomination 'use.'" *Id.* It further explained that the phrase "bona fide use in trade" requires that the mark "be affixed to the merchandise actually intended to bear the mark in commercial transactions." *Id.* at 1267. The court found that Blue Bell's addition of the TIME OUT mark to items bearing the label of another line of clothes was not a bona fide use because it was intended to reserve the mark for the future, not to identify a particular line of goods. It concluded that the first bona fide use of the mark was Farah's public shipment of clothes that were labeled with and designed for the TIME OUT mark.

Some seventeen years later, in *Zazú Designs v. L'Oreal, S.A.*, 979 F.2d 499 (7th Cir. 1992), the Seventh Circuit engaged in a similar analysis when it considered which of two shampoo makers first used the trademark "ZAZÚ." L'Oreal applied to register the ZAZÚ mark in June of 1986, and by August of that year had advertised and sold shampoo under that name across the nation. *Id.* at 501. In the previous year, a salon in suburban Chicago, named "Zazú Hair Designs" ("ZHD"), had begun developing a line of shampoo that it intended to bear the same mark. Between November of 1985 and February of 1986, ZHD sold some of its first samples to its customers and sold forty bottles to a hair stylist in Florida. The court found this latter shipment was "designed to interest the Floridian in the future marketing of the product line. These bottles could not have been sold to the public, because they lacked labels listing the ingredients and weight." *Id.* at 502. The *Zazú* court concluded that ZHD was "trying to reserve a mark for 'intended' exploitation. ZHD doled out a few samples in bottles lacking labeling necessary for sale to the public. Such transactions are the sort of pre-marketing maneuvers that . . . cases hold insufficient to establish rights in a trademark." Id. at 505.

These two cases illustrate the longstanding principle that, in the absence of federal registration, prior ownership of a mark is only established as of the first actual use of a mark in a genuine commercial transaction.

As long as there is a genuine use of the mark in commerce, however, ownership may be established even if the first uses are not extensive and do not result in deep market penetration or widespread recognition. As the *Blue Bell* court explained, "[t]he exclusive right to a trademark belongs to one who first uses it in connection with specified goods. Such use need not have gained wide public recognition, and even a single use in trade may sustain trademark rights if followed by continuous commercial utilization." 508 F.2d at 1265 (citations omitted). In an earlier case, the Fifth Circuit held that low volumes of door-to-door sales of metal and wood polish over a period of ten years were sufficient to establish priority, reasoning that "[t]he mere fact that a business is small and its trade modest does not necessarily militate against its being an established business capable of acquiring goodwill and rights in a trademark." *Sheila's Shine Prods., Inc. v. Sheila Shine, Inc.*, 486 F.2d 114, 123 (5th Cir. 1973). *See also Hydro-Dynamics, Inc.*, 811 F.2d at 1474 (recognizing that single bona fide shipment in commerce may support registration); *Kathreiner's Malzkaffee Fabriken v. Pastor Kneipp Medicine Co.*, 82 F. 321, 326 (7th Cir. 1897) (holding that for rights in a mark to accrue, "[i]t is not essential that its use has been long continued, or that the article should be widely known, or should have attained great reputation"); *Bell v. Streetwise Records, Ltd.*, 640 F. Supp. 575, 580 (D. Mass. 1986) (initial use of mark need not result in "instant success"); *E.I. Du Pont De Nemours & Co. v. Big Bear Stores, Inc.*, 161 U.S.P.Q. 50, 51 (1969) (finding that small volume of sales as part of test marketing plan were "sufficient to show a continuous use of the mark in question").

In other instances, however, courts have concluded that sporadic or minimal uses of a mark may indicate the mere intent to reserve a mark for later use rather than the present commercial utilization of the mark. For example, in *La Societe Anonyme des Parfums Le Galion v. Jean Patou, Inc.,* 495 F.2d 1265 (2d Cir. 1974), the Second Circuit considered a perfume manufacturer that recorded eighty-nine sales of perfume bearing a particular trademark over a period of twenty years. The court concluded that it could not "agree [with the district court] that such a meager trickle of business constituted the kind of bona fide use intended to afford a basis for trademark protection." *Id.* at 1272. In contrast to other cases where protection was warranted because "the trademark usage, although limited, was a part of an ongoing program to exploit the mark commercially," *id.,* the court found that the low-level sales in this case indicated a mere desire to warehouse the mark for potential use at sometime in the future. It explained that "'[t]rademark rights are not created by sporadic, casual, and nominal shipments of goods bearing a mark. There must be a trade in the goods sold under the mark or at least an active and public attempt to establish such a trade.'" *Id.* at 1274 (quoting *Clairol, Inc. v. Holland Hall Prods., Inc.,* 165 U.S.P.Q. 214, 217 (1970)).

On appeal, plaintiff discredits defendants' uses of the APR mark as part of a "word-of-mouth" marketing plan that targeted "personal friends," and asserts that such "secretive," "minimal," and "sporadic" uses are neither sufficiently commercial nor public to qualify as bona fide uses of a service mark. For the following reasons we disagree. First, we agree with the magistrate judge's finding that "whether or not this...word-of-mouth or 'relationship' marketing is the preferred or optimal way to conduct this type of business, it is not so atypical that no reasonable person could view it as 'commercial.'" In contrast to the internal shipments and pre-marketing consultations that courts held inadequate in such cases as *Blue Bell, Inc. and Zazú Designs,* defendants in the case before us used the APR mark on at least one fax, on at least one resume, and in numerous other solicitations, as they offered New APR's services to several employers doing business in Ohio. Defendants were not engaged in "pre-marketing maneuvers," the disingenuous uses of a trademark, or the mere attempt to reserve the APR mark for later utilization. Defendants used the APR mark as they attempted to complete genuine commercial transactions, with the understanding that they would be paid if an employee was hired. Second, these commercial uses also were sufficiently public to qualify for protection. The use of a mark "need not have gained wide public recognition" to establish priority, *Blue Bell, Inc.,* 508 F.2d at 1265, and there was evidence in this case that several large companies that did business in Ohio identified the APR mark with Heagren and his permanent employee placement services. Finally, we find that defendants' use of the APR mark over the course of 1993 and into 1994 was consistent and continuous, if not high-volume. Defendants' "trademark usage, although limited, was a part of an ongoing program to exploit the mark commercially." *La Societe Anonyme des Parfums Le Galion,* 495 F.2d at 1272. For these reasons, we conclude that defendants established both the bona fide use in commerce of the APR mark before plaintiff's first use on March 30, 1994 and the continuous use of that mark since then. Therefore, we affirm the trial court's determination that defendants established prior ownership rights to the APR mark. . . .

For the foregoing reasons, we affirm the trial court's determination that defendants established their prior use of the service marks at the center of this dispute. . . .

# Comments

1. *Relative Rights of Unregistered and Registered Users.* In *Allard Enterprises*, the plaintiff, Allard, who turned out to be the junior user of the service mark, sued Advanced Programming Resources, who turned out to be the senior user of the mark. The trial court permanently enjoined Allard from continuing to use its mark on competing service, despite the fact that Allard had registered the mark and Advanced Programming had not. Priority in use is of critical importance.

As the next chapter discusses, however, the rights of unregistered users do not extend beyond the geographic areas in which they have actually used their marks, though they have sometimes been allowed a "zone of natural expansion" if their business operations are expanding to new territory. Registered users are generally entitled to nationwide rights. Recognizing these relative rights, the Court of Appeals, in an omitted portion of the opinion, remanded the *Allard* case with instructions for the trial court to determine the areas in which Advanced Programming, the unregistered senior user, had continuously done business under the APR mark and modified the injunction to reflect the plaintiff's right to use of that mark in the rest of the nation.

2. *Use "in connection with" Goods and Services.* The rights to a mark apply only to the products or services in connection with which the mark was used. Both Allard and Heagren used the APR mark in connection with placement services for employees with computer and data processing skills. If another person had used the mark in a product or service market so unrelated that no confusion would result, neither would have any right to enjoin that use. In *Zazú Designs*, discussed in *Allard*, the plaintiff was the prior user of the ZAZÚ mark. The plaintiffs had sufficiently used it in connection with hair styling services in Illinois to acquire rights in that market, but that gave them no rights in the market for the hair care products marketed by the defendant.

3. *Extent of Use for Rights and for Registration.* Unlike most other countries, the right to register a trademark in the United States depends on use of the mark in commerce. This requirement prevents firms from reserving brand names they have no intent to use simply to prevent competitors from getting them. It also alerts rivals not to invest in establishing marks confusingly similar to marks already employed by another. Public use allows consumers to associate a mark with the good and is the means by which a supplier builds a reputation for its products or services. Because registered marks are published by the Patent and Trademark Office, public use plus publication gives rivals notice of the owner's use of the mark.

The amount of commercial activity required to establish "use" for the purpose of registration increased as a result of amendments to the Lanham Act in 1988. Before the amendments, "token" public use (such as a single sale or shipment to customers) plus publication was thought sufficient to satisfy the policy goals underlying the use requirement. The amendment requires more substantial use, as the discussion of *Blue Bell* and *Zazú* in *Allard Enterprises* indicates. "Use" now means use in the ordinary course of trade and contemplates commercial use common to the particular industry in question. The standard is flexible, so as to accommodate genuine trademark uses such as those made in small-area test markets, infrequent sales of very expensive or seasonal products, ongoing shipments of a new drug to clinical investigators from a company awaiting FDA approval, or the marketing of a drug to treat a rare disease that naturally involves few sales in the ordinary course of trade. How did the use that qualified for the purposes of registration in *Blue Bell* compare to the qualifying use in *Allard Enterprises*?

Zazú Hair Designs tried to rely on its use of the ZAZÚ mark on its shampoos for two purposes. The first was to establish itself as the senior unregistered user of the mark with rights superior to L'Oréal. The second was to register the ZAZÚ mark. That case considered the amount of use required for each purpose. To establish prior rights to an unregistered mark, the use of the mark "in commerce" must be more than just a token use, e.g., 40 bottles shipped to a friend. It must be enough to put other producers on notice that the mark has been taken and to establish a connection between the mark and the product. Zazú Hair Designs failed to meet this quantitative test for establishing common law rights because the product was not sold to the public. While it had sold a few bottles in its beauty shop, they had plain bottles to which its business card had been taped. Neither use was sufficient to put either producers or consumers on notice that the shop was using the mark in connection with hair care products.

By contrast, a token use was sufficient to register a mark prior to 1988, but the court in *Allard* recognized that after 1988, token use is no longer sufficient for registration. Under current law, the use must be in the ordinary course of trade and not merely to reserve a mark.

4. ***Abandonment and Renewal of Marks.*** In *Allard Enterprises*, Heagren picked up his employer's old mark after the employer abandoned it. Abandonment results in the loss of trademark rights against all users. Lanham Act §45 describes two ways in which abandonment may occur. The first way a mark may be abandoned is through nonuse with intent not to resume use, which may be inferred from the circumstances, such as nonuse for three consecutive years. The second way a mark may be abandoned is if the mark becomes generic. Abandonment may also result from uncontrolled or "naked" licensing. If a mark owner licenses another to use the mark but does not control the nature of that use, licensees may depart from the mark owner's quality standards, the public may be misled, and the trademark will fail to have the beneficial effect of signaling to consumers the nature of the goods offered.

The abandonment provision, which focuses on the owner's use of the mark, is designed to clear out the dead wood (marks lying around unused, cluttering the registry) and to make unused marks available for new owners. It was once estimated that 23 percent of marks older than six years are unused. See, Richard J. Taylor, *Loss of Trademark Rights Through Nonuse: A Comparative Worldwide Analysis*, 80 TRADEMARK RPTR. 197 (1990) (citing The United States Trademark Association Trademark Review Commission Report and Recommendations to USTA President and Board of Directors, 77 TMR 375, 408 (1987)).

A registration is in force for ten years, except that it may be cancelled by the Director of the PTO for failure to renew at the end of six years. 15 U.S.C. §1058 (Lanham Act §8). The renewal must identify the goods or services with respect to which a mark is still in use and support those claims with specimens or facsimiles showing current use or offer a special reason for nonuse. The length of time a registration remains in force and until a renewal is required may affect the number of unused marks on the registry. Proof of actual, as opposed to intended, use is required neither for registration nor renewal in most countries. Trademark rights in almost all countries outside the United States are gained solely through registration and do not require actual use.

> ### *PRACTICE PERSPECTIVE*
> ### Finding an Unused Mark
>
> Product suppliers often hire a marketing firm to choose a desirable mark and then investigate the availability of the mark before beginning to use it. The first step in this investigation is locating similar marks. The second is analyzing whether adoption of a mark similar to another's marks is likely to cause confusion. An informal approach to the first task is to check free government websites in a "knock out" search designed to eliminate easy-to-find registered users, such as
>
> *uspto.gov* for the United States;
>
> *patent.gov.uk/tm/dbase* for the United Kingdom;
>
> *strategis.ic.gc.ca* for Canada.
>
> *See lexnotes.com/sources/subs/tm.shtml#gov* for a more complete list of such sites. More formal and complete searches are available from commercial search firms such as Thompson & Thompson, *thomson-thomson.com*, and CCH Corsearch, *corsearch.com*. In early 2005, CCH Corsearch was quoting its rates for a basic "knock out" search of exact trademarks ranging from $180 per day to $305 for an "ultrarush" job. It described its comprehensive searches as including "newly filed trademark applications; active registrations and cancelled and abandoned marks; the most current and comprehensive state trademark data available; full text common law citations; [and] complete domain name information and Web page screen shots" — available at rates ranging from $505 for a report in three days to an ultrarush job at $1210.

## C. REGISTERING MARKS ON THE PRINCIPAL AND SUPPLEMENTAL REGISTERS

The initial requirements for registration of a mark are that the mark be used in commerce and be distinctive. The first part of this chapter discussed the distinctiveness requirements for protection of a mark. *Allard Enterprises* illustrated the use requirement for registration. Beyond that, there are numerous options for a mark owner. First, an applicant has a choice of applying for registration on either the principal or supplemental register. Actual use as a mark is required for registration on either. As discussed, a mark must also be distinctive to be protected as a mark. A mark may be inherently distinctive, as suggestive, arbitrary, and fanciful marks are, or acquire distinctiveness, as determined by the tests for whether a descriptive term has secondary meaning. A mark that is not distinctive is not registrable on the principal register. For the supplemental register, the test is not whether the mark *is* distinctive but whether it is *capable* of becoming distinctive. Descriptive marks without secondary meaning are capable of becoming distinctive, but generic marks are not. Registration on the supplemental registry does not give the protection registration on the principal registration does but is nevertheless useful. Among other purposes, it notifies others of the registrant's adoption of the mark.

Second, a person may apply for registration on the principal registry based on actual use of the mark or temporarily reserve a mark by filing an intent-to-use application. The temporary reservation allows a person to prepare and commit to marketing before actual use without fear that another will step in and use the mark first. Even under the intent-to-use process, however, the applicant gets no rights until it shows actual use as a source designator. The term for which application is made has to have been used as a source-indicating symbol and to distinguish the applicant's goods or services from those of others. There are innumerable alternative uses for symbols and words, such as for ornamentation or to give instruction or to describe a product or service, that have nothing to do with indicating source. Only source-indicating uses qualify for registration purposes.

Third, a person has a choice among different kinds of marks that service different purposes. The labels "trademark" and "service mark" apply to different types of businesses, but the marks are treated the same for all purposes. In addition, however, there are certification marks and collective marks. Certification marks are used by a certifying agency to verify and confirm that goods or services have particular characteristics, such as being organically grown or made in Wisconsin or meeting certain safety standards. Collective marks are used by members of an organization to indicate that the user is a member. These options have special purposes and special rules that distinguish them from trade and service marks.

To qualify as a registerable mark, a term must also meet a list of statutory requirements. In addition to being distinctive, it must, for instance, not be offensive or scandalous, confusingly similar to another mark, merely descriptive, misdescriptive, or deceptive.

These options and qualifications for registration are discussed next.

## 1. Intent-to-Use Applications

The toughening of the standards for actual use in 1988 was accompanied by a provision allowing for registration of plans to use marks, so called "intent to use" or "ITU" applications. Even under the rules governing ITU applications, more than token use in commerce is required before the mark becomes a registered mark. The application merely reserves rights temporarily. These applications are discussed in detail in this section.

Without a process for registering one's intent to use, intent alone cannot sensibly be a basis for priority. If one firm's investigation revealed that another firm is already using a mark on similar products or had registered the mark, it could choose another mark. Investigations prevent the duplication of costly development of trademarks. Even detailed investigation, however, might not reveal other firms' plans to use marks in the future. Even if investigation did reveal another's intent, the investigating firm would then have to wait to see if the other was serious about its plan. Under the registration process, some other users' intentions are revealed, but investigating firms still must wait to see if the other's plans come to fruition. *Eastman Kodak Co. v. Bell & Howell Document Management Products Co.* describes the intent-to-use process and the additional steps an applicant must take to obtain registration.

*STATUTE:* **Application for Registration Based on Intent to Use**
15 U.S.C.A. §1051(b), (d) (Lanham Act §1(b), (d))

## EASTMAN KODAK COMPANY v. BELL & HOWELL DOCUMENT MANAGEMENT PRODUCTS COMPANY
### 994 F.2d 1569 (Fed. Cir. 1993)

MICHEL, Circuit Judge.

...On October 12, 1990, Bell & Howell Document Management Products Company [B & H] filed intent-to-use applications, under 15 U.S.C. §1051(b), to register the numbers "6200," "6800" and "8100" on the Principal Register as trademarks for microfilm reader/printers. After initial examination of the applications, the trademark examining attorney approved the applications for publication in the PTO's *Official Gazette*.

Section 1051(b) allows an applicant who alleges a bona fide intent to use a mark to file an application seeking registration on the Principal Register. If, upon examination, the mark appears registrable, the PTO publishes it for opposition. If no opposer is successful, the PTO issues a notice of allowance. The applicant then has six months in which to file a statement that verifies that the mark is in use in commerce, the date of first use in commerce, the goods and services in connection with the mark are used in commerce, and the manner in which the mark is being used. The statement of use is then subject to another examination, in which the PTO considers how the mark is used and, if it is still satisfied that, as used, the mark is registrable, issues a certificate of registration.

Eastman Kodak Company [Kodak], a competitor of B & H in the manufacture and marketing of business equipment products, including microfilm reader/printers, timely filed a notice of opposition to registration of each of the three marks. Kodak alleged that the marks would be used solely as model designators for the reader/printers and therefore would be merely descriptive. Kodak argued that B & H had not shown that the marks had acquired secondary meaning and that, therefore, registration of the marks would be improper. The three opposition proceedings were consolidated before the Board.

B & H moved for summary judgment on the grounds that there were no genuine issues of material fact regarding the alleged mere descriptiveness of its applied-for number marks and, alternatively, that Kodak had no standing to oppose B & H's applications. Kodak filed a cross-motion for summary judgment. The Board determined that Kodak did have standing to oppose and that conclusion is not contested in this appeal.

On the issue of mere descriptiveness, the Board stated that it "believe[s] that it is possible for a numerical designation, which functions only in part to designate a model or grade, to be inherently distinctive and registrable without a showing of secondary meaning." *Eastman Kodak Co. v. Bell & Howell Document Management Prods. Co., Nos. 86,083, 86,093, and 86,101,* Slip Opinion at 5 (TTAB June 8, 1992). Due to the nature of intent-to-use applications, the number marks at issue had not been used at the time of the opposition proceeding. Accordingly, the Board held that it could not determine whether the numerical designations "are merely descriptive or if they are registrable without a showing of secondary meaning." *Id.* The Board concluded that in such situations, where the descriptiveness issue could not be resolved until use had begun, the opposition should be dismissed without prejudice to the initiation of a cancellation proceeding against the mark if the mark is registered after the statement of use is filed. Consequently, the Board denied Kodak's motion for summary judgment, granted B & H summary judgment on the descriptiveness issue, and dismissed the oppositions without prejudice. As a result, B & H received a notice of allowance.

The principal issue in this case is whether the Board's implied creation of a presumption in favor of the applicant for a numerical mark intended for use as more than a model designator is a reasonable interpretation of the Board's authority under the Lanham Act. We hold that it is. . . .

In the instant case, the Board's decision to grant B & H summary judgment and dismiss Kodak's opposition without prejudice, necessarily involved the Board's concluding that numerical designators are presumptively not merely descriptive under Lanham Act section 2(e), when applied for in an intent-to-use application under section 1(b). Section 1(b) sets forth the requirements for filing an intent-to-use application. Section 2(e) precludes registration of a trademark on the Principal Register that, *inter alia*, "[c]onsists of a mark which, . . . when used on or in connection with the goods of the applicant is merely descriptive or deceptively misdescriptive of them." Id. §1052(e). The statute on its face neither requires nor precludes the Board's interpretation.

Nor does the legislative history of the Trademark Law Revision Act of 1988 speak directly to this issue. The legislative history does demonstrate that Congress intended most marks applied for in an intent-to-use application (intent-to-use mark) to be reviewed for descriptiveness in the initial examination/pre-use stage of the intent-to-use application process. For example, Senate Report 515 states that "the absence of specimens at the time the application is filed will not affect examination on numerous fundamental issues of registrability (that is, descriptiveness, geographic or surname significance, or confusing similarity)." S. Rep. No. 515, 100th Cong., 2d Sess. 32 (1988), *reprinted in* 1988 U.S.C.C.A.N. 5577, 5595. With respect to the examination of the statement of use, which is filed after a notice of allowance has been issued, the Report states:

> The Patent and Trademark Office's examination of the statement of use will be only for the purpose of determining issues that could not have been fully considered during the initial examination of the application, that is, whether the person filing the statement of use is the applicant, whether the mark as used corresponds to the drawing submitted with the application, whether the goods or services were identified in the application and not subsequently deleted, and *whether the mark, as displayed in the specimens or facsimiles, functions as a mark*.

*Id.* at 34, 1988 U.S.C.C.A.N. at 5596 (emphasis added). As the highlighted phrase shows, Congress did intend the PTO to confirm, after the filing of the statement of use, that the intent-to-use mark, as displayed and used, actually "functions as a mark." Indeed, the statute provides: "Subject to *examination and acceptance* of the statement of use, the mark shall be registered. . . . Such examination may include an examination of the factors set forth in subsections (a) through (e) of section 1052." 15 U.S.C. §1051(d)(1) (emphasis added). And the legislative history itself emphasized that "[t]his provision [of the statute] permits the [PTO] to raise issues of registrability that might not be evident until the applicant makes available specimens showing the mark as used and/or clarifying the nature of the goods or services involved." H.R. Rep. No. 1028, 100th Cong., 2d Sess. 9 (1988). Thus, the statute and legislative history provide for the situation where, as here, the question of mere descriptiveness cannot be answered until after use has begun. . . .

Kodak argues, however, that the Board's interpretation is unreasonable because it would preclude asserting mere descriptiveness as a basis for denying registration of both word and number marks in intent-to-use applications. This argument is unavailing for several reasons. First, there are words and phrases that, as applied to certain goods, the examining attorney in the initial examination could certainly find to be prima facie merely descriptive. For example, an examining attorney could easily find that the term "reader/printer" applied to the microfilm reader/printers at issue here would be merely descriptive or that the term "slow-cooker" was merely descriptive of a Dutch oven. Furthermore, the examining attorney may also find numbers that are intended for use *solely* as model designators to be prima facie merely descriptive.

Second, Kodak's argument must assume that under circumstances such as these, after a notice of allowance is issued, intent-to-use marks will automatically be passed to registration. However, the statute provides for another examination of the mark after the statement of use is filed. 15 U.S.C. §1051(d)(1) ("Subject to examination and acceptance of the statement of use, the mark shall be registered in the Patent and Trademark Office. . . ."). Moreover, the statute contemplates the need, in certain circumstances, for a complete reexamination: "Such examination may include an examination of the factors set forth in subsections (a) through (e) of section 1052." *Id.* . . .

Unless the applicant originally claims use of the mark as purely a model designator, the examining attorney can make a determination of descriptiveness of numerical designators only after the statement of use has been filed. If, upon such further examination, the examining attorney determines that the mark is used in a merely descriptive manner, then the examining attorney must refuse registration because registration of a merely descriptive mark on the Principal Register would constitute "issuance of a registration in violation of the Act." Trademark Examination Guide §A.9.b. . . .

Because the Board's interpretation is consistent with the language and purposes of the statute, we hold that it is reasonable. . . .

## Comments

1. *Intent-to-Use Applications*. Trademark law offers two approaches to registration. The intent-to-use process allows an applicant to reserve a mark for six months, with extensions for good cause up to a total of 36 months. This relatively short time period may be enough to avoid wasting expenditures on a fight with competitors to be the first to actually use, but short enough to avoid people using the process for strategic reasons (such as tying up appealing marks). Showing progress on the development of the product and its marketing and legitimate reasons for the delay will aid in a showing of good cause. The requirement of a showing of "good cause" may also limit the strategic use of the process. Even where there is no strategic misuse of the process, the time limitation prevents even honest applicants from tying up distinct marks for undue lengths of time. *[handwritten margin note: can show good cause to extend intent to use]*

Ultimately, a mark must be used in commerce before it is registered, but the date on which the applicant filed its intent-to-use application is considered the "constructive" date of first use, even if the actual use occurred later. Employing the intent-to-use application process, a person can establish that he or she has national prior right to a mark as of that earlier date. Anyone who uses the mark after that intent-to-use application date is held to have had constructive notice of that applicant's priority.

Marks for which an applicant has filed an intent-to-use application are listed on a Patent and Trademark Office database so that other companies can see that someone has claimed the mark. If a company wants to use a lightening bolt as its mark in connection with the sale of golf clubs, for instance, it can look on the database to see if another has registered it or filed an intent-to-use application for that mark in connection with similar goods.

2. *Oppositions and Cancellation Petitions*. The *Eastman Kodak* case was initiated by Kodak, which "opposed" Bell & Howell's registration of the numerical marks. A party may file an opposition after another's application under either the intent-to-use or actual use provisions.

The court affirmed the Trademark Trial and Appeals Board's summary judgment against Kodak, but recognized that, even after Bell & Howell's ultimate registration of the numerical marks on the principal register, Kodak had a right to petition to "cancel" the registration. Parties who believe they would be damaged by registration have a right to file an opposition [15 U.S.C. §1063, (Lanham Act §13)], or file a petition for cancellation (15 U.S.C. §1064) based on a variety of grounds, including an objection that the mark is not registerable because it is merely descriptive, as in *Eastman Kodak.*

*STATUTE:* **Opposition to Registration**

15 U.S.C. §1063(a) (Lanham Act §13(a))

*STATUTE:* **Cancellation of Registration**

15 U.S.C. §1064(3), (5) (Lanham Act §14(3), (5))

**3. *Bona Fide Intention to Use.*** An intent-to-use application must include a statement of the applicant's domicile and citizenship, the goods in connection with which the applicant has a bona fide intention to use the mark, and a drawing of the mark. The applicant must also verify that it believes it is entitled to use the mark, that doing so will not cause confusion with another's mark, and that its intention to use the mark within the specified time period is bona fide.

An applicant may demonstrate that the application is or was bona fide by showing evidence of product development, market testing, and plans involving the promotion of the mark on the goods in connection with which the applicant intended to use the mark. There is no quantum of evidence required to show bona fide intent to use, but mere subjective statements without supporting evidence will not ordinarily be enough. For an example of bona fide intent as a matter of law, see *Lane Ltd. v. Jackson International Trading Co.*, 33 U.S.P.Q.2d 1351 (Trademark Tr. & App. Bd. 1994), where the intent-to-use applicant attempted to interest firms in the United States and abroad to import tobacco for the applicant's sale under the SMUGGLER mark, formed and implemented a business and licensing plan, and whose predecessor in interest had actually imported some tobacco.

Objective circumstances that cast doubt on whether the applicant had a bona fide intention to use the mark include the fact that the applicant has filed:

a. numerous intent-to-use applications to register the same mark for many more new products than are contemplated,

b. numerous intent-to-use applications for a variety of desirable trademarks intended to be used on [a] single new product,

c. numerous intent-to-use applications to register marks consisting of or incorporating descriptive terms relating to a contemplated new product,

d. numerous intent-to-use applications to replace applications which have lapsed because no timely declaration of use has been filed,

e. an excessive number of intent-to-use applications to register marks which ultimately were not actually used,

f. an excessive number of intent-to use applications in relation to the number of products the applicant is likely to introduce under the applied-for marks during the pendency of the applications, or

g. applications unreasonably lacking in specificity in describing the proposed goods.

*See* Senate Report No. 100-515, 100th Cong., 2d Session, at 23-24 (1988). Many of those methods are strategies people use to tie-up the rights to marks while deciding what mark to use or for keeping competitors from having rights to marks one will never use. Courts and the Patent and Trademark Office attempt to prevent those strategies in order to preserve the benefits of the intent-to-use process discussed in the previous note.

**4. *Pros and Cons of the Intent-to-Use Application System*.** Before 1988, an applicant for registration of a trademark in the United States had to actually use the mark in commerce before applying. This requirement led to competitors scrambling to be the "senior" user, the first to get the goods with the mark attached out to the consuming public. The constructive use system, a system offering an intent-to-use option, prevents the waste of expenditures on that race by at least one party who is bound to come in second (the "junior" user).

The intent-to-use system also prevents some litigation over who was the first user, but not all. A junior user can petition to cancel the senior user's mark on various grounds, including the claim that the registrant did not "use" the mark sufficiently to qualify for registration. In *Advertising to Women, Inc. v. Gianni Versace S.P.A.*, No. 98C15532, 2000 WL 1230461 (N.D. Ill. Aug. 24, 2000) (NO. 98 C 1553), Versace actually used the mark VERSACE'S BLONDE in connection with perfume after ATW's application for the BLONDE mark based on intent-to-use. When ATW sued Versace for infringement, Versace defended claiming that ATW's use was insufficient to qualify for registration because ATW had managed to sell its perfume to only one pharmacy. ATW argued that Versace's greater fame allowed Versace to foreclose ATW from all of the major stores, such as Saks, Nordstroms, and Neiman Marcus. The court denied both parties' motions for summary judgment, finding there were material issues of fact on whether ATW had met the use requirement and whether confusion would likely result from Versace's adoption of the VERSACE'S BLONDE mark.

There are recognized disadvantages to the constructive use system. One purpose was to eliminate token use, a trivial or commercially insignificant use of a mark in commerce to prevent others from having it or to tie up large numbers of distinctive and attractive marks. The system still allows for unused marks to remain unavailable for some period of time. A reported 25 percent of marks for which intent-to-use applications are filed are never used. The existence of a constructive use system may also make determining who has prior rights more difficult. Different entities are entitled to use the same marks for noncompeting goods where no confusion is likely to result. A seller of apples and a seller of blue jeans, for instance, may both use the drawing of a lightning bolt or the word "lightning" to market their goods. Until there is actual use of a mark, it is unclear precisely with what goods the mark will be connected, even though the applicant must describe those goods in the application.

# Problems

**2-5.** On September 23, 1994, Empire filed an intent-to-use application to use REAL WHEELS as a mark on small-scale toy vehicles. On January 3, 1995, before Empire had filed its verified statement of actual use, Warner-Vision filed an application for the REAL WHEELS mark based on actual use on home videos featuring motorized vehicles that were sold shrink-wrapped with toy vehicles in the same package. WarnerVision sought to enjoin Empire from using the REAL WHEELS mark in commerce on the grounds that it would cause confusion. Given the purposes of the intent-to-use provisions and the overarching desire to prevent confusion, should WarnerVision's injunction be granted? *See WarnerVision Entertainment, Inc. v. Empire of Carolina, Inc.*, 101 F.3d 259 (2d Cir. 1996).

**2-6.** Cyrus Milanian's business plan was to file intent-to-use applications for a series of trademarks for particular themes that he expected would be themes for a casino or resort hotel or theme park (e.g., a Titanic theme, a San Francisco theme), which he would then sell to businesses developing such projects. On his application, he described the business on which he would use the mark a little differently. He claimed on his application that he would use the service mark COLOSSEUM in connection with his service "Business management of resort hotels, casinos and theme parks." Caesar's World wants to use COLISEUM as a mark for its convention center in Las Vegas and objected that Milanian had no bona fide intent to use the mark in connection with the service he stated on his application. Does Caesar's World have a legitimate basis to oppose Milanian's registration? *See Caesar's World, Inc. v. Milanian*, 247 F. Supp. 2d 1171 (D. Nev. 2003).

### INTERNATIONAL PERSPECTIVE
### Trademark Registration in Foreign Countries

The first U.S. trademark law allowed registration of a mark based on intent to use. That law was struck down as unconstitutional by the United States Supreme Court in 1879 on the grounds that Congress was only empowered to regulate marks used in interstate commerce. From 1879 to the 1988 amendment of the Lanham Act to include the intent-to-use application, domestic applicants for U.S. trademark registration had to demonstrate actual use in commerce.

Most commercial foreign countries had signed the 1978 Trademark Registration Treaty, recognizing intent-to-use applications. The United States rejected that treaty. Applicants from some foreign countries with which the United States had treaties can rely on their home country registration or application rules rather than proving actual use when applying for U.S. trademark registration. If foreign countries allowed registration or application without use on the basis of intent to use, this old system would give foreign applicants an advantage over domestic applicants.

Congress was spurred to action by a 1984 opinion of the Trademark Trial and Appeals Board opinion in *Crocker National Bank v. Canadian Imperial Bank of Commerce*, 223 U.S.P.Q. 909 (TTAB 1984), holding that a foreign applicant did not even need to prove use anywhere in the world if its own country did not require that proof. Concerned with the disadvantaged domestic applicant, Congress finally adopted the Trademark Law Revision Act of 1988, eliminating the advantage based on a foreign intent-to-use application. As the *Allard* case indicates, however, Congress has not entirely abandoned the use requirement, leaving some foreign applicants, who can register at home without any showing of actual use, with an advantage over domestic applicants.

## 2. Registration on the Supplemental Register

A mark that does not meet all the requirements for registration on the *principal register* may be registered on the *supplemental register*. For the supplemental register, the test is not whether the mark is already distinctive of the applicant's goods or services, but whether it is *capable* of becoming distinctive. A mark that is ineligible for registration on the principal register because it is "merely descriptive" of the goods or services may be registered on the supplemental register. If the mark later becomes distinctive through use in commerce due, for instance, to the applicant's advertising and marketing efforts and their effect on the public, the mark then becomes eligible for registration on the principal register. Generic marks are incapable of becoming distinctive and are not registerable on the supplemental register. *Novartis Consumer Health Inc. v. McNeil-PPC Inc.* explores the role of the supplemental register in trademark law and the requirement for registration there as opposed to the principal register.

*STATUTE:* **Supplemental Register**
15 U.S.C. §1091(a), (c) (Lanham Act §23(a), (c))

### NOVARTIS CONSUMER HEALTH INC. v. McNEIL-PPC INC.
#### 53 U.S.P.Q. 1406 (D.N.J. 1999)

WALLS, J.
    . . . On January 20, 1999, Novartis sued McNeil for trademark infringement, false designation of origin and unfair competition based on defendant's unauthorized use of the mark Soft-Chews. Novartis is the manufacturer of the Triaminic brand of over-the-counter pharmaceutical products which includes cough, cold, allergy, and sinus products. McNeil, a division of Johnson & Johnson, is the manufacturer of the Tylenol brand of over-the-counter acetaminophen based pain relievers and fever reducers. Novartis manufactures a line of Triaminic products for children in the form of soft, chewable, fast-dissolving tablets under the Softchews mark.

Novartis is the owner of a registration on the Supplemental Register of the United States Patent and Trademark Office for its SOFTCHEWS mark for "cough, cold, allergy and sinus pharmaceutical preparation" which issued on June 4, 1996. McNeil has marketed a line of Tylenol pain-relieving and fever-reducing products for children under the mark Soft-Chews.

Plaintiff's mark softchews is registered with the PTO, not on the Principal Register, but on the Supplemental Register. Plaintiff's predecessor, Sandoz Corporation, had initially applied for registration of the term "soft chews" with the PTO on the Principal Register on April 5, 1995 on the basis of its intent-to-use the mark — it had not yet used the mark. On September 11, 1995, the PTO refused registration of the proposed mark on the Principal Register because it "merely describe[d] the goods." (PTO Office Action, Reynolds Decl. Ex. A.) The PTO explained that "[t]he proposed mark SOFT CHEWS appears to indicate that the goods are soft and for chewing." . . .

Novartis claims that McNeil's use of the term Soft-Chews is a copy or colorable imitation of its registered softchews mark in violation of Section 32(c) of the Lanham Act, 15 U.S.C. Section 1114(1). . . . Novartis also claims that McNeil's prominent use of Soft-Chews in its advertising and promotions conveys the misleading commercial impression to the public that McNeil's pharmaceutical products are affiliated, connected, or associated with those of Novartis and creates a false or misleading designation of origin in violation of Section 43(a)(1) of the Lanham Act, 15 U.S.C. Section 1125(a)(1). Plaintiff also claims reverse confusion — that defendant's use of the mark creates a likelihood of confusion and leads the public to believe that the plaintiff, not the defendant, is the trademark infringer. Finally, plaintiff claims that defendant has violated the New Jersey Unfair Competition statute, N.J.S.A. Section 56:4-1 and the New Jersey common law prohibiting trademark infringement and unfair competition.

Defendant McNeil argues that plaintiffs' claims under sections 32(c) and 43(a) of the Lanham Act fail because the softchews mark is not a valid and legally protectable mark and because there is no likelihood of confusion between Children's Tylenol Soft-Chews and Triaminic Softchews. Specifically, defendant McNeil contends that because Novartis registered softchews on the Supplemental Register, the mark is not entitled to any statutory presumption that it is a trademark and not a generic name. McNeil maintains that softchews is a generic term, or at best a descriptive one that has not acquired secondary meaning. Novartis argues that the mark is suggestive, that it has acquired secondary meaning, and that McNeil's use of the mark is likely to create confusion as to the origin of Novartis's products.

To prevail on a claim for trademark infringement or false designation of origin under Sections 32(c) or 43(a) of the Lanham Act, 15 U.S.C. Sections 1114(1), 1125(a), a plaintiff must establish that: "(1) the mark is valid and legally protectable; (2) the mark is owned by the plaintiff; and (3) the defendant's use of the mark to identify goods or services is likely to create confusion concerning the origin of the goods or services." *Fisons Horticulture, Inc. v. Vigoro Industries, Inc.*, 30 F.3d 466, 472, 473 (3d Cir. 1994). The requirements for a successful claim under the New Jersey Trademark Act, N.J.S.A. 56:4-1 or trademark infringement under New Jersey common law are the same. . . .

That plaintiff's mark is registered on the Supplemental Register rather than the Principal Register has definitive legal significance. Registration of a mark on the Principal Register provides "prima facie evidence of the validity of the registered mark and of the registration of the mark, of the registrant's ownership of the mark, and of the registrant's exclusive right to use the registered mark in commerce on or in connection with the goods or services specified in the certificate" of registration. 15 U.S.C. Section 1057(b). Registration of a mark on the Supplemental Register, however, does not entitle a mark to this statutory presumption. 15 U.S.C. Section 1094 ("applications for and registrations on the supplemental register shall not be subject to or receive the advantages of sections 1051(b), 1052(e), 1052(f), 1057(b), 1057(c), 1062(a), 1063 to 1068, inclusive, 1072, 1115 and 1124 of [Title 15]." Unlike Principal Registration, "Supplemental Registration creates no substantive rights." 3 J. Thomas McCarthy, *McCarthy on Trademarks and Unfair Competition* Section 19:37 at 19-75 (4th ed. 1998). However, one benefit conferred by Supplemental Registration is that "questions of validity, ownership and infringement of Supplemental Registrations are governed by federal law," and a suit for the infringement of a mark registered on the Supplemental Register may be brought in federal court, "along with a related claim of unfair competition." Id.

To be registered on the Principal Register, a mark must be a trademark, that is, "any word, name, symbol, or devise, or any combination thereof" which a person uses or has a bona fide intention to use in interstate commerce, "to identify and distinguish his or her goods, including a unique product, from those manufactured or sold by others and to indicate the source of the goods, even in that source is unknown." 15 U.S.C. Section 1127. A "trademark by which the goods of the applicant may be distinguished from the goods of others" may be registered on the Principal Register unless it, inter alia, "when used on or in connection with the goods of the applicant is merely descriptive or deceptively misdescriptive of them," or "comprises any matter that, as a whole, is functional." 15 U.S.C. Section 1052. "Eligibility for registration on the Supplemental Register, 15 U.S.C. Section 1091, requires that the term does not meet the requirements of registration on the Principal Register but is deemed capable of achieving an association with the source of the product." *In re Bush Brothers & Co.*, 884 F.2d 569 [12 USPQ2d 1058] (Fed. Cir. 1989); 15 U.S.C. Section 1091. In addition, to be registered on the Supplemental Register, a mark must be "in lawful use in commerce by the owner thereof, on or in connection with any goods or services." 15 U.S.C. Section 1091(a). A bona fide intent to use the mark in commerce does not satisfy the "use in commerce" requirement for registration on the Supplemental Register. 3 McCarthy, supra, Section 19:33 at 19-72 (4th ed. 1998). Although 15 U.S.C. Section 1095 provides that "[r]egistration of a mark on the supplemental register shall not constitute an admission that the mark has not acquired distinctiveness," there is nothing in the Lanham Act "to preclude Supplemental Registration from being deemed an admission against interest that the term is not inherently distinctive." Id. Section 19:35 at 19-73. The "very presence [of a mark] on the Supplemental Register indicates a preliminary determination that the mark is not distinctive of the applicant's goods." Id. Section 19:36 at 19-75.

If a mark has not been registered on the Principal Register, it may nonetheless be valid and legally protectable "if the public recognizes it as identifying the claimant's 'goods or services and distinguishing them from those of others.'" *A.J. Canfield Co. v. Honickman*, 808 F.2d 291, 296 (3d Cir. 1986). The validity of a mark which has not been registered on the Principal Register "depends on proof of secondary meaning, unless the unregistered mark is inherently distinctive." *Fisons*, 30 F.3d at 472.

. . . Because a mark not registered on the Principal Register has no presumption of validity or legal protectability, Novartis bears the burden to prove that softchews is descriptive and has acquired some secondary meaning or that it is suggestive. *Canfield*, 808 F.2d at 297.

. . . Here, plaintiff Novartis introduced a soft, chewable tablet form which differed from the other types of chewable tablets on the market in that it was softer than the hard chewable tablets. Novartis used the combination of two common terms descriptive of the soft and chewable characteristics of its new tablets to form the term "softchews." That the tablets also dissolve quickly and easily is inapposite because the distinguishing characteristic of Novartis's product is that it is soft and chewable. As Novartis has pointed out, a number of companies make tablets that dissolve quickly and sell them under marks such as: QUICKLETS, KIDMED, KIDMELT, WOW-TAB, ORASOLV, FLASH DOSE, and EZ CHEW. Novartis has introduced a product that differs from an established product class in a particular characteristic, and used a common descriptive term of that characteristic as the name of the product. The relevant product genus is soft, chewable tablets. . . .

Because softchews is a generic term, it follows that plaintiff does not have a legally protectable mark. Plaintiff cannot satisfy the requirements of a claim for trademark infringement, false designation of origin, or unfair competition under Sections 32(c) or 43(a) of the Lanham Act, 15 U.S.C. Sections 1114(1), 1125(a), under New Jersey common law, or under the New Jersey Trademark Act, N.J.S.A. 56:4-1. Defendant's motion for summary judgment to dismiss plaintiff's complaint is granted. . . .

## Comments

1. ***Purpose of Supplemental Registry***. Registration on the supplemental register allows a supplier who wishes ultimately to register a merely descriptive mark on the principal register to notify others of his adoption of the mark. The supplemental register is also a source of information for the PTO to use against subsequent applicants of similar marks. It also enables users of marks in the United States to register those marks under foreign laws honoring registration in the home country. Competitors are not entitled to file oppositions to marks on the supplemental register but may petition for cancellation if they believe they are or are likely to be damaged by registration on the supplemental register.

2. ***Legal Significance of Registration on the Supplemental Registry***. Registration on the supplemental register does not create any substantive rights to the mark. It creates no constructive use in areas outside of the territory of actual use, no prima facie presumption of validity of

the mark or of exclusive right to use the mark, no benefit of incontestability rules that protect marks registered on the principal registry and in continuous use for more than five years or the intent-to-use application process. On the other hand, as *Novartis* discusses, marks may be registered on the supplemental register without meeting the same requirements with respect to distinctiveness as for the principal register. Section 1052 (Lanham Act §2) lists kinds of marks, such as those that deceive the public, are merely descriptive, or are generic, that cannot be registered on the principal registry. The case illustrates that some of these apply to the supplemental registry while others do not. These prohibited types of marks are discussed in greater detail later in this chapter. Which of the prohibitions discussed in *Novartis* apply to both registries and which apply only to the principal registry? Did the SOFTCHEWS mark ever legitimately qualify for registry on the supplemental register?

3. *Reverse Confusion*. *Novartis* is a case of "reverse confusion." A typical infringement case involves a junior user using the senior user's mark with the result that consumers are likely to believe the junior user is selling goods made by the senior user. This is the usual case because the senior user's mark is generally better known and identified with the senior user. *See, e.g., Horizon Mills Corp.* and *Bristol-Myers*, earlier in this chapter. In a reverse confusion case, the junior user is often much larger than the senior user and better known than the senior user, or spends a great deal more capital in promoting the mark than does the senior user. The consequence of a junior user's use in a reverse confusion case is that consumers are likely to believe that the senior user is selling goods made by the junior user, or, as described in *Novartis*, "that the plaintiff, not the defendant, is the infringer."

4. *Elements of Infringement Claims*. While *Novartis* is concerned with the different rights of owners of marks registered on the principal register and those who register their marks on the supplemental register, it illustrates an important point about the elements of infringement claims. The elements of an infringement claim are identical for both registered and unregistered marks: The plaintiff's mark must be valid and legally protectable, the plaintiff must be entitled to the mark because of prior use, and the defendant's use of the mark must be likely to create confusion concerning the origin or source of the goods. These elements will be discussed in greater detail in the next chapter, but distinctiveness and priority of use, discussed in this chapter, are relevant to the first two elements. Federal and state statutory and common law trademark infringement claims are based on these elements.

## Problem

**2-7.** Generic marks are not registerable on either register, but descriptive marks without secondary meaning are registerable on the supplemental registry. *In re Bush Bros. & Co.*, 884 F.2d 569 (Fed. Cir. 1989), involves a denial of registration on the supplemental register by an examining attorney at the Patent and Trademark Office affirmed by the Trademark Trial and Appeals Board (TTAB). Bush Brothers applied for registration of the term "deluxe", for canned beans. Were the examining attorney and the TTAB correct to deny registration?

## 3. Nonqualifying Uses

Cases in this chapter have illustrated uses of a term that are not extensive enough to merit protection and junior uses that do not merit protection because of a senior user's priority. These reasons for nonqualification apply to marks used for both goods and services. Another reason why a term or device might not qualify for status as a registerable or protectible mark is that it is used for some purpose other than to designate source, such as for ornamentation or for a company's internal use as model numbers. The cases and materials in this section focus on additional issues involving nonqualifying uses. The first issue is what constitutes a "service." Service marks get the same protection as trademarks. While it is easy to determine what a "good" is, it is harder to determine what constitutes a qualifying service. The principal case, *In re Forbes*, explores this issue. Second, it is sometimes difficult to distinguish an individual who performs the services, for instance, a rock star, from the services the individual performs. Can David Letterman register THE DAVID LETTERMAN SHOW as a mark for use in connection with entertainment services? Third, can an individual or an organization like a museum receive trademark protection for his or her photograph of a photograph of the museum and prevent others from using that photograph? The notes following *In re Forbes* explore these issues.

### IN RE FORBES

**31 U.S.P.Q.2d 1315 (Trademark Tr. & App. Bd. 1994)**

QUINN, Administrative Trademark Judge.

An application has been filed by Forbes Inc. to register the mark NO GUTS. NO STORY. for "advertising services, namely, providing advertising space in a periodical."

The Trademark Examining Attorney has refused registration on the ground that applicant does not perform a "service" within the meaning of Section 45 of the Trademark Act, as amended, 15 U.S.C. 1127.

Applicant is engaged in the business of publishing magazines, of which the most prominent is a business magazine sold under the mark FORBES. Not unlike most magazines, *Forbes*, in addition to articles, editorials, etc., includes advertisements (which in small part, also comprise in the first issue of every month, classified advertisements) placed by others. Applicant solicits these advertisements by placing advertisements of its own in a variety of printed publications published by others. These advertisements do not serve to increase sales of applicant's magazines; rather, the advertisements serve to sell advertising space as they are directed to potential advertisers to persuade them to advertise their products and services in applicant's magazines. Of record are numerous advertisements placed by applicant in publications such as *The New York Times, Ad Age, Adweek, Automotive News, LA Style* and *Spy*. Each advertisement includes the applied-for mark, NO GUTS. NO STORY., and encourages others to run their ads in *Forbes*. One of the advertisements claims that *Forbes* is "the country's number one magazine in ad pages." The specimens of record are rate cards sent to potential advertisers.

The Examining Attorney contends, in refusing registration, that applicant's principal business is publishing magazines, that, thus, "applicant's magazines are the subject of the advertising and do not constitute separate services," and that applicant's providing advertising space to others in applicant's own publication is not a "service" which is separate from applicant's publishing services. In support of the refusal the Examining Attorney submitted excerpts retrieved from the NEXIS data base, which evidence, in the Examining Attorney's words, "demonstrates that advertising is an integral part of the existence of a magazine." (Office action, April 1, 1992, p. 2) Applicant argues, on the other hand, that providing advertising space for others in a periodical is not absolutely necessary to the publication of a periodical. Applicant emphasizes that its magazines are not the subjects of the advertisements; rather, it is the various goods and services of others that are being advertised in applicant's periodicals. Applicant contends that the Examining Attorney's reliance on earlier Board decisions is misplaced because, according to applicant, those cases no longer represent the current state of the law regarding the registrability of marks for advertising services. Applicant essentially argues that earlier Board precedent in this area is no longer good law in view of the Federal Circuit's subsequent decision in *In re Advertising & Marketing Development Inc.*, 821 F.2d 614, 2 USPQ2d 2010 (Fed. Cir. 1987).

In this case, the Board faces, yet again, the hard and often-asked question: what is a "service" as that term is understood under the Trademark Act? And, more specifically here, does applicant's activity of providing advertising space for others in its periodicals constitute a "service" in connection with which a service mark can be registered?

Section 3 of the Trademark Act provides for the registration of service marks. Section 45 of the Act defines, in relevant part, "service mark" as "any word, name, symbol, or device, or any combination thereof used by a person . . . to identify and distinguish the services of one person, including a unique service, from the services of others and to indicate the source of the services, even if that source is unknown."

The Federal Circuit has observed that

> [t]he Act does not define "services," nor does the legislative history provide such a definition. However, our predecessor court stated that *the term "services" was intended to have broad scope*, reasoning that "no attempt was made to define 'services' simply because of the plethora of services that the human mind is capable of conceiving." [emphasis added].

*In re Advertising & Marketing Development Inc.*, 2 USPQ2d at 2013, citing *American International Reinsurance Co., Inc. v. Airco, Inc.*, 570 F.2d 941, 197

USPQ 69, 71 (CCPA 1978), cert. denied, 439 U.S. 866, 200 USPQ 64 (1978). The Court, on another occasion, opined that the omission of a definition of "services" in the Act "suggest[s] that the term should be liberally construed." *American International Reinsurance Co.*, 197 USPQ at 71. Indeed, prior case law evidences the wide and diverse range of activities that have been held to be "services" sufficient to support a service mark registration. See J. T. McCarthy, *McCarthy on Trademarks and Unfair Competition*, Section 19.30 [1] (3d ed. 1992).

The Federal Circuit, in considering whether a designation functions as a service mark for advertising services, has pointed to the following factual considerations: (i) whether the advertising services are sufficiently separate from the subject of the advertising; and (ii) whether the mark has been used to identify the advertising services, not merely to identify the subject of the advertising. See, *In re Advertising & Marketing Development Inc.*, *supra*. In that decision the Federal Circuit found it instructive to view a service as "the performance of labor for the benefit of another." *Id.*, 2 USPQ2d at 2014.

The Board, in the past, has grappled with determining whether or not certain activities of a publisher constituted a "service." In the case of *In re Landmark Communications, Inc.*, 204 USPQ 692 (TTAB 1979) the applicant sought to register THE DAILY BREAK as a mark for services described as "educational and entertainment services comprising the collection, printing, presentation and distribution by means of a newspaper section of cultural and leisure information." The specimens of record were headings of a section of the applicant's newspaper showing, among other things, THE DAILY BREAK in prominent type. In affirming the refusal to register, the Board found that each of the services described in the application was a kind of feature commonly published in newspapers and that "these feature articles, stories and columns may be considered to be indispensable components of newspapers which readers expect and without which newspapers would not be sold." *Id.* at 698. The Board went on to say that a newspaper is a tangible commodity purchased because of the variety of reading material to be found therein and that readers would not consider a newspaper a collection of services. The Board concluded that the applicant sold goods, not services and that there was no significant economic difference between the applicant as a publisher of a periodical and the applicant as a provider of its alleged services.

Another case was *In re Hartford Courant Co.*, 231 USPQ 77 (TTAB 1986). In that case the applicant sought to register COURANT for "newspaper advertising services, including the design, layout and production of display advertisements for a newspaper." In affirming the refusal to register, the Board found that soliciting advertising for the applicant's own newspaper (*The Hartford Courant* is a large metropolitan daily newspaper) and the necessary activities of designing, laying out and producing those advertisements were activities which were part and parcel of the business of selling newspapers and would be expected by advertisers and other readers of the newspaper to be associated with any newspaper. In reaching this conclusion the Board viewed the sale of newspapers as the applicant's principal activity under the mark and found that the solicitation of advertising for one's own newspaper is not an activity qualitatively different from what any newspaper publisher does.

In the most recently decided Board case in this area of the law, *In re Home Builders Association of Greenville*, 18 USPQ2d 1313 (TTAB 1990), the applicant attempted to register NEW HOME BUYER'S GUIDE for "real estate advertisement services." Registration was refused, in relevant part, under Sections 2, 3 and 45 on the ground that the applied-for designation did not function as a service mark under the Act. The applicant provided its advertising services by soliciting others to place advertisements in a guide published by applicant. The guide essentially was a compilation of these advertisements placed by others (such as home builders, real estate agencies, mortgage lenders and various businesses in the home ownership industry). The Board reversed the refusal of registration, finding that the situation was similar to the one in *In re Advertising and Marketing*. Moreover, the Board stated as follows:

> [A]pplicant's business is advertising; the medium by which it accomplishes its advertising services is a publication, an advertising circular, filled with the advertisements it has solicited from its customers. That it renders its advertising services to its customers by publishing an advertising circular, instead of writing jingles or producing audio or video tapes, does not change the essential nature of its service from advertising to publishing.

The case now before us presents yet another variation on the familiar theme. Here, we have an applicant, engaged in publishing periodicals, seeking to register a mark for advertising services where the mark is different from any of the marks used to identify the periodicals, and where the advertising services essentially are rendered by the sale of advertising space in the periodicals.

We find that applicant's advertising services meet the test set out by the Federal Circuit in *In re Advertising & Marketing, supra*. In that case the Court found that "[applicant's] sale of advertising services to banks and automobile dealers is a wholly separate transaction from the banks' and automobile dealers' sale of financial services or automobiles to individuals." *Id*. [2 USPQ2d] at 2014. In the present case applicant's sale of advertising space in its periodicals to other businesses is a wholly separate transaction from those businesses' sale of goods and/or services. Although the Examining Attorney states that "the applicant's magazines are the subject of the advertising" (brief, p. 10), this clearly is not the case. The present case does not involve applicant's running an ad to promote sales of its own magazines; rather, it is the goods and/or services of others that are the subjects of the advertising. Cf.: *In re Dr Pepper Co.*, 836 F.2d 508, 5 USPQ2d 1207, 1209 (Fed. Cir. 1987) [ordinary promotional activities of one's own goods do not constitute a registrable service].

Applicant also must have used the mark to identify the services in connection with which registration of the mark is sought. Applicant's customers, which undoubtedly are businesses in many diverse fields, wishing to advertise their various goods and/or services would, upon reading the rate card (specimens of record), immediately associate the offer of advertising services with the prominently displayed words NO GUTS. NO STORY. Those words function to identify the source of the advertising services which involve the providing of advertising space in periodicals which are sold under marks different from the one sought to be registered here. The fact that customers for applicant's advertising services are, of course, aware that applicant renders its advertising services by providing space for their advertisements in applicant's *FORBES, EGG* and *FORBES VON BURDA* periodicals does not diminish the ability of a different mark, NO GUTS. NO STORY., to function as a service mark for those advertising services....

In the present application, the Examining Attorney "readily admit [s] that the solicitation of advertising is not necessary to the publication of a magazine." (brief, p. 11). Be that as it may, the point to be made here is that a determination of whether NO GUTS. NO STORY. functions as a service mark for advertising services turns on whether or not these services being rendered by applicant are separate from applicant's publishing activities. Although advertisers in and readers of applicant's periodicals know and expect that the publications contain advertising, that fact standing alone is of little importance, at least to our way of thinking, in determining whether the advertising services and publishing activities are separate activities or, rather, are integral activities. As we have done in the present case, it is important to look at other facts in making this determination. Here, these facts convince us that applicant is rendering advertising services under the mark it seeks to register because such services are sufficiently independent from applicant's publishing activities. Thus, applicant is rendering advertising services in connection with its mark NO GUTS. NO STORY. within the meaning of the Act.

Decision: The refusal to register is reversed.

## Comments

1. *Nonqualifying Marketing Uses.* In *In re Forbes*, the Judge relied on a Federal Circuit Court's definition of "service" as the "performance of labor for the benefit of another." Marketing that promotes one's own product is not "for the benefit of another." The Dr. Pepper Company sought to register PEPPERMAN to promote its Dr. Pepper soft drinks through a promotional contest awarding cash prizes to consumers who purchased the drinks. *See In re Dr. Pepper Co.*, 1 U.S.P.Q.2d 1421 (Trademark Tr. & App. Bd. 1986), *aff'd* 836 F.2d 508 (Fed. Cir. 1987). The TTAB denied the registration reasoning that where "an activity claimed to be a service is incidental to the sale of goods, the activity cannot be separately recognizable as a service unless it is shown that the activity constitutes something clearly different from, or over and above, any activity normally involved in promoting the sale of such goods." Running a promotional contest is not materially different from what would

normally be expected from one engaged in the sale of soft drinks; in fact, such promotions are quite common in that industry.

The question becomes a bit more complicated in the publishing world, where newspapers and magazines depend on both readers and advertisers for their revenues. The complication arises from the fact that the designation is used to generate revenues for the periodical and to promote the periodical as a good vehicle in which to place advertising; the designation is not being used to encourage people to buy the periodical. As discussed in *In re Forbes*, the Federal Circuit adopted a two-part test in its 1987 Advertising and Marketing opinion for whether designation functions as a service mark for an advertising service. Applying this test, why was the designation THE DAILY BREAK denied registration while NEW HOMES BUYER'S GUIDE and NO GUTS. NO STORY. were held to be registerable?

2. ***Uses Other Than as Source-Indicators***. Registration requires use as a mark to identify and distinguish the goods or services of one person from the goods and services of another and to indicate the source of goods or services; that is, the use must be as a *source indicator.* In *Eastman Kodak,* the intent-to-use case presented earlier in this chapter, Kodak's claim was that Bell & Howell intended only to use the model numbers to distinguish its own microfilm readers and printers from one another rather than from the readers and printers made by its competitors. If true, this would be one example of use of a mark for a purpose other than to indicate source. Numbers can be source designators, of course, as 4711 is a famous mark used by Mulhens Ltd. in association with it perfume and fragrance products and 7-ELEVEN is a famous mark used by 7-Eleven Inc. in association with its convenience stores.

The requirement that the mark be used as a source indicator arises in a variety of contexts. The three stripes on Adidas athletic shoes might be merely ornamentation or they might come to be recognized as being source indicators. *See In re Dassler,*134 U.S.P.Q. 265 (Trademark Tr. & App. Bd. 1962) (*see* Comment 1 following *Wal-Mart Stores, supra*). In *Rock & Roll Hall of Fame and Museum, Inc. v. Gentile Productions*, 134 F.3d 749, 755 (D. Ohio 1999), the Museum claimed that it used its building design as a mark. Claiming service mark infringement, the Museum tried to enjoin a professional photographer from marketing a poster featuring the Museum, which was designed by world famous architect I.M. Pei. The Museum was particularly concerned about competition with its own poster, sold in its Museum shop. It also sells paperweights, postcards, and t-shirts with various depictions of the Museum on them. The court recognized that a designation might serve both ornamental and source-identifying purposes, but found that the Museum had not used pictures of its building design with any consistency. Some uses represented the back of the building, which looks much different from the front. Some uses are photographs while others are drawings. The variety of depictions would prevent consumers from recognizing that these are source indicators rather than representations of the building or ornamentation for the paperweights and t-shirts. The court observed that "Consistent and repetitive use of a designation as an indicator of source is the hallmark of a trademark" that creates a consistent and distinct commercial impression.

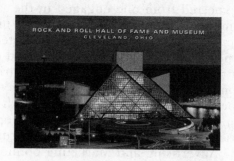

The *Rock & Roll Museum* case is similar to cases in which a party claimed exclusive rights to a famous person's likeness. In *Estate of Presley v. Russen,* 513 F. Supp. 1339, 1364 (D.N.J. 1981), the court concluded that, although one particular image of Elvis Presley had been used consistently as a mark by the Estate of Presley as a source indicator, "the available evidence [did] not support [the estate's] broad position" that all images of Presley served such a function. Similarly, in *Pirone v. McMillan, Inc.*, 894 F.2d 579, 583 (2d Cir. 1990), the court stated that "[e]ven if [the plaintiff] could show that it has established a trademark in a particular pictorial representation of [Babe] Ruth, such a trademark would not cover all photos taken of Ruth during his career, no matter how dissimilar."

3. **Nonqualifying Uses of Personal Names.** *In re Carson*, 197 U.S.P.Q. 554 (Trademark Tr. and App. Bd. 1977), involved entertainer Johnny Carson's attempt to register JOHNNY CARSON as a service mark for "rendering of entertainment to the general public by way of personal performances at shows such as by monologues, comedy routines, and the hosting of guest appearances of others." The examiner's objection was that the term referred only to the applicant as a person and was not used as a service mark. Carson offered specimens of his use of term. Whereas a page from a newspaper with a picture of Johnny Carson together with the words "JOHNNY CARSON is in the Congo Room at Del Webb's hotel Sahara with Bette Midler" did not show use as a service mark, advertisements using JOHNNY CARSON in connection with the words "in concert" and including information as to place and times of performances and as to where and for how much tickets may be purchased do constitute service mark use because the name is presented "in close association with a clear reference (i.e., "in concert") to the entertainment services to be performed by him." By contrast, the TTAB, in *In re Lee Trevino Enterprises, Inc.*, 182 U.S.P.Q. 253 (Trademark Tr. and App. Bd. 1974), concluded that the specimens offered by celebrated professional golfer, Lee Trevino, merely referred to him as an individual. The evidence included a publicity poster with captions such as "GOLF—THE COLORFUL APPROACH BY LEE TREVINO," "LIVELY LEE TREVINO WINS THE OPEN," "Trevino Wins Again," "Lee Trevino Defends His Title," "Trevino Wins National," and a promotional brochure "Meet the most colorful golfer to win the U.S. Open. His name is Lee Trevino!" in which reference is made to the availability

of Lee Trevino, the individual, for endorsements, advertisements, exhibitions of golf, and sales meetings.

## Problems

**2-8.** *In re Hartford Currant*, discussed in *Forbes*, was decided before the Federal Circuit articulated its two-part test. Is that case still good law under the Federal Circuit's test?

**2-9.** *In re Radio Corp. of Am.*, 205 F.2d 180 (CCPA 1953), involved an application by a seller of phonograph records to register the slogan THE MUSIC YOU WANT WHEN YOU WANT IT as a service mark. The service consisted of the seller supplying packaged radio programs containing a supply of phonograph records and advertising scripts to radio stations, which were paid by the record manufacturer to play the records and read the scripts advertising the records. Is the slogan registerable as a service mark?

**2-10.** *In re Orion Research Inc.*, 523 F.2d 1398, 1440 (CCPA 1975), involved an application by a seller of technical instruments to register a "ban lemons" designation, , as a service mark for the warranty on its goods that permitted a purchaser to elect repair or immediate replacement of defective goods. Is the symbol registerable as a service mark?

## 4. Registration of Certification and Collective Marks

In large part, certification and collective marks are treated the same way as trademarks and service marks. Owners of all types of marks may, for instance, bring infringement actions based on another's conflicting use. *See* Lanham Act §4. Certification and collective marks serve a different purpose from trademarks and service marks, however, because they are not source-indicating marks. As Lanham Act §45 indicates, certification marks are used to indicate that goods and services have certain qualities and characteristics and may not be used by the owner of the mark. Collective marks are used to indicate that the user is a member of an organization. Just as the owner of a trademark or service mark must keep others from using its mark to protect its source-indicating ability, the owner of a certification or collective mark must control other's use of its mark—limiting use to those whose goods do have the characteristics or membership the mark indicates.

The big distinction between certification marks and collective marks is that certification marks may not be used by their owners and collective marks can only be used by the members of an organization. The principal case in this section, *In re Florida Citrus Commission*, involves this issue. A certification mark does not require membership. It may certify regional or other origin, or that the goods or services were produced by a certain mode of manufacture, or have a certain quality, accuracy, or other characteristic. The use of certification and collective marks may, however, overlap. Standards of membership may require that a member meet certain quality standards or produce goods with certain characteristics. A certification mark is to certify that the work or labor on the goods or services was performed by members of a union or another organization. Collective marks may also indicate that the user is a member of a union or another organization.

Because the owner of a certification mark is a guarantor of a product or services characteristics, there are specific grounds for which a certification may be cancelled. *See* Lanham Act §14(5). The notes following *In re Florida Citrus Commission* discuss those grounds.

*STATUTE:* **Collective Marks and Certification Marks Registrable**
15 U.S.C. §1054 (Lanham Act §4)

*STATUTE:* **Cancellation of Certification Marks**
15 U.S.C. §1064(5) (Lanham Act §14(5))

*STATUTE:* **Collective and Certification Marks Defined**
15 U.S.C. §1127 (Lanham Act §45)

### IN RE FLORIDA CITRUS COMMISSION

**160 U.S.P.Q. 495 (Trademark Tr. & App. Bd. 1968)**

LEFKOWITZ, Member.

An application has been filed by the Florida Citrus Commission [an arm or branch of the government of the State of Florida] to register the following as a certification mark for oranges and orally ingestible products which are made from oranges, use of the mark as a certification mark since on or before March 23, 1964 being alleged.

It is alleged in the application that:

The certification mark is used by persons authorized by Applicant to certify that the goods bearing the mark are oranges grown within the State of Florida or are products which (1) are made from oranges grown within the State of Florida and (2) meet the Applicant's standards of identity.

Applicant is the owner of two subsisting registrations covering the designation "O.J.", per se, and the identical composite mark for which registration is sought herein as a service mark for services described as:

Creation and promotion of standards for, and the promotion of consumer purchases of, orange juice, canned orange juice, chilled orange juice, and frozen concentrated orange juice, made from oranges grown within the State of Florida.

The application contains the statement that "Applicant is not engaged in the production or marketing of any goods to which the mark is applied as a certification mark."

Registration has been refused on the ground that it is the practice of the Patent Office not to register the same mark both as a service mark and as a certification mark in view of Section 14(e)(2) of the Act of 1946 [now 14(5)(B)] which provides for the filing of a petition to cancel at any time in the case of a certification mark on the ground that the registrant engages in the production or marketing of any goods or services to which the certification mark is applied.

Applicant has appealed.

...A certification mark is a special creature created for a purpose uniquely different from that of an ordinary service mark or trademark as evidenced, inter alia, by the fact that Section 4 provides that a separate register be provided for such marks. It is a mark owned by one person and used by one or more parties on or in connection with their goods or services to certify quality, regional or other origin, and the like. As a consequence of the certification feature of the mark, it is a device which persons generally look for and many times are governed by in making their purchases. It is not unreasonable to assume that purchasers familiar with the use of a mark in connection with goods or services to certify quality, accuracy, or other characteristics of such goods or services will, upon encountering the identical mark on or in association with other goods or services, mistakenly attribute to it the same certification function as that to which they have been previously exposed. To permit the indiscriminate use of a certification mark with different goods or services will only lead to the dilution and impairment of the purpose and function of a certification mark as well as to practices wholly inconsistent with the public desirability of safeguarding the consuming public from confusion and damage not of its own making.

This is not intended to imply any devious intention on the part of applicant, the Florida Citrus Commission, in authorizing the use of its mark as a certification mark in the citrus fruit field and in using the identical mark itself as a service mark for services which it performs; but the standard to be applied in construing a portion of a Statute must necessarily have a general rather than a specific application. In order to effectuate the Congressional intent to maintain the true character of a certification mark and the unique function that it plays in the marketplace, it is our opinion that the owner of a certification mark cannot use the identical mark as a service mark or a trademark on or in connection with any goods or services that it markets or performs. A certification mark should be used only to certify. Any such other use is proscribed by both Section 4 and by Section 14(e)(2), the former as an ex parte bar to registration, and the latter as an inter partes ground for cancellation of an existing registration of a certification mark. . . .

The refusal of registration is affirmed.

# Comments

1. *Registration of Certification Marks*. A certification mark designates that a product or service, supplied by someone other than the owner of the mark, either has a certain geographic origin, such as Florida or the Cognac region of France, quality characteristics, such as made of pure dairy products or a certain kind of plastic, or labor provided by members of certain groups, such as the International Ladies Garment Workers Union. Certification is sometimes the only activity of a certification mark owner; the business of the Underwriters Laboratory is to certify the quality of goods. A person who owned a certification mark is not precluded from other activities, as the *Florida Citrus Commission* case indicates, though that person would need a different mark to designate the origin of its services or goods. The owner of a certification mark may not certify its own goods. Certification marks are "used by a person other than its owner."

2. *Cancellation of Certification Marks for "Own" Use or "Noncertifying" Use*. Just as source-indicating trademarks and service marks may be cancelled if they no longer serve their source-indicating function, certification marks may be cancelled if they do not serve their "characteristic-indicating" function. A certification mark is subject to cancellation, if, for instance, it is used by its owner to certify the owner's goods or to designate the owner as the source of the goods. E.I. du Pont de Nemours and Company uses TEFLON as a trademark to indicate that it is the source of a polymer used for coatings, films, finishes, and additives. It also owns the composite mark shown, which includes the word "Teflon," to certify that "the goods with which the mark is associated have been coated with material sold by applicant under its trademark TEFLON and that the coating has been applied in accordance with standards imposed by the applicant." DuPont cannot use the certification mark on its own TEFLON cookware, if it were to produce such a product, but it can own both of these marks. The appearance of the composite mark makes it clear to consumers that the mark is indicating a characteristic of the product rather than the source of the manufactured good.

**3. Cancellation of Certification Marks for Lack of Control.** Often a cancellation petition under Lanham Act §14(5) is based on a claim that the owner of the mark has not controlled the use of the mark, which means that consumers cannot rely on the mark as an indicator of the "regional or other origin, material, mode of manufacture, quality, accuracy, or other characteristic of the goods or services" displaying the mark. The purpose of the control requirement is to prevent consumers from being misled. The risk to the public is particularly great because a certification mark directly sets forth specific representations about the manufacturer and the qualities of the goods to which the mark is applied. It imposes an affirmative obligation on the mark holder to monitor the activities of those using the mark.

In *Midwest Plastic Fabricators Inc. v. Underwriters Laboratories Inc.,* 906 F.2d 1568 (Fed. Cir. 1990), Midwest appealed from denial of its petition to cancel the UL certification mark, ⓤⓛ, on the ground that the registrant, Underwriters Laboratories, did not control or was not able to exercise control over its use to certify that electrical equipment manufactured by others conformed to its safety requirements. In particular, Midwest claimed (1) that it tested its own products and, upon paying appropriate fees to Underwriters, applied the UL labels itself, and (2) that several of its competitors were applying the UL mark to products that did not conform to the established safety requirements according to tests by either independent laboratories or Underwriters' own laboratories. Each manufacturer certified by Underwriters is required to submit a sampling of each product and, once Underwriters determines the products to be in compliance and the manufacturer has established its own testing and inspection procedures, are thereafter permitted to apply the UL mark themselves, paying a fee to Underwriters for each label. Underwriters employed some 500 inspectors working out of 200 inspection centers throughout the United States who periodically inspected the manufacturers' factories and products. In the year in question, Underwriters conducted 438,000 inspections in approximately 38,900 factories and over 9 billion UL labels were issued covering approximately 12,500 different products. The Federal Circuit affirmed the Trademark Trial and Appeals Board's determination that a manufacturer's declaration that the marked product complies with UL standards is "a reasonable one designed to reflect the realities of the limitations involved in inspecting and certifying a large number of different products" and that Underwriters had "demonstrated considerable diligence in controlling the use of its marks; that while [Underwriters'] inspection and follow-up procedures are not 100% accurate or foolproof, we know of no such requirement." The Federal Circuit stated that the certification mark holder must take "reasonable steps, under all the circumstances of the case, to prevent the public from being misled," "such control as is practicable under all the circumstances of the case."

**4. Cancellation of a Certification Mark for Discrimination.** The "nondiscrimination" provision in Lanham Act §14(5) requires that the certification mark owner conduct the certification process in an impartial and inclusive fashion. The owner may not refuse to certify the goods or services of any party who meets and maintains the specified standards that the mark certifies. If, for instance, a certification mark certifies that the oranges are grown in the state of Florida, the Florida Citrus Commission must allow all Florida orange growers to apply the mark to their goods.

5. *Registration of Collective Marks*. Collective marks are owned by organizations and are membership indicators. They function in ways similar to certification marks but indicate a characteristic of the suppliers of goods and service (membership in a particular group) rather than a characteristic of the good or service itself. Collective and certification marks often overlap in their use. The most obvious overlap appears in the definition of certification marks as including membership in labor organizations. A collective mark may be used by all of the members to indicate that the organization is the source of the group, for instance, members of a dairy cooperative may all use the mark on their products to indicate their membership in the cooperative. Florists may all use the collective mark THIS BUD'S FOR YOU of their association to advertise their membership in the organization, as long as Anheuser-Busch, the producer of Budweiser beer, has no objections, which it did. *See Anheuser-Busch Inc. v. Florists Assn. of Greater Cleveland Inc.*, 29 U.S.P.Q.2d 1146 (TTAB 1993) (finding that confusion was likely because of the fame of the mark as applied to beer). Because a collective mark by definition excludes those who are not members, the nondiscrimination provision does not apply in the same way. A certifying organization composed of producers of maple syrup wishing to identify themselves by their geographic area may register the words "Vermont Maple Syrup" as a certification mark, in which case all producers of maple syrup in Vermont, whether members or not, must be allowed to use the mark. Alternatively, an organization of producers of maple syrup in Vermont could register "Vermont Maple Syrup Producers Association" as a collective mark and prohibit nonmembers from using the mark even if the nonmembers produced their syrup in Vermont.

# D. NONQUALIFYING TYPES OF MARKS

In addition to the general requirement that marks must be distinctive to be registrable, the Lanham Act §2 includes rules excluding specific types of marks. The policy reasons for most of these rules are obvious. Obscene and disparaging marks, for instance, are not registrable nor are deceptive marks. The challenge is understanding how the test for determining whether a mark falls into a particular prohibited category promotes the underlying policy. Part D of this chapter organizes nonqualifying types of marks into six categories: offensive, governmental, and personal marks; confusingly similar marks; deceptive, misdescriptive, and deceptively misdescriptive marks; descriptive and deceptive geographic marks; marks that are primarily a surname; and functional marks.

# 1. Offensive, Governmental, and Personal Marks

Lanham Act §2(a), (b), and (c) list a variety of types of offensive, governmental, and personal marks that are not registerable. Section 2(a) also prohibits deceptive marks, which are discussed in detail later in this chapter. Judges and factfinders must consider the commercial impression created by a mark in many procedural contexts, including the examination of proposed marks, of challenged marks, and of marks alleged to have been infringed. With that common ground, the analysis of marks falling under Section 2(a), (b), and (c) depends on the basis for the objection.

*STATUTE:* **Trademark Registrable on the Principal Register**
15 U.S.C. §1052(a), (b), (c) (Lanham Act §2(a), (b), (c))

When denying an application for a mark on the grounds that it is immoral or scandalous, the PTO has the burden of proof. The test varies, but often includes consideration of whether the mark is shocking to the sense of truth, decency, or propriety, disgraceful, offensive to the conscience or moral feelings, disreputable, or calls for condemnation, as in *Greyhound Corp. v. Both Worlds, Inc.*, 6 U.S.P.Q.2d 1635 (Trademark Tr. & App. Bd. 1988) (denying registration of defecating dog picture mark for apparel after opposition by Greyhound, user of racing dog mark for a variety of services and goods including bus transportation services). Because these tests are obviously highly subjective, the Trademark Trial and Appeals

Board has said that doubts should be resolved in favor of the applicant, as for the MOONIES mark granted registration in *In re Over Our Heads*, Inc., 16 U.S.P.Q.2d 1653 (Trademark Tr. & App. Bd. 1990). Evidence often consists of dictionary definitions that "distill the collective understanding of the community with respect to language," *see In re Boulevard Entertainment*, Inc., 334 F.3d 1336 (Fed. Cir. 2003) (denying registration of 1-800-JACKOFF for adult entertainment telephone number), because contemporary attitudes of a "substantial composite" of the general public rather than of the examiner are relevant. One should look to "ordinary and common meaning" of the term, by reference to Court and Board decisions in addition to dictionary definitions, as in *In re Old Glory Condom Corp.*, 26 U.S.P.Q.2d 1216 (Trademark Tr. & App. Bd. 1993) (holding stars and stripes design suggesting American flag for use in connection with condoms was not scandalous). It is always necessary to consider the proposed mark in the context of the marketplace as applied to the goods or services described in the application. Given that the mark was advertised with pictures of large roosters in its commercial context, the Board resolved doubts in favor of the applicant for the BIG PECKER BRAND for printed t-shirts in *In re Hershey*, 6 U.S.P.Q.2d 1470 (Trademark Tr. & App. Bd. 1988). The Federal Circuit reversed the denial of the mark BLACK TAIL used in connection with an adult entertainment magazine, *see In re Mavety Media Group Ltd.*, 33 F.3d 1367 (Fed. Cir. 1994). The court stated that the prohibition against scandalous marks was not an attempt to legislate morality, but, rather, a judgment by Congress that such marks not occupy the time, services, and use of funds of the federal government. It pointed to both nonvulgar ("rear end") as well as vulgar meanings (a female sexual partner) of the word "tail" and concluded that the Board must consider not just their own views, but the contemporary views of a substantial composite of the American public.

A disparaging mark is one that dishonors, belittles, or deprecates. Unlike scandalous marks, where the test is the reaction of American society as a whole, a disparagement test focuses on whether a substantial composite of those referred to, identified, or implicated in some recognizable manner by the mark would view the mark as disparaging. Again, the mark must be viewed in the context of the goods in connection with which it is used and the way the mark is used in the marketplace. In *Doughboy Industries, Inc. v. The Reese Chem. Co.*, 88 U.S.P.Q. 227 (Pat. Off. 1951), the Patent Office denied the registration for DOUGH-BOY for an anti-venereal preparation. The Patent Office observed that the mark DOUGH-BOY, a name for American soldiers in World War I, was disparaging *in connection with* an anti-venereal prophylactic preparation; particularly given its packaging, which featured depictions of American soldiers. If the mark is being examined for purposes of registration, the term must be considered disparaging at that time. If the mark is being challenged, either by a cancellation petition or in an infringement action, the term must have been considered disparaging at the time of registration. Whether the applicant or mark owner intended to disparage is irrelevant.

While the views of American society as a whole may be gleaned from dictionaries and encyclopedia, the views of an allegedly disparaged group are more difficult to determine. *In In re Hines*, 31 U.S.P.Q.2d 1685 (Trademark Tr. & App. Bd. 1994), the Board had denied registration for BUDDA BEACHWEAR, finding that "when Gautama Buddha, the founder of Buddhism, whose image is the subject of devotion of Buddhists each and every day, is featured in palm tree-emblazoned casual wear for commercial purposes, that use slights, depreciates and cheapens Buddha and Buddhism." On reconsideration after the decision in *In re Mavety Media Group Ltd.*, *supra*, the Board vacated its earlier decision and published the application for opposition because there was no evidence that Buddhists considered the mark disparaging. The BUDDA BEACHWEAR mark was abandoned March 6, 1996.

Objections to registration on the ground that the mark is scandalous must now include more than just evidence from general reference materials that refer to general views in America. In a cancellation proceeding the Board considered a variety of additional sources of information about whether Native Americans considered the Washington REDSKINS mark disparaging. On appeal from cancellation of the mark, the court found there was not enough evidence that Native Americans found the term offensive at the time of registration. *See Pro-Football Inc. v. Harjo*, 284 F. Supp. 2d 96 (D.D.C. 2003). A survey of public perspective on the word "redskin" showed that 46.2 percent of the general population and only 36.6 percent of Native Americans viewed the term as offensive. The court found that the views of the general population were irrelevant. The court also found that the views of the seven Native Americans who brought suit were irrelevant without independent or additional evidence. While some dictionaries indicated that the term "redskins" was "often offensive," "slang," or "offensive slang," there was no way to know why the dictionaries drew that conclusion or whether it meant that Native Americans found it offensive. The dictionaries also did not indicate whether the term was offensive when used in the context of a football team. And, on the whole, there was no evidence that, *at the time the marks were registered*, the term had a derogatory meaning.

The challenge to Pro-Football's REDSKINS mark arose through a petition for cancellation of registration under Lanham Act §14. The Patent and Trademark Office relies on both cancellation petitions and oppositions for raising issues it may not be able to foresee. Posting for opposition is a good way to give people who might be willing to collect evidence about disparaging an opportunity to do so. Publication for Opposition is an option favored by the TTAB because the examiners cannot be expected to appreciate the offensive content of all terms. Standing to oppose a disparaging mark is based on any damage indicating a real interest in the proceedings, not just the usual commercial damages. Two women were allowed to oppose registration of ONLY A BREAST IN THE MOUTH IS BETTER THAN A LEG IN THE HAND as a mark for a chicken restaurant in *Bromberg v. Carmel Self Service, Inc.*, 198 U.S.P.Q. 176 (Trademark Tr. & App. Bd. 1978). The TTAB denied the motion to dismiss the claim for lack of standing where the two women alleged that the mark was "disparaging to all people of a specific class, and in particular, women, in that it has false connotations and brings individuals, especially women, into contempt and disrepute; that the obvious double entendre of the mark indicates that it is lewd, lascivious, indecent, obscene, worthless, depraved, chauvinistic, degrading, and has no commercial value, and that the granting of a registration therefore unnecessarily lowers the standards of the United States Government."

The opinion in *Pro-Football* and the examples of scandalous marks both illustrate the sensitivity of the PTO to terms with multiple meanings and to the context in which the term is used. See the discussion of the BIG PECKER BRAND and BLACK TAIL in the section on scandalous marks. For instance, a petition for cancellation of the MEMPHIS MAFIA mark for entertainment services was denied in *Order Sons of Italy in America v. The Memphis Mafia*, 52 U.S.P.Q. 1364 (Trademark Tr. & App. Bd. 1999), where the TTAB held that "Mafia" has several meanings and that, in the context of the applicant's use, it would presumably mean an "exclusive, or small and powerful, group or clique."

### a. Flags, Coats of Arms, or Insignia

Section 2(a) prohibits marks that falsely suggest a connection with people, beliefs, institutions, or symbols. Marks that include flags, coats of arms, and insignia are prohibited if they "point uniquely" to the identity of a

particular government or governmental body. The Statue of Liberty is a symbol and not such a body, so it is not included, while the Patent and Trademark Office is. Lanham Act §2(b) prohibits copies or simulations of symbols, which means that the mark gives the appearance or effect of or has the characteristics of the flag, coat of arms, or insignia based on first impression gathered from visual comparison rather than a careful analysis and side-by-side impression. Thus, the TIMING THE WORLD mark used for watches and discussed in *In re Waltham Watch Co.*, 179 U.S.P.Q. 59

(Trademark Tr. & App. Bd. 1973) is not a simulation of the flags of identifiable governments because it is just a generalized collection of flags. The
ADVANCE SECURITY mark is not a simulation in *In re Advance Industrial
Security, Inc.*, 194 U.S.P.Q. 344 (Trademark Tr. & App. Bd. 1977), even
though it has a similar eagle and coat of arms resembling the coat of arms
of the United States, because the dominant impression of the entire mark
including the words is not one that would connect the ADVANCE SECUR-
ITY mark to the United States Government.

While it is fairly clear what flags and coats of arms are, the term
"insignia" is more troublesome. In *The United States Navy v. United States
Manufacturing Co.*, 2 U.S.P.Q. 2d 1254 (Trademark Tr. & App. Bd. 1987),
the Board held that "insignia" is to be interpreted restrictively to include
only insignia of the same general class as the flag and the coat of arms of
the United States. The mark USMC used in connection with prosthetic
components, which is the same as initials of the United States Marine
Corp used on equipment and uniforms, is registerable because the letters
are nothing like a flag or coat of arms and they identify people and things
associated with the particular branch of government rather than functioning as an insignia of national significance such as West Point or FBI. As with
other marks, the commercial impression depends on the context in which
the mark is used.

### b. Names, Portraits, Signatures

Lanham Act §2(c) prohibits marks consisting of a name, portrait, or signature of a living person or of a deceased President. Persons bringing suit
must have a cognizable or propriety interest in the name and the mark
must uniquely point to a particular living individual who has not given
consent. Sean Puffy Combs, a musician, has registered his signature
SEAN JOHN as a mark, Registration No. 2490545, for use with various
types of goods. In *Giuliano v. Manifattura Lane Gaetano Marzotto & Figli,
S.P.A*, 32 U.S.P.Q. 2d 1192 (Trademark Tr. & App. Bd. 1994), a party
raised the argument that the mark DUCA D'AOSTA should not have

been registered because it refers to a particular person who did not give his consent, specifically, Duca Amedeo Di Savoia Aosta. The Board first held that the party, who was an applicant for a similar mark, did not have standing to raise the claim because it had no proprietary interest in the Duca's name. Then it held that, even if the party did have standing, there was conflicting evidence as to whether there was such a living person. Furthermore, the fact that numerous people had held that title ("Duke of Aosta") might mean that the mark did not uniquely refer to a specific individual.

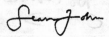

### c. "Falsely Suggests a Connection"

The Lanham Act provisions preventing registration of marks that falsely suggest a connection with particular people evolved out of the concepts of the rights of privacy and publicity, protecting an individual's control over the use of his "identity" or "persona." Denial of registration in these cases requires that (1) the mark is shown to be the same as or a close approximation of the name or identity in question, (2) the mark (or part of it) would be recognized as that name or identity, (3) the person is not connected with the good or service, and (4) that the connection would be considered by someone considering purchasing the good or service. Concluding that consumers would draw a false connection between the product and famous athlete Bo Jackson lead the TTAB to affirm denial of a combination mark including the words BO BALL and the outline of a football in *In re Sauer*, 27 U.S.P.Q.2d 1073 (Trademark Tr. & App. Bd. 1993). On the other hand, no specific person or institution was identified in the marks SPACE SHUTTLE used in connection with wine, *see Nat'l Aeronautics and Space Admin. v. Bully Hill Vineyards, Inc.*, 3 U.S.P.Q.2d 1671 (Trademark Tr. & App. Bd. 1987) (dismissing opposition) and INDIAN NATION LEATHER used in connection with equestrian equipment, *see In re Indian Nation*, 44 U.S.P.Q.2d 1539 (Trademark Tr. & App. Bd. 1997) (reversing refusal to register).

## 2. Confusingly Similar Marks and Concurrent Use

Trademark rights are usually defined by the product and geographic market within which they have been used. Registering a mark, however, gives rights that are national in scope. Registering a mark does not give exclusive rights to use the mark in all product markets. Section 1(a) of the Lanham Act requires that the applicant specify the goods in connection with which the mark will be used. That creates the possibility that another may use the same or a similar mark in another product market. Concurrent registration of two similar marks in different product markets is permitted under the conditions specified in §2(d) of the Lanham Act. *In re Coors Brewing Company* involves an attempt to register the mark BLUE MOON for use in connection with beer in the face of a similar registered mark used in connection with restaurant services.

*STATUTE:* **Concurrent Use**

15 U.S.C. §5052(d) (Lanham Act §2(d))

## IN RE COORS BREWING COMPANY

343 F.3d 1340 (Fed. Cir. 2003)

BRYSON, Circuit Judge.

In this trademark case, the Coors Brewing Company seeks to register the words "Blue Moon" and an associated design for a brand of beer. The examining attorney in the Patent and Trademark Office rejected Coors' application on the ground that the mark is likely to be confused with the registered mark "Blue Moon and design" for restaurant services. The Trademark Trial and Appeal Board upheld the examining attorney's rejection based on its findings that the two marks are similar and that restaurant services and beer are related goods and services. We uphold the Board's conclusion that the two marks are similar, but we hold that the Board erred in concluding that restaurant services and beer are related. We therefore reverse the Board's decision and remand for further proceedings....

The examining attorney initially refused to register Coors' mark under section 1052(d) on the ground that the proposed mark would be likely to be confused with three registrations, including [the mark "BLUE MOON and design" for restaurant services, which was registered on May 11, 1993, as Reg. No. 1,770,568 (the '568 mark)] and two registered marks for wine that contained the words "Blue Moon."...

On appeal, the Board disagreed with the examining attorney's ruling with respect to the two registered "Blue Moon" marks for wine. The Board concluded that even though beer and wine are sometimes sold by the same party under the same mark, the two beverages are not sufficiently related that the contemporaneous use of similar marks on the two products is likely to cause confusion as to source.

With respect to the registered "Blue Moon" mark for restaurant services, however, the Board took a different view. By a divided vote, the Board upheld the examining attorney's refusal to register Coors' mark on the ground that it was likely to cause confusion with the '568 mark. The Board majority first held that Coors' mark and the '568 mark convey a similar commercial impression because both contain the words "Blue Moon" and both contain a moon design. In addition, the Board majority found that beer and restaurant services are related, based on the evidence submitted by the examining attorney showing that (1) a number of brewpubs are also restaurants, (2) some restaurants that are not brewpubs nonetheless sell their own private label beer, and (3) some businesses have obtained registrations for beer and restaurant services under the same mark. The Board majority concluded that because beer and restaurant services are related, the examining attorney was correct to conclude that consumers were likely to assume that Coors' beer and the restaurant services offered by the '568 registrant emanated from the same source, even though there was no evidence that the '568 registrant brewed or served its own beer. . . .

*Confusion based on facts.*

The question whether there is a likelihood of confusion between a registered mark and a mark for which a registration application has been filed is an issue of law based on underlying facts. The legal conclusions of the Trademark Trial and Appeal Board are subject to de novo review, while the Board's factual findings must be sustained if they are supported by substantial evidence. To decide whether a likelihood of confusion has been shown in a particular case requires us to consider the factors summarized in *In re E.I. DuPont DeNemours & Co.*, 476 F.2d 1357, 1361 (CCPA 1973). The two *DuPont* factors at issue in this appeal are (1) the similarity of the marks, and (2) the similarity of the goods and services.

Evaluating the similarity between a registered mark and an applicant's mark requires examination of the appearance, sound, connotation, and commercial impression of the two marks. Applying those criteria in this case, we conclude that the Board's determination that Coors' mark and the registered '568 mark are similar is supported by substantial evidence.

The two marks are depicted below. . . . .

1. Both have moon + words.

2. Brewing Co. small font.

*Same*

*Diff*

Both marks contain the words "Blue Moon" in all capital letters, and those words are prominent in each mark. The Coors mark contains the disclaimed words "Brewing Co.," but because those words appear at the bottom of the mark in significantly smaller font, it was reasonable for the Board to find that those words do not significantly contribute to distinguishing the two marks.

Although both marks prominently display a full moon in conjunction with the words "Blue Moon," the two moon figures are quite different. The registered mark contains a cartoon-type design of a moon with a face and wearing sunglasses, while the Coors mark features a large circular arc suggestive of a full moon rising over a forest scene. Moreover, the other aspects of the Coors' design are quite different from the design of the

'568 mark. The Coors mark features a background consisting of a forest scene and stars, while the features of the '568 mark, other than the words "Blue Moon" and the moon wearing sunglasses, consist of a simple abstract design.

Although we uphold the Board's finding that the two marks are generally similar, principally because they both use the term "Blue Moon," we note that similarity is not a binary factor but is a matter of degree. Because there are significant differences in the design of the two marks, the finding of similarity is a less important factor in establishing a likelihood of confusion than it would be if the two marks had been identical in design or nearly indistinguishable to a casual observer. . . .

The pivotal portion of the Board's decision was its conclusion that beer and restaurant services are related and that, as a result, consumers would be likely to assume from the similarity of the two marks that Coors' beer and the registrant's restaurant services had the same source. In light of the Board's ruling that there is no likelihood of confusion between the registered "Blue Moon" marks for wine and Coors' "Blue Moon and design" mark for beer, it is clear that the Board's decision turned on its conclusion that beer and restaurant services are sufficiently related that the use of a similar mark for each would suggest to consumers that the two had a common source.

The Board acknowledged that, in *Jacobs v. International Multifoods Corp.*, 668 F.2d 1234, 1236 (CCPA 1982), our predecessor court held that the fact that restaurants serve food and beverages is not enough to render food and beverages related to restaurant services for purposes of determining the likelihood of confusion. Instead, as the Board noted, *Jacobs* provides that "[t]o establish likelihood of confusion a party must show *something more* than that similar or even identical marks are used for food products and for restaurant services." *Id.* (emphasis added). The Board therefore properly looked to other evidence to determine whether beer and restaurant services are related for purposes of assessing the likelihood of confusion. First, the Board relied on evidence from several references discussing the practice of some restaurants to offer private label or house brands of beer. Second, the Board cited articles showing that brewpubs, which brew their own beer, often feature restaurant services as well. Finally, the Board reviewed evidence of several third-party registrations showing that a single mark has been registered for beer and restaurant services. Based on that evidence, the Board concluded that beer and restaurant services are related and that consumers encountering a beer displaying a substantially similar mark as that used for a restaurant would be likely to conclude that the beer and the restaurant services came from the same source.

In light of the requirement that "something more" be shown to establish the relatedness of food and restaurant products for purposes of demonstrating a likelihood of confusion, the Board's finding that beer and restaurant services are related is not supported by substantial evidence. While the evidence produced by the examining attorney shows that some restaurants brew or serve their own private label beer, that evidence does not support the Board's conclusion that consumers are likely to conclude that beer and restaurant services with similar marks emanate from the same source. Coors introduced evidence that there are about 1,450 brewpubs, microbreweries, and regional specialty breweries in the United States, while there are approximately 815,000 restaurants. There was no contrary evidence introduced on those points. That means that even if all brewpubs, microbreweries, and regional specialty breweries featured restaurant services, those establishments would constitute only about 18 one-hundredths of one percent of all restaurants, or fewer than one in 500. While there was evidence that some restaurants sell private label beer, that evidence did not suggest that such restaurants are numerous. And although the Board had before it a few registrations for both restaurant services and beer, the very small number of such dual use registrations does nothing to counter Coors' showing that only a very small percentage of restaurants actually brew their own beer or sell house brands of beer; instead, the small number of such registrations suggests that it is quite uncommon for restaurants and beer to share the same trademark. Thus, the evidence before the Board indicates not that there is a substantial overlap between restaurant services and beer with respect to source, but rather that the degree of overlap between the sources of restaurant services and the sources of beer is *de minimis*. We therefore disagree with the Board's legal conclusion that Coors' beer and the registrant's restaurant services are sufficiently related to support a finding of a likelihood of confusion. The evidence of overlap between beer and restaurant services is so limited that to uphold the Board's finding of relatedness would effectively overturn the requirement of *Jacobs* that a finding of relatedness between food and restaurant services requires "something more" than the fact that restaurants serve food.

It is not unusual for restaurants to be identified with particular food or beverage items that are produced by the same entity that provides the restaurant services or are sold by the same entity under a private label. Thus, for example, some restaurants sell their own private label ice cream, while others sell their own private label coffee. But that does not mean that any time a brand of ice cream or coffee has a trademark that is similar to the registered trademark of some restaurant, consumers are likely to assume that the coffee or ice cream is associated with that restaurant. The *Jacobs* case stands for the contrary proposition, and in light of the very large number of restaurants in this country and the great variety in the names associated with those restaurants, the potential consequences of adopting such a principle would be to limit dramatically the number of marks that could be used by producers of foods and beverages....

For the reasons stated, we reverse the Board's decision upholding the examining attorney's refusal to register Coors' "Blue Moon and design" mark, and we remand to the Board for further consideration of Coors' application in light of this opinion.

## Comments

1. *Concurrent Use.* While registration of a mark gives nationwide exclusive rights, it is only a right to prevent others from using confusingly similar marks. The Patent and Trademark Office may register multiple similar marks as long as confusion, mistake, or deception are not likely to result. Any doubt about whether confusion would result is resolved against the

newcomer because the newcomer is in the best position to avoid confusion by adopting a different mark. There are many factors relevant to whether confusion is likely discussed in the next chapter, which looks at the elements of infringement claims in more detail. But before a mark has been registered, two parts of the confusion test are particularly relevant: whether the marks create a similar commercial impression and whether the goods or services of the two mark users are sufficiently related. Why is each relevant to the language of Lanham Act §2(d) and how did the two BLUE MOON marks fare under this two-part test?

] Test

## Problems

**2-11.** The party opposing registration had registered the word mark STEVE'S ICE CREAM for "ice cream consumed on or off the premises." The applicant, Steve's Hot Dogs, was attempting to register the composite mark shown here. Should registration be permitted under the two-part test of *Coors Brewing*? *See Steve's Ice Cream v. Steve's Hot Dogs*, 3 U.S.P.Q.2d 1477 (Trademark Tr. & App. Bd. 1987).

**2-12.** The party opposing registration in *In re Shell Oil Co.*, 992 F.2d 1204 (Fed. Cir. 1993) had registered the composite mark including the words RIGHT A WAY shown below to the left for use in connection with "distributorship services in the field of automotive parts." The applicant, Shell Oil Co., sought concurrent registration of the composite mark on the right for "service station oil and lubrication change services." Should concurrent registration be permitted? If so, what "conditions and limitation as to the mode or place of the use of the marks or the services in connection with which such marks are used" (*see* Lanham Act §2(d)) should the Patent and Trademark Office impose?

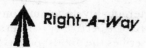 

## 3. Deceptive, Misdescriptive, and Deceptively Misdescriptive Marks

In separate parts of Section 2, the Lanham Act prohibits registration of deceptive marks and, unless there is proof of secondary meaning, marks that are deceptively misdescriptive of the goods or services in connection with which they are used. Recall from Part A of this chapter that merely descriptive marks are also unregistrable without proof of secondary meaning. *In re Phillips-Van Heusen Corp.* illustrates the more lenient standard for registering deceptively misdescriptive marks, how deceptive marks are different from deceptively misdescriptive marks, and how the elements of misdescriptiveness and deceptiveness are proved.

*STATUTE:* **Marks Registrable on the Principal Register**
15 U.S.C. §5052(a), (e)(1), (f) (Lanham Act §2(a), (e)(1), (f))

## IN RE PHILLIPS-VAN HEUSEN CORP.

### 63 U.S.P.Q. 1047 (Trademark Tr. & App. Bd. 2002)

HOHEIN, J.

Phillips-Van Heusen Corp. has filed an application to register the term "SUPER SILK" for "clothing, namely[,] dress shirts and sport shirts made of silk-like fabric."

Registration has been finally refused under Section 2(e)(1) of the Trademark Act, on the ground that, when used on or in connection with applicant's goods, the term "SUPER SILK" is deceptively misdescriptive of them. Registration also has been finally refused under Section 2(a) of the Trademark Act, on the basis that such term comprises deceptive matter in that it falsely and materially indicates that applicant's goods contain silk when, in fact, they do not.

Applicant has appealed. Briefs have been filed, but an oral hearing was not requested. We affirm the refusals to register.

Applicant does not appear to disagree with the Examining Attorney as to the proper standards for determining whether a mark is deceptively misdescriptive under Section 2(e)(1) and whether it is deceptive within the meaning of Section 2(a). Specifically, . . . a mark is deceptively misdescriptive if the following two-part test is met: (1) Does the mark misdescribe the goods or services? (2) Are consumers likely to believe the misrepresentation? A mark satisfying such criteria is additionally considered to be deceptive if the misrepresentation would be a material factor in the purchasing decision. Thus, as set forth in the leading case of *In re Budge Manufacturing Co. Inc.*, 857 F.2d 773, 8 USPQ2d 1259, 1260 (Fed. Cir. 1988), a mark must meet the following three-prong test to be adjudged deceptive:

(1) Is the term misdescriptive of the character, quality, function, composition or use of the goods [or services]? (2) If so, are prospective purchasers likely to believe that the misdescription actually describes the goods [or services]? (3) If so, is the misdescription likely to affect the decision to purchase?

Provided that the United States Patent and Trademark Office puts forth sufficient evidence to establish *prima facie* that each of the above elements is met, a mark is deceptive and thus is unregistrable under Section 2(a). . . .

As a starting point for analysis, we observe that in order for a term to misdescribe goods or services, the term must be merely descriptive, rather than suggestive, of a significant aspect of the goods or services which the goods or services plausibly possess but in fact do not. . . .

[W]hen considered in its entirety, the term "SUPER SILK" would in a laudatory fashion immediately describe, without conjecture or speculation, a significant quality, characteristic or feature of any articles of clothing, including dress shirts and sport shirts, made of silk fabric. Purchasers and potential customers for such goods would plainly understand, as asserted by the Examining Attorney, that because shirts, like other items of apparel, are commonly made of silk, the term "SUPER SILK" designates goods made of an excellent, first-rate, or superior grade of silk fabric and not, as suggested by applicant, those produced from "a fabric that is similar but superior *to* silk" (emphasis added).

However, because applicant's goods are identified as "clothing, namely[,] dress shirts and sport shirts made of silk-like fabric," it is clear that the term "SUPER SILK," which signifies an excellent, first-rate, or superior grade of silk fabric, misdescribes applicant's goods inasmuch as they are not made from silk fabric. Moreover, none of the variety of alternative meanings which applicant asserts for the term "SUPER SILK" in the abstract has any applicability to applicant's goods.[*] The first prong of the test for a deceptively misdescriptive term is therefore met, especially inasmuch as the record, as noted below, confirms that silk fabrics have several significant properties which are available in various grades or degrees, such that those with superior, excellent or first-rate quality would be viewed as super silk fabrics.

With respect to the second prong of the standard for what constitutes a deceptively misdescriptive term, the record clearly establishes that purchasers and prospective consumers for applicant's goods would be likely to believe the misrepresentation readily conveyed by the term "SUPER SILK." The Examining Attorney, in this regard, has introduced an article by the International Silk Association (U.S.A.), entitled "What is Silk...," which in addition to detailing the history of silk fibers, the care of silk fabrics and the types of silk weaves (grouped under the categories of "ROUGH-TEXTURED SILKS," "RAW" SILKS," "STIFF SILKS," "SOFT SILKS," "CRISP SILKS," "GLOSSY SILKS," "SHEER SILKS" and "VELVETS"), states in pertinent part that:

> *Qualities of Silk.* Silks may be woven on any type of loom made, into fabrics of any degree of crispness or softness, thickness or transparency. But all of these fabrics have in common the unique qualities that have made silk the most cherished of materials for 4,000 years. In the first place, they have the beauty that only this most beautiful of fibers can impart, whether they are woven to display all the natural gloss of the silk, or to glow with a soft, diffused lustre. They take dyes with a purity and clarity that makes possible a limitless range of color, from the softest, subtlest neutrals to the most brilliant deep tones. They print superbly; printed silks have clarity and depth to delight an artist. And silks have practical qualities which are unique.

Given the various degrees or grades which the properties of silk fabrics may have, it is indeed plausible, if not unavoidable, that customers and

---

[*] [The appellant identified a variety of meanings for "super" including, in addition to the interpretation as "of superfine grade or quality" or "of great worth, value, excellence or superiority," the alternative meanings "superintendent," "supervisor," "upper story of a beehive," and "watch." Appellant argued that, in addition to the fabric, "Silk" also refers to "the gown worn by a King's or Queen's counsel," and "the clothes worn by a jockey." — EDS.]

potential buyers of applicant's dress shirts and sports shirts made of silk-like fabric would believe that such goods, when marketed under the term "SUPER SILK," are made of an excellent, first-rate, or superior grade of genuine silk when, in fact, that is not the case. Accordingly, because both elements of the test for a deceptively misdescriptive term have been satisfied, registration of the term "SUPER SILK" is barred by Section 2 (e)(1) of the statute....

This brings us to consideration of the refusal under Section 2(a). Having found the term "SUPER SILK," for the reasons stated above, to be deceptively misdescriptive of applicant's "dress shirts and sport shirts made of silk-like fabric," the determinative issue for the purpose of whether such term is also unregistrable as deceptive is whether the misdescription is likely to affect the decision to purchase the goods. Applicant, in its brief, appears to essentially concede the materiality thereof, inasmuch as it notes that a silk shirt constitutes "a 'premium' garment":

> [T]he Examining Attorney...has stated that "silk shirts are generally higher priced than non-silk shirts," "consumers are willing to pay a premium for silk shirts," and "whether or not applicant's shirts contain silk is a material factor to consumers." This being said, it follows that consumers will exercise a high degree of care when purchasing silk shirts. A consumer who is taking care to purchase a "premium" garment will touch the fabric to feel its texture and try on the item to ensure a proper look, feel and fit before spending a "higher price."...

Although applicant concludes the above-quoted paragraph by asserting that "consumers will not purchase Applicant's shirts with the belief that they contain silk," applicant does not take issue with the Examining Attorney's contention that the presence or absence of silk in articles of apparel, including dress shirts and sport shirts, is a material consideration in a consumer's decision to purchase such items. In particular, applicant further acknowledges in its brief the desirability, and hence materiality, of whether clothing is made of silk by stating that, "[m]ost importantly, consumers who are looking to purchase a high priced silk garment will check the fiber content of an item to be sure they are getting what they desire."

The Examining Attorney, in his brief, insists that the term "SUPER SILK" is deceptive because, when used in connection with dress shirts and sport shirts made of silk-like fabric, the misrepresentation conveyed by such term "would materially affect the decision to purchase the goods." Specifically, the Examining Attorney states that:

> The excerpts from WHAT IS SILK...give ample testimony to the ancient pedigree and desirable qualities of silk. That silk shirts are generally higher priced than non-silk shirts shows that consumers regard shirts made of silk as more desirable....

Given that silk possesses such desirable attributes, it is plain that a term which indicates that shirts or other garments are made of silk is likely to affect the decision to purchase the goods. The term "SUPER SILK," which deceptively misdescribes applicant's dress shirts and sports shirts made of silk-like fabric as believably being made of an excellent, first-rate, or

superior grade of real silk, accordingly is also deceptive within the meaning of Section 2(a) of the statute.

Applicant appears to maintain, however, that any deception imparted by
the term "SUPER SILK" to its goods will be precluded by the fact that such
goods, when sold, are required by federal law to carry labels setting forth
the fiber content of the fabric from which the goods are made. According to
applicant's brief:     ⟹ G feels this irrelevant to mark

> The Federal Trade Commission ("FTC") requires that all textile and wool
> products contain a label listing the fiber content of the fabric. *See The Textile
> Fiber Products Identification Act*, 15 U.S.C. §§70, et seq. Applicant has been an
> eminent international manufacturer of various clothing products and acces-
> sories for over 100 years and has regularly complied with FTC guidelines.
> Because consumers exercising ordinary care will read Applicant's labels and
> tags, and such labels/tags will specify that the shirts do not contain silk, there
> is no way consumers will believe the shirts are made of silk. Further, Appli-
> cant contends that its mark SUPER SILK appears on the *same* label as the
> fabric content.

As support for its contention, applicant relies upon declarations which it
made of record from its president and a merchandise manager of another
apparel firm. Each declarant, among other things, states that consumers
"exercise care in purchasing clothing products" and that, as part of such
care, "consumers read the fiber content of a clothing item before purchasing the particular item."

Applicant presses the above contention despite citing, in its brief, *In re
Budge Manufacturing Co. Inc.*, *supra* at 1261, which specifically refuted such
an argument by stating, as to advertising and labeling which indicate the
actual fabric content of a product, that (citation omitted; emphasis in original):

> Misdescriptiveness of a term may be negated by its meaning in the context of
> the whole mark inasmuch as the combination is seen together and makes a
> unitary impression. The same is not true with respect to explanatory state-
> ments in advertising or on labels which purchasers may or may not note and
> which may or may not always be provided. The statutory provision bars
> registration of *a mark* comprising deceptive matter. Congress has said that
> the advantages of registration may not be extended to a mark which deceives
> the public. Thus, the mark standing alone must pass muster, for that is what
> the applicant seeks to register, not extraneous explanatory statements.

That applicant's dress shirts and sports shirts made of silk-like fabric will
disclose, when marketed under the term "SUPER SILK," the fact that the
fabric from which such goods are manufactured is not genuine silk is
accordingly irrelevant and immaterial.

*Decision:* The refusals under Sections 2(e)(1) and 2(a) are affirmed.

## Comments

1. ***Different Tests for §2(a) and (e)(1).*** It seems odd at first that there are
   different tests for marks that are allegedly deceptively misdescriptive
   and marks that are allegedly deceptive. The additional element,
   materiality, distinguishes deceptive from deceptively misdescriptive

marks. While the labels do not make it clear, the reason is that if the misdescription would not affect consumers' purchasing decisions, that is, is not material, registration should be more permissive. Lanham Act §2(f) describes circumstances under which deceptively misdescriptive marks may be registered. Deceptive marks may never be registered.

2. *Clarifying Tags, Words, Marketing.* While the commercial impression of the mark is relevant to determining the registrability of the mark, the manner in which the mark appears on the goods or the explanatory statements that accompany the mark are not considered in determining the commercial impression. The TTAB in *Phillips-Van Heusen* quotes from a leading opinion of the Court of Appeals for the Federal Circuit, *In re Budge Manufacturing Co. Inc.*, saying that the mark "standing alone" must pass muster. The statutory provision referred to by the Court of Appeals in *Budge* is support for this conclusion. Another rationale is that the PTO is in no position of provide constant monitoring of the manner in which the mark appears on the goods. It only approves the mark itself.

3. *Secondary Meaning for §2(e).* Deceptively misdescriptive marks may be registered if they have acquired secondary meaning while deceptive marks may not. Lanham Act §2(f) lists types of otherwise unregistrable marks that may be registrable with secondary meaning, including some of the types of marks in §2(e): merely descriptive, deceptively misdescriptive, primarily geographically descriptive, surnames.

## Problems

2-13. Is the mark APPLE used in connection with computer hardware deceptively misdescriptive? If so, is it deceptive?

2-14. *In re Paj, Inc.*, 2001 WL 227124 (March 7, 2001), involved an application for use of the mark DIAMONDLITE in connection with jewelry containing fake diamonds. The applicant relies on the COLLEGIATE DICTIONARY, MERRIAM-WEBSTER 2000, which defines "lite" as "containing less than the legal, standard, or usual weight," "of little importance," and "made with a lower calorie content or with less of some ingredient." Would registration of this mark be contrary to §2(a) (deceptive) or §2(e) (deceptively misdescriptive)?

2-15. The Trademark Trial and Appeals Board refused to register LOVEY LAMB for use in connection with synthetic (faux sheepskin) automobile seat covers. Do Lanham Act §2(a) and (d) both apply to bar registration? *See In re Budge Mfg. Co.* Inc., 857 F.2d 773 (Fed. Cir. 1988).

## 4. Descriptive and Deceptive Geographic Marks

Geographic marks include references to particular geographic areas, such as the state of Minnesota, the municipality of Roquefort, France, and the

North Pole. Geographic marks are regulated by three parts of the Lanham Act, which distinguishes deceptive marks (including deceptive geographic marks) from primarily geographically descriptive marks (registrable with secondary meaning), and primarily geographically deceptively misdescriptive marks (never registrable). *In re JT Tobacconists* discusses geographically descriptive marks and the "goods/place association" test. *Community of Roquefort v. William Faehndrich, Inc.* examines the policies underlying general prohibition of geographic marks in the context of a certification mark and the exception for indicators of regional origin. *In re California Innovations* applies the modern test for determining whether a mark is primarily geographically deceptively misleading. Be particularly alert to the changes resulting from the North American Free Trade Agreement (NAFTA).

*STATUTE:* **Marks Registrable on the Principal Register**
15 U.S.C. §5052(a), (e)(2), (3), (f) (Lanham Act §2(a), (e)(2), (3), (f))

## IN RE JT TOBACCONISTS
### 59 U.S.P.Q.2d 1080 (Trademark Tr. & App. Bd. 2001)

HOHEIN, J.

JT Tobacconists, a Minnesota corporation located in Minnetonka, Minnesota, has filed an application to register the mark "MINNESOTA CIGAR COMPANY" for "cigars; cigar cases not made of precious metal; [and] humidors".

Registration has been finally refused under Section 2(e)(2) of the Trademark Act, 15 U.S.C. §1052(e)(2), on the ground that, as applied to applicant's goods, the mark "MINNESOTA CIGAR COMPANY" is primarily geographically descriptive of them.

Applicant has appealed. Briefs have been filed, but an oral hearing was not requested. We affirm the refusal to register.

As a general proposition, in order for registration of a mark to be properly refused on the ground that it is primarily geographically descriptive of an applicant's goods or services, it is necessary to establish that (i) the primary significance of the mark is that of the name of a place generally known to the public and (ii) that the public would make a goods/place or services/place association, that is, believe that the goods or services for which the mark is sought to be registered originate in that place. Provided that these conditions are met, and the goods or services come from the place named by or in the mark, the mark is primarily geographically descriptive.

Moreover, where there is no genuine issue that the geographical significance of a term is its primary significance, and where the geographical place named by the term is neither obscure nor remote, a public association of the goods or services with the place may ordinarily be presumed from the fact that the applicant's goods or services come from the geographical place named in the mark. In addition, the presence of generic or highly descriptive terms in a mark which also contains a primarily geographically descriptive term does not serve to detract from the primary geographical significance of the mark as a whole.

In response to the first Office action, applicant's former attorney stated that "[t]he products which will be sold with the proposed mark will be either packaged or produced in Minnesota." Applicant's current attorney, in its initial brief, ratifies such statement by asserting that applicant has "begun selling its goods on the internet under the domain name: *www.minnesotacigarcompany.com*" and "confirming that the goods were at a minimum packaged and shipped from Minnesota." Applicant admits, therefore, that "the mark identifies the point of origin of the goods." Applicant further acknowledges in its initial brief that its "previous attorney . . . made the inartful statement [that] 'the primary significance of the mark is to identify the point of origin of the goods,'" but claims that the comment was made "in order to counter the assertion that the mark may be geographically deceptively misdescriptive if the goods will not originate in Minnesota." Applicant, although notably without any evidentiary support, additionally asserts on appeal that "[t]he actual primary significance [of the mark] is to suggest a level of excellence in procuring top quality cigars and cigar related products."

Applicant also argues, as perhaps its strongest point, that "geographic names are not always associated with the goods produced [in the location named by the mark,] making the reference to geography arbitrary" rather than descriptive. In particular, applicant maintains that:

> Tobacco is not grown in Minnesota, nor is Minnesota associated with the production of cigars. The potential purchasers absolutely will not associate the goods, cigars, with the geographic location. In addition, the potential and actual purchasers of the goods, cigars, do not perceive the mark *MINNESOTA CIGAR COMPANY* as identifying the geographic origin of the goods. Here, the name *MINNESOTA CIGAR COMPANY* as a geographic location has no significant relation to the production of cigars and is therefore arbitrary.

The Examining Attorney, on the other hand, argues that the primary significance of applicant's mark, as a whole, is that of a geographic location and that the purchasing public would make a goods/place association in that they would believe that applicant's goods originate in Minnesota. Specifically, as to the former, the Examining Attorney relies upon the definition of record of the word "Minnesota," which *The American Heritage Dictionary of the English Language* (3rd ed. 1992) lists as:

> A state of the Northern United States bordering on Lake Superior and on Manitoba and Ontario, Canada. It was admitted as the 32nd state in 1858. First explored by the French in the mid-17th century, the area became part of the United States through the Treaty of Paris (1783) and the Louisiana Purchase (1803). St. Paul is the capital and Minneapolis the largest city. Population, 4,387,029.

The addition, furthermore, of the words "CIGAR COMPANY," the Examining Attorney insists, "does not obviate a determination of geographic descriptiveness" because such words "are descriptive terms referring to the products provided by the applicant." The word "cigar," the Examining Attorney notes, is generic for applicant's cigars and merely descriptive of its cigar cases and humidors, while the word "company," being an entity designation, "is generic since the term is incapable of identifying the applicant's goods and distinguishing them from those of others." Consequently, and since "[t]he applicant has not disputed the genericness of *CIGAR COMPANY* for an...entity that is in the business of selling *cigars* and *cigar products*," the Examining Attorney insists that "the addition of this generic matter does not remove the mark from being primarily geographically descriptive."

As to whether the purchasing public would make a goods/place association by believing that applicant's goods have their origin in Minnesota, the Examining Attorney cites In re Nantucket Allserve Inc., 28 USPQ2d 1144 (TTAB 1993), for the proposition that, where "the primary significance of a mark is to indicate a geographic location which is neither obscure nor remote and the applicant's goods are manufactured or produced in the location indicated, then the public is likely to believe that the geographic term identifies the place from which the goods originate." Here, as noted above, not only is Minnesota neither obscure nor remote, but as the Examining Attorney points out, applicant has made an "admission that the goods are manufactured or produced in Minnesota." Therefore, absent sufficient incongruity between the place named in or by the mark and the goods marketed thereunder, the Examining Attorney maintains that a goods/place association must be presumed.

In particular, the Examining Attorney asserts that, unlike use of the mark "NORTH POLE" for goods, such as bananas, which could not possibly emanate from that geographic location, this case is not one in which applicant's goods have no significant or plausible relation to the State of Minnesota. To the contrary, the Examining Attorney stresses that applicant's goods do indeed "emanate from the geographic location [named in applicant's mark], in that the applicant's business is located in Minnesota, and the applicant has stated that...[its] products are packaged, produced and sold in Minnesota."

With respect to applicant's contention that tobacco is not grown in Minnesota and that such state is not associated with the production of cigars and/or cigar products, the Examining Attorney, citing In re Nantucket, Inc., 677 F.2d 95, 213 USPQ 889 (CCPA 1982), asserts that "[t]here is no requirement that the place identified in the mark be well known or noted for the goods...in order to find the existence of a goods/place association" under the statute. Instead, according to the Examining Attorney:

> To establish a goods/place association, the examining attorney must only show a "reasonable basis" for concluding that the public is likely to believe that the mark identifies the place from which the goods originate.

We agree with the Examining Attorney that the record in this case is sufficient to establish a *prima facie* case that the mark "MINNESOTA CIGAR COMPANY" is primarily geographically descriptive of applicant's cigars, cigar cases and humidors. Here, there simply is no doubt that the geographical significance of the term "MINNESOTA" is its primary significance, since such is its sole significance and, as one of the 50 states of the United States, Minnesota is plainly neither obscure nor remote. The additional presence in applicant's mark of the generic terminology "CIGAR COMPANY" for an entity in the business of selling cigars and related cigar products such as cigar cases and humidors does not detract from or otherwise alter the fact that the primary significance of the mark as a whole is geographical. Accordingly, the Examining Attorney has clearly established that the first element of the test for whether applicant's mark is primarily geographically descriptive of its goods is met.

For us, the dispositive issue in this case is whether the second prong of the primarily geographically descriptive test is satisfied, that is, would the purchasing public for applicant's goods make a goods/place association by believing that the goods for which the mark is sought to be registered originate in Minnesota. We find that they would, inasmuch as a public association of applicant's goods with the State of Minnesota may be presumed from the fact that, as conceded by applicant, its goods "at a minimum [are] packaged and shipped from Minnesota" and thus such term identifies the point of origin of the goods. There is simply no support for applicant's assertion that the primary significance of its mark "is to suggest a level of excellence in procuring top quality cigars and cigar related products." Applicant, moreover, has offered nothing, by way of argument or evidence, to demonstrate a sufficient incongruity between the place named in applicant's mark and the goods marketed thereunder.

Specifically, as to applicant's principal contention that its mark as a whole is arbitrary because, inasmuch as there is nothing to show that tobacco is grown in Minnesota or that such state is known for the production of tobacco products, there is no significant relationship between the State of Minnesota and the production of tobacco products, we note that cigars, cigar cases and humidors, unlike tobacco, are manufactured products which could have their origin practically anywhere. Therefore, while the purchasing public for applicant's goods may be unlikely to assume that the tobacco in applicant's cigars comes from a Northern state like Minnesota, since tobacco is traditionally associated with states which have a longer and milder growing season (such as Virginia and North Carolina), there is nothing in the record which even suggests that it would be incongruous or otherwise unexpected for the purchasing public to believe that products manufactured from tobacco, such as cigars, and/or containers for tobacco products, such as cigar cases and humidors, all of which are produced and shipped by applicant from its place of business in Minnesota, originate in the State of Minnesota. There is no requirement, as the Examining Attorney correctly points out, that the State of Minnesota be noted for cigars and cigar products in order for a mark such as "MINNESOTA CIGAR COMPANY" to be held primarily geographically descriptive, and prospective purchasers of applicant's goods would reasonably believe that applicant's goods, being products manufactured either from tobacco or for use with tobacco products, originate in the State of Minnesota, since such state is the geographic location from which applicant produces and sells its cigars, cigar cases and humidors. Accordingly, we find that a goods/place association exists in that customers for applicant's goods would believe that its cigars, cigar cases and humidors are manufactured in the State of Minnesota and that, because applicant's goods do indeed come from such state, its mark is primarily geographically descriptive of its goods within the meaning of the statute.

*Decision:* The refusal under Section 2(e)(2) is affirmed.

## COMMUNITY OF ROQUEFORT v. WILLIAM FAEHNDRICH, INC.

### 303 F.2d 494 (2d Cir. 1962)

KAUFMAN, Circuit Judge.

The Community of Roquefort (hereafter sometimes referred to as Community), a municipality in France, is the holder of a certification mark "Roquefort" for cheese, which is registered in the United States Patent Office under Section 4 of the Lanham Trade-Mark Act of 1946. Together with a French cheese exporter, another French agent, and an American cheese packaging concern, the Community filed a complaint against William Faehndrich, Inc. (hereafter referred to as Faehndrich), a New York cheese importer. The complaint alleged, inter alia, that Faehndrich was infringing the Community's "Roquefort" certification mark; and, in general, it sought to enjoin Faehndrich from selling cheese not produced in accordance with that mark but labeled or represented as "Imported Roquefort Cheese." Plaintiffs moved for summary judgment.... From a judgment in favor of the Community of Roquefort, and the issuance of a permanent injunction against continued infringement of the certification mark, the defendant Faehndrich appeals.

It appears that for centuries there has been produced and cured in the natural limestone caves in and about the municipality of Roquefort a sheep's milk blue-mold cheese, which has been marketed in this country for many years as "Roquefort Cheese." In an effort to protect themselves against unfair competition, producers of such French "Roquefort Cheese" frequently have asked our courts to prevent misleading use of the "Roquefort" designation. For similar reasons the Community of Roquefort, in 1953, obtained a certification mark so that the term "Roquefort," as applied to cheese, would be used exclusively:

> ***to indicate that the same has been manufactured from sheep's milk only, and had been cured in the natural caves of the Community of Roquefort, Department of Aveyron, France, in accordance with the historic methods and usages of production, curing and development which have been in vogue there for a long period of years.

Since that time the Community has been diligent in protecting the mark.

Nevertheless, in 1960, Faehndrich imported into the United States a quantity of sheep's milk blue-mold cheese, labeled "Imported Roquefort Cheese" (at Faehndrich's direction), which had been produced in Hungary and Italy. Of course, it was not (and could not be) produced by authority of the Community of Roquefort under its mark. When imported, Faehndrich's cheese was packaged in a manner clearly indicating the countries of origin. On the other hand, when Faehndrich prepared the cheese for resale, the labels prominently displaying the words "Product of Italy" and "Product of Hungary" were replaced with new wrappers printed "Imported Roquefort Cheese" and "Made from Pure Sheep's Milk Only" without any indication of origin. Hence, there was nothing on the wrappers which would suggest to the retail-buying public that Faehndrich's cheese came from Hungary or Italy.

In order to clarify our discussion of the single question presented by this appeal, i.e., whether Judge Metzner was correct in granting the

Community of Roquefort's motion for summary judgment, it will be helpful to summarize the law applicable to certification marks such as the mark involved in this case, and by way of explanation, to point out certain distinctions between trade-marks on the one hand, and certification marks on the other.

Until the Lanham Act of 1946, a geographical name could not be registered as a trade-mark. This prohibition operated to prevent a single producer from appropriating the name of a particular place or area in which he was located to the exclusion of other and similarly situated producers....

Section 2(e) of the Lanham Act continued to prohibit registration of a geographical name as a trade-mark, if "when applied to the goods of the applicant (it) is primarily geographically descriptive ***," 15 U.S.C.A. §1052(e)(2), unless such a name "has become distinctive of the applicant's goods ***," 15 U.S.C.A. §1052(f). Under the Lanham Act, therefore, if a geographical name acquires a secondary meaning, it can be registered as a trademark.

In addition to this extension of trade-mark law, the Lanham Act created an entirely new registered mark which was denominated a "certification mark."

> The term "certification mark" a mark used upon or in connection with the products *** of one or more persons other than the owner of the mark to certify regional or other origin, material, mode of manufacture, quality, accuracy or other characteristics of such goods ***. 15 U.S.C.A. §1127.

A geographical name does not require a secondary meaning in order to qualify for registration as a certification mark. It is true that section 1054 provides that certification marks are "subject to the provisions relating to the registration of trademarks, so far as they are applicable ***." But section 1052(c)(2), which prohibits registration of names primarily geographically descriptive, specifically excepts "indications of regional origin" registrable under section 1054. Therefore, a geographical name may be registered as a certification mark even though it is primarily geographically descriptive. This distinction, i.e., that a geographical name cannot be registered as a trade-mark unless it has secondary meaning, but can be registered as a certification mark without secondary meaning, has significance. A trade-mark gives a producer exclusive rights; but a certification mark, owned by a municipality, such as Roquefort, must be made available without discrimination "to certify the goods *** of any person who maintains the standards or conditions which such mark certifies." 15 U.S.C.A. §1064(d)(4).

On the other hand, a geographical name registered as a certification mark must continue to indicate the regional origin, mode of manufacture, etc. of the goods upon which it is used, just as a trade-mark must continue to identify a producer.

> When the meaning of a mark that had previously served as an indication of origin changes so that its principal significance to purchasers is that of indicating the nature or class of goods and its function as an indication of origin is subservient thereto, it is no longer a mark but rather is a generic term. Vandenburgh, Trademark Law and Procedure §9.20 (1959).

Therefore, if a geographical name which has been registered as a certification mark, identifying certain goods, acquires principal significance as a description of those goods, the rights cease to be incontestable and the mark is subject to cancellation.

*cum local Cert mark*

In the present case Faehndrich does not contest the validity of the mark's registration, as to which the Community's certificate of registration is prima facie proof. Instead, Faehndrich argues that there is a genuine issue of fact concerning the existence of generic meaning, i.e., whether the term "Roquefort" has acquired principal significance as a description of blue-mold sheep's milk regardless of its origin and without reference to the method of curing employed in the limestone caves of Roquefort, France.

*(vague) generic*

The difficulty with Faehndrich's position, however, is that nowhere in the affidavits submitted below on the motion for summary judgment is there any allegation of facts which suggests that such a genuine issue exists; nor does Faehndrich mark any allegation that is could prove such facts at a trial. The affidavits are barren of any allegations or facts that consumers understand the word "Roquefort" to mean nothing more than blue-mold cheese made with sheep's milk. Indeed, the Community's affidavits indicate the contrary. They allege that the only other cheese of this nature commercially sold in the United States, a product of Israel, is marketed as "Garden of Eden—Heavenly Cheese—Sheep's Milk Blue-Mold Cheese"; that a similar Tunisian product is marketed abroad as "Bleu de Brebis"; and that the same cheese which Faehndrich imports from Hungary and sells with the label "Imported Roquefort Cheese" is sold in Belgium as "Merinofort." Moreover, we have already noted that producers of French Roquefort cheese have diligently protected the name from unfair competition in this country.

*but show generic*

*P has history of protection*

The purpose of summary judgment is to dispose of cases in which "there is no genuine issue as to any material fact and *** the moving party is entitled to a judgment as a matter of law." Rule 56(c), Fed. R. Civ. P. 28 U.S.C.A.. Since the object is to discover whether one side has no real support for its version of the facts, the Rule specifically states that affidavits shall "set forth such facts as would be admissible in evidence." Rule 56(e), Fed. R. Civ. P. In view of this, we agree with Judge Metzner that Faehndrich "has failed to show *** that there is any possibility on a trial that he can raise an issue of fact" in regard to generic meaning.

Moreover, since Faehndrich's wrappers indisputably bore the inscription "Imported Roquefort Cheese," we believe that the District Court was justified in finding, as a matter of law, that appellant's use of an identical mark on substantially identical goods was "likely to cause confusion or mistake or to deceive purchasers as to the source of the origin of the goods." 15 U.S.C.A. §1114.

We are well aware of the dangers involved in haphazard use of summary judgment procedures. However, summary judgment cannot be defeated where there is no indication that a genuine issue of fact exists; to permit that would be to render this valuable procedure wholly inoperative and to place a "devastating gloss" on the rule.

Affirmed.

## IN RE CALIFORNIA INNOVATIONS, INC.

### 329 F.3d 1334 (Fed. Cir. 2003)

RADER, Circuit Judge.

California Innovations, Inc. (CA Innovations), a Canadian-based corporation, appeals the Trademark Trial and Appeal Board's refusal to register its mark—CALIFORNIA INNOVATIONS. Citing section 2(e)(3) of the Lanham Act, 15 U.S.C. §1052(e)(3) (2000), the Board concluded that the mark was primarily geographically deceptively misdescriptive. Because the Board applied an outdated standard in its analysis under §1052(e)(3), this court vacates the Board's decision and remands.

CA Innovations filed an intent-to-use trademark application, Serial No. 74/650,703, on March 23, 1995, for the composite mark CALIFORNIA INNOVATIONS and Design. The application sought registration for the following goods:

> automobile visor organizers, namely, holders for personal effects, and automobile trunk organizers for automotive accessories in International Class 12; backpacks in International Class 18; thermal insulated bags for food and beverages, thermal insulated tote bags for food or beverages, and thermal insulated wraps for cans to keep the containers cold or hot in International Class 21; and nylon, vinyl, polyester and/or leather bags for storage and storage pouches in International Class 22. . . .

The Lanham Act addresses geographical marks in three categories. The first category, §1052(a), identifies geographically deceptive marks:

> No trademark by which the goods of the applicant may be distinguished from the goods of others shall be refused registration on the principal register on account of its nature unless it—(a) Consists of or comprises immoral, *deceptive*, or scandalous matter; or matter which may disparage or falsely suggest a connection with persons, living or dead, institutions, beliefs, or national symbols, or bring them into contempt, or disrepute.

15 U.S.C. §1052(a) (2000) (emphasis added). Although not expressly addressing geographical marks, §1052(a) has traditionally been used to reject geographic marks that materially deceive the public. A mark found to be deceptive under §1052(a) cannot receive protection under the Lanham Act. To deny a geographic mark protection under §1052(a), the PTO must establish that (1) the mark misrepresents or misdescribes the goods, (2) the public would likely believe the misrepresentation, and (3) the misrepresentation would materially affect the public's decision to purchase the goods. This test's central point of analysis is materiality because that finding shows that the misdescription deceived the consumer.

The other two categories of geographic marks are (1) "primarily geographically descriptive" marks and (2) "primarily geographically deceptively misdescriptive" marks under §1052(e). The North American Free Trade Agreement [hereinafter NAFTA], as implemented by the NAFTA Implementation Act in 1993, has recently changed these two categories. Before the NAFTA changes, §1052(e) and (f) stated:

No trademark by which the goods of the applicant may be distinguished from the goods of others shall be refused registration on the principal register on account of its nature unless it —

(e) Consists of a mark which . . . (2) when used on or in connection with the goods of the applicant is primarily geographically descriptive or deceptively misdescriptive of them. . . .

(f) Except as expressly excluded in paragraphs (a)-(d) of this section, nothing in this chapter shall prevent the registration of a mark used by the applicant which has become distinctive of the applicant's goods in commerce.

The law treated these two categories of geographic marks identically. Specifically, the PTO generally placed a "primarily geographically descriptive" or "deceptively misdescriptive" mark on the supplemental register. Upon a showing of acquired distinctiveness, these marks could qualify for the principal register.

Thus, in contrast to the permanent loss of registration rights imposed on deceptive marks under §1052(a), pre-NAFTA §1052(e)(2) only required a temporary denial of registration on the principal register. Upon a showing of distinctiveness, these marks could acquire a place on the principal register. As permitted by pre-NAFTA §1052(f), a mark could acquire distinctiveness or "secondary meaning" by showing that "in the minds of the public, the primary significance of a product feature or term is to identify the source of the product rather than the product itself." *Inwood Labs., Inc. v. Ives Labs.*, 456 U.S. 844, 851 n. 11 (1982). . . .

Before NAFTA, the PTO identified and denied registration to a primarily geographically deceptively misdescriptive mark with a showing that (1) the primary significance of the mark was a generally known geographic location, and (2) "the public was likely to believe the mark identified the place from which the goods originate and that the goods did not come from there." *In re Loew's*, 769 F.2d 764, 768 (Fed. Cir. 1985). The second prong of the test represents the "goods-place association" between the mark and the goods at issue. This test raised an inference of deception based on the likelihood of a goods-place association that did not reflect the actual origin of the goods. A mere inference, however, is not enough to establish the deceptiveness that brings the harsh consequence of non-registrability under the amended Lanham Act. As noted, NAFTA and the amended Lanham Act place an emphasis on actual misleading of the public. . . .

Thus, due to the NAFTA changes in the Lanham Act, the PTO must deny registration under §1052(e)(3) if (1) the primary significance of the mark is a generally known geographic location, (2) the consuming public is likely to believe the place identified by the mark indicates the origin of the goods bearing the mark, when in fact the goods do not come from that place, and (3) the misrepresentation was a material factor in the consumer's decision.

As a result of the NAFTA changes to the Lanham Act, geographic deception is specifically dealt with in subsection (e)(3), while deception in general continues to be addressed under subsection (a). Consequently, this

court anticipates that the PTO will usually address geographically deceptive marks under subsection (e)(3) of the amended Lanham Act rather than
subsection (a). While there are identical legal standards for deception in
each section, subsection (e)(3) specifically involves deception involving
geographic marks.

CA Innovations unequivocally states in its opening brief that its "petition seeks review only of that portion of the [Board's] decision that pertains
to 'thermal insulated bags for food and beverages and thermal insulated
wraps for cans' " as identified in International Class 21 in the application.
Therefore, because of applicant's decision not to challenge the Board's
judgment with respect to all goods other than those identified in class
21, that part of the Board's decision is not affected by this opinion. . . .

> The parties agree that CA Innovations' goods do not originate in California.
> Under the first prong of the test—whether the mark's primary significance is
> a generally known geographic location—a composite mark such as the appli-
> cant's proposed mark must be evaluated as a whole. . . . It is not erroneous,
> however, for the examiner to consider the significance of each element
> within the composite mark in the course of evaluating the mark as a whole.

*Save Venice*, 259 F.3d at 1352 (citations omitted).

The Board found that "the word CALIFORNIA is a prominent part of
applicant's mark and is not overshadowed by either the word INNOVA-
TIONS or the design element." Although the mark may also convey the
idea of a creative, laid-back lifestyle or mindset, the Board properly recognized that such an association does not contradict the primary geographic
significance of the mark. Even if the public may associate California with a
particular life-style, the record supports the Board's finding that the primary meaning remains focused on the state of California. Nonetheless, this
court declines to review at this stage the Board's finding that CA Innovations' composite mark CALIFORNIA INNOVATIONS and Design is primarily geographic in nature. Rather the PTO may apply the entire new test
on remand.

The second prong of the test requires proof that the public is likely to
believe the applicant's goods originate in California. The Board stated that
the examining attorney submitted excerpts from the Internet and the
NEXIS database showing "some manufacturers and distributors of backpacks, tote bags, luggage, computer cases, and sport bags . . . headquar-
headquartered in California." The Board also acknowledged articles
"which make reference to companies headquartered in California which
manufacture automobile accessories such as auto organizers," as well as the
"very serious apparel and sewn products industry" in California.

A great deal of the evidence cited in this case relates to the fashion
industry, which is highly prevalent in California due to Hollywood's influence on this industry. However, clothing and fashion have nothing to do
with the products in question. At best, the record in this case shows some
general connection between the state of California and backpacks and
automobile organizers. However, because CA Innovations has limited its
appeal to insulated bags and wraps, the above referenced evidence is
immaterial. Therefore, this opinion has no bearing on whether the evidence of record supports a rejection of the application with regard to

any goods other than those identified in CA Innovations' application under International Class 21, namely insulated bags and wraps.

CA Innovations argues that the examining attorney provided no evidence at all concerning insulated bags for food and wraps for cans in California. The Government contends that the evidence shows some examples of a lunch bag, presumed to be insulated, and insulated backpacks. According to the government, the evidence supports a finding of a goods-place association between California and insulated bags and wraps. This court has reviewed the publications and listings supplied by the examining attorney. At best, the evidence of a connection between California and insulated bags and wraps is tenuous. Even if the evidence supported a finding of a goods-place association, the PTO has yet to apply the materiality test in this case. This court declines to address that issue and apply the new standard in the first instance. Accordingly, this court vacates the finding of the Board that CA Innovations' mark is primarily geographically deceptively misdescriptive, and remands the case for further proceedings. On remand, the Board shall apply the new three-prong standard....

Vacated and remanded.

## Comments

1. *Registrability of Geographic Marks*. Geographic marks may be denied registration on the ground that they are (a) primarily geographically descriptive, Lanham Act §2(e)(2) (*JT Tobacconists*) or (b) primarily geographically deceptively misdescriptive, Lanham Act §2(e)(3) (*California Innovations*). The second category is a special case of the prohibition of deceptive marks in Lanham Act §2(a). *Community of Roquefort* illustrates that the prohibition of primarily geographically descriptive marks does not apply to certification marks. *See* Comment 2 below. Geographic marks for wine and spirits receive special treatment, as a result of international treaties. *See* the International Perspective Note on page 118.

    The first two elements of the tests for whether marks are geographically descriptive or misdescriptive are nearly the same whether the primary significance of the mark is a generally known geographic location and whether consumers are likely to believe the goods in connection with which the mark is used originate in that place. For these two elements, the only difference is that for descriptive marks the belief is correct while for misdescriptive marks the belief is mistaken.

    The test for whether a mark is primarily geographically deceptively misdescriptive adds a third element: whether the misrepresentation is material. The addition of this element makes the three-part test for geographically misdescriptive align with the three-part test for deceptive. *See In re Phillips-Van Heusen Corp.*, above.

2. *Secondary Meaning and Geographic Descriptiveness.* Geographically descriptive trademarks and service marks, like merely descriptive marks without geographic significance, are registrable if they have acquired distinctiveness, that is, secondary meaning. As *Community of Roquefort* illustrates, however, geographically descriptive certification marks are registrable without a showing of secondary meaning. The

rationale is that the mark owner must nondiscriminatorily allow *all* producers meeting the geographic criteria to use the mark, so no qualifying producer is competitively disadvantaged. The same is not true for merely descriptive trade and service marks. Only the mark owner is allowed to use (or license) the mark and competitors may be disadvantaged by not being able to describe the qualities and characteristics of their goods.

FIGURE 1

Owners of all certification marks, including those that are geographically descriptive, must control use of the mark, *see* Lanham Act §14(5) (Cancellation of Certification Marks) and take care that the mark does not become generic. The French organization formed to protect regional designations of French wines opposed the registration of the mark CHABLIS WITH A TWIST by a California wine company. Its claim failed because the term "Chablis," which is the name of a wine-growing region in France, became generic when many vintners in the United States used the term to indicate a type of wine with the general characteristics of French Chablis. *See Institute Nat. des Appellations d'Origine v. Vintners International, Inc.*, 958 F.2d 1574 (Fed. Cir. 1992).

3. *Effect of NAFTA on Geographically Descriptive Marks*. When researching cases involving geographically descriptive marks, a lawyer must be alert to amendments to the Lanham Act that resulted from the North American Free Trade Agreement in 1993. Cases before that date apply an outdated test.

Before NAFTA, Lanham Act §2(e) listed two specific categories of geographic marks: primarily geographically descriptive marks and primarily geographically deceptively misdescriptive marks. The test for each type had only two elements and ignored the materiality of the geographic designation. Each type of geographic mark was registrable with secondary meaning. In addition, deceptive geographic marks were covered by §2(a) and could never be registered, even though that section did not refer specifically to geographic deception.

After the NAFTA amendments, there are still two specific categories of geographic marks with the same two labels. In *California Innovations*, the Federal Circuit interpreted those amendments as changing the rules for the second geographic category, primarily geographically deceptively misdescriptive marks. First, a three-part test with a materiality element identical to the §2(a) deceptiveness standard was adopted. Second, primarily geographically deceptively misdescriptive marks could never be registered.

Both the statute and the NAFTA amendments are silent on the status of geographically misdescriptive marks that are not material to consumers' purchasing decisions. In petitions for rehearing of *California Innovations*, both parties interpreted this as meaning that such marks could be registered without secondary meaning. An alternative view would be geographically misdescriptive marks should be treated like other misdescriptive marks under §2(e)(1)—registrable with secondary meaning. The motion for rehearing was denied.

4. *Services/Place Association.* To make a goods/place association, it is necessary to establish that the relevant public would reasonably identify or associate goods sold under a mark with the geographic place indicated by that mark because, to be deceived, the public must believe the goods came from that place. To make a services/place association, it is not enough that the location is known for performing the service. There must be some additional reason for the consumer to associate the services of the applicant with the geographic location invoked by the mark. For instance, San Francisco is known for its fine restaurants, but that is not enough to create a services/place association for a restaurant in Memphis, Tennessee with "San Francisco" in its mark. There must be some additional reason for consumers to believe the services have their origin in that location, such as the fact that the chef was trained there or the food came from there or that the menu was identical to a known San Franciscan menu. Geographic service marks are less likely to mislead consumers, especially for restaurants, which are the most ubiquitous types of services and particularly likely to employ geographic designations. Services, particularly restaurant services, are often rendered in the place where the consumer is located. In addition, the false association must be material for the mark to be primarily geographically deceptively misdescriptive, an element for which the same kind of enhanced evidence is relevant.

## Problems

**2-16.** *In re Municipal Capital Markets Corp.*, 51 U.S.P.Q. 2d 1369 (Trademark Tr. & App. Bd. 1999), involved an application by a Texas corporation to register the mark COOPERSTOWN for use in connection with restaurant services. Cooperstown is a town in central New York state known for the Baseball Hall of Fame; in fact, it is a synonym for the Baseball Hall of Fame. Does this mark pass the first part of the three-part test?

**2-17.** *In re MBNA America Bank, N.A.*, 340 F.3d 1328 (Fed. Cir. 2003), involved an examiner's refusal to register PHILADELPHIA CARD as a service mark for affinity credit card services. MBNA America Bank proposed a series of such credit cards to appeal to customers' regional pride and loyalty depicting scenes from those geographic areas. The various applications included service marks for at least 45 state names and 27 city names. Under which of the following sections of the Lanham Act is this mark invalid, if any: §2(a) deceptive, §2(e)(1) primarily geographically descriptive, §2(e) primarily geographically deceptively misdescriptive? Does it matter whether MBNA is a corporation based in Philadelphia or Los Angeles?

**2-18.**  *In re Les Halles de Paris J.V.*, 334 F.3d 1371 (Fed. Cir. 2003), involved a New York City restaurant that specialized in French kosher cuisine. The restaurant, Les Halles de Paris, sought to register the mark LE MARAIS for its restaurant services. There is a well-known part of Paris, France called "Le Marais." It is known as the Jewish quarter of Paris. Is this service mark registrable?

---

### INTERNATIONAL PERSPECTIVE
### Geographic Marks for Wines and Spirits

Lanham Act §2(a) gives special treatment to geographic marks first used in connection with wines or spirits after December 7, 1995, one year after international trade treaties growing out of the Trade Related Intellectual Property (TRIPs) negotiations went into force. If the mark identifies a place other than the origin of the goods, the mark is not registrable. The primary significance of the mark must be geographic and the genericide exception for certification mark discussed in Comment 2 above still applies. That means that NAPA VALLEY wine is treated differently from ARIZONA ice tea.

The disparate levels of protection under the TRIPs Agreement have drawn increasing criticism in formal [World Trade Organization] communications from many countries....One such communication states "[t]here is no systematic or logical explanation for the distinction made [between wines and spirits and other goods in] the TRIPs Agreement. This distinction ignores that geographical indications for categories of goods other than wines and spirits are equally important for trade."...

Extension advocates contend that due to the inherently weak standard of the misleading test... "[the TRIPs Agreement] enables free-riding by other producers on the renown of a geographical indication. A producer may use a geographical indication for his product, even if it does not originate in the territory purported, as long as the product's true origin is indicated on the label. Thus, a producer can profit from the use of a 'facour' geographical indication and argue at the same time that it is not misleading the consumer." Extension advocates also argue that "the use of geographical indications in translation or accompanied by expressions such as 'style,' 'type,' 'kind,' 'imitation,' or the like...should be prohibited [because TRIPs Agreement] puts...geographical indications at risk to become generic terms." They further contend that the "misleading test" "results in legal uncertainty as to the enforcement of protection for an individual geographical indication at the international level" because national courts' interpretations of the standard vary.

Steven A. Bowers, *Location, Location, Location: The Case Against Extending Geographical Indication Protection under the TRIPs Agreement*, 31 AIPLA QUARTERLY JOURNAL 129, 150 (2003) (citations omitted). Countries opposing extension argue that they did not see any justification for the special treatment in the first place and only agreed because of pressure from European Community wine-producing countries, given the level of protection already provided. They also cite the cost of implementing new laws to protect the large number of geographic indications used and the possible closing-off of future market access to emerging industries. *Id.* at 153-154.

## 5. Marks That Are Primarily a Surname

*STATUTE:* **Marks Registrable on the Principal Register**
15 U.S.C. §5052(a), (e)(4), (f) (Lanham Act §2(a), (e)(4), (f))

The Lanham Act prohibits registration of marks that are primarily a surname (last name) without secondary meaning. This prohibition is directed at marks consisting primarily of a word that is generally understood to be a surname, such as Kennedy, Nixon, or Clinton but perhaps not Ford (Reg. No. 0074530 for use in connection with automobiles and their parts), Johnson (Reg. No. 2694318 for use in connection with miniature outboard motors), or Bush (Reg. No. 2114947 for use in connection with the services of a musical group). The latter have well-known customary meanings in the English language. Surnames are registrable with secondary meaning, which is logical because secondary meaning means that the primary significance of the mark is not as a surname but rather as a source indicator. McDONALD'S used in connection with drive-in restaurant services is a familiar example.

A name is primarily a surname if the primary significance of the mark to consumers is that of a surname. The word "merely" in the statute is synonymous with "only," meaning that the question is whether the significance of the mark is "primarily only a surname." Consider the surnames of this book's authors. "Nard" is a flowering plant growing in the Himalayas from which an aromatic oil is produced. "Barnes" are large buildings for housing farm animals and implements. "Madison" is sometimes used as a given name, is the name of towns across the country (raising geographic issues), and is the name of a historical figure. When the mark in question consists of a surname and additional words, the question becomes what consumers would think of the mark as a whole.

Two examples illustrate the kinds of issues that arise. In the trademark infringement case *Lucien Piccard Watch Corp. v. Crescent Corp.,* 314 F. Supp. 329 (D.N.Y. 1970), the defendant moved for summary judgment on the grounds that the plaintiff's DA VINCI mark, used in connection with personal jewelry and leather products, was invalid because it falsely suggested a connection with a person living or dead and was primarily a surname. On the Lanham Act 2(a) objection, the court found that no consumer could reasonably believe that Leonardo Da Vinci was associated with the products. With respect to the "primarily a surname" contention, the court recognized that two people in the New York phone book used the surname Da Vinci, but concluded that, even though the mark did not suggest that the historical figure was associated with the products, the primary significance was an allusion to Leonardo Da Vinci rather than to the surname generally. In this respect, the mark was more like Rameses, Robin Hood, and Samson, which were registrable and unlike Webster, Longfellow, and Wayne, which were denied registration.

In *Lane Capital Management, Inc. v. Lane Capital Management,* Inc., 192 F.3d 337 (2d Cir. 1999), the parties had chosen identical names for their financial management services. Paul Fulenwider, the senior user, sued Douglas Lane for infringement. Lane, having chosen the business name because Lane is his surname, appealed the court's grant of summary judgment to Fulenwider arguing that the factfinder could find that consumers perceived Lane Capital Management to be primarily merely a surname with no secondary meaning.

Lane offered evidence that "Lane" was a common surname, but the court observed that "lane" also has a common dictionary meaning. Fulenwider claimed that he chose the name because it indicated a relatively straight and narrow path and that suggested a tightly controlled approach to investing. "Lane" was also Fulenwider's son's middle name and his father's nickname and middle name. The court found that alternative (nonsurname) meanings of the word "Lane" and its combination with other words was strong enough to negate its surname significance in the minds of consumers.

## 6. Functional Marks: Trade Dress and Product Design

One of the most controversial contemporary issues in trademark law is the scope and meaning of the Lanham Act §2(e)(5) prohibition on functional marks. Product designs and trade dress that have some utility raise two issues. The first is that, like generic marks, consumers might not see that they are source indicators. This issue was discussed in Part A of this chapter. The second is that giving a trademark monopoly on useful objects may conflict with patent law and its limited duration. The Supreme Court cases that follow, *Qualitex Co. v. Jacobson Products Co., Inc.* and *TrafFix Devices, Inc. v. Marketing Displays, Inc.* consider the functionality of product designs that are aesthetically useful (attractive to consumers because of their visual appeal) and practically useful (attractive to consumers because of their practical utility or to producers because of the cost advantages of the design), respectively. *TrafFix Devices* also discusses the relationship between trademark and patent law. The final case in this chapter, *Talking Rain Beverage Co., Inc. v. South Beach Beverage Co.*, is a modern application of the rules that have emerged from the Supreme Court's pronouncement on functionality.

STATUTE: **Marks Registrable on the Principal Register**
15 U.S.C. §5052(e)(5) (Lanham Act §2(e)(5))

## QUALITEX CO. v. JACOBSON PRODUCTS CO., INC.

### 514 U.S. 159 (1995)

Justice BREYER.

The question in this case is whether the Trademark Act of 1946 (Lanham Act) permits the registration of a trademark that consists, purely and simply, of a color. . . .

The case before us grows out of petitioner Qualitex Company's use (since the 1950's) of a special shade of green-gold color on the pads that it makes and sells to dry cleaning firms for use on dry cleaning presses. In 1989, respondent Jacobson Products (a Qualitex rival) began to sell its own press pads to dry cleaning firms; and it colored those pads a similar green gold. In 1991, Qualitex registered the special green-gold color on press pads with the Patent and Trademark Office as a trademark. Qualitex subsequently added a trademark infringement count, 15 U.S.C. §1114(1), to an unfair competition claim, §1125(a), in a lawsuit it had already filed challenging Jacobson's use of the green-gold color.

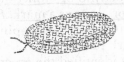 Registration No. 1,633,711 — Description of mark: The mark consists of a particular shade of green-gold applied to the top and side surfaces of the goods. The representation of the goods shown in phantom lining not a part of the mark and serves only to indicate position.

Qualitex won the lawsuit in the District Court. 21 U.S.P.Q.2d 1457 (CD Cal. 1991). But, the Court of Appeals for the Ninth Circuit set aside the judgment in Qualitex's favor on the trademark infringement claim because, in that Circuit's view, the Lanham Act does not permit Qualitex, or anyone else, to register "color alone" as a trademark. 13 F.3d 1297, 1300, 1302 (1994)....

We cannot find in the basic objectives of trademark law any obvious theoretical objection to the use of color alone as a trademark, where that color has attained "secondary meaning" and therefore identifies and distinguishes a particular brand (and thus indicates its "source"),.... It is the source-distinguishing ability of a mark — not its ontological status as color, shape, fragrance, word, or sign — that permits it to serve these basic purposes. And, for that reason, it is difficult to find, in basic trademark objectives, a reason to disqualify absolutely the use of a color as a mark.

Neither can we find a principled objection to the use of color as a mark in the important "functionality" doctrine of trademark law. The functionality doctrine prevents trademark law, which seeks to promote competition by protecting a firm's reputation, from instead inhibiting legitimate competition by allowing a producer to control a useful product feature. It is the province of patent law, not trademark law, to encourage invention by granting inventors a monopoly over new product designs or functions for a limited time after which competitors are free to use the innovation. If a product's functional features could be used as trademarks, however, a monopoly over such features could be obtained without regard to whether they qualify as patents and could be extended forever (because trademarks may be renewed in perpetuity). Functionality doctrine therefore would require, to take an imaginary example, that even if customers have come to identify the special illumination-enhancing shape of a new patented light bulb with a particular manufacturer, the manufacturer may not use that shape as a trademark, for doing so, after the patent had expired, would impede competition — not by protecting the reputation of the original bulb maker, but by frustrating competitors' legitimate efforts to produce an equivalent illumination-enhancing bulb. This Court consequently has explained that, "[i]n general terms, a product feature is functional," and cannot serve as a trademark, "if it is essential to the use or

*functioned it essential to use or perposs or effects cost or quality*

purpose of the article or if it affects the cost or quality of the article," that is, if exclusive use of the feature would put competitors at a significant non-reputation-related disadvantage. *Inwood Laboratories, Inc., supra*, 456 U.S., at 850, n. 10, 102 S. Ct., at 2186, n. 10. Although sometimes color plays an important role (unrelated to source identification) in making a product more desirable, sometimes it does not. And, this latter fact — the fact that sometimes color is not essential to a product's use or purpose and does not affect cost or quality — indicates that the doctrine of "functionality" does not create an absolute bar to the use of color alone as a mark. *In re Owens-Corning Fiberglas Corp.*, 774 F.2d 1116, 1123 (CA Fed. 1985) (pink color of insulation in wall "performs no nontrademark function")....

*Colors not always banned*

Having developed secondary meaning (for customers identified the green-gold color as Qualitex's), it identifies the press pads' source. And, the green-gold color serves no other function. (Although it is important to use *some* color on press pads to avoid noticeable stains, the [District Court] found "no competitive need in the press pad industry for the green-gold color, since other colors are equally usable." 21 U.S.P.Q.2d, at 1460.) Accordingly, unless there is some special reason that convincingly militates against the use of color alone as a trademark, trademark law would protect Qualitex's use of the green-gold color on its press pads....

The functionality doctrine, as we have said, forbids the use of a product's feature as a trademark where doing so will put a competitor at a significant disadvantage because the feature is "essential to the use or purpose of the article" or "affects [its] cost or quality." *Inwood Laboratories, Inc.*, 456 U.S., at 850, n. 10. The functionality doctrine thus protects competitors against a disadvantage (unrelated to recognition or reputation) that trademark protection might otherwise impose, namely, their inability reasonably to replicate important non-reputation-related product features. For example, this Court has written that competitors might be free to copy the color of a medical pill where that color serves to identify the kind of medication (*e.g.*, a type of blood medicine) in addition to its source. And, the federal courts have demonstrated that they can apply this doctrine in a careful and reasoned manner, with sensitivity to the effect on competition. Although we need not comment on the merits of specific cases, we note that lower courts have permitted competitors to copy the green color of farm machinery (because customers wanted their farm equipment to match) and have barred the use of black as a trademark on outboard boat motors (because black has the special functional attributes of decreasing the apparent size of the motor and ensuring compatibility with many different boat colors). The Restatement (Third) of Unfair Competition adds that, if a design's "aesthetic value" lies in its ability to "confe[r] a significant benefit that cannot practically be duplicated by the use of alternative designs," then the design is "functional." Restatement (Third) of Unfair Competition §17, Comment *c*, pp. 175-176 (1993). The "ultimate test of aesthetic functionality," it explains, "is whether the recognition of trademark rights would significantly hinder competition." *Id.*, at 176.

The upshot is that, where a color serves a significant nontrademark function—whether to distinguish a heart pill from a digestive medicine or to satisfy the "noble instinct for giving the right touch of beauty to common and necessary things," G. Chesterton, Simplicity and Tolstoy

61 (1912)—courts will examine whether its use as a mark would permit one competitor (or a group) to interfere with legitimate (nontrademark-related) competition through actual or potential exclusive use of an important product ingredient. That examination should not discourage firms from creating esthetically pleasing mark designs, for it is open to their competitors to do the same. But, ordinarily, it should prevent the anticompetitive consequences of Jacobson's hypothetical "color depletion" argument, when, and if, the circumstances of a particular case threaten "color depletion." . . .

Having determined that a color may sometimes meet the basic legal requirements for use as a trademark and that respondent Jacobson's arguments do not justify a special legal rule preventing color alone from serving as a trademark (and, in light of the District Court's here undisputed findings that Qualitex's use of the green-gold color on its press pads meets the basic trademark requirements), we conclude that the Ninth Circuit erred in barring Qualitex's use of color as a trademark. For these reasons, the judgment of the Ninth Circuit is reversed.

## Comments

1. ***The Range of Registrable "Nonword" Marks***. Words, whether invented or real, are the most obvious types of marks. Every case to this point has involved a word mark or a composite of words or letters and graphics. *Qualitex* reveals, however, that there is no legal requirement that words or graphics be used in a mark. "Symbols" and "devices" include "almost anything at all that is capable of conveying meaning."

   Consumers are more accustomed to the use of word marks (or composite marks) on labels, tags, or the good itself to indicate the source. Accordingly consumers may have to become acclimated to a particular nonword mark like color to realize that it is a source indicator. Nevertheless, consumers have come to associate the color pink with a particular brand of fiberglass insulation, the three-toned chime with a broadcasting company, and the fragrance of plumeria flowers with a particular kind of thread. Can any avid TV viewer deny the secondary meaning associating the theme song of their favorite show with the goods (the show itself) of the show's producers? The theme song "quickly and easily assures a potential customer that *this* item—the item with this mark—is made by the same producer as other similarly marked items that he or she liked (or disliked) in the past." Recall that nonfunctional trade dress that is not inherently distinctive and all nonfunctional product designs are registrable only with secondary meaning.

2. ***Aesthetic Functionality***. Lanham Act §2(e)(5) prohibits registration of marks that, as a whole, are functional. *Qualitex* involves a mark that is functional, if at all, only because it is aesthetically appealing. Product designs are potentially aesthetically functional if their appearance or ornamentation appeals to buyers. There are two related approaches to determining whether a design is aesthetically functional and not qualified for protection as a trademark. The source identification test

*Source indication Test ①*

considers whether the design feature serves any purpose other than to identify the supplier. If the feature is solely source identifying, the feature is protectible. If, on the other hand, the feature enhances the aesthetic appeal of the product, making it more appealing to consumers, particularly if the feature is essential to the product's commercial success, the feature is not protectible. If the primary significance to consumers of the design on hats or pins showing the logos of ski areas or sports teams is that the design indicates the source of the service or team, the design of the logo would be protectible. By contrast, if the primary significance of the design or pattern on the table china of a particular manufacturer is its aesthetic attractiveness, the design is not protectible under the source identification test.

*Test ②*

An alternative test is the competition test, which considers the existence of alternatives to the design feature in question and whether access to that design is necessary for effective competition. The Supreme Court recognized this approach in *Qualitex* where it concluded that, in light of the variety of other colors and designs available, the color of the pad did not give the manufacturer any non-reputation-related competitive advantage and therefore was protectible. Under this test, the competitive advantage of being the exclusive supplier of a particular china pattern may be related to the appearance of the china, if people select china for its aesthetic appeal, and the design would not be protectible. The competitive advantage of a sports team's emblem on a hat, by contrast, would be due to consumers' association of the emblem with the source of the product or service — a reputational advantage.

*Why cant hate other linear design?*

Examples of product features held to be aesthetically functional and therefore not protected include a popular pattern for hotel china because the design was the essential selling feature of the china, *Pagliero v. Wallace China Co.*, 198 F.2d 339, 340 (9th Cir. 1952), and an outdoor cube-shaped commercial lighting fixture because there were few alternatives compatible with certain building designs, *Keene Corp. v. Paraflex Indus. Inc.*, 653 F.2d 822 (3d Cir. 1981). Compare the aesthetic functionality of a handbag decorated with the Louis Vuitton logo. The court said that "If the Vuitton mark increases consumer appeal only because of the quality associated with Vuitton goods, or because of the prestige associated with owning a genuine Vuitton product, then the design is serving the legitimate function of a trademark; it is identifying the source of the product, and thus should be protected." *Vuitton et Fils S.A. v. J. Young Enterprises, Inc.*, 644 F.2d 769, 776 (9th Cir. 1981).

3. **Shade Confusion and Color Depletion**. Jacobson Products Co., the alleged infringer in *Qualitex*, argued that recognizing color as a mark would create confusion for courts and harm competition by limiting colors available for others. In an omitted portion of the opinion, the Court rejected both arguments.

Jacobson argued that it is for courts and competitors to distinguish different shades of color than different words or symbols, especially because colors change depending on the light (morning sun, twilight mist). Difficulty distinguishing colors would make it hard to determine whether an alleged infringer's mark was likely to cause confusion and harder for competitors to decide whether adopting a shade of a color would infringe. Jacobson added that the "shade confusion" problem is "more difficult" and "far different from" the "determination of the similarity of words or symbols." The Supreme Court concluded that there was nothing special about color, saying that courts regularly decide whether two words or phrases or symbols are sufficiently similar, in context, to confuse buyers and noting that there are legal standards to guide courts in making such comparisons. The Court cited as examples BONAMINE and DRAMAMINE both used for motion-sickness remedies; HUGGIES and DOUGIES both used for diapers; CHERACOL and SYRACOL, both used for cough syrup; and CYCLONE and TORNADO, both used for wire fences. The standards for deciding whether marks are confusing are discussed in the next chapter.

Jacobson also argued that, because colors are in limited supply, the supply will quickly be depleted as each competitor appropriates a particular color for its trademark. While there are thousands of colors, only some colors are usable in the context of particular products (pastels for power tools, for instance, might not be particularly appealing). When colors already used as trademarks deplete the supply, new competitors would be at a disadvantage because they are unable to find a suitable color, especially given the problem of "shade confusion." The Court concluded that normally there would be plenty of alternative colors and suggested that if color depletion arose, the doctrine of functionality would normally prevent the anticompetitive consequences. The following case examines the functionality doctrine in greater detail in a context that has practical rather than aesthetic functionality.

## TRAFFIX DEVICES, INC. v. MARKETING DISPLAYS, INC.

### 532 U.S. 23 (2001)

Justice KENNEDY.

Temporary road signs with warnings like "Road Work Ahead" or "Left Shoulder Closed" must withstand strong gusts of wind. An inventor named Robert Sarkisian obtained two utility patents for a mechanism built upon two springs (the dual-spring design) to keep these and other outdoor signs upright despite adverse wind conditions. The holder of the now-expired Sarkisian patents, respondent Marketing Displays, Inc. (MDI), established a successful business in the manufacture and sale of sign stands incorporating the patented feature. MDI's stands for road signs were recognizable to buyers and users (it says) because the dual-spring design was visible near the base of the sign.

This litigation followed after the patents expired and a competitor, TrafFix Devices, Inc., sold sign stands with a visible spring mechanism that looked like MDI's. MDI and TrafFix products looked alike because they were. When TrafFix started in business, it sent an MDI product abroad to have it reverse engineered, that is to say copied. Complicating matters, TrafFix marketed its sign stands under a name similar to MDI's. MDI used the name "WindMaster," while TrafFix, its new competitor, used "WindBuster."

MDI brought suit under the Trademark Act of 1946 (Lanham Act) against TrafFix for trademark infringement (based on the similar names), trade dress infringement (based on the copied dual-spring design), and unfair competition. . . .

We are concerned with the trade dress question. The District Court ruled against MDI on its trade dress claim. 971 F. Supp. 262 (E.D.Mich. 1997). After determining that the one element of MDI's trade dress at issue was the dual-spring design, it held that "no reasonable trier of fact could determine that MDI has established secondary meaning" in its alleged trade dress, id., at 269. In other words, consumers did not associate the look of the dual-spring design with MDI. As a second, independent reason to grant summary judgment in favor of TrafFix, the District Court determined the dual-spring design was functional. On this rationale secondary meaning is irrelevant because there can be no trade dress protection in any event. In ruling on the functional aspect of the design, the DistrictCourt noted that Sixth Circuit precedent indicated that the burden was on MDI to prove that its trade dress was nonfunctional, and not on TrafFix to show that it was functional (a rule since adopted by Congress) and then went on to consider MDI's arguments that the dual-spring design was subject to trade dress protection. Finding none of MDI's contentions persuasive, the District Court concluded MDI had not "proffered sufficient evidence which would enable a reasonable trier of fact to find that MDI's vertical dual-spring design is *non*-functional." 971 F. Supp., at 276. Summary judgment was entered against MDI on its trade dress claims.

The Court of Appeals for the Sixth Circuit reversed the trade dress ruling. 200 F.3d 929 (1999). The Court of Appeals held the District Court had erred in ruling MDI failed to show a genuine issue of material fact regarding whether it had secondary meaning in its alleged trade dress and had erred further in determining that MDI could not prevail in any event because the alleged trade dress was in fact a functional product configuration. The Court of Appeals suggested the District Court committed legal error by looking only to the dual-spring design when evaluating MDI's trade dress. Basic to its reasoning was the Court of Appeals' observation that it took "little imagination to conceive of a hidden dual-spring mechanism or a tri or quad-spring mechanism that might avoid infringing [MDI's] trade dress." *Ibid.* The Court of Appeals explained that "[i]f TrafFix or another competitor chooses to use [MDI's] dual-spring design, then it will have to find *some other way* to set its sign apart to avoid infringing [MDI's] trade dress." *Ibid.* It was not sufficient, according to the Court of Appeals, that allowing exclusive use of a particular feature such as the dual-spring design in the guise of trade dress would "hinde[r] competition somewhat." Rather, "[e]xclusive use of a feature must 'put competitors at a *significant* non-reputation-related disadvantage' before trade dress protection is denied on functionality grounds." *Ibid.* (quoting *Qualitex Co. v. Jacobson Products Co.*, 514 U.S. 159, 165 (1995)). In its criticism of the District Court's ruling on the trade dress question, the Court of Appeals took note of a split among Courts of Appeals in various other Circuits on the issue whether the existence of an expired utility patent forecloses the possibility of the patentee's claiming trade dress protection in the product's design. To resolve the conflict, we granted certiorari.

It is well established that trade dress can be protected under federal law. The design or packaging of a product may acquire a distinctiveness which serves to identify the product with its manufacturer or source; and a design or package which acquires this secondary meaning, assuming other requisites are met, is a trade dress which may not be used in a manner likely to cause confusion as to the origin, sponsorship, or approval of the goods. In these respects protection for trade dress exists to promote competition. As we explained just last Term, see *Wal-Mart Stores, Inc. v. Samara Brothers, Inc.*, 529 U.S. 205 (2000), various Courts of Appeals have allowed claims of trade dress infringement relying on the general provision of the Lanham Act which provides a cause of action to one who is injured when a person uses "any word, term name, symbol, or device, or any combination thereof . . . which is likely to cause confusion . . . as to the origin, sponsorship, or approval of his or her goods." 15 U.S.C. §1125(a)(1)(A). Congress confirmed this statutory protection for trade dress by amending the Lanham Act to recognize the concept. Title 15 U.S.C. §1125(a)(3) (1994 ed., Supp. V) provides: "In a civil action for trade dress infringement under this chapter for trade dress not registered on the principal register, the person who asserts trade dress protection has the burden of proving that the matter sought to be protected is not functional." This burden of proof gives force to the well-established rule that trade dress protection may not be claimed for product features that are functional. *Qualitex, supra*, at 164-165; *Two Pesos, Inc. v. Taco Cabana, Inc.*, 505 U.S. 763, 775 (1992). And in *Wal-Mart, supra*, we were careful to caution against misuse or overextension of trade dress. We noted that "product design almost invariably serves purposes other than source identification." *Id.*, at 213, 120 S. Ct. 1339.

Trade dress protection must subsist with the recognition that in many instances there is no prohibition against copying goods and products. In general, unless an intellectual property right such as a patent or copyright protects an item, it will be subject to copying. As the Court has explained, copying is not always discouraged or disfavored by the laws which preserve our competitive economy. *Bonito Boats, Inc. v. Thunder Craft Boats, Inc.*, 489 U.S. 141, 160, (1989). Allowing competitors to copy will have salutary effects in many instances. "Reverse engineering of chemical and mechanical articles in the public domain often leads to significant advances in technology." *Ibid.*

The principal question in this case is the effect of an expired patent on a claim of trade dress infringement. A prior patent, we conclude, has vital significance in resolving the trade dress claim. A utility patent is strong evidence that the features therein claimed are functional. If trade dress protection is sought for those features the strong evidence of functionality based on the previous patent adds great weight to the statutory presumption that features are deemed functional until proved otherwise by the party seeking trade dress protection. Where the expired patent claimed the features in question, one who seeks to establish trade dress protection must carry the heavy burden of showing that the feature is not functional, for instance by showing that it is merely an ornamental, incidental, or arbitrary aspect of the device.

In the case before us, the central advance claimed in the expired utility patents (the Sarkisian patents) is the dual-spring design; and the dual-spring design is the essential feature of the trade dress MDI now seeks to establish and to protect. The rule we have explained bars the trade dress claim, for MDI did not, and cannot, carry the burden of overcoming the strong evidentiary inference of functionality based on the disclosure of the dual-spring design in the claims of the expired patents.

The dual springs shown in the Sarkisian patents were well apart (at either end of a frame for holding a rectangular sign when one full side is the base) while the dual springs at issue here are close together (in a frame designed to hold a sign by one of its corners). As the District Court recognized, this makes little difference. The point is that the springs are necessary to the operation of the device. . . .

The rationale for the rule that the disclosure of a feature in the claims of a utility patent constitutes strong evidence of functionality is well illustrated in this case. The dual-spring design serves the important purpose of keeping the sign upright even in heavy wind conditions; and, as confirmed by the statements in the expired patents, it does so in a unique and useful manner. . . . The dual-spring design allows sign stands to resist toppling in strong winds. Using a dual-spring design rather than a single spring achieves important operational advantages. For example, the specifications of the patents note that the "use of a pair of springs . . . as opposed to the use of a single spring to support the frame structure prevents canting or twisting of the sign around a vertical axis," and that, if not prevented, twisting "may cause damage to the spring structure and may result in tipping of the device." U.S. Patent No. 3,646,696, col. 3. In the course of patent prosecution, it was said that "[t]he use of a pair of spring connections as opposed to a single spring connection . . . forms an important part of this combination" because it "forc[es] the sign frame to tip along the longitudinal axis of the elongated ground-engaging members." App. 218. The dual-spring design affects the cost of the device as well; it was acknowledged that the device "could use three springs but this would unnecessarily increase the cost of the device." *Id.*, at 217. These statements made in the patent applications and in the course of procuring the patents demonstrate the functionality of the design. MDI does not assert that any of these representations are mistaken or inaccurate, and this is further strong evidence of the functionality of the dual-spring design. . . .

Discussing trademarks, we have said "'[i]n general terms, a product feature is functional,' and cannot serve as a trademark, 'if it is essential to the use or purpose of the article or if it affects the cost or quality of the article.'" *Qualitex*, 514 U.S., at 165 (quoting *Inwood Laboratories, Inc. v. Ives Laboratories, Inc.*, 456 U.S. 844, 850, n. 10 (1982)). Expanding upon the meaning of this phrase, we have observed that a functional feature is one the "exclusive use of [which] would put competitors at a significant non-reputation-related disadvantage." 514 U.S., at 165, 115 S. Ct. 1300. The Court of Appeals in the instant case seemed to interpret this language to mean that a necessary test for functionality is "whether the particular product configuration is a competitive necessity." 200 F.3d, at 940. This was incorrect as a comprehensive definition. As explained in *Qualitex, supra*, and *Inwood, supra*, a feature is also functional when it is essential to the use or purpose of the device or when it affects the cost or quality of the device. The *Qualitex* decision did not purport to displace this traditional rule. Instead, it quoted the rule as *Inwood* had set it forth. It is proper to inquire into a "significant non-reputation-related disadvantage" in cases of esthetic functionality, the question involved in *Qualitex*. Where the design is functional under the *Inwood* formulation there is no need to proceed further to consider if there is a competitive necessity for the feature. In *Qualitex*, by contrast, esthetic functionality was the central question, there having been no indication that the green-gold color of the laundry press pad had any bearing on the use or purpose of the product or its cost or quality.

The Court has allowed trade dress protection to certain product features that are inherently distinctive. *Two Pesos*, 505 U.S., at 774. In *Two Pesos*, however, the Court at the outset made the explicit analytic assumption that the trade dress features in question (decorations and other features to evoke a Mexican theme in a restaurant) were not functional. *Id.*, at 767, n. 6. The trade dress in those cases did not bar competitors from copying functional product design features. In the instant case, beyond serving the purpose of informing consumers that the sign stands are made by MDI (assuming it does so), the dual-spring design provides a unique and useful mechanism to resist the force of the wind. Functionality having been established, whether MDI's dual-spring design has acquired secondary meaning need not be considered.

There is no need, furthermore, to engage, as did the Court of Appeals, in speculation about other design possibilities, such as using three or four springs which might serve the same purpose. Here, the functionality of the spring design means that competitors need not explore whether other spring juxtapositions might be used. The dual-spring design is not an arbitrary flourish in the configuration of MDI's product; it is the reason the device works. Other designs need not be attempted. . . .

The Lanham Act does not exist to reward manufacturers for their innovation in creating a particular device; that is the purpose of the patent law and its period of exclusivity. The Lanham Act, furthermore, does not protect trade dress in a functional design simply because an investment has been made to encourage the public to associate a particular functional feature with a single manufacturer or seller. The Court of Appeals erred in viewing MDI as possessing the right to exclude competitors from using a design identical to MDI's and to require those competitors to adopt a different design simply to avoid copying it. MDI cannot gain the exclusive right to produce sign stands using the dual-spring design by asserting that consumers associate it with the look of the invention itself. Whether a utility patent has expired or there has been no utility patent at all, a product design which has a particular appearance may be functional because it is "essential to the use or purpose of the article" or "affects the cost or quality of the article." *Inwood*, 456 U.S., at 850, n. 10. . . .

The judgment of the Court of Appeals is reversed, and the case is remanded for further proceedings consistent with this opinion.

## TALKING RAIN BEVERAGE CO., INC. v. SOUTH BEACH BEVERAGE CO.

### 349 F.3d 601 (9th Cir. 2003)

FISHER, Circuit Judge.

Talking Rain owns U.S. Trademark Registration No. 2,181,774, which covers the shape of a bottle that Talking Rain uses in its sales of flavored and unflavored water. Talking Rain claims that South Beach Beverage Company, Inc., and the South Beach Beverage Company, LLC (collectively "SoBe") use a bottle in sales of beverages that is confusingly similar to Talking Rain's trademarked bottle. Talking Rain sued SoBe, claiming trademark infringement and false designation of origin, in violation of §§32 and 43(a) of the Lanham Act and the Washington State Consumer Protection Act. SoBe counterclaimed, alleging that Talking Rain's bottle is functional and, accordingly, that its trademark registration is invalid and should be canceled.

Int. Cl.: 32
Prior U.S. Cls.: 43, 46 and 48                                          Reg. No. 2,181,774
**United States Patent and Trademark Office**          Registered Aug. 18, 1998

TRADEMARK
PRINCIPAL REGISTER

TALKING RAIN BEVERAGE CO., INC. (WASH-          THE MARK CONSISTS OF THE CONFIGU-
INGTON CORPORATION)                              RATION OF A BEVERAGE BOTTLE. THE
30520 SOUTHEAST 84TH                             DOTTED OUTLINE OF THE CAP IS NOT
PRESTON, WA 98050                                PART OF THE MARK IS MERELY INTENDED
                                                 TO REPRESENT THE BOTTLE AS VIEWED
                                                 ON THE SHELF.
FOR: USE AS A CONTAINER FOR FLA-                 SEC. 2(F).
VORED AND UNFLAVORED WATER, IN
CLASS 32 (U.S. CLS. 45, 46 AND 48).              SER. NO. 75-164,176, FILED 9-11-1996.
FIRST USE 3-1-1996; IN COMMERCE
3-1-1996.                                        CAROLYN GRAY, EXAMINING ATTORNEY

Talking Rain appeals from the district court's final judgment dismissing its complaint, granting SoBe's counterclaim to invalidate Talking Rain's federal trademark registration for its design and directing the Commissioner of Patents and Trademarks to cancel Talking Rain's federal trademark registration. . . .

Talking Rain's trademarked design and SoBe's bottle both resemble a typical "bike bottle." Specifically, the bottles have smooth sides and a recessed, grip area approximately two-thirds of the way up from the bottoms of the bottles. SoBe contends that it modeled its bottle after a traditional bike bottle. Talking Rain refers to its bottle as the "Grip Bottle" and has promoted the bottle under the slogan "Get a Grip!" Talking Rain acknowledges that its trademarked design, which it spent millions of dollars developing and promoting, also resembles a bike bottle. Both bottles fit easily into the bottle holders that are often used on bicycles. According to both parties, the recessed "grip" area also offers structural support, which helps a bottle retain its shape.

Talking Rain's bottles are made from polyester terephthalate, which is a transparent plastic. Talking Rain and its licensee, Santa Cruz Sports and

Nutrition, L.L.C., use the bottle in selling flavored and unflavored water. SoBe's bottles are made from polypropylene, which is a translucent plastic. SoBe uses its bottles in selling isotonic beverages, which are designed to prevent dehydration during exercise.

To succeed on its trademark claims under the Lanham Act, Talking Rain must meet three elements: (1) nonfunctionality, (2) distinctiveness and (3) likelihood of confusion. Talking Rain's state law claims also turn on whether it can establish these elements.

[handwritten marginal note: Test]

Talking Rain's trademark is presumptively valid because it has been registered. But if SoBe "can demonstrate through law, undisputed facts, or a combination thereof that the mark is invalid, the evidentiary bubble bursts and the plaintiff cannot survive summary judgment. In the face of sufficient and undisputed facts demonstrating functionality . . . the registration loses its evidentiary significance." *Id.* at 783. Thus, once the presumption of validity afforded a registered trademark has been rebutted, mere registration does not enable a trademark holder to survive summary judgment. . . .

A trademark is functional "when it is essential to the use or purpose of the device or when it affects the cost or quality of the device." *TrafFix Devices, Inc. v. Mktg. Displays, Inc.*, 532 U.S. 23, 33 (2001). To determine whether a product feature is functional, this circuit typically considers four factors: (1) whether advertising touts the utilitarian advantages of the design, (2) whether the particular design results from a comparatively simple or inexpensive method of manufacture, (3) whether the design yields a utilitarian advantage and (4) whether alternative designs are available. *See Disc Golf Ass'n v. Champion Discs, Inc.*, 158 F.3d 1002, 1006 (9th Cir. 1998).

[handwritten marginal note: Test for functions]

In applying the *Disc Golf* factors, we are mindful of the Supreme Court's recent pronouncement that once functionality is established, "[t]here is no need . . . to engage . . . in speculation about other design possibilities. . . ." *TrafFix*, 532 U.S. at 33, 121 S. Ct. 1255. Therefore, the existence of alternative designs cannot negate a trademark's functionality. But the existence of alternative designs may indicate whether the trademark itself embodies functional or merely ornamental aspects of the product.

The evidence in this case, even when viewed in the light most favorable to Talking Rain, establishes that Talking Rain's trademark is functional. First, Talking Rain's advertising touts its bottle's utilitarian features. Talking Rain, which refers to its bottle as the "Grip Bottle," argues that its "Get a Grip!" slogan involves a double-meaning because the slogan is a slang expression meaning "get in control." No matter the plausibility of Talking Rain's "double-entendre" argument, at least one meaning of its advertising is that the bottle is easy to grip. We are not required to ignore advertising that touts functional features just because those ads may include messages — subtle or otherwise — aimed at nonfunctional features.

Second, Talking Rain has acknowledged that manufacturing considerations explain why its bottle looks the way it does. In particular, the grip feature, aside from making the bottle easier to hold, offers structural support. Talking Rain misunderstands the functionality inquiry in contending that manufacturing considerations cut against a finding of functionality because the bottle was costly to design. Through its investment, Talking Rain learned that by adding a recessed/grip area, it could manufacture a plastic bottle with curved sides that would not collapse. Talking Rain's initiative is commendable, but to the extent its product design is functional, trademark law does not prohibit SoBe from also using this efficient manufacturing process. *See Tie Tech*, 296 F.3d at 785 ("The requirement of nonfunctionality is based on the judicial theory that *there exists a fundamental right to compete through imitation of a competitor's product*, which right can only be *temporarily* denied by the patent or copyright laws.") (internal quotation marks omitted) (emphasis in original); *Leatherman Tool Group, Inc. v. Cooper Indus., Inc.*, 199 F.3d 1009, 1012 (9th Cir. 1999) ("[I]t is not the purpose of unfair competition law, under the guise of either consumer protection or the protection of business good will, to implement a policy of encouraging innovative designs by protecting them once designed.") On the contrary, that the grip feature reflects a comparatively simple method of manufacturing a structurally sound bottle indicates that the trademarked bottle is functional.

Third, the bike bottle design yields a utilitarian advantage. SoBe contends that the bottle fits easily into a bicycle bottle holder and that the grip area helps the bottle to retain its shape for reuse. SoBe also contends that the grip area makes the bottle easier to grip, particularly for bicyclists and others who might use the bottle while exercising.

Talking Rain does not dispute these contentions. Instead, Talking Rain argues that its trademarked design is merely one of a number of possible designs for bike bottles. According to Talking Rain, SoBe could have achieved the same functionality by adopting a bike bottle design other than the design embodied by Talking Rain's trademark. But under the Supreme Court's decision in *TrafFix*, the mere existence of alternatives does not render a product nonfunctional.

Here, Talking Rain's advertising emphasizes functionality, the bottle's shape is motivated by manufacturing efficiencies and the bottle itself offers utilitarian advantages that non-bike bottles do not possess. Moreover, that recessed/grip areas appear to be common in the beverage industry tends to corroborate SoBe's assertion that the grip area is indeed functional and not arbitrary. Talking Rain points to no distinctive feature shared by Talking Rain's and SoBe's bottles, beyond the functional grip area. In short, the functional grip area *is* the essence of Talking Rain's claimed distinctiveness.

The first three *Disc Golf* factors support the district court's finding that Talking Rain's trademark is functional. Under *TrafFix*, the existence of alternative designs does not diminish these indicia of functionality. SoBe has overcome the presumption of nonfunctionality created by Talking Rain's trademark registration. Thus, we conclude that the district court correctly found that Talking Rain's trademark is functional and therefore invalid. The district court correctly granted summary judgment to SoBe on the federal and state law claims.

## Comments

*1. Functional Marks.* Functional marks, including trade dress, are not registrable. Two related policy reasons for this prohibition are

*Policy*

promoting competition and keeping items in the public domain available to all. Patent law determines which useful inventions deserve monopoly protection for a limited period of years. If trademark law were to take those useful characteristics of products that are in the public domain and protect them, potentially forever, competition would suffer because of the monopoly on that characteristic. Trademark law does not have criteria for deciding which inventions should receive monopoly protection as patent law does and would grant protection forever (or as long as the owner of the functional mark properly renewed the trademark). How does the test for what product features are functional relate to these policy reasons?

2. *Burden of Proof with Respect to Functionality*. For unregistered marks, the burden of proving that the mark is not functional is on the person seeking protection of the mark through an infringement action. For registered marks, the mark is presumed not to be functional and a person filing a cancellation petition or defending an infringement action has the burden of showing functionality. Even a mark that has achieved "incontestable status," special protection accorded to marks registered and used continuously for five consecutive years may be challenged on the basis that they are functional.

3. *Functionality, Alternatives, and Competitive Significance*. In *TrafFix*, the Supreme Court held that, once a trade dress is found to be functional, there is no need to consider "whether the particular product configuration is a competitive necessity." The Court held that the Court of Appeals erred in speculating about other design possibilities for the spring design, such as using three or four rather than two.

Consideration of whether competitors would be at a disadvantage without access to the product configuration in question arose from the Supreme Court's opinion in *Qualitex*, which said that a product feature is functional if it is essential to the use or purpose of the article or if it affects the cost or quality of the article, that is, if exclusive use of the feature would put competitors at a *significant non-reputation-related disadvantage*. The italicized words suggest that inquiry into the competitive significance of granting exclusive rights to it is essential. In *TrafFix* however, the Court limited consideration of the availability of alternatives to cases involving aesthetic functionality, saying that "[i]t is proper to inquire into a 'significant non-reputation-related disadvantage' in cases of aesthetic functionality, the question involved in *Qualitex*."

Subsequent to *TrafFix*, a number of lower courts have concluded that considering the availability of alternatives might help determine whether a product configuration is functional in cases where applying the other parts of the functionality test leaves an ambiguous result. These courts interpret the Supreme Court as having said that if a product's trade dress is functional, alternatives will not save it. But that does not mean alternatives cannot be used to determine whether it is functional in the first instance.

An example of how this approach works might be found in the facts of *K-Swiss Inc. v. USA Aisiqui Shoes Inc.*, 291 F. Supp. 2d 1116 (D. Cal. 2003). K-Swiss sued to enjoin Aisiqui from importing athletic shoes with the same five-stripe design employed by K-Swiss on its athletic shoes. Among other claims of functionality, Aisiqui argued that the stripes had a utilitarian advantage because they reinforced the speed-lacing eyelets, allowing greater form fitting and custom stabilization of the foot. K-Swiss responded that no other athletic shoe regularly sold in the market utilized the five-stripe design and others routinely used other designs so the five-stripe feature is primarily cosmetic. The court agreed that stripes may be placed on a shoe in many other con-figurations and that the loops, hooks, eyelets can be attached to the base shoe material in a variety of other ways to produce the same effect as the D-rings with the stripes. This factual conclusion might lead a court to conclude that the stripes are decorative rather than utilitarian. This consideration of alternatives would not run afoul of the Supreme Court's holding that the existence of alternatives cannot save a mark that has been found to be functional.

4. *Functionality and the Court of Appeals for the Federal Circuit.* Despite the Supreme Court's statements in *TrafFix*, the Court of Appeals for the Federal Circuit has not abandoned consideration of the competitive significance of the product feature. In 1982, the Court of Appeals for the Federal Circuit identified four factors relevant to determining func-tionality: (a) the existence of a utility patent disclosing the utilitarian advantages of the design, (b) advertising materials in which the origi-nator of the design touts the design's utilitarian advantages, (c) the availability to competitors of functionally equivalent designs, and (d) facts indicating that the design results in a comparatively simple or cheap method of manufacturing the product. *In re Morton-Norwich Pro-ducts, Inc.*, 671 F.2d 1332 (Fed. Cir. 1982) (involving the functionality of the design of a spray bottle for household cleaning products). The issue in *TrafFix* was the relevance of the third *Morton-Norwich* factor. In *Value Engineering, Inc., v. Rexnord Corp.*, 278 F.3d 1268 (Fed. Cir. 2002), decided after *TrafFix*, the Federal Circuit concluded that the Supreme Court's opinion in *TrafFix* had not altered the *Morton-Norwich* factors:

> An important policy underlying the functionality doctrine is the preservation of competition. As this court's predecessor noted in *Morton-Norwich*, the "effect upon competition 'is really the crux'" of the functionality inquiry and, accord-ingly, the functionality doctrine preserves competition by ensuring competitors "the right to compete effectively." As we stated in *Brunswick Corp. v. British Seagull Ltd.*, 35 F.3d 1527, 1531 (Fed.Cir.1994), "functionality rests on 'utility,' which is determined in light of 'superiority of design,' and rests upon the foun-dation of 'effective competition.'" The importance of competition was reaf-firmed in *Qualitex*, in which the Supreme Court focused on whether a feature "would put competitors at a significant non-reputation-related disadvantage." And when discussing the policy behind limiting trade dress protection, the Supreme Court in *TrafFix* noted that "[a]llowing competitors to copy will have salutary effects in many instances." ... Thus, in determining "function-ality," the Board must assess the effect registration of a mark would have on competition.

While competition might be essential to a finding of functionality, it seems contrary to the Supreme Court's opinion in *TrafFix* to allow the existence of alternatives to save a mark that was otherwise found to be functional.

# Problems

**2-19.** In *Publications Int'l Ltd. v. Landoll. Inc.*, 164 F.3d 377 (7th Cir. 1998), the court considered the protectibility of trade dress for a cookbook consisting of the following features: large pages making the book easier to lay flat on the counter, large-print font, a washable oil cloth cover, and large pictures of dishes. Is this trade dress protectable? *No ⇒ its functional*

**2-20.** In *Gateway Inc. v. Companion Products, Inc.*, 384 F.3d 503 (8th Cir. 2004), Gateway sued the manufacturer of "stretch pets" for trade dress infringement. Companion's stretch pets had animal heads with elastic bodies that would wrap around a computer monitor or case or television. Gateway complained that the "Cody Cow" version of the pets infringed the trade dress on its boxes, which are a black-and-white design resembling the hide of a Holstein dairy cow. Is Gateway's trade dress protectible? Consider both the distinctiveness and nonfunctionality requirements.

---

### *THEORETICAL PERSPECTIVE*
### Availability of Alternatives and Promoting Competition

Whether the availability of alternatives *should be* an important element of functionality depends on the underlying rationale of the prohibition on functional marks. If competition "is really the crux" of the functionality inquiry, then functional marks are like generic marks and permitting one person exclusive rights to the mark would prevent others from competing effectively. Competitors need generic words to refer to their products or services while competitors need access to unpatented functional designs to compete in the marketplace. From this perspective, the existence of many alternatives, alternative words to describe the class of products or alternative designs to accomplish the purpose, supports trademark protection of a work term or of trade dress. This is called the "competition theory" of functionality.

The opposing view is that trademark law may not give more protection to a utilitarian design than patent law. The rights to a mark that has trademark protection may last forever if the mark is regularly renewed. A utility patent lasts for only 20 years (14 years for a design patent), may not be renewed, and the patented invention is thereafter available for all to use. The United States Constitution grants Congress the power to protect inventions for "limited times." For trademarks to protect useful inventions forever might even be unconstitutional. The "identification theory" of functionality is that if the trade dress or design has any utilitarian purpose other than source identification, it should not be protected. From this perspective, the existence of alternatives is not relevant. If a useful item is not patentable or its patent has expired, it cannot be protected forever. Thus, the existence of alternatives is irrelevant under this view; alternatives cannot justify protecting useful, unpatentable designs.

Ironically, both approaches promote competition. From the first perspective, permitting registration of functional designs only if there are alternatives protects competition wherever protection is needed. From the second perspective, rewarding and encouraging invention and the disclosure of useful inventions only through limited-term patent monopolies encourages competition in the long run. The mandatory publication of a description of the invention and the finite term of the patent allows others to improve on the invention and eventually compete against the inventor.

# CHAPTER
# 3

# Rights of Trademark Owners

The scope of a supplier's trademark rights has geographic market and product or service market dimensions. The first step in the analysis of a conflict between users of similar marks is establishing who used it first. That analysis involves consideration of the geographic territory where they used the marks and of the nature of the products in connection with which they used them. A related question is whether their use was significant enough to support giving them rights. The first part of this chapter considers such conflicts.

Conflicting uses give rise to a variety of causes of action collectively labeled "unfair competition" claims. Trademark infringement is one type of unfair competition claim. Trademark infringement claims are based on proof that another's use of a mark creates a likelihood that consumers will be confused about who is the source of the goods or services in connection with which the mark is used. A related and broader legal theory is "passing off." A passing off claim may be based on any representation, not just use of another's mark, that is likely to cause confusion as to source.

The Lanham Act also provides special relief under the dilution theory for owners of famous marks, like McDONALD'S used in connection with food service or VICTORIA'S SECRET used in connection with women's lingerie. Dilution claims are based on proof that another's use of a similar mark will lessen the distinctiveness of a famous mark or diminish its selling power by, for instance, disparaging it. TOYS-R-US often complained about dilution when suppliers who did not compete with it in the toy market but simply used similar marks, such as COMPUTERS-R-US or BAGELS-R-US. The Kodak Company complains that use of marks resembling its KODAK mark (used in connection with camera film) by a movie theater calling itself KODAK XXX MOVIES would tarnish its mark's favorable association.

A recent addition to the Lanham Act prohibits "cybersquatting," which is bad faith registration and use for profit of an Internet domain name that is confusingly similar to another's mark. Cybersquatters or cyber-pirates sometimes register confusingly similar names in order either to attract unsuspecting visitors to their websites or to sell them to the mark owner.

Finally, some states recognize two legal theories that also fall under the classification of unfair competition: misappropriation and the right of publicity. Misappropriation claims involve allegations that the plaintiff has developed a resource at some expense, that the defendant has exploited that resource without compensating the plaintiff, and that it is good policy to allow the plaintiff an exclusive right to that resource. It fits some claims that do not fall explicitly under trademark, copyright, or patent law, areas in which federal statutes have determined the degree of protection for intellectual property is good policy. The type of misappropriation reflected in right of publicity actions involves well-known personalities who have invested time and energy in promoting their celebrity only to have others use their names or faces for promotional purposes without permission. Unlike state actions for trademark infringement, passing off, and dilution, misappropriation and publicity claims have no federal counterpart, though when there is confusion about source, a Lanham Act infringement or passing off claim may be accompanied by a misappropriation or right of publicity claim.

Every Lanham Act claim begins with proof that the claimant has a right to protect the mark in question. Chapter 2 explored the types of marks the law protects. This chapter begins with consideration of the geographic areas to which a mark owner's rights extend when the mark is unregistered and when it is registered. The chapter continues with a discussion of each type of unfair competition claim.

## A. GEOGRAPHIC EXTENT OF RIGHTS

The geographic extent of trademark rights depends on who used the mark first in a particular geographic area and who registered the mark. An unregistered user's rights are limited to the geographic area within which it has used the mark and sometimes a natural area for expansion of that use. Unregistered users in different geographic areas generally have rights in their own areas, regardless of whose use came first. When these unregistered users' geographic areas overlap, the senior user has exclusive rights. *National Association for Healthcare Communications, Inc. v. Central Arkansas Area Agency on Aging, Inc.* explores the rights of unregistered users.

While registration is not necessary for protection, it has the advantage of creating rights beyond the area of actual use, potentially to the entire nation. Thus, the geographic extent of rights depends on first user and first registration. We explore here the relationship between these two sources of geographic rights.

Either a junior user or a senior user may be the first to register and acquire these broad rights, but the geographic extent of rights is limited to parts of the nation where no one else continues to use the mark from a time prior to the registration. In *Peaches Entertainment Corp. v. Entertainment Repertoire Assocs., Inc.*, the senior user was the first to register and acquired rights to the entire nation except for the geographic area of pre-registration use by the junior user. In *Burger King v. Hoots*, the time priorities are similar, but the junior user acquired a state trademark registration before the senior user actually used the mark in that state. The notes following *Burger King* illustrate how a person who enters and begins using a registered mark in a geographic area after the date of registration may continue to use the mark in that area despite the prior registration, as long as that subsequent user's use is not likely to cause confusion about the source of its goods or services. This may occur when the registrant does not do any business in the subsequent user's geographic area.

These cases and comments are designed to illustrate the rights in each of four logical scenarios: (1) neither the senior nor the junior user registers the mark, (2) the senior user registers after the junior user begins use, (3) the junior user is the first to register, and (4) the senior user registers before the junior user begins use. In each of these four situations, both the junior user and the senior user may have some rights to use the mark. In the last scenario, the junior user's rights are, not surprisingly, very limited. Because chronology and geographic areas are critical to understanding the following cases, it will be helpful to keep a timeline of events as you read each case.

## NATIONAL ASSOC. FOR HEALTHCARE COMMUNICATIONS, INC. v. CENTRAL ARKANSAS AREA AGENCY ON AGING, INC.

### 257 F.3d 732 (8th Cir. 2001)

LOKEN, Circuit Judge.

This is an action under the Lanham Act and state law to determine which party has the superior right to use the service mark "CareLink" in Arkansas. The National Association for Healthcare Communications, Inc. ("Healthcom") was the first to use the mark nationally. It has a federal service mark registration pending but must rely in this case on its common law trademark rights as enforced under the Lanham Act. The Central Arkansas Area Agency on Aging, Inc. ("CA") was the first to use the mark in six counties in central Arkansas and has registered its mark under the Arkansas trademark statutes. The district court held that CA as first user prevailed in its six-county trade area and that CA's state registration entitled it to statewide relief. Accordingly, the court enjoined Healthcom from using the CareLink mark anywhere in Arkansas. Healthcom appeals....

Healthcom began marketing emergency response services under the CareLink service mark in 1991 or early 1992. From 1992 to 1995, Healthcom spent an estimated $50,000 attempting to sell its services in Arkansas. Despite these efforts, during this period Healthcom made only one $385 sale in Arkansas, to an end user who stopped using its CareLink service in April 1994. Healthcom had no Arkansas customers from April 1994 to September 1995, when it entered into a contract with North Arkansas Regional Medical Center in Harrison. By July 1999, Healthcom had contracts with seven Arkansas health care providers and served 350 individual subscribers. Healthcom estimated that its total Arkansas revenues in 1999 would be just over $82,000. Healthcom has *never* had a customer for its CareLink services located within the six-county region served by CA.

Healthcom applied for federal trademark registration on May 4, 1999, and its application is pending.

CA adopted the CareLink trade name and logo in early 1995 and has prominently displayed the logo on stationery, business cards, client information materials, and other publicity materials [in connection with its array of support services for elderly and disabled persons]. CA registered its CareLink mark with the Arkansas Secretary of State on March 23, 1995, and has used the mark in promoting all of its services, except hospice care. CA's annual revenues grew from $5,000,000 to $12,000,000 from early 1995 to mid-1999. Although CA derives most of its revenues from government grants, in 1999 it received approximately $138,000 in private donations and an estimated $250,000 from clients able to pay for its services. All of CA's clients reside in its six-county region, but its activities are publicized beyond central Arkansas through news coverage, telephone listings, advertisements, and a monthly column in an Arkansas newspaper for the elderly.

CA did not know of Healthcom's prior usage when it adopted the CareLink name and logo and received a state registration in early 1995. When CA learned that the North Arkansas Regional Medical Center was using Healthcom's CareLink mark for emergency response services in northern Arkansas, CA sent a cease-and-desist letter to that provider. The parties were unable to resolve the resulting dispute. Healthcom then commenced this action, alleging common law trademark infringement and unfair competition in violation of the Lanham Act, 15 U.S.C. §1125(a), and seeking an injunction barring CA from using the mark and cancellation of CA's state registration. CA counterclaimed, alleging unfair competition under the Lanham Act and trademark infringement under Ark. Code Ann. §4-71-212, and seeking an injunction prohibiting Healthcom from using its CareLink mark in Arkansas or, alternatively, in CA's six-county region....

Nearly a century ago, the Supreme Court established what is now called the *Tea Rose/Rectanus* doctrine — the first user of a common law trademark may not oust a later user's good faith use of an infringing mark in a market where the first user's products or services are not sold. *See United Drug Co. v. Theodore Rectanus Co.*, 248 U.S. 90, 100-01, 39 S. Ct. 48, 63 L. Ed. 141 (1918); *Hanover Star Milling Co. v. Metcalf*, 240 U.S. 403, 415, 36 S. Ct. 357, 60 L. Ed. 713 (1916). The rationale is a core principle of trademark law: the owner of a mark may not "monopolize markets that his trade has never reached and where the mark signifies not his goods but those of another." *Hanover Star Milling*, 240 U.S. at 416, 36 S. Ct. 357. That essential principle applies even when the first user has federally registered its mark under the Lanham Act, with one important modification: the owner of a *registered* mark has the right to expand its use into a new market unless an infringing user had penetrated that market *prior to registration*.

In this case we must apply the *Tea Rose/Rectanus* doctrine in resolving two distinct inquiries. First, we must determine whether Healthcom, as the first user of a CareLink common law mark elsewhere in the country, is entitled by reason of its own market penetration to oust CA from any area in Arkansas. Second, to the extent Healthcom failed to prove first use in Arkansas, we must determine whether CA, as owner of a state-registered mark used only in six counties, is entitled to statewide injunctive relief against Health-com's present use of its mark.

It is undisputed that, in early 1995, CA adopted the CareLink mark in good faith, without knowledge of Healthcom's prior use. To be entitled to injunctive relief against CA's subsequent good faith use, Healthcom must prove that its prior use of the mark penetrated the geographic market in question. In determining whether Healthcom achieved the necessary market penetration, we apply the factors identified in our often-cited *Sweetarts* cases:

> [Healthcom's] dollar value of sales at the time [CA] entered the market, number of customers compared to the population of the state, relative and potential growth of sales, and length of time since significant sales. Though the market penetration need not be large to entitle [Healthcom] to protection, it must be significant enough to pose the real likelihood of confusion among the consumers in that area.

*Sweetarts v. Sunline, Inc.*, 380 F.2d 923, 929 (8th Cir. 1967); *Sweetarts v. Sunline, Inc.*, 436 F.2d 705, 708 (8th Cir. 1971) (citation omitted). Where the first user's activities in a remote area are "so small, sporadic, and inconsequential" that its market penetration is *de minimis*, the first user is not entitled to protection against a later user's good faith adoption of the mark in that area. *Sweetarts*, 380 F.2d at 929. [handwritten: *Sweet Brl doctrine.*]

Healthcom argues that it penetrated the Arkansas market through its one sale to an end user in 1992, its seven provider-member contracts and 350 subscribers since the fall of 1995, and its continuous advertising and marketing efforts beginning in 1992. Healthcom errs in assuming without proof that the entire State of Arkansas is a single geographic market for these purposes. CA adopted its CareLink mark for use in six counties in central Arkansas, not the entire State. Healthcom has *never* made a sale in that area, nor has it even attempted to prove that CA's use of the mark in its region is causing a likelihood of confusion elsewhere in the State. For this reason alone, Healthcom has not penetrated CA's six-county trade area, and the district court properly denied Healthcom injunctive relief against CA's use in that area.

This leaves the question whether Healthcom is entitled to injunctive relief as a prior user with market penetration in any other part of Arkansas. We agree with the district court that Healthcom's one $385 sale long before CA's adoption of its mark was *de minimis* market penetration. That leaves Healthcom's reliance on later sales and continuous advertising. CA argues that sales in Arkansas after CA began using the mark are irrelevant, and that Healthcom's prior advertising may not be used to satisfy the *Sweetarts* market penetration test. Those are strong arguments. The issue is whether they warrant summary judgment.

*Sweetarts* expressly recognized that the market penetration issue is focused on the time when the later user entered the market. However, subsequent sales by the first user *may* establish a trend of increased sales justifying a finding of market penetration. Likewise, while "advertising alone is not sufficient to satisfy the significant market penetration test of *Sweetarts*," *Flavor Corp. of Am. v. Kemin Indus., Inc.*, 493 F.2d 275, 284 (8th Cir. 1974), we are not prepared to say as a matter of law that a first user's highly focused local advertising, followed by initial sales shortly after a later user enters the market, may never satisfy the *Sweetarts* test. Nevertheless, we need not decide whether CA is entitled to summary judgment on  the market penetration issue statewide because Healthcom presented no evidence that CA is presently likely to enter areas of Arkansas beyond its six-county region, and no evidence that any customers or potential customers of Healthcom are actually confused, or likely to be confused, by CA's use of its CareLink mark in serving a six-county region where Healthcom does no business. In these circumstances, the district court properly dismissed all of Healthcom's claims for relief.

Having concluded that Healthcom is not entitled to injunctive relief, we turn to CA's counterclaim for injunctive relief and the district court's grant of a statewide injunction. As we have explained, CA has superior common law rights in its six-county region, and it is a state-registered user of the CareLink mark. Therefore, under both the Lanham Act and the Arkansas trademark statute, CA is entitled to an injunction against an infringing use that is likely to cause confusion as to origin. In 1997, Healthcom attempted to sell its CareLink emergency response services to a health care provider in Little Rock, within CA's six-county territory. Healthcom concedes that the CareLink mark is entitled to trademark protection and that this kind of overlapping use of the parties' CareLink marks would create a likelihood of confusion among health care providers and end users. Therefore, the district court did not abuse its discretion in enjoining Healthcom from using a CareLink mark in CA's six-county region.

The question whether CA is entitled to a statewide injunction is far more difficult. The Arkansas trademark statute "provide[s] a system of state trademark registration and protection substantially consistent with the federal system of trademark registration and protection under the [Lanham Act]." Ark. Code Ann. §4-71-218(b). State registration confers the statewide right to use a service mark in  connection with the registered services, subject to defenses such as good faith prior use in a particular local market. Under the Lanham Act:

> the nationwide right conferred by registration does not entitle the owner to injunctive relief unless there is a present likelihood of confusion. Therefore, to enjoin a geographically remote infringer, the registered owner must prove that its trademarked products and the infringing products are being sold in the same geographic area, or that the owner has concrete plans to expand into the infringer's trade area.

*Minnesota Pet Breeders, Inc. v. Schell & Kampeter, Inc.,* 41 F.3d 1242, 1246 (8th Cir. 1994). Here, CA serves only the six-county region and presented no evidence of "concrete plans" to expand elsewhere in the State. Although both parties alleged there would be a likelihood of confusion if they used the CareLink mark in the same local area, neither presented evidence that the entire State is a single market for these kinds of services, or that health care providers or end users are confused by the use of two CareLink marks in different parts of the State. In these circumstances, CA did not establish its right to a statewide remedy under the *Pet Breeders* standard....

In summary, the absence of concrete evidence of likelihood of confusion outside of CA's six-county region makes it improvident to grant a statewide injunction on this record. Healthcom is now enjoined from using its Care-Link mark in CA's trade area. If CA never expands beyond that area, this injunction may be all the judicial action that is required. If CA does decide to expand, its statewide registration puts Healthcom at risk of being ousted. But any future prayer by CA for a broader injunction may raise issues that would be better resolved on a fuller fact record, such as whether Healthcom was the first user in any local market; whether the CareLink mark is descriptive and, if so, whether CA's mark has become incontestable or has acquired secondary meaning; precisely what services CA claims its registration covers; and whether there is likelihood of confusion between users of those services and users of Healthcom's emergency response services. . . .

We affirm the dismissal of Healthcom's claims and the grant of a permanent injunction barring Healthcom's use of its CareLink mark in CA's six-county trade area. We reverse the grant of a statewide injunction and remand to the district court for an appropriate modification of its Judgment dated January 31, 2000.

## Comments

1. *Healthcare's Geographic Rights.* Even though Healthcare applied for federal registration, its registration was still pending at the time of this suit and therefore had no effect on the geographic extent of its rights. Under the common law, "a mark, of itself, cannot travel to markets where there is no article to wear the badge and no trader to offer the article," so Healthcare's rights depended on its actual use throughout the nation and in various parts of Arkansas. Healthcare first argued that it had the exclusive right to the mark in the entire state. What is the basis for that argument and what statewide rights did the court grant to Healthcare? Healthcare then argued that it had exclusive rights outside of the six-county area in which CA had established its business. What is the basis for that argument and how did the court resolve the Healthcare infringement claim in that geographic market?

2. *CA's Geographic Rights.* CA claimed that it had superior rights to the mark in the six-county area because of its first use and well-established presence in the area. What rights did the court recognize in the six-county area? CA also claimed superior rights throughout the state because of its state registration. Under what circumstances would Healthcare be enjoined from use in other parts of the state?

3. *Good Faith Adoption of a Mark.* The rights of a junior user depend on its "good faith" adoption of the mark. Some courts interpret "good faith" as meaning "lack of prior knowledge of the other's use" and others interpret it as meaning "intent to reap the benefits of the other's good will" or "to carry out a purpose inimical to the interests of the other." The Lanham Act §22 states that registration on the principal register is constructive knowledge of the registrant's use. Under the first test, that would be enough to show lack of good faith. If the latter meaning is followed, then prior knowledge of the other's use is only some evidence of bad faith, but not dispositive.

4. *Applying the* **Tea Rose/Rectanus** *Doctrine.* The court began its analysis of geographic rights with reference to the *Tea Rose/Rectanus* doctrine, which embodies the principle that the first, good faith user in a particular geographic area has superior rights to use the mark in that market. If Chicago and San Diego are distinctly different markets for grocery stores, for instance, the first grocery store to use a trademark in Chicago will have rights in Chicago superior to those of a grocery store in San Diego that has been using the mark for decades, as long as the Chicago user adopted the mark in good faith. As the court in *Healthcare* observed, the underlying policy is that "the owner of a mark may not '*monopolize markets that his trade has never reached and where the mark signifies not his goods but those of another.*'" The related principle of "territoriality" states that priority of trademark rights in the United States depends on priority of use in this country, not in a foreign country. First use of a mark in Mexico does not normally give the user priority over a user in California.

In 2004, the Ninth Circuit Court of Appeals decided a case involving a priority dispute between a San Diego grocer and a Mexican grocery store chain, both of whom used the mark GIGANTE, meaning "giant" in Spanish. *See Grupo Giganta SA de CV v. Dallo & Co.*, 391 F.3d 1088 (2004). The Mexican company had used the mark widely in Mexico since 1962 but never in the United States. Dallo started using GIGANTE in San Diego in 1991. Following the territoriality principle, Dallo would have prior rights in San Diego.

The court, however, applied a "famous mark" exception, which recognizes that consumers in the United States might be confused by a domestic supplier's use of a foreigner's mark whose fame had reached the United States, as the GIGANTE mark had. The district court had held that if the foreigner's mark had acquired secondary meaning in the San Diego market, the foreign mark would have priority in San Diego. The court of appeals added that a substantial percentage of consumers in San Diego must be familiar with the foreign mark and that whether the domestic user had used the mark in good faith was also relevant. The basic focus of the Ninth Circuit's test was whether consumers in the domestic market were likely to be confused about the source of the goods or, in the context of the case, whether the mark signified to consumers in San Diego the goods of the domestic company, Dallo, or the Mexican company. While the "famous mark" exception may be an exception to the territoriality principle, it is not an exception to the general policy that consumer confusion is the central focus.

## PEACHES ENTERTAINMENT CORP. v. ENTERTAINMENT REPERTOIRE ASSOC., INC.

### 62 F.3d 690 (5th Cir. 1995)

STEWART, Circuit Judge.

...Peaches Entertainment Corporation, a retail music and video chain, operates twenty-one locations in six states. It is the owner of the federally registered service mark PEACHES for "retail tape and record services," the mark having been registered by a corporate predecessor, Lishon's Inc. ("Lishon's"), on July 6, 1976. Lishon's began using the mark in commerce in relation to music stores sometime in 1974.

Likewise, ERA owns a retail music and video store in New Orleans, Louisiana, which does business under the trade name PEACHES.[2] ERA first began to use the name PEACHES and a related graphic service mark in August 1975, when it opened stores in both Orleans and Jefferson Parish....

In 1992, when PEC learned of ERA's use of the mark PEACHES, it brought an infringement suit in federal court under the Lanham Trademark Act of 1946, seeking an injunction and damages. At that time, ERA was operating only one store in Orleans Parish, although the one store was extremely profitable. ERA defended on the grounds that it was an "intermediate junior user," entitled to exclusive use of the trademark within the territory that it had established prior to the federal registration of the mark. The district court agreed.

The triable issues that remained were limited to determining the extent of PEC's right to use the PEACHES service mark...

In 1946, Congress passed the Lanham Act in order to federalize the common law protection of trademarks used in interstate commerce. The Act was designed to protect both consumers' confidence in the quality and source of goods and services and protect businesses' goodwill in their products by creating a federal right of action for trademark infringement. Owners of a federally recognized trademark, service mark, or other collective mark[4] may bring suit in federal court for damages or injunctive relief against users of similar marks whose use is "likely to cause confusion, or to cause mistake, or to deceive." 15 U.S.C. §1114.

The basic scheme that creates rights under the Lanham Act is a national registration system. Under the common law, use of a distinctive mark in commerce only created a right through priority and market. *See United Drug Co. v. Theodore Rectanus Co.,* 248 U.S. 90, 97 (1918) ("There is no such thing as property in a trade-mark except as a right appurtenant to an established business or trade in connection with which the mark is employed."). The Lanham Act, however, changed the common law rule by allowing a user to acquire rights in a mark by registration. To complicate this process, however, Congress also created several defenses to a registered-user's rights. Significant to this case, junior users, parties who use a mark subsequent to another's use, may retain rights. If the use predates the senior user's registration, then the Act provides a defense if the mark "was adopted without knowledge of the registrant's prior use and has been continuously used by such party...from a date prior to registration of the mark..." 15 U.S.C. §1115(b)(5). The rights of a junior intermediate user, however, "apply only for the area in which such continuous prior use is proved." 15 U.S.C. §1115(b)(5). The junior user's area of continuous

---

2. The parties have stipulated that the owners of ERA were inspired to use the mark and name PEACHES after listening to a hit record by the Allman Brothers entitled "Eat a Peach."

4. Insofar as the applicable law here is concerned, the terms "service mark" and "trade mark" are synonymous.

prior use, which is frozen at the time the senior user obtains registration, becomes the junior user's trade territory.

The junior user may establish his trade territory by identifying the "zone of reputation" acquired for his mark. Provided that the junior user has significant sales in the areas the mark has gained reputation, these areas comprise the junior user's trade territory at the time the senior user obtained registration. Advertising alone cannot establish the junior user's trademark rights in an area....

The trial court identified ERA's trade territory, which was frozen at the time Lishon obtained registration of the PEACHES mark, using uncontroverted testimony regarding ERA's reputation, advertising and sales in the areas in which it concentrated its advertising....

In calculating ERA's trade area, the trial court made the following factual findings:

> In August 1, 1975, Smith and Rea began using the service mark PEACHES on exterior and interior signs, point-of-sale displays at its original locations in Gretna and on Elysian Fields and on bags for purchased merchandise. At that time it also began distributing flyers using the PEACHES service mark and word mark in various other forms of advertising is uncontroverted. In this vein, Rea testified that in *August 1975, ERA began advertising on numerous radio stations* in the metropolitan area of New Orleans, including WXEL (which is now WLTX-FM), WNNR (which is now WYAT), WYLD-AM and FM, WBOK, WTIX and WRNO-FM[.]...The coverage areas for the broadcast signals of the radio stations on which ERA advertised all include Orleans and Jefferson Parishes and most include all of the parishes south of New Orleans to the Gulf of Mexico, all of the parishes on the north shore of Lake Ponchartrain and across the state line well into Mississippi on the north and east, past Baton Rouge to the northwest, and past Lafayette to the west.

The trial court deduced that the market served continuously by ERA's PEACHES prior to Lishon's registration included the greater New Orleans area (i.e., Orleans Parish), and its contiguous parishes, Jefferson, Plaquemines, St. Bernard, St. Tammany, St. Charles and St. John the Baptist.

Our review of the record, and in particular the trial court's memorandum opinion, demonstrates that the trial court's determination of ERA's trade territory was based upon cumulative evidence regarding ERA's reputation. The trial court's determination was not made on the basis of the radio signals going out to various far-reaching areas, but rather on recognized sales coming in from particular localities. A comparison of the radio signals and the court-recognized trade territory reveals that the radio signals through which ERA advertised clearly went far beyond the seven parishes identified as ERA's trade territory. For example, some of the radio signals stretched to the Gulf of Mexico, while others penetrated Mississippi. Evidence adduced at trial magnifies the incongruity between ERA's sales and the radio signals. Harris Rea testified that ERA's PEACHES store survived despite the presence of two nearby Sound Warehouse stores because of ERA's ability to draw from a larger trade area than the PEACHES stores' immediate neighborhoods. He further testified that PEACHES' "reputation" and "customer loyalty" regularly drew customers from the following parishes: Orleans, Jefferson, St. Tammany, Tangipahoa,

St. John the Baptist, St. Charles, St. Bernard and Plaquemines. The trial court carefully tailored the trade territory to conform with evidence regarding ERA's sales; it did not rely solely on ERA's advertising evidence. Because ERA proved its reputation, advertising and sales in these seven parishes, the trial court delineated these parishes as ERA's trade territory. We cannot say that the trial court's factual finding of ERA's trade territory, which was fully supported by testimony and evidence at trial, was clearly erroneous.

Both parties appeal the restrictions placed on ERA's ability to expand within the trade area. PEC argues that ERA should be limited to the one store that is operating now, despite the fact that its trade area covers seven parishes. We find no support for this contention in the case law. As an intermediate junior user, ERA has the right to fully exploit the market potential of its trade area. *Dawn Donut Co. v. Hart's Food Stores,* 267 F.2d 358, 362 (2d Cir. 1959). PEC's rights are not affected by the opening of one store or one hundred stores as long as ERA does not infringe upon PEC's trademark outside of the seven parish trade area. We find PEC's argument to be without merit.

ERA appeals the portion of the district court's judgment that limits it from opening new stores outside of the Orleans and Jefferson Parish parts of the trade area. Harris Rea testified that ERA's specialization in ethnic music and its wide inventory of Louisiana music had gained it a loyal following. He also testified that gross revenues for the single store had been growing over the last few years despite competition from large franchise stores. As noted above, in 1991, gross revenues were $345,000. In 1992, they were $455,000. In 1993, they were $650,000. By July 31, 1994, gross revenues exceeded $750,000. He testified that gross revenues by square footage in 1994 was $417 dollars per square foot, which is approximately three times the industry average of $165 dollars per square foot.

Rea testified that in order to increase profitability in the future, he had planned to expand the size of his store in Orleans Parish as well as open new stores within the trade area. By opening new stores, he stated that he would be able to spread management costs over several stores and generate more sales for the same advertising dollar. Rea also testified that the new stores would make ERA eligible for volume discounts from record manufacturers and distributors.

Based on this uncontroverted evidence at trial, the district court stated in its memorandum opinion that:

> It appears incongruous for a court to limit an intermediate junior user to a specific retail location or a set of specific locations within its defined Trade Territory when the law is precisely to the effect that an intermediate junior user is entitled to freely use its mark within the confines of its established trade territory without interference by the registered owner of the mark. Accordingly, the Court is of the opinion that it is inappropriate to interfere with the ERA's use of its mark within its Trade Territory by delineating specific locations therein where the intermediate junior use is permitted [to] utilize its mark. [Footnote omitted.]

This conclusion comports perfectly with the principle that an intermediate junior user is entitled to fully exploit its trade area.

In its judgment, however, the district court limited the opening of new stores to the Orleans and Jefferson Parish, explaining its reason for the restriction:

> The court imposes such restriction for the sole purpose of avoiding the possibility of a prohibited expansion of the intermediate junior user's trade territory which would logically follow the establishment of additional retail locations approaching the outer boundaries of ERA's Trade Territory.

This restriction is unsupported by the record or law. There was no evidence adduced at trial indicating that a restriction on the physical location of an ERA store was required to prevent the expansion of ERA's trade area. In fact, the evidence at trial was that the opening of new stores was planned by ERA as a means of exploiting the existing trade area. This evidence was not contested by PEC. Neither the district court nor PEC cites any case that has allowed this type of restriction on the location of a store within a trade area, nor has our own research produced any case law that has imposed this type of restriction.

The district court reached the factual conclusion that ERA's trade area consisted of seven contiguous parishes in South Louisiana. This conclusion was fully supported by the evidence and testimony submitted at trial. Having reached that conclusion, it was error for the district court to restrict the location of any of ERA's future stores to Orleans and Jefferson Parish.

For the foregoing reasons, we REMAND the cause to the district court, and the district court is directed to MODIFY its judgment, consistent with this opinion, by removing the stricture prohibiting ERA from opening new stores outside of Orleans and Jefferson Parish. In all other respects, the judgment of the district court is AFFIRMED.

## Comments

1. *ERA's Rights Within Its Protected Trade Area.* An "intermediate junior user" has exclusive rights to a limited area despite using the mark after the senior user because it was the first in that limited area and began its use before the senior user's federal registration. Because ERA was an intermediate junior user, it had protectible rights within its trade area despite PEC's senior status as first user and its later federal registration. What factors determined the extent of ERA's trade area and its rights to expand its stores within that area?

2. *Junior and Senior Unregistered Users. Peaches Entertainment* involved an unregistered junior user, one whose first use came after the senior party's use but before the senior party's registration. That first use preserves the junior user's rights to its own trade area. The junior user who is the first to register takes its nationwide rights subject to the senior user's exclusive rights to its existing trade area. As long as the first person to use in a particular geographic area does not abandon its mark, its rights are recognized. Even when the registrant's mark acquires the status of an "incontestable" mark, that status does not interfere with the unregistered user's limited exclusive rights. Section 15 of

the Lanham Act subjects the registered mark holder's rights to "valid rights acquired under the law of any State or Territory by use of a mark or trade name continuing from a date prior to the date of registration under this chapter of such registered mark."

3. *Zones of Reputation and Penetration versus Zone of Natural Expansion.* In *Healthcare* and *Peaches Entertainment,* the courts focused on the equivalent zones of "reputation" and "penetration" to determine the scope of exclusive geographic rights. The *Sweetarts* factors, mentioned in *Healthcare,* are commonly applied in making this determination. "Freezing" the trade area to the market penetrated at the time of the other's registration protects the unregistered user's customers from confusion by excluding the senior user from that market. It also protects the unregistered user's goodwill, of which ERA in *Peaches Entertainment* apparently had a great deal.

Before federal registration granted national rights, some state courts entitled unregistered users of similar marks to trade areas defined by the area they had already penetrated plus a "zone of natural expansion" at the time of the other's use, which allowed for some flexibility in market definition. Courts would consider the nature of the party's business activity prior to the other's use including any previous expansion or lack thereof, its dominance in contiguous areas where it did not engage in marketing as well as growth trends in the area. The justification for being flexible about the zone of penetration was to protect consumers who had heard of the user and might believe that any entrant using the mark was that user and to allow the user to exploit the current full extent of its goodwill.

After the federal registration system granted national rights, courts began to limit the trade area to the area in which sales have already been made. Some courts have completely abandoned the zone of expansion concept. The First Circuit Court of Appeals, in *Raxton Corp. v. Anania Associates,* 635 F.2d 924 (1st Cir. 1980), examined the history of the natural expansion doctrine, found weak support for it in precedent and policy generally, and specifically rejected it as part of Massachusetts law, which it was applying in that case. On the other hand, the Fourth Circuit Court of Appeals, having held that the Lanham Act preempted state law from granting any rights to the entire state without actual use throughout the state and limited rights of the unregistered user to the area of actual use, defined the trade area for a Northern Virginia restaurant with three branches to include its zone of natural expansion. *See Spartan Food Systems, Inc., v. HFS Corporation,* 813 F.2d 1279 (4th Cir. 1987).

## BURGER KING V. HOOTS
### 403 F.2d 904 (7th Cir. 1968)

KILEY, Circuit Judge.

Defendants' appeal presents a conflict between plaintiffs' right to use the trade mark "Burger King," which plaintiffs have registered under the Federal Trade Mark Act, and defendants' right to use the same trade mark which defendants have registered under the Illinois Trade Mark Act. The district court resolved the conflict in favor of plaintiffs in this case of first impression in this Circuit. We affirm the judgment restraining the defendants from using the name "Burger King" in any part of Illinois except in their Mattoon, Illinois, market, and restraining plaintiffs from using their trade mark in the market area of Mattoon, Illinois.

Defendants do not challenge the district court's findings of fact and have not included testimony of witnesses at the trial in the record on appeal.

Plaintiff Burger King of Florida, Inc. opened the first "Burger King" restaurant in Jacksonville, Florida, in 1953. By 1955, fifteen of these restaurants were in operation in Florida, Georgia and Tennessee; in 1956 the number operating in Alabama, Kentucky and Virginia was twenty-nine; by 1957, in these states, thirty-eight restaurants were in operation.

In July, 1961, plaintiffs opened their first Illinois "Burger King" restaurant in Skokie, and at that time had notice of the defendants' prior registration of the same mark under the Illinois Trade Mark Act. Thereafter, on October 3, 1961, plaintiffs' certificate of federal registration of the mark was issued. Subsequently, plaintiffs opened a restaurant in Champaign, Illinois, and at the time of the trial in November, 1967, were operating more than fifty "Burger King" restaurants in the state of Illinois.

In 1957 the defendants, who had been operating an ice cream business in Mattoon, Illinois, opened a "Burger King" restaurant there. In July, 1959, they registered that name under Illinois law as their trade mark, without notice of plaintiffs' prior use of the same mark. On September 26, 1962, the defendants, with constructive knowledge of plaintiffs' federal trade mark, opened a second similar restaurant, in Charleston, Illinois.

Both parties have used the trade mark prominently, and in 1962 they exchanged charges of infringement in Illinois. After plaintiffs opened a restaurant in Champaign, Illinois, defendants sued in the state court to restrain plaintiffs' use of the mark in Illinois. Plaintiffs then brought the federal suit, now before us, and the defendants counter-claimed for an injunction, charging plaintiffs with infringement of their Illinois trade mark.

The district court concluded, from the unchallenged findings, that plaintiffs' federal registration is prima facie evidence of the validity of the registration and ownership of the mark; that plaintiffs have both a common-law and a federal right in the mark superior to defendants' in the area of natural expansion of plaintiffs' enterprise which "logically included" all of Illinois, except where defendants had actually adopted and used the mark, innocently, i.e., without notice and in good faith; and that the defendants had adopted and continuously used the mark in the Mattoon area innocently and were entitled to protection in that market.

We hold that the district court properly decided that plaintiffs' federal registration of the trade mark "Burger King" gave them the exclusive right to use the mark in Illinois except in the Mattoon market area in Illinois where the defendants, without knowledge of plaintiffs' prior use, actually used the mark before plaintiffs' federal registration. The defendants did not acquire the exclusive right they would have acquired by their Illinois registration had they actually used the mark throughout Illinois prior to the plaintiffs' federal registration.

We think our holding is clear from the terms of the Federal Trade Mark Act. Under 15 U.S.C. §1065 of the Act, plaintiffs, owners of the federally registered trade mark "Burger King," have the "incontestable" right to use the mark in commerce, except to the extent that such use infringes what valid right the defendants have acquired by their continuous use of the same mark prior to plaintiffs' federal registration.

Under 15 U.S.C. §1115(b), the federal certificate of registration is "conclusive evidence" of plaintiffs' "exclusive right" to use the mark. This Section, however, also provides a defense to an exclusive right to use a trade mark: If a trade mark was adopted without knowledge of the federal registrant's prior use, and has been continuously used, then such use "shall" constitute a defense to infringement, provided that this defense applies only for the area in which such continuous prior use is proved. Since the defendants have established that they had adopted the mark "Burger King" without knowledge of plaintiffs' prior use and that they had continuously used the mark from a date prior to plaintiffs' federal registration of the mark, they are entitled to protection in the area which that use appropriated to them.

Plaintiffs agree that the defendants as prior good faith users are to be protected in the area that they had appropriated. Thus, the question narrows to what area in Illinois the defendants have appropriated by virtue of their Illinois registration.

At common law, defendants were entitled to protection in the Mattoon market area because of the innocent use of the mark prior to plaintiffs' federal registration. They argue that the Illinois Trade Mark Act was designed to give more protection than they already had at common law, and that various provisions of the Illinois Act indicate an intention to afford Illinois registrants exclusive rights to use trade marks throughout the state, regardless of whether they actually used the marks throughout the state or not. However, the Act itself does not express any such intention. And no case has been cited to us, nor has our research disclosed any case in the Illinois courts deciding whether a registrant is entitled to state-wide protection even if he has used the mark only in a small geographical area.

Two decisions of this court, however, shed light on the defendants' argument. In Philco Corp. v. Phillips Mfg. Co., 133 F.2d 663 (7th Cir. 1943), this court, through Judge Kerner, discussed the 1905 and 1920 Trade Mark Acts, and decided that Congress had the constitutional power to legislate on "merits of trade mark questions," supra at 670 of 133 F.2d. It then stated that the policy of the Acts, to provide protection of federally registered marks used in interstate commerce, "may not be defeated or obstructed by State law" and that if state law conflicts with the policy it "must yield to the superior federal law." The court held that Philco's federal-registration rendered all questions of use and protection in interstate commerce questions of federal law, not state law. And in John Morrell & Co. v. Reliable Packing Co., 295 F.2d 314 (7th Cir. 1961), Judge Duffy states, at 317, "However, the Illinois registration carries no presumption of validity" — thus attributing greater value to a federal registration because of its "incontestability" feature, which is prima facie evidence of exclusivity in interstate commerce.

The competing federal and state statutes confirm the correctness of this court's statements. Under 15 U.S.C. §1115(b) of the Lanham Act, the federal certificate can be "conclusive evidence" of registrant's "exclusive right." And 15 U.S.C. §1127 of the Act provides that "The intent of this chapter is * * * to protect registered marks used in such commerce from interference by State * * * legislation." The Illinois Act, however, provides only that a certificate of registration "shall be admissible * * * evidence as competent and sufficient proof of the registration * * *." Ill.Rev.Stat. Ch. 140, §11 (1967).

Moreover, we think that whether or not Illinois intended to enlarge the common law with respect to a right of exclusivity in that state, the Illinois Act does not enlarge its right in the area where the federal mark has priority. Congress expanded the common law, however, by granting an exclusive right in commerce to federal registrants in areas where there has been no offsetting use of the mark. Congress intended the Lanham Act to afford nation-wide protection to federally-registered marks, and that once the certificate has issued, no person can acquire any additional rights superior to those obtained by the federal registrant....

We conclude that if we were to accept the defendants' argument we would be fostering, in clear opposition to the express terms of the Lanham Act, an interference with plaintiffs' exclusive right in interstate commerce to use its federal mark.

The undisputed continuous market for the defendants' "Burger King" products was confined to a twenty mile radius of Mattoon. There is no evidence before us of any intention or hope for their use of their Illinois mark beyond that market. Yet they seek to exclude plaintiffs from expanding the scope of their national exclusive right, and from operating fifty enterprises already begun in Illinois. This result would clearly burden interstate commerce.

The defendants argue also that unless they are given the right to exclusive use throughout Illinois, many persons from all parts of Illinois in our current mobile society will come in contact with the defendants' business and will become confused as to whether they are getting the defendants' product, as they intended.

We are not persuaded by this argument. Defendants have not shown that the Illinois public is likely to confuse the products furnished by plaintiffs and by defendants. We are asked to infer that confusion will exist from the mere fact that both trade marks co-exist in the state of Illinois. However, the district court found that the defendants' market area was limited to within twenty miles of their place of business. The court's decision restricted the use of the mark by plaintiffs and defendants to sufficiently distinct and geographically separate markets so that public confusion would be reduced to a minimum. The mere fact that some people will travel from one market area to the other does not, of itself, establish that confusion will result. Since the defendants have failed to establish on the record any likelihood of confusion or any actual confusion, they are not entitled to an inference that confusion will result.

For the reasons given, the judgment of the district court is affirmed.

# Comments

1. *Hoots' Rights.* Hoots asserted trademark rights in the Mattoon, Illinois market area despite its having adopted the mark in 1957, after Burger King of Florida's first use in 1953, and in Charleston, Illinois despite its first use there in 1962, after Burger King's 1961 federal registration of the mark. What was the basis for Hoots' claim in each area and what was Hoots' extent of rights in each area?

2. *Reverse Confusion.* In a traditional trademark infringement action, an established senior user attempts to prevent a junior user from free riding on the senior user's goodwill. By contrast, the label "reverse confusion" has been given to cases where a junior user's overwhelming use of a mark leads consumers to conclude that the senior user in a particular area is infringing on the junior user's mark. Consumers in Mattoon, Illinois, familiar with the famous mark of the corporate giant Burger King, might reasonably believe that the small business operated by Hoots was exploiting the larger company's mark despite the fact that Hoots used the mark first in Mattoon. The legal standards for the two types of cases are the same.

   The potential for strategic lawsuits arises in reverse confusion cases. Consider the position of a little-known senior user such as a local Colorado tire company with a local tire brand such as BIGFOOT. A major, nationally known tire company, Goodyear Tire, later decided to adopt the BIGFOOT mark for use in connection with its tires and spent millions to promote it. *Big O Tire Dealers, Inc. v. Goodyear Tire and Rubber Co.,* 408 F. Supp. 1219 (1976). The small senior user, who has a protectible right in its market area (and perhaps even nationwide if it was federally registered), can sue to enjoin the junior user. The junior user can either give up the value of the goodwill it has established through the millions of dollars spent in advertising or pay millions to the little-known senior user to buy the right to the BIGFOOT mark, or settle the suit. This puts the small senior user in a potentially remunerative bargaining position disproportionate to its size in the market.

   Remedies in Lanham Act suits are equitable in nature and thus may be limited to achieve justice when it appears that a small senior user is strategically exploiting its seniority. Two options for courts are to draft injunctions very narrowly, giving the small, relatively obscure senior user little in the way of protection or to limit damages to the necessarily small harm the senior user has suffered. The court's flexibility in awarding remedies in trademark suits is discussed in Chapter 4. Another option is to find that the small senior user has no rights at all. In *Lucent Information Management, Inc v. Lucent Technologies, Inc.,* 186 F.3d 311 (3d Cir. 1999), the huge junior user/first registrant of the LUCENT mark had national rights because the senior user's use was so minor and insignificant that there was no likelihood of confusion. The senior user had done only $323.50 in business in the three months before the junior user filed its intent-to-use application.

3. *State versus Federal Rights. Healthcare* left undecided the question of what rights the parties would have within the state of Arkansas if CA decided to expand. CA had acquired a state registration of its mark in March

1995. Healthcare had no significant Arkansas business before September 1995. Whatever rights Healthcare had were based on the fact that CA did not compete outside its six-county area. If neither party obtained a federal registration, CA's rights would depend entirely on state law. Justice Holmes was a champion of the view that a trade area should be defined by state boundaries, thinking it unfair to deny senior users the statewide fruits of its product identification. The realities of national marketing have made courts more reluctant to inhibit trade by granting an isolated user automatic statewide trademark rights, despite the difficulties in figuring out the boundaries of those smaller trade areas.

Healthcare had a federal registration pending at the time of the suit. Once that federal registration is granted, Healthcare is in a much stronger position to halt CA's expansion. As *Burger King* illustrates, state law yields to federal law and federal law governs all question of use and protection in interstate commerce. Similarly, a junior user who gets state registration of a mark after the senior user's federal registration gets no rights over the senior user by that state registration.

**4. Rights of Subsequent Junior Users.** Given the national scope of federal trademark rights, one might suspect that "subsequent junior users," those who adopt a mark after another has registered it, would have no rights whatsoever. The key to a trademark infringement action, however, if proof that the conflicting use is likely to cause confusion. If confusion is not likely, the subsequent junior user cannot be constrained by an infringement suit.

The most famous case illustrating the extremely limited rights of a subsequent junior user is *Dawn Donut Co. v. Hart's Food Stores, Inc.*, 267 F.2d 358 (2d Cir. 1959). In *Dawn Donut,* a wholesale distributor of mixes for donuts and other sweet baked goods had used and federally registered the trademarks DAWN and DAWN DONUT before the defendant, a retailer of donuts, started baking and distributing baked and fried goods under the DAWN mark in a 45-square-mile area around Rochester, New York. The senior user had done no business in that area for at least 16 years. Because confusion was not likely, the plaintiff could not enjoin the defendant from using its mark. The subsequent junior user's rights are extremely limited however, because any time the registrant wishes to enter that market, it may then enjoin the junior user. A more general interpretation of *Dawn Donuts* is that the plaintiff/registrant could enjoin the defendant's use at any time if it could prove that confusion was likely.

In a more recent case, *What-A-Burger of Virginia Inc. v. Whataburger, Inc. of Corpus Christi Texas*, 357 F.3d 441 (4th Cir. 2004), the Virginia firm sought a declaratory judgment that it was not infringing the registered trademark of the Texas firm. The Texas firm had federally registered the WHATABURGER mark in 1957 and there was insufficient evidence that the Virginia firm had used the mark before that date. As a result, the right to use the mark in Virginia belonged to the Texas firm. Consistent with *Dawn Donuts*, however, that does not mean the Texas firm can enjoin the Virginia firm's use. The Texas firm did not use the mark in Virginia so there was no confusion and no infringement. The Virginia firm argued that the Texas firm's many decades of delay in objecting to the Virginia firm's use meant the Texas firm could not object after waiting all these years. The Virginia firm argued that either the doctrine of laches (inequitable delay in asserting one's rights) or the doctrine of acquiescence (implicitly agreeing that the other could behave as they did) would prevent the Texas firm from ever objecting. The Fourth Circuit held that the Texas firm's right to object would not arise until there was confusion. Because the firms did not compete, there was no confusion and the Texas firm's right to object had not yet occurred. Accordingly, the Texas firm had not delayed in asserting its rights. Similarly, acquiescence assumes that there was infringing behavior to which the Texas firm expressly or impliedly consented. Because there was no confusion, there could be no infringement and no acquiescence.

## Problem

**3-1.** The plaintiff used the unregistered mark KISS FM for its radio broadcasting services starting in 1984 in Los Angeles, California, and in 2001 in Savannah, Georgia. Defendant started using the mark KISS 97.5 in Myrtle Beach, South Carolina, for similar services in 1985, KISS 104 in Savannah, Georgia, in 2000, and KISS 92.3 in Raleigh, North Carolina, in 2002. May Plaintiff enjoin defendant's use in Myrtle Beach? In Savannah? In Raleigh? How would it affect the plaintiff's rights if the plaintiff obtained a federal registration of the KISS FM mark in 1989? *See Citicasters Licenses, Inc. v. Cumulus Media, Inc.*, 189 F. Supp. 2d 1372 (D. Ga. 2002).

## B. INFRINGEMENT, CYBERSQUATTING, AND DILUTION

A person with an exclusive right to use a mark may bring infringement actions against others who use the mark in a way that confuses, causes mistakes, or deceives consumers. Lanham Act §32(1) describes the elements of a cause of action for infringement of a registered mark. The elements for a claim of infringement of an unregistered mark are identical in all respects, though the statutory authority for the action appears in Lanham Act §43(a).

The Lanham Act applies to confusion arising in a number of different ways. The traditional type of consumer confusion contemplated by the Lanham Act is "point of sale" confusion, where, for instance, a shopper in a grocery store sees a pound of butter with a kneeling Indian maiden on the box or the mark LAND OF LAKY and mistakenly assumes it is the butter sold by the Minnesota corporation Land O' Lakes Inc. The immediate harm to Land O' Lakes is loss of a sale to another butter maker. Post-sale confusion arises when one mark owner's potential or actual customers refuse to buy its goods or services in the future because they mistakenly associate it with the inferior quality of another supplier's product due to the use of a confusingly similar mark. A potential buyer may see a little car with a mark that looks like BMW's MINI mark broken down on the side of the road and think less of BMW's product quality. This would harm BMW's mark by interfering with future sales. *Lever Bros. v. American Bakeries Co., Inc.*, in Section B.1, introduces the test for infringement and confusion in a typical point-of-sale context. Similar facts might also lead to post-sale confusion.

**NEXXUS**

Pre-sale confusion, often called "initial interest confusion," occurs when one person uses a device similar to an owner's mark to create initial consumer interest, even if that confusion is dispelled before any sale occurs. Similar labeling might draw the consumer's eye to a competing product if, for instance, shampoo sold under the TE$^X_X$US mark were located near the shampoo sold under the more familiar NE$^X_X$US mark. If most consumers would recognize the difference before making a purchase, there is no point-of-sale confusion but the user of the TE$^X_X$US mark will have taken advantage of the goodwill established by the Nexxus Products Company. *Playboy Enterprises, Inc. v. Netscape Communications Corp.*, discussed briefly in Section B.2, involves the use of Playboy's mark by an Internet search engine to create banner ads for third parties whenever a person searches for Playboy on the Internet. This use of Playboy's mark capitalizes on the goodwill associated with the PLAYBOY mark. Cases where the mark is only used by the defendant in the internal operation of the search engine raise the question of whether the mark was "used in commerce" as required by the Lanham Act. *Government Employees Insurance Co. v. Google, Inc.*, discussed briefly in Section B.2 of this chapter, considers the various conclusions courts have reached on this issue.

While infringement actions protect consumers from being confused and suppliers from having their goodwill diminished, the dilution claim was originally intended only to protect the goodwill of mark owners. Even if another's use of a similar mark does not cause confusion, it may diminish its distinctiveness. The infringement cases in this section of the chapter will reveal that even though a mark, such as AUTUMN used in connection with bread, may be arbitrary, its strength might be weak if hundreds of others use or have used the word "autumn" in their marks. The more people using a term, the less consumers will identify the term with a single source. The source-indicating message in a mark may be "blurred" when more than one person uses a term, even if there is no confusion. The dilution claim addresses this concern.

In the state law from which the federal dilution action is derived, dilution of the goodwill or "selling power" of a mark may also result from another's use of the term in connection with inferior goods. A person who uses or sells inferior goods may create a negative association between the mark and all goods sold under similar marks. State dilution claims may be based on either this negative association, which is called "tarnishment," or the blurring of the mark. It is not clear whether federal claims under Lanham Act §43(c) may include tarnishment claims or are limited to proof of blurring. In Section B.3, *Wedgwood Homes, Inc. v. Lund* and *Moseley v. V Secret Catalogue, Inc.* illustrate the purpose of dilution claims and the differences between state and federal causes of action for dilution.

A related misuse of the Internet is *cybersquatting*. Cybersquatting occurs when someone registers with a company such as Network Solutions a domain name that is confusingly similar to a well-known trademark with the hope of selling it to the trademark owner. Domain names have legitimate and illegitimate uses. They are Internet "addresses" that identify sets of computers connected to the Internet and also identify trademark users who offer goods and services, often on the Internet. The potential for confusion arises when a domain name, such as "justdoitdirect.com" is similar to a trademark, such as Nike's JUST DO IT mark used in connection with clothing. If "justdoitdirect.com" leads to a site selling insurance, the impact is different than if it leads to a clothing seller competing with Nike. Whether confusion results from either use, however, depends on analysis of the familiar likelihood of confusion elements. It is a different story if the web address leads nowhere useful because the registrant is merely holding on to it hoping that Nike will want to buy it. The Lanham Act distinguishes among those whose registration of Internet addresses are legitimate with those whose registrations are illegitimate by looking at the intent of the domain name registrant. The brief discussion of *DaimlerChrysler v. The Net Inc.*, in Section B.4 of this chapter, considers Lanham Act §43(d), which prohibits bad faith cyber-piracy.

This part of the chapter ends with consideration of when secondary liability is imposed on those who assist in or benefit from another's infringing activity. If the direct infringers are small and numerous, imposing liability on those who assist the infringers may be a more effective means of policing trademark rights. *Hard Rock Licensing Corp. v. Concession Services, Inc.* involves an organizer of a flea market alleged to have assisted others to use the HARD ROCK CAFÉ mark on t-shirts without authorization.

## 1. Infringement and Likelihood of Confusion

Infringement claims can be brought to protect the source-indicating power of registered or unregistered marks. After a plaintiff proves that it has an exclusive right to use a mark in connection with particular goods or services in a geographic area, the key to proving an infringement claim is consumer confusion. Even though the relevant statutory sections, Lanham Act §§32(1) and 43(a), indicate that causing mistakes and deceiving consumers are also bases for infringement claims, courts usually simply focus on whether the other's use is likely to cause confusion. The case of *Lever Bros. v. American Bakeries Co., Inc.* and the materials that follow focus on the factors relevant to determining whether confusion is likely in a traditional infringement setting.

*STATUTE:* **Remedies; Infringement**
15 U.S.C. §1114(1) (Lanham Act §32(1))

*STATUTE:* **False designations of origin, false descriptions, and dilution forbidden**
15 U.S.C. §1125(a)(1) (Lanham Act §43(a)(1))

Infringement cases focus on whether a mark qualifies for protection, whether the complainant has an exclusive right to use the mark, and whether confusion is likely to result from concurrent use by the defendant. Each Federal Circuit Court of Appeal has is own multifactor test for whether confusion is likely. The basic thrust of each is similar and all are applied flexibly. The Courts of Appeal all recognize that the particular circumstances of a given product or service or of the market in which it is sold may make some factors more important than others and additional factors relevant. The principal cases in this and the following sections apply two of the most widely cited tests, named after the cases in which they were developed, the Second Circuit Court of Appeals' *Polaroid* test and the Ninth Circuit Court of Appeals' *Sleekcraft* test.

## LEVER BROS. v. AMERICAN BAKERIES CO., INC.
### 537 F. Supp. 248 (D.N.Y. 1982)

NEAHER, District Judge.

This action for injunctive relief against alleged infringement of plaintiff's trademark AUTUMN was tried by the court upon the facts. . . .

Plaintiff, Lever Brothers Company ("Lever"), is a Maine corporation having its principal place of business in New York City. Lever, which has conducted business in the United States since 1895, sells a variety of consumer products, including detergents, soaps, toothpaste and food products. Among its food products is margarine sold under the trade names AUTUMN, PROMISE and IMPERIAL, and such items as MRS. BUTTERWORTH'S syrup and pancake mix, LUCKY WHIP dessert topping and SPRY shortening. AUTUMN margarine, which came on the market in 1975, was developed and advertised as a natural margarine product, and in October 1975 Lever obtained a trademark registration for AUTUMN [shown above] without opposition.

Defendant, American Bakeries Company, Inc. ("American"), is a Delaware corporation having its principal place of business in Chicago, Illinois. American sells bread and other bakery products throughout the United States.

These are produced and distributed by a number of primary baking divisions utilizing the trade names Taystee, Merita, Langendorf and Cook Book.

The controversy between the parties arises out of American's decision in April 1977 to adopt AUTUMN GRAIN as a trade name for a grain-type bread it had developed to meet competition from others. The decision was made after a trademark search and advice from house counsel had cleared AUTUMN GRAIN for use. The search disclosed Lever's registration for AUTUMN, as well as similar registrations by others: AUTUMN GOLD (frozen turkeys), AUTUMN LEAVES (candy), AUTUMN CRISP (apples), AUTUMN CHERRY (wine), and AUTUMN WIND (whiskey)....

Lever's AUTUMN margarine is sold in two different forms, tub and stick, and the packaging for each prominently displays the AUTUMN trademark in a distinctive typeface. The primary color scheme for the packaging is red, white, brown and gold, representing the colors of autumn, and is designed to create the image of a "natural" margarine product. Lever's name appears in small type on the bottom panel of the packaging; therefore, the trademark forms the principal basis for consumer recognition.

Original marketing of AUTUMN margarine began in California in 1975 after initial sales in interstate commerce earlier that year from Lever's office in Edgewater, New Jersey to retail stores in Massachusetts and Maine. The initial marketing effort, however, was concentrated in Los Angeles because that area was known to have a relatively high interest in natural-type products. The promotion was accompanied by extensive television commercials and print advertising portraying the use of AUTUMN margarine on bread or crackers. The print advertisements also featured recipes using AUTUMN margarine for making bread and stuffing. The impact of the television advertising was tested by means of consumer surveys in which people were interviewed as to their recall of television commercials for AUTUMN margarine within 24 hours of the commercial. AUTUMN margarine scored a significantly high recall rating of approximately 30%, which compared favorably to the 20% rate for most food products.

That a considerable investment for advertising was made by Lever in promoting AUTUMN margarine is evident from the following table of expenditures for such purpose [showing expenditures totaling over $3.6 million].

Since AUTUMN margarine is generally sold to housewives, Lever's advertising of the product is directed to women, particularly those between the ages of 21 and 35. In both television commercials and print advertising, two basic themes are presented: that AUTUMN margarine is the first natural margarine, i.e., one free from artificial preservatives or coloring, and that it tastes good.

AUTUMN margarine, which generally retails for between 89 cents and 93 cents a package, is sold through two basic channels of trade: (1) directly to large supermarket chains; and (2) to wholesalers who, in turn, sell and distribute it to smaller retail accounts, usually chain supermarkets, independent supermarkets, and small grocery stores. Total sales of the product since 1975 have [exceeded $11.7 million].

American presently uses the mark AUTUMN GRAIN only on bread. The bread wrappers bear the mark in lettering almost identical with Lever's

AUTUMN mark except for color and the added expression "natural grains." Aside from the prominent designation "AUTUMN GRAIN Bread," the source of the product is identified by the "house mark" of the regional bakery, i.e., Merita, Langendorf, Taystee or Cook Book, displayed in white lettering in red ovals on the panels of the wrapper. American's name appears only inconspicuously on a side panel.

American's AUTUMN GRAIN bread is generally displayed and sold from "self-service" shelves in the same type of stores as AUTUMN margarine, i.e., retail grocery stores and supermarkets. Its sale is also promoted through advertisements in newspapers and television commercials, which are directed toward women, particularly housewives, and stress the "natural" qualities of its ingredients and taste.

Since April 1977, when it was introduced, American has sold some 50 to 60 million loaves of AUTUMN GRAIN bread, which wholesales at about 65 cents a loaf, for a total value of about $43,000,000. The majority of these sales occurred in the southeastern portion of the United States, in contrast to the bulk of AUTUMN margarine sales which have been made in California, Oregon and Washington. . . .

There is no question that the products involved in this trademark controversy, although different and noncompeting, are closely related in point of purchase and use. The crucial question is whether the use of AUTUMN on these differing but related products, and in their promotion, creates "any likelihood that an appreciable number of ordinarily prudent purchasers are likely to be misled, or indeed simply confused, as to the source of the goods in question." *Mushroom Makers, Inc. v. R. G. Barry Corp.*, 580 F.2d 44, 47 (2d Cir. 1978), cert. denied, 439 U.S. 1116 (1979). As pointed out by the District Court in Mushroom Makers, the fact that "the products are not identical does not foreclose relief to the senior owner (of the trademark) if they are sufficiently related to make confusion likely." 441 F. Supp. 1220, 1225 (S.D.N.Y.1977).

Factors to be considered in this Circuit in determining the senior user's right to relief where the products in question are non-competitive, but related, are outlined in *Polaroid Corp. v. Polarad Electronics Corp.*, 287 F.2d 492, 495 (2d Cir.), cert. denied, 368 U.S. 820 (1961):

> Where the products are different, the prior owner's chance of success is a function of many variables: the strength of his mark, the degree of similarity between the two marks, the proximity of the products, the likelihood that the prior owner will bridge the gap, actual confusion, and the reciprocal of defendant's good faith in adopting its own mark, the quality of defendant's product, and the sophistication of the buyers. Even this extensive catalogue does not exhaust the possibilities — the court may have to take still other variables into account.

#### (a) STRENGTH OF THE MARK

"The term 'strength' as applied to trademarks refers to the distinctive use of the mark, or more precisely, its tendency to identify the goods sold under the mark as emanating from a particular, although possibly anonymous, source." *McGregor-Doniger Inc. v. Inc.*, 599 F.2d 1126, 1131 (2d Cir. 1979). The strength or distinctiveness of a mark determines both the ease with which it may be established as a valid trademark and the degree of protection it will be accorded. An arbitrary or fanciful mark is considered the strongest type of mark and is therefore ordinarily entitled to a wider scope of protection from infringers. See 3 R. Callmann, *The Law of Unfair Competition Trademarks and Monopolies*, § 74.1 at 226 (3rd ed. 1969).

AUTUMN, albeit a common word, must be considered arbitrary when used in connection with a margarine product. According to Lever's evidence, which is uncontradicted, the word was chosen because it was not generic of the product and, more importantly, was suggestive of the "natural" quality of the margarine that Lever's advertising sought to promote. Lever's purpose in adopting the mark, however, cannot be controlling in determining its strength. The evidence also discloses that AUTUMN has been in common use as a mark for food and drink products dating back to 1932, long before Lever's use. As Callmann aptly points out, "a claim of priority is utterly inconsistent with common use." Id. at 228. Thus it cannot be said that the AUTUMN mark on margarine possesses such distinctiveness as to bar its use on a non-competitive food product.

### (b) DEGREE OF SIMILARITY

In determining the degree of similarity between two marks, the law does not require a microscopic examination or analysis of the elements of the marks. The purchasing public does not generally dissect a mark. Rather, the public is left with a general impression of the mark, and it is this impression which gives rise to the likelihood of consumer confusion.

Here, the packaging of the respective products unquestionably features AUTUMN as the primary word in virtually identical distinctive typeface. But as was explained in *McGregor-Doniger Inc. v. Drizzle Inc.*, *supra*, at 1133, "even close similarity between two marks is not dispositive of the issue of likelihood of confusion." Rather, the impact of the similarity must be appraised in light of the context in which the respective marks are generally presented.

Stressing the symbiotic relationship between bread and margarine, Lever points out that its television commercials and print advertising always feature AUTUMN margarine in conjunction with bread. The bread, however, is usually anonymous, and the advertisements are unlikely to create the impression that the margarine sponsor also produces bread. The packaging of the respective products would be the more likely source of confusion were it not for significant differences which overshadow the similarity in typeface. On Lever's cardboard package for both tub and stick margarine, "AUTUMN Natural Margarine" appears against the background of a picturesque farm scene. Depending upon the sensitivity of the consumer, this may engender thoughts of naturalness, freshness and wholesomeness, but hardly more. American's packaging, on the other hand, is the familiar bag wrapping generally used for bread, clearly depicting the name "AUTUMN GRAIN Bread," as opposed to merely AUTUMN. "Natural Grains" also appears on side panels of the wrapper, but similar expressions are common on bread wrappers, and cannot be viewed as a source of confusion with Lever's natural margarine.

In sum, although the packaging for both products share the common word AUTUMN in similar typeface, the context in which the marks appear is so dissimilar as to negate the likelihood of confusion on the part of purchasers. This conclusion is further supported by the prominent identification on the bread packages of American's regional bakery divisions, e.g., Merita, Tastee, Langendorf or Cook Book, which very likely are familiar to consumers in those regions.

*No confusion — ∆ uses familiar packge*

### (c) PROXIMITY OF THE PRODUCTS

The degree of proximity of the products must be considered here not because a consumer would purchase American's bread product as an alternative to AUTUMN margarine. Rather, as already indicated, it bears on the likelihood of consumers being confused as to the source of the respective products or that indirect harm will result to the senior user through loss of goodwill or tarnishment of reputation.

The factors to be considered regarding the "proximity" of non-competing goods were aptly stated by Callmann in his treatise on trademarks:

> The impression that non-competing goods are from the same origin may be conveyed by such differing considerations as the physical attributes or essential characteristics of the goods, with specific reference to their form, composition, texture or quality, the service or functions for which they are intended, the manner in which they are advertised, displayed or sold, the place where they are sold or the class of customers for whom they are designed and to whom they are sold. 3 R. Callmann, *supra*, § 82.2(c) at 807.

*factors for proximity*

Lever urges that a strong degree of proximity exists based upon the acknowledged fact that bread and margarine are naturally allied products in the minds of the consuming public. In fact, as previously noted, Lever uses them together to advertise and promote AUTUMN margarine. Specifically, Lever argues that bread and margarine are both sold in supermarkets, convenience stores and neighborhood groceries; that both products are low-priced essentials in the American diet; that the purchaser of a bread product will very likely purchase margarine; that both products are generally purchased from self-service racks or display cases without the aid of store assistants; and that most commonly, the consumer picks the products up without inquiring as to its source. Consequently, Lever contends, reliance upon the trademark in these off-the-shelves situations is great.

*P's claims But*

Nevertheless, the absence of any evidence of confusion on the part of consumers derogates from the significance of proximity. Although actual confusion need not be shown, where both products have been on the market for over three years, during which time 13 million packages of AUTUMN margarine and over 50 million loaves of AUTUMN GRAIN bread have been sold, the absence of even a single instance of confusion becomes significant. See *Mushroom Makers, Inc. v. R. G. Barry Corp.*, *supra*, at 48. Moreover, the various customer complaints in evidence from purchasers of AUTUMN GRAIN bread indicate no confusion as to the source of the product: the complaints were unerringly registered with American, not Lever. Pl. Exh. 108. The reason seems obvious. Despite their proximity, bread and margarine are different products accorded wholly distinct treatment in handling and sale. The products are invariably segregated, for margarine requires refrigeration and is found in the dairy section of a store, while bread is shelved separately in a baked goods section. The evidence shows, therefore, that the disparate nature of the goods, the source of origin information on the packages, the absence of actual confusion, and the distinct treatment by retailers prevent any likelihood of confusion caused by proximity.

### (d) QUALITY OF DEFENDANT'S PRODUCT

Lever contends that because of the close similarity of trademarks, consumer dissatisfaction with AUTUMN GRAIN bread may disparage Lever's product. Lever points to the concession of American's executive vice-president that American has no control over at least some of the bread it sells, particularly in Cook Book's Houston and Amarillo, Texas, plants, which are apparently operated by a third party. In our consideration of the proximity factor, however, we have pointed out that the few customers who had complaints about American's bread had no difficulty directing them to American.

Granted that the good reputation associated with a senior user's mark is a primary interest which our trademark laws seek to protect, the rule has no application here. The satisfactory quality of AUTUMN GRAIN bread is rather solidly demonstrated by American's sales of some 50 to 60 million loaves having a sales value of about $43,000,000, since the middle of 1977 when distribution began. Even assuming that a loaf of bread has a shorter life and is purchased more often than a package of margarine, American's sales certainly compare favorably with Lever's, whose sales of AUTUMN margarine total about $13,000,000 since 1975. Thus there is no basis in the evidence for finding that the continued sale of AUTUMN GRAIN bread would diminish the value of Lever's mark for margarine.

### (e) SOPHISTICATION OF THE BUYER

This element of the Polaroid test requires consideration of the sophistication — or naiveté — of the purchaser of the products in question. *Polaroid Corp. v. Polarad Electronics Corp., supra*, at 495. Again, Callmann states the issue well:

> The general impression of the ordinary purchaser, buying under the normally prevalent conditions of the market and given the attention such purchasers usually give in buying that class of goods, is the touchstone. 3 R. Callman, supra, §81.2 at 577.

The ordinary purchaser of bread and margarine will not stop to analyze the intricacies of trademarks or packaging. The typical market is such as to stimulate sales based on impulse, not introspection; purchase decisions are governed by appearances and general impressions, not in-depth analysis. Considering the nature of the goods, the bustling, self-service atmosphere of a typical supermarket in which over 5,000 trademarked items are presented, and the frequency of purchase, little more is required to conclude that the ordinary purchaser of AUTUMN margarine and AUTUMN GRAIN bread is a casual, unsophisticated buyer. Additionally, the low price of each item indicates that the normal buyer will exercise relatively less caution, making confusion more likely. See *Harold F. Ritchie, Inc. v. Chesebrough-Pond's, Inc.*, 281 F.2d 755, 762, n.19 (2d Cir. 1960).

### (f) Bridging the Gap

This expression describes "the senior user's interest in preserving avenues of expansion and entering into related fields." *Mushroom Makers, Inc. v. R. G. Barry Corp., supra*, at 1228. In this regard, Lever points out it has expanded several of its successful products into related markets. Further contending that it is not uncommon for both bread and margarine to be sold under the same mark, Lever cites its history of line extensions in other contexts:

| Original Product | Line Extension |
|---|---|
| DOVE toilet bar | DOVE dishwashing liquid |
| LUX toilet bar | LUX dishwashing liquid |
| ALL detergent | ALL liquid detergent |
| IMPERIAL margarine Diet | IMPERIAL margarine |
| MRS. BUTTERWORTH'S syrup | MRS. BUTTERWORTH'S pancake mix |

Unquestionably, an important purpose of the trademark laws is protection of legitimate potential and expansion into related fields. Nevertheless, Lever has failed to present evidence of the likelihood of bridging the gap in this instance. Its previous extensions fail to indicate a present likelihood because none involved products as distinct as bread and margarine. Nor does the evidence establish the likelihood that Lever will follow the example of its European parent in marketing a long shelf-life bread or even that it would adopt AUTUMN for such a product. In fact, at no point in its 85-year existence has Lever entered the baked goods market. Thus, the totality of evidence fails to show the likelihood that Lever will extend its AUTUMN line to the field into which American has entered.

### (g) Good Faith

American's adoption of AUTUMN in a logotype form virtually identical with that appearing on Lever's packaging raises an inference of intentional imitation. The inference is supported by the testimony of Raymond J. Lahvic, American's marketing vice-president, that manufacture of AUTUMN GRAIN packaging began six to eight weeks before house counsel had given trademark clearance. The trademark tracer report upon which he acted is dated April 17, 1977, and disclosed the registration of Lever's AUTUMN mark on October 21, 1975. Significantly, however, the report also revealed, as previously mentioned, a number of other registrations which used AUTUMN in combination with another word for a variety of food and drink products. Further, American's officials denied under oath that they were aware of Lever's AUTUMN mark when the initial decision was made to adopt AUTUMN GRAIN. These denials can be credited in light of the evidence that until 1979 AUTUMN margarine remained largely a test product in the Los Angeles area, whereas American developed AUTUMN GRAIN bread to compete with a grain-type bread marketed in North Carolina. Moreover, American rejected the use of HARVEST GRAIN because of prior registrations, which indicates defendant's process of decision was reasoned and in good faith. In these circumstances, the adoption of similar typeface on different packaging for distinct products cannot alone justify a finding of American's bad faith.

### CONCLUSION

As in Mushroom Makers there is no evidence that plaintiff has been or will be damaged by American's use of AUTUMN GRAIN. The court finds defendant's mark was adopted in good faith without intent to benefit from Lever's business reputation or to palm off or deceive the public as to origin of American's product. Nor is there any evidence that any purchasers of either party's product have been or will be in any way confused, deceived or misled. Since AUTUMN is a common word which has frequently been registered as a trademark for various food or beverage products prior to Lever's use, Lever does not have the right to preempt uses of the mark on other food products, particularly when, as here, the mark is coupled with a modifying word which precludes the likelihood of confusion. In the circumstances, considering the substantial investment American has made in its mark, the good will it has gained through substantial sales of its product and the absence of likelihood of any future confusion, it would be inequitable to bar American from further use of its mark.

Accordingly, the court concludes that plaintiff is not entitled to relief under 15 U.S.C. §§1114 or 1125; and having failed to prove the likelihood of injury to its business reputation or the distinctiveness of its mark, plaintiff has not met the statutory prerequisites to relief under N.Y. Gen. Bus. Law §368-d.

The Clerk of the Court is directed to enter judgment for defendant, and to forward copies of these findings of fact and conclusions of law to counsel for both parties.

## Comments

1. *Likelihood of Confusion Factors.* Each Federal Court of Appeals has adopted its own flexible list of factors, but there is a great deal of similarity among them. The table below indicates general agreement on six factors, though courts use different words to describe each factor:

   The Court of Appeals for the Federal Circuit has additional considerations in its test, derived from *In re E.I. Dupont De Nemours & Co.*, 476 F.2d 1357, 1357 (CCPA 1973), perhaps because of its jurisdiction over appeals from decisions by the TTAB. Those additional factors include

## Likelihood of Confusion Factors in the Federal Circuits

| | 1st | 2nd | 3rd | 4th | 5th | 6th | 7th | 8th | 9th | 10th | 11th |
|---|---|---|---|---|---|---|---|---|---|---|---|
| Similarity of Marks | YES | YES | YES | YES | YES | YES | YES | YES | YES | YES | YES |
| Similarity of Goods or Services | YES | YES | YES | YES | YES | YES | YES | YES | YES | YES | YES |
| Actual Confusion | YES | YES | YES | YES | YES | YES | YES | YES | YES | YES | YES |
| Extent of Applicant's Exclusive Rights/ Strength of Mark | YES | YES | YES | YES | YES | YES | YES | YES | YES | YES | YES |
| Conditions under which Sales are Made/Classes, Sophistication of Prospective Purchasers/ Price/ Similarity of Trade Channels/ Customers | YES | YES | YES | YES | YES | YES | YES | YES | YES | YES | YES |
| Intent/Good Faith | YES | YES | YES | YES | YES | YES | YES | YES | YES | YES | YES |
| Relationship between the Parties' Advertising | YES | | | YES | YES | YES | | | | YES | YES |
| Likelihood Plaintiff Will Bridge the Gap | | YES | YES | YES | | YES | | | YES | | |
| Time and Conditions of Concurrent Use w/o Actual Confusion | | | YES | | | | YES | | | | |

1. *Volkswagenwerk Aktiengesellschaft v. Wheeler*, 814 F.2d 812, 817 (1st Cir. 1987).
2. *Polaroid Corp. v. Polarad Elecs. Corp.*, 287 F.2d 492, 495 (2d Cir. 1961).
3. *Interpace Corp. v. Lapp, Inc.*, 721 F.2d 460, 462-463 (3d Cir. 1983).
4. *Shakespeare Co. v. Silstar Corp. of America, Inc.*, 110 F.3d 234, 241 (4th Cir. 1997).
5. *Elvis Presley Enterprises*, 141 F.3d 188, 194 (5th Cir. 1998).
6. *Frisch's Rests., Inc. v. Elby's Big Boy of Steubenville, Inc.*, 670 F.2d 642, 648 (6th Cir. 1982).
7. *Ty, Inc. v. Jones Group, Inc.*, 237 F.3d 891, 897-898 (7th Cir. 2000).
8. *Co-Rect Prods., Inc. v. Marvy! Adver. Photography, Inc.*, 780 F.2d 1324, 1330 (8th Cir. 1985).
9. *AMF Inc. v. Sleekcraft Boats*, 599 F.2d 341, 348-349 (9th Cir. 1979).
10. *King of the Mountain Sports, Inc. v. Chrysler Corp.*, 185 F.3d 1084 (10th Cir. 1999).
11. *Frehling Enters., Inc. v. Intern'l Select Group, Inc.*, 192 F.3d 1330, 1335 (11th Cir. 1999).

the number and nature of similar marks on similar goods, the variety of goods on which the mark is used, the extent of potential confusion, the fame of prior marks, and the market interface between the applicant and the owner of a prior mark.

Careful consideration of these factors reveals considerable overlap. For instance, the factors "Relationship between the Parties' Advertising" and "Market Interface between Applicant and Owner of Prior Mark" might both be included in the broad category "Conditions under which Sales are Made." As another example, recall that even though "Number and Nature of Similar Marks on Similar Goods" and "Variety of Good on Which Mark is Used" are not explicit parts of the *Polaroid* test, the court in *Lever Bros.* considered these factors in the context of its analysis of strength of the AUTUMN mark. For each factor discussed in *Lever Bros.*, the court considered conflicting arguments, revealing the types of evidence considered for each factor. The list of factors is flexible. Sometimes discussion of particular factors is combined. Sometimes an irrelevant factor is ignored. The opinion in *Lever Bros.* for instance combines consideration of similarity of marks and actual confusion for instance.

2. *Similarity of Marks and Products.* Liability for infringement depends on likelihood of confusion given all of the relevant factors and not on any particular degree of similarity of the marks and products. The Restatement (Second) of Unfair Competition §21 cmt. c, emphasizes that the similarity of the competing marks must be based on the commercial impression the marks create as they appear in the marketplace rather than the courtroom. A side-by-side comparison, for instance, is inappropriate if the goods are not sold side-by-side, as in the case of bread and butter. Tests for similarity look at appearance, pronunciation, verbal translation of the pictures or designs, and suggestions evoked by the marks. The general impression of the mark is important, rather than the details. A prospective purchaser does not carry a sample or specimen of a familiar article with him or her, only a mental picture of the indications of origin. Concurrent use of marks on products that are substitutes for one another, are sometimes used together as in *Lever Bros.*, or perform the same function are more likely to cause confusion than goods used by different people for different purposes.

3. *Actual Confusion.* Actual confusion is not essential to showing a likelihood of confusion, though less distinctive marks logically require greater proof of likely confusion. A less distinctive mark is a word, symbol, or device that consumers do not readily identify as source indicating. If a mark is not clearly a source indicator, consumers are unlikely to be confused about source even if two suppliers use identical marks. Consumers might, for instance, reasonably expect a term such as "slinky," to be used descriptively in connection with clingy fabric in women's clothing rather than as a source indicator. That is why descriptive marks are weak. If consumers interpret a term as descriptive rather than source indicating, confusion about source from concurrent use of the term is unlikely. Thus, weaker marks, such as descriptive and suggestive marks, might require more proof of confusion than stronger, arbitrary or fanciful marks.

Surveys are often used to determine whether confusion is likely to or has actually resulted from two people using similar marks. The court in *V&S Vin & Sprit Aktiebolag d/b/a/ Absolut Co. v. Cracovia Brands Inc.*, 2004 WL 42375 (D. Ill. Jan. 5, 2004) found that a survey showing 8 percent of people confused by the visual appearance of the marks ABSOLUT and ABSOLUWENT for vodka does not compel a finding for the plaintiff alleging confusion. The court referred to a number of other cases where surveys were used, including ones in which 10 percent confusion among consumers was "given significant weight," 11 percent "cannot be dismissed as insignificant, and 10 percent was "statistically significant." It also referred to a case where evidence showed 23 recent purchasers were confused about origin combined with survey evidence showing 7.7 percent of people perceived a business connection between the companies and 8.5 percent confused the name. The court in that case found the survey demonstrated "strong evidence of the likelihood of confusion." Misdirected phone calls and complaint letters are also offered as evidence of actual confusion, as discussed in *Lever Bros.* When the plaintiff's mark is strong and the defendant has not been using the allegedly infringing mark for long, a finding of likely confusion may be appropriate even without evidence of actual confusion.

4. *Strength of Marks.* The AUTUMN mark used in connection with margarine was classified as a strong mark, either arbitrary or suggestive. Classification alone is not the end of the analysis of strength, however, when evaluating the likelihood of confusion. If many others have used the word "autumn" in their marks, the mark is less distinctive. A search of the Patent and Trademark Office website, *http://www.uspto.gov/main/trademarks.htm*, reveals over 125 live marks using the word "autumn" and more than 150 marks using "autumn" that are expired, abandoned, or otherwise dead, including Lever Bros.' AUTUMN mark.

5. *Conditions of Sale.* When evaluating the likelihood of confusion from two people using a mark, courts take a realistic look at how consumers make purchases. Courts consider the general impression the marks create in the mind of an ordinary purchaser buying under normally prevalent conditions in markets and giving the degree of attention such purchasers usually give in buying that class of goods. If selections are made quickly and without much thought, in self-service settings, and if prices are low, buyers are less likely to pay close attention to the differences between two marks.

The relevance of buyer sophistication depends on the type of good or service in question. If the public-at-large is the consumer group, buyer sophistication is unlikely to be a key factor in the likelihood of confusion analysis. If the product or service is specialized or expensive or purchased only by experts, the buyer is likely to pay more attention to the mark and to be less confused by similar marks. The LEXIS computerized legal database company complained about Toyota's adoption of the LEXUS mark for luxury automobiles. Even aside from the differences in types of goods, confusion is unlikely because the respective buyers are likely to know in advance who supplies each and, if not, take care in making purchasing decisions. People buying machinery for a factory are more likely to pay attention to the details of the purchase than people buying paper clips in a drug store. Contractors who buy metal roofing panels are likely to be sophisticated, while home shoppers on the Internet for costume jewelry are likely to be unsophisticated, at least in the sense of taking great care with brand identification.

Price, sophistication of the purchaser, and nature of marketing are all considered. Even if current customers are sophisticated, a product might later be marketed to the general public. Cognac once had limited appeal in the United States but after mass marketing became a more popular beverage. Drinkers of Ouzo might be predominantly sophisticated Greeks or people of Greek descent who pay a great deal of attention to brands, but the owner of the mark in question has a right to try to expand its market to include others.

6. *Intent and Bad Faith.* An infringement claim does not require proof of intent; innocent infringement may be enjoined. Intent to confuse and bad faith may, however, indicate that confusion is likely. Courts presume that a person who adopts a similar mark intending to confuse consumers believed that it would be successful. "In other words, we presume that the person who sets out to infringe on another's trademark has more brains than scruples, and will likely succeed." *Sara Lee Corp. v. Kayser-Roth Corp.*, 81 F.3d 455 (4th Cir. 1996). *Lever Bros.* illustrates that knowledge of the other's mark is relevant to, but not dispositive of the intent issue.

7. *Bridging the Gap.* "Bridging the gap" refers to the likelihood (either actual or perceived) that the mark holder will expand its product (or service) line to include the product on which the alleged infringer used the mark. There are two justifications for including bridging the gap as a factor relevant to confusion. One is protecting the mark owner's interest in expanding and entering into new fields. For a registered mark owner with national rights, bridging the gap refers to expanding into supply of related products or services. *Lever Bros.* emphasized this view. For an unregistered mark owner, this might also mean expanding into new geographic areas. One might reasonably wonder why this is relevant to whether consumers are likely to be confused. The answer is that enjoining the defendant's use of a similar mark would prevent "future confusion" that would arise when the mark owner did expand.

Under this "interest in expansion" justification, evidence of the mark owner's actual expansion plans is relevant. If the mark owner has no plans to bridge the gap, this factor will weigh against confusion between different products or services. Courts do not universally recognize the interest in expansion and refer to the general policy of recognizing rights only for those products in connection with which a mark has actually been used in commerce. Bridging the gap is not a factor in all federal circuits' tests.

An opposing justification considers consumers' interests rather than mark owner's interests in expansion. Consumers might be confused by one person's use of a mark owned by another if the goods are dissimilar but related. Because the Lever Brothers Company makes many types of goods, consumers might reasonably think it has expanded into a new line of business. If consumers are familiar with the diversity of Lever

Brothers' products and history of expansion, they are more likely to be confused, believing that the defendant's product is the plaintiff's. Even if the plaintiff has no history of expansion or intention to bridge the gap between its product and the defendant's, consumers might think it has done so if the products are closely related or if other firms in the industry have expanded in that direction. Manufacturers of fashionable clothing, such as Ralph Lauren, frequently expand their product lines to include perfumes. Consumers, seeing a clothing manufacturer's mark on perfumes, might reasonably assume the clothing manufacturer produced it, even if the clothing manufacturer has never considered making fragrances.

Under this "related products" justification, evidence of the mark owner's actual expansion plans is relevant, but a court might find that this factor favors the plaintiff even without such plans. A mark owner is protected not only against its use on articles that compete with those to which it has applied the mark, but on those goods as might naturally be supposed to come from it. The more closely the products compete, the smaller the gap and the more likely there is confusion even without intent. If the products or services of the two parties are identical, there is no gap to bridge and this factor becomes irrelevant.

8. *Scope of Lanham Act §§32 and 43(a).* The Lanham Act provides for infringement actions for all types of registered marks in §32, trademarks, service marks, collective marks, and certification marks. Section 43(a) is even broader, applying to confusion resulting from use of "any word, term, name, symbol, or device, or combination thereof" whether registered or not. As for registered marks, the likelihood of confusion factors are applied flexibly, keeping in mind the context.

One type of "combination" of "devices" is trade dress, the general appearance of the packaging in which a product is sold or of the product itself. In *Phillip Morris USA Inc. v. Cowboy Cigarette, Inc.*, 2003 WL 22852243 (S.D.N.Y. 2003) (not published in the Federal Supplement), the court considered whether "Cowboy" cigarettes advertising using cowboy imagery infringed on Marlboro's trade dress. Since 1963, the great majority of advertisements for Marlboro cigarettes had prominently featured a cigarette-smoking cowboy integrated into a western motif. Although prior to that time other cigarette brands occasionally made use of a western motif, the advertisements of Marlboro were so saturated with such imagery that they came to be commonly referred to as the "Marlboro Man" and "Marlboro Country" ads. Since their entry into the marketplace in 2002, Cowboy cigarettes had been advertised using similar cowboy imagery. Such imagery also appeared on the Cowboy cigarette pack, which is, like the Marlboro cigarette pack, red and white, and prominently features a triangular wedge. Applying the *Polaroid* factors, the court found that Cowboy's trade dress infringed on Phillip Morris's trade dress.

9. *Confusion of Sponsorship, Endorsement, or Approval.* In the case of collective and certification marks, it is particularly important to remember the special purposes of those marks. For collective marks, an infringement action is used to protect the membership-signifying power of the mark. The analysis focuses on whether consumers will be confused about the

organization's sponsorship, endorsement, or approval of the use of the mark. For certification marks, an infringement action is used to protect the power of the mark to certify qualities and characteristics of the goods. The language of §43(a)(A) specifically applies to protecting indicia of "affiliation, connection, or association" between two people and to indicia of "sponsorship, or approval" by one person of the use of by another. As with trademarks and service marks, the commercial impression created by use of a mark depends on the realities of the marketplace.

To appreciate the test for sponsorship or approval, consider two cases with different results. In *Supreme Assembly, Order of Rainbow for Girls v. J.H. Ray Jewelry Co.*, 676 F.2d 1079 (5th Cir. 1982), Rainbow Girls, a fraternal organization for teenage girls, had established an "official jeweler" relationship with Stange Company by licensing Stange to provide all of Rainbow's jewelry requirements. J.H. Ray sold its own Rainbow Girl jewelry, which displayed the Order's trademarked rainbow and pot of gold emblem, at its retail stores without permission. Both Stange and Rainbow Girls complained, alleging misleading indication of sponsorship or approval. The court found that there was no evidence consumers would assume that such jewelry could only be manufactured with Rainbow's sponsorship or approval and there was no tradition of fraternal organizations exercising control over the manufacture of jewelry bearing their fraternal emblems. By contrast, the court in *Boston Professional Hockey Association, Inc. v. Dallas Cap & Emblem Manufacturing, Inc.*, 510 F.2d 1004 (5th Cir. 1975) found that "[i]t is not unreasonable to conclude, given the degree to which sports emblems are used to advertise teams and endorse products, that a consumer seeing the emblem or name of a team on or associated with a good or service would assume some sort of sponsorship or association between the product's seller and the team." The commercial impression a mark makes is formed by consumers' understanding of how such marks are typically used.

## Problems

**3-2.** Two New York City restaurants include "Patsy's" in their names. Patsy's Pizzeria opened in Harlem in 1933 and has five franchise locations throughout Manhattan, using the PATSY'S PIZZERIA mark, which it registered in 1996 for use in connection with restaurant services. Patsy's Italian Restaurant in midtown Manhattan opened in 1944 with a more complete

Italian style menu than Patsy's Pizzeria. In 1994, Patsy's Italian Restaurant started manufacturing, distributing, and selling pasta sauces in jars in retail stores nationwide and on the Internet under the PATSY'S PR SINCE 1944 mark, registered in 1995. Patsy's Italian Restaurant sells no pizza sauces. Patsy's Pizzeria began selling jars of pizza sauce in its own restaurants in 1999.

Patsy's Restaurant's pasta sauces are sold in clear glass jars with gold-colored screw-on lids and printed labels. The stylized "Patsy's" logo appears in large type in the upper center of the label, flanked by identical inward-facing profiles of a classical statue. In small type, the initials "PR" (apparently for "Patsy's Restaurant") appear enclosed in a circle as part of the logo. To the lower right of the logo appear the words "Since 1944," also in small type. The identification of the flavor of the sauce appears at the bottom of the label in white, uppercase, bold letters on a rectangular field of a different color than the label background. Gold borders line the top and bottom of the label. The background color of the label varies according to the flavor of the sauce. On one flavor of sauce, the label background is green.

The defendants' pizza sauces are sold in clear glass jars with gold-colored screw-on lids and printed labels. The upper portion of the defendants' jars are slightly more tapered than those of Patsy's Brand's. The word "Patsy's" appears in script at an angle in the center of the label. The words "Since 1933" appear to the lower right of the word "Patsy's." The label includes a registration symbol beside the "Patsy's" logo, even though the defendants do not have a federally registered trademark for use of a mark with sauces. The label also includes the design of a woman sipping from a wine glass that is identical to an image that appears on menus in Patsy's Pizzerias. The label states that the sauce is distributed by "Patsy's Restaurant, New York, New York"; the word "Pizzeria" does not appear on the label. The label has a green background and is bordered in gold at the top and bottom. The script typeface of the logo mirrors that used on the signs and menus in Patsy's Pizzerias, and the green color is the same as that used on the outside of the restaurant. If Patsy's Italian Restaurant petitions to cancel Patsy's Pizzeria's registered mark on the ground that it is likely to cause confusion with the PATSY'S PR SINCE 1944 mark and sues Patsy's Pizzeria alleging infringement of that mark by Patsy's Pizzeria's sales of sauce, who will prevail? *See Patsy's Brand, Inc. v. I.O.B. Realty, Inc.*, 317 F.3d 209 (2d Cir. 2003).

**3-3.** In 1992, Russell Simmons established Phat Fashions, L.L.C., the plaintiff corporation which manufactures and distributes urban and athletic apparel. Simmons, who is also the co-founder of "Def Jam Records," started the plaintiff corporation in order to sell apparel worn by popular rap and hip-hop artists whose music is produced by the record label. Plaintiff's products consist of t-shirts, jerseys, sweatshirts, slacks, jeans, jackets, shorts, caps, hats, backpacks, and sunglasses. The plaintiff's most prominent label and design is the registered mark PHAT FARM, which was first used in March 1993 and was registered for use on apparel with the United States Patent and Trademark Office (USPTO) on August 24, 1993. Since 1993, the plaintiff has obtained registrations for the use of other marks as subbrands of PHAT FARM, including PHAT THREADS, BABY PHAT, and PHAT. "PHAT" is understood to be an acronym for the words "Pretty Hot and Tempting." In 2003, an individual filed for trademark registration of a

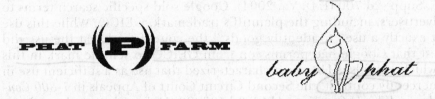

combined word and picture mark featuring the hindquarters of a donkey and the words "Phat Ass Jeans" used in connection with the sales of clothing. If Simmons filed an opposition to that mark, is it likely that he could establish a likelihood of confusion? The PHAT ASS JEANS mark was later abandoned, but for a related case, see *Phat Fashions, L.L.C. v. Phat Game Athletic Apparel, Inc.*, 2002 WL 570681 (D. Cal. March 20, 2002) (not published in the Federal Supplement).

## 2. Initial Interest Confusion

A type of infringement claim that has gotten a great deal of attention with the burgeoning popularity of the Internet is based on "initial interest" or "pre-sale" confusion. These claims involve situations in which one person uses another's source-indicating device to create initial consumer interest in its own product or service. While any confusion about whose good or service is being sold is dispelled before the sale, this use capitalizes on the mark owner's goodwill. Courts consider pre-sale confusion actionable when a consumer's response to the defendant's use results from the consumer erroneously believing that it is the mark owner who is using the mark.

*Playboy Enterprises, Inc. v. Netscape Communications Corp.*, 69 U.S.P.Q. 2d 1417 (9th Cir. 2004), is a classic Internet case involving initial interest confusion. In that case, Netscape allowed advertisers to target individuals with certain interests by linking ads to pre-identified search terms. Pop-up or banner ads for the advertisers would appear whenever a computer user searched for a term such as "playboy." Playboy claimed that consumers were confused about whether it was the sponsor of other websites' ads and computer users would click on the ad believing, incorrectly, that they were going to a Playboy-sponsored website. Applying the eight factors of the *Sleekcraft* likelihood of confusion test, the court found that there was a material issue of fact regarding whether confusion existed.

A related issue in Internet cases is whether the defendant's use of the mark is a "use in commerce" sufficient to be covered by the Lanham Act. The law is still developing in this area, but several examples might illustrate the issue. In *Government Employees Insurance Company v. Google, Inc.*, 330 F. Supp. 2d 700 (E.D. Va. 2004), Google sold specific search terms to its advertisers, including the plaintiff's trademark, GEICO. While this use is not exactly a use "to identify goods," the court found that the use did suggest that Google had permission from GEICO to sell the mark in this way, which was false. The court characterized that use as a sufficient use in commerce. By contrast, the Second Circuit Court of Appeals in *1-800 Contacts, Inc. v. WhenU.Com, Inc.*, 414 F.3d 400 (2005), found no trademark use under similar facts where there was no sale of access to any specific trademarks as links but rather sale of access to a directory of tens of thousands of search terms. In *1-800 Contacts* and in *U-Haul International Inc. v. WhenU.com Inc.*, discussed in *GEICO*, the courts held that online pop-up ads that cover-up or appear alongside Internet sites do not infringe the website owner's copyrights or trademarks. The courts concluded that computer software that triggers the display of pop-up ads using other's marks but never appears on the ads generated by the marks is not use in commerce. These cases illustrate that the outcomes depend heavily on the facts of specific cases.

The potential for initial interest confusion is not limited to the Internet and applies to a variety of circumstances in which a person uses another's mark to capitalize on the other's goodwill. Examples of non-Internet claims include: a manufacturer's claim that, because pens are sold in bulk over the telephone and buyers request pens by the AUDITOR mark, initial interest confusion results from the fact that a competitor used the mark "AUDITOR FINE POINT," despite the fact that when buyers received their pens they could see that the pens were made by the competitor, *see Lindy Pen Co., Inc. v. Bic Pen Corp.*, 796 F.2d 254 (9th Cir. 1986); and Mobil Oil Corporation's complaint that a competitor's use of the word PEGASUS as a mark caused initial interest confusion with Mobil's use of a depiction of a flying horse because "Pegasus" is the name of a mythological flying horse, *see Mobil Oil Corp. v. Pegasus Petroleum*, 818 F.2d 254 (2d Cir. 1989). The Sixth Circuit Court of Appeals recently held that initial interest confusion was not appropriate in a trade dress case involving a single-cutaway design for electric guitars. Even though consumers might confuse the parties' guitars from a distance or in a smoky bar, many marks may be confused from a distance and recognizing confusion in this instance would give too great a scope of protection. *Gibson Guitar Corp. v. Paul Reed Smith Guitars, LP*, 423 F.3d 539 (6th Cir. 2005).

A key distinction between initial interest confusion and traditional confusion appears to be that the initial confusion is dispelled once the buyer investigates further. In this respect, the theory of harm to consumers is similar to the harm that results from confusingly similar trade dress. For instance, Phillip Morris's claim that the cowboy motif and red and white packaging of cigarette packages sold by a competitor caused confusion between the competing cigarettes and its MARLBORO brand for which the rugged western "Marlboro Man" is the spokesman, *see Phillip Morris USA Inc. v. Cowboy Cigarette Inc.*, 2003 WL 22852243 (D.N.Y. Dec. 2, 2003); and Elvis Presley Enterprises' claim that another night club's exploitation of its ELVIS mark drew attention away from its own nightclub, *see Elvis Presley Enterprises, Inc. v. Capece*, 141 F.3d 188 (5th Cir. 1998). As *Playboy Enterprises* indicates, the same multifactor tests for whether confusion is likely are applied in such cases.

Commentators observe that an initially confused consumer who is not confused at the time of purchase was not all that attached to the original product in the first place and may have been using the mark simply to search for a category of goods. If so, initial interest confusion does not interfere with the trademark goal of reducing consumers' search costs. Such confusion does, however, increase search costs for consumers who really are looking for a particular brand because they must look extra carefully to see who is selling the product or service to which they are diverted. *See* Michael R. Grynberg, "The Road Not Taken: Initial Interest Confusion, Consumer Search Costs, and the Challenge of the Internet," 28 Seattle U.L. Rev. 97, 99-100 (2004).

## 3. Dilution

Dilution is a Lanham Act claim that does not involve confusing, misleading, or deceiving consumers. It is designed to protect the goodwill, the marketing value or selling power, associated with famous marks, regardless of whether consumers are confused. The underlying idea is that if many people use a mark like AMAZON, whether they compete with the owner of the famous mark or not, the mark's distinctiveness, its ability to call to mind the famous owner, is diminished. Though it has been part of state unfair competition law for many years, dilution was only added to the Lanham Act in 1995 and the federal law in this area is still developing.

Developments in the dilution area make this claim particularly controversial. Note that there are three assumptions underlying the belief that multiple noncompeting users will diminish a mark's selling power. First, there is the assumption that if one noncompeting person uses a famous mark, others will do so as well. This will slowly whittle away at the selling power of the mark. This assumption is significant because the owner may sue a single noncompeting user. Second, there is the assumption that when consumers see a famous mark in its marketing context they will assume that the source of the goods or services is the owner of the famous mark. This is significant because if consumers do not make the mental association, there is no diminution of the famous mark's distinctiveness. This mental association may be more likely for fanciful marks used by others, e.g., an EXXON bookstore, and less likely for famous marks based on words with other customary meanings, such as APPLE, e.g., an APPLE shampoo. Third, there is an assumption that the owner of the famous mark will or can be damaged by dilution. How the fact of damages resulting from another's noncompeting use can be proved is largely unknown. This is important because the Supreme Court opinion below requires proof of actual dilution. When reading the case in this section, consider the extent to which courts examine these assumptions.

This section includes a state case, *Wedgwood Homes, Inc. v. Lund,* and a U.S. Supreme Court case applying federal law, *Moseley v. V Secret Catalogue, Inc.* The state case applies a typical state statute and describes the origins, purposes, and contours of a dilution claim. The federal case interprets the provisions of Lanham Act §43(c). Focus on the differences between state and federal causes of action for dilution.

## WEDGWOOD HOMES, INC. v. LUND
### 659 P.2d 377 (Or. 1983)

ROBERTS, Justice.

This case presents for our consideration the extent of protection of trademarks and names provided by ORS 647.107, Oregon's antidilution statute. The statute provides:

> "Likelihood of injury to business reputation or of dilution of the distinctive quality of a mark registered under ORS 647.015, or a mark valid at common law, or a trade name valid at common law, shall be a ground for injunctive relief notwithstanding the absence of competition between the parties or the absence of confusion as to the source of goods or services."

Plaintiff, Wedgwood Homes of Portland, Inc., and its wholly owned subsidiary, Wedgwood Homes, Inc., sought to enjoin defendant from using "Wedgwood" in its assumed business names, Wedgwood Downs and Wedgwood Place. At trial plaintiff attempted to prove common law unfair competition as well as dilution of its trade name pursuant to ORS 647.107. We accept the facts as found by the trial court and Court of Appeals. Plaintiff has failed to show a likelihood of consumer confusion of the identities of plaintiff and defendant. Its cause of action for unfair competition therefore fails. The trial court nonetheless granted an injunction finding a likelihood of injury to business reputation or dilution of the distinctive quality of plaintiff's name under the statute. The Court of Appeals affirmed. We review to determine if there was "dilution" of the "distinctive quality" of plaintiff's name. The statute does not define either term. Neither this court nor the Court of Appeals has had occasion to construe the statute.

"Distinctive" is a term often used in the common law of trademarks. To qualify as a trademark a symbol must be "so distinctive that it is capable of performing the function of identifying and distinguishing the goods which bear the symbol." 1 J. McCarthy, Trademarks and Unfair Competition §3:1 (1973)....

We realize that the distinctiveness adequate to identify the origin of a product may be different from the distinctive quality deserving of protection from dilution. To this extent, the fact that a plaintiff may possess a distinctive tradename only begins our inquiry. The meaning of "distinctive quality" must take shape within the confines of the interests sought to be protected by the antidilution statute.

Traditionally, trademarks were the method by which the public identified a product's source. In modern times, trademarks have assumed a marketing function:

> The protection of trade-marks is the law's recognition of the psychological function of symbols. If it is true that we live by symbols, it is no less true that we purchase goods by them. A trade-mark is a merchandising short-cut which induces a purchaser to select what he wants, or what he has been led to believe he wants. The owner of a mark exploits this human propensity by making every effort to impregnate the atmosphere of the market with the drawing power of a congenial symbol. Whatever the means employed, the aim is the same — to convey through the mark, in the minds of potential customers, the desirability of the commodity upon which it appears. Once this is attained, the trade-mark owner has something of value. If another poaches upon the commercial magnetism of the symbol he has created, the owner can obtain legal redress. *Mishawaka Rubber & Woolen Manufacturing Co. v. S.S. Kresge Co.,* 316 U.S. 203, 205, 62 S. Ct. 1022, 1024, 86 L. Ed. 1381 (1942).

The antidilution statutes developed out of the growing recognition that trademarks now surpass the traditional identity role. "[T]he trademark functions on three different levels — as an indication of origin or ownership, as a guarantee of constancy, and as a medium of advertisement." 3 R. Callman, The Law of Unfair Competition, Trademarks and Monopolies §65 (3d ed. 1969). A mark may possess independent protectible value to the extent that it acquires advertising and selling power.

In the context of dilution, the protectible quality of a mark has been defined as the mark's power to evoke images of the product, that is, its favorable associational value in the minds of consumers. This attribute may be developed in a variety of ways, long use, consistent superior quality instilling consumer satisfaction, extensive advertising.

In application the existence of the mark's distinctive quality must be proven by demonstrating what the mark signifies to the consuming public. If the mark has come to signify plaintiff's product in the minds of a significant portion of consumers and if the mark evokes favorable images of plaintiff or its product it possesses the distinctive quality of advertising value — consumer recognition, association and acceptance — and will be entitled to protection from dilution.

Plaintiff has been engaged for the past 25 years in the development, construction and marketing of single and multiple family residential real estate in eastern Washington County. Plaintiff's substantial advertising programs seek to promote the quality, styling and flair of plaintiff's residential construction. Defendant has maintained dormitory style housing for the elderly in two retirement apartment complexes in eastern Washington County since 1977.

The trial court found that after 25 years' use plaintiff had established a secondary meaning in its name. Defendant does not dispute this conclusion but argues that the antidilution statute should be limited to marks which are coined, unique or truly famous. Relying on legislative history defendant contends that only the most distinctive marks deserve the enhanced protection afforded by ORS 647.107, and that because plaintiff's name is neither coined, unique nor nationally famous the statute should not be invoked on plaintiff's behalf.

We reject defendant's argument that the protection of the antidilution statute should apply to coined and unique words alone. As we have noted, marks may become distinctive in three ways: by use of coined words, by use of arbitrary words, or by acquisition of secondary meaning.

In light of the nature of the distinctive quality we have defined there is no reason to assume, as defendant's argument implies, that only coined marks possess advertising value. When first coined a mark will likely have no commercial value at all. Distinctive quality develops over time as consumer recognition and association is instilled. Moreover, defendant cannot dispute that a mark which has become distinctive through the acquisition of secondary meaning could be entitled to protection from dilution. Among examples of marks covered by the statute is Tiffany, a jewelry trademark, which acquired its distinctiveness through secondary meaning. It is our opinion that protection may be extended regardless of the manner by which a trademark becomes distinctive.

Likewise, we reject defendant's suggestion that the statute be limited to nationally famous marks. We see no reason why marks of national renown should enjoy protection while local marks should not. A small local firm may expend efforts and money proportionately as great as those of a large firm in order to establish its mark's distinctive quality. In both situations the interest to be protected and the damage to be prevented are the same. In summary, it is not the manner by which distinctiveness is acquired nor the span of a mark's notoriety but rather the degree of advertising value the mark has gained which determines the applicability of ORS 647.107.

At trial plaintiff demonstrated, by means of survey evidence, a high association between the words "Wedgwood" and "Homes" in the minds of consumers. Plaintiff has established that its name, Wedgwood, evokes its product, homes, in the minds of a large portion of the public where it does business. Plaintiff further showed that such an association was a positive one. The trial court observed, "Wedgwood Homes is a well recognized name in [eastern Washington County] which approaches a high degree of local fame." We recognize that this association has commercial value to plaintiff. For purposes of the antidilution statute plaintiff has demonstrated that its name possesses distinctive quality.

We must now resolve what dilution is and whether it occurred or was likely to occur in this case.

In *Pignons S.A. de Mecanique de Precision v. Polaroid Corporation*, 657 F.2d 482, 494-95 (1st Cir. 1981), the court illustrated the three situations where dilution may arise. The term may refer to injury to the value of the mark caused by actual or potential consumer confusion. It may also be applied to injury caused by use which detracts from the reputation associated with plaintiff's mark. Finally it may encompass any diminution in the uniqueness and individuality of the mark resulting from defendant's use of a similar mark.

The first definition is inapplicable because our statute recognizes an action for dilution "notwithstanding the absence of confusion as to the source of goods or services."

An action for potential detraction from or tarnishment of the reputation associated with plaintiff's mark may be recognized in our statute as "likelihood of injury to business reputation" or it may be encompassed within the meaning of dilution. We need not address that issue here. Although plaintiff attempted to show unfavorable associations cast upon its product's reputation by what plaintiff characterized as the inferior construction and design of defendant's buildings, the trial court found that such unfavorable associations were not proven.

We are left, then, with the third definition of dilution, a diminution in the uniqueness and individuality of the mark caused by another's use of the same or similar mark. We must consider whether a form of dilution is cognizable which does not depend on the relative quality of defendant's product or the undesirability of its association with plaintiff's product. We are persuaded that it is.

Where tradename owners have created a favorable association between their name and their product, they possess a valuable marketing tool. This aura of recognition enhances the value of plaintiff's name. Subsequent use of the name with a nonrelated product broadens the associations linking name and product in the minds of consumers of plaintiff's product and diminishes the specific association plaintiff seeks to foster. "[U]nrelated use erodes selling power by destroying the automatic identification of the trademark with the original product and the favorable images created by advertising." Greiwe, *Antidilution Statutes: A New Attack on Comparative Advertising*, 72 Trademark Rep. 178, 186 (1982). A second use may therefore be prevented by means of the antidilution statute. . . .

We hold that where a tradename possesses the distinctive quality of favorable associational value a second use may be enjoined under the statute whenever this is proven to be necessary in order to prevent the diminution of plaintiff's name as an advertising tool among consumers of plaintiff's product. In the case before us plaintiff has established that its name possesses the distinctive quality of positive associational value with its product. To a significant percentage of the consuming public of eastern Washington County, Wedgwood connotes homes. Defendant's use of the name in connection with retirement apartments expands the associations consumers are likely to connect with the name and thereby reduces the name's effectiveness in identifying and advertising plaintiff's product. On these facts plaintiff has adequately demonstrated dilution of the distinctive quality of its name.

The decision of the Court of Appeals is affirmed.

*STATUTE:* **Dilution of a Famous Mark**
15 U.S.C. §1125(c)(1) (Lanham Act §43(c)(1))

*STATUTE:* **Registration of Marks That Would Cause Dilution**
15 U.S.C. §1052(f) (Lanham Act §2(f))

## MOSELEY v. V SECRET CATALOGUE, INC.

### 537 U.S. 418 (2003)

Justice STEVENS.

In 1995 Congress amended §43 of the Trademark Act of 1946, 15 U.S.C. §1125, to provide a remedy for the "dilution of famous marks." That amendment, known as the Federal Trademark Dilution Act (FTDA), describes the factors that determine whether a mark is "distinctive and famous," and defines the term "dilution" as "the lessening of the capacity of a famous mark to identify and distinguish goods or services." The question we granted certiorari to decide is whether objective proof of actual injury to the economic value of a famous mark (as opposed to a presumption of harm arising from a subjective "likelihood of dilution" standard) is a requisite for relief under the FTDA.

Petitioners, Victor and Cathy Moseley, own and operate a retail store named "Victor's Little Secret" in a strip mall in Elizabethtown, Kentucky. They have no employees.

Respondents are affiliated corporations that own the VICTORIA'S SECRET trademark and operate over 750 Victoria's Secret stores, two of which are in Louisville, Kentucky, a short drive from Elizabethtown. In 1998 they spent over $55 million advertising "the VICTORIA'S SECRET brand—one of moderately priced, high quality, attractively designed lingerie sold in a store setting designed to look like a wom[a]n's bedroom." They distribute 400 million copies of the Victoria's Secret catalog each year, including 39,000 in Elizabethtown. In 1998 their sales exceeded $1.5 billion.

In the February 12, 1998, edition of a weekly publication distributed to residents of the military installation at Fort Knox, Kentucky, petitioners advertised the "GRAND OPENING Just in time for Valentine's Day!" of their store "VICTOR'S SECRET" in nearby Elizabethtown. The ad featured "Intimate Lingerie *for every woman*"; "Romantic Lighting"; "Lycra Dresses"; "Pagers"; and "Adult Novelties/Gifts." An army colonel, who saw the ad and was offended by what he perceived to be an attempt to use a reputable company's trademark to promote the sale of "unwholesome, tawdry merchandise," sent a copy to respondents. Their counsel then wrote to petitioners stating that their choice of the name "Victor's Secret" for a store selling lingerie was likely to cause confusion with the well-known VICTORIA'S SECRET mark and, in addition, was likely to "dilute the distinctiveness" of the mark. They requested the immediate discontinuance of the use of the name "and any variations thereof." In response, petitioners changed the name of their store to "Victor's Little Secret." Because that change did not satisfy respondents, they promptly filed this action in Federal District Court.

The complaint contained four separate claims: (1) for trademark infringement alleging that petitioners' use of their trade name was "likely to cause confusion and/or mistake in violation of 15 U.S.C. §1114(1)"; (2) for unfair competition alleging misrepresentation in violation of §1125(a); (3) for "federal dilution" in violation of the FTDA; and (4) for trademark infringement and unfair competition in violation of the common law of Kentucky. In the dilution count, the complaint alleged that petitioners' conduct was "likely to blur and erode the distinctiveness" and "tarnish the reputation" of the VICTORIA'S SECRET trademark....

Finding that the record contained no evidence of actual confusion between the parties' marks, the District Court concluded that "no likelihood of confusion exists as a matter of law" and entered summary judgment for petitioners on the infringement and unfair competition claims. Civ. Action No. 3:98CV-395-S, 2000 WL 370525 (W.D. Ky., Feb. 9, 2000). With respect to the FTDA claim, however, the court ruled for respondents.

Noting that petitioners did not challenge Victoria Secret's claim that its mark is "famous," the only question it had to decide was whether petitioners' use of their mark diluted the quality of respondents' mark. Reasoning from the premise that dilution "corrodes" a trademark either by "blurring its product identification or by damaging positive associations that have attached to it," "the court first found the two marks to be sufficiently similar to cause dilution, and then found "that Defendants' mark dilutes Plaintiffs' mark because of its tarnishing effect upon the Victoria's Secret mark." *Id.*, at 38a-39a. It therefore enjoined petitioners "from using the mark 'Victor's Little Secret' on the basis that it causes dilution of the distinctive quality of the Victoria's Secret mark." App. to Pet. for Cert. 38a-39a. The court did not, however, find that any "blurring" had occurred.

The Court of Appeals for the Sixth Circuit affirmed. 259 F.3d 464 (2001). In a case decided shortly after the entry of the District Court's judgment in this case, the Sixth Circuit had adopted the standards for determining dilution under the FTDA that were enunciated by the Second Circuit in *Nabisco, Inc. v. PF Brands, Inc.*, 191 F.3d 208 (1999). In order to apply those standards, it was necessary to discuss two issues that the District Court had not specifically addressed—whether respondents' mark is "distinctive," and whether relief could be granted before dilution has actually occurred. With respect to the first issue, the court rejected the argument that Victoria's Secret could not be distinctive because "secret" is an ordinary word used by hundreds of lingerie concerns. The court concluded that the entire mark was "arbitrary and fanciful" and therefore deserving of a high level of trademark protection. 259 F.3d, at 470. On the second issue, the court relied on a distinction suggested by this sentence in the House Report: "Confusion leads to immediate injury, while dilution is an infection, which if allowed to spread, will inevitably destroy the advertising value of the mark." H.R. Rep. No. 104-374, p. 3 (1995), U.S. Code Cong. & Admin. News 1995, pp. 1029, 1030. This statement, coupled with the difficulty of proving actual harm, lent support to the court's ultimate conclusion that the evidence in this case sufficiently established "dilution." 259 F.3d, at 475-477. In sum, the Court of Appeals held:

> While no consumer is likely to go to the Moseleys' store expecting to find Victoria's Secret's famed Miracle Bra, consumers who hear the name 'Victor's Little Secret' are likely automatically to think of the more famous store and link it to the Moseleys' adult-toy, gag gift, and lingerie shop. This, then, is a classic instance of dilution by tarnishing (associating the Victoria's Secret name with sex toys and lewd coffee mugs) and by blurring (linking the chain with a single, unauthorized establishment). Given this conclusion, it follows that Victoria's Secret would prevail in a dilution analysis, even without an exhaustive consideration of all ten of the *Nabisco* factors. *Id.*, at 477.[8]

---

8. The court had previously noted that the "Second Circuit has developed a list of ten factors used to determine if dilution has, in fact, occurred, while describing them as a 'nonexclusive list' to 'develop gradually over time' and with the particular facts of each

In reaching that conclusion the Court of Appeals expressly rejected the holding of the Fourth Circuit in *Ringling Bros.-Barnum & Bailey Combined Shows, Inc. v. Utah Div. of Travel Development,* 170 F.3d 449 (1999). In that case, which involved a claim that Utah's use on its license plates of the phrase "greatest *snow* on earth" was causing dilution of the "greatest *show* on earth," the court had concluded "that to establish dilution of a famous mark under the federal Act requires proof that (1) a defendant has made use of a junior mark sufficiently similar to the famous mark to evoke in a relevant universe of consumers a mental association of the two that (2) has caused (3) actual economic harm to the famous mark's economic value by lessening its former selling power as an advertising agent for its goods or services." *Id.,* at 461 (emphasis added). Because other Circuits have also expressed differing views about the "actual harm" issue, we granted certiorari to resolve the conflict. . . .

Because respondents did not appeal the District Court's adverse judgment on counts 1, 2, and 4 of their complaint, we decide the case on the assumption that the Moseleys' use of the name "Victor's Little Secret" neither confused any consumers or potential consumers, nor was likely to do so. Moreover, the disposition of those counts also makes it appropriate to decide the case on the assumption that there was no significant competition between the adversaries in this case. Neither the absence of any likelihood of confusion nor the absence of competition, however, provides a defense to the statutory dilution claim alleged in count 3 of the complaint. . . .

In 1988, when Congress adopted amendments to the Lanham Act, it gave consideration to an antidilution provision. . . .

The VICTORIA'S SECRET mark is unquestionably valuable and petitioners have not challenged the conclusion that it qualifies as a "famous mark" within the meaning of the statute. Moreover, as we understand their submission, petitioners do not contend that the statutory protection is confined to identical uses of famous marks, or that the statute should be construed more narrowly in a case such as this. Even if the legislative history might lend some support to such a contention, it surely is not compelled by the statutory text.

The District Court's decision in this case rested on the conclusion that the name of petitioners' store "tarnished" the reputation of respondents' mark, and the Court of Appeals relied on both "tarnishment" and "blurring" to support its affirmance. Petitioners have not disputed the relevance of tarnishment, presumably because that concept was prominent in litigation brought under state antidilution statutes and because it was mentioned in the legislative history. Whether it is actually embraced by the statutory text, however, is another matter. Indeed, the contrast between the state

---

case. Those factors are: distinctiveness; similarity of the marks; 'proximity of the products and the likelihood of bridging the gap;' 'interrelationship among the distinctiveness of the senior mark, the similarity of the junior mark, and the proximity of the products;' 'shared consumers and geographic limitations;' 'sophistication of consumers;' actual confusion; 'adjectival or referential quality of the junior use;' 'harm to the junior user and delay by the senior user;' and the 'effect of [the] senior's prior laxity in protecting the mark." *Id.,* at 476 (quoting *Nabisco,* 191 F.3d, at 217-222).

statutes, which expressly refer to both "injury to business reputation" and to "dilution of the distinctive quality of a trade name or trademark," and the federal statute which refers only to the latter, arguably supports a narrower reading of the FTDA.

The contrast between the state statutes and the federal statute, however, sheds light on the precise question that we must decide. For those state statutes, like several provisions in the federal Lanham Act, repeatedly refer to a "likelihood" of harm, rather than to a completed harm. The relevant text of the FTDA, provides that "the owner of a famous mark" is entitled to injunctive relief against another person's commercial use of a mark or trade name if that use *causes dilution* of the distinctive quality" of the famous mark. This text unambiguously requires a showing of actual dilution, rather than a likelihood of dilution.

This conclusion is fortified by the definition of the term "dilution" itself. That definition provides:

> The term "dilution" means the lessening of the capacity of a famous mark to identify and distinguish goods or services, regardless of the presence or absence of:
>
> (1) competition between the owner of the famous mark and other parties, or
> (2) likelihood of confusion, mistake, or deception. §1127.

The contrast between the initial reference to an actual "lessening of the capacity" of the mark, and the later reference to a "likelihood of confusion, mistake, or deception" in the second caveat confirms the conclusion that actual dilution must be established.

Of course, that does not mean that the consequences of dilution, such as an actual loss of sales or profits, must also be proved. To the extent that language in the Fourth Circuit's opinion in the *Ringling Bros.* case suggests otherwise, we disagree. We do agree, however, with that court's conclusion that, at least where the marks at issue are not identical, the mere fact that consumers mentally associate the junior user's mark with a famous mark is not sufficient to establish actionable dilution. As the facts of that case demonstrate, such mental association will not necessarily reduce the capacity of the famous mark to identify the goods of its owner, the statutory requirement for dilution under the FTDA. For even though Utah drivers may be reminded of the circus when they see a license plate referring to the "greatest *snow* on earth," it by no means follows that they will associate "the greatest show on earth" with skiing or snow sports, or associate it less strongly or exclusively with the circus. "Blurring" is not a necessary consequence of mental association. (Nor, for that matter, is "tarnishing.")

The record in this case establishes that an army officer who saw the advertisement of the opening of a store named "Victor's Secret" did make the mental association with "Victoria's Secret," but it also shows that he did not therefore form any different impression of the store that his wife and daughter had patronized. There is a complete absence of evidence of any lessening of the capacity of the VICTORIA'S SECRET mark to identify and distinguish goods or services sold in Victoria's Secret stores or advertised in its catalogs. The officer was offended by the ad, but it did not change his conception of Victoria's Secret. His offense was directed entirely at petitioners, not at respondents. Moreover, the expert retained by respondents had nothing to say about the impact of petitioners' name on the strength of respondents' mark.

Noting that consumer surveys and other means of demonstrating actual dilution are expensive and often unreliable, respondents and their *amici* argue that evidence of an actual "lessening of the capacity of a famous mark to identify and distinguish goods or services," §1127, may be difficult to obtain. It may well be, however, that direct evidence of dilution such as consumer surveys will not be necessary if actual dilution can reliably be proved through circumstantial evidence — the obvious case is one where the junior and senior marks are identical. Whatever difficulties of proof may be entailed, they are not an acceptable reason for dispensing with proof of an essential element of a statutory violation. The evidence in the present record is not sufficient to support the summary judgment on the dilution count. The judgment is therefore reversed, and the case is remanded for further proceedings consistent with this opinion.

## Comments

1. ***State and Federal Dilution***. *Wedgwood Homes* distinguishes the consumer interests protected by trademark infringement from commercial interests protected by antidilution laws. The likelihood of confusion that is so critical to infringement is not required for proof of dilution. The Lanham Act provides a federal cause of action for dilution, with three notable substantive differences in the law. First, while state statutes cover diminution of the marketing value of a mark by either tarnishment ("injury to business reputation") or blurring, the Lanham Act only refers to "dilution of the distinctive quality of the mark." Second, while state statutes require proof of a "likelihood of dilution," the Lanham Act requires "actual dilution." And, third, while state statutes protect "distinctive" marks and sometimes trade names, the Lanham Act protects only "famous" marks. The Lanham Act requires that the junior user begin use of the diluting mark after the senior mark has become famous. Some state statutes are silent on this point.

2. ***Blurring and Tarnishment***. The court's opinion in *Wedgwood Homes* was based on a finding of blurring, "diminution of the uniqueness and individuality of the mark caused by another's use of the same or similar mark." The plaintiff did not sufficiently prove the alleged "unfavorable associations" between the defendant's inferior quality construction and the plaintiff's good name necessary to show tarnishment. Unfavorable associations may be enjoined under statutes like the Oregon statute applied in *Wedgwood*. The Dallas Cowboy Cheerleaders organization was able to enjoin a pornographic film depicting performers in its uniforms engaged in "fundraising activities." The court in *Dallas Cowboys Cheerleaders, Inc. v. Pussycat Cinema, Ltd.*, 604 F.2d 200, 205 (2d Cir. 1979), reasoned that it would be "hard to believe that anyone who had seen defendants' sexually depraved film could ever thereafter disassociate it from plaintiff's cheerleaders. This association results in confusion which has a 'tendency to impugn [plaintiff's services] and injure

plaintiff's business reputation.'" A court evaluating a chemical company's slogan "where there's life there's bugs" held that slogan created "a peculiarly unwholesome association of ideas" with Budweiser beer's slogan "where there's life, there's Bud." *See Chemical Corp. of America v. Anheuser-Busch, Inc.*, 306 F.2d 433, 437 (5th Cir. 1962).

In *Victoria's Secret*, the Supreme Court did not explicitly hold that a tarnishment theory was unavailable under the Lanham Act, but suggested that it was unavailable, saying that, compared to state statutes, the language of the Lanham Act "arguably supports a narrower reading." Some legislative history supports a broader reading. Lower federal courts have cited *H.R. Rep.* No. 104-374 at 3 (1995), which says that the Act will "protect famous trade mark from subsequent uses that blur the distinctiveness of the mark or tarnish or disparage it."

3. *Likely and Actual Dilution.* The "likelihood of dilution" standard of state antidilution statutes is comfortably similar to the "likelihood of confusion" standard used for trademark infringement. The *Sleekcraft* and *Polaroid* tests consider the similarity of the marks as one factor in determining whether confusion is likely. The less similar the marks, the more evidence of actual confusion is needed. Thus, marks may be viewed on a sliding scale, with less similar marks requiring more proof of actual confusion. The ten factors relevant to proof of dilution referred to in footnote 8 of the Court's opinion in *Victoria's Secret*, the "*Nabisco* factors," look quite similar to the likelihood of confusion factors. Some courts and commentators have questioned the relevance of these factors under the Lanham Act, which requires that the defendant's use of the mark actually lessened the capability of the mark to identify and distinguish its goods or services.

The Supreme Court does not describe how actual dilution must be proved but refers to both direct evidence (such as consumer surveys) and circumstantial evidence (such as the fact that the marks are identical). The Court does refer to the Fourth Circuit's opinion in *Ringling Bros.-Barnum & Bailey Combined Shows, Inc, v. Utah Div. of Travel Development*, 170 F.3d 449 (1999), which held that "actual, consummated dilutive harm" could be proved by three general means: proof of actual loss of an actual loss of revenues not resulting from other causes, "skillfully constructed consumer survey[s] designed not just to demonstrate 'mental association' of the marks in isolation, but further consumer impressions from which actual harm and cause might rationally be inferred," and "relevant contextual factors such as the extent of the junior mark's exposure, the similarity of the marks, the firmness of the senior mark's hold." Post-*Victoria's Secret* opinions finding actual dilution have based their holdings on the identity of the marks, but lower courts are split on whether the identity of the marks *alone* is enough circumstantial evidence to show actual dilution.

Even if actual dilution may be shown by another's use of an identical mark, there remain two pertinent questions. The first is what "identical" means. The finding of identity may be context or media specific and is likely to be fact intensive. Marks that are textually identical may appear very different from one another in terms of font, size, and color, for instance, when used in dissimilar corporate logos. So whether the marks are used in printed text or on the Internet may determine whether marks are "identical" or "very similar." Textually identical marks may be pronounced differently when spoken, which may affect the finding of "identity" if radio is used as an advertising medium. In *Savin Corp. v. The Savin Group*, 391 F.3d 439 (2d Cir. 2004) (vacating dismissal of plaintiff's dilution claims and remanding), for instance, the SAVIN mark was identical in some contexts (when used on websites) but not others (when used in stylized graphics in print and on web pages). Both parties used similar block letter fonts, with one arm of the letter "V" slanted at a greater angle than the other, but the defendants' logo incorporated four squares, one slightly tilted, to the left of the name. The plaintiff used the mark in connection with the sales and services of photocopying machines. The defendant Savin Group was an engineering firm. The second question is how much weight should be given to a showing of identity. Courts have variously held that proof of identity is enough to (a) survive a motion for summary judgment, (b) present a *prima facie* case of actual dilution sufficient to go to the jury, or (c) enough evidence to satisfy the requirements of the Lanham Act if the other elements of the claim are satisfied. The Supreme Court has not addressed these questions.

**4. TTAB and Supreme Court Standards.** The TTAB doesn't require actual dilution in evaluating oppositions to intent-to-use applications. A likelihood of dilution is enough. In *NASDAQ Stock Market, Inc. v. Antarctica, S.R.L.*, 69 U.S.P.Q.2d 1718 (Trademark Tr. & App. Bd. 2003), the TTAB upheld opposition to an Italian company's attempt to trademark a composite mark including a stylized bird and the term "nasdaq" to use in connection with sporting goods. The Italian company claimed that "nasdaq" was an abbreviation for "Nuovi Articoli Sportivi Di Alta Qualita" which, in English, means "new, high-quality sporting goods." The NASDAQ stock exchange had used the mark since 1968 for gathering, processing, and providing securities information and providing securities trading services. The Board found that the NASDAQ mark was distinctive and famous and likely to be diluted by the Italian company's use. Because the junior mark had not been used in the marketplace, actual dilution would be impossible to prove.

5. *Actual Dilution and Actual Harm.* In *Victoria's Secret*, the Supreme Court stated that, while the plaintiff must prove actual dilution, the plaintiff does not have to prove the actual losses associated with dilution. To obtain an injunction, a plaintiff must prove the *existence* of harm but not the *extent* of the harm. To obtain damages for dilution, a plaintiff must prove the extent of the harm *plus* willful intent to cause dilution of the famous mark. *See* Lanham Act §43(c)(2). Remedies are discussed in more detail in the following chapter of this book.

6. *Distinctive and Famous Marks and Trade Names.* Both state and federal statutes protect registered and unregistered marks, but the Lanham Act does not extend protection to trade names. A trade name is a name used to identify a person's business or vocation, e.g., UAL Corporation or McDonald's Corporation, while a mark is used to identify and distinguish a person's goods or services from another person's and to indicate the source of the goods or services, UNITED AIRLINES or BIG MAC. However clear the distinction may seem in theory, it is complicated by the fact that many businesses use their trade names, Coca-Cola, Inc., as trade marks, COCA-COLA. For a trade name to be protected by the antidilution provisions of the Lanham Act, it must logically have the source-indicating properties of a mark.

For state antidilution law purposes, a mark must be distinctive, in the customary trademark sense of being capable of performing the function of identifying the source of the goods or services, source-identifying power, and, in addition, must have acquired "marketing power." *Wedgwood* lists a variety of ways in which a mark may develop this favorable associational value in the minds of consumers.

For Lanham Act purposes, §43(c) lists eight non-exclusive factors relevant to deciding whether a mark is famous for dilution purposes. The degree to which courts pay attention to these factors varies. Recall that the parties in *Victoria's Secret* simply assumed the mark was famous. Congress referred to DUPONT, KODAK, and BUICK as famous names in the legislative history to the Act. Courts have offered NETSCAPE, HARRY POTTER, and TYLENOL as examples of famous names.

The law about the degree of fame a mark must possess for Lanham Act purposes is still evolving. Some courts demand fame in a substantial portion of the country, while others permit fame in an area as small as a county, so-called "geographic niche fame." Some courts have held that proof of fame requires no more than proof of distinctiveness through secondary meaning while others say distinctiveness is just a threshold question, a necessary but not sufficient condition for fame. Some courts have suggested that fame within a product market subgroup is not enough if the second use is outside of that subgroup, "product niche fame." The mark TREK used for bicycles was held not famous despite its familiarity among bicycle enthusiasts and its appearance under Lance Armstrong, Tour de France winner, on a WHEATIES box. The second use was by the producer of stationary, elliptical, exercise machines. *See Thane International, Inc. v. Trek Bicycle Corp.*, 305 F.3d 894 (9th Cir. 2001). The court contrasted the minor fame of TREK with the fame of Mattel Corporation's BARBIE mark for a doll. BARBIE, the court stated, is enough of a cultural icon to be damned by feminists as exemplifying the view of women as "bimbos" and to be mocked in a top-forty hit by Aqua, a Danish band. *See Mattel, Inc. v. MCA Records, Inc.,* 28 F. Supp. 2d 1120 (D. Cal. 1998).

The Court of Appeals for the Federal Circuit stated that "fame," has a different meaning for infringement and dilution cases. In the former, it means fame among the class of customers and potential customers of a product or service rather than the general public. For dilution cases, "fame" means extensive public recognition and renown among the general public. *See Palm Bay Imports Inc. v. Veuve Clicquot Ponsardin Maison Fond(e en 1772,* 396 F.3d 1369 (Fed. Cir. 2005).

**7. Dilution in the European Community.** Many of these same issues are unresolved in the unfair competition law of the European Union. *See* J. Thomas McCarthy, *Dilution of a Trademark: European and United States Law Compared,* 94 TRADEMARK REPORTER 1163 (2004). The analogous law in the European Community applies to well-known marks, marks that have acquired a reputation in a member state. Article 5(2) of the European Community Trademark Directive allows trademark owners to object to others' use of identical or similar marks on goods or services that are not similar to the ones for which the trademark is registered *if the mark is used to take unfair advantage of or is detrimental to the distinctive character or reputation* of the mark.

## Problem

**3-4.** The differences between state and federal law have been controversial and have led to congressional hearings regarding amendments to the Lanham Act. One such proposed bill, the Trademark Dilution Act, introduced February 9, 2005 into the House of Representatives included the following sections:

(c) Dilution by Blurring; Dilution by Tarnishment.

(1) Injunctive Relief. Subject to the principles of equity, the owner of a famous mark that is distinctive inherently or through acquired distinctiveness, shall be entitled to an injunction against another person who, at any time after the owner's mark has become famous, commences use in commerce as a designation of source of the person's goods or services, a mark or trade name that is likely to cause dilution by blurring or dilution by tarnishment, regardless of the presence or absence of actual or likely confusion, of competition, or of actual economic injury.

(2) Definitions.

(A) For the purposes of paragraph (1), a mark is famous if it is widely recognized by the general consuming public of the United States as a designator of source of the goods or services of the mark's owner. In determining whether a mark possesses the requisite degree of recognition, the court may consider all relevant factors, including but not limited to the following:

(i) The duration, extent, and geographic reach of advertising and publicity of the mark, whether advertised or publicized by the owner or third parties.

(ii) The amount, volume, and geographic extent of sales of goods or services offered under the mark.

(iii) The extent of actual recognition of the mark.

(B) For the purposes of paragraph (1) "dilution by blurring" is association arising from the similarity between a designation of source and a famous mark that impairs the distinctiveness of the famous mark. In determining whether a designation of source is likely to cause dilution by blurring, the court may consider all relevant factors, including but not limited to the following:

(i) The degree of similarity between the designation of source and the famous mark.

(ii) The degree of inherent or acquired distinctiveness of the famous mark.

(iii) The extent to which the owner of the famous mark is engaging in substantially exclusive use of the mark.

(iv) The degree of recognition of the famous mark.

(v) Whether the user of the designation of source intended to create an association with the famous mark.

(vi) Any actual association between the designation of source and the famous mark.

(C) For the purposes of paragraph (1), "dilution by tarnishment" is association between a designation of source and a famous mark, arising from their similarity, that harms the reputation of the famous mark.

To what extent do these proposed amendments eliminate the differences between state and federal law and resolve differences among federal courts on interpreting the Lanham Act?

### *POLICY PERSPECTIVE*
### Likely and Actual Dilution

In the hearings on the proposed bill described above, the Chief Trademark Counsel for Eastman Kodak Company, David C. Stimson, included the following remarks in his testimony:

Kodak believes that the best way to assure the effectiveness of a federal dilution statute is to specifically incorporate a likelihood of dilution standard into the law.

Such a standard allows the trademark owner to stop the damage to the distinctiveness of its famous trademark before it becomes irreparable. It insures that the singular meaning of the trademark—its unique identification with the trademark owner alone and nobody else—will continue....

If Kodak were to be used as the name of a magazine containing photographs of child pornography the damage to Kodak's image as a family-oriented company that can be trusted with the pictures and memories of life's special moments is obvious. Obvious too is the damage to the KODAK trademark that would result from this misuse. However, if we were required to prove actual dilution, the sales of these magazines would continue and proliferate around the country. Even after we had shown actual dilution we never would be able to retrieve all those magazines. Our KODAK trademark would forever have been association by everyone who saw those magazines with child pornography, not with our company and the products which we so proudly sell.

See A Periodic Notification of AIPLA Activities and Current Developments in Intellectual Property Law, AIPLA REPORTS, April 28, 2004.

## POLICY PERSPECTIVE
### Trademark Infringement and Dilution

Trademark infringement claims are designed to protect both the mark owner and consumers who rely on a mark as a device that signals the qualities and characteristics of the goods and reduces consumers' costs of searching for goods that fill their needs. By contrast, trademark dilution claims are traditionally viewed as protecting only the mark owner's goodwill, the selling power of the mark. Dilution claims are not traditionally viewed as protecting consumers because it is not necessary to prove confusion.

There is an argument that dilution does protect consumers. Multiple users of a famous mark may create "noise" or "clutter," an erosion of the distinctiveness of the mark, even if the goods do not compete. This blurring of the mark distorts the signal consumers receive when viewing a famous mark. It no longer clearly refers to the original user of the famous mark and raises consumers' search costs. One noted commentator observed that "Whether this is significant risk in the real world is unknown and unproven." See J. Thomas McCarthy, Proving a Trademark Has Been Diluted: Theories or Facts?, 41 HOUSTON L. REV. 713, 727-728 (2004).

Trademark infringement law balances both the consumers' referential use of marks (to refer to or locate a particular brand of a good) and the owner's source-indicating (marketing) use against the public's customary use of the mark (the ordinary linguistic meaning of the device). If there is no appreciable consumer interest protected by dilution, dilution law balances only the owner's interest against the public interest. Logically, the balance should tip more in favor of the public in dilution cases than infringement cases, because there is less on one side of the scale.

If there is more interest in protecting the public interest in dilution cases, it ought to be harder to win a dilution claim than infringement claim. A dilution claim, however, does not require proof of confusion, where an infringement claim does. Perhaps the Lanham Act's requirements that the mark be famous and that there be proof of actual rather than likely dilution create the additional barriers necessary to protect the public domain.

---

### *INTERNATIONAL PERSPECTIVE*
### Comparative Treatment of Well-Known and Famous Marks

The fame of a mark must be established in each case, which can entail considerable expense for a mark owner confronting numerous imitators. Mexico simplified this procedure in 2005 by amendments to its intellectual property law that gives the Mexican Patent and Trademark Office (Instituto Mexicano de la Propriedad Industrial) the authority to declare and prepare a list of trademarks as well known or famous. A mark is "well known," for these purposes, when it is recognized within a determinate sector of the populace or certain commercial circles. Marks are "famous" if they are recognized by a majority of the public. The advantage of the declaration is that the owner of a well-known trademark may prevent the registration of similar trademarks without further proof of its notoriety if confusion is likely while the owner of a famous mark may prohibit registration of similar marks for all types of products and services. The status of "well known" or "famous" lasts for five years. *See* 69 PATENT, TRADEMARK & COPYRIGHT J. 700 (No. 1718 Apr. 29, 2005).

---

## 4. Cybersquatting

### *STATUTE:* Cyber Piracy Prevention
### 15 U.S.C. §1125(d) (Lanham Act §43(d))

Internet domain names are assigned by nongovernmental organizations on a first-come, first-served basis, without regard to potential conflicts between the registered domain names and trademark owners. The nongovernmental organizations are in no position to address these conflicts when assigning marks because of the difficulty in determining whether confusion or dilution is likely. The 1999 Anti-Cybersquatting Consumer Protection Act created a cause of action under the Lanham Act §43(d) aimed at the owners of domain names whose purpose is to profit by either diverting business from a mark owner or by selling that domain name to the mark owner.

*DaimlerChrysler v. The Net Inc.*, 388 F.3d 201 (6th Cir. 2004), is a recent example of the kind of conduct involved in cyber piracy. DaimlerChrysler sells a car under the registered trademark DODGE and has a domain name *4ADODGE.com* on which it marks its car. The defendant, a federal prisoner who had a variety of domain names quite similar to other trademarks, such as *cnn.org, espnet.com, themicrosoftnetwork.com*, and *ups.net*, also had a domain name *foradodge.com.* The anticybersquatting provisions of the Lanham Act create a cause of action for a trademark owner who can

*[handwritten margin note: Cybersquatting Test.]*

establish that (1) it has a valid trademark entitled to protection; (2) its mark is distinctive or famous; (3) the defendant's domain name is identical or confusingly similar to, or in the case of famous marks, dilutive of, the owner's mark; and (4) the defendant used, registered, or trafficked in the domain name (5) with a bad faith intent to profit.

In many cases brought under Lanham Act §43(d), the main question is the bad faith of the defendant. In cases such as *DaimlerChrysler*, bad faith is easily established. Reviewing the statutory factors relevant to determining bad faith the court found that:

*[handwritten margin note: Bad faith test]*

> 1) the defendants had no intellectual property rights in the "foradodge" name at the time of registration; 2) the domain name does not contain any variation of the names of the defendants; 3) the defendants have never *actually* used the site in connection with the bona fide offer of goods or services; 4) the defendants never claim that they used the site for any noncommercial or other "fair use;" 5) it can be inferred that the defendants intended to divert customers from the plaintiff's website from the fact that the defendants' "foradodge" domain name is phonetically identical to plaintiff's 4ADODGE mark; 6) the defendants provided misleading contact information as the site's registrant, initially listing the registrant as The Net Inc., of Hewlett, New York, while no such entity exists; 7) the defendants registered multiple sites, such as doj.com, espnet.com, ups.net, which are confusingly similar to names and marks of others; and finally 8) DODGE is a highly distinctive and famous mark.

The court concluded that no rational trier of fact could find that the defendant did not violate the anticybersquatting provisions of the Lanham Act and affirmed the district court's grant of a summary judgment motion to DaimlerChrysler.

The conflict between domain names and trademarks is also addressed by a private nonprofit organization authorized by the U.S. Department of Commerce to manage the domain name system called the Internet Corporation for Assigned Names and Numbers or ICANN. ICANN established the Uniform Domain Name Dispute Resolution Policy or UDRP as an administrative means for resolving disputes between trademark owners and alleged cybersquatters. Remedies are the same as those seen in *DaimlerChrysler*. A cybersquatter is typically enjoined from using the domain name and agrees to transfer the name to the trademark owner. Resolutions under UDRP are not binding, however, and the disputes may be independently brought before the courts.

## 5. Secondary Liability for Infringement

Each intellectual property law regime has provisions for holding people other than the direct infringer responsible for infringement. The standard under which secondary liability is imposed varies somewhat from one area to another. It is necessary to understand the details of each of two related secondary liability theories. These theories, contributory infringement and vicarious liability, have their origins in tort law, as does all of trademark and unfair competition law.

When reading the discussion of contributory infringement, keep in mind the tort rules governing liability under a concerted action theory.

According to the Restatement (Second) of Torts §876(b) (1979), a person will be subject to liability for harm arising from the tortious conduct of another if he knows that the other's conduct constitutes a breach of duty and gives substantial assistance or encouragement to the other so to conduct himself. Note how this concerted action theory is interpreted in the trademark infringement context.

The policies underlying vicarious liability in tort include the enterprise risk theory and the risk avoidance theory. Enterprise risk theory reflects the view that, even though the defendant's activity did not directly infringe, fairness requires that the defendant's activity ought to bear the costs associated with it. If operating flea markets creates traffic jams, for instance, the operators ought to pay the cost of preventing them. Risk avoidance theory argues that if the defendant is required to pay for harm associated with its activity, it will have an incentive to discover ways to minimize the harm. If flea market operators have to pay for the police officers needed to control traffic, they will have an incentive to find ways to avoid traffic jams. Note how these theories are translated into secondary liability for trademark infringement.

## HARD ROCK LICENSING CORP. v. CONCESSION SERVICES, INC.

### 955 F.2d 1143 (7th Cir. 1992)

CUDAHY, Circuit Judge.

#### ... I. A. THE PARTIES AND THEIR PRACTICES

In the summer of 1989, CSI owned and operated three "Swap-O-Rama" flea markets in the Chicago area: the Tri-State, in Alsip, Illinois; the Melrose Park, in Melrose Park, Illinois; and the Brighton Park, in Chicago itself. Although Parvez sold counterfeits at the Tri-State Swap-O-Rama and at Melrose Park, testimony at trial concentrated on the operations at the Tri-State. We too will refer mainly to the Tri-State Swap-O-Rama, although CSI's operations are apparently similar at all three flea markets.

CSI generates revenue from a flea market in four ways. First, it rents space to vendors for flat fees that vary by the day of the week and the location of the space. Second, CSI charges a reservation and storage fee to those vendors who want to reserve the same space on a month-to-month basis. Third, CSI charges shoppers a nominal 75 cents admission charge. Fourth, CSI runs concession stands inside the market. To promote its business, CSI advertises the markets, announcing "BARGAINS" to be had, but does not advertise the presence of any individual vendors or any particular goods.

Supervision of the flea markets is minimal. CSI posts a sign at the Tri-State prohibiting vendors from selling "illegal goods." It also has "Rules For Sellers" which prohibit the sale of food or beverages, alcohol, weapons, fireworks, live animals, drugs and drug paraphernalia and subversive or un-American literature. Other than these limitations, vendors can, and do, sell almost any conceivable item. Two off-duty police officers provide security and crowd control (an arrangement that does not apply to the other markets). These officers also have some duty to ensure that the vendors obey the Sellers' Rules. The manager of the Tri-State, Albert Barelli, walks around the flea market about five times a day, looking for problems and violations of the rules. No one looks over the vendors' wares before they enter the market and set up their stalls, and any examination after that is cursory. Moreover, Barelli does not keep records of the names and addresses of the vendors. The only penalty for violating the Seller's Rules is expulsion from the market.

James Pierski, the vice president in charge of CSI's flea markets, testified that CSI has a policy of cooperating with any trademark owner that notifies CSI of possible infringing activity. But there is no evidence that this policy has ever been carried into effect. Before this case, there have been a few seizures of counterfeit goods at Swap-O-Rama flea markets. In no case was CSI informed of a pending seizure, involved in a seizure or notified as to the ultimate disposition of the seized goods. On the other hand, CSI did not investigate any of the seizures, though it knew they had occurred.

Harry's is a small store in Darien, Illinois, owned and operated by Harry Spatero. The store sells athletic shoes, t-shirts, jackets with the names of professional sports teams and the like. Spatero testified that the store contains over 20,000 different items. When buying t-shirts, Harry's is somewhat indiscriminate. The store buys seconds, overruns and closeouts from a variety of sources. Harry's buys most of its t-shirts from Supply Brokers of Pennsylvania, a firm which specializes in buying up stocks from stores going out of business. Spatero testified that Supply Brokers sends him largely unidentified boxes of shirts which he may choose to return after looking them over. But Spatero testified that Harry's also bought shirts from people who came around in unmarked vans, offering shirts at a discount. The store kept no records of the sources of its inventory.

Hard Rock owns the rights to a variety of Hard Rock trademarks. The corporation grants licenses to use its trademarks to the limited partnerships that own and operate the various Hard Rock Cafe restaurants. These restaurants are the only authorized distributors of Hard Rock Cafe merchandise, but apparently this practice of exclusivity is neither publicized nor widely known. The shirts themselves are produced by Winterland Productions, which prints logos on blank, first quality t-shirts that it buys from Hanes, Fruit-of-the-Loom and Anvil. According to the manager of the Chicago Hard Rock Cafe, Scott Floersheimer, Winterland has an agreement with Hard Rock to retain all defective Hard Rock shirts. Thus, if Winterland performs as agreed, all legitimate Hard Rock shirts sold to the public are well-made and cleanly printed.

The Chicago Hard Rock Cafe has done very well from its business. Since 1986, it has sold over 500,000 t-shirts at an average gross profit of $10.12 per shirt.

B. *The Investigation:* National Investigative Services Corporation (NISCOR) carried out the search for counterfeit merchandise on Hard Rock's behalf. Another firm, Trademark Facts, Inc., trained NISCOR's investigators to recognize counterfeit merchandise. Recognizing counterfeit Hard Rock goods was apparently easy. Any shirt not sold in a Hard Rock

Cafe restaurant was, unless second-hand, counterfeit. Other than this, the investigators were instructed to check for the manufacturer of the t-shirt, a registration or trademark symbol, the quality of the printed design, the color of the design, the quality of the shirt stock and the price. But as to these latter factors (except for the price), Floersheimer testified that even he would have trouble distinguishing a good counterfeit from a legitimate t-shirt.

The investigators visited both the Melrose Park and the Tri-State Swap-O-Ramas and observed Iqbal Parvez (or his employees) offering more than a hundred Hard Rock t-shirts for sale. Cynthia Myers, the chief investigator on the project, testified that these shirts were obviously counterfeit. The shirts were poor quality stock, with cut labels and were being sold for $3 apiece (a legitimate Hard Rock shirt, we are told, goes for over $14). Harry's had four Hard Rock shirts for sale, sitting on a discount table for $3.99 each. The district court found that these too were of obviously low quality, with cut labels and cracked and worn designs. Nonetheless, both Parvez and Harry's were selling t-shirts made by approved manufacturers. Parvez was selling Hanes t-shirts, and Harry's was selling Fruit-of-the-Loom.

At no point before filing suit did Hard Rock warn Harry's or CSI (or Parvez, whose supplier Hard Rock was trying to track down) that the shirts were counterfeits.

C. *The District Court Proceedings:* Hard Rock brought suit against the defendants in September 1989, alleging violations of sections 32 and 43 of the Lanham Act. Pending trial, the court entered temporary restraining orders and then preliminary injunctions against both CSI and Harry's. Harry's got rid of its remaining Hard Rock t-shirts, and CSI told any vendors selling Hard Rock merchandise in its flea markets to get rid of their stock as well. There have been no more violations.

After a bench trial, the district court entered permanent injunctions against both defendants and ordered Harry's to pay treble damages based on Hard Rock's lost profits on four t-shirts (in sum, $120). Findings of Fact, Conclusions of Law and Order at 8 (Sept. 12, 1990) (hereinafter Mem. Op.). The court denied Hard Rock's request for attorney's fees.

The court's reasoning is crucial to the resolution of this appeal. Accordingly, we think it appropriate to quote from it at some length. The court concluded that both defendants were "guilty of willful blindness that counterfeit goods were being sold on [their] premises." *Id.* at 7. Another sentence follows, however, which somewhat dilutes the impact of the preceding finding: "Neither defendant took reasonable steps to detect or prevent the sale of Hard Rock Cafe counterfeit T-shirts on its premise [sic]." *Id.* This suggests mere negligence.

Willful blindness, the court said, "is a sufficient basis for a finding of violation of the Lanham Act." *Id.* As to CSI's argument that it did not actually sell the offending goods, the court observed that CSI is not "merely a landlord; it also advertises and promoted the activity on its premises, sells admission tickets to buyers and supervises the premises. Under these circumstances it must also take reasonable precautions against the sale of counterfeit products." *Id.*

## II.

The Lanham Trademark Act protects consumers from deceptive claims about the nature and origin of products. 15 U.S.C. §1114(1)(a) & (b) (use of mark violates Act if "likely to cause confusion, or to cause mistake, or to deceive"); 15 U.S.C. §1125(a)(1) (false designation of origin violates Act if "likely to cause confusion, or to cause mistake, or to deceive"). But the Lanham Act also protects trademarks as a form of intellectual property. In this case, the Act protects Hard Rock's investment in a fashionable image and a reputation for selling high quality goods. *See Inwood Laboratories, Inc. v. Ives Laboratories, Inc.,* 456 U.S. 844, 854 n. 14 (1982).

*Secondary Liability:* The most interesting issue in this case is CSI's liability for Parvez's sales. Hard Rock argues that CSI has incurred both contributory and vicarious liability for the counterfeits, and we take the theories of liability in that order.

It is well established that "if a manufacturer or distributor intentionally induces another to infringe a trademark, or if it continues to supply its product to one whom it knows or has reason to know is engaging in trademark infringement, the manufacturer or distributor is contributorially responsible for any harm done as a result of the deceit." *Id.* at 854. Despite this apparently definitive statement, it is not clear how the doctrine applies to people who do not actually manufacture or distribute the good that is ultimately palmed off as made by someone else. A temporary help service, for example, might not be liable if it furnished Parvez the workers he employed to erect his stand, even if the help service knew that Parvez would sell counterfeit goods. Thus we must ask whether the operator of a flea market is more like the manufacturer of a mislabeled good or more like a temporary help service supplying the purveyor of goods. To answer questions of this sort, we have treated trademark infringement as a species of tort and have turned to the common law to guide our inquiry into the appropriate boundaries of liability.

CSI characterizes its relationship with Parvez as that of landlord and tenant. Hard Rock calls CSI a licensor, not a landlord. Either way, the Restatement of Torts tells us that CSI is responsible for the torts of those it permits on its premises "knowing or having reason to know that the other is acting or will act tortiously...." Restatement (Second) of Torts §877(c) & cmt. d (1979). The common law, then, imposes the same duty on landlords and licensors that the Supreme Court has imposed on manufacturers and distributors. In the absence of any suggestion that a trademark violation should not be treated as a common law tort, we believe that the *Inwood Labs.* test for contributory liability applies. CSI may be liable for trademark violations by Parvez if it knew or had reason to know of them. But the factual findings must support that conclusion.

The district court found CSI to be willfully blind. Since we have held that willful blindness is equivalent to actual knowledge for purposes of the Lanham Act, this finding should be enough to hold CSI liable (unless clearly erroneous). But we very much doubt that the district court defined willful blindness as it should have. To be willfully blind, a person must suspect wrongdoing and deliberately fail to investigate. The district court, however, made little mention of CSI's state of mind and focused almost entirely on CSI's failure to take precautions against counterfeiting. In its conclusions of law, the court emphasized that CSI had a duty to take reasonable precautions. In short, it looks as if the district court found CSI to be negligent, not willfully blind.

This ambiguity in the court's findings would not matter if CSI could be liable for failing to take reasonable precautions. But CSI has no affirmative duty to take precautions against the sale of counterfeits. Although the "reason to know" part of the standard for contributory liability requires CSI (or its agents) to understand what a reasonably prudent person would understand, it does not impose any duty to seek out and prevent violations. We decline to extend the protection that Hard Rock finds in the common law to require CSI, and other landlords, to be more dutiful guardians of Hard Rock's commercial interests. Thus the district court's findings do not support the conclusion that CSI bears contributory liability for Parvez's transgressions.

Before moving on, we should emphasize that we have found only that the district court applied an incorrect standard. We have not found that the evidence cannot support the conclusion that CSI was in fact willfully blind. At the Tri-State, Barelli saw Parvez's shirts and had the opportunity to note that they had cut labels and were being sold cheap. Further, Barelli testified that he did not ask vendors whether their goods were counterfeit because they were sure to lie to him. One might infer from these facts that Barelli suspected that the shirts were counterfeits but chose not to investigate.

On the other hand, we do not wish to prejudge the matter. For it is undisputed that Hard Rock made no effort to broadcast the information that legitimate Hard Rock t-shirts could only be found in Hard Rock Cafes. Moreover, there does not seem to be any particular reason to believe that inexpensive t-shirts with cut labels are obviously counterfeit, no matter what logo they bear. The circumstantial evidence that Barelli suspected the shirts to be counterfeit is, at best, thin. On remand, the district court may choose to develop this issue more fully.

Perhaps recognizing that the district court's opinion is unclear, Hard Rock urges us to find CSI vicariously liable for Parvez's sales, regardless of its knowledge of the counterfeiting. Indeed, if we accept this theory, CSI is liable for Parvez's sales even if it was not negligent. *See, e.g., Shapiro, Bernstein & Co. v. H.L. Green Co.*, 316 F.2d 304, 309 (2d Cir. 1963).

We have recognized that a joint tortfeasor may bear vicarious liability for trademark infringement by another. This theory of liability requires a finding that the defendant and the infringer have an apparent or actual partnership, have authority to bind one another in transactions with third parties or exercise joint ownership or control over the infringing product. The case before us does not fit into the joint tortfeasor model, and Hard Rock does not argue that it does.

Instead, Hard Rock wants us to apply the more expansive doctrine of vicarious liability applicable to copyright violations. Under the test developed by the Second Circuit, a defendant is vicariously liable for copyright infringement if it has "the right and ability to supervise the infringing activity and also has a direct financial interest in such activities." *Gershwin Publishing Corp. v. Columbia Artists Management, Inc.*, 443 F.2d 1159, 1162

(2d Cir.1971) (hereinafter *CAMI*); *see also Dreamland Ball Room, Inc. v. Shapiro, Bernstein & Co.,* 36 F.2d 354, 355 (7th Cir.1929) (owner of dance hall liable for copyright violations by band hired to entertain paying customers); *Famous Music Corp. v. Bay State Harness Horse Racing & Breeding Ass'n,* 554 F.2d 1213, 1215 (1st Cir. 1977) (owner of racetrack liable for copyright violations by company hired to supply music over public address system). The purpose of the doctrine is to prevent an entity that profits from infringement from hiding behind undercapitalized "dummy" operations when the copyright owner eventually sues. *Shapiro, Bernstein,* 316 F.2d at 309.

The parties have argued vigorously about the application of this doctrine to the facts. But we need not decide the question; for the Supreme Court tells us that secondary liability for trademark infringement should, in any event, be more narrowly drawn than secondary liability for copyright infringement. If Hard Rock referred us to some principle of common law that supported its analogy to copyright, we would be more understanding of its claims. But it has not. Further, there is no hint that CSI is playing at the sort of obfuscation that inspired the Second Circuit to develop its more expansive form of vicarious copyright liability. Hard Rock must look to Congress to provide the level of protection it demands of CSI here.

In sum, we find that CSI may bear contributory liability for Parvez's unlawful sales, but we see no evidence on the record that would support a finding that CSI is vicariously liable. Accordingly, because the district court's findings fail to establish that CSI knew or had reason to know that Parvez was selling counterfeits, we must vacate the judgment against CSI and remand for further proceedings....

## Comments

1. *Secondary Liability for Trademark Infringement.* Plaintiffs have alternative theories on which to sue people other than the direct trademark infringer: contributory infringement and vicarious liability. Liability under each theory may be proved in a variety of ways. *Hard Rock* describes the elements of each theory. Both the direct and contributory infringer may be subject to the same remedies: injunction and damages.

2. *Contributory Infringement — The Knowledge Requirement.* One approach to proving contributory infringement requires proof that the defendant possesses the requisite degree of knowledge of the other's infringement. Relying on tort law, the court in *Hard Rock* described that sufficient degree of knowledge as "having reason to know," "actually knowing," or being "willfully blind." All three are subjective tests of the actor's state of mind. The latter two are completely subjective standards indicating the actor's conscious awareness of infringement. The first is a combination of a subjective and objective test involving the judgment of a reasonable person.

The Restatement (Second) of Torts §12(1) describes "having reason to know" as follows:

> The words "reason to know"...denote the fact that the actor has information from which a person of reasonable intelligence or the superior intelligence of the actor would infer that the fact in question exists.

This is a combination of a subjective element, what information the actor actually possessed, and an objective element, what inferences a reasonable person would make from those facts. "Having reason to know" is sometimes referred to as having "constructive knowledge." In tort law, all three knowledge standards are greater than a negligence standard that would require that the actor, judged by the reasonable person standard, "should know" of the infringement.

The District Court in *Hard Rock* emphasized that CSI had a duty to take reasonable precautions and failed to take precautions against counterfeiting. Is this consistent with a "should know" standard or a higher standard of knowledge? Given the degree of knowledge required by the Court of Appeals, did CSI meet the requisite standard? Did CSI meet the other requirement for contributory infringement?

3. *Contributory Infringement — Inducement.* CSI did not encourage, tempt, or persuade Parvez to sell counterfeit Hard Rock t-shirts, but contributory infringement may, in another case, be based on such inducement. A manufacturer of a pharmaceutical compound of quinine flavored with chocolate sold under the QUIN-COCO mark induced druggists to substitute its less expensive compound for an apparently identical compound made by the senior user of a similar mark, COCO-QUININE, without informing consumers. The evidence established that salespeople for the offending manufacturer suggested to pharmacists that, without danger of detection, prescriptions and orders for COCO-QUININE could be filled by substituting QUIN-COCO. Often, rather than making specific suggestions, the feasibility of such conduct was brought to the mind of the druggist by pointing out the identity of the two preparations and the enhanced profit to be made by selling QUIN-COCO because of its lower price. Either suggestion or insinuation may be sufficient to constitute inducement. *See William R. Warner & Co. v. Eli Lilly & Co.,* 265 U.S. 526 (1926) (finding that the marks were merely descriptive and concluding that inducing substitutions without informing consumers violated common law prohibitions on unfair competition).

4. *Contributory Infringement — Supplying a Product.* The standard rule for contributory infringement requires that the actor either "induce" or "continue to supply a product" with the requisite knowledge. The flea market in *Hard Rock* did not supply a product, but rather sold space. Where there is not a convenient product, such as a pharmaceutical compound, an "extent of control" test is often applied. Direct control and monitoring of the instrumentality used by the direct infringer permits a finding of contributory infringement.

The issue of control arose in *Lockheed Martin Corp v. Network Solutions, Inc.,* 194 F.3d 890 (9th Cir. 1999), where an aircraft manufacturer using the service mark SKUNK WORKS for its aircraft design and construction laboratories, sued NSI, the company in charge of registering Internet domain names alleging contributory infringement. After registering a name, NSI entered the combination and corresponding Internet Protocol (IP) address in its database permitting routing of an Internet user to the domain name registrant's computer. The registration and routing process involved 130,000 registrations per month and was mostly computerized with little human involvement, unless there was an error or a prohibited character string, such as variations on Olympic, Red Cross, NASA, or an obscene word. Third parties had registered domain names such as "skunkworks.net" and "skunkwerks.com." The court found that "NSI's rote translation service does not entail the kind of direct control and monitoring required to justify an extension of the 'supplies a product' requirement"; "NSI does not supply the domain-name combination any more than the Postal Service supplies a street address by performing the routine service of delivering the mail."

How does CSI's control over the pertinent instrumentality compare to that of NSI?

5. *Vicarious Liability.* Because the Lanham Act codifies and federalizes the common law torts of unfair competition, the tort doctrine of vicarious liability has carried over as one way to establish secondary liability. Most are familiar with this doctrine in its application to employer liability for the acts of an agent or employee but nonliability for acts of independent contractors. Vicarious liability for trademark infringement may be established by showing an agency relationship. Relevant, non-exclusive factors for establishing an agency relationship include: the principal's right to control the alleged agent; the alleged agent's duty to act primarily for the benefit of the principal; and the alleged agent's power to alter the legal relations of the principal. The three alternative ways of establishing vicarious liability for trademark infringement, proving (a) apparent or actual partnership, (b) authority to bind in third-party transactions, or (c) joint ownership or control over the infringing parties reflect the same principles used in tort law.

How do these alternatives differ from the expanded doctrine of vicarious liability used in copyright law for which Hard Rock argued? Under which version of the doctrine, if either, would CSI be vicariously liable?

## Problem

**3-5.** In addition to the direct infringement claims brought by Geico in the *Google* case, discussed in the context of initial interest confusion above, Geico further alleged that the operators of Internet search engines are secondarily liable under theories of contributory and vicarious liability. Geico alleged that defendants exercise significant control over the content of advertisements that appear on their search results pages and that advertisers themselves illegally used the GEICO mark in commerce by incorporating that mark into their advertisements. Geico claimed that the advertisers were the direct infringers because such ads were likely to deceive customers into believing that the advertisers provide accurate information about Geico products or are somehow related to Geico. Accepting as true the facts alleged by plaintiff regarding the inclusion of the marks in advertisements and defendants' overall control of their advertising program, may the operators of the Internet search engines be held secondarily liable under either theory? *See Government Employees Insurance Co. v. Google, Inc.*, 330 F. Supp. 2d 700 (E.D. Va. 2004).

# C. UNFAIR COMPETITION AND SECTION 43(a)

Lanham Act §43(a) applies to infringing uses of unregistered marks as well as other deceptive practices. The section does not mention "marks" specifically, but refers to "false designation[s] of origin." In addition, §43(a) applies to any other designations, descriptions, or representations of facts that are likely to confuse, cause mistakes, or deceive consumers. Because it applies to more than just use of marks, §43(a) creates causes of action for other means of misleading consumers. Other ways consumers might be misled include confusingly similar trade dress, infringing certification or collective marks, or by false advertising. All of these legal actions are embraced within the general category of legal theories called "unfair competition."

The broad language of Lanham Act §43 creates causes of action for unfair methods of competition that do not involve the use of other's marks or the confusion of customers. Many of these federal claims originated in state tort law and have state common law and statutory counterparts. A typical state statutory approach is reflected in the Illinois Deceptive Trade Practices statute reproduced below. The scope of such state statutes may exceed the scope of §43(a) by including types of practices governed by other federal statutes not directly related to intellectual property law. The provisions in subsections (9), (10), and (11) of the Illinois statute, for instance, describe unfair methods of competition that, in federal law, might come under the jurisdiction of the Federal Trade Commission's authority to prevent "unfair methods of competition in or affecting commerce, and unfair or deceptive acts or practices in or affecting commerce." 15 U.S.C. §45(a)(1). The extent of Federal Trade Commission jurisdiction is beyond the scope of this book.

*STATUTE:* **False Designations of Origin, False Descriptions, and Dilution Forbidden**

15 U.S.C. §1125(a) (Lanham Act §43(a))

*STATUTE:* **Deceptive Trade Practices**

815 Illinois Compiled Statutes 510/2 (2001)

(a) A person engages in a deceptive trade practice when, in the course of his or her business, vocation, or occupation, the person:

(1) passes off goods or services as those of another;

(2) causes likelihood of confusion or of misunderstanding as to the source, sponsorship, approval, or certification of goods or services;

(3) causes likelihood of confusion or of misunderstanding as to affiliation, connection, or association with or certification by another;

(4) uses deceptive representations or designations of geographic origin in connection with goods or services;

(5) represents that goods or services have sponsorship, approval, characteristics, ingredients, uses, benefits, or quantities that they do not have or that a person has a sponsorship, approval, status, affiliation, or connection that he or she does not have;

(6) represents that goods are original or new if they are deteriorated, altered, reconditioned, reclaimed, used, or secondhand;

(7) represents that goods or services are of a particular standard, quality, or grade or that goods are a particular style or model, if they are of another;

(8) disparages the goods, services, or business of another by false or misleading representation of fact;

(9) advertises goods or services with intent not to sell them as advertised;

(10) advertises goods or services with intent not to supply reasonably expectable public demand, unless the advertisement discloses a limitation of quantity;

(11) makes false or misleading statements of fact concerning the reasons for, existence of, or amounts of price reductions;

(12) engages in any other conduct which similarly creates a likelihood of confusion or misunderstanding.

This section presents cases dealing with legal theories of passing off and reverse passing off, and false advertising. Passing off occurs when one person makes representations that mislead consumers about the source of a product. The misrepresentation may be the unauthorized use of another's mark, as in trademark infringement cases, but Lanham Act §43(a) also includes deceptions that result from false and misleading representations of fact, which may be oral or written statements or conduct. Two types of confusion may result. Traditional passing off (or "palming off" as it is sometimes called) occurs when a person who is selling a product *it has made* represents that the product was made by another. Like an alleged infringer in a traditional trademark case, such a person is taking advantage of the other's reputation by misleading consumers into believing the product was manufactured by the other. The result is that a person engaged in passing off may divert trade from the other.

Reverse passing off occurs when a person who is selling a product *another has made* represents that it made the product. Reverse passing off diverts any reputational advantage associated with the quality of the goods that should have been obtained by the true maker of the goods. Because both types of confusion are related to the source of goods, passing off claims are often combined with infringement claims. State and federal passing off claims are often combined in a single action. The substantive legal standards are generally identical. The cases in this part of the chapter are all federal cases applying the language of §43(a)(1)(A) of the Lanham Act.

When the representation is made in the context of marketing, a false advertising claim may be added. Lanham Act §43(a)(1)(B) makes actionable misrepresentations of fact about one's own goods or another's goods "in commercial advertising or promotion." False advertising law is a large topic that extends beyond the bounds of intellectual property law. The use of misleading source-indicating marks, however, is a means of false advertising closely related to trademark law.

Lanham Act §43(a) provides protection for unregistered marks, for methods of indicating source that do not qualify as marks, and from false advertising. The passing off cases in Section C.1 of this chapter illustrate the breadth of such protection, which prevents confusion by misleading conduct, for instance, as well as from the use of generic terms that would not be protectable as trademarks. Cases and materials in Chapter 2 discussed the policy reasons behind denying trademark protection to generic terms as well as functional product trade dress and design. Those policies apply to §43(a) passing off claims as well. Cases in Section C.2 illustrate the extent to which unfair competition law protection of functional and design characteristics of products is limited by conflicts with patent law.

Reverse passing off involves a person's misrepresentation that it manufactured a product actually made by another. Cases in Section C.3 include a variety of examples of such misattribution of source. The case in Section C.4 illustrates that, when the product or service involves subject matter that may be copyrightable, misattribution claims under trademark law are denied because of conflicts with copyright law.

## 1. Passing Off and False Advertising

The Restatement (Third) of Unfair Competition §4 recognizes liability for "passing off" as follows:

> One is subject to liability to another . . . if, in connection with the marketing of goods or services, the actor makes a representation likely to deceive or mislead prospective purchasers by causing the mistaken belief that the actor's business is the business of the other, or that the actor is the agent, affiliate, or associate of the other, or that the goods or services that the actor markets are produced, sponsored, or approved by the other.

The Restatement language and equally broad language of Lanham Act §43(a)(1)(A) include misrepresentations in any form that are likely to deceive or mislead consumers, not just those in which involve using the another's mark. *Coca-Cola Co. v. Ed E. Dorris* illustrates the strict liability aspects of this rule in a case where the defendant tried not to mislead consumers.

Lanham Act §43(a)(1)(B) and numerous state statutes such as the Virginia statute excerpted above apply to misrepresentations of various sorts in advertising and promoting goods. *Forschner Group, Inc. v. Arrow Trading Co., Inc.* compares a passing off claim to a false advertising claim. Consistent with the difference between the two applicable sections of the Lanham Act, the passing off claim focuses on misrepresentations regarding source and the false advertising claim focuses on a specific type of false advertising, misrepresentation of geographic origin. *Forschner Group* also illustrates the important point that a passing off claim may succeed even if the source-designating device is not protectible as a trademark.

### COCA-COLA CO. v. ED E. DORRIS
#### 311 F. Supp. 287 (D. Ark. 1970)

OPEN HARRIS, Chief Judge.

This action is brought by The Coca-Cola Company, a corporation incorporated under the laws of the State of Delaware, having its principal place

of business in either New York, New York or Atlanta, Georgia, against Ed
E. Dorris, an individual doing business at 600 West 5th Avenue (Corner of
5th Avenue and Laurel Street) under the trade style DORRIS HOUSE #1,
and formerly engaged in operating a place of business at 2301 West 28th
Avenue under the trade style of DORRIS HOUSE #2, both in the City of
Pine Bluff, Arkansas; the said defendant being a citizen of said City and
State.

Plaintiff alleged that . . . defendant has substituted and passed off, and is
now substituting and passing off a product other than plaintiff's product
identified by the registered trademarks 'Coca-Cola' and 'Coke', when said
product is ordered; that these acts constitute trademark infringement and
unfair competition and result in irreparable injury and damage to the
plaintiff . . .

Plaintiff manufactures and sells throughout the United States and in
foreign countries, a soft drink syrup and beverage made therefrom
under its trademarks "Coca-Cola" and "Coke", which trademarks are
registered in the United States Patent Office and in the State of Arkansas.

Defendant filed an answer in which he denied the passing off, denied
trade-mark infringement and asked that the complaint be dismissed. In an
amended answer and counterclaim defendant alleged that he ceased serving plaintiff's product about May 18, 1965 and has made every reasonable
effort to advise the public that he does not sell plaintiff's product, that he
has instructed all of his employees to advise customers ordering Coca-Cola
and Coke that such product is not sold in defendant's establishment.
Defendant's counterclaim alleged that representatives of plaintiff had har-
assed him in an effort to force him to handle plaintiff's product and made
derogatory remarks about the product he was selling in lieu of Coca-Cola,
in an effort to damage his trade and business and that he had suffered
damage in excess of Ten Thousand ($10,000.00) Dollars.

The evidence shows that from January 27, 1966 through December 3,
1968, the defendant substituted another beverage in response to orders for
plaintiff's registered trademarked product, "Coke" or "Coca-Cola" at least
twenty-one (21) times at Dorris House #1 without informing the purchaser
of said substitution. Eight substitutions were in response to orders for Coke
and thirteen substitutions in response to orders for Coca-Cola. On one visit
defendant's attendant confirmed the order by saying "Coke", and on
another an attendant repeated "Coca-Cola". On at least four occasions
the attendants identified the beverage served by writing on the guest
checks "Coke". At Dorris House #2 there were three substitutions in
August, 1967, one in response to an order for Coke and two in response
to orders for Coca-Cola. In all instances at Dorris House #2 the beverage
served was identified by writing "Coke" on the guest checks. Defendant was
warned that these actions were infringing on plaintiff's registered trademarks and were unfair competition, by two personal visits made by the
representatives of the Trade Research Department of plaintiff and certified letters which followed said visits, and a third letter in lieu of another
personal protest. The substitutions were continued after said notices —
fifteen after the last visit and nine after the last letter.

Plaintiff has shown that the total shipments of Coca-Cola into Arkansas from 1923 through 1968 were in excess of sixty-eight million gallons of syrup. Plaintiff has shown that the total advertising expenditures for Coca-Cola was in excess of $750,000,000 from 1886 through 1968 in the United States. Defendant had signs posted in Dorris House #1 which read: "We do not serve coke or coca-cola. We serve 'Dorris House' Cola." Defendant's employees had been instructed to tell customers ordering Coke or Coca-Cola that they did not serve same, but served Dorris House Cola. The evidence clearly shows that such instructions were not carried out. Defendant produced twenty-six consumer witnesses including the Chief of Police of Pine Bluff, who was the former manager of Dorris House #2, two Baptist ministers, two newspaper reporters, and employees of local automobile agencies who testified that they knew the defendant did not handle Coca-Cola and had heard oral explanation given to customers ordering plaintiff's product, but no exact nor precise dates were given. Plaintiff's evidence is overwhelming in its exactness and uniformity as to specific times and dates of substitution and certainly proves a prima facie case of passing off.

Defendant's substitution of another product in response to a request for plaintiff's trademarked product "Coke" or "Coca-Cola", without verbal notice to the purchaser that the product served was not in fact that of the plaintiff and on occasion repeating the order, and writing the trademark "Coke" on guest checks is called palming off, passing off or substitution. Such acts are an infringement of plaintiff's lawfully registered trademarks and are unfair competition.

The signs placed in the defendant's place of business to the effect that he does not serve Coca-Cola are insufficient to constitute notice of the substitution of another product. The law does not place a burden on the customer to look for signs to ascertain what products are sold or are not sold in the retail outlet. The customer must be orally advised that the specified product is not available and be given the opportunity to accept or reject the substitute product. Nims, Unfair Competition and Trade-Marks 4th Ed. Page 962: "When a customer asks for the goods of one manufacturer, the substitution of the product of another is unfair competition. * * * substitution of any other goods is illegal, unless the customer understands that he is not getting what he ordered and assents thereto."

Defendant undertook in good faith to instruct his waitresses, attendants, and those serving his customers that only Dorris House Cola was being sold. It is well established however that good faith or lack of bad faith is no defense in unfair competition and trade-mark infringement actions. "The question is what is the commercial effect of what he is doing? If the effect would be to pass off his goods as those of plaintiff, then his honesty of purpose or the absence of any intention to deceive is no defense." Cutler, Passing Off (1907) 5-6.

Similarly, the owner of a business is responsible for the manner in which that business is operated, and for the actions of his agents, servants, and employees, even though such acts may be directly contrary to instructions. The Supreme Court of the United States has enunciated this to be the universal rule.

For the reasons stated herein, plaintiff is entitled to the injunctive relief sought. An order will be entered enjoining Ed E. Dorris, individually and doing business as Dorris House #1 and formerly doing business as Dorris House #2, enjoining and restraining said defendant, his agents, employees and servants, representatives, successors and assigns, and any and all persons acting by direction or under the authority of the defendant from passing off or substituting a soft drink of another manufacturer without oral explanation to the customer on calls or orders for "Coca-Cola" or "Coke" or from doing any other acts likely to infringe plaintiff's trademarks "Coca-Cola" or "Coke" or committing any other acts of unfair competition against the plaintiff....

## FORSCHNER GROUP, INC. v. ARROW TRADING CO. INC.

### 30 F.3d 348 (2d Cir. 1994)

Jacobs, Circuit Judge.

The phrase "Swiss Army knife" has never enjoyed trademark protection. This appeal considers chiefly whether that phrase is descriptive of geographic origin or product quality, and therefore protectible under the false advertising provision of the Lanham Act.

Victorinox Cutlery Company ("Victorinox") of Switzerland has manufactured multifunction pocketknives since 1892. Another Swiss firm, Wenger, S.A. ("Wenger"), has manufactured multifunction pocketknives since 1908. Since early in this century, these two Swiss firms have been the only purveyors of multifunction pocketknives to the Swiss Armed Forces. American soldiers returning from Europe after World War II coined the phrase Swiss Army knife to describe the intricate and ingenious pocketknives used by the Swiss military.

In 1950, plaintiff-appellee The Forschner Group, Inc. began importing pocketknives manufactured by Victorinox into the United States, and began calling them Swiss Army knives in 1958. The United States distributor of the Wenger knives, Precise Imports Corporation, is not a party to this litigation.

Early in 1992, defendant-appellant Arrow Trading Co., Inc. ("Arrow") began marketing in the United States an inexpensive and shoddy multifunction pocketknife manufactured in China. Arrow nevertheless referred to its knife as a Swiss Army knife and embossed the words "SWISS ARMY" on one side....

On September 22, 1992, Forschner filed a complaint in the Southern District of New York seeking to enjoin Arrow from marketing the Arrow knife as a Swiss Army knife. Although the complaint is not entirely clear, we read Count I to allege misrepresentation as to manufacturer or source under §43(a), 15 U.S.C. §1125(a)(1)(A) (1988), a claim which includes "passing off"; Count II to allege false advertising in respect of geographic origin and quality under §43(a), 15 U.S.C. §1125(a)(1)(B); and Count III to allege unfair competition under New York common law....

## A. 15 U.S.C. §1125(a)(1)(B) — FALSE ADVERTISING

The district court classified this action "as falling within the law of unfair competition or false advertising and not trademarks," *Forschner Group Inc. v. Arrow Trading Co.*, 833 F.Supp. 385, 388 (S.D.N.Y. 1993), and concluded that Arrow's use of the phrase Swiss Army knife constituted the "use[ ] in commerce" of a "false or misleading representation of fact" as to "qualities" or "geographic origin", in violation of section 43(a) of the Lanham Act. That section provides that:

*Geographic*

Any person who, on or in connection with any goods or services, or any container for goods, uses in commerce any word, term, name, symbol, or device, or any combination thereof, or any false designation of origin, false or misleading description of fact, or false or misleading representation of fact, which —

(A) is likely to cause confusion, or to cause mistake, or to deceive as to the affiliation, connection, or association of such person with another person, or as to the origin, sponsorship, or approval of his or her goods, services, or commercial activities by another person, or

(B) in commercial advertising or promotion, misrepresents the nature, characteristics, qualities, or geographic origin of his or her or another person's goods, services, or commercial activities,

shall be liable in a civil action by any person who believes that he or she is or is likely to be damaged by such act.

Relying on subsection (B), and survey evidence, the district court found that a Swiss Army knife is necessarily a high-quality knife manufactured in Switzerland, and therefore concluded that Arrow falsely designated the geographic origin and quality of its knife. The district court's analysis effectively affords Victorinox and Wenger trademark protection.

### GEOGRAPHIC ORIGIN

There is no doubt that injunctive relief under §43(a) of the Lanham Act is appropriate if needed to protect a geographically descriptive term. The district court relied upon a series of cases so holding. *See Black Hills Jewelry Mfg. Co. v. Gold Rush, Inc.*, 633 F.2d 746 (8th Cir. 1980) (affirming injunctive relief against use of BLACK HILLS GOLD or BLACK HILLS GOLD JEWELRY by manufacturers producing jewelry outside of the Black Hills of South Dakota); *Scotch Whiskey Ass'n v. Barton Distilling Co.*, 338 F. Supp. 595 (N.D. Ill. 1971), *aff'd in part, rev'd in part*, 489 F.2d 809 (7th Cir. 1973) (injunction against use of SCOTCH on whiskey not originating in Scotland). In these cases and others like them, injunctive relief was granted to producers in a particular place "who asserted their right to the use of a geographical designation in a suit against other producers who did not manufacture their goods in said area but nevertheless used the geographical designation in their name or label." *Black Hills*, 633 F.2d at 750....

Without deciding the unpresented issue of whether or not the phrase Swiss Army knife could have been exclusively appropriated as a trademark for a multifunction pocketknife if such an application had been made, we think it is clear that the phrase cannot be deemed a designation of geographic origin. If Victorinox or Wenger promoted a product as a

"Swiss pocketknife," the word "Swiss" could be said to denote geographic origin. We cannot, however, consider the word "Swiss" otherwise than as part of the phrase "Swiss Army." The fact that a composite phrase contains a geographic term does not necessarily mean that the phrase, viewed as a whole, is a geographic designation. The question is whether *the phrase* can be construed to mean that the product is made in a certain locale.

As used in the phrase Swiss Army knife, "Swiss" is read more naturally to modify "Army" than "knife" — and probably does. The phrase Swiss Army knife therefore denotes a knife of the type associated with the Swiss Army, rather than a military knife manufactured in Switzerland. . . . For these reasons, we hold that the phrase Swiss Army knife, as applied to a multifunction pocketknife manufactured outside Switzerland, is not a false designation of geographic origin. [The quality claims are tied to geographic claims because they derive from the reputation associated with Swiss companies and craftsmen. Because the geographic claim fails, the quality claim cannot] furnish an independent ground for false advertising liability under §43(a) of the Lanham Act.

### B.   15 U.S.C. §1125(a)(1)(A) — Passing Off

Arrow argues that if the phrase Swiss Army knife is not geographically descriptive, it is nothing more than a generic phrase denoting any multifunction pocketknife. A generic phrase, Arrow continues, is in the public domain for all to use. Accordingly, Arrow urges that we direct the district court to dismiss the complaint if we conclude — as we do — that the phrase Swiss Army knife is not geographically descriptive. We are not prepared to do so.

A phrase or term that is not geographically descriptive is not necessarily generic. Moreover, a phrase or term that is indeed generic is not without protection under §43(a) of the Lanham Act and New York common law. A judicial finding of genericness means only that courts will not recognize exclusive rights in the use of the generic phrase or term or impose trademark infringement liability upon subsequent users; such a finding does not close all avenues of relief. A manufacturer, for example, cannot use a generic term in a manner that constitutes a misrepresentation of manufacturer or source. *See Kellogg Co. v. National Biscuit Co.*, 305 U.S. 111, 114 (1938); *Murphy Door Bed Co. v. Interior Sleep Systems, Inc.*, 874 F.2d 95, 102 (2d Cir. 1989). Therefore, even if we assume (as Arrow contends) that the phrase Swiss Army knife is generic, Arrow may still have violated §43(a) of the Lanham Act or otherwise engaged in unfair competition.

"A generic term is one that refers, or has come to be understood as referring, to the genus of which the particular product is a species." *Abercrombie & Fitch Co. v. Hunting World, Inc.*, 537 F.2d 4, 9 (2d Cir. 1976). It is true, as Arrow notes, that generic names are not entitled to trademark protection. Nor is any one manufacturer entitled to the exclusive use of a generic name: "If the name of one manufacturer's product is generic, a competitor's use of that name, without more, does not give rise to an unfair competition claim under section 43(a) of the Lanham Act." *Blinded Veterans Ass'n v. Blinded Am. Veterans Found.*, 872 F.2d 1035, 1043 (D.C. Cir. 1989).

Forschner, however, is not seeking trademark protection for the phrase Swiss Army knife. Count I of Forschner's complaint points to Arrow's claim that it was using "Swiss Army" as a trademark under license and alleges that this "is likely to cause consumers and the trade to believe that defendant's knives are put out by, sponsored by or sold with the approval and/or authorization of a distributor of authentic Swiss made Swiss Army knives", in violation of §43(a) of the Lanham Act. Count III of the complaint alleges that "[t]he activities of [Arrow] and the dress of the knives offered by [Arrow] unfairly compete with Forschner and . . . are part of a plan by defendant to trade upon the goodwill and enviable reputation of Forschner and the authentic Swiss Army knives imported, sold and promoted by Forschner," in violation of New York common law. The district court had no occasion to address these causes of action, having determined that Forschner was entitled to relief on the false advertising claim asserted in Count II. Counts I and III, however, identify a separate danger—that consumers might mistake the Arrow knife for a multifunction pocketknife *manufactured by Victorinox or Wenger*. If there is a sufficient factual predicate for this allegation, injunctive relief is warranted irrespective of whether the phrase Swiss Army knife is generic.

Our determination that Arrow did not misrepresent the geographic origin or quality of its knife does not absolve Arrow of liability for other forms of misrepresentation or unfair competition, such as passing off: "The statutory prohibition against false designation of origin encompasses more than deceptions as to geographic origin; it extends, as well, to origin of source, sponsorship or affiliation." *Societe Des Produits Nestle, S.A. v. Casa Helvetia, Inc.*, 982 F.2d 633, 639 (1st Cir.1992). The language of subsection (A) of 15 U.S.C. §1125(a)(1) prohibits any misrepresentation likely to cause confusion as to the source or manufacturer of a product: "The use of a product or package design that is so similar to that of another producer that it is likely to confuse purchasers as to the product's source may constitute 'false designation of origin' within the meaning of [§43(a) of the Lanham] Act." *Inwood Laboratories, Inc. v. Ives Laboratories, Inc.*, 456 U.S. 844, 863 (1982). This type of false designation of origin is also actionable under the broad heading of unfair competition. Regardless of whether a term is trademarked, a plaintiff may show that the term name is so associated with its goods that "use of the same or similar [term] by another company constitutes a representation that its goods come from the same source." *Joshua Meier Co. v. Albany Novelty Mfg. Co.*, 236 F.2d 144, 147 (2d Cir. 1956).

Courts typically grant relief, injunctive or otherwise, for misrepresentations as to the source of a product where a formerly exclusive trademark is no longer protectible because it has become generic. *See, e.g., Murphy Door Bed*, 874 F.2d at 102 (misleading consumers as to source of product marketed under former trademark "Murphy Bed"); *King-Seeley Thermos Co. v. Aladdin Industries, Inc.*, 321 F.2d 577, 581 (2d Cir. 1963) (enjoining deceptive use of former trademark "thermos"). However, as the Supreme Court's decision in *Kellogg Co. v. National Biscuit Co.* demonstrates, relief is also available when the misrepresentation of source arises through the use of a phrase (like Swiss Army knife) that is generic *ab initio*.

In *Kellogg*, the National Biscuit Company sought to enjoin the Kellogg Company from using the term "shredded wheat." The Supreme Court found that "shredded wheat" is generic and that the National Biscuit

Company therefore did not have an exclusive right to use it. Nevertheless, since the National Biscuit Company had historically been the sole manufacturer of shredded wheat, there was an undeniable association in the public mind between that company and the term "shredded wheat." Accordingly, the Court recognized an obligation on the part of the Kellogg Company and other subsequent users "to use every reasonable means to prevent confusion," although not to the point of refraining from use. *Kellogg*, 305 U.S. at 115, 59 S. Ct. at 112.

The District of Columbia Circuit has summarized the *Kellogg* limitations on the use of generic terms, with emphasis on efforts by competitors to stimulate confusion or benefit from it:

> If a consumer confuses two manufacturers' shredded wheat cereal, for example, because both products share the same name and the consumer has a general appetite for crunchy, pillow-shaped wheat biscuits, there is no cause for judicial action. Such confusion results merely from the manufacturers' concurrent use of a generic term to designate their products, and the late entrant into the shredded wheat field cannot be said to have engaged in unfair competition. If, however, the consumer associates "shredded wheat" with a particular manufacturer, perhaps because that manufacturer enjoyed a de facto (or de jure) monopoly for many years, there is a risk that the consumer may erroneously assume that any product entitled "shredded wheat" comes from that manufacturer. *A second manufacturer may increase the risk of confusion by, for example, using a similar label, similar packaging, misleading advertisements, or simply by failing to state the product's source. Only when there is a likelihood that the newcomer might thus pass its product off as the original manufacturer's may a court require the newcomer to distinguish its product or to notify consumers explicitly that its product does not come from the original manufacturer.*

*Blinded Veterans Ass'n*, 872 F.2d at 1045 (emphasis added).

Assuming, arguendo, that the phrase Swiss Army knife is generic, *Kellogg* governs. A manufacturer such as Arrow cannot be prevented from using the phrase to denote its product. The district court, however, found that the phrase Swiss Army knife has come to be associated with two particular manufacturers. This finding is buttressed by the fact that we read the phrase Swiss Army knife as referring not to a military knife manufactured in Switzerland, but to a product used by the Swiss Army. Since Victorinox and Wenger are the only manufacturers who sell pocketknives to the Swiss Army, there is reason to associate the phrase Swiss Army knife with those two companies. Accordingly, Arrow must take "every reasonable precaution" to distinguish its Swiss Army knife from the Swiss Army knives produced by Victorinox and Wenger.

Arrow's use of the phrase Swiss Army knife is permissible only to the extent that such use does not engender a likelihood of confusion as to the source of Arrow's product. If Arrow wishes to market a Swiss Army knife, it may do so only in a manner that would not mislead the public into believing the knife was manufactured by Victorinox or Wenger.

Since the district court did not address the claims of misrepresentation of source or unfair competition alleged in Counts I and III, . . . we vacate the order of the district court and remand for further proceedings consistent with this opinion.

# Comments

1. *False Advertising and Passing Off under §43(a).* Lanham Act §43(a) makes misrepresentations of source and of facts actionable, with subsection (A) addressing confusion about the "origin, sponsorship, or approval of a person" and subsection (B) addressing confusion about "the nature, characteristics, qualities, or geographic origin" of goods and services. Although damages are available as a remedy, complainants in both *Coca-Cola* and *Forschner Group* sought injunctive relief.

   The plaintiffs in both cases might have had mixed motivations. The first motive in bringing the suit is to prevent confusion and to protect their goodwill. This motivation reflects the underlying policy of trademark law. The second motive is less honorable. Repeated suits may drive competitors out of business. If labeling a knife as "Swiss Army" is important to compete in part of the jackknife market, Forschner's suit effectively prevents anyone but Forschner and Wenger from doing so. Forschner and Wegner was awarded this protection even though the term is not trademarkable. Avoiding lawsuits may also require the Dorris House to change the brand of cola it serves. Coca-Cola might use lawsuits as a means of winning customers. It might even hire teams of investigators from its "Trade Research Department" to visit restaurants around the country. If two dominant suppliers of cola products in the country both send enforcers around the country, small suppliers of cola and house brands of cola face an uphill battle to win customers. Good faith attempts to encourage employees to clarify their customers' confusion are not a defense.

2. *False Advertising: Geographic Words and Phrases.* The false advertising provisions of §43(a)(B) apply to facts about the nature, characteristics, qualities, and geographic origin of goods, services, and commercial activities. As in the infringement context, the commercial impression of the entire representation is relevant to determining whether the representation is covered by statute. In *Canada Dry Ginger Ale, Inc. v. Lipsey,* 102 U.S.P.Q. 447, 448 (Comm'r of Patents 1954), the Commissioner of Patents found that the term "Royal Canadian" used in connection with soft drinks was not primarily geographic for trademark purposes because it signifies the Northwest Mounted Police, a military unit. On the other hand, the court in *Singer Mfg. Co. v. Birginal-Bigsby Corp.,* 319 F.2d 273, 275 (C.C.P.A. 1963), found that use of the term "American Beauty" on sewing machines was geographically descriptive because the term could be construed to mean an object of superior quality made in America. Would an argument that "American Beauty" also signifies a famous breed of roses make any difference to the court? Why did the court in *Forschner Group* find that "Swiss Army" was not a geographic designation?

3. *Passing Off and Infringement Compared.* The discussion of generic marks in *Forschner Group* illustrates the broad protection available under §43(a). Because trademark protection is unavailable for generic terms, no one can have an exclusive right to use them. Under appropriate circumstances, however, some users of an unprotectible term may have to distinguish themselves as a source from other sources. What was it about National Biscuit Company's use of the term "shredded wheat" that

required Kellogg to take "every reasonable step" to distinguish itself from National Biscuit Company? How does that apply to *Arrow*? The court in *Forschner Group* stated that a competitor's use of a generic term, without more, does not give rise to an unfair competition claim under §43(a). What else had Arrow done that justified limiting its right to use the term "Swiss Army"?

Defendants who use a term that does not qualify for trademark protection are not usually totally forbidden from using the term even if another uses it. Often an injunction can be fashioned to enable them to distinguish themselves and thereby prevent confusion. For instance, Kellogg may still use the term "shredded wheat" but may be required to accompany its use with a disclaimer stating in equal prominence "Not associated with the National Biscuit Company." The injunction must focus on practical means of avoiding confusion. If, however, there is no room for a readable disclaimer on the product, such as a jackknife, or the disclaimer does not call attention to itself, or consumers are unlikely to pay attention to the disclaimer, courts might require some other means of preventing confusion, including forbidding use altogether. Disclaimers are more likely to prevent the harm resulting from infringement than the harm resulting from dilution.

These rules also apply to other terms for which exclusive rights are denied such as surnames, geographic designations, and merely descriptive terms. For instance, "Stetson" is a well-known brand of cowboy hat. Even if "Stetson" were considered primarily a surname, junior users' right to use "Stetson" may require their use of qualifying language to prevent confusion. "Sardi's" is a well-known restaurant in the theater district of New York City. Even if "Sardi's" has no secondary meaning, another may be allowed to use this surname only with a disclaimer. A competitor's disclaimer would not be effective, however, for the use of the term "Waltham" (formerly a well-known brand of watches named after the town in Massachusetts where they were made) because the face of the watch is too small for a disclaimer consumers would notice.

## 2. Unfair Competition Law and Patent Law

Although the language of Lanham Act §43(a) is broad enough to cover many types of source-indicating devices that are not protectible as trademarks, its scope is not unlimited. The Supreme Court's opinions in *Sears, Roebuck & Co. v. Stiffel Co.* and its companion case, *Compco Corp. v. Day-Brite Lighting, Inc.*, illustrates the potential conflict between unfair competition rules protecting all types of source designators and patent law rules that limit exclusive rights to functional characteristics of product design.

## SEARS, ROEBUCK & CO. v. STIFFEL COMPANY

### 376 U.S. 973 (1964)

Mr. Justice BLACK delivered the opinion of the Court.

The question in this case is whether a State's unfair competition law can, consistently with the federal patent laws, impose liability for or prohibit the

copying of an article which is protected by neither a federal patent nor a copyright. The respondent, Stiffel Company, secured design and mechanical patents on a "pole lamp" — a vertical tube having lamp fixtures along the outside, the tube being made so that it will stand upright between the floor and ceiling of a room. Pole lamps proved a decided commercial success, and soon after Stiffel brought them on the market Sears, Roebuck & Company put on the market a substantially identical lamp, which it sold more cheaply, Sears' retail price being about the same as Stiffel's wholesale price. Stiffel then brought this action against Sears in the United States District Court for the Northern District of Illinois, claiming in its first count that by copying its design Sears had infringed Stiffel's patents and in its second count that by selling copies of Stiffel's lamp Sears had caused confusion in the trade as to the source of the lamps and had thereby engaged in unfair competition under Illinois law. There was evidence that identifying tags were not attached to the Sears lamps although labels appeared on the cartons in which they were delivered to customers, that customers had asked Stiffel whether its lamps differed from Sears', and that in two cases customers who had bought Stiffel lamps had complained to Stiffel on learning that Sears was selling substantially identical lamps at a much lower price.

The District Court, after holding the patents invalid for want of invention, went on to find as a fact that Sears' lamp was "a substantially exact copy" of Stiffel's and that the two lamps were so much alike, both in appearance and in functional details, "that confusion between them is likely, and some confusion has already occurred." On these findings the court held Sears guilty of unfair competition, enjoined Sears "from unfairly competing with (Stiffel) by selling or attempting to sell pole lamps identical to or confusingly similar to" Stiffel's lamp, and ordered an accounting to fix profits and damages resulting from Sears' "unfair competition."

The Court of Appeals affirmed. 313 F.2d 115. That court held that, to make out a case of unfair competition under Illinois law, there was no need to show that Sears had been "palming off" its lamps as Stiffel lamps; Stiffel had only to prove that there was a "likelihood of confusion as to the source of the products" — that the two articles were sufficiently identical that customers could not tell who had made a particular one. Impressed by the "remarkable sameness of appearance" of the lamps, the Court of Appeals upheld the trial court's findings of likelihood of confusion and some actual confusion, findings which the appellate court construed to mean confusion "as to the source of the lamps." The Court of Appeals thought this enough under Illinois law to sustain the trial court's holding of unfair competition, and thus held Sears liable under Illinois law for doing no more than copying and marketing an unpatented article. We granted certiorari to consider whether this use of a State's law of unfair competition is compatible with the federal patent law.

Before the Constitution was adopted, some States had granted patents either by special act or by general statute, but when the Constitution was adopted provision for a federal patent law was made one of the enumerated powers of Congress because, as Madison put it in The Federalist No. 43, the States "cannot separately make effectual provision" for either patents or copyrights. That constitutional provision is Art. I, § 8, cl. 8, which empowers Congress "To promote the Progress of Science and useful Arts, by securing for limited Times to Authors and Inventors the exclusive Right to their respective Writings and Discoveries." Pursuant to this constitutional authority, Congress in 1790 enacted the first federal patent and copyright law, and ever since that time has fixed the condition upon which patents and copyrights shall be granted. These laws, like other laws of the United States enacted pursuant to constitutional authority, are the supreme law of the land. When state law touches upon the area of these federal statutes, it is "familiar doctrine" that the federal policy "may not be set at naught, or its benefits denied" by the state law. *Sola Elec. Co. v. Jefferson Elec. Co.*, 317 U.S. 172, 173, 176 (1942). This is true, of course, even if the state law is enacted in the exercise of otherwise undoubted state power.

The grant of a patent is the grant of a statutory monopoly; indeed, the grant of patents in England was an explicit exception to the statute of James I prohibiting monopolies. Patents are not given as favors, as was the case of monopolies given by the Tudor monarchs, but are meant to encourage invention by rewarding the inventor with the right, limited to a term of years fixed by the patent, to exclude others from the use of his invention. During that period of time no one may make use, or sell the patented product without the patentee's authority. But in rewarding useful invention, the 'rights and welfare of the community must be fairly dealt with and effectually guarded.' *Kendall v. Winsor, 21 How. 322 (1859).* To that end the prerequisites to obtaining a patent are strictly observed, and when the patent has issued the limitations on its exercise are equally strictly enforced. To begin with, a genuine "invention" or "discovery" must be demonstrated "lest in the constant demand for new appliances the heavy hand of tribute be laid on each slight technological advance in an art." Once the patent issues, it is strictly construed, it cannot be used to secure any monopoly beyond that contained in the patent, the patentee's control over the product when it leaves his hands is sharply limited, and the patent monopoly may not be used in disregard of the antitrust laws. Finally, and especially relevant here, when the patent expires the monopoly created by it expires, too, and the right to make the article — including the right to make it in precisely the shape it carried when patented — passes to the public.

Thus the patent system is one in which uniform federal standards are carefully used to promote invention while at the same time preserving free competition. Obviously a State could not, consistently with the Supremacy Clause of the Constitution, extend the life of a patent beyond its expiration date or give a patent on an article which lacked the level of invention required for federal patents. To do either would run counter to the policy of Congress of granting patents only to true inventions, and then only for a limited time. Just as a State cannot encroach upon the federal patent laws directly, it cannot, under some other law, such as that forbidding unfair competition, give protection of a kind that clashes with the objectives of the federal patent laws.

In the present case the "pole lamp" sold by Stiffel has been held not to be entitled to the protection of either a mechanical or a design patent. An unpatentable article, like an article on which the patent has expired, is in the public domain and may be made and sold by whoever chooses to do so. What Sears did was to copy Stiffel's design and to sell lamps almost identical to those sold by Stiffel. This it had every right to do under the federal patent laws. That Stiffel originated the pole lamp and made it popular is immaterial. "Sharing in the goodwill of an article unprotected by patent or trade-mark is the exercise of a right possessed by all—and in the free exercise of which the consuming public is deeply interested." *Kellogg Co. v. National Biscuit Co.*, 305 U.S. 111, 122 (1938). To allow a State by use of its law of unfair competition to prevent the copying of an article which represents too slight an advance to be patented would be to permit the State to block off from the public something which federal law has said belongs to the public. The result would be that while federal law grants only 14 or 17 years' protection to genuine inventions, States could allow perpetual protection to articles too lacking in novelty to merit any patent at all under federal constitutional standards. This would be too great an encroachment on the federal patent system to be tolerated.

Sears has been held liable here for unfair competition because of a finding of likelihood of confusion based only on the fact that Sears' lamp was copied from Stiffel's unpatented lamp and that consequently the two looked exactly alike. Of course there could be "confusion" as to who had manufactured these nearly identical articles. But mere inability of the public to tell two identical articles apart is not enough to support an injunction against copying or an award of damages for copying that which the federal patent laws permit to be copied. Doubtless a State may, in appropriate circumstances, require that goods, whether patented or unpatented, be labeled or that other precautionary steps be taken to prevent customers from being misled as to the source, just as it may protect businesses in the use of their trademarks, labels, or distinctive dress in the packaging of goods so as to prevent others, by imitating such markings, from misleading purchasers as to the source of the goods. But because of the federal patent laws a State may not, when the article is unpatented and uncopyrighted, prohibit the copying of the article itself or award damages for such copying. The judgment below did both and in so doing gave Stiffel the equivalent of a patent monopoly on its unpatented lamp. That was error, and Sears is entitled to a judgment in its favor.

Reversed.

## COMPCO CORP. v. DAY-BRITE LIGHTING, INC.

### 376 U.S. 234 (1964)

Justice BLACK.

As in *Sears, Roebuck & Co. v. Stiffel Co.*, 376 U.S. 225, the question here is whether the use of a state unfair competition law to give relief against the copying of an unpatented industrial design conflicts with the federal patent laws. Both Compco and Day-Brite are manufacturers of fluorescent lighting fixtures of a kind widely used in offices and stores. Day-Brite in 1955 secured from the Patent Office a design patent on a reflector having cross-ribs claimed to give both strength and attractiveness to the fixture. Day-Brite also sought, but was refused, a mechanical patent on the same device. After Day-Brite had begun selling its fixture, Compco's predecessor began making and selling fixtures very similar to Day-Brite's. This action was then brought by Day-Brite. One count alleged that Compco had infringed Day-Brite's design patent; a second count charged that the public and the trade had come to associate this particular design with Day-Brite, that Compco had copied Day-Brite's distinctive design so as to confuse and deceive purchasers into thinking Compco's fixtures were actually Day-Brite's, and that by doing this Compco had unfairly competed with Day-Brite. The complaint prayed for both an accounting and an injunction.

The District Court held the design patent invalid; but as to the second count, while the court did not find that Compco had engaged in any deceptive or fraudulent practices, it did hold that Compco had been guilty of unfair competition under Illinois law. The court found that the overall appearance of Compco's fixture was "the same, to the eye of the ordinary observer, as the overall appearance" of Day-Brite's reflector, which embodied the design of the invalidated patent; that the appearance of Day-Brite's design had "the capacity to identify (Day-Brite) in the trade and does in fact so identify (it) to the trade"; that the concurrent sale of the two products was "likely to cause confusion in the trade"; and that "(a)ctual confusion has occurred." On these findings the court adjudged Compco guilty of unfair competition in the sale of its fixtures, ordered Compco to account to Day-Brite for damages, and enjoined Compco "from unfairly competing with plaintiff by the sale or attempted sale of reflectors identical to, or confusingly similar to" those made by Day-Brite. The Court of Appeals held there was substantial evidence in the record to support the District Court's finding of likely confusion and that this finding was sufficient to support a holding of unfair competition under Illinois law. Although the District Court had not made such a finding, the appellate court observed that "several choices of ribbing were apparently available to meet the functional needs of the product," yet Compco "chose precisely the same design used by the plaintiff and followed it so closely as to make confusion likely." 311 F.2d, at 30. A design which identifies its maker to the trade, the Court of Appeals held, is a "protectable" right under Illinois law, even though the design is unpatentable. We granted certiorari.

To support its findings of likelihood of confusion and actual confusion, the trial court was able to refer to only one circumstance in the record. A plant manager who had installed some of Compco's fixtures later asked Day-Brite to service the fixtures, thinking they had been made by Day-Brite. There was no testimony given by a purchaser or by anyone else that any customer had ever been misled, deceived, or "confused," that is, that anyone had ever bought a Compco fixture thinking it was a Day-Brite fixture. All the record shows, as to the one instance cited by the trial court, is that both Compco and Day-Brite fixtures had been installed in the same plant, that three years later some repairs were needed, and that the manager viewing the Compco fixtures — hung at least 15 feet above the floor and arranged end to end in a continuous line so that identifying marks were hidden — thought they were Day-Brite fixtures and asked Day-Brite to service them. Not only is this incident suggestive only of confusion after a purchase had been made, but also there is considerable evidence of the care taken by Compco to prevent customer confusion, including clearly labeling both the fixtures and the containers in which they were shipped and not selling through manufacturers' representatives who handled competing lines.

Notwithstanding the thinness of the evidence to support findings of likely and actual confusion among purchasers, we do not find it necessary in this case to determine whether there is "clear error" in these findings. They, like those in *Sears, Roebuck & Co. v. Stiffel Co.*, were based wholly on the fact that selling an article which is an exact copy of another unpatented article is likely to produce and did in this case produce confusion as to the source of the article. Even accepting the findings, we hold that the order for an accounting for damages and the injunction are in conflict with the federal patent laws. Today we have held in *Sears, Roebuck & Co. v. Stiffel Co.*, that when an article is unprotected by a patent or a copyright, state law may not forbid others to copy that article. To forbid copying would interfere with the federal policy, found in Art. I, §8, cl. 8, of the Constitution and in the implementing federal statutes, of allowing free access to copy whatever the federal patent and copyright laws leave in the public domain. Here Day-Brite's fixture has been held not to be entitled to a design or mechanical patent. Under the federal patent laws it is, therefore, in the public domain and can be copied in every detail by whoever pleases. It is true that the trial court found that the configuration of Day-Brite's fixture identified Day-Brite to the trade because the arrangement of the ribbing had, like a trademark, acquired a "secondary meaning" by which that particular design was associated with Day-Brite. But if the design is not entitled to a design patent or other federal statutory protection, then it can be copied at will.

As we have said in Sears, while the federal patent laws prevent a State from prohibiting the copying and selling of unpatented articles, they do not stand in the way of state law, statutory or decisional, which requires those who make and sell copies to take precautions to identify their products as their own. A State of course has power to impose liability upon those who, knowing that the public is relying upon an original manufacturer's reputation for quality and integrity, deceive the public by palming off their copies as the original. That an article copied from an unpatented article could be made in some other way, that the design is "nonfunctional" and not essential to the use of either article, that the configuration of the article copied may have a "secondary meaning" which identifies the maker to the trade, or that there may be "confusion" among purchasers as to which article is which or as to who is the maker, may be relevant evidence in applying a State's law requiring such precautions as labeling; however, and regardless of the copier's motives, neither these facts nor any others can furnish a basis for imposing liability for or prohibiting the actual acts of copying and selling. And of course a State cannot hold a copier accountable in damages for failure to label or otherwise to identify his goods unless his failure is in violation of valid state statutory or decisional law requiring the copier to label or take other precautions to prevent confusion of customers as to the source of the goods.

Since the judgment below forbids the sale of a copy of an unpatented article and orders an accounting for damages for such copying, it cannot stand.

Reversed.

## Comments

1. ***Constitutional Limits on Unfair Competition.*** The United States Constitution gives Congress power "[t]o promote the Progress of Science and useful Arts, by securing for limited times to Authors and inventors the exclusive Right to their respective Writings and Discoveries." This is the authority for granting copyright and patent monopolies for limited periods of time. The requirements for obtaining copyright or patent protection are quite different from the requirements for getting trademark or unfair competition rights. Trademark rights potentially last forever and, in that respect, provide more powerful protection. Where unfair competition law gives unlimited protection to a creation that is equivalent to what copyright or patent law is designed to protect, unfair competition law potentially comes into conflict with the federal statutes and the Constitution as well. These cases explore situations in which state unfair competition laws are preempted by federal intellectual property statutes or are unconstitutional. Like state unfair competition law, federal unfair competition law yields to copyright and patent laws when the laws are in conflict.

2. ***Copying, Marketing, and the Preemption by Patent Law.*** Federal patent law gives up to 20 years of protection in exchange for the disclosure of the details of how to make or use novel inventions. No state may create patent rights or extend the federal exclusive patent right to make, use, or sell (or offer to sell) an invention. Once an invention is in the public domain, anyone may copy it as Sears slavishly copied Stiffel's idea for a pole lamp and Compco copied the ribbing of Day-Brite's fluorescent lighting fixtures. Copying *alone* cannot be a violation of state law.

A state may, however, regulate marketing, by requiring labeling or otherwise preventing confusion about who is supplying the product. While copying alone cannot be a violation of state law, states can prohibit the selling of a copy that is mislabeled, falsely advertised, or sold with a misrepresentation as to source. Copying *plus* trademark infringement, for instance, can be prohibited. Some element in addition to copying is required. It is the infringement that is enjoined, not the copying. The lower courts in *Sears* impermissibly found unfair competition based only on the confusion likely to arise from Sears' selling "a substantially exact copy."

The lower courts in *Compco* similarly recognized exclusive rights to a design. Again the Court held that federal patent law preempts state law, forbidding states from granting exclusive rights to a design. Again, however, states can prohibit marketing of copies in a way that confuses buyers as to source. The additional pieces of evidence cited by the Supreme Court are examples of factors a state may consider in its regulation of marketing.

Proof of something more than copying applies to both the limited protection of generic terms (as in *Forschner Group*) and functional and design elements in *Sears* and *Compco*.

3. ***Lanham Act §43(a), Unfair Competition, and Patent Law.*** While federal patent law may preempt state unfair competition law, it cannot preempt another federal law, such as the Lanham Act. Yet the trademark law and patent law might conflict if a person could obtain protection through the passing off provisions of Lanham Act §43(a) for product designs. In *Sears* and *Compco*, the Supreme Court insisted that states require something more than mere copying in their unfair competition statutes. States may require labeling or other precautionary steps to prevent confusion. The Lanham Act prevents any conflict with patent law in a similar way, by requiring that the defendant have done something (in addition to copying) that results in confusion, such as passing off another's good as its own or passing off its goods as those of another.

*Crossbow, Inc. v. Dan-Dee Imports, Inc.*, 266 F. Supp. 335 (D.N.Y. 1967) was a Lanham Act §43(a) claim where the defendant engaged in a number of acts including copying the plaintiff's product design. The plaintiff produced and sold novelty glowing and blinking drink lights that are mounted on the side of a drinking glass, a device which is adapted for mounting on a glass. This act of mounting sets a trigger which causes the light to glow and then blink. In addition to copying the design, the defendant displayed one of the plaintiff's drink lights at a trade show as if it had been made by the defendant. The defendant also used similar packaging and accepted orders for the plaintiff's product (as in *Coca-Cola Co. v. Ed E. Dorris* in Section C.1 above). These additional acts suffice to distinguish simple copying from an act of unfair competition. The court issued a preliminary injunction restraining the defendant.

## 3. Reverse Passing Off

Passing off occurs when the defendant produced the goods and represents that the plaintiff had produced them. Reverse passing off is a variation in which the plaintiff produced the goods and the defendant represents that the defendant had made them. In regular passing-off cases, the source of the defendant's goods is misrepresented as being the plaintiff. Reverse passing off is a variation in which the source of the plaintiff's goods is misrepresented. A relative early case of reverse passing off involved an actor named Paul Smith who starred in a film called *Convoy Buddies*. When the film was distributed, the name of another actor, Bob Spencer, was substituted in the credits and advertising for Smith's name. This is reverse passing off because Smith was the source of the creative acting services while the distributor represented that Spencer had supplied them. *See Smith v. Montoro*, 648 F.2d 602 (9th Cir. 1981).

*Smith v. Montoro* also demonstrated the potential breadth of the Lanham Act's reach by identifying both "explicit" and "implied" versions of passing off:

> Express passing off occurs when an enterprise labels goods or services with a mark identical to that of another enterprise, or otherwise expressly misrepresents that the goods originated with another enterprise. Implied passing off occurs when an enterprise uses a competitor's advertising material, or a sample or photograph of the competitor's product, to impliedly represent that the product it is selling was produced by the competitor.

The infringement cases based on another's use of a confusingly similar mark are a type of express passing off. Implied passing off and reverse passing off may involve more subtle representations. In *Truck Equipment Service Co. v. Fruehauf*, 536 F.2d 1210 (8th Cir. 1976), the defendant, Fruehauf, used pictures of the plaintiff's semi-trailer truck when marketing its own truck. It did not use the other's mark or a confusingly similar mark, as in traditional infringement cases. The court found that this could be the basis for finding actual confusion. *Web Printing Controls Co., Inc. v. Oxy-Dry Corp.* is an example of express reverse passing off because it applies the reverse passing-off doctrine in a traditional setting involving the substitution of the plaintiff's mark on a machine with the defendant's. The opinion pays particularly close attention to the elements of a passing-off claim.

### WEB PRINTING CONTROLS CO., INC. v. OXY-DRY CORP.

#### 906 F.2d 1202 (7th Cir. 1990)

ESCHBACH, Senior Circuit Judge.

Section 43(a) of the Lanham Act, 15 U.S.C. §1125(a), is the main focus of this appeal. In the court below Web Printing Controls Company, Inc. (WPC) brought a "reverse passing off" claim against Oxy-Dry Corporation (Oxy-Dry). After a bench trial the district court entered judgment in Oxy-Dry's favor. The court found as true much of what WPC alleged. It believed, however, that where, as here, a plaintiff seeks to recover noninjunctive relief under the Lanham Act, the plaintiff must show injury caused by actual confusion; and it concluded that WPC failed to make such a showing. Because WPC failed to prove injury caused by actual confusion, the court held that WPC did not establish a violation of the Lanham Act, and, consequently, WPC could recover nothing. In our judgment, the lower court erred. To prove a *violation* of the Lanham Act, proof of injury caused by actual confusion is unnecessary....

WPC is a maker of certain high-tech printing equipment. It has a trademark, which it affixes to its products. In the late '70's WPC was a start-up company with a small share of the printing market and no sales force. To bolster its presence in this market, WPC entered into an oral marketing agreement with Oxy-Dry, which was an established and well-respected manufacturer and distributor in the printing market. The agreement provided for Oxy-Dry salesmen to sell WPC products. Oxy-Dry would handle all sales functions, make the deal with the customer, "buy" the products from WPC and "resell" them to the final customer at a mark-up. WPC would deliver the products and all associated technical services. By this arrangement WPC hoped to establish its product in the printing market and garner goodwill; Oxy-Dry hoped to make sales (and profits) and acquire knowledge of the high-tech market niche that WPC's products served.

In the course of this relationship Oxy-Dry obliterated, hid, or otherwise confused WPC's trademark, usually by attaching a combined Oxy-Dry/WPC trademark to WPC's products (over WPC's trademark) or by taking full credit, one way or another, for WPC's products. WPC complained about Oxy-Dry's practice, but in the end acquiesced, perhaps realizing that there was value in associating strongly with the Oxy-Dry name.

In 1980 WPC apparently changed its mind about the merits of acquiescing in Oxy-Dry's misbranding. The oral agreement between Oxy-Dry and WPC was reduced to writing; one of the clauses of the written agreement was that Oxy-Dry would sell WPC products only under the WPC trademark. It did not. Oxy-Dry continued to misbrand WPC's products, and it took steps to otherwise claim credit for the quality of those products. This time WPC did not acquiesce in Oxy-Dry's practice, and the relationship between the two was ended.

On its own, WPC took steps to secure its market. Although WPC had little evidence showing that Oxy-Dry's misbranding actually confused any customers, it spent large sums in a marketing campaign to make sure that none of its customers, or potential customers, were confused. The campaign seemed to work. WPC's sales post-Oxy-Dry grew quite well; this, despite Oxy-Dry's introduction of its own brand of competing, high-tech printing equipment.

In its thorough opinion, the lower court stated its belief that WPC had to prove five elements to "prevail on its claim": (1) Oxy-Dry misbranded WPC's goods; (2) the misbranding was "material"; (3) Oxy-Dry caused WPC's goods to enter interstate commerce; (4) the misbranding caused a likelihood of confusion; and (5) WPC was injured. The court found that the first three elements were proved, and it is clear that they were. Regarding the fourth element, "confusion," the court held that when a plaintiff seeks injunctive relief a "likelihood of confusion" is all that the plaintiff must prove, but when a plaintiff seeks monetary relief the confusion element merges with the fifth element, "injury": a plaintiff then must prove injury as a result of actual confusion in order to prevail. For this proposition the district court relied on *Schutt Mfg. Co. v. Riddell, Inc.*, 673 F.2d 202 (7th Cir. 1982). The district court found that WPC had brought forth some evidence of actual confusion, but not more than a *de minimis* amount. Moreover, the court found a lack of evidence showing that WPC was injured. Thus, the court held that WPC had failed to prove injury caused by actual confusion and, as a result, had failed to establish a violation of section 43(a) of the Lanham Act.

But the elements necessary to establish a *violation* of section 43(a) of the Lanham Act do not include any involving actual injury or actual confusion. As set out in 15 U.S.C. §1125(a), a violation of the Lanham Act is established upon proof only of the following: First, that the defendant used in connection with goods or services a false designation of origin or false description or representation. Second, that the defendant caused such goods and services to enter into commerce. Third, that the plaintiff is a person "who believes that he or she is likely to be damaged as a result thereof." In modern day parlance, and in the context of this suit, a violation of section 43(a) of the Lanham Act is shown by (1) Oxy-Dry's material misbranding of WPC's products, (2) Oxy-Dry's introduction of WPC's products into interstate commerce, and (3) the likelihood that consumers will be confused by Oxy-Dry's material misbranding. In the course of its opinion, the district court made clear that these three elements had been proven. Thus, WPC established a violation of the Lanham Act, its lack of proof on actual injury or actual confusion notwithstanding.

It seems to us that the district court confused a Lanham Act violation with a Lanham Act remedy. It confused the elements necessary to prove a breach of the law with elements necessary to justify a certain remedy for that breach. It mixed two stages of inquiry — violation of the law; remedies for the violation — that should be kept separate.

The inquiries should be kept separate because a violation of the Lanham Act can be remedied in more ways than one. The usual way, and the way which in this case riveted the court's attention, is by an award of damages. A plaintiff wishing to recover damages for a violation of the Lanham Act must prove the defendant's Lanham Act violation, that the violation caused actual confusion among consumers of the plaintiff's product, and, as a result, that the plaintiff suffered actual injury, i.e., a loss of sales, profits, or present value (goodwill). WPC did not prove the elements essential to a recovery of damages, of course, so to it that avenue of relief is foreclosed. Other avenues of relief, however, are not foreclosed. In the past, courts have fashioned wide-ranging relief for a violation of the Lanham Act, allowing remedies such as a recovery of defendant's profits, an award of costs of the action, and, in some exceptional cases, an award of attorney's fees. These remedies flow not from the plaintiff's proof of its injury or damage, but from its proof of the defendant's unjust enrichment or the need for deterrence, for example, or, in the case of costs, merely from its proof of the defendant's Lanham Act violation. To collapse the two inquiries of violation and remedy into one which asks only of the plaintiff's injury, as did the district court, is to read out of the Lanham Act the remedies that do not rely on proof of "injury caused by actual confusion." And this, of course, is improper....

Accordingly, we reverse the judgment of the district court. In so doing, however, we wish to disturb none of the court's findings of fact and as little as possible of its legal analysis. WPC has shown that Oxy-Dry violated section 43(a) of the Lanham Act. It has not shown, however, that it is entitled to a "grant of monetary damages." Whether it is entitled to a recovery of some or all of the defendant's profits, or to a recovery of its attorneys' fees or litigation costs, we do not decide. We leave those issues on remand for the district court.

# Comments

1. *The Harm Resulting from Passing Off and Reverse Passing Off.* Producers are likely to be harmed more directly by passing off than by reverse passing off. In passing off cases, a producer whose goods or services customers prefer, i.e., COKE or jackknives made by the suppliers of the Swiss Army, loses sales to another who falsely claims to be selling those goods or services. The true producer may also suffer harm to its goodwill if the substitute goods or services are inferior, for instance, the "inexpensive and shoddy" knives sold by Arrow Trading Company. In reverse passing-off cases, the true producer's goods or services are sold by the other, so there is no immediate diversion of trade, and there is no direct harm to reputation because, by definition, the true producer's identity is obscured. Reverse passing off may, however, deny the producer the reputational advantage from having supplied satisfactory goods or services. Only passing off results in the immediate loss of sales. Only passing off involves the direct harm to reputation resulting from inferior goods sold under the true producer's name. Reverse passing off may result in the eventual reduction in sales, but the loss is less certain. The actor in *Smith v. Montoro* may lose future jobs because viewers will not know whose brilliant performance it was in the film. Web Printing Controls might lose future customers to Oxy-Dry to buyers who believe Oxy-Dry made its machines.

2. *Proof of Commercial Detriment.* To recover compensation for lost sales under either passing off or reverse passing off, a plaintiff must prove that there was a loss of sales resulting from the misrepresentation. This is one type of noninjunctive remedy to which the court in *Web Printing* referred. Because the harms are more immediate for traditional passing off, it may be easier to prove damages under that theory. The other remedies available under either theory are an injunction and recovery of the profits the defendant has made by its unfair practice. For an injunction, the plaintiff must prove that the representation is likely to cause harm. For recovery of the defendant's profits, the plaintiff must prove that the misrepresentation caused the defendant to earn profits. Because an injunction may be obtained independently of damages, a plaintiff need not show actual confusion and actual loss of sales to show a violation of the Lanham Act. Remedies are discussed in more detail in Chapter 5.

# Problem

3-6. Brooks, a manufacturer of athletic shoes, sued Nike, a competing manufacturer, under §43(a). Nike paid athletes participating in public sports events to wear its shoes with its distinctive "swoosh" trademark. Nike knew that some of their sponsored athletes preferred other manufacturers' shoes for some purposes and doctored those other shoes by putting the "swoosh" logo on them. Brooks sought an injunction prohibiting Nike from authorizing, permitting, approving, or in any manner causing Nike's "swoosh stripe" trademark symbol or the "Nike" name to be placed or affixed on athletic shoes (including baseball and football shoes) manufactured or distributed by shoe manufacturers other than Nike. Is this a case of passing off or reverse passing off? Express or implied? *See Nike, Inc. v. Rubber Manufacturers Association, Inc.*, 509 F. Supp. 919 (D.N.Y. 1981).

## 4. Unfair Competition and Copyright Law

*Sears* and *Compco* are two of the leading Supreme Court cases discussing potential conflicts between unfair competition law and patent law. *Dastar Corp. v. Twentieth Century Fox Film Corp.* is a recent Supreme Court opinion case discussing a conflict between unfair competition and copyright law.

### DASTAR CORP. v. TWENTIETH CENTURY FOX FILM CORP.
#### 539 U.S. 23 (2003)

Justice SCALIA.

In this case, we are asked to decide whether §43(a) of the Lanham Act, 15 U.S.C. §1125(a), prevents the unaccredited copying of a work, and if so, whether a court may double a profit award under §1117(a), in order to deter future infringing conduct.

In 1948, three and a half years after the German surrender at Reims, General Dwight D. Eisenhower completed "Crusade in Europe," his written account of the allied campaign in Europe during World War II. Doubleday published the book, registered it with the Copyright Office in 1948, and granted exclusive television rights to an affiliate of respondent Twentieth Century Fox Film Corporation (Fox). Fox, in turn, arranged for Time, Inc., to produce a television series, also called Crusade in Europe, based on the book, and Time assigned its copyright in the series to Fox. The television series, consisting of 26 episodes, was first broadcast in 1949. It combined a soundtrack based on a narration of the book with film footage from the United States Army, Navy, and Coast Guard, the British Ministry of Information and War Office, the National Film Board of Canada, and unidentified "Newsreel Pool Cameramen." In 1975, Doubleday renewed the copyright on the book as the " 'proprietor of copyright in a work made for hire.' " Fox, however, did not renew the copyright on the Crusade television series, which expired in 1977, leaving the television series in the public domain.

In 1988, Fox reacquired the television rights in General Eisenhower's book, including the exclusive right to distribute the Crusade television series on video and to sub-license others to do so. Respondents SFM Entertainment and New Line Home Video, Inc., in turn, acquired from Fox the exclusive rights to distribute Crusade on video. SFM obtained the negatives of the original television series, restored them, and repackaged the series on videotape; New Line distributed the videotapes.

Enter petitioner Dastar. In 1995, Dastar decided to expand its product line from music compact discs to videos. Anticipating renewed interest in

World War II on the 50th anniversary of the war's end, Dastar released a video set entitled World War II Campaigns in Europe. To make Campaigns, Dastar purchased eight beta cam tapes of the *original* version of the Crusade television series, which is in the public domain, copied them, and then edited the series. Dastar's Campaigns series is slightly more than half as long as the original Crusade television series. Dastar substituted a new opening sequence, credit page, and final closing for those of the Crusade television series; inserted new chapter-title sequences and narrated chapter introductions; moved the "recap" in the Crusade television series to the beginning and retitled it as a "preview"; and removed references to and images of the book. Dastar created new packaging for its Campaigns series and (as already noted) a new title.

Dastar manufactured and sold the Campaigns video set as its own product. The advertising states: "Produced and Distributed by: *Entertainment Distributing*" (which is owned by Dastar), and makes no reference to the Crusade television series. Similarly, the screen credits state "DASTAR CORP presents" and "an ENTERTAINMENT DISTRIBUTING Production," and list as executive producer, producer, and associate producer, employees of Dastar. Supp. App. 2–3, 30. The Campaigns videos themselves also make no reference to the Crusade television series, New Line's Crusade videotapes, or the book. Dastar sells its Campaigns videos to Sam's Club, Costco, Best Buy, and other retailers and mail-order companies for $25 per set, substantially less than New Line's video set.

In 1998, respondents Fox, SFM, and New Line brought this action alleging that Dastar's sale of its Campaigns video set infringes Doubleday's copyright in General Eisenhower's book and, thus, their exclusive television rights in the book. Respondents later amended their complaint to add claims that Dastar's sale of Campaigns "without proper credit" to the Crusade television series constitutes "reverse passing off" in violation of §43(a) of the Lanham Act, and in violation of state unfair-competition law. App. to Pet. for Cert. 31a. On cross-motions for summary judgment, the District Court found for respondents on all three counts, *id.*, at 54a–55a, treating its resolution of the Lanham Act claim as controlling on the state-law unfair-competition claim because "the ultimate test under both is whether the public is likely to be deceived or confused," *id.*, at 54a. The court awarded Dastar's profits to respondents and doubled them pursuant to §35 of the Lanham Act, 15 U.S.C. §1117(a), to deter future infringing conduct by petitioner.

The Court of Appeals for the Ninth Circuit affirmed the judgment for respondents on the Lanham Act claim, but reversed as to the copyright claim and remanded. 34 Fed. Appx. 312, 316 (2002). (It said nothing with regard to the state-law claim.) With respect to the Lanham Act claim, the Court of Appeals reasoned that "Dastar copied substantially the entire *Crusade in Europe* series created by Twentieth Century Fox, labeled the resulting product with a different name and marketed it without attribution to Fox[, and] therefore committed a 'bodily appropriation' of Fox's series." *Id.*, at 314. It concluded that "Dastar's 'bodily appropriation' of Fox's original [television] series is sufficient to establish the reverse passing off." *Ibid.* The court also affirmed the District Court's award under the Lanham Act of twice Dastar's profits. We granted certiorari.

The Lanham Act was intended to make "actionable the deceptive and misleading use of marks," and "to protect persons engaged in . . . commerce against unfair competition." 15 U.S.C. §1127. While much of the Lanham Act addresses the registration, use, and infringement of trademarks and related marks, §43(a), 15 U.S.C. §1125(a) is one of the few provisions that goes beyond trademark protection. . . .

Thus, as it comes to us, the gravamen of respondents' claim is that, in marketing and selling Campaigns as its own product without acknowledging its nearly wholesale reliance on the Crusade television series, Dastar has made a "false designation of origin, false or misleading description of fact, or false or misleading representation of fact, which . . . is likely to cause confusion . . . as to the origin . . . of his or her goods." See, *e.g.*, Brief for Respondents 8, 11. That claim would undoubtedly be sustained if Dastar had bought some of New Line's Crusade videotapes and merely repackaged them as its own. Dastar's alleged wrongdoing, however, is vastly different: it took a creative work in the public domain—the Crusade television series—copied it, made modifications (arguably minor), and produced its very own series of videotapes. If "origin" refers only to the manufacturer or producer of the physical "goods" that are made available to the public (in this case the videotapes), Dastar was the origin. If, however, "origin" includes the creator of the underlying work that Dastar copied, then someone else (perhaps Fox) was the origin of Dastar's product. At bottom, we must decide what §43(a)(1)(A) of the Lanham Act means by the "origin" of "goods."

The dictionary definition of "origin" is "[t]he fact or process of coming into being from a source," and "[t]hat from which anything primarily proceeds; source." Webster's New International Dictionary 1720-1721 (2d ed. 1949). And the dictionary definition of "goods" (as relevant here) is "[w]ares; merchandise." *Id.*, at 1079. We think the most natural understanding of the "origin" of "goods"—the source of wares—is the producer of the tangible product sold in the marketplace, in this case the physical Campaigns videotape sold by Dastar. The concept might be stretched (as it was under the original version of §43(a)) to include not only the actual producer, but also the trademark owner who commissioned or assumed responsibility for ("stood behind") production of the physical product. But as used in the Lanham Act, the phrase "origin of goods" is in our view incapable of connoting the person or entity that originated the ideas or communications that "goods" embody or contain. Such an extension would not only stretch the text, but it would be out of accord with the history and purpose of the Lanham Act and inconsistent with precedent.

Section 43(a) of the Lanham Act prohibits actions like trademark infringement that deceive consumers and impair a producer's goodwill. It forbids, for example, the Coca-Cola Company's passing off its product as Pepsi-Cola or reverse passing off Pepsi-Cola as its product. But the brand-loyal consumer who prefers the drink that the Coca-Cola Company or PepsiCo sells, while he believes that that company produced (or at least stands behind the production of) that product, surely does not necessarily believe that that company was the "origin" of the drink in the sense that it was the very first to devise the formula. The consumer who buys a branded product does not automatically assume that the brand-name company is the same entity that came up with the idea for the product, or designed the product—and typically does not care whether it is. The words of the Lanham Act should not be stretched to cover matters that are typically of no consequence to purchasers.

It could be argued, perhaps, that the reality of purchaser concern is different for what might be called a communicative product—one that is valued not primarily for its physical qualities, such as a hammer, but for the intellectual content that it conveys, such as a book or, as here, a video. The purchaser of a novel is interested not merely, if at all, in the identity of the producer of the physical tome (the publisher), but also, and indeed primarily, in the identity of the creator of the story it conveys (the author). And the author, of course, has at least as much interest in avoiding passing-off (or reverse passing-off) of his creation as does the publisher. For such a communicative product (the argument goes) "origin of goods" in §43(a) must be deemed to include not merely the producer of the physical item (the publishing house Farrar, Straus and Giroux, or the video producer Dastar) but also the creator of the content that the physical item conveys (the author Tom Wolfe, or—assertedly—respondents).

The problem with this argument according special treatment to communicative products is that it causes the Lanham Act to conflict with the law of copyright, which addresses that subject specifically. The right to copy, and to copy without attribution, once a copyright has expired, like "the right to make [an article whose patent has expired]—including the right to make it in precisely the shape it carried when patented—passes to the public." *Sears, Roebuck & Co. v. Stiffel Co.,* 376 U.S. 225, 230 (1964); see also *Kellogg Co. v. National Biscuit Co.,* 305 U.S. 111, 121-122 (1938). "In general, unless an intellectual property right such as a patent or copyright protects an item, it will be subject to copying." *TrafFix Devices, Inc. v. Marketing Displays, Inc.,* 532 U.S. 23, 29 (2001). The rights of a patentee or copyright holder are part of a "carefully crafted bargain," *Bonito Boats, Inc. v. Thunder Craft Boats, Inc.,* 489 U.S. 141, 150-151 (1989), under which, once the patent or copyright monopoly has expired, the public may use the invention or work at will and without attribution. Thus, in construing the Lanham Act, we have been "careful to caution against misuse or overextension" of trademark and related protections into areas traditionally occupied by patent or copyright. *TrafFix,* 532 U.S., at 29. "The Lanham Act," we have said, "does not exist to reward manufacturers for their innovation in creating a particular device; that is the purpose of the patent law and its period of exclusivity." *Id.,* at 34. Federal trademark law "has no necessary relation to invention or discovery," *In re Trade-Mark Cases,* 100 U.S. 82, 94 (1879), but rather, by preventing competitors from copying "a source-identifying mark," "reduce[s] the customer's costs of shopping and making purchasing decisions," and "helps assure a producer that it (and not an imitating competitor) will reap the financial, reputation-related rewards associated with a desirable product," *Qualitex Co. v. Jacobson Products Co.,* 514 U.S. 159, 163-164 (1995). Assuming for the sake of argument that Dastar's representation of itself as the "Producer" of its videos amounted to a representation that it originated the creative work conveyed by the videos, allowing a cause of action under §43(a) for that representation would create a species of mutant copyright law that limits the public's "federal right to 'copy and to use,' " expired copyrights, *Bonito Boats, supra,* at 165.

When Congress has wished to create such an addition to the law of copyright, it has done so with much more specificity than the Lanham Act's ambiguous use of "origin." The Visual Artists Rights Act of 1990, §603(a), 104 Stat. 5128, provides that the author of an artistic work "shall have the right...to claim authorship of that work." 17 U.S.C. §106A(a)(1)(A). That express right of attribution is carefully limited and focused: It attaches only to specified "work[s] of visual art," §101, is personal to the artist, §§106A(b) and (e), and endures only for "the life of the author," at §106A(d)(1). Recognizing in §43(a) a cause of action for misrepresentation of authorship of noncopyrighted works (visual or otherwise) would render these limitations superfluous. A statutory interpretation that renders another statute superfluous is of course to be avoided.

Reading "origin" in §43(a) to require attribution of uncopyrighted materials would pose serious practical problems. Without a copyrighted work as the basepoint, the word "origin" has no discernable limits. A video of the MGM film Carmen Jones, after its copyright has expired, would presumably require attribution not just to MGM, but to Oscar Hammerstein II (who wrote the musical on which the film was based), to Georges Bizet (who wrote the opera on which the musical was based), and to Prosper Merimee (who wrote the novel on which the opera was based). In many cases, figuring out who is in the line of "origin" would be no simple task. Indeed, in the present case it is far from clear that respondents have that status. Neither SFM nor New Line had anything to do with the production of the Crusade television series—they merely were licensed to distribute the video version. While Fox might have a claim to being in the line of origin, its involvement with the creation of the television series was limited at best. Time, Inc., was the principal if not the exclusive creator, albeit under arrangement with Fox. And of course it was neither Fox nor Time, Inc., that shot the film used in the Crusade television series. Rather, that footage came from the United States Army, Navy, and Coast Guard, the British Ministry of Information and War Office, the National Film Board of Canada, and unidentified "Newsreel Pool Cameramen." If anyone has a claim to being the *original* creator of the material used in both the Crusade television series and the Campaigns videotapes, it would be those groups, rather than Fox. We do not think the Lanham Act requires this search for the source of the Nile and all its tributaries.

Another practical difficulty of adopting a special definition of "origin" for communicative products is that it places the manufacturers of those products in a difficult position. On the one hand, they would face Lanham Act liability for *failing* to credit the creator of a work on which their lawful copies are based; and on the other hand they could face Lanham Act liability for *crediting* the creator if that should be regarded as implying the creator's "sponsorship or approval" of the copy, 15 U.S.C. §1125(a)(1)(A). In this case, for example, if Dastar had simply "copied [the television series] as Crusade in Europe and sold it as Crusade in Europe," without changing the title or packaging (including the original credits to Fox), it is hard to have confidence in respondents' assurance that they "would not be here on a Lanham Act cause of action," Tr. of Oral Arg. 35.

Finally, reading §43(a) of the Lanham Act as creating a cause of action for, in effect, plagiarism—the use of otherwise unprotected works and inventions without attribution—would be hard to reconcile with our previous decisions. For example, in *Wal-Mart Stores, Inc. v. Samara Brothers, Inc.*, 529 U.S. 205 (2000), we considered whether product-design trade dress can ever be inherently distinctive. Wal-Mart produced "knockoffs" of children's clothes designed and manufactured by Samara Brothers, containing only "minor modifications" of the original designs. *Id.*, at 208. We concluded that the designs could not be protected under §43(a) without a showing that they had acquired "secondary meaning," *id.*, at 214, so that they " 'identify the source of the product rather than the product itself,' " *id.*, at 211. This carefully considered limitation would be entirely pointless if the "original" producer could turn around and pursue a reverse-passing-off claim under exactly the same provision of the Lanham Act. Samara would merely have had to argue that it was the "origin" of the designs that Wal-Mart was selling as its own line. It was not, because "origin of goods" in the Lanham Act referred to the producer of the clothes, and not the producer of the (potentially) copyrightable or patentable designs that the clothes embodied.

Similarly under respondents' theory, the "origin of goods" provision of §43(a) would have supported the suit that we rejected in *Bonito Boats*, 489 U.S. 141, where the defendants had used molds to duplicate the plaintiff's unpatented boat hulls (apparently without crediting the plaintiff). And it would have supported the suit we rejected in *TrafFix*, 532 U.S. 23: The plaintiff, whose patents on flexible road signs had expired, and who could not prevail on a trade-dress claim under §43(a) because the features of the signs were functional, would have had a reverse-passing-off claim for unattributed copying of his design.

In sum, reading the phrase "origin of goods" in the Lanham Act in accordance with the Act's common-law foundations (which were *not* designed to protect originality or creativity), and in light of the copyright and patent laws (which *were*), we conclude that the phrase refers to the producer of the tangible goods that are offered for sale, and not to the author of any idea, concept, or communication embodied in those goods. To hold otherwise would be akin to finding that §43(a) created a species of perpetual patent and copyright, which Congress may not do.

The creative talent of the sort that lay behind the Campaigns videos is not left without protection. The original film footage used in the Crusade television series could have been copyrighted, as was copyrighted (as a compilation) the Crusade television series, even though it included material from the public domain. Had Fox renewed the copyright in the Crusade television series, it would have had an easy claim of copyright infringement. And respondents' contention that Campaigns infringes Doubleday's copyright in General Eisenhower's book is still a live question on remand. If, moreover, the producer of a video that substantially copied the Crusade series were, in advertising or promotion, to give purchasers the impression that the video was quite different from that series, then one or more of the respondents might have a cause of action—not for reverse

passing off under the "confusion...as to the origin" provision of
§43(a)(1)(A), but for misrepresentation under the "misrepresents the nature, characteristics [or] qualities" provision of §43(a)(1)(B). For merely
saying it is the producer of the video, however, no Lanham Act liability
attaches to Dastar.

Because we conclude that Dastar was the "origin" of the products it sold
as its own, respondents cannot prevail on their Lanham Act claim. We thus
have no occasion to consider whether the Lanham Act permitted an award
of double petitioner's profits. The judgment of the Court of Appeals for the
Ninth Circuit is reversed, and the case is remanded for further proceedings
consistent with this opinion.

*It is so ordered.*

# Comments

1. ***Copying and Conflicts between Copyright Law and the Lanham Act.*** Copyright
law determines what "writings" and "works of authorship" are in the
public domain. "Writings" and "works of authorship" for copyright
purposes are interpreted broadly to embrace many forms of artistic
expression, including the books and movies involved in *Dastar*. After
the copyright on the original version of the Crusade television series
expired, Dastar edited those old videotapes and produced a shorter set
of videos of the series. *Sears* and *Compco* held that unfair competition law
may not prohibit copying of inventions and designs in the public
domain. A parallel analysis might conclude that that unfair competition
law may not prohibit copying of writings in the public domain.

The difficulty for the Supreme Court in *Dastar* is that the Lanham Act
prohibits representations that mislead consumers about the origin of
goods or services, and Dastar did not film, compile, assemble, or organize the original videos upon which its *Campaigns* series was based. If
"origin" means "authorship," Dastar misrepresented the origin of the
goods because Dastar was certainly not the sole author of the video. Its
contribution to authorship was only editing, which the Court described
as "arguably minor." If origin means authorship, the real authors would
have a perpetual right to have the work attributed to them, but copyright
law does not give that much protection. Once a work becomes part of the
public domain, anyone may copy it without attribution. Because of the
conflict between copyright and trademark law, the Court decided that
origin could not mean authorship.

The Court interpreted "origin" to refer "to the producer of the tangible goods that are offered for sale" and supported its conclusion by
reference to policy, statutory construction, and practicality. How did
each of those sources support its holding?

2. ***Misappropriation, §43(a), and Copyright Preemption.*** *Dastar* followed a
variety of cases in which plaintiffs relied on the unfair competition
tort of misappropriation to protect rights akin to copyright. State courts
gave unfair competition relief to the Metropolitan Opera, which complained that an unrelated person was recording its operatic radio broadcasts and selling phonorecords of those operas; to Capitol Records and

to Columbia Broadcasting System, which complained that unrelated persons were making "bootleg" tapes from phonorecords they had purchased at music stores and were selling them to others; and to Grove Press and the Hebrew Publishing Company, which complained that unrelated persons photocopied their published books and were intending to bind and sell them to others. The unfair competition remedies were held to be available without regard to whether the underlying material was copyrighted or copyrightable. *See Metropolitan Opera Ass'n v. Wagner-Nichols Recorder Corp.*, 101 N.Y.S.2d 483 (N.Y. Sup. Ct. 1950); *Capitol Records, Inc. v. Spies*, 264 N.E.2d 874 (Ill. App. Ct. 1970); *Columbia Broadcasting System, Inc. v. Melody Recordings, Inc.*, 341 A.2d 348 (N.J. Sup. Ct. 1975); *Grove Press, Inc. v. Collectors Publication, Inc.*, 264 F. Supp. 603 (Cal. D. Ct. 1967); and *Hebrew Publishing Company v. Scharfstein*, 43 N.E.2d 449 (N.Y. 1942). Subsequent to *Dastar*, courts relied on its holding to block Lanham Act claims by a film director complaining that the use of his narration script, edits, and score without credit; a producer complaining that a filmmaker and a film festival manager who failed to give him proper credit for his work on the movie; and a table leg maker's claim that a table leg it designed was used by another on a sample table submitted for a bid on a supply contract. *See, Williams v. UMG Recordings Inc.*, 281 F. Supp. 2d 1177 (C.D. Cal. 2003); *Carroll v. Kahn*, 68 U.S.P.Q.2d 1357 (D.N.Y. 2003) *Bretford Manufacturing Inc. v. Smith System Manufacturing Co.*, 68 U.S.P.Q.2d 1378 (N.D. Ill. 2003). Does *Dastar* cast doubts on or implicitly overrule the holding in *Smith v. Montoro*, discussed in the introduction to this section.

## Problem

**3-7.** In *Hustlers, Inc. v. Thomasson*, 307 F. Supp. 2d 1375 (N.D. Ga. 2004), the plaintiff, Hustlers, was a music publisher who acquired copyrights from musical artists, licensed them to others, and collected royalties. Thomasson was a song writer and performing artist for "The Outlaw" and Lynyrd Skynyrd bands who had conveyed all of his copyrights to Hustlers in exchange for a portion of the royalties on those songs. While his agreement with Hustlers was still in force, Thomasson formed his own music publishing company, Writers Justice, and directed a record company who was licensing his songs to send royalty payments to Writers Justice instead of Hustlers. That resulted in the record company listing Justice Writers as the publisher for the songs when Hustlers actually owned the copyrights. Hustlers filed a Lanham Act claim alleging that Thomasson falsely designated the origin of copyright ownership of those songs. Does *Dastar* prohibit this claim?

## D. THE GENERAL THEORY OF MISAPPROPRIATION

All aspects of intellectual property law discussed in this book reflect circumstances in which (1) a person has invested resources to develop a valuable resource and (2) a second person free rides on that investment without incurring comparable costs. A policy question arises in each of these cases as to whether it is appropriate to enjoin the second person's use. The choice is between giving exclusive monopoly rights to the first person or to permitting others to benefit from the first person's investment without paying. The legal theory called "misappropriation," reflects this view that one person ought not to get free benefits from another's investment.

This legal theory has been embodied in many rules applying to different types of property. The torts of conversion and crime of theft are classic examples of misappropriation of tangible property. Contract law also governs the rights of parties to benefit from the investments of others with whom they contract. Trademark, copyright, and patent infringement and misappropriation of ideas and trade secrets are examples of misappropriation of intangible property. Cybersquatting and dilution claims are just two of the specific unfair competition claims that reflect a misappropriation of another's investment. In each of these legal applications, the underlying policy question of when a party should have exclusive rights to a resource arises. In the specific examples above, the policy question is resolved by limiting remedies only to cases involving bad faith registration of domain names and only to dilution of famous marks, respectively.

The policy issue in all misappropriation cases involving intellectual property is deciding whether to grant rights and suffer the harms associated with monopoly, including higher prices, or deny rights and suffer the diminution of incentives to invest in creation of intangible resources. Granting exclusive rights provides an incentive to invest in the creation of assets and prevents the unjust enrichment associated with free riding. But recognizing exclusive rights restricts access to valuable information and restrains competition.

The state unfair competition theory of misappropriation has no parallel in federal law, despite originating in a federal case. The theory originated in *International News Service v. Associated Press*, 248 U.S. 215 (1918), in which Associated Press, a company that had collected and distributed news about the progress of World War I to its members at great expense (the first element), complained about a competitor, International News Service, copying that news as soon as it was released and distributing it to its own subscribers, without having incurred the costs of collection (the second element). The policy question was whether it is preferable to give the Associated Press an exclusive right to the news, which would reward their collection efforts, or permit the International News Service to copy it, thereby encouraging the dissemination of information. The U.S. Supreme Court gave the Associated Press a right to the exclusive use of the news for a limited period of time, until its initial value as a hot news story had passed.

This balance satisfied both policy goals of wide dissemination and incentive creation. The Supreme Court decided there was no federal general common law in *Erie R. Co. v. Tompkins*, 304 U.S. 64 (1938). As a result, the legal theory of misappropriation, as distinguished from its specific embodiment in the federal statutes applicable to tangible and intangible property described above, became exclusively a state law theory. While the

Lanham Act has codified and federalized some torts that originated in state law, such as passing off and antidilution law, it has never embraced a distinct misappropriation theory.

State courts have occasionally taken a broader view of misappropriation, applying the theory on an ad hoc basis where it seemed that policy required giving an exclusive right to an intangible property even where there was no specific statutory protection. For example, the Illinois Supreme Court gave the Dow Jones Company a right to prevent the Board of Trade of the City of Chicago from using the Dow Jones Industrial Average, a famous measure of the changing value of the stocks of the nation's largest companies, to sell stock options. *See Board of Trade of the City of Chicago v. Dow Jones & Co., Inc.*, 456 N.E.2d 84 (Ill. 1983). A California appellate court gave The United States Golf Association the right to prevent a software company from using the Association's golf handicapping formula in its handicapping software while the Third Circuit Court of Appeals, applying New Jersey law, denied the same plaintiff similar rights on the grounds that the parties were not competitors. *Compare The United States Golf Association v. Arroyo Software Corp.*, 81 Cal. Rptr. 2d Cal. App. 1999), *with U.S. Golf Association v. St. Andrews Systems, Data-Max, Inc.*, 749 F.2d 1028 (3d Cir. 1984).

The Restatement (Third) of Unfair Competition §38 would limit application of the general theory of misappropriation to that protection of intangibles already recognized in other specific areas, such as the law of trade secrets, patent, copyright, and trademark. There would be no role for a separate misappropriation theory. Federal unfair competition cases, like *Dastar Corp. v. Twentieth Century Fox Film Corp., Sears, Roebuck & Co. v. Stiffel Co.,* and *Compco Corp. v. Day-Brite Lighting, Inc.* limit application of state misappropriation law in unfair competition law while provisions of the copyright and patent acts and the United States Constitution limit application of state misappropriation law in those areas of intellectual property.

---

### *THEORETICAL PERSPECTIVE*
### Public Goods Theory and Misappropriation of Intellectual Property

As the following excerpt from the Restatement (Third) of Unfair Competition §38 cmt. b reveals, the underlying policy dilemma is created by the public goods nature of intellectual property:

> Unlike appropriations of physical assets, the appropriation of information or other intangible asset does not ordinarily deprive the originator of simultaneous use. The recognition of exclusive rights may thus deny to the public the full benefits of valuable ideas and innovations by limiting their distribution and exploitation. In addition, the principle of unjust enrichment does not demand restitution of every gain derived from the efforts of others. A small shop, for example, may freely benefit from the customers attracted by a nearby department store, a local manufacturer may benefit from increased demand attributable to the promotional efforts of a national manufacturer of similar goods, and a newspaper may benefit from reporting on the activities of local athletic teams. Similarly, the law has long recognized the right of a competitor to copy the successful products and business methods of others absent protection under patent, copyright, or trademark law.

Achieving a proper balance between protection and access is often a complicated and difficult undertaking. Because of the complexity and indeterminacy of the competing interests, rights in intangible trade values such as ideas, innovations, and information have been created primarily through legislation. The patent and copyright statutes illustrate the intricacy required to harmonize the competing public and private interests implicated in the recognition of rights in intangible trade values. Both statutes contain elaborate mechanisms intended to balance the interests in protection and access. Protection under the patent act, for example, is limited to innovations that are new, useful, and nonobvious to persons having ordinary skill in the art. The copyright act grants rights in works of authorship subject to a complex system of exemptions and limitations. Both statutes grant rights only for a limited term, after which the discovery or writing enters the public domain and may be freely appropriated by others.

The common law of unfair competition has generally recognized rights against the appropriation of intangible trade values only when the recognition of such rights is supported by other interests that justify protection, and then only when the scope of the resulting rights can be clearly defined....In the absence of such additional interests, the common law has resisted the recognition of general rights against the appropriation of information and other intangible trade values.

## E.  SECTION 43(a) AND THE STATE RIGHT OF PUBLICITY

The right of publicity is a state law claim with no exact federal counterpart. It grew out of the state tort of privacy. *White v. Samsung Electronics America, Inc.* illustrates elements typical of a state misappropriation claim: investment by Vanna White in marketing her celebrity status and exploitation of that status by another for commercial purposes. Some states permit right of publicity claims even without evidence of prior investment in celebrity by the plaintiff. *White* also includes a Lanham Act §43(a)(1)(A) claim that consumers would likely be confused about whether Ms. White was endorsing the product being advertised. Note the differences between these two claims.

### WHITE v. SAMSUNG ELECTRONICS AMERICA, INC.
#### 971 F.2d 1395 (9th Cir. 1992)

GOODWIN, Senior Circuit Judge.

This case involves a promotional "fame and fortune" dispute. In running a particular advertisement without Vanna White's permission, defendants Samsung Electronics America, Inc. (Samsung) and David Deutsch Associates, Inc. (Deutsch) attempted to capitalize on White's fame to enhance their fortune. White sued, alleging infringement of various intellectual property rights, but the district court granted summary judgment in favor of the defendants. We affirm in part, reverse in part, and remand.

Plaintiff Vanna White is the hostess of "Wheel of Fortune," one of the most popular game shows in television history. An estimated forty million people watch the program daily. Capitalizing on the fame which her participation in the show has bestowed on her, White markets her identity to various advertisers. . . .

The advertisement which prompted the current dispute was for Samsung video-cassette recorders (VCRs). The ad depicted a robot, dressed in a wig, gown, and jewelry which Deutsch consciously selected to resemble White's hair and dress. The robot was posed next to a game board which is instantly recognizable as the Wheel of Fortune game show set, in a stance for which White is famous. The caption of the ad read: "Longest-running game show. 2012 A.D." Defendants referred to the ad as the "Vanna White" ad. Unlike the other celebrities used in the campaign, White neither consented to the ads nor was she paid.

Following the circulation of the robot ad, White sued Samsung and Deutsch in federal district court under: (1) California Civil Code §3344; (2) the California common law right of publicity; and (3) §43(a) of the Lanham Act, 15 U.S.C. §1125(a). The district court granted summary judgment against White on each of her claims. White now appeals.

## I. SECTION 3344

White first argues that the district court erred in rejecting her claim under section 3344. Section 3344(a) provides, in pertinent part, that "[a]ny person who knowingly uses another's name, voice, signature, photograph, or likeness, in any manner, . . . for purposes of advertising or selling, . . . without such person's prior consent . . . shall be liable for any damages sustained by the person or persons injured as a result thereof."

White argues that the Samsung advertisement used her "likeness" in contravention of section 3344. In *Midler v. Ford Motor Co.*, 849 F.2d 460 (9th Cir. 1988), this court rejected Bette Midler's section 3344 claim concerning a Ford television commercial in which a Midler "sound-alike" sang a song which Midler had made famous. In rejecting Midler's claim, this court noted that "[t]he defendants did not use Midler's name or anything else whose use is prohibited by the statute. The voice they used was [another person's], not hers. The term 'likeness' refers to a visual image not a vocal imitation." *Id.* at 463.

In this case, Samsung and Deutsch used a robot with mechanical features, and not, for example, a manikin molded to White's precise features. Without deciding for all purposes when a caricature or impressionistic resemblance might become a "likeness," we agree with the district court that the robot at issue here was not White's "likeness" within the meaning of section 3344. Accordingly, we affirm the court's dismissal of White's section 3344 claim.

## II. RIGHT OF PUBLICITY

White next argues that the district court erred in granting summary judgment to defendants on White's common law right of publicity claim. In *Eastwood v. Superior Court*, 149 Cal. App. 3d 409, 198 Cal. Rptr. 342 (1983), the California court of appeal stated that the common law right

Test

of publicity cause of action "may be pleaded by alleging (1) the defendant's use of the plaintiff's identity; (2) the appropriation of plaintiff's name or likeness to defendant's advantage, commercially or otherwise; (3) lack of consent; and (4) resulting injury." *Id.* at 417, 198 Cal. Rptr. 342 (citing Prosser, Law of Torts (4th ed. 1971) §117, pp. 804-807). The district court dismissed White's claim for failure to satisfy *Eastwood*'s second prong, reasoning that defendants had not appropriated White's "name or likeness" with their robot ad. We agree that the robot ad did not make use of White's name or likeness. However, the common law right of publicity is not so confined.

The *Eastwood* court did not hold that the right of publicity cause of action could be pleaded only by alleging an appropriation of name or likeness. *Eastwood* involved an unauthorized use of photographs of Clint Eastwood and of his name. Accordingly, the *Eastwood* court had no occasion to consider the extent beyond the use of name or likeness to which the right of publicity reaches. That court held only that the right of publicity cause of action "may be" pleaded by alleging, *inter alia,* appropriation of name or likeness, not that the action may be pleaded *only* in those terms.

The "name or likeness" formulation referred to in *Eastwood* originated not as an element of the right of publicity cause of action, but as a description of the types of cases in which the cause of action had been recognized. The source of this formulation is Prosser, *Privacy*, 48 Cal. L. Rev. 383, 401-07 (1960), one of the earliest and most enduring articulations of the common law right of publicity cause of action. In looking at the case law to that point, Prosser recognized that right of publicity cases involved one of two basic factual scenarios: name appropriation, and picture or other likeness appropriation. *Id.* at 401-02, nn. 156-57.

Even though Prosser focused on appropriations of name or likeness in discussing the right of publicity, he noted that "[i]t is not impossible that there might be appropriation of the plaintiff's identity, as by impersonation, without the use of either his name or his likeness, and that this would be an invasion of his right of privacy." *Id.* at 401, n. 155. At the time Prosser wrote, he noted however, that "[n]o such case appears to have arisen." *Id.*

Since Prosser's early formulation, the case law has borne out his insight that the right of publicity is not limited to the appropriation of name or likeness. In *Motschenbacher v. R.J. Reynolds Tobacco Co.*, 498 F.2d 821 (9th Cir. 1974), the defendant had used a photograph of the plaintiff's race car in a television commercial. Although the plaintiff appeared driving the car in the photograph, his features were not visible. Even though the defendant had not appropriated the plaintiff's name or likeness, this court held that plaintiff's California right of publicity claim should reach the jury.

In *Midler,* this court held that, even though the defendants had not used Midler's name or likeness, Midler had stated a claim for violation of her California common law right of publicity because "the defendants . . . for their own profit in selling their product did appropriate part of her identity" by using a Midler sound-alike. *Id.* at 463-64.

In *Carson v. Here's Johnny Portable Toilets, Inc.*, 698 F.2d 831 (6th Cir. 1983), the defendant had marketed portable toilets under the brand name "Here's Johnny" — Johnny Carson's signature "Tonight Show" introduction—without Carson's permission. The district court had dismissed Carson's Michigan common law right of publicity claim because the defendants had not used Carson's "name or likeness." *Id.* at 835. In reversing the district court, the sixth circuit found "the district court's conception of the right of publicity...too narrow" and held that the right was implicated because the defendant had appropriated Carson's identity by using, *inter alia,* the phrase "Here's Johnny." *Id.* at 835-37.

These cases teach not only that the common law right of publicity reaches means of appropriation other than name or likeness, but that the specific means of appropriation are relevant only for determining whether the defendant has in fact appropriated the plaintiff's identity. The right of publicity does not require that appropriations of identity be accomplished through particular means to be actionable. It is noteworthy that the *Midler* and *Carson* defendants not only avoided using the plaintiff's name or likeness, but they also avoided appropriating the celebrity's voice, signature, and photograph. The photograph in *Motschenbacher* did include the plaintiff, but because the plaintiff was not visible the driver could have been an actor or dummy and the analysis in the case would have been the same.

Although the defendants in these cases avoided the most obvious means of appropriating the plaintiffs' identities, each of their actions directly implicated the commercial interests which the right of publicity is designed to protect. As the *Carson* court explained:

> [t]he right of publicity has developed to protect the commercial interest of celebrities in their identities. The theory of the right is that a celebrity's identity can be valuable in the promotion of products, and the celebrity has an interest that may be protected from the unauthorized commercial exploitation of that identity....If the celebrity's identity is commercially exploited, there has been an invasion of his right whether or not his "name or likeness" is used.

*Carson,* 698 F.2d at 835. It is not important *how* the defendant has appropriated the plaintiff's identity, but *whether* the defendant has done so. *Motschenbacher, Midler,* and *Carson* teach the impossibility of treating the right of publicity as guarding only against a laundry list of specific means of appropriating identity. A rule which says that the right of publicity can be infringed only through the use of nine different methods of appropriating identity merely challenges the clever advertising strategist to come up with the tenth.

Indeed, if we treated the means of appropriation as dispositive in our analysis of the right of publicity, we would not only weaken the right but effectively eviscerate it. The right would fail to protect those plaintiffs most in need of its protection. Advertisers use celebrities to promote their products. The more popular the celebrity, the greater the number of people who recognize her, and the greater the visibility for the product. The identities of the most popular celebrities are not only the most attractive for advertisers, but also the easiest to evoke without resorting to obvious means such as name, likeness, or voice.

Consider a hypothetical advertisement which depicts a mechanical robot with male features, an African-American complexion, and a bald head. The robot is wearing black hightop Air Jordan basketball sneakers, and a red basketball uniform with black trim, baggy shorts, and the number 23 (though not revealing "Bulls" or "Jordan" lettering). The ad depicts the robot dunking a basketball one-handed, stiff-armed, legs extended like open scissors, and tongue hanging out. Now envision that this ad is run on television during professional basketball games. Considered individually, the robot's physical attributes, its dress, and its stance tell us little. Taken together, they lead to the only conclusion that any sports viewer who has registered a discernible pulse in the past five years would reach: the ad is about Michael Jordan.

Viewed separately, the individual aspects of the advertisement in the present case say little. Viewed together, they leave little doubt about the celebrity the ad is meant to depict. The female-shaped robot is wearing a long gown, blond wig, and large jewelry. Vanna White dresses exactly like this at times, but so do many other women. The robot is in the process of turning a block letter on a game-board. Vanna White dresses like this while turning letters on a game-board but perhaps similarly attired Scrabble-playing women do this as well. The robot is standing on what looks to be the Wheel of Fortune game show set. Vanna White dresses like this, turns letters, and does this on the Wheel of Fortune game show. She is the only one. Indeed, defendants themselves referred to their ad as the "Vanna White" ad. We are not surprised.

Television and other media create marketable celebrity identity value. Considerable energy and ingenuity are expended by those who have achieved celebrity value to exploit it for profit. The law protects the celebrity's sole right to exploit this value whether the celebrity has achieved her fame out of rare ability, dumb luck, or a combination thereof. We decline Samsung and Deutsch's invitation to permit the evisceration of the common law right of publicity through means as facile as those in this case. Because White has alleged facts showing that Samsung and Deutsch had appropriated her identity, the district court erred by rejecting, on summary judgment, White's common law right of publicity claim.

### III. THE LANHAM ACT

White's final argument is that the district court erred in denying her claim under §43(a) of the Lanham Act, 15 U.S.C. §1125(a). The version of section 43(a) applicable to this case provides, in pertinent part, that "[a]ny person who shall...use, in connection with any goods or services...any false description or representation...shall be liable to a civil action...by any person who believes that he is or is likely to be damaged by the use of any such false description or designation." 15 U.S.C. §1125(a).

To prevail on her Lanham Act claim, White is required to show that in running the robot ad, Samsung and Deutsch created a likelihood of confusion.

This circuit recognizes several different multi-factor tests for determining whether a likelihood of confusion exists. None of these tests is correct to the exclusion of the others. Normally, in reviewing the district court's decision, this court will look to the particular test that the district court used. However, because the district court in this case apparently did not use any of the multi-factor tests in making its likelihood of confusion determination, and because this case involves an appeal from summary judgment and we review de novo the district court's determination, we will look for guidance to the 8-factor test enunciated in *AMF, Inc. v. Sleekcraft Boats,* 599 F.2d 341 (9th Cir. 1979). According to *AMF,* factors relevant to a likelihood of confusion include: (1) strength of the plaintiff's mark; (2) relatedness of the goods; (3) similarity of the marks; (4) evidence of actual confusion; (5) marketing channels used; (6) likely degree of purchaser care; (7) defendant's intent in selecting the mark; [and] (8) likelihood of expansion of the product lines. We turn now to consider White's claim in light of each factor.

*8 factor test*

In cases involving confusion over endorsement by a celebrity plaintiff, "mark" means the celebrity's persona. The "strength" of the mark refers to the level of recognition the celebrity enjoys among members of society. If Vanna White is unknown to the segment of the public at whom Samsung's robot ad was directed, then that segment could not be confused as to whether she was endorsing Samsung VCRs. Conversely, if White is well-known, this would allow the possibility of a likelihood of confusion. For the purposes of the *Sleekcraft* test, White's "mark," or celebrity identity, is strong.

In cases concerning confusion over celebrity endorsement, the plaintiff's "goods" concern the reasons for or source of the plaintiff's fame. Because White's fame is based on her televised performances, her "goods" are closely related to Samsung's VCRs. Indeed, the ad itself reinforced the relationship by informing its readers that they would be taping the "longest-running game show" on Samsung's VCRs well into the future.

The third factor, "similarity of the marks," both supports and contradicts a finding of likelihood of confusion. On the one hand, all of the aspects of the robot ad identify White; on the other, the figure is quite clearly a robot, not a human. This ambiguity means that we must look to the other factors for resolution.

The fourth factor does not favor White's claim because she has presented no evidence of actual confusion.

Fifth, however, White has appeared in the same stance as the robot from the ad in numerous magazines, including the covers of some. Magazines were used as the marketing channels for the robot ad. This factor cuts toward a likelihood of confusion.

Sixth, consumers are not likely to be particularly careful in determining who endorses VCRs, making confusion as to their endorsement more likely.

Concerning the seventh factor, "defendant's intent," the district court found that, in running the robot ad, the defendants had intended a spoof of the "Wheel of Fortune." The relevant question is whether the defendants "intended to profit by confusing consumers" concerning the endorsement of Samsung VCRs. *Toho,* 645 F.2d 788. We do not disagree that defendants intended to spoof Vanna White and "Wheel of Fortune." That does not preclude, however, the possibility that defendants also intended to confuse consumers regarding endorsement. The robot ad was one of a series of ads run by defendants which followed the same theme. Another ad in the series depicted Morton Downey Jr. as a presidential candidate in the year 2008. Doubtless, defendants intended to spoof presidential elections and Mr. Downey through this ad. Consumers, however, would likely believe, and would be correct in so believing, that Mr. Downey was paid for his permission and was endorsing Samsung products. Looking at the series of advertisements as a whole, a jury could reasonably conclude that beneath the surface humor of the series lay an intent to persuade consumers that celebrity Vanna White, like celebrity Downey, was endorsing Samsung products.

Finally, the eighth factor, "likelihood of expansion of the product lines," does not appear apposite to a celebrity endorsement case such as this.

Application of the *Sleekcraft* factors to this case indicates that the district court erred in rejecting White's Lanham Act claim at the summary judgment stage. In so concluding, we emphasize two facts, however. First, construing the motion papers in White's favor, as we must, we hold only that White has raised a genuine issue of material fact concerning a likelihood of confusion as to her endorsement. Whether White's Lanham Act claim should succeed is a matter for the jury. Second, we stress that we reach this conclusion in light of the peculiar facts of this case. In particular, we note that the robot ad identifies White and was part of a series of ads in which other celebrities participated and were paid for their endorsement of Samsung's products. . . .

## V.  CONCLUSION

In remanding this case, we hold only that White has pleaded claims which can go to the jury for its decision.

## Comments

1. *State Statutory and Common Law Rights.* Approximately a dozen states recognize a right of publicity by statute. More, but certainly not all, recognize the right as a matter of common law. Within those states recognizing the right, there is considerable variation on questions such as whether the right descends from a celebrity to his or her heirs and whether a person must have exploited his identity for commercial purposes while alive. Those states rejecting the right of publicity often cite First Amendment concerns.

The difference between the California statute and the California common law was crucial to the court's analysis in *White v. Samsung Electronics America, Inc*. While violation of the statute could be based only on use of certain manifestations of the celebrity's persona (name, likeness, etc.), the common law right was based on use of the celebrity's *identity* without regard to whether the name or likeness was used.

The evolution of the publicity tort also reflects these differences. The Restatement (Second) of Torts §652C recognized the interest in being free from another's appropriating the one's name or likeness. The Restatement (Third) of Unfair Competition §46 focuses directly on the commercial aspect of the person's identity:

> One who appropriates the commercial value of a person's identity by using without consent the person's name, likeness, *or other indicia of identity* for purposes of trade is subject to liability for the relief appropriate under the rules stated in §§48 and 49. (Emphasis added)

Sections 48 and 49 of the Restatement (Third) recognize the right to remedial relief in the form of an injunction or damages, as measured either by the plaintiff's loss or the defendant's ill-gotten gains.

2. *Commercial Use Focus.* While the California statute in *White* refers to use of the celebrity's name, likeness, etc. "for purposes of advertising or selling," the common law refers to use of the plaintiff's identity "to defendant's advantage, commercial or otherwise." In one case where the court thought this distinction made a difference, an artist had drawn charcoal sketches of The Three Stooges and printed them on t-shirts. *See Comedy III Productions, Inc. v. Gary Saderup, Inc.*, 106 Cal. Rptr. 2d 126 (2001). The statute in question had originally included only use "for purposes of advertising or solicitation." The defendant argued that use on t-shirts were not for that purpose. The court noted that the statute had been amended to include use "on or in products," which included the likeness placed on t-shirts.

The Restatement (Third) §46 reflects the broader common law view that a plaintiff must prove that the defendant used the name to obtain a commercial advantage. In *Doe v. TCI Cablevision*, 110 S.W.3d 363 (Mo. 2003), the Missouri Supreme Court interpreted this language as requiring that the defendant intended to derive commercial advantage from exploitation of the plaintiff's celebrity identity. It is not enough that the defendant incidentally derived commercial advantage. The defendant in *Doe* was the producer of the comic book *Spawn*, which is about a CIA assassin who died and made a deal with the devil to perform violent acts on earth. A character in the book was based on Tony Twist, a St. Louis Blues hockey player who made a reputation as a tough guy enforcer, who beat up on opposing players. Because the defendant admitted that the character was based on Twist and marketed the book to hockey fans, the jury could find that the defendant intended to derive commercial advantage.

3. *State and Federal Rights: Incomplete Overlap of §43(a) and Right of Publicity.* In the right of publicity discussion in *White*, there is no mention of facts establishing that consumers might be mislead or erroneously believe that Vanna White was endorsing Samsung's products. The focus is only on whether the defendants exploited her valuable identity. Such an analysis is critical, however, to the familiar Lanham Act §43(a) claim. In that part of the case, the court adapted the traditional likelihood of confusion factors for this celebrity endorsement context. While the outcome of the court's analysis of each claim was the same, reversing the grant of summary judgment to the defendant, the rationales and analyses were quite different.

### THEORY PERSPECTIVE
## Right of Publicity and First Amendment Concerns

The importance of celebrities in our culture suggests that giving a private right to their identities may raise First Amendment concerns. Public prominence invites creative comment, some of which may be done for commercial purposes. In a case involving the use of the likeness the comedy team known as "The Three Stooges" on t-shirts, the California Supreme Court acknowledged that "the right of publicity has the potential of censoring significant expression by suppressing alternative versions of celebrity images that are iconoclastic, irreverent, or otherwise attempt to redefine the celebrity's meaning." *See Comedy III Productions, Inc. v. Gary Saderup, Inc.*, 21 P.3d 797 (2001), citing Michael Madow, *Private Ownership of Public Image: Popular Culture and Publicity Rights*, 81 CAL. L. REV. 125 (1993). Madow observed that celebrities "symbolize individual aspirations, group identities, and cultural values" and thus are "important expressive and communicative resources." Id. at 128. The court struck the balance between First Amendment interests and the right of publicity in the *Three Stooges* case by concluding that Moe and Jerome (Curly) Howard and Larry Fein had invested a great deal in developing their celebrity while the t-shirt maker did little creative work that transformed the meaning of the celebrities in a way that should be protected as expression.

# 4

# Trademark Defenses

A trademark owner bringing an infringement action must establish that its mark is valid and that it has an exclusive right to use the mark. In a cancellation proceeding, a registered trademark owner must defend its mark's validity and its right to use the mark. Anyone who believes he will be damaged by the existing registration of a mark may bring a petition to cancel the registration. An owner's registered mark may be cancelled, according to Lanham Act §14, if the mark becomes generic, or is functional, or has been abandoned, or was otherwise obtained contrary to the provisions of Lanham Act §2, which specifies what types of marks are registrable. In both the infringement action and the cancellation proceeding, the fact of registration gives the mark holder evidentiary advantages over the owner of a nonregistered mark.

Under Lanham Act §33(a), the registration gives the trademark owner prima facie, but not conclusive, evidence of the validity of the mark and its exclusive right to use the mark in connection with specified goods or services. This evidentiary advantage may aid the owner's case regardless of whether it is the plaintiff in an infringement action—a so-called "offensive" use—or defending its mark in a cancellation proceeding—a "defensive" use.

*STATUTE:* **Registration on Principal Register as Evidence of Exclusive Right to Use Mark; Defenses**
15 U.S.C. §1115 (Lanham Act §33)

The evidentiary value of registration is increased if the trademark obtains "incontestability" status through five years on continuous use, as specified in Lanham Act §15. Incontestability serves as *conclusive* evidence of the mark's validity and the owner's right to use the mark. *See* Lanham Act §33b. The incontestability provision of Lanham Act §15 provides a defense available to mark owners in a cancellation proceeding. The first part of this chapter examines the incontestability provisions.

Alleged infringers may also take advantage of various defenses, which are available even if the mark they allegedly infringed was incontestable. These defenses are enumerated in Lanham Act §33(b). Many of those defenses have been discussed in previous chapters. Grounds for cancellation of a mark, such as fraudulent registration, abandonment of a mark, and genericide are also defenses. In addition, there are equitable defenses, which might arise if the plaintiff waited too long to assert its rights (laches) or misused its mark, such as to violate the antitrust laws. The defenses enumerated in Lanham Act §33 had a long prior history in the common law. Section B of this chapter focuses on the defense of fair use, which allows others to use a mark to describe their own goods or to refer to the mark owner's goods. The cases illustrate the breadth of common law development of the notion of what uses are "descriptive" and "fair."

# A. INCONTESTABILITY

*STATUTE:* **Incontestability of Right to Use Mark under
Certain Conditions**
15 U.S.C. §1065 (Lanham Act §15)

Lanham Act §33 describes the evidentiary value of the presumptions arising from the mere fact of registration (prima facie evidence) and from obtaining the status of incontestability (conclusive evidence) under Lanham Act §15. Courts generally recognized that parties could rely on the incontestability of their marks as conclusive evidence of validity and ownership defensively, to defend their marks in cancellation proceedings. The United States Courts of Appeal were split on whether a mark owner could use the presumptions arising from incontestable status both defensively in a cancellation proceeding and offensively in an infringement action. In the Supreme Court's opinion in *Park 'N Fly, Inc. v. Dollar Park and Fly, Inc.*, the Court resolved this split. In *Park 'N Fly*, the Court also considered the grounds on which a person charged with infringement could challenge the validity of an incontestable mark. Reviewing the provisions of Lanham Act §§15 and 33, the Supreme Court established the scope of protection given by incontestability status.

## PARK 'N FLY, INC. v. DOLLAR PARK AND FLY, INC.
### 469 U.S. 189 (1985)

Justice O'CONNOR.

In this case we consider whether an action to enjoin the infringement of an incontestable trade or service mark may be defended on the grounds that the mark is merely descriptive. We conclude that neither the language of the relevant statutes nor the legislative history supports such a defense.

Petitioner operates long-term parking lots near airports. After starting business in St. Louis in 1967, petitioner subsequently opened facilities in Cleveland, Houston, Boston, Memphis, and San Francisco. Petitioner applied in 1969 to the United States Patent and Trademark Office (Patent Office) to register a service mark consisting of the logo of an airplane and the words "Park 'N Fly." The registration issued in August 1971. Nearly six years later, petitioner filed an affidavit with the Patent Office to establish the incontestable status of the mark. As required by 15 U.S.C. §1065, the affidavit stated that the mark had been registered and in continuous use for five consecutive years, that there had been no final adverse decision to petitioner's claim of ownership or right to registration, and that no proceedings involving such rights were pending. Incontestable status provides, subject to the provisions of §15 and §33(b) of the Lanham Act, "conclusive evidence of the registrant's exclusive right to use the registered mark...." §33(b), 15 U.S.C. §1115(b).

Respondent also provides long-term airport parking services, but only has operations in Portland, Oregon. Respondent calls its business "Dollar Park and Fly." Petitioner filed this infringement action in 1978 in the United States District Court for the District of Oregon and requested the court permanently to enjoin respondent from using the words "Park and Fly" in connection with its business. Respondent counterclaimed and sought cancellation of petitioner's mark on the grounds that it is a generic term. Respondent also argued that petitioner's mark is unenforceable because it is merely descriptive. As two additional defenses, respondent maintained that it is in privity with a Seattle corporation that has used the expression "Park and Fly" since a date prior to the registration of petitioner's mark and that it has not infringed because there is no likelihood of confusion.

After a bench trial, the District Court found that petitioner's mark is not generic and observed that an incontestable mark cannot be challenged on the grounds that it is merely descriptive. The District Court also concluded that there was no evidence of privity between respondent and the Seattle corporation. Finally, the District Court found sufficient evidence of likelihood of confusion. The District Court permanently enjoined respondent from using the words "Park and Fly" and any other mark confusingly similar to "Park 'N Fly." The Court of Appeals for the Ninth Circuit reversed. The District Court did not err, the Court of Appeals held, in refusing to invalidate petitioner's mark. The Court of Appeals noted, however, that it previously had held that incontestability provides a defense against the cancellation of a mark, but it may not be used offensively to enjoin another's use. Petitioner, under this analysis, could obtain an injunction only if its mark would be entitled to continued registration without regard to its incontestable status. Thus, respondent could defend the infringement action by showing that the mark was merely descriptive. Based on its own examination of the record, the Court of Appeals then determined that petitioner's mark is in fact merely descriptive, and therefore respondent should not be enjoined from using the name "Park and Fly."

The decision below is in direct conflict with the decision of the Court of Appeals for the Seventh Circuit in *Union Carbide Corp. v. Ever-Ready Inc.*, 531 F.2d 366, cert. denied, 429 U.S. 830 (1976). We granted certiorari to resolve this conflict, 465 U.S. 1078 (1984), and we now reverse.

Congress enacted the Lanham Act in 1946 in order to provide national protection for trademarks used in interstate and foreign commerce. Previous federal legislation, such as the Federal Trademark Act of 1905, reflected the view that protection of trademarks was a matter of state concern and that the right to a mark depended solely on the common law. S. Rep. No. 1333, at 5. Consequently, rights to trademarks were uncertain and subject to variation in different parts of the country. Because trademarks desirably promote competition and the maintenance of product quality, Congress determined that "a sound public policy requires that trademarks should receive nationally the greatest protection that can be given them." *Id.*, at 6. Among the new protections created by the Lanham Act were the statutory provisions that allow a federally registered mark to become incontestable.

The provisions of the Lanham Act concerning registration and incontestability distinguish a mark that is "the common descriptive name of an article or substance" from a mark that is "merely descriptive." Marks that constitute a common descriptive name are referred to as generic. A generic term is one that refers to the genus of which the particular product is a species. Generic terms are not registrable, and a registered mark may be canceled at any time on the grounds that it has become generic. A "merely descriptive" mark, in contrast, describes the qualities or characteristics of a good or service, and this type of mark may be registered only if the registrant shows that it has acquired secondary meaning, *i.e.*, it "has become distinctive of the applicant's goods in commerce."

This case requires us to consider the effect of the incontestability provisions of the Lanham Act in the context of an infringement action defended on the grounds that the mark is merely descriptive. Statutory construction must begin with the language employed by Congress and the assumption that the ordinary meaning of that language accurately expresses the legislative purpose. With respect to incontestable trade or service marks, §33(b) of the Lanham Act states that "registration shall be conclusive evidence of the registrant's exclusive right to use the registered mark" subject to the conditions of §15 and certain enumerated defenses. Section 15 incorporates by reference subsections (c) and (e) of §14, 15 U.S.C. §1064 [now labeled subsections (3) and (5)]. An incontestable mark that becomes generic may be canceled at any time pursuant to §14(c) [now §14(3)]. That section also allows cancellation of an incontestable mark at any time if it has been abandoned, if it is being used to misrepresent the source of the goods or services in connection with which it is used, or if it was obtained fraudulently or contrary to the provisions of §4, 15 U.S.C. §1054, or §§2(a)-(c), 15 U.S.C. §§1052(a)-(c).

One searches the language of the Lanham Act in vain to find any support for the offensive/defensive distinction applied by the Court of Appeals. The statute nowhere distinguishes between a registrant's offensive and defensive use of an incontestable mark. On the contrary, §33(b)'s declaration that the registrant has an "exclusive right" to use the mark indicates that incontestable status may be used to enjoin infringement by others. A conclusion that such infringement cannot be enjoined renders meaningless the "exclusive right" recognized by the statute. Moreover, the language in three of the defenses enumerated in §33(b) clearly contemplates the use of incontestability in infringement actions by plaintiffs.

The language of the Lanham Act also refutes any conclusion that an incontestable mark may be challenged as merely descriptive. A mark that is merely descriptive of an applicant's goods or services is not registrable unless the mark has secondary meaning. Before a mark achieves incontestable status, registration provides prima facie evidence of the registrant's exclusive right to use the mark in commerce. The Lanham Act expressly provides that before a mark becomes incontestable an opposing party may prove any legal or equitable defense which might have been asserted if the mark had not been registered. Thus, §33(a) would have allowed respondent to challenge petitioner's mark as merely descriptive if the mark had not become incontestable. With respect to incontestable marks, however, §33(b) provides that registration is *conclusive* evidence of the registrant's exclusive right to use the mark, subject to the conditions of §15 and the seven defenses enumerated in §33(b) itself. Mere descriptiveness is not recognized by either §15 or §33(b) as a basis for challenging an incontestable mark.

The statutory provisions that prohibit registration of a merely descriptive mark but do not allow an incontestable mark to be challenged on this ground cannot be attributed to inadvertence by Congress. The Conference Committee rejected an amendment that would have denied registration to any descriptive mark, and instead retained the provisions allowing registration of a merely descriptive mark that has acquired secondary meaning. The Conference Committee agreed to an amendment providing that no incontestable right can be acquired in a mark that is a common descriptive, *i.e.,* generic, term. Congress could easily have denied incontestability to merely descriptive marks as well as to generic marks had that been its intention. . . .

Nothing in the legislative history of the Lanham Act supports a departure from the plain language of the statutory provisions concerning incontestability. Indeed, a conclusion that incontestable status can provide the basis for enforcement of the registrant's exclusive right to use a trade or service mark promotes the goals of the statute. The Lanham Act provides national protection of trademarks in order to secure to the owner of the mark the goodwill of his business and to protect the ability of consumers to distinguish among competing producers. National protection of trademarks is desirable, Congress concluded, because trademarks foster competition and the maintenance of quality by securing to the producer the benefits of good reputation. The incontestability provisions, as the proponents of the Lanham Act emphasized, provide a means for the registrant to quiet title in the ownership of his mark. The opportunity to obtain incontestable status by satisfying the requirements of §15 thus encourages producers to cultivate the goodwill associated with a particular mark. This function of the incontestability provisions would be utterly frustrated if the holder of an incontestable mark could not enjoin infringement by others so long as they established that the mark would not be registrable but for its incontestable status.

Respondent argues, however, that enforcing petitioner's mark would conflict with the goals of the Lanham Act because the mark is merely descriptive and should never have been registered in the first place. . . .

Respondent's argument that enforcing petitioner's mark will not promote the goals of the Lanham Act is misdirected. Arguments similar to those now urged by respondent were in fact considered by Congress in hearings on the Lanham Act. For example, the United States Department of Justice opposed the incontestability provisions and expressly noted that a merely descriptive mark might become incontestable. This result, the Department of Justice observed, would "go beyond existing law in conferring unprecedented rights on trade-mark owners," and would undesirably create an exclusive right to use language that is descriptive of a product. These concerns were answered by proponents of the Lanham Act, who noted that a merely descriptive mark cannot be registered unless the Commissioner finds that it has secondary meaning. Moreover, a mark can be challenged for five years prior to its attaining incontestable status. The supporters of the incontestability provisions further observed that a generic mark cannot become incontestable and that §33(b)(4) allows the nontrademark use of descriptive terms used in an incontestable mark.

The alternative of refusing to provide incontestable status for descriptive marks with secondary meaning was expressly noted in the hearings on the Lanham Act....Also mentioned was the possibility of including as a defense to infringement of an incontestable mark the "fact that a mark is a descriptive, generic, or geographical term or device." Hearings on S. 895 before the Subcommittee of the Senate Committee on Patents, 77th Cong., 2d Sess., 45, 47 (1942). Congress, however, did not adopt either of these alternatives. Instead, Congress expressly provided in §§33(b) and 15 that an incontestable mark could be challenged on specified grounds, and the grounds identified by Congress do not include mere descriptiveness....

We conclude that the holder of a registered mark may rely on incontestability to enjoin infringement and that such an action may not be defended on the grounds that the mark is merely descriptive. Respondent urges that we nevertheless affirm the decision below based on the "prior use" defense recognized by §33(b)(5) of the Lanham Act. Alternatively, respondent argues that there is no likelihood of confusion and therefore no infringement justifying injunctive relief. The District Court rejected each of these arguments, but they were not addressed by the Court of Appeals. That court may consider them on remand. The judgment of the Court of Appeals is reversed, and the case is remanded for further proceedings consistent with this opinion.

## Comments

*1. Goals of the Incontestability Provisions.* The Supreme Court compared the incontestability provision to the real property action to quiet title. An action to quiet title is a proceeding to establish a plaintiff's right to land by compelling another to establish their competing claim or be forever estopped from asserting it. In real property law, quieting title encourages a land owner to invest in developing the land by ensuring that he or she will be able to enjoy the benefits of that investment. The opportunity to obtain incontestable status by satisfying the requirements of Lanham Act §15 encourages registration because registration is necessary to obtain the conclusive presumption of validity and exclusive right to use the mark. Incontestability also encourages producers to cultivate the goodwill associated with their marks because the conclusive presumption provides greater protection for the investment against challenges by others. *Park 'N Fly* illustrates the greater protection provided to incontestable marks by preventing a challenge to the complainant's mark on the basis that it is merely descriptive.

Owning an incontestable mark may also help in the registration process. An organizer, arranger, and sponsor of sailing races filed an application to register RETURN OF THE TALL SHIPS as a mark for its services. The examining attorney found that the term "tall ships" was merely descriptive of the types of boats that sail in those races and required that the applicant disclaim any right to those words. The TTAB reversed the finding because the applicant also owned an incontestable mark for TALL SHIPS for identical services, which raised a conclusive presumption that the term was not merely descriptive. *See In re The American Sail Training Association*, 230 U.S.P.Q. 879 (Trademark Tr. and App. Bd. 1986). The services or goods to which the applicant intends to apply the mark must be identical or the PTO will consider the descriptiveness of the term *de novo*.

2. *Validity and Strength.* Incontestable status confers a conclusive presumption of validity and exclusive right to use a mark in connection with specified goods or services. In an infringement action, these elements are distinct from the question of whether the defendant's use of a term is likely to cause confusion. In all federal circuit courts, the strength of the plaintiff's mark is a factor in determining whether confusion is likely to occur. The "strength" of a mark is its tendency to identify the goods sold under the mark as emanating from a particular producer. Just because a mark is valid does not necessarily mean that it is strong. While some courts hold that incontestability status is some evidence of strength, most courts hold that the strength of a mark should be determined independently from whether the mark is incontestable. Thus, while PARK 'N FLY is a valid mark, it might get little protection from competitors' similar uses because it describes the services the mark owner supplies.

3. *Defenses and Rebuttals.* Courts use the term "defense" rather loosely in trademark law. These arguments should not be understood to be "affirmative defenses," as that term is typically used. For instance, the Supreme Court in *Park 'N Fly* identified two "additional defenses": (1) Dollar Park and Fly's assertion that it was in privity with a corporation whose use of the term "Park and Fly" was senior to the complainant's use and (2) Dollar Park and Fly's assertion that there was no likelihood of confusion. These are reasons why the complainant has no valid case because the complainant must prove a senior right to use the mark and that confusion is likely. These assertions are better understood as attempts to rebut the complainant's case.

In understanding the distinction between a defense and a rebuttal it may help to consider an analogy to another area of tort law. In a negligence case, a defendant may argue that it was not negligent. Because negligence is part of the plaintiff's case, the defendant's argument is a rebuttal of that claim. Such assertions are not "affirmative defenses." Affirmative defenses are assertions of facts and arguments that, if true, will defeat the complainant's claim even if all of the allegations in the complaint are true. In tort law, contributory or comparative negligence are affirmative defenses because they prevent (or reduce) the defendant's liability even if the plaintiff's allegations are true. The distinction between rebuttal arguments and affirmative defenses is not crucial to the issues raised in *Park 'N Fly* but the failure to distinguish among them has caused considerable confusion in applying the fair use defenses in §33(b)(4) that are discussed in the remainder of this chapter.

**4. *Exceptions to Incontestability.*** Obtaining incontestability status does not automatically eliminate all grounds on which a trademark may be challenged. A registered trademark may infringe on another's valid right, even if it is otherwise incontestable, and may be challenged on any of the grounds identified in Lanham Act §14(3) and (5). Lanham Act §14(3) includes the following bases for cancelling a trademark that also prevent a mark from obtaining incontestable status: the mark has become generic, is functional, has been abandoned, or was used to misrepresent the source of the goods or services. It also permits cancellation of marks that were obtained fraudulently or contrary to the provisions of Lanham Act §4, which describes when collective and certification marks are registrable, or Lanham Act §2(a), (b), or (c), prohibiting registration of certain trademarks and service marks such as marks consisting of immoral, deceptive, disparaging matter, flags, or names of living people without their consent. Lanham Act §14(5) describes when certification marks may be cancelled. Grounds on which a mark may be denied registration but do not prevent a mark from becoming incontestable include the fact that the mark is merely descriptive, deceptively misdescriptive, primarily geographically descriptive, or primarily a surname. In addition to these exceptions, a party charged with infringement of an incontestable mark may be able to rely on any of the nine "defenses or defects" listed in Lanham Act §33(b), some of which overlap with the exceptions (e.g., §33(b)(1), (2), (3), (5), (6), and (8)). The following section of this chapter focuses on Lanham Act §33(b)(4), a collection of "defenses" that fall under the broad category of "fair use."

## B. FAIR USE DEFENSES

A dominant goal of trademark law is preventing consumers from being confused about source. In addition, infringement and dilution actions protect the goodwill of mark owners, which encourages mark owners to invest in their reputation and the consistency of quality of their goods. The fair use provisions of Lanham Act §33(b)(4) reflect goals that may conflict with both consumers' interests in freedom from confusion about source and mark owners' interests in protecting the goodwill of their marks. Although §33(b)(4) is addressed to incontestable marks, the fair use defenses apply equally to unregistered marks, registered marks that are not incontestable, and trade dress.

*STATUTE:* **Incontestability; Defenses**
15 U.S.C. §1115(b)(4) (Lanham Act §33(b)(4))

Among the interests that may conflict with these goals are: promoting competition in product and service markets, informing consumers about the nature and characteristics of competing goods, and protecting freedom of expression. Each of these interests is reflected in the fair use defense. Conflicting uses arise in many ways, though most may be analyzed by one of the five approaches discussed in this section. The common thread in each type of fair use is that the alleged infringer has used a device to describe or comment on either its own goods or services or the mark owner's goods or services. Thus, all fit into the language of Lanham Act §33(b)(4) referring to use of a term "which is descriptive of and used fairly and in good faith only to describe" goods and services.

Different tests have emerged for each type of fair use. For each type, courts have found different ways to accommodate the policy considerations that compete with the basic goals of preventing confusion and protecting goodwill. Because the law is still evolving in the fair use area, it is essential to recognize the relevant policy considerations in each case. To understand each test, it helps to figure out whether the test creates a means for rebutting the mark owner's claim or an affirmative defense that absolves the alleged infringer of liability even if the mark owner's allegations are true.

## 1. Classic Fair Use

The fair use defense that fits the mold of "descriptive use" most closely is called "classic" fair use. In these cases, an alleged infringer has typically used words for their customary purpose, e.g., to describe the qualities or characteristics of its own product or service. The mark owner complains that the words are confusingly similar to its mark. For instance, the registered owner of the mark SUPERSWEET, used in connection with digital compact disks and digital DVDs, might complain if Hershey's used the words "super sweet" to describe one of its candy bars. The alleged infringer's response, as permitted by Lanham Act §33(b)(4), is that it is not using the term as a source-indicating mark but only to describe its goods, which it is entitled to do.

*Sunmark, Inc. v. Ocean Spray Cranberries, Inc.* considers the balance between preventing confusion and allowing other suppliers to use descriptive terms to inform consumers about their products. On one hand, trademark law is intended to prevent confusion about source and to protect the mark owner's goodwill. On the other hand, suppliers must be able to use the English language to describe their goods.

Courts have three logical options when designing rules governing fair use. They could (1) adopt a balancing test that considers the benefits and costs of permitting another to use a term descriptively; (2) consider the nature of the descriptive use when evaluating the likelihood of confusion; or (3) permit descriptive uses regardless of whether they were likely to cause confusion. Under either the first or third options, classic fair use is an affirmative defense that may absolve the alleged infringer of liability even if the mark owner proves the elements of an infringement claim. Under the second option, the classic fair use argument is used in rebuttal of the mark owner's claim. These three options are available in each of the five types of fair use defenses. Courts have not always chosen the same option for each type.

## SUNMARK, INC. v. OCEAN SPRAY CRANBERRIES, INC.
### 64 F.3d 1055 (7th Cir. 1995)

EASTERBROOK, Circuit Judge.

Sunmark produces *Swee*TARTS, a popular fruit-flavored sugar candy most often sold in a tablet form similar to a brightly colored aspirin. Ocean Spray Cranberries produces a variety of sugar-flavored cranberry juice drinks that they often advertise as tasting sweet and tart — or "sweet-tart." For want of a conjunction, Sunmark prays for an injunction; unhappy with the hyphenated version of the description, it has sued under the Lanham Act and the Illinois Anti-Dilution Act. After a three-day evidentiary hearing, a magistrate judge disparaged Sunmark's chances of prevailing on the merits. The district judge delivered a brief oral opinion that essentially adopted the magistrate judge's report, and he refused to grant a preliminary injunction.

Since 1963 *Swee*TARTS candy has been sold with this logo:

The "Swee" is rendered in bright blue, the "ARTS" in magenta; the "T" in the middle is divided between the two colors.

Ocean Spray has advertised its juices as "sweet-tart" sporadically since 1942. The two campaigns with the most media exposure drew objections from Sunmark or one of its predecessors (collectively Sunmark). A 1973 television commercial for Ocean Spray cranapple juice featured a Mounty and a maiden singing "Sweet-Tart" to the tune of "Sweetheart, Sweetheart, Sweetheart". Sunmark asked Ocean Spray to discontinue use of "sweet-tart." (The record does not reveal whether Nelson Eddy or the Royal Canadian Mounted Police registered a complaint. Now that the Mounties have appointed Disney as a marketing agent, Ocean Spray has more than Sunmark to be concerned about.) Ocean Spray responded that it saw no reason to quit using words it viewed as descriptive, and it continued running the commercials until the end of the campaign several months later. While it continued to use "sweet-tart" in newspaper advertising from time to time, Ocean Spray did not again use the term in any broadcast advertising until 1991.

That year Ocean Spray decided to distinguish its cranberry products from other juice drinks by making "sweet-tart" the centerpiece of its advertising. Television commercials featured actors' faces saying "sweet-tart" — sometimes with a pause, sometimes without — over a background jingle while the two words were superimposed on the screen. Sometimes color blocks surrounded the letters in sweet and tart, sometimes not. Sometimes the words were rendered in block letters, and sometimes tart was in oblique letters. The phrases "A Sweet Tart of a Deal", "Sweet-Tart Savings", and "Get the Sweet-Tart Taste of Ocean Spray" appeared in newspaper coupons. For two years, Sunmark and its predecessors negotiated with Ocean

Spray. Unwilling to accept the (minor) concessions Ocean Spray offered, Sunmark sued in 1993 under the Lanham Act and the Illinois Anti-Dilution Act. [This court rejected the state dilution claim because Sunmark failed to show that its descriptive mark had secondary meaning.]

The initial question is whether Ocean Spray used Sunmark's mark at all. If it employed the words "sweet" and "tart" simply as descriptions, and "otherwise than as a mark," it didn't, and there can be no violation of the Lanham Act under what is known as the fair use defense. This is a factual question, and therefore our review of the district court's findings is deferential. Section 1115(b)(4) also requires that the use be in good faith; Sunmark does not seriously dispute the district court's finding that Ocean Spray did not act in bad faith.

The district court found the words sweet and tart, and their conjunction, to be descriptive, although it acknowledged that the *Swee*TARTS logo cannot be called descriptive. Sunmark objects strenuously, arguing that sweet-tart is an oxymoron and therefore cannot be descriptive. Although an earlier litigation called the predecessor "Sweetarts" mark "uncommon, arbitrary, and distinct", *Sweetarts v. Sunline, Inc.*, 380 F.2d 923, 927 (8th Cir. 1967), the question in this litigation is not whether "sweet-tart" or the *Swee*TARTS logo is an arbitrary mark when used to describe Sunmark's candy — or, as in the eighth circuit's case, an entire corporation that sold many items including products not normally thought of as tart, like butter toffees and mixed chocolates. Instead the question is whether Ocean Spray has used "sweet-tart" descriptively, for a drink that has elements of both sweetness (it is sugared) and tartness (it is based on cranberries). Both sweet and tart are words of description in ordinary English, quite unlike words such as "Exxon" or "Kodak."

*[handwritten margin notes: "No", "Real ISSUE"]*

Under the Lanham Act it is irrelevant whether the *Swee*TARTS mark is itself descriptive, and the district court did not need to pursue the question. The potential descriptive nature of "sweet-tart" does not divest Sunmark of any rights to protect its mark "*Swee*TARTS", for that mark is incontestable under 15 U.S.C. §1065. "*Swee*TARTS" is no longer subject to challenge with respect to the products to which it applies, whether or not the mark is descriptive. . . .

That *Swee*TARTS is an incontestable mark for sugar candy does not make Sunmark the gatekeeper of these words for the whole food industry. Consider what would happen if a farm started selling apples under the FLUFFY APPLE mark. "Fluffy" is a fanciful description of an apple. Let us suppose it became well known, even incontestable, and that no one else could apply the word "fluffy" to an apple, or even to an orange. Would the vendor then be able to stop General Mills from advertising that you can make fluffy cakes from its batter? . . .

The question under §1115(b)(4) is whether "sweet-tart" is descriptive *as Ocean Spray uses it.* "Sweet" is adjectival. "Tart" is adjectival. Sunmark concedes that "sweet and tart" is descriptive. The district court found that "sweet-tart" meets the bill as well, at least for a product having both attributes. For a word or mark to be considered descriptive it merely needs to refer to a characteristic of the product. The eighth circuit put a great deal of weight on the fact that "sweet-tart" is not in the dictionary. Language often outpaces dictionaries; phrases such as "sports drink," and "hard drive" could not be found in a 1967 dictionary, but we would not be under an obligation to consider them arbitrary today. In 1990, a full year before Ocean Spray began the advertising campaign that Sunmark complains of here, eight *New York Times* writers used the phrase "sweet-tart" in eleven articles. In comparison, only three 1990 *New York Times* stories used the adjective "chocolatey", which does appear in the dictionary, and only one *New York Times* story in 1990 referred to the candy *SweeTarts*.

Is there anything more to the Lanham Act inquiry? "The use of a similar name by another to truthfully describe his own product does not constitute a legal or moral wrong, even if its effect be to cause the public to mistake the origin of the product." *William R. Warner & Co. v. Eli Lilly & Co.*, 265 U.S. 526, 528 (1924). True, a number of courts have implied that confusion is inconsistent with a fair use defense. But none of these cases acknowledges *William R. Warner* or asks how an accurate description can be objectionable. At all events, none of these cases dealt with unrelated products. *Zatarains Inc. v. Oak Grove Smokehouse, Inc.*, 698 F.2d 786, 791 (5th Cir.1983), for example, involved two products for frying fish, one with the mark FISH-FRI, the other identified as a "fish fry". When the products involved are similar, "likelihood of confusion" may amount to using a word in a "misleading" way, violating 15 U.S.C. §1125(a)(1) — not because the likelihood of confusion makes the use nondescriptive, but because the confusion about the product's source shows that the words are being used, de facto, as a mark. And the defense is available only to one who uses the words of description "otherwise than as a mark". . . .

Even if we assume that some of the ways Ocean Spray deployed "sweet-tart" to sell juices have the status of a trademark, Sunmark cannot prevail without demonstrating a likelihood of confusion. The district court found that Sunmark had not carried its burden on this subject. Likelihood of confusion in a trademark case is a factual issue; again, appellate review is deferential. The magistrate judge considered the evidence and concluded that Sunmark had not demonstrated a likelihood of confusion; the district judge agreed. We do not think this conclusion clearly erroneous. The whole of the evidence presented in the district court came from Ocean Spray's marketing surveys: three of the 257 people shown one of the actual commercials (or a mock-up of it) reported that "sweet-tart" in the commercial referred to the candy. (Interestingly enough, these three found this a reason to *dislike* the commercial, indicating that Ocean Spray has a market incentive not to associate its product with *Swee*TARTS.) Three of 257 is not much confusion; indeed, it is remarkably low given the normal state of human comprehension of advertising and corporate organization.

We wouldn't put great weight on this survey if Ocean Spray had been the one to emphasize it, since it was a test of the effectiveness of the advertising on consumers rather than the customary survey in trademark cases showing the packaging or product to consumers and asking: "Who makes this?" or "Are these two products made by the same firm?" But the Ocean Spray survey was the only evidence of confusion that Sunmark presented. That is weak support for a preliminary injunction when Sunmark had three years to obtain better data — if any were obtainable. Perhaps the advertising is confusing after all. It may be that Sunmark can present more evidence, and that after a trial the record will support Sunmark's claims; the current record does not....

Having canvassed all of this, we need not get into additional questions such as irreparable injury and the balance of harms from errors during the period between interlocutory and final decision. Sunmark has not reached first base.

AFFIRMED.

## Comments

1. *Use as a Mark versus Use Only to Describe.* Lanham Act §33(b)(4) presents three factors relevant to the fair use defense: (1) the alleged infringer must use the "name, term, or device" "otherwise than as a mark"; (2) the alleged infringer must use the term or device "only to describe" the goods and services; and (3) the alleged infringer must use the term "fairly and in good faith." The first issue presented, therefore, is whether the alleged infringer used the term "as a mark" or "only to describe." Was Ocean Spray attempting to have consumers associate the term "sweet-tart" with its product? Consider the variety of ways in which Ocean Spray made sweet-tart the centerpiece of its advertising. Is the term "sweet-tart" descriptive of Ocean Spray's goods? It does not matter whether the registered SWEETARTS trademark is descriptive or not; the issue is how Ocean Spray used the term. Even an arbitrary or fanciful mark may be used descriptively, as the court's "fluffy apple" example illustrates.

2. *Use That Is Fair and In Good Faith.* Although Lanham Act §33(b)(4) requires that the term be "used fairly and in good faith," courts typically combine discussion of fairness and good faith in all fair use contexts as if it were a single element. Courts equate a lack of good faith with the alleged infringer's intent to trade on the goodwill of the trademark holder by creating confusion as to source. For instance, Quaker Oats Company, the producer of Gatorade, used the slogan "Gatorade is Thirst Aid" in its advertising. When the owner of the THIRST AID mark objected, Quaker Oats responded that Gatorade does aid one's thirst so the term is used descriptively. In the infringement action, the court questioned the Quaker Oats Company's good faith noting the greater prominence given in advertisements to the term "Thirst Aid" than to Quaker Oats' own GATORADE mark. The rhyming in the slogan closely linked the term to the GATORADE mark, "increasing the misappropriation" of the plaintiff's mark. *See Sands, Taylor & Wood Co. v. Quaker Oats Co.*, 978 F.2d 947 (7th Cir. 1992).

Copying the typestyle, packaging, or labeling of the mark owner is also indicative of bad faith. A&P Imports, a mattress cover distributor, used the term "hygienic" on its covers, presumably to describe a characteristic of its goods. The term was, however, printed in the same typeface and located in the same place on the package as a manufacturer of competing mattress covers placed its registered HYGIENT mark and the covers were retailed side-by-side in the same size wrapper. The court held that the distributor was not entitled to use the descriptive fair use defense. *See Venetianaire Corp. v. A&P Import Co.*, 429 F.2d 1079 (2d Cir. 1970).

Observe how closely the good faith inquiry is tied to the issue of whether the term is used as a mark. The good faith inquiry led both appellate courts in the examples given above to uphold trial court findings that the term had been "used as a mark." "Use as a mark" is contrary to the requirements of the fair use defense and increases the likelihood of confusion.

**3. *Affirmative Defense or Rebuttal?*** In December 2004, the Supreme Court resolved a dispute among the federal circuit courts on how the descriptive fair use defense would be applied. The Ninth Circuit had held that to take advantage of the fair use defense, the alleged infringer must prove the absence of confusion. The Ninth Circuit's approach made a fair use claim an argument that rebuts the mark holder's evidence of confusion. Its logic was that use of a term "only to describe" cannot confuse consumers about source. By contrast, several federal circuit courts, including the Seventh Circuit in *Sunmark,* had held that the fair use defense applies even if there is some confusion. The Second Circuit had stated that any confusion resulting from a descriptive use was a risk assumed by the mark holder who selected a mark with descriptive attributes. The Seventh and Second Circuit's approach makes fair use an affirmative defense because there will be no infringement even if the mark holder can prove that confusion will result. In *KP Permanent Make-Up, Inc. v. Lasting Impression Inc.*, 328 F.3d 1061 (9th Cir. 2003), vacated and remanded, 543 U.S. ___, 125 S. Ct. 542 (2004), the Court held that the plaintiff must show likelihood of confusion as part of the prima facie case and that the defendant had no independent burden to show that there was no confusion when raising a fair use defense. In dictum, the Court observed that some possibility of confusion must be compatible with fair use to avoid someone having a complete monopoly of the descriptive meaning of words. It also observed, however, that the extent of likely consumer confusion might be relevant to assessing whether a defendant's descriptive use is objectively fair.

## Problem

**4-1.** A manufacturer of flat, cardboard, pine-tree-shaped air fresheners bearing the name "Little Tree," designed to hang from the mirror of automobiles, brought an action alleging that the manufacturer of Glade Plug-Ins room air fresheners infringed its mark, the pine tree shape. Glade Plug-Ins have a plastic casing that holds a replaceable fragrance cartridge of scented gel. When the unit is plugged in, the electrical current warms the gel, causing release of the fragrance into the air. During the Christmas holiday season, the manufacturer sells a pine-tree-scented, plug-in air freshener called "Holiday Pine Potpourri" under its GLADE PLUG-INS trademark. Assuming that the pine-tree shape is an incontestable trademark, would the manufacturer of Glade Plug-Ins be entitled to the fair use defense? *See Car-Freshener Corporation v. S.C. Johnson & Son, Inc.,* 70 F.3d 267 (2d Cir. 1995).

---

### THEORETICAL PERSPECTIVE
### Balancing Tests and Classic Fair Use

A logical alternative to the options presented by the Ninth Circuit's "rebuttal" approach to fair use and the Seventh and Second Circuits' "affirmative defense" approach is a balancing approach. A balancing approach considers the harms and benefits associated with descriptive use of another's mark. The potential harms from descriptive use are injury to the mark holder's goodwill by diminishing the source-identifying power of the mark and injury to consumers by source confusion. Harm to goodwill and confusion about source harms competition by discouraging mark holders from investing in the power of their marks to signal their products' qualities and characteristics. On the other hand, both sellers and consumers benefit and competition is enhanced by permitting descriptive use of trademarked terms. To compete effectively and to inform consumers about the qualities and characteristics of their products, sellers must be able to describe their products and have access to descriptive terms necessary to compete even if those terms are another's trademark. Consumers benefit from increased information and competition is enhanced by the ability of more sellers to compete effectively.

A balancing test for fair use would compare the harms resulting from damage to goodwill and to confused consumers to the benefits. The less the likely confusion and harm to goodwill and the more necessary the descriptive term is to effective competition, the more likely a court would find that the fair use defense protected the alleged infringer. The Supreme Court in *KP Permanent Make-Up* left open the possibility that a variety of factors, such as the likelihood of confusion, the commercial justification for the use, and the strength of the plaintiff's mark, could be considered when applying the fair use defense. Because the balancing approach would exculpate an alleged infringer even if some confusion was likely, it would be appropriately classified as an affirmative defense. *See* David Barnes & Teresa Laky, *Classic Fair Use: Confusion About Defenses,* 20 SANTA CLARA COMPUTER AND HIGH TECH. L.J. 833 (2004), for a complete discussion of the factors that might be considered in a balancing test.

---

## 2. Artistic or "First Amendment" Fair Use

Other types of fair use involve a person's use of another's mark to refer to the other or to the other's product. Examples of referential uses include artist Andy Warhol's use of CSC's CAMPBELL'S mark, used in connection with soups, to refer to an example of a common consumer item in a painting; a competing drug manufacturer's use of American Home Products' mark, ADVIL, used in connection with pain and cold medicines, to compare its product's efficacy, and Audi AG Corporation's use of Bose Corporation's BOSE mark, used in connection with speaker systems, to refer to a component of its AUDI automobiles.

Artistic or "First Amendment" fair use claims typically arise when an alleged infringer uses another's mark in producing an artistic work or when making fun of the mark holder or its product. One example of an artistic work using another's mark is the film "Debbie Does Dallas." The owner of the DALLAS COWBOYS CHEERLEADERS mark complained about advertising and scenes in the XXX-rated film depicting the movie's heroine in (and out of) a uniform strikingly similar to the mark holder's uniform and suggesting a connection with the mark holder. Similarly, the famous golfer, Tiger Woods, complained that use of his likeness in a painting infringed on his mark. Cases where mark holders complained about others making fun of their marks or products include the Mutual of Omaha insurance company complaining about use of "Mutant of Omaha" on t-shirts and coffee mugs, General Electric Company complaining about use of "Genital Electric" on clothing, and Coca-Cola Company complaining about "Enjoy Cocaine" on clothing in a logo similar to the familiar red and white Coca-Cola logo. As in all infringement cases, the mark holder's theory is that the alleged infringer's use of the trademark is likely to cause confusion about source or affiliation of the mark holder with the alleged infringer's product or service.

In the historical development of tests for artistic fair use, courts originally followed an "alternative avenues" approach, under which trademark rights were upheld as long as there were adequate alternative avenues of communication for the alleged infringer's message. In the "Debbie Does Dallas" case, the court found that the plaintiff had trademark rights in the uniform and that because there were numerous ways in which the makers of the movie could comment on "sexuality in athletics" without infringing the trademark, the district court did not violate the infringer's First Amendment rights by granting a preliminary injunction. In the "Mutant of Omaha" case, the court found that the t-shirt seller could use magazines, books, and films as alternatives ways to spread his anti-nuclear message. Some courts still follow this approach.

The modern approach to artistic fair use is illustrated in *Mattel, Inc. v. MCA Records, Inc.* The "artistic relevance" test is thought to be more accommodative of First Amendment interests. Consider whether it is a means of rebutting the plaintiff's evidence of confusion, whether confusion is irrelevant if there is a First Amendment interest, or whether the test is a balancing test.

## MATTEL, INC. v. MCA RECORDS, INC.
### 296 F.3d 894 (9th Cir. 2000)

KOZINSKI, Circuit Judge.

. . .

Barbie was born in Germany in the 1950s as an adult collector's item. Over the years, Mattel transformed her from a doll that resembled a "German street walker," as she originally appeared, into a glamorous, long-legged blonde. Barbie has been labeled both the ideal American woman and a bimbo. She has survived attacks both psychic (from feminists critical of her fictitious figure) and physical (more than 500 professional makeovers). She remains a symbol of American girlhood, a public figure who graces the aisles of toy stores throughout the country and beyond. With Barbie, Mattel created not just a toy but a cultural icon.

With fame often comes unwanted attention. Aqua is a Danish band that has, as yet, only dreamed of attaining Barbie-like status. In 1997, Aqua produced the song Barbie Girl on the album *Aquarium*. In the song, one bandmember impersonates Barbie, singing in a high-pitched, doll-like voice; another bandmember, calling himself Ken, entices Barbie to "go party." Barbie Girl singles sold well and, to Mattel's dismay, the song made it onto Top 40 music charts.

Mattel brought this lawsuit against the music companies who produced, marketed and sold Barbie Girl: MCA Records, Inc. [and others. Mattel appeals the District Court ruling that Barbie Girl is a fair use.]

A trademark is a word, phrase or symbol that is used to identify a manufacturer or sponsor of a good or the provider of a service. *New Kids on the Block v. News Am. Publ'g, Inc.*, 971 F.2d 302, 305 (9th Cir. 1992). It's the owner's way of preventing others from duping consumers into buying a product they mistakenly believe is sponsored by the trademark owner. A trademark "inform[s] people that trademarked products come from the same source," *Id.* at 305 n. 2. Limited to this core purpose — avoiding confusion in the marketplace — a trademark owner's property rights play well with the First Amendment. "Whatever first amendment rights you may have in calling the brew you make in your bathtub 'Pepsi' are easily outweighed by the buyer's interest in not being fooled into buying it." *Trademarks Unplugged*, 68 N.Y.U. L. Rev. 960, 973 (1993).

HA!

The problem arises when trademarks transcend their identifying purpose. Some trademarks enter our public discourse and become an integral part of our vocabulary. How else do you say that something's "the Rolls Royce of its class"? What else is a quick fix, but a Band-Aid? Does the average consumer know to ask for aspirin as "acetyl salicylic acid"? *See Bayer Co. v. United Drug Co.*, 272 F. 505, 510 (S.D.N.Y. 1921). Trademarks often fill in gaps in our vocabulary and add a contemporary flavor to our expressions. Once imbued with such expressive value, the trademark becomes a word in our language and assumes a role outside the bounds of trademark law.

Our likelihood-of-confusion test generally strikes a comfortable balance between the trademark owner's property rights and the public's expressive interests. But when a trademark owner asserts a right to control how we express ourselves—when we'd find it difficult to describe the product any other way (as in the case of aspirin), or when the mark (like Rolls Royce) has taken on an expressive meaning apart from its source-identifying function—applying the traditional test fails to account for the full weight of the public's interest in free expression.

The First Amendment may offer little protection for a competitor who labels its commercial good with a confusingly similar mark, but "[t]rademark rights do not entitle the owner to quash an unauthorized use of the mark by another who is communicating ideas or expressing points of view." *L.L. Bean, Inc. v. Drake Publishers, Inc.*, 811 F.2d 26, 29 (1st Cir. 1987). Were we to ignore the expressive value that some marks assume, trademark rights would grow to encroach upon the zone protected by the First Amendment. *See Yankee Publ'g, Inc. v. News Am. Publ'g, Inc.*, 809 F. Supp. 267, 276 (S.D.N.Y. 1992) ("[W]hen unauthorized use of another's mark is part of a communicative message and not a source identifier, the First Amendment is implicated in opposition to the trademark right."). Simply put, the trademark owner does not have the right to control public discourse whenever the public imbues his mark with a meaning beyond its source-identifying function. *See Anti-Monopoly, Inc. v. Gen. Mills Fun Group*, 611 F.2d 296, 301 (9th Cir. 1979) ("It is the source-denoting function which trademark laws protect, and nothing more.").

There is no doubt that MCA uses Mattel's mark: Barbie is one half of Barbie Girl. But Barbie Girl is the title of a song about Barbie and Ken, a reference that—at least today—can only be to Mattel's famous couple. We expect a title to describe the underlying work, not to identify the producer, and Barbie Girl does just that.

The Barbie Girl title presages a song about Barbie, or at least a girl like Barbie. The title conveys a message to consumers about what they can expect to discover in the song itself; it's a quick glimpse of Aqua's take on their own song. The lyrics confirm this: The female singer, who calls herself Barbie, is "a Barbie girl, in [her] Barbie world." She tells her male counterpart (named Ken), "Life in plastic, it's fantastic. You can brush my hair, undress me everywhere/Imagination, life is your creation." And off they go to "party." The song pokes fun at Barbie and the values that Aqua contends she represents. The female singer explains, "I'm a blond bimbo girl, in a fantasy world/Dress me up, make it tight, I'm your dolly.". . .

The Second Circuit has held that "in general the [Lanham] Act should be construed to apply to artistic works only where the public interest in avoiding consumer confusion outweighs the public interest in free expression." *Rogers v. Grimaldi,* 875 F.2d 994, 999 (2d Cir. 1989). *Rogers* considered a challenge by the actress Ginger Rogers to the film *Ginger and Fred.* The movie told the story of two Italian cabaret performers who made a living by imitating Ginger Rogers and Fred Astaire. Rogers argued that the film's title created the false impression that she was associated with it.

At first glance, Rogers certainly had a point. Ginger was her name, and Fred was her dancing partner. If a pair of dancing shoes had been labeled Ginger and Fred, a dancer might have suspected that Rogers was associated with the shoes (or at least one of them), just as Michael Jordan has endorsed Nike sneakers that claim to make you fly through the air. But *Ginger and Fred* was not a brand of shoe; it was the title of a movie and, for the reasons explained by the Second Circuit, deserved to be treated differently.

A title is designed to catch the eye and to promote the value of the underlying work. Consumers expect a title to communicate a message about the book or movie, but they do not expect it to identify the publisher or producer. If we see a painting titled "Campbell's Chicken Noodle Soup," we're unlikely to believe that Campbell's has branched into the art business. Nor, upon hearing Janis Joplin croon "Oh Lord, won't you buy me a Mercedes-Benz?," would we suspect that she and the carmaker had entered into a joint venture. A title tells us something about the underlying work but seldom speaks to its origin:

> Though consumers frequently look to the title of a work to determine what it is about, they do not regard titles of artistic works in the same way as the names of ordinary commercial products. Since consumers expect an ordinary product to be what the name says it is, we apply the Lanham Act with some rigor to prohibit names that misdescribe such goods. But most consumers are well aware that they cannot judge a book solely by its title any more than by its cover.

*Rogers,* 875 F.2d at 1000 (citations omitted).

*Rogers* concluded that literary titles do not violate the Lanham Act "unless the title has no artistic relevance to the underlying work whatsoever, or, if it has some artistic relevance, unless the title explicitly misleads as to the source or the content of the work." *Id.* at 999 (footnote omitted). We agree with the Second Circuit's analysis and adopt the *Rogers* standard as our own.

Applying *Rogers* to our case, we conclude that MCA's use of Barbie is not an infringement of Mattel's trademark. Under the first prong of *Rogers,* the use of Barbie in the song title clearly is relevant to the underlying work, namely, the song itself. As noted, the song is about Barbie and the values Aqua claims she represents. The song title does not explicitly mislead as to the source of the work; it does not, explicitly or otherwise, suggest that it was produced by Mattel. The *only* indication that Mattel might be associated with the song is the use of Barbie in the title; if this were enough to satisfy this prong of the *Rogers* test, it would render *Rogers* a nullity. We therefore agree with the district court that MCA was entitled to summary judgment on this ground. We need not consider whether the district court was correct in holding that MCA was also entitled to summary judgment because its use of Barbie was a . . . fair use. . . .

# Comments

1. ***Artistic Relevance Test.*** As *MCA* indicates, the two-pronged test from *Rogers v. Grimaldi* is the modern test for artistic fair use. Analytically, it is quite similar to the classic fair use test. Artistic relevance is a test to determine whether the use of the other's mark is relevant to the artistic expression. Its parallel in the classic fair use test is whether the trademarked term is used to describe the alleged infringer's goods or services.

   If the mark is relevant (or if the term is descriptive in a classic fair use test), then the second issue arises: Is the use expressly misleading? This second prong is parallel to the second part of the classic fair use test, which asks whether the use is in good faith. Both questions, being expressly misleading and in good faith, are relevant to the question of whether the alleged infringer's use will lead to confusion. An expressly misleading title, for instance, is similar to a descriptive use of another's mark in the same typeface, packaging, and labeling.

2. ***Balancing of Interests.*** The *Rogers v. Grimaldi* court described the artistic relevance test as a test that balances the public interest in avoiding consumer confusion and the public interest in free expression. The facts of both *Rogers* and *Mattel* indicate no likelihood of confusion. To see how a balancing would work, we would want to find a reported decision where the plaintiff's mark had only slight artistic relevance, was implicitly (but not explicitly) misleading, and confusion was somewhat likely to occur. We found no such cases.

3. ***Dilution and Fair Use.*** According to Lanham Act §43(c)(4), the fair use defenses also apply to dilution cases.

*STATUTE:* **Fair Use of Famous Marks Not Dilution**
15 U.S.C. §1125(c)(4) (Lanham Act §43(c)(4))

(4) The following shall not be actionable under this section:
   (A) Fair use of a famous mark by another person in comparative commercial advertising or promotion to identify the competing goods or services of the owner of the famous mark.
   (B) Noncommercial use of a mark.
   (C) All forms of news reporting and news commentary.

Mattel separately argued that MCA's song dilutes the BARBIE mark in two ways: It diminishes the mark's capacity to identify and distinguish Mattel products and it tarnishes the mark because the song is inappropriate for young girls. The three statutory exemptions are uses permitted even though they are potentially dilutive. Of those, only the "noncommercial use" in §43(c)(4)(C) exception might apply to MCA's use. The court in *MCA* stated the rule that speech is not "purely commercial" and is entitled to full First Amendment protection if it does more than propose a commercial transaction.

As an example of speech that did more than simply propose a commercial transaction, consider the facts of *Hoffman v. Capital Cities/ABC, Inc.,* 255 F.3d 1180 (9th Cir. 2001). In *Hoffman,* a magazine published an article featuring digitally altered images from famous films. Computer artists modified shots of Dustin Hoffman, Cary Grant, Marilyn Monroe, and others to put the actors in famous designers' spring fashions; a still of Hoffman from the movie "Tootsie" was altered so that he appeared to be wearing a Richard Tyler evening gown and Ralph Lauren heels. Hoffman, who had not given permission, sued under the Lanham Act. The court found that the article clearly served the commercial purpose of drawing attention to the for-profit magazine in which it appeared and for selling more copies, but included protected expression in its humorous and visual editorial comment on the firms and actors. The intertwining of commercial purpose with expressive elements resulted in the photographs receiving full First Amendment protections. MCA used Barbie's name to sell copies of the song, but also to lampoon the Barbie image and comment on the cultural values the band claimed she represents. Thus, MCA's use of the BARBIE mark was also exempt from the antidilution provision under the noncommercial use exception.

## 3. Comparative and Nominative Fair Use

Comparative and nominative fair uses involve using another's mark in order to refer to one's own product or service. As *August Storck K.G. v. Nabisco, Inc.* illustrates, comparative fair uses are often purely commercial and compare the alleged infringer's product or service to that of the mark holder. Comparative fair uses are descriptive, in the sense that the mark is being used to identify another's product for the ultimate purpose of describing the alleged infringer's product.

The label "nominative fair use" originate in the Court of Appeals for the Ninth Circuit and has since been adopted by a few other courts. Nominative fair uses include all cases in which a person uses another's mark to "name" or identify (refer to) the other's goods or services, including both commercial and noncommercial uses. A news report about an event at McDonald's or this casebook's reference to any company's trademark is a nominative use. The Ninth Circuit has used its nominative fair use test in cases that are purely comparative and descriptive as well as artistic. *Mattel Inc. v. Walking Mountain Productions* illustrates a noncomparative application of the nominative fair use test.

### AUGUST STORCK K.G. v. NABISCO, INC.
**59 F.3d 616 (7th Cir. 1995)**

EASTERBROOK, Circuit Judge.

"It happened a long time ago in the little village of Werther. There, the candymaker, Gustav Nebel, created his very finest candy, taking real butter, fresh cream, white and brown sugars, a pinch of salt, and lots of time. And because these butter candies tasted especially delicious, he called the candy 'Werther's Original', in honor of his little village of Werther." So reads the pitch on a bag of Werther's (R) Original candies. Nabisco surely developed its competing candy a different way—in a chemist's lab, followed by testing in focus groups. Nabisco concluded that Nebel used too

much sugar for modern tastes and worries; it substituted isomalt, hydrogenated glucose syrup, and acesulfame potassium. Its packaging of Life Savers (R) DelitesTM screams: *25% **LOWER IN CALORIES THAN WERTHERS (R) ORIGINAL\* CANDY.*** August Storck K.G., which makes and sells Werther's (R) Original, learned about Life Savers (R) DelitesTM from prototype trade samples; the candy is not scheduled for introduction until this coming August. Storck did not appreciate the comparison and filed this suit under the Lanham Act, 15 U.S.C. §§1114, 1125(a), arguing that Nabisco was about to infringe its trademark and trade dress. The district court issued a preliminary injunction, forbidding Nabisco to use the packaging it has devised. Nabisco tells us that if it must come up with new packaging the new candy cannot be introduced until 1996.

The prototype packaging for Life Savers (R) DelitesTM that Storck attached to the complaint used the words "Werther's Original" without either the (R) symbol or the asterisk that Nabisco will include in the product offered for sale. The asterisk refers to a disclaimer: "WERTHER'S (R) ORIGINAL is a registered trademark of and is made by August Storck KG. Storck does not make or license Life Savers DelitesTM." Nabisco assures us that it does not (and never did) plan to market a product without the (R) symbol or disclaimer, and that it told Storck so. Before the district judge issued the injunction, Nabisco gave him a copy of the consumer packaging. The judge remarked that if he had seen Nabisco's revised packaging earlier "the Court's ruling might have been different" — and then issued the injunction anyway. Yet Nabisco did not yield to the pressure of litigation, demonstrating in the process that an injunction is essential to prevent it from returning to its preferred practices; Nabisco's corporate policy calls for the use of an (R) symbol and disclaimer when mentioning rivals' products. That an injunction could have been appropriate to prevent the use of Storck's registered trademark without the symbol and disclaimer does not mean that it is appropriate once the judge learns that all prospect of an improper use has vanished. Quite the contrary, the injunction hampers a form of competition highly beneficial to consumers.

...It is hard to see how anyone could think that the Life Savers (R) DelitesTM package contains Werther's (R) Original candies or has anything to do with Storck's product. Life Savers (R), one of the most famous brand names in American life, is emblazoned on the package of Life Savers (R) DelitesTM; the candy-gulping public will quickly grasp that the point of the diagonal stripe containing the Werther's (R) Original name is to *dis-*

*tinguish* the two candies — to say that one is different from, and better than, the other. Trademarks designate the origin and quality of products. A use of a rival's mark that does not engender confusion about origin or quality is therefore permissible. The use is not just permissible in the sense that one firm is entitled to do everything within legal bounds to undermine a rival; it is beneficial to consumers. They learn at a glance what kind of product is for sale and how it differs from a known benchmark. Storck does not say that Nabisco's claim is false. That Life Savers (R) DelitesTM are 25% lower in calories than Werther's (R) Original candies is something consumers may want to know before deciding which candy to buy.

Both the FTC and the FDA encourage product comparisons. The FTC believes that consumers gain from comparative advertising, and to make the comparison vivid the Commission "encourages the naming of, or reference to competitors". 16 C.F.R. §14.15(b). A "comparison" to a mystery rival is just puffery; it is not falsifiable and therefore is not informative. Because comparisons must be concrete to be useful, the FDA's regulations implementing the Nutrition Labeling and Education Act of 1990, 21 U.S.C. §301 note, prefer that the object of a nutritional comparison be the market leader (a "comparison" to a product consumers do not recognize is as useless as a comparison to an anonymous rival) or an average of the three leading brands. 21 C.F.R. §101.13(j)(1)(ii)(A). Werther's (R) Original is the top selling butter cream hard candy, so Nabisco's claim follows the FDA's guideline.

Under the circumstances, the district judge's statement that the use of the Werther's (R) Original mark on the Life Savers (R) DelitesTM package creates a "possibility" of confusion cannot support an injunction. Many consumers are ignorant or inattentive, so some are bound to misunderstand no matter how careful a producer is. If such a possibility created a trademark problem, then all comparative references would be forbidden, and consumers as a whole would be worse off.

Likelihood of confusion in a trademark case is a factual issue, and appellate review is deferential. But the district court did not hold an evidentiary hearing. Nabisco and Storck informed us at oral argument that to this day no one has conducted the surveys customary in trademark cases, showing the packaging or product to consumers and asking: "Who makes this?" or "Are these two products made by the same firm?" Perhaps the packages are confusing after all; we make little of the disclaimer, which few consumers will read. But all the district court found — all that it could find on this record — is that Nabisco's packaging uses Storck's mark and that confusion is possible. That is not enough to postpone the introduction of a new product. When deciding whether to grant or withhold equitable relief a court must give high regard to the interest of the general public, which is a great beneficiary from competition. Although the benefits of competition do not justify the introduction of products that engender substantial confusion, when the plaintiff's showing is as thin as Storck's the interests of the public carry the day. Damages in trademark cases are hard to measure, but the possibility of compensation offers sufficient protection to a trademark owner, when an injunction bids fair to stifle competition and injure consumers in order to ward off occasional confusion. Even substantial deference to the district court's balancing of the equities cannot save an injunction when the judge overstates the private injury and disregards the public interest in competition....

The preliminary injunction is reversed. So that Nabisco may proceed with the introduction of Life Savers (R) DelitesTM on schedule, the mandate will issue today.

## MATTEL INC. v. WALKING MOUNTAIN PRODUCTIONS
### 353 F.3d 792 (9th Cir. 2003)

PREGERSON, Circuit Judge.

In the action before us, Plaintiff Mattel Corporation asks us to prohibit Defendant artist Thomas Forsythe from producing and selling photographs containing Mattel's "Barbie" doll. Most of Forsythe's photos portray a nude Barbie in danger of being attacked by vintage household appliances. Mattel argues that his photos infringe on their copyrights, trademarks, and trade dress. We have jurisdiction pursuant to 28 U.S.C. §1291 and affirm the district court's grant of summary judgment to Forsythe.

Thomas Forsythe, aka "Walking Mountain Productions," is a self-taught photographer who resides in Kanab, Utah. He produces photographs with social and political overtones. In 1997, Forsythe developed a series of 78 photographs entitled "Food Chain Barbie," in which he depicted Barbie in various absurd and often sexualized positions. Forsythe uses the word "Barbie" in some of the titles of his works. While his works vary, Forsythe generally depicts one or more nude Barbie dolls juxtaposed with vintage kitchen appliances. For example, "Malted Barbie" features a nude Barbie placed on a vintage Hamilton Beach malt machine. "Fondue a la Barbie" depicts Barbie heads in a fondue pot. "Barbie Enchiladas" depicts four Barbie dolls wrapped in tortillas and covered with salsa in a casserole dish in a lit oven.

In his declaration in support of his motion for summary judgment, Forsythe describes the message behind his photographic series as an attempt to "critique [ ] the objectification of women associated with

[Barbie], and [ ][to] lambast [ ] the conventional beauty myth and the societal acceptance of women as objects because this is what Barbie embodies." He explains that he chose to parody Barbie in his photographs because he believes that "Barbie is the most enduring of those products that feed on the insecurities of our beauty and perfection-obsessed consumer culture." Forsythe claims that, throughout his series of photographs, he attempts to communicate, through artistic expression, his serious message with an element of humor.

Forsythe's market success was limited. He displayed his works at two art festivals — the Park City Art Festival in Park City, Utah, and the Plaza Art Fair in Kansas City, Missouri. He promoted his works through a postcard, a business card, and a website. Forsythe printed 2000 promotional postcards depicting his work, "Barbie Enchiladas," only 500 of which were ever circulated. Of those that were circulated, some were distributed throughout his hometown of Kanab and some to a feminist scholar who used slides of Forsythe's works in her academic presentations. He also sold 180 of his postcards to a friend who owned a book store in Kanab so she could resell them in her bookstore and sold an additional 22 postcards to two other friends. Prior to this lawsuit, Forsythe received only four or five unsolicited calls inquiring about his work. The "Food Chain Barbie" series earned Forsythe total gross income of $3,659.

Forsythe also produced 1,000 business cards which depicted "Champagne Barbie." His name and self-given title "Artsurdist" were written on the card. He used these cards at fairs and as introductions to gallery owners.

Finally, Forsythe had a website on which he depicted low resolution pictures of his photographs. The website was not configured for online purchasing. "Tom Forsythe's Artsurdist Statement," in which he described his intent to critique and ridicule Barbie, was featured on his website. His website also contained a prominent link to his biography.

On August 23, 1999, Mattel filed this action in the United States District Court for the Central District of California (the "Los Angeles federal district court") against Forsythe, alleging that Forsythe's "Food Chain Barbie" series infringed Mattel's . . . trade dress. . . .

Mattel claims that it possesses a trade dress in the Superstar Barbie head and the doll's overall appearance. The district court concluded that there was no likelihood that the public would be misled into believing that Mattel endorsed Forsythe's photographs despite Forsythe's use of the Barbie figure.

Arguably, the Barbie trade dress also plays a role in our culture similar to the role played by the Barbie trademark — namely, symbolization of an unattainable ideal of femininity for some women. Forsythe's use of the Barbie trade dress, therefore, presumably would present First Amendment concerns similar to those that made us reluctant to apply the Lanham Act as a bar to the artistic uses of Mattel's Barbie trademark in both *MCA* and this case. But we need not decide how the *MCA/Rogers* First Amendment balancing might apply to Forsythe's use of the Barbie trade dress because we find, on a narrower ground, that it qualifies as nominative fair use.

In the trademark context, we recently held that a defendant's use is *classic* fair use where "a defendant has used the plaintiff's mark *only* to describe his own product, *and not at all to describe the plaintiff's product.*" *Cairns*, 292 F.3d at

1151 (emphasis in original). In contrast, a defendant's use of a plaintiff's mark is *nominative* where he or she "used the plaintiff's mark to describe the plaintiff's product, *even if the defendant's ultimate goal is to describe his own product.*" *Id.* (emphasis in original). The goal of a nominative use is generally for the "purposes of comparison, criticism [or] point of reference." *New Kids on the Block,* 971 F.2d at 306. These two mutually exclusive forms of fair use are equally applicable here in the trade dress context.

Applying these fair use standards to the trade dress context, we hold that a defendant's use is *classic* fair use where the defendant has used the plaintiff's dress to describe or identify the defendant's own product and not at all to describe or identify the plaintiff's product. Likewise, a defendant's use is *nominative* where he or she used the plaintiff's dress to describe or identify the plaintiff's product, even if the defendant's ultimate goal is to describe or identify his or her own product.

Forsythe's use of the Barbie trade dress is nominative. Forsythe used Mattel's Barbie figure and head in his works to conjure up associations of Mattel, while at the same time to identify his own work, which is a criticism and parody of Barbie. Where use of the trade dress or mark is grounded in the defendant's desire to refer to the plaintiff's product as a point of reference for defendant's own work, a use is nominative.

Fair use may be either nominative or classic. We recognize a fair use defense in claims brought under §1125 where the use of the trademark "does not imply sponsorship or endorsement of the product because the mark is used only to describe the thing, rather than to identify its source." *New Kids on the Block,* 971 F.2d at 306. Thus, we recently reiterated that, in the trademark context, nominative use becomes nominative *fair use* when a defendant proves three elements:

> First, the plaintiff's product or service in question must be one not readily identifiable without use of the trademark; second, only so much of the mark or marks may be used as is reasonably necessary to identify the plaintiff's product or service; and third, the user must do nothing that would, in conjunction with the mark, suggest sponsorship or endorsement by the trademark holder.

*Cairns,* 292 F.3d at 1151(quoting *New Kids on the Block,* 971 F.2d at 308).

Forsythe's use easily satisfies the first element; his use of the Barbie figure and head are reasonably necessary in order to conjure up the Barbie product in a photographic medium. It would have been extremely difficult for Forsythe to create a photographic parody of Barbie without actually using the doll.

Forsythe also satisfies the second element, which requires that a defendant only use so much of a trademark or trade dress as is reasonably necessary. As we recognized in *Cairns,* "[w]hat is 'reasonably necessary to identify the plaintiff's product' differs from case to case." *Id.* at 1154. Where identification "of the defendant's product depends on the description [or identification] of the plaintiff's product, more use of the plaintiff's trademark" or trade dress is reasonably necessary. *Id.* Given the photographic medium and Forsythe's goal of representing the social implications of Barbie, including issues of sexuality and body image, Forsythe's use of the Barbie torso and head is both reasonable and necessary.

It would be very difficult for him to represent and describe his photographic parodies of Barbie without using the Barbie likeness.

Though a "closer call than the first two elements" of the nominative fair use analysis, *id.* at 1155, the final element — that the user do nothing that would, in conjunction with use of the mark or dress, suggest sponsorship or endorsement by the trademark or trade dress holder — is satisfied here and weighs in Forsythe's favor. This element does not require that the defendant make an affirmative statement that their product is not sponsored by the plaintiff. . . .

We hold that Forsythe's use of Mattel's Barbie qualifies as nominative fair use. All three elements weigh in favor of Forsythe. Barbie would not be readily identifiable in a photographic work without use of the Barbie likeness and figure. Forsythe used only so much as was necessary to make his parodic use of Barbie readily identifiable, and it is highly unlikely that any reasonable consumer would have believed that Mattel sponsored or was affiliated with his work. The district court's grant of summary judgment to Forsythe on Mattel's trade dress infringement claim was, therefore, proper. . . .

## Comments

1. ***Comparative Fair Use.*** Comparative advertising use is a descriptive use because the mark holder's mark is used to describe, or to name, the mark holder's product. The comparative fair use defense does not fit literally under §33(b)(4) because that subsection requires that the use be "to describe the goods or services of *such party*" (emphasis added), referring to the party charged with infringement. Nevertheless, the comparative fair use defense is widely accepted. The general fair use doctrine has common law origins that precede the adoption of the specific language of §33(b)(4).

2. ***Balancing Test: How Much Confusion Would Be Tolerated?*** The court in *August Storck* clearly identifies the policy reasons underlying the comparative fair use defense, but is it an affirmative defense or a means of rebutting the mark holder's prima facie case? Many courts hold that, if any confusion is likely to result from the comparative use, it is not a fair use. Under this interpretation, comparative fair use is a way to rebut the mark holder's argument that confusion is likely. The court in *August Storck,* however, hints that some cases might involve a balancing, saying that while the benefits of comparative advertising would not justify substantial confusion "when the plaintiff's showing is as thin as Storck's the interest of the public must carry the day." Under this interpretation, comparative use might be more of an affirmative defense, where some confusion would be tolerated in order to promote competition.

3. ***Comparative Fair Use: The Good Faith Inquiry.*** Comparative advertising cases where the use has been held unfair are those where the alleged infringer uses the other's term in a way that makes it look like the infringer's own mark and confusion is likely. In *Pebble Beach Co. v. Tour 18 I, Ltd.*, 942 F. Supp. 1513 (S.D. Tex. 1996), for instance, the alleged infringer was a golf course that copied its individual holes from famous golf courses around the world and named the holes using the original trademarked names, such as "BAY HILL hole #6," "AUGUSTA

NATIONAL hole # 11," and "PEBBLE BEACH hole # 14." The infringer claimed that the use was merely comparative and should be interpreted as describing its own, supposedly identical holes. After an extensive analysis of the likelihood of confusion resulting from the use, however, the court found that the use of the mark in advertising and promotions was excessive and beyond that needed to describe the nature of the holes on the infringer's course. The infringer used disclaimers on some of its advertising materials, but they were inadequate to prevent consumers from thinking that the mark holders were associated with the infringer's course.

A contrary example appears in *Cumberland Packing Corp. v. Monsanto Co.*, 140 F. Supp. 2d 241 (E.D.N.Y. 2001), where the maker of Sweet 'n Low sued for the maker of "Sweetmate," a competing sugar substitute. The manufacturer of Sweetmate used the SWEET 'N LOW trademark on its packaging to point out that Sweetmate was identical in composition and less expensive. The mark holder complained that the typeface of its SWEET 'N LOW mark was much larger than most of the words on the alleged infringer's box, likely to be interpreted as a mark, and likely to cause confusion. The court found that the context in which it was used and the much larger typeface for the alleged infringer's SWEETMATE mark on the packaging made confusion unlikely and the comparative use fair. This analysis of fair use is similar to the analysis of that element in classic fair use cases, where the analysis of good faith is closely tied to the question of whether the term was used as a mark rather than simply to describe. Use "as a mark" is likely to lead to confusion and more likely to have been in bad faith.

4. *Nominative Fair Use.* Like comparative fair use, nominative fair use involves using the mark holder's mark to describe the mark holder's product. The general reason for nominative use is for purposes of comparison, criticism, or point of reference. Again, the use cannot be "as a mark" and the use must be "in good faith." The Ninth Circuit's nominative fair use test has three elements. How do these three elements compare with the elements of the classic fair use test? Is the nominative fair use test a rebuttal or an affirmative defense? Is it a balancing test in which some likelihood of confusion would be tolerated?

5. *Nominative Fair Use and Artistic Fair Use.* Comparing *Mattel Inc. v. Walking Mountain Productions* to *Mattel, Inc. v. MCA Records, Inc.*, one might wonder why the court in *Walking Mountain* did not apply the artistic fair use test. The court did consider the *Rogers v. Grimaldi* "artistic relevance" approach but preferred the nominative fair use test because, by avoiding the constitutional question, the case could be decided on a "narrower ground." How would the *Walking Mountain* case be decided under the artistic relevance test?

# Problems

**4-2.** In *Cairns v. Franklin Mint*, 292 F.3d 1139 (9th Cir. 2002), executors of the estate of Diana, Princess of Wales, claimed that the use of Princess

Diana's name and likeness on commercially sold jewelry, plates, and dolls and in advertising for those products falsely suggested that Princess Diana (or the estate) endorsed the products. The Franklin Mint moved for summary judgment based on nominative fair use. Should the motion be granted?

**4-3.** Wham-Inc. is a toy company that manufacturers the HACKY SACK, the FRISBEE, the HULA HOOP and, the subject of this case, the SLIP 'N SLIDE, a long patch of flexible and inflatable plastic. Instructions say the slide is to be used by children ages 5 to 12 and should be inflated then lubricated with water before use. In the movie *Dickie Roberts: Former Child Star*, actor David Spade, trying to recover his lost childhood, leaps onto an uninflated and unlubricated SLIP 'N SLIDE and comes to a quick and painful stop. He later lubricates the slide with a layer of cooking oil and slides way off the end of the slide, careens across the lawn, and collides with a picket fence. Wham-O complains that the characters identified the slide by its trademarked name and infringed its trademark. What fair use test applies and what is the result of applying that test? *See Wham-O v. Paramount Pictures Corp.*, 286 F. Supp. 2d 1254 (N.D. Cal. 2003). Compare *Caterpillar Inc. v. The Walt Disney Co.*, 287 F. Supp. 2d 913 (C.D. Ill. 2003), where the owner of the CATERPILLAR mark used on its earth mover complained of the villain's use of its bull dozer, with trademarks showing, in the *George of the Jungle 2* movie to destroy the hero George's home.

## 4. Fair Use on Reconditioned Goods

Fair use on reconditioned or rebuilt goods involves a remanufacturer using another's mark to describe the contents or original manufacturer of its goods. When sellers of used goods recondition, repair, or rebuild the goods before resale, the original manufacturers sometimes object to being associated with the resulting product by having their marks appear on the products. Permitting remanufacturers to apply the original mark informs consumers and enables them to buy recycled goods at a lower price than the new original goods. The potential harm to consumers is possible confusion about the quality and characteristics of the goods. This is accompanied by potential damage to the mark holder's goodwill. *Nitro Leisure Products, LLC v. Acushnet Co.* applies that traditional "misnomer" test, derived from *Champion Spark Plug Co. v. Sanders,* a classic Supreme Court case from 1947 that focuses on the qualities and characteristics of the goods after the reconditioning process.

### NITRO LEISURE PRODUCTS, LLC v. ACUSHNET CO.

341 F.3d 1356 (Fed. Cir. 2003)

LINN, Circuit Judge.

Acushnet Company ("Acushnet") appeals from the denial of its motion for a preliminary injunction by the United States District Court for the

Southern District of Florida. *In re Nitro Leisure Prods., L.L.C.,* No. 02-14008-CV-Middlebrooks (S.D. Fla. Aug. 9, 2002) (*"Order"*). Because the district court did not abuse its discretion in denying Acushnet's motion in view of Acushnet's failure to show a reasonable likelihood of success on the merits of its claims, we affirm.

Acushnet manufactures and sells golfing equipment, and in particular, golf balls. Acushnet owns and has federally registered the trademarks TITLEIST, ACUSHNET, PINNACLE, and PRO V1. Of particular interest in this case, Acushnet manufactures and markets new golf balls under the TITLEIST name and trademark, including the TITLEIST PRO V1, asserted by Acushnet to be the best selling golf ball in the United States since February 2001.

Nitro obtains and sells two categories of used golf balls at a discounted rate. The first category of balls are "recycled" balls. The recycled balls are those found in relatively good condition, needing little more than washing, and are repackaged for resale. Recycled balls represent approximately 30% of Nitro's sales. The second category includes balls that are found with stains, scuffs or blemishes, requiring "refurbishing." Nitro's refurbishing process includes cosmetically treating the balls by removing the base coat of paint, the clear coat layer, and the trademark and model markings without damaging the covers of the balls, and then repainting the balls, adding a clear coat, and reaffixing the original manufacturer's trademark. Nitro also applies directly to each "refurbished" ball the legend "USED & REFURBISHED BY SECOND CHANCE" or "USED AND REFURBISHED BY GOLFBALLSDIRECT.COM." In these statements, the terms "Second Chance" and "Golfballsdirect.com" refer to businesses of Nitro. Some, but not all, of the refurbished balls also bear a Nitro trademark. Nitro's refurbished balls are packaged in containers displaying the following disclaimer:

> ATTENTION USED/REFURBISHED GOLF BALLS: The enclosed contents of used/refurbished golf balls are USED GOLF BALLS. Used/Refurbished golf balls are subject to performance variations from new ones. These used/refurbished balls were processed via one or more of the following steps: stripping, painting, stamping and/or clear coating in our factory. This product has NOT been endorsed or approved by the original manufacturer and the balls DO NOT fall under the original manufacturer's warranty.

According to Nitro, there is a large market for used golf balls. In 2001, Nitro saw annual sales of approximately $10 million, including $4.8 million for refurbished balls. *Id.* . . .

On April 23, 2002, Acushnet moved for a preliminary injunction on its trademark . . . claims. As to the trademark claims, Acushnet concedes that it has no trademark claim with respect to "recycled" balls and does not object to those sales. As to the "refurbished" balls, however, Acushnet asserts that "Nitro's refurbishing process produces a golf ball that bears no resemblance to a genuine Acushnet product in performance, quality or appearance" and that "Nitro's refurbishing process so alters the basic composition of Acushnet's golf balls that 'it would be a misnomer to call the article by its original name.' " Following oral argument, the district court on August 9, 2002, issued its *Order,* concluding that Acushnet had failed to show a likelihood of success on the merits and denying preliminary injunctive relief...

Before this court, Acushnet seeks review of the denial of its motion for preliminary injunction...

Acushnet...argues that the district court failed to apply the correct legal standard to the trademark infringement claim. Acushnet asserts that the district court misapplied *Champion Spark Plug Co. v. Sanders*, 331 U.S. 125 (1947)....

To succeed in its request for a preliminary injunction on its trademark infringement claim, Acushnet must show, *inter alia*, a likelihood of success on the merits. This means that it must show a likelihood of success on its claim that the sale by Nitro of its refurbished golf balls bearing re-applied Acushnet trademarks is likely to cause confusion. In considering this issue, the district court looked to *Champion* — clear precedent in the used goods context — and concluded, on the record presented at this preliminary stage, that the differences between Acushnet's new golf balls and Nitro's refurbished golf balls were not so great as to be a misnomer and that it was not an act of infringement, warranting preliminary injunctive relief, for Nitro to re-apply Acushnet's trademarks to the Acushnet balls refurbished by Nitro and to re-sell those balls in packaging identifying them as used or refurbished.

In the present case, the dispute centers around the differences between new and refurbished Acushnet golf balls, thus implicating the "similarity of the products" factor [in the 11th Circuit's test for likelihood of confusion outlined in *Frehling Enters., Inc. v. Int'l Select Group, Inc.*, 192 F.3d 1330, 1335 (11th Cir. 1999)]. Specifically, the question presented is the propriety of the re-application by Nitro of the Acushnet trademark, without Acushnet's consent, to genuine Acushnet golf balls that have been used, subjected to Nitro's refurbishing process, and then re-sold by Nitro as refurbished balls....

Under 15 U.S.C. §§1114(1) and 1125(a)(1), any person who uses the trademark of another, without consent, in a manner that is likely to cause confusion, mistake, or to deceive may be liable in a civil action for trademark infringement. In the *Champion* case, a seminal opinion on the use of trademarks on used goods, the accused infringer collected genuine used Champion spark plugs, repaired and reconditioned the spark plugs, painted the spark plugs for aesthetic reasons, and resold the spark plugs, each labeled "Renewed." The issue before the Supreme Court was simply whether the lower courts erred in not requiring the accused infringer to remove Champion's trademark name from the repaired and reconditioned spark plugs. The Supreme Court acknowledged that, in some cases, used and repaired goods can be sold under the trademark of the original manufacturer, without "deceiv[ing] the public," so long as the accused infringer had attempted to restore "so far as possible" the original condition of the goods and full disclosure is made about the true nature of the goods, for example, as "used" or "repaired." *Id.* at 129-30. In *Champion*, the Supreme Court stated that "[w]hen the mark is used in a way that does not deceive the public we see no such sanctity in the word as to prevent its being used to tell the truth." *Id.* at 129.

The Supreme Court recognized that this standard results in the second-hand dealer getting some advantage from the trademark; however, this windfall is "wholly permissible so long as the manufacturer is not identified with the inferior qualities of the product." *Id.* at 130. This advantage is not inconsistent with the stated purposes of the Lanham Act. In passing the Lanham Act, Congress noted that the purpose was "to protect legitimate business and consumers of the country." 92 Cong. Rec. 7524 (1946). To fulfill this purpose, the Act "protect[s] the public so it may be confident that, in purchasing a product bearing a particular trade-mark which it favorably knows, it will get the product which it asks for and wants to get." S. Rep. No. 79-1333 at 3 (1946). Further, the owner of the trademark must have the energy and effort he expended in building goodwill in his trademark protected from misappropriation. However, so long as the customer is getting a product with the expected characteristics, and so long as the goodwill built up by the trademark owner is not eroded by being identified with inferior quality, the Lanham Act does not prevent the truthful use of trademarks, even if such use results in the enrichment of others.

The *Champion* court, while concluding that the facts of that case did not establish a likelihood of confusion, cautioned that there are limits on the use of a trademark by another on a used or repaired item. The Supreme Court explained that "[c]ases may be imagined where the reconditioning or repair would be so extensive or so basic that it would be a misnomer to call the article by its original name, even though the words 'used' or 'repaired' were added." 331 U.S. at 129. In *Champion*, the repair was such that it "[did] not give [the product] a new design," and the accused infringers had sought to restore the product "so far as possible, [to its] original condition," *id.* Thus, no infringement was found....

The *Champion* court recognizes that consumers do not expect used or refurbished goods to be the same as new goods and that for such goods, "material differences" do not necessarily measure consumer confusion. According to *Champion*, what is more telling on the question of likelihood of confusion in the context of used goods is whether the used or refurbished goods are so different from the original that it would be a misnomer for them to be designated by the original trademark....

The district court in this case properly assessed likelihood of confusion in concluding: (1) that on the evidence before it, the differences in the goods were nothing more than what would be expected for used golf balls; (2) that it was therefore not a misnomer to apply the Acushnet mark to the used Acushnet balls; and (3) that Acushnet had not established a likelihood of success on the merits of its trademark "likelihood of confusion" case. This is all that was required, and there is no basis to conclude that the district court applied the wrong test or otherwise abused its discretion....

Alternatively, Acushnet argues that the district court's reliance on *Champion* is misplaced. Acushnet attempts to distinguish *Champion*, arguing first that Nitro does not restore "so far as possible" the used balls to their original condition, but rather masks the balls' condition, and second, that by masking rather than restoring, Nitro makes it more likely that customers will associate inferior performance with Acushnet. Acushnet argues that, although there was repainting of the spark plugs in *Champion*, such painting was merely cosmetic. Acushnet contends that the district court failed to recognize that Nitro's process of stripping and repainting was more than cosmetic and changed the fundamental attributes of the reprocessed balls. Moreover, Acushnet argues that it is Nitro's refurbishing process, not normal wear and tear, that degraded the quality of Nitro's used golf balls. Acushnet thus asserts that *Champion* is distinguishable on its facts and should not apply. We disagree with Acushnet's distinctions.

First, while it is true that the spark plugs were repainted in *Champion*, the reconditioning also involved removing burned and pitted portions of the center electrodes, welding new metal to the side electrodes, wearing away the plug's porcelain insulators through sandblasting, and then cleaning and painting the spark plug. The refurbishing process in *Champion*, then, was not merely cosmetic, and cannot be distinguished from the present case on that basis. Second, *Champion* also held that the source of any inferiority, whether the reconditioning or the refurbishing, is irrelevant, stating that inferiority is immaterial as long as the original manufacturer "is not identified with the inferior qualities of the product *resulting from wear and tear or the reconditioning.*" *Champion*, 331 U.S. at 130, 67 S. Ct. 1136 (emphasis added). In the *Champion* case, the district court noted that there was no proof whether the inferior qualities stemmed from either "wear and tear prior to the discarding of the plug by the original user, or to the process of repair as conducted by the defendants." *Champion Spark Plug Co. v. Sanders*, 61 F. Supp. 247, 248-49 (E.D.N.Y. 1945). Acushnet's distinction on this point is similarly untenable.

In this case, the district court carefully considered the extent of the alterations made by Nitro. The district court also looked to a number of factors, outlined by the Ninth Circuit, to determine if the alterations resulted in a new product. *Order* at 9 ("These factors 'include the nature and extent of the alterations, the nature of the device and how it is designed . . ., whether a market has developed for service or spare parts . . . and, most importantly, whether end users of the product are likely to be misled as to the party responsible for the composition of the product.' *Karl Storz Endoscopy-America, Inc. v. Surgical Technologies, Inc.*, 285 F.3d 848, 856-57 (9th Cir. 2002)." The district court also considered: (a) evidence proffered by Nitro that the performance differences were not as extensive as claimed by Acushnet; (b) evidence of the use of disclaimers; and (c) evidence from customers of both Acushnet and Nitro on the question of confusion. On this record, the district court concluded that "Acushnet has not presented sufficient evidence to support its claim that the golf balls are so extensively repaired that they cannot be truly labeled with the Titleist marks." *Id.* at 9-10.

Because the district court properly considered the *Frehling* factors; fully and carefully assessed the differences between Acushnet's new golf balls and Nitro's refurbished golf balls in determining likelihood of confusion; and correctly looked to *Champion* for the applicable legal standard, we find no abuse of discretion in the district court's denial of Acushnet's requested preliminary injunction based on its trademark infringement claim. . . .

Acushnet makes a number of arguments that can be characterized as disagreements with the district court's findings of fact or the application of law to fact. In particular, Acushnet argues that the district court placed too much weight on the disclaimers Nitro placed on the packaging and golf balls; that the district court erroneously found that Acushnet and Nitro sell balls in different channels of trade; and that the district court failed to find customer confusion based on the evidence presented. A trial court's findings of fact must be upheld unless clearly erroneous. We have carefully considered Acushnet's arguments and the district court's findings of fact and discern no clear error . . .

# Comments

1. *Fair Use on Reconditioned Goods: The Misnomer Test.* Using another's mark on reconditioned goods is a descriptive use in the sense that the alleged infringer uses the term to describe or name the original source of the goods. In an infringement action, likelihood of confusion of source is always an element of the plaintiff's case. There is no question that the reconditioned goods in these cases originally came from the mark holder. The question is whether the qualities and characteristics of the reconditioned goods are so fundamentally altered that it would be a "misnomer" to say that the used goods came from the mark holder. The "similarity of the goods," a factor in establishing the likelihood of confusion, plays a slightly different role in reconditioned goods cases. In the usual infringement case, confusion (of source) is more likely if the products are similar. In reconditioned goods cases, confusion (of characteristics and qualities) is more likely if the original and reconditioned goods are dissimilar.

   The concern of the fair use test for reconditioned goods is that consumers accustomed to relying on the mark as an indicator of product quality and characteristics would be misled by the alleged infringer's use of the mark. A test that ensures that the manufacturer is not identified with any inferior quality of the product protects the manufacturer's goodwill and consumers. The reconditioner must "restore so far as possible" to the original condition and disclose the true nature of the goods. That may not be enough where reconditioning or repair are so extensive that it is inappropriate (a "misnomer") to describe the original manufacturer as the source.

2. *Full Disclosure Requirement.* The disclosure Nitro included in the container appears in the opinion. It tells consumers what was done to the balls and warns consumers that the original manufacturer does not endorse or approve the  product. Judge Newman dissented, strongly objecting to (1) the general idea of an unlicensed third party reapplying another's trademark and (2) the adequacy of disclosure. She was particularly concerned with the importance of the quality-indicating function of a trademark, which she described as a facet of the source-indicating function. Trademark law, she stated, bears the burden of protecting standards of quality and consumer confidence.

   The reconditioned balls in this case included those with scuff marks, cart path marks, and tree marks. The balls were refurbished by taking off the old base paint and clear coat top paint and repainting. Judge Newman objected that the repainting concealed the defects:

   > When the defects are concealed, that is not "full disclosure about the true nature" of the golf balls as the panel majority holds. Concealment is the

antithesis of full disclosure. In purchasing a used golf ball that has been repainted, the consumer is not provided with knowledge of concealed damage as well as surface changes. When the consumer purchases a used golf ball bearing the Titleist7 mark, the purchaser does not know if this is an almost-new golf ball that went from tee to lake on the first stroke, or a ball so badly cut that it was discarded. This is not the "full disclosure" accommodated by *Champion....* The record states that the Titleist7 balls are the premium balls in this market, and are recognized by the golfing public as of high and consistent quality and dependability. The producer of these products is entitled by law to protect the reputation and the value of its marks. Consumer expectations of quality should not be thwarted by an inappropriate balance of interests.

*3. Repackaged Goods and Component Parts.* Courts use the same logic when evaluating an alleged infringer's use of another's mark to describe the contents of its product. *Prestonettes Inc. v. Coty,* 264 U.S. 359 (1924), is a famous Supreme Court case in which a repackager of Coty's famous perfume was permitted to describe, truthfully, the contents of its goods. More recently, a maker of tuna salad was permitted to describe, truthfully, that it was "Made with Bumble Bee Tuna," without obtaining Bumble Bee's permission. *See Bumble Bee Seafoods L.L.C. v. UFS Industries, Inc.,* 71 U.S.P.Q.2d 1684 (S.D.N.Y. 2004). Even if the repackager modifies the mark holder's goods and produces an inferior product, e.g., tasteless tuna salad, a truthful use untainted by deception is permitted. Consumers must not, however, be deceived into thinking that the new article and the component part are from the same source.

# CHAPTER
# 5

# Trademark Remedies

## A. INTRODUCTION TO REMEDIES

The Lanham Act states that all remedies are equitable in nature. This permits courts great discretion in matching the remedy to the particular circumstances of individual cases. Section 34 states that injunctions may be awarded "according to principles of equity and upon such terms as the court may deem reasonable." The essential point to remember about injunctions is that they are specifically tailored to protect the rights violated and the interests affected. Their scope may be quite narrow or broad as the circumstances require.

Unlike other areas of law in which damages are a "legal" remedy, monetary recovery under the Lanham Act is governed by "equitable" principles. In contract and tort law, for instance, a plaintiff is entitled to recover all damages he or she can prove in well-defined compensatory categories. There is no such entitlement under the Lanham Act. Section 35 states that all monetary awards are "subject to the principles of equity" and that, if the dollar amounts for defendant's profits calculated according to standard formulas are inadequate or excessive, "the court may in its discretion enter judgment for such sum as the court shall find to be just." The essential point to remember for damages is that proof of infringement does not automatically entitle a plaintiff to any or all of the categories of monetary recovery or limit the plaintiff to recovery of what is provable.

*STATUTE:* **Injunctive Relief**
15 U.S.C.A. §1116(a) (Lanham Act §34(a))

*STATUTE:* **Recovery for Violation of Rights**
15 U.S.C.A. §1117 (Lanham Act §35(a))

Injunctions and monetary awards are the primary means through which trademark rights are enforced. The cases that follow focus on three important aspects of the preceding statutory excerpts: (1) injunctions and monetary recovery are both governed by equitable principles; (2) monetary recovery may include all of the following: the defendant's ill-gotten profits, the plaintiff's lost profits, costs, and attorneys' fees; and (3) monetary recovery must be a compensatory rather than punitive amount.

*Categories of Monetary Recovery.* Lanham Act §35(a) lists defendant's profits, plaintiff's damages, costs, and attorneys' fees as categories of recovery. The term "plaintiff's damages" does not refer to the total of plaintiff's monetary recovery as it does in other areas of law. It refers only to one component of possible recovery — the measure of profits the plaintiff has lost due to the Lanham Act violation. Loss of profits may result not only from lost sales (perhaps diverted to the infringer) but also increased costs of serving customers and damage to reputation arising from the confusion created by the infringer. Other types of monetary recovery available under the Lanham Act, an award of profits the defendant may have earned, for instance, have their own labels. Recovery of the defendant's profits, for instance, is called "an accounting." A plaintiff may demand damages and/or demand "an accounting."

The equitable nature of Lanham Act remedies and latitude given to courts by the Act means that the availability of a particular type of monetary recovery varies from case to case. For instance, a plaintiff may not recover both damages and the defendant's profits to the extent they overlap; a plaintiff may not recover attorneys' fees except in exceptional cases; and, if an injunction satisfies the court's sense of justice, the plaintiff may get no monetary recovery at all. These materials focus on general rules for when a plaintiff is likely to be awarded each type of recovery.

*Compensation and Not a Penalty.* Section 35 seems internally contradictory. First, it states that courts may award damages up to three times greater than the amount of actual damages proved. Second, it states that courts may increase awards based on defendant's profits above the amount proved. Finally, it states that these enhanced amounts must be compensation and not a penalty. This seems strange for two reasons. If a plaintiff recovers its own lost profits, based, perhaps, on sales diverted from the plaintiff to the defendant, how can plaintiff's recovery of defendant's profits also be compensatory? If the plaintiff proves its losses and defendant's gains, how can the court's enhanced amounts also be compensatory? Part of the explanation is that profits are hard to prove with any exactness and courts make adjustments to reflect that uncertainty. Another part is that, despite the compensatory language, courts make adjustments based on the degree of fault of the defendant and many other factors. These materials explore the rationales courts offer for their adjustments.

# B. SCOPE OF INJUNCTIVE RELIEF

Injunctive relief is tailored to the circumstances of each case. The scope of injunctions reflects, among other factors, the strength of the mark that was infringed or diluted and the likelihood that the defendant's activity will cause confusion or dilution in various product and geographic markets. These general principles apply to all types of marks, whether registered or not. *King-Seeley Thermos Co. v. Aladdin Industries, Inc.* illustrates some of the procedure for drafting and enforcing injunctions. *King-Seeley* also illustrates equitable considerations involved in tailoring injunctions to reflect the competing rights of mark owners and their competitors in a trade dress context. *Charles Jacquin et Cie, Inc. v. Destileria Serralles, Inc.* illustrates how a court may establish the geographic and product market scope of an injunction.

## KING-SEELEY THERMOS CO. v. ALADDIN INDUSTRIES, INC.

### 418 F.2d 31 (2d Cir. 1969)

FRIENDLY, Circuit Judge.

**" THERMOS "**

This appeal is from a denial by our colleague, Judge Anderson, sitting in the District Court for the District of Connecticut, of a motion by Aladdin Industries, Incorporated, to modify a judgment and an order previously made by him in an action for threatened trade-mark infringement brought against it some years ago by the predecessor of King-Seeley Thermos Co., 289 F. Supp. 155. The opinion leading to the judgment (hereafter the decree of injunction) is reported in 207 F. Supp. 9 (D. Conn. 1962); the other order (hereafter the policing order) was entered on December 30, 1963, and is not officially reported. We shall state only such facts and history as are necessary to understand the issues here presented.

The controversy stemmed from King-Seeley's assertion of a valid trade-mark in the word Thermos, which it and its predecessors had registered in the United States Patent Office beginning in 1908. The initial registration was for "Thermos" printed as such; subsequent registrations covered the word in logotype and solid capitals; none related to the word beginning with a lower-case "t." Learning from Aladdin that it was about to market its line of vacuum-insulated containers through use of the term "thermos," King-Seeley brought suit to enjoin this. Aladdin counterclaimed for a declaration of invalidity of the trade-mark. The court concluded that Aladdin had "sustained its burden of proof that the word 'thermos' is descriptive and generic and belongs in the public domain." However, the court also concluded that there was "an appreciable, though minority, segment of the consumer public which knows, recognizes and uses the plaintiff's trade-mark 'Thermos.'" 207 F.Supp. at 14. In an effort to allow Aladdin to make use of the generic term on the one hand and "to eliminate confusion and the possibility of deceit of * * * consumers" on the other, the court permitted Aladdin to use the word "thermos" in its literature, advertising and labels only under seven conditions. Id. at 14-15. The most important of these for present purposes were that the word must be entirely in lower case letters and be preceded "by the possessive of the name 'Aladdin' or, at its option, the possessive of 'Aladdin' plus one of defendant's brand names." In the decree the court retained jurisdiction "for the purpose of enabling either of the parties to this Final Judgment to apply to this Court at any time for such further orders and directions as may be necessary or appropriate for the construction or carrying out of this Final Judgment, or the modification or termination of any of the provisions thereof in the light of changed circumstances, or for the enforcement of compliance therewith or for the punishment of violations thereof." King-Seeley appealed, Aladdin did not, and we affirmed, 321 F.2d 577 (2 Cir. 1963).

Aladdin shortly complained to the district court with respect to publicity and policing letters issued by King-Seeley. Finding that King-Seeley and, to a lesser extent, Aladdin had distorted the judgment, Judge Anderson issued a further order on December 30, 1963. This laid down ground rules designed to insure that all advertising or publicity referring to the judicial decision should fairly represent it, and authorized King-Seeley to send out policing letters to persons who it had cause to believe were violating its trademark. These could take the form of a simple notice of infringement and request for discontinuance or could add a citation, a citation and the summary of the decision that had been approved for use in publicity, or a discussion accompanied by a copy of this court's opinion.

In the motion that gives rise to this appeal, Aladdin sought modifications both of the decree of injunction and of the policing order. It proposed that the conditions listed in the original decree be continued only with respect to labels on its products and that in literature, advertising and publicity releases it should be permitted to use "thermos" in solid capitals or with an initial capital "when such typography and/or capitalization are consistent with that of other generic or common words appearing therewith or are in accordance with ordinary rules of grammar," provided only that the material be identified as emanating from Aladdin or its representatives and that Aladdin should be prohibited, as it was in the decree of injunction, from using the words "genuine" or "original" or synonyms thereof relating or referring to "thermos." In support of this it urged that the decree of injunction had handicapped its use of the generic term in various ways, e.g., by preventing publication of testimonial letters from satisfied customers using only the word "thermos," curtailing press releases since newspaper editors tended to reject those which made too frequent mention of the manufacturer, and preventing such effective forms of advertising as "Who makes the best thermos?" It submitted that any possibility of harm to King-Seeley from such advertising or publicity could be avoided by identifying the source, without requirements so severe as those in the decree. Aladdin also sought a modification of the policing order to provide that King-Seeley should not have reasonable cause to believe its trademark rights had been violated by the use of the term "thermos" by persons other than Aladdin in type forms not permitted to Aladdin itself, where such third parties had not used the logotype "THERMOS" and the typographical form and/or capitalization were consistent with that for other generic words. In support of this Aladdin urged that King-Seeley, while ignoring advertisements where dealers used "Thermos" or "THERMOS" without any identification of source, sent policing letters whenever a dealer used the word in one of these forms and identified it with the product of a competitor, with the result that many

Aladdin dealers became confused and refrained from advertising which the decree permitted. Finally, Aladdin urged that the policing order be amended in conformity with the changes sought in the decree of injunction, by altering the approved summary of the decision to explain that most of the restrictions applied only to Aladdin's labeling, not to its publicity or advertising.

Judge Anderson denied both branches of the motion [relying on] United States v. Swift & Co., 286 U.S. 106 (1932) and United States v. United Shoe Machinery Corp., 391 U.S. 244 (1968)...

The true holding of Swift was stated in United Shoe, 391 U.S. at 248:

> Swift teaches that a decree may be changed upon an appropriate showing, and it holds that it may not be changed in the interests of the defendants if the purposes of the litigation as incorporated in the decree (the elimination of monopoly and restrictive practices) have not been fully achieved.

A case like this involves no such sharp conflict between wrong-doing and right-doing as did Swift. It presents rather the need for drawing the line between two kinds of right-doing, King-Seeley's legitimate interest in protecting its trademark insofar as this is valid and Aladdin's equally legitimate interest in being free to sell its products by use of a generic term, and their opposites, attempts by King-Seeley to extend its trademark beyond its legal bounds and efforts by Aladdin to encroach upon the protected area. "The source of the power to modify is of course the fact that an injunction often requires continuing supervision by the issuing court and always a continuing willingness to apply its power and processes on behalf of the party who obtained that equitable relief." System Federation v. Wright, 364 U.S. at 647. Aladdin can be regarded as having obtained equitable relief in the decree of injunction quite as much as King-Seeley. That King-Seeley was the plaintiff was mere accident; the issue could as well have been tendered in a suit by Aladdin for declaratory relief. In that event the decree would very likely have directed that King-Seeley refrain from threatening Aladdin with liability for infringement under the prescribed conditions and Aladdin would now be seeking to "impose new and additional restrictions" upon what King-Seeley could do. While changes in fact or in law afford the clearest bases for altering an injunction, the power of equity has repeatedly been recognized as extending also to cases where a better appreciation of the facts in light of experience indicates that the decree is not properly adapted to accomplishing its purposes. Here, as Aladdin points out, the decree was entered before any experience concerning Aladdin's use of "thermos" had been had.

We think therefore that the court imposed unduly rigid restrictions on its consideration of so much of Aladdin's motion as requested modification of the decree of injunction and that it was free to grant relief if Aladdin could show that, in the light of experience, the detailed provisions of the decree seriously and needlessly impeded its exploitation of the generic term and that modification was necessary to achieve the results intended, even though this would take the form of reducing the restrictions imposed upon it. We express no opinion what the decision should be when that criterion is applied. Although the showing seems sufficient to justify an exercise of discretion in Aladdin's favor, it did not compel this. While we hold there is power to modify an injunction even in the absence of changed conditions, the power should be sparingly exercised. "Firmness and stability must no doubt be attributed to continuing injunctive relief based on adjudicated facts and law, and neither the plaintiff nor the court should be subjected to the unnecessary burden of re-establishing what has once been decided." System Federation v. Wright, 364 U.S. 642, 647 (1961). We thus leave decision to Judge Anderson under the standard we have enunciated.

Aladdin concedes that the judge applied the correct standard in passing on the branch of its motion that sought to modify the policing order, and we would see no reason for interfering with his refusal to alter this if it stood alone. Since, however, a modification of the decree of injunction might require some changes in the policing order, we vacate the order denying this part of Aladdin's motion so that the judge may have freedom to make such modification of the policing order, if any, as may become appropriate.

The order denying Aladdin's motion is vacated and the cause remanded for further proceedings not inconsistent with this opinion.

## CHARLES JACQUIN ET CIE, INC. v. DESTILERIA SERRALLES, INC.
### 921 F.2d 467 (3d Cir. 1990)

NYGAARD, Circuit Judge.

In this Lanham Act case, appellant Charles Jacquin et Cie, Inc. ("Jacquin") alleged that Destileria Serralles, Inc. ("DSI") and Crown Marketing International ("Crown") infringed on its products' trade dress in violation of 15 U.S.C. §1125(a) and state common law....

Jacquin, a Pennsylvania corporation, produces alcoholic beverages, including cordials. DSI, a Puerto Rican corporation, produces rum and rum schnapps. Crown was a Florida partnership which distributed DSI's products in the continental United States. At the time of trial, Crown was no longer in business.

In 1968 Jacquin developed a bottle of a particular shape for its line of cordials. The bottle is 10 and ¾ inches high, with a beveled or tapered bottom. Jacquin has consistently used this same shape of bottle for all the cordials in its line. Jacquin promotes its cordials through billboards, print ads, and other materials. The district court found that approximately 75 per cent of Jacquin's promotional materials include the bottle as part of the advertisement.

In 1985, representatives of Peter Harvey Wines ("PHW") suggested to DSI that it produce a rum-based schnapps which PHW would market in the United States. The representatives of PHW suggested that the rum schnapps be sold in a bottle similar to the bottle used for Blackstone whiskey in Mexico. The Blackstone whiskey bottle has a beveled bottom. In 1986, DSI submitted a Blackstone whiskey bottle to Owens-Illinois, Inc., a bottle manufacturer, to use as a sample. DSI instructed Owens-Illinois to increase the height of the bottle to 10 inches and to make a few other minor adjustments.

The bottle developed by Owens-Illinois became the bottle DSI uses for Don Juan rum schnapps in the United States. The Don Juan bottle is shorter than Jacquin's, and Jacquin's bottle has a longer neck. The Don Juan bottle has an eight sided cross-section while the Jacquin's bottle has a four sided cross-section. However, the Don Juan bottle has a similar appearance to the Jacquin's bottle when viewed from the front, primarily because both have beveled bottoms.

In the fall of 1987, DSI sold 2,700 cases of Don Juan schnapps to Crown for distribution in the United States. Crown sold Don Juan in New York, Michigan, New Jersey, Massachusetts, Florida, Virginia, New Hampshire, Pennsylvania, Vermont and Maine. In February 1988, Jacquin sent a cease and desist letter to Crown, alleging that the Don Juan bottle infringed on Jacquin's distinctive trade dress. Later that year, DSI repurchased 1,421 unsold cases of Don Juan from Crown.

Jacquin filed suit alleging that the Don Juan bottle infringed on its trade dress in violation of section 43(a) of the Lanham Act, 15 U.S.C. §1125(a), and common law.

[A jury found that the trade dress had secondary meaning and that confusion of source was likely.]

The district court, after a thorough review of Jacquin's sales records, concluded that the bottle had acquired secondary meaning only in Pennsylvania, and issued an injunction prohibiting DSI from using its bottle for cordial or specialty beverages in Pennsylvania. Jacquin appeals. . . .

The district court fashioned an injunction to protect Jacquin's bottle in markets where it had established such market penetration that DSI's bottle would present a real likelihood of confusion among consumers. The court concluded that Jacquin only had significant market penetration in Pennsylvania. Jacquin argues that it was entitled to protection in other markets. . . .

The proper geographic scope of an injunction in a trademark infringement case is determined by examining the market penetration of the mark. An injunction is appropriate only if the market penetration is "significant enough to pose the real likelihood of confusion among the consumers in that area." *Natural Footwear Ltd. v. Hart, Schaffner & Marx*, 760 F.2d 1383, 1397 (3d Cir.) (1985). Market penetration of a trademark is determined by: "(1) the volume of sales of the trademarked product; (2) growth trends (both positive and negative) in the area; (3) the number of persons actually purchasing the product in relation to the potential number of customers; and (4) the amount of product advertising in the area." *Natural Footwear*, 760 F.2d at 1398-99.

We examine the market, as the district court did, by reference to state boundaries. Although state boundaries are not always appropriate delineators of markets, alcoholic beverages are distributed and regulated on a state-by-state basis, and state boundaries are uniquely proper for defining their markets. State markets are generally divided into "control" states, where the sale and distribution of alcohol is strictly regulated by the state, and "open" states, where state control is minimal. Jacquin sells its cordials in both "open" and "control" states.

In *Natural Footwear*, we reviewed the market penetration of a New Jersey based clothing manufacturer. We determined that we need only consider market penetration in two states outside of New Jersey, since the clothing manufacturer had failed to establish sales above $5,000 per year or a total of over 50 customers for any one year in any other states. Jacquin argues that, since its sales of cordials exceeds $5,000 per year in Alabama, Delaware, Iowa, Maryland, New Hampshire, New Jersey, North Carolina, Rhode Island, Vermont, Virginia, West Virginia, its market penetration is more than *de minimis* and it is entitled to protection in those states. Jacquin misunderstands our holding in *Natural Footwear*. Surpassing the *de minimis* threshold did not result in automatic protection for the clothing manufacturer in *Natural Footwear*. In fact, we held that the market penetration in the two states surpassing the *de minimis* threshold was insufficient to warrant protection.

Jacquin argues that it has also surpassed the threshold set out in *Wrist-Rocket Manufacturing Co., Inc. v. Saunders Archery Co.*, 578 F.2d 727, 733 (8th Cir.1978). In *Wrist-Rocket*, the court set a ratio of one sale of the product in question per 20,000 persons as a threshold for establishing secondary meaning. Jacquin's efforts to treat these cases as establishing bright line tests is misguided. Whether a volume of sales is significant will vary with the product and the market. The numbers that result in injunctive relief in one case may not be significant in another.

In determining that Jacquin had only established secondary meaning and likelihood of confusion in Pennsylvania, the district court relied primarily on the volume of sales prong of the *Natural Footwear* test. The district court summarized Jacquin's sales volume in the following chart:

| STATE | JACQUIN SALES | TOTAL SALES | PERCENTAGE |
|-------|---------------|-------------|------------|
| Alabama | 371 | 67,622 | 5.4 [sic .54] |
| Iowa | 311 | 213,095 | 0.14 |
| New Hampshire | 7,921 | 306,044 | 2.58 |
| North Carolina | 2,971 | 175,680 | 1.69 |
| Vermont | 315 | 82,469 | 0.38 |
| Virginia | 12,112 | 225,034 | 0.53 [sic −5.38] |
| West Virginia | 5,771 | 59,705 | 3.8 [sic 9.66] |
| Pennsylvania | 219,918 | 945,223 | 23.26 |

The district court concluded from these numbers that, since Jacquin's sales were less than three percent in all but two areas other than Pennsylvania, Jacquin's had failed to demonstrate "sufficient market penetration to warrant injunctive relief in any state but Pennsylvania." At 666.

There are several mathematical errors in the calculation of percentages in the above table. The correct percentages for Alabama, Virginia, and West Virginia are .54, 5.38, and 9.66, respectively. The first error is of little consequence, since the correct percentage reveals sales even lower than the district court believed. The second two errors, however, are more troubling. The correct percentages for Virginia and West Virginia indicate that sales in those states may well support a finding of market penetration sufficient to establish secondary meaning. The district court's findings in this respect are incomplete, since it is unclear what share of the market other cordials makers commanded. A three percent share may seem small in absolute terms, but if no other maker has more than a few percent share, three percent may be significant.

Since the district court crafted this injunction based on clearly erroneous fact findings, we will vacate the district court's injunction to the extent it limited protection to Pennsylvania. We will remand for the district court to make appropriate findings on Jacquin's market penetration in other states. We remand rather than conduct this analysis ourselves because it is not clear where the district court obtained some of the numbers it relied on. Jacquin submitted into evidence two annual reports of the National Alcoholic Beverage Control Association ("NABCA"), an industry group that compiles sales statistics for alcoholic beverages in several states. The sales summaries in those reports, however, do not correspond to the numbers in the chart the district court produced in its opinion.[6] It may be that...the numbers in the district court's opinion are the correct ones, but since we are unable to determine this from the record before us, we will remand.[7]

Jacquin [also] challenges the district court's injunction because it limited protection of Jacquin's trade dress to "cordials and specialties." Jacquin argues that protection should have been extended to the larger class of "spirits," which would include whiskeys, rums, vodkas, and gins as well as brandies and liqueurs. The district court limited the injunction because Jacquin had failed to present any evidence that its trade dress had acquired secondary meaning within the distilled spirits market as a whole or that consumers of distilled spirits, as opposed to the subset of consumers of cordials and specialties, would likely be confused by DSI's trade dress. The district court noted that the evidence at trial concerned only Jacquin's cordials sales, and did not address the distilled spirits market as a whole.

We stated the test for determining when an injunction should issue against infringing but non-competing products in *Scott Paper Co. v. Scott's Liquid Gold, Inc.*, 589 F.2d 1225 (3d Cir. 1978). Secondary meaning and likelihood of confusion are again the standards, but the analysis proceeds somewhat differently than when addressing geographic scope of protection. Makers of non-competing products may be enjoined from using a particular mark or trade dress where a consumer might assume that the

---

6. Apparently the district court relied on numbers supplied by Jacquin in its post-trial memorandum. Jacquin, however, has not included in this record the exhibit it submitted to the district court explaining how it calculated the numbers. Consequently, we cannot determine if Jacquin made some error, or relied on matters not in evidence, in calculating the totals.

7. Similarly, we can not determine why the district court did not credit the apparently uncontested testimony of Kevin O'Brien, Jacquin's vice-president in charge of national sales, on Jacquin's sales in the "open" states of New Jersey, Delaware, Maryland, and Rhode Island. App. p. 147. There may have been reason for the district court to discredit this testimony. On remand, the district court will have an opportunity to fully address this point.

non-competing product comes from the same source as the trademarked product. Ten factors should be considered in this regard: "(1) the degree of similarity between the owner's mark and the alleged infringing mark; (2) the strength of the owner's mark; (3) the price of the goods and other factors indicative of the care and attention expected of consumers when making a purchase; (4) the length of time the defendant has used the mark without evidence of actual confusion arising; (5) the intent of the defendant in adopting the mark; (6) the evidence of actual confusion; (7) whether the goods, though not competing, are marked through the same channels of trade and advertised through the same media; (8) the extent to which the targets of the parties' sales efforts are the same; (9) the relationship of the goods in the minds of consumers because of the similarity of function; (10) other facts suggesting that the consuming public might expect the prior owner to manufacture a product in the defendant's market, or that he is likely to expand into that market." *Interpace Corp. v. Lapp, Inc.*, 721 F.2d 460, 463 (3d Cir. 1983) (*citing Scott Paper*, 589 F.2d at 1229).

Applying this test to the evidence Jacquin introduced, we conclude that the district court properly limited this injunction to cordials and specialties. First, Jacquin's bottle and DSI's bottle are similar in outline, but the similarity of the bottle designs is lessened considerably when the bottles are viewed with their complete labeling. Jacquin only asserted secondary meaning in the shape of the bottle. In determining the secondary meaning and likelihood of confusion, however, we need to view the total package as a consumer would. As for the strength of Jacquin's trade dress, the district court found that it was prominent in only a few markets.

Jacquin presented no evidence to establish the third factor, the care with which consumers select cordials or distilled spirits. Indeed, Jacquin presented no consumer evidence whatsoever. It presented no consumer surveys to show consumer expectations or actual confusion, so likewise neither the fourth nor sixth factor favors Jacquin. The only evidence of DSI's intent in adopting its bottle shape was the testimony that the bottle was modeled on the Blackstone whiskey bottle.

As to the seventh factor, there was evidence that, at least in the control states, all distilled spirits are marketed through the same channels and advertised similarly. Jacquin, however, has not demonstrated that the targets of its sales efforts for cordials are the same as any sales efforts DSI might direct toward consumers of other distilled spirits. Similarly, Jacquin introduced no surveys or other evidence showing that consumers would find that distilled spirits such as rum and vodka have a similar function as cordials. Finally, other facts indicate that consumers likely would not be confused by DSI using its bottle for rum or other distilled spirits. Jacquin does sell other distilled spirits, but does not package them in the same bottle as it uses for cordials. Evaluating all the factors of the *Scott Paper* test, we conclude that the district court did not abuse its discretion by limiting injunctive relief to cordials and specialties....

We will affirm the district court's injunction to the extent that it limited protection to cordials and specialties, however, we will vacate and remand the portion of the injunction that limited protection to Pennsylvania for further proceedings in accordance with this opinion. Each side shall bear its own costs.

## Comments

1. **The Equitable Nature of Injunctions.** *King-Seeley* is noteworthy because injunctive relief is given to King-Seeley even though the THERMOS mark had become generic. Even though a generic mark may not be registered, the injunction serves to prevent confusion. The idea that generic marks get some slight protection is not new. The opinion in *Forschner Group Inc. v. Arrow Trading Co., Inc.*, reproduced in Chapter 3, protected the original importers of "Swiss Army knives" even though the phrase could not have trademark protection.

   The narrow scope of the injunction in *King-Seeley* reflects the narrow scope of rights to a generic mark. In the original injunction, Aladdin was permitted to use the formerly trademarked term "thermos," but only in lowercase letters preceded by the possessive of the word "Aladdin." The appellant court viewed favorably Aladdin's request to expand its rights to the term. Infringement warnings sent by the user of a mark to competitors ("policing letters") must reflect the specific nature of any injunction that has been issued. The narrow scope of the injunction reflected the court's view that both parties had rights that deserved equitable recognition. What were the respective rights of the parties? Will both parties to an infringement action always have similar rights to be balanced?

2. **Intent as an Equitable Consideration.** In *United States v. Swift*, discussed in *King-Seeley*, the Court concluded that the defendants had abused their powers so grossly and persistently that their conduct should be subjected to extraordinary restraints and denied the defendants' request for a modification of a broad injunction. Courts agree that injunctions can be therapeutic as well as protective, so an injunction may be broader if the infringer has engaged in deliberate wrongdoing or attempted to come as close to the line where confusion is likely as possible. A broader injunction might mean adopting a "safe distance" rule, which, as the label suggests, enjoins the infringer from conduct that comes anywhere close to the line of causing confusion. The last opinion in this chapter, *Tamko Roofing Products, Inc. v. Ideal Roofing Company, Ltd.*, applies this rule to a case where the infringer used the mark H25 to compete with the plaintiff's registered mark HERITAGE 25. In *King-Seeley*, by contrast, the court was very sympathetic to Aladdin's legitimate interest in using the generic term "thermos" and drafted the injunction very narrowly.

3. **Injunctive Protection of Trade Dress.** Generally, trade dress is protectable if it is not functional and is distinctive (either inherently or as a result of the acquisition of secondary meaning). As with other types of marks, the more distinctive the trade dress, the broader will be the scope of the injunction. Strong marks get strong protection. In *Ambrit, Inc. v. Kraft, Inc.*, 812 F.2d 1531 (11th Cir. 1983), Ambrit sought protection for trade dress consisting of a polar bear figure on a silver foil wrapper with royal blue lettering and an artic sun image used on its chocolate-covered Klondike ice cream bar. The court found that this was only a moderately strong mark because it was suggestive (of cold, which is a characteristic of the ice cream bar) and contained elements similar though not identical to those used in the trade dress of at least eight other sellers of frozen desserts. Kraft produced Polar B'ars, a competing five-ounce

chocolate-covered ice cream bar and used a polar bear and a silver foil wrapper as its trade dress. The court declined to recognize that Ambrit had any exclusive right to the polar bear figure, but did have a right to prevent confusion resulting from others' use of trade dress creating the same overall impression. The court enjoined only Kraft's use of the polar bear on five-ounce ice cream bars (leaving it free to use the bear on other products) because Ambrit's trade dress had only moderate strength as a source indicator. In support of this limitation, the court noted that Kraft had intentionally designed its trade dress to resemble Ambrit's. Despite the fact that Ambrit had no exclusive right to the bear, the court focused on the restrictions necessary to prevent confusion. The proper scope of any injunction would reflect the strength of the mark and the likelihood of confusion from others' use. In addition, an injunction may be therapeutic as well as protective. When a party has "transgressed the governing legal standards, a court of equity is free to proscribe activities that, standing alone, would have been unassailable." *Id.* at 1548.

4. *Geographic and Product Market Scope of Injunctions.* The discussion of the scope of rights in Chapter 2 illustrated the principle that confusion can occur only in markets where awareness of the mark owner's use has penetrated. *See National Assoc. for Healthcare Communications, Inc. v. Central Arkansas Area Agency on Aging, Inc.* As *Charles Jacquin* illustrates, the scope of injunctions also reflects this principle. The court in *Charles Jacquin* relied on the four-factor *Natural Footwear* test for geographic market penetration. Compare that test to the *Sweetarts* test used in the *National Assoc. for Healthcare,* which considered the dollar value of the plaintiff's sales at the time the other entered the market, the number of customers of the plaintiff compared to the population of the state, the relative and potential growth of the plaintiff's sales, and length of time since significant sales.

Neither the geographic area nor the range of products to which the injunction applies is determined by a bright line test. The key is the potential for confusion. While the court in *Charles Jacquin* used the geographic market penetration test to determine consumers' exposure to the plaintiff's mark and define the geographic scope of the injunction, it used the likelihood of confusion test to define the product market scope. The individual factors in that test are used to determine the boundaries of how the infringer will be permitted to market its product and which of the infringer's products should be covered by the injunction. The focus is on what marketing methods and products are likely to cause confusion.

**5. *Standards for Granting Injunctions.*** When deciding whether an injunction is appropriate, courts consider (1) whether the party requesting a permanent injunction has shown actual success on the merits (or a likelihood of success on the merits for a preliminary injunction), (2) whether that party will suffer irreparable injury if the injunction is not granted, (3) whether the granting of the injunction will cause even greater harm to the other party, and (4) whether an injunction is in the public interest. The Restatement (Third) of Unfair Competition §35(2) identifies eight factors a court might consider given that injunctive and monetary relief in trademark cases are equitable remedies: (a) the nature of the interest to be protected; (b) the nature and extent of the wrongful conduct; (c) the relative adequacy to the plaintiff of an injunction and of other remedies; (d) the relative harm likely to result to the legitimate interests of the defendant if an injunction is granted and to the legitimate interests of the plaintiff if an injunction is denied; (e) the interests of third persons and of the public; (f) any unreasonable delay by the plaintiff in bringing suit or otherwise asserting its rights; (g) any related misconduct on the part of the plaintiff; and (h) the practicality of framing and enforcing the injunction.

# C. MONETARY RECOVERY

This section introduces several of the approaches taken by courts to determine the availability and amount of monetary awards for damages, accountings, and attorneys' fees. There is wide room for creative "lawyering" in the remedies portion of an infringement action. This section provides the basic vocabulary necessary to understand those disputes.

*Maltina Corp. v. Cawy Bottling Co.* deals with burden of proof and accounting issues presented when calculating a plaintiff's lost profits and a defendant's ill-gotten profits. As Lanham Act §35 indicates, courts may consider equitable factors when deciding the proper amount of monetary recovery, particularly whether to award an accounting, discussed in *Maltin*, and attorneys' fees. Attorneys' fees are awarded only in "exceptional" cases. *Tamko Roofing Products, Inc. v. Ideal Roofing Company, Ltd.* describes the standards for determining whether an award of attorneys' fees is appropriate, for determining whether a party's conduct before and during litigation was oppressive, and for establishing the amount of fees.

## MALTINA CORP. v. CAWY BOTTLING CO.

### 613 F.2d 582 (5th Cir. 1980)

JOHNSON, Circuit Judge.

### I. THE FACTS

Cawy Bottling Company (Cawy), defendant below, appeals from the judgment of the district court in favor of the plaintiffs Maltina Corporation and Julio Blanco-Herrera in their trademark infringement action. The district court enjoined Cawy from further infringement, awarded the plaintiffs $35,000 actual damages, and ordered the defendant to account for $55,050 of gross profit earned from the sale of infringing products.

Julio Blanco-Herrera fled to this country from Cuba in late 1960 after that country nationalized the company of which he was president and, along with his family, majority stockholder. Before that year, this company was one of the largest breweries and beverage distributors in Cuba. Among its products was malta, a dark, non-alcoholic carbonated beverage brewed similar to beer. The Cuban company distributed malta under the trademarks "Malta Cristal" and "Cristal" in Cuba and in the United States. The Cuban company had registered the marks both in Cuba and the United States. When Blanco-Herrera arrived in the United States, he formed the Maltina Corporation and assigned the "Cristal" trademark to it. He attempted to produce and distribute "Cristal" in this country, but despite his efforts Maltina Corporation was never able to obtain sufficient financial backing to produce more than $356 worth of "Cristal".

Cawy Bottling, however, had an altogether different experience in producing malta. At the outset, it attempted to register the "Cristal" trademark so that it might be utilized in marketing the product. This attempt was rejected by the Patent Office because of plaintiffs' prior registration. After this attempted registration and with the knowledge of the plaintiffs' ownership of the trademark, Cawy began producing and distributing malta under the "Cristal" label in February 1968.

In 1970 the plaintiffs sued Cawy under 15 U.S.C. §1117 for trademark infringement and unfair competition. They sought an injunction against further use of their mark, damages, and an accounting. The district court dismissed the suit on the ground that Cuba's confiscation of the assets of Blanco-Herrera's Cuban corporation made Blanco-Herrera's assignment of the "Cristal" mark to the Maltina Corporation invalid. This Court reversed, holding Cuba's confiscation decree did not extend to the "Cristal" mark registered by the United States Patent Office. Maltina Corp. v. Cawy Bottling Co., 462 F.2d 1021 (5th Cir.), cert. denied, 409 U.S. 1060 (1972). On remand, the district court determined that the plaintiffs had a valid trademark. Cawy appealed, and we affirmed. Maltina Corp. v. Cawy Bottling Co., 491 F.2d 1391 (1974) (per curiam).

At trial on the merits, from which this appeal is taken, the district court determined that Cawy had infringed the plaintiffs' mark and assigned the case to a magistrate for determination of what recovery was appropriate under 15 U.S.C. Section 1117. Before holding a hearing the magistrate wrote a memorandum to the district court stating that he thought that the plaintiffs were entitled to an injunction but not to an accounting for defendant's profits.

After holding the hearing, however, the magistrate changed his recommendation. He noted that Cawy designed its "Cristal" label to resemble the label used by Maltina's predecessor in Cuba. He found that Cawy intended to exploit the reputation and good will of the "Cristal" mark and to deceive and mislead the Latin community into believing that the "Cristal" once sold in Cuba was now being sold in the United States. The magistrate further found that Cawy willfully infringed the plaintiffs' mark and had been unjustly enriched to the detriment of plaintiffs' reputation and good will. He recommended that Cawy account to the plaintiffs for the profit it earned from the infringement, and he directed Cawy to report its sales of "Cristal" and associated costs to the plaintiffs for determination of its profits. The magistrate also found Cawy's infringement damaged the reputation and good will of the plaintiffs in the amount of $35,000. He recommended that Cawy compensate plaintiffs in that amount.

The district court, after a complete and independent review of the record, adopted the magistrate's recommendations as its order. As more fully discussed below, the district court eventually found Cawy liable to the plaintiffs for its gross profits from the sale of "Cristal", $55,050. The court entered judgment against Cawy for $55,050 gross profits plus $35,000 damages and enjoined Cawy from any further infringement of the plaintiffs' mark.

Cawy presents three arguments on appeal. First, it argues that an accounting was inappropriate. Second, that if an accounting was appropriate, the district court erred in awarding to the plaintiff Cawy's entire gross profits from the sales of "Cristal". Third, Cawy argues that the award of $35,000 actual damages cannot stand in the absence of any evidence to support it. We accept this final contention, but reject the first two. Cawy does not complain on appeal of the district court's enjoining it from further infringement of the plaintiffs' mark.

## II.  WAS AN ACCOUNTING APPROPRIATE?

Section 1117, 15 U.S.C., entitles a markholder to recover, subject to the principles of equity, the profits earned by a defendant from infringement of the mark. The courts have expressed two views of the circumstances in which an accounting is proper under 15 U.S.C. Section 1117. Some courts view the award of an accounting as simply a means of compensating a markholder for loss or diverted sales. Other courts view an accounting not as compensation for lost or diverted sales, but as redress for the defendant's unjust enrichment and as a deterrent to further infringement. See Maier Brewing Co. v. Fleischman Distilling Corp., 390 F.2d 117, 121 (9th Cir.) cert. denied, 391 U.S. 966 (1968). In this case, the plaintiffs never sold any appreciable amount of "Cristal" in the United States so they cannot claim that Cawy diverted any of their sales. Accordingly, we must decide whether diversion of sales is a prerequisite to an award of an accounting. We hold that it is not.

In Maier Brewing, the Ninth Circuit awarded an accounting to a plaintiff who was not in direct competition with a defendant and who, accordingly, had not suffered any diversion of sales from the defendant's infringement. The court noted that the defendant had willfully and deliberately infringed. It reasoned that awarding an accounting would further Congress' purpose in enacting 15 U.S.C. Section 1117 of making infringement unprofitable. This Court is in accord with this reasoning. The Fifth Circuit has not addressed the issue whether an accounting only compensates for diverted sales or whether an accounting serves the broader functions of remedying an infringer's unjust enrichment and deterring future infringement. A recent opinion by this Court, however, recognizes that a trademark is a protected property right. This recognition of a trademark as property is consistent with the view that an accounting is proper even if the defendant and plaintiff are not in direct competition, and the defendants' infringement has not diverted sales from the plaintiff. The Ninth Circuit in Maier Brewing noted that the infringer had used the markholder's property to make a profit and that an accounting would force the infringer to disgorge its unjust enrichment. Here, the only valuable property Blanco-Herrera had when he arrived in this country was his right to the "Cristal" mark. Cawy used this property, and an accounting is necessary to partially remedy its unjust enrichment.

The district court relied, in part, on W. E. Bassett Co. v. Revlon, Inc., 435 F.2d 656 (2nd Cir. 1970), in ordering an accounting. That case held that an accounting should be granted "if the defendant is unjustly enriched, if the plaintiff sustained damages from the infringement, or if an accounting is necessary to deter a willful infringer from doing so again." Id. at 664. Revlon sold a cuticle trimmer embossed with a "Cuti-Trim" mark "in the teeth of the patent office's refusal to register" that mark. Id. at 662. This was willful infringement that an accounting would deter in the future. In the instant case, the district court found that Cawy's "infringement was willful and that such infringement resulted in (Cawy) being unjustly enriched...." Cawy used the "Cristal" mark after the patent office refused to register it. This clearly and explicitly supports the finding of willful infringement. An injunction alone will not adequately deter future infringement. In short, we find the district court properly ordered Cawy to account to the plaintiffs for the profits it earned from its willful infringement. This accounting serves two purposes: remedying unjust enrichment and deterring future infringement.

### III.  DID THE DISTRICT COURT ERR IN REQUIRING CAWY TO ACCOUNT FOR ITS ENTIRE GROSS PROFIT FROM THE SALE OF "CRISTAL"?

The district court ordered Cawy to account to the plaintiffs for $55,050, the entire gross profit (total revenue less cost of goods sold) from the sale of "Cristal". The district court did not allow Cawy to deduct overhead and other expenses. These expenses would have produced a net loss from the sale of "Cristal" and, if allowed, would have enabled Cawy to escape liability to the plaintiffs for its infringement.

Under 15 U.S.C. Section 1117, the plaintiff has the burden of showing the amount of the defendant's sales of the infringing product. The defendant has the burden of showing all elements of cost and other deductions. In this case, the court ordered Cawy to report its total sales of "Cristal" and associated costs to the plaintiffs. If the plaintiffs objected to Cawy's estimate of its net profits from "Cristal", they were to file their objection with the court. The record on appeal reflects that Cawy submitted three exhibits showing its net loss on "Cristal" sales. These exhibits are set out in the below. The plaintiffs filed their objections to Cawy's figures with the court. They accepted Cawy's estimate of gross revenues from the sale of "Cristal" and the cost of goods sold. Thus, they met the burden of proving the amount of sales of the infringing product. The plaintiffs, however, did not accept other deductions claimed by Cawy. Cawy claimed deductions for "EXPENSES SPECIFICALLY IDENTIFIED WITH MALTA CRISTAL", as set out in Exhibit 2. Plaintiffs objected to these claimed deductions because Cawy did not show they were actually spent on "Cristal". Cawy also claimed deductions for general overhead, apportioned to "Cristal" on the basis of the ratio of "Cristal" sales to Cawy's total sales. Exhibit 3 displays these claimed overhead deductions. The plaintiffs objected to the overhead deductions because the infringing product constituted only a small percentage of the defendant's business.

**Defendant's Exhibit 1.**
Net Loss on Sales of Malta Cristal

|  | 1969 | 1970 | 1971 | 1972 | 1973 | 1974 | 1975 | TOTAL |
|---|---|---|---|---|---|---|---|---|
| Revenues from sales of Malta Cristal | $40,032 | $41,705 | $83,861 | $ 60,119 | $31,099 | $14,666 | — | $271,482 |
| Less cost of goods sold | 31,883 | 34,059 | 67,285 | 46,438 | 25,209 | 11,558 | — | 216,432 |
| **GROSS PROFIT** | **$ 8,149** | **$ 7,646** | **$16,576** | **$ 13,681** | **$ 5,890** | **$ 3,108** | — | **$ 55,050** |
| Less expenses per Exhibit 2 | 8,165 | 6,479 | 10,175 | 17,870 | 17,007 | 9,353 | 500 | 69,549 |
| Per Exhibit 3 | 6,683 | 4,250 | 7,859 | 6,448 | 3,199 | 1,762 | — | 30,201 |
| **TOTAL EX-PENSES** | **$14,848** | **$10,729** | **$18,034** | **$ 24,318** | **$ 20,206** | **$11,115** | **$ 500** | **$ 99,750** |
| **(NET LOSS)** | **$ (6,699)** | **$ (3,083)** | **$ (1,458)** | **$(10,637)** | **$(14,316)** | **$ (8,007)** | **$(500)** | **$(44,700)** |

**Defendant's Exhibit 2.**
Expenses Specifically Identified with Malta Cristal

|  | 1969 | 1970 | 1971 | 1972 | 1973 | 1974 | 1975 | TOTAL |
|---|---|---|---|---|---|---|---|---|
| Advertising | $2,277 | $1,723 | $4,299 | $13,080 | $13,124 | $6,510 | — | $41,013 |
| Sales commissions | 3,137 | 3,172 | 5,505 | 4,116 | 1,732 | 752 | — | 18,414 |
| Legal fees | 2,130 | 1,500 | 200 | 483 | 1,988 | 709 | — | 7,010 |
| Telephone and telegraph | 43 | 84 | 171 | 191 | 163 | 13 | — | 665 |
| Other | 578 | — | — | — | — | 1,369 | 500 | 2,447 |
| **Total** | **$8,165** | **$6,479** | **$10,175** | **$17,870** | **$17,007** | **$9,353** | **$500** | **$69,549** |

**Defendant's Exhibit 3.**

Expenses Related to Malta Cristal Allocated Based on Sales Ratio

| | 1969 | 1970 | 1971 | 1972 | 1973 | 1974 | 1975 | TOTAL |
|---|---|---|---|---|---|---|---|---|
| Malta Cristal cases sold | 15,139 | 15,439 | 30,151 | 21,471 | 10,849 | 5,238 | –0– | 98,287 |
| Total number of cases sold | 176,458 | 228,000 | 276,424 | 288,500 | 296,590 | 314,485 | –0– | 1,580,457 |
| Ratio of Malta's cases to total cases sold | 8.58% | 6.77% | 10.91% | 7.44% | 3.66% | 1.67% | — | 6.22% |
| **Expenses Related to Malta** | | | | | | | | |
| 1. Repairs and mainte-nance | $1,323 | $524 | $762 | $1,256 | $663 | $1,091 | — | $5,619 |
| 2. Rent | 6,864 | 6,864 | 7,938 | — | — | — | — | 21,666 |
| 3. Building depreciation | — | — | — | 3,073 | 3,073 | 3,073 | — | 9,219 |
| 4. Interest— mostly build-ing | — | — | — | 11,958 | 14,408 | 13,758 | — | 40,124 |
| 5. Taxes other than payroll | 4,932 | 8,065 | 5,645 | 12,456 | 11,964 | 10,791 | — | 53,853 |
| 5. Payroll taxes | 7,718 | 6,282 | 8,582 | 6,624 | 6,859 | 6,787 | — | 42,852 |
| 6. Trucks' expenses | 7,238 | 6,301 | 12,502 | 13,083 | 9,482 | 8,668 | — | 57,274 |
| 7. Utilities | 1,620 | — | 509 | — | — | — | — | 2,129 |
| 8. Indirect labor | 23,156 | 9,360 | 9,360 | 11,305 | 12,480 | 12,450 | — | 78,111 |
| 9. Officers' salaries | 17,500 | 13,000 | 13,000 | 13,000 | 13,000 | 31,750 | — | 101,250 |
| 10. Office expenses | 403 | 665 | — | 1,046 | 767 | 1,503 | — | 4,384 |
| 11. Sales promotion | 808 | 95 | 275 | 1,513 | — | 82 | — | 2,773 |
| 12. Insurance | 3,536 | 5,031 | 6,967 | 6,566 | 8,722 | 8,265 | — | 39,087 |
| 13. Uniforms | 916 | 926 | 1,119 | 1,129 | 1,180 | 1,483 | — | 6,753 |
| 14. Traveling | — | 2,613 | 2,255 | 324 | 820 | 2,938 | — | 8,950 |
| 15. Account-ing fees | 165 | 970 | 800 | 1,485 | — | 2,875 | — | 6,295 |
| 16. Miscella-neous | 1,714 | 2,088 | 2,320 | 1,843 | 3,980 | — | — | 11,945 |
| TOTAL EXPENSES | $77,893 | $62,784 | $72,034 | $86,661 | $87,398 | $105,514 | — | $492,284 |
| MALTA TO TOTAL RATIO | 8.58% | 6.77% | 10.91% | 7.44% | 3.66% | 1.67% | — | |
| **MALTA RELATED TOTAL EXPENSES** | **$6,683** | **$4,250** | **$7,859** | **$6,448** | **$3,199** | **$1,762** | **—** | **$30,201** |

Cawy responded to the plaintiffs' objections by asserting that it did have "specific and detailed figures and corroborating sales slips, invoices and the like to support" its claims of expenses attributable to "Cristal". Cawy failed, however, to submit any of this corroboration to the district court.

The district court, after noting that Cawy had the burden of establishing deductions from gross profits, disallowed Cawy's claims of expenses specifically attributable to "Cristal" as set forth in Exhibit 2. The court stated that it could not determine whether the advertising, sales commissions, legal fees, telephone, and other expenses claimed by Cawy related to "Cristal" sales or to the sales of other products. It then held that Cawy failed to sustain its burden of proof with respect to those claimed expenses. We cannot say that the district court erred in its holding. The record on appeal, like the record before the district court, simply affords no support for the contention that the claimed "EXPENSES SPECIFICALLY IDENTIFIED WITH MALTA CRISTAL" actually related to "Cristal" sales. Furthermore, Cawy's claims of deductions of legal fees, as the district court noted, would not be allowable in any case. While we cannot tell whether these fees related to this suit; if they did, they would not be deductible.

The district court also disallowed Cawy's deductions of a proportionate part of its overhead expenses as set forth in Exhibit 3. Quoting from Societee Anonyme v. Western Distilling Co., 46 F. 921 (C.C.E.D. Mo. 1891), the district court noted, "It appears that 'the unlawful venture increased the gross profits without swelling the gross expenses'." It then held that Cawy failed to sustain its burden of showing the propriety of allowing deductions for overhead. Again, we must agree with the district court that Cawy failed to meet its burden of showing its expenses in the absence from the record on appeal of any evidence that Cawy's production of "Cristal" actually increased its overhead expenses. Furthermore, we note that a proportionate share of overhead is not deductible when the sales of an infringing product constitute only a small percentage of total sales. Here, on the average, infringing sales constituted just over 6% of total sales. Accordingly, we think it unlikely, especially in the absence of any evidence to the contrary, that Cawy's production of "Cristal" increased its overhead expenses.

The district court properly ordered Cawy to account for its entire gross profit from the sale of "Cristal". Cawy failed to meet its burden of showing that the overhead and other expenses that it claimed in Exhibits 2 and 3 actually related to the production of "Cristal".

## IV. DID THE DISTRICT COURT ERR IN AWARDING THE PLAINTIFFS $35,000 AS ACTUAL DAMAGES FOR CAWY'S INFRINGEMENT?

The district court awarded the plaintiffs $35,000 as actual damages from Cawy's infringement. The record, however, is wholly devoid of support for this figure. Accordingly, we must reverse as to this element.

The plaintiffs have never been able to get sufficient financial backing to produce more than a very small amount of "Cristal" in the United States. That inability makes proof of actual damages from Cawy's infringement unlikely. In any event, the plaintiffs have had an opportunity to show their damages and have failed to do so. This Court concludes that plaintiffs should not have another opportunity to show their damages just as Cawy should not have another opportunity to prove its expenses.

In the ten years since the plaintiffs filed their original petition, this case has been before us three times. All litigation must end. We remand only for entry of judgment in accordance with this opinion.

## Comments

1. *Causation and Monetary Recovery.* Tort law causation principles apply to claims for monetary relief in trademark cases. If a plaintiff seeks damages, the plaintiff must prove that the defendant's conduct caused harm such as a diversion of trade that reduced profits. If there is no evidence that consumers were confused, it is difficult to infer that the defendant took business away from the plaintiff. Evidence of intentional deception by the defendant may support a conclusion that consumers were confused. Thus, courts often require evidence either of actual confusion or intent to confuse to justify an award of damages.

If a plaintiff seeks and is otherwise entitled to an accounting, however, the defendant has the burden of showing that its profits were not caused by its infringing activity. If, for instance, the defendant can prove that some of its sales would have occurred even if it had not infringed on the plaintiff's mark, the plaintiff is not entitled to that portion of the defendant's profits.

2. *Damages, Lost Profits.* The Fifth Circuit in *Maltina* reversed the award of $35,000 in actual damages (lost profit) because there was no evidence supporting that loss. Plaintiffs often have great difficulty proving their lost profits because those losses were too speculative. The plaintiff's business must have enough of a track record to provide a foundation for calculating lost profits. In *Zazú Designs v. L'Oreal*, which is discussed in Chapter 2, the Zazú hair salon claimed it would have made $4 profit per bottle on the 25,000 bottles of shampoo it ordered before L'Oreal allegedly infringed its trademark. The Seventh Circuit Court of Appeals objected to the trial court's award of $100,000 in lost profits because there was no evidence of how much Zazú could have sold, either in their own salon or to others. Just ordering the bottles was not enough proof; "people who want damages have to prove them, using methodologies that need not be intellectually sophisticated but must not insult the intelligence."

One way to measure actual damages when parties compete is to compare the plaintiff's profits during the "infringing period" to a "base period" before the infringement. The trademark owner in *Borg-Warner Corp. v. York-Shipley, Inc.*, 136 U.S.P.Q. 255 (D. Ill. 1963), adequately projected sales of its heating equipment from the base to the infringing period. It estimated lost profits on those sales by referring to records of costs incurred to produce such equipment. While the infringer attempted to prove that the lost sales were due to other factors, such as personnel changeover and problems with supply, that evidence was unconvincing.

Lanham Act §29 provides that a registered trademark owner who does not display the mark with an R enclosed in a circle, ®, or the words "Registered in U.S. Patent and Trademark Office," may not recover profits or damages without proof the defendant had actual notice of the registration.

3. *Recovery of Lost Profits as well as Defendant's Profits.* The amount finally awarded in *Maltina* reflects the defendant's ill-gotten profits rather than the plaintiff's lost profits. The court held that it was not necessary for a plaintiff to prove that sales were diverted from the plaintiff to the defendant to recover the defendant's profits. One rationale for permitting plaintiffs to recover the defendant's profits from the infringing activity is that it is difficult for plaintiffs to prove their own losses. To the extent the defendant earned profits by diverting trade from the plaintiff, the defendant's profits might be a good estimate of the plaintiff's actual damages. Section 35(a) of the Lanham Act, however, connects these two types of monetary awards with a conjunction, allowing recovery, in appropriate cases, of both defendant's profits and any damages sustained by the plaintiff. What kind of cases would those be?

Both types of monetary recovery may be allowed where lost profit amounts are difficult to prove. In *United Phosphorus, Ltd. v. Midland Fumigant, Inc.*, 205 F.3d 1219 (10th Cir. 2000), the plaintiff, United, had offered documentary and testimonial evidence that it had suffered over $4 million in damages. As part of those losses, United's expert calculated lost profits of $376,346 and Midland's profits from infringement at $385,520. Midland claimed that the jury award of $761,866 (the sum) was double-recovery. Because the jury could have believed the evidence of $4 million in actual damages, the appellate court found that permitting recovery of both lost profits and defendant's profits was permissible. A trademark owner's actual damages may also exceed its past lost profits because it may also have lost opportunities to grow and expand its future sales. While difficult to prove, lost future profits are also potentially recoverable.

Where there is accurate evidence of both plaintiff's actual damages and defendant's profits from infringement *and* the defendant's sales were to customers that would have purchased from the plaintiff, an award of both damages and an accounting might be inappropriate. If, for instance, Cawy had diverted $35,000 in profits from Maltina to itself, awarding Maltina $35,000 plus Cawy's profits double-counts that $35,000 in lost profit. Allowing plaintiff to recover both measures would result in overcompensation, which sounds like the kind of "penalty" the statute prohibits. One solution in such cases is to deduct from the total the amount of overlap, that is, subtract the loss profit due to diverted sales.

4. *Willfulness and Accounting for Profits.* The Federal Circuit Courts of Appeal appear to be split on the question of whether willfulness is a prerequisite to an accounting or just one factor to consider. The three well-recognized justifications for an award of defendant's ill-gotten gains are: compensation (to make up for the plaintiff's difficulty in proving damages), deterrence (to discourage knowing infringement), and unjust enrichment (to return to the plaintiff profits that rightly were

due to the plaintiff's goodwill and unjustly held by the defendant). Willfulness is a natural component of the deterrence and unjust enrichment rationales.

The most common approach is to consider willfulness along with other considerations, such as the degree of certainty that the defendant benefited from the unlawful conduct; availability and adequacy of other remedies; the role of a particular defendant in effectuating the infringement; plaintiffs delay in asserting its rights; and plaintiff's unclean hands. *See George Basch Co., Inc. v. Blue Coral, Inc.,* 968 F.2d 1532 (2d Cir. 1992). The *Tamko* case, which follows, also identifies relevant equitable factors.

**5.** *Proof of Defendant's Revenues and Costs.* Lanham Act §34 requires a plaintiff seeking recovery of the defendant's profits to prove only the defendant's sales revenues from the infringing activity. The burden then shifts to the defendant to prove the cost of producing those sales. Those costs are deducted from revenues to determine the defendant's profits. In *Maltina,* those costs are referred to as the "cost of goods sold." In addition to the cost of producing its infringing malta, Cawy Bottling incurred costs, listed in Exhibit 3, producing other products. Those costs are not deductible.

The general rule for calculating the defendant's ill-gotten profits is that costs resulting from the infringing activity are deducted from revenues resulting from the infringing activity. Costs the defendant would have incurred even without the infringing activity are not deducted. Expenses that would have been incurred even without the infringing activity are called "fixed costs" or "overhead costs." They are the costs of running the enterprise as a whole. The increased expenses resulting from the infringing activity are called "variable costs." Variable costs are deducted from sales revenues, but fixed costs are not. The court in *Maltina* noted that "a proportionate share of overhead is not deductible when the sales of an infringing product constitute only a small percentage of total sales." The logic underlying this short-hand rule is that if the infringing activity is only a small portion of the defendant's business, the infringing activity is not likely to have increased overhead costs. If the defendant had only produced the infringing product, all of its expenses would have resulted from the infringing activity and would be deductible. The real question is whether any of the overhead expenses were caused by the production and sale of the infringing goods.

In *Maltina*, variable costs are shown in Line 2 of Exhibit 1. Cawy also argued for two additional deductions: "Expenses Specifically Identified with Malta Cristal," shown in Exhibit 2, and "Expenses Related to Malta Cristal Allocated Based on Sales Ratio," shown in Exhibit 3. Which costs did the court allow Cawy to deduct? Which are variable and which are fixed costs?

**6.** *Corrective Advertising.* To minimize its future losses, a plaintiff may request compensation for corrective advertising. Goodyear Tire infringed Big O Tire's trademark BIGFOOT used in connection with its tires. *See Big O Tire Dealers, Inc. v. Goodyear Tire & Rubber Co.,* 561 F.2d 1365 (10th Cir. 1977). Unable to prove with sufficient precision what its lost profits were, Big O argued that it could only be put in the position it occupied prior to the infringement by conducting a corrective advertising campaign. Goodyear had spent $10 million for national advertising of its infringing BIGFOOT tires. Big O offered two justifications for the jury award of $2.8 million, 28 percent of the amount Goodyear had spent. First, Big O sold tires in 14 of the 50 states, which is 28 percent of the states. Second, the Federal Trade Commission often requires businesses that engage in misleading advertising to spend 25 percent of their advertising budget on corrective advertising. The Court of Appeals for the Tenth Circuit recognized these arguments, but corrected the math and arrived at a proper figure of $678,302, which is 25 percent of 28 percent of Goodyear's $10 million.

Awards for corrective advertising must reflect the underlying realities of each case. The Seventh Circuit reversed the award of $1 million for corrective advertising in *Zazú Designs*, discussed in *Allard Enterprises, Inc. v. Advanced Programming Resources, Inc.* and comments following in Chapter 2, despite the fact that it was 20 percent of the amount spent by the infringer, L'Oreal. The court observed that corrective advertising is a method of "repair" of the damage done. If a car worth $4,000 is damaged by another's negligence, the car's owner may not recover more than $4,000 in repair costs and must establish that there is no less expensive way to be made whole, such as buying a replacement. Zazú had not proved that its mark had any reputational value (and was like a car worth nothing) or that restoring its old mark would be less expensive than adopting a new one. The realities of the case made the award of $1 million for corrective advertising "an arbitrary number; an award of $6 $\frac{7}{8}$ would be neither more nor less supportable."

7. *Reasonable Royalties as an Estimate of Damages*. Where such an estimate was available, some courts have relied on reasonable royalties to estimate a plaintiff's damages. It might be feasible to estimate lost royalties where the plaintiff routinely licenses its trademark to owners of franchises, such as individual BURGER KING restaurants. It is also feasible to estimate lost royalties where the defendant has refused a licensing offer before engaging in the infringing conduct. In *Boston Professional Hockey Association v. Dallas Cap & Emblem Manufacturing, Inc.*, 597 F.2d 71 (5th Cir. 1979), the defendant, seeking to manufacture embroidered embodiments of the team symbols of the members of the National Hockey League, offered $15,000 for a three-year, non-exclusive license. The plaintiff rejected the offer and the defendant used the team symbols anyway. The court used this $15,000 figure in structuring part of its damage award. Royalties normally received for the use of a mark may be a proper measure if that measure comports with the equitable limitations of the Lanham Act §35 and bears a rational relationship to the rights appropriated by the defendant.

## Problems

5-1. Texas Pig Stands, Inc. sued Hard Rock Café for including on its menu an item called "Pig Sandwich," which was a registered trademark of the plaintiff. Texas Pig Stands, Inc. [TPS] opened its first "Pig Stand" in Dallas, Texas on September 15, 1921 and within a few years had opened 100 more Pig Stands from California to New York. It used the term "pig sandwich" the entire time to describe its barbecued pork sandwich and as part of its sign, menus, and promotional items. Consumers all identified the term "pig sandwich" with the "Pig Stands" owned by TPS and no one else marketed their sandwiches as "pig sandwiches." In 1924, TPS registered as a trademark and service mark the words "Pig Sandwich" and "a picture of a pig in a natural walking position, head down, with the words 'Pig Sandwich' extending from shoulder to hind leg, midway of the body of the hog." Most Pig Stands were closed during the next 60 years. The last Pig Stand in Dallas was closed in September 1985. By 1989, there were fewer than ten Pig Stands operating in Texas and none outside of Texas.

The Hard Rock Café offered a barbecued pork sandwich with the name "pig sandwich" at the Hard Rock Café in Jackson, Tennessee in 1982 and later introduced the pig sandwich in its restaurants in New York and Stockholm, Sweden. In November 1986, Hard Rock Café opened a restaurant in Dallas, Texas, featuring the pig sandwich on its menu. TPS notified Hard Rock in writing on October 20, 1987 of its claim to rights to the term "pig sandwich" and demanded that Hard Rock cease its infringement. As the court in this case reported, "Hard Rock refused to cease using it and instead chose to stay in its house and let TPS try to blow it down." In 1989, TPS sued for trademark and service mark infringement and two unfair competition claims, passing off/reverse passing off and misappropriation. TPS sought an injunction on use of the term "pig sandwich" throughout the United States as well as damages and an accounting. Assuming there was a likelihood of confusion, to which of these remedies is TPS entitled? *See Texas Pig Stands, Inc. v. Hard Rock Café International, Inc.*, 951 F.2d 684 (5th Cir. 1992).

**5-2.** S.C. Johnson is a manufacturer of many types of household cleaning products. In 1958, S.C. Johnson & Son, Inc. began to market an aerosol furniture wax and polish under the trademark PLEDGE with a distinctive label, which acquired secondary meaning as an indicator of source. Exhibit 1, below, shows S.C. Johnson's revenues and profits from sales of PLEDGE for the years 1960 to 1969. Drop Dead is a competing manufacturer of many types of household cleaning products. In 1966, Drop Dead Co., Inc. infringed S.C. Johnson's trade dress by marketing a competing wax and polish under the trademark PROMISE with a label that closely copied the PLEDGE label. Exhibit 2, below, details Drop Dead's revenues from sales of PROMISE with the infringing label from 1964 to 1967, when it adopted a noninfringing trade dress, and from 1968 to 1969. Exhibit 2 also details Drop Dead's costs for each of those years. What is the proper monetary award for both damages and an accounting? *See S.C. Johnson & Son, Inc. v. Drop Dead Co., Inc.*, 144 U.S.P.Q. 257 (S.D. Cal. 1965).

**Exhibit 1.**

S.C. Johnson's Revenues and Profits from PLEDGE
(All numbers in thousands)

|  | 1960 | 1961 | 1962 | 1963 | 1964 | 1965 | 1966 | 1967 | 1968 | 1969 |
|---|---|---|---|---|---|---|---|---|---|---|
| Sales (No. of cans) | 10 | 20 | 30 | 40 | 50 | 60 | 60 (70) | 50 (80) | 70 (90) | 100 |
| Revenues ($) | 30 | 60 | 90 | 120 | 150 | 180 | 180 (210) | 150 (240) | 210 (270) | 300 |
| Cost of goods sold ($) | 5 | 10 | 15 | 20 | 25 | 30 | 30 (35) | 25 (40) | 35 (45) | 50 |
| Profits ($) | 25 | 50 | 75 | 100 | 125 | 150 | 150 (175) | 125 (200) | 175 (225) | 250 |

**Exhibit 2.**

Drop Dead's Sales and Costs
(All numbers in thousands)

|  | 1964 | 1965 | 1966 | 1967 | 1968 | 1969 |
|---|---|---|---|---|---|---|
| Sales (No. of cans) | 5 | 5 | 15 | 25 | 5 | 5 |
| Revenues from PROMISE | 15 | 15 | 45 | 75 | 15 | 15 |
| Advertising for all products | 5 | 5 | 5 | 5 | 5 | 5 |
| Salaries of company executives | 5 | 5 | 5 | 5 | 5 | 5 |
| Cost of labels, cans, and content for PROMISE | 2.5 | 2.5 | 7.5 | 12.5 | 2.5 | 2.5 |

## TAMKO ROOFING PRODUCTS, INC. v. IDEAL ROOFING COMPANY, LTD.

### 282 F.3d 23 (1st Cir. 2002)

LYNCH, Circuit Judge.

Tamko Roofing Products, Inc. won its trademark infringement case against Ideal Roofing Company, Ltd. after a six-day jury trial. The district court . . . ordered Ideal to pay Tamko's attorneys' fees, which amounted to a sum larger than the profits, and issued a permanent injunction. Ideal now appeals each of these district court actions. . . .

Tamko and Ideal each manufacture and sell roofing products. Tamko manufactures and sells asphalt roofing products, including shingles, in the United States and Canada. Ideal is based in Ottawa, Canada, and manufactures metal roofing and siding products, which it sells in Canada and the United States.

Since 1975, Tamko has been using the trademark "Heritage" in its roofing products business. By 1997, when Ideal began to use the Heritage mark, Tamko had registered ten marks in the Heritage family with the USPTO, including "The American Heritage Series" mark, and two Heritage family trademarks in Canada. Tamko has vigorously defended the Heritage marks, and has successfully enforced its trademark rights.

In April 1997, Ideal selected the trademark "Heritage Series" for hidden fastener metal roofing panels, a new product it introduced to the market later that year. Ideal's "Heritage Series" mark used very similar cursive script to Tamko's "The American Heritage Series" mark....

After the close of the trial [in which the jury found that Ideal willfully infringed Tamko's valid trademarks], the judge [awarded attorneys' fees and] permanently enjoined Ideal from "using the term Heritage, Heritage Series, H Series, or any name or mark confusingly similar to Heritage."

[Ideal] does not contest the jury's findings, but disputes the district court's rulings. Ideal argues, first, that Tamko should not have been awarded attorneys' fees because there was no evidence to support the court's findings that "exceptional circumstances" existed. In the alternative, Ideal argues that even if attorneys' fees were justified, the district court erred in calculating the fees....Ideal [also] argues that the scope of the district court's permanent injunction was too broad in that it enjoined it from using the term "H Series," which is not one of Tamko's registered trademarks.

The district court awarded over $500,000 in attorneys' fees and expenses to Tamko. Ideal protests that no fees at all should have been awarded since this was not an "exceptional case," a requirement under section 35 of the Lanham Act, for an attorneys' fees award. The district court erred, Ideal says, by using an incorrect legal standard to determine exceptional circumstances and by concluding that the evidence supported such an award. The court's error of law, Ideal argues, is that fees may only be awarded in circumstances where the defendant acted deceitfully or with a degree of culpability; it claims the court's error of fact is that there was no such deceit or culpability here. Finally, Ideal argues that even if some award of attorneys' fees was justified, the sum awarded is too high....

The Lanham Act provides: "The court in exceptional cases may award reasonable attorneys fees to the prevailing party." 15 U.S.C. §1117(a). Ideal asserts that the district court erred by essentially converting the jury finding of willful infringement, without more, into a court finding of exceptional circumstances justifying a fee award. In truth, the district court referred to both the jury finding of willfulness and to other record evidence before it, so there was no automatic conversion of a jury willfulness finding into a finding of exceptional circumstances. The district court said nothing one way or the other as to whether there was bad faith or fraud on Ideal's part.

Under the statute, the decision to award fees is committed to the district court, not the jury. Ideal says that the trial court failed to make the necessary findings. Where the facts of record amply explain the decision, we will not find that the mere failure of the trial judge to be more explicit amounts to an abuse of discretion.

Because the Lanham Act does not further explain the term "exceptional cases," this court and others have turned to the legislative history for a working definition. In exceptional cases, attorneys' fees may be appropriate in circumstances where the acts of infringement were " 'malicious,' 'fraudulent,' 'deliberate,' or 'willful.' " S. Rep. 93-1400, at 5 (1974). The legislative history also explains that attorneys' fees may be awarded "when equitable considerations justify such awards," *id.* at 6, and so the list of four (for example, "malicious") may not be exclusive.

Ideal urges this court to adopt the "bad faith" standard utilized by some circuits. Other circuits hold that willfulness alone is an adequate basis for the award of attorneys' fees. While conceding that an award may be made if the acts of infringement are willful, Ideal argues that "willful" must mean more than just voluntary and intentional. Ideal grafts on another requirement that the infringing act must be fraudulent or malicious; for example, the act must be done with an intent to deceive or confuse the public, by palming off inferior goods as though they were trademark holder's goods, or through "deliberate pirating."

Ideal's argument confuses sufficient conditions for an attorneys' fees award with necessary conditions for such an award. Fraud or bad faith may justify an attorneys' fees award in some cases,[7] but a finding of bad faith or fraud is not a necessary precondition. Willfulness short of bad faith or fraud will suffice when equitable considerations justify an award and the district court supportably finds the case exceptional. There are two reasons we reject a bad faith or fraud requirement as a precondition to an award of attorneys' fees. First, the legislative history of section 35 links such exceptional cases to situations where the acts are malicious or fraudulent or deliberate or willful, and where equity justifies the award. Congress's list does not stop with "malicious" or "fraudulent," and we are loath to strip "deliberate" and "willful" of meaning. Second, the purpose of the attorneys' fees amendment to the Lanham Act was to provide for an award in exceptional cases in which equity called for an award in the sound discretion of the district judge. We would be hard pressed to say that such a case can never arise unless there is fraud or bad faith. As an example, one circuit has approved an award of fees in a case where there was no bad faith in the infringement but the subsequent litigation was oppressive and meant to delay.

Still, awards may be made only in exceptional cases. In *Volkswagenwerk Aktiengesellschaft v. Wheeler*, 814 F.2d 812, 821 (1st Cir. 1987), this court reversed an award where the plaintiff did not plead attorneys' fees in its complaint, defendant had no statutory constructive notice of plaintiff's claim of ownership of the marks because neither the trade name nor design mark were registered, and it would have been inequitable to visit an award on the defendant's small local automobile shop. Other circuits have identified as counseling against an award the following factors: the area of law is unclear and defendants might reasonably think they did not infringe, there is a close legal question as to whether there is any trademark violation, defendant had no intent to deceive or confuse the public, the defendant made a concerted effort to create a non-infringing mark, the plaintiff suf-

---

7. Nonetheless, it is also possible that a finding of bad faith by one party might not justify an award if equity required otherwise: for example, in a case where there is equivalent bad faith by the other party.

fered no actual damage. We agree that these are factors to be considered as part of a case-specific multi-factored analysis.

Here, there was adequate evidence of exceptional, willful behavior, both in the infringing acts and in Ideal's conduct after Tamko brought the infringement to Ideal's attention. We outline just some of the pertinent conduct.

1. Within several days of a 1997 trade show attended by Ideal, where Tamko's Heritage Mark was prominently displayed, Ideal adopted the Heritage name and told its advertising agency not to do a trademark search, which is usually done. Neither Ideal nor its patent attorney did a trademark search.

2. The other two names considered by Ideal for its new product were substantially similar to marks owned by other companies.

3. Ideal used an elaborate cursive script for its "Heritage Series" mark, very similar to the one used in Tamko's mark "The American Heritage Series" (which was displayed in a 1996 Tamko brochure).

4. Ideal's metal roofing competes directly with Tamko's asphalt roofing for steep-slope roofs and Ideal tried to increase its market in the residential marketplace, which is asphalt's primary market.

5. Ideal did not respond to the March 9, 1999 letter from Tamko, which notified Ideal of its infringement. Tamko sent another letter on March 26, 1999. Ideal responded and suggested a lengthy two-year phase out. When Tamko informed Ideal that the USPTO rejected a trademark application for Heritage for another company's metal roofing panels, Ideal still refused to stop its use of the mark.

6. Before filing suit, Tamko gave Ideal notice on August 17, 1999; Ideal asked for a one-year phase out.

7. In August 1999, Ideal nonetheless reprinted one of its brochures that continued the use of the Heritage Series name.

8. On February 29, 2000, the district court issued a preliminary injunction against Ideal, enjoining it from further use of the mark.

9. Nonetheless, Ideal used the brochures containing the mark in a trade show in mid-March 2000, after the preliminary injunction had issued against it.

10. Despite the preliminary injunction, Ideal continued to use the mark on its web site, which was accessed by users in the United States.

11. On May 15, 2000, the magistrate judge issued a report and recommendation, which found that Ideal was in contempt for violation of the preliminary injunction. The district court adopted the report and recommendation and held Ideal in contempt on May 26, 2000.

12. Ideal did not come into compliance with the preliminary injunction until June 13, 2000; in the course of its noncompliance it incurred fines of $3,000.

It is the totality of the circumstances, rather than a particular item alone, that suffices for an award of attorneys' fees. For example, mere failure to conduct a trademark search before using a mark may evidence nothing more than carelessness, and so may not warrant an award of fees. In combination, the facts above warrant the district court's conclusion that the initial infringement and continuing infringement, even in the face of court orders, was deliberate and willful and that equity required an award of fees.

The district court determined the amount of attorneys' fees under the commonly used lodestar method, in which the number of hours reasonably spent by the attorneys on the case is multiplied by a reasonable hourly rate. Tamko submitted a supporting declaration by an experienced trademark attorney. It also submitted detailed time records from lead counsel, house counsel, and local counsel. The court considered the time and labor required, the skill required, the nature and length of the professional relationship with the client, and time limitations imposed by the client. It is clear from the court's October 6, 2000 order that it reviewed the materials in some detail.

Because Ideal did not file any opposition to Tamko's attorneys' fees request and materials, it may well have forfeited this issue for appeal. Ideal argues that because the size of the award is substantially larger than the award of profits in this case, an injustice might result if this court does not review the amount of fees. Neither the statute nor the legislative history limits the award of fees to an amount less than the award of profits or damages. To the contrary, the legislative intent was partly to encourage the enforcement of trademark rights in cases where "the measurable damages are nominal." S. Rep. 93-1400. When a trademark is infringed, trademark owners have more at stake than just the damages or loss of profits in that case. Their failure to enforce their rights may result in the weakening of these rights over time. The cost of enforcing the rights may well be larger than the lost profits in any particular case. In all events, the district court appears carefully to have scrutinized Tamko's filing, and it articulated a clear understanding of the applicable lodestar principles. Given these facts, and given Ideal's failure to furnish the district court with any reasons why Tamko's fee application should have been pared down, we do not think that this is an issue that requires further review....

Although Ideal's counsel on appeal have striven mightily, the trial record dooms the appeal. The judgment is *affirmed*. Costs are awarded to Tamko.

## Comments

1. *Recovery of Attorneys' Fees*. Trademark plaintiffs and defendants may recover attorneys' fees in exceptional cases, as defined in Lanham Act §35. Some courts use the phrase "oppressive" to describe conduct by the opposing party that is "willful, malicious, fraudulent, or deliberate." Ideal's conduct went beyond simply its intent to adopt a mark confusingly similar to Tamko's. As outlined by the court, the conduct included numerous instances in which Ideal delayed its compliance with Tamko's reasonable requests and the court's orders to desist. The court in *Tamko Roofing* also identified circumstances that weigh against an award of attorneys' fees. Whether a case is "exceptional" is an individualized determination.

An award of attorneys' fees is generally based on evidence of a defendant's disregard of the plaintiff's rights rather than more generalized policy reasons for increasing the liability of the defendant. In *Texas Pig Stands, Inc. v. Hard Rock Café International, Inc.*, 951 F.2d 684 (5th Cir. 1992), which was the basis for the problem following *George Basch Co. Inc. v. Blue Coral, Inc.*, above, the appellate court reversed a trial court holding that Texas Pig Stands was entitled to recover attorneys' fees from Hard Rock Café because "the larger, guilty company can more easily absorb the loss than the smaller, innocent one. If plaintiff had to pay its own fees, it would suffer for having to protect its trademark and service mark rights." The Federal Circuit Court for the Fifth Circuit observed that "This noble sentiment, perhaps fitting for Sherwood Forest, does not meet the congressional standard of 'exceptional'" and that the parties' relative economic position should not enter into the determination. Similarly, promoting the goal of deterring others, in the absence of evidence of oppressiveness, does not justify awarding attorneys' fees.

2. *Amounts of Attorneys' Fees.* Under common law and many statutory schemes, attorneys' fees are determined by the "lodestar" method. A lodestar is a guiding star used as a reference point in navigation or astronomy, or, more generally, something that serves as a model or guide. The reference point from which fee calculations are adjusted is a reasonable number of hours multiplied by a reasonable hourly fee. Various factors justify adjusting this fee, including not only those mentioned in *Tamko Roofing* but also the novelty and difficulty of the questions involved; whether the attorney was made to forgo other employment as a result of accepting the case; the customary fee for the work involved; whether the fee was fixed or contingent; the amount of damages involved and the results obtained; the experience, reputation, and ability of the attorney; the desirability or undesirability of the case; the sizes of awards in similar cases; and the total of investigators' fees, costs of travel, telephone, mailing, photocopying, and computerized legal research.

3. *Recovery of Costs of the Action.* Lanham Act §35(a) also permits recovery of "the costs of the action." These may include such items as fees of the court clerk, marshal, and reporter, filing and docket fees, and fees for copies of papers necessarily obtained for use in the case. Recovery is based on equitable considerations similar to those involved in recovery of attorneys' fees.

# TRADEMARK STATUTES

## THE LANHAM ACT (Selected Portions)
### 15 U.S.C. §§1051 et seq.

### §1051 (§1). Application for registration; verification

(a) Application for use of trademark

(1) The owner of a trademark used in commerce may request registration of its trademark on the principal register hereby established by paying the prescribed fee and filing in the Patent and Trademark Office an application and a verified statement, in such form as may be prescribed by the Director, and such number of specimens or facsimiles of the mark as used as may be required by the Director.

(2) The application shall include specification of the applicant's domicile and citizenship, the date of the applicant's first use of the mark, the date of the applicant's first use of the mark in commerce, the goods in connection with which the mark is used, and a drawing of the mark.

(3) The statement shall be verified by the applicant and specify that—

(A) the person making the verification believes that he or she, or the juristic person in whose behalf he or she makes the verification, to be the owner of the mark sought to be registered;

(B) to the best of the verifier's knowledge and belief, the facts recited in the application are accurate;

(C) the mark is in use in commerce; and

(D) to the best of the verifier's knowledge and belief, no other person has the right to use such mark in commerce either in the identical form thereof or in such near resemblance thereto as to be likely, when used on or in connection with the goods of such other person, to cause confusion, or to cause mistake, or to deceive, except that, in the case of every application claiming concurrent use, the applicant shall—

(i) state exceptions to the claim of exclusive use; and

(ii) shall specify, to the extent of the verifier's knowledge—

(I) any concurrent use by others;

(II) the goods on or in connection with which and the areas in which each concurrent use exists;

(III) the periods of each use; and

(IV) the goods and area for which the applicant desires registration.

(4) The applicant shall comply with such rules or regulations as may be prescribed by the Director. The Director shall promulgate rules prescribing the requirements for the application and for obtaining a filing date herein.

(b) Application for bona fide intention to use trademark

(1) A person who has a bona fide intention, under circumstances showing the good faith of such person, to use a trademark in commerce may request registration of its trademark on the principal register hereby established by paying the prescribed fee and filing in the Patent

and Trademark Office an application and a verified statement, in such form as may be prescribed by the Director.

(2) The application shall include specification of the applicant's domicile and citizenship, the goods in connection with which the applicant has a bona fide intention to use the mark, and a drawing of the mark.

(3) The statement shall be verified by the applicant and specify —

(A) that the person making the verification believes that he or she, or the juristic person in whose behalf he or she makes the verification, to be entitled to use the mark in commerce;

(B) the applicant's bona fide intention to use the mark in commerce;

(C) that, to the best of the verifier's knowledge and belief, the facts recited in the application are accurate; and

(D) that, to the best of the verifier's knowledge and belief, no other person has the right to use such mark in commerce either in the identical form thereof or in such near resemblance thereto as to be likely, when used on or in connection with the goods of such other person, to cause confusion, or to cause mistake, or to deceive.

Except for applications filed pursuant to section 1126 of this title, no mark shall be registered until the applicant has met the requirements of subsections (c) and (d) of this section.

(4) The applicant shall comply with such rules or regulations as may be prescribed by the Director. The Director shall promulgate rules prescribing the requirements for the application and for obtaining a filing date herein.

(c) Amendment of application under subsection (b) to conform to requirements of subsection (a). At any time during examination of an application filed under subsection (b) of this section, an applicant who has made use of the mark in commerce may claim the benefits of such use for purposes of this chapter, by amending his or her application to bring it into conformity with the requirements of subsection (a) of this section.

(d) Verified statement that trademark is used in commerce

(1) Within six months after the date on which the notice of allowance with respect to a mark is issued under section 1063(b)(2) of this title to an applicant under subsection (b) of this section, the applicant shall file in the Patent and Trademark Office, together with such number of specimens or facsimiles of the mark as used in commerce as may be required by the Director and payment of the prescribed fee, a verified statement that the mark is in use in commerce and specifying the date of the applicant's first use of the mark in commerce and those goods or services specified in the notice of allowance on or in connection with which the mark is used in commerce. Subject to examination and acceptance of the statement of use, the mark shall be registered in the Patent and Trademark Office, a certificate of registration shall be issued for those goods or services recited in the statement of use for which the mark is entitled to registration, and notice of registration shall be published in the Official Gazette of the Patent and Trademark Office. Such examination may include an examination of the factors set forth in subsections (a) through (e) of section 1052 of this title. The

notice of registration shall specify the goods or services for which the mark is registered.

(2) The Director shall extend, for one additional 6-month period, the time for filing the statement of use under paragraph (1), upon written request of the applicant before the expiration of the 6-month period provided in paragraph (1). In addition to an extension under the preceding sentence, the Director may, upon a showing of good cause by the applicant, further extend the time for filing the statement of use under paragraph (1) for periods aggregating not more than 24 months, pursuant to written request of the applicant made before the expiration of the last extension granted under this paragraph. Any request for an extension under this paragraph shall be accompanied by a verified statement that the applicant has a continued bona fide intention to use the mark in commerce and specifying those goods or services identified in the notice of allowance on or in connection with which the applicant has a continued bona fide intention to use the mark in commerce. Any request for an extension under this paragraph shall be accompanied by payment of the prescribed fee. The Director shall issue regulations setting forth guidelines for determining what constitutes good cause for purposes of this paragraph.

(3) The Director shall notify any applicant who files a statement of use of the acceptance or refusal thereof and, if the statement of use is refused, the reasons for the refusal. An applicant may amend the statement of use.

(4) The failure to timely file a verified statement of use under paragraph (1) or an extension request under paragraph (2) shall result in abandonment of the application, unless it can be shown to the satisfaction of the Director that the delay in responding was unintentional, in which case the time for filing may be extended, but for a period not to exceed the period specified in paragraphs (1) and (2) for filing a statement of use.

## §1052 (§2). Trademarks registrable on principal register; concurrent registration

No trademark by which the goods of the applicant may be distinguished from the goods of others shall be refused registration on the principal register on account of its nature unless it—

(a) Consists of or comprises immoral, deceptive, or scandalous matter; or matter which may disparage or falsely suggest a connection with persons, living or dead, institutions, beliefs, or national symbols, or bring them into contempt, or disrepute; or a geographical indication which, when used on or in connection with wines or spirits, identifies a place other than the origin of the goods and is first used on or in connection with wines or spirits by the applicant on or after one year after the date on which the WTO Agreement (as defined in section 3501(9) of Title 19) enters into force with respect to the United States.

(b) Consists of or comprises the flag or coat of arms or other insignia of the United States, or of any State or municipality, or of any foreign nation, or any simulation thereof.

(c) Consists of or comprises a name, portrait, or signature identifying a particular living individual except by his written consent, or the name, signature, or portrait of a deceased President of the United States during the life of his widow, if any, except by the written consent of the widow.

(d) Consists of or comprises a mark which so resembles a mark registered in the Patent and Trademark Office, or a mark or trade name previously used in the United States by another and not abandoned, as to be likely, when used on or in connection with the goods of the applicant, to cause confusion, or to cause mistake, or to deceive: *Provided*, That if the Director determines that confusion, mistake, or deception is not likely to result from the continued use by more than one person of the same or similar marks under conditions and limitations as to the mode or place of use of the marks or the goods on or in connection with which such marks are used, concurrent registrations may be issued to such persons when they have become entitled to use such marks as a result of their concurrent lawful use in commerce prior to (1) the earliest of the filing dates of the applications pending or of any registration issued under this chapter; (2) July 5, 1947, in the case of registrations previously issued under the Act of March 3, 1881, or February 20, 1905, and continuing in full force and effect on that date; or (3) July 5, 1947, in the case of applications filed under the Act of February 20, 1905, and registered after July 5, 1947. Use prior to the filing date of any pending application or a registration shall not be required when the owner of such application or registration consents to the grant of a concurrent registration to the applicant. Concurrent registrations may also be issued by the Director when a court of competent jurisdiction has finally determined that more than one person is entitled to use the same or similar marks in commerce. In issuing concurrent registrations, the Director shall prescribe conditions and limitations as to the mode or place of use of the mark or the goods on or in connection with which such mark is registered to the respective persons.

(e) Consists of a mark which (1) when used on or in connection with the goods of the applicant is merely descriptive or deceptively misdescriptive of them, (2) when used on or in connection with the goods of the applicant is primarily geographically descriptive of them, except as indications of regional origin may be registrable under section 1054 of this title, (3) when used on or in connection with the goods of the applicant is primarily geographically deceptively misdescriptive of them, (4) is primarily merely a surname, or (5) comprises any matter that, as a whole, is functional.

(f) Except as expressly excluded in subsections (a), (b), (c), (d), (e)(3), and (e)(5) of this section, nothing in this chapter shall prevent the registration of a mark used by the applicant which has become distinctive of the applicant's goods in commerce. The Director may accept as prima facie evidence that the mark has become distinctive, as used on or in connection with the applicant's goods in commerce, proof of substantially exclusive and continuous use thereof as a mark by the applicant in commerce for the five years before the date on which the claim of distinctiveness is made. Nothing in this section shall prevent the registration of a mark which, when used on or in connection with the goods of the applicant, is primarily geographically deceptively misdescriptive of them, and which became distinctive of the applicant's goods in commerce before December 8, 1993.

A mark which when used would cause dilution under section 1125(c) of this title may be refused registration only pursuant to a proceeding brought under section 1063 of this title. A registration for a mark which when used would cause dilution under section 1125(c) of this title may be canceled pursuant to a proceeding brought under either section 1064 of this title or section 1092 of this title.

### §1053 (§3). Service marks registrable

Subject to the provisions relating to the registration of trademarks, so far as they are applicable, service marks shall be registrable, in the same manner and with the same effect as are trademarks, and when registered they shall be entitled to the protection provided in this chapter in the case of trademarks. Applications and procedure under this section shall conform as nearly as practicable to those prescribed for the registration of trademarks.

### §1054 (§4). Collective marks and certification marks registrable

Subject to the provisions relating to the registration of trademarks, so far as they are applicable, collective and certification marks, including indications of regional origin, shall be registrable under this chapter, in the same manner and with the same effect as are trademarks, by persons, and nations, States, municipalities, and the like, exercising legitimate control over the use of the marks sought to be registered, even though not possessing an industrial or commercial establishment, and when registered they shall be entitled to the protection provided in this chapter in the case of trademarks, except in the case of certification marks when used so as to represent falsely that the owner or a user thereof makes or sells the goods or performs the services on or in connection with which such mark is used. Applications and procedure under this section shall conform as nearly as practicable to those prescribed for the registration of trademarks.

### §1055 (§5). Use by related companies affecting validity and registration

Where a registered mark or a mark sought to be registered is or may be used legitimately by related companies, such use shall inure to the benefit of the registrant or applicant for registration, and such use shall not affect the validity of such mark or of its registration, provided such mark is not used in such manner as to deceive the public. If first use of a mark by a person is controlled by the registrant or applicant for registration of the mark with respect to the nature and quality of the goods or services, such first use shall inure to the benefit of the registrant or applicant, as the case may be.

### §1056 (§6). Disclaimer of unregistrable matter

(a) Compulsory and voluntary disclaimers

The Director may require the applicant to disclaim an unregistrable component of a mark otherwise registrable. An applicant may voluntarily disclaim a component of a mark sought to be registered.

(b) Prejudice of rights

No disclaimer, including those made under subsection (e) of section 1057 of this title, shall prejudice or affect the applicant's or registrant's rights then existing or thereafter arising in the disclaimed matter, or his right of registration on another application if the disclaimed matter be or shall have become distinctive of his goods or services.

### §1057 (§7). Certificates of registration

(a) Issuance and form

Certificates of registration of marks registered upon the principal register shall be issued in the name of the United States of America, under the seal of the Patent and Trademark Office, and shall be signed by the Director or have his signature placed thereon, and a record thereof shall be kept in the Patent and Trademark Office. The registration shall reproduce the mark, and state that the mark is registered on the principal register under this chapter, the date of the first use of the mark, the date of the first use of the mark in commerce, the particular goods or services for which it is registered, the number and date of the registration, the term thereof, the date on which the application for registration was received in the Patent and Trademark Office, and any conditions and limitations that may be imposed in the registration.

(b) Certificate as prima facie evidence

A certificate of registration of a mark upon the principal register provided by this chapter shall be prima facie evidence of the validity of the registered mark and of the registration of the mark, of the registrant's ownership of the mark, and of the registrant's exclusive right to use the registered mark in commerce on or in connection with the goods or services specified in the certificate, subject to any conditions or limitations stated in the certificate.

(c) Application to register mark considered constructive use

Contingent on the registration of a mark on the principal register provided by this chapter, the filing of the application to register such mark shall constitute constructive use of the mark, conferring a right of priority, nationwide in effect, on or in connection with the goods or services specified in the registration against any other person except for a person whose mark has not been abandoned and who, prior to such filing —

    (1) has used the mark;

    (2) has filed an application to register the mark which is pending or has resulted in registration of the mark; or

    (3) has filed a foreign application to register the mark on the basis of which he or she has acquired a right of priority, and timely files an application under section 1126(d) of this title to register the mark which is pending or has resulted in registration of the mark.

### §1058 (§8). Duration

(a) In general

Each registration shall remain in force for 10 years, except that the registration of any mark shall be canceled by the Director for failure to comply with the provisions of subsection (b) of this section, upon the expiration of the following time periods, as applicable:

(1) For registrations issued pursuant to the provisions of this chapter, at the end of 6 years following the date of registration.

(2) For registrations published under the provisions of section 1062(c) of this title, at the end of 6 years following the date of publication under such section.

(3) For all registrations, at the end of each successive 10-year period following the date of registration.

(b) Affidavit of continuing use

During the 1-year period immediately preceding the end of the applicable time period set forth in subsection (a) of this section, the owner of the registration shall pay the prescribed fee and file in the patent and trademark office—

(1) an affidavit setting forth those goods or services recited in the registration on or in connection with which the mark is in use in commerce and such number of specimens or facsimiles showing current use of the mark as may be required by the Director; or

(2) an affidavit setting forth those goods or services recited in the registration on or in connection with which the mark is not in use in commerce and showing that any such nonuse is due to special circumstances which excuse such nonuse and is not due to any intention to abandon the mark.

## §1063 (§13). Opposition to registration

(a) Any person who believes that he would be damaged by the registration of a mark upon the principal register, including as a result of dilution under section 1125(c) of this title, may, upon payment of the prescribed fee, file an opposition in the Patent and Trademark Office, stating the grounds therefor, within thirty days after the publication under subsection (a) of section 1062 of this title of the mark sought to be registered. Upon written request prior to the expiration of the thirty-day period, the time for filing opposition shall be extended for an additional thirty days, and further extensions of time for filing opposition may be granted by the Director for good cause when requested prior to the expiration of an extension. The Director shall notify the applicant of each extension of the time for filing opposition. An opposition may be amended under such conditions as may be prescribed by the Director.

(b) Unless registration is successfully opposed—

(1) a mark entitled to registration on the principal register based on an application filed under section 1051(a) of this title or pursuant to section 1126 of this title shall be registered in the Patent and Trademark Office, a certificate of registration shall be issued, and notice of the registration shall be published in the Official Gazette of the Patent and Trademark Office; or

(2) a notice of allowance shall be issued to the applicant if the applicant applied for registration under section 1051(b) of this title.

## §1064 (§14). Cancellation of registration

A petition to cancel a registration of a mark, stating the grounds relied upon, may, upon payment of the prescribed fee, be filed as follows by any person who believes that he is or will be damaged, including as a result of dilution under section 1125(c) of this title, by the registration of a mark on the principal register established by this chapter, or under the Act of March 3, 1881, or the Act of February 20, 1905:

(1) Within five years from the date of the registration of the mark under this chapter.

(2) Within five years from the date of publication under section 1062(c) of this title of a mark registered under the Act of March 3, 1881, or the Act of February 20, 1905.

(3) At any time if the registered mark becomes the generic name for the goods or services, or a portion thereof, for which it is registered, or is functional, or has been abandoned, or its registration was obtained fraudulently or contrary to the provisions of section 1054 of this title or of subsection (a), (b), or (c) of section 1052 of this title for a registration under this chapter, or contrary to similar prohibitory provisions of such prior Acts for a registration under such Acts, or if the registered mark is being used by, or with the permission of, the registrant so as to mis-represent the source of the goods or services on or in connection with which the mark is used. If the registered mark becomes the generic name for less than all of the goods or services for which it is registered, a petition to cancel the registration for only those goods or services may be filed. A registered mark shall not be deemed to be the generic name of goods or services solely because such mark is also used as a name of or to identify a unique product or service. The primary significance of the registered mark to the relevant public rather than purchaser moti-vation shall be the test for determining whether the registered mark has become the generic name of goods or services on or in connection with which it has been used.

(4) At any time if the mark is registered under the Act of March 3, 1881, or the Act of February 20, 1905, and has not been published under the provisions of subsection (c) of section 1062 of this title.

(5) At any time in the case of a certification mark on the ground that the registrant (A) does not control, or is not able legitimately to exercise control over, the use of such mark, or (B) engages in the production or marketing of any goods or services to which the certification mark is applied, or (C) permits the use of the certification mark for purposes other than to certify, or (D) discriminately refuses to certify or to con-tinue to certify the goods or services of any person who maintains the standards or conditions which such mark certifies:

*Provided,* That the Federal Trade Commission may apply to cancel on the grounds specified in paragraphs (3) and (5) of this section any mark registered on the principal register established by this chapter, and the prescribed fee shall not be required.

Nothing in paragraph (5) shall be deemed to prohibit the registrant from using its certification mark in advertising or promoting recogni-tion of the certification program or of the goods or services meeting the certification standards of the registrant. Such uses of the certification mark shall not be grounds for cancellation under paragraph (5), so long as the registrant does not itself produce, manufacture, or sell any of the certified goods or services to which its identical certification mark is applied.

### §1065 (§15). Incontestability of right to use mark under certain conditions

Except on a ground for which application to cancel may be filed at any time under paragraphs (3) and (5) of section 1064 of this title, and except to the extent, if any, to which the use of a mark registered on the principal register infringes a valid right acquired under the law of any State or Territory by use of a mark or trade name continuing from a date prior to the date of registration under this chapter of such registered mark, the right of the registrant to use such registered mark in commerce for the goods or services on or in connection with which such registered mark has been in continuous use for five consecutive years subsequent to the date of such registration and is still in use in commerce, shall be incontestable: *Provided,* That—

(1) there has been no final decision adverse to registrant's claim of ownership of such mark for such goods or services, or to registrant's right to register the same or to keep the same on the register; and

(2) there is no proceeding involving said rights pending in the Patent and Trademark Office or in a court and not finally disposed of; and

(3) an affidavit is filed with the Director within one year after the expiration of any such five-year period setting forth those goods or services stated in the registration on or in connection with which such mark has been in continuous use for such five consecutive years and is still in use in commerce, and other matters specified in paragraphs (1) and (2) of this section; and

(4) no incontestable right shall be acquired in a mark which is the generic name for the goods or services or a portion thereof, for which it is registered.

Subject to the conditions above specified in this section, the incontestable right with reference to a mark registered under this chapter shall apply to a mark registered under the Act of March 3, 1881, or the Act of February 20, 1905, upon the filing of the required affidavit with the Director within one year after the expiration of any period of five consecutive years after the date of publication of a mark under the provisions of subsection (c) of section 1062 of this title.

The Director shall notify any registrant who files the above-prescribed affidavit of the filing thereof.

### §1072 (§22). Registration as constructive notice of claim of ownership

Registration of a mark on the principal register provided by this chapter or under the Act of March 3, 1881, or the Act of February 20, 1905, shall be constructive notice of the registrant's claim of ownership thereof.

## §1091 (§23). Supplemental register

(a) Marks registerable

In addition to the principal register, the Director shall keep a continuation of the register provided in paragraph (b) of section 1 of the Act of March 19, 1920, entitled "An Act to give effect to certain provisions of the convention for the protection of trademarks and commercial names, made and signed in the city of Buenos Aires, in the Argentine Republic, August 20, 1910, and for other purposes", to be called the supplemental register. All marks capable of distinguishing applicant's goods or services and not registrable on the principal register provided in this chapter, except those declared to be unregistrable under subsections (a), (b), (c), (d), and (e)(3) of section 1052 of this title, which are in lawful use in commerce by the owner thereof, on or in connection with any goods or services may be registered on the supplemental register upon the payment of the prescribed fee and compliance with the provisions of subsections (a) and (e) of section 1051 of this title so far as they are applicable. Nothing in this section shall prevent the registration on the supplemental register of a mark, capable of distinguishing the applicant's goods or services and not registrable on the principal register under this chapter, that is declared to be unregistrable under section 1052(e)(3) of this title, if such mark has been in lawful use in commerce by the owner thereof, on or in connection with any goods or services, since before December 8, 1993.

(b) Application and proceedings for registration

Upon the filing of an application for registration on the supplemental register and payment of the prescribed fee the Director shall refer the application to the examiner in charge of the registration of marks, who shall cause an examination to be made and if on such examination it shall appear that the applicant is entitled to registration, the registration shall be granted. If the applicant is found not entitled to registration the provisions of subsection (b) of section 1062 of this title shall apply.

(c) Nature of mark

For the purposes of registration on the supplemental register, a mark may consist of any trademark, symbol, label, package, configuration of goods, name, word, slogan, phrase, surname, geographical name, numeral, device, any matter that as a whole is not functional, or any combination of any of the foregoing, but such mark must be capable of distinguishing the applicant's goods or services.

## §1111 (§29). Notice of registration; display with mark; recovery of profits and damages in infringement suit

Notwithstanding the provisions of section 1072 of this title, a registrant of a mark registered in the Patent and Trademark Office, may give notice that his mark is registered by displaying with the mark the words "Registered in U.S. Patent and Trademark Office" or "Reg. U.S. Pat. & Tm. Off." or the letter R enclosed within a circle, thus ®; and in any suit for infringement under this chapter by such a registrant failing to give such notice of registration, no profits and no damages shall be recovered under the provisions of this chapter unless the defendant had actual notice of the registration.

### §1114 (§32). Remedies; infringement; innocent infringement by printers and publishers

(1) Any person who shall, without the consent of the registrant —
    (a) use in commerce any reproduction, counterfeit, copy, or colorable imitation of a registered mark in connection with the sale, offering for sale, distribution, or advertising of any goods or services on or in connection with which such use is likely to cause confusion, or to cause mistake, or to deceive; or
    (b) reproduce, counterfeit, copy, or colorably imitate a registered mark and apply such reproduction, counterfeit, copy, or colorable imitation to labels, signs, prints, packages, wrappers, receptacles or advertisements intended to be used in commerce upon or in connection with the sale, offering for sale, distribution, or advertising of goods or services on or in connection with which such use is likely to cause confusion, or to cause mistake, or to deceive, shall be liable in a civil action by the registrant for the remedies hereinafter provided. Under subsection (b) hereof, the registrant shall not be entitled to recover profits or damages unless the acts have been committed with knowledge that such imitation is intended to be used to cause confusion, or to cause mistake, or to deceive.

### §1115 (§33). Registration on principal register as evidence of exclusive right to use mark; defenses

(a) Evidentiary value; defenses
    Any registration issued under the Act of March 3, 1881, or the Act of February 20, 1905, or of a mark registered on the principal register provided by this chapter and owned by a party to an action shall be admissible in evidence and shall be prima facie evidence of the validity of the registered mark and of the registration of the mark, of the registrant's ownership of the mark, and of the registrant's exclusive right to use the registered mark in commerce on or in connection with the goods or services specified in the registration subject to any conditions or limitations stated therein, but shall not preclude another person from proving any legal or equitable defense or defect, including those set forth in subsection (b) of this section, which might have been asserted if such mark had not been registered.
(b) Incontestability; defenses
    To the extent that the right to use the registered mark has become incontestable under section 1065 of this title, the registration shall be conclusive evidence of the validity of the registered mark and of the registration of the mark, of the registrant's ownership of the mark, and of the registrant's exclusive right to use the registered mark in commerce. Such conclusive evidence shall relate to the exclusive right to use the mark on or in connection with the goods or services specified in the affidavit filed under the provisions of section 1065 of this title, or in the renewal application filed under the provisions of section 1059 of this title if the goods or services specified in the renewal are fewer in number, subject to any conditions or limitations in the registration or in such affidavit or renewal application. Such conclusive evidence of the

right to use the registered mark shall be subject to proof of infringement as defined in section 1114 of this title, and shall be subject to the following defenses or defects:

(1) That the registration or the incontestable right to use the mark was obtained fraudulently; or

(2) That the mark has been abandoned by the registrant; or

(3) That the registered mark is being used by or with the permission of the registrant or a person in privity with the registrant, so as to misrepresent the source of the goods or services on or in connection with which the mark is used; or

(4) That the use of the name, term, or device charged to be an infringement is a use, otherwise than as a mark, of the party's individual name in his own business, or of the individual name of anyone in privity with such party, or of a term or device which is descriptive of and used fairly and in good faith only to describe the goods or services of such party, or their geographic origin; or

(5) That the mark whose use by a party is charged as an infringement was adopted without knowledge of the registrant's prior use and has been continuously used by such party or those in privity with him from a date prior to (A) the date of constructive use of the mark established pursuant to section 1057(c) of this title, (B) the registration of the mark under this chapter if the application for registration is filed before the effective date of the Trademark Law Revision Act of 1988, or (C) publication of the registered mark under subsection (c) of section 1062 of this title: *Provided, however,* That this defense or defect shall apply only for the area in which such continuous prior use is proved; or

(6) That the mark whose use is charged as an infringement was registered and used prior to the registration under this chapter or publication under subsection (c) of section 1062 of this title of the registered mark of the registrant, and not abandoned: *Provided, however,* That this defense or defect shall apply only for the area in which the mark was used prior to such registration or such publication of the registrant's mark; or

(7) That the mark has been or is being used to violate the antitrust laws of the United States; or

(8) That the mark is functional; or

(9) That equitable principles, including laches, estoppel, and acquiescence, are applicable.

### §1116 (§34). Injunctive relief

(a) Jurisdiction; service

The several courts vested with jurisdiction of civil actions arising under this chapter shall have power to grant injunctions, according to the principles of equity and upon such terms as the court may deem reasonable, to prevent the violation of any right of the registrant of a mark registered in the Patent and Trademark Office or to prevent a violation under subsection (a), (c), or (d) of section 1125 of this title.

### §1117 (§35). Recovery for violation of rights

(a) Profits; damages and costs; attorney fees

When a violation of any right of the registrant of a mark registered in the Patent and Trademark Office, a violation under section 1125(a) or (d) of this title, or a willful violation under section 1125(c) of this title, shall have been established in any civil action arising under this chapter, the plaintiff shall be entitled, subject to the provisions of sections 1111 and 1114 of this title, and subject to the principles of equity, to recover (1) defendant's profits, (2) any damages sustained by the plaintiff, and (3) the costs of the action. The court shall assess such profits and damages or cause the same to be assessed under its direction. In assessing profits the plaintiff shall be required to prove defendant's sales only; defendant must prove all elements of cost or deduction claimed. In assessing damages the court may enter judgment, according to the circumstances of the case, for any sum above the amount found as actual damages, not exceeding three times such amount. If the court shall find that the amount of the recovery based on profits is either inadequate or excessive the court may in its discretion enter judgment for such sum as the court shall find to be just, according to the circumstances of the case. Such sum in either of the above circumstances shall constitute compensation and not a penalty. The court in exceptional cases may award reasonable attorney fees to the prevailing party.

### §1125 (§43). False designations of origin, false descriptions, and dilution forbidden

(a) Civil action

(1) Any person who, on or in connection with any goods or services, or any container for goods, uses in commerce any word, term, name, symbol, or device, or any combination thereof, or any false designation of origin, false or misleading description of fact, or false or misleading representation of fact, which—

> (A) is likely to cause confusion, or to cause mistake, or to deceive as to the affiliation, connection, or association of such person with another person, or as to the origin, sponsorship, or approval of his or her goods, services, or commercial activities by another person, or
>
> (B) in commercial advertising or promotion, misrepresents the nature, characteristics, qualities, or geographic origin of his or her or another person's goods, services, or commercial activities,

shall be liable in a civil action by any person who believes that he or she is or is likely to be damaged by such act.

(2) As used in this subsection, the term "any person" includes any State, instrumentality of a State or employee of a State or instrumentality of a State acting in his or her official capacity. Any State, and any such instrumentality, officer, or employee, shall be subject to the provisions of this chapter in the same manner and to the same extent as any nongovernmental entity.

(3) In a civil action for trade dress infringement under this chapter for trade dress not registered on the principal register, the person who asserts trade dress protection has the burden of proving that the matter sought to be protected is not functional.

(b) Importation

Any goods marked or labeled in contravention of the provisions of this section shall not be imported into the United States or admitted to entry at any customhouse of the United States. The owner, importer, or consignee of goods refused entry at any customhouse under this section may have any recourse by protest or appeal that is given under the customs revenue laws or may have the remedy given by this chapter in cases involving goods refused entry or seized.

(c) Remedies for dilution of famous marks

(1) The owner of a famous mark shall be entitled, subject to the principles of equity and upon such terms as the court deems reasonable, to an injunction against another person's commercial use in commerce of a mark or trade name, if such use begins after the mark has become famous and causes dilution of the distinctive quality of the mark, and to obtain such other relief as is provided in this subsection. In determining whether a mark is distinctive and famous, a court may consider factors such as, but not limited to —

(A) the degree of inherent or acquired distinctiveness of the mark;

(B) the duration and extent of use of the mark in connection with the goods or services with which the mark is used;

(C) the duration and extent of advertising and publicity of the mark;

(D) the geographical extent of the trading area in which the mark is used;

(E) the channels of trade for the goods or services with which the mark is used;

(F) the degree of recognition of the mark in the trading areas and channels of trade used by the marks' owner and the person against whom the injunction is sought;

(G) the nature and extent of use of the same or similar marks by third parties; and

(H) whether the mark was registered under the Act of March 3, 1881, or the Act of February 20, 1905, or on the principal register.

(2) In an action brought under this subsection, the owner of the famous mark shall be entitled only to injunctive relief as set forth in section 1116 of this title unless the person against whom the injunction is sought willfully intended to trade on the owner's reputation or to cause dilution of the famous mark. If such willful intent is proven, the owner of the famous mark shall also be entitled to the remedies set forth in sections 1117(a) and 1118 of this title, subject to the discretion of the court and the principles of equity.

(3) The ownership by a person of a valid registration under the Act of March 3, 1881, or the Act of February 20, 1905, or on the principal register shall be a complete bar to an action against that person, with respect to that mark, that is brought by another person

under the common law or a statute of a State and that seeks to prevent dilution of the distinctiveness of a mark, label, or form of advertisement.

(4) The following shall not be actionable under this section:

(A) Fair use of a famous mark by another person in comparative commercial advertising or promotion to identify the competing goods or services of the owner of the famous mark.

(B) Noncommercial use of a mark.

(C) All forms of news reporting and news commentary.

(d) Cyberpiracy prevention

(1)(A) A person shall be liable in a civil action by the owner of a mark, including a personal name which is protected as a mark under this section, if, without regard to the goods or services of the parties, that person

(i) has a bad faith intent to profit from that mark, including a personal name which is protected as a mark under this section; and

(ii) registers, traffics in, or uses a domain name that—

(I) in the case of a mark that is distinctive at the time of registration of the domain name, is identical or confusingly similar to that mark;

(II) in the case of a famous mark that is famous at the time of registration of the domain name, is identical or confusingly similar to or dilutive of that mark; or

(III) is a trademark, word, or name protected by reason of section 706 of Title 18 or section 220506 of Title 36.

(B)(i) In determining whether a person has a bad faith intent described under subparagraph (a), a court may consider factors such as, but not limited to

(I) the trademark or other intellectual property rights of the person, if any, in the domain name;

(II) the extent to which the domain name consists of the legal name of the person or a name that is otherwise commonly used to identify that person;

(III) the person's prior use, if any, of the domain name in connection with the bona fide offering of any goods or services;

(IV) the person's bona fide noncommercial or fair use of the mark in a site accessible under the domain name;

(V) the person's intent to divert consumers from the mark owner's online location to a site accessible under the domain name that could harm the goodwill represented by the mark, either for commercial gain or with the intent to tarnish or disparage the mark, by creating a likelihood of confusion as to the source, sponsorship, affiliation, or endorsement of the site;

(VI) the person's offer to transfer, sell, or otherwise assign the domain name to the mark owner or any third party for financial gain without having used, or having an intent to use, the domain name in the bona fide offering of any goods or services, or the person's prior conduct indicating a pattern of such conduct;

(VII) the person's provision of material and misleading false contact information when applying for the registration of the domain name, the person's intentional failure to maintain accurate contact information, or the person's prior conduct indicating a pattern of such conduct;

(VIII) the person's registration or acquisition of multiple domain names which the person knows are identical or confusingly similar to marks of others that are distinctive at the time of registration of such domain names, or dilutive of famous marks of others that are famous at the time of registration of such domain names, without regard to the goods or services of the parties; and

(IX) the extent to which the mark incorporated in the person's domain name registration is or is not distinctive and famous within the meaning of subsection (c)(1) of this section.

(ii) Bad faith intent described under subparagraph (A) shall not be found in any case in which the court determines that the person believed and had reasonable grounds to believe that the use of the domain name was a fair use or otherwise lawful.

(C) In any civil action involving the registration, trafficking, or use of a domain name under this paragraph, a court may order the forfeiture or cancellation of the domain name or the transfer of the domain name to the owner of the mark.

(D) A person shall be liable for using a domain name under subparagraph (A) only if that person is the domain name registrant or that registrant's authorized licensee.

(E) As used in this paragraph, the term "traffics in" refers to transactions that include, but are not limited to, sales, purchases, loans, pledges, licenses, exchanges of currency, and any other transfer for consideration or receipt in exchange for consideration.

### §1127 (§45). Construction and definitions; intent of chapter

In the construction of this chapter, unless the contrary is plainly apparent from the context —

The term "related company" means any person whose use of a mark is controlled by the owner of the mark with respect to the nature and quality of the goods or services on or in connection with which the mark is used.

The terms "trade name" and "commercial name" mean any name used by a person to identify his or her business or vocation.

The term "trademark" includes any word, name, symbol, or device, or any combination thereof —

(1) used by a person, or

(2) which a person has a bona fide intention to use in commerce and applies to register on the principal register established by this chapter, to identify and distinguish his or her goods, including a unique

product, from those manufactured or sold by others and to indicate the source of the goods, even if that source is unknown.

The term "service mark" means any word, name, symbol, or device, or any combination thereof—

(1) used by a person, or

(2) which a person has a bona fide intention to use in commerce and applies to register on the principal register established by this chapter, to identify and distinguish the services of one person, including a unique service, from the services of others and to indicate the source of the services, even if that source is unknown. Titles, character names, and other distinctive features of radio or television programs may be registered as service marks notwithstanding that they, or the programs, may advertise the goods of the sponsor.

The term "certification mark" means any word, name, symbol, or device, or any combination thereof—

(1) used by a person other than its owner, or

(2) which its owner has a bona fide intention to permit a person other than the owner to use in commerce and files an application to register on the principal register established by this chapter, to certify regional or other origin, material, mode of manufacture, quality, accuracy, or other characteristics of such person's goods or services or that the work or labor on the goods or services was performed by members of a union or other organization.

The term "collective mark" means a trademark or service mark—

(1) used by the members of a cooperative, an association, or other collective group or organization, or

(2) which such cooperative, association, or other collective group or organization has a bona fide intention to use in commerce and applies to register on the principal register established by this chapter, and includes marks indicating membership in a union, an association, or other organization.

The term "mark" includes any trademark, service mark, collective mark, or certification mark.

The term "use in commerce" means the bona fide use of a mark in the ordinary course of trade, and not made merely to reserve a right in a mark. For purposes of this chapter, a mark shall be deemed to be in use in commerce—

(1) on goods when—

(A) it is placed in any manner on the goods or their containers or the displays associated therewith or on the tags or labels affixed thereto, or if the nature of the goods makes such placement impracticable, then on documents associated with the goods or their sale, and

(B) the goods are sold or transported in commerce, and

(2) on services when it is used or displayed in the sale or advertising of services and the services are rendered in commerce, or the services are rendered in more than one State or in the United States and a foreign country and the person rendering the services is engaged in commerce in connection with the services.

A mark shall be deemed to be "abandoned" if either of the following occurs:

(1) When its use has been discontinued with intent not to resume such use. Intent not to resume may be inferred from circumstances. Nonuse for 3 consecutive years shall be prima facie evidence of abandonment. "Use" of a mark means the bona fide use of such mark made in the ordinary course of trade, and not made merely to reserve a right in a mark.

(2) When any course of conduct of the owner, including acts of omission as well as commission, causes the mark to become the generic name for the goods or services on or in connection with which it is used or otherwise to lose its significance as a mark. Purchaser motivation shall not be a test for determining abandonment under this paragraph.

The term "dilution" means the lessening of the capacity of a famous mark to identify and distinguish goods or services, regardless of the presence or absence of—

(1) competition between the owner of the famous mark and other parties, or

(2) likelihood of confusion, mistake, or deception.

A "counterfeit" is a spurious mark which is identical with, or substantially indistinguishable from, a registered mark.

The term "domain name" means any alphanumeric designation which is registered with or assigned by any domain name registrar, domain name registry, or other domain name registration authority as part of an electronic address on the Internet.

The term "Internet" has the meaning given that term in section 230(f)(1) of Title 47.

Words used in the singular include the plural and vice versa.

# CHAPTER
# 6

# Acquiring Copyrights

## INTRODUCTION

Copyright law offers legal protection to the fruits of human creativity so that the public as a whole may benefit from it. This goal of copyright is reflected in the Constitutional provision that authorizes Congress to enact a copyright statute: "The Congress shall have the Power . . . To promote the Progress of Science and useful Arts, by securing for limited Times to Authors and Inventors the exclusive Right to their respective Writings and Discoveries." U.S. Const., Art. I, §8, cl. 8. The purpose of this chapter and the three chapters that follow it is to break that very broad portrait down into smaller and more nuanced components. This chapter deals with how copyright interests arise in the first place. What forms of "creativity" are governed by copyright? How does legal protection get attached to those forms? Who is entitled to a copyright, and when? Chapter 7 addresses enforcing copyrights against accused infringers and others. Copyright law, like trademark law, has expanded in recent years beyond core or traditional notions of protection, so Chapter 7 also addresses enforcement options related to but beyond traditional copyright infringement, particularly the Digital Millennium Copyright Act. Chapter 8 takes up defenses to copyright infringement. Copyright law is statutory, meaning that the rights of copyright owners are defined by the Copyright Act and are subject to exceptions and limitations also provided there, particularly the doctrines of "first sale" and "fair use." Chapter 9 describes the remedies available to a copyright owner (and others) proving violations of the exclusive rights provided by the Copyright Act.

Copyright law today is governed by the Copyright Revision Act of 1976, a comprehensive revision and restatement of copyright law that took effect on January 1, 1978. For purposes of this chapter and the next three, that statute will be referred to as "the Copyright Act," or sometimes just "the 1976 Act." Though Congress has amended the 1976 Act many times, its basic framework for analyzing copyright law remains intact. Copyright protection arises automatically so long as a given "work of authorship" meets three broad criteria: the work must be original, it must be fixed in some tangible form, and it must consist of "expression," rather than "ideas." The copyright owner acquires certain exclusive rights — to reproduce, distribute,

327

and publicly perform or display copyrighted "works" — so that those who exercise any of those rights without the copyright owner's permission may be enjoined and/or are liable for damages. These exclusive rights are subject to important limitations designed to ensure that the public policies that guide copyright law benefit readers, consumers, and new authors as well as existing authors. The public — the primary beneficiary of the copyright system — must retain both the ability to benefit from existing copyrighted works, and the ability to use those works to create new ones.

The statutory character of modern copyright law is worth some emphasis here. The 1976 Act is merely the latest in a long line of copyright statutes. The first American copyright act was passed by Congress in 1790. Its English precursor, generally regarded as the first modern copyright statute, was the Statute of Anne, 8 Anne c.19, which took effect in 1710 and granted "authors or their assigns" the exclusive right of publication of "books" for 14 years from the date of publication, with the possibility of an additional 14 years if the author were living at the expiration of that term. From the beginning, modern copyright's statutory basis created a potential conflict with the notion of the author's common law right to prevent unauthorized publication of the work, or what is known by the shorthand "common law copyright." In cases brought on each side of the Atlantic shortly after enactment of the English Statute of Anne and the American Copyright Act of 1790, the question arose: With respect to works that had earned statutory copyright protection, did the author's common law copyright survive as well? The question had important practical implications. In connection with contracting to publish the work, the author typically assigned the copyright to the publisher. A continuing system of common law copyright would vest these publishers with perpetual copyright interests enforceable against infringers, in addition to statutory remedies available for a limited term. On both continents, however, it was decided that when a work became subject to statutory copyright, common law rights, if any existed, were extinguished. According to the House of Lords, and later the Supreme Court of the United States, statutory copyright when applicable, displaced common law copyright. *See Donaldson v. Becket*, 4 Burr. 2408, 98 Eng. Rep. 257 (H.L. 1774); *Wheaton v. Peters*, 33 U.S. (8 Pet.) 591 (1834).

---

The original Copyright Act of 1790 granted legal protection only to "maps, charts, and books." Copyright protection today, of course, deals with far more than that. The central notion, expressed in §102(a) of the Copyright Act, is protection for "original works of authorship fixed in any tangible medium of expression." The first three sections of this chapter investigate the three core concepts in this phrase: Section B deals with originality. Section C deals with fixation. Section D deals with expression. Sections E and F note some important qualifications and limitations on copyrightability, which derive from the same policies that animate protection for original expression fixed in tangible form. Under the predecessor to the current Copyright Act, copyright protection also required compliance with certain statutory formalities. The revision in 1976 abolished many but not all of those requirements, so that some formalities persist in copyright law, even though they carry less force than they did previously. This chapter addresses them in Section G.

Once it has been determined that a work of authorship is eligible for copyright protection, two important questions remain. One is the question of ownership. Given the multiplicity of ways in which creative works are produced, who owns the copyright? Section H considers that question. The second question is how long the right persists. Unlike real estate and most forms of ordinary tangible property, copyright ownership does not last forever. The Constitution provides that copyrights, like patents, may be provided "for limited Times." Section I discusses the variety of rules that Congress has developed to manage the duration of copyrights.

---

### POLICY PERSPECTIVE
### The Theories and Policies of Copyright Law

Despite its historical pedigree, today there remains a significant degree of debate, both in academic commentary and even in Supreme Court opinions, regarding the precise public policy underpinnings of copyright law. The following reviews the basic theories and policies surrounding intellectual property law.

- Utilitarian theories: Intellectual property law exists to maximize the welfare of society as a whole. The law grants legal rights to developers of new, creative, and innovative works to allow them to profit from exploiting those works, creating incentives to produce material that otherwise would be undersupplied because others could use or profit from it without investing themselves. (In practice, the distribution of these rights and their transferability — to publishers and distributors — enables the development of economic structures for developing, publishing, and consuming creative and innovative works that assure that participants at each level receive financial returns that encourage their participation.) At the same time, because the exclusive rights offered by copyright encourage copyright owners to behave, in effect, as monopolists with respect to their works, copyright law acts to limit the costs of those monopolies. Specifically, the law offers the public sufficient rights of access and use to ensure that creative and innovative work can in fact benefit society as a whole. Intellectual property law in general and copyright law in particular manifest a careful balance between the interests of authors and the interests of the audience.
- Personal autonomy theories: Intellectual property rights may exist as society's expression of the inherent value of the human person and of human creativity, both of which are represented directly in an individual's creative expression. Granting a creator or innovator exclusive rights in a new work is the equivalent of granting a human being control over his or her mind and body. This approach is more pronounced in copyright law, which at times recognizes the inherent worth or dignity of the "author," than in patent or trademark law.
- Labor desert: The proposition that authors "earn" property rights in their creative output can be traced to John Locke, who theorized in his

*Second Treatise of Government* (1689) that property rights were vested in individuals as they mixed their own labor and effort, to which they were entitled, with material drawn from the domain of the common or the unowned. This proposition is subject to the famous "Lockean proviso," which provides that the property right that results is subject to the limitation that following any resulting property right "there is enough and as good left in common for others."

It has also been observed that copyright exists today largely because of the persistence of historical forms. (Similarly, the Scottish philosopher David Hume suggested that property rights in general exist largely as a matter of social convention.) Copyright's English origins lay in resistance to government censorship and to monopolistic behavior by publishers and printers. As the Crown's control over printing waned and competitive publishing markets emerged, both in England and in the United States, justifications for copyright law shifted in favor of utilitarian theories and in particular in favor of incentive arguments. Modern copyright law remains attentive to risks that copyright owners may use their exclusive rights for censorial ends, or to enable anticompetitive behavior, and personality-based and labor/desert theories remain important objects of analysis for both courts and scholars. The co-existence of multiple theoretical justifications for copyright suggests, in part, that we currently lack a comprehensive, persuasive account of the law. Yet the basic framework of exclusive copyright rights persists, along with limitations and exceptions of equally long-standing and sometimes fragile theoretical justifications.

From time to time copyright lawmaking reflects concern for values that are not clearly derived from or related to intellectual property law as a whole. One of those is the First Amendment to the Constitution. Creating and distributing a creative work may be understood as a form of free speech; restrictions on that activity based on liability for copyright infringement might be judged to be a restriction on speaking freely that conflicts, at least potentially, with the First Amendment obligation not to regulate speech except in specialized circumstances. Possible conflicts between copyright law and the First Amendment have come before the Supreme Court twice, most recently and directly in *Eldred v. Ashcroft*, 537 U.S. 186 (2003), a challenge to the Sonny Bono Copyright Term Extension Act of 1998. In its opinion in *Eldred*, the Court concluded that any possible conflicts between copyright law and the First Amendment were adequately addressed in the context of existing doctrine. The right to speak freely does not provide an independent defense to a claim of copyright infringement, and copyright's potential impact on speech does not justify any heightened judicial review for congressional copyright legislation.

A second concern is the public domain, which is of obvious concern to intellectual property law as a whole but which appears to have become of special concern in copyright law over the last 30 years, as the scope of copyright has expanded and lengthened. "The public domain" has no generally accepted or specialized meaning in the law.

In different formulations it encompasses material that cannot be protected by copyright law, or by any law; material that is eligible for protection or that has been protected in the past, but that is not protected today; and rights and interests of users and consumers of copyrighted material in using copyrighted content without the consent of copyright owners. Whatever the specific formulation, the animating concern is the same, that what we refer to as "the public domain" may represent an interest in ensuring that some material remain available for the public to use — whether as authors themselves, or as consumers, teachers, students, and citizens.

As you read the next four chapters, scrutinize the theoretical justifications for copyright's various rules and doctrines and consider the extent to which rule and theory match.

## A. REQUIREMENTS FOR COPYRIGHT PROTECTION

### 1. Originality and Authorship

Only "original works of authorship" are eligible for copyright protection, according to §102(a) of the Copyright Act. Even before this phrase entered the statutory lexicon, "originality" was a prerequisite for copyright protection, as the courts interpreted the Constitutional mandate. In *The Trade-Mark Cases*, 100 U.S. 82 (1879), the Court held that Congress could not use its copyright authority to legislate protection for trademarks. Copyright, it said, was reserved only for work that is "original . . . and founded on the creative powers of the mind." *Id.* at 94. The term "original" is thus central to copyright law and policy. Yet nowhere in the Constitution or in the copyright statutes has the term ever been defined. The following cases chronicle the evolving interpretations that courts have given the term.

*STATUTE:* **Subject Matter of Copyright: In General**
17 U.S.C. §102(a)

### *C𝛼* BURROW-GILES LITHOGRAPHIC CO. v. SARONY *( P )*
**111 U.S. 53 (1884)**

MILLER, J.

This is a writ of error to the circuit court for the southern district of New York. Plaintiff is a lithographer, and defendant a photographer, with large business in those lines in the city of New York. The suit was commenced by an action at law in which Sarony was plaintiff and the lithographic company was defendant, the plaintiff charging the defendant with violating his copyright in regard to a photograph, the title of which is "Oscar Wilde, No. 18." A jury being waived, the court made a finding of facts on which a judgment in favor of the plaintiff was rendered for the sum of $600 for the plates and 85,000 copies sold and exposed to sale, and $10 for copies found in his possession, as penalties under section 4965 of the Revised Statutes. Among the finding of facts made by the court the following presents the principal question raised by the assignment of errors in the case:

"(3) That the plaintiff, about the month of January, 1882, under an agreement with Oscar Wilde, became and was the author, inventor, designer, and proprietor of the photograph in suit, the title of which is 'Oscar Wilde, No. 18,' being the number used to designate this particular photograph and of the negative thereof; that the same is a useful, new, harmonious, characteristic, and graceful picture, and that said plaintiff made the same at his place of business in said city of New York, and within the United States, entirely from his own original mental conception, to which he gave visible form by posing the said Oscar Wilde in front of the camera, selecting and arranging the costume, draperies, and other various accessories in said photograph, arranging the subject so as to present graceful outlines, arranging and disposing the light and shade, suggesting and evoking the desired expression, and from such disposition, arrangement, or representation, made entirely by the plaintiff, he produced the picture in suit, Exhibit A, April 14, 1882, and that the terms 'author,' 'inventor,' and 'designer,' as used in the art of photography and in the complaint, mean the person who so produced the photograph."

Other findings leave no doubt that plaintiff had taken all the steps required by the act of congress to obtain copyright of this photograph, and section 4952 names photographs, among other things, for which the author, inventor, or designer may obtain copyright, which is to secure him the sole privilege of reprinting, publishing, copying, and vending the same. That defendant is liable, under that section and section 4965, there can be no question if those sections are valid as they relate to photographs.

* * *

The constitutional question is not free from difficulty. The eighth section of the first article of the constitution is the great repository of the powers of congress, and by the eighth clause of that section congress is authorized 'to promote the progress of science and useful arts, by securing, for limited times to authors and inventors the exclusive right to their respective writings and discoveries.' The argument here is that a photograph is not a writing nor the production of an author. Under the acts of congress designed to give effect to this section, the persons who are to be benefited are divided into two classes — authors and inventors. The monopoly which is granted to the former is called a copyright: that given to the latter, letters patent, or, in the familiar language of the present day, *patent-right*. We have then copyright and patent-right, and it is the first of these under which plaintiff asserts a claim for relief. It is insisted, in argument, that a photograph being a reproduction, on paper, of the exact features of some natural object, or of some person, is not a writing of which the producer is the author. Section 4952 of the Revised Statutes places photographs in the same class as things which may be copyrighted with "books, maps, charts, dramatic or musical compositions, engravings, cuts, prints, paintings, drawings, statues, statuary, and models or designs intended to be perfected as works of the fine arts.". . . .

The first congress of the United States, sitting immediately after the formation of the constitution, enacted that the "author or authors of any map, chart, book, or books, being a citizen or resident of the United States, shall have the sole right and liberty of printing, reprinting, publishing, and vending the same for the period of fourteen years from the recording of the title thereof in the clerk's office, as afterwards directed." 1 St. p. 124, §1. This statute not only makes maps and charts subjects of copyright, but mentions them before books in the order of designation. The second section of an act to amend this act, approved April 29, 1802, (2 St. 171,) enacts that from the first day of January thereafter he who shall invent and design, engrave, etch, or work, or from his own works shall cause to be designed and engraved, etched, or worked, any historical or other print or prints, shall have the same exclusive right for the term of 14 years from recording the title thereof as prescribed by law.

By the first section of the act of February 3, 1831, (4 St. 436,) entitled 'An act to amend the several acts respecting copyright, musical compositions, and cuts, in connection with prints and engravings,' are added, and the period of protection is extended to 28 years. The caption or title of this act uses the word "copyright" for the first time in the legislation of congress.

The construction placed upon the constitution by the first act of 1790 and the act of 1802, by the men who were contemporary with its formation, many of whom were members of the convention which framed it, is of itself entitled to very great weight, and when it is remembered that the rights thus established have not been disputed during a period of nearly a century, it is almost conclusive. Unless, therefore, photographs can be distinguished in the classification of this point from the maps, charts, designs, engravings, etchings, cuts, and other prints, it is difficult to see why congress cannot make them the subject of copyright as well as the others. These statutes certainly answer the objection that books only, or writing, in the limited sense of a book and its author, are within the constitutional provision. Both these words are susceptible of a more enlarged definition than this. An author in that sense is "he to whom anything owes its origin; originator; maker; one who completes a work of science or literature." So, also, no one would now claim that the word "writing" in this clause of the constitution, though the only word used as to subjects in regard to which authors are to be secured, is limited to the actual script of the author, and excludes books and all other printed matter. By writings in that clause is meant the literary productions of those authors, and congress very properly has declared these to include all forms of writing, printing, engravings, etchings, etc., by which the ideas in the mind of the author are given visible expression. The only reason why photographs were not included in the extended list in the act of 1802 is, probably, that they did not exist, as photography, as an art, was then unknown, and the scientific principle on which it rests, and the chemicals and machinery by which it is operated, have all been discovered long since that statute was enacted. . . .

We entertain no doubt that the constitution is broad enough to cover an act authorizing copyright of photographs, so far as they are representatives of original intellectual conceptions of the author.

But it is said that an engraving, a painting, a print, does embody the intellectual conception of its author, in which there is novelty, invention, originality, and therefore comes within the purpose of the constitution in securing its exclusive use or sale to its author, while a photograph is the mere mechanical reproduction of the physical features or outlines of some object, animate or inanimate, and involves no originality of thought or any novelty in the intellectual operation connected with its visible reproduction in shape of a picture. That while the effect of light on the prepared plate may have been a discovery in the production of these pictures, and patents could properly be obtained for the combination of the chemicals, for their application to the paper or other surface, for all the machinery by which the light reflected from the object was thrown on the prepared plate, and for all the improvements in this machinery, and in the materials, the remainder of the process is merely mechanical, with no place for novelty, invention, or originality. It is simply the manual operation, by the use of these instruments and preparations, of transferring to the plate the visible representation of some existing object, the accuracy of this representation being its highest merit. This may be true in regard to the ordinary production of a photograph, and that in such case a copyright is no protection. On the question as thus stated we decide nothing.

In regard, however, to the kindred subject of patents for invention, they cannot, by law, be issued to the inventor until the novelty, the utility, and the actual discovery or invention by the claimant have been established by proof before the commissioner of patents; and when he has secured such a patent, and undertakes to obtain redress for a violation of his right in a court of law, the question of invention, of novelty, of originality is always open to examination. Our copyright system has no such provision for previous examination by a proper tribunal as to the originality of the book, map, or other matter offered for copyright. A deposit of two copies of the article or work with the librarian of congress, with the name of the author and its title page, is all that is necessary to secure a copyright. It is therefore much more important that when the supposed author sues for a violation of his copyright, the existence of those facts of originality, of intellectual production, of thought, and conception on the part of the author should be proved than in the case of a patent-right. In the case before us we think this has been done.

The third finding of facts says, in regard to the photograph in question, that it is a "useful, new, harmonious, characteristic, and graceful picture, and that plaintiff made the same * * * entirely from his own original mental conception, to which he gave visible form by posing the said Oscar Wilde in front of the camera, selecting and arranging the costume, draperies, and other various accessories in said photograph, arranging the subject so as to present graceful outlines, arranging and disposing the light and shade, suggesting and evoking the desired expression, and from such disposition, arrangement, or representation, made entirely by plaintiff, he produced the picture in suit." These findings, we think, show this photograph to be an original work of art, the product of plaintiff's intellectual invention, of which plaintiff is the author, and of a class of inventions for which the constitution intended that congress should secure to him the exclusive right to use, publish, and sell, as it has done by section 4952 of the Revised Statutes.

\* \* \*

The judgment of the circuit court is accordingly affirmed.

## Comments

1. *Is a Photograph a Writing?* The Constitution authorizes copyright in "writings," and the copyright statute as it stood at the time of this opinion granted copyright in photographs, among other things. The Court notes that there was no reason to distinguish photographs, as a class of writings, from "maps, charts, designs, engravings, etchings, cuts, and other prints," all of which were already the subject of copyright and had been from the earliest days of the statute, without objection. Going further, the opinion remarks that "writing" is not limited to the actual words inscribed by an author, but includes all forms of recording by which "the ideas in the mind of the author are given visible expression." Originality, in short, lies in formulating mental images of reality and transferring them to fixed form, and not in mere reproductions. This formulation, which focuses on the "creative" author, is not particularly troublesome in the context of pre-mechanical arts. As machine-based expression developed (via still and motion picture cameras), conflicts between this "creative soul" conception of copyright and the mechanical character of artistic output surfaced with greater frequency. Just as photographs were not anticipated by the drafters of the early nineteenth-century copyright statute, Justice Miller could not anticipate computer technology, in which "the ideas in the mind of the author" are inscribed in electronic memory — forms "visible," or readable, only to computer programs themselves.

2. *Is a Photograph the Production of an Author?* The Constitution limits the grant of copyright to works that have an "author." What does it mean to be an "author" of a work? The "author" of a work might be the person who records the "ideas" of the mind, or it might be the person who supplies those ideas themselves. The Court notes that a photograph may realize the "intellectual conception" of the photographer. In the

case of nineteenth-century photographs, the actual production of a photograph involved the efforts of a number of people, including assistants who worked lighting and camera equipment, and the "photographer," who may not have pressed the shutter but who may have supervised the production. Should a studio photograph, composed in view of an "artistic" judgment analogous to that involved in a painting or an engraving, be distinguished from a photograph of nature or an "unposed" scene, in which the photographer's goal is to capture the "truth" of the underlying reality? The Court suggests that such a distinction might be sustained, and that the latter sort of photographs might not be "original" enough to support a copyright.

3. *The Skills of the Photographer.* Photography is a more varied discipline than this duality suggests. Consider the haunting photographs of nature produced by Ansel Adams, who was known not only for his images of New Mexico and the Yosemite Valley but also for the exacting darkroom techniques that he perfected to produce them. Or the Dust Bowl photographs of Dorothea Lange, whose images of migrant families were, technologically speaking, little more than snapshots; the fashion photography of Irving Penn, who brought both Hell's Angels and fashion models into his studio; or the photojournalism of Robert Capa, who covered wars on several continents. If "originality" is interpreted strictly to mean an image formed in the author's mind, and then transferred to some "writing," not all of these photographers would receive copyrights for their works, since not all of them formed a working "idea" in their minds before shooting or processing a particular photograph. Or did they?

## BLEISTEIN v. DONALDSON LITHOGRAPHING CO.

### 188 U.S. 239 (1903)

Mr. Justice HOLMES delivered the opinion of the court.

This case comes here from the United States circuit court of appeals for the sixth circuit by writ of error. Act of March 3, 1891. It is an action brought by the plaintiffs in error to recover the penalties prescribed for infringements of copyrights. The alleged infringements consisted in the copying in reduced form of three chromolithographs prepared by employees of the plaintiffs for advertisements of a circus owned by one Wallace. Each of the three contained a portrait of Wallace in the corner, and lettering bearing some slight relation to the scheme of decoration, indicating the subject of the design and the fact that the reality was to be seen at the circus. One of the designs was of an ordinary ballet, one of a number of men and women, described as the Stirk family, performing on bicycles, and one of groups of men and women whitened to represent statues. The circuit court directed a verdict for the defendant on the ground that the chromolithographs were not within the protection of the copyright law, and this ruling was sustained by the circuit court of appeals.

\* \* \*

. . . . [W]e come at once to the ground of decision in the courts below. That ground was not found in any variance between pleading and proof, such as was put forward in argument, but in the nature and purpose of the designs.

We shall do no more than mention the suggestion that painting and engraving, unless for a mechanical end, are not among the useful arts, the progress of which Congress is empowered by the Constitution to promote. The Constitution does not limit the useful to that which satisfies immediate bodily needs. *Burrow-Giles Lithographing Co. v. Sarony*, 111 U. S. 53. It is obvious also that the plaintiff's case is not affected by the fact, if it be one, that the pictures represent actual groups, — visible things. They seem from the testimony to have been composed from hints or description, not from sight of a performance. But even if they had been drawn from the life, that fact would not deprive them of protection. The opposite proposition would mean that a portrait by Velasquez or Whistler was common property because others might try their hand on the same face. Others are free to copy the original. They are not free to copy the copy. The copy is the personal reaction of an individual upon nature. Personality always contains something unique. It expresses its singularity even in handwriting, and a very modest grade of art has in it something irreducible, which is one man's alone. That something he may copyright unless there is a restriction in the words of the act.

If there is a restriction it is not to be found in the limited pretensions of these particular works. The least pretentious picture has more originality in it than directories and the like, which may be copyrighted. The amount of training required for humbler efforts than those before us is well indicated by Ruskin. "If any young person, after being taught what is, in polite circles, called 'drawing,' will try to copy the commonest piece of real *work*, — suppose a lithograph on the title page of a new opera air, or a woodcut in the cheapest illustrated newspaper of the day, — they will find themselves entirely beaten." Elements of Drawing, first ed. 3. There is no reason to doubt that these prints in their ensemble and in all their details, in their design and particular combinations of figures, lines, and colors, are the original work of the plaintiffs' designer. If it be necessary, there is express testimony to that effect. It would be pressing the defendant's right to the verge, if not beyond, to leave the question of originality to the jury upon the evidence in this case. . . .

We assume that the construction of Rev. Stat. §4952, allowing a copyright to the "author, designer, or proprietor . . . of any engraving, cut, print . . . [or] chromo" is affected by the act of 1874 (18 Stat. at L. 78, 79, chap. 301, §3). That section provides that, "in the construction of this act, the words 'engraving,' 'cut,' and 'print' shall be applied only to pictorial illustrations or works connected with the fine arts." We see no reason for taking the words "connected with the fine arts" as qualifying anything except the word "works," but it would not change our decision if we should assume further that they also qualified "pictorial illustrations," as the defendant contends.

These chromolithographs are "pictorial illustrations." The word "illustrations" does not mean that they must illustrate the text of a book, and that the etchings of Rembrandt or Müller's engraving of the Madonna di San Sisto could not be protected today if any man were able to produce them. Again, the act, however construed, does not mean that ordinary posters are not good enough to be considered within its scope. The antithesis to "illustrations or works connected with the fine arts" is not works of little merit or of humble degree, or illustrations addressed to the less educated classes; it is "prints or labels designed to be used for any other articles of manufacture." Certainly works are not the less connected with the fine arts because their pictorial quality attracts the crowd, and therefore gives them a real use, — if use means to increase trade and to help to make money. A picture is none the less a picture, and none the less a subject of copyright, that it is used for an advertisement. And if pictures may be used to advertise soap, or the theatre, or monthly magazines, as they are, they may be used to advertise a circus. Of course, the ballet is as legitimate a subject for illustration as any other. A rule cannot be laid down that would excommunicate the paintings of Degas.

Finally, the special adaptation of these pictures to the advertisement of the Wallace shows does not prevent a copyright. That may be a circumstance for the jury to consider in determining the extent of Mr. Wallace's rights, but it is not a bar. Moreover, on the evidence, such prints are used by less pretentious exhibitions when those for whom they were prepared have given them up.

It would be a dangerous undertaking for persons trained only to the law to constitute themselves final judges of the worth of pictorial illustrations, outside of the narrowest and most obvious limits. At the one extreme, some works of genius would be sure to miss appreciation. Their very novelty would make them repulsive until the public had learned the new language in which their author spoke. It may be more than doubted, for instance, whether the etchings of Goya or the paintings of Manet would have been sure of protection when seen for the first time. At the other end, copyright would be denied to pictures which appealed to a public less educated than the judge. Yet if they command the interest of any public, they have a commercial value, — it would be bold to say that they have not an aesthetic and educational value, — and the taste of any public is not to be treated with contempt. It is an ultimate fact for the moment, whatever may be our hopes for a change. That these pictures had their worth and their success is sufficiently shown by the desire to reproduce them without regard to the plaintiffs' rights. We are of opinion that there was evidence that the plaintiffs have rights entitled to the protection of the law.

The judgment of the Circuit Court of Appeals is reversed; the judgment of the Circuit Court is also reversed and the cause remanded to that court with directions to set aside the verdict and grant a new trial.

[Dissenting opinion of Justice HARLAN, joined by MCKENNA, J., omitted.]

## Comments

1. *Originality*. The first issue taken up by the Court is whether copyright is barred by the fact that the chromolithograph is an image taken from nature, in this case the circus performers of the Stirk family. The Court adopts a definition of originality that differs slightly from the *Burrow-Giles* formulation: "The copy is the personal reaction of an individual upon nature. Personality always contains something unique. It expresses its singularity even in handwriting, and a very modest grade of art has in it something irreducible, which is one man's alone." "The copy," to adopt the somewhat confusing terminology of copyright, is the original work, what the artist produces. Here, originality appears to lie in the very act of producing the tangible work, rather than in the act of forming an intellectual creation in the mind, then transferring it to written form.

2. *The Fine Arts*. Having cleared the Constitutional hurdle, the question for the Court is whether copyright is authorized by statute. The question is whether chromolithographs designed to advertise a circus production are works "connected with the fine arts." (The statute appears to grant copyright protection to "pictorial illustrations" whether or not connected with the fine arts, but the Court assumes that the "fine arts" limitation applies to this case.) The Court concludes that what has come to be known as copyright's "nondiscrimination" principle — "It would be a dangerous undertaking for persons trained only to the law to constitute themselves final judges of the worth of pictorial illustrations, outside of the narrowest and most obvious limits" — prevents it from concluding that works of art used in connection with advertising are less deserving of copyright than works of art displayed in museums or produced for collectors. The Court treats the fact that someone sought to reproduce the circus posters as sufficient evidence of their commercial value, and it equates that commercial value with aesthetic or educational value for purposes of copyright.

3. *Copyright's Public Policy*. *Bleistein* highlights a quandary that continues to pervade copyright. Given the underlying incentive purpose of the statute, what sorts of works, and what sorts of authors, should copyright encourage? In a dissenting opinion not included here, Justice Harlan takes a narrower view of copyright's domain. By focusing on authentic "fine art," he narrows the field of eligible authors and works to "true" art. Justice Holmes's formulation, that originality consists of anything that is not copied, has the effect of democratizing copyright policy. Anyone, whether or not trained as an artist, has the potential to produce a work that is eligible for copyright. (Note that Justice Holmes, in analyzing the constitutional goals of copyright, links copyright with constitutional support of the "useful arts." Modern scholars, and more recent opinions of the Supreme Court, align the "useful arts" with patent law,

and link copyright with the progress of "science." *See Eldred v. Ashcroft*, 537 U.S. 186 (2003).)

**4.** *"Originality" as Variation.* In *Alfred E. Bell & Co. v. Catalda Fine Arts, Inc.*, 191 F.2d 99 (2d Cir. 1951), the Court of Appeals for the Second Circuit was confronted with the question of copyright in mezzotint engravings—works produced by a laborious process of tracing, engraving, and coloring exact reproductions of preexisting works of fine art. The court concluded that these works were copyrightable. Instead of focusing on the labor involved in producing these works, the court relied on the ground that a comparison between the preexisting work and the chromolithographic reproduction yielded a "distinguishable variation" between it and its source. In dicta, the court went one step further, concluding that such a copyrightable variation may arise even unintentionally, that is, even if the "author" did not intend to produce a copyrightable work.

**5.** *Reproductions of Public Domain Material.* The chromolithographs at issue in *Alfred E. Bell* were reproductions of public domain works of art. Granting copyright on reproductions of public domain works of art may encourage distribution of copies of those works to audiences that otherwise might not be able to afford access to the originals, by giving a copyright-based incentive to their producers. Think of paintings and sculptures located in museums around the world and the cost of producing photographs and models of those works of art. If the originals are truly in the public domain, then copyright on a reproduction does not prevent anyone else from making a competing reproduction, so the grant of copyright, in theory, does not entail any offsetting costs. Recall Justice Holmes's admonition in *Bleistein*: "Others are free to copy the original. They are not free to copy the copy." On the other hand, if reproductions can be copyrighted upon a showing of a "trivial variation," as in *Alfred E. Bell*, then the first copyist to obtain a copyright in a reproduction may be able to use that copyright to discourage other copyists, and therefore increase the cost of the reproduction above a competitive level. How, then, should copyright law measure the copyrightability of reproductions, translations, and modernizations of public domain material? Consider that issue in the context of the following problem.

## Problem

**6-1.** The Frack Gallery houses one of the world's great collections of nineteenth-century pre-modern paintings. Under the terms of the will of Luther Frack, who amassed the collection and founded the gallery, the building that houses the collection is located far from the urban art centers of New York and London and is open to the public only one day per month. The Frack has however invested several million dollars in producing color transparencies and ultra-high-resolution digital reproductions of its entire collection on CD-ROM, which it sells to art historians, researchers, and to the public, via a catalog. These transparencies and digital reproductions are produced using state-of-the-art industrial technology and extraordinary measures to ensure absolute faithfulness to the original works of art. When the Frack Gallery discovered that Brooklyn Art Co. was operating a website offering copies of the Frack Gallery's digital reproductions for 99 cents per download, it sued Brooklyn Art for copyright infringement. Brooklyn has refused to disclose how it acquired the digital reproductions. Assume that Brooklyn is liable for copyright infringement if the Frack Gallery's digital reproductions are original (and therefore copyrightable). Are the reproductions original? *See Bridgeman Art Library v. Corel Corp.*, 25 F. Supp. 2d 421 (S.D.N.Y. 1998).

## FEIST PUBLICATIONS v. RURAL TELEPHONE SERVICE
### 499 U.S. 340 (1991)

Justice O'CONNOR delivered the opinion of the Court.

This case requires us to clarify the extent of copyright protection available to telephone directory white pages.

### I

Rural Telephone Service Company, Inc., is a certified public utility that provides telephone service to several communities in northwest Kansas. It is subject to a state regulation that requires all telephone companies operating in Kansas to issue annually an updated telephone directory. Accordingly, as a condition of its monopoly franchise, Rural publishes a typical telephone directory, consisting of white pages and yellow pages. The white pages list in alphabetical order the names of Rural's subscribers, together with their towns and telephone numbers. The yellow pages list Rural's business subscribers alphabetically by category and feature classified advertisements of various sizes. Rural distributes its directory free of charge to its subscribers, but earns revenue by selling yellow pages advertisements.

Feist Publications, Inc., is a publishing company that specializes in area-wide telephone directories. Unlike a typical directory, which covers only a particular calling area, Feist's area-wide directories cover a much larger geographical range, reducing the need to call directory assistance or consult multiple directories. The Feist directory that is the subject of this litigation covers 11 different telephone service areas in 15 counties and contains 46,878 white pages listings — compared to Rural's approximately 7,700 listings. Like Rural's directory, Feist's is distributed free of charge and includes both white pages and yellow pages. Feist and Rural compete vigorously for yellow pages advertising.

As the sole provider of telephone service in its service area, Rural obtains subscriber information quite easily. Persons desiring telephone service must apply to Rural and provide their names and addresses; Rural then assigns them a telephone number. Feist is not a telephone company, let alone one with monopoly status, and therefore lacks independent access to any subscriber information. To obtain white pages listings for its area-wide directory, Feist approached each of the 11 telephone companies operating in northwest Kansas and offered to pay for the right to use its white pages listings.

Of the 11 telephone companies, only Rural refused to license its listings to Feist. Rural's refusal created a problem for Feist, as omitting these listings would have left a gaping hole in its area-wide directory, rendering it less attractive to potential yellow pages advertisers. . . .

Unable to license Rural's white pages listings, Feist used them without Rural's consent. Feist began by removing several thousand listings that fell outside the geographic range of its area-wide directory, then hired personnel to investigate the 4,935 that remained. These employees verified the data reported by Rural and sought to obtain additional information. As a result, a typical Feist listing includes the individual's street address; most of Rural's listings do not. Notwithstanding these additions, however, 1,309 of the 46,878 listings in Feist's 1983 directory were identical to listings in Rural's 1982-1983 white pages. Four of these were fictitious listings that Rural had inserted into its directory to detect copying.

Rural sued for copyright infringement in the District Court for the District of Kansas taking the position that Feist, in compiling its own directory, could not use the information contained in Rural's white pages. Rural asserted that Feist's employees were obliged to travel door-to-door or conduct a telephone survey to discover the same information for themselves. Feist responded that such efforts were economically impractical and, in any event, unnecessary because the information copied was beyond the scope of copyright protection. The District Court granted summary judgment to Rural, explaining that "[c]ourts have consistently held that telephone directories are copyrightable" and citing a string of lower court decisions. 663 F. Supp. 214, 218 (1987). In an unpublished opinion, the Court of Appeals for the Tenth Circuit affirmed "for substantially the reasons given by the district court." App. to Pet. for Cert. 4a. We granted certiorari to determine whether the copyright in Rural's directory protects the names, towns, and telephone numbers copied by Feist.

## II

### A

This case concerns the interaction of two well-established propositions. The first is that facts are not copyrightable; the other that compilations of facts generally are. Each of these propositions possesses an impeccable pedigree. That there can be no valid copyright in facts is universally understood. The most fundamental axiom of copyright law is that "[n]o author may copyright his ideas or the facts he narrates." *Harper & Row, Publishers, Inc. v. Nation Enterprises,* 471 U.S. 539, 556 (1985). Rural wisely concedes this point, noting in its brief that "[f]acts and discoveries, of course, are not themselves subject to copyright protection." Brief for Respondent 24. At the same time, however, it is beyond dispute that compilations of facts are within the subject matter of copyright. Compilations were expressly mentioned in the Copyright Act of 1909, and again in the Copyright Act of 1976.

There is an undeniable tension between these two propositions. Many compilations consist of nothing but raw data—*i.e.,* wholly factual information not accompanied by any original written expression. On what basis may one claim a copyright in such a work? Common sense tells us that

100 uncopyrightable facts do not magically change their status when gathered together in one place. Yet copyright law seems to contemplate that compilations that consist exclusively of facts are potentially within its scope.

The key to resolving the tension lies in understanding why facts are not copyrightable. The *sine qua non* of copyright is originality. To qualify for copyright protection, a work must be original to the author. See *Harper & Row, supra,* at 547-549. Original, as the term is used in copyright, means only that the work was independently created by the author (as opposed to copied from other works), and that it possesses at least some minimal degree of creativity. 1 M. Nimmer & D. Nimmer, Copyright §§2.01[A], [B] (1990) (hereinafter Nimmer). To be sure, the requisite level of creativity is extremely low; even a slight amount will suffice. The vast majority of works make the grade quite easily, as they possess some creative spark, "no matter how crude, humble or obvious" it might be. *Id.,* §1.08[C][1]. Originality does not signify novelty; a work may be original even though it closely resembles other works so long as the similarity is fortuitous, not the result of copying. To illustrate, assume that two poets, each ignorant of the other, compose identical poems. Neither work is novel, yet both are original and, hence, copyrightable.

Originality is a constitutional requirement. The source of Congress' power to enact copyright laws is Article I, §8, cl. 8, of the Constitution, which authorizes Congress to "secur[e] for limited Times to Authors . . . the exclusive Right to their respective Writings." In two decisions from the late 19th century — *The Trade-Mark Cases,* 100 U.S. 82 (1879); and *Burrow-Giles Lithographic Co. v. Sarony,* 111 U.S. 53 (1884) — this Court defined the crucial terms "authors" and "writings." In so doing, the Court made it unmistakably clear that these terms presuppose a degree of originality.

In *The Trade-Mark Cases,* the Court addressed the constitutional scope of "writings." For a particular work to be classified "under the head of writings of authors," the Court determined, "originality is required." 100 U.S., at 94. The Court explained that originality requires independent creation plus a modicum of creativity: "[W]hile the word *writings* may be liberally construed, as it has been, to include original designs for engraving, prints, &c., it is only such as are *original,* and are founded in the creative powers of the mind. The writings which are to be protected are *the fruits of intellectual labor,* embodied in the form of books, prints, engravings, and the like." *Ibid.* (emphasis in original).

In *Burrow-Giles,* the Court distilled the same requirement from the Constitution's use of the word "authors." The Court defined "author," in a constitutional sense, to mean "he to whom anything owes its origin; originator; maker." 111 U.S., at 58 (internal quotation marks omitted). As in *The Trade-Mark Cases,* the Court emphasized the creative component of originality. It described copyright as being limited to "original intellectual conceptions of the author," 111 U.S., at 58, and stressed the importance of requiring an author who accuses another of infringement to prove "the existence of those facts of originality, of intellectual production, of thought, and conception." *Id.,* at 59-60.

The originality requirement articulated in *The Trade-Mark Cases* and *Burrow-Giles* remains the touchstone of copyright protection today. It is the very "premise of copyright law." *Miller v. Universal City Studios, Inc.*, 650 F.2d 1365, 1368 (5th Cir. 1981)....

It is this bedrock principle of copyright that mandates the law's seemingly disparate treatment of facts and factual compilations. "No one may claim originality as to facts." [Nimmer] §2.11[A], p. 2-157. This is because facts do not owe their origin to an act of authorship. The distinction is one between creation and discovery: The first person to find and report a particular fact has not created the fact; he or she has merely discovered its existence. To borrow from *Burrow-Giles*, one who discovers a fact is not its "maker" or "originator." 111 U.S., at 58. "The discoverer merely finds and records." Nimmer §2.03[E]....

Factual compilations, on the other hand, may possess the requisite originality. The compilation author typically chooses which facts to include, in what order to place them, and how to arrange the collected data so that they may be used effectively by readers. These choices as to selection and arrangement, so long as they are made independently by the compiler and entail a minimal degree of creativity, are sufficiently original that Congress may protect such compilations through the copyright laws. Thus, even a directory that contains absolutely no protectible written expression, only facts, meets the constitutional minimum for copyright protection if it features an original selection or arrangement.

This protection is subject to an important limitation. The mere fact that a work is copyrighted does not mean that every element of the work may be protected. Originality remains the *sine qua non* of copyright; accordingly, copyright protection may extend only to those components of a work that are original to the author. Thus, if the compilation author clothes facts with an original collocation of words, he or she may be able to claim a copyright in this written expression. Others may copy the underlying facts from the publication, but not the precise words used to present them. In *Harper & Row*, for example, we explained that President Ford could not prevent others from copying bare historical facts from his autobiography, see 471 U.S., at 556-557, but that he could prevent others from copying his "subjective descriptions and portraits of public figures." *Id.*, at 563. Where the compilation author adds no written expression but rather lets the facts speak for themselves, the expressive element is more elusive. The only conceivable expression is the manner in which the compiler has selected and arranged the facts. Thus, if the selection and arrangement are original, these elements of the work are eligible for copyright protection. No matter how original the format, however, the facts themselves do not become original through association.

This inevitably means that the copyright in a factual compilation is thin. Notwithstanding a valid copyright, a subsequent compiler remains free to use the facts contained in another's publication to aid in preparing a competing work, so long as the competing work does not feature the same selection and arrangement. As one commentator explains it: "[N]o matter how much original authorship the work displays, the facts and ideas it exposes are free for the taking....[T]he very same facts and ideas may be divorced from the context imposed by the author, and restated or reshuffled by second comers, even if the author was the first to discover the facts or to propose the ideas." [Ginsburg, *Creation and Commercial Value*:

*Copyright Protection of Works of Information*, 90 COLUM. L. REV. 1865, 1868 (1990)].

It may seem unfair that much of the fruit of the compiler's labor may be used by others without compensation. As Justice Brennan has correctly observed, however, this is not "some unforeseen byproduct of a statutory scheme." *Harper & Row*, 471 U.S., at 589 (dissenting opinion). It is, rather, "the essence of copyright," *ibid.*, and a constitutional requirement. The primary objective of copyright is not to reward the labor of authors, but "[t]o promote the Progress of Science and useful Arts." Art. I, §8, cl. 8. To this end, copyright assures authors the right to their original expression, but encourages others to build freely upon the ideas and information conveyed by a work. *Harper & Row, supra*, 471 U.S., at 556-557. This principle, known as the idea/expression or fact/expression dichotomy, applies to all works of authorship. As applied to a factual compilation, assuming the absence of original written expression, only the compiler's selection and arrangement may be protected; the raw facts may be copied at will. This result is neither unfair nor unfortunate. It is the means by which copyright advances the progress of science and art.

\* \* \*

This, then, resolves the doctrinal tension: Copyright treats facts and factual compilations in a wholly consistent manner. Facts, whether alone or as part of a compilation, are not original and therefore may not be copyrighted. A factual compilation is eligible for copyright if it features an original selection or arrangement of facts, but the copyright is limited to the particular selection or arrangement. In no event may copyright extend to the facts themselves.

**B**

As we have explained, originality is a constitutionally mandated prerequisite for copyright protection. The Court's decisions announcing this rule predate the Copyright Act of 1909, but ambiguous language in the 1909 Act caused some lower courts temporarily to lose sight of this requirement.

The 1909 Act embodied the originality requirement, but not as clearly as it might have. See Nimmer §2.01. The subject matter of copyright was set out in §§3 and 4 of the Act. Section 4 stated that copyright was available to "all the writings of an author." 35 Stat. 1076. By using the words "writings" and "author"—the same words used in Article I, §8, of the Constitution and defined by the Court in *The Trade-Mark Cases* and *Burrow-Giles*—the statute necessarily incorporated the originality requirement articulated in the Court's decisions. It did so implicitly, however, thereby leaving room for error.

\* \* \*

Most courts construed the 1909 Act correctly, notwithstanding the less-than-perfect statutory language. They understood from this Court's decisions that there could be no copyright without originality. As explained in the Nimmer treatise: "The 1909 Act neither defined originality, nor even expressly required that a work be 'original' in order to command protection. However, the courts uniformly inferred the requirement from the fact that copyright protection may only be claimed by 'authors'.... It was reasoned that since an author is 'the ... creator, originator' it follows that a work is not the product of an author unless the work is original." Nimmer §2.01 (footnotes omitted) (citing cases).

But some courts misunderstood the statute....

Making matters worse, these courts developed a new theory to justify the protection of factual compilations. Known alternatively as "sweat of the brow" or "industrious collection," the underlying notion was that copyright was a reward for the hard work that went into compiling facts....

The "sweat of the brow" doctrine had numerous flaws, the most glaring being that it extended copyright protection in a compilation beyond selection and arrangement—the compiler's original contributions—to the facts themselves. Under the doctrine, the only defense to infringement was independent creation. A subsequent compiler was "not entitled to take one word of information previously published," but rather had to "independently wor[k] out the matter for himself, so as to arrive at the same result from the same common sources of information." *Id.*, at 88-89 (internal quotation marks omitted). "Sweat of the brow" courts thereby eschewed the most fundamental axiom of copyright law—that no one may copyright facts or ideas....

Without a doubt, the "sweat of the brow" doctrine flouted basic copyright principles. Throughout history, copyright law has "recognize[d] a greater need to disseminate factual works than works of fiction or fantasy." *Harper & Row*, 471 U.S., at 563. But "sweat of the brow" courts took a contrary view; they handed out proprietary interests in facts and declared that authors are absolutely precluded from saving time and effort by relying upon the facts contained in prior works. In truth, "[i]t is just such wasted effort that the proscription against the copyright of ideas and facts ... [is] designed to prevent." *Rosemont Enterprises, Inc. v. Random House, Inc.*, 366 F.2d 303, 310 (2d Cir. 1966). "Protection for the fruits of such research ... may in certain circumstances be available under a theory of unfair competition. But to accord copyright protection on this basis alone distorts basic copyright principles in that it creates a monopoly in public domain materials without the necessary justification of protecting and encouraging the creation of 'writings' by 'authors.'" Nimmer §3.04, p. 3-23 (footnote omitted).

## C

.... In enacting the Copyright Act of 1976, Congress dropped the reference to "all the writings of an author" and replaced it with the phrase "original works of authorship." 17 U.S.C. §102(a)....

To ensure that the mistakes of the "sweat of the brow" courts would not be repeated, Congress took additional measures. For example, §3 of the 1909 Act had stated that copyright protected only the "copyrightable component parts" of a work, but had not identified originality as the basis for distinguishing those component parts that were copyrightable from those that were not. The 1976 Act deleted this section and replaced it with

§102(b), which identifies specifically those elements of a work for which copyright is not available: "In no case does copyright protection for an original work of authorship extend to any idea, procedure, process, system, method of operation, concept, principle, or discovery, regardless of the form in which it is described, explained, illustrated, or embodied in such work." Section 102(b) is universally understood to prohibit any copyright in facts. *Harper & Row, supra,* at 547, 556. As with §102(a), Congress emphasized that §102(b) did not change the law, but merely clarified it: "Section 102(b) in no way enlarges or contracts the scope of copyright protection under the present law. Its purpose is to restate...that the basic dichotomy between expression and idea remains unchanged." H.R. Rep., at 57; S. Rep., at 54, U.S. Code Cong. & Admin. News 1976, p. 5670.

Congress took another step to minimize confusion by deleting the specific mention of "directories...and other compilations" in §5 of the 1909 Act. As mentioned, this section had led some courts to conclude that directories were copyrightable *per se* and that every element of a directory was protected. In its place, Congress enacted two new provisions. First, to make clear that compilations were not copyrightable *per se,* Congress provided a definition of the term "compilation." Second, to make clear that the copyright in a compilation did not extend to the facts themselves, Congress enacted §103.

The definition of "compilation" is found in §101 of the 1976 Act. It defines a "compilation" in the copyright sense as "a work formed by the collection and assembling of preexisting materials or of data *that* are selected, coordinated, or arranged *in such a way that* the resulting work as a whole constitutes an original work of authorship" (emphasis added).

The purpose of the statutory definition is to emphasize that collections of facts are not copyrightable *per se*. It conveys this message through its tripartite structure, as emphasized above by the italics. The statute identifies three distinct elements and requires each to be met for a work to qualify as a copyrightable compilation: (1) the collection and assembly of pre-existing material, facts, or data; (2) the selection, coordination, or arrangement of those materials; and (3) the creation, by virtue of the particular selection, coordination, or arrangement, of an "original" work of authorship....

The third requirement...emphasizes that a compilation, like any other work, is copyrightable only if it satisfies the originality requirement ("an *original* work of authorship"). Although §102 states plainly that the originality requirement applies to all works, the point was emphasized with regard to compilations to ensure that courts would not repeat the mistake of the "sweat of the brow" courts by concluding that fact-based works are treated differently and measured by some other standard. As Congress explained it, the goal was to "make plain that the criteria of copyrightable subject matter stated in section 102 apply with full force to works...containing preexisting material." H.R. Rep., at 57; S. Rep., at 55, U.S. Code Cong. & Admin. News 1976, p. 5670.

The key to the statutory definition is the second requirement. It instructs courts that, in determining whether a fact-based work is an original work of authorship, they should focus on the manner in which the collected facts have been selected, coordinated, and arranged. This is a straightforward application of the originality requirement. Facts are never original, so the compilation author can claim originality, if at all, only in the way the facts are presented. To that end, the statute dictates that the principal focus should be on whether the selection, coordination, and arrangement are sufficiently original to merit protection.

Not every selection, coordination, or arrangement will pass muster. This is plain from the statute. It states that, to merit protection, the facts must be selected, coordinated, or arranged "in such a way" as to render the work as a whole original. This implies that some "ways" will trigger copyright, but that others will not. Otherwise, the phrase "in such a way" is meaningless and Congress should have defined "compilation" simply as "a work formed by the collection and assembly of preexisting materials or data that are selected, coordinated, or arranged." That Congress did not do so is dispositive. . . .

As discussed earlier, however, the originality requirement is not particularly stringent. A compiler may settle upon a selection or arrangement that others have used; novelty is not required. Originality requires only that the author make the selection or arrangement independently (*i.e.*, without copying that selection or arrangement from another work), and that it display some minimal level of creativity. Presumably, the vast majority of compilations will pass this test, but not all will. There remains a narrow category of works in which the creative spark is utterly lacking or so trivial as to be virtually nonexistent. See generally *Bleistein v. Donaldson Lithographing Co.*, 188 U.S. 239, 251 (1903) (referring to "the narrowest and most obvious limits"). Such works are incapable of sustaining a valid copyright.

Even if a work qualifies as a copyrightable compilation, it receives only limited protection. This is the point of §103 of the Act. Section 103 explains that "[t]he subject matter of copyright . . . includes compilations," §103(a), but that copyright protects only the author's original contributions — not the facts or information conveyed:

> The copyright in a compilation . . . extends only to the material contributed by the author of such work, as distinguished from the preexisting material employed in the work, and does not imply any exclusive right in the preexisting material." §103(b).

As §103 makes clear, copyright is not a tool by which a compilation author may keep others from using the facts or data he or she has collected. "The most important point here is one that is commonly misunderstood today: copyright . . . has no effect one way or the other on the copyright or public domain status of the preexisting material." H.R. Rep., at 57; S. Rep., at 55, U.S. Code Cong. & Admin. News 1976, p. 5670. The 1909 Act did not require, as "sweat of the brow" courts mistakenly assumed, that each subsequent compiler must start from scratch and is precluded from relying on research undertaken by another. Rather, the facts contained in existing works may be freely copied because copyright protects only the elements that owe their origin to the compiler — the selection, coordination, and arrangement of facts. . . .

### III

There is no doubt that Feist took from the white pages of Rural's directory a substantial amount of factual information. At a minimum, Feist copied the names, towns, and telephone numbers of 1,309 of Rural's subscribers. Not all copying, however, is copyright infringement. To establish infringement, two elements must be proven: (1) ownership of a valid copyright, and (2) copying of constituent elements of the work that are original. The first element is not at issue here; Feist appears to concede that Rural's directory, considered as a whole, is subject to a valid copyright because it contains some foreword text, as well as original material in its yellow pages advertisements.

The question is whether Rural has proved the second element. In other words, did Feist, by taking 1,309 names, towns, and telephone numbers from Rural's white pages, copy anything that was "original" to Rural? Certainly, the raw data does not satisfy the originality requirement. Rural may have been the first to discover and report the names, towns, and telephone numbers of its subscribers, but this data does not "'ow[e] its origin'" to Rural. *Burrow-Giles*, 111 U.S., at 58. Rather, these bits of information are uncopyrightable facts; they existed before Rural reported them and would have continued to exist if Rural had never published a telephone directory. . . .

Rural essentially concedes the point by referring to the names, towns, and telephone numbers as "preexisting material." Brief for Respondent 17. Section 103(b) states explicitly that the copyright in a compilation does not extend to "the preexisting material employed in the work."

The question that remains is whether Rural selected, coordinated, or arranged these uncopyrightable facts in an original way. As mentioned, originality is not a stringent standard; it does not require that facts be presented in an innovative or surprising way. It is equally true, however, that the selection and arrangement of facts cannot be so mechanical or routine as to require no creativity whatsoever. The standard of originality is low, but it does exist. As this Court has explained, the Constitution mandates some minimal degree of creativity, see *The Trade-Mark Cases*, 100 U.S., at 94; and an author who claims infringement must prove "the existence of . . . intellectual production, of thought, and conception." *Burrow-Giles, supra*, 111 U.S., at 59-60.

The selection, coordination, and arrangement of Rural's white pages do not satisfy the minimum constitutional standards for copyright protection. As mentioned at the outset, Rural's white pages are entirely typical. Persons desiring telephone service in Rural's service area fill out an application and Rural issues them a telephone number. In preparing its white pages, Rural simply takes the data provided by its subscribers and lists it alphabetically by surname. The end product is a garden-variety white pages directory, devoid of even the slightest trace of creativity.

Rural's selection of listings could not be more obvious: It publishes the most basic information—name, town, and telephone number—about each person who applies to it for telephone service. This is "selection" of a sort, but it lacks the modicum of creativity necessary to transform mere selection into copyrightable expression. Rural expended sufficient effort to make the white pages directory useful, but insufficient creativity to make it original.

We note in passing that the selection featured in Rural's white pages may also fail the originality requirement for another reason. Feist points out that Rural did not truly "select" to publish the names and telephone numbers of its subscribers; rather, it was required to do so by the Kansas Corporation Commission as part of its monopoly franchise. *See* 737 F. Supp., at 612. Accordingly, one could plausibly conclude that this selection was dictated by state law, not by Rural.

Nor can Rural claim originality in its coordination and arrangement of facts. The white pages do nothing more than list Rural's subscribers in alphabetical order. This arrangement may, technically speaking, owe its origin to Rural; no one disputes that Rural undertook the task of alphabetizing the names itself. But there is nothing remotely creative about arranging names alphabetically in a white pages directory. It is an age-old practice, firmly rooted in tradition and so commonplace that it has come to be expected as a matter of course. It is not only unoriginal, it is practically inevitable. This time-honored tradition does not possess the minimal creative spark required by the Copyright Act and the Constitution.

We conclude that the names, towns, and telephone numbers copied by Feist were not original to Rural and therefore were not protected by the copyright in Rural's combined white and yellow pages directory. As a constitutional matter, copyright protects only those constituent elements of a work that possess more than a *de minimis* quantum of creativity. Rural's white pages, limited to basic subscriber information and arranged alphabetically, fall short of the mark. As a statutory matter, 17 U.S.C. §101 does not afford protection from copying to a collection of facts that are selected, coordinated, and arranged in a way that utterly lacks originality. Given that some works must fail, we cannot imagine a more likely candidate. Indeed, were we to hold that Rural's white pages pass muster, it is hard to believe that any collection of facts could fail.

Because Rural's white pages lack the requisite originality, Feist's use of the listings cannot constitute infringement. This decision should not be construed as demeaning Rural's efforts in compiling its directory, but rather as making clear that copyright rewards originality, not effort. As this Court noted more than a century ago, "'great praise may be due to the plaintiffs for their industry and enterprise in publishing this paper, yet the law does not contemplate their being rewarded in this way.'" [*Baker v. Selden*, 101 U.S. 99, 105 (1880)].

The judgment of the Court of Appeals is *Reversed*.

## Comments

1. *Statutory versus Constitutional Holding.* The text of the copyright statute at issue in the earlier cases in this section did not include the term "original," but the Copyright Act of 1976, which applied in *Feist*, does so. As a result, the Court might have resolved this case on statutory grounds, by concluding that Rural's telephone directory did not meet

the "originality" standard of the statute, and leaving untouched the older body of cases that deal with "originality" as a constitutional matter. Among other things, however, that approach might have created two "originality" thresholds in copyright law, a lower Constitutional threshold for older works produced under the Copyright Act of 1909 and a higher statutory threshold for works produced under the Copyright Act of 1976. Justice O'Connor's opinion consciously avoids this path, setting a consistent "minimal creativity" standard as a constitutional matter for all works, whenever they were produced.

2. **Rural's Incentives.** If the decision not to grant a copyright to Rural Telephone were to undermine its incentive to produce telephone directories, then perhaps the Court erred by setting the threshold for copyrightability too high. But Rural Telephone was a regulated public utility which was required by state law to produce a white pages directory of telephone listings. Copyright protection for the directory, in other words, would not affect Rural's incentives in any way.

3. **Originality as Minimal Creativity.** The Court constructs a two-step standard for copyrightability. The first step asks whether the work displays "minimal creativity," in the sense that it is at least slightly distinctive over and above any preexisting material on which it relies, or which it borrows. Only a "modicum" of creativity is required; it is enough that the alleged creativity not be "mechanical or routine." *Feist* does not articulate precisely how much creativity is enough and how much is not enough; all that the law tells us for sure is that the alphabetical version of the white pages telephone directory is "commonplace" and therefore not sufficiently creative. Notably, it is commonplace specifically because this is how we all expect phone directories to be arranged, and it is the form in which telephone directories are most useful. Consider whether "reverse lookup" telephone directories, in which listings are arranged numerically by telephone number, are similarly "commonplace."

4. **Originality as Independent Production.** The second step of *Feist*'s originality standard focuses on the author, and the manner in which the work was prepared. This step is "independent creation." The allegedly copyrighted material must "owe its origin" to the author and must not have been copied from some other source. The Court thus adopts portions of both the *Bleistein* originality formulation (originality means lack of copying) and the *Sarony* formulation (originality as creativity in the mind).

5. **Copyright in Compilations of Preexisting Material: Selection, Coordination, and Arrangement.** The result in *Feist* follows from two premises. First, Rural Telephone cannot copyright individual telephone numbers. *Feist* introduces the distinction between copyrightable "expression" and uncopyrightable "fact." A telephone number is a "fact," and facts, according to the Court, cannot satisfy the demand that copyrightable works be original; that is, under the *Feist* standard, facts are not minimally creative. The distinction between fact and expression is a foundational principle for all of copyright. Second, Rural Telephone cannot copyright its collection of telephone numbers, which copyright

law would characterize as a "compilation" under the definition in §101 of the Copyright Act, which the Court quotes. A compilation collects preexisting material or data of some sort, but it must satisfy the same "originality" standard that any work must satisfy in order to be copyrighted. That standard can be satisfied in at least one of three ways: the preexisting material may be selected in a creative way, arranged in a creative way, or "coordinated" in a creative way. In this case, the white pages telephone directory satisfies none of those standards.

6. *"Sweat of the Brow" Arguments and Copyright Policy.* The Court clearly intends *Feist* as a strong endorsement of the incentive function of copyright law and as a rejection of labor-desert theories of copyright. Nonetheless, it is easy to read *Feist*'s two-step originality standard as restating the policy endorsing "sweat of the brow" justifications for copyright protection, and some courts following *Feist* have, at times, appeared to do just that. Those cases are considered below in the context of copyrightable compilations of fact. The distinction that the Court appears to be drawing, however, is the distinction between earning copyright solely by virtue of the time and energy applied to producing the work, which constitutes an invalid "sweat of the brow" justification, and receiving copyright by virtue of an application of *creative* time and/or energy, which is legitimate. An "author" is one who not only works hard at producing a work, but who works hard in applying some measure of minimally creative judgment or skill. From the perspective of copyright policy, the incentive that the standard supplies is designed to encourage production of works that represent "Progress" in the Constitutional sense. Mere recreations of existing works do not increase the store of society's knowledge, even incrementally, since presumably society already has access to that material. Works of authorship that are new, even incrementally new, do tend to increase that store, and thus satisfy the Constitutional command.

**COMPARATIVE PERSPECTIVE**
**Database Protection**

The Court's decision in *Feist* has been widely interpreted by commercial database publishers, such publishers of stock price information, telephone directories, real estate listings, statistics from professional sports leagues, and legal reference materials, as sounding the death knell for legal protection for their products. In the United States, therefore, commercial database publishers have aggressively pursued a two-pronged legal strategy. First, they rely heavily on alternative legal doctrines, such as shrinkwrap and "clickwrap" contracts with end users, and the doctrine of "hot news" misappropriation from tort law, to prevent reuse of information in their databases. Second, they have lobbied Congress to enact new legislation to provide a federal cause of action against the unauthorized extraction and use of information contained in a valuable database. To date, however, these efforts to secure new legislation have been unsuccessful.

In Europe, however, producers and vendors of databases have been more successful. In 1996, the European Union adopted what has become known as the EU Database Directive, Directive 96/9/EC of the European Parliament and of the Council of March 11, 1996 on the Legal Protection of Databases, 1996 O.J. (L 77) 20, which requires that EU member nations enact two forms of protection for databases. The Directive is premised explicitly on a "sweat of the brow" rationale rejected in *Feist*. A qualifying database is one that involves a substantial investment in obtaining, verifying, or presenting the contents of the database. The first form of protection tracks the standard in *Feist*. States must provide copyright protection for databases that constitute the author's "own intellectual creation" by virtue of the selection or arrangement of their contents. Second is a "sui generis" right: States must provide the right to prevent unauthorized extraction or re-utilization of the contents of the database.

Importantly, the Directive contains a reciprocity provision, so that the benefits of the Directive extend only to nationals or residents of EU Member States, to firms incorporated and having their principal offices in a Member State, and to nationals or residents of countries that offer comparable protection to databases produced by nationals or residents of the EU. In other words, unless the United States provides protection for databases comparable to that provided under the Database Directive, EU database rights are not available to U.S. database producers.

To date, litigation under the legislation enacted in light of the EU Database Directive has been infrequent. In an important recent case, an English Court of Appeal interpreted U.K. database law narrowly, permitting a private bookmaking firm to use race listings produced by the British Horseracing Board. Data regarding the horses, the court noted, was compiled and published by the Horseracing Board, but did not originate with it. *See The British Horseracing Board Ltd. v. William Hill Organization Ltd.*, [2005] EWCA Civ. 863.

## 2. Fixation

*STATUTE:* **Definitions — "Copies," "Fixed," "Phonorecords," "Transmit"**
17 U.S.C. §101

English precursors to modern copyright law used the term "copie," which referred both to the legal right to publish a book and to the physical manuscript itself. The publisher typically owned both. (Today, a modern analogy might be the "copy" produced by advertising agencies.) Modern copyright is organized around the intangible rights in the author's creative output, but for both historical and policy reasons the law remains concerned that this output be constituted in tangible form before those intangible rights attach.

The creative work must be "fixed" in what copyright law today refers to as a "tangible medium of expression," or what has historically been referred to as a "copy." In short, the original of a copyrighted work is referred to as a "copy," and (confusingly) absent a copy, there is no original copyrighted work.

Enforcing copyright in tangible versions of creative works serves copyright policy in a number of ways. It encourages authors to reduce their expressive output to forms that are easily and cheaply distributed to readers and other consumers, thereby supporting the distribution of creative output through society. It serves an evidentiary purpose, by allowing courts and prospective licensees of the work to confirm that the author has, in fact, produced a work of creative authorship. It also prevents opportunism by authors, by ensuring that what they claim as their copyrightable work does not change over time. Fixation serves a jurisdictional purpose, by reserving federal statutory copyright exclusively for works that are "fixed." State common law copyright, to the extent that it is effective, applies only to works that are not "fixed." Finally, copyright's focus on tangible works is at least partly a historical convention. Copyright originated in books, and books, by their nature, have traditionally been tangible things.

### HISTORICAL PERSPECTIVE
### The Origins of Modern Copyright Law

Like all intellectual property law, copyright law is a modern adaptation of legal principles that go back centuries, to technical developments of the late Middle Ages and to the spread of commerce and learning that sparked what we know today as the Enlightenment.

The technical developments were the invention of movable type and the printing press by Johannes Gutenberg in the mid-1400s and the importation of the printing press into England by Caxton, near the end of that century. The printing press led to the rise of the printed book, and soon it led to the availability to non-elite audiences of printed materials of all sorts. Two developments followed. Printers (what today we would call publishers) discovered opportunities for profit, both in publishing new books and in pirating copies of existing ones. Governments discovered that broad distribution of printed materials carried the seeds of both theological and secular challenges to royal authority. Though there was early government regulation of publishing and printing in Germany and in Venice in the sixteenth century, for purposes of American copyright law it was the English experience that laid the foundations for modern law. English common law recognized the right of an author to prevent the unauthorized publication of his manuscript. The common law was beyond the authority of the Crown, however. Beginning in the early 1500s, royal printing privileges were granted to favored printers, and in 1557 the Stationers Company of London, an existing guild of printers and booksellers, was granted a royal charter, giving it the exclusive right to the "copie," that is, both the right to print and publish books, and to the physical books themselves. According to the charter of the Stationers Company, no book could be printed or sold in the kingdom unless its title was entered in its Register under the name of a member of the Company (rather than in the name of the author). Even without the royal imprimatur, the point of this provision, to preserve monopoly power to members of the Stationers, was clear. As with all royal decrees, enforcement was vested in the Court of the Star Chamber; a book had to be approved by a royal censor before it could be entered in the Register. This gave full effect to the purpose of the royal privilege. In sum, the English antecedents of "copyright" lie in a government-sanctioned monopoly deployed to censor seditious and heretical works.

The Star Chamber was abolished in 1640, and the control of publishing vested in the Stationers Company diminished with Parliament's passage of a series of Licensing Acts, beginning in 1643. The Licensing Acts retained the condition that the right to publish depended on prior approval of the government (so that registration of books in the Register of the Stationers was still required), and the law continued to forbid publication of seditious or heretical material. As the Age of Enlightenment dawned, the discomfiting effects of monopoly and the censorial nature of the Licensing Acts encouraged Parliament to let the licensing regime expire entirely in 1692.

The Stationers Company petitioned for a new Licensing Act, but the statute that Parliament passed, which took effect in 1710, gave it far less than it asked for and set the stage for the copyright law that we know today. The Statute of Anne, which vested the exclusive right of publication of "books" in "authors or their assigns," began with the phrase: "An Act for the Encouragement of Learning, by Vesting the Copies of Printed Books in the Authors or Purchasers of such Copies, during the Times therein mentioned."

## WILLIAMS ELECTRONICS, INC. v. ARTIC INTERNATIONAL, INC.

### 685 F.2d 870 (3d Cir. 1982)

SLOVITER, Circuit Judge.

Defendant Artic International, Inc. appeals from the district court's entry of a final injunction order permanently restraining and enjoining it from infringing plaintiff's copyrights on audiovisual works and a computer program relating to the electronic video game DEFENDER.

Plaintiff-appellee Williams Electronics, Inc. manufactures and sells coin-operated electronic video games. A video game machine consists of a cabinet containing, inter alia, a cathode ray tube (CRT), a sound system, hand controls for the player, and electronic circuit boards. The electronic circuitry includes a microprocessor and memory devices, called ROMs (R ead O nly M emory), which are tiny computer "chips" containing thousands of data locations which store the instructions and data of a computer program. The microprocessor executes the computer program to cause the game to operate. Judge Newman of the Second Circuit described a similar type of memory device as follows: "The (ROM) stores the instructions and data from a computer program in such a way that when electric current passes through the circuitry, the interaction of the program stored in the (ROM) with the other components of the game produces the sights and sounds of the audiovisual display that the player sees and hears. The memory devices determine not only the appearance and movement of the (game) images but also the variations in movement in response to the player's operation of the hand controls." *Stern Electronics, Inc. v. Kaufman,* 669 F.2d 852, 854 (2d Cir. 1982).

In approximately October 1979 Williams began to design a new video game, ultimately called DEFENDER, which incorporated various original and unique audiovisual features. The DEFENDER game was introduced to the industry at a trade show in 1980 and has since achieved great success in the marketplace. One of the attractions of video games contributing to their phenomenal popularity is apparently their use of unrealistic fantasy creatures, a fad also observed in the popularity of certain current films. In the DEFENDER game, there are symbols of a spaceship and aliens who do battle with symbols of human figures. The player operates the flight of and weapons on the spaceship, and has the mission of preventing invading aliens from kidnapping the humans from a ground plane.

Williams obtained three copyright registrations relating to its DEFENDER game: one covering the computer program, Registration No. TX 654-755, effective date December 11, 1980; the second covering the audiovisual effects displayed during the game's "attract mode",[2] Registration No. PA 97-373, effective date March 3, 1981; and the third covering the audiovisual effects displayed during the game's "play mode",[3] Registration No. PA 94-718, effective date March 11, 1981. Readily visible copyright notices for the DEFENDER game were placed on the game cabinet, appeared on the CRT screen during the attract mode and at the beginning of the play mode, and were placed on labels which were attached to the outer case of each memory device (ROM). In addition, the Williams program provided that the words "Copyright 1980-Williams Electronics" in code were to be stored in the memory devices, but were not to be displayed on the CRT at any time.

Defendant-appellant Artic International, Inc. is a seller of electronic components for video games in competition with Williams. The district court made the following relevant findings which are not disputed on this appeal. Artic has sold circuit boards, manufactured by others, which contain electronic circuits including a microprocessor and memory devices (ROMs). These memory devices incorporate a computer program which is virtually identical to Williams' program for its DEFENDER game. The result is a circuit board "kit" which is sold by Artic to others and which, when connected to a cathode ray tube, produces audiovisual effects and a

2. The "attract mode" refers to the audiovisual effects displayed before a coin is inserted into the game. It repeatedly shows the name of the game, the game symbols in typical motion and interaction patterns, and the initials of previous players who have achieved high scores.

3. The "play mode" refers to the audiovisual effects displayed during the actual play of the game, when the game symbols move and interact on the screen, and the player controls the movement of one of the symbols (e.g., a spaceship).

game almost identical to the Williams DEFENDER game including both the attract mode and the play mode. The play mode and actual play of Artic's game, entitled "DEFENSE COMMAND", is virtually identical to that of the Williams game, i.e., the characters displayed on the cathode ray tube including the player's spaceship are identical in shape, size, color, manner of movement and interaction with other symbols. Also, the attract mode of the Artic game is substantially identical to that of Williams' game, with minor exceptions such as the absence of the Williams name and the substitution of the terms "DEFENSE" and/or "DEFENSE COMMAND" for the term "DEFENDER" in its display. Based on the evidence before it, the district court found that the defendant Artic had infringed the plaintiff's computer program copyright for the DEFENDER game by selling kits which contain a computer program which is a copy of plaintiff's computer program, and that the defendant had infringed both of the plaintiff's audiovisual copyrights for the DEFENDER game by selling copies of those audiovisual works.

In the appeal before us, defendant does not dispute the findings with respect to copying but instead challenges the conclusions of the district court with respect to copyright infringement and the validity and scope of plaintiff's copyrights. . . .

. . . . Essentially, defendant Artic attacks the validity and the scope of the copyrights which it has been found by the district court to have infringed. Plaintiff possesses certificates of registration issued by the Copyright Office. Under the Copyright Act, these certificates constitute prima facie evidence of the validity of plaintiff's copyright. 17 U.S.C. §410(c). Defendant, therefore, has the burden of overcoming this presumption of validity.

With respect to the plaintiff's two audiovisual copyrights, defendant contends that there can be no copyright protection for the DEFENDER game's attract mode and play mode because these works fail to meet the statutory requirement of "fixation." . . . Defendant claims that the images in the plaintiff's audiovisual game are transient, and cannot be "fixed." Specifically, it contends that there is a lack of "fixation" because the video game generates or creates "new" images each time the attract mode or play mode is displayed, notwithstanding the fact that the new images are identical or substantially identical to the earlier ones.

We reject this contention. The fixation requirement is met whenever the work is "sufficiently permanent or stable to permit it to be . . . reproduced, or otherwise communicated" for more than a transitory period. Here the original audiovisual features of the DEFENDER game repeat themselves over and over. . . . . [T]he rejection of a similar contention by the Second Circuit is also applicable here. The court stated:

> The (video game's) display satisfies the statutory definition of an original "audiovisual work," and the *memory devices of the game satisfy the statutory requirement of a "copy" in which the work is "fixed."* The Act defines "copies" as "material objects . . . in which a work is fixed by any method now known or later developed, and from which the work can be perceived, reproduced, or otherwise communicated, either directly or with the aid of a machine or device" and specifies that a work is "fixed" when "its embodiment in a copy . . . is sufficiently permanent or stable to permit it to be perceived, reproduced, or otherwise communicated for a period of more than transitory duration." 17 U.S.C. App. §101 (1976). *The audiovisual work is permanently*

*embodied in a material object, the memory devices,* from which it can be perceived with the aid of the other components of the game.

*Stern Electronics, Inc. v. Kaufman,* 669 F.2d at 855-56 (footnote omitted; emphasis added).

Defendant also apparently contends that the player's participation withdraws the game's audiovisual work from copyright eligibility because there is no set or fixed performance and the player becomes a co-author of what appears on the screen. Although there is player interaction with the machine during the play mode which causes the audiovisual presentation to change in some respects from one game to the next in response to the player's varying participation, there is always a repetitive sequence of a substantial portion of the sights and sounds of the game, and many aspects of the display remain constant from game to game regardless of how the player operates the controls. See *Stern Electronics, Inc. v. Kaufman,* 669 F.2d at 855-56. Furthermore, there is no player participation in the attract mode which is displayed repetitively without change.

* * *

For the above reasons, the district court's order granting the injunction will be affirmed....

## Comments

1. **Fixation as Physical Stability.** The concept of "fixation" has at least two possible senses. One sense is that the work of authorship is attached to an unchanging physical thing (other than the human brain). The text of a book is fixed in this sense, in that the words are attached permanently to pages, which are bound together to form the book. In the same sense, the audiovisual work challenged in *Williams Electronics* is attached, in a remote sense, to a computer chip inside the video game console. Note that this connection is at least one step more abstract than the connection of text to page. Text is attached to page as ink is attached to paper; the work of authorship is embedded in the ink itself. The audiovisual work that the game player perceives is produced by a computer program, which translates the ones and zeroes of the program's computer code into sounds and images. The ones and zeroes of the computer program itself are "fixed" in the computer chip; the work of authorship is fixed in the computer program. One might ask, then, why the plaintiff did not characterize its work as a copyrightable computer program, which clearly was fixed in computer memory, rather than as an audiovisual work. The answer may be that when the case was filed, the copyrightability of computer programs, and particularly of computer programs driving video games, was not yet settled under the Copyright Act of 1976. Moreover, before a court unfamiliar with computer technology, focusing on the extent to which the two parties' games *looked and sounded the same* carried substantial appeal.

2. **Fixation as Temporal Stability.** The second sense of "fixation" is that the work of authorship is static over time. Each time we read, or hear, or listen to the work, we perceive the same thing. A book obviously does not

change between readings. A motion picture unfolds in the same sequence each time we watch it. The court in *Williams Electronics* concludes that the "attract mode" and "play mode" of the Defender video game are "fixed" in a temporal sense because "the original audio-visual features of the DEFENDER game repeat themselves over and over." Yet each time the player encounters the game, whether in attract mode or play mode, the actual sequence of images changes. It may be that each game "mode" consists of a copyrightable collection of images and sounds, which is fixed in the game's computer memory.

3. **The Authority of the Author.** "Fixation" for copyright purposes occurs only when the work is fixed by or under the authority of the author. Does the participation of the reader, listener, or game player in creating the work deprive its author of copyright protection, or create copyright interests in the reader, listener, or player? The *Williams Electronics* court says "no," since much of the audio and video portions of the game repeat regardless of how the player interacts with the game. Works of authorship that consist wholly or partly of improvisation, such as extemporaneous speaking, or dance, or jazz, are much less likely to do so. Such "unfixed" works are not eligible for federal statutory copyright unless they are video or audiotaped under the authority of the author, and even then, the copyright in the work as recorded will be stronger than a copyright in the underlying composition or choreography. For certain "unfixed" works, such as televised sporting events, that are extremely valuable commercially, Congress has adapted the Copyright Act to provide protection. The statutory definition of "fixed" includes a provision for fixation of a work that is "transmitted," so long as the recording and the transmission occur simultaneously.

*[handwritten margin note: Jazz, dance + extempore speech — No unfixed.]*

4. **The Perceptibility of the Work in the Fixed Copy.** The audiovisual work that is "fixed" in *Williams Electronics* is perceptible to humans, but the computer program that stores and generates that audiovisual work is perceptible only to machines. The definition of "fixed" in the Copyright Act, coupled with the definition of "copies," makes it clear that a work of authorship may be fixed for purposes of the statute even if it is only perceptible via some mechanical process, and even if it exists only for a "transitory" period of time.

5. **Copies and Phonorecords.** For all types of copyrightable works except sound recordings, works of authorship fixed in a tangible medium of expression constitute "copies" as that term is defined by §101 of the Copyright Act. Sound recordings (such as musical recordings, or books on tape), when fixed in a tangible medium, become "phonorecords" under §101. The distinction is important in the context of popular music. Copyrightable works known as musical compositions are fixed in "copies" (such as sheet music); copyrightable works known as sound recordings are fixed in "phonorecords" (such as .mp3 computer files, compact discs, cassettes, and vinyl records). As you will see later, actual recordings of copyrighted songs typically embody two copyrighted works simultaneously; the composition, owned by the songwriter, and the recording, owned by the record producer. At least this is where copyright interests begin; in the music industry, copyrights are typically assigned to publishing companies and recording companies.

## 3. Expression

*STATUTE:* **Subject Matter of Copyright: In General**
17 U.S.C.§102(b)

Copyright protection in any work of authorship is limited to the "expression" that the work contains. Other material, such as "ideas," and "facts," must be distinguished and reserved in the public domain. Although this distinction is a fundamental principle of copyright, the law recognizes several different rationales for it. Only "expression" is properly considered to be the "creative" output of an author. Only "expression" requires the incentive of copyright protection for its production. "Ideas," and "facts," for example, preexist "creative" efforts or would exist without them. Moreover, future authors may, and do, incorporate preexisting ideas and facts into their own new works, and permitting copyright to extend to that material would unduly interfere with their future creativity.

## BAKER v. SELDEN
### 101 U.S. 99 (1880)

Mr. Justice BRADLEY delivered the opinion of the court.

Charles Selden, the testator of the complainant in this case, in the year 1859 took the requisite steps for obtaining the copyright of a book, entitled "Selden's Condensed Ledger, or Book-keeping Simplified," the object of which was to exhibit and explain a peculiar system of book-keeping. In 1860 and 1861, he took the copyright of several other books, containing additions to and improvements upon the said system. The bill of complaint was filed against the defendant, Baker, for an alleged infringement of these copyrights. The latter, in his answer, denied that Selden was the author or designer of the books, and denied the infringement charged, and contends on the argument that the matter alleged to be infringed is not a lawful subject of copyright.

The parties went into proofs, and the various books of the complainant, as well as those sold and used by the defendant, were exhibited before the examiner, and witnesses were examined to both sides. A decree was rendered for the complainant, and the defendant appealed.

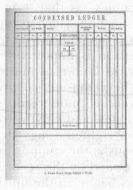

The book or series of books of which the complainant claims the copyright consists of an introductory essay explaining the system of book-keeping referred to, to which are annexed certain forms or banks, consisting of
ruled lines, and headings, illustrating the system and showing how it is to
be used and carried out in practice. This system effects the same results as
book-keeping by double entry; but, by a peculiar arrangement of columns
and headings, presents the entire operation, of a day, a week, or a month,
on a single page, or on two pages facing each other, in an account-book.
The defendant uses a similar plan so far as results are concerned; but
makes a different arrangement of the columns, and uses different headings. If the complainant's testator had the exclusive right to the use of the
system explained in his book, it would be difficult to contend that the
defendant does not infringe it, notwithstanding the difference in his
form of arrangement; but if it be assumed that the system is open to public
use, it seems to be equally difficult to contend that the books made and sold
by the defendant are a violation of the copyright of the complainant's book
considered merely as a book explanatory of the system. Where the truths of
a science or the methods of an art are the common property of the whole
world, any author has the right to express the one, or explain and use the
other, in his own way. As an author, Selden explained the system in a
particular way, It may be conceded that Baker makes and uses account-
books arranged on substantially the same system; but the proof fails to
show that he has violated the copyright of Selden's book, regarding the
latter merely as an explanatory work; or that he has infringed Selden's
right in any way, unless the latter became entitled to an exclusive right
in the system.

The evidence of the complainant is principally directed to the object of
showing that Baker uses the same system as that which is explained and
illustrated in Selden's books. It becomes important, therefore, to determine whether, in obtaining the copyright of his books, he secured the
exclusive right to the use of the system or method of book-keeping
which the said books are intended to illustrate and explain. It is contended
that he has secured such exclusive right, because no one can use the system
without using substantially the same ruled lines and headings which he was
appended to his books in illustration of it. In other words, it is contended
that the ruled lines and headings, given to illustrate the system, are a part
of the book, and, as such, are secured by the copyright; and that no one can
make or use similar ruled lines and headings, or ruled lines and headings
made and arranged on substantially the same system, without violating the
copyright. And this is really the question to be decided in this case. Stated
in another form, the question is, whether the exclusive property in a system
of book-keeping can be claimed, under the law or copyright, by means of a
book in which that system is explained? The complainant's bill, and the
case made under it, are based on the hypothesis that it can be.

It cannot be pretended, and indeed it is not seriously urged, that the
ruled lines of the complainant's account-book can be claimed under any
special class of objects, other than books, named in the law of copyright
existing in 1859. The law then in force was that of 1831, and specified only
books, maps, charts, musical compositions, prints, and engravings. An

account-book, consisting of ruled lines and blank columns, cannot be called by any of these names unless by that of a book.

There is no doubt that a work on the subject of book-keeping, though only explanatory of well-known systems, may be the subject of a copyright; but, then, it is claimed only as a book. Such a book may be explanatory either of old systems, or of an entirely new system; and, considered as a book, as the work of an author, conveying information on the subject of book-keeping, and containing detailed explanations of the art, it may be a very valuable acquisition to the practical knowledge of the community. But there is a clear distinction between the book, as such, and the art which it is intended to illustrate. The mere statement of the proposition is so evident, that it requires hardly any argument to support it. The same distinction may be predicated of every other art as well as that of book-keeping. A treatise on the composition and use of medicines, be they old or new; on the construction and use of ploughs, or watches, or churns; or on the mixture and application of colors for painting or dyeing; or on the mode of drawing lines to produce the effect of perspective, — would be the subject of copyright; but no one would contend that the copyright of the treatise would give the exclusive right to the art or manufacture described therein. The copyright of the book, if not pirated from other works, would be valid without regard to the novelty, or want of novelty, of its subject-matter. The novelty of the art or thing described or explained has nothing to do with the validity of the copyright. To give to the author of the book an exclusive property in the art described therein, when no examination of its novelty has ever been officially made, would be a surprise and a fraud upon the public. That is the province of letters-patent, not of copyright. The claim to an invention or discovery of an art or manufacture must be subjected to the examination of the Patent Office before an exclusive right therein can be obtained; and it can only be secured by a patent from the government.

* * *

The copyright of a book on perspective, no matter how many drawings and illustrations it may contain, gives no exclusive right to the modes of drawing described, though they may never have been known or used before. By publishing the book, without getting a patent for the art, the latter is given to the public. The fact that the art described in the book by illustrations of lines and figures which are reproduced in practice in the application of the art, makes no difference. Those illustrations are the mere language employed by the author to convey his ideas more clearly. Had he used words of description instead of diagrams (which merely stand in the place of words), there could not be the slightest doubt that others, applying the art to practical use, might lawfully draw the lines and diagrams which were in the author's mind, and which he thus described by words in his book.

The copyright of a work on mathematical science cannot give to the author an exclusive right to the methods of operation which he propounds, or to the diagrams which he employs to explain them, so as to prevent an engineer from using them whenever occasion requires. The very object of publishing a book on science or the useful arts is to communicate to the world the useful knowledge which it contains. But this object would be frustrated if the knowledge could not be used without incurring the guilt of piracy of the book. And where the art it teaches cannot be used without employing the methods and diagrams used to illustrate the book, or such as are similar to them, such methods and diagrams are to be considered as necessary incidents to the art, and given therewith to the public; not given for the purpose of publication in other works explanatory of the art, but for the purpose of practical application.

Of course, these observations are not intended to apply to ornamental designs, or pictorial illustrations addressed to the taste. Of these it may be said, that their form is their essence, and their object, the production of pleasure in their contemplation. This is their final end. They are as much the product of genius and the result of composition, as are the lines of the poet or the historian's period. On the other hand, the teachings of science and the rules and methods of useful art have their final end in application and use; and this application and use are what the public derive from the publication of a book which teaches them. But as embodied and taught in a literary composition or book, their essence consists only in their statement. This alone is what is secured by the copyright. The use by another of the same methods of statement, whether in words or illustrations, in a book published for teaching the art, would undoubtedly be an infringement of the copyright.

*Science is dissimilar to ornamental designs.*

Recurring to the case before us, we observe that Charles Selden, by his books, explained and described a peculiar system of book-keeping, and illustrated his method by means of ruled lines and blank columns, with proper headings on a page, or on successive pages. Now, whilst no one has a right to print or publish his book, or any material part thereof, as a book intended to convey instruction in the art, any person may practise and use the art itself which he has described and illustrated therein. The use of the art is a totally different thing from a publication of the book explaining it. The copyright of a book on book-keeping cannot secure the exclusive right to make, sell, and use account-books prepared upon the plan set forth in such book. Whether the art might or might not have been patented, is a question which is not before us. It was not patented, and is open and free to the use of the public. And, of course, in using the art, the ruled lines and headings of accounts must necessarily be used as incident to it.

The plausibility of the claim put forward by the complainant in this case arises from a confusion of ideas produced by the peculiar nature of the art described in the books which have been made the subject of copyright. In describing the art, the illustrations and diagrams employed happen to correspond more closely than usual with the actual work performed by the operator who uses the art. Those illustrations and diagrams consist of ruled lines and headings of accounts; and it is similar ruled lines and headings of accounts which, in the application of the art, the book-keeper makes with his pen, or the stationer with his press; whilst in most other cases the diagrams and illustrations can only be represented in concrete forms of wood, metal, stone, or some other physical embodiment. But the principle is the same in all. The description of the art in a book, though entitled to the benefit of copyright, lays no foundation for an exclusive claim to the art itself. The object of the one is explanation; the object of the other is use. The former may be secured by copyright. The latter can only be secured, if it can be secured at all, by letters-patent.

* * *

The conclusion to which we have come is, that blank account-books are not the subject of copyright; and that the mere copyright of Selden's book did not confer upon him the exclusive right to make and use account-books, ruled and arranged as designated by him and described and illustrated in said book.

The decree of the Circuit Court must be reversed, and the cause remanded with instructions to dismiss the complainant's bill; and it is
*So ordered.*

## Comments

1. ***The Idea/Expression Distinction.*** *Baker v. Selden* is routinely cited for the common proposition that copyright protects only the author's expression. Ideas, separable from expression, lie in the public domain and are free for anyone to use. A more precise reading of the case, however, suggests a variety of possible, narrower interpretations. Why did Selden's claim fail? There are a number of possibilities. First, the plaintiff may have improperly claimed a copyright in the system of double-entry bookkeeping. As a system, Selden's work was classified as an idea, and the Court rightly concludes that copyright cannot protect ideas. Second, the plaintiff may have claimed a copyright in Selden's version of double-entry bookkeeping, but the expression of that system in Selden's book (particularly in its illustrations and diagrams) was so intertwined with that system that a copyright could not be sustained, even though the defendant copied the illustrations and diagrams. In modern terms, this argument resembles the notion of merger, discussed below. Third, Selden may have been entitled to a copyright in the text describing his system, but the defendant copied only the accompanying forms, and not that text. In other words, there was no copying of the very thing that Selden claimed to have copyrighted. Fourth, to the extent that the plaintiff alleged a copyright interest in the forms themselves, those forms may not have been protectable by copyright.

2. ***Blank Forms Rule.*** The last interpretation of *Baker v. Selden* comes down to modern copyright law as the Blank Forms Rule, which rejects copyright in forms that are designed only to receive information, not to convey it. *See* 37 C.F.R. §202.1(c) (2005) (noting that "[b]lank forms, such as time cards, graph paper, account books, diaries, bank checks, scorecards, address books, report forms, order forms and the like, which are designed for recording information and do not in themselves convey information" cannot be copyrighted).

3. ***Copyright, Patent, and Functionality.*** The Court in *Baker* makes much of the fact that Selden is attempting to use copyright law to protect subject matter — a functional system — that ordinarily is the province of patent, with its heightened examination requirements and burdens as to novelty and non-obviousness. As we see below, copyright uses a number of different doctrinal devices to try to maintain the line between subject

matter that belongs in the copyright system and subject matter that belongs in the patent system. Copyright addresses "expressive" subject matter; patent law, in the language of the current Patent Act, covers any "new and useful process, machine, manufacture, or composition of matter." 35 U.S.C. §101. Under patent law as it existed at the time, it is not clear that Selden would have been entitled to a patent, since his system was far from the sort of mechanical or industrial process that dominated nineteenth-century patent law. Given the result in this case, therefore, it is likely that Selden was left with neither copyright nor patent protection. Today, however, a modern Selden might be able to obtain a patent, given the express endorsement of patenting inventions dealing with "business methods" in *State Street Bank & Trust Co. v. Signature Financial Group, Inc.,* 149 F.3d 1368 (Fed. Cir. 1998).

## NICHOLS v. UNIVERSAL PICTURES CORP.
### 45 F.2d 119 (2d Cir. 1930)

L. HAND, Circuit Judge.

The plaintiff is the author of a play, "Abie's Irish Rose," which it may be assumed was properly copyrighted under section five, subdivision (d), of the Copyright Act, 17 USCA §5(d). The defendant produced publicly a motion picture play, "The Cohens and The Kellys," which the plaintiff alleges was taken from it. As we think the defendant's play too unlike the plaintiff's to be an infringement, we may assume, arguendo, that in some details the defendant used the plaintiff's play, as will subsequently appear, though we do not so decide. It therefore becomes necessary to give an outline of the two plays.

"Abie's Irish Rose" presents a Jewish family living in prosperous circumstances in New York. The father, a widower, is in business as a merchant, in which his son and only child helps him. The boy has philandered with young women, who to his father's great disgust have always been Gentiles, for he is obsessed with a passion that his daughter-in-law shall be an orthodox Jewess. When the play opens the son, who has been courting a young Irish Catholic girl, has already married her secretly before a Protestant minister, and is concerned to soften the blow for his father, by securing a favorable impression of his bride, while concealing her faith and race. To accomplish this he introduces her to his father at his home as a Jewess, and lets it appear that he is interested in her, though he conceals the marriage. The girl somewhat reluctantly falls in with the plan; the father takes the bait, becomes infatuated with the girl, concludes that they must marry, and assumes that of course they will, if he so decides. He calls in a rabbi, and prepares for the wedding according to the Jewish rite.

Meanwhile the girl's father, also a widower, who lives in California, and is as intense in his own religious antagonism as the Jew, has been called to New York, supposing that his daughter is to marry an Irishman and a Catholic. Accompanied by a priest, he arrives at the house at the moment when the marriage is being celebrated, but too late to prevent it and the two fathers, each infuriated by the proposed union of his child to a heretic, fall into unseemly and grotesque antics. The priest and the rabbi become friendly, exchange trite sentiments about religion, and agree that the match is good. Apparently out of abundant caution, the priest celebrates the marriage for a third time, while the girl's father is inveigled away. The second act closes with each father, still outraged, seeking to find some way by which the union, thus trebly insured, may be dissolved.

The last act takes place about a year later, the young couple having meanwhile been abjured by each father, and left to their own resources. They have had twins, a boy and a girl, but their fathers know no more than that a child has been born. At Christmas each, led by his craving to see his grandchild, goes separately to the young folks' home, where they encounter each other, each laden with gifts, one for a boy, the other for a girl. After some slapstick comedy, depending upon the insistence of each that he is right about the sex of the grandchild, they become reconciled when they learn the truth, and that each child is to bear the given name of a grandparent. The curtain falls as the fathers are exchanging amenities, and the Jew giving evidence of an abatement in the strictness of his orthodoxy.

"The Cohens and The Kellys" presents two families, Jewish and Irish, living side by side in the poorer quarters of New York in a state of perpetual enmity. The wives in both cases are still living, and share in the mutual animosity, as do two small sons, and even the respective dogs. The Jews have a daughter, the Irish a son; the Jewish father is in the clothing business; the Irishman is a policeman. The children are in love with each other, and secretly marry, apparently after the play opens. The Jew, being in great financial straits, learns from a lawyer that he has fallen heir to a large fortune from a great-aunt, and moves into a great house, fitted luxuriously. Here he and his family live in vulgar ostentation, and here the Irish boy seeks out his Jewish bride, and is chased away by the angry father. The Jew then abuses the Irishman over the telephone, and both become hysterically excited. The extremity of his feelings make the Jew sick, so that he must go to Florida for a rest, just before which the daughter discloses her marriage to her mother.

On his return the Jew finds that his daughter has borne a child; at first he suspects the lawyer, but eventually learns the truth and is overcome with anger at such a low alliance. Meanwhile, the Irish family who have been forbidden to see the grandchild, go to the Jew's house, and after a violent scene between the two fathers in which the Jew disowns his daughter, who decides to go back with her husband, the Irishman takes her back with her baby to his own poor lodgings. The lawyer, who had hoped to marry the Jew's daughter, seeing his plan foiled, tells the Jew that his fortune really belongs to the Irishman, who was also related to the dead woman, but offers to conceal his knowledge, if the Jew will share the loot. This the Jew repudiates, and, leaving the astonished lawyer, walks through the rain to his enemy's house to surrender the property. He arrives in great defection, tells the truth, and abjectly turns to leave. A reconciliation ensues, the Irishman agreeing to share with him equally. The Jew shows some interest in his grandchild, though this is at most a minor motive in the reconciliation, and the curtain falls while the two are in their cups, the Jew insisting that in the firm name for the business, which they are to carry on jointly, his name shall stand first.

It is of course essential to any protection of literary property, whether at common-law or under the statute, that the right cannot be limited literally to the text, else a plagiarist would escape by immaterial variations. That has never been the law, but, as soon as literal appropriation ceases to be the test, the whole matter is necessarily at large, so that, as was recently well said by a distinguished judge, the decisions cannot help much in a new case. When plays are concerned, the plagiarist may excise a separate scene; or he may appropriate part of the dialogue. Then the question is whether the part so taken is 'substantial,' and therefore not a 'fair use' of the copyrighted work; it is the same question as arises in the case of any other copyrighted work. But when the plagiarist does not take out a block in suit, but an abstract of the whole, decision is more troublesome. Upon any work, and especially upon a play, a great number of patterns of increasing generality will fit equally well, as more and more of the incident is left out. The last may perhaps be no more than the most general statement of what the play is about, and at times might consist only of its title; but there is a point in this series of abstractions where they are no longer protected, since otherwise the playwright could prevent the use of his 'ideas,' to which, apart from their expression, his property is never extended. Nobody has ever been able to fix that boundary, and nobody ever can. In some cases the question has been treated as though it were analogous to lifting a portion out of the copyrighted work; but the analogy is not a good one, because, though the skeleton is a part of the body, it pervades and supports the whole. In such cases we are rather concerned with the line between expression and what is expressed. As respects plays, the controversy chiefly centers upon the characters and sequence of incident, these being the substance.

We did not in *Dymow v. Bolton*, 11 F.(2d) 690, hold that a plagiarist was never liable for stealing a plot; that would have been flatly against our ruling in *Dam v. Kirk La Shelle Co.*, 175 F. 902, and *Stodart v. Mutual Film Co.*, 249 F. 513, affirming my decision in (D.C.) 249 F. 507; neither of which we meant to overrule. We found the plot of the second play was too different to infringe, because the most detailed pattern, common to both, eliminated so much from each that its content went into the public domain; and for this reason we said, "this mere subsection of a plot was not susceptible of copyright." But we do not doubt that two plays may correspond in plot closely enough for infringement. How far that correspondence must go is another matter. Nor need we hold that the same may not be true as to the characters, quite independently of the "plot" proper, though, as far as we know such a case has never arisen. If Twelfth Night were copyrighted, it is quite possible that a second comer might so closely imitate Sir Toby Belch or Malvolio as to infringe, but it would not be enough that for one of his characters he cast a riotous knight who kept wassail to the discomfort of the household, or a vain and foppish steward who became amorous of his mistress. These would be no more than Shakespeare's "ideas" in the play, as little capable of monopoly as Einstein's Doctrine of Relativity, or Darwin's theory of the Origin of Species. It follows that the less developed the characters, the less they can be copyrighted; that is the penalty an author must bear for marking them too indistinctly.

In the two plays at bar we think both as to incident and character, the defendant took no more — assuming that it took anything at all — than the law allowed. The stories are quite different. One is of a religious zealot who insists upon his child's marrying no one outside his faith; opposed by another who is in this respect just like him, and is his foil. Their difference in race is merely an obbligato to the main theme, religion. They sink their differences through grandparental pride and affection. In the other, zealotry is wholly absent; religion does not even appear. It is true that the parents are hostile to each other in part because they differ in race; but the marriage of their son to a Jew does no apparently offend the Irish family at all, and it exacerbates the existing animosity of the Jew, principally because he has become rich, when he learns it. They are reconciled through the honesty of the Jew and the generosity of the Irishman; the grandchild has nothing whatever to do with it. The only matter common to the two is a quarrel between a Jewish and an Irish father, the marriage of their children, the birth of grandchildren and a reconciliation.

If the defendant took so much from the plaintiff, it may well have been because her amazing success seemed to prove that this was a subject of enduring popularity. Even so, granting that the plaintiff's play was wholly original, and assuming that novelty is not essential to a copyright, there is no monopoly in such a background. Though the plaintiff discovered the vein, she could not keep it to herself; so defined, the theme was too generalized an abstraction from what she wrote. It was only a part of her "ideas."

Nor does she fare better as to her characters. It is indeed scarcely credible that she should not have been aware of those stock figures, the low comedy Jew and Irishman. The defendant has not taken from her more than their prototypes have contained for many decades. If so, obviously so to generalize her copyright, would allow her to cover what was not original with her. But we need not hold this as matter of fact, much as we might be justified. Even though we take it that she devised her figures out of her brain de novo, still the defendant was within its rights.

There are but four characters common to both plays, the lovers and the fathers. The lovers are so faintly indicated as to be no more than stage properties. They are loving and fertile; that is really all that can be said of them, and anyone else is quite within his rights if he puts loving and fertile lovers in a play of his own, wherever he gets the cue. The Plaintiff's Jew is quite unlike the defendant's. His obsession in his religion, on which depends such racial animosity as he has. He is affectionate, warm and patriarchal. None of these fit the defendant's Jew, who shows affection for his daughter only once, and who has none but the most superficial interest in his grandchild. He is tricky, ostentatious and vulgar, only by misfortune redeemed into honesty. Both are grotesque, extravagant and quarrelsome; both are fond of display; but these common qualities make up only a small part of their simple pictures, no more than any one might lift if he chose. The Irish fathers are even more unlike; the plaintiff's a mere symbol for religious fanaticism and patriarchal pride, scarcely a character at all. Neither quality appears in the defendant's, for while he goes to get his grandchild, it is rather out of a truculent determination not to be forbidden, than from pride in his progeny. For the rest he is only a grotesque hobbledehoy, used for low comedy of the most conventional sort, which any one might borrow, if he chanced not to know the exemplar.

The defendant argues that the case is controlled by my decision in *Fisher v. Dillingham* (D.C.) 298 F. 145. Neither my brothers nor I wish to throw doubt upon the doctrine of that case, but it is not applicable here. We assume that the plaintiff's play is altogether original, even to an extent that in fact it is hard to believe. We assume further that, so far as it has been anticipated by earlier plays of which she knew nothing, that fact is immaterial. Still, as we have already said, her copyright did not cover everything that might be drawn from her play; its content went to some extent into the public domain. We have to decide how much, and while we are as aware as any one that the line, wherever it is drawn, will seem arbitrary, that is no excuse for not drawing it; it is a question such as courts must answer in nearly all cases. Whatever may be the difficulties a priori, we have no question on which side of the line this case falls. A comedy based upon conflicts between Irish and Jews, into which the marriage of their children enters, is no more susceptible of copyright than the outline of Romeo and Juliet.

The plaintiff has prepared an elaborate analysis of the two plays, showing a "quadrangle" of the common characters, in which each is represented by the emotions which he discovers. She presents the resulting parallelism as proof of infringement, but the adjectives employed are so general as to be quite useless. Take for example the attribute of 'love' ascribed to both Jews. The plaintiff has depicted her father as deeply attached to his son, who is his hope and joy; not so, the defendant, whose father's conduct is throughout not actuated by any affection for his daughter, and who is merely once overcome for the moment by her distress when he has violently dismissed her lover. "Anger" covers emotions aroused by quite different occasions in each case; so do "anxiety," "despondency" and "disgust." It is unnecessary to go through the catalogue for emotions are too much colored by their causes to be a test when used so broadly. This is not the proper approach to a solution; it must be more ingenuous, more like that of a spectator, who would rely upon the complex of his impressions of each character.

*   *   *

Decree affirmed.

## Comments

1. **Substantial Similarity.** *Nichols*, like *Baker v. Selden*, is a classic case in the history of American copyright jurisprudence. In most accounts, *Nichols* occupies a leading role in the story of "substantial similarity," or the standard that a plaintiff must meet to prove that a defendant has infringed a copyrighted work by imitation rather than literal reproduction. "Substantial similarity" is discussed in detail in the first part of Chapter 7. The case appears here, however, because upon close reading Judge Hand neither offers a legal standard for determining whether "substantial similarity" between two works exists, nor uses a precise standard to decide the facts of the case. The key passage is the following:

   > Upon any work, and especially upon a play, a great number of patterns of increasing generality will fit equally well, as more and more of the incident is left out. The last may perhaps be no more than the most general statement of what the play is about, and at times might consist only of its title; but there is a

point in this series of abstractions where they are no longer protected, since otherwise the playwright could prevent the use of his 'ideas,' to which, apart from their expression, his property is never extended. Nobody has ever been able to fix that boundary, and nobody ever can.

Instead, Judge Hand offers an ingenious and detailed accounting of the stories, plots ("incident"), and characters of the two works, characterizing them in terms sufficiently distinct that one cannot help but conclude that whatever the defendant "copied," it copied only material that was too broad or general to be protectable by copyright.

2. ***The Abstractions Test and Traditional Literary Works.*** Two important points emerge from Judge Hand's approach. One is that the line between unprotected idea and protected expression is one that need not be drawn by the author as part of the creation or publication of the work. Instead, it can be (and typically is) drawn as part of the process of litigating a particular claim of infringement. Two is that this line, wherever it exists, may lie at many places within a given work. Note that Judge Hand independently investigates the possibly protected status of the plot and of the characters of *Abie's Irish Rose*; overly detailed borrowing of either one might have sustained a valid claim by the plaintiff. The "abstractions" analysis therefore maps nicely onto traditional dramatic and literary works, including novels and plays, in which copyrighted expression might exist at a minimum of three levels: character, story, and plot. *See, e.g., Twentieth Century-Fox Film Corp. v. MCA, Inc.*, 715 F.2d 1327 (9th Cir. 1983) (reversing summary judgment for the defendant in a lawsuit by the producers of the original *Star Wars* motion picture against the producers of the original *Battlestar Galactica* television program).

3. ***The Abstractions Test and Other Works.*** Because the abstractions test was developed in connection with literary works, courts have tried to adapt it to nontraditional literary works, such as copyrighted computer programs. *See Whelan Associates, Inc. v. Jaslow Dental Laboratory, Inc.*, 797 F.2d 1222 (3d Cir. 1986) (endorsing claim of infringement of the "structure, sequence, and organization" of a computer program); *Computer Associates Int'l, Inc. v. Altai, Inc.*, 982 F.2d 693 (2d Cir. 1992) (rejecting *Whelan* in favor of "abstraction, filtration, comparison" analysis to separate idea from expression in computer programs). One pair of commentators has noted that while the abstractions test in principle might be applied to any type of copyrightable work, using it in the nondramatic context and across different types of works runs a risk of comparing apples to oranges. *See* Dan L. Burk & Mark A. Lemley, *Quantum Patent Mechanics*, 9 Lewis & Clark L. Rev. 29, 36 (2005).

4. ***Competitive Concerns.*** In *Herbert Rosenthal Jewelry Corp. v. Kalpakian*, 446 F.2d 738 (9th Cir. 1971), the Court of Appeals for the Ninth Circuit refused to enforce a copyright on a jeweled bee pin against another, similar jeweled bee pin, departing from the conventional principle that each work contains an "idea" than must be distilled from its "expression." The court wrote:

> The critical distinction between "idea" and "expression" is difficult to draw. As Judge Hand candidly wrote, "Obviously, no principle can be stated as to when an imitator has gone beyond copying the 'idea,' and has borrowed its 'expression.'" *Peter Pan Fabrics, Inc. v. Martin Weiner Corp.*, 274 F.2d 487,

489 (2d Cir. 1960). At least in close cases, one may suspect, the classification the court selects may simply state the result reached rather than the reason for it. In our view, the difference is really one of degree as Judge Hand suggested in his striking 'abstraction' formulation in *Nichols v. Universal Pictures Corp.*, 45 F.2d 119, 121 (2d Cir. 1930). The guiding consideration in drawing the line is the preservation of the balance between competition and protection reflected in the patent and copyright laws.

What is basically at stake is the extent of the copyright owner's monopoly — from how large an area of activity did Congress intend to allow the copyright owner to exclude others? We think the production of jeweled bee pins is a larger private preserve than Congress intended to be set aside in the public market without a patent. A jeweled bee pin is therefore an 'idea' that defendants were free to copy. Plaintiff seems to agree, for it disavows any claim that defendants cannot manufacture and sell jeweled bee pins and concedes that only plaintiff's particular design or 'expression' of the jeweled bee pin 'idea' is protected under its copyright. The difficulty, as we have noted, is that on this record the 'idea' and its 'expression' appear to be indistinguishable. There is no greater similarity between the pins of plaintiff and defendants than is inevitable from the use of jewel-encrusted bee forms in both.

The *Kalpakian* court's formulation of copyright's competition concern co-exists with other formulations. The ban on copyright ownership of ideas is consistent with society's interest in the free exchange of ideas, grounded in the First Amendment. *See Harper & Row, Publishers, Inc. v. Nation Enterprises*, 471 U.S. 539 (1985) (concluding that the idea/expression distinction is part of copyright's accommodation of the First Amendment interest in free speech). It is also consistent with the incentive structure that underlies copyright. It may be true that no economic incentive is needed to encourage the production of new ideas, but incentives are needed to promote the development of new forms of those ideas — their expression. Finally, and consistent with that incentive-based policy, since copyright can only be granted in works of creative authorship, it might be correct to say that ideas have no specific author. They emanate from social and historical conditions that serve as the foundations for new creativity. As Isaac Newton famously wrote, "If I have seen further, it is by standing on the shoulders of giants."

## Problem

**6-2.** Ruth is a sculptor who produces glass-in-glass works. Inspired by what she saw at the Monterey Bay Aquarium in California in 1999, she started to produce sculptures that consist of a full-size sculpted, glass jellyfish encased in a round, clear glass "shroud," somewhat narrower at the base than at the top, and with a rounded top. She has produced hundreds of these sculptures, in different sizes and using different colors for the jellyfish, and has registered her designs with the Copyright Office. Each sculpture sells for several hundred dollars. Ruth sells them in galleries and in museum and aquarium gift shops around the country.

Ruth's Sculpture                    Paul's Sculpture

Paul, also a sculptor, saw one of Ruth's sculptures in 2003 and realized that he could produce a version of it more cheaply. Paul contracted with an industrial glassmaking factory to help him produce his glass-in-glass jelly-fish sculptures, and he sells them for $99 each. In Ruth's suit for copyright infringement against Paul, Ruth's evidence included testimony that purchasers for aquarium gift shops, and gallery owners and customers, frequently confused Paul's sculptures for Ruth's. If Ruth's sculpture is copyrightable, she can prevail against Paul. Is it? *See Satava v. Lowry,* 323 F.3d 805 (9th Cir. 2003).

# B. LIMITATIONS ON COPYRIGHTABILITY

Copyright law begins with such broad concepts of eligibility for protection — originality; fixation; expression — that it is not surprising that the law has developed a range of doctrinal devices to police those boundaries. Courts generally apply these devices after making an initial determination that the foundational thresholds for copyright protection, described in Section A, have been met. This section describes two tools that copyright law uses to limit the expanse of copyright's subject matter: the related doctrines of merger and scènes à faire; and the prohibition on copyright in systems, processes, and "methods of operation."

## 1. Merger and Scènes à Faire

*STATUTE:* **Subject Matter of Copyright: Compilations and Derivative Works**
17 U.S.C. §103

*STATUTE:* **Definitions — "Compilation," "Collective Work"**
17 U.S.C. §101

### CCC INFORMATION SERVICES, INC. v. MACLEAN HUNTER MARKET REPORTS, INC.

**44 F.3d 61 (2d Cir. 1994)**

LEVAL, Circuit Judge.

The appellant, publisher of a compendium of its projections of used car valuations, seeks to establish copyright infringement on the part of a competitor, which copied substantial portions of appellant's compendium into the computer data base of used car valuations it offers to its customers. Arising in the wake of the Supreme Court's decision in *Feist Publications, Inc. v. Rural Telephone Serv. Co.*, 499 U.S. 340 (1991), this appeal raises the question of the scope of protection afforded by the copyright law to such compilations of informational matter. Finding no infringement, the district court granted summary judgment to the appellee. In our view, the copyright law offers more substantial protection to such compilations than envisioned in the district court's ruling. We therefore reverse.

### Background

*The Red Book.* The appellant is Maclean Hunter Market Reports, Inc. ("Maclean"). Since 1911, Maclean, or its predecessors, have published the *Automobile Red Book — Official Used Car Valuations* (the "Red Book"). The Red Book, which is published eight times a year, in different versions for each of three regions of the United States (as well as a version for the State of Wisconsin), sets forth the editors' projections of the values for the next six weeks of "average" versions of most of the used cars (up to seven years old) sold in that region. These predicted values are set forth separately for each automobile make, model number, body style, and engine type. Red Book also provides predicted value adjustments for various options and for mileage in 5,000 mile increments.

The valuation figures given in the Red Book are not historical market prices, quotations, or averages; nor are they derived by mathematical formulas from available statistics. They represent, rather, the Maclean editors' predictions, based on a wide variety of informational sources and their professional judgment, of expected values for "average" vehicles for the upcoming six weeks in a broad region. The introductory text asserts, "You, the subscriber, must be the final judge of the actual value of a particular vehicle. Any guide book is a supplement to and not a substitute for expertise in the complex field of used vehicle valuation."

*CCC's computer services.* Appellee CCC Information Services, Inc. ("CCC"), is also in the business of providing its customers with information as to the valuation of used vehicles. Rather than publishing a book, however, CCC provides information to its customers through a computer data base. Since at least 1988, CCC has itself been systematically loading major portions of the Red Book onto its computer network and republishing Red Book information in various forms to its customers.[3]

CCC utilizes and resells the Red Book valuations in several different forms. CCC's "VINguard Valuation Service" ("VVS") provides subscribers with the average of a vehicle's Red Book valuation and its valuation in the NADA Official Used Car Guide (the "Bluebook"), the other leading valuation book, published by the National Automobile Dealers Association

---

3. In 1981, CCC unsuccessfully attempted to secure a license from Maclean to use Red Book valuations on its on-line services. In 1984, CCC wrote to the publisher of the Red Book to inform it that it was being "ripped off" because another computer averaging service was using Red Book's figures.

("NADA"). The offer of this average of Red Book and Bluebook satisfies a market because the laws of certain states use that average figure as a minimum for insurance payments upon the "total loss" of a vehicle. CCC's "Computerized Valuation Service" ("CVS"), while it primarily provides its subscribers with CCC's independent valuation of used cars, also provides customers with the Red Book/Bluebook average and the Red Book values standing alone.

It is uncontested that CCC earns significant revenues through the sale of its services, in which it both directly and indirectly resells the figures it copies every few weeks from the Red Book. As the court found below, since 1988 numerous Red Book customers have canceled their subscriptions, opting instead to purchase CCC's services.

*Proceedings below.* CCC brought this action in 1991, seeking, inter alia, a declaratory judgment that it incurred no liability to Maclean under the copyright laws by taking and republishing material from the Red Book. Maclean counterclaimed alleging infringement....

Both sides moved for summary judgment, and the motions were referred for report and recommendation to Magistrate Judge Arthur H. Latimer. Magistrate Judge Latimer recommended to the district court that CCC's motion for summary judgment be granted. Judge Latimer found (1) that the Red Book employed no originality or creativity in the selection, coordination or arrangement of data, and therefore did not constitute a protected "original work of authorship," 17 U.S.C.A. §101 (West 1977); (2) that the Red Book valuations were facts, or interpretations of facts, and were, therefore, not protected by copyright; (3) that, even if the entries were not facts, copyright protection was nonetheless precluded by the doctrine of "merger of idea and expression," because each entry in the Red Book is an idea—the idea of the value of the particular vehicle—and that idea is necessarily communicated by a dollar figure; and (4) that the Red Book had been placed in the public domain by being "incorporated into governmental regulations." District Judge Nevas then "approved, adopted and ratified" the Magistrate Judge's recommended ruling, and judgment was entered in CCC's favor.

* * *

*The idea-expression dichotomy and the merger of necessary expression with the ideas expressed.* CCC's strongest argument is that it took nothing more than ideas, for which the copyright law affords no protection to the author. According to this argument, (1) each entry in the Red Book expresses the authors' *idea* of the value of a particular vehicle; (2) to the extent that "expression" is to be found in the Red Book's valuations, such expression is indispensable to the statement of the idea and therefore merges with the idea, so that the expression is also not protectible, and; (3) because each of Red Book's valuations could freely be taken without infringement, all of them may be taken without infringement. This was one of the alternate bases of the district court's ruling in CCC's favor.

The argument is not easily rebutted, for it does build on classically accepted copyright doctrine. It has been long accepted that copyright protection does not extend to ideas; it protects only the means of expression employed by the author....

It is also well established that, in order to protect the immunity of ideas from private ownership, when the expression is essential to the statement of the idea, the expression also will be unprotected, so as to insure free public access to the discussion of the idea. *See* [*Kregos v. Associated Press*, 937 F.2d 700, 705 (2d Cir. 1991)]; *Herbert Rosenthal Jewelry Corp. v. Kalpakian*, 446 F.2d 738, 742 (9th Cir. 1971) ("When the 'idea' and its 'expression' are ... inseparable, copying the 'expression' will not be barred, since protecting the 'expression' in such circumstances would confer a monopoly of the 'idea' upon the copyright owner free of the conditions and limitations imposed by the patent law.").

We nonetheless believe the district court erred in granting judgment to CCC. We reach this conclusion based on the need to balance the conflicts and contradictions that pervade the law of copyright, and the need, where elements of the copyright law conflict, to determine, as a policy judgment, which of its commands prevails over the other.

The fundamental principle of copyright, as expressed in the Copyright Clause of the Constitution, is to promote the advance of knowledge by granting authors exclusive rights to their writings. As the Supreme Court said in *Mazer* [*v. Stein*, 347 U.S. 201 (1954)], "The economic philosophy behind the clause empowering Congress to grant patents and copyrights is the conviction that encouragement of individual effort by personal gain is the best way to advance public welfare through the talents of authors and inventors in 'Science and useful Arts.'" 347 U.S. at 219. The financial incentives to authors consist of exclusive rights to their writings, that may be sold or licensed for money, so that authors may earn a living from the creations that benefitted the public.

From an early time, however, courts, taking a different approach from that taken in the patent law, developed a theory which almost directly contradicted the original theory of copyright. The new theory was that ideas are too important to the advancement of knowledge to permit them to be under private ownership, and that open public debate, which is essential to a free democratic society, requires free access to the ideas to be debated. Judicially created doctrine thus led to a drastic limitation on the scope of copyright protection.[12] Ideas were not to be protected; only the manner of their "expression." This limitation came to be known as the "idea-expression" dichotomy.

The contradiction between these imperatives, one calling for the protection of creations that will advance the progress of knowledge, the second requiring that these same creations be free of protection, has understandably given rise to bewildering problems of interpretation as to whether copying has been of protected expression or of the unprotected ideas underlying the expression....

---

12. This doctrine is codified in section 102(b) of the Copyright Act, which provides that "[i]n no case does copyright protection for an original work of authorship extend to any idea, procedure, process, system, method of operation, concept, principle, or discovery, regardless of the form in which it is described, explained, illustrated, or embodied in such work." 17 U.S.C.A. §102(b) (West 1977).

This conflict between these contradictory thrusts recurs at the level of several more particular applications of the copyright law. Among them is the issue raised by this appeal of the protection, if any, to be accorded to compilations. For if CCC's argument prevails, for reasons explained below, virtually nothing will remain of the protection accorded by the statute to compilations, notwithstanding the express command of the copyright statute.

Given the nature of compilations, it is almost inevitable that the original contributions of the compilers will consist of *ideas*. Originality in *selection*, for example, will involve the compiler's idea of the utility to the consumer of a limited selection from the particular universe of available data. One compiler might select out of a universe of all businesses those that he believes will be of interest to the Chinese-American community, *see* [*Key Publications, Inc. v. Chinatown Today Publishing Enterprises, Inc.*, 945 F.2d 509, 514 (2d Cir. 1991)], another will select those statistics as to racehorses or pitchers that are believed to be practical to the consumer in helping to pick winners, *see Kregos*, 937 F.2d at 706-07, another will offer a list of restaurants he suggests are the best, the most elegant, or offer the best value within a price range. Each of these exercises in selection represents an *idea*.

In other compilations, the original contribution of the compiler will relate to ideas for the coordination, or arrangement of the data. Such ideas for arrangement are generally designed to serve the consumers' needs, making the data more useful by increasing the ease of access to those data that answer the needs of the targeted customers, or dividing the data in ways that will efficiently serve the needs of more diverse groups of customers. For example, a listing of New York restaurants might be broken down by geographic areas of the city, specialty or type (e.g., seafood, steaks and chops, vegetarian, kosher, Chinese, Indian); price range; handicapped accessibility, etc.

It is apparent that virtually any independent creation of the compiler as to selection, coordination, or arrangement will be designed to add to the usefulness or desirability of his compendium for targeted groups of potential customers, and will represent an idea. In the case of a compilation, furthermore, such structural ideas are likely to be expressed in the most simple, unadorned, and direct fashion. If, as CCC argues, the doctrine of merger permits the wholesale copier of a compilation to take the individual expression of such ideas, so as to avoid the risk that an idea will improperly achieve protection, then the protection explicitly conferred on compilations by Section 103 of the U.S. Copyright Act will be illusory.

We addressed precisely this problem in *Kregos*, 937 F.2d 700. The plaintiff Kregos had created a form to be used to help predict the outcome of a baseball game by filling in nine statistics of the competing pitchers. The defendant contended, in terms similar to CCC's argument, that the copyright owner's idea was the utility of the nine selected statistics in helping a fan predict the outcome, and that the idea was merged in the expression of it—in the copyrighted form that listed those nine statistics. Judge Newman wrote:

> In one sense, every compilation of facts can be considered to represent a merger of an idea with its expression. Every compiler of facts has the idea

> that his particular selection of facts is useful. If the compiler's idea is identi-
> fied at that low level of abstraction, then the idea would always merge into the
> compiler's expression of it. Under that approach, there could never be a
> copyrightable compilation of facts.

*Kregos*, 937 F.2d at 706.

Recognizing that the purpose of the doctrine of merger of expression
with idea is to insure that protection not extend to ideas, the *Kregos* opinion
went on to describe different categories of ideas. It distinguished between,
on the one hand, those ideas that undertake to advance the understanding
of phenomena or the solution of problems, such as the identification of the
symptoms that are the most useful in identifying the presence of a particular disease; and those like the pitching form there at issue, that do not
undertake to explain phenomena or furnish solutions, but are infused with
the author's taste or opinion. *Kregos* postulated that the importance of
keeping ideas free from private ownership is far greater for ideas of the
first category, directed to the understanding of phenomena or the solving
of problems, than for those that merely represent the author's taste or
opinion and therefore do not materially assist the understanding of future
thinkers. As to the latter category, the opinion asserted that, so long as the
selections reflected in the compilation "involve matters of taste and personal opinion, there is no serious risk that *withholding the merger doctrine*,"
937 F.2d at 707 (emphasis added), would inflict serious injury on the policy
underlying the rule that forbids granting protection to an idea. This was in
contrast to analyses belonging to the first category — building blocks of
understanding — as to which "protecting the [necessary] 'expression' of
the selection would clearly risk protecting the idea of the analysis." *Id* at
707. Because Kregos's idea was of the soft type infused with taste or opinion, the court withheld application of the merger doctrine, permitting
Kregos to exercise ownership. It accomplished this by assigning to the idea
a different level of abstraction from the expression of it, so that the merger
doctrine would not apply and the copyright owner would not lose protection. ("His 'idea,' for purposes of the merger doctrine, remains the general
idea that statistics can be used to assess pitching performance rather than
the precise idea that his selection yields a determinable probability of
outcome." 937 F.2d at 707.)

*Kregos*, thus, makes a policy judgment as between two evils. Unbridled
application of the merger doctrine would undo the protection the copyright law intends to accord to compilations. Complete failure to apply it,
however, would result in granting protection to useful ideas. *Kregos* adopts
a middle ground. In cases of wholesale takings of compilations, a *selective*
application of the merger doctrine, withholding its application as to soft
ideas infused with taste and opinion, will carry out the statutory policy to
protect innovative compilations without impairing the policy that requires
public access to ideas of a more important and useful kind.

Application of the *Kregos* approach to our facts leads us to the conclusion
that the district court should, as in *Kregos*, have "*withheld*" the merger
doctrine. As a matter of copyright policy, this was not an appropriate
instance to apply the merger doctrine so as to deprive Red Book of

copyright protection. The consequences of giving CCC the benefit of the merger doctrine are too destructive of the protection the Act intends to confer on compilations, without sufficient benefit to the policy of copyright that seeks to preserve public access to ideas.

In the first place, the takings by CCC from the Red Book are of virtually the entire compendium. This is not an instance of copying of a few entries from a compilation. This copying is so extensive that CCC effectively offers to sell its customers Maclean's Red Book through CCC's data base. CCC's invocation of the merger doctrine to justify its contention that it has taken no protectible matter would effectively destroy all protection for Maclean's compilation.[26]

Secondly, the valuations copied by CCC from the Red Book are not ideas of the first, building-block, category described in *Kregos*, but are rather in the category of approximative statements of opinion by the Red Book editors. To the extent that protection of the Red Book would impair free circulation of any ideas, these are ideas of the weaker category, infused with opinion; the valuations explain nothing, and describe no method, process or procedure. Maclean Hunter makes no attempt, for example, to monopolize the basis of its economic forecasting or the factors that it weighs; the Red Book's entries are no more than the predictions of Red Book editors of used car values for six weeks on a rough regional basis. As noted above, Red Book specifies in its introduction that "[y]ou, the subscriber, must be the final judge of the actual value of a particular vehicle. Any guide book is a supplement to and not a substitute for expertise in the complex field of used vehicle valuation." This language is remarkably similar to our observation in *Kregos*, that the author "has been content to select categories of data that he obviously believes have some predictive power, but has left it to all sports page readers to make their own judgments as to the likely outcomes from the sets of data he has selected." 937 F.2d at 707.

The balancing of interests suggested by *Kregos* leads to the conclusion that we should reject CCC's argument seeking the benefit of the merger doctrine. Because the ideas contained in the Red Book are of the weaker, suggestion-opinion category, a withholding of the merger doctrine would not seriously impair the policy of the copyright law that seeks to preserve free public access to ideas. If the public's access to Red Book's valuations is slightly limited by enforcement of its copyright against CCC's wholesale copying, this will not inflict injury on the opportunity for public debate, nor restrict access to the kind of idea that illuminates our understanding of the phenomena that surround us or of useful processes to solve our problems. In contrast, if the merger doctrine were applied so as to bar

---

26. In this circuit, consideration of the merger doctrine takes place in light of the alleged copying to determine if infringement has occurred, rather than in analyzing the copyrightability of the original work. This approach is applauded by Nimmer as the "better view." 13.03[B] at 13-76 to -78. As we noted in *Kregos*, "[a]ssessing merger in the context of alleged infringement will normally provide a more detailed and realistic basis for evaluating the claim that protection of expression would inevitably accord protection to an idea." *Kregos*, 937 F.2d at 705. In the instant case, for example, it is of consequence that we are confronted with wholesale copying *of* a compilation rather than some more limited copying *from* a compilation.

Maclean's enforcement of its copyright against CCC's wholesale takings, this would seriously undermine the protections guaranteed by §103 of the Copyright Act to compilations that employ original creation in their selection, coordination, or arrangement. It would also largely vitiate the inducements offered by the copyright law to the makers of original useful compilations.

\* \* \*

### CONCLUSION

Because Maclean has demonstrated a valid copyright, and an infringement thereof, we direct the entry of judgment in Maclean's favor. We remand to the district court for further proceedings.

## Comments

1. *The Nature of CCC's Claim.* The court's analysis makes it difficult to distinguish the different arguments advanced by the parties. In asserting that MacLean did not have a valid copyright interest, was CCC arguing that each price, for each make and model of automobile, was unprotectible? Or was it asserting that the collection of automobile prices in MacLean's directory was unprotectible? On what basis did the court conclude that MacLean did have a valid copyright? As to the individual automobile prices, the court noted, "The district court was simply mistaken in its conclusion that the Red Book valuations were, like the telephone numbers in *Feist,* preexisting facts that had merely been discovered by the Red Book editors." As to the book as a whole, the court reasoned: "We find that the selection and arrangement of data in the Red Book displayed amply sufficient originality to pass the low threshold requirement to earn copyright protection."

2. **Kregos *and the Expression of Useful Ideas.*** As the court illustrates in its extended discussion of *Kregos v. Associated Press,* copyright law struggles to analyze arguably "original" or "creative" expressions of what are, at bottom, concepts that describe things we use. The form in *Kregos* selected various statistical categories that were useful in predicting the outcomes of baseball games. The criteria selected by MacLean were useful in measuring the value of a used car. The merger doctrine can be used to police this boundary. To the extent that the selection of data *is* the useful method itself, the merger doctrine should bar copyright in the selection, because granting the copyright would effectively grant the owner a monopoly over both the selection and the method, rather than promote competition in different forms of implementing the method. Where the method can be implemented in more than one way, *Kregos* and *CCC Information Service* agree that the merger doctrine does not apply.

3. *Is There More Than One Price for a Used Car?* The cases turn on the court's characterization of the method, and on the method's susceptibility to

multiple forms of expression. The court in *CCC Information Service* relies on the *Kregos* court's distinction between methods based on what might be called "objective" facts, and methods based on what might be called "subjective" facts, or opinions. The merger doctrine takes on greater importance in the former category because of the public policy that no one should be able to obtain a copyright monopoly on facts. A copyright on "objective" facts would prevent authors and creators from developing and distributing new theories about those facts. The merger doctrine is less problematic in the context of methods based on "subjective" facts, because the underlying data is "created" or "authored" in the first place. If that is the case, then the competitive risks associated with allowing copyright on the expression are smaller. Note that MacLean's Red Book competes with at least one well-known alternative: the Kelley Blue Book.

4. **The Burden of Feist.** *Feist Publications* teaches that "sweat of the brow" arguments are invalid as public policy justifications in copyright cases. Disputes involving "compilation works," where the creativity of the author lies in how underlying material is selected, coordinated, and arranged, nonetheless naturally tend to pull litigants and courts toward "sweat" based claims. At the core of MacLean's argument lies the point that MacLean spent a lot of time and money assembling the Red Book, and it is fundamentally unfair for CCC to appropriate that labor wholesale, as a free-rider. The court is sympathetic to the claim, expressing skepticism of CCC's position that "because each of Red Book's valuations could freely be taken without infringement, all of them may be taken without infringement." The difficulty in cases involving compilations, then, is articulating the balance between appropriate levels of protection and incentive for creators of compilation works, on the one hand, and fair provision for those who rely on and reuse facts and ideas, on the other hand, in terms that do not depend on the discredited "sweat of the brow" theory.

5. **Fact-Based Works and Thin Copyright.** Even where works based on fact constitute protectible copyright subject matter, the resulting copyright is "thin," meaning that infringement is likely to be found only if the defendant literally copied all or substantially all of the plaintiff's work. The finding that copyright protection applies, in other words, does not end the law's interest in ensuring that the costs to competition of the copyright monopoly are not excessive.

6. **When Should the Merger Doctrine be Applied?** Though *CCC Information Service* is presented here as a limit on copyrightability, the Second Circuit takes the position that the merger doctrine, and its cousin, the doctrine of scènes à faire, operate as defenses to a claim of copyright infringement, to be pleaded and proved by the accused infringer, rather than as bars to copyrightability in the first place, with the burden of proof lying on the copyright owner. Some courts take the position that merger and scènes à faire render a work uncopyrightable. *See Mason v. Montgomery Data, Inc.*, 967 F.2d 135, 138 n.5 (5th Cir. 1992).

7. **Scènes à Faire.** The doctrine of scènes à faire refers to the unprotectability of incidents, characters, or settings which are as a practical matter

indispensable, or at least standard in the treatment of a given topic. In *Incredible Technologies, Inc. v. Virtual Technologies, Inc.,* 400 F.3d 1007 (7th Cir. 2005), the court affirmed a district court's refusal to enjoin distribution of a "video golf" arcade game that used imagery and video features that closely resembled the plaintiff's game:

> In presenting a realistic video golf game, one would, by definition, need golf courses, clubs, a selection menu, a golfer, a wind meter, etc. Sand traps and water hazards are a fact of life for golfers, real and virtual. The menu screens are standard to the video arcade game format, as are prompts showing the distance remaining to the hole. As such, the video display is afforded protection only from virtually identical copying.
>
> Given that certain items are necessary to making the game realistic, the differences in the presentation are sufficient to make [the plaintiff's] chances of success on the merits unlikely. Global VR [the defendant's game] has "real" courses and "real" golfers; Golden Tee's courses [in the plaintiff's game] are imaginary and its golfers generic. In the Global VR game, a golf bag appears on the screen as the player chooses a club for the shot he intends to play. Global VR offers a "grid" mapping the green as a guide for putting. Golden Tee has no such device. Also, the Global VR game has a helicopter that whirls overhead from time to time. Both games mimic condescending real television golf announcers, but the announcers use different phrases: "the fairway would be over there" and "I don't think that's going to help a whole lot" in Global VR versus "That can only hurt," "You've got to be kidding," and "You can lead a ball to water but..." from the Golden Tee announcers. Judge Kennelly did not abuse his discretion on this point....

8. ***The Difference Between Merger and Scènes à Faire.*** Merger and scènes à faire are frequently invoked simultaneously, and both operate to limit copyright protection based on utilitarian or functional dimensions of the work of authorship. The two doctrines work from opposite perspectives, however. Merger derives from the inherent character of the idea in question, so that it is capable of being presented in only one or (perhaps) a small handful of ways. To apply the merger doctrine, the law has to adopt the perspective of the author and ask whether the author had any meaningful choice in deciding how to express a particular idea. The law thus protects later authors in relying on common underlying material. Scènes à faire likewise reflects the notion that certain ideas can be expressed in only a limited number of ways, but it locates that limitation not in the inherent character of the idea, but in the expectations of the audience as to certain expressive forms. These might be characterized as the conventions of a genre. The audience has come to expect certain plot devices, stock or standard characters, images, sounds, or expressive techniques. It may be the case that a given work that lacks those features simply would not achieve any communicative effect. Alternatively, it may be that the communicative effect of invoking those stock or standard features is so great that the benefit to creators and consumers clearly outweighs any possible cost to the originators of those features. The policy of the law thus protects readers, listeners, and viewers

in maintaining levels of comprehensibility in the culture they encounter. For example, successful parodists frequently invoke the conventions of a genre in order to poke fun at them. Consider the conventions of a Western movie — the hero in the white hat and the villain in the black hat; the noble, lone lawman and the hostile townsfolk — and then consider how the wildly successful parody of Western films, Mel Brooks's *Blazing Saddles*, both adopts and distinguishes them. Examine your own favorite films, television programs, or video games and distinguish conventions of the genre from original features added by the producers.

## 2. Methods of Operation

*STATUTE:* **Subject Matter of Copyright: In General**
17 U.S.C. §102(b)

## LOTUS DEV. CORP. v. BORLAND INTERNATIONAL, INC.
### 49 F.3d 807 (1st Cir. 1995)

STAHL, Circuit Judge.

This appeal requires us to decide whether a computer menu command hierarchy is copyrightable subject matter. In particular, we must decide whether, as the district court held, plaintiff-appellee Lotus Development Corporation's copyright in Lotus 1-2-3, a computer spreadsheet program, was infringed by defendant-appellant Borland International, Inc., when Borland copied the Lotus 1-2-3 menu command hierarchy into its Quattro and Quattro Pro computer spreadsheet programs. *See Lotus Dev. Corp. v. Borland Int'l, Inc.*, 788 F. Supp. 78 (D. Mass. 1992) ("*Borland I*"); *Lotus Dev. Corp. v. Borland Int'l, Inc.*, 799 F. Supp. 203 (D. Mass. 1992) ("*Borland II*"); *Lotus Dev. Corp. v. Borland Int'l, Inc.*, 831 F. Supp. 202 (D. Mass. 1993) ("*Borland III*"); *Lotus Dev. Corp. v. Borland Int'l, Inc.*, 831 F. Supp. 223 (D. Mass. 1993) ("*Borland IV*").

### I.
#### BACKGROUND

Lotus 1-2-3 is a spreadsheet program that enables users to perform accounting functions electronically on a computer. Users manipulate and control the program via a series of menu commands, such as "Copy," "Print," and "Quit." Users choose commands either by highlighting them on the screen or by typing their first letter. In all, Lotus 1-2-3 has 469 commands arranged into more than 50 menus and submenus.

\* \* \*

Borland released its first Quattro program to the public in 1987, after Borland's engineers had labored over its development for nearly three years. Borland's objective was to develop a spreadsheet program far superior to existing programs, including Lotus 1-2-3. In Borland's words, "[f]rom the time of its initial release . . . Quattro included enormous innovations over competing spreadsheet products."

The district court found, and Borland does not now contest, that Borland included in its Quattro and Quattro Pro version 1.0 programs "a *virtually identical* copy of the entire 1-2-3 menu tree." *Borland III,* 831 F. Supp. at 212 (emphasis in original). In so doing, Borland did not copy any of Lotus's underlying computer code; it copied only the words and structure of Lotus's menu command hierarchy. Borland included the Lotus menu command hierarchy in its programs to make them compatible with Lotus 1-2-3 so that spreadsheet users who were already familiar with Lotus 1-2-3 would be able to switch to the Borland programs without having to learn new commands or rewrite their Lotus macros.

\* \* \*

[T]he district court held that with its Key Reader, Borland had infringed Lotus's copyright. The district court also rejected Borland's affirmative defenses. . . . The district court then entered a permanent injunction against Borland, from which Borland appeals.

This appeal concerns only Borland's copying of the Lotus menu command hierarchy into its Quattro programs and Borland's affirmative defenses to such copying. Lotus has not cross-appealed; in other words, Lotus does not contend on appeal that the district court erred in finding that Borland had not copied other elements of Lotus 1-2-3, such as its screen displays.

## II.

### DISCUSSION

On appeal, Borland does not dispute that it factually copied the words and arrangement of the Lotus menu command hierarchy. Rather, Borland argues that it "lawfully copied the unprotectable menus of Lotus 1-2-3." Borland contends that the Lotus menu command hierarchy is not copyrightable because it is a system, method of operation, process, or procedure foreclosed from protection by 17 U.S.C. §102(b).

\* \* \*

Borland argues that the Lotus menu command hierarchy is uncopyrightable because it is a system, method of operation, process, or procedure foreclosed from copyright protection by 17 U.S.C. §102(b). Section 102(b) states: "In no case does copyright protection for an original work of authorship extend to any idea, procedure, process, system, method of operation, concept, principle, or discovery, regardless of the form in which it is described, explained, illustrated, or embodied in such work." Because we conclude that the Lotus menu command hierarchy is a method of operation, we do not consider whether it could also be a system, process, or procedure.

We think that "method of operation," as that term is used in §102(b), refers to the means by which a person operates something, whether it be a car, a food processor, or a computer. Thus a text describing how to operate something would not extend copyright protection to the method of operation itself; other people would be free to employ that method and to describe it in their own words. Similarly, if a new method of operation is used rather than described, other people would still be free to employ or describe that method.

We hold that the Lotus menu command hierarchy is an uncopyrightable "method of operation." The Lotus menu command hierarchy provides the means by which users control and operate Lotus 1-2-3. If users wish to copy material, for example, they use the "Copy" command. If users wish to print material, they use the "Print" command. Users must use the command terms to tell the computer what to do. Without the menu command hierarchy, users would not be able to access and control, or indeed make use of, Lotus 1-2-3's functional capabilities.

The Lotus menu command hierarchy does not merely explain and present Lotus 1-2-3's functional capabilities to the user; it also serves as the method by which the program is operated and controlled.... The Lotus menu command hierarchy is also different from the Lotus screen displays, for users need not "use" any expressive aspects of the screen displays in order to operate Lotus 1-2-3; because the way the screens look has little bearing on how users control the program, the screen displays are not part of Lotus 1-2-3's "method of operation."[10] The Lotus menu command hierarchy is also different from the underlying computer code, because while code is necessary for the program to work, its precise formulation is not. In other words, to offer the same capabilities as Lotus 1-2-3, Borland did not have to copy Lotus's underlying code (and indeed it did not); to allow users to operate its programs in substantially the same way, however, Borland had to copy the Lotus menu command hierarchy. Thus the Lotus 1-2-3 code is not an uncopyrightable "method of operation."[11]

The district court held that the Lotus menu command hierarchy, with its specific choice and arrangement of command terms, constituted an "expression" of the "idea" of operating a computer program with commands arranged hierarchically into menus and submenus. *Borland II*, 799 F. Supp. at 216. Under the district court's reasoning, Lotus's decision to employ hierarchically arranged command terms to operate its program could not foreclose its competitors from also employing hierarchically arranged command terms to operate their programs, but it did foreclose them from employing the specific command terms and arrangement that Lotus had used. In effect, the district court limited Lotus 1-2-3's "method of operation" to an abstraction.

Accepting the district court's finding that the Lotus developers made some expressive choices in choosing and arranging the Lotus command terms, we nonetheless hold that that expression is not copyrightable because it is part of Lotus 1-2-3's "method of operation." We do not think that "methods of operation" are limited to abstractions; rather, they are the means by which a user operates something. If specific words

10. As they are not before us on appeal, we take no position on whether the Lotus 1-2-3 screen displays constitute original expression capable of being copyrighted.

11. Because the Lotus 1-2-3 code is not before us on appeal, we take no position on whether it is copyrightable. We note, however, that original computer codes generally are protected by copyright.

are essential to operating something, then they are part of a "method of operation" and, as such, are unprotectable. This is so whether they must be highlighted, typed in, or even spoken, as computer programs no doubt will soon be controlled by spoken words.

The fact that Lotus developers could have designed the Lotus menu command hierarchy differently is immaterial to the question of whether it is a "method of operation." In other words, our initial inquiry is not whether the Lotus menu command hierarchy incorporates any expression. Rather, our initial inquiry is whether the Lotus menu command hierarchy is a "method of operation." Concluding, as we do, that users operate Lotus 1-2-3 by using the Lotus menu command hierarchy, and that the entire Lotus menu command hierarchy is essential to operating Lotus 1-2-3, we do not inquire further whether that method of operation could have been designed differently. The "expressive" choices of what to name the command terms and how to arrange them do not magically change the uncopyrightable menu command hierarchy into copyrightable subject matter.

\* \* \*

In many ways, the Lotus menu command hierarchy is like the buttons used to control, say, a video cassette recorder ("VCR"). A VCR is a machine that enables one to watch and record video tapes. Users operate VCRs by pressing a series of buttons that are typically labelled "Record, Play, Reverse, Fast Forward, Pause, Stop/Eject." That the buttons are arranged and labeled does not make them a "literary work," nor does it make them an "expression" of the abstract "method of operating" a VCR via a set of labeled buttons. Instead, the buttons are themselves the "method of operating" the VCR.

When a Lotus 1-2-3 user chooses a command, either by highlighting it on the screen or by typing its first letter, he or she effectively pushes a button. Highlighting the "Print" command on the screen, or typing the letter "P," is analogous to pressing a VCR button labeled "Play."

Just as one could not operate a buttonless VCR, it would be impossible to operate Lotus 1-2-3 without employing its menu command hierarchy. Thus the Lotus command terms are not equivalent to the labels on the VCR's buttons, but are instead equivalent to the buttons themselves. Unlike the labels on a VCR's buttons, which merely make operating a VCR easier by indicating the buttons' functions, the Lotus menu commands are essential to operating Lotus 1-2-3. Without the menu commands, there would be no way to "push" the Lotus buttons, as one could push unlabeled VCR buttons. While Lotus could probably have designed a user interface for which the command terms were mere labels, it did not do so here. Lotus 1-2-3 depends for its operation on use of the precise command terms that make up the Lotus menu command hierarchy....

### III.
#### CONCLUSION

Because we hold that the Lotus menu command hierarchy is uncopyrightable subject matter, we further hold that Borland did not infringe Lotus's copyright by copying it. Accordingly, we need not consider any of Borland's affirmative defenses. The judgment of the district court is *Reversed.*

BOUDIN, *Circuit Judge,* concurring.

\* \* \*

Requests for the protection of computer menus present the concern with fencing off access to the commons in an acute form. A new menu may be a creative work, but over time its importance may come to reside more in the investment that has been made by *users* in learning the menu and in building their own mini-programs — macros — in reliance upon the menu. Better typewriter keyboard layouts may exist, but the familiar QWERTY keyboard dominates the market because that is what everyone has learned to use. The QWERTY keyboard is nothing other than a menu of letters.

Thus, to assume that computer programs are just one more new means of expression, like a filmed play, may be quite wrong. The "form" — the written source code or the menu structure depicted on the screen — look hauntingly like the familiar stuff of copyright; but the "substance" probably has more to do with problems presented in patent law or, as already noted, in those rare cases where copyright law has confronted industrially useful expressions. Applying copyright law to computer programs is like assembling a jigsaw puzzle whose pieces do not quite fit.

\* \* \*

The present case is an unattractive one for copyright protection of the menu. The menu commands (*e.g.,* "print," "quit") are largely for standard procedures that Lotus did not invent and are common words that Lotus cannot monopolize. What is left is the particular combination and sub-grouping of commands in a pattern devised by Lotus. This arrangement may have a more appealing logic and ease of use than some other configurations; but there is a certain arbitrariness to many of the choices.

If Lotus is granted a monopoly on this pattern, users who have learned the command structure of Lotus 1-2-3 or devised their own macros are locked into Lotus, just as a typist who has learned the QWERTY keyboard would be the captive of anyone who had a monopoly on the production of such a keyboard. Apparently, for a period Lotus 1-2-3 has had such sway in the market that it has represented the *de facto* standard for electronic spreadsheet commands. So long as Lotus is the superior spreadsheet — either in quality or in price — there may be nothing wrong with this advantage.

But if a better spreadsheet comes along, it is hard to see why customers who have learned the Lotus menu and devised macros for it should remain captives of Lotus because of an investment in learning made by the users and not by Lotus. Lotus has already reaped a substantial reward for being first; assuming that the Borland program is now better, good reasons exist for freeing it to attract old Lotus customers: to enable the old customers to take advantage of a new advance, and to reward Borland in turn for making a better product. If Borland has not made a better product, then customers will remain with Lotus anyway.

Thus, for me the question is not whether Borland should prevail but on what basis. Various avenues might be traveled, but the main choices are between holding that the menu is not protectable by copyright and devising a new doctrine that Borland's use is privileged. No solution is perfect and no intermediate appellate court can make the final choice.

To call the menu a "method of operation" is, in the common use of those words, a defensible position. After all, the purpose of the menu is not to be admired as a work of literary or pictorial art. It is to transmit directions from the user to the computer, *i.e., to operate* the computer. The menu is also a "method" in the dictionary sense because it is a "planned way of doing something," an "order or system," and (aptly here) an "orderly or systematic arrangement, sequence or the like." *Random House Webster's College Dictionary* 853 (1991).

* * *

In sum, the majority's result persuades me and its formulation is as good, if not better, than any other that occurs to me now as within the reach of courts. Some solutions (*e.g.,* a very short copyright period for menus) are not options at all for courts but might be for Congress. In all events, the choices are important ones of policy, not linguistics, and they should be made with the underlying considerations in view.

## Comments

1. *Section 102(b).* Section II of *Lotus* describes §102(b) of the Copyright Act as the statutory implementation of the venerable idea/expression principle. *Lotus v. Borland* illustrates, however, that the categorical language of the statute does not capture all of the problems created by functional devices, particularly when those devices are implemented in forms that are typically compatible with copyright. The Lotus menu command hierarchy was embodied in a computer program, and it is accepted that computer programs are copyrightable literary works, since in at least one form, they are composed of text. Yet the menu command hierarchy serves only a functional purpose: It makes it easier to use the program. That kind of advance may warrant recognition and encouragement through intellectual property law, but as the court notes, functional advances are typically the province of patent law, not copyright. As a matter of public policy, then, and as the court confirms with its discussion of *Baker v. Selden,* §102(b) serves partly to differentiate between copyrightable subject matter and patentable subject matter.

2. *When is a Computer Program Like a Videocassette Recorder?* The majority opinion highlights an important issue in copyright jurisprudence, reasoning by analogy and metaphor. Recall that the core principles of copyright were developed in an era in which authors and publishers relied entirely on a single format: the printed page, bound into books, or formatted as maps or charts. As forms and formats have expanded, the scope of copyright law has expanded as well, but the underlying policies of the law still implicitly assume that authors and publishers, and readers, follow well-understood and established patterns of activity. The copyright implications of the computer program known as the elec-

tronic spreadsheet, therefore, depend in part on the lawyers' and the judges' selection of the "right" analogy or metaphor. As a preliminary matter, bear in mind that the spreadsheet software at issue in *Lotus v. Borland* ran on the DOS operating system, so that users had to rely on text-based commands and keyboard shortcuts. There was no computer mouse or graphical interface to guide them. The *Lotus* court concludes that operating a spreadsheet is something like operating a VCR, and that no one should "own" that kind of information. Borland undoubtedly benefited from the fact that one of the seminal copyright cases, *Baker v. Selden*, concluded that methods of using a system of double-entry bookkeeping—a cousin of the statistical methods embedded in Lotus 1-2-3—could not be copyrighted.

3. *Judge Boudin's Concurrence.* Judge Boudin reasons that the real problem in the case is how to articulate a clear problem of public policy in terms that copyright doctrine will recognize. The public policy problem is that consumers of the Lotus 1-2-3 product who learn how to use keyboard macros for that product will be deterred from switching from Lotus 1-2-3 to superior products offered by competitors unless they can re-use their acquired skills, and rely on those macros, in the competitors' products. Economists refer to the obstacles faced by consumers in this situation as "switching costs," and they characterize the situation of the unhappy consumers as "lock-in." Lock-in may be natural, and even efficient, particularly if the market has identified a technological standard or practice. Lotus, however, is trying to use copyright law to enforce a lock-in effect that benefits Lotus alone, at the possible expense of better technology. Copyright ought not to support this sort of anticompetitive result. The concurrence reminds us to be flexible in adapting the doctrinal tools of copyright law in light of its policy objectives.

4. **Lotus v. Borland** *at the Supreme Court.* The Supreme Court granted certiorari in *Lotus v. Borland* but affirmed the judgment, without an opinion, by a 4-to-4 vote, Justice Stevens not participating. *See Lotus Development Corp. v. Borland Int'l, Inc.,* 516 U.S. 233 (1996).

## C. CLASSIFYING COPYRIGHTABLE WORKS

Section 102(a) not only provides the basic framework for copyright protection—original works of authorship, fixed in a tangible medium of expression—but it also provides a set of non-exclusive categories of copyrightable work. This is a significant departure from copyright's historical practice, which limited copyright protection to forms of copyrighted works identified by name in the statute. The Copyright Act of 1909, for example, granted protection to "all writings of an author" in §4, but in §5 it provided that an application to register a work with the Copyright Office had to specify the precise character of the work. The categories provided by §5 of the statute included book, periodical, lecture or sermon, "reproductions of a work of art," and "Drawings or plastic works of a scientific or technical character," among other things. With the 1976 Act, Congress deliberately chose a legal framework that was open-ended in order to avoid future problems of accommodating the law to new media and technologies.

Nonetheless, while the proper classification of a work of authorship does not affect its copyrightability, classification retains some significance, even under current law. This section illustrates that point in two ways. First, it discusses the importance of the distinction between the copyrighted work of authorship and the tangible medium, or "copy," in which the work is fixed. Second, it reviews three particularly troublesome statutory categories: pictorial, graphic, and sculptural works; derivative works; and compilations and collective works.

## 1. Distinguishing the Work of Authorship from the Copy

Copyright lawyers must remember the sense of the metaphysical that attaches to much of intellectual property law. Like the "invention" in patent law and the "mark" in trademark law, the "work of authorship" in copyright law is an intangible artifact of the law, rather than a physical artifact of nature. The law is designed in the first instance to encourage and protect the author's creativity, not the publisher's binding and packaging. Copyright protects a "literary work," for example, but not the book that encases it.

> **STATUTE:** **Ownership of Copyright as Distinct from**
> **Ownership of Material Object**
> 17 U.S.C. §202

In *Matthew Bender & Co. v. West Publishing Co.*, 158 F.3d 693 (1998), the West Publishing Company, proprietor not only of the electronic Westlaw service but of the hard-bound series of case reporters that preceded it, sued HyperLaw, Inc., which produced and marketed a CD-ROM compilation of judicial opinions that had previously appeared in West's copyrighted reporters. West specifically objected to HyperLaw's inclusion of notations in each case that indicated page breaks in the West originals; use of this "star pagination" system constituted infringement of West's copyright in its compilations of the opinions. The court of appeals affirmed a lower court decision that granted summary judgment to HyperLaw, on the primary ground that HyperLaw's product created no actionable "copy" of the West compilation. As an alternative ground for its conclusion, the court noted in a footnote that West's entire claim failed because of its reliance on its pagination of the West reporters. Pagination is an artifact of reproduction of the work in a physical medium, rather than a product of creativity. Under the principle reflected in §202 of the Copyright Act, that the intangible work of authorship is copyrightable but the tangible artifact is not, West's claim failed because "star pagination" was no part of the "work of authorship" that West was entitled to protect. David Nimmer, editor of the leading copyright treatise *Nimmer on Copyright* and one of the defense attorneys in this case, wrote later that the defense team did not even think of this theory until after the case was briefed in the trial court. It was raised in the defense briefs on appeal, but West did not reply to it. *See* David Nimmer, *Copyright in the Dead Sea Scrolls: Authorship and Originality*, 38 HOUS. L. REV. 1, 98-99 (2001).

## 2. The Statutory Categories

*STATUTE:* **Subject Matter of Copyright: In General**
17 U.S.C. §102(a)

*STATUTE:* **Definitions — "Architectural Works," "Audiovisual Works,"
"Literary Works," "Sound Recordings"**
17 U.S.C. §101

The statutory categories included in §102(a) include some, such as "literary works," which are specially defined in §101, and others, such as "musical works" and "dramatic works," which are not. Still other classifications, for derivative and compilation works, appear in §103. The proper classification of a work may have important consequences. For example, as the *Nichols* opinion and its progeny illustrate, *literary* works, because they tend to rely on narrative devices, are particularly susceptible to Judge Hand's "abstractions" analysis. In other instances, the classification of a work determines the scope of the author's exclusive rights. The owner of the copyright in an "architectural work" cannot prevent members of the public from photographing the work, "if the building in which the work is embodied is located in or ordinarily visible from a public place." 17 U.S.C. §120(a). The owner of a sound recording copyright does not enjoy the full array of exclusive rights otherwise provided to copyright owners; most important, the owner of the sound recording copyright does not have the exclusive right to publicly perform the work. 17 U.S.C. §114. In practice, this means that when recordings of copyrighted songs are played on the radio, the owner of the copyright in the song, which is a musical work, is entitled to a royalty. The owner of the copyright in the recording, which is a sound recording, is not entitled to a royalty.

This section of the chapter describes the classification issues associated with three particularly troublesome classes of works: pictorial, graphic, and sculptural works (usually known as "PGS" works); derivative works; and compilations and collective works.

### a. Pictorial, Graphic, and Sculptural Works

You have already seen a number of instances where copyright law has grappled with distinguishing between creative expression to be protected by copyright law, on the one hand, and useful or functional expression to be protected by other sources of law, on the other hand. This distinction is illustrated here via the definition of and scope of protection afforded to PGS works. There are two questions to consider. The first is whether Congress is empowered to authorize copyright in these works in the first place. In *Mazer v. Stein,* 347 U.S. 201 (1954), a case that challenged the copyrightability of a sculpture that was sold as the base of a lamp, the Supreme Court implicitly answered this question in the affirmative. The Court in *Mazer* concluded that the lamp bases in question constituted "writings of an author" within the meaning of the Copyright Act of 1909, despite their status as mass-produced commercial objects. Its judgment was heavily influenced by the interpretation of the Copyright Office that these sorts of works would constitute "works of art" as the Office defined that phrase. Enactment of the revised Copyright Act in 1976, and the Court's adoption of the constitutional "minimal creativity" standard in *Feist*, rendered further analysis of the constitutional question moot. There is little doubt today that whatever the applicability of trademark and patent law to "expressive" objects, they are eligible for copyright protection. The second question is how to distinguish between works that tend toward the "artistic," or what might be referred to colloquially as "applied art," and works that tend toward the "useful," or what might be referred to as "industrial design." The former ought to be copyrightable. The latter ought to remain outside of copyright, and protectable via trademark or patent law.

*STATUTE:* **Definitions — "Pictorial, Graphic, and Sculptural Works," "Useful Article"**
17 U.S.C. §101

*STATUTE:* **Scope of Exclusive Rights in Pictorial, Graphic, and Sculptural Works**
17 U.S.C. §113

## BRANDIR INTERNATIONAL, INC. v. CASCADE PACIFIC LUMBER CO.

**834 F.2d 1142 (2d Cir. 1987)**

OAKES, Circuit Judge.

In passing the Copyright Act of 1976 Congress attempted to distinguish between protectable "works of applied art" and "industrial designs not subject to copyright protection." *See* H.R. Rep. No. 1476, 94th Cong., 2d Sess. 54, *reprinted in* 1976 U.S. Code Cong. & Admin. News 5659, 5667 (hereinafter H.R. Rep. No. 1476). The courts, however, have had difficulty framing tests by which the fine line establishing what is and what is not copyrightable can be drawn. Once again we are called upon to draw such a line, this time in a case involving the "RIBBON Rack," a bicycle rack made of bent tubing that is said to have originated from a wire sculpture. (A photograph of the rack is contained in the appendix to this opinion.)....The Register of Copyright, named as a third-party defendant under the statute, 17 U.S.C. §411, but electing not to appear, denied copyrightability. In the subsequent suit brought in the United States District Court for the Southern District of New York, Charles S. Haight, Jr., Judge, the district court granted summary judgment on...the copyright...

claim[] to defendant Cascade Pacific Lumber Co., d/b/a Columbia Cascade Co., manufacturer of a similar bicycle rack.

Against the history of copyright protection well set out in the majority opinion in *Carol Barnhart Inc. v. Economy Cover Corp.*, 773 F.2d 411, 415-18 (2d Cir. 1985), and in Denicola, *Applied Art and Industrial Design: A Suggested Approach to Copyright in Useful Articles,* 67 Minn. L. Rev. 707, 709-17 (1983), Congress adopted the Copyright Act of 1976. The "works of art" classification of the Copyright Act of 1909 was omitted and replaced by reference to "pictorial, graphic, and sculptural works." 17 U.S.C. §102(a)(5). According to the House Report, the new category was intended to supply "as clear a line as possible between copyrightable works of applied art and uncopyrighted works of industrial design." H.R. Rep. No. 1476, at 55, U.S. Code Cong. & Admin. News 1976, p. 5668. The statutory definition of "pictorial, graphic, and sculptural works" states that "the design of a useful article, as defined in this section, shall be considered a pictorial, graphic, or sculptural work only if, and only to the extent that, such design incorporates pictorial, graphic, or sculptural features that can be identified separately from, and are capable of existing independently of, the utilitarian aspects of the article." 17 U.S.C. §101. The legislative history added gloss on the criteria of separate identity and independent existence in saying:

> On the other hand, although the shape of an industrial product may be aesthetically satisfying and valuable, the Committee's intention is not to offer it copyright protection under the bill. Unless the shape of an automobile, airplane, ladies' dress, food processor, television set, or any other industrial product contains some element that, physically or conceptually, can be identified as separable from the utilitarian aspects of that article, the design would not be copyrighted under the bill.

H.R. Rep. No. 1476, at 55, U.S. Code Cong. & Admin. News 1976, p. 5668.

As courts and commentators have come to realize, however, the line Congress attempted to draw between copyrightable art and noncopyrightable design "was neither clear nor new." Denicola, *supra,* 67 Minn. L. Rev. at 720. One aspect of the distinction that has drawn considerable attention is the reference in the House Report to "*physically or conceptually*" (emphasis added) separable elements.... [I]n *Kieselstein-Cord v. Accessories by Pearl, Inc.,* 632 F.2d 989, 993 (2d Cir. 1980), this court accepted the idea that copyrightability can adhere in the "conceptual" separation of an artistic element. Indeed, the court went on to find such conceptual separation in reference to ornate belt buckles that could be and were worn separately as jewelry. *Kieselstein-Cord* was followed in *Norris Industries, Inc. v. International Telephone & Telegraph Corp.,* 696 F.2d 918, 923-24 (11th Cir. 1983), although there the court upheld the Register's refusal to register automobile wire wheel covers, finding no "conceptually separable" work of art.

In *Carol Barnhart Inc. v. Economy Cover Corp.,* 773 F.2d 411 (2d Cir. 1985), a divided panel of this circuit affirmed a district court grant of summary judgment of noncopyrightability of four life-sized, anatomically correct human torso forms. *Carol Barnhart* distinguished *Kieselstein-Cord,* but it surely did not overrule it. The distinction made was that the ornamented surfaces of the *Kieselstein-Cord* belt buckles "were not in any respect required by their utilitarian functions," but the features claimed to be aesthetic or artistic in the *Carol Barnhart* forms were "inextricably intertwined with the utilitarian feature, the display of clothes." 773 F.2d at 419. As Judge Newman's dissent made clear, the *Carol Barnhart* majority did not dispute "that 'conceptual separability' is distinct from 'physical separability' and, when present, entitles the creator of a useful article to a copyright on its design." 773 F.2d at 420.

"Conceptual separability" is thus alive and well, at least in this circuit. The problem, however, is determining exactly what it is and how it is to be applied. Judge Newman's illuminating discussion in dissent in *Carol Barnhart, see* 773 F.2d at 419-24, proposed a test that aesthetic features are conceptually separable if "the article...stimulate[s] in the mind of the beholder a concept that is separate from the concept evoked by its utilitarian function." *Id.* at 422. This approach has received favorable endorsement by at least one commentator, W. Patry, *Latman's The Copyright Law* 43-45 (6th ed. 1986), who calls Judge Newman's test the "temporal displacement" test. It is to be distinguished from other possible ways in which conceptual separability can be tested, including whether the primary use is as a utilitarian article as opposed to an artistic work, whether the aesthetic aspects of the work can be said to be "primary," and whether the article is marketable as art, none of which is very satisfactory. But Judge Newman's test was rejected outright by the majority as "a standard so ethereal as to amount to a 'nontest' that would be extremely difficult, if not impossible, to administer or apply." 773 F.2d at 419 n. 5.

Perhaps the differences between the majority and the dissent in *Carol Barnhart* might have been resolved had they had before them the Denicola article on *Applied Art and Industrial Design: A Suggested Approach to Copyright in Useful Articles, supra.* There, Professor Denicola points out that although the Copyright Act of 1976 was an effort "'to draw as clear a line as possible,'" in truth "there is no line, but merely a spectrum of forms and shapes responsive in varying degrees to utilitarian concerns." 67 Minn. L. Rev. at 741. Denicola argues that "the statutory directive requires a distinction between works of industrial design and works whose origins lie outside the design process, despite the utilitarian environment in which they appear." He views the statutory limitation of copyrightability as "an attempt to identify elements whose form and appearance reflect the unconstrained perspective of the artist," such features not being the product of industrial design. *Id.* at 742. "Copyrightability, therefore, should turn on the relationship between the proffered work and the process of industrial design." *Id.* at 741. He suggests that "the dominant characteristic of industrial design is the influence of nonaesthetic, utilitarian concerns" and hence concludes that copyrightability "ultimately should depend on the extent to which the work reflects artistic expression uninhibited by functional considerations."[2] *Id.*

2. Professor Denicola rejects the exclusion of all works created with some utilitarian application in view, for that would not only overturn *Mazer v. Stein*, 347 U.S. 201 (1954), on which much of the legislation is based, but also "a host of other eminently sensible decisions, in favor of an intractable factual inquiry of questionable relevance." 67 Minn. L. Rev. at 741. He adds that "[a]ny such categorical approach would also undermine the legislative determination to preserve an artist's ability to exploit utilitarian markets." *Id.* (*citing* 17 U.S.C. §113(a) (1976)).

To state the Denicola test in the language of conceptual separability, if design elements reflect a merger of aesthetic and functional considerations, the artistic aspects of a work cannot be said to be conceptually separable from the utilitarian elements. Conversely, where design elements can be identified as reflecting the designer's artistic judgment exercised independently of functional influences, conceptual separability exists.

We believe that Professor Denicola's approach provides the best test for conceptual separability and, accordingly, adopt it here for several reasons. First, the approach is consistent with the holdings of our previous cases. In *Kieselstein-Cord*, for example, the artistic aspects of the belt buckles reflected purely aesthetic choices, independent of the buckles' function, while in *Carol Barnhart* the distinctive features of the torsos — the accurate anatomical design and the sculpted shirts and collars — showed clearly the influence of functional concerns. Though the torsos bore artistic features, it was evident that the designer incorporated those features to further the usefulness of the torsos as mannequins. Second, the test's emphasis on the influence of utilitarian concerns in the design process may help, as Denicola notes, to "alleviate the de facto discrimination against nonrepresentational art that has regrettably accompanied much of the current analysis." *Id.* at 745.[3] Finally, and perhaps most importantly, we think Denicola's test will not be too difficult to administer in practice. The work itself will continue to give "mute testimony" of its origins. In addition, the parties will be required to present evidence relating to the design process and the nature of the work, with the trier of fact making the determination whether the aesthetic design elements are significantly influenced by functional considerations.

Turning now to the facts of this case, we note first that Brandir contends, and its chief owner David Levine testified, that the original design of the RIBBON Rack stemmed from wire sculptures that Levine had created, each formed from one continuous undulating piece of wire. These sculptures were, he said, created and displayed in his home as a means of personal expression, but apparently were never sold or displayed elsewhere. He also created a wire sculpture in the shape of a bicycle and states that he did not give any thought to the utilitarian application of any of his sculptures until he accidentally juxtaposed the bicycle sculpture with one of the self-standing wire sculptures. It was not until November 1978 that Levine seriously began pursuing the utilitarian application of his sculptures, when a friend, G. Duff Bailey, a bicycle buff and author of numerous articles about urban cycling, was at Levine's home and informed him that the sculptures would make excellent bicycle racks, permitting bicycles to be parked under the overloops as well as on top of the underloops. Following this meeting, Levine met several times with Bailey and others, completing the designs for the RIBBON Rack by the use of a vacuum cleaner hose, and

---

3. We are reminded . . . that we judges should not let our own view of styles of art interfere with the decisionmaking process in this area. Denicola suggests that the shape of a Mickey Mouse telephone is copyrightable because its form is independent of function, and "[a] telephone shape owing more to Arp, Brancusi, or Moore than Disney may be equally divorced from utilitarian influence." 67 Minn. L. Rev. at 746. This is true, of course, of the artist Christo's "Running Fence," approved (following Professor Nimmer) as an example of conceptual separability in *Keiselstein-Cord*, 632 F.2d at 993.

submitting his drawings to a fabricator complete with dimensions. The Brandir RIBBON Rack began being nationally advertised and promoted for sale in September 1979.

\* \* \*

Applying Professor Denicola's test to the RIBBON Rack, we find that the rack is not copyrightable. It seems clear that the form of the rack is influenced in significant measure by utilitarian concerns and thus any aesthetic elements cannot be said to be conceptually separable from the utilitarian elements. This is true even though the sculptures which inspired the RIBBON Rack may well have been — the issue of originality aside — copyrightable.

Brandir argues correctly that a copyrighted work of art does not lose its protected status merely because it subsequently is put to a functional use. The Supreme Court so held in *Mazer v. Stein*, 347 U.S. 201 (1954), and Congress specifically intended to accept and codify *Mazer* in section 101 of the Copyright Act of 1976. *See* H.R. Rep. No. 1476 at 54-55. The district court thus erred in ruling that, whatever the RIBBON Rack's origins, Brandir's commercialization of the rack disposed of the issue of its copyrightability.

Had Brandir merely adopted one of the existing sculptures as a bicycle rack, neither the application to a utilitarian end nor commercialization of that use would have caused the object to forfeit its copyrighted status. Comparison of the RIBBON Rack with the earlier sculptures, however, reveals that while the rack may have been derived in part from one of more "works of art," it is in its final form essentially a product of industrial design. In creating the RIBBON Rack, the designer has clearly adapted the original aesthetic elements to accommodate and further a utilitarian purpose. These altered design features of the RIBBON Rack, including the spacesaving, open design achieved by widening the upper loops to permit parking under as well as over the rack's curves, the straightened vertical elements that allow in- and above-ground installation of the rack, the ability to fit all types of bicycles and mopeds, and the heavy-gauged tubular construction of rustproof galvanized steel, are all features that combine to make for a safe, secure, and maintenance-free system of parking bicycles and mopeds. Its undulating shape is said in *Progressive Architecture*, January 1982, to permit double the storage of conventional bicycle racks. Moreover, the rack is manufactured from 2-⅜–inch standard steam pipe that is bent into form, the six-inch radius of the bends evidently resulting from bending the pipe according to a standard formula that yields bends having a radius equal to three times the nominal internal diameter of the pipe.

Brandir argues that its RIBBON Rack can and should be characterized as a sculptural work of art within the minimalist art movement. Minimalist sculpture's most outstanding feature is said to be its clarity and simplicity, in that it often takes the form of geometric shapes, lines, and forms that are pure and free of ornamentation and void of association. As Brandir's expert put it, "The meaning is to be found in, within, around and outside the work of art, allowing the artistic sensation to be experienced as well as intellectualized." People who use Foley Square in New York City see in the form of minimalist art the "Tilted Arc," which is on the plaza at 26 Federal Plaza. Numerous museums have had exhibitions of such art, and the school of minimalist art has many admirers.

It is unnecessary to determine whether to the art world the RIBBON Rack properly would be considered an example of minimalist sculpture. The result under the copyright statute is not changed. Using the test we have adopted, it is not enough that, to paraphrase Judge Newman, the rack may stimulate in the mind of the reasonable observer a concept separate from the bicycle rack concept. While the RIBBON Rack may be worthy of admiration for its aesthetic qualities alone, it remains nonetheless the product of industrial design. Form and function are inextricably intertwined in the rack, its ultimate design being as much the result of utilitarian pressures as aesthetic choices. Indeed, the visually pleasing proportions and symmetricality of the rack represent design changes made in response to functional concerns. Judging from the awards the rack has received, it would seem in fact that Brandir has achieved with the RIBBON Rack the highest goal of modern industrial design, that is, the harmonious fusion of function and aesthetics. Thus there remains no artistic element of the RIBBON Rack that can be identified as separate and "capable of existing independently, of, the utilitarian aspects of the article." Accordingly, we must affirm on the copyright claim.

* * *

Winter, Circuit Judge, concurring in part and dissenting in part:

...I respectfully dissent from the majority's discussion and disposition of the copyright claim.

My colleagues, applying an adaptation of Professor Denicola's test, hold that the aesthetic elements of the design of a useful article are not conceptually separable from its utilitarian aspects if "[f]orm and function are inextricably intertwined" in the article, and "its ultimate design [is] as much the result of utilitarian pressures as aesthetic choices." Applying that test to the instant matter, they observe that the dispositive fact is that "in creating the Ribbon Rack, [Levine] has clearly adapted the *original* aesthetic elements to accommodate and further a utilitarian purpose." (emphasis added). The grounds of my disagreement are that: (1) my colleagues' adaptation of Professor Denicola's test diminishes the statutory concept of "conceptual separability" to the vanishing point; and (2) their focus on the process or sequence followed by the particular designer makes copyright protection depend upon largely fortuitous circumstances concerning the creation of the design in issue.

With regard to "conceptual separability," my colleagues deserve considerable credit for their efforts to reconcile *Carol Barnhart Inc. v. Economy Cover Corp.*, 773 F.2d 411 (2d Cir. 1985) with *Kieselstein-Cord v. Accessories by Pearl, Inc.*, 632 F.2d 989 (2d Cir. 1980). In my view, these cases are not reconcilable. *Carol Barnhart* paid only lip service to the fact that the "conceptual separability" of an article's aesthetic utilitarian aspects may render the design of a "useful article" a copyrightable "sculptural work." 17 U.S.C. §101 (1982). Actually, the *Carol Barnhart* majority applied a test of physical separability. They thus stated:

What distinguishes [the *Kieselstein Cord*] buckles from the Barnhart forms is that the ornamented surfaces of the buckles were not in any respect required by their utilitarian functions; the artistic and aesthetic features could thus be conceived of as having been *added to, or superimposed upon,* an otherwise utilitarian article. The unique artistic design was wholly unnecessary to performance of the utilitarian function. In the case of the Barnhart forms, on the other hand, the features claimed to be aesthetic or artistic, e.g., the life-size configuration of the breasts and the width of the shoulders are inextricably intertwined with the utilitarian feature, the display of clothes.

773 F.2d at 419 (emphasis added). In contrast, *Kieselstein-Cord* focused on the fact that the belt buckles at issue could be perceived as objects other than belt buckles:

We see in appellant's belt buckles conceptually separable sculptural elements, as apparently have the buckles' wearers who have used them as ornamentation for parts of the body other than the waist.

632 F.2d at 993.

My colleagues' adaptation of the Denicola test tracks the *Carol Barnhart* approach, whereas I would adopt that taken in *Kieselstein-Cord,* which allows for the copyrightability of the aesthetic elements of useful articles even if those elements simultaneously perform utilitarian functions.[1] The latter approach received its fullest elaboration in Judge Newman's dissent in *Carol Barnhart,* where he explained that "[f]or the [artistic] design features to be 'conceptually separate' from the utilitarian aspects of the useful article that embodies the design, the article must stimulate in the mind of the beholder a concept that is separate from the concept evoked by its utilitarian function." 773 F.2d at 422 (Newman, J., dissenting).

In other words, the relevant question is whether the design of a useful article, however intertwined with the article's utilitarian aspects, causes an ordinary reasonable observer to perceive an aesthetic concept not related to the article's use. The answer to this question is clear in the instant case because any reasonable observer would easily view the Ribbon Rack as an ornamental sculpture. Indeed, there is evidence of actual confusion over whether it is strictly ornamental in the refusal of a building manager to accept delivery until assured by the buyer that the Ribbon Rack was in fact a bicycle rack. Moreover, Brandir has received a request to use the Ribbon Rack as environmental sculpture, and has offered testimony of art experts who claim that the Ribbon Rack may be valued solely for its artistic features. As one of those experts observed: "If one were to place a Ribbon Rack on an island without access, or in a park and surround the work with a barrier, . . . its status as a work of art would be beyond dispute."

My colleagues also allow too much to turn upon the process or sequence of design followed by the designer of the Ribbon Rack. They thus suggest that copyright protection would have been accorded "had Brandir merely

---

1. Indeed, *Kieselstein-Cord* approved Professor Nimmer's example of Christo's "Running Fence" as an object whose sculptural features were conceptually, but not physically, separable from its utilitarian aspects. 632 F.2d at 993; *see* 1 *Nimmer on Copyright* §2.08[B] at 2-96.1 & n. 112.2 (1987). The fact that the Running Fence's aesthetic features were "inextricably intertwined" with its functional aspects, however, creates doubt as to whether it is a copyrightable "sculptural work" under *Carol Barnhart* or the instant decision.

adopted...as a bicycle rack" an enlarged version of one of David Levine's original sculptures rather than one that had wider upper loops and straightened vertical elements. I cannot agree that copyright protection for the Ribbon Rack turns on whether Levine serendipitously chose the final design of the Ribbon Rack during his initial sculptural musings or whether the original design had to be slightly modified to accommodate bicycles. Copyright protection, which is intended to generate incentives for designers by according property rights in their creations, should not turn on purely fortuitous events. For that reason, the Copyright Act expressly states that the legal test is how the final article is perceived, not how it was developed through various stages....

I therefore dissent from the decision so far as it relates to copyrightability....

## Comments

1. **Kieselstein-Cord** *and* **Carol Barnhart.** *Brandir* is the culmination of a remarkable trio of cases decided by the Second Circuit on the question of "conceptual separability." In *Kieselstein-Cord v. Accessories by Pearl, Inc.*, 632 F.2d 989 (2d Cir. 1980), the court approved copyright protection for silver belt buckles that adopted the abstract forms of modern sculpture; the court noted that the "conceptual separability" of the aesthetic elements of the buckles was supported, among other ways, by the fact that the buckles had been accepted into the permanent collection of the Metropolitan Museum of Art. In *Carol Barnhart Inc. v. Economy Cover Corp.*, 773 F.2d 411 (2d Cir. 1985), the court rejected the notion that mannequins used for clothing displays could be copyrighted, noting that any "expressive" dimension to the mannequins at issue could not be distinguished from their function.

2. *Tests for Separability.* There is no doubt in *Brandir* that the Ribbon Rack is a "pictorial, graphic, and sculptural work," and that it is also a "useful article." Both definitions must be satisfied in order for the court to confront the issue that divides the majority and dissent: whether the utilitarian features of the article can be separated from its pictorial, graphic, and sculptural (that is, artistic) features. The court divides over two issues. The first is whether "separability" of useful and artistic features must be "physical," so that the useful features must have an independent physical existence, or whether "conceptual" separability, in which the "artistic" features of the work may be constituted as a sort of virtual thing, may also suffice. The second is the character of the evidence that may be relied on to demonstrate "conceptual" separability. The majority, following Professor Denicola, would rely on the design process of the author; the dissent, claiming inspiration in the text of the statute, would rely instead on evidence distilled from the market.

3. *The Author's Purpose and the Nondiscrimination Principle.* Recall Justice Holmes's statement in *Bleistein* of the "nondiscrimination" principle in copyright law. Is admitting PGS works into copyright an all-or-nothing proposition? If not, how should courts and Congress draw the line between what is copyrightable, and what is not? As the issue was framed

in *Mazer v. Stein*, the question was "an artist's right to copyright a work of art intended to be reproduced for lamp bases." *Mazer,* 347 U.S. at 205. The Court concluded there that if the work was copyrightable in the first place, the fact that it was subsequently adapted as a lamp would not change its copyrightable status. In *Brandir*, however, the artist's purpose is all but determinative of copyrightability. Under what circumstances, if any, should an author's intent to create a work of art (or, conversely, to create an item for industrial use, or for mass consumption, or for some other purpose) be relevant to whether it is entitled to protection under the copyright laws, and when should intent be irrelevant? It is often the case that a product developed for one purpose finds another through use. Apparently artistic items like sculpture may be adapted for functional purposes, like lamp bases. Apparently functional items, such as tables and chairs, may be considered fine art by museums and other collectors.

4. *Sources of Evidence.* As the dissent points out, a test for conceptual separability that focuses on the creator's design process may lead to granting or withholding copyright protection based on a variety of fortuitous events, including the sequence of events that unfolded in the studio, and the extent to which the creator maintained contemporaneous records of the design process. The idiosyncratic and potentially unreliable character of litigation oriented around what the creator did is likely to be no more or less idiosyncratic than litigation oriented around alternatives—though the idiosyncrasies will differ. Consider the "reasonable observer" standard proposed by the dissent, and consider the credibility problems associated with obtaining evidence—whether from lay or expert witnesses—of what the "reasonable observer" thinks. Or, consider the sort of evidence that helped to persuade the court in *Kieselstein-Cord*—that artistic experts, such as museum curators, think that an object is "aesthetic" enough to be treated as art. The history of twentieth- (and now twenty-first-) century art teaches us to be skeptical of any arguments premised on an expert's view of what is "art." Finally, consider possible reliance on more "objective" forms of evidence, such as sales and royalties derived from "functional" domains (such as cities buying bicycle racks, or department stores buying belt buckles), which could be compared with revenues from more "artistic" domains (such as galleries). At the end of the day, it is difficult to conclude that Professor Denicola's standard is less reliable than any other.

5. *Is it a Useful Article?* If a PGS work does not constitute a "useful article," then there is no need to perform a separability analysis; the work is entitled to copyright so long as it otherwise meets the default standards of originality and fixation. The statute defines a useful article as "an article having an intrinsic utilitarian function that is not merely to portray the appearance of the article or to convey information." Maps and globes, for example, are "articles" that are not "useful" within the meaning of this definition. Though they have an intrinsic utilitarian function, their purpose is to convey information. The issue of "usefulness" has led courts to some improbable distinctions. Though ordinary mannequins of humans are useful articles, animal mannequins used for taxidermy are not. *See Superior Form Builders, Inc. v. Dan Chase Taxidermy*

*Supply Co., Inc.,* 74 F.3d 488 (4th Cir. 1996). Halloween costumes are ordinarily useful articles, *see Whimsicality, Inc. v. Rubie's Costume Co., Inc.,* 891 F.2d 452 (2d Cir. 1989), though the Second Circuit held in a recent opinion that a complaint that alleged that "plush, sculpted animal costumes are not useful articles" should have survived a pretrial motion to dismiss. *See Chosun Intern., Inc. v. Chrisha Creations, Ltd.,* 413 F.3d 324 (2d Cir. 2005). Halloween masks, standing alone, are not "useful articles." *See Masquerade Novelty v. Unique Industries,* 912 F.2d 663 (3d Cir. 1990). And in *Poe v. Missing Persons,* 745 F.2d 1238 (9th Cir. 1984), the court confronted whether what appeared to be a woman's swimsuit made of triangles of opaque plastic was in fact a swimsuit (and therefore a useful article), or instead a work of conceptual art. It remanded the case for factfinding by the trial court.

## Problem

**6-3.** Plantation Productions (PP) develops and markets techniques and tools for the hair design industry. One aspect of PP's business is the design and development of mannequin heads. In the mid-1990s, PP wanted to develop a mannequin that would imitate the "hungry look" of high-fashion, runway models. PP's designers believed that this mannequin could be marketed as a premium item to cutting-edge hair-stylists and to stylists involved in hair design competitions. The designers created an original plaster sculpture of a female human head, entitled "Tara." Wax molds of Tara were made and sent to PP's manufacturer in Hong Kong. The manufacturer created exact reproductions of Tara in polyvinyl chloride (PVC), then used the PVC form to create Tara mannequins using a liquid that expands and hardens into foam. Early versions of the Tara mannequin included a slight manufacturing error, so that the mannequin's hairline was too high on the forehead. The error was corrected by etching a new, lower hairline and covering the first with hair; later copies of the Tara mannequin had the single, correct hairline. The process of creating the Tara sculpture and developing the mannequin based on the sculpture took approximately 18 months. At a trade show in Chicago in 1998, TenOaks, a wholesaler of beauty products founded by Rhett, displayed its own "Melanie" mannequin, which was very close in appearance to PP's Tara. In addition to the strikingly similar facial features, Melanie also exhibited a double hairline that the early Tara mannequins possessed. In PP's lawsuit against Rhett for copyright infringement, Rhett argued that the Tara mannequin is not copyrightable. Is it? *See Pivot Point Intern., Inc. v. Charlene Products, Inc.,* 372 F.3d 913 (7th Cir. 2004).

### b. Derivative Works

The definition of "derivative works" in the Copyright Act feeds two distinct parts of the statute. For purposes of this chapter, on acquiring copyright interests, the meaning of "derivative works" defines the scope of rights that an author can acquire in a work that is derived from or based on some other work. The scope is defined by the expressive elements the author has contributed to an existing work. For purposes of the next chapter, on enforcing copyright interests, the meaning of "derivative works" defines part of the copyright owner's exclusive rights, specifically, the exclusive right to prepare derivative works. In short, an author may both obtain rights in a derivative work that she prepared herself, and also prevent anyone from preparing a derivative work without her permission.

*STATUTE:* **Subject Matter of Copyright: Compilations and Derivative Works**
17 U.S.C. §103

*STATUTE:* **Definition — "Derivative Work"**
17 U.S.C. §101

## GRACEN v. BRADFORD EXCHANGE

### 698 F.2d 300 (7th Cir. 1983)

POSNER, Circuit Judge.

This appeal brings up to us questions of some novelty, at least in this circuit, regarding implied copyright licenses and the required originality for copyrighting a derivative work.

In 1939 MGM produced and copyrighted the movie "The Wizard of Oz." The central character in the movie, Dorothy, was played by Judy Garland. The copyright was renewed by MGM in 1966 and is conceded, at least for purposes of this case, to be valid and in effect today. In 1976 MGM licensed Bradford Exchange to use characters and scenes from the movie in a series of collectors' plates. Bradford invited several artists to submit paintings of Dorothy as played by Judy Garland, with the understanding that the artist who submitted the best painting would be offered a contract for the entire series. Bradford supplied each artist with photographs from the movie and with instructions for the painting that included the following: "We do want *your* interpretation of these images, but your interpretation must evoke all the warm feeling the people have for the film and its actors. So, *your* Judy/Dorothy must be very recognizable as everybody's Judy/Dorothy."

Figure 7

Jorie Gracen, an employee in Bradford's order-processing department, was permitted to join the competition. From photographs and her recollections of the movie (which she had seen several times) she made a painting of Dorothy as played by Judy Garland; Figure 1 at the end of this opinion is a reproduction of a photograph of Miss Gracen's painting (an inadequate one, because the original is in color). Bradford exhibited it along with the other contestants' paintings in a shopping center. The passersby liked Miss Gracen's the best, and Bradford pronounced her the winner of the competition and offered her a contract to do the series, as well as paying her, as apparently it paid each of the other contestants, $200. But she did not like the contract terms and refused to sign, and Bradford turned to another artist, James Auckland, who had not been one of the original contestants. He signed a contract to do the series and Bradford gave him Miss Gracen's painting to help him in doing his painting of Dorothy. The record does not indicate who has her painting now.

Figure 1

Gracen's counsel describes Auckland's painting of Dorothy as a "piratical copy" of her painting. Bradford could easily have refuted this charge, if it is false, by attaching to its motion for summary judgment a photograph of its Dorothy plate, but it did not, and for purposes of this appeal we must assume that the plate is a copy of Miss Gracen's painting. This is not an absurd supposition. Bradford, at least at first, was rapturous about Miss Gracen's painting of Dorothy. It called Miss Gracen "a true prodigy." It said that hers "was the one painting that conveyed the essence of Judy's character in the film . . . the painting that left everybody saying, 'That's Judy in Oz.'" Auckland's deposition states that Bradford gave him her painting with directions to "clean it up," which he understood to mean: do the same thing but make it "a little more professional."

Miss Gracen also made five drawings of other characters in the movie, for example the Scarecrow as played by Ray Bolger. Auckland's affidavit states without contradiction that he had not seen any of the drawings when he made his paintings of those characters. Pictures of the plates that were made from his paintings are attached to the motion for summary judgment filed by MGM and Bradford, but there is no picture of his Dorothy plate, lending some support to the charge that it is a "piratical copy." But apparently the other plates are not copies at all.

Auckland completed the series, and the plates were manufactured and sold. But Miss Gracen meanwhile had obtained copyright registrations on her painting and drawings, and in 1978 she brought this action for copyright infringement against MGM, Bradford, Auckland, and the manufacturer of the plates. MGM and Bradford counterclaimed, alleging among other things that Miss Gracen had infringed the copyright on the movie by showing her drawings and a photograph of her painting to people whom she was soliciting for artistic commissions.

The district court granted summary judgment against Miss Gracen on both the main claim and the counterclaim. It held that she could not copyright her painting and drawings because they were not original and that she had infringed MGM's copyright. . . .

\* \* \*

. . . The initial issue is . . . the scope of [Miss Gracen's] implied license from Bradford. Even if she was authorized to exhibit her derivative works, she may not have been authorized to copyright them. Bradford was licensed to use MGM's copyright in its series of collectors' plates but not to copyright the derivative works thus created. A copyright owner is naturally reluctant to authorize a licensee to take out copyrights on derivative works — copyrights that might impede him in making his own derivative works or in licensing others to do so. And it would have made no more sense for Bradford, the licensee, to arm Miss Gracen, its sublicensee, with a weapon — the right to copyright her derivative works — that she could use to interfere with Bradford's efforts to get another artist to do the plates if it could not cut a deal with her. The affidavits submitted with the motions for summary judgment deny that Miss Gracen was authorized to copyright derivative works based on the movie and are not contradicted on this point. (In contrast, they do not deny that she was authorized to exhibit her painting of Dorothy.)

We are reluctant to stop here, though, and uphold the dismissal of the complaint on the basis of an issue of fact that the district judge did not address, and that we therefore may have got wrong, so we shall go on and consider his ground for dismissal of the complaint — that Miss Gracen's painting and drawings are not original enough to be copyrightable.

Miss Gracen reminds us that judges can make fools of themselves pronouncing on aesthetic matters. But artistic originality is not the same thing as the legal concept of originality in the Copyright Act. Artistic originality indeed might inhere in a detail, a nuance, a shading too small to be apprehended by a judge. A contemporary school of art known as "Super Realism" attempts with some success to make paintings that are indistinguishable to the eye from color photographs. See Super Realism: A Critical Anthology (Battcock ed. 1975). These paintings command high prices; buyers must find something original in them. Much Northern European painting of the Renaissance is meticulously representational, see, e.g., Gombrich, The Story of Art 178-80 (13th ed. 1978), and therefore in a sense — but not an aesthetic sense — less "original" than Cubism or Abstract Expressionism. A portrait is not unoriginal for being a good likeness.

But especially as applied to derivative works, the concept of originality in copyright law has as one would expect a legal rather than aesthetic function—to prevent overlapping claims. See [*L. Batlin & Son v. Snyder*, 536 F.2d 486, 491-92 (2d Cir. 1976)]. Suppose Artist A produces a reproduction of the Mona Lisa, a painting in the public domain, which differs slightly from the original. B also makes a reproduction of the Mona Lisa. A, who has copyrighted his derivative work, sues B for infringement. B's defense is that he was copying the original, not A's reproduction. But if the difference between the original and A's reproduction is slight, the difference between A's and B's reproductions will also be slight, so that if B had access to A's reproductions the trier of fact will be hard-pressed to decide whether B was copying A or copying the Mona Lisa itself. Miss Gracen's drawings illustrate the problem. They are very similar both to the photographs from the movie and to the plates designed by Auckland. Auckland's affidavit establishes that he did not copy or even see her drawings. But suppose he had seen them. Then it would be very hard to determine whether he had been copying the movie stills, as he was authorized to do, or copying her drawings.

The painting of Dorothy presents a harder question. A comparison of Figures 1 and 2 reveals perceptible differences. A painting (except, perhaps, one by a member of the Super Realist school mentioned earlier) is never identical to the subject painted, whether the subject is a photograph, a still life, a landscape, or a model, because most painters cannot and do not want to achieve a photographic likeness of their subject. Nevertheless, if the differences between Miss Gracen's painting of Dorothy and the photograph of Judy Garland as Dorothy were sufficient to make the painting original in the eyes of the law, then a painting by an Auckland also striving, as per his commission, to produce something "very recognizable as everybody's Judy/Dorothy" would look like the Gracen painting, to which he had access; and it would be difficult for the trier of fact to decide whether Auckland had copied her painting or the original movie stills. True, the background in Miss Gracen's painting differs from that in Figure 2, but it is drawn from the movie set. We do not consider a picture created by superimposing one copyrighted photographic image on another to be "original"—always bearing in mind that the purpose of the term in copyright law is not to guide aesthetic judgments but to assure a sufficiently gross difference between the underlying and the derivative work to avoid entangling subsequent artists depicting the underlying work in copyright problems.

We are speaking, however, only of the requirement of originality in derivative works. If a painter paints from life, no court is going to hold that his painting is not copyrightable because it is an exact photographic likeness. If that were the rule photographs could not be copyrighted—the photographs of Judy Garland in "The Wizard of Oz," for example—but of course they can be. The requirement of originality is significant chiefly in connection with derivative works, where if interpreted too liberally it would paradoxically inhibit rather than promote the creation of such works by giving the first creator a considerable power to interfere with the creation of subsequent derivative works from the same underlying work.

. . . If Miss Gracen had painted Judy Garland from life, her painting would be copyrightable even if we thought it *kitsch;* but a derivative work must be substantially different from the underlying work to be copyrightable. This is the test of *L. Batlin & Son, Inc. v. Snyder, supra,* 536 F.2d at

491, a decision of the Second Circuit—the nation's premier copyright court—sitting en banc. Earlier Second Circuit cases discussed in *Batlin* that suggest a more liberal test must be considered superseded.

We agree with the district court that under the test of *Batlin* Miss Gracen's painting, whatever its artistic merit, is not an original derivative work within the meaning of the Copyright Act....

The judgment dismissing the complaint is therefore affirmed....

## Comments

1. **The Distinguishable Variation Standard.** In *L. Batlin & Son, Inc. v. Snyder*, 536 F.2d 486 (2d Cir. 1976) (en banc), cited by the Court of Appeals in *Gracen*, the court addressed the copyrightability of a plastic replica of the classic, antique (and public domain) cast iron "Uncle Sam" bank. The court concluded that the plastic bank could not be copyrighted (and, therefore, that its producer could not prevent distribution of a competing plastic Uncle Sam bank), because the several minor differences between the cast iron original and the plastic copy did not amount to "at least some substantial variation, not merely a trivial variation such as might occur in the translation to a different medium."

2. **The Impact of Feist.** *Batlin* was decided in 1976, before the Supreme Court articulated the "minimal creativity" standard for copyrightability in *Feist*. Is *Gracen*, which relies on *Batlin*, consistent with *Feist*? Does *Gracen* establish a higher standard for copyrighting derivative works? The court recognizes that Gracen's painting is minimally "creative" but is nonetheless not copyrightable. The logic of the court's reasoning is straightforward: Assume the existence of an original copyrighted work A, and a derivative work prepared from that work B. Consider the work, C, of a third creator, which is similar both to A and B. The creator of C may want to obtain appropriate permission before setting out to work. If A and B are too much alike, however, then C cannot figure out in advance whether to get permission from either creator, or both. C's creator may end up paying too much or be discouraged from working at all. The same problem might arise in litigation: If A and B are too similar, C's creator might be liable twice for what is, in effect, the same infringement. The rule of *Gracen* avoids this problem by ensuring that B cannot be copyrighted unless it is more than minimally distinguishable from A.

3. **Patent Law Compared.** The treatment of derivative works in copyright law is substantially different than the treatment of modifications and improvements in patent law. Since no copyright is available for derivative works prepared without the copyright owner's permission, copyright law effectively forces the would-be creator of a derivative work to bargain with the original author for permission, compensation, and ownership. The patent doctrine of "blocking patents" provides that the inventor of an improved or modified version of an existing patented invention may obtain an independent patent for the improvement or modification. The improvement patent cannot be practiced without

simultaneously practicing the prior invention, which requires the improver to bargain with the original inventor. But the improver has some bargaining leverage, since the original patentee cannot practice the improvement without the improver's permission. If the improvement increases the value of the original invention, then both patentees will have an incentive to bargain with one another. *See* Robert P. Merges, *Intellectual Property Rights and Bargaining Breakdown: The Case of Blocking Patents,* 62 TENN. L. Rev. 75 (1994).

**4. *Lawful Use of Source Material.*** Addressing the scope of copyright in derivative works, §103(b) provides, "protection for a work employing pre-existing material in which copyright subsists does not extend to any part of the work in which such material has been used unlawfully." What is "lawful" use? This might consist of use of material in the public domain, for which no permission is needed. Note that the source material in *Batlin* was in the public domain. Or, the source material might be protected by copyright. The court in *Gracen* assumes that Jorie Gracen's painting of Judy Garland was created with the permission of the copyright holder. In both cases, therefore, the plaintiff's work was eligible for copyright protection; the issue confronting the court was whether the work was sufficiently original. It is conceivable that the creator of a derivative work might claim a copyright based on lawful "fair" use of the underlying work. Such a theory was rejected in *Sobhani v. @Radical.Media Inc.*, 257 F. Supp. 2d 1234 (C.D. Cal. 2003), in which the court reasoned that Congress intended to equate "lawfulness" under §103 with the permission of the copyright owner. If the creator of the derivative work does not incorporate prior work "lawfully," then that creator owns no valid copyright. *See Pickett v. Prince*, 207 F.3d 402 (7th Cir. 2000) (rejecting claim asserted against Prince by the creator of a guitar shaped like Prince's copyrighted "symbol," where the creator worked without Prince's permission). What happens to copyright in the unauthorized derivative? As a practical matter, the original creator controls disposition of the unauthorized derivative. But ownership of the copyright to that work falls into a sort of copyright black hole. The derivative creator does not own a copyright in the work, by application of §103(b). The original creator does not own a copyright to the work, because the original creator did not create that work and is not its author.

## Problem

**6-4.** Wonder Toys, producer of the internationally famous Lovey doll, sued Radio City Music Hall for copyright infringement. Radio City produced dolls based on the famous Rockettes dance troupe, and Wonder Toys claimed that facial features from the Rockettes dolls were substantially similar to one, particular version of the Lovey doll and infringed Wonder Toys's copyright. Radio City admitted that it had copied the eyes, nose, and mouth of the Lovey doll, specifically the doll's widely spaced eyes, upturned nose, and bow lips, but it argued that those features were not protected by the Lovey copyright. Radio City introduced evidence that many dolls on the market today include those features. The uncontradicted evidence shows that Wonder Toys first independently created the Lovey doll in 1958 and since then has regularly produced revisions and adjustments to the Lovey face in order to appeal to the changing tastes of its customers. Is Wonder Toys's Lovey doll a copyrightable work of authorship? *See Mattel, Inc. v. Goldberger Doll Manufacturing Co.*, 365 F.3d 133 (2d Cir. 2004).

## D. FORMALITIES

The history of copyright law in the United States is a history of steady reduction in the number and type of formal actions that an author must take in order to acquire a valid copyright. Under the original Copyright Act of 1790, copyright was available only if the author recorded the title of the work with the clerk of the district court where the author resided, prior to publication of the work, to be followed by newspaper publication of the fact of the clerk's action and delivery of a copy of the work to the Secretary of State within six months of publication of the work. The Copyright Act of 1909 confirmed a change in practice that evolved over the intervening century, particularly with the establishment of the United States Copyright Office (which took over the recording function of local court clerks) in 1870. Copyright was obtained by publishing the work, so long as the publication was accompanied by an appropriate notice of copyright. The 1909 statute also provided that certain works that were not reproduced for publication, such as lectures or motion picture screenplays, could obtain federal copyright protection via registration with the Copyright Office. In all cases, federal copyright protection required deposit of copies of the work with the Copyright Office, which during the nineteenth century became the leading source of new material for the collections of the Library of Congress. If a creative work was published but lacked the requisite notice of copyright, the penalty was strict: The author forfeited any possible copyright, and the work passed immediately into the public domain.

With the formation of the Berne Convention in 1886, a comprehensive framework for international copyright law, a different model emerged. With respect to the minimum standards of protection for works governed by copyright, Article 5, §5 of the Convention stipulated that "The enjoyment and the exercise of these rights shall not be subject to any formality." This provision was intended to distinguish the approach taken by countries that subscribed to the convention from the notice-and-publication approach of the United States. Though the United States did not join the Berne Convention until 1989, membership was widely anticipated during the negotiations that preceded enactment of the 1976 Act. Accordingly, the notice-and-publication regime for obtaining copyright protection was dropped as part of the 1976 revision, in favor of a regime that granted copyright protection to an author automatically upon creation of a work of creative authorship. Among other important effects, this change dramatically increased the number of works created in the United States that are subject to the federal copyright system. Before the 1976 Act, only published works and certain registered unpublished works were subject to that system. Authors of unpublished works retained rights established under state law, including state common law copyright. Under the 1976 Act, and continuing today, both unpublished and published works are subject to federal copyright, so long as they are fixed in a tangible medium of expression.

Notice, publication, and deposit of copies of copyrighted works retain some important effects, however, even under the current statute. First, it is important to note that whether a given work is protected by copyright is determined in the first place by the legal standards in place at the time that the work was created (if the work was created after January 1, 1978) or published (if the work was created before January 1, 1978). Since there are thousands of works published before 1978 that are still protected by copyright, notice-and-publication standards are still relevant as to those works. Second, though the validity of a copyright under the current statute does not depend on including a copyright notice, or on publication of the work, notice of copyright *was* required, subject to certain exceptions, for works published between 1978 (when the new statute came into effect) and March 1, 1989 (when the United States joined the Berne Convention). Third, even today, authors and publishers who include notice of copyright on their published works earn certain benefits under the statute, including access to enhanced remedies for infringement, and registration of copyrighted works with the Copyright Office is a prerequisite to filing most lawsuits for copyright infringement.

### COMPARATIVE PERSPECTIVE
### The Development of International Copyright Law

The Berne Convention grew out of the maturing of international trade in copyrighted works during the 1800s, as developing countries (such as the United States) imported books and other materials from more mature societies (such as England). In the absence of a workable international regime of copyright protection, there was no way for authors of these works to prevent piracy by publishers in the importing countries. In 1886, however, at a meeting in Berne, Switzerland promoted by the French novelist Victor Hugo, a small group of countries adopted the Berne Convention for the Protection of Literary and Artistic Works, known as the Berne Convention, which established a framework for international copyright law. Though it is a treaty, the Berne Convention is not itself a source of law; rather, it provides that countries that are signatories must provide certain minimum standards of protection within their domestic copyright law, and, importantly, that each Berne member nation must offer domestic copyright protection to authors of other Berne member nations on the same basis that it offers copyright protection to its own nationals. These are known as principles of "minimum standards," and "national treatment," respectively. Along with other international intellectual property treaties, today the Berne Convention is administered by the World Intellectual Property Organization, or WIPO, headquartered in Geneva.

The United States was an observer at the original Berne negotiations but did not join the Convention itself for more than a century, in 1989. By that time, the United States had gone from being an importer of copyrighted materials from other countries to a major exporter, and the interests of American authors and publishers in copyright protection abroad had grown dramatically. American adherence to Berne had been anticipated for some time, however, and the Copyright Revision Act of 1976 embodied most of the changes to American copyright law that were needed to bring the United States into compliance with Berne.

Though the Berne Convention was significant as a matter of international diplomacy, it still lacked (and lacks) an effective enforcement mechanism. The enforceability of national copyright obligations changed, however, in 1994, as part of the Uruguay Round of negotiations on the General Agreement on Tariffs and Trade, or GATT, the major treaty governing trade relations around the world. That round established the World Trade Organization (WTO), which has the authority, among other things, to adjudicate disputes between nations arising under WTO rules. The Uruguay Round also saw adoption of the WTO Agreement on Trade-Related Aspects of Intellectual Property Rights, or TRIPs, which specifically incorporated international intellectual property rules into the WTO framework and made member noncompliance with TRIPs standards a basis for WTO sanctions. For copyright law, the TRIPs agreement borrowed Berne Convention standards nearly wholesale, thus at last creating a meaningful enforcement mechanism for international copyright norms.

## 1. Notice

*STATUTE:* **Notice of Copyright: Visually Perceptible Ccopies**
17 U.S.C. §401

*STATUTE:* **Notice of Copyright: Omission of Notice on Certain Copies and Phonorecords**
17 U.S.C. §405

The importance of notice of copyright varies depending on when the work was produced. For works produced after the implementation of the Copyright Act of 1976, but before the effective date of the Berne Convention Implementation Act in 1989, the work of authorship is automatically eligible for copyright protection, but *published* works must be accompanied by proper notice. Failure as to notice renders the copyright invalid and leaves the copyright plaintiff without a remedy. For works produced after March 1, 1989, the omission of notice is not fatal to copyright protection.

Instead, the absence of notice may limit the remedies available to a plaintiff successful against an infringer who lacked notice, *see* 17 U.S.C. §405(b) (actual or statutory damages not available). In addition to serving as a deterrent to some infringers, therefore, a copyright notice attached to the work preserves the maximum range of remedies available to the copyright owner.

The continuing importance of copyright notice in the remedial context serves as a reminder of the underlying public policies involved. One policy concerns the interests of the public. Enforcing copyright, or (under current law) the maximum remedies for copyright only for works accompanied by public notice, is fair to defendants accused of infringement and especially to individuals and firms that want to exercise reasonable caution to avoid being accused of copyright infringement. A counterpart policy concerns copyright owners themselves. It is reasonable to believe that an author or publisher who expects to exploit a copyrighted work for profit signals that expectation to society by investing at least a modest effort in protecting the copyright in the first place. This serves to reinforce a distinction between valuable and less valuable works and to encourage copyright owners to invest in works that they believe are worth more.

The Copyright Act of 1909 included elaborate provisions regarding both the form of notice and its placement within a given copyrighted work, meaning that copyright protection could be defeated not only by omission of notice entirely but also by inclusion of a notice that was defective in form or in placement on the work. The 1976 Act relaxed those requirements. *See* 17 U.S.C. §401(b) (describing elements of form of copyright notice). To create an effective notice, the current statute requires only that the notice be placed in a location that gives "reasonable notice" of the claim of copyright. *See* 17 U.S.C. §401(c). In case of omission, however, §405(a) allows a generous five-year period for curing errors regarding notice. (The Copyright Act of 1909 provided that accidental omission of a proper copyright notice would not invalidate the copyright, but it included no provision for curing the omission.)

The consequences of improper notice may be substantial. In *Charles Garnier, Paris v. Andin Int'l, Inc.*, 36 F.3d 1214 (1st Cir. 1994), a jewelry designer sold copyrighted earrings for the first time in 1988 but failed to include notice of copyright on the earrings themselves. Upon discovery of infringement by the defendant, Garnier revised its manufacturing process to include notice, and tried to cure the omission as to earrings in retailers' inventories by sending letters to its 50 largest customers, reminding them of Garnier's copyright interest. Also, for two years prior to that time, Garnier distributed "story cards" to its customers, for distribution with the earrings, that referred to Garnier's copyrighted design. The court held that these efforts to cure the omission of copyright notice were insufficient, and it affirmed a judgment for the accused infringer.

In *Charles Garnier, Paris*, which interprets §405, the questions are twofold. First, when does that five-year period begin to run, and second, what constitute satisfactory efforts to cure? If the cure is both timely and satisfactory, it operates retrospectively, restoring proper notice as of the date the work was initially published. As to the running of the five-year period, there is the concern that a copyright owner might deliberately omit a copyright notice in order to lull potential competitors into infringing activities. In the case of deliberate omission, then, the five-year period begins to run immediately upon publication of the work. As to the adequacy of the cure itself, the copyright owner's effort to provide notice must be merely "reasonable," not perfect, but that effort must both follow discovery of the inadequate notice, and must be directed to affixing notice to copies of the work themselves. Publicly disseminating notice of the copyright interest, as Garnier tried to do, is insufficient both under the language of the statute and as a matter of public policy: Garnier's "story cards" might have provided adequate notice to its retail customers and to individuals who bought Garnier designs through those customers. But if the Garnier earrings were resold later, subsequent purchasers would have no way to be aware of Garnier's copyright claim absent notice affixed to the jewelry.

Determining whether a copyright owner has complied with the relevant notice requirements of the copyright statute is particularly complex when a work embodies previously published material. A modern computer program, for example, may incorporate copyrighted material that was published as part of an earlier version of that same program. Indeed, a modern program may incorporate material from a succession of earlier versions of that program. Determining the copyright status of the most recent version of that program may require independent examination of compliance with notice rules with respect to each earlier version of the work. *See, e.g., Montgomery v. Noga*, 168 F.3d 1282 (11th Cir. 1999) (concluding that later-released version of computer program constituted a copyrightable derivative work even though prior versions fell into the public domain following publication without notice).

## 2. Registration and Deposit

*STATUTE:* **Deposit of Copies or Phonorecords for Library of Congress**
17 U.S.C. §407

*STATUTE:* **Copyright Registration in General**
17 U.S.C. §408

Though both registration and deposit involve submitting copies of the work to appropriate federal offices, they are distinct requirements of the statute. Registration of copyright with the United States Copyright Office (over which the "Register of Copyrights" presides) is permissive. Since the United States joined the Berne Convention in 1989, registration is not required to secure a valid copyright.

However, registration has its benefits, and under some circumstances it is required. First, issuance of a certificate of registration within five years of publication of the work provides prima facie evidence of the validity of the copyright and of the facts stated in the certificate. *See* 17 U.S.C. §410(c). The validity of the copyright may still be challenged, but the defendant in a copyright infringement lawsuit ordinarily will bear the burden of proof on this point. Attorneys' fees and statutory damages (as an alternative to actual damages and lost profits) may be recoverable in copyright infringement lawsuits, but these remedies are barred with respect to infringement that occurred before registration of the copyright. *See* 17 U.S.C. §412. Second, for works created in the United States or by American authors, issuance of a certificate of registration for the work is a jurisdictional prerequisite to filing a lawsuit for copyright infringement. *See* 17 U.S.C. §411(a). The mechanics of registration are simple. Registration requires completion of a simple form, payment of a small fee, and submission of one or more copies of the work being registered (the number and form of the copies will vary somewhat depending on the character of the work). Registration forms are available for download via the Copyright Office website, at *http://www.copyright.gov/*. The Copyright Office does examine applications for registration, but its review is not as searching as the examination process for patents is designed to be, and there is no mechanism for opposing another party's application for registration, as with federally registered trademarks.

The deposit requirement has no function related to copyright validity or infringement actions. Section 407 requires that copies of works published in the United States be deposited with the Copyright Office, "for the use or disposition of the Library of Congress," of which the Copyright Office is a part. The express purpose of this requirement and its predecessors is to enhance the collection of the Library of Congress, thereby making copyrighted works available to the public. In this respect American copyright law has been a spectacular success. Failure to comply with this statute does not affect the validity of the copyright. Instead, the Copyright Office has the authority to levy a small fine.

## 3. Publication

*STATUTE:* **Definition — "Publication"**

17 U.S.C. §101

### ESTATE OF MARTIN LUTHER KING, JR. v. CBS, INC.

**194 F.3d 1211 (11th Cir. 1999)**

Anderson, Chief Judge.

The Estate of Martin Luther King, Jr., Inc. brought this copyright infringement action against CBS, Inc. after CBS produced a video documentary that used, without authorization, portions of civil rights leader Dr. Martin Luther King's famous "I Have a Dream" speech at the March on Washington on August 28, 1963. The district court granted summary judgment to CBS on the ground that Dr. King had engaged in a general publication of the speech, placing it into the public domain. We now reverse.

### I. FACTS

The facts underlying this case form part of our national heritage and are well-known to many Americans. On the afternoon of August 28, 1963, the Southern Christian Leadership Conference ("SCLC") held the March on Washington ("March") to promote the growing civil rights movement. The events of the day were seen and heard by some 200,000 people gathered at the March, and were broadcast live via radio and television to a nationwide audience of millions of viewers. The highlight of the March was a rousing speech that Dr. Martin Luther King, Jr., the SCLC's founder and president, gave in front of the Lincoln Memorial ("Speech"). The Speech contained the famous utterance, "I have a dream...," which became symbolic of the civil rights movement. The SCLC had sought out wide press coverage of the March and the Speech, and these efforts were successful; the Speech was reported in daily newspapers across the country, was broadcast live on radio and television, and was extensively covered on television and radio subsequent to the live broadcast.

On September 30, 1963, approximately one month after the delivery of the Speech, Dr. King took steps to secure federal copyright protection for the Speech under the Copyright Act of 1909, and a certificate of registration of his claim to copyright was issued by the Copyright Office on October 2, 1963. Almost immediately thereafter, Dr. King filed suit in the Southern District of New York to enjoin the unauthorized sale of recordings of the Speech and won a preliminary injunction on December 13, 1963.

For the next twenty years, Dr. King and the Estate enjoyed copyright protection in the Speech and licensed it for a variety of uses, and renewed the copyright when necessary. In 1994, CBS entered into a contract with the Arts & Entertainment Network to produce a historical documentary series entitled "The 20th Century with Mike Wallace." One segment was devoted to "Martin Luther King, Jr. and The March on Washington." That episode contained material filmed by CBS during the March and extensive footage of the Speech (amounting to about 60% of its total content). CBS, however, did not seek the Estate's permission to use the Speech in this manner and refused to pay royalties to the Estate. The instant litigation ensued.

On summary judgment, the district court framed the issue as "whether the public delivery of Dr. King's speech...constituted a general publication of the speech so as to place it in the public domain." 13 F. Supp. 2d at 1351. After discussing the relevant case law, the district court held that Dr. King's "performance coupled with such wide and unlimited reproduction and dissemination as occurred concomitant to Dr. King's speech during the March on Washington can be seen only as a general publication which thrust the speech into the public domain." *Id.* at 1354.[1] Thus, the district court granted CBS's motion for summary judgment. The Estate now appeals to this Court.

## II. DISCUSSION

\* \* \*

Because of the dates of the critical events, the determinative issues in this case are properly analyzed under the Copyright Act of 1909 ("1909 Act"), rather than the Copyright Act of 1976 ("1976 Act") that is currently

---

1. The district court noted that there potentially was some additional evidence of general publication. First, the SCLC published a newsletter of wide circulation containing the full text of the Speech. Second, an advance text of the Speech may have been freely available to the public in a press tent at the March. However, the district court disregarded both of these items of evidence because the procedural posture of the case was one of summary judgment, and "material facts [were] in dispute as to whether the use of Dr. King's speech in the newsletter was authorized and also as to the actual availability of the advance text." 13 F. Supp. 2d at 1353 n. 5.

in effect. The question is whether Dr. King's attempt to obtain statutory copyright protection on September 30, 1963 was effective, or whether it was a nullity because the Speech had already been forfeited to the public domain via a general publication.

Under the regime created by the 1909 Act, an author received state common law protection automatically at the time of creation of a work. This state common law protection persisted until the moment of a general publication. When a general publication occurred, the author either forfeited his work to the public domain, or, if he had therebefore complied with federal statutory requirements, converted his common law copyright into a federal statutory copyright.

In order to soften the hardship of the rule that publication destroys common law rights, courts developed a distinction between a "general publication" and a "limited publication." [*Brown v. Tabb*, 714 F.2d 1088, 1091 (11th Cir. 1983).] Only a general publication divested a common law copyright. A general publication occurred "when a work was made available to members of the public at large without regard to their identity or what they intended to do with the work." *Id.* Conversely, a non-divesting limited publication was one that communicated the contents of a work to a select group and for a limited purpose, and without the right of diffusion, reproduction, distribution or sale. The issue before us is whether Dr. King's delivery of the Speech was a general publication.

Numerous cases stand for the proposition that the performance of a work is not a general publication. *See, e.g., Ferris v. Frohman*, 223 U.S. 424, 433 (1912) ("The public representation of a dramatic composition, not printed and published, does not deprive the owner of his common-law right. . . . [T]he public performance of the play is not an abandonment of it to the public use."); *Nutt v. National Inst. Incorporated for the Improvement of Memory*, 31 F.2d 236, 238 (2d Cir. 1929) ("The author of a literary composition, as a lecture, may profit from public delivery, but that does not constitute the kind of publication which deprives him of the protection of the copyright statute. . . .").

It appears from the case law that a general publication occurs only in two situations. First, a general publication occurs if tangible copies of the work are distributed to the general public in such a manner as allows the public to exercise dominion and control over the work. Second, a general publication may occur if the work is exhibited or displayed in such a manner as to permit unrestricted copying by the general public. However, the case law indicates that restrictions on copying may be implied, and that express limitations in that regard are deemed unnecessary.

The case law indicates that distribution to the news media, as opposed to the general public, for the purpose of enabling the reporting of a contemporary newsworthy event, is only a limited publication. For example, in *Public Affairs Assoc., Inc. v. Rickover*, 284 F.2d 262 (D.C. Cir. 1960), the court said that general publication occurs only when there is "a studied effort not only to secure publicity for the contents of the addresses through the channels of information, but to *go beyond customary sources of press or broadcasting* in distributing the addresses to any interested individual." *Id.* at 270 (emphasis added). Although the *Rickover* court ultimately held that a general publication had occurred, it contrasted the "limited use of the addresses by the press for fair comment," i.e., limited publication, with "the unlimited distribution to anyone who was interested," i.e., general publication. *Id.* at 271. This rule comports with common sense; it does not force an author whose message happens to be newsworthy to choose between obtaining news coverage for his work and preserving his common-law copyright. As the dissenting judge in the *Rickover* case remarked (which remark was entirely consistent with the majority opinion in the case), "[t]here is nothing in the law which would compel this court to deprive the creator of the right to reap financial benefits from these efforts because, at the time of their creation, they had the added virtue of being newsworthy events of immediate public concern." *Rickover,* 284 F.2d at 273 (Washington, J., dissenting).

With the above principles in mind, in the summary judgment posture of this case and on the current state of this record, we are unable to conclude that CBS has demonstrated beyond any genuine issue of material fact that Dr. King, simply through his oral delivery of the Speech, engaged in a general publication making the Speech "available to members of the public at large without regard to their identity or what they intended to do with the work." *Brown,* 714 F.2d at 1091. A performance, no matter how broad the audience, is not a publication; to hold otherwise would be to upset a long line of precedent. This conclusion is not altered by the fact that the Speech was broadcast live to a broad radio and television audience and was the subject of extensive contemporaneous news coverage. We follow the above cited case law indicating that release to the news media for contemporary coverage of a newsworthy event is only a limited publication.[4] . . . .

The district court held that "the circumstances in this case take the work in question outside the parameters of the 'performance is not a publication' doctrine." 13 F. Supp. 2d at 1351. These circumstances included "the overwhelmingly public nature of the speech and the fervent intentions of

---

4. We emphasize the summary judgment posture of this case, which necessitates that we disregard evidence that may be important or even dispositive at trial. In other words, in this summary judgment posture, we consider only the evidence with respect to which there is no genuine issue of material fact. This evidence includes only the fact of the oral delivery of the Speech to a large audience and the fact that the sponsors of the event including Dr. King sought and successfully obtained live broadcasts on radio and television and extensive contemporary coverage in the news media. In this regard, we do not consider at this stage of the litigation two potentially important pieces of evidence brought to our attention by CBS. First, an advance text of the Speech was apparently available in a press tent on the day of the speech. According to an eyewitness affidavit submitted by CBS, members of the public at large — not merely the press — were permitted access to the press tent and were given copies of the advance text. However, the Estate has proffered affidavits which contradict the statements of the CBS witness, and suggest that access was controlled by the SCLC within reasonable means. Moreover, the Estate argues that much of the content of the Speech was generated extemporaneously by Dr. King and was not contained in this advance text — an argument that we do not consider but that can be explored by the district court. Finding genuine issues of material fact with respect to the availability of the advance text to the general public, the district court disregarded CBS's allegations in this regard. We agree, and do likewise.

Second, CBS has produced a September 1963 issue of the SCLC's newsletter in which the text of the Speech was reprinted in its entirety, with no copyright notice. The newsletter was widely circulated to the general public. Indeed, at oral argument, the Estate conceded that this reprinting of the Speech and wide distribution of the newsletter would constitute a general publication, if it were authorized by Dr. King. However, the Estate has raised the issue that Dr. King did not authorize this reprinting and distribution of the Speech. Finding genuine issues of fact in this regard, the district court disregarded this evidence. We agree, and do likewise. . . .

the March organizers to draw press attention." *Id.* Certainly, the Speech was one of a kind—a unique event in history. However, the features that make the Speech unique—e.g., the huge audience and the Speech's significance in terms of newsworthiness and history—are features that, according to the case law, are not significant in the general versus limited publication analysis. With respect to the huge audience, the case law indicates that the general publication issue depends, not on the number of people involved, but rather on the fact that the work is made available to the public without regard to who they are or what they propose to do with it. *See Brown v. Tabb,* 714 F.2d 1088, 1091-92 (11th Cir. 1983). For this proposition, *Brown* cited [*Burke v. National Broadcasting Co., Inc.,* 598 F.2d 688 (1st Cir. 1979)] at 691 ("[G]eneral publication depends on the author making the work available to those interested, and not on the number of people who actually express an interest.")....In the instant case, the district court acknowledged that "[t]he size of the audience before which a work is performed cannot be the basis for a court's finding that a general publication has occurred." 13 F. Supp. 2d at 1352.

With respect to the significance of the Speech in terms of newsworthiness and history, the case law again suggests that this feature should not play a substantial role in the analysis. As noted above, the D.C. Circuit in *Rickover* indicated that the wide press distribution of the speeches at issue there would not alone have constituted a general publication....Also supporting this proposition is the case law above cited to the effect that size of the audience is not significant.

\* \* \*

Because there exist genuine issues of material fact as to whether a general publication occurred, we must reverse the district court's grant of summary judgment for CBS. It would be inappropriate for us to address CBS's other arguments, e.g., fair use and the First Amendment, because the district court did not address them, and because the relevant facts may not yet be fully developed. Of course, we express no opinion on the eventual merits of this litigation. The judgment of the district court is reversed and remanded for further proceedings not inconsistent with this opinion.

[Opinion of COOK, Senior District Judge, concurring in part and dissenting in part, and opinion of RONEY, Senior Circuit Judge, dissenting, omitted.]

## Comments

1. *The Relevance of "Publication" under the 1976 Act.* The court in *Estate of Martin Luther King* reviews and applies the common law meaning of "publication" because that is the law that would have applied to Dr. King at the time that he prepared and delivered the speech, in 1963. The Copyright Act of 1976 abolished the distinction between "published" and "unpublished" works of authorship for purposes of obtaining copyright protection. Today, all creative works fixed in a tangible medium are automatically protected by copyright law, whether they are published or not. "Publication" of a work retains some remaining

significance under the 1976 Act, however, and the statute includes a definition of "publication" in §101 that closely tracks the common law meaning described in *Estate of Martin Luther King.* Works created between January 1, 1978 (the effective date of the 1976 Act) and March 1, 1989 (when the United States fully acceded to the Berne Convention) had to include a proper copyright notice to receive copyright protection—but only if they were published. Unpublished works created during that period received copyright protection even in the absence of notice.

2. *The Copyrightability of "I Have a Dream."* If "I Have a Dream" was never published, how could it have been protected by the federal copyright system? The answer is that the Copyright Act of 1909 included a special provision for federal copyright registration of certain unpublished works, including "lectures" and other works "not reproduced for sale." Copyright Act of 1909, §12. Dr. King promptly registered "I Have a Dream" with the Copyright Office, and the speech was therefore entitled to full protection in copyright against unauthorized reproduction.

3. *Widespread Availability of "Published" Works.* Paradoxically, the court can conclude that Dr. King's speech was not "published," given the specialized meaning given that term in copyright law, despite the fact that the speech was heard both by hundreds of thousands of people who were present at its delivery, and by millions more who were listening by radio and television. The speech has not achieved its iconic, newsworthy status in retrospect. It was recognized at the time as a signal moment in the Civil Rights Movement of the 1960s. Nonetheless, the court's opinion accurately tracks the basic framework of publication jurisprudence. It is widely accepted that performance of a work of authorship does not constitute "publication" of any works of authorship on which that performance is based. *See* Copyright Act of 1909, §1(d). Performance of a play does not constitute "publication" of the play; performance of a motion picture (such as by showing it in a movie theater) does not constitute "publication" of the underlying screenplay; performance of a song (via live or radio performance) does not constitute "publication" of the underlying musical composition. Distribution of phonorecords does not publish the musical works on which the recordings are based. *See ABKCO Music, Inc. v. LaVere,* 217 F.3d 684 (9th Cir. 2000). On the other hand, publication of a derivative work that is based on an unpublished work, such as a motion picture based on an unpublished screenplay, publishes as much of the underlying work as is incorporated into the published version. *See Batjac Productions Inc. v. GoodTimes Home Video Corp.,* 160 F.3d 1223 (9th Cir. 1998).

4. *General Publication and Limited Publication.* The consequences of publication-without-notice were dramatic. Since notice was omitted, the work was no longer eligible for federal copyright protection. Since the work was published, the work was no longer eligible for common law copyright protection. In effect, the work fell into the public domain. In light of those consequences, courts developed methods of mitigating those effects. One of the most important methods is illustrated in *Estate of Martin Luther King*: the distinction between general publication and

limited publication. "Limited publication" is a misnomer, since legally speaking, "limited" publication — distribution of copies of the work to a limited audience, and for a limited purpose — is equated with no publication at all. This concept enabled authors to distribute modest numbers of a work without worrying about the presence or form of a copyright notice. "General publication" is the term applied to what the law treats as "publication," distribution of copies through means broad enough to require proper notice.

5. *Investing Publication and Divesting Publication.* A second technique for moderating the impact of the doctrine of publication was to distinguish between "investing" publication and "divesting" publication. Whether or not a work was "published" for copyright purposes could arise in one of two ways. In the first case, an accused infringer might allege that a work had been published, but the author or publisher failed to include an appropriate notice. This scenario was called "divesting" publication, because if publication did in fact occur, the omission of notice meant that the author was divested of a copyright. In the second case, an author or publisher who distributed a work to a narrow audience, but with a proper notice, might argue that a defendant had infringed. This scenario was called "investing" publication, because the plaintiff argued that publication did in fact occur, triggering the existence of federal copyright protection. On the whole, courts tended to apply more lenient standards to the publication issue when the question was "investing" publication (so that authors or publishers would obtain valid copyrights), and stricter standards to the issue when the question was "divesting" publication (so that authors and publishers would be less likely to lose copyrights). *See American Vitagraph, Inc. v. Levy*, 659 F.2d 1023 (9th Cir. 1981).

# E. OWNERSHIP

*STATUTE:* **Ownership of Copyright**
17 U.S.C. §201

Section 201 confirms what has been implicit in the discussion above of creativity and originality: Ownership of a copyright vests immediately and automatically in the author of a copyrightable work. In the case of individual authors, that proposition is relatively straightforward and intuitive; more complex problems arise in the context of collaborative authorship, and authorship in the context of structured enterprises — firms that employ people to produce creative work.

Application of the baseline individual authorship principle is not unproblematic, however. On occasion, disputes over copyright ownership arise between individuals who assert their claim based on their "creative" contribution to a problem, as against individuals who actually created a work using "creative" input from others. Generally, courts have held that copyright in a work of authorship belongs to the individual responsible for its "creative" content, and not to a party whose contribution was to take that "creative" input and convert it, through some mechanical process, into fixed form. For example, in *Lindsay v. The Wrecked and Abandoned Vessel*

*R.M.S. Titanic,* 1999 WL 816163, 52 U.S.P.Q.2d 1609 (S.D.N.Y., Oct 13, 1999), the plaintiff was a filmmaker who asserted ownership of copyright in documentary film footage shot of the wreck of the *Titanic,* against the company that owned salvage rights to the vessel and that contracted with the plaintiff to produce the film. The salvage firm moved to dismiss the plaintiff's lawsuit, and the court denied the motion, noting that "where a plaintiff alleges that he exercised such a high degree of control over a film operation — including the type and amount of lighting used, the specific camera angles to be employed, and other detail-intensive artistic elements of a film — such that the final product duplicates his conceptions and visions of what the film should look like, the plaintiff may be said to be an 'author' within the meaning of the Copyright Act." *See also Andrien v. Southern Ocean County Chamber of Commerce,* 927 F.2d 132, 135 (3d Cir. 1991) ("a party can be considered an author when his or her expression of an idea is transposed by mechanical or rote transcription into tangible form under the authority of the party").

Frequently, however, original works of authorship are produced by groups of people rather than by individuals. The Copyright Act addresses these situations using two basic frameworks, one for collaborations among creative individuals working essentially side by side, and the second for works produced by employees and others who are hired or commissioned to produce copyrightable works. The first is discussed in Section E.1, below, and the second is discussed in Section E.2.

## 1. Collaboration and Joint Works

*STATUTE:* **Definition — "Joint Work"**
17 U.S.C. §101

### AALMUHAMMED v. LEE
**202 F.3d 1227 (9th Cir. 2000)**

KLEINFELD, Circuit Judge.

This is a copyright case involving a claim of coauthorship of the movie *Malcolm X.* We reject the "joint work" claim but remand for further proceedings on a quantum meruit claim.

### I. FACTS

In 1991, Warner Brothers contracted with Spike Lee and his production companies to make the movie *Malcolm X,* to be based on the book, *The Autobiography of Malcolm X.* Lee co-wrote the screenplay, directed, and co-produced the movie, which starred Denzel Washington as Malcolm X. Washington asked Jefri Aalmuhammed to assist him in his preparation for the starring role because Aalmuhammed knew a great deal about Malcolm X and Islam. Aalmuhammed, a devout Muslim, was particularly knowledgeable about the life of Malcolm X, having previously written, directed, and produced a documentary film about Malcolm X.

Aalmuhammed joined Washington on the movie set. The movie was filmed in the New York metropolitan area and Egypt. Aalmuhammed presented evidence that his involvement in making the movie was very extensive. He reviewed the shooting script for Spike Lee and Denzel Washington and suggested extensive script revisions. Some of his script revisions were included in the released version of the film; others were filmed but not included in the released version. Most of the revisions Aalmuhammed made were to ensure the religious and historical accuracy and authenticity of scenes depicting Malcolm X's religious conversion and pilgrimage to Mecca.

Aalmuhammed submitted evidence that he directed Denzel Washington and other actors while on the set, created at least two entire scenes with new characters, translated Arabic into English for subtitles, supplied his own voice for voice-overs, selected the proper prayers and religious practices for the characters, and edited parts of the movie during post production. Washington testified in his deposition that Aalmuhammed's contribution to the movie was "great" because he "helped to rewrite, to make more authentic." Once production ended, Aalmuhammed met with numerous Islamic organizations to persuade them that the movie was an accurate depiction of Malcolm X's life.

Aalmuhammed never had a written contract with Warner Brothers, Lee, or Lee's production companies, but he expected Lee to compensate him for his work. He did not intend to work and bear his expenses in New York and Egypt gratuitously. Aalmuhammed ultimately received a check for $25,000 from Lee, which he cashed, and a check for $100,000 from Washington, which he did not cash.

During the summer before *Malcolm X*'s November 1992 release, Aalmuhammed asked for a writing credit as a co-writer of the film, but was turned down. When the film was released, it credited Aalmuhammed only as an "Islamic Technical Consultant," far down the list. In November 1995, Aalmuhammed applied for a copyright with the U.S. Copyright Office, claiming he was a co-creator, co-writer, and co-director of the movie. The Copyright Office issued him a "Certificate of Registration," but advised him in a letter that his "claims conflict with previous registrations" of the film.

On November 17, 1995, Aalmuhammed filed a complaint against Spike Lee, his production companies, and Warner Brothers (collectively "Lee"), as well as Largo International, N.V., and Largo Entertainment, Inc. (collectively "Largo"), and Victor Company of Japan and JVC Entertainment, Inc. (collectively "Victor"). The suit sought declaratory relief and an accounting under the Copyright Act. In addition, the complaint alleged breach of implied contract, quantum meruit, and unjust enrichment, and federal (Lanham Act) and state unfair competition claims. The district court dismissed some of the claims under Rule 12(b)(6) and the rest on summary judgment.

## II. ANALYSIS

### A. COPYRIGHT CLAIM

Aalmuhammed claimed that the movie *Malcolm X* was a "joint work" of which he was an author, thus making him a co-owner of the copyright. He sought a declaratory judgment to that effect, and an accounting for profits. He is not claiming copyright merely in what he wrote or contributed, but rather in the whole work, as a co-author of a "joint work." The district court granted defendants summary judgment against Mr. Aalmuhammed's copyright claims. We review de novo.

* * *

Aalmuhammed argues that he established a genuine issue of fact as to whether he was an author of a "joint work," *Malcolm X*. The Copyright Act does not define "author," but it does define "joint work":

> A "joint work" is a work prepared by two or more authors with the intention that their contributions be merged into inseparable or interdependent parts of a unitary whole.

... The statutory language establishes that for a work to be a "joint work" there must be (1) a copyrightable work, (2) two or more "authors," and (3) the authors must intend their contributions be merged into inseparable or interdependent parts of a unitary whole. A "joint work" in this circuit "requires each author to make an independently copyrightable contribution" to the disputed work.[9] *Malcolm X* is a copyrightable work, and it is undisputed that the movie was intended by everyone involved with it to be a unitary whole. It is also undisputed that Aalmuhammed made substantial and valuable contributions to the movie, including technical help, such as speaking Arabic to the persons in charge of the mosque in Egypt, scholarly and creative help, such as teaching the actors how to pray properly as Muslims, and script changes to add verisimilitude to the religious aspects of the movie. Speaking Arabic to persons in charge of the mosque, however, does not result in a copyrightable contribution to the motion picture. Coaching of actors, to be copyrightable, must be turned into an expression in a form subject to copyright. The same may be said for many of Aalmuhammed's other activities. Aalmuhammed has, however, submitted evidence that he rewrote several specific passages of dialogue that appeared in *Malcolm X*, and that he wrote scenes relating to Malcolm X's Hajj pilgrimage that were enacted in the movie. If Aalmuhammed's evidence is accepted, as it must be on summary judgment, these items would have been independently copyrightable. Aalmuhammed, therefore, has presented a genuine issue of fact as to whether he made a copyrightable contribution. All persons involved intended that Aalmuhammed's contributions would be merged into interdependent parts of the movie as a unitary whole. Aalmuhammed maintains that he has shown a genuine issue of fact for each element of a "joint work."

But there is another element to a "joint work." A "joint work" includes "two or more authors."[11] Aalmuhammed established that he contributed substantially to the film, but not that he was one of its "authors." We hold that authorship is required under the statutory definition of a joint work, and that authorship is not the same thing as making a valuable and copyrightable contribution. We recognize that a contributor of an expression may be deemed to be the "author" of that expression for purposes of determining whether it is independently copyrightable. The issue we

9. *Ashton-Tate Corp. v. Ross*, 916 F.2d 516, 521 (9th Cir. 1990).
11. 17 U.S.C. §101.

deal with is a different and larger one: is the contributor an author of the joint work within the meaning of 17 U.S.C. §101.

By statutory definition, a "joint work" requires "two or more authors." The word "author" is taken from the traditional activity of one person sitting at a desk with a pen and writing something for publication. It is relatively easy to apply the word "author" to a novel. It is also easy to apply the word to two people who work together in a fairly traditional pen-and-ink way, like, perhaps, Gilbert and Sullivan. In the song, "I Am the Very Model of a Modern Major General," Gilbert's words and Sullivan's tune are inseparable, and anyone who has heard the song knows that it owes its existence to both men, Sir William Gilbert and Sir Arthur Sullivan, as its creative originator. But as the number of contributors grows and the work itself becomes less the product of one or two individuals who create it without much help, the word is harder to apply.

Who, in the absence of contract, can be considered an author of a movie? The word is traditionally used to mean the originator or the person who causes something to come into being, or even the first cause, as when Chaucer refers to the "Author of Nature." For a movie, that might be the producer who raises the money. Eisenstein thought the author of a movie was the editor. The "auteur" theory suggests that it might be the director, at least if the director is able to impose his artistic judgments on the film. Traditionally, by analogy to books, the author was regarded as the person who writes the screenplay, but often a movie reflects the work of many screenwriters. Grenier suggests that the person with creative control tends to be the person in whose name the money is raised, perhaps a star, perhaps the director, perhaps the producer, with control gravitating to the star as the financial investment in scenes already shot grows.[13] Where the visual aspect of the movie is especially important, the chief cinematographer might be regarded as the author. And for, say, a Disney animated movie like "The Jungle Book," it might perhaps be the animators and the composers of the music.

The Supreme Court dealt with the problem of defining "author" in new media in *Burrow-Giles Lithographic Co. v. Sarony* [111 U.S. 53 (1884)]. The question there was, who is the author of a photograph: the person who sets it up and snaps the shutter, or the person who makes the lithograph from it. Oscar Wilde, the person whose picture was at issue, doubtless offered some creative advice as well. The Court decided that the photographer was the author, quoting various English authorities: "the person who has superintended the arrangement, who has actually formed the picture by putting the persons in position, and arranging the place where the people are to be — the man who is the effective cause of that"; "'author' involves originating, making, producing, as the inventive or master mind, the thing which is to be protected"; "the man who really represents, creates, or gives effect to the idea, fancy, or imagination." The Court said that an "author," in the sense that the Founding Fathers used the term in the Constitution, was "'he to whom anything owes its origin; originator; maker; one who completes a work of science or literature.'"

---

13. *See* Richard Grenier, *Capturing the Culture*, 206-07 (1991).

Answering a different question, what is a copyrightable "work," as opposed to who is the "author," the Supreme Court held in *Feist Publications* [*v. Rural Telephone Service Co., Inc.,* 499 U.S. 340 (1991)] that "some minimal level of creativity" or "originality" suffices. But that measure of a "work" would be too broad and indeterminate to be useful if applied to determine who are "authors" of a movie. So many people might qualify as an "author" if the question were limited to whether they made a substantial creative contribution that that test would not distinguish one from another. Everyone from the producer and director to casting director, costumer, hairstylist, and "best boy" gets listed in the movie credits because all of their creative contributions really do matter. It is striking in *Malcolm X* how much the person who controlled the hue of the lighting contributed, yet no one would use the word "author" to denote that individual's relationship to the movie. A creative contribution does not suffice to establish authorship of the movie.

*Burrow-Giles*, in defining "author," requires more than a minimal creative or original contribution to the work. *Burrow-Giles* is still good law, and was recently reaffirmed in *Feist Publications*. *Burrow-Giles* and *Feist Publications* answer two distinct questions: who is an author, and what is a copyrightable work. *Burrow-Giles* defines author as the person to whom the work owes its origin and who superintended the whole work, the "master mind."[22] In a movie this definition, in the absence of a contract to the contrary, would generally limit authorship to someone at the top of the screen credits, sometimes the producer, sometimes the director, possibly the star, or the screenwriter — someone who has artistic control. After all, in *Burrow-Giles* the lithographer made a substantial copyrightable creative contribution, and so did the person who posed, Oscar Wilde, but the Court held that the photographer was the author.

The Second and Seventh Circuits have likewise concluded that contribution of independently copyrightable material to a work intended to be an inseparable whole will not suffice to establish authorship of a joint work.[24] Although the Second and Seventh Circuits do not base their decisions on the word "authors" in the statute, the practical results they reach are consistent with ours. These circuits have held that a person claiming to be an author of a joint work must prove that both parties intended each other to be joint authors. In determining whether the parties have the intent to be joint authors, the Second Circuit looks at who has decision making authority, how the parties bill themselves, and other evidence.

In *Thomson v. Larson*, an off-Broadway playwright had created a modern version of *La Boheme*, and had been adamant throughout its creation on being the sole author. He hired a drama professor for "dramaturgical assistance and research," agreeing to credit her as "dramaturg" but not author, but saying nothing about "joint work" or copyright.[28] The playwright tragically died immediately after the final dress rehearsal, just before his play became the tremendous Broadway hit, *Rent*. The dramaturg

---

22. *Burrow-Giles,* 111 U.S. at 61 (quoting *Nottage v. Jackson,* 11 Q.B.D. 627 (1883)).

24. *Thomson v. Larson,* 147 F.3d 195, (2d Cir. 1998); *Erickson v. Trinity Theatre, Inc.,* 13 F.3d 1061 (7th Cir. 1994); *Childress v. Taylor,* 945 F.2d 500 (2d Cir. 1991).

28. *Thomson v. Larson,* 147 F.3d 195, 197 (2d Cir. 1998).

then sued his estate for a declaratory judgment that she was an author of *Rent* as a "joint work," and for an accounting. The Second Circuit noted that the dramaturg had no decision making authority, had neither sought nor was billed as a co-author, and that the defendant entered into contracts as the sole author. On this reasoning, the Second Circuit held that there was no intent to be joint authors by the putative parties and therefore it was not a joint work.

Considering *Burrow-Giles*, the recent cases on joint works (especially the thoughtful opinion in *Thomson v. Larson*), and the Gilbert and Sullivan example, several factors suggest themselves as among the criteria for joint authorship, in the absence of contract. First, an author "superintend[s]" the work by exercising control. This will likely be a person "who has actually formed the picture by putting the persons in position, and arranging the place where the people are to be-the man who is the effective cause of that,"[37] or "the inventive or master mind" who "creates, or gives effect to the idea."[38] Second, putative coauthors make objective manifestations of a shared intent to be coauthors, as by denoting the authorship of *The Pirates of Penzance* as "Gilbert and Sullivan." We say objective manifestations because, were the mutual intent to be determined by subjective intent, it could become an instrument of fraud, were one coauthor to hide from the other an intention to take sole credit for the work. Third, the audience appeal of the work turns on both contributions and "the share of each in its success cannot be appraised."[40] Control in many cases will be the most important factor.

The best objective manifestation of a shared intent, of course, is a contract saying that the parties intend to be or not to be co-authors. In the absence of a contract, the inquiry must of necessity focus on the facts. The factors articulated in this decision and the Second and Seventh Circuit decisions cannot be reduced to a rigid formula, because the creative relationships to which they apply vary too much. Different people do creative work together in different ways, and even among the same people working together the relationship may change over time as the work proceeds.

Aalmuhammed did not at any time have superintendence of the work. Warner Brothers and Spike Lee controlled it. Aalmuhammed was not the person "who has actually formed the picture by putting the persons in position, and arranging the place...."[42] Spike Lee was, so far as we can tell from the record. Aalmuhammed, like Larson's dramaturg, could make extremely helpful recommendations, but Spike Lee was not bound to accept any of them, and the work would not benefit in the slightest unless Spike Lee chose to accept them. Aalmuhammed lacked control over the work, and absence of control is strong evidence of the absence of co-authorship.

Also, neither Aalmuhammed, nor Spike Lee, nor Warner Brothers, made any objective manifestations of an intent to be coauthors. Warner

37. *Burrow-Giles v. Sarony*, 111 U.S. at 61 (quoting *Nottage v. Jackson*, 11 Q.B. Div. 627 (1883)).
38. *Id.*
40. *Edward B. Marks Music Corp. v. Jerry Vogel Music Co., Inc.*, 140 F.2d 266, 267 (2d Cir. 1944) (Hand, J.), *modified*, 140 F.2d 268 (1944).
42. *Burrow-Giles v. Sarony*, 111 U.S. 53, 61 (1883).

Brothers required Spike Lee to sign a "work for hire" agreement, so that even Lee would not be a co-author and co-owner with Warner Brothers. It would be illogical to conclude that Warner Brothers, while not wanting to permit Lee to own the copyright, intended to share ownership with individuals like Aalmuhammed who worked under Lee's control, especially ones who at the time had made known no claim to the role of co-author. No one, including Aalmuhammed, made any indication to anyone prior to litigation that Aalmuhammed was intended to be a co-author and co-owner.

Aalmuhammed offered no evidence that he was the "inventive or master mind" of the movie. He was the author of another less widely known documentary about Malcolm X, but was not the master of this one. What Aalmuhammed's evidence showed, and all it showed, was that, subject to Spike Lee's authority to accept them, he made very valuable contributions to the movie. That is not enough for co-authorship of a joint work.

The Constitution establishes the social policy that our construction of the statutory term "authors" carries out. The Founding Fathers gave Congress the power to give authors copyrights in order "[t]o promote the progress of Science and useful arts." Progress would be retarded rather than promoted, if an author could not consult with others and adopt their useful suggestions without sacrificing sole ownership of the work. Too open a definition of author would compel authors to insulate themselves and maintain ignorance of the contributions others might make. Spike Lee could not consult a scholarly Muslim to make a movie about a religious conversion to Islam, and the arts would be the poorer for that.

\* \* \*

Because the record before the district court established no genuine issue of fact as to Aalmuhammed's co-authorship of *Malcolm X* as a joint work, the district court correctly granted summary judgment dismissing his claims for declaratory judgment and an accounting resting on co-authorship.

\* \* \*

## Comments

*1. Who is an Author?* Recall that "authorship," under *Feist*, requires only that the "author" contribute independently generated material that manifests "minimal" creativity. If that standard were applied to Aalmuhammed's claim, it seems likely that Aalmuhammed would have a valid claim of copyright, at least with respect to material that he created. Joint authorship appears to require more, largely because a successful claim of joint authorship leads to a finding that each joint author co-owns an undivided, equal share of the entire copyright. If Aalmuhammed were to prove that he was a joint author of *Malcolm X,* in other words, he would co-own a 50 percent share (with Warner Brothers) of the copyright in the entire film. Joint authors in copyright, like joint tenants in property law, have independent authority to rent or license the work, subject to a duty to account to other joint owners for their respective shares of any income. In joint authorship cases, therefore, courts are often leery of granting joint authorship status to a party in the absence of clear evidence that the parties intended to stand in a joint ownership relationship. In *Thomson v. Larson*, 147 F.3d 195 (2d Cir. 1998), cited by the *Aalmuhammed* court, the Second Circuit looked to "objective" indications of the parties' intent to become joint authors. In *Aalmuhammed*, the court looks not only for objective evidence of intent but also for evidence that Aalmuhammed qualifies as an "author" with "superintendence of the work," that is, is in a position of supreme creative authority over the composition of the work. Since Aalmuhammed lacks that status, he cannot be a joint author, notwithstanding the creativity of his independent contribution to the film.

2. *Authorship and Hollywood.* Courts may resist the notion that casual or minimal creative contributions to a collaborative work render all contributors "joint authors" for copyright purposes, but does the "superintendence" standard that the court adopts in *Aalmuhammed* make it *too* difficult for an excluded collaborator to obtain fair recognition in copyright for a contribution to a large project? How many "superintendents" of a work can there be? In the film industry, this question is typically worked out carefully before production of a movie starts. By contract, all hands on the project typically waive any intellectual property claims to the final product, and copyright usually ends up with the production company that leads the financing for the project. On the one hand, this seems entirely fair and appropriate, and consistent with the outcome in *Aalmuhammed*: Given the hundreds of actors and other creative contributors to the typical film, it would be enormously disruptive for any given supporting player to be able to make a credible claim of "joint authorship" that could interfere with the anticipated profitability of the final film. On the other hand, note that neither Warner Brothers nor Spike Lee required that Aalmuhammed sign an agreement waiving any copyright claim, though they presumably had every opportunity to do so. As a matter of public policy, it might be argued that ruling for Aalmuhammed, while disruptive to the marketing of *Malcolm X*, would teach the rest of Hollywood a valuable lesson regarding the importance of obtaining appropriate releases. And in fact, audio-visual works like motion pictures are recognized as contractual "works made for hire," discussed in the next part, below.

3. *The Real Creative Mastermind.* The court intimates that Warner Brothers, which contracted with Spike Lee to make *Malcolm X*, is the "inventive or master mind" of the movie, as Warner Brothers held the purse strings for the film's budget. This is certainly true up to a point, but it also seems to be at odds with the court's emphasis on *creative* supervision of the work. Spike Lee, of course, has earned a prized reputation for being one of the most innovative and creatively independent filmmakers of the present generation. If *Malcolm X* had a *creative* mastermind, certainly Spike Lee, despite his having to answer to Warner Brothers, deserves that title.

4. *Recognizing Creativity versus Creating Incentives to Produce Complex Works.* The court's standard highlights a pair of divisions in both law and practice. The first is between economic control of a complex project and

creative control of that project. If those two sources of control are located in different places, as they are here (and as they are frequently, in a variety of creative domains), which should the law prefer in allocating copyright ownership? Locating copyright in the creator is consistent with copyright traditions that focus on *creative* incentives; locating copyright in the financier is consistent with copyright traditions that focus on *economic* incentives. The second, related distinction is between actual creative contributions to a collaborative project, and nominal or formal supervision and control over that project. Again, to the extent that these two functions do not reside in one place or person, which should the court prefer? Preferring the actual creative contributor is consistent with traditional support for the producer of original output; preferring the supervisor recognizes the reality that production of large creative projects requires encouraging people to undertake possibly risky coordination activities. Even if Warner Brothers had not been the producer of *Malcolm X*, and Spike Lee had been the legal "creative mastermind," it was impossible for Lee to make every creative decision on that film. Film aficionados may recognize Spike Lee as a creative genius, but in fact his "creativity" lies partly in his ability to supervise the creative work of others.

## Problem

**6-5.** Edgar and Johnny produce comic books. Edgar writes scripts; Johnny also writes scripts, but he also illustrates and publishes the books. In 1995, shortly after forming his own publishing company, Johnny began publishing a series of comic books titled "Hellfire," which he wrote and illustrated himself. The scripts for Hellfire were criticized for being weak, so Johnny invited Edgar, a freelance comic book scriptwriter, to write four scripts for the series. The two friends did not sign a written agreement. Their arrangement was entirely oral. In his scripts for Hellfire, Edgar introduced two new characters suggested by Johnny: a sage, which Edgar's scripts called Rex, and an evil wizard, which Edgar called Wanda. Before Edgar wrote the scripts, Johnny described the characters he wanted: The sage should appear to be a drunken bum, who is wasting away in an alley, but who turns out to be a wise seer who can guide the main character, Hellfire, through various challenges by teaching him about his special powers. Johnny described the evil wizard as a character from centuries before the present day, who encounters an ancestor of Hellfire by appearing as a damsel in distress before revealing her true character, then confronting and being killed by Hellfire. Edgar's scripts incorporated these suggestions; Johnny inked and colored the characters along with the rest of the books, and published them. After comic books based on Edgar's four scripts were complete, Edgar and Johnny had a falling out, and they stopped working together. Johnny continued to publish the Hellfire series, however, and the series continued to incorporate the Rex and Wanda characters. Edgar sued Johnny for an accounting of profits from later books that used those characters. Are Edgar and Johnny joint authors of the Rex and Wanda characters? *See Gaiman v. McFarlane*, 360 F.3d 644 (7th Cir. 2004).

## 2. Works Made for Hire

STATUTE: Definitions — "Work Made for Hire"
17 U.S.C. §101

### COMMUNITY FOR CREATIVE NON-VIOLENCE v. REID

#### 490 U.S. 730 (1989)

Justice MARSHALL delivered the opinion of the Court.

In this case, an artist and the organization that hired him to produce a sculpture contest the ownership of the copyright in that work. To resolve this dispute, we must construe the "work made for hire" provisions of the Copyright Act of 1976 (Act or 1976 Act), 17 U.S.C. §§101 and 201(b), and in particular, the provision in §101, which defines as a "work made for hire" a "work prepared by an employee within the scope of his or her employment" (hereinafter §101(1)).

### I

Petitioners are the Community for Creative Non-Violence (CCNV), a nonprofit unincorporated association dedicated to eliminating homelessness in America, and Mitch Snyder, a member and trustee of CCNV. In the fall of 1985, CCNV decided to participate in the annual Christmastime Pageant of Peace in Washington, D.C., by sponsoring a display to dramatize the plight of the homeless. As the District Court recounted:

> "Snyder and fellow CCNV members conceived the idea for the nature of the display: a sculpture of a modern Nativity scene in which, in lieu of the traditional Holy Family, the two adult figures and the infant would appear as contemporary homeless people huddled on a streetside steam grate. The family was to be black (most of the homeless in Washington being black); the figures were to be life-sized, and the steam grate would be positioned atop a platform 'pedestal,' or base, within which special-effects equipment would be enclosed to emit simulated 'steam' through the grid to swirl about the figures. They also settled upon a title for the work — 'Third World America' — and a legend for the pedestal: 'and still there is no room at the inn.'"
> 652 F. Supp. 1453, 1454 (DC 1987).

Snyder made inquiries to locate an artist to produce the sculpture. He was referred to respondent James Earl Reid, a Baltimore, Maryland, sculptor. In the course of two telephone calls, Reid agreed to sculpt the three human figures. CCNV agreed to make the steam grate and pedestal for the statue. Reid proposed that the work be cast in bronze, at a total cost of approximately $100,000 and taking six to eight months to complete. Snyder rejected that proposal because CCNV did not have sufficient funds, and because the statue had to be completed by December 12 to be included in the pageant. Reid then suggested, and Snyder agreed, that the sculpture would be made of a material known as "Design Cast 62," a synthetic substance that could meet CCNV's monetary and time constraints, could be tinted to resemble bronze, and could withstand the elements. The parties agreed that the project would cost no more than $15,000, not including

Reid's services, which he offered to donate. The parties did not sign a written agreement. Neither party mentioned copyright.

After Reid received an advance of $3,000, he made several sketches of figures in various poses. At Snyder's request, Reid sent CCNV a sketch of a proposed sculpture showing the family in a crèche like setting: the mother seated, cradling a baby in her lap; the father standing behind her, bending over her shoulder to touch the baby's foot. Reid testified that Snyder asked for the sketch to use in raising funds for the sculpture. Snyder testified that it was also for his approval. Reid sought a black family to serve as a model for the sculpture. Upon Snyder's suggestion, Reid visited a family living at CCNV's Washington shelter but decided that only their newly born child was a suitable model. While Reid was in Washington, Snyder took him to see homeless people living on the streets. Snyder pointed out that they tended to recline on steam grates, rather than sit or stand, in order to warm their bodies. From that time on, Reid's sketches contained only reclining figures.

Throughout November and the first two weeks of December 1985, Reid worked exclusively on the statue, assisted at various times by a dozen different people who were paid with funds provided in installments by CCNV. On a number of occasions, CCNV members visited Reid to check on his progress and to coordinate CCNV's construction of the base. CCNV rejected Reid's proposal to use suitcases or shopping bags to hold the family's personal belongings, insisting instead on a shopping cart. Reid and CCNV members did not discuss copyright ownership on any of these visits.

On December 24, 1985, 12 days after the agreed-upon date, Reid delivered the completed statue to Washington. There it was joined to the steam grate and pedestal prepared by CCNV and placed on display near the site of the pageant. Snyder paid Reid the final installment of the $15,000. The statue remained on display for a month. In late January 1986, CCNV members returned it to Reid's studio in Baltimore for minor repairs. Several weeks later, Snyder began making plans to take the statue on a tour of several cities to raise money for the homeless. Reid objected, contending that the Design Cast 62 material was not strong enough to withstand the ambitious itinerary. He urged CCNV to cast the statue in bronze at a cost of $35,000, or to create a master mold at a cost of $5,000. Snyder declined to spend more of CCNV's money on the project.

In March 1986, Snyder asked Reid to return the sculpture. Reid refused. He then filed a certificate of copyright registration for "Third World

America" in his name and announced plans to take the sculpture on a more modest tour than the one CCNV had proposed. Snyder, acting in his capacity as CCNV's trustee, immediately filed a competing certificate of copyright registration.

Snyder and CCNV then commenced this action against Reid and his photographer, Ronald Purtee, seeking return of the sculpture and a determination of copyright ownership. The District Court granted a preliminary injunction, ordering the sculpture's return. After a 2-day bench trial, the District Court declared that "Third World America" was a "work made for hire" under §101 of the Copyright Act and that Snyder, as trustee for CCNV, was the exclusive owner of the copyright in the sculpture. 652 F. Supp., at 1457. The court reasoned that Reid had been an "employee" of CCNV within the meaning of §101(1) because CCNV was the motivating force in the statue's production. Snyder and other CCNV members, the court explained, "conceived the idea of a contemporary Nativity scene to contrast with the national celebration of the season," and "directed enough of [Reid's] effort to assure that, in the end, he had produced what they, not he, wanted." *Id.*, at 1456.

The Court of Appeals for the District of Columbia Circuit reversed and remanded, holding that Reid owned the copyright because "Third World America" was not a work for hire. 846 F.2d 1485, 1494 (1988). Adopting what it termed the "literal interpretation" of the Act as articulated by the Fifth Circuit in *Easter Seal Society for Crippled Children & Adults of Louisiana, Inc. v. Playboy Enterprises*, 815 F.2d 323, 329 (1987), the court read §101 as creating "a simple dichotomy in fact between employees and independent contractors." 846 F.2d, at 1492. Because, under agency law, Reid was an independent contractor, the court concluded that the work was not "prepared by an employee" under §101(1). Nor was the sculpture a "work made for hire" under the second subsection of §101 (hereinafter §101(2)): sculpture is not one of the nine categories of works enumerated in that subsection, and the parties had not agreed in writing that the sculpture would be a work for hire. The court suggested that the sculpture nevertheless may have been jointly authored by CCNV and Reid, and remanded for a determination whether the sculpture is indeed a joint work under the Act.

We granted certiorari to resolve a conflict among the Courts of Appeals over the proper construction of the "work made for hire" provisions of the Act. We now affirm.

II

A

The Copyright Act of 1976 provides that copyright ownership "vests initially in the author or authors of the work." 17 U.S.C. §201(a). As a general rule, the author is the party who actually creates the work, that is, the person who translates an idea into a fixed, tangible expression entitled to copyright protection. §102. The Act carves out an important exception, however, for "works made for hire." If the work is for hire, "the employer or other person for whom the work was prepared is considered the author" and owns the copyright, unless there is a written agreement to the contrary. §201(b). Classifying a work as "made for hire" determines not only the initial ownership of its copyright, but also the copyright's duration, §302(c), and the owners' renewal rights, §304(a), termination rights, §203(a), and right to import certain goods bearing the copyright, §601(b)(1). The contours of the work for hire doctrine therefore carry profound significance for freelance creators—including artists, writers, photographers, designers, composers, and computer programmers—and for the publishing, advertising, music, and other industries which commission their works.

Section 101 of the 1976 Act provides that a work is "for hire" under two sets of circumstances:

> (1) a work prepared by an employee within the scope of his or her employment; or
>
> (2) a work specially ordered or commissioned for use as a contribution to a collective work, as a part of a motion picture or other audiovisual work, as a translation, as a supplementary work, as a compilation, as an instructional text, as a test, as answer material for a test, or as an atlas, if the parties expressly agree in a written instrument signed by them that the work shall be considered a work made for hire.

Petitioners do not claim that the statue satisfies the terms of §101(2). Quite clearly, it does not. Sculpture does not fit within any of the nine categories of "specially ordered or commissioned" works enumerated in that subsection, and no written agreement between the parties establishes "Third World America" as a work for hire.

The dispositive inquiry in this case therefore is whether "Third World America" is "a work prepared by an employee within the scope of his or her employment" under §101(1). The Act does not define these terms. In the absence of such guidance, four interpretations have emerged. The first holds that a work is prepared by an employee whenever the hiring party retains the right to control the product. See *Peregrine v. Lauren Corp.*, 601 F. Supp. 828, 829 (Colo. 1985); *Clarkstown v. Reeder*, 566 F. Supp. 137, 142 (S.D.N.Y. 1983). Petitioners take this view. A second, and closely related, view is that a work is prepared by an employee under §101(1) when the hiring party has actually wielded control with respect to the creation of a particular work. This approach was formulated by the Court of Appeals for the Second Circuit, *Aldon Accessories Ltd. v. Spiegel, Inc.*, 738 F.2d 548 (1984), and adopted by the Fourth Circuit, *Brunswick Beacon, Inc. v. Schock-Hopchas Publishing Co.*, 810 F.2d 410 (1987), the Seventh Circuit, *Evans Newton, Inc. v. Chicago Systems Software*, 793 F.2d 889 (1986), and, at times, by petitioners. A third view is that the term "employee" within §101(1) carries its common-law agency law meaning. This view was endorsed by the Fifth Circuit in *Easter Seal Society for Crippled Children & Adults of Louisiana, Inc. v. Playboy Enterprises*, 815 F.2d 323 (1987), and by the Court of Appeals below. Finally, respondent and numerous *amici curiae* contend that the term "employee" only refers to "formal, salaried" employees. The Court of Appeals for the Ninth Circuit recently adopted this view. See *Dumas v. Gommerman*, 865 F.2d 1093 (1989).

The starting point for our interpretation of a statute is always its language. The Act nowhere defines the terms "employee" or "scope of employment." It is, however, well established that "[w]here Congress uses terms that have accumulated settled meaning under . . . the common law, a court must infer, unless the statute otherwise dictates, that Congress means to incorporate the established meaning of these terms." *NLRB v. Amax Coal Co.*, 453 U.S. 322, 329 (1981). In the past, when Congress has used the term "employee" without defining it, we have concluded that Congress intended to describe the conventional master-servant relationship as understood by common-law agency doctrine. See, *e.g., Kelley v. Southern Pacific Co.*, 419 U.S. 318, 322-323 (1974); *Baker v. Texas & Pacific R. Co.*, 359 U.S. 227, 228, (1959) (*per curiam*); *Robinson v. Baltimore & Ohio R. Co.*, 237 U.S. 84, 94 (1915). Nothing in the text of the work for hire provisions indicates that Congress used the words "employee" and "employment" to describe anything other than " 'the conventional relation of employer and employé.' " *Kelley, supra,* 419 U.S., at 323, quoting *Robinson, supra,* 237 U.S., at 94. On the contrary, Congress' intent to incorporate the agency law definition is suggested by §101(1)'s use of the term, "scope of employment," a widely used term of art in agency law. See Restatement (Second) of Agency §228 (1958) (hereinafter Restatement).

In past cases of statutory interpretation, when we have concluded that Congress intended terms such as "employee," "employer," and "scope of employment" to be understood in light of agency law, we have relied on the general common law of agency, rather than on the law of any particular State, to give meaning to these terms. See, *e.g., Kelley,* 419 U.S., at 323-324, and n. 5; *id.,* at 332 (Stewart, J., concurring in judgment); *Ward v. Atlantic Coast Line R. Co.*, 362 U.S. 396, 400 (1960); *Baker, supra,* 359 U.S., at 228. This practice reflects the fact that "federal statutes are generally intended to have uniform nationwide application." *Mississippi Band of Choctaw Indians v. Holyfield,* 490 U.S. 30, 43 (1989). Establishment of a federal rule of agency, rather than reliance on state agency law, is particularly appropriate here given the Act's express objective of creating national, uniform copyright law by broadly pre-empting state statutory and common-law copyright regulation. See 17 U.S.C. §301(a). We thus agree with the Court of Appeals that the term "employee" should be understood in light of the general common law of agency.

In contrast, neither test proposed by petitioners is consistent with the text of the Act. The exclusive focus of the right to control the product test on the relationship between the hiring party and the product clashes with the language of §101(1), which focuses on the relationship between the hired and hiring parties. The right to control the product test also would distort the meaning of the ensuing subsection, §101(2). Section 101 plainly creates two distinct ways in which a work can be deemed for hire: one for works prepared by employees, the other for those specially ordered or commissioned works which fall within one of the nine enumerated categories and are the subject of a written agreement. The right to control the product test ignores this dichotomy by transforming into a work for hire under §101(1) any "specially ordered or commissioned" work that is subject to the supervision and control of the hiring party. Because a party who hires a "specially ordered or commissioned" work by definition has a right to specify the characteristics of the product desired, at the time the commission is accepted, and frequently until it is completed, the right to control the product test would mean that many works that could satisfy §101(2) would already have been deemed works for hire under §101(1). Petitioners' interpretation is particularly hard to square with §101(2)'s enumeration of the nine specific categories of specially ordered or commissioned works eligible to be works for hire, *e.g.*, "a contribution to a collective work," "a part of a motion picture," and "answer material for a test." The unifying feature of these works is that they are usually prepared at the instance, direction, and risk of a publisher or producer. By their very nature, therefore, these types of works would be works by an employee under petitioners' right to control the product test.

The actual control test, articulated by the Second Circuit in *Aldon Accessories,* fares only marginally better when measured against the language and structure of §101. Under this test, independent contractors who are so controlled and supervised in the creation of a particular work are deemed "employees" under §101(1). Thus work for hire status under §101(1) depends on a hiring party's *actual* control of, rather than *right* to control, the product. Under the actual control test, a work for hire could arise under §101(2), but not under §101(1), where a party commissions, but does not actually control, a product which falls into one of the nine enumerated categories. Nonetheless, we agree with the Court of Appeals for the Fifth Circuit that "[t]here is simply no way to milk the 'actual control' test of *Aldon Accessories* from the language of the statute." *Easter Seal Society,* 815 F.2d, at 334. Section 101 clearly delineates between works prepared by an employee and commissioned works. Sound though other distinctions might be as a matter of copyright policy, there is no statutory support for an additional dichotomy between commissioned works that are actually controlled and supervised by the hiring party and those that are not.

We therefore conclude that the language and structure of §101 of the Act do not support either the right to control the product or the actual control approaches.[8] The structure of §101 indicates that a work for hire can arise through one of two mutually exclusive means, one for employees and one for independent contractors, and ordinary canons of statutory interpretation indicate that the classification of a particular hired party should be made with reference to agency law.

This reading of the undefined statutory terms finds considerable support in the Act's legislative history. The Act, which almost completely revised existing copyright law, was the product of two decades of negotiation by representatives of creators and copyright-using industries, supervised by the Copyright Office and, to a lesser extent, by Congress. Despite

---

8. We also reject the suggestion of respondent and *amici* that the §101(1) term "employee" refers only to formal, salaried employees. While there is some support for such a definition in the legislative history, the language of §101(1) cannot support it. The Act does not say "formal" or "salaried" employee, but simply "employee." Moreover, respondent and those *amici* who endorse a formal, salaried employee test do not agree upon the content of this test. Compare, *e.g.*, Brief for Respondent 37 (hired party who is on payroll is an employee within §101(1)) with Tr. of Oral Arg. 31 (hired party who receives a salary or commissions regularly is an employee within §101(1)); and Brief for Volunteer Lawyers for the Arts, Inc., et al. as *Amici Curiae* 4 (hired party who receives a salary *and* is treated as an employee for Social Security and tax purposes is an employee within §101(1)). Even the one Court of Appeals to adopt what it termed a formal, salaried employee test in fact embraced an approach incorporating numerous factors drawn from the agency law definition of employee which we endorse. See *Dumas,* 865 F.2d, at 1104.

the lengthy history of negotiation and compromise which ultimately produced the Act, two things remained constant. First, interested parties and Congress at all times viewed works by employees and commissioned works by independent contractors as separate entities. Second, in using the term "employee," the parties and Congress meant to refer to a hired party in a conventional employment relationship. These factors militate in favor of the reading we have found appropriate.

* * *

...[T]he legislative history of the Act is significant for several reasons. First, the enactment of [a 1965 compromise between representatives publishers' interests and representatives of authors' interests] with only minor modifications demonstrates that Congress intended to provide two mutually exclusive ways for works to acquire work for hire status: one for employees and the other for independent contractors. Second, the legislative history underscores the clear import of the statutory language: only enumerated categories of commissioned works may be accorded work for hire status. The hiring party's right to control the product simply is not determinative. Indeed, importing a test based on a hiring party's right to control, or actual control of, a product would unravel the "'carefully worked out compromise aimed at balancing legitimate interests on both sides.'" H.R. Rep. No. 2237, *supra,* at 114, quoting Supplemental Report, at 66.

We do not find convincing petitioners' contrary interpretation of the history of the Act. They contend that Congress, in enacting the Act, meant to incorporate a line of cases decided under the 1909 Act holding that an employment relationship exists sufficient to give the hiring party copyright ownership whenever that party has the right to control or supervise the artist's work. See, *e.g., Siegel v. National Periodical Publications, Inc.,* 508 F.2d 909, 914 (2d Cir. 1974); *Picture Music, Inc. v. Bourne, Inc.,* 457 F.2d 1213, 1216 (2d Cir. 1972); *Scherr v. Universal Match Corp.,* 417 F.2d 497, 500 (2d Cir. 1969); *Brattleboro Publishing Co. v. Winmill Publishing Corp.,* 369 F.2d 565, 567-568 (2d Cir. 1966). In support of this position, petitioners note: "Nowhere in the 1976 Act or in the Act's legislative history does Congress state that it intended to jettison the control standard or otherwise to reject the pre-Act judicial approach to identifying a work for hire employment relationship." Brief for Petitioners 20, citing *Aldon Accessories,* 738 F.2d, at 552.

We are unpersuaded. Ordinarily, "Congress' silence is just that — silence." *Alaska Airlines, Inc. v. Brock,* 480 U.S. 678, 686 (1987). Petitioners' reliance on legislative silence is particularly misplaced here because the text and structure of §101 counsel otherwise. Furthermore, the structure of the work for hire provisions was fully developed in 1965, and the text was agreed upon in essentially final form by 1966. At that time, however, the courts had applied the work for hire doctrine under the 1909 Act exclusively to traditional employees. Indeed, it was not until after the 1965 compromise was forged and adopted by Congress that a federal court for the first time applied the work for hire doctrine to commissioned works. See, *e.g., Brattleboro Publishing Co., supra,* at 567-568. Congress certainly could not have "jettisoned" a line of cases that had not yet been decided.

Finally, petitioners' construction of the work for hire provisions would impede Congress' paramount goal in revising the 1976 Act of enhancing predictability and certainty of copyright ownership. See H. R. Rep. No. 94-1476, *supra*, at 129. In a "copyright marketplace," the parties negotiate with an expectation that one of them will own the copyright in the completed work. *Dumas*, 865 F.2d, at 1104-1105, n. 18. With that expectation, the parties at the outset can settle on relevant contractual terms, such as the price for the work and the ownership of reproduction rights.

To the extent that petitioners endorse an actual control test, CCNV's construction of the work for hire provisions prevents such planning. Because that test turns on whether the hiring party has closely monitored the production process, the parties would not know until late in the process, if not until the work is completed, whether a work will ultimately fall within §101(1). Under petitioners' approach, therefore, parties would have to predict in advance whether the hiring party will sufficiently control a given work to make it the author. "If they guess incorrectly, their reliance on 'work for hire' or an assignment may give them a copyright interest that they did not bargain for." *Easter Seal Society*, 815 F.2d, at 333. This understanding of the work for hire provisions clearly thwarts Congress' goal of ensuring predictability through advance planning. Moreover, petitioners' interpretation "leaves the door open for hiring parties, who have failed to get a full assignment of copyright rights from independent contractors falling outside the subdivision (2) guidelines, to unilaterally obtain work-made-for-hire rights years after the work has been completed as long as they directed or supervised the work, a standard that is hard not to meet when one is a hiring party." Hamilton, Commissioned Works as Works Made for Hire Under the 1976 Copyright Act: Misinterpretation and Injustice, 135 U. Pa. L. Rev. 1281, 1304 (1987).

In sum, we must reject petitioners' argument. Transforming a commissioned work into a work by an employee on the basis of the hiring party's right to control, or actual control of, the work is inconsistent with the language, structure, and legislative history of the work for hire provisions. To determine whether a work is for hire under the Act, a court first should ascertain, using principles of general common law of agency, whether the work was prepared by an employee or an independent contractor. After making this determination, the court can apply the appropriate subsection of §101.

We turn, finally, to an application of §101 to Reid's production of "Third World America." In determining whether a hired party is an employee under the general common law of agency, we consider the hiring party's right to control the manner and means by which the product is accomplished. Among the other factors relevant to this inquiry are the skill required; the source of the instrumentalities and tools; the location of the work; the duration of the relationship between the parties; whether the hiring party has the right to assign additional projects to the hired party; the extent of the hired party's discretion over when and how long to work; the method of payment; the hired party's role in hiring and paying assistants; whether the work is part of the regular business of the hiring party; whether the hiring party is in business; the provision of employee benefits; and the tax treatment of the hired party. See Restatement §220(2) (setting forth a nonexhaustive list of factors relevant to determining whether a hired party is an employee). No one of these factors is determinative.

Examining the circumstances of this case in light of these factors, we agree with the Court of Appeals that Reid was not an employee of CCNV but an independent contractor. True, CCNV members directed enough of Reid's work to ensure that he produced a sculpture that met their specifications. But the extent of control the hiring party exercises over the details of the product is not dispositive. Indeed, all the other circumstances weigh heavily against finding an employment relationship. Reid is a sculptor, a skilled occupation. Reid supplied his own tools. He worked in his own studio in Baltimore, making daily supervision of his activities from Washington practicably impossible. Reid was retained for less than two months, a relatively short period of time. During and after this time, CCNV had no right to assign additional projects to Reid. Apart from the deadline for completing the sculpture, Reid had absolute freedom to decide when and how long to work. CCNV paid Reid $15,000, a sum dependent on "completion of a specific job, a method by which independent contractors are often compensated." *Holt v. Winpisinger,* 811 F.2d 1532, 1540 (1987). Reid had total discretion in hiring and paying assistants. "Creating sculptures was hardly 'regular business' for CCNV." 846 F.2d, at 1494, n. 11. Indeed, CCNV is not a business at all. Finally, CCNV did not pay payroll or Social Security taxes, provide any employee benefits, or contribute to unemployment insurance or workers' compensation funds.

Because Reid was an independent contractor, whether "Third World America" is a work for hire depends on whether it satisfies the terms of §101(2). This petitioners concede it cannot do. Thus, CCNV is not the author of "Third World America" by virtue of the work for hire provisions of the Act. However, as the Court of Appeals made clear, CCNV nevertheless may be a joint author of the sculpture if, on remand, the District Court determines that CCNV and Reid prepared the work "with the intention that their contributions be merged into inseparable or interdependent parts of a unitary whole." 17 U.S.C. §101. In that case, CCNV and Reid would be co-owners of the copyright in the work.

For the aforestated reasons, we affirm the judgment of the Court of Appeals for the District of Columbia Circuit.

## Comments

*1. The Fate of "Third World America."* The effect of the Supreme Court's opinion is to affirm the conclusion of the Court of Appeals that CCNV did not own the copyright to the sculpture as a work made for hire. It leaves open the possibility that CCNV and Reid might be "joint authors" of the copyright. On remand to the district court, the parties settled the case, dividing ownership so that CCNV retained ownership of the sculpture and Reid received the copyright and the right to make three-dimensional copies. Neither party anticipated the problems that would result from this arrangement, since nothing in copyright law expressly guarantees that the owner of a copyright must have access to the work itself. Reid, who wanted to make reproductions of his copyrighted sculpture, asked CCNV for permission to make a mold of the piece, and CCNV refused. The parties returned to court, which fashioned an equitable remedy that allowed Reid what the court characterized as akin to "an implied easement of necessity" to enable him to exercise his rights under the settlement. *See CCNV v. Reid*, 1991 WL 370138 (D.D.C. Oct. 16, 1991); *CCNV v. Reid*, 1991 Copr. L. Dec. (CCH) ¶26,753 (D.D.C. Jan. 7, 1991).

2. *Predictability through Advance Planning.* The Court emphasizes predictability in rejecting an "actual control" test for determining whether the employer/employee provisions of the work-made-for-hire standard have been satisfied. Instead, the Court borrows the common law agency standard, which mandates evaluation of a number of factors:

- the hiring party's right to control the manner and means by which the product is accomplished;
- the skill required;
- the source of the instrumentalities and tools;
- the location of the work;
- the duration of the relationship between the parties;
- whether the hiring party has the right to assign additional projects to the hired party;
- the extent of the hired party's discretion over when and how long to work;
- the method of payment;
- the hired party's role in hiring and paying assistants;
- whether the work is part of the regular business of the hiring party;
- whether the hiring party is in business;
- the provision of employee benefits; and
- the tax treatment of the hired party.

It is not clear that a 13-factor test provides more clarity and predictability than a single-factor test. It is true, however, that the multifactor agency test does look to more of the sorts of considerations that do go into structuring a relationship on an "employee" rather than "independent contractor" basis. Employees often receive health, retirement, and other benefits from their employers; independent contractors rarely do. Employees are required by law to deduct income and other taxes from employee paychecks; they rarely do so — in fact, they often refuse to do so — in the cases of independent contractors. Employees are usually paid on a periodic basis (weekly, bimonthly, monthly, etc.); independent contractors are often paid on a project-by-project basis.

3. *Specially Commissioned Works and the Signed Writing Requirement.* A work may constitute a "work made for hire" in one of two ways under §101. As the Court discusses in *CCNV v. Reid*, the work may be prepared by an employee within the scope of the employee's duties. Alternatively, the work may be a specially commissioned work, falling within one of the categories listed in the statute, so long as *both* parties (the commissioning party, and the creative party) agree, in a signed writing, that the result of the effort will constitute a work made for hire. The types of works eligible for treatment as works made for hire under this nonemployee definition, including contributions to collective works and to audiovisual works, including motion pictures, may be understood as contexts in which the collaborative character of authorship is clear, and the benefits of concentrating copyright ownership in a single author, in order to provide the economic incentive to produce the work in the first place, are substantial. Not all works of authorship that seem to meet this threshold are part of the work-made-for-hire definition for specially commissioned works. Computer programs, for example, are frequently the products of collaborative activity, yet are not part of the definition.

4. *Works Made for Hire and the Employment Contract.* Even if a work does not qualify as a work made for hire under *Reid*'s multi-factor standard, in many settings it is common, even routine, for employers or hiring parties working with independent contractors to demand that the contractor assign copyright interests in the project to the employer, as part of a written contract. In the short term, the result of this transfer is the same as the result under a work-made-for-hire analysis, since in both cases the hiring party obtains ownership of the copyright. In the longer term, however, the result is different. Under a work-made-for-hire arrangement, the hiring party is considered the author of the work. Under an assignment of copyright arrangement, the independent contractor retains the status of author; the hiring party receives the copyright under contract. This contract constitutes a *transfer* of a copyright interest for statutory purposes, and under rules governing termination of transfers (discussed in the next part of the chapter), that transfer may be terminated some time in the future, and the original author may recover the original copyright interest. The importance of this distinction was underscored in 1999 and 2000. In 1999, at the behest of the recording industry, Congress added the phrase "sound recordings" to the list in §101(2) of works eligible for treatment as "works made for hire" even in the absence of an employment relationship. Recording artists were outraged; several testified in Congress objecting to the change. In 2000, Congress repealed the amendment. As a result, a sound recording made by a musician constitutes a "work made for hire" owned by the recording company only if the recording artist is an employee within the meaning of *Reid*. Otherwise, the recording company may receive the copyright in the recording via a contractual transfer, which is subject to future termination under §203.

## 3. Duration, Renewal, Transfers, and Termination

*STATUTE:* **Termination of Transfers and Licenses Granted by the Author**
17 U.S.C. §203

*STATUTE:* **Duration of Copyright: Works Created on or after January 1, 1978**
17 U.S.C. §302

*STATUTE:* **Duration of Copyright: Works Created But Not Published or Copyrighted before January 1, 1978**
17 U.S.C. §303

*STATUTE:* **Duration of Copyright: Subsisting Copyrights**
17 U.S.C. §304

The Copyright Clause authorizes Congress to enact copyright protection that will last "for limited Times." Copyright is thus limited not only in scope but in duration. Unlike trademark protection, which can last indefinitely so long as the mark is used by the trademark owner, copyright protection expires. At that point, the work passes into the public domain, where anyone is free to use the work, for any purpose, without seeking the author's permission. The term of copyright therefore plays a potentially vital role in ensuring that a steady supply of new works passes ultimately into the hands of the public.

The first Copyright Act, in 1790, offered protection for a term of 14 years from publication, plus the prospect of an additional 14 years if the author survived to renew the copyright. In 1831, Congress extended the term of copyright to an initial term of 28 years from publication, plus a renewal of 14 years. The 1909 Act extended copyright still further, granting copyright owners a 28-year baseline and a renewal of an additional 28 years. The 1976 Act replaced this dual system of initial terms plus renewals with a single, unitary term for new works, using a baseline of life of the author, plus 50 years, the minimum standard adopted in the Berne Convention (Article 7). Moreover, to bring copyright term under the old dual system approximately into line with copyright term under the new unitary system, in 1976 Congress added 19 years to unexpired renewal terms. In 1998, Congress passed the Sonny Bono Copyright Term Extension Act, which added 20 years to the term of all copyrights then in existence (including 20 years added to renewal terms), and also extended the baseline for new works to life of the author, plus 70 years.

Under the Copyright Act of 1909, the renewal system was understood as economic protection for the author. The renewal term created a new estate, free of any licenses or transfers of copyright interests that the author had granted during the initial term. If an author made a bad deal during the initial term, selling or licensing the copyright on terms that later turned out to be unfavorable given the unexpected popularity of the work, the renewal term gave the author a second bite at the apple, the power to negotiate a higher fee. In *Stewart v. Abend*, 495 U.S. 207 (1990), for example, the Supreme Court held that the owner of the renewal copyright in the short story "It Had to Be Murder" could sue Alfred Hitchcock and Jimmy Stewart, the producers of the derivative work "Rear Window," for copyright infringement. "Rear Window" was produced in reliance on permission granted during the initial copyright term. *Stewart* illustrates how the renewal system generated some risks, and some unfairness, for producers (and consumers) of works based on permission granted in the initial term. Authors had the power to sell (and publishers would typically acquire) both initial and renewal terms simultaneously, but the renewal interest was contingent and vested only if the author survived to register the renewal with the Copyright Office.

The unitary system created by the 1976 Act for new works eliminated those hazards, though it created a new one, by eliminating the ability to determine in advance when a copyright would expire. Congress also wanted to be sensitive to the "second bite at the apple" opportunity that the renewal system had offered authors. It therefore created a "termination right," allowing copyright owners the statutory right at a point in the distant future to terminate transfers of copyright interests, and to recover those interests for themselves. Today, therefore, the unitary-term-plus-termination-right roughly approximates the previous dual system, both in purpose, and (in theory) in duration.

Determining how long a copyright lasts is a matter of applying the detailed provisions of three sections of the Copyright Act: §§302, 303, and 304. To figure out which section applies and the term of copyright that results, you need to know three pieces of information: First, when the work was *created*; second, whether and when the work was *published*; and third, if the copyright was *renewed* following its initial term.

For *works created on or after January 1, 1978*, apply §302 to determine the term of copyright:

- A copyright in a work created by a single author lasts for the life of the author plus 70 years.
- A copyright in a joint work (other than works made for hire) lasts for the life of the last surviving author plus 70 years.
- A copyright in a work made for hire, anonymous work, or pseudonymous work lasts for 120 years from the year of creation or 95 years from the year of publication, whichever expires *first*.

For *works created before January 1, 1978*, apply §§303 and 304 to determine the term of copyright. For works published or copyrighted before January 1, 1978, apply §304; for works created but not published or copyrighted before January 1, 1978, apply §303.

For *works published or copyrighted before January 1, 1978*:

- The initial term of copyright is 28 years.
- The renewal term of copyright is 67 years, for a total potential copyright term of 95 years.
- However: filing a renewal certificate to qualify for the renewal term was made optional in 1992, meaning that renewal of the copyright term was made automatic. Automatic renewal, however, could apply only to copyrights still in their initial term (i.e., works published not more than 28 years before 1992). Therefore,

> For works published or copyrighted before January 1, 1978 but after 1964, the total copyright term is 95 years.

> For works published or copyrighted before January 1, 1978 and before 1964, the total copyright term is 28 years, plus an additional 67 years *if a renewal certificate was timely filed.*

For *works created but not published or copyrighted before January 1, 1978*:

- The term of copyright is the term provided by §302, i.e., life of the author plus 70 years, or (for works made for hire, anonymous, and pseudonymous works), 120 years from creation or 95 years from publication, whichever expires first).
- However, in no case does a copyright for a work in this category expire before December 31, 2002, and if the work is published (by or with the authority of the copyright owner) before that date, then in no case does a copyright for a work in this category expire before December 31, 2047.

The paradoxical effect of these provisions is clearest when considering older works. By virtue of the dual system of copyrights, 1923 becomes a salient date. Any work published *before 1923* is now in the public domain, because its maximum 56-year term expired before the 1976 Act took effect in 1978. Any work created *after 1923* may still be copyrighted today, if the appropriate renewal certificate was filed. Any work created *but not published before 1923*, including diaries and letters from centuries ago, *may still be protected by copyright law today, if they were published in the United States before December 31, 2002.* As "works of authorship fixed in a tangible medium of expression," legal protection for these works is governed by federal statutory copyright, and not by older common law copyright.

Termination rights are governed by two sections of the Copyright Act, §§203 and 304. These sections apply to transfers or grants of copyright interests. Assignment or sale of copyrights, and licensing copyright interests, are the two most common forms of transfers. (Chapter 8 discusses copyright licensing in more detail.) Copyright interests can pass by will, but the termination rules do not apply to wills. In addition, as you read in connection with works made for hire, the termination of transfer rules do not apply to works made for hire. Termination rights can be exercised by the author or by the author's successors. Selecting the correct section requires knowing *when the transfer occurred.*

For *transfers made on or after January 1, 1978*, apply §203:

- Termination can be effected at any time during a five-year window that begins at the end of 35 years from the date of the grant, or transfer. Appropriate prior notice of the intent to terminate must be given to the grantee and recorded in the Copyright Office. To protect the legitimate interests of the grantee, derivative works prepared under the authority of the original grant can continue to be used, subject to any conditions (such as payment of royalties) included in that grant.

For *transfers made prior to January 1, 1978,* apply §304(c) and (d):

- Only transfers conveying an interest *in the renewal term* can be terminated. Subsection (c) applies to transfers of interests in the 19 years added to the renewal term by the 1976 Act. Subsection (d) applies to transfers to interests in the 20 years added to the renewal term in 1998, by the Sonny Bono Copyright Term Extension Act. Notice requirements and protection for existing derivative uses are similar to those under §203. The termination window, however, is different. Under §304(c), the five-year termination window opens 56 years from the date when copyright was first secured. Under §304(d), a *second* five-year window opens 75 years from the date copyright was first secured. Section 304(d) is available only if the rights granted by §304(c) expired before the Sonny Bono statute took effect in 1998, and if §304(c) rights were not exercised.

### COMPARATIVE PERSPECTIVE
### The Duration of Copyright

The Sonny Bono Copyright Term Extension Act of 1998 was challenged on constitutional grounds. In *Eldred v. Ashcroft*, 537 U.S. 186 (2003), the plaintiff, Eric Eldred, a publisher of public domain works, argued that Congress had exceeded its authority. He made two arguments. First, he argued that Congress exceeded its authority to enact copyright legislation under the Copyright Clause, on the ground that the extension of the copyright term for previously produced works violated the "limited Times" provision of that clause. Second, he argued that the extension violated the First Amendment, since it interfered with the plaintiff's ability to publish works that he anticipated would fall into the public domain. The Supreme Court, in a 7-to-2 decision, rejected both arguments, on the ground that the statute was a permissible exercise of Congress's authority.

Eldred's challenge to the extension of the term of copyright was the culmination of a long, international battle over the "right" policy for the length of copyright. In 1993, the European Union adopted a Directive mandating that EU member countries extend the term of copyright in their respective national laws, from the life-of-the-author-plus-50-years baseline required under the Berne Convention, to the life-plus-70 term that later appeared in American legislation. In passing the Sonny Bono statute, Congress noted that it was responding to the desire of American authors and publishers to "keep up with" their European competitors. The Court majority in *Eldred* took note of this development in concluding that Congress had a rational basis for enacting the statute. On the other hand, the Court majority seemed to make it clear it was skeptical of the merits of Congress's choice, a position that may reflect the well-known fact that term extension in Congress was partly the product of heavy lobbying by copyright-owning industries, and particularly by the motion picture industry. The two dissenters, Justices Stevens and Breyer, each would have been less deferential to Congress, on the premise that the benefits conferred by the statute are sizable, and private (particularly concerning their retrospective character), and the costs conferred, in terms of added licensing and permission fees for older works not in the public domain, are sizable, yet public. Notably, before Justice Breyer became a federal appellate judge, he served on the faculty of Harvard Law School and published an early law review article that used economic reasoning to express skepticism about overly strong copyright protection. *See* Stephen Breyer, *The Uneasy Case for Copyright: A Study of Copyright in Books, Photocopies, and Computer Programs*, 84 HARV. L. REV. 281 (1970).

# Enforcing Copyrights

This chapter explores how copyright owners enforce the rights they acquire against copyright infringers and those who contribute to or support copyright infringement. You have already seen how copyright's statutory character defines how copyright interests arise. Enforcement, like acquisition, is a matter of applying and interpreting the Copyright Act. Copyright law offers owners not an unlimited "property" right but instead a menu of exclusive rights, listed in §106. Under that section, the copyright owner has no obligation to publish or distribute the work, but has the sole right to determine whether, and under what circumstances, others may do so. That menu of rights, moreover, is limited by a variety of defenses, which are the subjects of Chapter 8.

In copyright law, as in many areas of the law, the scope of the legal interest, as a matter of what the right "is," cannot always be separated neatly into the context of enforcement, that is, how the right is enforced. As you proceed through this chapter, consider the extent to which issues that are resolved under various doctrines of "infringement" might alternatively be handled as questions of initial entitlement to copyright, which you encountered in Chapter 6. You have already seen how defining the scope of a copyright typically takes place during litigation against accused infringers, rather than as part of the creative process itself. *Feist Publications v. Rural Telephone Service,* which enforced the distinction between copyrightable expression and uncopyrightable facts in the context of a telephone directory, is a good example. In that respect, copyright law is quite unlike patent law, which (as Chapters 10 through 13 explain) involves obtaining a patent via a formal process conducted before the United States Patent and Trademark Office. Copyright is also distinct from the mixed system of trademark law, under which trademark owners may obtain certain rights by registering their marks with the United States Patent and Trademark Office but can also exercise rights under the Lanham Act in the absence of registration.

This chapter considers several ways in which the copyright owner may enforce rights in a copyright. The first and most important is the lawsuit for direct infringement of the copyright, which is pursued against an individual or firm which has exercised one or more of the copyright owner's exclusive rights, without the necessary permission. Direct infringement is explored in Section A. The second is the lawsuit for secondary liability for infringement, in which the defendant is alleged to be liable for direct infringement committed by someone else. Claims based on secondary liability may be broken down further into two categories: contributory liability, in which the defendant substantially contributed to the infringement, and vicarious liability, in which the defendant is held responsible for another's infringement on account of the legal relationship between the infringer and the defendant. Secondary liability is considered in Section B. A more recent development is liability under a relatively new statute, the Digital Millennium Copyright Act of 1998, which was enacted in anticipation of various challenges of digital technology used to create, distribute, and protect copyrighted works. Title I of this statute offers legal protection to copyright owners and others who use "technological protection measures" to limit access to or use of copyrighted works. Section C of this chapter addresses enforcement of those rights. Section D briefly considers the possibility that copyright law, or related law, might be used to protect interests of the author apart from interests in the work of authorship itself, such as the author's identity or reputation. These interests are sometimes known as "moral" rights.

## A. DIRECT INFRINGEMENT

*STATUTE:* **Exclusive Rights in Copyrighted Works**
17 U.S.C. §106

*STATUTE:* **Infringement of Copyright**
17 U.S.C. §501

Copyright infringement is often characterized as based on "strict liability," rather than liability based on negligence or intentional misconduct, but this characterization can be misleading. It is true that proof of copyright infringement does not require proof of a defendant's *scienter*, or state of mind, but it does require proof of two other, somewhat related things: First the defendant must have copied the plaintiff's copyrighted work, rather than created it independently. This requirement is often known as "copying in fact." Plaintiffs in copyright infringement cases typically satisfy this element in one of two ways, either by showing that the infringer actually reproduced the plaintiff's work, often via a mechanical or electronic process, or by showing that the infringer had access to the plaintiff's work and that the infringer's work is "substantially similar" to the plaintiff's work. To ease the burden of confusing terminology, this form of similarity is sometimes known as "probative similarity." Second, in addition to "copying in fact," the plaintiff must prove that the defendant's work is "substantially similar" to the plaintiff's work. This test is sometimes referred to as the question of "improper appropriation." The phrase and concept "substantial similarity" appear twice, but courts use "substantial similarity" in different ways. With respect to copying, substantial similarity relies on objective criteria, sometimes characterized as "extrinsic," to identify the temporal and spatial proximity between the plaintiff's work and the defendant's work. With respect to improper appropriation, substantial similarity depends on additional criteria, sometimes characterized as "subjective" or "intrinsic," as part of determining whether the proximity between the parties' works, identified under point one, is wrongful as a matter of copyright law. The second question asks, in short, whether the copyist defendant copied *too much* of the plaintiff's work. The next two parts of this section address problems of copying, in Section A.1, and improper appropriation, in Section A.2.


## 1. Copying or Independent Creation?

*STATUTE:* **Exclusive Rights in Copyrighted Works**
17 U.S.C. §106(1)

*STATUTE:* **Definitions — "Copies," "Fixed"**
17 U.S.C. §101

The defendant in a suit for direct infringement cannot have infringed unless the defendant "copied" the plaintiff's work. The paradigmatic claim of infringement, which involves infringement of the right "to reproduce the copyrighted work in copies" under §106(1), is a straightforward analysis of "copying": the defendant reproduced the plaintiff's work verbatim, and the defendant reproduced the plaintiff's work in tangible form, that is, in "copies." The fact that the defendant derived these "copies" from the plaintiff's work is difficult to contest.

The requirement that the infringer have "copied" the plaintiff's work applies to all of the subsections of §106, not only to the reproduction right under §106(1). Claims under §106(1) present the clearest examples of how courts handle arguments in which the defendant denies having copied the plaintiff's work. (Of course, the defendant may admit to having copied the work but will deny that the copy is otherwise infringing — because the work is not protected by copyright, or because a defense or exception applies, or because a comparison of the two creations shows that they are not only not identical, but that they are not sufficiently similar to be infringing. The first of these arguments was reviewed in Chapter 6; the second is the subject of Chapter 8; and the third is addressed in the next part of this chapter.) If the defendant denies having copied the plaintiff's work, the plaintiff may establish "copying" by proving two elements: First, that the defendant had "access" to the plaintiff's work, and second, that in light of this access, the defendant's work is "substantially similar" to the plaintiff's work. In combination, this evidence tends to show that the defendant *in fact* copied the plaintiff's work. Keep two important distinctions in mind, however. First, the *fact* that the defendant copied the plaintiff's work does not translate automatically into a conclusion that the defendant *infringed* the plaintiff's copyright. The plaintiff has more to prove, as you will see. Second, the phrase "substantial similarity" in the context of *copying-in-fact* is confusingly identical to the phrase "substantial similarity" in the second context, *infringing copying*. (Sometimes, to limit the confusion, the concept of similarity in the context of actual copying is referred to as "probative similarity.") Unfortunately, there is little else to be done about the linguistic identity except to recognize that here, as in many places in copyright, the law makes do with substantially less than perfect precision.

## THREE BOYS MUSIC CORP. v. BOLTON
### 212 F.3d 477 (9th Cir. 2000)

D.W. NELSON, Circuit Judge.

In 1994, a jury found that Michael Bolton's 1991 pop hit, "Love Is a Wonderful Thing," infringed on the copyright of a 1964 Isley Brothers' song of the same name. The district court denied Bolton's motion for a new trial and affirmed the jury's award of $5.4 million.

Bolton, his co-author, Andrew Goldmark, and their record companies ("Sony Music") appeal, arguing that the district court erred in finding that: (1) sufficient evidence supported the jury's finding that the appellants had access to the Isley Brothers' song; [and] (2) sufficient evidence supported the jury's finding that the songs were substantially similar. . . .

We affirm.

### I. BACKGROUND

The Isley Brothers, one of this country's most well-known rhythm and blues groups, have been inducted into the Rock and Roll Hall of Fame. They helped define the soul sound of the 1960s with songs such as "Shout," "Twist and Shout," and "This Old Heart of Mine," and they mastered the funky beats of the 1970s with songs such as "Who's That Lady," "Fight the Power," and "It's Your Thing." In 1964, the Isley Brothers wrote and recorded "Love is a Wonderful Thing" for United Artists. The Isley Brothers received a copyright for "Love is a Wonderful Thing" from the Register of Copyrights on February 6, 1964. The following year, they switched to the famous Motown label and had three top-100 hits including "This Old Heart of Mine."

Hoping to benefit from the Isley Brothers' Motown success, United Artists released "Love is a Wonderful Thing" in 1966. The song was not released on an album, only on a 45-record as a single. Several industry publications predicted that "Love is a Wonderful Thing" would be a hit—"Cash Box" on August 27, 1966, "Gavin Report" on August 26, 1966, and "Billboard" on September 10, 1966. On September 17, 1966, Billboard listed "Love is a Wonderful Thing" at number 110 in a chart titled "Bubbling Under the Hot 100." The song was never listed on any other Top 100 charts. In 1991, the Isley Brothers' "Love is a Wonderful Thing" was released on compact disc. See Isley Brothers, *The Isley Brothers — The Complete UA Sessions,* (EMI 1991).

Michael Bolton is a singer/songwriter who gained popularity in the late 1980s and early 1990s by reviving the soul sound of the 1960s. Bolton has orchestrated this soul-music revival in part by covering old songs such as Percy Sledge's "When a Man Love a Woman" and Otis Redding's "(Sittin' on the) Dock of the Bay." Bolton also has written his own hit songs. In early 1990, Bolton and Goldmark wrote a song called "Love Is a Wonderful Thing." Bolton released it as a single in April 1991, and as part of Bolton's album, "Time, Love and Tenderness." Bolton's "Love Is a Wonderful Thing" finished 1991 at number 49 on Billboard's year-end pop chart.

On February 24, 1992, Three Boys Music Corporation filed a copyright infringement action for damages against the appellants under 17 U.S.C. §§101 *et seq.* (1988). The parties agreed to a trifurcated trial. On April 25, 1994, in the first phase, the jury determined that the appellants had infringed the Isley Brothers' copyright. At the end of second phase five days later, the jury decided that Bolton's "Love Is a Wonderful Thing" accounted for 28 percent of the profits from "Time, Love and Tenderness." The jury also found that 66 percent of the profits from commercial uses of the song could be attributed to the inclusion of infringing elements. On May 9, 1994, the district court entered judgment in favor of the Isley Brothers based on the first two phases.

\* \* \*

On December 5, 1996, the district court adopted the findings of the Special Master's Amended Report about the allocation of damages (third phase). In the final judgment entered against the appellants, the district court ordered Sony Music to pay $4,218,838; Bolton to pay $932,924; Goldmark to pay $220,785; and their music publishing companies to pay $75,900. They timely appealed.

## II. Discussion

Proof of copyright infringement is often highly circumstantial, particularly in cases involving music. A copyright plaintiff must prove (1) ownership of the copyright; and (2) infringement—that the defendant copied protected elements of the plaintiff's work. *See Smith v. Jackson,* 84 F.3d 1213, 1218 (9th Cir. 1996) (citation omitted). Absent direct evidence of copying, proof of infringement involves fact-based showings that the defendant had "access" to the plaintiff's work and that the two works are "substantially similar." *Id.*

\* \* \*

### Access

Proof of access requires "an opportunity to view or to copy plaintiff's work." *Sid and Marty Krofft Television Productions, Inc. v. McDonald's Corp.,* 562 F.2d 1157, 1172 (9th Cir. 1977). This is often described as providing a "reasonable opportunity" or "reasonable possibility" of viewing the plaintiff's work. 4 Melville B. Nimmer & David Nimmer, *Nimmer on Copyright,* §13.02[A], at 13-19 (1999); *Jason v. Fonda,* 526 F. Supp. 774, 775 (C.D. Cal. 1981), *aff'd,* 698 F.2d 966 (9th Cir. 1982). We have defined reasonable access as "more than a 'bare possibility.'" *Jason,* 698 F.2d at 967. Nimmer has elaborated on our definition: "Of course, reasonable opportunity as here used, does not encompass any bare possibility in the sense that anything is possible. Access may not be inferred through mere speculation or conjecture. There must be a reasonable possibility of viewing the plaintiff's work—not a bare possibility." 4 Nimmer, §13.02[A], at 13-19. "At times, distinguishing a 'bare' possibility from a 'reasonable' possibility will present a close question." *Id.* at 13-20.

Circumstantial evidence of reasonable access is proven in one of two ways: (1) a particular chain of events is established between the plaintiff's work and the defendant's access to that work (such as through dealings with a publisher or record company) or (2) the plaintiff's work has been widely disseminated. *See* 2 Paul Goldstein, *Copyright: Principles, Law, and Practice* §8.3.1.1, at 90-91 (1989). Goldstein remarks that in music cases the "typically more successful route to proving access requires the plaintiff to show that its work was widely disseminated through sales of sheet music, records, and radio performances." 2 Goldstein, §8.3.1.1, at 91. Nimmer, however, cautioned that "[c]oncrete cases will pose difficult judgments as to where along the access spectrum a given exploitation falls." 4 Nimmer, §13.02[A], at 13-22.

Proof of widespread dissemination is sometimes accompanied by a theory that copyright infringement of a popular song was subconscious. Subconscious copying has been accepted since Learned Hand embraced it in a 1924 music infringement case: "Everything registers somewhere in our memories, and no one can tell what may evoke it.... Once it appears that another has in fact used the copyright as the source of this production, he has invaded the author's rights. It is no excuse that in so doing his memory has played him a trick." *Fred Fisher, Inc. v. Dillingham*, 298 F. 145, 147-48 (S.D.N.Y. 1924). In *Fred Fisher,* Judge Hand found that the similarities between the songs "amount[ed] to identity" and that the infringement had occurred "probably unconsciously, what he had certainly often heard only a short time before." *Id.* at 147.

In modern cases, however, the theory of subconscious copying has been applied to songs that are more remote in time. *ABKCO Music, Inc. v. Harrisongs Music, Ltd.,* 722 F.2d 988 (2d Cir. 1983) is the most prominent example. In *ABKCO,* the Second Circuit affirmed a jury's verdict that former Beatle George Harrison, in writing the song "My Sweet Lord," subconsciously copied The Chiffons' "He's So Fine," which was released six years earlier. Harrison admitted hearing "He's So Fine" in 1963, when it was number one on the Billboard charts in the United States for five weeks and one of the top 30 hits in England for seven weeks. The court found: "the evidence, standing alone, 'by no means compels the conclusion that there was access . . . it does not compel the conclusion that there was not.'" *Id.* (quoting *Heim v. Universal Pictures Co.,* 154 F.2d 480, 487 (2d Cir. 1946)). In *ABKCO,* however, the court found that "the similarity was so striking and where access was found, the remoteness of that access provides no basis for reversal." *Id.* . . .

The Isley Brothers' access argument was based on a theory of widespread dissemination and subconscious copying. They presented evidence supporting four principal ways that Bolton and Goldmark could have had access to the Isley Brothers' "Love is a Wonderful Thing":

(1) Bolton grew up listening to groups such as the Isley Brothers and singing their songs. In 1966, Bolton and Goldmark were 13 and 15, respectively, growing up in Connecticut. Bolton testified that he had been listening to rhythm and blues music by black singers since he was 10 or 11, "appreciated a lot of Black singers," and as a youth was the lead singer in a band that performed "covers" of popular songs by black singers. Bolton also testified that his brother had a "pretty good record collection."

(2) Three disk jockeys testified that the Isley Brothers' song was widely disseminated on radio and television stations where Bolton and Goldmark

grew up. First, Jerry Blavitt testified that the Isley Brothers' "Love is a Wonderful Thing" was played five or six times during a 13-week period on the television show, "The Discophonic Scene," which he said aired in Philadelphia, New York, and Hartford-New Haven. Blavitt also testified that he played the song two to three times a week as a disk jockey in Philadelphia and that the station is still playing the song today. Second, Earl Rodney Jones testified that he played the song a minimum of four times a day during an eight to 14 to 24 week period on WVON radio in Chicago, and that the station is still playing the song today. Finally, Jerry Bledsoe testified that he played the song on WUFO radio in Buffalo, and WWRL radio in New York was playing the song in New York in 1967 when he went there. Bledsoe also testified that he played the song twice on a television show, "Soul," which aired in New York and probably in New Haven, Connecticut, where Bolton lived.

(3) Bolton confessed to being a huge fan of the Isley Brothers and a collector of their music. Ronald Isley testified that when Bolton saw Isley at the Lou Rawls United Negro College Fund Benefit concert in 1988, Bolton said, "I know this guy. I go back with him. I have all his stuff." Angela Winbush, Isley's wife, testified about that meeting that Bolton said, "This man needs no introduction. I know everything he's done."

(4) Bolton wondered if he and Goldmark were copying a song by another famous soul singer. Bolton produced a work tape attempting to show that he and Goldmark independently created their version of "Love Is a Wonderful Thing." On that tape of their recording session, Bolton asked Goldmark if the song they were composing was Marvin Gaye's "Some Kind of Wonderful." The district court, in affirming the jury's verdict, wrote about Bolton's Marvin Gaye remark:

> This statement suggests that Bolton was contemplating the possibility that the work he and Goldmark were creating, or at least a portion of it, belonged to someone else, but that Bolton wasn't sure who it belonged to. A reasonable jury can infer that Bolton mistakenly attributed the work to Marvin Gaye, when in reality Bolton was subconsciously drawing on Plaintiff's song.

The appellants contend that the Isley Brothers' theory of access amounts to a "twenty-five-years-after-the-fact-subconscious copying claim." Indeed, this is a more attenuated case of reasonable access and subconscious copying than *ABKCO*. In this case, the appellants never admitted hearing the Isley Brothers' "Love is a Wonderful Thing." That song never topped the Billboard charts or even made the top 100 for a single week. The song was not released on an album or compact disc until 1991, a year after Bolton and Goldmark wrote their song. Nor did the Isley Brothers ever claim that Bolton's and Goldmark's song is so "strikingly similar" to the Isley Brothers' that proof of access is presumed and need not be proven.

Despite the weaknesses of the Isley Brothers' theory of reasonable access, the appellants had a full opportunity to present their case to the jury. Three rhythm and blues experts (including legendary Motown songwriter Lamont Dozier of Holland-Dozier-Holland fame) testified that they never heard of the Isley Brothers' "Love is a Wonderful Thing." Furthermore, Bolton produced copies of "TV Guide" from 1966 suggesting that the television shows playing the song never aired in Connecticut. Bolton also pointed out that 129 songs called "Love is a Wonderful Thing" are registered with the Copyright Office, 85 of them before 1964.

The Isley Brothers' reasonable access arguments are not without merit. Teenagers are generally avid music listeners. It is entirely plausible that two Connecticut teenagers obsessed with rhythm and blues music could remember an Isley Brothers' song that was played on the radio and television for a few weeks, and subconsciously copy it twenty years later. Furthermore, Ronald Isley testified that when they met, Bolton said, "I have all his stuff." Finally, as the district court pointed out, Bolton's remark about Marvin Gaye and "Some Kind of Wonderful" indicates that Bolton believed he may have been copying someone else's song.

Finally, with regard to access, we are mindful of Judge Frank's words of caution in *Arnstein v. Porter:* "The judge characterized plaintiff's story as 'fantastic'; and in the light of the references in his opinion to defendant's deposition, the judge obviously accepted the defendant's denial of access and copying....[Y]et plaintiff's credibility, even as to those improbabilities, should be left to the jury." *Arnstein,* 154 F.2d at 469....

Although we might not reach the same conclusion as the jury regarding access, we find that the jury's conclusion about access is supported by substantial evidence. We are not establishing a new standard for access in copyright cases; we are merely saying that we will not disturb the jury's factual and credibility determinations on this issue.

### B. SUBSTANTIAL SIMILARITY

Under our case law, substantial similarity is inextricably linked to the issue of access. In what is known as the "inverse ratio rule," we "require a lower standard of proof of substantial similarity when a high degree of access is shown." *Smith,* 84 F.3d at 1218 (citing *Shaw v. Lindheim,* 919 F.2d 1353, 1361-62 (9th Cir. 1990); *Krofft,* 562 F.2d at 1172). Furthermore, in the absence of any proof of access, a copyright plaintiff can still make out a case of infringement by showing that the songs were "strikingly similar." *See Smith,* 84 F.3d at 1220.

Proof of the substantial similarity is satisfied by a two-part test of extrinsic similarity and intrinsic similarity. *See Krofft,* 562 F.2d at 1164. Initially, the extrinsic test requires that the plaintiff identify concrete elements based on objective criteria. The extrinsic test often requires analytical dissection of a work and expert testimony. Once the extrinsic test is satisfied, the factfinder applies the intrinsic test. The intrinsic test is subjective and asks "whether the ordinary, reasonable person would find the total concept and feel of the works to be substantially similar." *Pasillas v. McDonald's Corp.,* 927 F.2d 440, 442 (9th Cir. 1991) (internal quotations omitted)....

### 1. EVIDENCE OF SUBSTANTIAL SIMILARITY

Bolton and Goldmark argue that there was insufficient evidence of substantial similarity because the Isley Brothers' expert musicologist, Dr. Gerald Eskelin, failed to show that there was copying of a *combination* of unprotectible elements. On the contrary, Eskelin testified that the two songs shared a combination of five unprotectible elements: (1) the title hook phrase (including the lyric, rhythm, and pitch); (2) the shifted cadence; (3) the instrumental figures; (4) the verse/chorus relationship; and (5) the fade ending. Although the appellants presented testimony from their own expert musicologist, Anthony Ricigliano, he conceded that there were similarities between the two songs and that he had not found the combination of unprotectible elements in the Isley Brothers' song "anywhere in the prior art." The jury heard testimony from both of these experts and "found infringement based on a unique compilation of those elements." We refuse to interfere with the jury's credibility determination, nor do we find that the jury's finding of substantial similarity was clearly erroneous.

### 2. INDEPENDENT CREATION

Bolton and Goldmark also contend that their witnesses rebutted the Isley Brothers' prima facie case of copyright infringement with evidence of independent creation. By establishing reasonable access and substantial similarity, a copyright plaintiff creates a presumption of copying. The burden shifts to the defendant to rebut that presumption through proof of independent creation.

The appellants' case of independent creation hinges on three factors: the work tape demonstrating how Bolton and Goldmark created their song, Bolton and Goldmark's history of songwriting, and testimony that their arranger, Walter Afanasieff, contributed two of five unprotectible elements that they allegedly copied. The jury, however, heard the testimony of Bolton, Goldmark, Afanasieff, and Ricigliano about independent creation. The work tape revealed evidence that Bolton may have subconsciously copied a song that he believed to be written by Marvin Gaye. Bolton and Goldmark's history of songwriting presents no direct evidence about this case. And Afanasieff's contributions to Bolton and Goldmark's song were described by the appellants' own expert as "very common." Once again, we refuse to disturb the jury's determination about independent creation. The substantial evidence of copying based on access and substantial similarity was such that a reasonable juror could reject this defense.

### 3. INVERSE-RATIO RULE

Although this may be a weak case of access and a circumstantial case of substantial similarity, neither issue warrants reversal of the jury's verdict. An amicus brief on behalf of the recording and motion picture industries warns against watering down the requirements for musical copyright infringement. This case presents no such danger. The Ninth Circuit's inverse-ratio rule requires a lesser showing of substantial similarity if there is a strong showing of access. In this case, there was a weak showing of access. We have never held, however, that the inverse ratio rule says a weak showing of access requires a stronger showing of substantial similarity. Nor are we redefining the test of substantial similarity here; we merely find that there was substantial evidence from which the jury could find access and substantial similarity in this case.

\* \* \*

AFFIRMED.

## Comments

1. *Actual Copying*. Where the defendant denies having copied the plaintiff's copyrighted work, the court must apply the "access and substantial similarity" framework in order to determine whether an inference of actual copying, or copying-in-fact, is justified. One could imagine a legal regime in which proof of actual copying is irrelevant. The question of infringement could be decided simply by comparing the defendant's work to the plaintiff's copyrighted work. Patent law works essentially on this principle. Even innocent and independent use of a patented invention will subject the defendant to liability. In copyright law, however, "independent creation" is a valid defense to a claim of infringement. The law of copyright infringement thus represents the flip side of the rules for obtaining a valid copyright in the first place. Unlike patent law, which grants only one valid patent to any given invention (even if multiple inventors independently develop the same thing), copyright law recognizes the possibility that multiple authors will independently produce the identical (or nearly identical) expressive work, and that if they do so, each may independently demonstrate the necessary originality to support a copyright. Judge Learned Hand famously expressed this point as follows: "[I]f by some magic a man who had never known it were to compose anew Keats's Ode on a Grecian Urn, he would be an 'author,' and, if he copyrighted it, others might not copy that poem, though they might of course copy Keats's." *Sheldon v. Metro-Goldwyn Pictures Corporation*, 81 F.2d 49, 54 (2d Cir. 1936).

2. *The Inverse-Ratio Rule*. *Three Boys Music Corp.* recognizes and applies the majority rule that copying-in-fact requires at least some evidence of both access and substantial (or probative) similarity, even if in the particular case a strong showing of access might be paired with a relative weak showing of similarity, and vice versa. The Seventh Circuit Court of Appeals has pioneered the concept of "striking similarity," under which the resemblance between two works may be so strong that the similarity itself provides evidence of access, and the plaintiff need not produce independent evidence on the latter point. *See Selle v. Gibb*, 71 F.2d 896 (7th Cir. 1984). In *Ty, Inc. v. GMA Accessories, Inc.*, 132 F.3d 1167 (7th Cir. 1997), Ty, Inc., the manufacturer of the Beanie Babies line of stuffed animals, obtained an injunction under the Copyright Act against GMA, arguing that GMA's stuffed "Preston the Pig" infringed Ty's "Squealer." The court affirmed the injunction, noting that GMA's stuffed pig was strikingly similar to Ty's pig and not to any real-life or public domain pig, and that this similarity itself was sufficient to justify an inference of copying.

3. *Subconscious Copying*. The doctrine of "striking similarity" is not the only challenge to an independent creation defense. As the court points out in *Three Boys Music Corp.*, copying may be actionable even though it is *subconscious*. *Bright Tunes Music Corp. v. Harrisongs Music, Ltd.*, 420 F. Supp. 177 (S.D.N.Y. 1976), aff'd sub nom. *ABKCO Music, Inc. v. Harrisongs Music, Ltd.*, 722 F.2d 988 (2d Cir. 1983), involved the claim that the former Beatle George Harrison infringed *He's So Fine*, a pop tune by the Chiffons, in his song, *My Sweet Lord*. The district court

concluded that an inference of copying was justified even if that copying was "subconscious":

> What happened? I conclude that the composer, in seeking musical materials to clothe his thoughts, was working with various possibilities. As he tried this possibility and that, there came to the surface of his mind a particular combination that pleased him as being one he felt would be appealing to a prospective listener; in other words, that this combination of sounds would work. Why? Because his subconscious knew it already had worked in a song his conscious mind did not remember. Having arrived at this pleasing combination of sounds, the recording was made, the lead sheet prepared for copyright and the song became an enormous success. Did Harrison deliberately use the music of He's So Fine? I do not believe he did so deliberately. Nevertheless, it is clear that My Sweet Lord is the very same song as He's So Fine with different words, and Harrison had access to He's So Fine. This is, under the law, infringement of copyright, and is no less so even though subconsciously accomplished.

*Id.* at 180-181.

4. ***Dissection and the Role of Expert Witnesses***. Though both copying-in-fact and the ultimate question of infringement depend on the concept of similarity between the parties' works, in practice "similarity" is approached differently for each purpose. In the context of copying-in-fact, it is appropriate to "dissect" the works into their constituent elements, to examine (and compare) those elements independently of their place in the work as a whole, and to bring expert testimony to bear on the likelihood that similarities between those elements arose as a result of copying. In the context of infringing similarity, or improper appropriation, "dissection" of the works is ordinarily not permitted. The works are compared in their whole form. Ordinarily, expert testimony at this stage is not permitted. The question of similarity is measured by a lay audience, represented by the jury.

---

### POLICY PERSPECTIVE
### The Reproduction Right under §106(1) and
### Copies in Computer Memory

A single unauthorized copy of a copyrighted work may infringe the copyright owner's exclusive right under §106(1), the right to reproduce the work in copies. To infringe under §106(1), that "copy" must be "fixed," according to the nested definitions in §101. Traditionally, the fixation requirement for infringing copies related to a variety of public policies: tangible copies of copyrighted works were relatively hard to make (thus, a copyist is likely an infringer) and relatively easy to identify (thus, the court's evidentiary task is simplified), and they substituted for the copies that were authorized by the copyright holder (thus, the copyright owner's injury is relatively clear). In *MAI Systems Corp. v. Peak Computer, Inc.*, 991 F.2d 511 (9th Cir. 1993), the Court of Appeals for the Ninth Circuit applied the "fixation" requirement under §106(1) to the preparation of an electronic copy of a copyrighted computer program in the computer's RAM (Random Access Memory) during the "boot up" process that followed switching on the computer. Since the unauthorized copy was located in the computer's RAM, it was automatically deleted when the computer was turned off. Despite the temporary character of the copy, and despite the fact that the copy is present solely for the purpose of enabling a user to use the machine, the court concluded that this copy was sufficiently "fixed" to meet the definition of "fixation" in §101.

The technology involved in the *MAI Systems* case has passed into the dustbin of technology history, but the contemporary implications of the case remain far-reaching. Ordinary operation of a computer involves thousands of potentially infringing "reproductions" of copyrighted works, even temporary reproductions, including both computer programs and other data files. (Operation of the Internet, which involves reproduction of copyrighted works on a mass scale not only in each end user's computer but in thousands of hubs, routers, and switches unseen to the ordinary user, illustrates how the problem instantly becomes one of enormous practical importance.) The holding of *MAI Systems* treats each of these "reproductions" as potentially infringing.

Computer programs raise a variety of issues in copyright law, some of which (like RAM copying) were not wholly appreciated when the copyright revision process concluded with the Copyright Act of 1976. But Congress was aware of the coming computer revolution, and instead of dealing with computer programs in the Act, it appointed a special commission, the Commission on New Technological Uses (known by the acronym CONTU), to investigate the copyright issues posed by computer technology and to report its findings to Congress. CONTU ultimately made two recommendations, which were both adopted by Congress in amendments to the Copyright Act that were enacted in 1980: First, the Act added a definition of "computer program" in §101. Second, the Act added §117, which clarified that a copy of a copyrighted computer program might be used legitimately with a particular computer by an "owner" of that copy, and adapted or modified, if necessary, to run on that computer, even if doing so technically involved preparation of a "copy" of that program. The changes were intended to confirm the basic copyrightability of computer programs and to enable ordinary use of those programs without fear of copyright infringement. However, since computer software developers now "license" their programs to users, who do not "own" copies, §117 is largely irrelevant to day-to-day use of most computer programs.

Given the expansive definition of "copying" in *MAI Systems*, courts have looked to other ways to limit the scope of liability for infringement in the case of literal reproduction of computer programs. In *Religious Technology Center v. Netcom On-Line Communication Services, Inc.*, 907 F. Supp. 1361 (N.D. Cal. 1995), a federal district court ruled that a host of Usenet newsgroups was not liable for preparing infringing copies of a copyrighted test, where the host's computer systems automatically created and forwarded electronic copies of messages posted by newsgroup subscribers. The *Netcom* court's requirement that allegedly infringing reproduction by a service provider be "volitional" was adopted in *CoStar Group, Inc. v. LoopNet, Inc.*, 373 F.3d 544 (4th Cir. 2004), in which the owner of copyrighted photographs of commercial real estate sued an Internet service provider (ISP) that hosted a website onto which the ISP's subscribers posted copies. The court of appeals affirmed an order granting summary judgment in favor of the ISP on the question of direct infringement, following *Netcom*. Alternatively, one scholar has suggested that courts avoid reliance on problematic extensions of *MAI Systems* to mere temporary digital copies by analyzing digital reproduction cases under the copyright owner's exclusive right to display the work publicly. *See* R. Anthony Reese, *The Public Display Right: The Copyright Act's Neglected Solution to the Controversy Over RAM "Copies,"* 2001 U. Ill. L. Rev. 83.

## 2. Infringing Copying — Misappropriation

Liability for copyright infringement has always extended beyond the literal scope of the precise words or images of the copyrighted work owned by the plaintiff. The difficult question has been where and how to draw the line between a modification so slight that liability for infringement should be imposed nonetheless, and modifications so substantial that the creator of the new work should be immune from the claim of the predecessor. Given the fact that the scope of a valid copyright interest need not be defined precisely until the point at which a claim is litigated, the problem arises in several different guises. An infringing defendant might incorporate only a portion of an underlying copyrighted work into a larger new work. Or, the infringer might incorporate all of the underlying work into a larger creation. Finally, the defendant's work might retain the same scale as the original, neither expanding it nor contracting it but presenting that work in altered form. Section 106, which governs all of these contexts, does not address the question of infringement by "substantial similarity." Each of the rights enumerated in that section speaks only of infringement of "the copyrighted work."

### TUFENKIAN IMPORT/EXPORT VENTURES, INC. v. EINSTEIN MOOMJY, INC.

#### 338 F.3d 127 (2d Cir. 2003)

CALABRESI, Circuit Judge.

This copyright infringement case involves two textile designs, each of which combines, with modifications, the "primary border" and the "half field" of two unrelated public domain carpets, one a classical Indian Agra and the other a Persian antique. Viewed uncritically, the two designs at issue are substantially similar. For the defendant's rug to infringe upon the plaintiff's design, however, the defendant's composition must be substantially similar to that which is original in the plaintiff's expression.

Battilossi               Blau Indian Agra               Floral Heriz

The district court found no infringement, concluding as a matter of law that whatever substantial similarity there may be emerges from unprotected public domain materials in the allegedly infringed design. We disagree.

## BACKGROUND

In March 1995, James Tufenkian, a designer and manufacturer of Tibetan style carpets, filed a copyright registration for the "Floral Heriz" ("Heriz") carpet design that is the subject of this lawsuit. He had composed the Heriz two years earlier by scanning into his computer two public domain images, one of the "Battilossi" carpet (a Persian antique), the other of the "Blau" carpet (an Indian Agra, designed by Dorris Blau). The field of the Battilossi rug is a dense, bilateral symmetrical design of stylized branching-vine, leaf and flower motifs. Tufenkian selected roughly the central third of the upper half of this Battilossi field. From this dense pattern, he culled out a number of motifs. He then stretched the field slightly in one direction and used the thus modified design as the entire field of the Heriz. In the process, Tufenkian created an asymmetrical pattern, for he used only an off-center portion of what had been a symmetrical design. From the Blau, he took the principal border, which, with modifications, became the major border of the Heriz. Finally, he added two minor borders of his own creation. One of these consists of stick-figure animals, the other of even simpler, castle-like figures.

Tufenkian describes his principal creative contributions as: (1) combining two unrelated rug styles; (2) designing and adding the minor borders; (3) selectively removing entire design motifs from the Battilossi so as to create a more 'open' aesthetic from those remaining; (4) converting the symmetrical Battilossi image into a design "with no central focus" (by copying from only half of the Battilossi field); and (5) elongating the Battilossi pattern.

Sometime in 1995, Appellee Bashian retained Appellee Nichols-Marcy, who had worked for Tufenkian, to oversee the designing of the "Bromley 514" ("Bromley"). Nichols-Marcy and his Nepalese contractors began

— Bromley Hall   Tibetan (514) Black—T112
Country of Origin: Nepal
Sizes: 4x6, 6x9, 8x10, 9x12, 10x14

Bromley

work on the Bromley in early 1996, two years after the Heriz was first marketed. These designers were familiar with the Heriz, and the appellees do not challenge the district court's determination that some copying of the Heriz actually occurred.

Nonetheless, the appellees contend that the Heriz's extensive use of designs taken from the public domain combined with the Bromley's distinctiveness precludes a finding of infringement. In the latter regard, they point to the following as instances of their own creative work that distinguishes the Bromley from the Heriz: (1) addition of a second "beetle" (or "flower") element to the field, placed in a roughly symmetrical position to an existing "beetle" shape so as to give the Bromley a more balanced feel than the Heriz; (2) retention of a "leaf shape" from the Battilossi that Tufenkian did not include in the Heriz; (3) removal of a vine-like line segment from the Battilossi that Tufenkian had retained; and (4) greater modification of the Blau border design, with "different shapes at different angles."

In November 1999, Tufenkian initiated this lawsuit, claiming copyright infringement and seeking various injunctive and monetary remedies. Both parties moved for summary judgment on the issue of copyright infringement....

The district court evaluated infringement by comparing the two designs' "total concept and feel" (or "overall aesthetic"). In so doing the court applied what we have called the "more discerning observer" test. *Boisson v. Banian, Ltd.*, 273 F.3d 262, 271 (2d Cir. 2001), a test intended to emphasize that substantial similarity must exist between the defendant's allegedly infringing design and the *protectible* elements in the plaintiff's design. Noting that "the prominent public domain elements incorporated into Floral Heriz ...play a significant role in the overall appearance of plaintiff's work," the district court "factor[ed] out" those elements from the substantial similarity comparison, explaining that to do otherwise "would grant plaintiff protection to public domain elements that the public has a right to copy." [*Tufenkian Imp./ Exp. Ventures, Inc. v. Einstein Moomjy, Inc.*, 237 F. Supp. 2d 376, 387 (S.D.N.Y. 2002)]. Nonetheless, the court specified that the Heriz contained various 'protectible elements' including: "[the] removal of certain elements to create open space, the asymmetrical pattern, the elongation of the design adapted from the body of the Battilossi rug, the creation of the castle and stick figure animal borders, and the ordering and placement of all of these elements into a harmonious whole...." *Id.* The district court further stated that it would also factor out "those elements which are original to defendants," among these the fact that "defendants incorporated flower elements in the center field not found in plaintiff's design."[3] *Id.* at 387-88.

Having identified the plaintiff's and the defendants' original contributions, the district court concluded that a finding of lack of infringement was "ineluctabl[e]": "[t]he Bromley 514's overall aesthetic is due to the public domain sources and to defendants' own efforts," rather than to any copying of protectible aspects of the Heriz. *Id.* at 388. To illustrate the lack of substantial similarity, the district court recited a number of differences between the rugs, including the fact that "[d]efendants' design is symmetrical, while plaintiff's is asymmetrical, a difference which creates substantial changes in the total concept and feel of the two works, given that both are substantial copies of the public domain Battilossi." *Id.* While the district court "appreciate[d] that defendants did copy, in modified form, a few elements original to plaintiff," the court concluded that "those elements (especially in their modified form) do not change the different total concept and feel of the two works." *Id.*

## DISCUSSION

\* \* \*

### B. THE TEST FOR COPYRIGHT INFRINGEMENT

"Copyright infringement is established when the owner of a valid copyright demonstrates unauthorized copying." *Castle Rock Entm't, Inc. v. Carol Publ'g Group, Inc.*, 150 F.3d 132, 137-38 (2d Cir. 1998) (internal quotation marks omitted). To demonstrate unauthorized copying, the plaintiff must first "show that his work was actually copied"; second, he must establish "substantial similarity" or that "the copying amounts to an improper or unlawful appropriation," i.e., (i) that it was protected expression in the earlier work that was copied and (ii) that the amount that was copied is "more than de minimis." *Id.* at 137-38. . . . In the appeal before us, however, the defendants do not mount a fair use defense, nor do they contest the district court's findings of ownership and actual copying. Substantial similarity is therefore the only issue we face. But substantial similarity, we emphasize again, must be to that which is protected in the plaintiff's work.

### C. THE SCOPE OF COPYRIGHT PROTECTION: ORIGINAL EXPRESSION

"[O]riginality is 'the *sine qua non* of copyright,'" *Boisson*, 273 F.3d at 268 (quoting *Feist Publ'ns, Inc. v. Rural Tel. Serv. Co.*, 499 U.S. 340, 345 (1991)). It is universally true, however, that even works which express enough originality to be protected also contain material that is not original, and hence that may be freely used by other designers. This is not simply an artifact of

---

3. In the end, however, an element added by the defendant figured prominently in the court's finding of non-infringement. The defendants' rug has a second anchoring beetle or flower element in the field, which imparts a balanced feel to the design, in contrast to the plaintiff's more "asymmetric" creation.

some rather lenient caselaw on the originality requirement. The principle is more fundamental: all creative works draw on the common wellspring that is the public domain.

In this pool are not only elemental "raw materials," like colors, letters, descriptive facts, and the catalogue of standard geometric forms, but also earlier works of art that, due to the passage of time or for other reasons, are no longer copyright protected. Thus the public domain includes, for example, both the generic shape of the letter "L" and all of the elaborately more specific "L's" from the hundreds of years of font designs that have fallen into the public domain. *See Boisson*, 273 F.3d at 269-71 (considering copyright infringement in "alphabet quilts," and treating the letters of the alphabet and the spectrum of colors as belonging to the public domain).

### D. CONUNDRUMS OF INFRINGEMENT BY INEXACT COPIES

It has long been settled that "no plagiarist can excuse the wrong by showing how much of his work he did not pirate," *Sheldon v. Metro-Goldwyn Pictures Corp.*, 81 F.2d 49, 56 (2d Cir. 1936) (Hand, J.), and this aphorism applies equally to exact reproduction of visual works. As a result, a would-be appropriator who wishes to test the limits of copyright law gains nothing from "adding on" to what she has precisely reproduced. But she might prevail insofar as her work transforms the copied expression into a design that in some respects resembles the original, yet does not actually excerpt ("cut and paste") a more-than-de-minimis protected portion of the original. Such designs may be termed "inexact copies," in recognition of the fact that they alter the prior image yet mimic its structure in some fashion.[5] Jurists have long been vexed by the task of precisely identifying that which separates inexact copies that infringe from those that do not.

In recent years we have often found it productive to assess claims of inexact-copy infringement by comparing the contested design's "total concept and overall feel" with that of the allegedly infringed work. Because this was the method used by the district court, and because the appellant sharply disputes the district court's "total concept and feel" analysis, a few remarks on the history and application of this test are in order.

Our circuit first employed the "total feel" nomenclature in a case involving children's books. *See Reyher v. Children's Television Workshop*, 533 F.2d 87, 91-92 (2d Cir. 1976). *Reyher* characterized this Court's previous treatment of inexact copying of books, movies, and plays as concerned with the "the 'pattern' of the work[, i.e.,] the sequence of events and the development of the interplay of characters." *Id.* at 91 (quoting Zechariah Chafee, *Reflections on the Law of Copyright*, 45 Colum. L. Rev. 503, 513-14 (1945)). But the children's books at issue in *Reyher* were "necessarily less complex" than the works we had previously submitted to "pattern" analysis, and, moreover, the sequence of events in the plaintiff's book consisted of little

---

5. Our intention in using the term "inexact copies" is to describe a manner of visual copying analogous to the textual copying that is described in Nimmer as "non-literal." Melville B. Nimmer & David Nimmer, 4 Nimmer on Copyright §13.03[A][1] (2003). We recognize, of course, that these designs may feature much that is new, in addition to whatever may be said to be original in the "inexact copy." Terming such a design an "inexact copy" is simply a means of drawing attention to the portion of the design that is relevant to a charge of infringement.

more than "scenes a faire" attendant to an underlying idea that was shared with the defendant's work. *Id.* at 91-92. In all respects other than the sequence of events, the works were very different:

> Reyher's book presents a picture of family life in the Russian Ukraine and develops the characters of the little girl and her mother. The [defendant's] story is barren of meaningful setting or character development in its attempt to present its theme. The two stories are not similar in mood, details or characterization.

*Id.* at 92. Summarizing, we said the works differed in their "total feel." *Id.*

In *Reyher*, "total feel" functioned as a shorthand way of explaining that—while a children's story whose sequence of events is not protected might nonetheless be infringed by other forms of inexact copying—no such copying was present in the allegedly infringing work.

Some commentators have worried that the "total concept and feel" standard may "invite[] an abdication of analysis," because "feel" can seem a "wholly amorphous referent." Melville B. Nimmer & David Nimmer, 4 Nimmer on Copyright §13.03[A][1][c] (2003). Likewise, one may wonder whether a copyright doctrine whose aspiration is to protect a work's "concept" could end up erroneously protecting "ideas." But our caselaw is not so incautious. Where we have described possible infringement in terms of whether two designs have or do not have a substantially similar "total concept and feel," we generally have taken care to identify precisely the particular aesthetic decisions—original to the plaintiff and copied by the defendant—that might be thought to make the designs similar in the aggregate.... Thus in *Knitwaves v. Lollytogs Ltd.*, we explained:

> Lollytogs has chosen to feature the same two fall symbols that Knitwaves used, leaves and squirrels. Not only do Lollytogs' renderings of these symbols substantially resemble Knitwaves' renderings, but Lollytogs has employed them in virtually the same manner as Knitwaves has (as felt appliques stitched to the sweaters' surface); on strikingly similar backgrounds ("shadow-striped" for the Leaf Sweater, and four-paneled for the Squirrel Cardigan); and in virtually the same color scheme.

71 F.3d 996, 1004 (2d Cir. 1995). *Cf. Boisson*, 273 F.3d at 273-74 (finding infringement on the basis of protectible and similar combinations of letters, colors and patterns in two alphabet rugs—in sum, on the basis of the "enormous amount of sameness" between the two designs).

Essentially, the total-concept-and-feel locution functions as a reminder that, while the infringement analysis must *begin* by dissecting the copyrighted work into its component parts in order to clarify precisely what is not original, infringement analysis is not *simply* a matter of ascertaining similarity between components viewed in isolation. For the defendant may infringe on the plaintiff's work not only through literal copying of a portion of it, but also by parroting properties that are apparent only when numerous aesthetic decisions embodied in the plaintiff's work of art—the excerpting, modifying, and arranging of public domain compositions, if any, together with the development and representation of wholly new motifs and the use of texture and color, etc.—are considered in relation to one another. The court, confronted with an allegedly infringing work, must analyze the two works closely to figure out in what respects, if any, they are similar, and then determine whether these similarities are due to protected aesthetic expressions original to the allegedly infringed work, or whether the similarity is to something in the original that is free for the taking.

## II.

The appellant charges that, in comparing the two designs' total concept and feel, the district court improperly factored out public domain elements from the Heriz and the Bromley. As the above discussion of doctrine indicates, however, the court was surely correct to factor such elements out. For copying is not unlawful if what was copied from the allegedly infringed work was not protected, for example, if the copied material had itself been taken from the public domain. This principle applies, moreover, whether the copied, unprotected expression at issue is a selection, coordination, or arrangement of elements, or whether it is the exact design itself.

But in its comparison of the two rugs, the district court failed to consider — apart from total concept and feel — whether *material portions* of the Bromley infringed on corresponding parts of the Heriz. Here the court erred. *See generally* 3 Nimmer on Copyright §13.03[A][1][c] ("'[T]otal concept and feel' should not be viewed as a *sine qua non* for infringement — similarity that is otherwise actionable cannot be rendered defensible simply because of a different 'concept and feel.'"(footnotes omitted)).

What makes this case perplexing is that, to the judicial observer who has a passing familiarity with carpet design, many of the plaintiff's expressive choices may seem to be rather mechanical or conventional acts, which might be deemed to be either non-original or else so weakly original that their copying would appropriate no more than a de minimis amount of protected expression.[10] Consider, for example, the cropping and elongating of the Battilossi half-field so as to create a typical "longer than wide" field for the Heriz; the use of one primary and two minor borders; the proportions between borders and field; and the design of the outer minor border. On the other hand, the record contains little evidence of what is conventional (and hence, by analogy to "scenes a faire," unprotected) in these respects.

Even the Heriz's pairing of the Battilossi half-field with the Blau-derived border was, arguably, a fairly simple exercise. One might contend that the pairing is too minor to surmount even the low threshold for copyright protection, or else conclude that it is protected only against very close copies.[11] The question of infringement thus might be thought to

---

10. Furthermore, one apparently original element in the plaintiff's design — the inner minor border — is not closely reproduced in the Bromley. True, like the Heriz, the Bromley uses a stick-figure motif in its inner border, but the Bromley stick figures are not particularly similar to their counterparts in the Heriz.

11. In suggesting these possibilities, we note only that they are arguable, and we express no opinion as to whether the arguments, if made, would prove correct. We do believe, however, that the district court probably erred in categorically dismissing as an unprotected "idea" the plaintiff's combination of the Battilossi half-field and Blau-ish border. The plaintiff's *particular* combination of these two rugs is an expression, albeit one protected by a thin copyright.

turn on subtle differences in the Heriz and Bromley adaptations of the Blau border.

Whether the Bromley infringes on the Heriz, however, need not depend on variation between the primary borders, or on a determination of the extent to which various features of the Heriz design are conventions. There is one substantial respect in which the creator of the Heriz made distinctly idiosyncratic and particular design decisions—decisions whose effect permeates the entire field of the Heriz—and in this respect the Bromley is a virtually exact copy of the Heriz. The plaintiff not only cropped and elongated the Battilossi half-field, he also *selectively eliminated* numerous design motifs, creating a more open, less busy aesthetic.

Of course, mere simplification of an ornate public domain carpet into a mass market knock-off may not be protectible. But the plaintiff's half-field modification was not a uniform or homogeneous simplification akin to removing all serifs from a font, blurring the petals on all flowers, or eliminating every third leaf on a stem. Rather, the plaintiff seems to have engaged in a selective and particularized culling of a leaf here, a complex of leaves and flowers there, and so forth. And close visual inspection of the two rugs confirms that the Bromley precisely mimics the Heriz in nearly all of these choices.

This non-mechanical adaptation of individually unprotectible elements from the public domain is precisely the type of "original selection" that the Supreme Court indicated was protectible expression in *Feist*. There, the Court clarified that a telephone directory contained protectible expression insofar as the compiler had "selected, coordinated, or arranged [its] uncopyrightable facts in an original way." 499 U.S. at 362. The Court cautioned, however, that the protection given is "thin," *id.* at 349, because the scope of the copyright "is limited to the particular selection or arrangement," and a "subsequent [author] remains free to use [the public domain elements] to aid in preparing a competing work, so long as the competing work does not feature the same selection and arrangement," *id.* at 349-51.

We conclude that this is one of those relatively unusual cases in which the infringing work has copied the original and "particular" or "same" selections embodied in the allegedly infringed upon work. The number of motifs present (or absent) in the Bromley field which mirror those the Heriz selected (or deleted) in an original way from the Battilossi is overwhelming. And the structural layout of these elements is essentially the same in both designs.

It should be noted that while the Bromley field is based on a near-exact copy of the Heriz's original selections from the Battilossi, the Bromley does depart from the Heriz in one salient respect. Specifically, the Bromley field has a second, anchoring "beetle" or "flower" element, which conveys a sense of balance that is absent in the Heriz. This addition, and the resulting faux symmetry, was important to the district court's determination that the "total concept and feel" of the Bromley was not substantially similar to that of the Heriz. Whatever the possible relevance of the Bromley's second beetle element to a comparison of the two rugs' "overall feel"—an issue we need not decide today—this addition does not alter the fact that the rest of the Bromley field is a near-exact copy of the Heriz field, and therefore infringing. To hold otherwise would be rather like holding that one who closely copies a long poem can do so without prima facie infringement if she replaces one (admittedly significant) stanza with verse of her own invention and thereby alters the poem's "feel."

## III.

For the foregoing reasons, we hold that the Bromley is substantially similar to the Heriz. We therefore VACATE the judgment of the district court and REMAND for further proceedings.

## Comments

1. **Copyrightability and Substantial Similarity.** The standard test for evaluating "substantial similarity" as a question of improper appropriation, and a test that for historical reasons is closely associated with the Court of Appeals for the Second Circuit, involves a form of nonexpert evaluation. The leading standard asks "whether an average lay observer would recognize the alleged copy as having been appropriated from the copyrighted work." *Ideal Toy Corp. v. Fab-Lu Ltd.*, 360 F.2d 1021, 1022 (2d Cir. 1966). An earlier version of that principle, still applied in some cases, frames the question as follows: The parties' works are "substantially similar" if "the ordinary observer, unless he set out to detect the disparities [between the parties' works], would be disposed to overlook them, and regard their aesthetic appeal as the same." *Peter Pan Fabrics, Inc. v. Martin Weiner Corp.*, 274 F.2d 487, 489 (2d Cir. 1960). As the court notes in *Tufenkian*, in either case, this analysis frequently involves a comparison of the works' "total concept and feel." *See Eden Toys, Inc. v. Marshall Field & Co.*, 675 F.2d 498, 500 (2d Cir. 1982).

2. **The Average Lay Observer Standard Applied.** Among the most interesting applications of the "average lay observer" standard is *Steinberg v. Columbia Pictures Industries, Inc.*, 663 F. Supp. 706 (S.D.N.Y. 1987). Saul Steinberg, the creator of an iconic poster of parochial New Yorkers' view of the United States, with Manhattan dominating the foreground and the rest of the country appearing in low relief in the background, sued the producers of the motion picture *Moscow on the Hudson*, who borrowed a similar perspective for a promotional poster. The coloring, lettering, and bird's eye perspective of the two works was similar. The *Moscow on the Hudson* poster represented Manhattan as the focal point of the foreground, and the rest of the world (looking east, to Moscow) as the background. The art director for the film testified that he directed the artist to use the Steinberg poster to achieve a New York "look." The district court granted summary judgment for Steinberg. Though it noted that there could be no liability "for using the *idea* of a map of the world from an egocentrically myopic perspective," *id.* at 712, it held that the poster met the Second Circuit's "average lay observer" standard for infringement by "substantial similarity":

> Even at first glance, one can see the striking stylistic relationship between the posters, and since style is one ingredient of 'expression,' this relationship is significant. Defendants' illustration was executed in the sketchy,

whimsical style that has become one of Steinberg's hallmarks. . . . [¶] The strongest similarity is evident in the rendering of the New York City blocks. Both artists chose a vantage point that looks directly down a wide two-way cross street that intersects two avenues before reaching a river. Despite defendants' protestations, this is not an inevitable way of depicting blocks in a city with a grid-like street system, particularly since most New York City cross streets are one-way. . . . [¶] While not all of the details are identical, many of them could be mistaken for one another; for example, the depiction of the water towers, and the cars, and the red sign above a parking lot, and even many of the individual buildings. The shapes, windows, and configurations of various edifices are substantially similar.

*Steinberg*, 663 F. Supp. at 712-713. The court rejected the argument that "only a small proportion of [the defendant's] design could possibly be considered similar," because "this case involves the entire protected work and an iconographically, as well as proportionately, significant portion of the allegedly infringing work." *Id.* at 713. Noting the irrelevance of the addition of the eastward perspective, or the depiction of Moscow, the court quoted approvingly from Judge Hand's well-known opinion in *Sheldon v. Metro-Goldwyn Pictures Corp.*, 81 F.2d 49, 56 (2d Cir. 1936), that "no plagiarist can excuse the wrong by showing how much of his work he did not pirate."

3. ***The Discerning Observer.*** The court in *Tufenkian* applies what it characterizes as a "more discerning observer" standard for determining substantial similarity. The question is whether the two works share the same "total concept and feel" from the perspective of this more sophisticated viewer. The modification is appropriate in cases where the plaintiff's work is based largely on public domain sources, so that copying of those sources is not mistaken for copying from the plaintiff's work. *See Boisson v. Banian, Ltd.*, 273 F.3d 262 (2d Cir. 2001). Application of the "ordinary observer" standard has also been found appropriate in cases where the plaintiff's work is marketed primarily to a specialized audience, so that the "ordinary observer" in these cases is deemed to be a member of that audience, and expert testimony may be appropriate to demonstrate how that audience would perceive the works. *See, e.g., Computer Assocs. Int'l, Inc. v. Altai, Inc.*, 982 F.2d 693, 713 (2d Cir. 1992) (infringement of copyrighted computer programs); *Lyons Partnership, L.P. v. Morris Costumes, Inc.*, 243 F.3d 789, 802-803 (4th Cir. 2001) (infringement of Halloween costumes for children).

4. ***Copyright's Balancing Act.*** In applying different standards for substantial similarity, courts are wrestling with several concerns. There is the inevitably fact-specific nature of substantial similarity analysis. There is the concern that facts and ideas should remain in the public domain and free for others to use. And there is the interest of the creative compiler in drawing on public domain elements to produce a creative and protectable work of authorship. Under any standard, a court must take care to ensure that a defendant is not penalized for copying material that is free to be copied. "Substantial similarity" is intended to identify substantial similarity of protected material. Drawing that distinction is easier in theory than it is in practice. In *Tufenkian*, the court

removes public domain elements from the plaintiff's work before applying a "total concept and feel" analysis, but it then concludes that the defendant is liable precisely because of its calculated adaptation and modification of public domain elements contained in the plaintiff's pattern.

---

The next case illustrates an alternative to the improper appropriation standards developed in the Court of Appeals for the Second Circuit. In at least some circumstances, the Court of Appeals for the Ninth Circuit approaches the question of infringement by substantially similar copying using what it refers to as "extrinsic" and "intrinsic" tests. As you read this case, note that in some respects these two tests appear to track the copying-plus-improper-appropriation framework discussed above, and in some respects, they offer a different approach.

## SHAW v. LINDHEIM
### 919 F.2d 1353 (9th Cir. 1990)

ALARCON, Circuit Judge.

Lou Shaw and Eastbourne Productions, Inc. (Shaw) appeal from a grant of summary judgment in favor of Richard Lindheim, Michael Sloan, and three entertainment corporations (defendants). On appeal, Shaw argues that the district court erred in finding that, as a matter of law, there was no substantial similarity between his script entitled "The Equalizer" and defendants' pilot script for their "Equalizer" television series. Because a reasonable trier of fact could have found that the two works are substantially similar, Shaw argues, the district court erred in dismissing his copyright and Lanham Act claims on summary judgment. We reverse and remand.

### STATEMENT OF THE CASE

Lou Shaw is a well-known writer and producer in the entertainment industry in Los Angeles. At one time during the 1976-1977 television season, there were eight network television programs on the air that Shaw had created, written for, or produced.[1] In February 1978, Shaw entered into an option contract with Richard Lindheim, an executive in the Dramatic Programming Division of NBC Television, that granted NBC the option to develop "The Equalizer," a pilot script created by Shaw, into a television series. Shaw delivered the script to Lindheim on July 27, 1978. Lindheim read Shaw's script. Because NBC declined to produce it, all rights in the script reverted back to Shaw.

Lindheim left NBC in 1979 and began work for Universal Television. In 1981, Lindheim wrote a television series treatment entitled "The Equal-

---

1. These series were "Quincy," "Nancy Drew," "McCloud," "Columbo," "Switch," "Maude," "Six Million Dollar Man," and "Barnaby Jones." Shaw has also been a writer for such television mainstays as "Mission: Impossible," "Ironside," "Love American Style," and "The Munsters."

izer." Lindheim admits that he copied the title of his treatment from Shaw's script. In 1982, defendant Michael Sloan expanded Lindheim's treatment, and the revised version became the pilot script for defendants' Equalizer series, which was broadcast on CBS beginning in 1985.

On November 19, 1987, Shaw filed an action for copyright infringement and unfair competition, alleging that defendants' pilot script and series were substantially similar to the script he had submitted. On August 8, 1988, defendants moved for summary judgment. On October 28, 1988, the district court found that there was no substantial similarity between the two works as a matter of law and granted summary judgment on Shaw's copyright and Lanham Act claims. Shaw timely appeals....

## DISCUSSION

### I. COPYRIGHT CLAIM

Copyright law protects an author's expression; facts and ideas within a work are not protected. To establish a successful copyright infringement claim, Shaw must show that he owns the copyright and that defendant copied protected elements of the work. Because, in most cases, direct evidence of copying is not available, a plaintiff may establish copying by showing that the infringer had access to the work and that the two works are substantially similar. The defendants conceded Shaw's ownership of the original Equalizer script and their access to the script for purposes of the summary judgment motion. As a result, the only issue before the district court on the copyright claim was whether defendants' version of the Equalizer is substantially similar to Shaw's original script.

Any test for substantial similarity is necessarily imprecise:

> Upon any work, and especially upon a play, a great number of patterns of increasing generality will fit equally well, as more and more of the incident is left out. The last may perhaps be no more than the most general statement of what the play is about and at times might consist of only its title; but there is a point in this series of abstractions where they are no longer protected, since otherwise the playwright could prevent the use of his "ideas," to which, apart from their expression, his property is never extended.

*Sid & Marty Krofft Television Prods. Inc. v. McDonald's Corp.*, 562 F.2d 1157, 1163 (9th Cir. 1977) (quoting *Nichols v. Universal Pictures Corp.*, 45 F.2d 119, 121 (2d Cir. 1930). It is thus impossible to articulate a definitive demarcation that measures when the similarity between works involves copying of protected expression; decisions must inevitably be ad hoc. *Id.* at 1164.

### A. THE KROFFT FRAMEWORK

The Ninth Circuit employs a two-part test for determining whether one work is substantially similar to another. Established in *Sid & Marty Krofft Television Prods. Inc. v. McDonald's Corp.*, 562 F.2d 1157, 1164 (9th Cir. 1977), the test permits a finding of infringement only if a plaintiff proves *both* substantial similarity of general ideas under the "extrinsic test" and substantial similarity of the protectable expression of those ideas under the "intrinsic test." *Krofft*, 562 F.2d at 1164.

### 1. SCOPE OF THE *KROFFT* TESTS

*Krofft* defined the extrinsic test as a "test for similarity of ideas" under which "analytic dissection and expert testimony are appropriate." 562 F.2d at 1164. The intrinsic test, according to *Krofft,* should measure "substantial similarity in expressions...depending on the response of the ordinary reasonable person....[I]t does not depend on the type of external criteria and analysis which marks the extrinsic test." *Id.* In decisions under the intrinsic test, "analytic dissection and expert testimony are not appropriate." *Id.*

Relying on this language, panels applying *Krofft* to literary works have included a lengthy list of concrete elements under the extrinsic test. Whereas *Krofft* listed "the type of artwork involved, the materials used, the subject matter, and the setting for the subject" as criteria for consideration under the extrinsic test, *id.,* a series of opinions beginning with the district court opinion in *Jason v. Fonda,* 526 F. Supp. 774 (C.D. Cal. 1981), *aff'd and incorporated by reference,* 698 F.2d 966 (9th Cir. 1982), have listed "plot, themes, dialogue, mood, setting, pace, and sequence" as extrinsic test criteria. 526 F. Supp. at 777; *see also Litchfield v. Spielberg,* 736 F.2d 1352, 1356 (9th Cir. 1984) (repeating this list); *Berkic v. Crichton,* 761 F.2d 1289, 1293 (9th Cir. 1985) (same); [*Narell v. Freeman,* 872 F.2d 907, 912 (9th Cir. 1989)] (adding "characters" to the list and transforming "sequence" into "sequence of events").

Now that it includes virtually every element that may be considered concrete in a literary work, the extrinsic test as applied to books, scripts, plays, and motion pictures can no longer be seen as a test for mere similarity of ideas. Because the criteria incorporated into the extrinsic test encompass all objective manifestations of creativity, the two tests are more sensibly described as objective and subjective analyses of *expression,* having strayed from *Krofft*'s division between expression and ideas. Indeed, a judicial determination under the intrinsic test is now virtually devoid of analysis, for the intrinsic test has become a mere subjective judgment as to whether two literary works are or are not similar.

### 2. THE DISTRICT COURT'S APPLICATION OF *KROFFT*

An example of how the absence of legal analysis may frustrate appellate review of the intrinsic test is the district court's order in this matter. The district court found, after extensive analysis, that reasonable minds might conclude that plaintiffs' and defendants' works were substantially similar as to the objective characteristics of theme, plot, sequence of events, characters, dialogue, setting, mood, and pace. Nevertheless, the court made a subjective determination under the intrinsic test that *no* reasonable juror could determine that the works had a substantially similar total concept and feel. The district court order reads in part:

2. *Application of the Extrinsic Test*
Under the first part of *Krofft*'s two-part test, the plaintiff must prove that the general ideas in both the plaintiffs' and defendants' works are substantially similar....

....

a. Theme

The theme of both works revolves around the main character, the Equalizer,—"a man who will equalize the odds, a lone man working outside the system to protect his underdog clients and to resolve their predicaments as a part of his rough notion of justice."...Beyond the defendants' superficial evaluation of the themes of both works, one discovers some similarity. For example, plaintiffs' lead character describes his job as "the greatest thing a man could do with his life...[that is] help give somebody an even shot, shake up the odds a little;" while defendants' lead character tells a client that his job is to "Equalize the odds. Put the odds in your favor."

b. Plot

A comparison of the plots of both works reveals significant similarities and differences. For example, both works involve a cover up/blackmail conspiracy and a woman who is in jeopardy, however, in defendants' work the main character takes on two cases whereas plaintiffs' Equalizer has only one client. A review of plaintiffs' expert's analysis reveals substantial similarities between the respective works, yet, as defendants point out many of these comparisons are taken out of order or context. For example, both works involve a criminal organization that blackmails a public official. The defendants' Equalizer, however, involves a tight blackmail ring, operated out of the corporate headquarters of a telecommunication company in New York city, whereas plaintiffs' criminal organization is described as a Mafia that controls the Boyle Heights Chicano Community of Los Angeles.

Despite these dissimilarities, the respective plots do parallel each other. Dr. Seger's declaration illustrates how the plots in both scripts share a common sequence and rhythm.

c. Characters and Dialogue

Both parties' scripts have similar lead characters. In defendants' story, McCall, the former spy turned Equalizer is motivated by past wrongs and seems intent on helping any underprivileged person who faces insurmountable odds. Plaintiffs' lead character, Jericho, also seeks to prevent injustice, however, as defendants point out his motivations are often unclear. Both leads are well educated, wealthy and have expensive tastes. The most striking similarity between the McCall and Jericho is their self-assuredness, and unshakable faith in the satisfactory outcome of any difficult situation.

Although certain characters (such as Erica in plaintiffs' script) are not duplicated in defendants' work, their absence is not of major significance when considering both stories in their entirety. Instead many of defendants' characters share similar traits with plaintiffs' characters. Examples include the clients, Tracy Rollins and Colleen Randall; the candidates, Kale and Blanding; the cover up villains, Rivera and Morgan; the former colleagues/inside contacts, Fleming and Brahms. Such a parallel may go unnoticed, however, when considering the overall format of each work.

The dialogue in the respective works do share some striking similarities. Plaintiffs' expert has set forth, side-by-side, dialogue from a variety of characters which almost match.

Utilizing the extrinsic test adopted in *Krofft* it appears that reasonable minds might differ as to the substantial similarity between the protected *ideas* of the respective works.

3. *Application of the Intrinsic Test*

The second step of the *Krofft* analysis requires the trier of fact to decide whether there is substantial similarity in the expression of the ideas so as to constitute copyright infringement. *Krofft,* 562 F.2d at 1164. This second step is called the intrinsic or audience test, because it depends on the response of the ordinary reasonable person. *Id.* The Court must determine whether reasonable minds can differ as to whether defendants' Equalizer captured the total "concept and feel" of plaintiffs' scripts....

... Reasonable minds could not differ as to whether the total concept and feel of the respective Equalizer works is substantially similar [under the intrinsic test]. Although general similarities between the works exist, plaintiffs have failed to establish that enough protected *expression* is infringed to warrant denial of defendants' Motion for Summary Judgment.

The district court's decision to grant summary judgment solely on a subjective assessment under *Krofft*'s intrinsic test conflicts with the prescriptions of *Krofft*. In *Krofft*, this court stated that the outcome of the extrinsic test "may often be decided as a matter of law." 562 F.2d at 1164. In contrast, "[i]f there is substantial similarity in ideas, then *the trier of fact* must decide [under the intrinsic test] whether there is substantial similarity in the expressions of the ideas so as to constitute infringement." *Id.* (emphasis added); *see also id.* at 1166 ("[T]he intrinsic test for expression is uniquely suited for determination by *the trier of fact*." (emphasis added)). Professor Nimmer has also noted that "the second step in the [*Krofft*] analytic process requires that *the trier of fact* then decide 'whether there is substantial similarity in the expressions of the ideas so as to constitute infringement.'" 3 M. Nimmer, *Nimmer on Copyright* §13.03 [E][3], at 62.14 (1989) [hereinafter *Nimmer on Copyright*].

### 3. *KROFFT* AND THE SUMMARY JUDGMENT STANDARD

\* \* \*

We must determine in this matter whether a party that demonstrates a triable issue of fact under the extrinsic test has made a sufficient showing of substantial similarity to defeat a summary judgment motion. As noted above, the extrinsic test focuses on "specific similarities between the plot, theme, dialogue, mood, setting, pace, characters, and sequence of events.... 'the actual concrete elements that make up the total sequence of events and the relationships between the major characters.'" *Narell*, 872 F.2d at 912 (quoting *Berkic*, 761 F.2d at 1293). These are the measurable, objective elements that constitute a literary work's expression. Because these elements are embodied in the extrinsic test, we hold that it is improper for a court to find, as the district court did, that there is no substantial similarity as a matter of law after a writer has satisfied the extrinsic test. To conclude otherwise would allow a court to base a grant of summary judgment on a purely subjective determination of similarity.... *2 part test*

\* \* \*

Given the variety of possible expression and the objective criteria available under the extrinsic test to analyze a literary work's expression, as distinct from the ideas embodied in it, the intrinsic test cannot be the sole basis for a grant of summary judgment. Once a court has established that a triable question of objective similarity of expression exists, by analysis of each element of the extrinsic test, its inquiry should proceed no further. What remains is a subjective assessment of the "concept and feel" of two works of literature—a task no more suitable for a judge than for a jury. This subjective assessment is not a legal conclusion; rather it involves the audience in an interactive process with the author of the work in question, and calls on us "to transfer from our inward nature a human interest and a semblance of truth sufficient to procure for these shadows of imagination that willing suspension of disbelief for the moment, which constitutes poetic faith." S.T. Coleridge, *Biographia Literaria*, ch. 14, *reprinted in 5 English Literature: The Romantic Period* (A. Reed ed. 1929). This interactive assessment is by nature an individualized one that will provoke a varied response in each juror, for what "makes the unskillful laugh, cannot but make the judicious grieve." W. Shakespeare, *Hamlet*, Act III, scene ii, ll. 27-28. It is not the district court's role, in ruling on a motion for a summary judgment, to limit the interpretive judgment of each work to that produced by its own experience.

A determination that a bee fashioned by a jeweler, or a stuffed animal produced by a toymaker, embodies an idea—the form of a natural creature—that cannot be separated from its expression, primarily involves the observer's physical senses. Where idea and expression merge, a court is well-suited to make the required determination of similarity on a motion for summary judgment. A comparison of literary works, on the other hand, generally requires the reader or viewer to engage in a two-step process. The first step involves the objective comparison of concrete similarities; the second employs the subjective process of comprehension, reasoning, and understanding. The imagery presented in a literary work may also engage the imagination of the audience and evoke an emotional response. Because each of us differs, to some degree, in our capability to reason, imagine, and react emotionally, subjective comparisons of literary works that are objectively similar in their expression of ideas must be left to the trier of fact.

For these reasons, a showing of substantial similarity with reference to the eight objective components of expression in the extrinsic test applied to literary works creates a genuine issue for trial. If a district court concludes, after analyzing the objective criteria under the extrinsic test, that reasonable minds might differ as to whether there is substantial similarity between the protected expression of ideas in two literary works, and the record supports the district court's conclusion, there is a triable issue of fact that precludes summary judgment. This rule is necessary because our expansion of the extrinsic test as applied to literary works has incorporated all objective elements of expression, leaving a mere subjective assessment of similarity for the intrinsic test. Because such an assessment may not properly be made as a matter of law, it is for the trier of fact to determine whether the intrinsic test is satisfied.[2] Accordingly, our decision in this matter turns on whether Shaw has raised a triable issue of fact under *Krofft*'s extrinsic test.

### B. THE EXTRINSIC TEST

#### 1. ROLE OF ACCESS

Although access was not an issue before the district court for purposes of the defendants' summary judgment motion, we must consider defendants'

---

2. This is not to say that summary judgment on the issue of *expression* is never proper. When a plaintiff demonstrates an issue of fact as to the objective components of expression now embodied in the extrinsic test, however, it is improper to grant summary judgment based on a subjective assessment under the intrinsic test alone.

access to Shaw's script in determining substantial similarity. The holding in *Krofft* itself rested in part on a finding that the defendants' "degree of access justifies a lower standard of proof to show substantial similarity." 562 F.2d at 1172. As we stated in *Krofft*:

> No amount of proof of access will suffice to show copying if there are no similarities. This is not to say, however, that where clear and convincing evidence of access is presented, the quantum of proof required to show substantial similarity may not be lower than when access is shown merely by a preponderance of the evidence.

*lower proof of similar, eg when clear access*

. . . Because no subsequent decision has disturbed the access rule established in *Krofft*, we believe that it is the law of this circuit. Thus, defendants' admission that they had access to Shaw's script is a factor to be considered in favor of Shaw.

### 2. EFFECT OF IDENTICAL TITLE ON SUBSTANTIAL SIMILARITY

The fact that the two works have identical titles also weighs in Shaw's favor. In *Arnstein v. Porter*, 154 F.2d 464 (2d Cir. 1946), the Second Circuit held that "[a] title cannot be copyrighted." *Id.* at 474. This is true in the sense that titles, in and of themselves, cannot claim statutory copyright. 1 M. Nimmer, *Nimmer on Copyright*, §2.16, at 2-186 (1989). Nevertheless, "[i]f the copying of a title is not an act of copyright infringement, it may . . . have copyright significance as one factor in establishing whether the substance of plaintiff's work (not the title) has been copied." *Id.* at 2-188. As the Seventh Circuit has stated, "the title of a copyrighted work should be taken into account when the same title is applied to a work [allegedly] copied from it." *Wihtol v. Wells*, 231 F.2d 550, 553 (7th Cir. 1956). Thus, we acknowledge and consider defendants' admitted copying of Shaw's title in determining whether there is substantial similarity of protected expression between the two works.

*Copy title is evid*

### 3. THE EXTRINSIC TEST APPLIED

As noted earlier, a court applying the extrinsic test must compare "the individual features of the works to find specific similarities between the plot, theme, dialogue, mood, setting, pace, characters, and sequence of events." *Narell*, 872 F.2d at 912. "The test focuses not on basic plot ideas, which are not protected by copyright, but on 'the actual concrete elements that make up the total sequence of events and the relationships between the major characters.'" *Narell*, 872 F.2d at 912 (quoting *Berkic*, 761 F.2d at 1293). Our study of the two scripts at issue reveals the following objective similarities in protected expression under the extrinsic test:

#### a) THEME

As the district court noted, the theme of both works revolves around the character of the Equalizer — "a man who will equalize the odds, a lone man working outside the system." This, in itself, is but an unprotectible idea — the same could be said of literary characters from Aladdin to Zorro. Yet the similarity in theme extends beyond this basic idea — the Equalizer in each script solicits clients requiring assistance that conventional law enforcement cannot offer, and each lead character describes his role as to "equalize" or "shake up" the odds. Defendants point to differences in their pilot, contending that their Equalizer is motivated by his dissatisfaction with prior covert government employment and his desire to renew his relationship with his estranged wife and son. These themes, although different, are secondary and do little to erode the similarity between the central themes embodied in the titles of the two works. " 'No plagiarist can excuse the wrong by showing how much of his work he did not pirate.' " *Nimmer on Copyright* §13.03[B][1] [a], at 13-48 to 13-49 (quoting *Sheldon v. Metro-Goldwyn Pictures Corp.*, 81 F.2d 49 (2d Cir. 1936). The similarity in themes in the two works before the court extends to elements of protectable expression.

### b) PLOT/SEQUENCE OF EVENTS

Shaw provides a list of "26 strikingly similar events" that he claims appear in both works in substantially the same sequence. Examination of this list after a reading of both scripts, however, reveals that it is, for the most part, a compilation of "random similarities scattered throughout the works" that this court discounted in *Litchfield*. 736 F.2d at 1356. Shaw's list misrepresents the order and similarity of many of these events, and relies heavily on "scenes à faire")— that is, scenes that flow naturally from a basic plot premise. *Berkic*, 761 F.2d at 1293. Indeed, defendants provide a list of similarities between "The Wizard of Oz" and "Star Wars" that is virtually as compelling as Shaw's.

Shaw's overexuberance, however, does not change the fact that many of the events in the two works are substantially similar. Both works involve a criminal organization that blackmails a candidate for public office. Both organizations attempt to kill a prospective Equalizer client, who has discovered their operation, by means of an oncoming truck. In both scripts, henchmen for the criminal organization interrupt the Equalizer's initial meeting with the client, chase and shoot at the Equalizer and the client, and are foiled as the Equalizer saves the client. In both scripts, the uninvited Equalizer appears at a party in a tuxedo. In both, the Equalizer confronts the candidate/blackmail victim after a campaign speech. After thwarting the leader of the criminal conspiracy, the Equalizer rushes to save a female client from danger. The Equalizer's actions in both scripts result in the candidate/blackmail victim's withdrawal from the political race.

Even if none of these plot elements is remarkably unusual in and of itself, the fact that both scripts contain all of these similar events gives rise to a triable question of substantial similarity of protected expression. As the district court noted, "the respective plots parallel each other....[T]he plots in both scripts share a common sequence and rhythm." "Where plot is...properly defined as 'the "sequence of events" by which the author expresses his "theme" or "idea," ' it constitutes a pattern which is sufficiently concrete so as to warrant a finding of substantial similarity if it is common to both plaintiff's and defendant's works." *Nimmer on Copyright* §1303[A], at 13-31 (quoting *Shipman v. RKO Radio Pictures, Inc.*, 100 F.2d 533, 537 (2d Cir. 1938)).

### c) MOOD, SETTING AND PACE

Both works are fast-paced, have ominous and cynical moods that are lightened by the Equalizer's victory, and are set in large cities. These similarities are common to any action adventure series, however, and do not weigh heavily in our decision.

### d) CHARACTERS AND DIALOGUE

As the district court noted, both the dialogue and the characters in the respective works share some striking similarities. A particularly glaring example of similar personal traits is revealed by a comparison of the principal characters in both works. As the district court found, both scripts have "similar lead characters.... Both leads are well dressed, wealthy and have expensive tastes. The most striking similarity is their self-assuredness, and unshakeable faith in the satisfactory outcome of any difficult situation." Although James Bond may have the Equalizers' demeanor and the Ghostbusters may have their penchant for unpopular assignments, the totality of the similarities between the two characters goes beyond the necessities of the "Equalizer" theme and belies any claim of literary accident. We find that defendants' copying of the Equalizer character and other characters extends to elements of protected expression. Because the similarities between the principals in each script and among the other common characters point to copying of more than a general theme or plot idea, they support the district court's finding that Shaw raised a triable issue of fact regarding substantial similarity under the extrinsic test.

### 4. CONCLUSION

We conclude that Shaw has satisfied the extrinsic test for literary works and thus has presented a triable issue of fact regarding substantial similarity of protected expression. "Even if a copied portion be relatively small in proportion to the entire work, if qualitatively important, the finder of fact may properly find substantial similarity." [*Baxter v. MCA, Inc.*, 812 F.2d 421, 425 (9th Cir. 1987).] A reasonable trier of fact could find that the similarity between Shaw's script and defendants' pilot is not so general as to be beyond the protections of copyright law. Because Shaw has produced a triable issue of fact under the extrinsic test, we reverse the district court's grant of summary judgment on Shaw's copyright claim.

\* \* \*

## Comments

1. *The Extrinsic and Intrinsic Tests, and Copying-and-Improper Appropriation, Compared.* For a copyright infringement plaintiff to prevail on a claim of infringement by substantially similar copying, both the Second Circuit and the Ninth Circuit require proof of access to the plaintiff's work and appropriation of protected expression. The courts diverge, however, not only in their terminology but in how they divide those substantive principles into procedural burdens. The Second Circuit requires proof of copying in fact, which requires both proof of access and proof of

"substantial similarity"—measured under an "objective" standard. A plaintiff that satisfies both burdens is entitled to present the case of improper appropriation to the jury, under a "subjective" standard of "substantial similarity," though that "subjective" standard requires that the jury apply the perspective of an "average lay observer." In the Ninth Circuit, once the plaintiff proves that the defendant had access to the plaintiff's work, the case turns to the question of improper appropriation, that is, copying by "substantial similarity," which has two subparts. If the plaintiff raises a triable issue of fact as to "substantial similarity of ideas," or "extrinsic" copying, then the plaintiff is entitled to present the case of "intrinsic" copying, or substantial similarity of expression, to the jury.

2. *Lay and Expert Witnesses.* Recall the discussion at the outset of this section regarding the distinction between copying-in-fact in which the court must determine whether or not the defendant produced the allegedly infringing work independent of the plaintiff, and improper appropriation, in which the court must determine whether the defendant, having copied the plaintiff's work, copied so much that the defendant's work is deemed infringing. "Dissection" of the work and expert testimony are ordinarily appropriate with respect to the first question; no dissection, and evaluation from the perspective of the ordinary or lay observer, are ordinarily appropriate with respect to the second. With respect to the use of expert testimony, the Ninth Circuit's development of the "extrinsic/intrinsic" standards for infringement by substantial similarity, announced in *Sid & Marty Krofft Television Prods. Inc. v. McDonald's Corp.*, 562 F.2d 1157, 1164 (9th Cir. 1977), and followed in *Shaw*, tracks that distinction. Under the *Krofft* test, once access to the plaintiff's work is shown, the plaintiff must prove both substantial similarity of the ideas contained in the work under the "extrinsic test" (as to which dissection and expert testimony are appropriate) and substantial similarity of the work's protectable expression under the "intrinsic test." Under the intrinsic test, no dissection is permitted, and appropriation is determined based on the response of the ordinary reasonable person.

3. *The "Ordinary Reasonable Person."* Given the determination that the plaintiff has met its burden with respect to the extrinsic test (comparison of ideas, or objective elements of the copyrighted work), how is the trier of fact supposed to proceed? In *Krofft*, the court quoted *Twentieth Century Fox Film Corp. v. Stonesifer*, 140 F.2d 579, 582 (9th Cir. 1944): "The two works involved in this appeal should be considered and tested, not hypercritically or with meticulous scrutiny, but by the observations and impressions of the average reasonable reader and spectator." The court also noted the relevance of the "total concept and feel" standard of *Roth Greeting Cards v. United Card Co.*, 429 F.2d 1106, 1110 (9th Cir. 1976).

4. *Copying Unprotected Ideas.* The distinction between unprotectable ideas and protectable expression is fundamental to copyright doctrine. Observe that under the approach followed by the Ninth Circuit, proof of a triable issue of fact regarding the substantial similarity of the ideas in the defendant's work and the plaintiff's work—a circumstance that presumably is entirely permitted under copyright law—warrants the

court's handing the question of substantial similarity of expression to the trier of fact.

5. *Extrinsic and Intrinsic Tests and Literary Works.* The court in *Shaw* limits its rule — that satisfaction of the "extrinsic test for substantial similarity" creates a triable issue of fact with regard to the "intrinsic test" — to literary works. The extrinsic/intrinsic framework has been borrowed and applied to other kinds of copyrighted works. *See, e.g., Taylor Corp. v. Four Seasons Greetings, LLC,* 403 F.3d 958 (8th Cir. 2005) (greeting cards); *Three Boys Music Corp. v. Bolton,* 212 F.3d 477 (9th Cir. 2000) (musical composition).

## 3. The Right to Prepare Derivative Works

*STATUTE:* **Exclusive Rights in Copyrighted Works**
17 U.S.C. §106(2)

*STATUTE:* **Definition — "Derivative Work"**
17 U.S.C. §101

The original copyright statute of 1790 included only the rights to "print, publish, republish, and vend" the copyrighted work; it did not include the author's exclusive right to adapt or modify the work. The first form of an adaptation right was added to the statute in 1870, when Congress offered authors the exclusive right to translate the copyrighted work. The adaptation right was expanded in the 1909 revision and codified in 1976 at §106(2) as the exclusive right "to prepare derivative works based upon the copyrighted work." You have already seen that under certain circumstances, authorized "derivative" works may be copyrighted independently of works or other materials on which they are based, so long as they are sufficiently creative and original. The definition of "derivative work" supplied in §101 of the Copyright Act, and relied on in Chapter 6, remains applicable here: A derivative work is a work of authorship that is based on a preexisting work, or constitutes an adaptation or transformation of a preexisting work. Unauthorized derivative works may infringe an author's copyright, even if they contain otherwise copyrightable creativity and originality. In many cases, what constitutes a derivative work is an easy matter, and authors and producers have little difficulty negotiating licenses that authorize the preparation of derivative works. Movies made from copyrighted novels are almost invariably licensed by publishers or authors as authorized derivative works. In other cases, however, it is unclear what constitutes an infringing derivative work, and what, if anything, this right offers authors in addition to the exclusive right in §106(1) to reproduce the copyrighted work in (substantially similar) copies.

### MICRO STAR v. FORMGEN, INC.
#### 154 F.3d 1107 (9th Cir. 1998)

KOZINSKI, Circuit Judge.

Duke Nukem routinely vanquishes Octabrain and the Protozoid Slimer. But what about the dreaded Micro Star?

## I

FormGen Inc., GT Interactive Software Corp. and Apogee Software, Ltd. (collectively FormGen) made, distributed and own the rights to Duke Nukem 3D (D/N-3D), an immensely popular (and very cool) computer game. D/N-3D is played from the first-person perspective; the player assumes the personality and point of view of the title character, who is seen on the screen only as a pair of hands and an occasional boot, much as one might see oneself in real life without the aid of a mirror. Players explore a futuristic city infested with evil aliens and other hazards. The goal is to zap them before they zap you, while searching for the hidden passage to the next level. The basic game comes with twenty-nine levels, each with a different combination of scenery, aliens, and other challenges. The game also includes a "Build Editor," a utility that enables players to create their own levels. With FormGen's encouragement, players frequently post levels they have created on the Internet where others can download them. Micro Star, a computer software distributor, did just that: It downloaded 300 user-created levels and stamped them onto a CD, which it then sold commercially as Nuke It (N/I). N/I is packaged in a box decorated with numerous "screen shots," pictures of what the new levels look like when played.

Micro Star filed suit in district court, seeking a declaratory judgment that N/I did not infringe on any of FormGen's copyrights. FormGen counterclaimed, seeking a preliminary injunction barring further production and distribution of N/I. Relying on *Lewis Galoob Toys, Inc. v. Nintendo of Am., Inc.*, 964 F.2d 965 (9th Cir. 1992), the district court held that N/I was not a derivative work and therefore did not infringe FormGen's copyright. The district court did, however, grant a preliminary injunction as to the screen shots, finding that N/I's packaging violated FormGen's copyright by reproducing pictures of D/N-3D characters without a license. The court rejected Micro Star's fair use claims. Both sides appeal their losses.

\* \* \*

## III

To succeed on the merits of its claim that N/I infringes FormGen's copyright, FormGen must show (1) ownership of the copyright to D/N-3D, and (2) copying of protected expression by Micro Star. FormGen's copyright registration creates a presumption of ownership, and we are satisfied that FormGen has established its ownership of the copyright. We therefore focus on the latter issue.

FormGen alleges that its copyright is infringed by Micro Star's unauthorized commercial exploitation of user-created game levels. In order to understand FormGen's claims, one must first understand the way D/N-3D works. The game consists of three separate components: the game engine, the source art library and the MAP files.[2] The game engine is the heart of the computer program; in some sense, it *is* the program. It tells the computer when to read data, save and load games, play sounds and project images onto the screen. In order to create the audiovisual display

---

2. So-called because the files all end with the extension ".MAP". Also, no doubt, because they contain the layout for the various levels.

for a particular level, the game engine invokes the MAP file that corresponds to that level. Each MAP file contains a series of instructions that tell the game engine (and, through it, the computer) what to put where. For instance, the MAP file might say scuba gear goes at the bottom of the screen. The game engine then goes to the source art library, finds the image of the scuba gear, and puts it in just the right place on the screen.[3] The MAP file describes the level in painstaking detail, but it does not actually contain any of the copyrighted art itself; everything that appears on the screen actually comes from the art library. Think of the game's audiovisual display as a paint-by-numbers kit. The MAP file might tell you to put blue paint in section number 565, but it doesn't contain any blue paint itself; the blue paint comes from your palette, which is the low-tech analog of the art library, while you play the role of the game engine. When the player selects one of the N/I levels, the game engine references the N/I MAP files, but still uses the D/N-3D art library to generate the images that make up that level.

FormGen points out that a copyright holder enjoys the exclusive right to prepare derivative works based on D/N-3D. *See* 17 U.S.C. §106(2) (1994). According to FormGen, the audiovisual displays generated when D/N-3D is run in conjunction with the N/I CD MAP files are derivative works that infringe this exclusivity. Is FormGen right? The answer is not obvious.

The Copyright Act defines a derivative work as

a work based upon one or more preexisting works, such as a translation, musical arrangement, dramatization, fictionalization, motion picture version, sound recording, art reproduction, abridgment, condensation, or any other form in which a work may be recast, transformed, or adapted. A work consisting of editorial revisions, annotations, elaborations, or other modifications which, as a whole, represent an original work of authorship, is a "derivative work."

*Id.* §101. The statutory language is hopelessly overbroad, however, for "[e]very book in literature, science and art, borrows and must necessarily borrow, and use much which was well known and used before." *Emerson v. Davies,* 8 F. Cas. 615, 619 (C.C.D. Mass. 1845) (No. 4436), *quoted in 1 Nimmer on Copyright,* §3.01, at 3-2 (1997). To narrow the statute to a manageable level, we have developed certain criteria a work must satisfy in order to qualify as a derivative work. One of these is that a derivative work must exist in a "concrete or permanent form," *Galoob,* 964 F.2d at 967 (internal quotation marks omitted), and must substantially incorporate protected material from the preexisting work. Micro Star argues that N/I is not a derivative work because the audiovisual displays generated when D/N-3D is run with N/I's MAP files are not incorporated in any concrete or permanent form, and the MAP files do not copy any of D/N-3D's protected expression. It is mistaken on both counts.

3. Actually, this is all a bit metaphorical. Computer programs don't actually go anywhere or fetch anything. Rather, the game engine receives the player's instruction as to which game level to select and instructs the processor to access the MAP file corresponding to that level. The MAP file, in turn, consists of a series of instructions indicating which art images go where. When the MAP file calls for a particular art image, the game engine tells the processor to access the art library for instructions on how each pixel on the screen must be colored in order to paint that image.

The requirement that a derivative work must assume a concrete or permanent form was recognized without much discussion in *Galoob*. There, we noted that all the Copyright Act's examples of derivative works took some definite, physical form and concluded that this was a requirement of the Act. *See Galoob*, 964 F.2d at 967-68. Obviously, N/I's MAP files themselves exist in a concrete or permanent form; they are burned onto a CD-ROM. But what about the audiovisual displays generated when D/N-3D runs the N/I MAP files—i.e., the actual game level as displayed on the screen? Micro Star argues that, because the audiovisual displays in *Galoob* didn't meet the "concrete or permanent form" requirement, neither do N/I's.

In *Galoob*, we considered audiovisual displays created using a device called the Game Genie, which was sold for use with the Nintendo Entertainment System. The Game Genie allowed players to alter individual features of a game, such as a character's strength or speed, by selectively "blocking the value for a single data byte sent by the game cartridge to the [Nintendo console] and replacing it with a new value." *Galoob*, 964 F.2d at 967. Players chose which data value to replace by entering a code; over a billion different codes were possible. The Game Genie was dumb; it functioned only as a window into the computer program, allowing players to temporarily modify individual aspects of the game.

Nintendo sued, claiming that when the Game Genie modified the game system's audiovisual display, it created an infringing derivative work. We rejected this claim because "[a] derivative work must incorporate a protected work in some concrete or permanent form." *Galoob*, 964 F.2d at 967 (internal quotation marks omitted). The audiovisual displays generated by combining the Nintendo System with the Game Genie were not incorporated in any permanent form; when the game was over, they were gone. Of course, they could be reconstructed, but only if the next player chose to reenter the same codes.[4]

Micro Star argues that the MAP files on N/I are a more advanced version of the Game Genie, replacing old values (the MAP files in the original game) with new values (N/I's MAP files). But, whereas the audiovisual displays created by Game Genie were never recorded in any permanent form, the audiovisual displays generated by D/N-3D from the N/I MAP files are in the MAP files themselves. In *Galoob*, the audiovisual display was defined by the original game cartridge, not by the Game Genie; no one could possibly say that the data values inserted by the Game Genie described the audiovisual display. In the present case the audiovisual display that appears on the computer monitor when a N/I level is played is described—in exact detail—by a N/I MAP file.

This raises the interesting question whether an exact, down to the last detail, description of an audiovisual display (and—by definition—we know

---

4. A low-tech example might aid understanding. Imagine a product called the Pink Screener, which consists of a big piece of pink cellophane stretched over a frame. When put in front of a television, it makes everything on the screen look pinker. Someone who manages to record the programs with this pink cast (maybe by filming the screen) would have created an infringing derivative work. But the audiovisual display observed by a person watching television through the Pink Screener is not a derivative work because it does not incorporate the modified image in any permanent or concrete form. The Game Genie might be described as a fancy Pink Screener for video games, changing a value of the game as perceived by the current player, but never incorporating the new audiovisual display into a permanent or concrete form.

that MAP files do describe audiovisual displays down to the last detail) counts as a permanent or concrete form for purposes of *Galoob*. We see no reason it shouldn't. What, after all, does sheet music do but describe in precise detail the way a copyrighted melody sounds?.... Similarly, the N/I MAP files describe the audiovisual display that is to be generated when the player chooses to play D/N-3D using the N/I levels. Because the audiovisual displays assume a concrete or permanent form in the MAP files, *Galoob* stands as no bar to finding that they are derivative works.

In addition, "[a] work will be considered a derivative work only if it would be considered an infringing work if the material which it has derived from a preexisting work had been taken without the consent of a copyright proprietor of such preexisting work." *Mirage Editions v. Albuquerque A.R.T. Co.*, 856 F.2d 1341, 1343 (quoting 1 *Nimmer on Copyright* §3.01 (1986)) (internal quotation marks omitted). "To prove infringement, [FormGen] must show that [D/N-3D's and N/I's audiovisual displays] are substantially similar in both ideas and expression." *Litchfield v. Spielberg*, 736 F.2d 1352, 1356 (9th Cir. 1984) (emphasis omitted). Similarity of ideas may be shown by comparing the objective details of the works: plot, theme, dialogue, mood, setting, characters, etc. Similarity of expression focuses on the response of the ordinary reasonable person, and considers the total concept and feel of the works. FormGen will doubtless succeed in making these showings since the audiovisual displays generated when the player chooses the N/I levels come entirely out of D/N-3D's source art library.

Micro Star further argues that the MAP files are not derivative works because they do not, in fact, incorporate any of D/N-3D's protected expression. In particular, Micro Star makes much of the fact that the N/I MAP files reference the source art library, but do not actually contain any art files themselves. Therefore, it claims, nothing of D/N-3D's is reproduced in the MAP files. In making this argument, Micro Star misconstrues the protected work. The work that Micro Star infringes is the D/N-3D story itself—a beefy commando type named Duke who wanders around post-Apocalypse Los Angeles, shooting Pig Cops with a gun, lobbing hand grenades, searching for medkits and steroids, using a jetpack to leap over obstacles, blowing up gas tanks, avoiding radioactive slime. A copyright owner holds the right to create sequels, and the stories told in the N/I MAP files are surely sequels, telling new (though somewhat repetitive) tales of Duke's fabulous adventures. A book about Duke Nukem would infringe for the same reason, even if it contained no pictures.[5] ...

## IV

Because FormGen will likely succeed at trial in proving that Micro Star has infringed its copyright, we reverse the district court's order denying a preliminary injunction and remand for entry of such an injunction. Of course, we affirm the grant of the preliminary injunction barring Micro Star from selling N/I in boxes covered with screen shots of the game.

---

5. We note that the N/I MAP files can only be used with D/N-3D. If another game could use the MAP files to tell the story of a mousy fellow who travels through a beige maze, killing vicious saltshakers with paper-clips, then the MAP files would not incorporate the protected expression of D/N-3D because they would not be telling a D/N-3D story.

# Comments

*handwritten margin notes: "Inspired doesn't infringe need →"*

1. **Substantial Similarity of the Derivative Work.** To infringe the adaptation right, a derivative work must incorporate some copyrighted portion of the original work. A work that is merely inspired by or based on a prior work, but that is not substantially similar to protected expression contained in that work, does not infringe. *See Litchfield v. Spielberg*, 736 F.2d 1352, 1357 (9th Cir. 1984).

*handwritten margin notes: "106(1) need fixed  106(2) no fixed req."*

2. **Fixation of the Infringing Derivative Work.** Infringement of the §106(1) reproduction right requires that the infringer reproduce the work "in copies," providing a clear requirement that the infringing work be fixed in some tangible form. Section 106(2), by contrast, contains no such express requirement, prompting the conclusion that a work might infringe this right even if it were not fixed in a "copy." The House Report accompanying the 1976 Act made this distinction explicit:

> The exclusive right to prepare derivative works...overlaps the exclusive right of reproduction to some extent. It is broader than that right, however, in the sense that reproduction requires fixation in copies or phonorecords, whereas the preparation of a derivative work, such as a ballet, pantomime, or improvised performance, may be an infringement even though nothing is ever fixed in tangible form....
>
> [T]o constitute a violation of section 106(2), the infringing work must incorporate a portion of the copyrighted work in some form; for example, a detailed commentary on a work or a programmatic musical composition inspired by a novel would not normally constitute infringements under this clause.

H.R. Rep. No. 94-1476, 94th Cong., 2d Sess. 62 (1976), *reprinted in* 1976 U.S.C.C.A.N. 5659, 5675. Commentators and courts have noted, however, that a literal application of the statute, together with this legislative history, would lead to absurd results. For example, in the absence of a fixation requirement for infringement of §106(2), then merely imagining a variation of a copyrighted work would constitute a prima facie violation of copyright law. *See* Jessica Litman, *The Exclusive Right to Read*, 13 CARDOZO ARTS & ENT. L.J. 29, 38 n. 44 (1994). *Nimmer on Copyright*, the authoritative treatise on copyright law, agrees that a fixation requirement should apply to infringement of the §106(2) right. The authors' reasoning relies on the assumption that the phrase "derivative work" in §101 should be interpreted consistently. "Derivative works" must be fixed to be protected as copyrightable works; therefore the plain language of the statute requires that "derivative works" must be fixed to infringe §106(2). *See* 2 Melville B. Nimmer & David Nimmer, *Nimmer on Copyright*, §8.09[A] (2003). The court in *Micro Star* acknowledges that a prior panel of the Ninth Circuit reached this conclusion, based on the definition of "derivative work" in §101, in *Lewis Galoob Toys, Inc. v. Nintendo of Am., Inc.*, 964 F.2d 965 (9th Cir. 1992), and it concludes that if a "fixation" requirement applies in *Micro Star*, then that requirement is satisfied.

3. **The Copyrighted Work.** What is the copyrighted work that is infringed by *Micro Star*? Copyright infringement analysis ordinarily begins by

identifying the work of authorship that the copyright owner is trying to protect from infringement, and the scope of the owner's rights under §106 depends on the character of that work. The court does not clearly identify the copyrighted work of authorship that is infringed by Micro Star's unauthorized distribution of derivative works. The scope of rights under §106 may vary, depending on how the work of authorship is characterized. In *Micro Star*, for example, the work of authorship may reside in the audiovisual presentation of the game as users play it. That characterization raises questions regarding the fixation of the original work, and regarding ownership of creative authorship contributed by users. FormGen's copyright interest may be limited as a result. Alternatively, the work of authorship may reside in the computer coding that underlies the game engine, MAP files, and source art library. FormGen clearly owns valid copyrights to each of those, and there should be no doubt regarding fixation. Yet Micro Star copied little or none of that material. Finally, the copyrighted work might be characterized as the audiovisual work that results from the interaction of the original CD with the original MAP files, a work that the court characterizes as "the D/N-3D story itself—a beefy commando type named Duke who wanders around post-Apocalypse Los Angeles, shooting Pig Cops with a gun, lobbing hand grenades, searching for medkits and steroids, using a jetpack to leap over obstacles, blowing up gas tanks, avoiding radioactive slime."

4. ***The Infringing Work.*** That final characterization of the work makes the court's analysis an easy one: Even though Micro Star did not copy or modify any of the computer code that underlies Duke Nukem 3D, it did create a modified combination of the original CD and new MAP files, and that modified combination is fixed in a combination of the original CD and the new Micro Star CD. In footnote 5 of its opinion, the court expressly links its "sequel" analysis to this precise combination of the new MAP files and the original CD: "We note that the N/I MAP files can only be used with D/N-3D. If another game could use the MAP files to tell the story of a mousy fellow who travels through a beige maze, killing vicious saltshakers with paper-clips, then the MAP files would not incorporate the protected expression of D/N-3D because they would not be telling a D/N-3D story." The case therefore offers an important illustration of how courts (and lawyers) may use the tools of copyright doctrine flexibly in order to achieve what they believe are appropriate outcomes from the perspective of copyright policy.

5. ***Consumer Uses and New Markets.*** Courts in copyright cases often struggle with challenging issues by drawing parallels to copyright paradigms, that is, to books. That seems to be where the court rests its analysis, on analyzing Duke Nukem 3D as a form of literature. If the original Duke Nukem 3D video game were properly regarded as a story, should FormGen own the exclusive right to prepare sequels? On this point, the court makes what is best understood as a policy argument, grounded in economic theory. Because consumer demand for sequels is connected directly to consumer demand for the original work, then an author who holds the copyright to a story also should hold the exclusive right to make sequels. Protecting the author's exclusive right to authorize sequels enhances the incentives for that author to create the work in the first place. Professor Paul Goldstein

argues that markets for derivative versions of the work presumptively lie within the copyright owner's exclusive rights because anticipated returns from those markets affect authors' and publishers' initial decisions regarding whether and when to invest in creating and distributing the work. *See* Paul Goldstein, *Derivative Rights and Derivative Works in Copyright*, 30 J. COPYRIGHT SOC. 209 (1983).

To what extent should this economic rationale reach beyond initial investment decisions, to new, later-developed markets for adaptations or versions of a work? In *Castle Rock Entertainment, Inc. v. Carol Publishing Group, Inc.*, 150 F.3d 132 (2d Cir. 1998), the Court of Appeals for the Second Circuit concluded that an unauthorized book of trivia questions about the *Seinfeld* television series infringed the copyright in the television show. The court observed, however, that not only was there no evidence that publication of the plaintiff's "The Seinfeld Aptitude Test" harmed the profitability of the *Seinfeld* television series, but that *Seinfeld*'s audience grew following publication. Determination to challenge the book seems to have arisen not from harm to the market for the television series itself but from potential harm to a distinct market for books based on the television series.

6. *The Need for an Adaptation Right.* Given the breadth of "substantial similarity" doctrines and the relative ease with which courts identify the existence of fixed "copies," the broad scope of the reproduction right under §106(1) suggests that the adaptation right under §106(2) might be superfluous. (A century ago, however, the law's sense of what constituted an infringing "copy" was far narrower, and the value of an added right to adapt or translate the work was clearer. In *White-Smith Music Publ'g Co. v. Apollo*, 209 U.S. 1 (1908), the Supreme Court ruled that a player piano roll that embodied a copyrighted musical composition was not an infringing "copy" of the original work, because humans could not read or hear the work by examining the piano roll itself. Shortly thereafter, the Copyright Act of 1909 granted the copyright owner the exclusive right to "make any other version" of the copyrighted work.) Examining the language of the statute and the legislative history, Professor Tyler Ochoa has suggested one way to accommodate the adaptation right with the rest of §106: "[W]hat Congress intended was to prohibit the public performance of an unfixed derivative work, as well as the reproduction, public distribution, public performance or public display of a fixed derivative work." *See* Tyler T. Ochoa, *Copyright, Derivative Works and Fixation: Is* Galoob *a Mirage, or Does the* Form(Gen) *of the Alleged Derivative Work Matter?*, 20 SANTA CLARA COMPUTER & HIGH TECH. L.J. 991, 1044 (2004). The copyright owner's exclusive rights of distribution (§106(3)), public performance (§106(4)), and public display (§106(5)) are discussed in Sections A.4 and A.5, below.

## Problem

**7-1.** Nicholas Bushman developed a talking, animatronic stuffed bear that he called "Fuzzy the Bear." Fuzzy had the appearance of a typical stuffed bear, but inside there were motors that controlled movements of its arms, legs, and mouth that were synchronized with sounds played on a very small tape recorder installed in the bear's back that accommodated standard mini-cassettes. Each Fuzzy the Bear toy came with four prerecorded tapes. Each tape included a "content" track that included a Fuzzy the Bear story for children, written by Nicholas Bushman, and a "command" track that sent cues to the mechanical motors to synchronize Fuzzy's movements with the story. Operating Fuzzy the Bear with one of these tapes created the impression that the bear could "talk." The tape recorder could be opened, and tapes replaced, by removing a strip of the bear's furry covering. Bushman obtained a copyright registration for Fuzzy the Bear as an "audio-visual work." California Novelties sold a series of mini-cassettes for use with Fuzzy the Bear, which were prerecorded with public domain fairy tales and which also included "command" tracks that triggered Fuzzy's robotic movements. Bushman sued California Novelties for copyright infringement. Did California Novelties produce an unauthorized derivative work? *See Worlds of Wonder, Inc. v. Vector Intercontinental, Inc.*, 653 F. Supp. 135 (N.D. Ohio 1986).

## 4. The Right to Distribute Copies of the Work

*STATUTE:* **Exclusive Rights in Copyrighted Works**
17 U.S.C. §106(3)

*STATUTE:* **Definition — "Copies"**
17 U.S.C. §101

In many cases, infringement of the copyright owner's exclusive right to reproduce the work in copies will simultaneously infringe the exclusive right to distribute copies of the work, but in some important cases the copyright owner will rely solely on the latter. These involve cases where the infringer is not itself a producer of the infringing work, but, as in the case of a bookstore that stocks copies of an infringing reproduction, merely offers the work for sale.

## HOTALING v. CHURCH OF JESUS CHRIST OF LATTER-DAY SAINTS

**118 F.3d 199 (4th Cir. 1997)**

BUTZNER, Senior Circuit Judge.
   In this appeal we hold that a library distributes a published work, within the meaning of the Copyright Act, 17 U.S.C. §§101 *et seq.,* when it places an unauthorized copy of the work in its collection, includes the copy in its catalog or index system, and makes the copy available to the public. Because the district court ruled that these actions, by themselves, were insufficient to constitute distribution, we reverse the district court's summary judgment for the library and remand this case for further proceedings.

* * *

# I

We present the facts in the light most favorable to the plaintiffs, Donna Hotaling, William Hotaling, Jr., James Maher, and Dorothy Sherwood (collectively the Hotalings). The Hotalings compiled and copyrighted a number of genealogical research materials. The validity of the copyrights is not at issue at this stage of the litigation. The Hotaling research materials were published in microfiche form and marketed by All-Ireland Heritage, Inc. At some point, most likely between 1985 and 1989, the defendant, the Church of Jesus Christ of Latter-Day Saints (Church), acquired a single legitimate copy of the microfiche and added it to its main library's collection in Salt Lake City, Utah. Sometime before 1992, the Church made microfiche copies of the works without the Hotalings' permission and sent the copies to several of its branch libraries, located throughout the country. The legitimately acquired copy had a black background, and the copies that were made by the Church had purple backgrounds.

In July, 1991, Donna Hotaling learned that the Church was making copies and placing them in its branch libraries. She contacted the Church and demanded that it stop this activity. After receiving her complaint, the Church recalled and destroyed many of the copies that it had made. According to the affidavits submitted by the Church, it did not make any copies after 1991, and there is no evidence to contradict that assertion.

In 1992, All-Ireland Heritage, Inc., sued the Church for copyright infringement based on the Church's copying and distribution of the Hotaling works. The district court dismissed the action because All-Ireland Heritage, Inc., did not own the copyright. As a result of the lawsuit, the Church became concerned that nine of its branch libraries might still possess copies of the Hotaling works. In October, 1993, the Church sent a memorandum to those branch libraries asking them to search their microfiche inventories for copies of the works. Six libraries found and returned one microfiche copy each. Upon receipt, the main library destroyed these copies.

In 1994, Donna Hotaling visited a branch library in Rhode Island. During her visit, she discovered a paper copy of one of the Hotaling works. According to the Rhode Island library director, a patron made the copy and left it in an infrequently used section of the library. The director had been unaware, and believes the other staff members had been unaware, of the copy's existence. When the copy was discovered, the director destroyed it. Prior to April 1992, the Rhode Island library had returned to the Church's main library the microfiche from which the patron apparently had made the paper copy.

In 1995, Donna Hotaling went to the Church's main library in Salt Lake City. There she observed that the library maintained a microfiche copy of the Hotaling works in its collection. She examined a portion of the microfiche and noticed that it had a purple background. The Church acknowledges that the single copy it keeps in its collection is one that it made. The library retained this copy, the Church explains, because the copy it originally acquired was destroyed inadvertently.

In August, 1995, the Hotalings filed this suit. Following discovery, the Church moved for summary judgment, arguing that the record did not include any evidence of an infringing act within the three year statute of limitations. The district court granted the motion, and the Hotalings appealed.

* * *

III

A copyright infringement is a violation of "any of the exclusive rights of the copyright owner." 17 U.S.C. §501(a). One of those exclusive rights is the right "to distribute copies . . . of the copyrighted work to the public by sale or other transfer of ownership, or by rental, lease, or lending[.]" 17 U.S.C. §106(3). Generally, as permitted by what is known as the first-sale doctrine, the copyright owner's right to distribute a copyrighted work does not prevent the owner of a lawful copy of the work from selling, renting, lending, or otherwise disposing of the lawful copy. 17 U.S.C. §109(a). For example, a library may lend an authorized copy of a book that it lawfully owns without violating the copyright laws. *See* H.R. Rep. No. 94-1476, §109, at 79 (1976), *reprinted in* 1976 U.S.C.C.A.N. 5659, 5693 and *excerpted following* 17 U.S.C.A. §109. However, distributing unlawful copies of a copyrighted work does violate the copyright owner's distribution right and, as a result, constitutes copyright infringement. In order to establish "distribution" of a copyrighted work, a party must show that an unlawful copy was disseminated "to the public." 17 U.S.C. §106(3).

The Hotalings assert that the Church's libraries infringed their copyrights by distributing unauthorized copies of their works to the public. The libraries did not record public use of the microfiche. Consequently, the Hotalings concede that the record does not contain any evidence showing specific instances within the limitations period in which the libraries loaned the infringing copies to members of the public. But, they argue that proving the libraries held unauthorized copies in their collections, where they were available to the public, is sufficient to establish distribution within the meaning of the statute.

The Church, on the other hand, argues that holding a work in a library collection that is open to the public constitutes, at most, an offer to distribute the work. In order to establish distribution, the Church argues, the evidence would need to show that a member of the public accepted such an offer.

On this issue, we agree with the Hotalings. When a public library adds a work to its collection, lists the work in its index or catalog system, and makes the work available to the borrowing or browsing public, it has completed all the steps necessary for distribution to the public. At that point, members of the public can visit the library and use the work. Were this not to be considered distribution within the meaning of §106(3), a copyright holder would be prejudiced by a library that does not keep records of public use, and the library would unjustly profit by its own omission.

IV

The Church argues that, even if holding a copyrighted work in a library's collection does constitute distribution within the meaning of the statute, there is no evidence showing that, within the limitations period,

unauthorized copies of the Hotaling works were available to the public at
any of its libraries. In response, the Hotalings point to the copy Donna
Hotaling examined in Salt Lake City in 1995, the paper copy she found in
Rhode Island in 1994, and the six copies that were returned and destroyed
in 1993.

The Hotalings presented sufficient evidence to create a genuine issue
over whether the copy Donna Hotaling examined in Salt Lake City was
being distributed to the public in 1995. According to Donna Hotaling's
personal observations, that copy was part of the library's collection, listed
in the card file, and available to the public. In addition, she asserts that the
copy she inspected had a purple background. Based on this evidence, a
reasonable jury could conclude that the library held an unauthorized copy
of the Hotaling works in its publicly-accessible collection within the limitations period. Because the evidence is sufficient to show that this potentially
infringing copy was being distributed to the public as recently as 1995, it
provides a timely basis for Hotaling's suit.

* * *

## VI

The Hotalings presented evidence that suggests the Church distributed
at its main library one potentially infringing copy of the Hotaling works to
the public within the limitations period. For that reason, dismissal of the
suit based on the statute of limitations was inappropriate. Accordingly, we
reverse and remand to the district court for adjudication of the Hotalings'
surviving claim....

*REVERSED AND REMANDED.*

K.K. HALL, Circuit Judge, dissenting.

I respectfully dissent. The statute specifically identifies the sorts of "distribution" that violate a copyright, and none of them fit this situation.

The owner of a copyright does not possess an exclusive right to "distribute" the work in any conceivable manner; instead, it has the exclusive
right "to distribute copies . . . of the copyrighted work to the public *by sale or
other transfer of ownership, or by rental, lease, or lending*[.]" 17 U.S.C. §106(3).
The Church did not sell or give an infringing copy to anyone. The Church
did not "rent" or "lease" a copy; indeed, the public may use the Church's
libraries and all of their contents for free.

"Lending" is the only remaining candidate. Because they are for
research, the libraries do not permit materials to be checked out and
used by a member of the public off-premises. Do the libraries nonetheless
"lend" a work each time a patron consults it? I think not. The patron might
report that he "used" or "looked at" the work, but he would not likely say
that it had been "lent" to him.

Moreover, in this case, the plaintiffs do not even have any evidence that
anyone used or looked at an infringing copy during the limitations period.
The majority suggests that such evidence might have existed had the
libraries — unlike all or nearly all others — recorded each and every use
of its millions of volumes. It might have, but it does not.

In closing, I should say that I have some sympathy for the result
reached by the majority. A library's allowing on-premises public use of

an unauthorized copy should probably infringe a copyright. Nonetheless, I believe that current law does not deem this sort of use an infringing "distribution," and that, in any event, there is no evidence of such use in this case.

I would affirm the judgment of the district court.

## Comments

1. *Making a Work Available for Distribution.* The court in *Hotaling* concludes that making a copy of a work available for distribution is sufficient to establish liability under §106(3). Does making a copy of a work available jeopardize the copyright owner's legitimate interests to the same extent that selling unauthorized copies does? Consider *A&M Records, Inc. v. Napster, Inc.*, 239 F.3d 1004 (9th Cir. 2001). The defendant was Napster, Inc., which distributed the original free MusicShare or "Napster" file sharing software. Napster, Inc. was alleged to be liable for infringement by its users. User infringement consisted, in part, of logging in to the Napster system; logging in automatically copied the file names of the user's .mp3 audio files to Napster servers, where those names could be searched by other Napster users. If the search revealed a match, the Napster servers allowed the two users to connect directly, and the .mp3 file could be uploaded (by the first user) and downloaded (by the second user). The court concluded that the first user was violating the distribution rights of owners in the copyrighted music: "Napster users who upload file names to the search index for others to copy violate plaintiffs' distribution rights." *Id.* at 1014.

2. *Limitations and Exceptions.* As the reproduction right under §106(1) is subject to the limitation of §117, for computer programs, the distribution right under §106(3) is subject to a variety of limitations and exceptions, chiefly privileges for libraries established by §108 and the first sale doctrine of §109. Procedurally, these are usually characterized as defenses to liability for infringement, and they are discussed in greater depth in the next chapter.

3. *The Importation Right.* Section 106(3) grants the copyright owner the exclusive right to distribute copies of the work. Section 602 of the Copyright Act grants a related right: the power to prevent the unauthorized importation of copies of the work into the United States: "Importation into the United States, without the authority of the owner of copyright under this title, of copies or phonorecords of a work that have been acquired outside the United States is an infringement of the exclusive right to distribute copies or phonorecords under section 106, actionable under section 501." The statute contains limited exceptions for copies for private use and for not-for-profit use. The Supreme Court has held, however, that §602 does not apply to importation of copies that were lawfully produced in the United States, then sold abroad and eventually re-imported into the United States — so-called "grey market" copies. *Quality King Distributors, Inc. v. L'anza Research International, Inc.*, 523 U.S. 135 (1998). The defendant's business in that case was premised on the fact that the plaintiff's goods — hair care products bearing copyrighted labels — were offered for sale overseas at prices significantly

lower than their domestic prices. The defendant was able to purchase the goods overseas and resell them in the United States at prices below their "authorized" price offered by the plaintiff, and still earn a profit.

## Problem

**7-2.** In 1994, Fire Safety Appliances (FSA) developed and registered copyrights in three volumes of digital "clip art" files for use by members of the emergency services industries. Joe Van Buren, a volunteer firefighter and computer consultant who manages the website for the South Hills Emergency Response District (SHERD), copied all three volumes of FSA's clip art onto the computer server that hosts the SHERD website and created links to each FSA clip art item on the SHERD home page, so that individual police, fire, and EMS departments in the SHERD territory could use that clip art if they chose to. The SHERD home page and all files to which it links are hosted on a server that is owned and operated by a commercial website hosting service, Running Rabbit, Inc. Did SHERD violate FSA's exclusive right to distribute FSA's works when it copied them to the Running Rabbit server? *See Marobie-FL, Inc. v. National Association of Fire Equipment Distributors*, 983 F. Supp. 1167 (N.D. Ill. 1997).

## 5. The Public Display and Public Performance Rights

Owners of copyrights in certain types of works of authorship are granted the exclusive rights to publicly perform and publicly display the copyrighted work, under §106(4) and (5) of the Copyright Act. In general, the scope of the exclusive right corresponds roughly to the ordinary manner in which an author, artist, or publisher would expect to make money from the work. Paintings, photographs, and sculpture may be put on display, and customers may be charged admission for the privilege of viewing them. Orchestras and theater companies perform symphonies and plays in concert halls and theaters and likewise usually expect to charge admission. Not all works of authorship can be performed or displayed, so that the rights granted in these subsections do not apply to all copyrighted works. As a preliminary matter, then, the copyrighted work must be classified in order to determine whether either of these rights, or both, might apply. Some of the exclusions are intuitive; there is no exclusive right of public performance for a pictorial, graphic, or sculptural work, for example. Some, however, represent accommodations of the public interest (for example, owners of copyrights in architectural works do not have a public display right), and some represent conscious decisions by Congress to limit the scope of the copyright monopoly. Owners of copyrights in sound recordings (such as the CD version of a popular song) do not have a general public performance right. In practice, this means that broadcasters owe copyright royalties to owners of musical composition copyrights (the songwriters) but not to owners of recordings (recording companies and recording artists). In addition, and importantly, these two rights apply only to *public* performances and displays.

*STATUTE:* **Exclusive Rights in Copyrighted Works**
17 U.S.C. §106(4), (5)

*STATUTE:* **Definitions — "Display," "Perform," "Publicly," "Transmit"**
17 U.S.C. §101

## COLUMBIA PICTURES INDUS. v. REDD HORNE, INC.
### 749 F.2d 154 (3d Cir. 1984)

RE, Chief Judge.

In this copyright infringement case, defendants appeal from an order of the United States District Court for the Western District of Pennsylvania which granted the plaintiffs' motion for summary judgment, and enjoined defendants from exhibiting plaintiffs' copyrighted motion pictures....

\* \* \*

### THE FACTS

Maxwell's Video Showcase, Ltd., operates two stores in Erie, Pennsylvania. At these two facilities, Maxwell's sells and rents video cassette recorders and prerecorded video cassettes, and sells blank video cassette cartridges. These activities are not the subject of the plaintiffs' complaint. The copyright infringement issue in this case arises from defendants' *exhibition* of video cassettes of the plaintiffs' films, or what defendants euphemistically refer to as their "showcasing" or "in-store rental" concept.

Each store contains a small showroom area in the front of the store, and a "showcase" or exhibition area in the rear. The front showroom contains video equipment and materials for sale or rent, as well as dispensing machines for popcorn and carbonated beverages. Movie posters are also displayed in this front area. In the rear "showcase" area, patrons may view any of an assortment of video cassettes in small, private booths with space for two to four people. There are a total of eighty-five booths in the two stores. Each booth or room is approximately four feet by six feet and is carpeted on the floor and walls. In the front there is a nineteen inch color television and an upholstered bench in the back.

The procedure followed by a patron wishing to utilize one of the viewing booths or rooms is the same at both facilities. The customer selects a film from a catalogue which contains the titles of available films. The fee charged by Maxwell's depends on the number of people in the viewing room, and the time of day. The price is $5.00 for one or two people before 6 p.m., and $6.00 for two people after 6 p.m. There is at all times a $1.00 surcharge for the third and fourth person. The fee also entitles patrons to help themselves to popcorn and soft drinks before entering their assigned rooms. Closing the door of the viewing room activates a signal in the counter area at the front of the store. An employee of Maxwell's then places the cassette of the motion picture chosen by the viewer into one of the video cassette machines in the front of the store and the picture is transmitted to the patron's viewing room. The viewer may adjust the light in the room, as well as the volume, brightness, and color levels on the television set.

Access to each room is limited to the individuals who rent it as a group. Although no restriction is placed on the composition of a group, strangers are not grouped in order to fill a particular room to capacity. Maxwell's is open to any member of the public who wishes to utilize its facilities or services.

Maxwell's advertises on Erie radio stations and on the theatre pages of the local newspapers. Typically, each advertisement features one or more motion pictures, and emphasizes Maxwell's selection of films, low prices, and free refreshments. The advertisements do not state that these motion pictures are video-cassette copies. At the entrance to the two Maxwell's facilities, there are also advertisements for individual films, which resemble movie posters.

### INFRINGEMENT OF PLAINTIFFS' COPYRIGHT

It may be stated at the outset that this is not a case of unauthorized taping or video cassette piracy. The defendants obtained the video cassette copies of plaintiffs' copyrighted motion pictures by purchasing them from either the plaintiffs or their authorized distributors. The sale or rental of these cassettes to individuals for home viewing is also not an issue. Plaintiffs do not contend that in-home use infringes their copyright.

The plaintiffs' complaint is based on their contention that the exhibition or showing of the video cassettes in the private booths on defendants' premises constitutes an unauthorized public performance in violation of plaintiffs' exclusive rights under the federal copyright laws.

It is acknowledged that it is the role of the Congress, not the courts, to formulate new principles of copyright law when the legislature has determined that technological innovations have made them necessary. In the words of Justice Stevens, "Congress has the constitutional authority and the institutional ability to accommodate fully the varied permutations of competing interests that are inevitably implicated by such new technology." [*Sony Corp. v. Universal City Studios, Inc.*, 464 U.S. 417, 431 (1984).] A defendant, however, is not immune from liability for copyright infringement simply because the technologies are of recent origin or are being applied to innovative uses. Although this case involves a novel application of relatively recent technological developments, it can nonetheless be readily analyzed and resolved within the existing statutory framework.

\* \* \*

It is undisputed that the defendants were licensed to exercise the right of distribution. A copyright owner, however, may dispose of a copy of his work while retaining all underlying copyrights which are not expressly or impliedly disposed of with that copy. Thus, it is clear that the plaintiffs have retained their interest in the other four enumerated rights. *See* M. Nimmer, 2 Nimmer on Copyright §8.01[A], at 8-11 to 8-12 (1983). Since the rights granted by section 106 are separate and distinct, and are severable from one another, the grant of one does not waive any of the other exclusive rights. Thus, plaintiffs' sales of video cassette copies of their copyrighted motion pictures did not result in a waiver of any of the other exclusive rights enumerated in section 106, such as the exclusive right to perform their motion pictures publicly. In essence, therefore, the fundamental question is whether the defendants' activities constitute a public performance of the plaintiffs' motion pictures. We agree with the conclusion of the district court that these activities constitute a public performance, and are an infringement.

"To perform a work means . . . in the case of a motion picture or other audiovisual work, to show its images in any sequence or to make the sounds accompanying it audible." 17 U.S.C. §101 (1982). Clearly, playing a video cassette results in a sequential showing of a motion picture's images and in making the sounds accompanying it audible. Thus, Maxwell's activities constitute a performance under section 101.

The remaining question is whether these performances are public. Section 101 also states that to perform a work "publicly" means "[t]o perform . . . it at a place open to the public or at any place where a substantial number of persons outside of a normal circle of a family and its social acquaintances is gathered." *Id.* The statute is written in the disjunctive, and thus two categories of places can satisfy the definition of "to perform a work publicly." The first category is self-evident; it is "a place open to the public." The second category, commonly referred to as a semi-public place, is determined by the size and composition of the audience.

The legislative history indicates that this second category was added to expand the concept of public performance by including those places that, although not open to the public at large, are accessible to a significant number of people. *See* H.R. Rep. No. 1476, 94th Cong., 2d Sess. 64, *reprinted in,* 1976 U.S. Code Cong. & Ad. News 5659, 5677-78 (hereafter cited as *House Report*). Clearly, if a place is public, the size and composition of the audience are irrelevant. However, if the place is not public, the size and composition of the audience will be determinative.

We find it unnecessary to examine the second part of the statutory definition because we agree with the district court's conclusion that Maxwell's was open to the public. On the composition of the audience, the district court noted that "the showcasing operation is not distinguishable in any significant manner from the exhibition of films at a conventional movie theater." 568 F. Supp. at 500. Any member of the public can view a motion picture by paying the appropriate fee. The services provided by Maxwell's are essentially the same as a movie theatre, with the additional feature of privacy. The relevant "place" within the meaning of section 101 is each of Maxwell's two stores, not each individual booth within each store. Simply because the cassettes can be viewed in private does not mitigate the essential fact that Maxwell's is unquestionably open to the public.

The conclusion that Maxwell's activities constitute public performances is fully supported by subsection (2) of the statutory definition of public performance:

> (2) to transmit or otherwise communicate a performance . . . of the work to a place specified by clause (1) or to the public, by means of any device or process, whether the members of the public capable of receiving the performance . . . receive it in the same place or in separate places and at the same time or at different times.

17 U.S.C. §101 (1982). As explained in the House Report which accompanies the Copyright Revision Act of 1976, "a performance made available by transmission to the public at large is 'public' even though the recipients are not gathered in a single place.... The same principles apply whenever the potential recipients of the transmission represent a limited segment of the public, such as the occupants of hotel rooms...." *House Report, supra,* at 64-65, U.S. Code Cong. & Admin. News, p. 5678. Thus, the transmission of a performance to members of the public, even in private settings such as hotel rooms or Maxwell's viewing rooms, constitutes a public performance. As the statutory language and legislative history clearly indicate, the fact that members of the public view the performance at different times does not alter this legal consequence.

Professor Nimmer's examination of this definition is particularly pertinent: "*if the same copy*...of a given work is repeatedly played (*i.e.,* 'performed') by different members of the public, albeit at different times, this constitutes a 'public' performance." 2 M. Nimmer, §8.14[C] [3], at 8-142 (emphasis in original). Indeed, Professor Nimmer would seem to have envisaged Maxwell's when he wrote:

> one may anticipate the possibility of theaters in which patrons occupy separate screening rooms, for greater privacy, and in order not to have to await a given hour for commencement of a given film. These too should obviously be regarded as public performances within the underlying rationale of the Copyright Act.

*Id.* at 8-142. Although Maxwell's has only one copy of each film, it shows each copy repeatedly to different members of the public. This constitutes a public performance.

*         *         *

The judgment of the district court, therefore, will be affirmed.

## Comments

1. *"Performance" or "Display."* Issues under the public performance and public display rights require a two-stage analysis. The first question is whether there is a "performance" or "display" by the defendant. The definitions of the two concepts in §101 are similar, except that the "display" of a work generally means the visual presentation of a static form or image, and the "performance" of a work generally means that the presentation is dynamic. A statue or painting is displayed; a motion picture is performed. The more challenging question involves changing technology. As the law has evolved to recognize infringing "copies" of copyrighted works in forms that operated mechanically, the definitions of "performance" and "display" recognize that the infringement may occur by means of a "device or process." This language was adopted in response to the decision of the Supreme Court in *Twentieth Century Music Corp. v. Aiken,* 422 U.S. 151 (1975). George Aiken, the owner of a Pittsburgh delicatessen, was accused of copyright infringement by virtue of a radio that played music over four speakers in the store. The Court held

that his turning on the radio did not make him a "performer" of the music. Rather, he was the audience.

2. *The "Homestyle" Exception.* By virtue of the definitions now found in the Copyright Act, current law treats Aiken and other music-playing business owners as "performers." Congress has tried to accommodate the interests of small business owners, such as bars, shops, and restaurants, in other ways. In what is known as the "homestyle" exception to the public performance right, public performances via "a single receiving apparatus of a kind commonly used in private homes" are exempt from liability, so long as certain additional conditions are met, including the square footage of the business in which the radio is being played, and the number of speakers or television monitors does not exceed a statutory number. The precise rules are quite precise and followed exacting negotiations in Congress between copyright-owning interests and small business owners. *See* 17 U.S.C. §110(5). In 2000 a Dispute Resolution Panel of the World Trade Organization, which adjudicates international disputes regarding national compliance with international trade law (including the TRIPs Agreement on intellectual property rights), ruled that the square-footage and space limitations prescribed by §110(5) violated United States obligations under TRIPs rules because in practice, the exception applied so broadly that it unfairly prejudiced the normal economic interests of copyright holders. The Copyright Act has not been amended. The United States subsequently settled the dispute via a payment to the European Union to compensate performers.

3. *"Public."* The second question is whether the performance or display is "public." This is the question that concerned the court in *Redd Horne.* The statute contains two alternative definitions of "public." Public may be measured according to the characteristics of the location itself. Or, public may be measured by the number of people present to hear (or see) a copyrighted work, and the relationship among them. In *Redd Horne,* the court concludes that the first standard applies. Notably, however, the court chooses to emphasize the fact that each store as a whole is "open to the public," rather than the possibility that each individual viewing booth might be a place open only to a "normal circle of a family and its social acquaintances."

4. *Public Performance by Transmission.* The holding in *Redd Horne* appears to depend in part on the particular technical mechanism used to "perform" the copyrighted motion pictures. Each individual viewing booth included only a television for viewing videotapes running on a player in the front of the store, plus furniture for sitting and watching the films. Should the outcome change if the location of the machines changes, or if the furnishings change? In *Columbia Pictures Industries, Inc. v. Aveco, Inc.,* 800 F.2d 59 (3d Cir. 1986), the defendant re-structured the in-store rental business. Customers rented video tapes at a desk in the store and took the tapes to individual viewing booths that were outfitted with individual video players. The court held that despite the absence of a "transmission" as in *Redd Horne,* and despite the fact that customers played the tapes, the defendant was still engaged in a "public performance." In *Columbia Pictures Industries, Inc. v. Professional Real Estate*

*Investors, Inc.*, 866 F.2d 278 (9th Cir. 1989), however, the defendant was a hotel that rented videodiscs to guests for viewing on in-room equipment. In this case, the court concluded that the relevant "place" for "public performance" purposes was the hotel room itself, and it held that hotel rooms were not places "open to the public."

5. *Tailored Rights for Sound Recordings and Architectural Works.* The Copyright Act defines "sound recordings" in §101 as "works that result from the fixation of a series of musical, spoken, or other sounds, but not including the sounds accompanying a motion picture or other audiovisual work, regardless of the nature of the material objects, such as disks, tapes, or other phonorecords, in which they are embodied." (Under §101, a "phonorecord" is the fixed object that embodies a copyrighted work that consists of sounds.) The recording of a popular musical composition is a copyrightable work that is distinct from the copyrighted composition. Sound recordings were not made eligible for statutory copyright protection until 1971, and owners of sound recording copyrights do not receive the full array of exclusive rights under §106. The reproduction right under §106(1) is limited, for example, to "the right to duplicate the sound recording in the form of phonorecords or copies that directly or indirectly recapture the actual sounds fixed in the recording." 17 U.S.C. §114(b). Under §114(b) a recording artist does not need a license to replicate a recording by re-recording an identical version with new musical performers. Duplicating the original recording using mechanical or digital equipment, however, is prohibited.

Originally, owners of copyrights in sound recordings were not granted public performance rights. Congress amended §106 in 1995 to authorize a public performance right for sound recording copyrights in "digital audio transmissions," i.e., for digital downloading and digital music subscription services. 17 U.S.C. §106(6). Rights in sound recording copyrights are more fully specified in §114. You will read more about them in Chapter 8, in connection with compulsory and statutory licensing of copyrighted works.

Section 101 defines an "architectural work" as "the design of a building as embodied in any tangible medium of expression, including a building, architectural plans, or drawings. The work includes the overall form as well as the arrangement and composition of spaces and elements in the design, but does not include individual standard features." Architectural work copyrights were added to the Copyright Act in 1990. Because architectural works are frequently embodied in buildings, the Copyright Act includes two important limitations on the exclusive rights of the owner of a copyright in an architectural work. The right of public display cannot be used to prevent photographing an architectural work (or displaying or distributing those photographs), if the work is located in or ordinarily visible from a public place. 17 U.S.C. §120(a). Both tourists and professional photographers have the right under §120(a) to take photographs of copyrighted buildings, so long as the building is in a public place, or can ordinarily been seen from a public place. Finally, the owner of a building that embodies a copyrighted work has the right to modify or even destroy the building, which limits the copyright owner's exclusive right to prepare derivative works. 17 U.S.C. §120(b).

---

### COMPARATIVE PERSPECTIVE
### Patent Infringement and Trademark Infringement Compared

Despite the conceptual relationship among the three major doctrines of intellectual property law, each one includes a distinct set of rights. In understanding copyright law, take care not to "borrow" analyses and concepts from trademark and patent law uncritically. As described in the first section of this chapter, copyright law provides copyright owners with a specific set of exclusive rights. Patent law provides a set of exclusive rights to the patent owner that is likewise enumerated (in 35 U.S.C. §271), but which are different in important ways from the copyright owner's rights. The patentee possesses the exclusive rights to make, use, sell, offer to sell, and import the patented invention. Trademark law does not provide trademark owners with an exclusive right. Instead, trademark law offers protection against use of a mark that creates a likelihood of confusion with the trademark owner's mark, or that (in some circumstances) dilutes the owner's mark. *See* 15 U.S.C. §§1114, 1125.

---

## B. SECONDARY LIABILITY

Copyright owners, like many parties injured by wrongful conduct, often cannot find the parties who directly caused the harm, or cannot or do not want to sue them. Direct infringers in copyright cases may have no assets to pay a judgment, or they may be customers of the copyright owner whose ongoing good will is more important to the copyright owner, as a practical matter, than an injunction or damage award based on copyright law. To take account of these and related circumstances, copyright law authorizes copyright owners to pursue relief against those who participate in and support infringing activity, but who are not themselves direct infringers. Secondary, or indirect, liability for copyright infringement comes in two forms: contributory liability and vicarious liability. Copyright owners frequently allege both claims in suits against third parties that assist or enable copyright infringement, but the two doctrines have distinct pleading and proof requirements. Contributory liability applies to a party that substantially participates in an activity, knowing that copyright infringement is the probable result. Vicarious liability does not require active participation by the accused defendant, merely that the indirect infringer has benefited financially from the infringement, while having the power to control the activity that produced it. (A recent case, *Metro-Goldwyn-Mayer Studios v. Grokster, Ltd.*, has introduced the prospect of a third form of relief: liability for "inducing" copyright infringement. The *Grokster* case appears in the materials below.) One thing that all theories of indirect liability share is the fundamental principle that there can be no secondary liability unless someone is identified as a primary (direct) infringer. The direct infringer need not be a party to the lawsuit. In fact, it may be preferable as a strategic matter not to sue the direct infringer and then to point to that infringer's "empty chair" in the courtroom. The named defendant, isolated in this way, may be more easily characterized as a culpable wrongdoer.

## FONOVISA, INC. v. CHERRY AUCTION, INC.
### 76 F.3d 259 (9th Cir. 1996)

SCHROEDER, Circuit Judge.

This is a copyright and trademark enforcement action against the operators of a swap meet, sometimes called a flea market, where third-party vendors routinely sell counterfeit recordings that infringe on the plaintiff's copyrights and trademarks. The district court dismissed on the pleadings, holding that the plaintiffs, as a matter of law, could not maintain any cause of action against the swap meet for sales by vendors who leased its premises. . . . We reverse.

### BACKGROUND

The plaintiff and appellant is Fonovisa, Inc., a California corporation that owns copyrights and trademarks to Latin/Hispanic music recordings. Fonovisa filed this action in district court against defendant-appellee, Cherry Auction, Inc., and its individual operators (collectively "Cherry Auction"). For purposes of this appeal, it is undisputed that Cherry Auction operates a swap meet in Fresno, California, similar to many other swap meets in this country where customers come to purchase various merchandise from individual vendors. The vendors pay a daily rental fee to the swap meet operators in exchange for booth space. Cherry Auction supplies parking, conducts advertising and retains the right to exclude any vendor for any reason, at any time, and thus can exclude vendors for patent and trademark infringement. In addition, Cherry Auction receives an entrance fee from each customer who attends the swap meet.

There is also no dispute for purposes of this appeal that Cherry Auction and its operators were aware that vendors in their swap meet were selling counterfeit recordings in violation of Fonovisa's trademarks and copyrights. Indeed, it is alleged that in 1991, the Fresno County Sheriff's Department raided the Cherry Auction swap meet and seized more than 38,000 counterfeit recordings. The following year, after finding that vendors at the Cherry Auction swap meet were still selling counterfeit recordings, the Sheriff sent a letter notifying Cherry Auction of the on-going sales of infringing materials, and reminding Cherry Auction that they had agreed to provide the Sheriff with identifying information from each vendor. In addition, in 1993, Fonovisa itself sent an investigator to the Cherry Auction site and observed sales of counterfeit recordings.

\* \* \*

The copyright claims are brought pursuant to 17 U.S.C. §§101 *et seq.* Although the Copyright Act does not expressly impose liability on anyone other than direct infringers, courts have long recognized that in certain circumstances, vicarious or contributory liability will be imposed. *See Sony Corp. of America v. Universal City Studios, Inc.,* 464 U.S. 417, 435 (1984) (explaining that "vicarious liability is imposed in virtually all areas of the law, and the concept of contributory infringement is merely a species of the broader problem of identifying circumstances in which it is just to hold one individually accountable for the actions of another").

\* \* \*

### VICARIOUS COPYRIGHT INFRINGEMENT

The concept of vicarious copyright liability was developed in the Second Circuit as an outgrowth of the agency principles of respondeat superior. The landmark case on vicarious liability for sales of counterfeit recordings is *Shapiro, Bernstein and Co. v. H.L. Green Co.,* 316 F.2d 304 (2d Cir. 1963). In *Shapiro,* the court was faced with a copyright infringement suit against the owner of a chain of department stores where a concessionaire was selling counterfeit recordings. Noting that the normal agency rule of respondeat superior imposes liability on an employer for copyright infringements by an employee, the court endeavored to fashion a principle for enforcing copyrights against a defendant whose economic interests were intertwined with the direct infringer's, but who did not actually employ the direct infringer.

The *Shapiro* court looked at the two lines of cases it perceived as most clearly relevant. In one line of cases, the landlord-tenant cases, the courts had held that a landlord who lacked knowledge of the infringing acts of its tenant and who exercised no control over the leased premises was not liable for infringing sales by its tenant. *See, e.g., Deutsch v. Arnold,* 98 F.2d 686 (2d Cir. 1938). In the other line of cases, the so-called "dance hall cases," the operator of an entertainment venue was held liable for infringing performances when the operator (1) could control the premises and (2) obtained a direct financial benefit from the audience, who paid to enjoy the infringing performance. *See, e.g., Dreamland Ball Room, Inc. v. Shapiro, Bernstein & Co.,* 36 F.2d 354 (7th Cir. 1929).

From those two lines of cases, the *Shapiro* court determined that the relationship between the store owner and the concessionaire in the case before it was closer to the dance-hall model than to the landlord-tenant model. It imposed liability even though the defendant was unaware of the infringement. *Shapiro* deemed the imposition of vicarious liability neither unduly harsh nor unfair because the store proprietor had the power to cease the conduct of the concessionaire, and because the proprietor derived an obvious and direct financial benefit from the infringement. The test was more clearly articulated in a later Second Circuit case as follows: "even in the absence of an employer-employee relationship one may be vicariously liable if he has the right and ability to supervise the

infringing activity and also has a direct financial interest in such activities."
*Gershwin Publishing Corp. v. Columbia Artists Management, Inc.*, 443 F.2d
1159, 1162 (2d Cir. 1971)....

The district court in this case agreed with defendant Cherry Auction that
Fonovisa did not, as a matter of law, meet either the control or the financial
benefit prong of the vicarious copyright infringement test articulated in
*Gershwin, supra.* Rather, the district court concluded that based on the
pleadings, "Cherry Auction neither supervised nor profited from the vendors' sales." 847 F. Supp. at 1496. In the district court's view, with respect
to both control and financial benefit, Cherry Auction was in the same position as an absentee landlord who has surrendered its exclusive right of
occupancy in its leased property to its tenants.

This analogy to absentee landlord is not in accord with the facts as
alleged in the district court and which we, for purposes of appeal, must
accept. The allegations below were that vendors occupied small booths
within premises that Cherry Auction controlled and patrolled. According
to the complaint, Cherry Auction had the right to terminate vendors for
any reason whatsoever and through that right had the ability to control the
activities of vendors on the premises. In addition, Cherry Auction promoted the swap meet and controlled the access of customers to the swap
meet area. In terms of control, the allegations before us are strikingly
similar to those in *Shapiro* and *Gershwin.*

In *Shapiro,* for example, the court focused on the formal licensing agreement between defendant department store and the direct infringer-con-
cessionaire. There, the concessionaire selling the bootleg recordings had a
licensing agreement with the department store (H.L. Green Company) that
required the concessionaire and its employees to "abide by, observe and
obey all regulations promulgated from time to time by the H.L. Green
Company," and H.L. Green Company had the "unreviewable discretion"
to discharge the concessionaires' employees. 316 F.2d at 306. In practice,
H.L. Green Company was not actively involved in the sale of records and
the concessionaire controlled and supervised the individual employees.
Nevertheless, H.L. Green's ability to police its concessionaire—which parallels Cherry Auction's ability to police its vendors under Cherry Auction's
similarly broad contract with its vendors—was sufficient to satisfy the control requirement.

In *Gershwin,* the defendant lacked the formal, contractual ability to control the direct infringer. Nevertheless, because of defendant's "pervasive
participation in the formation and direction" of the direct infringers,
including promoting them (i.e. creating an audience for them), the
court found that defendants were in a position to police the direct infringers and held that the control element was satisfied. 443 F.2d at 1163. As
the promoter and organizer of the swap meet, Cherry Auction wields the
same level of control over the direct infringers as did the *Gershwin* defendant.

The district court's dismissal of the vicarious liability claim in this case
was therefore not justified on the ground that the complaint failed to allege
sufficient control.

We next consider the issue of financial benefit. The plaintiff's allegations
encompass many substantive benefits to Cherry Auction from the

infringing sales. These include the payment of a daily rental fee by each of the infringing vendors; a direct payment to Cherry Auction by each customer in the form of an admission fee, and incidental payments for parking, food and other services by customers seeking to purchase infringing recordings.

Cherry Auction nevertheless contends that these benefits cannot satisfy the financial benefit prong of vicarious liability because a commission, directly tied to the sale of particular infringing items, is required. They ask that we restrict the financial benefit prong to the precise facts presented in *Shapiro*, where defendant H.L. Green Company received a 10 or 12 per cent commission from the direct infringers' gross receipts. Cherry Auction points to the low daily rental fee paid by each vendor, discounting all other financial benefits flowing to the swap meet, and asks that we hold that the swap meet is materially similar to a mere landlord. The facts alleged by Fonovisa, however, reflect that the defendants reap substantial financial benefits from admission fees, concession stand sales and parking fees, all of which flow directly from customers who want to buy the counterfeit recordings at bargain basement prices. The plaintiff has sufficiently alleged direct financial benefit.

Our conclusion is fortified by the continuing line of cases, starting with the dance hall cases, imposing vicarious liability on the operator of a business where infringing performances enhance the attractiveness of the venue to potential customers. In *Polygram* [*Intern. Pub., Inc. v. Nevada/ TIG, Inc.*, 855 F. Supp. 1314 (D. Mass. 1984)], for example, direct infringers were participants in a trade show who used infringing music to communicate with attendees and to cultivate interest in their wares. 855 F. Supp. at 1332. The court held that the trade show participants "derived a significant financial benefit from the attention" that attendees paid to the infringing music. *Id.* In this case, the sale of pirated recordings at the Cherry Auction swap meet is a "draw" for customers, as was the performance of pirated music in the dance hall cases and their progeny.

Plaintiffs have stated a claim for vicarious copyright infringement.

### CONTRIBUTORY COPYRIGHT INFRINGEMENT

Contributory infringement originates in tort law and stems from the notion that one who directly contributes to another's infringement should be held accountable. *See Sony v. Universal City*, 464 U.S. at 417; 1 Neil Boorstyn, Boorstyn On Copyright §10.06[2], at 10-21 (1994) ("In other words, the common law doctrine that one who knowingly participates in or furthers a tortious act is jointly and severally liable with the prime tortfeasor, is applicable under copyright law"). Contributory infringement has been described as an outgrowth of enterprise liability, *see* 3 Nimmer §1204[a] [2], at 1275; and imposes liability where one person knowingly contributes to the infringing conduct of another. The classic statement of the doctrine is in *Gershwin*, 443 F.2d 1159, 1162: "[O]ne who, with knowledge of the infringing activity, induces, causes or materially contributes to the infringing conduct of another, may be held liable as a 'contributory' infringer."

There is no question that plaintiff adequately alleged the element of knowledge in this case. The disputed issue is whether plaintiff adequately alleged that Cherry Auction materially contributed to the infringing activity. We have little difficulty in holding that the allegations in this case are sufficient to show material contribution to the infringing activity. Indeed, it would be difficult for the infringing activity to take place in the massive quantities alleged without the support services provided by the swap meet. These services include, *inter alia*, the provision of space, utilities, parking, advertising, plumbing, and customers.

Here again Cherry Auction asks us to ignore all aspects of the enterprise described by the plaintiffs, to concentrate solely on the rental of space, and to hold that the swap meet provides nothing more. Yet Cherry Auction actively strives to provide the environment and the market for counterfeit recording sales to thrive. Its participation in the sales cannot be termed "passive," as Cherry Auction would prefer.

The district court apparently took the view that contribution to infringement should be limited to circumstances in which the defendant "expressly promoted or encouraged the sale of counterfeit products, or in some manner protected the identity of the infringers." 847 F. Supp. 1492, 1496. Given the allegations that the local sheriff lawfully requested that Cherry Auction gather and share basic, identifying information about its vendors, and that Cherry Auction failed to comply, the defendant appears to qualify within the last portion of the district court's own standard that posits liability for protecting infringers' identities. Moreover, we agree with the Third Circuit's analysis in *Columbia Pictures Industries, Inc. v. Aveco, Inc.*, 800 F.2d 59 (3rd Cir. 1986) that providing the site and facilities for known infringing activity is sufficient to establish contributory liability.

\* \* \*

The judgment of the district court is REVERSED and the case is REMANDED FOR FURTHER PROCEEDINGS.

## Comments

1. *Statutory Authority for Secondary Liability.* Both vicarious liability and contributory liability are well-established doctrines of tort law, and as the opinion in *Fonovisa* illustrates, tort principles under both doctrines are applied to copyright law. (For a helpful introduction to the tort law behind copyright's secondary liability doctrines, see Alfred C. Yen, *Internet Service Provider Liability for Subscriber Copyright Infringement, Enterprise Liability, and the First Amendment.* 88 GEO. L.J. 1833 (2000).) The Copyright Act itself, however, offers only indirect statutory authority for claims of "contributory" or "vicarious" copyright infringement. The first line of §106 states that the copyright owner has the exclusive rights to do "and to authorize" each of the acts listed in that section. The House Report that accompanied the statute states, "Use of the phrase 'to authorize' is intended to avoid any questions as to the liability of contributory infringers. For example, a person who lawfully acquires an authorized copy of a motion picture would be an infringer if he or she engages in the business of renting it to others for purposes of unauthorized public performance." H.R.

Rep. No. 94-1476, 94th Cong., 2d Sess. 62 (1976), *reprinted in* 1976 U.S.C.C.A.N. 5659, 5675.

2. *Control and Supervision.* The concept of "control" for purposes of vicarious liability and the concept of "knowledge" for purposes of contributory liability are distinct, though closely related. "Control" represents the character of the legal relationship between the direct infringer and the third party, and it runs along a spectrum between "actual supervision" (as a company may and does supervise its employees, for whose work the company is liable) and the more formal "right to control" (the position taken by the court in *Fonovisa*, looking to the terms of the contracts between the swap meet operator and individual vendors). "Knowledge" is determined by the extent of the interweaving of the direct infringer's activities and the activities of the third party, rather than by their legal relationship. As with "control," knowledge typically is best measured on a spectrum, ranging from knowledge of the character of the direct infringer or nature of the direct infringer's business, to knowledge of the infringing or innocent character of each transaction. Frequently, however, courts look to the same evidence in evaluating each element.

3. *Financial Benefit. Fonovisa* ruled that a copyright plaintiff may adequately allege the existence of a "financial benefit" from the infringement if it alleged facts showing that the availability of infringing material acts as a "draw" for customers. In *Ellison v. Robertson*, 357 F.3d 1072 (9th Cir. 2004), the Court of Appeals for the Ninth Circuit elaborated on that standard, finding that Harlan Ellison, the author of copyrighted novels and stories, had not proved the existence of a causal relationship between the availability of unauthorized copies of his works on USENET newsgroups carried by America Online, on the one hand, and the attractiveness of subscribing to AOL, on the other hand. Affirming summary judgment in AOL's favor with respect to a claim of vicarious liability, the court wrote: "We note that there is no evidence that indicates that AOL customers either subscribed because of the available infringing material or canceled subscriptions because it was no longer available. While a causal relationship might exist between AOL's profits from subscriptions and the infringing activity taking place on its USENET servers, Ellison has not offered enough evidence for a reasonable juror so to conclude." *Id.* at 1079.

4. *A Preview of Liability for "Inducing" Copyright Infringement.* For its definition of contributory copyright infringement, the court in *Fonovisa* quotes from *Gershwin Publishing Corp. v. Columbia Artists Management, Inc.*, 443 F.2d 1159, 1162 (2d Cir. 1971): "[O]ne who, with knowledge of the infringing activity, induces, causes or materially contributes to the infringing conduct of another, may be held liable as a 'contributory' infringer." As you read the Supreme Court's opinion in *Metro-Goldwyn-Mayer Studios v. Grokster, Ltd.* consider whether each of these three characterizations — "induces, causes, or materially contributes" — is an independent ground for relief, or whether the three terms are synonyms for one another and for the underlying concept of "contribution" to direct infringement by a third party.

## Note on *Sony Corp. of America v. Universal City Studios, Inc.*

Whether the mere sale of a device that can be used to violate the Copyright Act triggers secondary liability for copyright infringement is a question that came to the Supreme Court in *Sony Corp. of America v. Universal City Studios, Inc.*, 464 U.S. 417 (1984), in which Sony's sales of the Betamax videotape recorder were challenged because consumers used VTRs to record copyrighted broadcast television programming. Finding no clear standard in the Copyright Act, in a 5-to-4 decision the Court majority borrowed a rule from the Patent Act. Under 35 U.S.C. §271(d), a defendant which sells a part or device that might be used in connection with a patented invention is not liable for contributory patent infringement if the part or device is "a staple article or commodity of commerce suitable for substantial noninfringing use." The Court therefore ruled that selling the VTR did not make Sony liable for infringing use of the VTR if the VTR was "capable of substantial noninfringing uses." The Court majority found that noninfringing use in "time-shifting," private videotaping of over-the-air television broadcasting for later replay, which the Court concluded constituted "fair use." (The fair use doctrine and its relationship to enforcement of copyrights are considered in greater length in Chapter 8.)

## Problems

**7-3.** Alpert Records sued Mixit, Inc. and Party Time Co. for copyright infringement. Alpert's evidence established that Mixit sells empty audio cassette cartridges, spools of blank recording tape, audio duplicating equipment, and "time-loaded" audio tapes. A "time-loaded" audio tape is a tape that runs for a certain time period that is specified by the customer. For example, a customer would order 10,000 tapes with a playing time of 27 minutes and 45 seconds, and Mixit would then assemble 10,000 cassette tapes of that length out of blank recording tape and empty cassette cartridges using tape-loading machines. Party Time Co. also sells empty audio cassette cartridges, blank recording tape, and audio duplicating equipment, but it sells audio tape only in fixed lengths: 20 minutes of playing time; 30 minutes; 40 minutes; and so on, up to 2 hours. Each sale by Party Time is accompanied by a single sheet of instructions that explain how to cut audio tape to create an audio cassette with a specified fixed playing time. Party Time's tape is considerably less expensive than Mixit's time-loaded tapes. Between 1990 and 1992, Mixit sold time-loaded audio tapes, and Party Time sold fixed-length audio tape, to three individuals, not sued as defendants, who used the materials to produce illegal counterfeit copies of Alpert's copyrighted recordings. Are Party Time and Mixit liable for copyright infringement? *See A & M Records, Inc. v. Abdallah*, 948 F. Supp. 1449 (C.D. Cal. 1996).

**7-4.** Until the rise of electronic commerce on the Internet in the late 1990s, few cases were litigated under the *Sony* standard, leaving mostly unanswered the various questions left open by the case. Among other things, did the "substantial noninfringing uses" standard apply to claims for both contributory and vicarious copyright infringement? Or, as some argued, did the standard apply only to claims for contributory infringement, on the theory that the existence of "substantial noninfringing uses" deprived a copyright owner of the argument that a defendant "knew" that the device was used in concert with copyright infringement? Did the "substantial noninfringing use" standard refer to qualitatively significant uses, or quantitatively significant uses, or both? Did those uses have to be supported by present evidence, or was the mere possibility of future noninfringing uses sufficient? The Supreme Court had an opportunity to address these questions recently in *Grokster*, a case involving an Internet "file sharing" technology.

## METRO-GOLDWYN-MAYER STUDIOS, INC. v. GROKSTER, LTD.
### ____ U.S. ____, 125 S. Ct. 2764 (2005)

Justice SOUTER delivered the opinion of the Court.

The question is under what circumstances the distributor of a product capable of both lawful and unlawful use is liable for acts of copyright infringement by third parties using the product. We hold that one who distributes a device with the object of promoting its use to infringe copyright, as shown by clear expression or other affirmative steps taken to foster infringement, is liable for the resulting acts of infringement by third parties.

### I
### A

Respondents, Grokster, Ltd., and StreamCast Networks, Inc., defendants in the trial court, distribute free software products that allow computer users to share electronic files through peer-to-peer networks, so called because users' computers communicate directly with each other, not through central servers. The advantage of peer-to-peer networks over information networks of other types shows up in their substantial and growing popularity. Because they need no central computer server to mediate the exchange of information or files among users, the high-bandwidth communications capacity for a server may be dispensed with, and the need for costly server storage space is eliminated. Since copies of a file (particularly a popular one) are available on many users' computers, file requests and retrievals may be faster than on other types of networks, and since file exchanges do not travel through a server, communications can take place between any computers that remain connected to the network without risk that a glitch in the server will disable the network in its entirety. Given these benefits in security, cost, and efficiency, peer-to-peer networks are employed to store and distribute electronic files by universities, government agencies, corporations, and libraries, among others.

Other users of peer-to-peer networks include individual recipients of Grokster's and StreamCast's software, and although the networks that they enjoy through using the software can be used to share any type of digital file, they have prominently employed those networks in sharing copyrighted music and video files without authorization. A group of copyright holders (MGM for short, but including motion picture studios, recording companies, songwriters, and music publishers) sued Grokster and StreamCast for their users' copyright infringements, alleging that they knowingly and intentionally distributed their software to enable users to reproduce and distribute the copyrighted works in violation of the Copyright Act, 17 U.S.C. §101 *et seq.* (2000 ed. and Supp. II). MGM sought damages and an injunction.

Discovery during the litigation revealed the way the software worked, the business aims of each defendant company, and the predilections of the users. Grokster's eponymous software employs what is known as FastTrack technology, a protocol developed by others and licensed to Grokster. StreamCast distributes a very similar product except that its software, called Morpheus, relies on what is known as Gnutella technology. A user who downloads and installs either software possesses the protocol to send requests for files directly to the computers of others using software compatible with FastTrack or Gnutella. On the FastTrack network opened by the Grokster software, the user's request goes to a computer given an indexing capacity by the software and designated a supernode, or to some other computer with comparable power and capacity to collect temporary indexes of the files available on the computers of users connected to it. The supernode (or indexing computer) searches its own index and may communicate the search request to other supernodes. If the file is found, the supernode discloses its location to the computer requesting it, and the requesting user can download the file directly from the computer located. The copied file is placed in a designated sharing folder on the requesting user's computer, where it is available for other users to download in turn, along with any other file in that folder.

In the Gnutella network made available by Morpheus, the process is mostly the same, except that in some versions of the Gnutella protocol there are no supernodes. In these versions, peer computers using the protocol communicate directly with each other. When a user enters a search request into the Morpheus software, it sends the request to computers connected with it, which in turn pass the request along to other connected peers. The search results are communicated to the requesting computer, and the user can download desired files directly from peers' computers. As this description indicates, Grokster and StreamCast use no servers to intercept the content of the search requests or to mediate the file transfers conducted by users of the software, there being no central point through which the substance of the communications passes in either direction.

Although Grokster and StreamCast do not therefore know when particular files are copied, a few searches using their software would show what is available on the networks the software reaches. MGM commissioned a statistician to conduct a systematic search, and his study showed that nearly 90% of the files available for download on the FastTrack system were copyrighted works. Grokster and StreamCast dispute this figure, raising methodological problems and arguing that free copying even of copyrighted works may be authorized by the rightholders. They also argue that potential noninfringing uses of their software are significant in kind, even if infrequent in practice. Some musical performers, for example, have gained new audiences by distributing their copyrighted works for free across peer-to-peer networks, and some distributors of unprotected content have used peer-to-peer networks to disseminate files, Shakespeare being an example. Indeed, StreamCast has given Morpheus users the opportunity to download the briefs in this very case, though their popularity has not been quantified.

As for quantification, the parties' anecdotal and statistical evidence entered thus far to show the content available on the FastTrack and Gnutella networks does not say much about which files are actually downloaded by users, and no one can say how often the software is used to obtain copies of unprotected material. But MGM's evidence gives reason to think that the vast majority of users' downloads are acts of infringement, and because well over 100 million copies of the software in question are known to have been downloaded, and billions of files are shared across the Fast-Track and Gnutella networks each month, the probable scope of copyright infringement is staggering.

Grokster and StreamCast concede the infringement in most downloads, and it is uncontested that they are aware that users employ their software primarily to download copyrighted files, even if the decentralized Fast-Track and Gnutella networks fail to reveal which files are being copied, and when. From time to time, moreover, the companies have learned about their users' infringement directly, as from users who have sent e-mail to each company with questions about playing copyrighted movies they had downloaded, to whom the companies have responded with guidance. And MGM notified the companies of 8 million copyrighted files that could be obtained using their software.

Grokster and StreamCast are not, however, merely passive recipients of information about infringing use. The record is replete with evidence that from the moment Grokster and StreamCast began to distribute their free software, each one clearly voiced the objective that recipients use it to download copyrighted works, and each took active steps to encourage infringement.

After the notorious file-sharing service, Napster, was sued by copyright holders for facilitation of copyright infringement, StreamCast gave away a software program of a kind known as OpenNap, designed as compatible with the Napster program and open to Napster users for downloading files from other Napster and OpenNap users' computers. Evidence indicates that "[i]t was always [StreamCast's] intent to use [its OpenNap network] to be able to capture email addresses of [its] initial target market so that [it] could promote [its] StreamCast Morpheus interface to them," indeed, the OpenNap program was engineered "'to leverage Napster's 50 million user base.'"

StreamCast monitored both the number of users downloading its Open-Nap program and the number of music files they downloaded. It also used the resulting OpenNap network to distribute copies of the Morpheus software and to encourage users to adopt it. Internal company documents indicate that StreamCast hoped to attract large numbers of former Napster users if that company was shut down by court order or otherwise, and that StreamCast planned to be the next Napster. A kit developed by StreamCast to be delivered to advertisers, for example, contained press articles about StreamCast's potential to capture former Napster users, and it introduced itself to some potential advertisers as a company "which is similar to what Napster was." It broadcast banner advertisements to users of other Napster-compatible software, urging them to adopt its OpenNap. An internal e-mail from a company executive stated: " 'We have put this network in place so that when Napster pulls the plug on their free service . . . or if the Court orders them shut down prior to that . . . we will be positioned to capture the flood of their 32 million users that will be actively looking for an alternative.' "

Thus, StreamCast developed promotional materials to market its service as the best Napster alternative. One proposed advertisement read: "Napster Inc. has announced that it will soon begin charging you a fee. That's if the courts don't order it shut down first. What will you do to get around it?" Another proposed ad touted StreamCast's software as the "# 1 alternative to Napster" and asked "[w]hen the lights went off at Napster . . . where did the users go?"[7] StreamCast even planned to flaunt the illegal uses of its software; when it launched the OpenNap network, the chief technology officer of the company averred that "[t]he goal is to get in trouble with the law and get sued. It's the best way to get in the new[s]."

The evidence that Grokster sought to capture the market of former Napster users is sparser but revealing, for Grokster launched its own Open-Nap system called Swaptor and inserted digital codes into its Web site so that computer users using Web search engines to look for "Napster" or "[f]ree filesharing" would be directed to the Grokster Web site, where they could download the Grokster software. And Grokster's name is an apparent derivative of Napster.

StreamCast's executives monitored the number of songs by certain commercial artists available on their networks, and an internal communication indicates they aimed to have a larger number of copyrighted songs available on their networks than other file-sharing networks. The point, of course, would be to attract users of a mind to infringe, just as it would be with their promotional materials developed showing copyrighted songs as examples of the kinds of files available through Morpheus. Morpheus in fact allowed users to search specifically for "Top 40" songs, which were inevitably copyrighted. Similarly, Grokster sent users a newsletter promoting its ability to provide particular, popular copyrighted materials.

In addition to this evidence of express promotion, marketing, and intent to promote further, the business models employed by Grokster and StreamCast confirm that their principal object was use of their software to download copyrighted works. Grokster and StreamCast receive no revenue from users, who obtain the software itself for nothing. Instead, both companies generate income by selling advertising space, and they stream the advertising to Grokster and Morpheus users while they are employing the programs. As the number of users of each program increases,

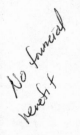

---

7. The record makes clear that StreamCast developed these promotional materials but not whether it released them to the public. Even if these advertisements were not released to the public and do not show encouragement to infringe, they illuminate StreamCast's purposes.

advertising opportunities become worth more. While there is doubtless some demand for free Shakespeare, the evidence shows that substantive volume is a function of free access to copyrighted work. Users seeking Top 40 songs, for example, or the latest release by Modest Mouse, are certain to be far more numerous than those seeking a free Decameron, and Grokster and StreamCast translated that demand into dollars.

Finally, there is no evidence that either company made an effort to filter copyrighted material from users' downloads or otherwise impede the sharing of copyrighted files. Although Grokster appears to have sent e-mails warning users about infringing content when it received threatening notice from the copyright holders, it never blocked anyone from continuing to use its software to share copyrighted files. StreamCast not only rejected another company's offer of help to monitor infringement, but blocked the Internet Protocol addresses of entities it believed were trying to engage in such monitoring on its networks.

## B

After discovery, the parties on each side of the case cross-moved for summary judgment. The District Court limited its consideration to the asserted liability of Grokster and StreamCast for distributing the current versions of their software. . . . The District Court held that those who used the Grokster and Morpheus software to download copyrighted media files directly infringed MGM's copyrights, a conclusion not contested on appeal, but the court nonetheless granted summary judgment in favor of Grokster and StreamCast as to any liability arising from distribution of the then current versions of their software. Distributing that software gave rise to no liability in the court's view, because its use did not provide the distributors with actual knowledge of specific acts of infringement.

The Court of Appeals affirmed. In the court's analysis, a defendant was liable as a contributory infringer when it had knowledge of direct infringement and materially contributed to the infringement. But the court read *Sony Corp. of America v. Universal City Studios, Inc.*, 464 U.S. 417 (1984), as holding that distribution of a commercial product capable of substantial noninfringing uses could not give rise to contributory liability for infringement unless the distributor had actual knowledge of specific instances of infringement and failed to act on that knowledge. The fact that the software was capable of substantial noninfringing uses in the Ninth Circuit's view meant that Grokster and StreamCast were not liable, because they had no such actual knowledge, owing to the decentralized architecture of their software. The court also held that Grokster and StreamCast did not materially contribute to their users' infringement because it was the users themselves who searched for, retrieved, and stored the infringing files, with no involvement by the defendants beyond providing the software in the first place.

The Ninth Circuit also considered whether Grokster and StreamCast could be liable under a theory of vicarious infringement. The court held against liability because the defendants did not monitor or control the use of the software, had no agreed-upon right or current ability to supervise its use, and had no independent duty to police infringement. We granted certiorari.

## II

### A

MGM and many of the *amici* fault the Court of Appeals's holding for upsetting a sound balance between the respective values of supporting creative pursuits through copyright protection and promoting innovation in new communication technologies by limiting the incidence of liability for copyright infringement. The more artistic protection is favored, the more technological innovation may be discouraged; the administration of copyright law is an exercise in managing the trade-off.

\* \* \*

The argument for imposing indirect liability in this case is, however, a powerful one, given the number of infringing downloads that occur every day using StreamCast's and Grokster's software. When a widely shared service or product is used to commit infringement, it may be impossible to enforce rights in the protected work effectively against all direct infringers, the only practical alternative being to go against the distributor of the copying device for secondary liability on a theory of contributory or vicarious infringement.

One infringes contributorily by intentionally inducing or encouraging direct infringement, and infringes vicariously by profiting from direct infringement while declining to exercise a right to stop or limit it.[9] Although "[t]he Copyright Act does not expressly render anyone liable for infringement committed by another," *Sony Corp. v. Universal City Studios*, 464 U.S., at 434, these doctrines of secondary liability emerged from common law principles and are well established in the law, *id.*, at 486 (Blackmun, J., dissenting).

### B

\* \* \*

The parties and many of the *amici* in this case think the key to resolving it is the *Sony* rule and, in particular, what it means for a product to be "capable of commercially significant noninfringing uses." [*Sony Corp. of America v. Universal City Studios, Inc.*, 464 U.S. 417, 442 (1984)]. MGM advances the argument that granting summary judgment to Grokster and StreamCast as to their current activities gave too much weight to the value of innovative technology, and too little to the copyrights infringed by users of their software, given that 90% of works available on one of the networks was shown to be copyrighted. Assuming the remaining 10% to be its noninfringing

---

9. We stated in *Sony Corp. of America v. Universal City Studios, Inc.*, 464 U.S. 417 (1984), that " 'the lines between direct infringement, contributory infringement and vicarious liability are not clearly drawn'....[R]easoned analysis of [the *Sony* plaintiffs' contributory infringement claim] necessarily entails consideration of arguments and case law which may also be forwarded under the other labels, and indeed the parties...rely upon such arguments and authority in support of their respective positions on the issue of contributory infringement," *id.*, at 435, n. 17 (quoting *Universal City Studios, Inc. v. Sony Corp.*, 480 F. Supp. 429, 457-458 (C.D. Cal. 1979)). In the present case MGM has argued a vicarious liability theory, which allows imposition of liability when the defendant profits directly from the infringement and has a right and ability to supervise the direct infringer, even if the defendant initially lacks knowledge of the infringement. Because we resolve the case based on an inducement theory, there is no need to analyze separately MGM's vicarious liability theory.

use, MGM says this should not qualify as "substantial," and the Court should quantify Sony to the extent of holding that a product used "principally" for infringement does not qualify. As mentioned before, Grokster and StreamCast reply by citing evidence that their software can be used to reproduce public domain works, and they point to copyright holders who actually encourage copying. Even if infringement is the principal practice with their software today, they argue, the noninfringing uses are significant and will grow.

We agree with MGM that the Court of Appeals misapplied *Sony*, which it read as limiting secondary liability quite beyond the circumstances to which the case applied. *Sony* barred secondary liability based on presuming or imputing intent to cause infringement solely from the design or distribution of a product capable of substantial lawful use, which the distributor knows is in fact used for infringement. The Ninth Circuit has read *Sony*'s limitation to mean that whenever a product is capable of substantial lawful use, the producer can never be held contributorily liable for third parties' infringing use of it; it read the rule as being this broad, even when an actual purpose to cause infringing use is shown by evidence independent of design and distribution of the product, unless the distributors had "specific knowledge of infringement at a time at which they contributed to the infringement, and failed to act upon that information." 380 F.3d, at 1162 (internal quotation marks and alterations omitted). Because the Circuit found the StreamCast and Grokster software capable of substantial lawful use, it concluded on the basis of its reading of *Sony* that neither company could be held liable, since there was no showing that their software, being without any central server, afforded them knowledge of specific unlawful uses.

This view of *Sony*, however, was error, converting the case from one about liability resting on imputed intent to one about liability on any theory. Because *Sony* did not displace other theories of secondary liability, and because we find below that it was error to grant summary judgment to the companies on MGM's inducement claim, we do not revisit *Sony* further, as MGM requests, to add a more quantified description of the point of balance between protection and commerce when liability rests solely on distribution with knowledge that unlawful use will occur. It is enough to note that the Ninth Circuit's judgment rested on an erroneous understanding of *Sony* and to leave further consideration of the *Sony* rule for a day when that may be required.

C

*Sony*'s rule limits imputing culpable intent as a matter of law from the characteristics or uses of a distributed product. But nothing in *Sony* requires courts to ignore evidence of intent if there is such evidence, and the case was never meant to foreclose rules of fault-based liability derived from the common law.[10] *Sony Corp. v. Universal City Studios*, 464 U.S., at 439 ("If vicarious liability is to be imposed on Sony in this case, it

---

10. Nor does the Patent Act's exemption from liability for those who distribute a staple article of commerce, 35 U.S.C. §271(c), extend to those who induce patent infringement, §271(b).

must rest on the fact that it has sold equipment with constructive knowledge" of the potential for infringement). Thus, where evidence goes beyond a product's characteristics or the knowledge that it may be put to infringing uses, and shows statements or actions directed to promoting infringement, *Sony's* staple-article rule will not preclude liability.

The classic case of direct evidence of unlawful purpose occurs when one induces commission of infringement by another, or "entic[es] or persuad[es] another" to infringe, Black's Law Dictionary 790 (8th ed. 2004), as by advertising. Thus at common law a copyright or patent defendant who "not only expected but invoked [infringing use] by advertisement" was liable for infringement "on principles recognized in every part of the law." [*Kalem Co. v. Harper Brothers*, 222 U.S. 55, 62-63 (1911)] (copyright infringement).

The rule on inducement of infringement as developed in the early cases is no different today. Evidence of "active steps . . . taken to encourage direct infringement," *Oak Industries, Inc. v. Zenith Electronics Corp.*, 697 F. Supp. 988, 992 (N.D. Ill. 1988), such as advertising an infringing use or instructing how to engage in an infringing use, show an affirmative intent that the product be used to infringe, and a showing that infringement was encouraged overcomes the law's reluctance to find liability when a defendant merely sells a commercial product suitable for some lawful use.

For the same reasons that *Sony* took the staple-article doctrine of patent law as a model for its copyright safe-harbor rule, the inducement rule, too, is a sensible one for copyright. We adopt it here, holding that one who distributes a device with the object of promoting its use to infringe copyright, as shown by clear expression or other affirmative steps taken to foster infringement, is liable for the resulting acts of infringement by third parties. We are, of course, mindful of the need to keep from trenching on regular commerce or discouraging the development of technologies with lawful and unlawful potential. Accordingly, just as *Sony* did not find intentional inducement despite the knowledge of the VCR manufacturer that its device could be used to infringe, mere knowledge of infringing potential or of actual infringing uses would not be enough here to subject a distributor to liability. Nor would ordinary acts incident to product distribution, such as offering customers technical support or product updates, support liability in themselves. The inducement rule, instead, premises liability on purposeful, culpable expression and conduct, and thus does nothing to compromise legitimate commerce or discourage innovation having a lawful promise.

### III

### A

The only apparent question about treating MGM's evidence as sufficient to withstand summary judgment under the theory of inducement goes to the need on MGM's part to adduce evidence that StreamCast and Grokster communicated an inducing message to their software users. The classic instance of inducement is by advertisement or solicitation that broadcasts a message designed to stimulate others to commit violations. MGM claims that such a message is shown here. It is undisputed that StreamCast beamed onto the computer screens of users of Napster-compatible programs ads urging the adoption of its OpenNap program, which was designed, as its name implied, to invite the custom of patrons of Napster, then under attack in the courts for facilitating massive infringement. Those who accepted StreamCast's OpenNap program were offered software to perform the same services, which a factfinder could conclude would readily have been understood in the Napster market as the ability to download copyrighted music files. Grokster distributed an electronic newsletter containing links to articles promoting its software's ability to access popular copyrighted music. And anyone whose Napster or free file-sharing searches turned up a link to Grokster would have understood Grokster to be offering the same file-sharing ability as Napster, and to the same people who probably used Napster for infringing downloads; that would also have been the understanding of anyone offered Grokster's suggestively named Swaptor software, its version of OpenNap. And both companies communicated a clear message by responding affirmatively to requests for help in locating and playing copyrighted materials.

In StreamCast's case, of course, the evidence just described was supplemented by other unequivocal indications of unlawful purpose in the internal communications and advertising designs aimed at Napster users ("When the lights went off at Napster...where did the users go?"). Whether the messages were communicated is not to the point on this record. The function of the message in the theory of inducement is to prove by a defendant's own statements that his unlawful purpose disqualifies him from claiming protection (and incidentally to point to actual violators likely to be found among those who hear or read the message). Proving that a message was sent out, then, is the preeminent but not exclusive way of showing that active steps were taken with the purpose of bringing about infringing acts, and of showing that infringing acts took place by using the device distributed. Here, the summary judgment record is replete with other evidence that Grokster and StreamCast, unlike the manufacturer and distributor in *Sony,* acted with a purpose to cause copyright violations by use of software suitable for illegal use.

Three features of this evidence of intent are particularly notable. First, each company showed itself to be aiming to satisfy a known source of demand for copyright infringement, the market comprising former Napster users. StreamCast's internal documents made constant reference to Napster, it initially distributed its Morpheus software through an OpenNap program compatible with Napster, it advertised its OpenNap program to Napster users, and its Morpheus software functions as Napster did except that it could be used to distribute more kinds of files, including copyrighted movies and software programs. Grokster's name is apparently derived from Napster, it too initially offered an OpenNap program, its software's function is likewise comparable to Napster's, and it attempted to divert queries for Napster onto its own Web site. Grokster and StreamCast's efforts to supply services to former Napster users, deprived of a mechanism to copy and distribute what were overwhelmingly infringing files, indicate a principal, if not exclusive, intent on the part of each to bring about infringement.

Second, this evidence of unlawful objective is given added significance by MGM's showing that neither company attempted to develop filtering tools or other mechanisms to diminish the infringing activity using their software. While the Ninth Circuit treated the defendants' failure to develop such tools as irrelevant because they lacked an independent duty to monitor their users' activity, we think this evidence underscores Grokster's and StreamCast's intentional facilitation of their users' infringement.[12]

Third, there is a further complement to the direct evidence of unlawful objective. It is useful to recall that StreamCast and Grokster make money by selling advertising space, by directing ads to the screens of computers employing their software. As the record shows, the more the software is used, the more ads are sent out and the greater the advertising revenue becomes. Since the extent of the software's use determines the gain to the distributors, the commercial sense of their enterprise turns on high-volume use, which the record shows is infringing. This evidence alone would not justify an inference of unlawful intent, but viewed in the context of the entire record its import is clear.

The unlawful objective is unmistakable.

### B

In addition to intent to bring about infringement and distribution of a device suitable for infringing use, the inducement theory of course requires evidence of actual infringement by recipients of the device, the software in this case. As the account of the facts indicates, there is evidence of infringement on a gigantic scale, and there is no serious issue of the adequacy of MGM's showing on this point in order to survive the companies' summary judgment requests. Although an exact calculation of infringing use, as a basis for a claim of damages, is subject to dispute, there is no question that the summary judgment evidence is at least adequate to entitle MGM to go forward with claims for damages and equitable relief.

\* \* \*

In sum, this case is significantly different from *Sony* and reliance on that case to rule in favor of StreamCast and Grokster was error. *Sony* dealt with a claim of liability based solely on distributing a product with alternative lawful and unlawful uses, with knowledge that some users would follow the unlawful course. The case struck a balance between the interests of protection and innovation by holding that the product's capability of substantial lawful employment should bar the imputation of fault and consequent secondary liability for the unlawful acts of others.

MGM's evidence in this case most obviously addresses a different basis of liability for distributing a product open to alternative uses. Here, evidence of the distributors' words and deeds going beyond distribution as such shows a purpose to cause and profit from third-party acts of copyright infringement. If liability for inducing infringement is ultimately found, it

---

12. Of course, in the absence of other evidence of intent, a court would be unable to find contributory infringement liability merely based on a failure to take affirmative steps to prevent infringement, if the device otherwise was capable of substantial noninfringing uses. Such a holding would tread too close to the *Sony* safe harbor.

will not be on the basis of presuming or imputing fault, but from inferring a patently illegal objective from statements and actions showing what that objective was.

There is substantial evidence in MGM's favor on all elements of inducement, and summary judgment in favor of Grokster and StreamCast was error. On remand, reconsideration of MGM's motion for summary judgment will be in order.

The judgment of the Court of Appeals is vacated, and the case is remanded for further proceedings consistent with this opinion.

*It is so ordered.*

[Concurring opinions of Justice GINSBURG and Justice BREYER omitted.]

## Comments

1. *The Meaning of* **Grokster**. The Court appears to hold that the producer of a device that is "capable" of "substantial noninfringing use" may be liable for copyright infringement by users of the device if the producer acted with "culpable intent." The further implications of the Court's decision are speculative at best. Among other things, the opinion raises the following questions:

   a. Consider a case in which the only evidence of "intent" consists of the device itself, which uncontradicted expert testimony discloses could have been designed in a way that mitigated or eliminated the risk of its use for copyright infringement. An example might be a peer-to-peer networking program designed by a university computer science researcher that can be used to swap music files or scholarly articles, but that does nothing to determine the copyright status of its swapped content. Is the producer of that device indirectly liable for copyright infringement?

   b. How should the "culpable intent" standard be applied if a device is produced and distributed with malign intent, but is adopted and used enthusiastically and innocently by consumers, to reproduce public domain material, for example? What result if the opposite occurs, and a device produced by a good faith innovator is appropriated for use primarily by a ring of copyright pirates?

   c. If you were counsel to a small technology company, in light of *Grokster* how would you counsel your client, including both its business development team and its engineering team, regarding how to design its new products? Regarding its recordkeeping and internal communications processes? Similarly, if you were counsel to a major research university, how would you counsel your science and engineering faculty? The graduate students working for those faculty?

2. *Noninfringing Uses.* In a concurring opinion, Justice Breyer identified a number of noninfringing uses for this technology:

   > Such legitimate noninfringing uses are coming to include the swapping of: *research information* (the initial purpose of many peer-to-peer networks); *public domain films* (*e.g.*, those owned by the Prelinger Archive); *historical recordings and digital educational materials* (*e.g.*, those stored on the

Internet Archive); *digital photos* (OurPictures, for example, is starting a P2P photo-swapping service); *"shareware"* and *"freeware"* (*e.g.,* Linux and certain Windows software); *secure licensed music and movie files* (Intent MediaWorks, for example, protects licensed content sent across P2P networks); *news broadcasts past and present* (the BBC Creative Archive lets users "rip, mix and share the BBC"); *user-created audio and video files* (including "podcasts" that may be distributed through P2P software); *and all manner of free "open content" works collected by Creative Commons* (one can search for Creative Commons material on StreamCast).

3. *Inducement as an Independent Basis for Liability.* The Court's opinion leaves unclear whether "inducement" of copyright infringement is now a third basis for secondary liability for copyright infringement, alongside vicarious and contributory liability, or whether "inducement" is a species of contributory liability. As a species of contributory liability, an "inducement" claim presumably remains subject to the "substantial noninfringing use" defense provided by *Sony*. As an independent basis for liability, an "inducement" claim may not be subject to the *Sony* defense.

## C. THE DIGITAL MILLENNIUM COPYRIGHT ACT

Although Congress recognized the coming importance of computer technology when it passed the Copyright Act in 1976, the first direct encounter between copyright interests and developers of digital technology took place in the late 1980s, with the introduction of Digital Audio Tape (DAT) technology by Sony. Rather than pursue litigation after the introduction of a novel recording technology, as it did with videotape recording, the entertainment industry pursued legislation that would preempt threats from copyright infringement. The result was the Audio Home Recording Act (AHRA) of 1992, which mandates that DAT recorders and tapes incorporate a Serial Copy Management System that limits consumers' ability to make tape-to-tape copies. The AHRA requires that producers of DAT recorders and blank tapes pay a small royalty on each device and tape into a fund managed by the Copyright Office to compensate copyright owners injured by distribution of DAT technology. *See* 17 U.S.C. §§1001, *et. seq.* With the dramatic growth of the Internet and electronic commerce during the 1990s, publishing interests again raised the spectre of large-scale copying of their works via digital reproduction. They pointed to emerging research on "trusted systems" of computing that would encrypt copyrighted works and enable fine-grained, person-by-person metering of use of and payment for digital forms of information. They urged that the law create incentives to develop and use this technology and protect the interests of those who deployed it. Given the nature of the Internet, moreover, the issues were global. In late 1996, the World Intellectual Property Organization (WIPO) Copyright Treaty was negotiated, requiring its signatories, including the United States, to "provide adequate legal protection and effective legal remedies against the circumvention of effective technological measures that are used by authors in connection with the exercise of their rights" (Article 11), among other things. Two years later, in 1998, Congress passed the Digital Millennium Copyright Act, a complex statute that implements protection for "technological measures" and includes a variety of additional protections to copyright owners that use technological means to prevent unauthorized access to and use of copyrighted works.

## 1. Anti-Circumvention and Technological Protection Measures

*STATUTE:* **Circumvention of Copyright Protection Systems**
17 U.S.C. §1201(a), (b), (c)

### REALNETWORKS, INC. v. STREAMBOX, INC.
No. 2:99CV02070, 2000 WL 127311 (W.D. Wash. Jan. 18, 2000)

PECHMAN, J.

#### INTRODUCTION

Plaintiff RealNetworks, Inc. ("RealNetworks") filed this action on December 21, 1999. RealNetworks claims that Defendant Streambox has violated provisions of the Digital Millennium Copyright Act ("DMCA"), 17 U.S.C. §1201 *et seq.*, by distributing and marketing products known as the Streambox VCR and the Ripper. RealNetworks also contends that another Streambox product, known as the Ferret, is unlawfully designed to permit consumers to make unauthorized modifications to a software program on which RealNetworks holds the copyright. . . .

The Court, having considered the papers and pleadings filed herein and having heard oral argument from the parties, concludes that a preliminary injunction should be entered to enjoin the manufacture, distribution, and sale of the Streambox VCR and the Ferret during the pendency of this action. The Court does not conclude that a preliminary injunction should be entered with respect to the Ripper. . . .

#### FINDINGS OF FACT
##### REALNETWORKS

RealNetworks is a public company based in Seattle, Washington that develops and markets software products designed to enable owners of audio, video, and other multimedia content to send their content to users of personal computers over the Internet.

RealNetworks offers products that enable consumers to access audio and video content over the Internet through a process known as "streaming." When an audio or video clip is "streamed" to a consumer, no trace of the clip is left on the consumer's computer, unless the content owner has permitted the consumer to download the file.

Streaming is to be contrasted with "downloading," a process by which a complete copy of an audio or video clip is delivered to and stored on a consumer's computer. Once a consumer has downloaded a file, he or she can access the file at will, and can generally redistribute copies of that file to others.

In the digital era, the difference between streaming and downloading is of critical importance. A downloaded copy of a digital audio or video file is essentially indistinguishable from the original, and such copies can often be created at the touch of a button. A user who obtains a digital copy may supplant the market for the original by distributing copies of his or her own. To guard against the unauthorized copying and redistribution of their content, many copyright owners do not make their content available for downloading, and instead distribute the content using streaming technology in a manner that does not permit downloading.

\* \* \*

### REALNETWORKS' PRODUCTS

The RealNetworks' products at issue in this action include the "RealProducer," the "RealServer" and the "RealPlayer." These products may be used together to form a system for distributing, retrieving and playing digital audio and video content via the Internet.

Owners of audio or video content may choose to use a RealNetworks product to encode their digital content into RealNetworks' format. Once encoded in that format, the media files are called RealAudio or RealVideo (collectively "RealMedia") files.

After a content owner has encoded its content into the RealMedia format, it may decide to use a "RealServer" to send that content to consumers. A RealServer is software program that resides on a content owner's computer that holds RealMedia files and "serves" them to consumers through streaming.

The RealServer is not the only available means for distributing RealMedia files. RealMedia files may also be made available on an ordinary web server instead of a RealServer. An end-user can download content from an ordinary web server using nothing more than a freely available Internet browser such as Netscape's Navigator or Microsoft's Internet Explorer.

To download streaming content distributed by a RealServer, however, a consumer must employ a "RealPlayer." The RealPlayer is a software program that resides on an end-user's computer and must be used to access and play a streaming RealMedia file that is sent from a RealServer.

### REALNETWORKS' SECURITY MEASURES

RealNetworks' products can be used to enable owners of audio and video content to make their content available for consumers to listen to or view, while at the same time securing the content against unauthorized access or copying.

The first of these measures, called the "Secret Handshake" by RealNetworks, ensures that files hosted on a RealServer will only be sent to a RealPlayer. The Secret Handshake is an authentication sequence which only RealServers and RealPlayers know. By design, unless this authentication sequence takes place, the RealServer does not stream the content it holds.

By ensuring that RealMedia files hosted on a RealServer are streamed only to RealPlayers, RealNetworks can ensure that a second security measure, which RealNetworks calls the "Copy Switch," is given effect. The Copy Switch is a piece of data in all RealMedia files that contains the content owner's preference regarding whether or not the stream may be copied by end-users. RealPlayers are designed to read this Copy Switch and obey the content owner's wishes. If a content owner turns on the Copy Switch in a particular Real-Media file, when that file is streamed, an end-user can use the RealPlayer to save a copy of that RealMedia file to the user's computer. If a content owner does not turn on the Copy Switch in a RealMedia file, the RealPlayer will not allow an end-user to make a copy of that file. The file will simply "evaporate" as the user listens to or watches it stream.

Through the use of the Secret Handshake and the Copy Switch, owners of audio and video content can prevent the unauthorized copying of their content if they so choose.

Content owners who choose to use the security measures described above are likely to be seeking to prevent their works from being copied without their authorization. RealNetworks has proferred declarations from copyright owners that they rely on RealNetworks security measures to protect their copyrighted works on the Internet. Many of these copyright owners further state that if users could circumvent the security measures and make unauthorized copies of the content, they likely would not put their content up on the Internet for end-users.

* * *

Copyright owners also use Real Networks' technology so that end-users can listen to, but not record, music that is on sale, either at a Web site or in retail stores. Other copyright owners enable users to listen to content on a "pay-per-play" basis that requires a payment for each time the end-user wants to hear the content. Without the security measures afforded by Real-Networks, these methods of distribution could not succeed. End-users could make and redistribute digital copies of any content available on the Internet, undermining the market for the copyrighted original.

* * *

### Streambox

Defendant Streambox, Inc. is a Washington corporation which provides software products for processing and recording audio and video content, including but not limited to content which is streamed over the Internet. Streambox also maintains a searchable database of Internet web addresses of various audio and video offerings on the Internet. The Streambox products at issue in this case are known as the Streambox VCR, the Ripper, and the Ferret.

### Streambox VCR

The Streambox VCR enables end-users to access and download copies of RealMedia files that are streamed over the Internet. While the Streambox VCR also allows users to copy RealMedia files that are made freely available for downloading from ordinary web servers, the only function relevant to this case is the portions of the VCR that allow it to access and copy Real-Media files located on RealServers.

In order to gain access to RealMedia content located on a RealServer, the VCR mimics a RealPlayer and circumvents the authentication procedure, or Secret Handshake, that a RealServer requires before it will stream content. In other words, the Streambox VCR is able to convince the RealServer into thinking that the VCR is, in fact, a RealPlayer.

Having convinced a RealServer to begin streaming content, the Streambox VCR, like the RealPlayer, acts as a receiver. However, unlike the RealPlayer, the VCR ignores the Copy Switch that tells a RealPlayer whether an end-user is allowed to make a copy of (i.e., download) the RealMedia file as it is being streamed. The VCR thus allows the end-user to download RealMedia files even if the content owner has used the Copy Switch to prohibit end-users from downloading the files.

The only reason for the Streambox VCR to circumvent the Secret Handshake and interact with a RealServer is to allow an end-user to access and make copies of content that a copyright holder has placed on a RealServer in order to secure it against unauthorized copying. In this way, the Streambox VCR acts like a "black box" which descrambles cable or satellite broadcasts so that viewers can watch pay programming for free. Like the cable and satellite companies that scramble their video signals to control access to their programs, RealNetworks has employed technological measures to ensure that only users of the RealPlayer can access RealMedia content placed on a RealServer. RealNetworks has gone one step further than the cable and satellite companies, not only controlling access, but also allowing copyright owners to specify whether or not their works can be copied by end-users, even if access is permitted. The Streambox VCR circumvents both the access control and copy protection measures....

Streambox's marketing of the VCR notes that end-users can "[d]ownload RealAudio and RealMedia files as easily as you would any other file, then reap the benefits of clean, unclogged streams straight from your hard drive" and that the product can be used by "savvy surfers who enjoy taking control of their favorite Internet music/video clips."

\* \* \*

### STREAMBOX RIPPER

Streambox also manufactures and distributes a product called the Streambox Ripper. The Ripper is a file conversion application that allows conversion (adaptation) of files from RealMedia format to other formats such as .WAV, .RMA, and MP3. The Ripper also permits conversion of files between each of these formats, i.e., .WAV to .WMA and .WAV to MP3.

The Ripper operates on files which are already resident on the hard disk of the user's computer. The Ripper permits users to convert files that they have already created or obtained (presumably through legitimate means) from one format to another.

Streambox has proffered evidence that one potential use of the Ripper would be to permit copyright owners to translate their content directly from the RealMedia format into other formats that they may wish to utilize for their own work. Streambox has provided examples of various content owner who need a way to convert their own RealMedia files into different formats, such as .WAV for editing, or .WMA to accommodate those users who wish to access the content with a Windows Media Player instead of a

RealPlayer. In addition, content which is freely available, such as public domain material and material which users are invited and even encouraged to access and copy, may be converted by the Ripper into a different file format for listening at a location other than the user's computer....

## CONCLUSIONS OF LAW

...The Court finds that RealNetworks has standing to pursue DMCA claims under 17 U.S.C. §1203, which affords standing to "any person" allegedly injured by a violation of sections 1201 and 1202 of the DMCA....

### REALNETWORKS HAS DEMONSTRATED A REASONABLE LIKELIHOOD OF SUCCESS ON ITS DMCA CLAIMS WITH RESPECT TO THE STREAMBOX VCR

The DMCA prohibits the manufacture, import, offer to the public, or trafficking in any technology, product, service, device, component, or part thereof that: (1) is primarily designed or produced for the purpose of circumventing a technological measure that effectively "controls access to" a copyrighted work or "protects a right of a copyright owner;" (2) has only limited commercially significant purpose or use other than to circumvent such technological protection measures; or (3) is marketed for use in circumventing such technological protection measures. 17 U.S.C. §§1201(a)(2), 1201(b).

### PARTS OF THE VCR ARE LIKELY TO VIOLATE SECTIONS 1201(a)(2) AND 1201(b)

Under the DMCA, the Secret Handshake that must take place between a RealServer and a RealPlayer before the RealServer will begin streaming content to an end-user appears to constitute a "technological measure" that "effectively controls access" to copyrighted works. *See* 17 U.S.C. §1201(a)(3)(B) (measure "effectively controls access" if it "requires the application of information or a process or a treatment, with the authority of the copyright holder, to gain access to the work"). To gain access to a work protected by the Secret Handshake, a user must employ a RealPlayer, which will supply the requisite information to the RealServer in a proprietary authentication sequence.

In conjunction with the Secret Handshake, the Copy Switch is a "technological measure" that effectively protects the right of a copyright owner to control the unauthorized copying of its work. *See* 17 U.S.C. §1201(b)(2)(B) (measure "effectively protects" right of copyright holder if it "prevents, restricts or otherwise limits the exercise of a right of a copyright owner"); 17 U.S.C. §106(a) (granting copyright holder exclusive right to make copies of its work). To access a RealMedia file distributed by a RealServer, a user must use a RealPlayer. The RealPlayer reads the Copy Switch in the file. If the Copy Switch in the file is turned off, the RealPlayer will not permit the user to record a copy as the file is streamed. Thus, the Copy Switch may restrict others from exercising a copyright holder's exclusive right to copy its work.

Under the DMCA, a product or part thereof "circumvents" protections afforded a technological measure by "avoiding, bypassing, removing, deactivating or otherwise impairing" the operation of that technological measure. 17 U.S.C. §§1201(b)(2)(A), 1201(a)(2)(A). Under that definition, at least a part of the Streambox VCR circumvents the technological measures RealNetworks affords to copyright owners. Where a RealMedia file is stored on a RealServer, the VCR "bypasses" the Secret Handshake to gain access to the file. The VCR then circumvents the Copy Switch, enabling a user to make a copy of a file that the copyright owner has sought to protect.

Given the circumvention capabilities of the Streambox VCR, Streambox violates the DMCA if the product or a part thereof: (i) is primarily designed to serve this function; (ii) has only limited commercially significant purposes beyond the circumvention; or (iii) is marketed as a means of circumvention. 17 U.S.C. §§1201(a)(2)(A-C), 1201(b)(b)(A-C). These three tests are disjunctive. *Id.* A product that meets only one of the three independent bases for liability is still prohibited. Here, the VCR meets at least the first two.

The Streambox VCR meets the first test for liability under the DMCA because at least a part of the Streambox VCR is primarily, if not exclusively, designed to circumvent the access control and copy protection measures that RealNetworks affords to copyright owners. 17 U.S.C. §§1201(a)(2)(A), 1201(b)(c)(A).

The second basis for liability is met because portion of the VCR that circumvents the Secret Handshake so as to avoid the Copy Switch has no significant commercial purpose other than to enable users to access and record protected content. 17 U.S.C. §1201(a)(2)(B), 1201(b)(d)(B). There does not appear to be any other commercial value that this capability affords.

Streambox's primary defense to Plaintiff's DMCA claims is that the VCR has legitimate uses. In particular, Streambox claims that the VCR allows consumers to make "fair use" copies of RealMedia files, notwithstanding the access control and copy protection measures that a copyright owner may have placed on that file.

The portions of the VCR that circumvent the secret handshake and copy switch permit consumers to obtain and redistribute perfect digital copies of audio and video files that copyright owners have made clear they do not want copied. For this reason, Streambox's VCR is not entitled to the same "fair use" protections the Supreme Court afforded to video cassette recorders used for "time-shifting" in *Sony Corp. v. Universal City Studios, Inc.*, 464 U.S. 417 (1984).

The *Sony* decision turned in large part on a finding that substantial numbers of copyright holders who broadcast their works either had authorized or would not object to having their works time-shifted by private viewers. *See Sony*, 464 U.S. at 443, 446. Here, by contrast, copyright owners have specifically chosen to prevent the copying enabled by the Streambox VCR by putting their content on RealServers and leaving the Copy Switch off.

Moreover, the *Sony* decision did not involve interpretation of the DMCA. Under the DMCA, product developers do not have the right to distribute products that circumvent technological measures that prevent consumers from gaining unauthorized access to or making unauthorized copies of works protected by the Copyright Act. Instead, Congress specifically prohibited the distribution of the tools by which such circumvention could be accomplished. The portion of the Streambox VCR that circumvents the technological measures that prevent unauthorized access to and duplication of audio and video content therefore runs afoul of the DMCA.

* * *

Streambox also argues that the VCR does not violate the DMCA because the Copy Switch that it avoids does not "effectively protect" against the unauthorized copying of copyrighted works as required by §1201(a)(3)(B). Streambox claims this "effective" protection is lacking because an enterprising end-user could potentially use other means to record streaming audio content as it is played by the end-user's computer speakers. This argument fails because the Copy Switch, in the ordinary course of its operation when it is on, restricts and limits the ability of people to make perfect digital copies of a copyrighted work. The Copy Switch therefore constitutes a technological measure that effectively protects a copyright owner's rights under section. 1201(a)(3)(B).

In addition, the argument ignores the fact that before the Copy Switch is even implicated, the Streambox VCR has already circumvented the Secret Handshake to gain access to a unauthorized RealMedia file. That alone is sufficient for liability under the DMCA. *See* 17 U.S.C. §1201(i)(e).

* * *

### REALNETWORKS HAS NOT DEMONSTRATED THAT IT IS REASONABLY LIKELY TO SUCCEED ON ITS DMCA CLAIM WITH RESPECT TO THE RIPPER

RealNetworks also alleges that Streambox's marketing and distribution of the Ripper violates section 1201(b) (but not section 1201(a)(2)) of the DMCA.

RealNetworks maintains that the primary purpose and only commercially significant use for the Ripper would be to enable consumers to prepare unauthorized "derivatives" of copyrighted audio or video content in the RealMedia format in violation of 17 U.S.C. §106(2).

The Ripper has legitimate purposes and commercially significant uses. For example, the Ripper may be used by content owners, including copyright holders, to convert their content from the RealMedia format to other formats. Streambox has submitted evidence that at least some content owners would use the Ripper for this legitimate purpose. The Ripper may also be used by consumers to convert audio and video files that they acquired with the content owner's permission from RealMedia to other formats. RealNetworks has not demonstrated that it is likely to succeed on its claims that the Ripper violates sections 1201(b)(1)(A) or (B) of the DMCA.

RealNetworks' DMCA claims with respect to the Ripper rely largely on its argument that the proprietary RealMedia format constitutes a technological measure that effectively protects a right of a copyright owner because it prevents end-users from making derivative works based on audio or video content that a consumer obtains in RealMedia format. RealNetworks did not offer this argument in any detail in its opening memorandum.

There is little evidence that content owners use the RealMedia format as a "technological measure" to prevent end-users from making derivative works. In any case, RealNetworks has not introduced evidence that a substantial number of content owners would object to having end-users convert RealMedia files that they legitimately obtain into other formats.

* * *

In light of Streambox's demonstration that the Ripper has legitimate and commercially significant uses, RealNetworks has not shown that it is likely to succeed on its DMCA claims with respect to the product.

Even if RealNetworks had raised a "serious question" about the Ripper's alleged violation of the DMCA, RealNetworks has not demonstrated that the balance of hardships tips sharply in its favor. As noted above, RealNetworks has not submitted evidence that the sale of the Ripper would cause it to lose customers or goodwill. By contrast, enjoining the Ripper would deprive Streambox of the ability to market a potentially valuable product with legitimate uses....

## CONCLUSION

Consistent with the findings of fact and conclusions of law above, the Court hereby ORDERS that:

> During the pendency of this action, Defendant Streambox, Inc. and its officers, agents, servants, employees and attorneys, and those persons in active concert and participation with Streambox, Inc. who receive actual notice of this Preliminary Injunction, are restrained and enjoined from manufacturing, importing, licensing, offering to the public, or offering for sale:
> a) versions of the Streambox VCR or similar products that circumvent or attempt to circumvent RealNetworks' technological security measures, and from participating or assisting in any such activity;....

Plaintiff's motion for a preliminary injunction with respect to the Streambox Ripper is DENIED.

# Comments

**1. Summary of the DMCA's Anti-Circumvention Provisions.** The DMCA anticipates "technological measures" with either or both of two functions. A "technological measure" might prevent unauthorized *access* to a copyrighted work. *See* 17 U.S.C. §1201(a)(1)(A). In that case, both *circumventing* such an access control is prohibited, and *trafficking in* or *distributing* technology that can be used to circumvent an access control is prohibited. The *RealNetworks* case involved the first type of "technological measure," one that is designed to prevent unauthorized access to a copyrighted work. *See* 17 U.S.C. §1201(a)(1)(A). Section 1201 prohibits both the act of circumventing such a measure, as well as "trafficking in" or distributing technology used for circumventing such measures. A second type of technological measure covered by §1201 is the technological measure that protects a *right* of a copyright owner, under §106, such as the exclusive right to reproduce or distribute the work. Circumventing this second sort of technological measure is not itself prohibited, since the unauthorized exercise of a right of a copyright owner is itself an act of copyright infringement, and there is no need for an additional layer of liability. However, the DMCA prohibits *trafficking in* or *distributing* technology used to circumvent such technological measures. *See* 17 U.S.C. §1201(b)(1)(A).

2. *What Constitutes Circumvention?* Section 1201 defines "to circumvent" a "technological measure" as "to descramble a scrambled work, to decrypt an encrypted work, or otherwise to avoid, bypass, remove, deactivate, or impair a technological measure, without the authority of the copyright owner." 17 U.S.C. §1201(a)(3)(A). Did the Streambox VCR allow users to "circumvent" the Copy Switch within the meaning of this phrase? Or did the Streambox VCR communicate signals that the Copy Switch was designed to respond to? In *Egilman v. Keller & Heckman, LLP*, 401 F. Supp. 2d 105 (D.D.C. 2005), the court rejected a DMCA claim under §1201(a) (which addresses direct circumvention, rather than trafficking in circumvention technology) against a law firm that accessed a computer database via unauthorized use of a valid password. The court noted: "[U]sing a username/password combination as intended—by entering a valid username and password, albeit without authorization—does not constitute circumvention under the DMCA." *Id.* at 113. *See also I.M.S. Inquiry Mgmt. Sys., Ltd. v. Berkshire Info. Sys., Inc.*, 307 F. Supp. 2d 521 (S.D.N.Y. 2004) (unauthorized use of password generated by plaintiff does not constitute "circumvention" for DMCA purposes).

3. *Exceptions and Limitations.* Section 1201 enumerates a number of specific limitations and exceptions to liability under the DMCA's anti-circumvention provisions, including exceptions for law enforcement (§1201(e)), for good faith research into computer security (§1201(j)), and limited protection for libraries (§1201(d)) and for using reverse engineering techniques to create complementary computer programs (§1201(f)). Section 1201(c)(1) provides that nothing in that section "shall affect rights, remedies, limitations, or defenses to copyright infringement, including fair use, under this title."

4. *Standing to Pursue a DMCA Anti-Circumvention Claim.* Unlike §106 of the Copyright Act, which makes clear that certain exclusive rights belong to the copyright owner, the anti-circumvention provisions of the DMCA are not so limited. Section 1203(a) of the Copyright Act provides that a civil action may be brought by "Any person injured by a violation of section 1201 or 1202." Note that the plaintiff in *RealNetworks* is not a copyright owner offended by the use of the Streambox VCR to capture its streamed copyrighted content, but the producer of a "technological measure" which is concerned about the integrity of its product.

5. *What Constitutes a Technological Measure?* Consider the definition in 17 U.S.C. §1201(a)(3)(B), which defines the circumstances under which a "technological measure" "effectively controls access to a work." (Consider as well the counterpart definition in 17 U.S.C. §1201(b)(2)(B).) Nothing in that section requires that the copyright owner or plaintiff use a sophisticated encryption or "trusted" technology. In *RealNetworks*, the court concludes that two different features of the RealNetworks system constitute "effective" technological measures: One is the "Secret Handshake" that confirms that a consumer's player is authorized to receive streamed content; the second (which is relevant to the "Ripper") is the RealMedia file format itself.

6. *Analog VCR versus Digital VCR.* RealNetworks illustrates the distinction between liability standards under background copyright law and those imposed by the DMCA. Under background copyright law, the "analog"

VCR, such as the Sony Betamax, is legal provided that it is "capable of substantial noninfringing use." Distribution of the digital StreamBox VCR, by contrast, which offers comparable functionality, nonetheless triggers liability under §1201(a) of the DMCA because, in the words of the court, it "(i) is primarily designed to [be used for circumvention]; (ii) has only limited commercially significant purposes beyond the circumvention; or (iii) is marketed as a means of circumvention." *See* 17 U.S.C. §1201(a)(2).

7. ***Concern for Competition.*** The DMCA has been controversial virtually since it was enacted. In response to arguments about protecting authors and publishers of digital work from Internet-based piracy, opponents raise the possibility that in an age of copyrighted, digital technology represented in ordinary, everyday objects, competitors may use the DMCA's anti-circumvention rules to suppress competition, rather than preserve incentives to produce copyrighted works. Two recent courts have agreed. In *Lexmark Intern., Inc. v. Static Control Components, Inc.*, 387 F.3d 522 (6th Cir. 2004), the court reversed a preliminary injunction granted to a manufacturer of computer printers. The plaintiff argued that a competing producer of print cartridges violated the DMCA when it copied a small computer program that enabled cartridges to function with the printers. In *Chamberlain Group, Inc. v. Skylink Technologies, Inc.*, 381 F.3d 1178 (Fed. Cir. 2004), the court affirmed a grant of summary judgment in favor of an aftermarket producer of universal garage door openers, which was accused of violating the DMCA by distributing transmitters that copied the plaintiff's digital codes in order to be compatible with its openers.

8. ***Constitutional Challenges to the DMCA.*** The relative complexity of the DMCA; the ambiguity of its relationship to traditional defenses to claims of copyright infringement, such as fair use and first sale, and to defenses to secondary liability, such as *Sony*'s "substantial noninfringing use" standard; and the fact that it includes criminal as well as civil penalties, prompted litigation over the constitutional validity of the DMCA. Challenges have been raised under both the First Amendment and the Fifth Amendment. Those constitutional challenges have been rejected. *See Universal City Studios, Inc. v. Corley*, 273 F.3d 429 (2d Cir. 2001) (affirming application of DMCA anti-circumvention rules to "DeCSS" computer code used to play region-coded DVDs on personal computers not loaded with industry-licensed CSS technology).

## 2. Protection for Copyright Management Information

### *STATUTE:* **Integrity of Copyright Management Information**
#### 17 U.S.C. §1202 (a), (b), (c)

In addition to its anti-circumvention provisions, the DMCA enacted protection for "copyright management information" accompanying copyrighted works. Like the anti-circumvention provisions, this part of the statute has its roots in the WIPO Copyright Treaty. "Copyright management information" may consist of the title of the work and the names of the author and copyright owner, as well as terms and conditions for using the work, "conveyed in connection with copies or phonorecords of a work." 17 U.S.C. §1202(c). It is a violation of §1202 to "intentionally remove or alter any copyright management information." 17 U.S.C. §1202(b)(1), and to knowingly "provide copyright management information that is false," 17 U.S.C. §1202(a)(1), among other things. The statute has multiple purposes: It is designed to prevent counterfeiting; to facilitate copyright owners' efforts to track and charge for particular uses of copyrighted works by individual users; and to ensure that authors and copyright owners receive appropriate recognition in connection with copyrighted works. In the latter regard, it is consistent with other efforts to recognize so-called "moral rights" in American copyright law. *See* Section D, *infra*.

The few cases interpreting the statute, however, have been reluctant to find the degree of "intent" or "knowledge" required to find a violation. *See, e.g., Gordon v. Nextel Communications and Mullen Advertising, Inc.*, 345 F.3d 922 (6th Cir. 2003); *Kelly v. Arriba Soft Corp.*, 77 F. Supp. 2d 1116 (C.D. Cal. 1999), *aff'd in part, rev'd in part on other grounds*, 336 F.3d 811 (9th Cir. 2003). What constitutes "copyright management information" also has been narrowly defined. *See IQ Group, Ltd. v. Wiesner Pub., LLC*, 409 F. Supp. 2d 587 (D.N.J. 2006).

# D. MORAL RIGHTS

Section 106 of the Copyright Act does not expressly grant owners of American copyrights so-called "moral rights," borrowed from the French "droit moral," commonly associated with Continental copyright systems. (Exclusive rights to exploit the work for profit are known generally as "economic rights.") Continental copyright

> focuses on the author and his personal relationship to his work. Continental doctrine views copyright essentially as the protection of the author's individual character and spirit as expressed in his literary or artistic creation. Although a work may be commercially exploited, it is not simply a commodity—and many commentators would say that it is not a commodity at all. Instead, the work is seen, partially or wholly, as an extension of the author's personality, the means by which he seeks to communicate to the public.

Neil Netanel, *Alienability Restrictions and the Enhancement of Author Autonomy in United States and Continental Copyright Law*, 12 Cardozo Arts & Ent. L.J. 1, 7 (1994). Under French law, for example, "moral rights" include the right of the author to claim or disclaim authorship of the work (*droit à la paternité*), the right of the author to the integrity of the work—to object to distortion, modification, or destruction that injures the reputation of the author (*droit au respect de l'oeuvre*), the right to determine when and how to publish the work (*droit de divulgation*), the right to withdraw or repurchase unsold copies of the work if it no longer represents the author's views (*droit de retrait ou de repentir*), and the right of the artist to a royalty upon resale of the work (*droit de suite*). Article 6bis of the Berne Convention obligates signatory countries to protect certain moral rights of the author:

(1) Independently of the author's economic rights, and even after the transfer of the said rights, the author shall have the right to claim authorship of the work and to object to any distortion, mutilation or other modification of, or other derogatory action in relation to, the said work, which would be prejudicial to his honor or reputation.

Given its historic emphasis on copyright's function in protecting authorial incentives in order to produce works that benefit the public as a whole, American law has long resisted the notion of moral rights and their orientation toward the inherent worth of the author's "natural" right. When the United States joined the Berne Convention, Congress declared that existing United States law was sufficient to satisfy Article 6bis, given various provisions of state law, common law principles of libel, defamation, misrepresentation, and unfair competition; the Lanham Act; and "various provisions of the Copyright Act." *See* S. Rep. No. 352, 100th Cong., 2d Sess. 9-10 (1988), *reprinted in* 1988 U.S.C.C.A.N. 3706, 3714-15.

The Copyright Act does include one limited "moral rights" provision, the Visual Artists Rights Act of 1990, or VARA, codified at 17 U.S.C. §106A. VARA applies only to works "of visual art," which is a term of art under §101, with relatively narrow scope:

A "work of visual art" is —

> (1) a painting, drawing, print, or sculpture, existing in a single copy, in a limited edition of 200 copies or fewer that are signed and consecutively numbered by the author, or, in the case of a sculpture, in multiple cast, carved, or fabricated sculptures of 200 or fewer that are consecutively numbered by the author and bear the signature or other identifying mark of the author; or
>
> (2) a still photographic image produced for exhibition purposes only, existing in a single copy that is signed by the author, or in a limited edition of 200 copies or fewer that are signed and consecutively numbered by the author.

The author of a qualifying "work of visual art" is granted the right of attribution; the right to prevent any intentional distortion, mutilation, or modification of the work that would be prejudicial to the author's reputation; and for a still-narrower class of works of "recognized stature," the right to prevent destruction of the work. As with all "moral rights," rights under VARA belong to the author, rather than to the copyright owner (if different), and they attach not to the intangible "work of authorship" embedded in a tangible medium, but inhere in the tangible copy (or copies) themselves. The author can waive rights under VARA, in writing, but cannot transfer them to someone else. VARA rights generally last for the life of the author.

## Note on *Gilliam v. American Broadcasting Companies, Inc.*

Though American copyright law does not recognize "moral rights" in a broad sense, at times courts have looked for ways to recognize the author's interest in reputation or integrity of the work. In *Gilliam v.*

*American Broadcasting Companies, Inc.*, 538 F.2d 14 (2d Cir. 1976), the members of the Monty Python comedy troupe sued the ABC broadcast television network, which had acquired the rights to broadcast episodes of "Monty Python's Flying Circus" on American television. ABC edited the initial episode, however, removing what it considered to be offensive and obscene material. Arguing that the changes violated the integrity of their copyrighted scripts, the members of Monty Python sued to enjoin further broadcasts of edited versions of "Monty Python's Flying Circus." The trial court declined to enter the relief, but the court of appeals reversed, noting that the reputation of Monty Python was likely to be damaged by broadcasts of their work that were not funny, and that this harm was properly characterized either as infringement of the Python copyrights by modification of the works beyond the editing permitted by the relevant licensing agreements, or as infringement of rights available under §43(a) of the Lanham Act. In either case, the court noted, the cognizable injury was one recognized under Continental legal systems as an injury to the author's "moral right."

In a concurring opinion in *Gilliam*, Judge Gurfein noted that the Lanham Act may offer more direct protection for an author's reputation interests. As you saw in Chapters 2 through 5, trademark law as a whole is concerned with ensuring that trademark-related information guides accurate information about product sources to consumers. In *Dastar Corp. v. Twentieth Century Fox Film Corp.*, 539 U.S. 23 (2003), which you read in Chapter 3, the Supreme Court held that unfair competition provisions of the Lanham Act could not be used by the owner of an expired copyright in a public domain work to limit distribution of the work by a competitor—even where the competitor characterized itself as the "producer" of the work in its packaging. The plaintiff, Twentieth Century Fox Film Corp., was the successor to the original producer of a television series based on General Dwight Eisenhower's book about World War II. After the copyright to the television series expired, the defendant, Dastar, repackaged the television series for sales on videotape, without identifying Fox or its predecessor as the original source of the work. The Court concluded:

> Assuming for the sake of argument that Dastar's representation of itself as the "Producer" of its videos amounted to a representation that it originated the creative work conveyed by the videos, allowing a cause of action under §43(a) for that representation would create a species of mutant copyright law that limits the public's "federal right to 'copy and to use,'" expired copyrights.

*Id.* at 34. The Lanham Act, the Court noted, was "*not* designed to protect originality or creativity." *Id.* at 37. The decision has been interpreted by some courts as precedent for the view that trademark law can never be used to expand the economic rights granted by the Copyright Act, thus limiting the potential value of trademark law as a resource for authors interested in protecting their "moral" rights. *See, e.g., General Universal Systems, Inc. v. Lee*, 379 F.3d 131 (5th Cir. 2004). More generally, to the extent that American law should recognize authors' moral rights more broadly than it does today, the limited scope and impact of VARA and the limited applicability of trademark law have been urged as bases for more comprehensive federal lawmaking on behalf of authors. *See, e.g.,* Roberta Rosenthal Kwall, *The Attribution Right in the United States: Caught in the Crossfire between Copyright and Section 43(A),* 77 WASH. L. REV. 985 (2002) (urging enactment of federal statute providing authors with a right of attribution).

# Defenses to Copyright Infringement

The exclusive rights of the copyright owner are not absolute. You have already encountered some limitations on those rights. Some limitations inhere in the structure of §102 and in the initial scope of copyright interests, such as the idea/expression dichotomy. Others inhere in the structure and application of §106, which defines the exclusive rights of the copyright owner. In addition to these limitations, claims of copyright infringement are subject to a number of independent defenses found in other parts of the Copyright Act. Those defenses are the subjects of this chapter.

Section A of this chapter addresses a topic that is technically and importantly a defense to a claim of copyright infringement, but which is particularly significant in providing the foundation for the transactional nature of most copyright law practice. The most important defense to a claim of infringement is that the copyright owner authorized the allegedly infringing use. In transactional setting, this defense becomes the framework for licensing copyrighted works. Section B focuses on fair use, which permits some possibly infringing uses of copyrighted works without the copyright owner's consent, and without compensation, in contexts such as criticism, research, and teaching. Like the defense of authorization, the defense of fair use applies to all possible claims of copyright infringement. Section C deals with a defense that applies only to claims of infringement of the exclusive right to distribute copies of the work: the doctrine of first sale, which protects the right of the owner of a copy of a work to re-sell that copy, or to give it away. The first sale doctrine reflects the distinction that the law draws between the intangible work of authorship protected by copyright and the tangible medium of expression in which the work is embodied. Section D describes a set of legal mechanisms that are unique among the doctrines of intellectual property law reviewed in this book: provisions for compulsory licensing of copyrights. Under certain circumstances, the law permits exploitation of copyrights that would otherwise constitute infringement, so long as the party using the work meets certain statutory conditions and compensates the copyright owner according to statutory rules. The use of the copyright in such a case is automatically sanctioned by the Copyright Act, rather than cleared in advance, or afterward, by the copyright owner.

# A. COPYRIGHT LICENSING

*STATUTE:* **Infringement of Copyright**
17 U.S.C. §501(a)

*STATUTE:* **Definition — "Copyright Owner"**
17 U.S.C. §101

Section 106 grants the copyright owner the ability to do and to authorize certain acts in connection with the copyrighted work. The first question in any suit for copyright infringement, therefore, is whether the copyright owner has authorized the allegedly infringing activity. If the copyright owner has granted permission, then no action can be maintained. In all cases, permission is a question of the intent of the copyright owner. Valid permission need not be part of a bargained-for contract. As in contract law, however, manifestations of the owner's intent may be express, or they may be implied.

The Act also contains a definition of "copyright owner" in §101 which makes clear that ownership of the copyright in a work of authorship, and ownership of the different exclusive rights provided in §106, may be divided among more than one person or firm. As a result of licenses, bargains, and outright assignments, the reproduction right for a given copyrighted work, found in §106(1), may be owned by one person, for example, and the public display right, found in §106(5), may be owned by another. Obtaining valid permission to use a copyrighted work involves confirming that the party granting the permission has the authority to do so.

As a practical matter, in the vast majority of instances, permission to use a copyrighted work is part of an express contract. In some copyright industries, obtaining the right to use a copyrighted work for certain purposes is part of what is called a "permissions" process. For example, if your professor supplements your casebook with photocopied excerpts of articles or copies of other materials, in all likelihood the professor went through some form of administrative process to get permission to reproduce and distribute those materials, or to "clear" them with the appropriate copyright interest, and to arrange for compensation to be paid. Many copyright industries use the term "license" to refer to the permission granted by the copyright owner (in the common law of property, a "license" by a property owner constitutes a defense to a claim of trespass). Since permissions and licenses are typically given in exchange for consideration, in the form of royalties, colloquially, "licenses" constitute both the grant of rights to use the work as well as the contracts that usually embody the exchange. What this chapter characterizes doctrinally as a defense to copyright infringement also represents the major method by which copyright owners exploit their work for profit. Licensing and infringement are two sides of the same coin.

In practice, understanding copyright licensing and its implications for copyright infringement litigation closely resembles the analogous art of interpreting contracts. Copyright owners have the power to grant permission to use the work — that is, to try to exploit the work, usually commercially — in nearly any form, format, place, time, and manner that they wish, so long as the permission they grant lies within the scope of their exclusive rights under §106.

Copyright licenses may take two forms. Copyright owners may grant an express license to do some of the things covered by §106 (to reproduce, distribute, modify, publicly perform, and/or publicly display the work, in some specified context). In the case of the express license, good lawyers will usually be careful to specify the rights granted and the contexts involved—but as in any case involving a legal document, questions may arise requiring interpretation of the language in light of unforeseen circumstances. Those questions are addressed in Section A.1, below. Copyright licenses also may be implied under the circumstances of a particular use of a work, or under the circumstances of the use of a particular copy of a work. Section A.2 addresses how and when implied licenses arise.

## 1. Express Licenses

### RANDOM HOUSE v. ROSETTA BOOKS

150 F. Supp. 2d 613 (S.D.N.Y. 2001), aff'd, 283 F.3d 490 (2d Cir. 2002)

STEIN, District Judge.

* * *

In the year 2000 and the beginning of 2001, Rosetta Books contracted with several authors to publish certain of their works—including *The Confessions of Nat Turner* and *Sophie's Choice* by William Styron; *Slaughterhouse-Five, Breakfast of Champions, The Sirens of Titan, Cat's Cradle,* and *Player Piano* by Kurt Vonnegut; and *Promised Land* by Robert B. Parker—in digital format over the internet. On February 26, 2001 Rosetta Books launched its ebook business, offering those titles and others for sale in digital format. The next day, Random House filed this complaint accusing Rosetta Books of committing copyright infringement and tortiously interfering with the contracts Random House had with Messrs. Parker, Styron and Vonnegut by selling its ebooks. It simultaneously moved for a preliminary injunction prohibiting Rosetta from infringing plaintiff's copyrights.

#### A. EBOOKS

Ebooks are "digital book[s] that you can read on a computer screen or an electronic device." (Hrg. at 13; http:// www.rosettabooks.com/pages/about_ebooks.html) Ebooks are created by converting digitized text into a format readable by computer software. The text can be viewed on a desktop or laptop computer, personal digital assistant or handheld dedicated ebook reading device. Rosetta's ebooks can only be read after they are downloaded into a computer that contains either Microsoft Reader, Adobe Acrobat Reader, or Adobe Acrobat eBook Reader software.

Included in a Rosetta ebook is a book cover, title page, copyright page and "eforward" all created by Rosetta Books. Although the text of the ebook is exactly the same as the text of the original work, the ebook contains various features that take advantage of its digital format. For example, ebook users can search the work electronically to find specific words and phrases. They can electronically "highlight" and "bookmark" certain text, which can then be automatically indexed and accessed through hyperlinks. They can use hyperlinks in the table of contents to jump to specific chapters.

Users can also type electronic notes which are stored with the related text. These notes can be automatically indexed, sorted and filed. Users can also change the font size and style of the text to accommodate personal preferences; thus, an electronic screen of text may contain more words, fewer words, or the same number of words as a page of the original published book. In addition, users can have displayed the definition of any word in the text. In one version of the software, the word can also be pronounced aloud.

Rosetta's ebooks contain certain security features to prevent users from printing, emailing or otherwise distributing the text. Although it is technologically possible to foil these security features, anyone who does so would be violating the licensing agreement accompanying the software.

### B. RANDOM HOUSE'S LICENSING AGREEMENTS

While each agreement between the author and Random House differs in some respects, each uses the phrase "print, publish and sell the work in book form" to convey rights from the author to the publisher.

\* \* \*

### B. OWNERSHIP OF A VALID COPYRIGHT

Two elements must be proven in order to establish a prima facie case of infringement: "(1) ownership of a valid copyright, and (2) copying of constituent elements of the work that are original." *Feist Publications, Inc. v. Rural Tel. Serv. Co.*, 499 U.S. 340, 361 (1991). In this case, only the first element—ownership of a valid copyright—is at issue, since all parties concede that the text of the ebook is identical to the text of the book published by Random House.

\* \* \*

### 1. CONTRACT INTERPRETATION OF LICENSING AGREEMENTS — LEGAL STANDARDS

Random House claims to own the rights in question through its licensing agreements with the authors. Interpretation of an agreement purporting to grant a copyright license is a matter of state contract law. All of the agreements state that they "shall be interpreted according to the law of the State of New York."

In New York, a written contract is to be interpreted so as to give effect to the intention of the parties as expressed in the contract's language. The court must consider the entire contract and reconcile all parts, if possible, to avoid an inconsistency.

\* \* \*

Relying on "the language of the license contract and basic principles of interpretation," [*Boosey & Hawkes Music Publishers, Ltd. v. Walt Disney Co.*,

145 F.3d 481, 487 n. 3 (2d Cir. 1998)], as instructed to do so by *Boosey* and [*Bartsch v. Metro-Goldwyn-Mayer, Inc.*, 391 F.2d 150 (2d Cir. 1968)], this Court finds that the most reasonable interpretation of the grant in the contracts at issue to "print, publish and sell the work in book form" does not include the right to publish the work as an ebook. At the outset, the phrase itself distinguishes between the pure content—i.e. "the work"—and the format of display—"in book form." The *Random House Webster's Unabridged Dictionary* defines a "book" as "a written or printed work of fiction or nonfiction, usually on sheets of paper fastened or bound together within covers" and defines "form" as "external appearance of a clearly defined area, as distinguished from color or material; the shape of a thing or person." *Random House Webster's Unabridged Dictionary* (2001), available in searchable form at http://www.allwords.com.

Manifestly, paragraph # 1 of each contract—entitled either "grant of rights" or "exclusive publication right"—conveys certain rights from the author to the publisher. In that paragraph, separate grant language is used to convey the rights to publish book club editions, reprint editions, abridged forms, and editions in Braille. This language would not be necessary if the phrase "in book form" encompassed all types of books. That paragraph specifies exactly which rights were being granted by the author to the publisher. Indeed, many of the rights set forth in the publisher's form contracts were in fact not granted to the publisher, but rather were reserved by the authors to themselves. For example, each of the authors specifically reserved certain rights for themselves by striking out phrases, sentences, and paragraphs of the publisher's form contract. This evidences an intent by these authors not to grant the publisher the broadest rights in their works.

\* \* \*

Not only does the language of the contract itself lead almost ineluctably to the conclusion that Random House does not own the right to publish the works as ebooks, but also a reasonable person "cognizant of the customs, practices, usages and terminology as generally understood in the particular trade or business," [*Sayers v. Rochester Telephone Corp. Supplemental Management Pension Plan*, 7 F.3d 1091, 1095 (2d Cir. 1993)], would conclude that the grant language does not include ebooks. "To print, publish and sell the work in book form" is understood in the publishing industry to be a "limited" grant. *See Field v. True Comics*, 89 F. Supp. 611, 613-14 (S.D.N.Y. 1950); *see also* Melville B. Nimmer & David Nimmer, *Nimmer on Copyright*, §10.14[C] (2001) (citing *Field*).

\* \* \*

Because Random House cannot establish a prima facie case of copyright infringement, it is not likely to succeed on the merits and is not entitled to a presumption of irreparable harm. Random House has made no showing of irreparable harm; therefore, it cannot meet the test for obtaining a preliminary injunction. Even if it could show such harm, and could be considered to have presented sufficiently serious questions about the merits to make them a fair ground for litigation, the balance of hardships does not tip decidedly in Random House's favor. Random House fears that Rosetta's ebooks will harm its goodwill with its customers and cause direct competition in Random House's own efforts to establish its ebook business. Rosetta worries that a preliminary injunction will effectively put its new company out of business because it will impede its ability to publish any works previously licensed to other publishers. While both parties present valid concerns, Random House has not demonstrated that its concerns decidedly outweigh Rosetta's.

## CONCLUSION

Employing the most important tool in the armamentarium of contract interpretation — the language of the contract itself — this Court has concluded that Random House is not the beneficial owner of the right to publish the eight works at issue as ebooks. This is neither a victory for technophiles nor a defeat for Luddites. It is merely a determination, relying on neutral principles of contract interpretation, that because Random House is not likely to succeed on the merits of its copyright infringement claim and cannot demonstrate irreparable harm, its motion for a preliminary injunction should be denied.

# Comments

1. *The Language of the License.* Copyright licensing cases, just like contracts cases, typically start with the language of the license. In *Random House*, the key passage from each of the relevant agreements is the author's conveyance to the publisher of the right to "print, publish and sell the work[s] in book form." If this phrase included the right to distribute electronic "book" versions of the works, then the authors gave up that right, and Random House should prevail, since the authors had nothing left to convey to Rosetta Books. If this phrase did not include "electronic" books, however, then the authors retained ebook rights and had the authority to sell those rights later.

2. *Rules of Contract Interpretation.* The court concludes that its use of dictionary definitions, its assessment of the internal structure of the license agreements, and usage of "book form" in other cases and in treatises on the entertainment industry are all consistent with "neutral principles of contract interpretation." Suppose, however, that the case had arisen as a commercial contract dispute, rather than as a suit for copyright infringement. What principles of contract interpretation might be applied? There is, for example, the proposition that trade usage is typically relevant to explain ambiguous contract terms. *See* Restatement (2d) Contracts §§219-223 (1981). Trade usage is ordinarily proved through the testimony of experts in some relevant trade. There is also the maxim of *contra proferentem*, under which ambiguous contract terms may be interpreted against the interest of the party who drafted or supplied them. *See* Restatement (2d) Contracts §206 (1981). There is the body of contract law that addresses interpretation of contracts in light of claims of that one or both parties was mistaken at the time of contracting, and as a result failed to anticipate how the contract would be applied in the future. *See* Restatement (2d) Contracts §§152, 154 (1981) (asking

whether the adversely affected party bore the risk of a mistake). And there is the issue of "omitted terms": When the parties to a contract have not agreed with respect to a term that is essential to a determination of their rights and duties, a term that is reasonable under the circumstances may be supplied by the court. *See* Restatement (2d) Contracts §204 (1981). It is always possible for parties to avoid these problems by limiting the risks of ambiguity. One way to do so in a copyright license is to include an express provision covering exploitation of the work via future or unknown and undeveloped technologies.

3. *The Mechanics of Copyright Licensing.* Copyright law does not regulate the form and format of transfers of interests in copyrights, with one important exception: A "transfer of copyright ownership," which §101 of the Act defines as a conveyance of any of the exclusive rights of the copyright owner other than a non-exclusive license, is effective only if it is in writing and signed by the owner of the rights conveyed or transferred. Note that this copyright Statute of Frauds differs from the related writing requirement found in the work made for hire doctrine. Under the portion of the work made for hire doctrine that authorizes works made for hire via an arrangement expressed in writing, both sides of the transaction — the person performing the work, and the person or firm that becomes the copyright owner — must sign the relevant writing. Under §204 of the Act, however, an effective transfer of copyright ownership must be signed only by one party. This distinction confirms that an effective conveyance of an interest in a copyright, such as a license or grant of permission, may be unilateral. It need not be part of a bargain.

## POLICY PERSPECTIVE
### New Use Problems

*Random House* and other so-called "new use" cases appear to ask metaphysical questions, such as "is an ebook a 'book'?," though in practical terms they concern how to allocate profits from markets not anticipated in the original bargain. Public policy offers different approaches to this question. On the one hand, it might be argued that success of the work in the new market is derived from the author's creativity, and the original publisher should retain profits from that market. On the other hand, it might be argued that this unforeseen market was not part of the original author's (or publisher's) calculus in deciding whether to produce or publish the work, and it resulted from new efforts to develop and exploit new markets. Any profit from new markets would constitute an unnecessary and undeserved windfall to the original publisher and should belong instead to the newcomer. The distinction has important implications for allocating the burden of negotiating for inclusion, or exclusion, of new uses from copyright licenses.

Other "new use" cases reflect both points of view, even while they occasionally seem to approach the issues (such as "what is television?") in metaphysical terms. In *Boosey & Hawkes Music Publishers,*

*Ltd. v. The Walt Disney Company*, 145 F.3d 481 (2d Cir. 1998), the question was whether a copyright license signed in 1939 that authorized Disney to use Stravinsky's "The Rite of Spring" in "one motion picture" was sufficient to enable Disney to release *Fantasia* (the original "motion picture") on videotape. The court ruled that "neutral principles of contract interpretation" dictated that the license was "more reasonably read to include than to exclude a motion picture distributed in video format." The court noted that a "nascent" market for home viewing of feature films was recognized in 1939. In *Herbert L. Cohen v. Paramount Pictures Corp.*, 845 F.2d 851 (9th Cir. 1988), however, the court confronted a license signed in 1969 that authorized the use of the plaintiff's musical composition in a motion picture that could be shown in theaters and "by means of television." The defendant distributed copies of the film on videocassette. The court ruled that "the license must be construed in accordance with the purpose underlying federal copyright law." That purpose, it found, would be frustrated "were we to construe this license—with its limiting language—as granting a right in a medium that had not been introduced to the domestic market at the time the parties entered into the agreement." It noted that VCRs for home use were not invented or known in 1969, and therefore could not have been the subject of the original bargain.

## 2. Implied Licenses

Copyright licenses may be "exclusive" or "non-exclusive." Under an exclusive license, the licensee is the sole party authorized to exploit the copyrighted work in the manner prescribed by the license. Under a non-exclusive license, the copyright owner retains the power to grant licenses to others, even to others who might compete with the first licensee. Well-drafted express licenses will specify which form of license is involved; in fact, as the next case illustrates, an exclusive license is a form of transfer of copyright ownership that is enforceable only if it is properly memorialized. Because of the writing requirement for exclusive licenses, non-exclusive licenses may arise expressly, or they may be implied in light of relevant facts and circumstances.

### EFFECTS ASSOCIATES, INC. v. COHEN
#### 908 F.2d 555 (9th Cir. 1990)

KOZINSKI, Circuit Judge.

What we have here is a failure to compensate. Larry Cohen, a low-budget horror movie mogul, paid less than the agreed price for special effects footage he had commissioned from Effects Associates. Cohen then used this footage without first obtaining a written license or assignment of the copyright; Effects sued for copyright infringement. We consider whether a transfer of copyright without a written agreement, an arrangement apparently not uncommon in the motion picture industry, conforms with the requirements of the Copyright Act.

## FACTS

This started out as a run-of-the-mill Hollywood squabble. Defendant Larry Cohen wrote, directed and executive produced "The Stuff," a horror movie with a dash of social satire: Earth is invaded by an alien life form that looks (and tastes) like frozen yogurt but, alas, has some unfortunate side effects — it's addictive and takes over the mind of anyone who eats it. Marketed by an unscrupulous entrepreneur, the Stuff becomes a big hit. An industrial spy hired by ice cream manufacturers eventually uncovers the terrible truth; he alerts the American people and blows up the yogurt factory, making the world safe once again for lovers of frozen confections.

In cooking up this gustatory melodrama, Cohen asked Effects Associates, a small special effects company, to create footage to enhance certain action sequences in the film. In a short letter dated October 29, 1984, Effects offered to prepare seven shots, the most dramatic of which would depict the climactic explosion of the Stuff factory. Cohen agreed to the deal orally, but no one said anything about who would own the copyright in the footage.

Cohen was unhappy with the factory explosion Effects created, and he expressed his dissatisfaction by paying Effects only half the promised amount for that shot. Effects made several demands for the rest of the money (a little over $8,000), but Cohen refused. Nevertheless, Cohen incorporated Effects's footage into the film and turned it over to New World Entertainment for distribution. Effects then brought this copyright infringement action, claiming that Cohen (along with his production company and New World) had no right to use the special effects footage unless he paid Effects the full contract price....

The district court initially dismissed the suit, holding that it was primarily a contract dispute and, as such, did not arise under federal law. In an opinion remarkable for its lucidity, we reversed and remanded, concluding that plaintiff was "master of his claim" and could opt to pursue the copyright infringement action instead of suing on the contract. *Effects Assocs., Inc. v. Cohen,* 817 F.2d 72, 73 (9th Cir. 1987). We recognized that the issue on remand would be whether Effects had transferred to Cohen the right to use the footage.

On remand, the district court granted summary judgment to Cohen on the infringement claim, holding that Effects had granted Cohen an implied license to use the shots. Accordingly, the court dismissed the remaining state law claims, allowing Effects to pursue them in state court. We review the district court's grant of summary judgment de novo.

## DISCUSSION
### 4. TRANSFER OF COPYRIGHT OWNERSHIP

The law couldn't be clearer: The copyright owner of "a motion picture or other audiovisual work" has the exclusive rights to copy, distribute or display the copyrighted work publicly. 17 U.S.C. §106 (1988). While the copyright owner can sell or license his rights to someone else, section 204 of the Copyright Act invalidates a purported transfer of ownership unless it is in writing. 17 U.S.C. §204(a) (1988). Here, no one disputes that Effects is the copyright owner of the special effects footage used in "The Stuff," and that defendants copied, distributed and publicly displayed this footage without written authorization.

Cohen suggests that section 204's writing requirement does not apply to this situation, advancing an argument that might be summarized, tongue in cheek, as: Moviemakers do lunch, not contracts. Cohen concedes that "[i]n the best of all possible legal worlds" parties would obey the writing requirement, but contends that moviemakers are too absorbed in developing "joint creative endeavors" to "focus upon the legal niceties of copyright licenses." Thus, Cohen suggests that we hold section 204's writing requirement inapplicable here because "it [i]s customary in the motion picture industry...not to have written licenses." To the extent that Cohen's argument amounts to a plea to exempt moviemakers from the normal operation of section 204 by making implied transfers of copyrights "the rule, not the exception," we reject his argument.

Common sense tells us that agreements should routinely be put in writing. This simple practice prevents misunderstandings by spelling out the terms of a deal in black and white, forces parties to clarify their thinking and consider problems that could potentially arise, and encourages them to take their promises seriously because it's harder to backtrack on a written contract than on an oral one. Copyright law dovetails nicely with common sense by requiring that a transfer of copyright ownership be in writing. Section 204 ensures that the creator of a work will not give away his copyright inadvertently and forces a party who wants to use the copyrighted work to negotiate with the creator to determine precisely what rights are being transferred and at what price. Most importantly, section 204 enhances predictability and certainty of copyright ownership — "Congress' paramount goal" when it revised the Act in 1976. *Community for Creative Non-Violence* [*v. Reid*, 490 U.S. 730, 749 (1989)]. Rather than look to the courts every time they disagree as to whether a particular use of the work violates their mutual understanding, parties need only look to the writing that sets out their respective rights.

Section 204's writing requirement is not unduly burdensome; it necessitates neither protracted negotiations nor substantial expense. The rule is really quite simple: If the copyright holder agrees to transfer ownership to another party, that party must get the copyright holder to sign a piece of paper saying so. It doesn't have to be the Magna Charta; a one-line pro forma statement will do.

\* \* \*

### B. NONEXCLUSIVE LICENSES

Although we reject any suggestion that moviemakers are immune to section 204, we note that there is a narrow exception to the writing requirement that may apply here. Section 204 provides that all transfers of copyright ownership must be in writing; section 101 defines transfers of ownership broadly, but expressly removes from the scope of section 204 a "nonexclusive license." The sole issue that remains, then, is whether Cohen had a nonexclusive license to use plaintiff's special effects footage.

The leading treatise on copyright law states that "[a] nonexclusive license may be granted orally, or may even be implied from conduct." 3 M. Nimmer & D. Nimmer, *Nimmer on Copyright* §10.03[A], at 10-36 (1989). Cohen relies on the latter proposition; he insists that, although Effects never gave him a written or oral license, Effects's conduct created an implied license to use the footage in "The Stuff."

Cohen relies largely on our decision in *Oddo v. Ries,* 743 F.2d 630 (9th Cir. 1984). There, we held that Oddo, the author of a series of articles on how to restore Ford F-100 pickup trucks, had impliedly granted a limited non-exclusive license to Ries, a publisher, to use plaintiff's articles in a book on the same topic. We relied on the fact that Oddo and Ries had formed a partnership to create and publish the book, with Oddo writing and Ries providing capital. Oddo prepared a manuscript consisting partly of material taken from his prior articles and submitted it to Ries. Because the manuscript incorporated pre-existing material, it was a derivative work; by publishing it, Ries would have necessarily infringed the copyright in Oddo's articles, unless Oddo had granted him a license. We concluded that, in preparing and handing over to Ries a manuscript intended for publication that, if published, would infringe Oddo's copyright, Oddo "impliedly gave the partnership a license to use the articles insofar as they were incorporated in the manuscript, for without such a license, Oddo's contribution to the partnership venture would have been of minimal value." *Id.*

The district court agreed with Cohen, and we agree with the district court: *Oddo* controls here. Like the plaintiff in *Oddo,* Effects created a work at defendant's request and handed it over, intending that defendant copy and distribute it.[6] To hold that Effects did not at the same time convey a license to use the footage in "The Stuff" would mean that plaintiff's contribution to the film was "of minimal value," a conclusion that can't be squared with the fact that Cohen paid Effects almost $56,000 for this footage. Accordingly, we conclude that Effects impliedly granted nonexclusive licenses to Cohen and his production company to incorporate the special effects footage into "The Stuff" and to New World Entertainment to distribute the film.

## CONCLUSION

We affirm the district court's grant of summary judgment in favor of Cohen and the other defendants. We note, however, that plaintiff doesn't leave this court empty-handed. Copyright ownership is comprised of a

6. As the district court found, "every objective fact concerning the transaction at issue supports a finding that an implied license existed." Order Granting Summary Judgment (Aug. 26, 1988) at 2. Effects's copyright registration certificate states that the footage is to be used in "The Stuff," so does the letter agreement of October 29, 1984, and Effects's President James Danforth agreed at his deposition that this was his understanding. Also, Effects delivered the film negatives to Cohen, never warning him that cutting the negatives into the film would constitute copyright infringement. While delivery of a copy "does not *of itself* convey any rights in the copyrighted work," 17 U.S.C. §202 (1988) (emphasis added), it is one factor that may be relied upon in determining that an implied license has been granted.

bundle of rights; in granting a nonexclusive license to Cohen, Effects has given up only one stick from that bundle—the right to sue Cohen for copyright infringement. It retains the right to sue him in state court on a variety of other grounds, including breach of contract. Additionally, Effects may license, sell or give away for nothing its remaining rights in the special effects footage. Those rights may not be particularly valuable, of course: "The Stuff" was something less than a blockbuster, and it remains to be seen whether there's a market for shots featuring great gobs of alien yogurt oozing out of a defunct factory. On the other hand, the shots may have much potential for use in music videos. In any event, whatever Effects chooses to do with the footage, Cohen will have no basis for complaining. And that's an important lesson that licensees of more versatile film properties may want to take to heart.

## Comments

1. *Implied Licenses and the Copyright Owner's Intent.* Ordinarily, the grant of a license or permission to use a copyrighted work, and the scope of that license or permission, is a question of the copyright holder's intent. The court here infers intent to permit reproduction and distribution of the copyrighted footage from Effects Associates' delivering the footage to Cohen, along with several additional facts: Cohen requested that Effects Associates produce the footage; Effects Associates reasonably believed that the footage was valuable; and Effects Associates necessarily knew that Cohen intended to incorporate the footage into a larger finished film.

2. *Other Rights, Other Remedies.* In reading *Cohen*, it is important to distinguish the two legal claims involved. Effects Associates had a single grievance. The grievance was that it had prepared special effects footage without being paid the money that it had bargained for. The court divides that grievance into two parts. To the extent that Effects Associates simply wanted to be paid, Cohen breached a promise. That contract claim, as the court notes, remains to be decided in state court. To the extent that Effects Associates did not want Cohen to use the footage, Cohen allegedly infringed Effects Associates' copyright. The court concludes that delivery of the footage to Cohen manifested Effects Associates' intent that the footage be used. The resulting implied license defeated the copyright claim.

3. *Writing Requirements and Certainty.* Among the benefits of requirements that certain transactions be recorded in writing is that they encourage parties and lawyers to channel transactions into forms that are easily recognizable and testable by other parties, and by courts. The court relies on this rationale in concluding that any possible transfer of the copyright or exclusive license in *Cohen* is invalid, given the absence of a signed writing. Is the court's resolution of the implied license issue consistent with its interest in certainty? In the absence of a writing, and in the absence of an express oral license, the court might have concluded that Cohen had no permission to use the footage, and that Effects Associates should prevail on the copyright infringement claim.

*4. Implied Licenses and Balancing the Interests of Authors and Audience. Cohen* is a case in which litigation over the meaning of a license ensues because of the failure of two commercial interests to undertake even minimal planning regarding copyright interests. Questions of implied licenses may arise in other contexts where prior bargaining over the scope of §106 is unlikely, such as consumer contexts. One way to understand *Cohen*, then, is as an effort to accommodate the legitimate interests of authors with the legitimate interests of readers, consumers, and users. Effects Associates has a valid grievance, but that grievance is not so severe that it should be able to exercise the power that copyright grants authors to enjoin unauthorized exercise of §106 rights. Cohen obtains what amounts to a compulsory license: it is entitled to use the footage and, separately, it is required to pay a royalty to Effects Associates. The copyright owner's intent serves as a proxy for the real public policy interests that the court is balancing.

This perspective on implied licenses takes on particular importance in the context of the Internet. Since they are fixed in tangible media and contain at least modest creativity, most web pages constitute copyrightable works. A web user who browses and reads those pages typically makes temporary copies of those works automatically, in the computer's temporary memory (RAM), by following URLs and links. (Recall from Chapter 7 that *MAI Systems v. Peak Computer* would treat such a copy as "fixed" for §106 purposes.) Commentators generally agree that browsing may nominally infringe copyrights in web pages, but should be excused under the doctrine of implied license. *See, e.g.,* Joseph P. Liu, *Owning Digital Copies: Copyright Law and the Incidents of Copy Ownership,* 42 Wm. & Mary L. Rev. 1245, 1168-1169 (2001). Owners of websites retain the authority to exclude some or all unwanted users from accessing their sites by using password schemes and other technologies, for example.

# Problem

**8-1.** In 1980, Joyce wrote a book titled *Victim of Love,* an account of an axe murder of a housewife in Tyler, Texas in 1979. Late in 1980, Joyce signed a contract with Longhorn Press (LP) to publish the manuscript. That contract also included a grant of certain additional rights, including:

> The Author hereby grants and assigns solely and exclusively to the Publisher throughout the world during the full term of copyright and all renewals thereof the book and volume publishing right in the English language throughout the world in [Victim of Love] along with the following rights; abridgement, syndication, radio broadcasting, television, mechanical recording and rendition, projection, Braille, microfilm, translation, dramatic, and motion pictures; ancillary commercial promotion rights, together with the right to grant licenses for the exercise of and/or to dispose of any or all of the rights granted.

LP published the book version of *Victim of Love*, and it entered into a contract with Tucson Pictures to produce a motion picture adaptation of the book. The motion picture version, titled "Forty Whacks," was produced and broadcast on the NBC television network in 1986. Shortly afterward, Joyce read a notice in an entertainment trade publication that Tucson Pictures was planning to release "Forty Whacks" on home video, for both domestic and international distribution. If Tucson Pictures proceeds with its plan to distribute "Forty Whacks" on home video, is it liable to Joyce for copyright infringement? *See Bloom v. Hearst Entertainment, Inc.*, 33 F.3d 518 (5th Cir. 1994).

## B. FAIR USE

*STATUTE:* **Limitations on Exclusive Rights: Fair Use**
17 U.S.C. §107

Section 107 provides that certain uses of copyrighted works are *not* infringements of the copyright owner's exclusive rights. Nonetheless, it is generally agreed that a claim that a use is "fair" is a defense to a charge of infringement, with the burdens of pleading and proving the claim falling on the alleged infringer. The doctrine of fair use was not part of the original copyright statute, either in its pre-American English form, or in the Copyright Act of 1790. Rather, early copyright law recognized a claim of "fair abridgement," by which a defendant could be found not to infringe by having demonstrated his own "invention, learning, and judgment" in the production of a modified work. *See Cary v. Kearsley*, 170 Eng. Rep. 679 (K.B. 1803). By the middle of the nineteenth century, however, American copyright jurisprudence shifted its focus from the benefits produced by the accused infringer to the injury inflicted upon the original author. In his seminal opinion in *Folsom v. Marsh*, 9 F. Cas. 342 (C.C.D. Mass. 1841) (No. 4901), Supreme Court Justice Joseph Story articulated a framework for analysis that largely survives in §107. Addressing a claim that a biographer of George Washington had improperly copied certain of Washington's copyrighted letters, Story wrote: "In short, we must often, in deciding questions of this sort, look to the nature and objects of the selections made, the quantity and value of the materials used, and the degree in which the use may prejudice the sale, or diminish the profits, or supersede the objects, of the original work." Fair use thus entered the law, where it remained uncodified until the 1976 Act brought the doctrine formally within the statute. Section 107 today consists largely of the same four factors that Justice Story articulated in *Folsom*.

Given the extremely long duration of copyrights and the imprecise line between protected expression and unprotected fact and idea, fair use occupies a central place in the day-to-day administration of copyright's balance between the incentives it offers authors and publishers, and rights to access and re-use copyrighted works that are preserved to readers, consumers, and users. The doctrine gives courts an important resource for dealing with social, economic, and technical change in the world of copyright.

## 1. Criticism, Parody, and Other "Exemplary" Uses

The heart of fair use, and the source of much criticism of the doctrine, lies in the relationship among the four factors suggested in §107 and the overall purposes of the doctrine. As the quotation above from *Folsom* suggests, part of the justification for fair use is the lack of injury to the copyright holder, and part of the justification is enabling certain purposes and uses of copyrighted material. The cases explore whether these justifications are in tension with one another, or are complementary, in any particular context.

### HARPER & ROW, PUBLISHERS, INC. v. NATION ENTERPRISES
#### 471 U.S. 539 (1985)

Justice O'CONNOR delivered the opinion of the Court.

\* \* \*

In February 1977, shortly after leaving the White House, former President Gerald R. Ford contracted with petitioners Harper & Row and Reader's Digest, to publish his as yet unwritten memoirs. The memoirs were to contain "significant hitherto unpublished material" concerning the Watergate crisis, Mr. Ford's pardon of former President Nixon and "Mr. Ford's reflections on this period of history, and the morality and personalities involved." In addition to the right to publish the Ford memoirs in book form, the agreement gave petitioners the exclusive right to license prepublication excerpts, known in the trade as "first serial rights." Two years later, as the memoirs were nearing completion, petitioners negotiated a prepublication licensing agreement with Time, a weekly news magazine. Time agreed to pay $25,000, $12,500 in advance and an additional $12,500 at publication, in exchange for the right to excerpt 7,500 words from Mr. Ford's account of the Nixon pardon. The issue featuring the excerpts was timed to appear approximately one week before shipment of the full length book version to bookstores. Exclusivity was an important consideration; Harper & Row instituted procedures designed to maintain the confidentiality of the manuscript, and Time retained the right to renegotiate the second payment should the material appear in print prior to its release of the excerpts.

Two to three weeks before the Time article's scheduled release, an unidentified person secretly brought a copy of the Ford manuscript to Victor Navasky, editor of The Nation, a political commentary magazine. Mr. Navasky knew that his possession of the manuscript was not authorized and that the manuscript must be returned quickly to his "source" to avoid discovery. He hastily put together what he believed was "a real hot news story" composed of quotes, paraphrases, and facts drawn exclusively from the manuscript. Mr. Navasky attempted no independent commentary, research or criticism, in part because of the need for speed if he was to "make news" by "publish[ing] in advance of publication of the Ford book." The 2,250-word article, reprinted in the Appendix to this opinion, appeared on April 3, 1979. As a result of The Nation's article, Time canceled its piece and refused to pay the remaining $12,500.

Petitioners brought suit in the District Court for the Southern District of New York, alleging conversion, tortious interference with contract, and violations of the Copyright Act. After a 6-day bench trial, the District Judge found that "A Time to Heal" was protected by copyright at the time of The Nation publication and that respondents' use of the copyrighted material constituted an infringement under the Copyright Act, §§106(1), (2), and (3), protecting respectively the right to reproduce the work, the right to license preparation of derivative works, and the right of first distribution of the copyrighted work to the public. The District Court rejected respondents' argument that The Nation's piece was a "fair use" sanctioned by §107 of the Act. Though billed as "hot news," the article contained no new facts. The magazine had "published its article for profit," taking "the heart" of "a soon-to-be-published" work. This unauthorized use "caused the *Time* agreement to be aborted and thus diminished the value of the copyright." 557 F. Supp., at 1072. Although certain elements of the Ford memoirs, such as historical facts and memoranda, were not *per se* copyrightable, the District Court held that it was "the totality of these facts and memoranda collected together with Ford's reflections that made them of value to The Nation, [and] this...totality...is protected by the copyright laws." *Id.*, at 1072-1073. The court awarded actual damages of $12,500.

A divided panel of the Court of Appeals for the Second Circuit reversed. The majority recognized that Mr. Ford's verbatim "reflections" were original "expression" protected by copyright. But it held that the District Court had erred in assuming the "coupling [of these reflections] with uncopyrightable fact transformed that information into a copyrighted 'totality.'" 723 F.2d 195, 205 (2d Cir. 1983). The majority noted that copyright attaches to expression, not facts or ideas. It concluded that, to avoid granting a copyright monopoly over the facts underlying history and news, "'expression' [in such works must be confined] to its barest elements —the ordering and choice of the words themselves." *Id.*, at 204. Thus similarities between the original and the challenged work traceable to the copying or paraphrasing of uncopyrightable material, such as historical facts, memoranda and other public documents, and quoted remarks of third parties, must be disregarded in evaluating whether the second author's use was fair or infringing.... Examining the four factors enumerated in §107, the majority found the purpose of the article was "news reporting," the original work was essentially factual in nature, the 300 words appropriated were insubstantial in relation to the 2,250-word piece, and the impact on the market for the original was minimal as "the evidence [did] not support a finding that it was the very limited use of expression *per se* which led to Time's decision not to print the excerpt." The Nation's borrowing of verbatim quotations merely "len[t] authenticity to this politically significant material...complementing the reporting of the facts." 723 F.2d, at 208. The Court of Appeals was especially influenced by the "politically significant" nature of the subject matter and its conviction that it is not "the purpose of the Copyright Act to impede that harvest of knowledge so necessary to a democratic state" or "chill the activities of the press by forbidding a circumscribed use of copyrighted words." *Id.*, at 197, 209.

## II

We agree with the Court of Appeals that copyright is intended to increase and not to impede the harvest of knowledge. But we believe the Second Circuit gave insufficient deference to the scheme established by the Copyright Act for fostering the original works that provide the seed and substance of this harvest. The rights conferred by copyright are designed to assure contributors to the store of knowledge a fair return for their labors.

...As we noted last Term: "[This] limited grant [contained in Article I, §8 of the Constitution] is a means by which an important public purpose may be achieved. It is intended to motivate the creative activity of authors and inventors by the provision of a special reward, and to allow the public access to the products of their genius after the limited period of exclusive control has expired." *Sony Corp. of America v. Universal City Studios, Inc.*, 464 U.S. 417, 429 (1984). "The monopoly created by copyright thus rewards the individual author in order to benefit the public." *Id.*, at 477 (dissenting opinion). This principle applies equally to works of fiction and nonfiction. The book at issue here, for example, was two years in the making, and began with a contract giving the author's copyright to the publishers in exchange for their services in producing and marketing the work. In preparing the book, Mr. Ford drafted essays and word portraits of public figures and participated in hundreds of taped interviews that were later distilled to chronicle his personal viewpoint. It is evident that the monopoly granted by copyright actively served its intended purpose of inducing the creation of new material of potential historical value.

Section 106 of the Copyright Act confers a bundle of exclusive rights to the owner of the copyright. Under the Copyright Act, these rights—to publish, copy, and distribute the author's work—vest in the author of an original work from the time of its creation. In practice, the author commonly sells his rights to publishers who offer royalties in exchange for their services in producing and marketing the author's work. The copyright owner's rights, however, are subject to certain statutory exceptions. Among these is §107 which codifies the traditional privilege of other authors to make "fair use" of an earlier writer's work. In addition, no author may copyright facts or ideas. The copyright is limited to those aspects of the work—termed "expression"—that display the stamp of the author's originality.

Creation of a nonfiction work, even a compilation of pure fact, entails originality. The copyright holders of "A Time to Heal" complied with the relevant statutory notice and registration procedures. Thus there is no dispute that the unpublished manuscript of "A Time to Heal," as a whole, was protected by §106 from unauthorized reproduction. Nor do respondents dispute that verbatim copying of excerpts of the manuscript's original form of expression would constitute infringement unless excused as fair use. Yet copyright does not prevent subsequent users from copying from a prior author's work those constituent elements that are not original—for example, quotations borrowed under the rubric of fair use from other copyrighted works, facts, or materials in the public domain—as long as such use does not unfairly appropriate the author's original contributions. Perhaps the controversy between the lower courts in this case over copyrightability is more aptly styled a dispute over whether The Nation's appropriation of unoriginal and uncopyrightable elements encroached on the originality embodied in the work as a whole. Especially in the realm of factual narrative, the law is currently unsettled regarding the ways in which uncopyrightable elements combine with the author's original contributions to form protected expression.

We need not reach these issues, however, as The Nation has admitted to lifting verbatim quotes of the author's original language totaling between 300 and 400 words and constituting some 13% of The Nation article. In using generous verbatim excerpts of Mr. Ford's unpublished manuscript to lend authenticity to its account of the forthcoming memoirs, The Nation effectively arrogated to itself the right of first publication, an important marketable subsidiary right. For the reasons set forth below, we find that this use of the copyrighted manuscript, even stripped to the verbatim quotes conceded by The Nation to be copyrightable expression, was not a fair use within the meaning of the Copyright Act.

### III

\* \* \*

Perhaps because the fair use doctrine was predicated on the author's implied consent to "reasonable and customary" use when he released his work for public consumption, fair use traditionally was not recognized as a defense to charges of copying from an author's as yet unpublished works. Under common-law copyright, "the property of the author . . . in his intellectual creation [was] absolute until he voluntarily part[ed] with the same." *American Tobacco Co. v. Werckmeister,* 207 U.S. 284, 299 (1907). This absolute rule, however, was tempered in practice by the equitable nature of the fair use doctrine. In a given case, factors such as implied consent through *de facto* publication on performance or dissemination of a work may tip the balance of equities in favor of prepublication use. See Copyright Law Revision—Part 2: Discussion and Comments on Report of the Register of Copyrights on General Revision of the U.S. Copyright Law, 88th Cong., 1st Sess., 27 (H.R. Comm. Print 1963) (discussion suggesting works disseminated to the public in a form not constituting a technical "publication" should nevertheless be subject to fair use). But it has never been seriously disputed that "the fact that the plaintiff's work is unpublished . . . is a factor tending to negate the defense of fair use." *Ibid.* Publication of an author's expression before he has authorized its dissemination seriously infringes the author's right to decide when and whether it will be made public, a factor not present in fair use of published works. Respondents contend, however, that Congress, in including first publication among the rights enumerated in §106, which are expressly subject to fair use under §107, intended that fair use would apply *in pari materia* to published and unpublished works. The Copyright Act does not support this proposition.

The Copyright Act represents the culmination of a major legislative reexamination of copyright doctrine. Among its other innovations, it eliminated publication "as a dividing line between common law and statutory protection," House Report, at 129 U.S. Code Cong. & Admin. News 1976, p. 5745, extending statutory protection to all works from the time of their creation. It also recognized for the first time a distinct statutory right of first publication, which had previously been an element of the common-law protections afforded unpublished works. The Report of the House Committee on the Judiciary confirms that "Clause (3) of section 106, establishes the exclusive right of publications.... Under this provision the copyright owner would have the right to control the first public distribution of an authorized copy...of his work." *Id.,* at 62 U.S. Code Cong. & Admin. News 1976, p. 5675.

Though the right of first publication, like the other rights enumerated in §106, is expressly made subject to the fair use provision of §107, fair use analysis must always be tailored to the individual case. *Id.,* at 65. The nature of the interest at stake is highly relevant to whether a given use is fair. From the beginning, those entrusted with the task of revision recognized the "overbalancing reasons to preserve the common law protection of undisseminated works until the author or his successor chooses to disclose them." Copyright Law Revision, Report of the Register of Copyrights on the General Revision of the U.S. Copyright Law, 87th Cong., 1st Sess., 41 (Comm. Print 1961). The right of first publication implicates a threshold decision by the author whether and in what form to release his work. First publication is inherently different from other §106 rights in that only one person can be the first publisher; as the contract with Time illustrates, the commercial value of the right lies primarily in exclusivity. Because the potential damage to the author from judicially enforced "sharing" of the first publication right with unauthorized users of his manuscript is substantial, the balance of equities in evaluating such a claim of fair use inevitably shifts.

\* \* \*

...We conclude that the unpublished nature of a work is "[a] key, though not necessarily determinative, factor" tending to negate a defense of fair use. Senate Report, at 64.

\* \* \*

## IV

Fair use is a mixed question of law and fact. Where the district court has found facts sufficient to evaluate each of the statutory factors, an appellate court "need not remand for further factfinding...[but] may conclude as a matter of law that [the challenged use] do[es] not qualify as a fair use of the copyrighted work." [*Pacific & Southern Co. v. Duncan,* 744 F.2d 1490, 1495 (11th 1984).] Thus whether The Nation article constitutes fair use under §107 must be reviewed in light of the principles discussed above. The factors enumerated in the section are not meant to be exclusive: "[S]ince the doctrine is an equitable rule of reason, no generally applicable definition is possible, and each case raising the question must be decided on its own facts." House Report, at 65, U.S. Code Cong. & Admin. News 1976, p. 5678. The four factors identified by Congress as especially relevant in determining whether the use was fair are: (1) the purpose and character of the use; (2) the nature of the copyrighted work; (3) the substantiality of the portion used in relation to the copyrighted work as a whole; (4) the effect on the potential market for or value of the copyrighted work. We address each one separately.

*Purpose of the Use.* The Second Circuit correctly identified news reporting as the general purpose of The Nation's use. News reporting is one of the examples enumerated in §107 to "give some idea of the sort of activities the courts might regard as fair use under the circumstances." Senate Report, at 61. This listing was not intended to be exhaustive, see *ibid.*; §101 (definition of "including" and "such as"), or to single out any particular use as presumptively a "fair" use. The drafters resisted pressures from special interest groups to create presumptive categories of fair use, but structured the provision as an affirmative defense requiring a case-by-case analysis. "[W]hether a use referred to in the first sentence of section 107 is a fair use in a particular case will depend upon the application of the determinative factors, including those mentioned in the second sentence." Senate Report, at 62. The fact that an article arguably is "news" and therefore a productive use is simply one factor in a fair use analysis.

We agree with the Second Circuit that the trial court erred in fixing on whether the information contained in the memoirs was actually new to the public. As Judge Meskill wisely noted, "[c]ourts should be chary of deciding what is and what is not news." 723 F.2d, at 215 (dissenting). . . . The Nation has every right to seek to be the first to publish information. But The Nation went beyond simply reporting uncopyrightable information and actively sought to exploit the headline value of its infringement, making a "news event" out of its unauthorized first publication of a noted figure's copyrighted expression.

The fact that a publication was commercial as opposed to nonprofit is a separate factor that tends to weigh against a finding of fair use. "[E]very commercial use of copyrighted material is presumptively an unfair exploitation of the monopoly privilege that belongs to the owner of the copyright." *Sony Corp. of America v. Universal City Studios, Inc.*, 464 U.S., at 451. In arguing that the purpose of news reporting is not purely commercial, The Nation misses the point entirely. The crux of the profit/nonprofit distinction is not whether the sole motive of the use is monetary gain but whether the user stands to profit from exploitation of the copyrighted material without paying the customary price.

In evaluating character and purpose we cannot ignore The Nation's stated purpose of scooping the forthcoming hardcover and Time abstracts. The Nation's use had not merely the incidental effect but the *intended purpose* of supplanting the copyright holder's commercially valuable right of first publication. Also relevant to the "character" of the use is "the propriety of the defendant's conduct." 3 Nimmer §13.05[A], at 13-72. "Fair use presupposes 'good faith' and 'fair dealing.'" *Time Inc. v. Bernard Geis Associates*, 293 F. Supp. 130, 146 (S.D.N.Y. 1968), quoting Schulman,

Fair Use and the Revision of the Copyright Act, 53 Iowa L. Rev. 832 (1968). The trial court found that The Nation knowingly exploited a purloined manuscript. Unlike the typical claim of fair use, The Nation cannot offer up even the fiction of consent as justification. Like its competitor news-weekly, it was free to bid for the right of abstracting excerpts from "A Time to Heal." Fair use "distinguishes between 'a true scholar and a chiseler who infringes a work for personal profit.'" [*Wainwright Securities Inc. v. Wall Street Transcript Corp.*, 558 F.2d 91, 94 (2d Cir. 1977)], quoting from Hearings on Bills for the General Revision of the Copyright Law before the House Committee on the Judiciary, 89th Cong., 1st Sess., ser. 8, pt. 3, p. 1706 (1966) (statement of John Schulman).

*Nature of the Copyrighted Work.* Second, the Act directs attention to the nature of the copyrighted work. "A Time to Heal" may be characterized as an unpublished historical narrative or autobiography. The law generally recognizes a greater need to disseminate factual works than works of fiction or fantasy.... Some of the briefer quotes from the memoirs are arguably necessary adequately to convey the facts; for example, Mr. Ford's charac-terization of the White House tapes as the "smoking gun" is perhaps so integral to the idea expressed as to be inseparable from it. But The Nation did not stop at isolated phrases and instead excerpted subjective descrip-tions and portraits of public figures whose power lies in the author's indi-vidualized expression. Such use, focusing on the most expressive elements of the work, exceeds that necessary to disseminate the facts.

The fact that a work is unpublished is a critical element of its "nature." Our prior discussion establishes that the scope of fair use is narrower with respect to unpublished works. While even substantial quotations might qualify as fair use in a review of a published work or a news account of a speech that had been delivered to the public or disseminated to the press, the author's right to control the first public appearance of his expression weighs against such use of the work before its release. The right of first publication encompasses not only the choice whether to publish at all, but also the choices of when, where, and in what form first to publish a work.

In the case of Mr. Ford's manuscript, the copyright holders' interest in confidentiality is irrefutable; the copyright holders had entered into a con-tractual undertaking to "keep the manuscript confidential" and required that all those to whom the manuscript was shown also "sign an agreement to keep the manuscript confidential." While the copyright holders' con-tract with Time required Time to submit its proposed article seven days before publication, The Nation's clandestine publication afforded no such opportunity for creative or quality control. It was hastily patched together and contained "a number of inaccuracies." A use that so clearly infringes the copyright holder's interests in confidentiality and creative control is difficult to characterize as "fair."

*Amount and Substantiality of the Portion Used.* Next, the Act directs us to examine the amount and substantiality of the portion used in relation to the copyrighted work as a whole. In absolute terms, the words actually quoted were an insubstantial portion of "A Time to Heal." The District Court, however, found that "[T]he Nation took what was essentially the heart of the book." 557 F. Supp., at 1072. We believe the Court of Appeals erred in overruling the District Judge's evaluation of the qualitative nature of the taking. A Time editor described the chapters on the pardon as "the most interesting and moving parts of the entire manuscript." The portions actually quoted were selected by Mr. Navasky as among the most powerful passages in those chapters. He testified that he used verbatim excerpts because simply reciting the information could not adequately convey the "absolute certainty with which [Ford] expressed himself," or show that "this comes from President Ford," or carry the "definitive quality" of the original. In short, he quoted these passages precisely because they qualitatively embodied Ford's distinctive expression.

As the statutory language indicates, a taking may not be excused merely because it is insubstantial with respect to the *infringing* work. As Judge Learned Hand cogently remarked, "no plagiarist can excuse the wrong by showing how much of his work he did not pirate." *Sheldon v. Metro-Goldwyn Pictures Corp.*, 81 F.2d 49, 56 (2d Cir. 1936). Conversely, the fact that a substantial portion of the infringing work was copied verbatim is evidence of the qualitative value of the copied material, both to the originator and to the plagiarist who seeks to profit from marketing someone else's copyrighted expression.

Stripped to the verbatim quotes, the direct takings from the unpublished manuscript constitute at least 13% of the infringing article. The Nation article is structured around the quoted excerpts which serve as its dramatic focal points. In view of the expressive value of the excerpts and their key role in the infringing work, we cannot agree with the Second Circuit that the "magazine took a meager, indeed an infinitesimal amount of Ford's original language." 723 F.2d, at 209.

*Effect on the Market.* Finally, the Act focuses on "the effect of the use upon the potential market for or value of the copyrighted work." This last factor is undoubtedly the single most important element of fair use. "Fair use, when properly applied, is limited to copying by others which does not materially impair the marketability of the work which is copied." 1 Nimmer §1.10[D], at 1-87. The trial court found not merely a potential but an actual effect on the market. Time's cancellation of its projected serialization and its refusal to pay the $12,500 were the direct effect of the infringement. The Court of Appeals rejected this factfinding as clearly erroneous, noting that the record did not establish a causal relation between Time's nonperformance and respondents' unauthorized publication of Mr. Ford's *expression* as opposed to the facts taken from the memoirs. We disagree. Rarely will a case of copyright infringement present such clear-cut evidence of actual damage. Petitioners assured Time that there would be no other authorized publication of *any* portion of the unpublished manuscript prior to April 23, 1979. *Any* publication of material from chapters 1 and 3 would permit Time to renegotiate its final payment. Time cited The Nation's article, which contained verbatim quotes from the unpublished manuscript, as a reason for its nonperformance. . . . [O]nce a copyright holder establishes with reasonable probability the existence of a causal connection between the infringement and a loss of revenue, the burden properly shifts to the infringer to show that this damage would have occurred had there been no taking of copyrighted expression. Petitioners established a prima facie case of actual damage that respondents failed to rebut. . . .

More important, to negate fair use one need only show that if the challenged use "should become widespread, it would adversely affect the *potential* market for the copyrighted work." *Sony Corp. of America v. Universal City Studios, Inc.,* 464 U.S., at 451 (emphasis added). This inquiry must take account not only of harm to the original but also of harm to the market for derivative works. "If the defendant's work adversely affects the value of any of the rights in the copyrighted work (in this case the adaptation [and serialization] right) the use is not fair." 3 Nimmer §13.05[B], at 13-77–13-78 (footnote omitted).

It is undisputed that the factual material in the balance of The Nation's article, besides the verbatim quotes at issue here, was drawn exclusively from the chapters on the pardon. The excerpts were employed as featured episodes in a story about the Nixon pardon—precisely the use petitioners had licensed to Time. The borrowing of these verbatim quotes from the unpublished manuscript lent The Nation's piece a special air of authenticity—as Navasky expressed it, the reader would know it was Ford speaking and not The Nation. Thus it directly competed for a share of the market for prepublication excerpts. . . .

Placed in a broader perspective, a fair use doctrine that permits extensive prepublication quotations from an unreleased manuscript without the copyright owner's consent poses substantial potential for damage to the marketability of first serialization rights in general. "Isolated instances of minor infringements, when multiplied many times, become in the aggregate a major inroad on copyright that must be prevented." [Senate Report, at 65.]

## V

The Court of Appeals erred in concluding that The Nation's use of the copyrighted material was excused by the public's interest in the subject matter. It erred, as well, in overlooking the unpublished nature of the work and the resulting impact on the potential market for first serial rights of permitting unauthorized prepublication excerpts under the rubric of fair use. Finally, in finding the taking "infinitesimal," the Court of Appeals accorded too little weight to the qualitative importance of the quoted passages of original expression. In sum, the traditional doctrine of fair use, as embodied in the Copyright Act, does not sanction the use made by The Nation of these copyrighted materials. Any copyright infringer may claim to benefit the public by increasing public access to the copyrighted work. But Congress has not designed, and we see no warrant for judicially imposing, a "compulsory license" permitting unfettered access to the unpublished copyrighted expression of public figures.

The Nation conceded that its verbatim copying of some 300 words of direct quotation from the Ford manuscript would constitute an infringement unless excused as a fair use. Because we find that The Nation's use of these verbatim excerpts from the unpublished manuscript was not a fair use, the judgment of the Court of Appeals is reversed, and the case is remanded for further proceedings consistent with this opinion.

*It is so ordered.*

[Dissenting opinion of Justice BRENNAN, joined by WHITE, J., and MARSHALL, J., omitted.]

## Comments

1. **The Supreme Court and Fair Use.** *Harper & Row* was not the first Supreme Court opinion to address fair use. That distinction belongs to *Sony Corp. of America v. Universal City Studios*, 464 U.S. 417 (1984), decided a year earlier and cited by the Court. (*Sony* appears below, in part 2.) *Sony*, however, involved a relatively novel issue: unauthorized reproduction of copyrighted works by consumers. *Harper & Row* asked the Supreme Court for the first time to analyze a traditional fair use problem involving unauthorized use by a competitor (the plaintiff's characterization) or by a "creative" successor (the defendant's characterization).

2. **Applying the Four Statutory Factors.** The heart of traditional fair use analysis is application of each of the four non-exclusive factors listed in the statute. Unfortunately, nothing in the text or the history of the statute suggests precisely how any of the factors should be handled, nor how to sum up or balance the results of analyzing each factor separately. That leaves a great deal of room for courts to adapt the factors to the circumstances of the case (in fact, note that in *Harper & Row*, the district court found for the plaintiff and the Court of Appeals found for the defendant). Given the oft-repeated statement that fair use is "a mixed question of law and fact," appellate courts are not reluctant to engage in factual analysis, without deference to trial courts. Be sure you understand how Justice O'Connor's majority opinion handles each of the four fair use factors.

3. **Nonstatutory Factors.** By noting that fair use considerations shall "include" certain factors, §107 anticipates that its factors are not exclusive of other considerations, including, among other things, the types of uses that the statute lists in its first sentence ("criticism, comment, news reporting, teaching (including multiple copies for classroom use), scholarship, or research,"). What other factors might be relevant to determining whether a given use is "fair"? The legislative history of §107 notes that the doctrine is designed as an "equitable rule of reason," which might be interpreted as license for applying it as an all-purpose "fairness" doctrine, or merely that fair use is designed to be flexible and contextual. Consider the majority opinion again. It appears to be colored by the perception that *The Nation* acted in bad faith, acquiring its copy of *A Time to Heal* by illicit, if not illegal, means. If the Copyright Act is guided primarily by policy considerations that focus on incentives to produce and distribute creative works, including new creative works based on preexisting works, "good faith" and "bad faith" may be less important than an assessment of the effects of the arguably fair use on social welfare. For example of an analysis of fair use that consciously avoids a "bad faith" inquiry on these grounds, see *Ty, Inc. v. Publications Intern. Ltd.*, 292 F.3d 512 (7th Cir. 2002) (Posner, J.), which is discussed in the Comments following *Campbell v. Acuff-Rose Music, Inc.*, below.

4. *The Right of First Publication.* The majority is persuaded by the notion that *The Nation* appropriated the copyright owner's "right of first publication." In other words, had *A Time to Heal* been published at the time of *The Nation*'s article, the majority implies that the use might have been found noninfringing. Where does the first publication right appear in §106? Before the 1976 Act took effect, the author of an unpublished work retained a nonstatutory exclusive right to publish the work. Recall that one of the purposes of the Copyright Act of 1976 was to bring unpublished works in fixed form within the scope of statutory copyright, presumably bringing them also within reach of the fair use doctrine. To what extent should the distinction in prior law between published and unpublished works persist under the 1976 Act? Application of fair use to unpublished works has been of particular concern to historians and biographers, who frequently make use of unpublished letters in their work. *See Salinger v. Random House, Inc.,* 811 F.2d 90, 96-97 (2d Cir. 1987) (rejecting fair use claim by biographer of J.D. Salinger). Congress amended §107 in 1992 to add the following sentence: "The fact that a work is unpublished shall not itself bar a finding of fair use if such finding is made upon consideration of all the above factors." Some courts, however, continue to count the fact that a copyrighted work is unpublished as a factor weighing against fair use.

5. *Presumptions and Commercial Use.* The *Harper & Row* Court's discussion of the first fair use factor, and particularly the following excerpt, has been influential:

> The fact that a publication was commercial as opposed to nonprofit is a separate factor that tends to weigh against a finding of fair use. "[E]very commercial use of copyrighted material is presumptively an unfair exploitation of the monopoly privilege that belongs to the owner of the copyright." *Sony Corp. of America v. Universal City Studios, Inc.,* 464 U.S., at 451. In arguing that the purpose of news reporting is not purely commercial, The Nation misses the point entirely. The crux of the profit/nonprofit distinction is not whether the sole motive of the use is monetary gain but whether the user stands to profit from exploitation of the copyrighted material without paying the customary price.

Bear in mind the fact that journalists, critics, and historians — three paradigmatic "fair users" of copyrighted works — regularly sell their own work for profit. What does it mean, then, for unauthorized "commercial" use of a copyrighted work to be "presumptively" unfair? Perhaps this statement must be read in conjunction with the notion of "the customary price." Journalistic use of a copyrighted work may be noninfringing against a background norm that accepts that newspapers are profit-making enterprises. Legal arguments based on "custom," however, are tricky. Identifying a relevant custom, and proving that it exists in the context of a legal dispute, requires borrowing materials from social science and relying on expert testimony.

6. *The Effect on the Market.* The meaning of "effect on the market" in §107 is unclear. At minimum, §107 contemplates that a use is not fair if the accused infringer directly competes with the copyright owner for sales of copies of the work. In *Harper & Row,* the Court locates harm to

the plaintiff's market in Time, Inc.'s refusal to pay in full for serialization rights to *A Time to Heal*. Market injury, for purposes of the fourth fair use factor, thus may consist of injury to the market for a derivative version of the work, rather than to the market for copies of the original work. Identifying relevant markets is a particularly difficult question in fair use cases, because the statute anticipates that certain markets for the work, under certain conditions, may be "effected" by the defendant's use without triggering a finding of infringement. The statute does not provide any explicit guidance for drawing a distinction between market injury that weighs against fair use, and market injury that does not.

7. ***Qualitative versus Quantitative Comparisons.*** *A Time to Heal* includes more than 400 pages of text. *The Nation* published excerpts that included 300 of its words, in total, which the majority opinion characterizes as the "heart" of the work. Note not only how unauthorized reproduction may be qualitatively as well as quantitatively significant, but note further the implications of this statement for purposes of ordinary "substantial similarity" analysis. Stripped of the fair use debate, *Harper & Row* boils down to the claim that *The Nation* engaged in copyright infringement by publishing 300 words out of a 400-plus-page manuscript.

8. ***Fair Use and the First Amendment.*** The Court rejects the proposition that the public interest and/or the First Amendment qualify as independent grounds for deeming a use of a copyrighted work to be noninfringing. Both arguments are subsumed by the fair use inquiry and by the idea/expression distinction. The Court's reluctance to consider First Amendment arguments in the context of copyright disputes reappears in *Eldred v. Ashcroft*, 537 U.S. 186 (2003), which rejected a challenge to Congress's extension of the term of copyright in the Sonny Bono Copyright Term Extension Act of 1998.

## CAMPBELL v. ACUFF-ROSE MUSIC, INC.
### 510 U.S. 569 (1994)

Justice SOUTER delivered the opinion of the Court.

We are called upon to decide whether 2 Live Crew's commercial parody of Roy Orbison's song, "Oh, Pretty Woman," may be a fair use within the meaning of the Copyright Act of 1976, 17 U.S.C. §107 (1988 ed. and Supp. IV). Although the District Court granted summary judgment for 2 Live Crew, the Court of Appeals reversed, holding the defense of fair use barred by the song's commercial character and excessive borrowing. Because we hold that a parody's commercial character is only one element to be weighed in a fair use enquiry, and that insufficient consideration was given to the nature of parody in weighing the degree of copying, we reverse and remand.

### I

In 1964, Roy Orbison and William Dees wrote a rock ballad called "Oh, Pretty Woman" and assigned their rights in it to respondent Acuff-Rose Music, Inc. Acuff-Rose registered the song for copyright protection.

Petitioners Luther R. Campbell, Christopher Wongwon, Mark Ross, and David Hobbs are collectively known as 2 Live Crew, a popular rap music group. In 1989, Campbell wrote a song entitled "Pretty Woman," which he later described in an affidavit as intended, "through comical lyrics, to satirize the original work...." On July 5, 1989, 2 Live Crew's manager informed Acuff-Rose that 2 Live Crew had written a parody of "Oh, Pretty Woman," that they would afford all credit for ownership and authorship of the original song to Acuff-Rose, Dees, and Orbison, and that they were willing to pay a fee for the use they wished to make of it. Enclosed with the letter were a copy of the lyrics and a recording of 2 Live Crew's song. Acuff-Rose's agent refused permission, stating that "I am aware of the success enjoyed by 'The 2 Live Crews', but I must inform you that we cannot permit the use of a parody of 'Oh, Pretty Woman.'" Nonetheless, in June or July 1989, 2 Live Crew released records, cassette tapes, and compact discs of "Pretty Woman" in a collection of songs entitled "As Clean As They Wanna Be." The albums and compact discs identify the authors of "Pretty Woman" as Orbison and Dees and its publisher as Acuff-Rose.

Almost a year later, after nearly a quarter of a million copies of the recording had been sold, Acuff-Rose sued 2 Live Crew and its record company, Luke Skyywalker Records, for copyright infringement. The District Court granted summary judgment for 2 Live Crew, reasoning that the commercial purpose of 2 Live Crew's song was no bar to fair use; that 2 Live Crew's version was a parody, which "quickly degenerates into a play on words, substituting predictable lyrics with shocking ones" to show "how bland and banal the Orbison song" is; that 2 Live Crew had taken no more than was necessary to "conjure up" the original in order to parody it; and that it was "extremely unlikely that 2 Live Crew's song could adversely affect the market for the original." 754 F. Supp. 1150, 1154-1155, 1157-1158 (M.D. Tenn. 1991). The District Court weighed these factors and held that 2 Live Crew's song made fair use of Orbison's original.

The Court of Appeals for the Sixth Circuit reversed and remanded. Although it assumed for the purpose of its opinion that 2 Live Crew's song was a parody of the Orbison original, the Court of Appeals thought the District Court had put too little emphasis on the fact that "every commercial use...is presumptively...unfair," *Sony Corp. of America v. Universal City Studios, Inc.*, 464 U.S. 417, 451 (1984), and it held that "the admittedly commercial nature" of the parody "requires the conclusion" that the first of four factors relevant under the statute weighs against a finding of fair use. 972 F.2d, at 1435, 1437. Next, the Court of Appeals determined that, by "taking the heart of the original and making it the heart of a new work," 2 Live Crew had, qualitatively, taken too much. *Id.*, at 1438. Finally, after noting that the effect on the potential market for the original (and the market for derivative works) is "undoubtedly the single most important element of fair use," *Harper & Row, Publishers, Inc. v. Nation Enterprises*, 471 U.S. 539, 566 (1985), the Court of Appeals faulted the District Court for "refus[ing] to indulge the presumption" that "harm for purposes of the fair use analysis has been established by the presumption attaching to commercial uses." 972 F.2d, at 1438-1439. In sum, the court concluded that its "blatantly commercial purpose...prevents this parody from being a fair use." *Id.*, at 1439.

We granted certiorari to determine whether 2 Live Crew's commercial parody could be a fair use.

## II

\* \* \*

### A

The first factor in a fair use enquiry is "the purpose and character of the use, including whether such use is of a commercial nature or is for non-profit educational purposes." §107(1). This factor draws on Justice Story's formulation, "the nature and objects of the selections made." [*Folsom v. Marsh,* 9 F. Cas. 342, 348 (No. 4,901) (C.C.D. Mass. 1841).] The enquiry here may be guided by the examples given in the preamble to §107, looking to whether the use is for criticism, or comment, or news reporting, and the like, see §107. The central purpose of this investigation is to see, in Justice Story's words, whether the new work merely "supersede[s] the objects" of the original creation, *Folsom v. Marsh, supra,* at 348; or instead adds something new, with a further purpose or different character, altering the first with new expression, meaning, or message; it asks, in other words, whether and to what extent the new work is "transformative." [Leval, Toward a Fair Use Standard, 103 Harv. L. Rev. 1105, 1111 (1990) (hereinafter Leval).] Although such transformative use is not absolutely necessary for a finding of fair use, the goal of copyright, to promote science and the arts, is generally furthered by the creation of transformative works. Such works thus lie at the heart of the fair use doctrine's guarantee of breathing space within the confines of copyright, and the more transformative the new work, the less will be the significance of other factors, like commercialism, that may weigh against a finding of fair use.

...Suffice it to say now that parody has an obvious claim to transformative value, as Acuff-Rose itself does not deny. Like less ostensibly humorous forms of criticism, it can provide social benefit, by shedding light on an earlier work, and, in the process, creating a new one. We thus line up with the courts that have held that parody, like other comment or criticism, may claim fair use under §107. See, *e.g., Fisher v. Dees,* 794 F.2d 432 (9th Cir. 1986) ("When Sonny Sniffs Glue," a parody of "When Sunny Gets Blue," is fair use); *Elsmere Music, Inc. v. National Broadcasting Co.,* 482 F. Supp. 741 (S.D.N.Y.), aff'd, 623 F.2d 252 (2d Cir. 1980) ("I Love Sodom," a "Saturday Night Live" television parody of "I Love New York," is fair use).

The germ of parody lies in the definition of the Greek *parodeia,* quoted in Judge Nelson's Court of Appeals dissent, as "a song sung alongside another." 972 F.2d, at 1440, quoting 7 Encyclopedia Britannica 768 (15th ed. 1975). Modern dictionaries accordingly describe a parody as a "literary or artistic work that imitates the characteristic style of an author or a work for comic effect or ridicule,"[12] or as a "composition in prose or verse in which the characteristic turns of thought and phrase in an author or class of authors are imitated in such a way as to make them appear ridiculous."[13] For the purposes of copyright law, the nub of the definitions,

---

12. American Heritage Dictionary 1317 (3d ed. 1992).
13. 11 Oxford English Dictionary 247 (2d ed. 1989).

and the heart of any parodist's claim to quote from existing material, is the use of some elements of a prior author's composition to create a new one that, at least in part, comments on that author's works. If, on the contrary, the commentary has no critical bearing on the substance or style of the original composition, which the alleged infringer merely uses to get attention or to avoid the drudgery in working up something fresh, the claim to fairness in borrowing from another's work diminishes accordingly (if it does not vanish), and other factors, like the extent of its commerciality, loom larger.[14] Parody needs to mimic an original to make its point, and so has some claim to use the creation of its victim's (or collective victims') imagination, whereas satire can stand on its own two feet and so requires justification for the very act of borrowing.[15]

The fact that parody can claim legitimacy for some appropriation does not, of course, tell either parodist or judge much about where to draw the line. Like a book review quoting the copyrighted material criticized, parody may or may not be fair use, and petitioners' suggestion that any parodic use is presumptively fair has no more justification in law or fact than the equally hopeful claim that any use for news reporting should be presumed fair. The Act has no hint of an evidentiary preference for parodists over their victims, and no workable presumption for parody could take account of the fact that parody often shades into satire when society is lampooned through its creative artifacts, or that a work may contain both parodic and nonparodic elements. Accordingly, parody, like any other use, has to work its way through the relevant factors, and be judged case by case, in light of the ends of the copyright law.

Here, the District Court held, and the Court of Appeals assumed, that 2 Live Crew's "Pretty Woman" contains parody, commenting on and criticizing the original work, whatever it may have to say about society at large. As the District Court remarked, the words of 2 Live Crew's song copy the original's first line, but then "quickly degenerat[e] into a play on words, substituting predictable lyrics with shocking ones...[that] derisively demonstrat[e] how bland and banal the Orbison song seems to them." 754 F. Supp., at 1155 (footnote omitted). Judge Nelson, dissenting below, came to the same conclusion, that the 2 Live Crew song "was clearly intended to ridicule the white-bread original" and "reminds us that sexual congress with nameless streetwalkers is not necessarily the stuff of romance and is not necessarily without its consequences. The singers (there are several) have the same thing on their minds as did the lonely man with

14. A parody that more loosely targets an original than the parody presented here may still be sufficiently aimed at an original work to come within our analysis of parody. If a parody whose wide dissemination in the market runs the risk of serving as a substitute for the original or licensed derivatives, it is more incumbent on one claiming fair use to establish the extent of transformation and the parody's critical relationship to the original. By contrast, when there is little or no risk of market substitution, whether because of the large extent of transformation of the earlier work, the new work's minimal distribution in the market, the small extent to which it borrows from an original, or other factors, taking parodic aim at an original is a less critical factor in the analysis, and looser forms of parody may be found to be fair use, as may satire with lesser justification for the borrowing than would otherwise be required.

15. Satire has been defined as a work "in which prevalent follies or vices are assailed with ridicule," 14 Oxford English Dictionary, *supra*, at 500, or are "attacked through irony, derision, or wit," American Heritage Dictionary, *supra*, at 1604.

the nasal voice, but here there is no hint of wine and roses." 972 F.2d, at 1442. Although the majority below had difficulty discerning any criticism of the original in 2 Live Crew's song, it assumed for purposes of its opinion that there was some.

We have less difficulty in finding that critical element in 2 Live Crew's song than the Court of Appeals did, although having found it we will not take the further step of evaluating its quality. The threshold question when fair use is raised in defense of parody is whether a parodic character may reasonably be perceived.[16] Whether, going beyond that, parody is in good taste or bad does not and should not matter to fair use. As Justice Holmes explained, "[i]t would be a dangerous undertaking for persons trained only to the law to constitute themselves final judges of the worth of [a work], outside of the narrowest and most obvious limits. At the one extreme some works of genius would be sure to miss appreciation. Their very novelty would make them repulsive until the public had learned the new language in which their author spoke." *Bleistein v. Donaldson Lithographing Co.*, 188 U.S. 239, 251 (1903).

While we might not assign a high rank to the parodic element here, we think it fair to say that 2 Live Crew's song reasonably could be perceived as commenting on the original or criticizing it, to some degree. 2 Live Crew juxtaposes the romantic musings of a man whose fantasy comes true, with degrading taunts, a bawdy demand for sex, and a sigh of relief from paternal responsibility. The later words can be taken as a comment on the naiveté of the original of an earlier day, as a rejection of its sentiment that ignores the ugliness of street life and the debasement that it signifies. It is this joinder of reference and ridicule that marks off the author's choice of parody from the other types of comment and criticism that traditionally have had a claim to fair use protection as transformative works.

The Court of Appeals, however, immediately cut short the enquiry into 2 Live Crew's fair use claim by confining its treatment of the first factor essentially to one relevant fact, the commercial nature of the use. The court then inflated the significance of this fact by applying a presumption ostensibly culled from *Sony*, that "every commercial use of copyrighted material is presumptively...unfair...." *Sony*, 464 U.S., at 451. In giving virtually dispositive weight to the commercial nature of the parody, the Court of Appeals erred.

The language of the statute makes clear that the commercial or nonprofit educational purpose of a work is only one element of the first factor enquiry into its purpose and character. Section 107(1) uses the term "including" to begin the dependent clause referring to commercial use, and the main clause speaks of a broader investigation into "purpose and character." As we explained in *Harper & Row*, Congress resisted attempts to narrow the ambit of this traditional enquiry by adopting categories of presumptively fair use, and it urged courts to preserve the breadth of their traditionally ample view of the universe of relevant evidence. Accordingly, the mere fact that a use is educational and not for profit does not insulate it

---

16. The only further judgment, indeed, that a court may pass on a work goes to an assessment of whether the parodic element is slight or great, and the copying small or extensive in relation to the parodic element, for a work with slight parodic element and extensive copying will be more likely to merely "supersede the objects" of the original.

from a finding of infringement, any more than the commercial character of a use bars a finding of fairness. If, indeed, commerciality carried presumptive force against a finding of fairness, the presumption would swallow nearly all of the illustrative uses listed in the preamble paragraph of §107, including news reporting, comment, criticism, teaching, scholarship, and research, since these activities "are generally conducted for profit in this country." *Harper & Row, supra,* at 592 (Brennan, J., dissenting). Congress could not have intended such a rule, which certainly is not inferable from the common-law cases, arising as they did from the world of letters in which Samuel Johnson could pronounce that "[n]o man but a blockhead ever wrote, except for money." 3 Boswell's Life of Johnson 19 (G. Hill ed. 1934).

*Sony* itself called for no hard evidentiary presumption. There, we emphasized the need for a "sensitive balancing of interests," 464 U.S., at 455, n. 40, noted that Congress had "eschewed a rigid, bright-line approach to fair use," *id.,* at 449, n. 31, and stated that the commercial or nonprofit educational character of a work is "not conclusive," *id.,* at 448-449, but rather a fact to be "weighed along with other[s] in fair use decisions," *id.,* at 449, n. 32, (quoting House Report, p. 66) U.S. Code Cong. & Admin. News 1976, pp. 5659, 5679. The Court of Appeals's elevation of one sentence from *Sony* to a *per se* rule thus runs as much counter to *Sony* itself as to the long common-law tradition of fair use adjudication. Rather, as we explained in *Harper & Row, Sony* stands for the proposition that the "fact that a publication was commercial as opposed to nonprofit is a separate factor that tends to weigh against a finding of fair use." 471 U.S., at 562. But that is all, and the fact that even the force of that tendency will vary with the context is a further reason against elevating commerciality to hard presumptive significance. The use, for example, of a copyrighted work to advertise a product, even in a parody, will be entitled to less indulgence under the first factor of the fair use enquiry than the sale of a parody for its own sake, let alone one performed a single time by students in school.

### B

The second statutory factor, "the nature of the copyrighted work," §107(2), draws on Justice Story's expression, the "value of the materials used." *Folsom v. Marsh,* 9 F. Cas., at 348. This factor calls for recognition that some works are closer to the core of intended copyright protection than others, with the consequence that fair use is more difficult to establish when the former works are copied. We agree with both the District Court and the Court of Appeals that the Orbison original's creative expression for public dissemination falls within the core of the copyright's protective purposes. This fact, however, is not much help in this case, or ever likely to help much in separating the fair use sheep from the infringing goats in a parody case, since parodies almost invariably copy publicly known, expressive works.

### C

The third factor asks whether "the amount and substantiality of the portion used in relation to the copyrighted work as a whole," §107(3) (or, in Justice Story's words, "the quantity and value of the materials used," *Folsom v. Marsh, supra*, at 348) are reasonable in relation to the purpose of the copying. Here, attention turns to the persuasiveness of a parodist's justification for the particular copying done, and the enquiry will harken back to the first of the statutory factors, for, as in prior cases, we recognize that the extent of permissible copying varies with the purpose and character of the use. The facts bearing on this factor will also tend to address the fourth, by revealing the degree to which the parody may serve as a market substitute for the original or potentially licensed derivatives.

The District Court considered the song's parodic purpose in finding that 2 Live Crew had not helped themselves overmuch. The Court of Appeals disagreed, stating that "[w]hile it may not be inappropriate to find that no more was taken than necessary, the copying was qualitatively substantial. . . . We conclude that taking the heart of the original and making it the heart of a new work was to purloin a substantial portion of the essence of the original." 972 F.2d, at 1438.

The Court of Appeals is of course correct that this factor calls for thought not only about the quantity of the materials used, but about their quality and importance, too. In *Harper & Row*, for example, the Nation had taken only some 300 words out of President Ford's memoirs, but we signaled the significance of the quotations in finding them to amount to "the heart of the book," the part most likely to be newsworthy and important in licensing serialization. 471 U.S., at 564-566, 568 (internal quotation marks omitted). We also agree with the Court of Appeals that whether "a substantial portion of the infringing work was copied verbatim" from the copyrighted work is a relevant question, see *id.*, at 565, for it may reveal a dearth of transformative character or purpose under the first factor, or a greater likelihood of market harm under the fourth; a work composed primarily of an original, particularly its heart, with little added or changed, is more likely to be a merely superseding use, fulfilling demand for the original.

Where we part company with the court below is in applying these guides to parody, and in particular to parody in the song before us. Parody presents a difficult case. Parody's humor, or in any event its comment, necessarily springs from recognizable allusion to its object through distorted imitation. Its art lies in the tension between a known original and its parodic twin. When parody takes aim at a particular original work, the parody must be able to "conjure up" at least enough of that original to make the object of its critical wit recognizable. What makes for this recognition is quotation of the original's most distinctive or memorable features, which the parodist can be sure the audience will know. Once enough has been taken to assure identification, how much more is reasonable will depend, say, on the extent to which the song's overriding purpose and character is to parody the original or, in contrast, the likelihood that the parody may serve as a market substitute for the original. But using some characteristic features cannot be avoided.

We think the Court of Appeals was insufficiently appreciative of parody's need for the recognizable sight or sound when it ruled 2 Live Crew's use unreasonable as a matter of law. It is true, of course, that 2 Live Crew copied the characteristic opening bass riff (or musical phrase) of the original, and true that the words of the first line copy the Orbison lyrics. But if quotation of the opening riff and the first line may be said to go to the "heart" of the original, the heart is also what most readily conjures up the song for parody, and it is the heart at which parody takes aim. Copying does not become excessive in relation to parodic purpose merely because the portion taken was the original's heart. If 2 Live Crew had copied a significantly less memorable part of the original, it is difficult to see how its parodic character would have come through.

This is not, of course, to say that anyone who calls himself a parodist can skim the cream and get away scot free. In parody, as in news reporting, context is everything, and the question of fairness asks what else the parodist did besides go to the heart of the original. It is significant that 2 Live Crew not only copied the first line of the original, but thereafter departed markedly from the Orbison lyrics for its own ends. 2 Live Crew not only copied the bass riff and repeated it, but also produced otherwise distinctive sounds, interposing "scraper" noise, overlaying the music with solos in different keys, and altering the drum beat. This is not a case, then, where "a substantial portion" of the parody itself is composed of a "verbatim" copying of the original. It is not, that is, a case where the parody is so insubstantial, as compared to the copying, that the third factor must be resolved as a matter of law against the parodists.

Suffice it to say here that, as to the lyrics, we think the Court of Appeals correctly suggested that "no more was taken than necessary," 972 F.2d, at 1438, but just for that reason, we fail to see how the copying can be excessive in relation to its parodic purpose, even if the portion taken is the original's "heart." As to the music, we express no opinion whether repetition of the bass riff is excessive copying, and we remand to permit evaluation of the amount taken, in light of the song's parodic purpose and character, its transformative elements, and considerations of the potential for market substitution sketched more fully below.

### D

The fourth fair use factor is "the effect of the use upon the potential market for or value of the copyrighted work." §107(4). It requires courts to consider not only the extent of market harm caused by the particular actions of the alleged infringer, but also "whether unrestricted and widespread conduct of the sort engaged in by the defendant . . . would result in a substantially adverse impact on the potential market" for the original. Nimmer §13.05[A] [4], p. 13-102.61 (footnote omitted). The enquiry "must take account not only of harm to the original but also of harm to the market for derivative works." *Harper & Row, supra*, 471 U.S. at 568.

Since fair use is an affirmative defense, its proponent would have difficulty carrying the burden of demonstrating fair use without favorable evidence about relevant markets. In moving for summary judgment, 2 Live Crew left themselves at just such a disadvantage when they failed to address the effect on the market for rap derivatives, and confined themselves to uncontroverted submissions that there was no likely effect on the market for the original. . . .

No "presumption" or inference of market harm that might find support in *Sony* is applicable to a case involving something beyond mere duplication for commercial purposes. *Sony*'s discussion of a presumption contrasts a context of verbatim copying of the original in its entirety for commercial purposes, with the noncommercial context of *Sony* itself (home copying of television programming). In the former circumstances, what *Sony* said simply makes common sense: when a commercial use amounts to mere duplication of the entirety of an original, it clearly "supersede[s] the objects," *Folsom v. Marsh, supra,* at 348, of the original and serves as a market replacement for it, making it likely that cognizable market harm to the original will occur. But when, on the contrary, the second use is transformative, market substitution is at least less certain, and market harm may not be so readily inferred. Indeed, as to parody pure and simple, it is more likely that the new work will not affect the market for the original in a way cognizable under this factor, that is, by acting as a substitute for it ("supersed[ing] [its] objects"). This is so because the parody and the original usually serve different market functions.

We do not, of course, suggest that a parody may not harm the market at all, but when a lethal parody, like a scathing theater review, kills demand for the original, it does not produce a harm cognizable under the Copyright Act. Because "parody may quite legitimately aim at garroting the original, destroying it commercially as well as artistically," B. Kaplan, An Unhurried View of Copyright 69 (1967), the role of the courts is to distinguish between "[b]iting criticism [that merely] suppresses demand [and] copyright infringement[, which] usurps it." *Fisher v. Dees,* 794 F.2d, at 438.

This distinction between potentially remediable displacement and unremediable disparagement is reflected in the rule that there is no protectible derivative market for criticism. The market for potential derivative uses includes only those that creators of original works would in general develop or license others to develop. Yet the unlikelihood that creators of imaginative works will license critical reviews or lampoons of their own productions removes such uses from the very notion of a potential licensing market. "People ask . . . for criticism, but they only want praise." S. Maugham, Of Human Bondage 241 (Penguin ed. 1992). Thus, to the extent that the opinion below may be read to have considered harm to the market for parodies of "Oh, Pretty Woman," see 972 F.2d, at 1439, the court erred.

In explaining why the law recognizes no derivative market for critical works, including parody, we have, of course, been speaking of the later work as if it had nothing but a critical aspect (*i.e.,* "parody pure and simple"). But the later work may have a more complex character, with effects not only in the arena of criticism but also in protectible markets for derivative works, too. In that sort of case, the law looks beyond the criticism to the other elements of the work, as it does here. 2 Live Crew's song comprises not only parody but also rap music, and the derivative market for rap music is a proper focus of enquiry, see *Harper & Row, supra,* 471 U.S., at 568. Evidence of substantial harm to it would weigh against a finding of fair use, because the licensing of derivatives is an important economic incentive to the creation of originals. See 17 U.S.C. §106(2) (copyright owner has rights to derivative works). Of course, the only harm to derivatives that need concern us, as discussed above, is the harm of market substitution. The fact that a parody may impair the market for derivative uses by the very effectiveness of its critical commentary is no more relevant under copyright than the like threat to the original market.

Although 2 Live Crew submitted uncontroverted affidavits on the question of market harm to the original, neither they, nor Acuff-Rose, introduced evidence or affidavits addressing the likely effect of 2 Live Crew's parodic rap song on the market for a nonparody, rap version of "Oh, Pretty Woman." And while Acuff-Rose would have us find evidence of a rap market in the very facts that 2 Live Crew recorded a rap parody of "Oh, Pretty Woman" and another rap group sought a license to record a rap derivative, there was no evidence that a potential rap market was harmed in any way by 2 Live Crew's parody, rap version. The fact that 2 Live Crew's parody sold as part of a collection of rap songs says very little about the parody's effect on a market for a rap version of the original, either of the music alone or of the music with its lyrics. The District Court essentially passed on this issue, observing that Acuff-Rose is free to record "whatever version of the original it desires," 754 F. Supp., at 1158; the Court of Appeals went the other way by erroneous presumption. Contrary to each treatment, it is impossible to deal with the fourth factor except by recognizing that a silent record on an important factor bearing on fair use disentitled the proponent of the defense, 2 Live Crew, to summary judgment. The evidentiary hole will doubtless be plugged on remand.

### III

It was error for the Court of Appeals to conclude that the commercial nature of 2 Live Crew's parody of "Oh, Pretty Woman" rendered it presumptively unfair. No such evidentiary presumption is available to address either the first factor, the character and purpose of the use, or the fourth, market harm, in determining whether a transformative use, such as parody, is a fair one. The court also erred in holding that 2 Live Crew had necessarily copied excessively from the Orbison original, considering the parodic purpose of the use. We therefore reverse the judgment of the Court of Appeals and remand the case for further proceedings consistent with this opinion.

*It is so ordered.*

### APPENDIX A TO OPINION OF THE COURT

#### "OH, PRETTY WOMAN" BY ROY ORBISON AND WILLIAM DEES

Pretty Woman, walking down the street,
Pretty Woman, the kind I like to meet,
Pretty Woman, I don't believe you, you're not the truth,
No one could look as good as you
Mercy
Pretty Woman, won't you pardon me,
Pretty Woman, I couldn't help but see,
Pretty Woman, that you look lovely as can be
Are you lonely just like me?
Pretty Woman, stop a while,
Pretty Woman, talk a while,
Pretty Woman give your smile to me
Pretty Woman, yeah, yeah, yeah

Pretty Woman, look my way,
Pretty Woman, say you'll stay with me
'Cause I need you, I'll treat you right
Come to me baby, Be mine tonight
Pretty Woman, don't walk on by,
Pretty Woman, don't make me cry,
Pretty Woman, don't walk away,
Hey, O.K.
If that's the way it must be, O.K.
I guess I'll go on home, it's late
There'll be tomorrow night, but wait!
What do I see
Is she walking back to me?
Yeah, she's walking back to me!
Oh, Pretty Woman.

### APPENDIX B TO OPINION OF THE COURT

#### "PRETTY WOMAN" AS RECORDED BY 2 LIVE CREW

Pretty woman walkin' down the street
Pretty woman girl you look so sweet
Pretty woman you bring me down to that knee
Pretty woman you make me wanna beg please
Oh, pretty woman
Big hairy woman you need to shave that stuff
Big hairy woman you know I bet it's tough
Big hairy woman all that hair it ain't legit
'Cause you look like 'Cousin It'
Big hairy woman
Bald headed woman girl your hair won't grow
Bald headed woman you got a teeny weeny afro
Bald headed woman you know your hair could look nice
Bald headed woman first you got to roll it with rice
Bald headed woman here, let me get this hunk of biz for ya
Ya know what I'm saying you look better than rice a roni
Oh bald headed woman
Big hairy woman come on in
And don't forget your bald headed friend
Hey pretty woman let the boys
Jump in
Two timin' woman girl you know you ain't right
Two timin' woman you's out with my boy last night
Two timin' woman that takes a load off my mind
Two timin' woman now I know the baby ain't mine
Oh, two timin' woman
Oh pretty woman

[Concurring opinion of Justice KENNEDY omitted.]

## Comments

*1. Parody and Satire. Campbell* is sometimes cited for the proposition
that parody (criticizing a work itself) is fair use, but satire (using a

copyrighted work to criticize someone or something else) is not. Read the opinion closely; the Court concludes that a parody — where "a parodic character may reasonably be perceived" — constitutes a "transformative" use of a copyrighted work, which counts in favor of the accused infringer under the first fair use factor. But the Court leaves open the possibility that upon consideration of all four factors, satire may nonetheless be "fair" and noninfringing.

2. *Transformative Use and the Heart of the Work.* Recall that in *Harper & Row*, the Court critiqued the defendant for having appropriated the "heart" of *A Time to Heal*. In *Campbell*, the Court notes that in some contexts, reproducing the "heart" of a copyrighted work is not only fair use, but may be indispensable: "When parody takes aim at a particular original work, the parody must be able to 'conjure up' at least enough of that original to make the object of its critical wit recognizable. What makes for this recognition is quotation of the most distinctive or memorable features of the original, which the parodist can be sure the audience will know." The distinction can be drawn only on a case-by-case basis. While *Campbell* offers a standard — "transformative" use — for distinguishing between fair and unfair uses of the "heart" of a work, consider how effective that standard is in practice. Presumably, the dissenters in *Harper & Row* would have concluded that *The Nation* "transformed" the copyrighted work when using it journalistically. Neither opinion contains much guidance for deciding when a work is sufficiently "transformed," leading to the suspicion that courts may simply manipulate the contents of their analysis of the four fair use factors to support conclusions that fair use should protect certain "favored" uses.

3. *The Nature of the Transformation.* The Court equivocates on what constitutes effective "transformation" for purposes of the first statutory factor. Is it the case that the work itself must be transformed, so that the defendant is accused of having prepared an unauthorized derivative work? This was clearly the posture of *Campbell* itself. Or is it the case that a work might be suitably "transformed" by being used, in unmodified form, in the context of a preferred statutory purpose, such as news reporting, criticism, teaching, or research? In Chapter 6 you encountered a related equivocation, between the originality of the work itself and the creativity of the process used to develop the work, in copyrightability analysis under *Feist Publications, Inc. v. Rural Telephone Service*.

4. *Markets for Derivative Works.* Given how readily each of the four fair use factors can be characterized to suit multiple perspectives, perhaps a better reading of *Campbell* is its endorsement of the distinction between uses of copyrighted works that *substitute* for the original work, and uses that do not. Under this view, copyright infringement constitutes a form of unfair competition; fair use is a form of legitimate competition. Implicit in this formulation, however, is the presumption that there are "natural" limits to markets for copyrighted works. It is logical to suppose that protected markets for derivative versions of copyrighted works do have limits. Otherwise, it is conceivable that there could be a licensing market for *any* use of a copyrighted work, *any* unlicensed use could constitute infringement, and the test for infringement would simply swallow the fair use defense. But *Campbell* does not suggest precisely

where or how to establish those limits. The Court concludes that while genuine criticism, including parody, tends to harm the market for the work, the market for criticism is simply not one that the copyright law is intended to protect. On the other hand, the Court is not willing to conclude that 2 Live Crew's version of "Oh, Pretty Woman" is in fact protected as fair use. Instead, the Court remands the case for consideration of whether 2 Live Crew appropriated a market for a derivative rap version of the Roy Orbison classic.

5. *Presumptions and Commercial Use.* In *Campbell*, the Court retreats — in part — from its earlier strong statements that commercial re-use of copyrighted works is presumptively infringing. "Commercial" use under the first factor is re-located as one of several fair use factors, rather than first among many. However, it appears that the commercial/noncommercial distinction retains an important practical effect. In the case of an accused infringing use that is characterized as "commercial," the defendant retains the burden of both pleading and proving that the use is fair, since harm to the plaintiff's market may be presumed. In the case of an accused infringing use that is characterized as "noncommercial," the defendant bears the burden of proving fair use, but the copyright owner must prove the existence of market harm in order to obtain relief.

6. *Permission — Denied.* Still another reading of *Campbell* focuses on the mechanics of asking for and receiving permission to use the copyrighted work. An economically rational copyright owner should be willing to license profitable uses of the copyrighted work. However, even rational copyright owners likely will not grant permission to use their work in cases of "market failure" — where willing buyers and willing sellers are unable to reach private agreements. This is likely to be true in at least two contexts. One is the sort of situation present in *Campbell*, the copyright owner who is unwilling to license the work to the critic. In this situation, fears of censorship may be well founded. In this case, as the Court notes, fair use serves as a legal mechanism for authorizing a use of the work that is socially productive, but that the copyright owner is unlikely to develop. In *Campbell*, 2 Live Crew asked for permission to make a derivative version of "Oh, Pretty Woman," but the copyright owner rejected the request. In the circumstances of this case, that refusal to license was not treated as a factor favoring infringement. The second situation is where transactions costs of various sorts interfere with the ability of the copyright owner and potential licensees to locate and negotiate licensing terms with one another, given a proposed use that would not ordinarily substitute for the original. Users may be too numerous, or the scope of their individual interests may be too small, to warrant the copyright owner's energy. Licensing fees typically charged by the copyright owner for commercial uses may exceed amounts typically budgeted (if any amounts are budgeted) by researchers, journalists, or teachers, for example. Here, censorship concerns are less important than logistical concerns. Fair use enables a welfare-enhancing use of the work, where logistics alone may otherwise interfere.

Both parts of this perspective on fair use, with its focus on market logic, are well illustrated by *Ty, Inc. v. Publications Intern. Ltd.*, 292 F.3d

512 (7th Cir. 2002). The plaintiff, Ty, Inc., is the producer of the wildly successful "Beanie Babies" line of stuffed animals. The defendant produced a collectors' guide that included color photos of the Beanie Babies. Ty sued for copyright infringement, arguing that the photographs constituted unauthorized derivatives of the copyrighted stuffed animals. The trial court granted summary judgment for the plaintiff, but the court of appeal reversed, noting that the collectors' guides were a form of criticism, which does not usurp the copyright owner's market for the work:

> Book reviews and parodies are merely examples of types of work that quote or otherwise copy from copyrighted works yet constitute fair use because they are complements of (though sometimes negative complements, as in the case of a devastating book review) rather than substitutes for the copyrighted original. The commonest type is simply a quotation from a copyrighted work in a book or article on the same or a related subject. The complementary effect may be quite weak, but the quotation is unlikely to reduce the demand for the copyrighted work; nor could the copyright owner command a license fee commensurate with the costs of transacting with the copier. Such copying is therefore fair use.

*Id.* at 518. Moreover, as the court observed, "Ty wants to suppress criticism of its product in these guides." *Id.* at 521. Despite its strong intimation that the defendant's use was not infringing, the court remanded the case for trial on the fair use defense.

7. *Fair Use as an Affirmative Defense. Campbell* confirms what has been the long-standing practice of the federal courts, treating fair use as an affirmative defense to be raised and proved by the accused infringer, rather than as an element of infringement to be negated by the copyright owner. Fair use is sometimes treated, accordingly, as "merely" a defense, rather than as a "right" of the accused infringer. Given the close conceptual connection between the role of fair use as protecting parody and criticism, and First Amendment doctrine protecting criticism and other free speech from government interference, some recent courts have advocated treating fair use as the equivalent of a right protected under the First Amendment. *See Suntrust Bank v. Houghton Mifflin Co.,* 268 F.3d 1257 (11th Cir. 2001) (vacating preliminary injunction against publication of *The Wind Done Gone*, a parody of *Gone With the Wind*).

8. *After* **Campbell.** On remand, 2 Live Crew and Acuff-Rose Music settled the case rather than litigate the question of markets for derivative rap versions of "Oh, Pretty Woman." Acuff-Rose dropped its lawsuit, and 2 Live Crew paid a licensing fee for use of the composition.

### *COUNSELING PERSPECTIVE*
### Fair Use and Copyright Counseling

In Section A of this chapter you read about some of the key legal issues confronting lawyers and parties who are negotiating over licensing copyrighted works. Fair use complicates this problem considerably, because it raises a preliminary question. Is a license or permission necessary in the first place, or might the use be legitimately characterized as "fair"? The fact-specific character of most fair use litigation makes this judgment especially precarious. As a practical matter, virtually all copyright lawyers err on the side of caution, urging their clients to secure appropriate permission rather than run the risk of being sued for copyright infringement and the further risk of an adverse determination by a court. Whether or not this is troublesome depends on one's perspective on public policy. Ambiguity in the law discourages reliance on fair use, which means that fair use remains a relatively narrow exception reserved for the extraordinary case, usually in litigation. Investments in creating and distributing new works are channeled primarily through licensing activity. Greater clarity in fair use might encourage more reliance on the doctrine in the course of investment and creative decisions, broadening fair use somewhat and reducing the importance of licensing accordingly.

## Problem

**8-2.** For several years, Video Palace compiled movie trailers onto videotape for home video retailers to display in their stores. To obtain the right to distribute the trailers, Video Palace entered into contracts with various entertainment companies. It entered into such an agreement with Warner Brothers (WB), among others, in 1990, and under that agreement Warner Brothers eventually provided Video Palace with over 500 trailers for its movies. In 1997, Video Palace entered the electronic commerce world and began to operate VideoPalace.net. The company maintains a database accessible from VideoPalace.net, which contains movie trailers Video Palace has received throughout the years. Video Palace's Internet clients are retail websites selling home videos, which use VideoPalace.net to display trailers to site visitors. Site visitors access trailers by clicking on a button labeled "preview" for a particular film that the site offers for sale. The trailer is then "streamed" for the visitor to view (streaming prevents the visitor from downloading or storing the trailer). Video Palace's Internet clients pay a fee to have the trailers streamed based on the number of megabytes shown to site visitors. Video Palace has agreements to stream trailers with approximately 25 online retailers, including Yahoo!, Amazon, and Best Buy. Because Video Palace's agreement with Warner Brothers did not extend to use of WB trailers on the Internet, at WB's request Video Palace removed trailers previously received from WB from the online database. Video Palace subsequently used digital editing equipment to create its own "clip previews" from WB motion pictures. Each "clip preview" consists of displaying the WB trademark and title of the motion picture, one or two scenes from the first part of the film, and then the title again. These previews do not include voiceover narration and music often found in trailers shown in theaters. WB produces trailers for use on its own website, and licenses trailers to third-party websites such as barnesandnoble.com. WB has sued Video Palace for copyright infringement. Is Video Palace's use a fair use? *See Video Pipeline, Inc. v. Buena Vista Home Entertainment, Inc.*, 342 F.3d 191 (3d Cir. 2003).

## 2. "Ordinary" and "Personal" Use

In a number of places in copyright law, you have seen how developments in technology — photography and computer programs among them — have challenged traditional understandings and applications of the law. Fair use is no exception. Before the dawn of "personal computing," first photocopying and then videotape recording put inexpensive reproduction technology in the hands of consumers for the first time. The next case represents not only the first time that the Supreme Court addressed the fair use doctrine — note that it was decided a year before *Harper & Row* — but also the first major confrontation between copyright owners and consumers, rather than competitors.

### SONY CORP. OF AMERICA v. UNIVERSAL CITY STUDIOS, INC.
#### 464 U.S. 417 (1984)

Justice STEVENS delivered the opinion of the Court.

Petitioners manufacture and sell home video tape recorders. Respondents own the copyrights on some of the television programs that are broadcast on the public airwaves. Some members of the general public use video tape recorders sold by petitioners to record some of these broadcasts, as well as a large number of other broadcasts. The question presented is whether the sale of petitioners' copying equipment to the general public violates any of the rights conferred upon respondents by the Copyright Act.

Respondents commenced this copyright infringement action against petitioners in the United States District Court for the Central District of California in 1976. Respondents alleged that some individuals had used Betamax video tape recorders (VTR's) to record some of respondents' copyrighted works which had been exhibited on commercially sponsored television and contended that these individuals had thereby infringed respondents' copyrights. Respondents further maintained that petitioners were liable for the copyright infringement allegedly committed by Betamax consumers because of petitioners' marketing of the Betamax VTR's. Respondents sought no relief against any Betamax consumer. Instead, they sought money damages and an equitable accounting of profits from petitioners, as well as an injunction against the manufacture and marketing of Betamax VTR's.

After a lengthy trial, the District Court denied respondents all the relief they sought and entered judgment for petitioners. The United States Court of Appeals for the Ninth Circuit reversed the District Court's judgment on respondent's copyright claim, holding petitioners liable for contributory infringement and ordering the District Court to fashion appropriate relief. We granted certiorari. . . . We now reverse.

An explanation of our rejection of respondents' unprecedented attempt to impose copyright liability upon the distributors of copying equipment requires a quite detailed recitation of the findings of the District Court. In summary, those findings reveal that the average member of the public uses a VTR principally to record a program he cannot view as it is being televised and then to watch it once at a later time. This practice, known as "time-shifting," enlarges the television viewing audience. For that reason, a significant amount of television programming may be used in this manner without objection from the owners of the copyrights on the programs. For the same reason, even the two respondents in this case, who do assert objections to time-shifting in this litigation, were unable to prove that the practice has impaired the commercial value of their copyrights or has created any likelihood of future harm. Given these findings, there is no basis in the Copyright Act upon which respondents can hold petitioners liable for distributing VTR's to the general public. The Court of Appeals' holding that respondents are entitled to enjoin the distribution of VTR's, to collect royalties on the sale of such equipment, or to obtain other relief, if affirmed, would enlarge the scope of respondents' statutory monopolies to encompass control over an article of commerce that is not the subject of copyright protection. Such an expansion of the copyright privilege is beyond the limits of the grants authorized by Congress.

## I

The two respondents in this action, Universal Studios, Inc. and Walt Disney Productions, produce and hold the copyrights on a substantial number of motion pictures and other audiovisual works. In the current marketplace, they can exploit their rights in these works in a number of ways: by authorizing theatrical exhibitions, by licensing limited showings on cable and network television, by selling syndication rights for repeated airings on local television stations, and by marketing programs on prerecorded videotapes or videodiscs. Some works are suitable for exploitation through all of these avenues, while the market for other works is more limited.

Petitioner Sony manufactures millions of Betamax video tape recorders and markets these devices through numerous retail establishments, some of which are also petitioners in this action. Sony's Betamax VTR is a mechanism consisting of three basic components: (1) a tuner, which receives electromagnetic signals transmitted over the television band of the public airwaves and separates them into audio and visual signals; (2) a recorder, which records such signals on a magnetic tape; and (3) an adapter, which converts the audio and visual signals on the tape into a composite signal that can be received by a television set.

* * *

The respondents and Sony both conducted surveys of the way the Betamax machine was used by several hundred owners during a sample period in 1978. Although there were some differences in the surveys, they both showed that the primary use of the machine for most owners was "time-shifting," — the practice of recording a program to view it once at a later time, and thereafter erasing it. Time-shifting enables viewers to see programs they otherwise would miss because they are not at home, are occupied with other tasks, or are viewing a program on another station at the time of a broadcast that they desire to watch. Both surveys also showed, however, that a substantial number of interviewees had accumulated libraries of tapes. Sony's survey indicated that over 80% of the interviewees watched at least as much regular television as they had before owning a Betamax. Respondents offered no evidence of decreased television viewing by Betamax owners.

Sony introduced considerable evidence describing television programs that could be copied without objection from any copyright holder, with special emphasis on sports, religious, and educational programming. For example, their survey indicated that 7.3% of all Betamax use is to record sports events, and representatives of professional baseball, football, basketball, and hockey testified that they had no objection to the recording of their televised events for home use.

Respondents offered opinion evidence concerning the future impact of the unrestricted sale of VTR's on the commercial value of their copyrights. The District Court found, however, that they had failed to prove any likelihood of future harm from the use of VTR's for time-shifting. *Id.,* at 469.

\* \* \*

The two respondents in this case do not seek relief against the Betamax users who have allegedly infringed their copyrights. Moreover, this is not a class action on behalf of all copyright owners who license their works for television broadcast, and respondents have no right to invoke whatever rights other copyright holders may have to bring infringement actions based on Betamax copying of their works. As was made clear by their own evidence, the copying of the respondents' programs represents a small portion of the total use of VTR's. It is, however, the taping of respondents own copyrighted programs that provides them with standing to charge Sony with contributory infringement. To prevail, they have the burden of proving that users of the Betamax have infringed their copyrights and that Sony should be held responsible for that infringement.

[The Court held, by analogy to patent law, that "the contributory infringement doctrine is grounded on the recognition that adequate protection of a monopoly may require the courts to look beyond actual duplication of a device or publication to the products or activities that make such duplication possible. The staple article of commerce doctrine must strike a balance between a copyright holder's legitimate demand for effective — not merely symbolic — protection of the statutory monopoly, and the rights of others freely to engage in substantially unrelated areas of commerce. Accordingly, the sale of copying equipment, like the sale of other articles of commerce, does not constitute contributory infringement if the product is widely used for legitimate, unobjectionable purposes. Indeed, it need merely be capable of substantial noninfringing uses."]

## IV

The question is thus whether the Betamax is capable of commercially significant noninfringing uses. In order to resolve that question, we need not explore *all* the different potential uses of the machine and determine whether or not they would constitute infringement. Rather, we need only consider whether on the basis of the facts as found by the district court a significant number of them would be non-infringing. Moreover, in order to resolve this case we need not give precise content to the question of how much use is commercially significant. For one potential use of the Betamax plainly satisfies this standard, however it is understood: private, noncommercial time-shifting in the home. It does so both (A) because respondents have no right to prevent other copyright holders from authorizing it for their programs, and (B) because the District Court's factual findings reveal that even the unauthorized home time-shifting of respondents' programs is legitimate fair use.

### AUTHORIZED TIME SHIFTING

[The Court reviewed testimony supporting time-shifting from representatives of professional sports leagues, religious broadcasters, and Fred Rogers, of Mr. Rogers' Neighborhood.]

### UNAUTHORIZED TIME-SHIFTING

Even unauthorized uses of a copyrighted work are not necessarily infringing. An unlicensed use of the copyright is not an infringement unless it conflicts with one of the specific exclusive rights conferred by the copyright statute. Moreover, the definition of exclusive rights in §106 of the present Act is prefaced by the words "subject to sections 107 through 118." Those sections describe a variety of uses of copyrighted material that "are not infringements of copyright notwithstanding the provisions of §106." The most pertinent in this case is §107, the legislative endorsement of the doctrine of "fair use."

That section identifies various factors that enable a Court to apply an "equitable rule of reason" analysis to particular claims of infringement.[31] Although not conclusive, the first factor requires that "the commercial or nonprofit character of an activity" be weighed in any fair use decision. If the Betamax were used to make copies for a commercial or profit-making purpose, such use would presumptively be unfair. The contrary presumption is appropriate here, however, because the District Court's findings plainly establish that time-shifting for private home use must be characterized as a noncommercial, nonprofit activity. Moreover, when one considers the nature of a televised copyrighted audiovisual work, see 17 U.S.C. §107(2), and that timeshifting merely enables a viewer to see such a work which he had been invited to witness in its entirety free of charge,

---

31. The House Report expressly stated that the fair use doctrine is an "equitable rule of reason" in its explanation of the fair use section:

> Although the courts have considered and ruled upon the fair use doctrine over and over again, no real definition of the concept has ever emerged. Indeed, since the doctrine is an equitable rule of reason, no generally applicable definition is possible, and each case raising the question must be decided on its own facts. . . .

the fact that the entire work is reproduced, see *id.*, at §107(3), does not have its ordinary effect of militating against a finding of fair use.

This is not, however, the end of the inquiry because Congress has also directed us to consider "the effect of the use upon the potential market for or value of the copyrighted work." *Id.*, at §107(4). The purpose of copyright is to create incentives for creative effort. Even copying for noncommercial purposes may impair the copyright holder's ability to obtain the rewards that Congress intended him to have. But a use that has no demonstrable effect upon the potential market for, or the value of, the copyrighted work need not be prohibited in order to protect the author's incentive to create. The prohibition of such noncommercial uses would merely inhibit access to ideas without any countervailing benefit.

Thus, although every commercial use of copyrighted material is presumptively an unfair exploitation of the monopoly privilege that belongs to the owner of the copyright, noncommercial uses are a different matter. A challenge to a noncommercial use of a copyrighted work requires proof either that the particular use is harmful, or that if it should become widespread, it would adversely affect the potential market for the copyrighted work. Actual present harm need not be shown; such a requirement would leave the copyright holder with no defense against predictable damage. Nor is it necessary to show with certainty that future harm will result. What is necessary is a showing by a preponderance of the evidence that *some* meaningful likelihood of future harm exists. If the intended use is for commercial gain, that likelihood may be presumed. But if it is for a noncommercial purpose, the likelihood must be demonstrated.

In this case, respondents failed to carry their burden with regard to home time-shifting....

\* \* \*

...[T]he District Court restated its overall conclusion several times, in several different ways. "Harm from time-shifting is speculative and, at best, minimal." *Ibid.* "The audience benefits from the time-shifting capability have already been discussed. It is not implausible that benefits could also accrue to plaintiffs, broadcasters, and advertisers, as the Betamax makes it possible for more persons to view their broadcasts." *Ibid.* "No likelihood of harm was shown at trial, and plaintiffs admitted that there had been no actual harm to date." *Id.*, at 468-469. "Testimony at trial suggested that Betamax may require adjustments in marketing strategy, but it did not establish even a likelihood of harm." *Id.*, at 469. "Television production by plaintiffs today is more profitable than it has ever been, and, in five weeks of trial, there was no concrete evidence to suggest that the Betamax will change the studios' financial picture." *Ibid.*

The District Court's conclusions are buttressed by the fact that to the extent time-shifting expands public access to freely broadcast television programs, it yields societal benefits. Earlier this year, in *Community Television of Southern California v. Gottfried*, ___ U.S. ___, 103 S. Ct. 885, 891-892 (1983), we acknowledged the public interest in making television broadcasting more available. Concededly, that interest is not unlimited. But it supports an interpretation of the concept of "fair use" that requires the copyright holder to demonstrate some likelihood of harm before he may condemn a private act of time-shifting as a violation of federal law.

When these factors are all weighed in the "equitable rule of reason" balance, we must conclude that this record amply supports the District Court's conclusion that home time-shifting is fair use. In light of the findings of the District Court regarding the state of the empirical data, it is clear that the Court of Appeals erred in holding that the statute as presently written bars such conduct.

In summary, the record and findings of the District Court lead us to two conclusions. First, Sony demonstrated a significant likelihood that substantial numbers of copyright holders who license their works for broadcast on free television would not object to having their broadcasts time-shifted by private viewers. And second, respondents failed to demonstrate that time-shifting would cause any likelihood of nonminimal harm to the potential market for, or the value of, their copyrighted works. The Betamax is, therefore, capable of substantial noninfringing uses. Sony's sale of such equipment to the general public does not constitute contributory infringement of respondent's copyrights. . . .

It may well be that Congress will take a fresh look at this new technology, just as it so often has examined other innovations in the past. But it is not our job to apply laws that have not yet been written. Applying the copyright statute, as it now reads, to the facts as they have been developed in this case, the judgment of the Court of Appeals must be reversed.

*It is so ordered.*

[Dissenting opinion of Justice BLACKMUN, joined by MARSHALL, J., POWELL, J., and REHNQUIST, J., is omitted.]

## Comments

1. *The Procedural Context of* Sony. The fair use issue arises in *Sony* in the context of the broader issue of indirect liability. The defendant, Sony, is liable for distributing the Betamax VTR only if there are direct infringers using the VTR to infringe the plaintiff's copyrights. As a class, those direct infringers are VTR users. To ensure testimony at trial that would be favorable to Universal, Universal arranged to have a "friendly" VTR user (William Griffiths, a client of Universal's law firm) named as a defendant in the case, with the promise that no judgment would be enforced against him. Given the Court's adoption of the rule that no indirect liability will lie if the accused device is "capable of substantial noninfringing uses" (recall the discussion of this standard in Chapter 7), the question is whether the VTR has "substantial noninfringing uses." *Fair* uses qualify as both "noninfringing" and, in this case, "substantial," rendering it lawful for Sony to sell the Betamax.

2. *The Limits of* Sony. The Court appears to draw a clear distinction between lawful use of the Betamax for time-shifting, which constitutes fair use, and infringing use of the Betamax for "librarying," or building a library of recorded programming. (Note that the Court does not address application of this distinction to cable programming.) What, precisely, is the

basis of the majority's conclusion? In part, the Court relies on the conclusion that "time-shifting for private home use must be characterized as
a noncommercial, nonprofit activity," a point that emphasizes the role
of fair use in private, personal decisions regarding when and how to
read, watch, or listen to copyrighted works. In part, also, the Court
concludes that the plaintiffs "failed to demonstrate that time-shifting
would cause any likelihood of nonminimal harm to the potential market
for, or the value of, their copyrighted works."

3. **The Audio Home Recording Act and Personal Use.** Consumer interests in
personal and private use of copyrighted works have found expression in
one other place in the Copyright Act. In 1992, as part of the Audio
Home Recording Act (AHRA) (recall the discussion of this statute in
Chapter 7), Congress enacted §1008 of the Copyright Act, which
provides:

> No action may be brought under this title alleging infringement of copy-
> right based on the manufacture, importation, or distribution of a digital
> audio recording device, a digital audio recording medium, an analog
> recording device, or an analog recording medium, or based on the non-
> commercial use by a consumer of such a device or medium for making
> digital musical recordings or analog musical recordings.

This statute thus creates statutory immunity for the noncommercial
consumer creation of "digital musical recordings or analog musical
recordings" using an analog recording device or medium (for example,
a cassette or reel-to-reel tape deck) or a digital audio recording device or
medium (for example, a DAT recorder or tape). As a result, it appears
that the Copyright Act now permits the long-standing practice of making "mix tapes" to entertain friends at parties. How broadly this statute
applies, however, is unclear. The statute defines "digital audio recording medium" and "digital audio recording device" tightly, so as to
exclude general purpose computers. *See* 17 U.S.C. §1001(3), (4). Burning CDs of one's own music collection, therefore, may not be protected
under §1008, though one could argue that it is protected as fair use.
Section 1008 has been interpreted only once by a federal appellate
court, in *Recording Indus. Ass'n of Am. v. Diamond Multimedia Sys., Inc.*,
180 F.3d 1072 (9th Cir. 1999). That court considered whether the Diamond Rio, an early MP3 player, was a "digital audio recording device"
subject to the technology and royalty obligations created by the AHRA.
The court concluded that it was not, and noted that the operation of the
device was consistent with the purpose of the AHRA, which was to facilitate personal use. "The Rio merely makes copies in order to render
portable, or 'space-shift,' those files that already reside on a user's hard
drive. . . . Such copying is a paradigmatic noncommercial personal use."
*Id.* at 1079.

4. **Commercial Use and Presumptions of Unfairness.** In dissent in *Sony*, Justice
Blackmun emphasized that traditional applications of the fair use doctrine centered on uses that were "productive," and that time-shifting is
not consistent with this approach. *Campbell v. Acuff-Rose Music Co.*,
decided nearly a decade after *Sony*, represents something of a vindica-
tion for Justice Blackmun's emphasis on "productive" use, but it also

represents a retreat from the strong statement in *Sony* that "[i]f the Betamax were used to make copies for a commercial or profit-making purpose, such use would presumptively be unfair." Under *Campbell*, the "commercial" character of the defendant's use is one factor to be weighed along with all other evidence.

5. *The Market Failure Rationale for Fair Use.* The most lasting influence of *Sony* on fair use jurisprudence has been its discussion of market harm. According to the majority, time-shifting constituted fair use because the copyright owners failed to demonstrate that time-shifting injured markets for broadcast television programming. In an influential article published as the Court was considering its decision, Professor Wendy Gordon articulated a "market failure" rationale for fair use decision-making. *See* Wendy J. Gordon, *Fair Use as Market Failure: A Structural and Economic Analysis of the* Betamax *Case and its Predecessors,* 82 COLUM. L. REV. 1600 (1982). She argued that courts in copyright cases ordinarily should defer to market processes and should be reluctant to excuse copyright infringement as fair use if doing so would interfere with an existing licensing or permissions market, or would interfere with a market that was likely to emerge. Fair use remained appropriate in cases where the use was socially desirable but unlikely to occur via market processes, and where allowing the fair use to proceed would not substantially injure the copyright owner's incentives. Examples of those cases would include circumstances where the copyright owner was likely to refuse consent to the use in order to suppress the work of the "fair user," and where other strong public interests, such as those in teaching, research, and political debate, outweighed copyright concerns.

## Problem

**8-3.** Worksafe Publishing produced a teaching text for avoiding repetitive stress injuries (RSI), such as carpal tunnel syndrome, called "Hands Free." Hands Free, which was published in 1998, includes text and hand-drawn illustrations that describe positions for computer users to employ in order to avoid injuries. In 2001, Bell Computer Corporation decided to include a booklet with each computer that it sold and shipped to a customer that described techniques for ergonomically safe use of the computer. Bell called its booklet, "Safe to Work." During the production of Safe to Work, the manager in charge of the project, Sarah Alden, reviewed Hands Free. The finished version of Safe to Work, which was first distributed with Bell computers in 2002, contained four illustrations and seven phrases that were similar to photographs and phrases in Hands Free. For example, Hands Free contained a hand-drawn illustration of a computer-user's hands, angled wrists, and lower arms positioned over a keyboard, with a caption reading "Angled-Wrist Position — Incorrect." Safe to Work contained a similar photograph with a caption reading "Angled-wrist position — No." Worksafe sued Bell for copyright infringement. Worksafe produced evidence that during 2001, Worksafe offered to sell copies of Hands Free to Bell for distribution with Bell computers, but Bell declined the offer. There was no evidence, however, that Sarah Alden was aware of this negotiation. Bell offered evidence that Hands Free is over 100 pages long and contains 88 photographs in all. Bell also offered evidence that because of widespread publicity over corporate liability for repetitive stress injuries among computer users, by 2000 corporate managers were generally expected to be aware of RSI problems and to know how to train users to avoid them. Is Bell's use of the Worksafe photographs a fair use? *See Compaq Computer Corp. v. Ergonome Inc.,* 387 F.3d 403 (5th Cir. 2004).

---

### COMPARATIVE PERSPECTIVE
### Fair Use and Fair Dealing

Among national copyright systems around the world, only the United States offers a doctrine of "fair use" as a flexible, general-purpose exception to copyright infringement. In the United Kingdom, Australia, and Canada, for example, claims of copyright infringement are subject to the more limited defense of "fair dealing," which permits use of limited portions of copyrighted works for research or private study, for news reporting, and for the purpose of criticism and review. (Australian authorities have begun to consider the possibility of enacting a U.S.-style fair use statute.) "Fair dealing" provisions are clearly consistent with international copyright obligations under the Berne Convention, which acknowledges that national copyright law may include exceptions to the copyright owner's exclusive rights so long as the exceptions meet a three-step test. Under Article 9(2) of the Convention, exceptions and limitations on the rights of copyright owners be confined (1) to certain special cases, (2) which do not conflict with normal exploitation of the work, and (3) do not unreasonably prejudice the legitimate interests of the right holder. Section 107 has never been challenged on the ground that it is inconsistent with this standard, but some scholars have argued that it is, and that international copyright regimes should be amended to permit other countries to develop fair use–style defenses to infringement claims. *See* Ruth Okediji, *Toward an International Fair Use Doctrine,* 39 COLUM. J. TRANSNAT'L L. 75 (2000).

---

## C. FIRST SALE

*STATUTE:* **Limitations on Exclusive Rights: Effect of Transfer of Particular Copy or Phonorecord**
17 U.S.C. §109(a), (b), (c)

In Chapter 6 you encountered the distinction between the intangible "work of authorship" which is protected by copyright, and the tangible medium in which the work is fixed, which is governed by other law. Section 202 of the Act confirms that distinction, and it appears in one additional place in copyright law, known as the "first sale" doctrine, codified in §109. Though the phrase "first sale" does not appear in the Copyright Act, the colloquialism is appropriate. The essence of the doctrine is that once the copyright owner has sold a particular copy of the work, the owner of that copy may lawfully dispose of it, by gift, resale, or rental, without interference by the copyright owner. Because any of those actions might constitute "distributing" copies of the copyrighted work, "first sale" under §109 provides a defense to a claim of infringement under §106(3), the distribution right, but not to other claims of infringement based on other rights of a copyright holder. Owners of lawfully obtained copies of the work are still prohibited from reproducing the work or preparing derivative works without the permission of the copyright owner.

Like fair use, first sale was first codified in the Copyright Act of 1976. The origins of the rule, however, are much older. The principle that underlies first sale has its origins in the common law proposition that restraints on alienation of chattels are disfavored. Its modern form is usually traced to the Supreme Court's decision in *Bobbs-Merrill Co. v. Straus*, 210 U.S. 339 (1908), in which the Court refused to enforce a notice printed inside the front cover of a book that stated, "The price of this book at retail is $1 net. No dealer is licensed to sell it at a less price, and a sale at a less price will be treated as an infringement of the copyright." The notice was deemed to exceed the exclusive right to "vend" the book granted by the copyright statute of the time, and to interfere with the purchaser's ability to resell the book.

The first sale doctrine recognizes copyright owners' legitimate interests in exploiting their works in ways other than selling copies, and it also recognizes developments in technology. First, while §109(a) provides a defense to the infringement of the distribution right, §109(c) includes a counterpart defense to claims of infringement of the public display right, for owners of works, such as paintings, photographs, and sculptures, intended to be "consumed" via display to the public. If you own a lawfully obtained copy of a painting, you may display it publicly in a gallery or a museum or elsewhere to a live audience. Second, §109(b) withdraws part of the first sale defense with respect to copies of computer programs and sound recordings: Neither class of copyrighted works may be disposed of "by rental, lease, or lending" for purposes of "direct or indirect commercial advantage." The original logic of this exception was that consumers who "rented" copies of computer programs and record albums could easily make their own copies before returning the rental versions to the store. Software rental and record rental, in short, created an undue risk of infringement. Section 109(b) does not apply to audiovisual works, so movie rental businesses can rely on §109(a). And §109(b) does not apply to not-for-profit libraries, so your local public library can lend copies of movies and compact discs.

Recall from Chapter 7 that each of the exclusive rights of the copyright owner must be assessed separately in order to determine whether copyright infringement has occurred. For that reason, the fact that the first sale doctrine may provide a defense to a claimed violation of the distribution right does not necessarily mean that the same conduct has not violated another of the copyright owner's exclusive rights. The statute does not explain how to resolve conflicts of this sort.

## LEE v. A.R.T. CO.
### 125 F.3d 580 (7th Cir. 1997)

EASTERBROOK, Circuit Judge.

Annie Lee creates works of art, which she sells through her firm Annie Lee & Friends. Deck the Walls, a chain of outlets for modestly priced art, is among the buyers of her works, which have been registered with the Register of Copyrights. One Deck the Walls store sold some of Lee's notecards and small lithographs to A.R.T. Company, which mounted the works on ceramic tiles (covering the art with transparent epoxy resin in the process) and resold the tiles. Lee contends that these tiles are derivative works, which under 17 U.S.C. §106(2) may not be prepared without the permission of the copyright proprietor. She seeks both monetary and injunctive relief. Her position has the support of two cases holding that A.R.T.'s business violates the copyright laws. *Muñoz v. Albuquerque A.R.T. Co.*, 38 F.3d 1218 (9th Cir. 1994), affirming without published opinion, 829 F. Supp. 309 (D. Alaska 1993); *Mirage Editions, Inc. v. Albuquerque A.R.T. Co.*, 856 F.2d 1341 (9th Cir. 1988). *Mirage Editions*, the only full appellate discussion, dealt with pages cut from books and mounted on tiles; the court of appeals' brief order in *Muñoz* concludes that the reasoning of *Mirage Editions* is equally applicable to works of art that were sold loose. Our district court disagreed with these decisions and entered summary judgment for the defendant. 925 F. Supp. 576 (N.D. Ill.1996).

Now one might suppose that this is an open and shut case under the doctrine of first sale, codified at 17 U.S.C. §109(a). A.R.T. bought the work legitimately, mounted it on a tile, and resold what it had purchased. Because the artist could capture the value of her art's contribution to the finished product as part of the price for the original transaction, the economic rationale for protecting an adaptation as "derivative" is absent. An alteration that includes (or consumes) a complete copy of the original lacks economic significance. One work changes hands multiple times, exactly what §109(a) permits, so it may lack legal significance too. But §106(2) creates a separate exclusive right, to "prepare derivative works", and Lee believes that affixing the art to the tile is "preparation," so that A.R.T. would have violated §106(2) even if it had dumped the finished tiles into the Marianas Trench. For the sake of argument we assume that this is so and ask whether card-on-a-tile is a "derivative work" in the first place.

"Derivative work" is a defined term:

A "derivative work" is a work based upon one or more preexisting works, such as a translation, musical arrangement, dramatization, fictionalization, motion picture version, sound recording, art reproduction, abridgment, condensation, or any other form in which a work may be recast, transformed, or adapted. A work consisting of editorial revisions, annotations, elaborations, or other modifications which, as a whole, represent an original work of authorship, is a "derivative work".

17 U.S.C. §101. The district court concluded that A.R.T.'s mounting of Lee's works on tile is not an "original work of authorship" because it is no different in form or function from displaying a painting in a frame or placing a medallion in a velvet case. No one believes that a museum violates §106(2) every time it changes the frame of a painting that is still under copyright, although the choice of frame or glazing affects the impression the art conveys, and many artists specify frames (or pedestals for sculptures) in detail. *Muñoz* and *Mirage Editions* acknowledge that framing and other traditional means of mounting and displaying art do not infringe authors' exclusive right to make derivative works. Nonetheless, the ninth circuit held, what A.R.T. does creates a derivative work because the epoxy resin bonds the art to the tile. Our district judge thought this a distinction without a difference, and we agree. If changing the way in which a work of art will be displayed creates a derivative work, and if Lee is right about what "prepared" means, then the derivative work is "prepared" when the art is mounted; what happens later is not relevant, because the violation of the §106(2) right has already occurred. If the framing process does not create a derivative work, then mounting art on a tile, which serves as a flush frame, does not create a derivative work. What is more, the ninth circuit erred in assuming that normal means of mounting and displaying art are easily reversible. A painting is placed in a wooden "stretcher" as part of the framing process; this leads to some punctures (commonly tacks or staples), may entail trimming the edges of the canvas, and may affect the surface of the painting as well. Works by Jackson Pollock are notoriously hard to mount without damage, given the thickness of their paint. As a prelude to framing, photographs, prints, and posters may be mounted on stiff boards using wax sheets, but sometimes glue or another more durable substance is employed to create the bond.

Lee wages a vigorous attack on the district court's conclusion that A.R.T.'s mounting process cannot create a derivative work because the change to the work "as a whole" is not sufficiently original to support a copyright. Cases such as *Gracen v. The Bradford Exchange, Inc.*, 698 F.2d 300 (7th Cir. 1983), show that neither A.R.T. nor Lee herself could have obtained a copyright in the card-on-a-tile, thereby not only extending the period of protection for the images but also eliminating competition in one medium of display. After the ninth circuit held that its mounting process created derivative works, A.R.T. tried to obtain a copyright in one of its products; the Register of Copyrights sensibly informed A.R.T. that the card-on-a-tile could not be copyrighted independently of the note card itself. But Lee says that this is irrelevant — that a change in a work's appearance may infringe the exclusive right under §106(2) even if the alteration is too trivial to support an independent copyright. Pointing to the word "original" in the second sentence of the statutory definition, the district judge held that "originality" is essential to a derivative work. This understanding has the support of both cases and respected commentators. E.g., *L. Batlin & Son, Inc. v. Snyder*, 536 F.2d 486 (2d Cir. 1976); Melville B. Nimmer & David Nimmer, 1 *Nimmer on Copyrights* §3.03 (1997). Pointing to the fact that the first sentence in the statutory definition omits any reference to originality, Lee insists that a work may be derivative despite the mechanical nature of the transformation. This view, too, has the support of both cases and respected commentators.

Fortunately, it is not necessary for us to choose sides. Assume for the moment that the first sentence recognizes a set of non-original derivative works. To prevail, then, Lee must show that A.R.T. altered her works in one of the ways mentioned in the first sentence. The tile is not an "art reproduction"; A.R.T. purchased and mounted Lee's original works. That leaves the residual clause: "any other form in which a work may be recast, transformed, or adapted." None of these words fits what A.R.T. did. Lee's works were not "recast" or "adapted." "Transformed" comes closer and gives the ninth circuit some purchase for its view that the permanence of the bond between art and base matters. Yet the copyrighted note cards and lithographs were not "transformed" in the slightest. The art was bonded to a slab of ceramic, but it was not changed in the process. It still depicts exactly what it depicted when it left Lee's studio.[1] If mounting works a "transformation," then changing a painting's frame or a photograph's mat equally produces a derivative work. Indeed, if Lee is right about the meaning of the definition's first sentence, then *any* alteration of a work, however slight, requires the author's permission. We asked at oral argument what would happen if a purchaser jotted a note on one of the note cards, or used it as a coaster for a drink, or cut it in half, or if a collector applied his seal (as is common in Japan); Lee's counsel replied that such changes prepare derivative works, but that as a practical matter artists would not file suit. A definition of derivative work that makes criminals out of art collectors and tourists is jarring despite Lee's gracious offer not to commence civil litigation.

If Lee (and the Ninth Circuit) are right about what counts as a derivative work, then the United States has established through the back door an extraordinarily broad version of authors' moral rights, under which artists may block any modification of their works of which they disapprove. No European version of *droit moral* goes this far. Until recently it was accepted wisdom that the United States did not enforce any claim of moral rights; even bowdlerization of a work was permitted unless the modifications produced a new work so different that it infringed the exclusive right under §106(2). The Visual Artists Rights Act of 1990, Pub. L. 101-650, 104 Stat. 5089, 5123-33, moves federal law in the direction of moral rights, but the cornerstone of the new statute, 17 U.S.C. §106A, does not assist Lee. Section 106A(a)(3)(A) gives an artist the right to "prevent any intentional distortion, mutilation, or other modification of that work which would be prejudicial to his or her honor or reputation". At oral argument Lee's lawyer disclaimed any contention that the sale of her works on tile has damaged her honor or reputation. What is more, §106A applies only to a "work of visual art", a new term defined in §101 to mean either a unique work or part of a limited edition (200 copies or fewer) that has been "signed and consecutively numbered by the author". Lee's note cards and lithographs are not works of visual art under this definition, so she could not invoke §106A even if A.R.T.'s use of her works to produce kitsch had damaged her

---

1. Scholarly disapproval of *Mirage Editions* has been widespread. Goldstein §5.3 at 5:81-82; Nimmer & Nimmer §3.03; Wendy J. Gordon, *On Owning Information: Intellectual Property and the Restitutionary Impulse*, 78 Va. L. Rev. 149, 255 n. 401 (1992).

reputation. It would not be sound to use §106(2) to provide artists with exclusive rights deliberately omitted from the Visual Artists Rights Act. We therefore decline to follow *Muñoz* and *Mirage Editions*.
AFFIRMED.

## Comments

1. *Transformation and Derivative Works.* Is the court in *Lee* correct that a derivative work necessarily transforms the original work on which it is based? Consider the following from the definition of "derivative work" in §101: "A 'derivative work' is a work based upon one or more preexisting works. . . . A work consisting of editorial revisions, annotations, elaborations, or other modifications which, as a whole, represent an original work of authorship, is a 'derivative work'." Has A.R.T. created a "work" that is "based upon" a preexisting work? Alternatively, has A.R.T. created a "work" that consists of "elaborations" which, "as a whole, represent an original work of authorship"? The court is understandably eager to avoid a result that would impose copyright liability on frame shops, but it may not give appropriate deference to the statutory language, and to the "minimal creativity" standard from *Feist Publications, Inc. v. Rural Telephone Service*. Chapter 7 noted that authorized derivative works may be copyrightable if they embody sufficient creativity, but recall from that discussion that courts have sometimes required that copyrightable derivative works demonstrate a higher level of creativity than nonderivative works. *Lee* may reflect a comparable effort to manage competing policy imperatives contained in different portions of the Copyright Act.

2. **Mirage Editions, Inc. v. Albuquerque A.R.T. Co.** The court in *Lee* disagrees with the reasoning of the Court of Appeals for the Ninth Circuit, in *Mirage Editions, Inc. v. Albuquerque A.R.T. Co.,* 856 F.2d 1341 (9th Cir. 1988). In *Mirage Editions*, the defendant purchased a book containing prints of the graphic art of Patrick Nagel, cut individual pages of prints from the book, mounted the individual pages on ceramic tiles, and sold the tiles to the public. The court found that the defendant prepared unauthorized derivative works based on the copyrighted prints. "By removing the individual images from the book and placing them on the tiles, perhaps the appellant has not accomplished reproduction. We conclude, though, that appellant has certainly recast or transformed the individual images by incorporating them into its tile-preparing process." *Id.* at 1344. The court specifically rejected the proposition that the first sale doctrine barred the claim.

3. *Rights in the Work and Rights in the Object.* The exclusive right to prepare derivative works is addressed to the intangible work that is protected by copyright. The first sale doctrine, as a defense to a claim of infringement of the distribution right, is addressed to the tangible object that embodies the copyrighted work. Had the court in *Lee* (and the court in *Mirage Editions*) relied on the distinction between work and object that is confirmed by §202 of the Copyright Act, they might have avoided mistaking the physical modification of the object for transformation of the copy-

righted expression. Had they done so, they might have avoided having to reconcile the derivative works right under §106(2) and the first sale doctrine under §109(a).

# D. COMPULSORY LICENSES AND REGULATORY COPYRIGHT

Those sections of the Copyright Act that define eligibility for copyright, the exclusive rights of the copyright owner, and defenses to claims of copyright infringement are relatively few in number, and they are relatively brief. The vast bulk of the text of the Copyright Act is dedicated to administration of what one commentator refers to as "regulatory copyright": detailed specification of the rights and obligations of copyright owners in industry- and market-specific contexts that are implemented largely either via administrative processes or through litigation outside the boundaries of "ordinary" suits for copyright infringement. *See* Joseph P. Liu, *Regulatory Copyright*, 83 N. CAR. L. REV. 87 (2004). This section describes the major regulatory provisions of the Copyright Act: "mechanical" licenses for creation of cover recordings of musical compositions; compulsory licenses for transmission of copyrighted works through cable and satellite television systems; and special exemptions for certain uses of copyrighted works by not-for-profit and charitable organizations. As you read these materials, consider the ways in which each provision of the statute serves the various policies and goals of the Copyright Act that you have encountered so far. In addition, consider how compulsory licensing may be used to serve additional purposes, such as reducing the costs associated with exploiting and getting access to copyrighted works; limiting the risk of anticompetitive behavior; and providing special subsidies to certain institutions, actors, and/or markets.

## 1. Compulsory Licenses

Under certain limited circumstances, copyright owners have no power to object to reuse of their copyrighted works. Qualifying users may reproduce, transmit, or otherwise exploit the works, provided they comply with various obligations — most importantly, payment of appropriate compensation — specified by statute. The mechanics of compensation involve royalty rates set by statute or by Copyright Office regulation; payments collected by the Copyright Office; and royalties distributed to qualifying copyright interests. These "compulsory" licenses have made their way into the Copyright Act for a variety of reasons, each having to do with the specifics of the affected industry. What they share, however, is a concern that litigation to enforce the copyright owner's exclusive rights, which is copyright's standard mechanism for assuring a balance between the incentives of copyright owners and access and reuse privileges of copyright users and consumers, will not deal adequately with concerns that copyright's monopoly should remain limited in scope.

### a. Mechanical Licensing

The oldest compulsory license in the Copyright Act appears in §115 and is known generally as "mechanical" licensing, after the technology that gave rise to it as part of the Copyright Act of 1909. "Mechanical" licensing grew out of *White-Smith Music Publ'g Co. v. Apollo Co*, 209 U.S. 1 (1908), noted in Chapter 7 in connection with the development of the copyright owner's exclusive right to prepare derivative works. *White-Smith* determined that makers of player piano rolls did not infringe copyrights in musical compositions encoded on those rolls. The Court's ruling was predicated on the notion that piano rolls did not constitute "copies" of copyrighted musical compositions. The copyright statute was subsequently revised to provide that owners of copyrighted musical works have the exclusive right to make such "mechanical" reproductions of their works (in player piano rolls, vinyl phonograph records, and other "phonorecords"), but Congress was also concerned that one piano roll company, the Aeolian Company, might secure a monopoly over the market for piano rolls. Accordingly, Congress implemented a compulsory license system: Any piano roll manufacturer could use any copyrighted musical composition without securing prior permission of the copyright owner, so long as the work had previously been licensed for mechanical reproduction, and so long as the producer of the new mechanical version paid a statutory royalty to the copyright owner, then set at 2 cents per copy.

Today, the "mechanical" licensing provision in §115 works very much in the same way. Section 115 qualifies the reproduction right and the distribution right for nondramatic musical works, that is, for stand-alone songs, rather than for music incorporated into a dramatic work, such as an opera. (Importantly, however, the license applies only to the copyright in the musical composition. Rights to publicly perform the sound recording in the mechanical reproduction, which are significant in the case of digital reproduction, must be licensed separately.) Once phonorecords of such a work have been distributed to the public under the authority of the copyright owner, then any person may make and distribute phonorecords of the work (that is to say, copies of "cover" versions of the song, not reproductions of the recording), including CDs and cassette tapes, so long as the purpose is to produce phonorecords for public use (i.e., for consumer purchase and enjoyment). This "mechanical" licensing scheme also includes the right to make "digital phonorecord deliveries," or DPDs, which include downloadable digital files, but not streamed music.

Section 115 is sometimes known as the "cover recording" right, because the compulsory license includes the right to arrange the work "to the extent necessary to conform it to the style or manner of interpretation of the performance involved, but the arrangement shall not change the basic melody or fundamental character of the work, the different version...." 17 U.S.C. §115(a)(2). The maker of the cover recording does not obtain a copyright in this version of the work, unless the original copyright owner consents. To obtain a compulsory license under this section, the maker of the cover recording must give prior notice to the copyright owner of the intention to produce the recording and must make quarterly payments of royalties fixed by statute. As of January 1, 2006, those rates are 9.1 cents or 1.75 cents per minute of playing time or fraction thereof, for each phonorecord made and distributed, whichever is greater. 17 U.S.C. §115(b), (c)(2). So long as proper notice is given and royalty payments are made, the copyright owner may not object to creation and distribution of the cover recording, unless a change in musical genre produces a new version of the work that changes "the basic melody or fundamental character of the work."

### *POLICY PERSPECTIVE*
### Cover Recordings

The cover recording right is sometimes cited as a model example of how copyright law balances the interests of creators in compensation and incentives, and the interests of consumers and later creators in access and production of new work. The full picture, however, may be more complex.

On the one hand, the cover recording right has been celebrated by some artists and critics because it gives new recording artists simple and inexpensive access to songs that may already have been made popular by previous artists. Some of the most powerful, successful, and/or simply fun popular recordings of the last 30 years are covers: Jimi Hendrix's cover of Bob Dylan's "All Along the Watchtower;" the Talking Heads' cover of "Take Me to the River," written by Al Green and Mabon Hodges and originally recorded by Al Green; and the White Stripes's cover of Dolly Parton's "Jolene," for example. For a recent example of this perspective on the cover recording right, see Lawrence Lessig, FREE CULTURE: HOW BIG MEDIA USES TECHNOLOGY AND THE LAW TO LOCK DOWN CULTURE AND CONTROL CREATIVITY 56-58 (2005).

On the other hand, some critics have argued that the cover recording right has enabled mainstream pop artists, particularly white artists, to capitalize unfairly on songs and songwriting produced initially by niche artists, particularly African-American artists working in jazz and R&B genres. The cover recording right allows later artists to pay relatively low, fixed royalties to the original songwriter, and to keep all of the profits from the cover recording. This was particularly true during the 1950s. More recent examples of covers of R&B works by established white pop artists include Rita Coolidge's cover of Jackie Wilson's "Your Love Keeps Lifting Me Higher," written by Gary L. Jackson, Carl Smith, and Rayard Miner and first recorded by Jackie Wilson, and Michael Bolton's cover of "Sittin' on the Dock of the Bay," written by Otis Redding and Steve Cropper and first recorded by Otis Redding. For more on this perspective on the history of cover recordings, see Siva Vaidhyanathan, COPYRIGHTS AND COPYWRONGS: THE RISE OF INTELLECTUAL PROPERTY AND HOW IT THREATENS CREATIVITY 132-140 (2001).

In practice, few makers of cover recordings exercise the statutory rights created by §115. Instead, most cover recordings are produced via voluntary licenses administered by a private company, the Harry Fox Agency, which serves as an agent for music publishers (who own or license most music composition copyrights from composers) and which administers licenses for mechanical reproductions as well as for other uses authorized by the publishers. Harry Fox maintains a website at *http://www.harryfox.com* and offers both publishers and licensees a number of administrative advantages over complying with the statutory requirements specified in §115. First, for licensees, it simplifies the task of locating and contacting copyright owners, and making royalty payments. Second, for music publishers, it simplifies the task of keeping track of notices and incoming royalty obligations. Rates charged by Harry Fox typically mirror or (if authorized by the copyright owner) fall just below those specified in the Copyright Act.

## Note on the Digital Performance Right in Sound Recordings Act

In 1995, Congress amended §106, adding a new §106(6) that provides a limited public performance right for owners of sound recording copyrights. Sound recordings still lack a general public performance right. That means, for example, that radio stations must pay royalties to the owners of songwriting copyrights (for performance of their musical compositions) but not to performers or other owners of recording copyrights (for performance of their sound recordings). In §106(6), under the Digital Performance Right in Sound Recordings Act (DPRSRA) of 1995, copyright owners were granted a public performance right in "digital audio transmissions," primarily as a means of helping copyright owners stop record piracy. The scope of this right is detailed in §114 of the Copyright Act.

For sound recordings performed by "digital audio transmission," §114 sets up a three-tiered system for determining whether a compulsory license applies, on the one hand, or whether the work is subject to a copyright owner's exclusive right, and therefore to voluntary licensing, on the other hand. Digital transmissions are categorized according to the likelihood that the transmissions are likely to affect sales of phonorecords. "Broadcast" transmissions, which are least likely to affect sales, are outside the scope of the §106(6) right. No royalties need be paid for these. Transmissions that have the potential to affect sales are subject to a compulsory license (referred to as a "statutory" license by the statute); these consist of digital services that are not "interactive" (so that recipients cannot specify or anticipate what music will be played) and are subject to a variety of additional restrictions. Transmissions that are the most likely to affect sales, or "interactive" transmissions, are within the scope of the §106(6) right and are not subject to a compulsory license, meaning that the copyright owner retains the full authority to enter into voluntary licenses. *See* 17 U.S.C. §114(b)-(j).

Reliance on the tiered system in §114 by Internet music services is complicated by the fact that §114 applies only to the sound recording copyright. Digital transmissions of recorded music involve rights in musical compositions, which are not governed by §114 and therefore must be licensed separately, as well as sound recording copyrights. Yet §115, which deals with mechanical licenses for musical compositions, applies only to distribution of "cover" recordings; it does not offer a licensing scheme for firms that would simply like to distribute existing music online. At present, there is no "one-stop-shopping" for Internet music services that would like to license all necessary rights to make recorded music available on the Internet. Acquiring those rights is expensive and time-consuming.

## Note on Collective Rights Organizations

The Harry Fox Agency is an example of a "Collective Rights Organization," or CRO. CROs are private entities which were developed to solve problems associated with administering copyright interests on a large scale, or what economists refer to as "transactions costs" problems, where the time and expense associated with an individual copyright owner's identifying and negotiating voluntary licenses for sometimes modest royalties likely outweigh possible profits from the activity. *See* Robert P. Merges, *Contracting into Liability Rules: Intellectual Property Rights and Collective Rights Organizations*, 84 CAL. L. REV. 1293 (1996). In addition to the Harry Fox Agency, the best known CROs in copyright are the three performing rights organizations: ASCAP (American Society of Composers, Authors, and Publishers), established in 1913 (*http://www.ascap.com*); BMI (Broadcast Music, Inc.), established in 1939 (*http://www.bmi.com*); and SESAC, Inc., founded in 1930 (*http://www.sesac.com*). These organizations are not created by statute, though they are recognized as "performing rights societies" in §101 of the Copyright Act, and they do not administer rights subject to compulsory licenses. Instead, they license public performance rights on behalf of songwriters and music publishers for enormous catalogs of music and for a breathtaking variety of venues where that music is publicly performed—from radio and television stations to restaurants, bars, sports stadiums, shopping malls, elevators, and funeral homes. The performing rights societies offer both blanket licenses to all or large portions of their respective catalogs, as well as licenses for the public performance of individual compositions.

Blanket licenses offered by performing rights societies may be characterized as market-allocating agreements among competitors (the owners of music composition copyrights), and as such they have attracted the attention of federal antitrust enforcement authorities. Since 1941, both ASCAP and BMI have operated under the auspices of consent decrees supervised by federal district courts. The decrees regulate the terms under which each organization makes licenses available, assures that the organizations charge reasonable license fees, and provide that the organizations may require only that songwriters and publishers grant them non-exclusive licenses, giving them flexibility to join—and leave—the organization.

## b. Cable and Satellite Systems

The Copyright Act includes two detailed licensing provisions for systems that retransmit broadcast television signals. The compulsory license for cable retransmission, at 17 U.S.C. §111, was enacted as part of the 1976 Act on the heels of actions by the Federal Communications Commission (FCC) to limit cable system transmission of distant network television signals. The statute also followed a pair of Supreme Court opinions holding that retransmission of broadcast television signals by Community Antenna Television (CATV) systems, precursors of today's cable systems, did not constitute "public performance" of copyrighted television programming under the 1909 Copyright Act. *See Fortnightly Corp. v. United Artists Television, Inc.,* 392 U.S. 390 (1968); *Teleprompter Corp. v. Columbia Broadcasting System, Inc.,* 415 U.S. 394 (1974). Because the Supreme Court's rulings effectively granted cable system operators immunity from liability under copyright law, while the FCC's actions limited cable operators' ability to transmit broadcast content, the 1976 Act involved a compromise among broadcasters, cable system operators, and providers of copyrighted content: Transmission of broadcast television programming over these systems is covered by the public performance right, but those transmissions are subject to a compulsory license. So long as cable operators submit periodic accountings of their use of broadcast material, they may carry broadcast content, including both material originated locally and material originated by broadcast networks. The compulsory license also applies to non-network signals that are not originated locally, such as broadcasts of sporting events. As to those signals the license requires payment of a fee, specified in the statute, collected by the Copyright Office and distributed to suppliers of copyrighted material. Cable systems are simultaneously subject to regulation by the FCC, applying the Communications Act, and must observe non-copyright-related rules including "must carry" obligations with respect to local broadcast stations; blackouts for sporting events; syndication exclusivity; and nonduplication of network programming.

In 1988, Congress added a compulsory license for operators of satellite television systems, which appears at 17 U.S.C. §119. The compulsory license of §111 was extended to allow retransmission of network signals by satellite systems serving "unserved households," largely in rural areas, which could not receive sufficiently strong over-the-air signals from local broadcast stations. In 1999, Congress renewed §119, grandfathering in existing satellite television customers (many of whom were receiving satellite service in urban areas using newer, more compact satellite dishes, in violation of the "unserved household" requirement). At the same time, it authorized satellite carriers to retransmit local television broadcasts into local market areas without paying royalties. *See* 17 U.S.C. §122. Network and superstation broadcasts are subject to the compulsory license. At the same time, Congress added the rule (in the Communications Act) that if a satellite provider retransmits any local broadcast station, it must carry all of them. If a provider wants to limit the local broadcasts that it carries, it can do so by negotiating private, voluntary retransmission agreements.

Following extended and detailed negotiations among satellite providers, providers of copyrighted content, broadcasters, and cable system operators (who compete with satellite providers), the compulsory license for satellite providers was renewed again in late 2004 and extended until 2010, adding provisions to cover certain satellite retransmission of digital network signals.

## 2. Special Exemptions for Libraries, Not-for-Profit Organizations, and Intermediaries

The Copyright Act has numerous provisions designed to ensure that certain markets or industries function more profitably or effectively in the face of the broad set of exclusive rights set out in §106. Earlier, in Chapter 7, you encountered §117, which is designed to permit use of copyrighted computer programs when computer users reproduce the work in copies. Section 121 permits certain reproduction and distribution of previously published copyrighted works in formats for use by the blind or disabled. Section 116, the so-called "jukebox" license, was originally adopted as part of the 1909 Copyright Act, which made performance of a mechanical reproduction of a musical composition via a "coin-operated machine" exempt from the public performance right. This exemption from royalty obligations effectively created the jukebox industry. It was replaced with a compulsory license for jukeboxes in the 1976 Act. The current form of §116 encourages private industry negotiations regarding royalty rates. Section 118 grants public broadcasters the right to use certain copyrighted works under royalty rates to be established by the Copyright Office and offers a limited exemption from the antitrust laws for purposes of enabling public broadcasters to bargain collectively with copyright owners, in lieu of an administrative rate-setting proceeding. Section 112 authorizes the creation of certain "ephemeral" reproductions of copyrighted works in the course of transmitting them, a right that is particularly important to broadcasters.

Section 108 creates a set of exemptions from copyright infringement liability for libraries and archives, permitting limited reproduction and distribution of copies of copyrighted works for researchers and library patrons, and for preservation purposes, under conditions intended not to deprive copyright owners of legitimate economic expectations. "Interlibrary loan" arrangements, for example, are specifically recognized as lawful under this section, but "systematic" reproduction of copyrighted works by libraries and archives is prohibited.

Section 110 of the Copyright Act includes a series of exemptions from liability for public performances or displays of copyright works in contexts that might be characterized, generally, as noncommercial. Section 110(1) addresses "face-to-face teaching activities of a nonprofit educational institution." Section 110(2) addresses "distance learning" and includes provisions, added in 2002, designed to accommodate distance education via digital computer networks. Section 110(3) addresses display and performance of copyrighted works as part of religious services. Section 110(4) addresses use of copyrighted works for educational, religious, or charitable purposes, so long as there is no admission charge for the event at which the work is performed or displayed. Section 110(5) consists of the so-called "homestyle" exemption for performance and display of copyrighted musical works via a radio or stereo of the sort commonly found in private homes, limited to businesses and stereo equipment of a certain size and designed for small businesses that play music or television in their stores. The statute contains additional exemptions for agricultural and horticultural organizations (§110(6)); for playing music in music stores (§110(7)); for certain performances for the blind, deaf, or other disabled individuals (§110(8) and (9)); and for veterans' and fraternal organizations (§110(10)).

## Note on U.S. Compliance with TRIPs and the Berne Convention

As a member of the Berne Convention, the United States must ensure that its menu of compulsory licenses and special exemptions is consistent with its obligations to ensure minimum levels of protection for copyright owners. The Berne Convention authorizes member countries to limit the public performance right through compulsory license and other compensation systems, referred to in the treaty at "equitable remuneration." Berne Convention, art. 11bis(2). Article 10bis(2) provides for certain special exemptions: "It shall be a matter for legislation in the countries of the Union . . . to the extent justified by the purpose, of literary or artistic works by way of illustration in publications, broadcasts or sound or visual recordings for teaching, provided such utilization is compatible with fair practice." Also, recall from the discussion of fair use and fair dealing, *supra,* that in Article 9(2) the Berne Convention provides a "three-step" test for evaluating limitations and exceptions to the rights of the copyright owner. Those rights may be limited to certain special cases, which do not conflict with a normal exploitation of the work and do not unreasonably prejudice the legitimate interest of the right holder. This three-step test is incorporated into Article 13 of the TRIPs Agreement on intellectual property obligations in international trade law.

Under both the Berne Convention and the TRIPs Agreement, compliance with these standards is largely a matter of national law, but TRIPs includes an enforcement mechanism—complaints by World Trade Organization members, addressed to a WTO Dispute Resolution Panel—that may raise the cost of national legislation. As you read in Chapter 7, in connection with the exclusive right of public performance, one American exception, the §110(5) "homestyle" exemption for performance of nondramatic musical works, was challenged by the European Union in proceedings before the WTO. The finding in favor of the European Union resulted in a settlement payment by the United States, but not in a change to American law.

## Note on Safe Harbors for ISPs Under the Digital Millennium Copyright Act

The Copyright Act addresses a separate class of exempt institutions in §512, which deals with the liability of service providers on the Internet. Section 512 was part of the Digital Millennium Copyright Act of 1998, whose "anticircumvention" provisions you encountered earlier in Chapter 7. Under §512, "service providers" are given immunity from liability for monetary damages and for most injunctive relief in four circumstances, each of which is intended to address situations where the service provider is, in effect, "passively" or automatically supplying information to consumers rather than actively reproducing copyrighted material without permission. Granting immunity to these "intermediaries" on the Internet is, among other things, a way to ensure that the smooth functioning of the Internet is not interrupted by a constant flow of claims of copyright infringement directed to those who are not active participants in infringing activity.

Section 512(a) provides immunity for "transmitting, routing, or providing connections for, material through a system or network controlled or operated by or for the service provider, or by reason of the intermediate and transient storage of that material in the course of such transmitting, routing, or providing connections...." Internet service providers, in short, are not liable for copyright infringement merely on account of their function as "conduits," providing automated access to material on the Internet in response to consumer requests, such as mouse clicks.

Section 512(b) provides immunity for liability "by reason of the intermediate and temporary storage of material on a system or network controlled or operated by or for the service provider...." Service providers that provide "caching" capability that allows Internet content to be delivered to consumers quickly and effectively are reproducing copyrighted works in the course of doing so, but are not liable for copyright infringement.

Section 512(c) provides immunity for infringement "by reason of the storage at the direction of a user of material that resides on a system or network controlled or operated by or for the service provider...." A service provider that simply hosts Internet content supplied by customers is not liable, ordinarily, for copyright infringement committed by its customers.

Section 512(d) provides immunity for infringement "by reason of the provider referring or linking users to an online location containing infringing material or infringing activity, by using information location tools, including a directory, index, reference, pointer, or hypertext link...." This subsection is designed to address indexes of material on the World Wide Web and search engines.

Each of these four "safe harbors" comes with important conditions and limitations, and whether the service provider is a "service provider" for purposes of §512 must be investigated under the definition of "service provider" given in §512(k).

Because the framework of §512 safe harbors is built around the concept that "passive" service providers should not be liable for copyright infringement, litigation under §512 has focused on the extent of service providers' engagement with selecting and posting content supplied by others, and their knowledge of infringing activity. All four safe harbors require that service providers post and enforce policies regarding termination of repeat copyright infringers using their services, and §512(c) and (d), in particular, are available to service providers only so long as they disable access to infringing content upon complaint from the copyright owner. However, note that §512 operates alongside standards for both direct infringement as well as for indirect copyright infringement. In *CoStar Group, Inc. v. LoopNet, Inc.*, 373 F.3d 544 (4th Cir. 2004), the court held that a website that hosted infringing photographs of real estate listings was protected under §512(c) (material posted at the direction of a user) despite the fact that the site exercised some "gatekeeping" review of each photograph before posting it on the site.

# CHAPTER
# 9

---

# Remedies for Copyright Infringement

Section 501 of the Copyright Act provides that any violation of the exclusive rights of the copyright owner constitutes an infringement of copyright. The Act provides several remedial tools for the copyright owner. The first is equitable relief, often regarded in practice as the primary or default remedy, though formally in copyright and elsewhere, injunctions are available only so long as legal relief—damages—is inadequate. Section A below reviews the availability of injunctive relief in copyright cases. Section B describes mechanisms for recovering money from infringers, in the form of actual damages or lost profits, or both, as well as "statutory damages." Statutory damages, an award of damages within a range specified by the Act, exist partly to offset the fact that there is no provision for punitive or treble damages in copyright law, and partly to account for cases in which proof of actual damages may be difficult. Section C addresses other remedial options available to the prevailing copyright owner, even in the absence of a successful copyright infringement lawsuit: seizure, impoundment, and destruction of infringing articles. Section D discusses various related aspects of the copyright infringement lawsuit, including parties, timing, jurisdiction, criminal copyright enforcement, and remedies available under statutes related to the Copyright Act, particularly the Digital Millennium Copyright Act.

*STATUTE:* **Infringement of Copyright**
17 U.S.C. §501(a), (b)

*STATUTE:* **Registration and Infringement Actions**
17 U.S.C. §411(a)

As you read in Chapter 6, the United States has mostly done away with formal prerequisites to obtaining copyright interests. Formalities have not disappeared entirely, however. Before filing a lawsuit for copyright infringement, the copyright owner must comply with an important procedural prerequisite. Under §411 of the Copyright Act, when the suit for infringement is based on a United States work, copyright in that work must be registered with the Copyright Office. The registration requirement is jurisdictional. If the plaintiff has not registered its copyright, the court must and will dismiss the case. The limitation of §411 to United States works brings the United States into compliance with its obligations under the Berne Convention. Owners of non-United States works may file claims for copyright infringement in the United States without registering their works with the Copyright Office.

# A. INJUNCTIVE RELIEF

*STATUTE:* **Remedies for Infringement: Injunctions**
17 U.S.C. §502

Prevailing plaintiffs in copyright infringement lawsuits are not entitled to injunctions as a matter of right (in fact, §502, speaking of a court's authority to enter injunctive relief, uses the permissive "may"), but as a practical matter an injunction against further infringement is often the copyright owner's preferred remedy, and sometimes its only one. The scope of the injunction is as important as the fact of the injunction. Copyright owners that want courts to enter injunctions must request equitable relief, and they typically request relief that takes a specific form. The form that the relief takes—provisional or preliminary relief; permanent relief; forbidding certain types of reproduction or distribution, but not others—must be supported by appropriate showings of facts that go to the traditional elements of equitable relief: the inadequacy of legal relief, and the weighing of the hardships in favor of the plaintiff.

## ABKCO MUSIC, INC. v. STELLAR RECORDS, INC.
### 96 F.3d 60 (2d Cir. 1996)

OWEN, District Judge.

This is an appeal from an order of the District Court for the Southern District of New York (Batts, *J.*), entered on August 10, 1995, preliminarily enjoining defendant-appellant Performance Tracks, Inc. ("Tracks") from publishing without authority the lyrics to copyrighted songs owned by plaintiffs-appellees ABKCO Music Inc. and ABKCO Music and Records Inc. ("ABKCO"), thus prohibiting Tracks from distributing its compact discs containing the copyrighted songs. We affirm.

Although this presents a case of first impression in terms of the technology at issue, the applicable legal principles are well-settled. ABKCO owns the copyrights to seven musical compositions by Mick Jagger and Keith Richards of the Rolling Stones, including the rock-and-roll classics "Satisfaction (I Can't Get No)," "Jumping Jack Flash," and "Brown Sugar." Despite many requests, ABKCO has never licensed these famous songs for use in the "karaoke" or "sing-along" industry.

Tracks, a newcomer in the music field, is in the sing-along industry. It uses a new technology to encode on a compact disc ("CD") not only the audio rendition of a song, but also the contemporaneous video display of a song's lyrics. Thus, for a user who has a CD player with a video output, the lyrics of the songs can be displayed on a video screen in "real time" as the songs are playing so that the viewer can sing the lyrics along with the recorded artist. No other image or information appears, and the user cannot print the lyrics from the screen or control the speed of the music or lyrics. The Tracks discs, called "Compact Discs + Graphics" ("CD+G's"), will provide audio playback alone when played on standard CD players. These CD+G's are similar in purpose to the more familiar karaoke laser discs, which are quite popular in this country and abroad for entertainment at parties and nightclubs. Like the CD+G's, karaoke discs display song lyrics against video images, enabling people to sing in time to the music. The primary difference between traditional karaoke discs and CD+G's is that CD+G's display only the lyrics, whereas karaoke discs display some video image, such as a sun-drenched beach, behind the song lyrics. Under the Copyright Act of 1976, 17 U.S.C. §101 *et seq.*, the producers and distributors of karaoke versions of songs must acquire synchronization or "synch" licenses from the copyright owners of the songs to legally manufacture karaoke discs; a copyright owner may negotiate, if so disposed, the karaoke use of a song and the terms of the authorizing synch license with a karaoke maker.

Tracks did not secure synchronization licenses from ABKCO, but instead, viewing its products as "phonorecords," obtained "compulsory licenses" for the compositions, pursuant to the Copyright Act, 17 U.S.C. §115, which permits the manufacture and distribution of new "cover" versions of copyrighted musical works as long as the licensee follows the statutory notice requirements and pays the proper royalty fees....

\* \* \*

Tracks sent ABKCO a CD+G entitled "Songs of the Rolling Stones" containing the compositions, as well as notices of its intention to obtain compulsory licenses for the compositions. ABKCO thereupon informed Tracks that the Rolling Stones CD+G infringed on its copyrights of the compositions, and shortly thereafter initiated this action.

On July 5, 1995, ABKCO obtained a temporary restraining order. Thereafter, on August 10, 1995, Judge Deborah A. Batts, ruling from the bench, granted a preliminary injunction enjoining Tracks from "further publishing the lyrics of plaintiff's copyrighted Rolling Stones songs without authorization to do so," concluding that the visual depiction of the lyrics constituted an unauthorized publication of the lyrics, infringing ABKCO's copyrights. Tracks appeals pursuant to 28 U.S.C. §1292(a)(1).

It is well-settled in this circuit that a preliminary injunction requires a showing of (1) irreparable harm and (2) either (a) a likelihood of success on the merits or (b) sufficiently serious questions about the merits to make them a fair ground for litigation and a balance of hardships tipping decidedly toward the party requesting relief. To demonstrate likelihood of success, ABKCO must establish *prima facie* a copyright infringement by showing that it owns valid copyrights and that Tracks has engaged in unauthorized copying. As to irreparable harm, generally when a copyright plaintiff makes out a *prima facie* showing of infringement, irreparable harm may be presumed.

Our review of an order granting or denying a preliminary injunction is generally limited to whether there has been an abuse of discretion, which usually involves either the application of an incorrect legal standard or reliance on clearly erroneous findings of fact.

Tracks asserts as error, first, the district court's conclusion that the CD+G's visual display of song lyrics constitutes an unauthorized reproduction in violation of 17 U.S.C. §106 because the visual feature of the CD+G's is not within the ambit of the compulsory license provisions of 17 U.S.C. §115, and second, the court's holding that the irreparable harm requirement had been satisfied.

In granting the preliminary injunction, the court below properly found that Tracks' compulsory licenses do not give it the right to publish the compositions' lyrics on a screen. Song lyrics enjoy independent copyright protection as "literary works," [1 Melville B. Nimmer & David Nimmer, *Nimmer on Copyright* §2.05[B] (1995)], and the right to print a song's lyrics is exclusively that of the copyright holder under 17 U.S.C. §106(1). Thus, while a compulsory license permits the recording of a "cover" version of a song, it does not permit the inclusion of a copy of the lyrics. That requires the separate permission of the copyright holder.

\* \* \*

A time-honored method of facilitating singing along with music has been to furnish the singer with a printed copy of the lyrics. Copyright holders have always enjoyed exclusive rights over such copies. While projecting lyrics on a screen and producing printed copies of the lyrics, of course, have their differences, there is no reason to treat them differently for purposes of the Copyright Act.

\* \* \*

Lastly, Tracks contends that the injunction issued by the court below was erroneously granted without an adequate demonstration of irreparable harm. Tracks asserts "[i]t is a dramatic leap in logic to argue that the addition of the lyrics to an indisputably permissible activity [rerecording a copyrighted composition pursuant to the compulsory license provisions of 17 U.S.C. §115] somehow instantly creates irreparable harm to the copyright holders." We disagree. It is precisely this addition of the lyrics to be projected on the screen that renders the CD+G's potentially lucrative for Tracks, and at the same time, if not enjoined, would leave ABKCO with a difficult reconstruction of damages should that issue arise at a later time, and would put ABKCO at the risk of disadvantageous exploitation of its artists in ways it would not have authorized. In any event, in a copyright infringement case, once a *prima facie* case of infringement has been demonstrated, irreparable harm is normally presumed, and substantial deference is given to a district court finding of irreparable harm. Thus, the court below, having a sound legal and factual basis for its assessment of a likelihood of success of on the merits, was justified in relying on the presumption of irreparable harm.

CONCLUSION

For the foregoing reasons, the order of the district court granting the preliminary injunction is affirmed.

# Comments

1. *Presumption of Irreparable Harm.* At stake in *ABKCO Music* is an order granting a preliminary injunction in favor of the copyright owner. The court adheres to the rule, followed nearly universally in copyright cases, that a demonstration of likelihood of success on the merits (which follows from a showing of a prima facie case of infringement) produces a presumption of irreparable harm, and thus leads virtually automatically to entry of injunctive relief.

2. *Preliminary Injunction Standards Generally.* In general, entry of a preliminary injunction is appropriate once four tests have been met: (i) whether the plaintiff will have an adequate remedy at law or will be irreparably harmed if the injunction does not issue; (ii) whether the threatened injury to the plaintiff outweighs the threatened harm the injunction might inflict on the defendant; (iii) whether the plaintiff has at least a reasonable likelihood of success on the merits; and (iv) whether the granting of a preliminary injunction will disserve the public interest. *See Atari, Inc. v. North American Philips Consumer Electronics Corp.,* 672 F.2d 607, 613 (7th Cir. 1982). So long as the court indulges the presumption in favor of irreparable injury, a plausible claim of copyright infringement leads almost inexorably to entry of a preliminary injunction. On the one hand, as the court recognizes in *ABKCO Music,* failure to enter an injunction on facts where infringement seems clear would lead, in effect, to a sort of compulsory license in favor of the infringer, who remains at liberty to use the plaintiff's copyrighted work — even in circumstances in which the plaintiff might legitimately object — so long as appropriate compensation is paid. On the other hand, it is reasonable to be concerned that injunctions might thus be entered too easily, and too frequently, even in cases in which infringement turns out to be clear. In many circumstances, an infringing defendant will be able to compensate the copyright owner for the harm, and an injunction, particularly a broad one, runs the risk of interfering with a range of activity that is broader than the infringement itself.

## UNIVERSAL CITY STUDIOS, INC. v. REIMERDES

111 F. Supp. 2d 294 (S.D.N.Y. 2000), aff'd sub nom. Universal City Studios, Inc. v. Corley, 273 F.3d 429 (2d Cir. 2001)

KAPLAN, District Judge.

Plaintiffs, eight major United States motion picture studios, distribute many of their copyrighted motion pictures for home use on digital versatile disks ("DVDs"), which contain copies of the motion pictures in digital form. They protect those motion pictures from copying by using an encryption system called CSS. CSS-protected motion pictures on DVDs may be viewed only on players and computer drives equipped with licensed technology that permits the devices to decrypt and play — but not to copy — the films.

Late last year, computer hackers devised a computer program called DeCSS that circumvents the CSS protection system and allows CSS-protected motion pictures to be copied and played on devices that lack the licensed decryption technology. Defendants quickly posted DeCSS on their Internet web site, thus making it readily available to much of the world. Plaintiffs promptly brought this action under the Digital Millennium Copyright Act (the "DMCA") to enjoin defendants from posting DeCSS and to prevent them from electronically "linking" their site to others that post DeCSS. Defendants responded with what they termed "electronic civil disobedience" — increasing their efforts to link their web site to a large number of others that continue to make DeCSS available.

Defendants contend that their actions do not violate the DMCA and, in any case, that the DMCA, as applied to computer programs, or code, violates the First Amendment.[2] This is the Court's decision after trial, and the decision may be summarized in a nutshell.

Defendants argue first that the DMCA should not be construed to reach their conduct, principally because the DMCA, so applied, could prevent those who wish to gain access to technologically protected copyrighted works in order to make fair — that is, non-infringing — use of them from doing so. They argue that those who would make fair use of technologically protected copyrighted works need means, such as DeCSS, of circumventing access control measures not for piracy, but to make lawful use of those works.

Technological access control measures have the capacity to prevent fair uses of copyrighted works as well as foul. Hence, there is a potential tension between the use of such access control measures and fair use. Defendants are not the first to recognize that possibility. As the DMCA made its way through the legislative process, Congress was preoccupied with precisely this issue. Proponents of strong restrictions on circumvention of access control measures argued that they were essential if copyright holders were to make their works available in digital form because digital works otherwise could be pirated too easily. Opponents contended that strong anti-circumvention measures would extend the copyright monopoly inappropriately and prevent many fair uses of copyrighted material.

Congress struck a balance. The compromise it reached, depending upon future technological and commercial developments, may or may not prove ideal. But the solution it enacted is clear. The potential tension to which defendants point does not absolve them of liability under the statute. There is no serious question that defendants' posting of DeCSS violates the DMCA.

Defendants' constitutional argument ultimately rests on two propositions — that computer code, regardless of its function, is "speech" entitled

---

2. Shortly after the commencement of the action, the Court granted plaintiffs' motion for a preliminary injunction barring defendants from posting DeCSS. *Universal City Studios, Inc. v. Reimerdes,* 82 F. Supp. 2d 211 (S.D.N.Y. 2000). Subsequent motions to expand the preliminary injunction to linking and to vacate it were consolidated with the trial on the merits. This opinion reflects the Court's findings of fact, conclusions of law and decision on the merits....

to maximum constitutional protection and that computer code therefore essentially is exempt from regulation by government. But their argument is baseless.

Computer code is expressive. To that extent, it is a matter of First Amendment concern. But computer code is not purely expressive any more than the assassination of a political figure is purely a political statement. Code causes computers to perform desired functions. Its expressive element no more immunizes its functional aspects from regulation than the expressive motives of an assassin immunize the assassin's action.

In an era in which the transmission of computer viruses—which, like DeCSS, are simply computer code and thus to some degree expressive— can disable systems upon which the nation depends and in which other computer code also is capable of inflicting other harm, society must be able to regulate the use and dissemination of code in appropriate circumstances. The Constitution, after all, is a framework for building a just and democratic society. It is not a suicide pact.

* * *

## IV. RELIEF

### A. INJURY TO PLAINTIFFS

The DMCA provides that "[a]ny person injured by a violation of section 1201 or 1202 may bring a civil action in an appropriate United States court for such violation."[259] For the reasons set forth above, plaintiffs obviously have suffered and, absent effective relief, will continue to suffer injury by virtue of the ready availability of means of circumventing the CSS access control system on their DVDs. Defendants nevertheless argue that they have not met the injury requirement of the statute. Their contentions are a farrago of distortions.

They begin with the assertion that plaintiffs have failed to prove that decrypted motion pictures actually are available. To be sure, plaintiffs might have done a better job of proving what appears to be reasonably obvious. They certainly could have followed up on more of the 650 movie titles listed on the web site described above to establish that the titles in fact were available. But the evidence they did adduce is not nearly as meager as defendants would have it. Dr. Shamos [an expert witness for the plaintiffs] did pursue and obtain a pirated copy of a copyrighted, [compressed] motion picture from someone he met in an Internet chat room. An MPAA investigator downloaded between five and ten such copies. And the sudden appearance of listings of available motion pictures on the Internet promptly after DeCSS became available is far from lacking in evidentiary significance. In any case, in order to obtain the relief sought here, plaintiffs need show only a threat of injury by reason of a violation of the statute.[261] The Court finds that plaintiffs overwhelmingly have established a clear threat of injury by reason of defendants' violation of the statute.

259. 17 U.S.C. §1203(a).

261. The statute expressly authorizes injunctions to prevent or restrain violations, 17 U.S.C. §1203(b)(1), thus demonstrating that the requisite injury need only be threatened.

Defendants next maintain that plaintiffs exaggerate the extent of the threatened injury. They claim that the studios in fact believe that DeCSS is not a threat. But the only basis for that contention is a couple of quotations from statements that the MPAA or one or another studio made (or considered making but did not in fact issue) to the effect that it was not concerned about DeCSS or that it was inconvenient to use. These statements, however, were attempts to "spin" public opinion. They do not now reflect the actual state of affairs or the studios' actual views, if they ever did.

Third, defendants contend that there is no evidence that any decrypted movies that may be available, if any there are, were decrypted with DeCSS. They maintain that "[m]any utilities and devices...can decrypt DVDs equally well and often faster and with greater ease than by using DeCSS." This is a substantial exaggeration. There appear to be a few other so-called rippers, but the Court finds that DeCSS is usable on a broader range of DVDs than any of the others. Further, there is no credible evidence that any other utility is faster or easier to use than DeCSS. Indeed, the Court concludes that DeCSS is the superior product, as evidenced by the fact that the web site promoting DivX as a tool for obtaining usable copies of copyrighted movies recommends the use of DeCSS, rather than anything else, for the decryption step and that the apparent availability of pirated motion pictures shot up so dramatically upon the introduction of DeCSS.

### B. PERMANENT INJUNCTION AND DECLARATORY RELIEF

Plaintiffs seek a permanent injunction barring defendants from posting DeCSS on their web site and from linking their site to others that make DeCSS available.

The starting point, as always, is the statute. The DMCA provides in relevant part that the court in an action brought pursuant to its terms "may grant temporary and permanent injunctions on such terms as it deems reasonable to prevent or restrain a violation...."[268] Where statutes in substance so provide, injunctive relief is appropriate if there is a reasonable likelihood of future violations absent such relief and, in cases brought by private plaintiffs, if the plaintiff lacks an adequate remedy at law.

In this case, it is quite likely that defendants, unless enjoined, will continue to violate the Act. Defendants are in the business of disseminating information to assist hackers in "cracking" various types of technological security systems. And while defendants argue that they promptly stopped posting DeCSS when enjoined preliminarily from doing so, thus allegedly demonstrating their willingness to comply with the law, their reaction to the preliminary injunction in fact cuts the other way. Upon being enjoined from posting DeCSS themselves, defendants encouraged others to "mirror" the information — that is, to post DeCSS — and linked their own web site to mirror sites in order to assist users of defendants' web site in obtaining DeCSS despite the injunction barring defendants from providing it directly. While there is no claim that this activity violated the letter of the preliminary injunction, and it therefore presumably was not contumacious, and while its status under the DMCA was somewhat uncertain, it was

268. 17 U.S.C. §1203(b)(1).

a studied effort to defeat the purpose of the preliminary injunction. In consequence, the Court finds that there is a substantial likelihood of future violations absent injunctive relief.

There also is little doubt that plaintiffs have no adequate remedy at law. The only potential legal remedy would be an action for damages under Section 1203(c), which provides for recovery of actual damages or, upon the election of the plaintiff, statutory damages of up to $2,500 per offer of DeCSS. Proof of actual damages in a case of this nature would be difficult if not virtually impossible, as it would involve proof of the extent to which motion picture attendance, sales of broadcast and other motion picture rights, and sales and rentals of DVDs and video tapes of movies were and will be impacted by the availability of DVD decryption technology. Difficulties in determining what constitutes an "offer" of DeCSS in a world in which the code is available to much of the world via Internet postings, among other problems, render statutory damages an inadequate means of redressing plaintiffs' claimed injuries. Indeed, difficulties such as this have led to the presumption that copyright and trademark infringement cause irreparable injury, i.e., injury for which damages are not an adequate remedy. The Court therefore holds that the traditional requirements for issuance of a permanent injunction have been satisfied. Yet there remains another point for consideration.

Defendants argue that an injunction in this case would be futile because DeCSS already is all over the Internet. They say an injunction would be comparable to locking the barn door after the horse is gone. And the Court has been troubled by that possibility. But the countervailing arguments overcome that concern.

To begin with, any such conclusion effectively would create all the wrong incentives by allowing defendants to continue violating the DMCA simply because others, many doubtless at defendants' urging, are doing so as well. Were that the law, defendants confronted with the possibility of injunctive relief would be well advised to ensure that others engage in the same unlawful conduct in order to set up the argument that an injunction against the defendants would be futile because everyone else is doing the same thing.

Second, and closely related, is the fact that this Court is sorely "troubled by the notion that any Internet user . . . can destroy valuable intellectual property rights by posting them over the Internet."[273] While equity surely should not act where the controversy has become moot, it ought to look very skeptically at claims that the defendant or others already have done all the harm that might be done before the injunction issues.

The key to reconciling these views is that the focus of injunctive relief is on the defendants before the Court. If a plaintiff seeks to enjoin a defendant from burning a pasture, it is no answer that there is a wild fire burning in its direction. If the defendant itself threatens the plaintiff with irreparable harm, then equity will enjoin the defendant from carrying out the threat even if other threats abound and even if part of the pasture already is burned.

---

273. *Religious Technology Center v. Netcom On-Line Communication Services, Inc.*, 923 F. Supp. 1231, 1256 (N.D. Cal. 1995).

These defendants would harm plaintiffs every day on which they post DeCSS on their heavily trafficked web site and link to other sites that post it because someone who does not have DeCSS thereby might obtain it. They thus threaten plaintiffs with immediate and irreparable injury. They will not be allowed to continue to do so simply because others may do so as well. In short, this Court, like others than have faced the issue, is "not persuaded that modern technology has withered the strong right arm of equity."[274] Indeed, the likelihood is that this decision will serve notice on others that "the strong right arm of equity" may be brought to bear against them absent a change in their conduct and thus contribute to a climate of appropriate respect for intellectual property rights in an age in which the excitement of ready access to untold quantities of information has blurred in some minds the fact that taking what is not yours and not freely offered to you is stealing. Appropriate injunctive and declaratory relief will issue simultaneously with this opinion.

* * *

# Comments

1. *The Merits of* **Reimerdes.** *Universal City Studios v. Reimerdes* is not a copyright infringement lawsuit; it is a case brought under §1201(a) of the Digital Millennium Copyright Act, which forbids "trafficking" in devices that permit circumvention of technological measures that control access to copyrighted works. The defendants were found liable both for hosting copies of the DeCSS computer program on their own website, and for posting hyperlinks on websites to sites that offered DeCSS for download. To the court, this amounted to "trafficking" in technology that enabled consumers to watch DVDs on devices that lacked the "CSS" computer code that is licensed by the motion picture industry to producers of "authorized" DVD playback devices. CSS-enabled DVD players do not prevent consumers from reproducing DVDs, but they do include technology that supports worldwide "region coding" of DVDs by the film industry. DVDs purchased in one region are playable only on players that CSS-enabled and coded for that region.

2. *The Scope of the Injunction in* **Reimerdes.** Having found a violation of the DMCA, and noting that the DMCA authorizes injunctive relief against violators, the question before the court concerns the scope of the injunction. The defendants are barred from doing two things: First, they are prohibited from hosting copies of the DeCSS computer program on their own website, where it might be downloaded. Second, they are prohibited from maintaining links on their website to other sites that host copies of the DeCSS program for download. While the scope of the injunction is quite broad, particularly to the extent that it prohibits posting hyperlinks to other websites, the court has two legitimate concerns. First, it is concerned about its jurisdiction to award any relief to the plaintiff. Second, and related, it is concerned about its ability to

---

274. *Com-Share, Inc. v. Computer Complex, Inc.*, 338 F. Supp. 1229, 1239 (E.D. Mich. 1971).

grant effective relief. Similar concerns may arise in copyright infringement cases. In *Intellectual Reserve, Inc. v. Utah Lighthouse Ministry, Inc.*, 75 F. Supp. 2d 1290 (D. Utah 1999), having found that the defendant infringed the plaintiff's copyright by posting infringing text on its website, the court enjoined the defendant not only from posting that text, but also from posting addresses of other websites where the infringing text could be found.

In both cases, enjoining a defendant from posting website addresses, whether or not in the form of hyperlinks, edges away from a prohibition on causing injury to the value of the plaintiff's copyrights, and, since the prohibition on linking amounts to a restriction on the contents of webpages, edges toward a prohibition on speaking. The defendants in *Reimerdes* raise First Amendment objections to liability under any theory, on the ground that creation and distribution of computer code constitutes "speech," at least in the context of the computer science community. The court is untroubled by the argument. Some scholars have urged, however, that injunctions in copyright cases, and preliminary injunctions in particular, are the equivalents of prior restraints on speech, and should be treated by courts with equivalent skepticism. *See* Mark A. Lemley & Eugene Volokh, *Freedom of Speech and Injunctions in Intellectual Property Cases*, 48 DUKE L.J. 147 (1998).

## Note on *Suntrust Bank v. Houghton Mifflin Co.*

One recent case has confronted possible conflicts between remedies for copyright infringement and First Amendment interests. In *Suntrust Bank v. Houghton Mifflin Co.*, 268 F.3d 1257 (11th Cir. 2001), the accused infringer was Alice Randall, who wrote *The Wind Done Gone*, which she characterized as a parody of Margaret Mitchell's classic novel, *Gone With the Wind*, told from the perspective of a slave on Tara, the O'Hara plantation. The owner of the Mitchell copyright, Suntrust Bank, sued Randall's publisher for copyright infringement and sought an injunction prohibiting distribution of her book. The trial court granted a preliminary injunction. The Court of Appeals for the Eleventh Circuit vacated the injunction, noting that *The Wind Done Gone* was likely protected as a parody under the fair use doctrine. The court's opinion began with a lengthy analysis of the importance of protecting First Amendment principles in the context of copyright law. While the merits of the decision rested on the court's analysis of the four fair use factors, the court noted that it proceeded with the fair use argument "cognizant of the First Amendment protections interwoven into copyright law." *Id.* at 1265. *See generally Harper & Row Publishers, Inc. v. Nation Enterprises*, 471 U.S. 539, 558-560 (1985) (noting that First Amendment interests in copyright are appropriately addressed via the substantive mechanisms of the fair use doctrine and the idea/expression distinction).

The Supreme Court has also noted the need to protect free speech interests in the context of copyright's remedial structure. In *Campbell v.*

*Acuff-Rose Music, Inc.*, 510 U.S. 569 (1994), which set forth the framework for claims of "parodic" fair use on which the court relied in *Suntrust Bank*, the Supreme Court wrote: "[T]he goals of copyright law, 'to stimulate the creation and publication of edifying matter,'... are not always best served by automatically granting injunctive relief when parodists are found to have gone beyond the bounds of fair use." *Campbell*, 510 U.S. at 578 n.10. In one other case, not involving fair use, the Supreme Court repeated the suggestion that injunctive relief ought not to be granted to victorious copyright plaintiffs as a matter of right. In *New York Times Co., Inc. v. Tasini*, 533 U.S. 483 (2001), in which the Court held that the *New York Times* and other publishers exceeded their authority to "revise" collective works when they caused articles prepared by freelance journalists to appear in online electronic databases, the Court took care to note that its ruling that the freelance articles were used improperly did not mean, necessarily, that the articles would have to be removed from the databases:

> [I]t hardly follows from today's decision that an injunction against the inclusion of these Articles in the Databases (much less all freelance articles in any databases) must issue. The parties (Authors and Publishers) may enter into an agreement allowing continued electronic reproduction of the Authors' works; they, and if necessary the courts and Congress, may draw on numerous models for distributing copyrighted works and remunerating authors for their distribution.

*Id.* at 505. Both cases echo a suggestion found in an opinion by the Court of Appeals for the Ninth Circuit, *Abend v. MCA, Inc.*, 863 F.2d 1465, 1479 (9th Cir. 1988), aff'd sub nom. *Stewart v. Abend*, 495 U.S. 207 (1990). *Stewart* involved interpretation of the rules found in the 1909 Copyright Act for renewal of copyright. Alfred Hitchcock and Jimmy Stewart, producers of the classic film *Rear Window*, had obtained the rights to the short story on which the film was based but, because the story author died before renewing the copyright, they did not own rights in the renewal term. Just as the market for videotapes was taking off, the successor to the renewal rights sued to enjoin further distribution of the film. On the theory that the renewal term created a new "estate" free of encumbrances created during the initial term, the copyright owner prevailed. Given the fame and artistic merits of the movie, and the slight (to nonexistent) fame and artistic merits of the short story, the court found "special circumstances" that would cause "great injustice" to the defendants and "public injury" were an injunction to issue.

## Problem

**9-1.** In 2004, the author Gene O'Connor published a sensational biography of Ted Turner, founder of CNN, former husband of Jane Fonda, and international sailing star. *The New Yorker* magazine quickly filed a copyright infringement action against O'Connor alleging that the book infringed copyrights which *The New Yorker* owned on a series of three articles entitled

"The Ted Turner Story" which appeared in *The New Yorker* in late 2003. Together with its lawsuit, *The New Yorker* filed a motion for a preliminary injunction restraining the sale, publication, distribution, and advertisement of the biography, pending final determination of the action. The three *New Yorker* articles contained roughly 15,000 words in total and would have, if published in book form, filled some 40 book pages. O'Connor's biography consisted of more than 100,000 words and more than 250 pages. There can be little doubt that some parts of *The New Yorker* articles—including numerous quotations of historical events in which Ted Turner participated, attributed to the author of the articles, and a total of over 1,000 words—were copied in O'Connor's biography. O'Connor maintained that the rest of the biography was based entirely on his independent research. Is *The New Yorker* entitled to the preliminary relief that it has requested? *See Rosemont Enters., Inc. v. Random House, Inc.*, 366 F.2d 303 (2d Cir. 1966).

# B. DAMAGES

In an appropriate case, a copyright owner prevailing on a copyright infringement claim may obtain both injunctive relief as to prospective infringement and financial compensation for harm already inflicted. How to measure that harm is complicated by the numerous ways in which copyrighted works can be used. For example, a copyrighted work may be incorporated into a new work without the copyright owner's permission, leading to a finding of infringement, but raising a question of calculating harm; the new work may be financially profitable for several reasons, including incorporation of the infringing material, because of other, noninfringing content, or for a combination of reasons. The damages provisions of the Copyright Act attempt to give parties and courts the flexibility to deal with these complexities. Section 504(b) provides that an infringer is liable for "the actual damages suffered by him or her as a result of the infringement, and any profits of the infringer that are attributable to the infringement and are not taken into account in computing the actual damages." Section 504(c) allows the plaintiff to elect to recover statutory damages instead, a choice that may be sensible in cases where proof of actual damages is difficult, or where an award of actual damages and profits is not adequate to deter future wrongful conduct.

## 1. Actual Damages and Profits

*STATUTE:* **Remedies for Infringement: Damages and Profits**
17 U.S.C. §504(a), (b)

In awarding actual damages and profits, the purpose of the law is to award damages that actually compensate the copyright owner. Doing so may involve some complex accounting.

## HAMIL AMERICA INC. v. GFI
### 193 F.3d 92 (2d Cir. 1999)

OAKES, Senior Circuit Judge.

### I. INTRODUCTION

Hamil America, Inc. sued GFI (a Division of Goldtex, Inc.), SGS Studio, Inc. and J.C. Penney Company, Inc. for copyright infringement. According to Hamil America, GFI copied one of Hamil America's floral fabric patterns, SGS manufactured garments using the infringing GFI fabric and sold the garments to J.C. Penney, and J.C. Penney sold the garments in its retail stores. Hamil America prevailed at trial and was awarded damages against all three defendants. GFI, SGS, and J.C. Penney appeal the district court's finding of liability for infringement and its calculation of damages. Hamil America cross-appeals the district court's calculation of damages, arguing that the district court should have awarded damages for profits that Hamil America presumably would have earned had other customers not purchased GFI's infringing pattern. Because the district court erroneously prohibited GFI from deducting any overhead expenses in the calculation of its profits, we reverse in part and remand for recalculation of damages. We affirm on all other issues.

### II. BACKGROUND

Hamil America and GFI are companies doing business in the garment industry. Each sells printed fabric to manufacturers that, in turn, create garments for sale to wholesalers or retailers.

In 1993, Tabitha Kim created an original floral design for Hamil America which was designated Pattern No. 96. Kim transferred her copyright rights in the design to Hamil America. Hamil America produced and sold fabric printed with Pattern No. 96 in various color combinations, or "colorways." One of the color combinations, designated colorway 575, featured clusters of small white and yellow flowers with blue centers on a red background.

SGS is a garment manufacturer. J.C. Penney is a retailer that sells, among other things, garments made by SGS. In June 1994, SGS purchased fabric samples of Hamil America Pattern No. 96 in four colorways, including colorway 575. SGS showed the fabric samples to J.C. Penney, along with other fabric samples obtained from other fabric vendors, to allow J.C. Penney to choose fabric patterns to be used for garments that SGS would manufacture for J.C. Penney. J.C. Penney selected six patterns out of the various patterns shown to it by SGS, including Hamil America Pattern No. 96 in colorway 575 and five GFI patterns.

SGS made sample garments from these six fabric patterns and supplied them to J.C. Penney. J.C. Penney used the sample garments for intra-company marketing and outside advertising. It showed a garment made with Hamil America Pattern No. 96 to buyers in its individual stores and featured a garment made with Hamil America Pattern No. 96 in its newspaper advertising.

SGS then manufactured garments for J.C. Penney. It was more expensive for SGS to use Hamil America fabric than GFI fabric: Hamil America fabric in Pattern No. 96 cost $5 per yard, whereas GFI fabric cost only $3.60 per yard. According to Hamil America, SGS wanted GFI to develop and manufacture a fabric pattern that SGS could substitute for Hamil America Pattern No. 96 in colorway 575, so that SGS could fulfill the J.C. Penney order for garments made from that pattern at a lower cost to SGS.

In October 1994, GFI hired Jae Wang, a freelance artist frequently employed by GFI, to create a fabric pattern that GFI would sell to SGS. In the same month, SGS ordered two yards of Pattern No. 96 in colorway 575 from Hamil America to be shipped to SGS on a rush basis. According to Hamil America, Wang copied, or "knocked-off," Hamil America Pattern No. 96. Wang's design was designated GFI Pattern No. 330. SGS substituted GFI Pattern No. 330 for Hamil America Pattern No. 96 in the garments it manufactured for J.C. Penney.

Hamil America learned of the infringement from Beaver Raymond, one of its Texas manufacturing customers. Raymond asked Howard Goldstein, Hamil America's sales manager, why garments made with Hamil America Pattern No. 96 were being sold at J.C. Penney. Raymond showed Goldstein a garment that Raymond had purchased at J.C. Penney in Dallas, Texas. The garment was made with GFI Pattern No. 330, although Raymond believed that the garment was made with Hamil America Pattern No. 96 because the patterns were so similar. Goldstein then purchased another garment made with GFI Pattern No. 330 at the J.C. Penney store in Dallas.

In April 1995, Hamil America registered Pattern No. 96 with the United States Copyright Office and was granted a registration number, VA 642-546. Hamil America sued GFI for copyright infringement, claiming Hamil America Pattern No. 96 was infringed by GFI Pattern No. 330. Hamil America also sued SGS and J.C. Penney because they each sold garments manufactured with GFI's infringing fabric. After a non-jury trial, the district court found that the defendants willfully infringed Hamil America's copyright. In March 1998, the court entered judgment in favor of Hamil America against all defendants, and awarded damages in the amount of $201,049 from GFI, $28,836 from SGS, and $67,106 from J.C. Penney.

GFI, SGS, and J.C. Penney appeal the district court's finding of liability for infringement and its calculation of damages. Hamil America cross-appeals the district court's calculation of damages, arguing that the district court should have awarded damages for profits that Hamil America presumably would have earned had other customers not purchased GFI's infringing pattern.

### III. DISCUSSION

\* \* \*

Because the "actual copying" prong of the infringement test requires a fact-intensive inquiry, the district court's determination as to whether the defendant actually copied the plaintiff's copyright material warrants our deference. This is particularly true when the district court must make a credibility determination. The court below was well-situated to gauge the credibility of the witnesses who testified as to whether the appellants willfully copied Hamil America's pattern. In addition, as we discuss below, the many similarities between the patterns are probative of copying. The district court's finding of willful infringement was not clearly erroneous, and the first part of the infringement test was satisfied.

\* \* \*

Viewed under the ordinary observer standard, it is clear to us that GFI's Pattern No. 330 and Hamil America's Pattern No. 96 are substantially similar. Both patterns depict small clusters of flowers and leaves. The shapes of the flower petals and the leaves are virtually identical, and feature similar defining line work and highlights in the flowers and leaves. Both patterns depict leaves that do not appear to be attached to any of the flowers. Both patterns are "tossed," which means that they have no top or bottom and are non-directional, and appear in repeat.

The intended uses of both fabric patterns further support a finding of substantial similarity. . . . Likewise, Hamil America Pattern No. 96 and GFI Pattern No. 330 were to be used in garments, and the slight differences between the two patterns fade away when they are viewed from a distance. Giving due weight, as we must, to the scrutiny that observers would give to the patterns *as used,* we conclude that the patterns are substantially similar. This conclusion is substantiated by the fact that when Raymond saw the garment made with GFI Pattern No. 330, he immediately assumed that it was made with Hamil America Pattern No. 96.

\* \* \*

. . . Here, GFI has duplicated Hamil America's selection of clustered flowers and leaves, its coordination of these elements in particular spatial combinations, and its arrangement of these design elements on a tossed pattern that appears in repeat. Given the similarity of the "total concept and feel" of the fabric patterns, we are not convinced by the appellants' recitation of differences.

Because GFI Pattern No. 330 is substantially similar to Hamil America Pattern No. 96, we affirm the district court's holding that the appellants infringed Hamil America's copyright.

### C. Damages

We next turn to the issue of damages. Under the current Copyright Act, a copyright owner can elect to recover either "actual damages and profits" under 17 U.S.C. §504(b), or "statutory damages" under 17 U.S.C. §504(c). 17 U.S.C. §504(c)(1). At Hamil America's request, the district court awarded damages under 17 U.S.C. §504(b). Hamil America could recover "the actual damages suffered by [it] as a result of the infringement, *and* any profits of the infringer that are attributable to the infringement and are not taken into account in computing the actual damages." 17 U.S.C. §504(b) (emphasis added). These two methods of recovery available under §504(b) serve two distinct purposes: "[d]amages are awarded to compensate the copyright owner for losses from the infringement, and profits are awarded to prevent the infringer from unfairly benefitting from a wrongful act." H.R. Rep. No. 94-1476, at 161 (1976), reprinted in 17 U.S.C.A. §504 at 146 (West 1996).

The parties contend that the district court erred with respect to both damages calculations permitted under §504(b). The appellants argue that the court erred by disallowing deductions for overhead and other fixed expenses from the profits generated from the sales of the infringing fabric. Hamil America cross-appeals the calculation of its own actual damages, arguing that it was entitled to recover profits that it presumably would have earned had other customers not purchased GFI's infringing pattern. We address each issue in turn.

### 1. CALCULATION OF THE INFRINGERS' PROFITS

Section 504(b) of the Copyright Act authorizes a copyright owner to recover the infringer's profits. That section expressly provides that "[i]n establishing the infringer's profits, the copyright owner is required to present proof only of the infringer's gross revenue, and the infringer is required to prove his or her deductible expenses and the elements of profit attributable to factors other than the copyrighted work." 17 U.S.C. §504(b). Put another way, the infringer's profits are calculated as the gross sales of infringing goods minus the costs that the infringer proves are attributable to the production and sale of those goods.

In compliance with this statutory procedure, Hamil America submitted proof of GFI's gross revenue from the sale of the infringing dress patterns, and GFI submitted a schedule of its deductible expenses that included both the actual costs of production of the infringing pattern as well as its general, or "fixed," overhead expenses. The district court rejected GFI's submission to the extent that it sought deductions for overhead expenses, stating that GFI "would have had general administrative expenses of 'X' amount whether [it] sold [the infringing] goods or not." The court also rejected certain specific expenses, such as country club dues, on the ground that they were not "incremental costs of producing [the infringing] fabric." The court asked GFI to adduce the "actual cost of the goods, what it actually cost [GFI] to manufacture [the] specific items." The district court accepted GFI's amended cost schedule, which showed only the variable costs of producing and selling the infringing pattern, and which excluded general overhead items such as rent, insurance, and depreciation.

GFI argues that the district court erred in excluding an allocation of general overhead expenses in its calculation of GFI's profits and that we must remand for recalculation of damages. We agree.

Our analysis begins with *Sheldon v. Metro-Goldwyn Pictures Corp.*, 106 F.2d 45 (2d Cir. 1939) (L. Hand, *J.*), in which a motion picture studio infringed the copyright on a certain play. The district court allowed a deduction for overhead expenses based on the ratio that the cost of producing the infringing movie bore to the total costs of the movie studio. On appeal, the copyright holder argued that the infringers should not have been permitted any deduction for overhead expenses absent a showing that the overhead had been increased by the production of the infringing movie, which was only one of forty produced by the studio. This court affirmed, noting generally that, " '[o]verhead' which does not assist in the production of the infringement should not be credited to the infringer; that which does, should be; it is a question of fact in all cases." *Id.* at 54.

Turning to the specific facts of the *Sheldon* case, the court applied its general rule as follows:

> In the case at bar the infringing picture was one of over forty made by the defendants, using the same supervising staff and organization, which had to be maintained if the business was to go on at all. Without them no picture could have been produced; they were as much a condition upon the production of the infringing picture as the scenery, or the plaintiffs' play itself.

*Id.* The court thus concluded that certain categories of general overhead expenses — in this case, those relating to creating and maintaining a "supervising staff and organization" — were appropriately deducted from gross revenue. The court then considered various methods of allocating those overhead expenses to the production of the infringing movie, and selected the method that was most fair, accurate, and practical in light of the infringing company's structure and products. Given the impossibility of determining the overhead costs that were directly related to the production of the infringing motion picture, the court permitted a deduction of a portion of overhead expenses based on the cost of production of the motion picture:

> [T]o make a perfect allocation one would have to examine what part of the time of all the employees whose pay went into the "overhead", was given to each picture; and so of the other expenses. That was obviously impossible. It is on the whole more likely that a given picture required that proportion of the general services represented by its cost of production, than that each picture shared those services equally.... The [cost of production] solution appears to us as nearly right as was practically possible.

*Id.* at 52-53.

The court therefore affirmed the district court's use of an estimate of overhead expenses based on the cost of production — notwithstanding the absence of particularized findings as to the use of those expenses for things that specifically contributed to the infringing picture — because of the "extravagant labor" necessary to determine the incremental contribution of individual property to the infringing picture:

> It was better...to compute this item by assuming that the infringing picture used that proportion of the whole plant which its cost of production bore to the cost of production of all pictures made that year, than to attempt any allocation of buildings and other property according to their actual use for the picture. The second method would have been incredibly difficult in application, involving as it would a different proportional use of each bit of property concerned.

*Id.* at 54. In adopting this pragmatic approach, the court implicitly rejected the need for a detailed analysis of an infringer's ledgers.

*Sheldon* thus contemplates a two-step procedure for deducting overhead expenses from an infringer's profits. The first step is to determine what overhead expense categories (such as rent, business, entertainment, personnel and public relations) are actually implicated by the production of the infringing product. Once a sufficient nexus is shown between a category of overhead and the production or sale of the infringing product, a court need not scrutinize for inclusion or exclusion particular items within the overhead category. For example, if "entertainment expenses" is a category of overhead implicated in the line of business that produced or sold the infringing product, then country club dues included within that category should not be singled out for exclusion, as they were by the district court here. Rather, the court should limit its inquiry to the sufficiency of the nexus between the expense category and production of the infringing product.

The second step is to arrive at a fair, accurate, and practical method of allocating the implicated overhead to the infringement. The infringer has the burden of "offering a fair and acceptable formula for allocating a given portion of overhead to the particular infringing items in issue." 4 Melville B. Nimmer and David Nimmer, *Nimmer on Copyright* §14.03 [B], at 14-39 (1996). The reasonableness of the proffered overhead allocation formula is a question of fact in all cases.[5]

\* \* \*

Despite the clear precedent on the deduction of overhead expenses established by *Sheldon* . . . , the district court here prohibited GFI from deducting any overhead whatsoever unless GFI could show that its overhead was actually increased by its production of Pattern No. 330. *See* [*Hamil America, Inc. v. SGS Studio, Inc. et al.*, 1998 WL 19991 (S.D.N.Y. Jan. 21, 1998)], at \*3 ("[T]he Court must examine the facts to determine those incremental cost[s] of the infringer that were increased as a direct result of the production and sale of the infringing goods . . . and to separate them from those fixed costs that would have been incurred in any event."). The court appears to have based its holding at least in part on the fact that the infringement by GFI was willful, relying on cases from other jurisdictions suggesting that willful or deliberate infringers may not deduct overhead when calculating the profit the plaintiff is entitled to recover.

Unlike the district court, we are not prepared to abandon the teachings of *Sheldon* in favor of a hard and fast rule denying all overhead deductions to willful infringers. But we share the district court's concern that willful infringers should not be permitted to subsidize the sale of legitimate goods with the sale of infringing goods by "passing part of its fixed cost on to the copyright holder." *See id.* at \*2. We also recognize that "a rule of liability which merely takes away profits from an infringement would offer little discouragement to infringers." *F.W. Woolworth Co. v. Contemporary Arts,* 344 U.S. 228, 233 (1952). We therefore conclude that *Sheldon*'s two-step approach must be applied with particular rigor in the case of willful infringement.

---

5. Some methods of allocating overhead to the infringement proffered in previous cases include: the production cost of the infringing product as a percentage of the total production costs, *see Sheldon,* 106 F.2d at 52; the number of infringing products as a percentage of total products, *see Wilkie v. Santly Bros.*, 139 F.2d 264, 265 (2d Cir. 1943); and the dollar sales from the infringing product as a percentage of total dollar sales, *but see Gaste v. Kaiserman,* 863 F.2d 1061, 1071 (2d Cir. 1988) (rejecting the dollar sales method).

Every infringer shoulders the burden of demonstrating a "sufficient nexus between each expense claimed and the sales of the unlawful goods," [*Manhattan Indus. v. Sweater Bee by Banff, Ltd.*, 885 F.2d 1, 8 (2d Cir. 1989)], before it may deduct any overhead expenses from its profits. When infringement is found to be willful, the district court should give extra scrutiny to the categories of overhead expenses claimed by the infringer to insure that each category is directly and validly connected to the sale and production of the infringing product. Unless a strong nexus is established, the court should not permit a deduction for the overhead category.

An infringer also bears the burden of proposing a fair and acceptable formula for allocating a portion of overhead expenses to the infringing items at issue. The district court must determine that the particular allocation formula is optimal and sound, and all presumptions are drawn against the infringer. The allocation formula of a willful infringer should be held to a particularly high standard of fairness, and the court should not hesitate to reject a formula which allows the willful infringer to deduct more of its overhead than was directly implicated in the manufacture of the infringing product.

Because the district court erred under *Sheldon* in applying a blanket prohibition of all overhead deductions, we reverse on this issue and remand for a recalculation of GFI's profits. In that proceeding, GFI, as a willful infringer, must demonstrate a direct and valid nexus between each claimed overhead expense category and the production of GFI Pattern No. 330 and propose a fair and acceptable formula for allocating a portion of overhead to the pattern's production. The district court, applying the heightened scrutiny appropriate in cases of willful infringement, will have the latitude to adopt or reject certain categories of overhead, and to accept, reject, or amend GFI's overhead allocation formula. Of course, if the resulting calculation causes the district court to reconsider its finding that Hamil America "will be fully compensated on its claims," *see Hamil America, Inc.*, 1998 WL 19991, at *3, the court could award Hamil America its "actual damages" in lieu of, or in addition to, GFI's recalculated profits. *See* 17 U.S.C. §504(b).

### 2. HAMIL AMERICA'S LOST PROFITS

Hamil America raises one issue on cross-appeal: whether the district court erred when it determined that Hamil America could not recover for lost profits that it might have earned from sales to those of its customers who purchased GFI's infringing design. It relies on three facts: (1) Hamil America and GFI had several shared customers; (2) the shared customers bought samples of Hamil America Pattern No. 96 with the probable intention to purchase more Hamil America fabric; and (3) the shared customers did not purchase the fabric from Hamil America after the less expensive version offered by GFI appeared on the market. Hamil America reasons that it is entitled to damages for lost profits, as it would have sold Pattern No. 96 to the shared customers had GFI not made the infringing pattern. It argues that it is entitled to a total judgment against GFI in the amount of $240,782, rather than the $201,049 that was awarded by the district court.

GFI argued below that Hamil America should not recover lost profits, because the shared customers would not have purchased the fabric at Hamil America's above-market prices. GFI also pointed out that those customers purchased GFI's fabric several months after they had purchased Hamil America's samples, and concluded that the commercial failure of Hamil America's pattern "had nothing to do with the availability of [GFI's] pattern."

The district court agreed that the shared customers may well have declined to purchase Hamil America's fabric, due to its higher price, and held that Hamil America could not recover the alleged lost profits. The court further noted that Hamil America could not recover both for its hypothetical sales to the shared customers and for GFI's actual sales to those same customers.[7] The court elected to measure GFI's actual profits from sales to the shared customers, rather than speculate as to what Hamil America might have earned had it sold Pattern No. 96 to the shared customers.

As Nimmer states, "[i]n the absence of convincing evidence as to the volume of sales that plaintiff would have obtained but for the infringement, the measure of lost profits may be rejected as too speculative." *Nimmer on Copyright* §14.02[A], at 14-11 (citing *Odegard, Inc. v. Costikyan Classic Carpets, Inc.*, 963 F. Supp. 1328, 1341 (S.D.N.Y. 1997)). The district court rejected Hamil America's request for lost profits as too speculative. In our view, this conclusion was not clearly erroneous. In the absence of more reliable evidence of Hamil America's lost profits, the district court was entitled to rely on the less abstract calculation of damages from GFI's sales to the shared customers. We therefore affirm on this issue.

## IV. CONCLUSION

Because the district court erroneously prohibited GFI from deducting any overhead expenses in the calculation of its profits, we reverse in part and remand for recalculation of damages....

## Comments

*1. Shifting Burdens.* The court in *Hamil America* follows the rule that calculating the infringer's profits involves proof submitted by plaintiff of the

---

7. Hamil America properly conceded below that "it may not recover its profit on these alleged sale[s] and defendant[s]' profit on the sale to these companies." *Hamil America, Inc.*, 1998 WL 19991, at *3. A copyright plaintiff may recover its own lost profits, which are part of the plaintiff's "actual damages," as well as the defendant's profits. But a "plaintiff may not recover damages that have already been taken into account in computing its actual damages." *Nimmer on Copyright*, §14.03, at 14-29. Thus, "[a] plaintiff may not recover its full lost profits plus all of the defendant's profits, for this would constitute a forbidden double recovery." *Id.* §14.02[A], at 14-10 (citing *Taylor v. Meirick*, 712 F.2d 1112 (7th Cir. 1983)). Thus, if Hamil America were in fact entitled to recover lost profits, it would have had to set off its recovery for GFI's profits by those profits already taken into account to determine Hamil America's lost profits, because Hamil America could not recover twice. Hamil America properly performed this analysis below, when Hamil America contended that it had lost profits of $149,823, and that GFI's profits not taken in account in computing Hamil America's lost profits were $90,959, for a total judgment against GFI in the amount of $240,782.

infringer's gross revenue, followed by deductions offered by the infringer of overhead and profit not attributable to the infringement. (Copyright courts have recognized that calculations of gross profit may include both direct profit from exploiting the copyrighted work itself, and indirect profit from exploitation of the work as part of a larger enterprise. *See Frank Music Corp. v. Metro-Goldwyn-Mayer, Inc.*, 886 F.2d 1545 (9th Cir. 1989) (noting that the district court did not err when it included indirect profits from the hotel and gaming operations of a defendant which infringed the copyright in a Broadway musical by including excerpts in a live production at a casino).) Allowing the infringer to deduct overhead expenses related to unlawful products might force the copyright owner, in effect, to subsidize production of infringing articles and, as a result, not receive full compensation for the infringement. The court is sensitive to that concern, particularly in light of the fact that the defendant was found to have acted willfully. The further implications of a finding of willfulness are considered in the next part of this chapter, regarding statutory damages.

2. *Compensating the Injured Plaintiff.* Recovery of the infringer's profits is partly intended to compensate the injured copyright owner, to the extent that the infringer made sales to customers who otherwise would have obtained the work from the copyright owner. For those sales, deducting the infringer's overhead related to production of the infringing articles makes the copyright owner whole, without providing overcompensation. If Hamil America had made sales of its own products to customers who bought infringing reproductions instead, Hamil, too, would have had its profits reduced by overhead expenses.

3. *Avoiding Unjust Enrichment of the Infringer.* Using the infringer's profits as a measure of the copyright owner's lost profits also serves two additional, related purposes of the Copyright Act's damages provisions: to prevent unjust enrichment by the infringer, and to deter further infringement in the future. These two goals may not be entirely consistent. To the extent that unjust enrichment is the goal, deducting overhead expenses seems appropriate, so long as the overhead expenses are in fact increased by the fact that the defendant engaged in the infringing activity. But the law might achieve a greater deterrent effect by not permitting deduction of overhead under any circumstances, or at least in cases of willful infringement—where, presumably, the need for deterrence is greatest.

4. *Licensing Markets and Actual Damages.* Suppose that the defendant's infringing use of the plaintiff's work does not deprive the plaintiff of any sales, royalties, or expected profits. There is no existing licensing market for the work, other than the expectation that the defendant itself should have paid the copyright owner for use of the work, and the defendant does not earn any indirect profits that were caused by the use. The defendant argues, therefore, that the plaintiff should recover neither actual damages (because there are none) nor the infringer's profits (because no causal link has been shown). Should the plaintiff nonetheless recover damages based on a "reasonable" licensing value for the work? The Patent Act, 35 U.S.C. §284, provides that a patent owner is entitled to damages "adequate to compensate for the infringe-

ment, but in no event less than a reasonable royalty," but the Copyright Act contains no equivalent provision. Nonetheless, in *Davis v. The Gap, Inc.*, 246 F.3d 152 (2d Cir. 2001), the court ruled that the plaintiff was entitled to actual damages in the form of a "fair licensing fee" for the unauthorized use of his copyrighted eyeglass frame in an advertisement for a clothing retailer. The plaintiff had no evidence that he had lost any sales on account of the infringement, and there was no evidence that the defendant had earned any profits that were traceable to the infringement. Prior to the infringement, the plaintiff had earned only one "fee," $50, from placing a pair of his eyeglasses on a model at a fashion show.

5. *Tracing Profits.* Often, the most complex portion of a copyright infringement lawsuit involves tracing the unauthorized use of a copyrighted work to profits realized by an infringer from activities other than exploiting the work itself. These "indirect profits" cases, which follow the burden shifting rules noted above in Comment 1, present particularly difficult problems of proving causation. In *Cream Records, Inc. v. Jos. Schlitz Brewing Co.*, 754 F.2d 826 (9th Cir. 1985), the defendant used a small portion of the copyrighted musical composition "The Theme from Shaft" to advertise its malt liquor, without a license from the copyright owner. The plaintiff claimed a percentage of the profits derived from sales of malt liquor during the relevant time period, basing its calculation on a percentage of the defendant's annual advertising budget and the failure of the defendant to introduce evidence that its profits were unrelated to the infringement. The court of appeals approved the district court's substitution of a different (smaller) figure, noting that so long as the plaintiff met its burden of proving that the defendant's profits were at least partly caused by the infringement, all that was required of the award was that it consist of a "reasonable approximation" of those profits. The importance of causation to the plaintiff's case was underscored in *Polar Bear Productions, Inc. v. Timex Corp.*, 384 F.3d 700 (9th Cir. 2004), in which the defendant re-used copyrighted film footage produced by the plaintiff, in connection with promotional efforts for its watches. When the plaintiff alleged an indirect profits claim of between $1.7 and $3.2 million in profits earned on the defendant's sale of watches, and the jury's award totaled $2.1 million, the court vacated the award on the ground that the bulk of the total—"enhanced brand prestige" resulting from association of Timex watches with the extreme sport portrayed in the film—was not supported by evidence of a causal link between the infringement and the revenue derived from the prestige.

## 2. Statutory Damages

STATUTE: **Remedies for Infringement: Damages and Profits**
17 U.S.C. §504(c)

At any time during the infringement lawsuit, but before entry of final judgment, the copyright plaintiff may elect an award of statutory damages. The reason, often, is that an award of actual damages and/or the infringer's profits is difficult to prove. Alternatively, infringement may be clear but the amount of actual damages, while clear, may be small. This is especially likely to be true for infringement by consumers, or via other apparently not-for-profit uses. Or, particularly in a case of willful infringement, the fact that the court has discretion to impose statutory damages across a broad range may produce a deterrent effect that the copyright owner finds particularly valuable. While judges are frequently the arbiters of statutory damage awards in copyright infringement cases, the plaintiff in an infringement action has the right, under the Seventh Amendment to the Constitution, to have its claim for statutory damages tried to a jury. *See Feltner v. Columbia Pictures Television, Inc.*, 523 U.S. 340 (1998).

Though the copyright plaintiff has broad discretion regarding whether and when to elect an award of statutory damages, there is one procedural requirement. Under §412, no award of statutory damages is available for infringement that occurs after the publication of a work and before its registration, unless registration occurs within three months following publication. In short, particularly for works of commercial value, timely registration ensures that the copyright owner reserves the maximum range of remedial options.

## ENGEL v. WILD OATS, INC.
### 644 F. Supp. 1089 (S.D.N.Y. 1986)

ROBERT L. CARTER, District Judge.

Plaintiff in this copyright infringement action is Mary Engel, daughter and executrix of the estate of the late Ruth Orkin Engel, a renowned photographer. Defendants are Ocean Atlantic Textile Screen Printing, Inc., which manufactures T-shirts and other garments and goes by the acronym "Wild Oats," and New World Sales, Inc. ("New World Sales"), which sells Wild Oats garments on a contractual basis. Also named as defendants are the officers and directors of both companies.

The late Ms. Engel is perhaps best known for her still-life color photographs of Central Park. Plaintiff has alleged that without permission Wild Oats reprinted on some of its T-shirts and sweat shirts one of these photographs from the late Ms. Engel's book *More Pictures from My Window*. Defendants concede liability for copyright infringement, leaving damages as the issue before the court.

At a hearing on damages, Mary Engel testified to her mother's stature and reputation in the fine art of photography. Plaintiff did not, however, produce evidence of either her actual damages or defendants' net profits resulting from the infringement. Injury to her mother's reputation, plaintiff asserts, is not readily ascertainable.

Jerry Klause, the president and majority stockholder of Wild Oats, testified on behalf of all defendants. He stated that with 104 employees, Wild Oats produces 360,000 shirts per month. His company has not previously been sued for copyright infringement. However, soon after plaintiff brought the infringing shirt design to Mr. Klause's attention, the director of the Wild Oats art department admitted to having produced the design from a photograph, explaining that he had found the photograph in a book. Wild Oats produced a total of approximately 2,500 shirts that bear the infringing design. Mr. Klause also offered into evidence production reports showing net profits and sales commissions on the 2,500 shirts at $1,878.52.

Defendants argue that this number controls plaintiff's damages because it reflects both the ascertained profits of the infringers and the apparent absence of injury to plaintiff. In fact, according to defendants, even if statutory damages are appropriate, the ascertained net profits are the proper guide to the court's determination of damages.

Plaintiff disagrees. She argues that it is her absolute right to elect the statutory remedy. And in her view this remedy is inherently open to the court's discretion, not controlled by the net profits figure, because her damages are not readily ascertainable. Plaintiff requests the statutory maximum of $50,000 for willful infringement or, in the alternative, the maximum of $10,000 for unwillful infringement. *See* 17 U.S.C. §504(c). She also seeks attorneys' fees and costs, and permanent injunctive relief against the infringement.

### DISCUSSION

The victim of a copyright infringement who seeks damages is entitled to choose between two remedies. She may pursue the actual damages she has suffered plus the infringer's additional profits; or she may elect statutory damages to be determined, within specified limits, "as the court considers just." 17 U.S.C. §§504(b)-504(c). The choice of remedies belongs to the plaintiff, as the plain language of section 504 says, and she may exercise her choice at any time before the final judgment. However, once the plaintiff elects statutory damages, that remedy is generally exclusive.

Plaintiff has exercised her right to elect statutory damages. The only task at this point is to determine a just award. The court takes up the task with the frank acknowledgment that its discretion on this subject is anything but narrow. Indeed, the court's "discretion and sense of justice are controlling" subject only to the specific statutory limits. Congress surely did not grant this discretion unthinkingly. On the contrary, flexibility in fashioning an appropriate award when actual damages and profits are unclear is entirely consonant with the broader goal of providing the copyright owner with "a potent arsenal of remedies against the infringer," *Sony Corp. v. Universal City Studios*, 464 U.S. 417, 432 (1984). And it is equally consonant with the parallel goal of discouraging further infringement.

With these general considerations in mind the court must disagree with defendants' suggestion that their estimate of the profits derived from infringement should control the determination of statutory damages. The infringers' profits are a factor to consider, but only one among others.

Other factors include the nature of the copyright, the difficulty of proving actual damages, the circumstances of the infringement, and in particular whether the infringement was willful. The importance of this last factor should be emphasized because it is the one that may affect the statutory limits on damages: While the floor on statutory damages is $250, the ceiling is $10,000 for unwillful infringement but $50,000 if the infringement is willful.

The court finds that the infringement by Wild Oats was willful. The preponderance of the evidence indicates that the art director at Wild Oats copied the late Ms. Engel's photograph from the copyrighted book *More Pictures from My Window*. The art director knew or should have known that the unauthorized reprinting of a photograph from the book was a copyright violation. Although the court finds no direct proof of the art director's actual knowledge of the copyright infringement, the compelling circumstantial evidence of his reckless disregard for, if not actual knowledge of, plaintiff's rights in the photograph is sufficient to establish willfulness.

The court also takes note of circumstances apart from Wild Oats's willfulness surrounding the infringement in this case. The nature of plaintiff's copyright — ownership of a rarefied, artistic subject matter — is unusually susceptible to damage when reproduced on the rather less rarefied medium of a T-shirt or sweat shirt. The scale of the infringement was not slight as defendants have distributed approximately 2,500 shirts in the open market. At the same time, the extent of plaintiff's actual damages is virtually impossible to ascertain. The harm of the infringement to the late Ms. Engel's artistic reputation, in the form of lost revenues from her works, may become evident only over the years to come.

In light of all of these circumstances, the court has determined that $20,000 is the proper award of damages in this case. The award is adequate both to compensate plaintiff for her losses and to remind defendants and other would-be infringers of the seriousness of copyright violations.

\* \* \*

## Comments

1. *The Range of Statutory Damages.* Section 504(c) has been amended to increase the range of amounts at issue in a claim for statutory damages to not less than $750 and not more than $30,000, with a total cap of $150,000 for willful infringement.

2. *Willfulness as an Alternative to Punitive Damages.* Copyright law does not provide for an award of punitive damages, but §504(c) authorizes courts to increase the award of statutory damages from $30,000 to up to $150,000 per work upon a finding of "willfulness." (Conversely, in a proceeding for statutory damages, the court has the discretion to reduce an award of statutory damages against an "innocent infringer" to not less than $200, and in certain limited cases, to remit damages entirely.) The meaning of "willfulness" in copyright continues to be the subject of interpretation. According to a recent opinion of the Court of Appeals for the Second Circuit, "To prove 'willfulness' under the Copyright Act, the plaintiff must show (1) that the defendant was actually aware of the infringing activity, or (2) that the defendant's actions were the result of 'reckless disregard' for, or 'willful blindness' to, the copyright holder's rights." *Island Software and Computer Service, Inc. v. Microsoft Corp.*, 413 F.3d 257 (2d Cir. 2005). In *Island Software*, the court noted that the district court should not have entered summary judgment in favor of the copyright owner on the question of willfulness, since the evidence did not demonstrate actual knowledge of the infringing activity, and a

reasonable jury might interpret the infringer's testimony in favor of either party.

3. ***Compensation or Punishment?*** The role of willfulness determinations in calculating statutory damages confirms that remedies for copyright infringement are designed not merely to compensate copyright owners for losses due to unauthorized exploitation of their works. Those remedies may also serve a deterrent function:

> [A] rule of liability which merely takes away the profits from an infringement would offer little discouragement to infringers. It would fall short of an effective sanction for enforcement of the copyright policy. The statutory rule, formulated after long experience, not merely compels restitution of profit and reparation for injury but also is designed to discourage wrongful conduct. . . . Even for uninjurious and unprofitable invasions of copyright the court may, if it deems just, impose a liability within statutory limits to sanction and vindicate the statutory policy.

*F.W. Woolworth Co. v. Contemporary Arts, Inc.*, 344 U.S. 228, 233 (1952).

4. ***Statutory Damages and the Right to Jury Trial.*** In *Feltner v. Columbia Pictures Television, Inc.*, 523 U.S. 340 (1998), the Supreme Court held that the Seventh Amendment guarantee of a right to a jury trial applies to claims for statutory damages for copyright infringement. A copyright infringement plaintiff that elects the statutory damages remedy may also, therefore, elect to have the claim for damages tried to a jury — rather than only to the court, as in *Engel*. Despite the fact that *Feltner* concluded that §504(c) of the Copyright Act is unconstitutional to the extent that it fails to allow the plaintiff to elect a jury trial, the statute has not been amended.

---

Section 504(c) provides that the copyright owner may elect an award of statutory damages "for all infringements involved in the action, with respect to any one work." This raises the question: What constitutes a work, for purposes of an award of statutory damages?

## COLUMBIA PICTURES TELEVISION v. KRYPTON BROADCASTING OF BIRMINGHAM, INC.

### 106 F.3d 284 (9th Cir. 1997)

BRUNETTI, Circuit Judge.

C. Elvin Feltner is the owner of Krypton International Corporation, which in turn owns three television stations in the southeast. Columbia Pictures Television licensed several television shows to the three stations, including "Who's the Boss?," "Silver Spoons," "Hart to Hart," and "T.J. Hooker." After the stations became delinquent in paying royalties, Columbia attempted to terminate the licensing agreements. The stations continued to broadcast the programs, and Columbia filed suit. During the course of the litigation, Columbia dropped all causes of action except its copyright claims against Feltner. The district court found Feltner vicariously and contributorily liable for copyright infringement on the part of the Krypton defendants, granted summary judgment in favor of Columbia on liability, and, after a bench trial, awarded Columbia $8,800,000 in statutory damages and over $750,000 in attorneys fees and costs. In this appeal, Feltner and Krypton International challenge several of the district court's rulings.

\* \* \*

## VII.  CALCULATION OF THE NUMBER OF INFRINGEMENTS

### A. THE STATIONS WERE SEPARATE INFRINGERS.

Section 504(c)(1) of the Act provides that statutory damages may be awarded "for all infringements involved in the action, with respect to any one work, for which any one infringer is liable individually, or for which any two or more infringers are liable jointly and severally...." Thus, when statutory damages are assessed against one defendant or a group of defendants held to be jointly and severally liable, each work infringed may form the basis of only one award, regardless of the number of separate infringements of that work. However, "where separate infringements for which two or more defendants are not jointly liable are joined in the same action, separate awards of statutory damages would be appropriate." H.R. Rep. No. 94-1476, 94th Cong., 2d Sess., at 162, *reprinted in* 1976 U.S. Code Cong. and Admin. News 5778.

By finding that "the 'Who's the Boss?' episodes broadcast by WNFT are separate acts of infringement from the episodes broadcast by WTVX," the district court impliedly found that WNFT and WTVX were not joint tortfeasors with respect to the broadcasting of these episodes.

\* \* \*

...Feltner has failed to demonstrate that the finding was erroneous.

### B. EACH EPISODE WAS A SEPARATE WORK.

As mentioned, §504(c)(1) of the Act provides that statutory damages may be awarded "for all infringements involved in the action, with respect to any one work." Section 504(c)(1) further provides that "for purposes of this subsection, all the parts of a compilation or derivative work constitute one work." The district court found that each infringed episode of the television series constituted a separate work for purposes of §504(c)(1). Feltner argues that each series, and not each episode, constitutes a work.

The two courts to have addressed whether each episode of a television series constitutes a separate work have both held in the affirmative. *Gamma Audio & Video, Inc. v. Ean-Chea*, 11 F.3d 1106, 1116-17 (1st Cir. 1993). Feltner attempts to distinguish these cases by arguing that the episodes at issue are not separate works because they do not have independent economic value.

While Feltner correctly states the proper test to apply in analyzing whether each episode is a separate work, *see Gamma Audio*, 11 F.3d at 1117 (focusing on whether each television episode "has an independent economic value and is, in itself, viable"); *Walt Disney Co. v. Powell*, 897 F.2d 565, 569 (D.C. Cir. 1990) (stating that "separate copyrights are not distinct unless they can 'live their own copyright life'"), the facts upon which

Feltner bases his argument — that the episodes are licensed as a series — were addressed and rejected in *Gamma Audio*.

In *Gamma Audio*, the district court found that the episodes were a single work because the copyright holder sold only complete sets of the series to video stores. The First Circuit found this unpersuasive. Instead, the court found significant "the fact that (1) viewers who rent the tapes from their local video stores may rent as few or as many tapes as they want, may view one, two, or twenty episodes in a single setting, and may never watch or rent all of the episodes; and (2) each episode in the . . . series was separately produced." 11 F.3d at 1117.

*[handwritten margin note: each episode is its own work]*

In this case, the different episodes were broadcast over the course of weeks, months, and years. From this fact, it was reasonable for the district court to conclude that, as in *Gamma Audio*, viewers may watch as few or as many episodes as they want, and may never watch all of the episodes. Additionally, it was clear from the record that the episodes could be repeated and broadcast in different orders. Nor does Feltner contest that the episodes were separately written, produced, and registered. Thus, this case comes squarely within the holdings of *Gamma Audio* and *Twin Peaks*.

Feltner also contends that each series was an anthology, a type of "compilation" under §504(c). Feltner argues that the question of whether the episodes amounted to a "collective whole" was a factual one. Thus, argues Feltner, the district court's refusal to allow Feltner to produce evidence on the issue, which would have consisted of a license agreement and expert testimony that "programs of this nature are considered to be anthologies," was error.

Even were Feltner allowed to prove that the programs were considered to be "anthologies," he would still have to show that they consisted of "separate and independent works . . . assembled into a collective whole." As mentioned, the evidence was uncontroverted that the episodes were broadcast over the course of weeks, months, or even years, and could be repeated and rearranged at the option of the broadcaster. Because this evidence supports the conclusion that the episodes were not "assembled into a collective whole," it was not error for the district court to reject Feltner's contention that each series was a "compilation" under §504(c).

The district court did not err in calculating the number of infringements.

\* \* \*

## Comments

*1. **Flexibility and Statutory Purpose.*** Statutory damages are awarded on the basis of the number of works infringed, rather than on the basis of the number of infringements of each work. Nonetheless, the "independent economic value" standard that the court follows in *Columbia Pictures Television* allows courts substantial flexibility. That flexibility shows up elsewhere in the Copyright Act where courts must decide "what is the work." Even in the context of television series, for example, "the work" may consist of the series as a whole, rather than the individual episode.

In *Castle Rock Entertainment, Inc. v. Carol Publishing Group, Inc.*, 150 F.3d 132 (2d Cir. 1998), noted in Chapter 7, the Court of Appeals for the Second Circuit ruled that a book of trivia questions titled "The Seinfeld Aptitude Test" infringed a valid copyright in the *Seinfeld* television series taken as a whole. In *Tin Pan Apple, Inc. v. Miller Brewing Co., Inc.*, No. 88 Civ. 4085 (CSH), 1994 WL 62360 (S.D.N.Y. Feb. 24, 1994), the court denied the defendants' motion for summary judgment in a case alleging that they had infringed musical composition and sound recording copyrights in a song titled "Stick Em" by the Fat Boys, and specifically in the lyrics, "Brrr" and "Hugga-Hugga." In *Country Road Music, Inc. v. Mp3.com, Inc.*, 279 F. Supp. 2d 325 (S.D.N.Y. 2003), involving unauthorized reproduction of musical recordings via the creation of an online digital music storage service, the court concluded that the appropriate unit for statutory damage analysis was the CD, since the defendant had both copied and intended to distribute entire CDs, rather than the individual musical composition. The court relied on §504(c)(1), which provides that "For the purposes of this subsection, all the parts of a compilation or derivative work constitute one work." This language limits the possibility of double recovery by copyright owners who own copyrights to a CD (which is a compilation work), for example, as well as to individual recordings included on the CD.

2. ***Pretty Soon, You're Talking Real Money.*** Do not be misled by the relatively small amounts recited in §504(c). In the appropriate case, statutory damages can reach lofty levels. To paraphrase the late Senator Everett Dirksen, a million here, a million there, and pretty soon you're talking real money. In *Lowry's Reports, Inc. v. Legg Mason, Inc.*, 302 F. Supp. 2d 455 (D. Md. 2004), involving the unauthorized reproduction and distribution of a stock market newsletter by a subscriber that made additional copies for its employees, the court affirmed a jury verdict finding that the defendant had infringed 240 separate works, that the infringement was willful, and that the statutory damages award should be $19,725,270. The plaintiff had placed its actual damages at $6.8 million; the defendant argued that actual damages were limited to $59,000.

# C. ADDITIONAL REMEDIES

In addition to injunctive relief and damages, the Copyright Act grants additional remedies to copyright owners: seizure and impoundment of infringing articles and tools used to produce them, and attorneys' fees. In certain cases, these can be powerful tools for putting a stop to infringing activity and deterring future infringement.

## 1. Seizure and Impoundment

Section 503 of the Copyright Act provides that in connection with a pending suit for copyright infringement, a court may impound copies and phonorecords alleged to have been made or used in violation of the copyright owner's rights, as well as any means by which the allegedly infringing copies were produced. The court may order their disposition upon a final judgment of infringement, meaning that they are subject to being destroyed. Under §509, in the case of criminal liability for copyright infringement, all infringing copies and phonorecords and their means of production may be seized and forfeited to the United States.

Copyright owners may also obtain seizure and impoundment of infringing articles without having to file a lawsuit, if the seizure applies to the unauthorized importation of infringing articles. Section 603(c) of the Copyright Act provides that unauthorized importation of infringing goods renders the items subject to seizure as forfeiture as property imported in violation of American customs laws. By regulation, §603(c) applies only to copyrighted works that have been registered; once registration is accomplished, the copyright owner records the copyright with the Customs Service. The relevant port director is then empowered to seize each item "which he determines is an infringing copy or phonorecord of a copyrighted work protected by Customs." 19 C.F.R. §133.42(c) (2005).

## 2. Attorneys' Fees

Section 505 grants courts discretion to award attorneys' fees and costs to prevailing parties, but it contains no standards to guide that discretion. As with an election of statutory damages, §412 provides that recovery of fees is subject to a requirement of timely registration. The standards for awarding attorneys' fees in copyright cases were refined in extended litigation involving a rock 'n' roll singer-songwriter. The claim in the case, *Fantasy, Inc. v. Fogerty*, began in 1985, when Fantasy sued John Fogerty, formerly the lead singer of Creedence Clearwater Revival, for copyright infringement. Fantasy alleged that Fogerty's solo work "The Old Man Down the Road" infringed the copyright on another of his songs, "Run Through the Jungle," recorded by Creedence, which Fantasy owned. Three years later, the jury returned a verdict in favor of Fogerty. Fogerty moved for a reasonable attorney's fee under 17 U.S.C. §505. The district court denied the request, on the ground that prevailing defendants in copyright cases were entitled to attorneys' fees only if the lawsuit was frivolous or prosecuted in bad faith, and Fantasy's lawsuit was neither. That ruling was affirmed by the Ninth Circuit, in *Fantasy, Inc. v. Fogerty*, 984 F.2d 1524 (9th Cir. 1993), known as "*Fogerty I*," but the Supreme Court reversed and remanded in *Fogerty v. Fantasy, Inc.*, 510 U.S. 517 (1994), known as "*Fogerty II*." The Court held that §505 permits district courts to exercise their discretion and award attorneys' fees to prevailing defendants on a like basis with prevailing plaintiffs, even in the absence of a finding of frivolity or bad faith, in order to promote the underlying purposes of the Copyright Act. Following further proceedings in the trial court on the question of attorneys' fees, the case was again appealed to the Ninth Circuit. In *Fantasy, Inc. v. Fogerty*, 94 F.3d 553 (9th Cir. 1996) (known as "*Fantasy III*"), that court ruled that the trial court's discretion — as to both prevailing plaintiffs and prevailing defendants — should be informed by non-exclusive factors including those listed in *Lieb v. Topstone Indus., Inc.*, 788 F.2d 151 (3d Cir. 1986) (frivolousness, motivation, the objective unreasonableness of the factual and the legal components of the case, and the need to advance considerations of compensation and deterrence); the degree of success obtained in the litigation; the presence or absence of culpability in bringing, pursuing, or defending the lawsuit; and the purposes of the Act—which include both encouraging claims to enforce rights under the Act as well as encouraging successful defense of meritless claims.

## D. OTHER REMEDIAL CONCERNS

### 1. The Civil Procedure of Copyright

Suits for copyright infringement are subject to a variety of special procedural limitations specified by statute.

#### a. Standing

Throughout this chapter, access to copyright remedies has been linked to "copyright owners." Section 501(b) of the Copyright Act provides a more precise definition: A suit for copyright infringement may be instituted by a legal or a beneficial owner of an exclusive right under a copyright. This means both that an exclusive licensee of a copyright interest may sue for infringement of the licensee's exclusive rights, *see Eden Toys v. Florelee Undergarment Co.*, 697 F.2d 27 (2d Cir. 1983), and that "beneficial owners," who have given up legal title in exchange for royalties based on a percentage of sales or license income, likewise have standing to sue for infringement of the copyright. The statutory language does not include claims for infringement brought by assignees of causes of action for infringement, who have neither legal nor beneficial ownership of a right under the copyright. In *Silvers v. Sony Pictures Entertainment, Inc.*, 402 F.3d 881 (9th Cir. 2005) (en banc), the plaintiff, a screenwriter, sued a motion picture production company for infringement of the copyright in her screenplay. The script was prepared initially as a work-made-for-hire for a production company. When another motion picture studio released a feature film that allegedly infringed the copyright, the production company that owned the copyright executed an Assignment of Claims and Causes of Action in favor of the screenwriter. The screenwriter filed suit. The defendant moved to dismiss the Complaint on the ground that she lacked standing under §501(b). The district court denied the motion and certified the issue for interlocutory appeal. The Court of Appeals for the Ninth Circuit reversed, ruling that the specification of proper plaintiffs in §501(b) constituted an exclusive listing of parties eligible to bring infringement suits.

#### b. Subject Matter Jurisdiction

Federal courts have exclusive subject matter jurisdiction over copyright infringement actions. Section 1338(a) of Title 28 provides:

The district courts shall have original jurisdiction of any civil action arising under any Act of Congress relating to patents, plant variety protection, copyrights and trademarks. Such jurisdiction shall be exclusive of the courts of the states in patent, plant variety protection and copyright cases.

An action that pleads a claim for copyright infringement clearly constitutes an action "arising under" the Copyright Act. From time to time, however, copyright plaintiffs may couple a claim for copyright infringement with a claim against the same defendant that nominally arises under state law, such as a claim for breach of a license agreement. In such a case, it may appear that the copyright claim is added merely to invoke federal jurisdiction over what is "really" a state law matter. Or, the plaintiff may try to avoid federal court altogether by pleading the claim entirely as a matter of state law. In either instance, the question may then arise: Has the plaintiff pleaded a claim that "arises under" the Copyright Act? The relevant standard is supplied by *T.B. Harms Co. v. Eliscu*, 339 F.2d 823 (2d Cir. 1964), which states that a claim "arises under" the Copyright Act if it seeks a remedy expressly provided by the Act (such as a suit for infringement, or for statutory royalties), or asserts a claim requiring construction of the Act. In the case of a properly pleaded claim of copyright infringement coupled with a proper state law claim, federal jurisdiction will lie with respect to the copyright infringement claim, and the state law claim also may be decided by the federal court under its "supplemental" jurisdiction. *See* 28 U.S.C. §1367.

## c. Timing, the Statute of Limitations, and Declaratory Judgments

Recall from earlier in this chapter that a suit for copyright infringement cannot be initiated until and unless a certificate of registration has been issued. (Section 411 also provides that if the Register refuses registration, the copyright owner can initiate a lawsuit so long as the Register is given notice of the complaint, together with a copy.) Claims for infringement have a statute of limitations: Section 507(b) provides that "[n]o civil action shall be maintained under the provisions of this title unless it is commenced within three years after the claim accrued." "Accrual" of a copyright infringement claim occurs when the copyright owner has actual or constructive knowledge of the cause of action. *See Polar Bear Productions, Inc. v. Timex Corp.*, 384 F.3d 700, 706-707 (9th Cir. 2004). Even though an application for copyright registration is not subject to the searching scrutiny ordinarily given to patent applications, processing an application may take several months. The prospective copyright plaintiff should take care not to delay unnecessarily in submitting an application.

At times, the plaintiff may not be the copyright owner seeking a remedy for infringement, but an individual or firm that is concerned prospectively about liability for infringement. Filing an action for a declaratory judgment is appropriate, under the United States Code, in the case of an "actual controversy." *See* 28 U.S.C. §2201. An "actual controversy" for declaratory judgment purposes exists if (i) there is a threat of other action by the copyright owner that creates a reasonable apprehension that an infringement suit will be filed (a cease-and-desist letter from the copyright owner will usually satisfy this requirement), and (ii) the declaratory plaintiff has engaged in conduct that could constitute infringement, or taken concrete steps with the intent to do so. *See Diagnostic Unit Inmate Council v. Films Inc.*, 88 F.3d 651, 653 (8th Cir. 1996).

### d. Parties

Section 501 grants owners of exclusive rights in copyright, including exclusive licensees, the right to pursue claims of copyright infringement. While it might appear initially that any individual or entity that infringes one or more rights under §106 is potentially liable as a defendant, in fact there is an important class of potential defendants that may be immune from suit: state governments. In *Florida Prepaid Postsecondary Educ. Expense Board v. College Savings Bank*, 527 U.S. 627 (1999), and *College Savings Bank v. Florida Prepaid Postsecondary Educ. Expense Board*, 527 U.S. 666 (1999), issued on the same day, the Supreme Court held that the Eleventh Amendment to the Constitution, which grants sovereign immunity to the states for suits filed in federal court, bars suits against states in federal court for violations of the patent and trademark laws, respectively. In *Chavez v. Arte Publico Press*, 204 F.3d 601 (5th Cir. 2000), the Fifth Circuit concluded that the *College Savings Bank* cases dictate the same result with respect to copyright claims.

Under the Fourteenth Amendment, under certain circumstances Congress may abrogate sovereign immunity and authorize federal courts to hear certain claims against state governments. Commentators and legislators have proposed a variety of statutory solutions to the problem created by the *College Savings Bank* cases, consistent with this limited authority, but to date no comprehensive reform has been adopted.

## 2. Criminal Penalties

*STATUTE:* **Criminal Offenses**

17 U.S.C. §506

*STATUTE:* **Definition — "Financial Gain"**

17 U.S.C. §101

Criminal copyright remedies were first added to the Copyright Act in 1897, when infringing public performances and presentations of copyrighted dramatic or musical works, when made willfully and for profit, were made misdemeanors. In the 1909 Copyright Act, willful and for-profit infringement was made the basis for criminal liability with respect to all types of works and infringement. The 1976 Act changed the basis for liability slightly. Criminal liability attached when the infringement was done "willfully and for purposes of commercial advantage or financial gain." Since 1976, the criminal provisions of the Act have been amended further. While the "willfulness" requirement has been retained, criminal copyright infringements may now be classed as felonies, and infringements may be characterized as based on the number of infringing copies made or sold within a limited time period, as well as based on their "commercial" character. This last change was made in response to the development of networks of people trading unauthorized copies of computer programs, rather than selling them. Penalties for criminal copyright infringement include prison terms of up to five years and fines of up to $250,000. *See* 18 U.S.C. §2319.

## UNITED STATES v. MORAN
### 757 F. Supp. 1046 (D. Neb. 1991)

RICHARD G. KOPF, United States Magistrate Judge.

The parties have consented to try this misdemeanor case before me. Trial was held on January 15, 1991, and briefs were received on January 23, 1991. I now find that the defendant is not guilty of the alleged willful infringement of a copyrighted video cassette in violation of 17 U.S.C. §506(a).

### I. FACTS

Dennis Moran (Moran), the defendant, is a full-time Omaha, Nebraska, police officer and the owner of a "mom-and-pop" movie rental business which rents video cassettes of copyrighted motion pictures to the public. On April 14, 1989, agents of the Federal Bureau of Investigation (FBI) executed a court-ordered search warrant on the premises of Moran's business. The FBI seized various video cassettes appearing to be unauthorized copies of copyrighted motion pictures, including "Bat 21," "Big," "Crocodile Dundee II," "The Fourth Protocol," "Hell-Bound: Hellraiser II," and "Mystic Pizza." The parties have stipulated that these six motion pictures are validly copyrighted motion pictures. The parties have further stipulated that each of the six motion pictures was distributed to Moran, with the permission of the copyright holder, between February 1, 1989, and April 14, 1989. The parties have further stipulated that at least one of the movies identified was reproduced by Moran onto a video cassette, without the authorization of the copyright holder, placed into inventory for rental, and subsequently rented.

At the time the FBI executed the search warrant, Moran was fully cooperative. He told the FBI agents he put the "duped" copies out for rental and held the "originals" back because he feared the "original" motion pictures would be stolen or damaged. Moran told the FBI agents at the time they executed the warrant that he believed this practice was legal as long as he had purchased and was in possession of the "original" motion picture. Moran further advised the FBI agents that he would affix to the "duped" copies title labels for the copyrighted motion pictures and a copy of the FBI copyright warning label commonly found on video cassette tapes. Moran advised the FBI agents that he put the title labels and FBI warning on the tapes to stop customers from stealing or duplicating the tapes.

Moran testified at trial. He indicated that he had been employed as an Omaha, Nebraska, police officer for approximately twenty-two-and-a-half years, including service as a narcotics investigator and as a bodyguard to the mayor of the City of Omaha. Moran has a reputation for honesty among his associates.

Moran testified that he began to "insure" copyrighted video cassettes, meaning that he duplicated copyrighted video cassettes which he had validly purchased from distributors, when he realized copyrighted tapes were being vandalized. Moran testified he was under the impression that "insuring" tapes was legal whereas "pirating" tapes was not. For practical purposes, Moran defined "insuring" versus "pirating" as meaning that he could duplicate a copyrighted tape provided he had purchased the copyrighted tape and did not endeavor to rent both the copyrighted tape and the duplicate he had made. Moran testified that he formulated his belief about "insuring" versus "pirating" when talking with various colleagues in the business and from reading trade publications. However, Moran was not able to specifically identify the source of his information.

There was no persuasive evidence that Moran made multiple copies of each authorized version of the copyrighted material. The evidence indicates that Moran purchased more than one copyrighted tape of the same movie, but the persuasive evidence also reveals that Moran made only one copy of each copyrighted tape he purchased. There was no persuasive evidence that Moran endeavored to rent both the copyrighted tape and the duplicate. When Moran made the unauthorized copy, he put the unauthorized copy in a package made to resemble as closely as possible the package containing the original copyrighted motion picture Moran had purchased from an authorized distributor.

## II. LAW

Moran makes two arguments. First, Moran argues that the government must prove that he had the specific intent to violate the law, that is, he knew that what he was doing was illegal and he committed the act nevertheless. Secondly, Moran argues that he did not have the specific intent to violate the law and, as a consequence, should be found not guilty.

In pertinent part 17 U.S.C. §506(a) punishes as a criminal any "person who infringes a copyright willfully and for purposes of commercial advantage or private financial gain." Pursuant to 17 U.S.C. §106(3), the owner of a copyright has the exclusive right to "distribute copies...of the copyrighted work to the public by sale or other transfer of ownership, or by rental, lease, or lending." The "exclusive right" of the owner of a copyright is subject to a variety of exceptions.

### A.

It must first be determined whether the word "willfully," as used in 17 U.S.C. §506(a), requires a showing of "bad purpose" or "evil motive" in the sense that there was an "intentional violation of a known legal duty." Adopting the research of the Motion Picture Association of America, the government argues that the term "willful" means only "an intent to copy and not to infringe." On the other hand, Moran argues that the use of the word "willful" implies the kind of specific intent required to be proven in federal tax cases, which is to say, a voluntary, intentional violation of a known legal duty.

The general rule is, of course, that ignorance of the law or mistake of the law is no defense to a criminal prosecution. However, when the term "willfully" is used in complex statutory schemes, such as federal criminal tax statutes, the term "willful" means a "voluntary, intentional violation of a known legal duty." *Cheek v. United States,* 498 U.S. 192 (1991) (holding in a criminal tax prosecution that a good faith misunderstanding of the law or a good faith belief that one is not violating the law negates willfulness, whether or not the claimed belief or misunderstanding is objectively reasonable). . . .

Apparently no case has compared and analyzed the competing arguments, i.e., whether the word "willfully" requires either a showing of specific intent, as suggested by Moran, or the more generalized intent suggested by the government. Indeed, a leading text writer acknowledges that there are two divergent lines of cases, one of which requires specific intent and another which does not. 3 M. Nimmer & D. Nimmer, *Nimmer on Copyright,* §15.01 at 15-5 n. 13 (1990) (hereinafter *Nimmer*). As pointed out by the government, some courts have suggested that "willful" only means an intent to copy, not to infringe. On the other hand, as suggested by Moran, other courts have seemingly required evidence of specific intent. At least two courts have specifically approved jury instructions essentially stating that an act of infringement done "willfully" means an act voluntarily and purposely done with specific intent to do that which the law forbids, that is to say, with bad purpose either to disobey or disregard the law. None of the cases recognize that there are divergent lines of cases on this point, and none of the cases endeavor to explain why one line of cases is more compelling than the other.

I am persuaded that under 17 U.S.C. §506(a) "willfully" means that in order to be criminal the infringement must have been a "voluntary, intentional violation of a known legal duty." *Cheek,* 498 U.S. at 201. I am so persuaded because I believe that in using the word "willful" Congress intended to soften the impact of the common-law presumption that ignorance of the law or mistake of the law is no defense to a criminal prosecution by making specific intent to violate the law an element of federal criminal copyright offenses. I came to this conclusion after examining the use of the word "willful" in the civil copyright infringement context and applying that use to the criminal statute.

In the civil context there is "strict liability" for infringement, even where the infringement was "innocent." In this connection, a plaintiff in a civil case need not prove actual damages, but rather may seek what are called statutory damages. The term "willful" is used in the context of statutory damages, and it is instructive to compare the definition of the term "willful," as used in the civil context regarding statutory damages, with the definition of the term "willful" used in the criminal context.

In the statutory damage context, a civil plaintiff is generally entitled to recover no less than $250.00 nor more than $10,000.00 per act of infringement. 17 U.S.C. §504(c)(1). But where the infringement is committed "willfully," the court in its discretion may increase the award of statutory damages up to a maximum of $50,000.00 per act of infringement. 17 U.S.C. §504(c)(2). On the other hand, in the case of "innocent infringement," if the defendant sustains the burden of proving he/she was not aware, and had no reason to believe, that his/her acts constituted an infringement of the copyright, and the court so finds, the court may in its discretion reduce the applicable minimum to $100.00 per act of infringement. 17 U.S.C. §504(c)(2).

As noted text writers have concluded, the meaning of the term "willful," used in 17 U.S.C. §504, must mean that the infringement was with knowledge that the defendant's conduct constituted copyright infringement. Otherwise, there would be no point in providing specially for the reduction of awards to the $100.00 level in the case of "innocent" infringement since any infringement which was nonwillful would necessarily be innocent.

\* \* \*

There is nothing in the text of the criminal copyright statute, the overall scheme of the copyright laws, or the legislative history to suggest that Congress intended the word "willful," when used in the criminal statute, to mean simply, as the government suggests, an intent to copy. Rather, since Congress used "willful" in the civil damage copyright context to mean that the infringement must take place with the defendant being knowledgeable that his/her conduct constituted copyright infringement, there is no compelling reason to adopt a less stringent requirement in the criminal copyright context. Accordingly, I find that "willfully," when used in 17 U.S.C. §506(a), means a "voluntary, intentional violation of a known legal duty."

### B.

Having determined that the standard enunciated by the Supreme Court in *Cheek*, 498 U.S. 192, applies, it is important to recognize that the rule does not require that a defendant's belief that his conduct is lawful be judged by an objective standard. Rather, the test is whether Moran truly believed that the copyright laws did not prohibit him from making one copy of a video cassette he had purchased in order to "insure" against vandalism. In other words, the test is not whether Moran's view was objectively reasonable, but rather, whether Moran truly believed that the law did not proscribe his conduct. Of course, the more unreasonable the asserted belief or misunderstanding, the more likely it is that the finder of fact will consider the asserted belief or misunderstanding to be nothing more than simple disagreement with known legal duties imposed by the law, and will find that the government has carried its burden of proving knowledge.

Most of the government's argument that it proved beyond a reasonable doubt that Moran violated the criminal copyright statute, even if the word "willfully" is defined as Moran suggests, is based upon the assumption that Moran's beliefs must be "objectively" reasonable. As indicated above, Moran's beliefs need not have been objectively reasonable; rather, if Moran truly believed that he was not subject to the copyright laws, then his subjective belief would defeat a finding that he "willfully" violated the statute.

First, I note that I had an opportunity to observe Moran when he testified. Moran struck me as an honest, albeit naive, person. I was left with the definite impression that Moran was befuddled and bewildered by the criminal prosecution.

Second, although Moran is a local police officer of long standing, there is nothing in his background to suggest any particular sophistication about business matters, and there is no evidence to suggest that he has any particular knowledge about the intricacies of the copyright laws. When confronted by FBI agents upon the execution of the search warrant, Moran was entirely cooperative. On the day the search warrant was executed, he told his story in the same way he now tells his story.

Third, Moran said he had heard from others and read in various publications that it was legally appropriate to engage in the practice he called "insuring." Moran could not cite the specific source of his information. In this regard, I note that the copyright laws permit libraries and archives to replace a copyrighted article that is damaged, deteriorated, lost, or stolen, if the library or archives have, after reasonable effort, determined that an unused replacement cannot be obtained at a fair price. 17 U.S.C. §108(c). While Moran obviously did not operate his business as a library or archives, the government's assertion that the practice of "insuring" is patently unreasonable is belied by the recognition that under certain circumstances certain users of copyrighted materials may lawfully engage in copying activity which is similar to Moran's conduct.

Fourth, Moran testified that he made only one copy of the original motion picture purchased from the authorized distributor. The government doubts his testimony, but offers no persuasive evidence to contradict it. Moreover, Moran testified that he never rented both the original copyrighted version of the video cassette purchased from the authorized distributor and the copy he made. Instead, he testified that he always held back the original motion picture. Once again, the government doubts this testimony in its brief, but offers no persuasive evidence to the contrary. Furthermore, the evidence indicates that Moran purchased more than one authorized cassette of a particular motion picture, but made only one duplicate for each authorized cassette purchased.

This evidence suggests that Moran was not acting with a willful intention to violate the copyright laws because if he had such an intention it would make absolutely no sense to purchase multiple authorized video cassettes and then make only one duplicate of each authorized cassette. It would have been far simpler, and certainly more lucrative, for Moran to purchase one authorized cassette of a particular motion picture and make multiple copies from the authorized version. In this way Moran would have had to pay only one fee. The fact that Moran seems to have consistently followed the practice of buying an authorized version, but making only one copy of it, suggests that he was acting in accordance with his belief that to duplicate an authorized version in order to "insure it" was lawful so long as only one copy was made and the authorized version and copy were not both rented.

Fifth, the government argues that Moran must have known that what he was doing constituted a copyright infringement because he had before him the FBI warning label and in fact affixed such labels to the unauthorized copies he made. In pertinent part, the FBI warning states, "Federal law provides severe civil and criminal penalties for the *unauthorized* reproduction, distribution or exhibition of copyrighted motion pictures and video tapes" (emphasis added). Moran explained that he thought these warning labels applied to the renting public, not to him. The use of the word "unauthorized" on the warning label suggested to Moran that vendors who had purchased an authorized version were not subject to the legal restrictions expressed in the warning to the extent that the practice of "insuring" was legal. As Moran suggests, the FBI warning label does not specifically address the claim of legality professed by Moran. Accordingly, Moran's failure to heed the warning label is not determinative.

Sixth, the government further argues that Moran's effort to place the unauthorized copy into a video cassette package displaying a label on its spine and an FBI warning label suggests a sinister motivation. I disagree. Moran's testimony, as I understood it, indicated that when he made a copy he endeavored to make the duplicate look like the original in all respects. After all, the whole purpose of the practice of "insuring" was to use the unauthorized copy in lieu of the original when renting to the public. It was perfectly consistent with Moran's view of the law to make the unauthorized copy look as nearly as possible like the authorized version.

In summary, when Moran's actions were viewed from the totality of the circumstances, the government failed to convince me beyond a reasonable doubt that Moran acted willfully. Moran is a long-time street cop who was fully cooperative with law enforcement authorities. He is obviously not sophisticated and, at least from the record, his business operation of renting movies to the public was not large or sophisticated. Rather, Moran's business appears to have been of the "mom-and-pop" variety. Moran's practice of "insuring," while obviously shifting the risk of loss from Moran to the copyright holder, was conducted in such a way as not to maximize profits, which one assumes would have been his purpose if he had acted willfully. For example, Moran purchased multiple authorized copies of the same movie, but he made only one unauthorized copy for each authorized version purchased. This suggests that Moran truly believed that what he was doing was in fact legal. I therefore find Moran not guilty.

## Comments

1. **Scienter** *in Copyright.* *Moran* responds to the concern that there should be a meaningful distinction between criminal copyright infringement, which incorporates the traditional principle that criminal liability depends on a finding of *scienter*, or intent, and the oft-stated maxim that civil copyright infringement is a strict liability offense, for which no "intent to infringe" is required. Recall, further, that "willfulness" may be relevant in a civil infringement lawsuit, if the copyright owner seeks statutory damages. A finding of "willful" infringement permits the court to increase the range of recoverable damages. A finding of "innocent" infringement permits the court to reduce that range.

2. *Criminal Enforcement of the Copyright Act.* Partly in response to pressure from the entertainment and computer software industries, in recent years the U.S. Department of Justice has substantially increased the amount of resources devoted to investigating and prosecuting criminal copyright infringement. Much of this effort is devoted to ensuring that consumers are aware of the penalties for criminal copyright infringe-

ment. For example, in 2004 and in cooperation with music, motion picture, and computer software industry associations, the FBI released an "Anti-Piracy Warning" seal, described at *http://www.fbi.gov/ipr/*, that may be affixed to copies of CDs, DVDs, and computer disks, warning consumers of criminal penalties associated with copyright infringement. Large-scale piracy rings remain a priority for prosecutors. The Justice Department has collected and increased resources for addressing "cybercrime," including criminal copyright infringement, involving use of the Internet. The Justice Department maintains a website at *http://www.usdoj.gov/criminal/cybercrime/* that summarizes its ongoing activity in this area.

## 3. Remedies for Violations of Related Rights

The manner in which the Copyright Act fixes the rights and remedies of copyright owners for violations of the exclusive rights provided in §106 should be contrasted with the remedial provisions of other parts of Title 17: the anticircumvention provisions of the DMCA; and the limited "moral rights" protection afforded under the Visual Artists Rights Act.

### a. Digital Millennium Copyright Act

Chapter 7 described the substantive provisions of the Digital Millennium Copyright Act's prohibition on "circumvention" of technological measures which guard against unauthorized access to and exploitation of copyrighted works. That chapter noted that the structure of the substantive rights offered by the DMCA extends beyond those offered by §106, a change in the law that Congress concluded was warranted in light of the technical and marketplace conditions created by the Internet. The remedial structure of the DMCA, too, differs from the default remedial structure of the Copyright Act.

Section 1203(a) provides, "Any person injured by a violation of section 1201 or 1202 may bring a civil action in an appropriate United States district court for such violation." This section was among the first to be applied following the enactment of the DMCA. *RealNetworks, Inc. v. Streambox, Inc.*, No. 2:99CV02070, 2000 WL 127311 (W.D. Wash. Jan. 18, 2000), noted in Chapter 7, involved a claim for relief under §1201 that was brought not by a copyright owner, but by the developer of a technical scheme for implementing a "technological measure" protected under the DMCA.

The range of civil remedies available under §1203 is broad. In addition to equitable relief, actual damages, lost profits, and statutory damages (§1203(b)), the court may order provisional relief "impounding, on such terms as it deems reasonable, of any device or product that is in the custody or control of the alleged violator and that the court has reasonable cause to believe was involved in a violation," (§1203(b)(2)), and as part of a final judgment, may order "the remedial modification or the destruction of any device or product involved in the violation that is in the custody or control

of the violator or has been impounded under paragraph (2)."
(§1203(b)(6).) In addition, the court has the power to reduce or remit
damages entered against any party that proves that it was an "innocent"
offender (§1203(c)(5)(A)). The statute provides that the court shall remit
damages entirely against certain nonprofit institutions that prove that they
were innocent offenders (§1203(c)(5)(B)).

The DMCA also includes criminal penalties. Willful violation of §§1201
or 1202, "for purposes of commercial advantage or private financial gain"
is punishable by a fine of up to $500,000 or a sentence of up to five years, or
both, for the first offense, a fine of up to $1,000,000 or a sentence of up to
ten years, or both, for any subsequent offense. *See* 17 U.S.C. §1204. The
criminal penalties of the DMCA are thus more severe than those applicable
to copyright infringement itself. The statute of limitations is likewise
longer: prosecutions must be brought with five years of the date that the
cause of action accrues.

### b. Visual Artists Rights Act

Chapter 7 also reviewed the Visual Artists Rights Act, a limited exception to
the general principle that American copyright law does not offer "moral
rights" to authors. The VARA grants authors limited rights to claim authorship of a work and to prevent mutilation or destruction of their works.
Section 106A, however, specifically provides that rights under VARA are
granted only to the author of the work, whether or not the author is the
copyright owner. *See* 17 U.S.C. §106A(b). The author's rights under this
section last for a term consisting of the life of the author (rather than life of
the author plus 70 years, the term that applies to copyrights), and while
these rights may be waived, in writing, they may not be assigned or transferred. *See* 17 U.S.C. §106A(d), (e).

# COPYRIGHT STATUTES

## THE COPYRIGHT REVISION ACT of 1976 (Selected Portions)

### 17 U.S.C. §§101 et seq.

### 17 U.S.C. §101. Definitions

"Audiovisual works" are works that consist of a series of related images which are intrinsically intended to be shown by the use of machines, or devices such as projectors, viewers, or electronic equipment, together with accompanying sounds, if any, regardless of the nature of the material objects, such as films or tapes, in which the works are embodied.

A "collective work" is a work, such as a periodical issue, anthology, or encyclopedia, in which a number of contributions, constituting separate and independent works in themselves, are assembled into a collective whole.

A "compilation" is a work formed by the collection and assembling of preexisting materials or of data that are selected, coordinated, or arranged in such a way that the resulting work as a whole constitutes an original work of authorship. The term "compilation" includes collective works.

"Copies" are material objects, other than phonorecords, in which a work is fixed by any method now known or later developed, and from which the work can be perceived, reproduced, or otherwise communicated, either directly or with the aid of a machine or device. The term "copies" includes the material object, other than a phonorecord, in which the work is first fixed.

"Copyright owner", with respect to any one of the exclusive rights comprised in a copyright, refers to the owner of that particular right.

A "derivative work" is a work based upon one or more preexisting works, such as a translation, musical arrangement, dramatization, fictionalization, motion picture version, sound recording, art reproduction, abridgment, condensation, or any other form in which a work may be recast, transformed, or adapted. A work consisting of editorial revisions, annotations, elaborations, or other modifications which, as a whole, represent an original work of authorship, is a "derivative work".

To "display" a work means to show a copy of it, either directly or by means of a film, slide, television image, or any other device or process or, in the case of a motion picture or other audiovisual work, to show individual images nonsequentially.

A work is "fixed" in a tangible medium of expression when its embodiment in a copy or phonorecord, by or under the authority of the author, is sufficiently permanent or stable to permit it to be perceived, reproduced, or otherwise communicated for a period of more than transitory duration. A work consisting of sounds, images, or both, that are being transmitted, is "fixed" for purposes of this title if a fixation of the work is being made simultaneously with its transmission.

A "joint work" is a work prepared by two or more authors with the intention that their contributions be merged into inseparable or interdependent parts of a unitary whole.

637

"Literary works" are works, other than audiovisual works, expressed in words, numbers, or other verbal or numerical symbols or indicia, regardless of the nature of the material objects, such as books, periodicals, manuscripts, phonorecords, film, tapes, disks, or cards, in which they are embodied.

To "perform" a work means to recite, render, play, dance, or act it, either directly or by means of any device or process or, in the case of a motion picture or other audiovisual work, to show its images in any sequence or to make the sounds accompanying it audible.

"Phonorecords" are material objects in which sounds, other than those accompanying a motion picture or other audiovisual work, are fixed by any method now known or later developed, and from which the sounds can be perceived, reproduced, or otherwise communicated, either directly or with the aid of a machine or device. The term "phonorecords" includes the material object in which the sounds are first fixed.

"Pictorial, graphic, and sculptural works" include two-dimensional and three-dimensional works of fine, graphic, and applied art, photographs, prints and art reproductions, maps, globes, charts, diagrams, models, and technical drawings, including architectural plans. Such works shall include works of artistic craftsmanship insofar as their form but not their mechanical or utilitarian aspects are concerned; the design of a useful article, as defined in this section, shall be considered a pictorial, graphic, or sculptural work only if, and only to the extent that, such design incorporates pictorial, graphic, or sculptural features that can be identified separately from, and are capable of existing independently of, the utilitarian aspects of the article.

"Publication" is the distribution of copies or phonorecords of a work to the public by sale or other transfer of ownership, or by rental, lease, or lending. The offering to distribute copies or phonorecords to a group of persons for purposes of further distribution, public performance, or public display, constitutes publication. A public performance or display of a work does not of itself constitute publication.

To perform or display a work "publicly" means—

(1) to perform or display it at a place open to the public or at any place where a substantial number of persons outside of a normal circle of a family and its social acquaintances is gathered; or

(2) to transmit or otherwise communicate a performance or display of the work to a place specified by clause (1) or to the public, by means of any device or process, whether the members of the public capable of receiving the performance or display receive it in the same place or in separate places and at the same time or at different times.

"Sound recordings" are works that result from the fixation of a series of musical, spoken, or other sounds, but not including the sounds accompanying a motion picture or other audiovisual work, regardless of the nature of the material objects, such as disks, tapes, or other phonorecords, in which they are embodied.

To "transmit" a performance or display is to communicate it by any device or process whereby images or sounds are received beyond the place from which they are sent.

Useful article: intrinsic utilitarian function

A "work made for hire" is—

(1) a work prepared by an employee within the scope of his or her employment; or

(2) a work specially ordered or commissioned for use as a contribution to a collective work, as a part of a motion picture or other audiovisual work, as a translation, as a supplementary work, as a compilation, as an instructional text, as a test, as answer material for a test, or as an atlas, if the parties expressly agree in a written instrument signed by them that the work shall be considered a work made for hire. For the purpose of the foregoing sentence, a "supplementary work" is a work prepared for publication as a secondary adjunct to a work by another author for the purpose of introducing, concluding, illustrating, explaining, revising, commenting upon, or assisting in the use of the other work, such as forewords, afterwords, pictorial illustrations, maps, charts, tables, editorial notes, musical arrangements, answer material for tests, bibliographies, appendixes, and indexes, and an "instructional text" is a literary, pictorial, or graphic work prepared for publication and with the purpose of use in systematic instructional activities.

## 17 U.S.C. §102 Subject matter of copyright: In general

(a) Copyright protection subsists, in accordance with this title, in original works of authorship fixed in any tangible medium of expression, now known or later developed, from which they can be perceived, reproduced, or otherwise communicated, either directly or with the aid of a machine or device. Works of authorship include the following categories:

(1) literary works;
(2) musical works, including any accompanying words;
(3) dramatic works, including any accompanying music;
(4) pantomimes and choreographic works;
(5) pictorial, graphic, and sculptural works;
(6) motion pictures and other audiovisual works;
(7) sound recordings; and
(8) architectural works.

(b) In no case does copyright protection for an original work of authorship extend to any idea, procedure, process, system, method of operation, concept, principle, or discovery, regardless of the form in which it is described, explained, illustrated, or embodied in such work.

## 17 U.S.C. §103 Subject matter of copyright: Compilations and derivative works

(a) The subject matter of copyright as specified by section 102 includes compilations and derivative works, but protection for a work employing preexisting material in which copyright subsists does not extend to any part of the work in which such material has been used unlawfully.

(b) The copyright in a compilation or derivative work extends only to the material contributed by the author of such work, as distinguished from the preexisting material employed in the work, and does not imply any exclusive right in the preexisting material. The copyright in such work is independent of, and does not affect or enlarge the scope, duration, ownership, or subsistence of, any copyright protection in the preexisting material.

## 17 U.S.C. §106 Exclusive rights in copyrighted works

Subject to sections 107 through 122, the owner of copyright under this title has the exclusive rights to do and to authorize any of the following:

(1) to reproduce the copyrighted work in copies or phonorecords;

(2) to prepare derivative works based upon the copyrighted work;

(3) to distribute copies or phonorecords of the copyrighted work to the public by sale or other transfer of ownership, or by rental, lease, or lending;

(4) in the case of literary, musical, dramatic, and choreographic works, pantomimes, and motion pictures and other audiovisual works, to perform the copyrighted work publicly;

(5) in the case of literary, musical, dramatic, and choreographic works, pantomimes, and pictorial, graphic, or sculptural works, including the individual images of a motion picture or other audiovisual work, to display the copyrighted work publicly; and

(6) in the case of sound recordings, to perform the copyrighted work publicly by means of a digital audio transmission.

## 17 U.S.C. §107 Limitations on exclusive rights: Fair use

Notwithstanding the provisions of sections 106 and 106A, the fair use of a copyrighted work, including such use by reproduction in copies or phonorecords or by any other means specified by that section, for purposes such as criticism, comment, news reporting, teaching (including multiple copies for classroom use), scholarship, or research, is not an infringement of copyright. In determining whether the use made of a work in any particular case is a fair use the factors to be considered shall include—

(1) the purpose and character of the use, including whether such use is of a commercial nature or is for nonprofit educational purposes;

(2) the nature of the copyrighted work;

(3) the amount and substantiality of the portion used in relation to the copyrighted work as a whole; and

(4) the effect of the use upon the potential market for or value of the copyrighted work.

The fact that a work is unpublished shall not itself bar a finding of fair use if such finding is made upon consideration of all the above factors.

## 17 U.S.C. §109 Limitations on exclusive rights: Effect of transfer of particular copy or phonorecord

(a) Notwithstanding the provisions of section 106 (3), the owner of a particular copy or phonorecord lawfully made under this title, or any person authorized by such owner, is entitled, without the authority of the copyright owner, to sell or otherwise dispose of the possession of that copy or phonorecord. Notwithstanding the preceding sentence, copies or phonorecords of works subject to restored copyright under section 104A that are manufactured before the date of restoration of copyright or, with respect to reliance parties, before publication or service of notice under section 104A (e), may be sold or otherwise disposed of without the authorization of the owner of the restored copyright for purposes of direct or indirect commercial advantage only during the 12-month period beginning on—

(1) the date of the publication in the Federal Register of the notice of intent filed with the Copyright Office under section 104A (d)(2)(A), or

(2) the date of the receipt of actual notice served under section 104A (d)(2)(B), whichever occurs first.

(b) (1) (A) Notwithstanding the provisions of subsection (a), unless authorized by the owners of copyright in the sound recording or the owner of copyright in a computer program (including any tape, disk, or other medium embodying such program), and in the case of a sound recording in the musical works embodied therein, neither the owner of a particular phonorecord nor any person in possession of a particular copy of a computer program (including any tape, disk, or other medium embodying such program), may, for the purposes of direct or indirect commercial advantage, dispose of, or authorize the disposal of, the possession of that phonorecord or computer program (including any tape, disk, or other medium embodying such program) by rental, lease, or lending, or by any other act or practice in the nature of rental, lease, or lending. Nothing in the preceding sentence shall apply to the rental, lease, or lending of a phonorecord for nonprofit purposes by a nonprofit library or nonprofit educational institution. The transfer of possession of a lawfully made copy of a computer program by a nonprofit educational institution to another nonprofit educational institution or to faculty, staff, and students does not constitute rental, lease, or lending for direct or indirect commercial purposes under this subsection.

(B) This subsection does not apply to—

(i) a computer program which is embodied in a machine or product and which cannot be copied during the ordinary operation or use of the machine or product; or

(ii) a computer program embodied in or used in conjunction with a limited purpose computer that is designed for playing video games and may be designed for other purposes.

(2) (A) Nothing in this subsection shall apply to the lending of a computer program for nonprofit purposes by a nonprofit library, if each copy of a computer program which is lent by such library has affixed to the packaging containing the program a warning of copyright in accordance with requirements that the Register of Copyrights shall prescribe by regulation.

(B) Not later than three years after the date of the enactment of the Computer Software Rental Amendments Act of 1990, and at such times thereafter as the Register of Copyrights considers appropriate, the Register of Copyrights, after consultation with representatives of copyright owners and librarians, shall submit to the Congress a report stating whether this paragraph has achieved its intended purpose of maintaining the integrity of the copyright system while providing nonprofit libraries the capability to fulfill their function. Such report shall advise the Congress as to any information or recommendations that the Register of Copyrights considers necessary to carry out the purposes of this subsection.

(3) Nothing in this subsection shall affect any provision of the antitrust laws. For purposes of the preceding sentence, "antitrust laws" has the meaning given that term in the first section of the Clayton Act and includes section 5 of the Federal Trade Commission Act to the extent that section relates to unfair methods of competition.

(4) Any person who distributes a phonorecord or a copy of a computer program (including any tape, disk, or other medium embodying such program) in violation of paragraph (1) is an infringer of copyright under section 501 of this title and is subject to the remedies set forth in sections 502, 503, 504, 505, and 509. Such violation shall not be a criminal offense under section 506 or cause such person to be subject to the criminal penalties set forth in section 2319 of title 18.

(c) Notwithstanding the provisions of section 106 (5), the owner of a particular copy lawfully made under this title, or any person authorized by such owner, is entitled, without the authority of the copyright owner, to display that copy publicly, either directly or by the projection of no more than one image at a time, to viewers present at the place where the copy is located.

## 17 U.S.C. §201 Ownership of copyright

(a) Initial Ownership. — Copyright in a work protected under this title vests initially in the author or authors of the work. The authors of a joint work are coowners of copyright in the work.

(b) Works Made for Hire. — In the case of a work made for hire, the employer or other person for whom the work was prepared is considered the author for purposes of this title, and, unless the parties have expressly agreed otherwise in a written instrument signed by them, owns all of the rights comprised in the copyright.

(c) Contributions to Collective Works. — Copyright in each separate contribution to a collective work is distinct from copyright in the collective work as a whole, and vests initially in the author of the contribution. In the absence of an express transfer of the copyright or of any rights under it, the owner of copyright in the collective work is presumed to have acquired only the privilege of reproducing and distributing the contribution as part of that particular collective work, any revision of that collective work, and any later collective work in the same series.

## 17 U.S.C. §202 Ownership of copyright as distinct from ownership of material object

Ownership of a copyright, or of any of the exclusive rights under a copyright, is distinct from ownership of any material object in which the work is embodied. Transfer of ownership of any material object, including the copy or phonorecord in which the work is first fixed, does not of itself convey any rights in the copyrighted work embodied in the object; nor, in the absence of an agreement, does transfer of ownership of a copyright or of any exclusive rights under a copyright convey property rights in any material object.

### 17 U.S.C. §302 Duration of copyright: Works created on or after January 1, 1978

(a) In General. — Copyright in a work created on or after January 1, 1978, subsists from its creation and, except as provided by the following subsections, endures for a term consisting of the life of the author and 70 years after the author's death.

(b) Joint Works. — In the case of a joint work prepared by two or more authors who did not work for hire, the copyright endures for a term consisting of the life of the last surviving author and 70 years after such last surviving author's death.

(c) Anonymous Works, Pseudonymous Works, and Works Made for Hire. — In the case of an anonymous work, a pseudonymous work, or a work made for hire, the copyright endures for a term of 95 years from the year of its first publication, or a term of 120 years from the year of its creation, whichever expires first. If, before the end of such term, the identity of one or more of the authors of an anonymous or pseudonymous work is revealed in the records of a registration made for that work under subsections (a) or (d) of section 408, or in the records provided by this subsection, the copyright in the work endures for the term specified by subsection (a) or (b), based on the life of the author or authors whose identity has been revealed. Any person having an interest in the copyright in an anonymous or pseudonymous work may at any time record, in records to be maintained by the Copyright Office for that purpose, a statement identifying one or more authors of the work; the statement shall also identify the person filing it, the nature of that person's interest, the source of the information recorded, and the particular work affected, and shall comply in form and content with requirements that the Register of Copyrights shall prescribe by regulation.

### 17 U.S.C. §303 Duration of copyright: Works created but not published or copyrighted before January 1, 1978

(a) Copyright in a work created before January 1, 1978, but not theretofore in the public domain or copyrighted, subsists from January 1, 1978, and endures for the term provided by section 302. In no case, however, shall the term of copyright in such a work expire before December 31, 2002; and, if the work is published on or before December 31, 2002, the term of copyright shall not expire before December 31, 2047.

### 17 U.S.C. §401 Notice of copyright: Visually perceptible copies

(a) General Provisions. — Whenever a work protected under this title is published in the United States or elsewhere by authority of the copyright owner, a notice of copyright as provided by this section may be placed on publicly distributed copies from which the work can be visually perceived, either directly or with the aid of a machine or device.

(b) Form of Notice. — If a notice appears on the copies, it shall consist of the following three elements:

(1) the symbol © (the letter C in a circle), or the word "Copyright", or the abbreviation "Copr."; and

(2) the year of first publication of the work; in the case of compilations, or derivative works incorporating previously published material, the year date of first publication of the compilation or derivative work is sufficient. The year date may be omitted where a pictorial, graphic, or sculptural work, with accompanying text matter, if any, is reproduced in or on greeting cards, postcards, stationery, jewelry, dolls, toys, or any useful articles; and

(3) the name of the owner of copyright in the work, or an abbreviation by which the name can be recognized, or a generally known alternative designation of the owner.

(c) Position of Notice. — The notice shall be affixed to the copies in such manner and location as to give reasonable notice of the claim of copyright. The Register of Copyrights shall prescribe by regulation, as examples, specific methods of affixation and positions of the notice on various types of works that will satisfy this requirement, but these specifications shall not be considered exhaustive.

(d) Evidentiary Weight of Notice. — If a notice of copyright in the form and position specified by this section appears on the published copy or copies to which a defendant in a copyright infringement suit had access, then no weight shall be given to such a defendant's interposition of a defense based on innocent infringement in mitigation of actual or statutory damages, except as provided in the last sentence of section 504 (c)(2).

## 17 U.S.C. §411 Registration and infringement actions

(a) Except for an action brought for a violation of the rights of the author under section 106A (a), and subject to the provisions of subsection (b), no action for infringement of the copyright in any United States work shall be instituted until registration of the copyright claim has been made in accordance with this title. In any case, however, where the deposit, application, and fee required for registration have been delivered to the Copyright Office in proper form and registration has been refused, the applicant is entitled to institute an action for infringement if notice thereof, with a copy of the complaint, is served on the Register of Copyrights. The Register may, at his or her option, become a party to the action with respect to the issue of registrability of the copyright claim by entering an appearance within sixty days after such service, but the Register's failure to become a party shall not deprive the court of jurisdiction to determine that issue.

## 17 U.S.C. §501 Infringement of copyright

(a) Anyone who violates any of the exclusive rights of the copyright owner as provided by sections 106 through 122 or of the author as provided in section 106A (a), or who imports copies or phonorecords into the United States in violation of section 602, is an infringer of the copyright or right of the author, as the case may be. For purposes of this chapter (other than section 506), any reference to copyright shall be deemed to include the rights conferred by section 106A (a). As used in this subsection, the term "anyone" includes any State, any instrumentality of a State, and any officer or employee of a State or instrumentality of a State acting in his or her official capacity. Any State, and any such instrumentality, officer, or employee, shall be subject to the provisions of this title in the same manner and to the same extent as any nongovernmental entity.

(b) The legal or beneficial owner of an exclusive right under a copyright is entitled, subject to the requirements of section 411, to institute an action for any infringement of that particular right committed while he or she is the owner of it. The court may require such owner to serve written notice of the action with a copy of the complaint upon any person shown, by the records of the Copyright Office or otherwise, to have or claim an interest in the copyright, and shall require that such notice be served upon any person whose interest is likely to be affected by a decision in the case. The court may require the joinder, and shall permit the intervention, of any person having or claiming an interest in the copyright.

### 17 U.S.C. §502 Remedies for infringement: Injunctions

(a) Any court having jurisdiction of a civil action arising under this title may, subject to the provisions of section 1498 of title 28, grant temporary and final injunctions on such terms as it may deem reasonable to prevent or restrain infringement of a copyright.

(b) Any such injunction may be served anywhere in the United States on the person enjoined; it shall be operative throughout the United States and shall be enforceable, by proceedings in contempt or otherwise, by any United States court having jurisdiction of that person. The clerk of the court granting the injunction shall, when requested by any other court in which enforcement of the injunction is sought, transmit promptly to the other court a certified copy of all the papers in the case on file in such clerk's office.

### 17 U.S.C. §504 Remedies for infringement: Damages and profits

(a) In General. — Except as otherwise provided by this title, an infringer of copyright is liable for either —

   (1) the copyright owner's actual damages and any additional profits of the infringer, as provided by subsection (b); or
   (2) statutory damages, as provided by subsection (c).

(b) Actual Damages and Profits. — The copyright owner is entitled to recover the actual damages suffered by him or her as a result of the infringement, and any profits of the infringer that are attributable to the infringement and are not taken into account in computing the actual damages. In establishing the infringer's profits, the copyright owner is required to present proof only of the infringer's gross revenue, and the infringer is required to prove his or her deductible expenses and the elements of profit attributable to factors other than the copyrighted work.

[handwritten margin note: No double counting]

(c) Statutory Damages. —

   (1) Except as provided by clause (2) of this subsection, the copyright owner may elect, at any time before final judgment is rendered, to recover, instead of actual damages and profits, an award of statutory damages for all infringements involved in the action, with respect to any one work, for which any one infringer is liable individually, or for which any two or more infrin-

gers are liable jointly and severally, in a sum of not less than $750 or more than $30,000 as the court considers just. For the purposes of this subsection, all the parts of a compilation or derivative work constitute one work.

(2) In a case where the copyright owner sustains the burden of proving, and the court finds, that infringement was committed willfully, the court in its discretion may increase the award of statutory damages to a sum of not more than $150,000. In a case where the infringer sustains the burden of proving, and the court finds, that such infringer was not aware and had no reason to believe that his or her acts constituted an infringement of copyright, the court in its discretion may reduce the award of statutory damages to a sum of not less than $200. The court shall remit statutory damages in any case where an infringer believed and had reasonable grounds for believing that his or her use of the copyrighted work was a fair use under section 107, if the infringer was:

(i) an employee or agent of a nonprofit educational institution, library, or archives acting within the scope of his or her employment who, or such institution, library, or archives itself, which infringed by reproducing the work in copies or phonorecords; or

(ii) a public broadcasting entity which or a person who, as a regular part of the nonprofit activities of a public broadcasting entity (as defined in subsection (g) of section 118) infringed by performing a published nondramatic literary work or by reproducing a transmission program embodying a performance of such a work.

### 17 U.S.C. §506 Criminal offenses

(a) Criminal Infringement. — Any person who infringes a copyright willfully either —

(1) for purposes of commercial advantage or private financial gain, or

(2) by the reproduction or distribution, including by electronic means, during any 180-day period, of 1 or more copies or phonorecords of 1 or more copyrighted works, which have a total retail value of more than $1,000, shall be punished as provided under section 2319 of title 18, United States Code. For purposes of this subsection, evidence of reproduction or distribution of a copyrighted work, by itself, shall not be sufficient to establish willful infringement.

(b) Forfeiture and Destruction. — When any person is convicted of any violation of subsection (a), the court in its judgment of conviction shall, in addition to the penalty therein prescribed, order the forfeiture and destruction or other disposition of all infringing copies or phonorecords and all implements, devices, or equipment used in the manufacture of such infringing copies or phonorecords.

### 17 U.S.C. §1201 Circumvention of copyright protection systems

(a) Violations Regarding Circumvention of Technological Measures. —

(1)

(A) No person shall circumvent a technological measure that effectively controls access to a work protected under this title. The prohibition contained in the preceding sentence shall take effect at the end of the 2-year period beginning on the date of the enactment of this chapter.

(B) The prohibition contained in subparagraph (A) shall not apply to persons who are users of a copyrighted work which is in a particular class of works, if such persons are, or are likely to be in the succeeding 3-year period, adversely affected by virtue of such prohibition in their ability to make noninfringing uses of that particular class of works under this title, as determined under subparagraph (C).

(C) During the 2-year period described in subparagraph (A), and during each succeeding 3-year period, the Librarian of Congress, upon the recommendation of the Register of Copyrights, who shall consult with the Assistant Secretary for Communications and Information of the Department of Commerce and report and comment on his or her views in making such recommendation, shall make the determination in a rulemaking proceeding for purposes of subparagraph (B) of whether persons who are users of a copyrighted work are, or are likely to be in the succeeding 3-year period, adversely affected by the prohibition under subparagraph (A) in their ability to make noninfringing uses under this title of a particular class of copyrighted works. In conducting such rulemaking, the Librarian shall examine —

(i) the availability for use of copyrighted works;

(ii) the availability for use of works for nonprofit archival, preservation, and educational purposes;

(iii) the impact that the prohibition on the circumvention of technological measures applied to copyrighted works has on criticism, comment, news reporting, teaching, scholarship, or research;

(iv) the effect of circumvention of technological measures on the market for or value of copyrighted works; and

(v) such other factors as the Librarian considers appropriate.

(D) The Librarian shall publish any class of copyrighted works for which the Librarian has determined, pursuant to the rulemaking conducted under subparagraph (C), that noninfringing uses by persons who are users of a copyrighted work are, or are likely to be, adversely affected, and the prohibition contained in subparagraph (A) shall not apply to such users with respect to such class of works for the ensuing 3-year period.

(E) Neither the exception under subparagraph (B) from the applicability of the prohibition contained in subparagraph (A), nor any determination made in a rulemaking conducted under subparagraph (C), may be used as a defense in any action to enforce any provision of this title other than this paragraph.

(2) No person shall manufacture, import, offer to the public, provide, or otherwise traffic in any technology, product, service, device, component, or part thereof, that —

(A) is primarily designed or produced for the purpose of circumventing a technological measure that effectively controls access to a work protected under this title;

(B) has only limited commercially significant purpose or use other than to circumvent a technological measure that effectively controls access to a work protected under this title; or

(C) is marketed by that person or another acting in concert with that person with that person's knowledge for use in circumventing a technological measure that effectively controls access to a work protected under this title.

(3) As used in this subsection —

(A) to "circumvent a technological measure" means to descramble a scrambled work, to decrypt an encrypted work, or otherwise to avoid, bypass, remove, deactivate, or impair a technological measure, without the authority of the copyright owner; and

(B) a technological measure "effectively controls access to a work" if the measure, in the ordinary course of its operation, requires the application of information, or a process or a treatment, with the authority of the copyright owner, to gain access to the work.

(b) Additional Violations. —

(1) No person shall manufacture, import, offer to the public, provide, or otherwise traffic in any technology, product, service, device, component, or part thereof, that —

(A) is primarily designed or produced for the purpose of circumventing protection afforded by a technological measure that effectively protects a right of a copyright owner under this title in a work or a portion thereof;

(B) has only limited commercially significant purpose or use other than to circumvent protection afforded by a technological measure that effectively protects a right of a copyright owner under this title in a work or a portion thereof; or

(C) is marketed by that person or another acting in concert with that person with that person's knowledge for use in circumventing protection afforded by a technological measure that effectively protects a right of a copyright owner under this title in a work or a portion thereof.

(2) As used in this subsection —

(A) to "circumvent protection afforded by a technological measure" means avoiding, bypassing, removing, deactivating, or otherwise impairing a technological measure; and

(B) a technological measure "effectively protects a right of a copyright owner under this title" if the measure, in the ordinary course of its operation, prevents, restricts, or otherwise limits the exercise of a right of a copyright owner under this title.

(c) Other Rights, Etc., Not Affected. —

(1) Nothing in this section shall affect rights, remedies, limitations, or defenses to copyright infringement, including fair use, under this title.

(2) Nothing in this section shall enlarge or diminish vicarious or contributory liability for copyright infringement in connection with any technology, product, service, device, component, or part thereof.

(3) Nothing in this section shall require that the design of, or design and selection of parts and components for, a consumer electronics, telecommunications, or computing product provide for a response to any particular technological measure, so long as such part or component, or the

product in which such part or component is integrated, does not otherwise fall within the prohibitions of subsection (a)(2) or (b)(1).

(4) Nothing in this section shall enlarge or diminish any rights of free speech or the press for activities using consumer electronics, telecommunications, or computing products.

### 17 U.S.C. §1202 Integrity of copyright management information

(a) False Copyright Management Information. — No person shall knowingly and with the intent to induce, enable, facilitate, or conceal infringement —

(1) provide copyright management information that is false, or
(2) distribute or import for distribution copyright management information that is false.

(b) Removal or Alteration of Copyright Management Information. —

No person shall, without the authority of the copyright owner or the law —

(1) intentionally remove or alter any copyright management information,

(2) distribute or import for distribution copyright management information knowing that the copyright management information has been removed or altered without authority of the copyright owner or the law, or

(3) distribute, import for distribution, or publicly perform works, copies of works, or phonorecords, knowing that copyright management information has been removed or altered without authority of the copyright owner or the law, knowing, or, with respect to civil remedies under section 1203, having reasonable grounds to know, that it will induce, enable, facilitate, or conceal an infringement of any right under this title.

(c) Definition. — As used in this section, the term "copyright management information" means any of the following information conveyed in connection with copies or phonorecords of a work or performances or displays of a work, including in digital form, except that such term does not include any personally identifying information about a user of a work or of a copy, phonorecord, performance, or display of a work:

(1) The title and other information identifying the work, including the information set forth on a notice of copyright.

(2) The name of, and other identifying information about, the author of a work.

(3) The name of, and other identifying information about, the copyright owner of the work, including the information set forth in a notice of copyright.

(4) With the exception of public performances of works by radio and television broadcast stations, the name of, and other identifying information about, a performer whose performance is fixed in a work other than an audiovisual work.

(5) With the exception of public performances of works by radio and television broadcast stations, in the case of an audiovisual work, the name of, and other identifying information about, a writer, performer, or director who is credited in the audiovisual work.

(6) Terms and conditions for use of the work.

(7) Identifying numbers or symbols referring to such information or links to such information.

(8) Such other information as the Register of Copyrights may prescribe by regulation, except that the Register of Copyrights may not require the provision of any information concerning the user of a copyrighted work.

# CHAPTER
# 10

# Acquiring Patent Rights

## INTRODUCTION

Patent law strives to strike a balance between the promotion of technological innovation and the dissemination of and access to its fruits. It does this by offering a potential financial reward as an inducement to invent, to disclose, and to invest with the goal of bringing the claimed invention to market. These goals are consistent with Article I, Section 8, Clause 8 of the Constitution, which empowers Congress to "promote the progress of the useful arts." This constitutional provision is utilitarian in its structure and purpose, meaning that the patent laws are ultimately designed to benefit society.

This utilitarian goal is important because the patent system, as discussed in Chapter 1, is more important to some industries than others and the patents are obtained for a variety of reasons. And whether a patent on a given technology benefits society is a complex question that depends on the technology and industry in question. As two commentators recently noted:

> In some areas, patent rights certainly are economically and socially productive in generating invention, spreading technological knowledge, inducing innovation and commercialization, and providing some degree of order in the development of broad technological prospects. However, in many areas of technology this is not the case. In a number of these, strong broad patent rights entail major economic costs while generating insufficient additional social benefits. And in some strong broad patents are simply counterproductive. One needs to be discriminating and cautious on this front.[1]

Moreover, while the private value of patents has increased,[2] our understanding of patent law's relationship to economic welfare remains

---

1. Robert Mazzoleni & Richard R. Nelson, *The Benefits and Costs of Strong Patent Protection: A Contribution to the Current Debate*, 27 RESEARCH POLICY 273, 281 (1998).
2. *See* Robert P. Merges, *As Many As Six Impossible Patents Before Breakfast: Property Rights for Business Concepts and Patent System Reform*, 14 BERKELEY TECH. L.J. 577, 603 (1999) (noting the "increase in the private value of patents since the early 1980s").

incomplete.[3] Nonetheless, scholars have begun to add resolution to this patent/economic welfare puzzle as reflected in the increasing amount of empirical and social science scholarship. Much of the scholarship that forms the empirical current has examined the relationship between patent law and innovation practices of firms in various industries, including research and development decisionmaking and the extent to which divergent industries rely on the patent system or other appropriability mechanisms;[4] the role of juries in patent cases;[5] Federal Circuit voting patterns;[6] patent filing;[7] litigation trends;[8] and patent law's effect on innovation in specific technologies.[9] A good deal of the social science work is law and economics oriented, focusing on the important normative issues of proprietary claim scope and patentability standards in the context of innovation policy;[10] and patent law's relationship to R & D,[11] and innovation.[12]

---

There are primarily three types of patents: utility, design, and plant. An overwhelming majority of patents are utility, and therefore, with the exception of two lengthy notes at the end of this chapter discussing design and plant patents, this and the remaining patent law chapters pertain exclusively to utility patents.[13] Unlike trademark law, there is no such thing as common law patent rights. Nor do patent rights subsist upon fixation in a

3. *See* William M. Landes & Richard A. Posner, THE ECONOMIC STRUCTURE OF INTELLECTUAL PROPERTY LAW 310 (2003) ("Although there are powerful economic reasons in favor of creating property rights in inventions, there are also considerable social costs and whether the benefits exceed the costs is impossible to answer with confidence on the basis of present knowledge"); Richard Brunell, *Appropriability in Antitrust: How Much is Enough?*, 69 ANTITRUST L.J. 1, 4 (2001) ("[I]f the vast economics literature on intellectual property conveys one message, it is that the relationship between intellectual property protection and economic welfare is unclear").

4. *See* Wesley M. Cohen et al., *Protecting Their Intellectual Assets: Appropriability Conditions and Why U.S. Manufacturing Firms Patent (or Not)* 24 (Nat'l Bureau of Econ. Research, Working Paper No. 7552, 2000).

5. *See, e.g.*, Kimberly A. Moore, *Judges, Juries, and Patent Cases: An Empirical Peek Inside the Black Box*, 99 MICH. L. REV. 365 (2000) (illustrating patent holders' success rates in jury and bench trials).

6. *See, e.g.*, John R. Allison & Mark A. Lemley, *How Federal Circuit Judges Vote in Patent Validity Cases*, 27 FLA. ST. U. L. REV. 745 (2000) (chronicling patent validity decisions).

7. *See, e.g.*, John R. Allison & Mark A. Lemley, *The Growing Complexity of the Patent System*, 82 B.U. L. REV. 77 (2002).

8. *See, e.g.*, Jean O. Lanjouw & Mark Schankerman, *Protecting Intellectual Property Rights: Are Small Firms Handicapped*, 47 J.L. & ECON. 45 (2004) (studying patent litigation and settlements and concluding firms with small patent portfolios are at higher litigation risk); Josh Lerner, *Patenting in the Shadow of Competitors*, 38 J.L. & ECON. 463 (1995) (analyzing patenting patterns of firms with differing litigation costs).

9. *See, e.g.*, John P. Walsh, Ashish Arora & Wesley Cohen, *Effects of Research Tool Patents and Licensing on Biomedical Innovation*, in PATENTS IN THE KNOWLEDGE-BASED ECONOMY 285-340 (The National Academies Press 2003); Julie E. Cohen & Mark A. Lemley, *Patent Scope and Innovation in the Software Industry*, 89 CAL. L. REV. 1 (2001).

10. *See, e.g.*, Robert P. Merges & Richard R. Nelson, *On the Complex Economics of Patent Scope*, 90 COLUM. L. REV. 839 (1990) (concluding that law should favor a competitive environment for improvements rather than one dominated by the pioneer firm).

11. *See, e.g.*, Ashish Arora, Marco Ceccagnoli & Wesley M. Cohen, *R&D and the Patent Premium* (National Bureau of Econ. Research Working Paper No. 9431, 2003).

12. For a nice overview of the empirical literature, *see* Bronwyn H. Hall, *Business Method Patents, Innovation, and Policy* (Competition Policy Center, Univ. of California, Berkeley, May 4, 2003) (Working Paper No. CPC03-39).

13. Thus, unless expressly noted otherwise, utility patent is implied when the word "patent" is used in this book.

tangible medium of expression as provided for by copyright law. Rather, a United States patent can only be acquired by filing a patent application with the United States Patent and Trademark Office (PTO), a federal agency established in 1836 that is under the Department of Commerce. Not all patent applications result in issued patents. (In 2004, 46 percent of filed applications issued as patents.)

Over the past 30 years, there has been a significant increase in patent filings and, naturally, a corresponding increase in issuances. For instance, 104,329 utility patent applications were filed in 1980 resulting in 61,819 issued patents, whereas in 2004 the PTO received 356,943 and issued 164,293. *See http://www.uspto.gov/.* Figure 10.1 reflects the dramatic increase in patent filings and grants over the past three decades.

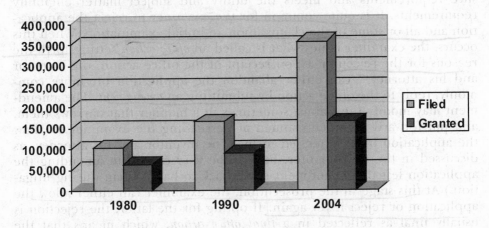

**Figure 10.1. Patent Filings**

The patent application (and issued patent) is comprised of two parts: (1) written description; and (2) claims. It is common among patent professionals and courts to refer to the written description as the specification or to use the two terms interchangeably. The claims are considered to be the most important part of the patent document because the claims delineate the patent owner's property right. To borrow real property terminology, the claims set forth the metes and bounds of the patentee's proprietary interest. The specification, on the other hand, contains an extensive disclosure of the claimed invention and can be viewed as a teaching device, informing its reader of the particulars of the claimed invention. As the United States Court of Appeals for the Federal Circuit has noted, "specifications teach, and claims claim."

To obtain patent protection, an inventor must file a patent application with the PTO. Importantly, patent applications are published 18 months after filing, but only for applicants who are also seeking protection outside of the United States. The process of applying for a patent is called *patent prosecution*, and the record of the prosecution proceedings before the PTO is called the *prosecution history* (sometimes referred to as file history). The proceeding is *ex parte*, meaning that the prosecution is only between the applicant and the examiner. Although there are opportunities for third parties to submit information to the examiner regarding the patentability of the application in question, these opportunities are not constructed to optimize a legitimate challenge. But there have been reform efforts in Congress calling for the implementation of an inter partes, post-grant opposition proceeding, whereby third parties would be able to challenge issued patents within either nine months of the grant or reissue of a patent.

Once filed, the application is examined by a patent examiner that is trained in the technology to which the claimed invention pertains. The examiner usually conducts a search of the prior art to determine if the claimed invention is novel and non-obvious. (Prior art is technical information in the form of prior patents, publications, and knowledge.) The examiner will also determine whether the application satisfies the disclosure requirements and meets the utility and subject matter eligibility requirements. It is quite common for the examiner to reject the application and all or some of the claims upon an initial examination. When this occurs, the examiner issues what is called an *office action* setting forth the reasons for the rejection. Upon receipt of the office action, the inventor and his attorney[14] can either abandon the application or, more commonly, reply to the office action by submitting an *amendment*. The amendment may modify the claims, sometimes in a manner that narrows them, and put forward arguments aimed at persuading the examiner to allow the application in its amended form. (The inventor and his attorney, as discussed in the next chapter, have to be very careful in amending the application lest the amendment come back to haunt them during litigation.) At this stage in the prosecution, the examiner can either allow the application or reject it yet again. If opting for the latter, the rejection is usually final as reflected in a *final office action*, which means that the inventor's options are more limited than they were after receipt of the initial office action. The inventor's choices are to make a request for continuing examination, appeal the decision to the Board of Patent Appeals and Interferences (a PTO administrative body), file another application, or abandon the application.

Patent claim drafting is a difficult endeavor that takes many years of practice to achieve a high level of competency. Indeed, as discussed in the next chapter, poorly drafted claims can be particularly costly if the patent is subject to licensing negotiations or eventually litigated. To illustrate the difficulty of claim drafting, consider the following invention, something familiar to most students: a pizza box. How would you draft a claim to cover the fundamental features of this invention? Keep in mind you want to draft a claim with an eye toward litigation, meaning that you want a claim that provides the maximum amount of protection, but does not overlap with the prior art.

---

14. Attorneys representing clients before the PTO must be licensed to practice before the PTO, which means they must have passed the patent bar exam. *See http://www.uspto. gov/ web/offices/dcom/gcounsel/oed.htm* for more information about the patent bar. One does not have to be an attorney to sit for the patent bar and represent clients before the PTO. Nonattorneys who practice before the PTO are called patent agents.

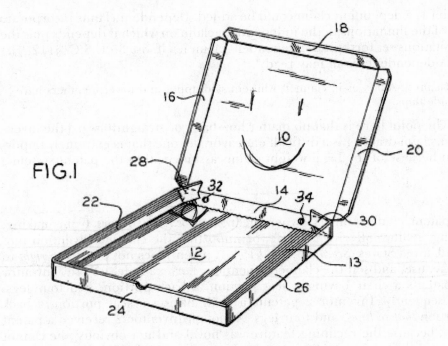

**Figure 10.2. Pizza Box U.S. Patent 4,441,626**

The following is an excerpt from the specification of the patent:

As shown in FIG. 1, a pizza box constructed in accordance with the teachings of this invention comprises upper and lower members having a top panel **10**, a bottom panel **12** and a central panel **14**. The top panel **10** and the bottom panel **12** include side panels **16, 18, 20, 22, 24, 26** and various side flaps **28, 30**, to complete the folding and assembly of the box.

According to the invention, means are provided for venting the box at holes **32** and **34**. Research has found that proper ventilation should be attained inside the box to keep the pizza hot and still retain good crust quality, when approximately one square inch of ventilation is provided for each cubic foot of volume, to acquire a paper balance between heat and steam.

There is a great deal of prior art showing many of the features of FIG. 1 (e.g., upper and lower members with a central plane), but none of the prior art discloses flaps and ventilation holes together in a single pizza box. Think about the features of FIG. 1 you want to protect, while also keeping in mind that you have to draft a claim that avoids the prior art. A sample claim may look like the following:

Claim 1: A box comprising upper and lower members that open and close relative to each other, a plurality of side panels, and a central panel having holes for ventilation, said upper and lower members having side flaps.

There are many ways to draft this claim. One could modify "box" with the word "pizza," but recall you want to claim as broadly as the prior art would allow. Moreover, instead of claiming "holes for ventilation," one could claim "means for ventilation" and disclose the means (i.e., the holes) in the specification. Also, instead of claiming the "side flaps" in claim 1, a dependent claim could be added. Dependent claims incorporate all of the limitations in the independent claim on which it depends plus the limitations set forth in the dependent claim itself. *See* 35 U.S.C. §112, ¶¶3, 4. A dependent claim may read:

> Claim 2: A box as in claim 1, wherein said upper and lower members have side flaps.

The point here is that no matter how basic or straightforward the invention, claim drafting is a difficult endeavor, yet one that is extremely important because of the legal weight claims assume within the patent system.

---

A patent confers on its owner the right to exclude others from making, using, selling, offering for sale, or importing the claimed invention into the United States. *See* 35 U.S.C. §154. A patent does not provide a *right* to make, use, and sell the claimed invention. For example, let's say Inventor 1 patents a chair having a seat portion, a back portion, and four legs. Subsequently, Inventor 2 patents a chair having a seat portion, a back portion *that reclines,* and four legs. Although Inventor 2 received a patent (say, because the reclining feature was novel and not obvious), he cannot practice his claimed invention because it would infringe Inventor 1's patent. Infringement exists here because Inventor 2's chair has all of the limitations of Inventor 1's patent claim (i.e., a seat portion, a back portion, and four legs). While the reclining feature may have allowed Inventor 2 to patent his chair in the light of Inventor 1's patent, the reclining feature does not save Inventor 2 from infringement. By the same token, Inventor 1 cannot practice Inventor 2's claimed invention. But there is a way out of this congestion. Assuming Inventor 2's invention is an improvement over Inventor 1's with greater commercial potential, each party has the motivation to enter into a cross-licensing agreement permitting each to practice their respective claimed inventions.

For patent applications filed after June 8, 1995, the patent term is 20 years from the filing date of the earliest referenced application. The patent term for applications filed *before* June 8, 1995, is (1) 17 years from date of issuance; *or* (2) 20 years measured from the filing date of the earliest referenced application, whichever is greater.

This chapter explores the most important patentability requirements, namely the disclosure requirements (discussed in Section A); statutory bars and novelty (discussed in Sections B and C, respectively); non-obviousness (discussed in Section D); utility (discussed in Section E); and statutory subject matter (discussed in Section F). Before moving on to the details of the patentability requirements, a short explanation on the sequencing of the following materials is in order. The sections are sequenced to present patent law's "big picture" first. Section 112 is covered initially because the disclosure requirements are at the heart of the patent system: what must the inventor disclose to society before society grants the inventor a right to exclude—the essence of the *quid pro quo.* Moreover, §112's demand for a technological disclosure upon which others can improve is fundamental to the constitutional goal of promoting the progress of the useful arts. After the disclosure requirements, the statutory bars are presented because the driving policy behind §102(b)'s on-sale and public-use bars is timeliness of disclosure, namely the promotion of *early* disclosure. From a policy perspective, §112 is about what should be disclosed and §102(b) is about when one should disclose it. Novelty, non-obviousness, utility, and subject matter requirements are explored thereafter. These three requirements are certainly important and replete with policy implications. Indeed, they demand a substantive contribution to society from the inventor and, like §112, form part of the *quid pro quo*. But their policy focus is narrower than §§112 and 102(b)'s, and thus they are covered only after the student has an appreciation for patent law's broad policy goals.

# A. DISCLOSING AND CLAIMING THE INVENTION

The disclosure requirements of §112 are perhaps the most important of any of the patentability requirements. By requiring the patent applicant to claim the invention with clarity and to teach (or enable) other persons having ordinary skill in the art to make and use the claimed invention, patent law seeks to facilitate the dissemination of technical information and improvement activity on the claimed invention. Moreover, the disclosure requirements force the patentee to give the public fair notice of what the patentee and the PTO have agreed constitute the metes and bounds of the claimed invention. Thus, the disclosure requirements are at the heart of patent law and its goal of promoting the progress of the useful arts. The *O'Reilly* case reflects these goals.

*STATUTE:* **Specification**
35 U.S.C. §112, ¶¶1 & 2

## O'REILLY v. MORSE
### 56 U.S. 62 (1854)

Mr. Chief Justice TANEY delivered the opinion of the court.

\* \* \*

[In a patent issued to Morse in 1840 and reissued in 1848, Morse described "a new and useful apparatus for, and a system of, transmitting intelligence between distant points by means of electro-magnetism, which puts in motion machinery for producing sounds or signs, and recording said signs upon paper or other suitable material." The patent described "the instruments and . . . mode of their operation," including the famed "Code." The patent continued and set forth the now famous claim eight:]

Eighth. I do not propose to limit myself to the specific machinery, or parts of machinery, described in the foregoing specifications and claims; the essence of my invention being the use of the motive power of the electric or galvanic current, which I call electro-magnetism, however developed, for making or printing intelligible characters, letters, or signs, at any distances, being a new application of that power, of which I claim to be the first inventor or discoverer.

\* \* \*

We perceive no well-founded objection to the description which is given of the whole invention and its separate parts, nor to his right to a patent for the first seven inventions set forth in the specification of his claims. The difficulty arises on the eighth.

\* \* \*

It is impossible to misunderstand the extent of this claim. He claims the exclusive right to every improvement where the motive power is the electric or galvanic current, and the result is the marking or printing intelligible characters, signs, or letters at a distance.

If this claim can be maintained, it matters not by what process or machinery the result is accomplished. For aught that we now know some future inventor, in the onward march of science, may discover a mode of writing or printing at a distance by means of the electric or galvanic current, without using any part of the process or combination set forth in the plaintiff's specification. His invention may be less complicated — less liable to get out of order — less expensive in construction, and in its operation. But yet if it is covered by this patent the inventor could not use it, nor the public have the benefit of it without the permission of this patentee.

Nor is this all, while he shuts the door against inventions of other persons, the patentee would be able to avail himself of new discoveries in the properties and powers of electro-magnetism which scientific men might bring to light. For he says he does not confine his claim to the machinery or parts of machinery, which he specifies; but claims for himself a monopoly in its use, however developed, for the purpose of printing at a distance. New discoveries in physical science may enable him to combine it with new agents and new elements, and by that means attain the object in a manner superior to the present process and altogether different from it. And if he can secure the exclusive use by his present patent he may vary it with every new discovery and development of the science, and need place no description of the new manner, process, or machinery, upon the records of the patent office. And when his patent expires, the public must apply to him to learn what it is. In fine he claims an exclusive right to use a manner and process which he has not described and indeed had not invented, and therefore could not describe when he obtained his patent. The court is of the opinion that the claim is too broad, and not warranted by law.

No one, we suppose will maintain that Fulton could have taken out a patent for his invention of propelling vessels by steam, describing the process and machinery he used, and claimed under it the exclusive right to use the motive power of steam, however developed, for the purpose of propelling vessels. It can hardly be supposed that under such a patent he could have prevented the use of the improved machinery which science has since introduced; although the motive power is steam, and the result is the propulsion of vessels. Neither could the man who first discovered that steam might, by a proper arrangement of machinery, be used as a motive power to grind corn or spin cotton, claim the right to the exclusive use of steam as a motive power for the purpose of producing such effects.

Again, the use of steam as a motive power in printing-presses is comparatively a modern discovery. Was the first inventor of a machine or process of this kind entitled to a patent, giving him the exclusive right to use steam as a motive power, however developed, for the purpose of marking or printing intelligible characters? Could he have prevented the use of any other press subsequently invented where steam was used? Yet so far as patentable rights are concerned both improvements must stand on the same principles. Both use a known motive power to print intelligible marks or letters; and it can make no difference in their legal rights under the patent laws, whether the printing is done near at hand or at a distance. Both depend for success not merely upon the motive power, but upon the machinery with which it is combined. And it has never, we believe, been supposed by any one, that the first inventor of a steam printing-press, was entitled to the exclusive use of steam, as a motive power, however developed, for marking or printing intelligible characters.

Indeed, the acts of the patentee himself are inconsistent with the claim made in his behalf. For in 1846 he took out a patent for his new improvement of local circuits, by means of which intelligence could be printed at intermediate places along the main line of the telegraph; and he obtained a reissued patent for this invention in 1848. Yet in this new invention the electric or galvanic current was the motive power, and writing at a distance the effect. The power was undoubtedly developed, by new machinery and new combinations. But if his eighth claim could be sustained, this improvement would be embraced by his first patent. And if it was so embraced, his patent for the local circuits would be illegal and void. For he could not take out a subsequent patent for a portion of his first invention, and thereby extend his monopoly beyond the period limited by law.

\* \* \*

. . . Professor Morse has not discovered, that the electric or galvanic current will always print at a distance, no matter what may be the form of the machinery or mechanical contrivances through which it passes. You may use electro-magnetism as a motive power, and yet not produce the described effect, that is, print at a distance intelligible marks or signs. To produce that effect, it must be combined with, and passed through, and operate upon, certain complicated and delicate machinery, adjusted and arranged upon philosophical principles, and prepared by the highest mechanical skill. And it is the high praise of Professor Morse, that he has been able, by a new combination of known powers, of which electro-magnetism is one, to discover a method by which intelligible marks or signs may be printed at a distance. And for the method or process thus discovered, he is entitled to a patent. But he has not discovered that the electro-magnetic current, used as motive power, in any other method, and with any other combination, will do as well.

\* \* \*

It is a well-settled principle of law, that the mere change in the form of the machinery (unless a particular form is specified as the means by which the effect described is produced) or an alteration in some of its unessential parts; or in the use of known equivalent powers, not varying essentially the machine, or its mode of operation or organization, will not make the new machine a new invention. It may be an improvement upon the former; but that will not justify its use without the consent of the first patentee.

\* \* \*

Mr. Justice Wayne, Mr. Justice NELSON, and Mr. Justice GRIER, dissent from the judgment of the court on the question of costs.

Mr. Justice GRIER.

. . . The . . . point, in which I cannot concur with the opinion of the majority, arises in the construction of the eighth claim of complainant's first patent, as finally amended.

\* \* \*

The great art of printing, which has changed the face of human society and civilization, consisted in nothing but a new application of principles known to the world for thousands of years. No one could say it consisted in the type or the press, or in any other machine or device used in performing some particular function, more than in the hands which picked the types or worked the press. Yet if the inventor of printing had, under this narrow construction of our patent law, claimed his art as something distinct from his machinery, the doctrine now advanced, would have declared it unpatentable to its full extent as an art, and that the inventor could be protected in nothing but his first rough types and ill-contrived press.

\* \* \*

To say that a patentee, who claims the art of writing at a distance by means of electro-magnetism, necessarily claims all future improvements in the art, is to misconstrue it, or draws a consequence from it not fairly to be inferred from its language. An improvement in a known art is as much the subject of a patent as the art itself; so, also, is an improvement on a known machine. Yet, if the original machine be patented, the patentee of an improvement will not have a right to use the original. This doctrine has not been found to retard the progress of invention in the case of machines; and I can see no reason why a contrary one should be applied to an art.

\* \* \*

The word telegraph is derived from the Greek, and signifies "to write afar off or at a distance." It has heretofore been applied to various contrivances or devices, to communicate intelligence by means of signals or semaphores, which speak to the eye for a moment. But in its primary and literal signification of writing, printing, or recording at a distance, it never was invented, perfected, or put into practical operation till it was done by Morse. He preceded Steinheil, Cook, Wheatstone, and Davy in the successful application of this mysterious power or element of electro-magnetism to this purpose; and his invention has entirely superseded their inefficient contrivances. It is not only "a new and useful art," if that term means any thing, but a most wonderful and astonishing invention, requiring tenfold more ingenuity and patient experiment to perfect it, than the art of printing with types and press, as originally invented.

\* \* \*

Now the patent law requires an inventor, as a condition precedent to obtaining a patent, to deliver a written description of his invention or discovery, and to particularly specify what he claims to be his own invention or discovery. If he has truly stated the principle, nature and extent of his art or invention, how can the court say it is too broad, and impugn the validity of his patent for doing what the law requires as a condition for obtaining it? And if it is only in case of a machine that the law requires the inventor to specify what he claims as his own invention and discovery, and to distinguish what is new from what is old, then this eighth claim is superfluous and cannot affect the validity of his patent, provided his art is new and useful, and the machines and devices claimed separately, are of his own invention. If it be in the use of the words "however developed" that the claim is to be adjudged too broad, then it follows that a person using any other process for the purpose of developing the agent or element of electro-magnetism, than the common one now in use, and described in the patent, may pirate the whole art patented.

\* \* \*

## Comments

1. *Section 112's Disclosure Requirements.* There are four disclosure requirements in §112: (1) enablement; (2) best mode; (3) written description; and (4) clear claiming. Each of these requirements is discussed in the following comments.

2. *Enablement and Claim Scope. Morse* held claim 8 invalid because the breadth of this claim was not commensurate with the specification. Recall, claim 8 read: "I do not propose to limit myself to the specific machinery [that is set forth in claims 1 through 7]; . . . the essence of my invention being the use of motive power of the electric or galvanic current . . . *however developed*." (Emphasis added.) The specification did not disclose all uses and improvements of the motive power of the electric or galvanic current. Morse claimed more than he actually invented.

   *Morse* demonstrates the importance of determining optimal claim scope. The Court employed the enablement requirement to limit Morse to his first seven claims. The Court was very concerned that Morse's claim 8 would easily capture future improvements or alternatives that Morse did not invent or describe in his patent. But determining the proper scope of Morse's patent (or any patent) is very difficult. (*See* the Policy Perspective on page 667.) A court must ascertain how much improvement activity patentees such as Morse should be able to capture vis-à-vis improver-competitors. Morse, by all accounts, made a significant inventive contribution, something upon which the dissent focused in urging the majority to provide Morse with a broader proprietary scope. According to the dissent, Morse's invention was "not only 'a new and useful art,' but a most wonderful and astonishing invention, requiring tenfold more ingenuity and patient experiment to perfect it, than the art of printing with types and press, as originally invented."

3. *Enablement and "Undue Experimentation": Determining Compliance.* The scope of enablement is that which is disclosed in the specification coupled with what is known to a person having ordinary skill in the art. The test for compliance with the enablement requirement is whether "undue experimentation" is required to make and use the claimed invention. In determining what constitutes undue experimentation, the Federal Circuit has applied a standard of reasonableness. The test is not merely quantitative because a significant amount of routine experimentation is permitted. The court will consider several factors in determining whether undue experimentation is needed, including: (1) the quantity of experimentation necessary, (2) the amount of direction or guidance presented, (3) presence or absence of working examples, (4) the nature of the invention, (5) the state of the prior art, (6) the relative skill of those in the art, (7) the predictability or unpredictability of the art, and (8) the breadth of the claims.

## COMPARATIVE PERSPECTIVE
### The Enablement Requirement in Europe and TRIPs

Both the European Patent Convention and TRIPs set forth an enablement requirement. Article 83 of the European Patent Convention reads:

*Disclosure of the invention*

The European patent application must disclose the invention in a manner sufficiently clear and complete for it to be carried out by a person skilled in the art.

Article 29 of TRIPs states:
Conditions on Patent Applicants

1. Members shall require that an applicant for a patent shall disclose the invention in a manner sufficiently clear and complete for the invention to be carried out by a person skilled in the art.

---

Instead of "undue experimentation," some countries, such as the United Kingdom, ask if the specification requires the skilled artisan to "go beyond routine." In *Mentor v. Hollister*, [1991] FSR 557, 561-562, for example, Justice Aldous wrote:

This section [Article 83 of the EPC transposed into section 14 of the 1977 English Patent Act] requires the skilled man to be able to perform the invention, but does not lay down the limits as to the time and energy that the skilled man must spend seeking to perform the invention before it is insufficient. Clearly there must be a limit. The subsection, by using the words "clearly enough and completely enough," contemplates that patent specifications need not set out every detail necessary for performance, but can leave the skilled man to use his skill to perform the invention. In so doing he must seek success he should not be required to carry out any prolonged research, enquiry or experiment. He may need to carry out the ordinary methods of trial and error, which involve no inventive step and generally are necessary in applying the particular discovery to produce a practical result.

The section requires the skilled man to be able to perform the invention. Such a man is the ordinary addressee of the patent. He must be assumed to be possessed of the common general knowledge in the art and the necessary skill and expertise to apply that knowledge. He is the man of average skill and intelligence, but is not expected to be able to exercise any invention.

4. *Enablement Measured at Time of Filing.* The language of §112 does not clearly resolve the question of at what time the disclosure must be "enabling" — that is, sufficient to enable one with ordinary skill in the art to make and use the claimed invention. Nevertheless, the Federal Circuit has held that the sufficiency of the patent's disclosure must be judged as of its filing date. Information that is developed or becomes available after that date cannot be considered in determining the sufficiency of the disclosure. The principle reason for this rule is that the filing date is proof of an inventor's latest date of invention, a date of crucial importance in American patent law because a patent is awarded to the party who can prove he was the first to invent the claimed invention. Proving date of invention is also important because the earlier one can show date of invention the more likely it is that there will be less prior art available to competitors and the PTO. Proving date of invention is discussed in Section C.1, *infra*.

5. *Best Mode Requirement.* The best mode requirement of §112, ¶1 dictates that in addition to providing an enabling disclosure, the patentee must disclose the best way (or mode) of practicing the claimed invention. (The best mode is sometimes referred to as the preferred embodiment in patent documents.) For example, the inventor claims "a method of making chemical X wherein A and B are heated between 100-110°C." If the patentee knows, *at the time of filing*, that heating at 107°C provides optimal results, he must disclose that information. The purpose of the best mode requirement is to prevent inventors from obtaining patent protection while concealing (as a trade secret, for example) from the public preferred embodiments of their claimed invention. The Federal Circuit has developed a two-part test for determining compliance with the best mode requirement. The first part is subjective, and asks whether at the time of filing the inventor knew of a mode of making and using his invention that he considered best. If the answer to this question is yes, the second part of test, which is objective, is reached. This part of the test compares what the inventor knew with what he disclosed by framing the question as follows: Is the disclosure adequate to enable one of ordinary skill in the art to practice the best mode or has the inventor "concealed" his preferred mode? Interestingly, there is no

duty to update the best mode after the application has been filed. Arguably, this lack of duty to update is inconsistent with the underlying policies of the disclosure requirements.

Lastly, there are some things, commonly referred to as "production details," that do not need to be disclosed. There are two types of production details. First, so-called commercial considerations such as the equipment on hand or prior relationships with suppliers are not required to be disclosed. These are considerations that do not relate to the quality of the claimed invention. The second type of production detail are qualitatively significant vis-à-vis the claimed invention, but are deemed routine, such as details of production of which those of ordinary skill in the art are aware.

The best mode requirement is unique to the United States, and serves as a potential pitfall for foreign applicants. Because of the outlier status of the United States on this issue, and the dubious value of requiring a best mode, the most recent legislation on patent reform would eliminate the best mode requirement. *See* H.R. 2795. Article 29 of TRIPs permits signatory countries to have a best mode requirement, but does not require such. Article 29.1 states:

*Article 29 Conditions on Patent Applicants*

1. Members . . . **may** require the applicant to indicate the best mode for carrying out the invention known to the inventor at the filing date. . . . (Emphasis added.)

**6.** ***Written Description Requirement.*** The first paragraph of §112 provides that the "specification shall contain *a written description of the invention.* . . ." The written description requirement (WD) serves a signaling function, permitting third parties to ascertain whether the inventor had "possession" of the claimed invention at the time of the original filing date. The policy underlying the requirement becomes clear when we consider the significance of the filing date. The filing date is deemed constructive reduction to practice, which is the applicant's latest date of invention. In this capacity, the WD requirement assures the applicant's claimed invention is entitled to a particular priority date (date of invention) and "prevent[s] an applicant from later asserting that he invented that which he did not." *Amgen, Inc. v. Hoechst Marion Roussel, Inc.,* 314 F.3d 1313, 1330 (Fed. Cir. 2003).

The WD requirement is most often at issue when an applicant amends his claims during prosecution or by filing subsequent applications, while trying to retain his original filing date. For instance, in the well-known case of *Vas-Cath Inc. v. Mahurkar,* 935 F.2d 1555 (Fed. Cir. 1991) Mahurkar appealed a partial summary judgment ruling in favor of Vas-Cath that declared Mahurkar's two utility patents invalid due to prior activity. The district court concluded that Mahurkar's patents were not entitled to a filing date of an earlier filed application, which had the same drawings as the two patents, because the earlier-filed application did not provide a "written description of the invention." To antedate the prior activity, Mahurkar needed to prove his two patents were entitled to an earlier priority date. The Federal Circuit reversed, and held that the drawings could provide enough support to satisfy the written description requirement.

The test for compliance with the WD requirement is "whether the disclosure of the application relied upon 'reasonably conveys to the artisan that the inventor had possession at that time of the later claimed subject matter.'" But the specification does not have to disclose "*in haec verba*" (verbatim) support to satisfy the requirement. For instance, in *Application of Wertheim*, 541 F.2d 257, 265 (CCPA 1976), the patent claimed a particular range, "at least 35%," that was narrower than what was disclosed in the specification, which read "25% to 60%." The CCPA held that the specification supported the claim even though the precise range claimed was not exactly set forth in the specification.

This "possession" test suggests that the written description and enablement requirements are closely related, and indeed they are. The key difference, however, is that written description focuses on what the applicant actually invented, proof of which requires a level of specificity in the specification that may be unnecessary for enablement purposes. *See In re Ruschig*, 379 F.2d 990, 995 (CCPA 1967) ("[T]he question is not whether [one skilled in the art] would be so enabled but whether the specification discloses the compound to him, specifically, as something appellants actually invented."). Thus, it is possible for a specification to enable a skilled artisan to make and use claimed subject matter yet fall short of satisfying the written description requirement. As the Court of Customs and Patent Appeals noted in *In re DiLeone*, 436 F.2d 1404, 1405 (CCPA 1971), a specification that only discloses compound A with no broadening language "might very well enable one skilled in the art to make and use compounds B and C; yet the class consisting of A, B and C has not been described." Thus, an applicant who later amends his claims to add B and C may comply with enablement, but not WD.

Interestingly, the WD requirement has recently been applied to *originally* filed, un-amended claims, particularly claims related to biotechnology inventions, where priority was not at issue. In *Regents of the Univ. of California v. Eli Lilly & Co.*, 119 F.3d 1559 (Fed. Cir. 1997), for example, the University of California (UC) claimed in its '525 patent a cDNA sequence for vertebrate or mammalian insulin. But at the time the '525 was filed, UC only ascertained and isolated the cDNA sequence in rats, not humans. The Federal Circuit invalidated the vertebrate claims, holding that the '525 patent's disclosure of the cDNA sequence of the insulin gene of a rat did not adequately describe the cDNA sequence of the insulin gene of every vertebrate. According to the court, the WD requirement demands more than a functional recitation of the DNA; it demands a "precise definition" of the DNA itself "such as by structure, formula, chemical name, or physical properties," not a mere wish or plan for obtaining the claimed chemical invention." *Id.* at 1566. In *Enzo Biochem v. Gen-Probe, Inc.*, 323 F.3d 956, 964 (Fed. Cir. 2002), the court refined its *Eli Lilly* decision, noting that not all functional descriptions of genetic material run afoul of the WD requirement. The court stated that the WD requirement may be satisfied if it is known in the art that the disclosed function is sufficiently correlated to a particular, known structure. *See also Amgen, Inc. v. Hoechst Marion Roussel, Inc.*, 314 F.3d 1313, 1332-1333 (Fed. Cir. 2003) (noting that

*Enzo* "clarified" *Eli Lilly* holding); *Moba, B.V. v. Diamond Automation, Inc.*, 325 F.3d 1306, 1320 (Fed. Cir. 2003) (same). It should be noted that when applied in a non-priority context, the WD requirement looks very close to the enablement requirement. Indeed, some Federal Circuit judges have expressed concern about this doctrinal overlap. *See Enzo Biochem*, 323 F.3d at 976 n.2 (Rader, J., dissenting from denial of petition to rehear case en banc).

7. **Definiteness Requirement.** Section 112, ¶2 requires that the patent particularly point out and distinctly claim the invention. This requirement, known as the "definiteness" requirement, serves two purposes. First, a distinctly drafted claim puts the public, particularly the patentee's competitors, on notice of where the patentee's proprietary boundaries reside thereby informing the competitors of what activity may constitute infringement; and second, a distinctly drafted claim distinguishes the invention from the prior art, in other words, it sets forth what exactly the invention is. In the late nineteenth century, the Supreme Court in *Bates v. Coe*, 98 U.S. 31, 39 (1878), captured the policies underlying the notice function:

> Accurate description of the invention is required by law, for several important purposes: (1) That the government may know what is granted, and what will become public property when the term of the monopoly expires; (2) That licensed persons desiring to practice the invention may know during the term how to make, construct, and use the invention; [and] (3) That other inventors may know what part of the field of invention is unoccupied.

Certainty and security in property rights are paramount concerns in any property rights regime, including IP. *See* Terry L. Anderson & Peter J. Hill, THE NOT SO WILD, WILD WEST 206 (2004) (stating "[w]ell-defined and secure property rights for intellectual property are a key to economic growth in the modern world").

An assertion of indefiniteness "requires an analysis of whether those persons skilled in the art would understand the bounds of the claim when read in light of the specification," *Credle v. Bond*, 25 F.3d 1566, 1576 (Fed. Cir. 1994), and the "degree of precision necessary for adequate claims is a function of the nature of the subject matter." *Miles Laboratories, Inc. v. Shandon Inc.*, 997 F.2d 870, 875 (Fed. Cir. 1993). Thus, a patentee does not have to "define his invention with mathematical precision" to comply with the definiteness requirement; indeed, terms of degree such as "substantially" are frequently and property used in claim drafting. In short, only claims "not amenable to construction" or "insolubly ambiguous" are indefinite. *See Datamize LLC v. Plumtree Software, Inc.*, 417 F.3d 1342 (Fed. Cir. 2005) (finding claim term "aesthetically pleasing" indefinite).

Reflecting this reluctance to demand precision is the case of *Bancorp Services, L.L.C. v. Hartford Life Insurance Co.*, 359 F.3d 1367 (Fed. Cir. 2004). Bancorp owned a patent related to a system for administering and tracking the value of life insurance policies in several accounts. All of the independent claims of the patent referred to "surrender value protected investment credits," and it is this phrase that Hartford asserted was indefinite. Hartford argued that the term was not defined in the patent and it does not have a commonly understood meaning by persons having ordinary skill in the art. The court agreed with Hartford that "surrender value protected investment credits" was not defined in the patent and Bancorp did not provide an industry publication that defines the term. Nevertheless, said the court, "the components of the term have well-recognized meanings, which allow the reader to infer the meaning of the entire phrase with reasonable confidence." The court, citing the presumption of validity that accompanies issued patents, expressed a reluctance to invalidate claims that are not "insolubly ambiguous." For the court, a claim is not indefinite "if the meaning of the claim is discernible, even though the task may be formidable and the conclusion may be one over which reasonable persons will disagree." Another case where the court was reluctant to invalidate a claim based on indefiniteness was *Athletic Alternatives v. Prince Mfg.*, 73 F.3d 1573 (Fed. Cir. 1996). There the court believed the claim language in question was subject to two interpretations, one narrower than the other, but both enabled by the specification. In this situation, the court adopted the narrower interpretation instead of invalidating the claim. The court based its decision on the notice function of the patent claim. That is, a PHOSITA faced with this scenario will know that a court will opt for a narrow interpretation.

## POLICY PERSPECTIVE
### Optimal Claim Scope and Patent Law's Delicate Balance

The *O'Reilly* case involved one of the two great communication inventions of the nineteenth century, Morse's telegraph (the other was the telephone). *O'Reilly* demonstrates that the purpose of the disclosure requirement is not only to provide the public with the benefits of a technological disclosure, but also to delineate the proprietary boundaries or scope of the patent owner's rights. The Court was very concerned that Morse's claim 8 would easily capture future improvements or alternatives that Morse did not invent or describe in his patent. But determining the proper scope of Morse's patent (or any patent) is very difficult. A court must ascertain how much improvement activity patentees such as Morse should be able to capture vis-à-vis improver-competitors. Because of Morse's inventive contribution, Justice Grier and the dissent were willing to provide Morse with broader claim scope whereas Chief Justice Taney and the majority thought such scope would be ill-advised given the nature of Morse's disclosure.

Thus, a critical and difficult balance must be struck keeping in mind patent law's incentives to invent and commercialize, coordination of improvement activity, and transaction costs (i.e., the costs associated with identifying owners of patents, negotiating licensing terms, etc.). A narrower claim scope may allow for more vigorous improvement activity and competition, but detract from the incentive to invent in the first instance or to see a product through to commercialization. A particular concern is that future innovators may unduly benefit from the first invention's disclosure that allows for enabling follow-on research and lower research costs. In contrast, a broader claim scope my lend itself to efficient coordination of improvement activity and allow a patentee to efficiently commercialize the claimed invention, but may limit competition and the pace of technological advancement due to high transaction costs. Suzanne Scotchmer succinctly captures the aforementioned scope dilemma when she writes, "the challenge is to reward early innovators fully for the technological foundation they provide to later innovators, but to reward later innovators adequately for their improvements and new products as well." Suzanne Scotchmer, *Standing on the Shoulders of Giants: Cumulative Research and the Patent Law*, 5 J. ECON. PERSPECTIVES 29, 30 (Winter 1991). *See also* Robert P. Merges & Richard Nelson, *On the Complex Economics of Patent Scope*, 90 COLUM. L. REV. 839 (1990); Edmund W. Kitch, *The Nature and Function of the Patent System*, 20 J.L. & ECON. 265 (1977).

   In the mid-1990s, the House of Lords addressed the issue of claim scope and enablement in *Biogen Inc. v. Medeva* [1997] RPC 1996. Lord Hoffmann, arguably the U.K.'s most prominent jurist on matters of intellectual property, wrote that "the concept of an enabling disclosure is central to the law of patents." Citing the *Morse* case, he continued:

> If the patentee has hit upon a new product which has a beneficial effect but cannot demonstrate that there is a common principle by which that effect will be shared by other products of the same class, he will be entitled to a patent for that product but not for the class, even though some may subsequently turn out to have the same beneficial effect. On the other hand, if he has disclosed a beneficial property which is common to the class, he will be entitled to a patent for all products of that class (assuming them to be new) even though he has not himself made more than one or two of them....
>
> The patent may claim results which it does not enable, such as making a wide class of products when it enables only one of those products and discloses no principle which would enable others to be made. Or it may claim every way of achieving a result when it enables only one way and it is possible to envisage other ways of achieving that result which make no use of the invention.
>
> I suppose it could be said that Samuel Morse had shown that electric telegraphy could be done. The Wright Brothers showed that heavier-than-air flight was possible, but that did not entitle them to a monopoly of heavier-than-air flying machines. It is inevitable in a young science, like electricity in the early nineteenth century or flying at the turn of the last century or recombinant DNA technology in the 1970s, that dramatically new things will be done for the first time. The technical contribution made in such cases deserves to be recognised. But care is needed not to stifle further research and healthy competition by allowing the first person who has found a way of achieving an obviously desirable goal to monopolise every other way of doing so. (*See* Merges & Nelson, *On the Complex Economics of Patent Scope*, 90 COLUM. L. REV. 839 (1990).)

# B. STATUTORY BARS

Section 102(b) is a *statutory bar* provision. Under §102(b), even if the inventor is the first to invent something new, he may be statutorily barred if he or a third party sells, offers for sale, publicly uses, patents, or describes in a printed publication the claimed invention (or an obvious variation thereof) more than one year before the filing date of the patent application. The date that is one year before the filing date is known as the *critical date.* Thus, this statutory provision focuses on when the applicant *filed* the patent application.

What are the policies underlying the statutory bar provision? The Federal Circuit has named the following: (1) the policy "against removing inventions from the public which the public has justifiably come to believe are freely available to all as a consequence of prolonged sales activity"; (2) the policy "favoring prompt and widespread disclosure of new inventions to the public"; (3) the policy preventing "the inventor from commercially exploiting the exclusivity of his invention substantially beyond the" statutory term; and (4) the policy giving "the inventor a reasonable amount of time following sales activity (set by statute as one year) to determine whether a patent is a worthwhile investment." *General Electric Co. v. United States*, 654 F.2d 55, 61 (Ct. Cl. 1981).

*STATUTE:* **Conditions for Patentability; Novelty and Loss of Right to Patent**
35 U.S.C. §102(b)

## 1. On-Sale Bar

### SPACE SYSTEMS/LORAL, INC. v. LOCKHEED MARTIN CORP.

#### 271 F.3d 1076 (Fed. Cir. 2001)

NEWMAN, Circuit Judge.

Space Systems/Loral, Inc. (herein "SSL") appeals the decision of the United States District Court for the Northern District of California, granting summary judgment in favor of Lockheed Martin Corporation based on the court's ruling of invalidity of SSL's United States Patent No. 4,537,375. Because the district court misapplied the law of "on sale," 35 U.S.C. §102(b), we reverse the summary judgment and remand for further proceedings.

#### BACKGROUND

The '375 patent is directed to an attitude control system for maintaining the position and orientation of a satellite. A satellite in orbit may drift out of position due to influences such as gravitational effects of the sun and moon and pressure from the solar wind, generally called "disturbance transients." To return the satellite to its correct orbit and orientation various on-board devices are employed, such as momentum/reaction wheels or thrusters, which are small rocket engines. Such corrective maneuvers are called "station keeping." Imbalances in thruster power or misalignments with respect to the satellite's center of mass, which may change as fuel is consumed, tend to introduce new errors in position or orientation during station keeping maneuvers. Such new errors require further correction after the primary correcting maneuver is made. The novel method of station keeping described in the '375 patent is called the "prebias" technique. By this technique a correction for thruster imbalances is made before the primary station keeping maneuver is performed, using data stored from previous maneuvers. If any attitude inaccuracies remain they are subjected to a further correction, but as a result of the prebias step substantially less fuel is required overall than would be consumed without the prebias compensatory action. Conservation of on-board fuel prolongs the effective life of a satellite. . . . The district court held that the invention claimed in the '375 patent was on sale more than one year before the patent application was filed, rendering the patent invalid pursuant to §102(b). Since the '375 application date is April 21, 1983, the "critical date" for the on sale bar is April 21, 1982.

The relevant events are not in dispute. Ford Aerospace and Communications Corp., a predecessor of SSL and the initial assignee of the '375 patent, entered into a contract with Société Nationale Industrielle Aerospatiale, a French company that had contracted with the Arab Satellite Communications Organization to develop the "Arabsat" satellite system. Ford was responsible for several aspects of the Arabsat system, including the satellite attitude control system.

Dr. Fred Chan, a Ford employee, conceived of the prebias method of satellite station keeping as a potential improvement over the design that was originally intended to be used. On March 19, 1982 Ford sent Aerospatiale a document entitled "Engineering Change Proposal" (ECP) which described the prebiasing idea and how Dr. Chan proposed to achieve it, by the steps of storing an estimated disturbance torque, performing a first thruster modulation in response to the stored value, detecting the net position error, and then performing a second modulation in response to the net position error and the stored value. Included were Dr. Chan's rough drawings, along with an estimate of the cost of developing the system. The district court held that this submission was an invalidating on sale event. Applying *Pfaff v. Wells Electronics, Inc.,* 525 U.S. 55, (1998), the court ruled that the ECP was a commercial offer of sale, and that the invention was ready for patenting because "SSL admitt[ed] that Dr. Chan had legal conception of every element of every claim of the '375 patent at the time the ECP was submitted to Aerospatiale." The court held that it was irrelevant that the inventor was uncertain whether the system could be made to work.

### DISCUSSION

In this case there was no dispute as to what transpired; the issue was whether the criteria of the on sale bar were met. In *Pfaff, supra,* the Supreme Court held that the on sale bar arises when the invention is both (1) ready for patenting and (2) the subject of a commercial offer for sale. SSL states that neither of these criteria was met. SSL states that at the time the engineering proposal was sent to Aerospatiale and for many months thereafter, Dr. Chan's idea was not ready for patenting for its feasibility was not yet known and it had not been enabled. Dr. Chan testified that at the time he sent the proposal to Aerospatiale he had conceived of the idea but he did not know whether he could make it work. He testified that the method for generating a value had to be developed, and that he was not sure he could establish a stable control loop. He stated that it was not until many months later, after development and testing of an engineering model, that he determined that the idea would work.

Lockheed presented no evidence disputing Dr. Chan's testimony, and does not assign error to the district court's statement that it could not conclude as a matter of law that the engineering proposal was an "enabling disclosure." Instead, Lockheed states that the bar arises, as a matter of law, "if an inventor offers for sale a product which has reached the 'conception stage.'" Lockheed stresses that "Because SSL had conceived the invention as of March 19, 1982, it could have filed a patent application—the invention was ready for patenting." Lockheed states that conception embraces enablement, and since SSL conceded conception at the time of the Engineering Change Proposal, it also conceded enablement. Thus Lockheed led the district court into error, for the district court ruled that all that is required for an invention to be ready for patenting is "legal conception of every element of every claim." The court described "legal conception" as a mental act, and held that it is not necessary to enable an invention that is fully conceived, in order for the invention to be ready for patenting. Lockheed states that this is the law of *Pfaff*. That is incorrect.

In *Pfaff* the Court explained that two ways to show that an invention is ready for patenting are if it has been actually reduced to practice, or if "prior to the critical date the inventor had prepared drawings or other descriptions of the invention that were sufficiently specific to enable a person skilled in the art to practice the invention." 525 U.S. at 67-68. The Court noted that it must be "clear that no aspect of the invention was developed after the critical date." *Id.* at 68 n. 14.

Lockheed argues that Dr. Chan's rough drawings showed the essential principles of the invention, although in lesser detail than was later available and included in the patent application. SSL responds that many months of development were required in order to learn the information that was essential to an operable invention, and that the drawings do not show an enabled invention. Lockheed states that its position that conception alone suffices in order to satisfy the *Pfaff* requirement of ready for patenting is supported by the Court's statements in *Pfaff* that "invention . . . refers to the inventor's conception rather than to a physical embodiment of [the] idea," 525 U.S. at 60. However, the Court in defining "invention" was not saying that conception alone equals "ready for patenting." The Court later explained that "The word 'invention' must refer to a concept that is complete, rather than merely one that is 'substantially complete.' It is true that reduction to practice ordinarily provides the best evidence that an invention is complete . . . it does not follow that proof of reduction to practice is necessary in every case." 525 U.S. at 66.

The Court thus held that reduction to practice was not necessary in every case; but the Court did not hold that a conception, having neither a reduction to practice nor an enabling description, is ready for patenting as a matter of law. To be "ready for patenting" the inventor must be able to prepare a patent application, that is, to provide an enabling disclosure as required by 35 U.S.C. §112. *See Robotic Vision Systems, Inc. v. View Engineering, Inc.*, 249 F.3d 1307, 1313 (Fed. Cir. 2001). For a complex concept such as the prebias technique, wherein the inventor himself was uncertain whether it could be made to work, a bare conception that has not been enabled is not a completed invention ready for patenting. Although conception can occur before the inventor has verified that his idea will work, *see Burroughs Wellcome Co. v. Barr Labs., Inc.*, 40 F.3d 1223, 1228 (Fed. Cir. 1994), when development and verification are needed in order to prepare a patent application that complies with §112, the invention is not yet ready for patenting.

Lockheed argues that since Dr. Chan's proposal included the system's four steps that are set forth in the claim, the idea was "ready for patenting" as a matter of law, even if it were not then enabled. However, the patent statute requires an enabling disclosure of how to make and use the invention. The fact that a concept is eventually shown to be workable does not retrospectively convert the concept into one that was "ready for patenting" at the time of conception. As we have observed, the Court recognized this distinction when it stated in *Pfaff* that the on sale bar does not arise when there is "additional development after the offer for sale." 525 U.S. at 68 n. 14. The district court erred in ruling that the prebias invention was ready for patenting upon conception as communicated in the engineering proposal. The judgment based thereon can not stand; thus we need not reach the question of whether a commercial offer of sale was made.

## Comments

1. **The "On-Sale" Bar Test.** The on-sale bar is only concerned with on-sale activity more than one year before the filing date of the application in question. As *Space Systems* stated, the Supreme Court in *Pfaff v. Wells Electronics, Inc.* established a two-part test for determining whether the claimed invention was on sale under §102(b). First, "the product must be the subject of a commercial offer for sale"; second, "the invention must be ready for patenting."

2. **"Commercial Offer for Sale."** The *Space Systems* court did not have to decide whether a commercial offer for sale was made because it held the invention was not ready for patenting. Prior to *Pfaff* there was some confusion as to what constituted an offer under §102(b), and the *Pfaff* court did not address the issue. But the Federal Circuit has subsequently defined commercial offer for sale by applying traditional contract principles. The court held that "the offer must meet the level of an offer for sale in the contract sense as understood by the commercial community." *Group One, Ltd. v. Hallmark Cards, Inc.*, 254 F.3d 1041, 1046-1047 (Fed. Cir. 2001).

3. **Subject Matter of the Sale.** It is important to remember that *Pfaff* did not remove the requirement that the subject matter of the commercial offer for sale be something within the scope of the claim. In other words, for the on-sale bar to apply, the subject matter of the offer for sale must either fully anticipate or render obvious what is eventually claimed.

For example, in *Sparton v. United States*, 399 F.3d 1321 (Fed. Cir. 2005), the Navy entered into a contract with Sparton for the procurement of a sonobuoy, a device that is used to detect, locate, and classify the source of underwater sounds, such as those generated by submarines. Sparton subsequently submitted an Engineering Change Proposal (ECP) to the Navy under its existing contract, proposing to incorporate dual depth operating capability into the existing sonobuoy by modifying the design. The sonobuoy device described in the ECP included a *multi-piece release plate* for either retaining or deploying the sonobuoy internal components within or from the sonobuoy housing. But shortly after the ECP was issued, Sparton developed, and later tested, a sonobuoy having a *single-piece release plate*. This single-piece release plate performed better than previous release plates and was ultimately used in the sonobuoy Sparton delivered to the Navy under the contract.

Sparton obtained two patents that each contained claim limitations drawn to a single-piece release plate for a sonobuoy. In 1992, Sparton filed suit in the Claims Court against the United States to recover money damages for the government's unlicensed use of Sparton's patented inventions. The government maintained that the patents were invalid under §102(b)'s on-sale bar. The Federal Circuit held that the patented invention was not the subject of the offer for sale prior to the critical date. According to the court, the offer for sale was the submission of an ECP incorporating dual depth operating capability. The ECP included a description of the dual depth sonobuoy deployment design, including drawings. This description and drawings contained a release plate mechanism. But the court noted that:

> [t]he parties disagree as to what type of release plate was identified. The specific release plate mechanism proposed in the ECP is not relevant to our analysis, because, as the Claims Court noted, the government concedes, and the parties do not dispute, the release plate mechanism described in the [patents-in-suit] is not the release plate that was part of the original design proposed in the ECP; in other words, the...contract does not include a release plate that meets the description of the release plate limitation of the claimed inventions. This fact is of utmost importance, as both sides agree that what was offered in the ECP was not the patented invention.... Accordingly, there is nothing to suggest that prior to the critical date of March 29, 1972, Sparton made an offer for anything other than dual-depth sonobuoys having the release plate mechanism described in the ECP.

*Id.* at 1323.

4. ***Assignments and Licenses.*** An inventor who sells his patent rights (assigns the invention) to raise money to develop and perfect the invention does not invoke the on-sale bar. There is a distinction between offering for sale the patent itself and what is claimed in the patent. The former, which provides its owner with the right to exclude, does not invoke §102(b). This rule reflects the business realities ordinarily surrounding a corporation's patent prosecution. Also, a transfer of know-how requiring further development or an offer to license the patent does not typically give rise to the on-sale bar because §102(b) bars a sale, not a license, of the patented product, and a license usually involves prospec-

tive activity. Of course, just calling something a "license" does not make it so, particularly if the "license" masks a sale that would immediately transfer the product to the "buyer" as if it were sold.

5. *"Ready for Patenting."* The Supreme Court affirmed that an invention need not be reduced to practice in order to be subject to the on-sale bar. But the Court disapproved of the Federal Circuit's "totality of circumstances" and "substantial completion" tests, suggesting that these tests were impermissibly indefinite. According to the Court, the invention has to be "ready for patenting," and this can be shown by proof of (1) reduction to practice, or (2) a description of the claimed invention that was sufficiently specific to enable a person skilled in the art to practice the invention. One way to measure (2), as the court in *Space Systems* noted, is to ask if the inventor is able to prepare a patent application that would comply with the enabling disclosure of §112. The invention in *Space Systems* was not ready for patenting.

6. *Seller's Knowledge.* The *Space Systems* court seemed to rely in part on the fact that at the time the alleged offer was made, Dr. Chan was uncertain about whether the claimed invention worked. But with respect to the inventor's (or seller's) knowledge of the product offered for sale, the Federal Circuit has adopted more of an objective test. The court has held a §102(b) offer will exist even though the offer does not specifically identify the characteristics of the claimed invention or even though the seller and buyer do not recognize the significance of the characteristics at the time of the offer. *See Abbott Laboratories v. Geneva Pharmaceuticals, Inc.*, 182 F.3d 1315, 1318-1319 (Fed. Cir. 1999). The point here is that the seller attempted to commercially exploit the claimed invention. *See also Robotic Vision Systems, Inc. v. View Engineering, Inc.*, 249 F.3d 1307, 1312 (Fed. Cir. 2001) (stating "[n]otably absent from [the *Pfaff*] test is a requirement that an inventor have complete confidence that his invention will work for its intended purpose....We did not hold that lack of skepticism regarding the 'workability of an invention' was an evidentiary requirement. It will be a rare case indeed in which an inventor has no uncertainty concerning the workability of his invention before he has reduced it to practice").

## 2. Public-Use Bar

### EGBERT v. LIPPMANN
#### 104 U.S. 333 (1882)

Mr. Justice WOODS.

This suit was brought for an alleged infringement of the complainant's patent, No. 5216, dated Jan. 7, 1873, for an improvement in corset-springs.

The original letters bear date July 17, 1866, and were issued to Samuel H. Barnes. The reissue was made to the complainant, under her then name, Frances Lee Barnes, executrix of the original patentee.

* * *

The evidence on which the defendants rely to establish a prior public use of the invention consists mainly of the testimony of the complainant.

She testifies that Barnes invented the improvement covered by his patent between January and May, 1855; that between the dates named the witness and her friend Miss Cugier were complaining of the breaking of their corset-steels. Barnes, who was present, and was an intimate friend of the witness, said he thought he could make her a pair that would not break. At their next interview he presented her with a pair of corset-steels which he himself had made. The witness wore these steels a long time. In 1858 Barnes made and presented to her another pair, which she also wore a long time. When the corsets in which these steels were used wore out, the witness ripped them open and took out the steels and put them in new corsets. This was done several times.

...[T]hese steels embodied the invention afterwards patented by Barnes and covered by the reissued letters-patent on which this suit is brought.

Joseph H. Sturgis, another witness for complainant, testifies that in 1863 Barnes spoke to him about two inventions made by himself, one of which was a corset-steel, and that he went to the house of Barnes to see them. Before this time, and after the transactions testified to by the complainant, Barnes and she had intermarried. Barnes said his wife had a pair of steels made according to his invention in the corsets which she was then wearing, and if she would take them off he would show them to witness. Mrs. Barnes went out, and returned with a pair of corsets and a pair of scissors, and ripped the corsets open and took out the steels. Barnes then explained to witness how they were made and used.

\* \* \*

We observe, in the first place, that to constitute the public use of an invention it is not necessary that more than one of the patented articles should be publicly used. The use of a great number may tend to strengthen the proof, but one well-defined case of such use is just as effectual to annul the patent as many....

We remark, secondly, that, whether the use of an invention is public or private does not necessarily depend upon the number of persons to whom its use is known. If an inventor, having made his device, gives or sells it to another, to be used by the donee or vendee, without limitation or restriction, or injunction of secrecy, and it is so used, such use is public, even though the use and knowledge of the use may be confined to one person.

We say, thirdly, that some inventions are by their very character only capable of being used where they cannot be seen or observed by the public eye. An invention may consist of a lever or spring, hidden in the running gear of a watch, or of a rachet, shaft, or cog-wheel covered from view in the recesses of a machine for spinning or weaving. Nevertheless, if its inventor sells a machine of which his invention forms a part, and allows it to be used without restriction of any kind, the use is a public one. So, on the other hand, a use necessarily open to public view, if made in good faith solely to test the qualities of the invention, and for the purpose of experiment, is not a public use within the meaning of the statute. *Elizabeth v. Pavement Company*.

Tested by these principles, we think the evidence of the complainant herself shows that for more than two years before the application for the original letters there was, by the consent and allowance of Barnes, a public use of the invention, covered by them. He made and gave to her two pairs of corset-steels, constructed according to his device, one in 1855 and one in 1858. They were presented to her for use. He imposed no obligation of secrecy, nor any condition or restriction whatever. They were not presented for the purpose of experiment, nor to test their qualities. No such claim is set up in her testimony. The invention was at the time complete, and there is no evidence that it was afterwards changed or improved. The donee of the steels used them for years for the purpose and in the manner designed by the inventor. They were not capable of any other use. She might have exhibited them to any person, or made other steels of the same kind, and used or sold them without violating any condition or restriction imposed on her by the inventor.

According to the testimony of the complainant, the invention was completed and put into use in 1855. The inventor slept on his rights for eleven years. Letters-patent were not applied for till March, 1866. In the mean time, the invention had found its way into general, and almost universal, use. A great part of the record is taken up with the testimony of the manufacturers and venders of corset-steels, showing that before he applied for letters the principle of his device was almost universally used in the manufacture of corset-steels. It is fair to presume that having learned from this general use that there was some value in his invention, he attempted to resume, by his application, what by his acts he had clearly dedicated to the public.

* * *

We are of opinion that the defense of two years' public use, by the consent and allowance of the inventor, before he made application for letters-patent, is satisfactorily established by the evidence.

Mr. Justice MILLER dissenting.

The sixth section of the act of July 4, 1836, c. 357, makes it a condition of the grant of a patent that the invention for which it was asked should not, at the time of the application for a patent, "have been in public use or on sale with the consent or allowance" of the inventor or discoverer. Section fifteen of the same act declares that it shall be a good defense to an action for infringement of the patent, that it had been in public use or on sale with the consent or allowance of the patentee before his application. This was afterwards modified by the seventh section of the act of March 3, 1839, c. 88, which declares that no patent shall be void on that ground unless the prior use has been for more than two years before the application.

This is the law under which the patent of the complainant is held void by the opinion just delivered. The previous part of the same section requires that the invention must be one "not known or used by others" before the discovery or invention made by the applicant. In this limitation, though in the same sentence as the other, the word "public" is not used, so that the use by others which would defeat the applicant, if without his consent, need not be public; but where the use of his invention is by his consent or allowance, it must be public or it will not have that affect.

The reason of this is undoubtedly that, if without his consent others have used the machine, composition, or manufacture, it is strong proof that he was not the discoverer or first inventor. In that case he was not entitled to a patent. If the use was with his consent or allowance, the fact that such consent or allowance was first obtained is evidence that he was the inventor, and claimed to be such. In such case, he was not to lose his right to a patent, unless the use which he permitted was such as showed an intention of abandoning his invention to the public. It must, in the language of the act, be in public use or on sale. If on sale, of course the public who buy can use it, and if used in public with his consent, it may be copied by others. In either event there is an end of his exclusive right of use or sale.

The word public is, therefore, an important member of the sentence. A private use with consent, which could lead to no copy or reproduction of the machine, which taught the nature of the invention to no one but the party to whom such consent was given, which left the public at large as ignorant of this as it was before the author's discovery, was no abandonment to the public, and did not defeat his claim for a patent. If the little steep spring inserted in a single pair of corsets, and used by only one woman, covered by her outer-clothing, and in a position always withheld from public observation, is a public use of that piece of steel, I am at a loss to know the line between a private and a public use.

The opinion argues that the use was public, because, with the consent of the inventor to its use, no limitation was imposed in regard to its use in public. It may be well imagined that a prohibition to the party so permitted against exposing her use of the steel spring to public observation would have been supposed to be a piece of irony. An objection quite the opposite of this suggested by the opinion is, that the invention was incapable of a public use. That is to say, that while the statute says the right to the patent can only be defeated by a use which is public, it is equally fatal to the claim, when it is permitted to be used at all, that the article can never be used in public....

## Comments

1. *Section 102(b)'s Predecessor.* The *Ebert* court applied §102(b)'s predecessor. The 1836 Patent Act barred a patent if the invention was, "at the time of his application, in public use or on sale with consent or allowance" of the inventor. The 1839 Patent Act broke new ground and introduced a period of "grace" by providing that pre-application purchase, sale, or use would not invalidate a patent "except on proof...that such purchase, sale, or prior use has been for more than two years prior to such application for a patent." Note that the 1839 Act did away with the "consent or allowance" language. Two additional changes brought the statutory provision into its current form. In 1897, Congress specified that the public use or sale must be "in this country," but added patenting and description in a printed publication anywhere as bars. In 1939, exactly a century after the two-year grace period was introduced, Congress lowered the period to one year.
2. *How Public Must "Public Use" Be?* It is clear from the pertinent Supreme Court decisions that very little use and very little publicity are required to constitute a public use under 35 U.S.C. §102(b). In *Egbert*, the use was

by a donee of apparently a single embodiment of the invention. The Court emphasized that "one well defined case of public use is just as effectual to annul the patent as many."

"Public" use means use of the product or process "in its natural and intended way" — even though the invention may in fact be hidden from public view with such use. Again, in *Egbert*, corset steels were apparently hidden inside the corset, and of course, the corset in use was hidden from public view by the woman's clothing. At least one person other than the inventor knew of the invention. For a comprehensive discussion of the public-use bar, see *Invitrogen Corp. v. Biocrest Mfg., L.P.*, 424 F.3d 1374, 2005 WL 2443864 (Fed. Cir. 2005).

3. ***Private Uses.*** To escape the public-use bar the utilization must be private, under the inventor's control, and not for commercial purposes. Despite *Egbert*, courts continue to exclude, under §102(b), purely private uses of an invention by the inventor or uses under the conditions of confidentiality. In *Moleculon Research Corp. v. CBS, Inc.*, 793 F.2d 1261 (Fed. Cir. 1986), the invention was a puzzle, popularly known as "Rubik's Cube." While a graduate student, the inventor had constructed several models of his invention, which he displayed and explained to roommates and another graduate student. Later, after beginning employment, he showed another model to his employer. Upholding the district court's finding that the uses were private, the Federal Circuit distinguished *Egbert*: The uses were either by or under the inventor's control and the inventor "had not given over the invention for free and unrestricted use by another person." *Id.* at 1266.

4. ***Commercial Products, Secret Production.*** What if the invention is used for a commercial purpose but under conditions of deliberate secrecy? Judge Hand faced this question in *Metallizing Engineering Co. v. Kenyon Bearing & Auto Parts Co.*, 153 F.2d 516 (2d Cir. 1946), which established that *commercial* exploitation by the inventor of a machine or process constitutes a public use even though the machine or process is held secret. As Judge Hand stated in this regard, an inventor "forfeits his right regardless of how little the public may have learned about the invention." As a result of Judge Hand's opinion in *Metallizing*, it is now well-established that commercial exploitation by the inventor of a machine or process constitutes a public use even though the machine or process is held secret.

5. ***Third-Party Public Use and On-Sale Activity.*** Section 102(b) makes no distinction between inventor and third-party activity. Thus, §102(b) is applicable when a third party, unbeknownst to the inventor, publicly uses or sells the invention. Moreover, it is irrelevant under §102(b) if the invention were pirated or fraudulently obtained by a third party who then used or offered the invention for sale. A barring event can arise from any source. See *Lorenz v. Colgate-Palmolive Co.*, 167 F.2d 423 (3d Cir. 1948).

Third-party activity was not always regarded this way. As Justice Story stated in *Pennock v. Dialogue*, 27 U.S. (2 Pet.) 1, 18 (1829), "it can scarcely be supposed, that the legislature had within its contemplation such [third-party] knowledge and use." And Judge Hand, in *Metallizing*, distinguished between inventor and third-party "exploitation." The

1836 Act codified *Pennock* by requiring the "consent and allowance" of the inventor before third-party public use would invalidate a patent. This requirement was removed in the 1839 Act, but any harshness to the inventor was somewhat ameliorated by implementing, for the first time, a grace period.

6. *No Need for Statutory Bars in First-to-File System.* Importantly, if the United States adopts a first-to-file system, there will no longer be a need for statutory bars because the policy of favoring prompt disclosure would be furthered by the incentives inherent in a first-to-file system. Although what constitutes a "use" and "sale" will likely remain important in determining novelty.

## Problem

**10-1.** Dr. Cullis invented a sealless centrifuge for separating blood into its components and filed a patent application claiming the sealless centrifuge on May 14, 1976. Unbeknownst to Cullis, Dr. Jacques Sito, a research scientist for the National Institutes of Health (NIH), was working with a centrifuge in connection with studying isolated heart preservation by perfusion, which involved the pumping of whole blood and platelet-rich plasma that had been separated from whole blood through a heart. The centrifuge Sito had been using damaged platelets in the blood and he found that the damage was caused by rotating seals in the centrifuge. So Sito designed and began using a sealless centrifuge on January 4, 1975. Sito had no relationship or connection with Cullis, the inventor named in the '089 patent.

The centrifuge that Sito was using met all the limitations of the representative claims of Cullis' application. Sito testified that the centrifuge worked as a separator as soon as he operated it, which verified that it would work for its intended purpose as a centrifugal blood processing apparatus and method as recited in the claims. Sito further testified that others at NIH came into his laboratory and observed the centrifuge in operation, including co-workers, who were under a strict duty to maintain it as confidential.

Is Sito's use a public use under §102(b)? *See Baxter International, Inc. v. COBE Laboratories, Inc.*, 88 F.3d 1054 (Fed. Cir. 1996).

---

### COMPARATIVE PERSPECTIVE
### Statutory Bars in Europe and Japan

The patent laws throughout most of the world, including Japan and the countries of the European Patent Convention, embrace something called "absolute novelty." This doctrine allows for a grace period in very limited circumstances. Consider Articles 54 and 55 of the EPC:

## Article 54

(1) An invention shall be considered to be new if it does not form part of the state of the art.

(2) The state of the art shall be held to comprise everything made available to the public by means of a written or oral description, by use, or in any other way, before the date of filing of the European patent application.

## Article 55

(1) For the application of Article 54 a disclosure of the invention shall not be taken into consideration if it occurred no earlier than six months preceding the filing of the European patent application and if it was due to, or in consequence of:

(a) an evident abuse in relation to the applicant or his legal predecessor, or

(b) the fact that the applicant or his legal predecessor has displayed the invention at an official, or officially recognised, international exhibition falling within the terms of the Convention on international exhibitions signed at Paris on 22 November 1928 and last revised on 30 November 1972.

Thus, the European Patent Convention has a six-month grace period only for disclosures made against the inventor's will (e.g., the invention was stolen or a breach of fiduciary relationship) or if the inventor disclosed at an "officially recognized" exhibition. Disclosures by the inventor himself (other than exhibitions) are novelty defeating.

Japanese patent law also permits a grace period of six months in limited circumstances. The exceptions to absolute novelty are disclosures made by the inventor and disclosures that originate from the inventor's disclosure, disclosures "against the will" of the inventor; and similar to the EPC, disclosures made at certain recognized exhibitions. But third-party, independent disclosures defeat patent rights under Japanese patent law. *See* §§29 and 30 of the Japan Patent Act.

## 3. Experimental Use

### LOUGH v. BRUNSWICK CORPORATION
#### 86 F.3d 1113 (Fed. Cir. 1996)

LOURIE, Circuit Judge.

Brunswick Corporation, d/b/a Mercury Marine, appeals from the final judgment of the United States District Court for the Middle District of Florida in which the court denied Brunswick's Motion for Judgment as a Matter of Law and its Motion for New Trial after a jury verdict of infringement of U.S. Patent 4,848,775, owned by the inventor Steven G. Lough....Because the court erred in denying Brunswick's Motion for Judgment as a Matter of Law, we reverse in part and vacate in part.

## BACKGROUND

Stern drives are marine propulsion devices for boats in which the engine is located inside the boat and is coupled to an outdrive, which includes a propeller located outside the boat ("inboard/outboard boat")....

In 1986, Steven G. Lough worked as a repairman for a boat dealership in Sarasota, Florida. While repairing Brunswick inboard/outboard boats, he noticed that the upper seal assembly in the stern drives often failed due to corrosion....

Lough determined that the corrosion in the upper seal assembly occurred due to contact between the annular seal...and the bell housing aperture.... He designed a new upper seal assembly that isolated the annular seal... from the aluminum bell housing...in order to prevent such corrosion.

After some trial and error with his grandfather's metal lathe, he made six usable prototypes in the spring of 1986. He installed one prototype in his own boat at home. Three months later, he gave a second prototype to a friend who installed it in his boat. He also installed prototypes in the boat of the owner of the marina where he worked and in the boat of a marina customer. He gave the remaining prototypes to longtime friends who were employees at another marina in Sarasota. Lough did not charge anyone for the prototypes. For over a year following the installation of these prototypes, Lough neither asked for nor received any comments about the operability of the prototypes. During this time, Lough did not attempt to sell any seal assemblies.

On June 6, 1988, Lough filed a patent application entitled "Liquid Seal for Marine Stern Drive Gear Shift Shafts," which issued as the '775 patent on July 18, 1989....

After learning of Lough's invention, Brunswick designed its own improved upper seal assembly.... In addition to a bushing with an upper and lower portion, Brunswick's upper seal assembly included its own patented gap technology.... Brunswick incorporated its new upper seal assembly in its "Alpha One" inboard/outboard boat. In addition, it sold this seal assembly as a replacement part under its "Quicksilver" line of replacement parts.

Lough sued Brunswick on June 12, 1993, alleging infringement of the '775 patent. Brunswick counterclaimed for a declaratory judgment of patent noninfringement, invalidity, and/or unenforceability. A jury found that Brunswick failed to prove that Lough's invention was in public use before the critical date on June 6, 1987, one year prior to the filing date of the '775 patent. The jury also found that Brunswick infringed claims 1-4 of the '775 patent, both literally and under the doctrine of equivalents. Based on its infringement finding, the jury awarded Lough $1,500,000 in lost profits. After trial, Brunswick filed a Motion for Judgment as a Matter of Law in which it argued, inter alia, that the claimed invention was invalid because it had been in public use before the critical date. Brunswick also filed a Motion for New Trial on damages. The court denied Brunswick's motions without any comment.... Brunswick appeals.

## DISCUSSION

* * *

Brunswick challenges, *inter alia*, the court's denial of its motion for JMOL on the issue of public use. Brunswick argues that the district court erred in denying its motion for JMOL because the uses of Lough's prototypes prior to the critical date were not experimental. Brunswick asserts that Lough did not control the uses of his prototypes by third parties before the critical date, failed to keep records of the alleged experiments, and did not place the parties to whom the seals were given under any obligation of secrecy. Based on this objective evidence, Brunswick argues that the uses of Lough's prototypes before the critical date were not "experimental." Therefore, Brunswick contends that the jury's verdict was incorrect as a matter of law and that the court erred in denying its JMOL motion.

Lough counters that the tests performed with the six prototypes were necessary experiments conducted in the course of completing his invention. He argues that when the totality of circumstances is properly viewed, the evidence supports the jury's conclusion that those uses were experimental. Lough maintains that a number of factors support the jury's experimental use conclusion, including evidence that he received no compensation for the prototypes, he did not place the seal assemblies on sale until after he filed his patent application, and he gave the prototypes only to his friends and personal acquaintances who used them in such a manner that they were unlikely to be seen by the public. He further argues that, to verify operability of the seal assemblies, prototypes had to be installed by mechanics of various levels of skill in boats that were exposed to different conditions. Thus, he asserts that the court did not err in denying Brunswick's JMOL motion. We disagree with Lough.

One is entitled to a patent unless, inter alia, "the invention was . . . in public use . . . in this country, more than one year prior to the date of the application for patent in the United States." 35 U.S.C. §102(b) (1994). We have defined "public use" as including "any use of [the claimed] invention by a person other than the inventor who is under no limitation, restriction or obligation of secrecy to the inventor." *In re Smith*, 714 F.2d 1127, 1134 (Fed. Cir. 1983) (*citing Egbert v. Lippmann*, 104 U.S. 333, 336 (1881)). An evaluation of a question of public use depends on "how the totality of the circumstances of the case comports with the policies underlying the public use bar." *Tone Bros. v. Sysco Corp.*, 28 F.3d 1192, 1198 (Fed. Cir. 1994). These policies include:

> (1) discouraging the removal, from the public domain, of inventions that the public reasonably has come to believe are freely available; (2) favoring the prompt and widespread disclosure of inventions; (3) allowing the inventor a reasonable amount of time following sales activity to determine the potential economic value of a patent; and (4) prohibiting the inventor from commercially exploiting the invention for a period greater than the statutorily prescribed time.

*Id.*, 28 F.3d 1192, 1198. A patentee may negate a showing of public use by coming forward with evidence that its use of the invention was experimental.

Neither party disputes that Lough's prototypes were in use before the critical date. Thus, both parties agree that the issue presented on appeal is whether the jury properly decided that the use of Lough's six prototypes in 1986, prior to the critical date, constituted experimental use so as to negate the conclusion of public use. Whether an invention was in public use prior to the critical date within the meaning of §102(b) is a question of law. *Manville Sales Corp. v. Paramount Sys., Inc.*

"The use of an invention by the inventor himself, or of any other person under his direction, by way of experiment, and in order to bring the invention to perfection, has never been regarded as [a public] use." *City of Elizabeth v. American Nicholson Pavement Co.*, 97 U.S. 126, 134 (1877). This doctrine is based on the underlying policy of providing an inventor time to determine if the invention is suitable for its intended purpose, in effect, to reduce the invention to practice. . . .

To determine whether a use is "experimental," a question of law, the totality of the circumstances must be considered, including various objective indicia of experimentation surrounding the use, such as the number of prototypes and duration of testing, whether records or progress reports were made concerning the testing, the existence of a secrecy agreement between the patentee and the party performing the testing, whether the patentee received compensation for the use of the invention, and the extent of control the inventor maintained over the testing. . . . The last factor of control is critically important, because, if the inventor has no control over the alleged experiments, he is not experimenting. If he does not inquire about the testing or receive reports concerning the results, similarly, he is not experimenting.

In order to justify a determination that legally sufficient experimentation has occurred, there must be present certain minimal indicia. The framework might be quite formal, as may be expected when large corporations conduct experiments, governed by contracts and explicit written obligations. When individual inventors or small business units are involved, however, less formal and seemingly casual experiments can be expected. Such less formal experiments may be deemed legally sufficient to avoid the public use bar, but only if they demonstrate the presence of the same basic elements that are required to validate any experimental program. . . . The question framed on this appeal is whether Lough's alleged experiments lacked enough of these required indicia so that his efforts cannot, as a matter of law, be recognized as experimental.

Here, Lough either admits or does not dispute the following facts. In the spring of 1986, he noted that the upper seal assembly in Brunswick inboard/outboard boats was failing due to galvanic corrosion between the annular seal and the aperture provided for the upper seal assembly in the aluminum bell housing. He solved this problem by isolating the annular seal from the aluminum bell housing in order to prevent corrosion. After some trial and error, Lough made six prototypes. He installed the first prototype in his own boat. Lough testified at trial that after the first prototype had been in his boat for three months and he determined that it worked, he provided the other prototypes to friends and acquaintances in order to find out if the upper seal assemblies would work as well in their boats as it had worked in his boat. Lough installed one prototype in the boat of his friend, Tom Nikla. A prototype was also installed in the boat of Jim Yow, co-owner of the dealership where Lough worked. Lough installed a fourth prototype in one of the dealership's customers who had considerable problems with corrosion in his stern drive unit. The final two prototypes were given to friends who were employed at a different marina in

Florida. These friends installed one prototype in the boat of Mark Liberman, a local charter guide. They installed the other prototype in a demonstration boat at their marina. Subsequently, this boat was sold. Neither Lough nor his friends knew what happened with either the prototype or the demonstration boat after the boat was sold. After providing the five prototypes to these third parties, Lough did not ask for any comments concerning the operability of these prototypes.

Accepting that the jury found these facts, which either were undisputed or were as asserted by Lough, it cannot be reasonably disputed that Lough's use of the invention was not "experimental" so as to negate a conclusion of public use. It is true that Lough did not receive any compensation for the use of the prototypes. He did not place the seal assembly on sale before applying for a patent. Lough's lack of commercialization, however, is not dispositive of the public use question in view of his failure to present objective evidence of experimentation. Lough kept no records of the alleged testing. *See Paragon Podiatry Lab., Inc. v. KLM Lab., Inc.*, 984 F.2d 1182, 1188 (Fed. Cir. 1993) ("[W]hen further combined with other factors, such as the inventor's failure to keep test records, the entire surrounding circumstances point to only one possible legal conclusion — that the sales [of the patented device] were commercial in nature and fall within the statutory bar"). Nor did he inspect the seal assemblies after they had been installed by other mechanics. *See In re Hamilton*, 882 F.2d 1576, 1581-83 (Fed. Cir. 1989) (lack of involvement by inventor in alleged testing is an important factor in determining that use was not experimental). He provided the seal assemblies to friends and acquaintances, but without any provision for follow-up involvement by him in assessment of the events occurring during the alleged experiments, and at least one seal was installed in a boat that was later sold to strangers. Thus, Lough did not maintain any supervision and control over the seals during the alleged testing. . . .

Lough argues that other evidence supports a finding that his uses were experimental, including his own testimony that the prototypes were installed for experimental purposes and the fact that the prototypes were used in such a manner that they were unlikely to be seen by the public. However, "the expression by an inventor of his subjective intent to experiment, particularly after institution of litigation, is generally of minimal value." *TP Laboratories*, 724 F.2d at 972. In addition, the fact that the prototypes were unlikely to be seen by the public does not support Lough's position. As the Supreme Court stated in *Egbert v. Lippmann*:

> [S]ome inventions are by their very character only capable of being used where they cannot be seen or observed by the public eye. An invention may consist of a lever or spring, hidden in the running gear of a watch, or of a rachet, shaft, or cog-wheel covered from view in the recesses of a machine for spinning or weaving. Nevertheless, if its inventor sells a machine of which his invention forms a part, and allows it to be used without restriction of any kind, the use is a public one.

104 U.S. at 336. Moreover, those to whom he gave the prototypes constituted "the public," in the absence of meaningful evidence of experimentation. Thus, we find Lough's reliance on this additional evidence to be of minimal

value when viewed in light of the totality of the other circumstances surrounding the alleged experimentation.

We therefore hold that the jury had no legal basis to conclude that the
uses of Lough's prototypes were experimental and that the prototypes were
not in public use prior to the critical date. Our holding is consistent with
the policy underlying the experimental use negation, that of providing an
inventor time to determine if the invention is suitable for its intended
purpose, *i.e.*, to reduce the invention to practice. Lough's activities clearly
were not consistent with that policy. We do not dispute that it may have
been desirable in this case for Lough to have had his prototypes installed
by mechanics of various levels of skill in boats that were exposed to different conditions. Moreover, Lough was free to test his invention in boats of
friends and acquaintances to further verify that his invention worked for its
intended purpose; however, Lough was required to maintain some degree
of control and feedback over those uses of the prototypes if those tests were
to negate public use. . . . Lough's failure to monitor the use of his prototypes
by his acquaintances, in addition to the lack of records or reports from
those acquaintances concerning the operability of the devices, compel
the conclusion that, as a matter of law, he did not engage in experimental
use. Lough in effect provided the prototype seal assemblies to members of
the public for their free and unrestricted use. The law does not waive
statutory requirements for inventors of lesser sophistication. When one
distributes his invention to members of the public under circumstances
that evidence a near total disregard for supervision and control concerning
its use, the absence of these minimal indicia of experimentation require a
conclusion that the invention was in public use.

We conclude that the jury's determination that Lough's use of the invention was experimental so as to defeat the assertion of public use was incorrect as a matter of law. The court thus erred in denying Brunswick's JMOL
motion on the validity of claims 1-4 of the '775 patent under §102(b).

\* \* \*

# Comments

1. *Distinguishing Between Public and Experimental Use.* The experimental use
doctrine balances two policies. The first is to allow the inventor time to
test and perfect his invention and to assess its utility in operation, which
results in social benefits. The second is to prevent inventors from
extending the statutory period of exclusivity by delaying filing for a
patent while commercially exploiting the invention. This balance is
achieved through application of a "reasonable purpose" test: The
inventor's *purpose* in undertaking activity that would otherwise constitute a public use must be one of experimentation, not commercial
exploitation; and, further, the scope and length of the activity must
be reasonable in terms of that purpose. If the purpose was experimental
and the activity reasonable, it does not matter that the inventor benefits
incidentally from the activity.

   Given the broad definition of public use, it is not surprising that
disputes about application of the public-use bar focus more often on

the experimental use issue than on whether a use was otherwise public. The statutory language ("public use") does not exclude experimental uses, but beginning with *Pennock v. Dialogue* in 1829 and later *City of Elizabeth*, the courts recognized that such use by an inventor should not create a bar. The doctrine is a difficult one to apply to actual cases. It is frequently invoked by patent holders to avoid the statutory bar, but is rarely sustained by the courts. (In fact, *City of Elizabeth* is the only Supreme Court case in which the Court excused public-use or on-sale activity on the basis of the experimental use doctrine.)

2. ***Defining and Applying Standards for Experimentation.*** Applying the experimental use doctrine is no simple task. Consider the list of experimental factors set forth in *Lough*, such as [1] "number of prototypes and duration of testing" [2] "whether records or progress reports were made concerning the testing" [3] "the existence of a secrecy agreement between the patentee and the party performing the testing" [4] "whether the patentee received compensation for the use of the invention" and [5] "the extent of control the inventor maintained over the testing." The court emphasized that the control factor "is critically important, because if the inventor has no control over the alleged experiments, he is not experimenting." Importantly, the experimental use exception only applies to claimed features of the invention.

In *City of Elizabeth*, Nicholson invented a process for constructing wooden block pavement. He tested the invention in its intended environment for six years, but the Court held Nicholson was engaged in public use. A number of factors contributed to the holding in *City of Elizabeth*. First, the nature of the invention (road paving) was such that any testing necessarily had to be to some extent in public. Second, for similar reasons, the testing had to be for a substantial period of time (long-term durability being the object of road paving). Third, the section of paving was at least to some extent under the control of the inventor. It was laid on private land belonging to a company of which the inventor was an officer. Fourth, the inventor regularly inspected the road during the period of use to determine its performance. In *Lough*, experimental use was not found because the court thought that, despite no commercialization efforts, recordkeeping and inventor control were lacking.

3. ***When Does Experimental Use End?*** The Federal Circuit has stated on numerous occasions that experimental use ends when the invention is reduced to practice. And a public-use bar may not be overcome even though the invention may be later refined or improved. But the environment in which the invention will be used must be taken into consideration. For example, in the *City of Elizabeth*, Nicholson had to test the pavement in its intended environment. As Judge Hand noted in *Aerovox Corp. v. Polymet Mfg.*, 67 F.2d 860, 863 (2d Cir. 1933), "it did not appear that Nicholson, the inventor, delayed for any other reason than to learn how well his pavement would wear; apparently it was already as good as he hoped to make it." In this regard, consider *Manville Sales Corp. v. Paramount Systems, Inc.*, 917 F.2d 544 (Fed. Cir. 1990). In *Manville*, the court held that a public-use bar did not arise when the inventor installed the invention, an iris arm luminaire pole, in a highway rest stop for testing in Wyoming winter weather conditions, even though the inventor previously tested the invention in a R&D center. According to the court: "Prior to its testing in

the winter environment, there really was no basis for confidence by the inventor that the invention would perform as intended, and hence no proven invention to disclose.... When durability in an outdoor environment is inherent to the purpose of an invention, then further testing to determine the invention's ability to serve that purpose will not subject the invention to a section 102(b) bar." *Id.* at 550-551.

## Problem

**10-2.** In May 1989 Axle Corp. became interested in developing an improved tie rod tool for a rack and pinion steering control system. On or about December 12, 1989, Axle Corp. delivered the prototype tool to four different automobile repair shops in Omaha, Nebraska. Axle Corp. did not receive any payment for those tools. Upon distributing the tool, Axle Corp. also did not require any of the mechanics to enter into a formal confidentiality agreement and no restrictions were placed on the use of the prototype tool by the mechanics. Also, there was no documentation regarding the actual testing of the prototype tool.

At trial, Axle Corp. presented the testimony of Mr. Danny Williams, co-inventor of the patent-in-suit and an engineer at Axle Corp. Williams testified that he needed to know whether the prototype tool would fit in the confined location of the tie rod in different automobile models. Williams also stated that, under company protocol, he and other engineers at Axle Corp. would have contacted the mechanics who were given the prototype tool every two to four weeks by telephone or in person to receive testing feedback. Williams further testified that he modified the design of the retainer in the prototype tool and added additional wrench disc sizes based on comments he received from the outside mechanics. Finally, Williams explained that although there was no formal confidentiality agreement between Axle Corp. and the mechanics who were given the prototype tools, Axle Corp. had prior working relationships with those mechanics.

On June 26, 1992, over 30 months after the first prototype tool was delivered, Axle Corp. filed the application leading to the patent-in-suit. Is there experimental use? Are the mechanics members of the public? *See Lisle Corp. v. A.J. Mfg. Co.*, 398 F.3d 1306 (Fed. Cir. 2005).

## 4. "Printed Publication"

### IN RE KLOPFENSTEIN
#### 380 F.3d 1345 (Fed. Cir. 2004)

PROST, Circuit Judge.

Carol Klopfenstein and John Brent appeal a decision from the Patent and Trademark Office's Board of Patent Appeals and Interferences ("Board") upholding the denial of their patent application. The Board upheld the Patent and Trademark Office's ("PTO's") initial denial of their application on the ground that the invention described in the patent application had already been described in a printed publication more than one year before the date of the patent application. We affirm.

## BACKGROUND

### A.

The appellants applied for a patent on October 30, 2000. Their patent application, Patent Application Serial No. 09/699,950 ("the '950 application"), discloses methods of preparing foods comprising extruded soy cotyledon fiber ("SCF"). The '950 application asserts that feeding mammals foods containing extruded SCF may help lower their serum cholesterol levels while raising HDL cholesterol levels. The fact that extrusion reduces cholesterol levels was already known by those of ordinary skill in the art that worked with SCF. What was not known at the time was that double extrusion increases this effect and yielded even stronger results.

In October 1998, the appellants, along with colleague M. Liu, presented a printed slide presentation ("Liu" or "the Liu reference") entitled "Enhancement of Cholesterol-Lowering Activity of Dietary Fibers By Extrusion Processing" at a meeting of the American Association of Cereal Chemists ("AACC"). The fourteen-slide presentation was printed and pasted onto poster boards. The printed slide presentation was displayed continuously for two and a half days at the AACC meeting.

In November of that same year, the same slide presentation was put on display for less than a day at an Agriculture Experiment Station ("AES") at Kansas State University.

Both parties agree that the Liu reference presented to the AACC and at the AES in 1998 disclosed every limitation of the invention disclosed in the '950 patent application. Furthermore, at neither presentation was there a disclaimer or notice to the intended audience prohibiting note-taking or copying of the presentation. Finally, no copies of the presentation were disseminated either at the AACC meeting or at the AES, and the presentation was never catalogued or indexed in any library or database.

### B.

On October 24, 2001, nearly one year after its filing, the '950 patent application was rejected by the PTO examiner. The examiner found all of the application's claims anticipated by the Liu reference or obvious in view of Liu and other references. Shortly thereafter, the appellants amended the claims of the '950 patent and described the circumstances under which the Liu reference had been displayed to the AACC and at the AES. The appellants argued that the Liu reference was not a "printed publication" because no copies were distributed and because there was no evidence that the reference was photographed. The examiner rejected these arguments and issued a final office action on April 10, 2002 rejecting the claims of the '950 application. The appellants then appealed to the Board.

Before the Board, the appellants again advanced their argument that the lack of distribution and lack of evidence of copying precluded the Liu reference from being considered a "printed publication." The appellants further contended that the Liu reference was also not a "printed publication" because it was not catalogued or indexed in any library or database. The Board rejected the appellants' arguments and affirmed the decision of the PTO examiner, finding the Liu reference to be a "printed publication." The Board affirmed on the grounds that the full invention of the '950 application was made publicly accessible to those of ordinary skill in the art by the Liu reference and that this introduction into the public domain of disclosed material via printed display represented a "printed publication" under 35 U.S.C. §102(b).

## DISCUSSION

### A.

The only question in this appeal is whether the Liu reference constitutes a "printed publication" for the purposes of 35 U.S.C. §102(b). As there are no factual disputes between the parties in this appeal, the legal issue of whether the Liu reference is a "printed publication" will be reviewed de novo.

### B.

The appellants argue on appeal that the key to establishing whether or not a reference constitutes a "printed publication" lies in determining whether or not it had been disseminated by the distribution of reproductions or copies and/or indexed in a library or database. They assert that because the Liu reference was not distributed and indexed, it cannot count as a "printed publication" for the purposes of 35 U.S.C. §102(b). To support their argument, they rely on several precedents from this court and our predecessor court on "printed publications." They argue that *In re Cronyn*, *In re Hall*, *Massachusetts Institute of Technology v. AB Fortia*, ("*MIT*"), and *In re Wyer*, among other cases, all support the view that distribution and/or indexing is required for something to be considered a "printed publication."[2]

We find the appellants' argument unconvincing and disagree with their characterization of our controlling precedent. Even if the cases cited by the appellants relied on inquiries into distribution and indexing to reach their holdings, they do not limit this court to finding something to be a "printed publication" *only* when there is distribution and/or indexing. Indeed, the key inquiry is whether or not a reference has been made "publicly accessible." As we have previously stated,

> The statutory phrase "printed publication" has been interpreted to mean that before the critical date the reference must have been sufficiently accessible to the public interested in the art; dissemination and public accessibility are the keys to the legal determination whether a prior art reference was "published."

*In re Cronyn*, 890 F.2d at 1160.[3] For example, a public billboard targeted to those of ordinary skill in the art that describes all of the limitations of an invention and that is on display for the public for months may be neither "distributed" nor "indexed"—but it most surely is "sufficiently accessible

---

2. Appellants acknowledge that our precedent considers the term "printed publication" to be a unitary concept that may not correspond exactly to what the term "printed publication" meant when it was introduced into the patent statutes in 1836. *In re Wyer*, 655 F.2d at 226. Indeed, the question to be resolved in a "printed publication" inquiry is the extent of the reference's "accessibility to at least the pertinent part of the public, of a perceptible description of the invention, in whatever form it may have been recorded." *Id*.

3. While the *Cronyn* court held "dissemination" to be necessary to finding something to be a "printed publication", the court there used the word "disseminate" in its literal sense, i.e. "make widespread" or "to foster general knowledge of." *Webster's Third New International Dictionary* 656 (1993). The court did not use the word in the narrower sense the appellants have employed it, which requires distribution of reproductions or photocopies.

to the public interested in the art" and therefore, under controlling precedent, a "printed publication." Thus, the appellants' argument that "distribution and/or indexing" are the key components to a "printed publication" inquiry fails to properly reflect what our precedent stands for.

Furthermore, the cases that the appellants rely on can be clearly distinguished from this case. *Cronyn* involved college students' presentations of their undergraduate theses to a defense committee made up of four faculty members. Their theses were later catalogued in an index in the college's main library. The index was made up of thousands of individual cards that contained only a student's name and the title of his or her thesis. The index was searchable by student name and the actual theses themselves were neither included in the index nor made publicly accessible. We held that because the theses were only presented to a handful of faculty members and "had not been cataloged [sic] or indexed in a meaningful way," they were not sufficiently publicly accessible for the purposes of 35 U.S.C. §102(b). *In re Cronyn*, 890 F.2d at 1161.

In *Hall*, this court determined that a thesis filed and indexed in a university library did count as a "printed publication." The *Hall* court arrived at its holding after taking into account that copies of the indexed thesis itself were made freely available to the general public by the university more than one year before the filing of the relevant patent application in that case. But the court in *Hall* did not rest its holding merely on the indexing of the thesis in question. Instead, it used indexing as a factor in determining "public accessibility." As the court asserted:

> The ["printed publication"] bar is grounded on the principle that once an invention is in the public domain, it is no longer patentable by anyone.... Because there are many ways in which a reference may be disseminated to the interested public, "public accessibility" has been called the touchstone in determining whether a reference constitutes a "printed publication" bar under 35 U.S.C. §102(b).

*In re Hall*, 781 F.2d at 898-99.

In *MIT*, a paper delivered orally to the First International Cell Culture Congress was considered a "printed publication." In that case, as many as 500 persons having ordinary skill in the art heard the presentation, and at least six copies of the paper were distributed. The key to the court's finding was that actual copies of the presentation were distributed. The court did not consider the issue of indexing. The *MIT* court determined the paper in question to be a "printed publication" but did not limit future determinations of the applicability of the "printed publication" bar to instances in which copies of a reference were actually offered for distribution. *MIT*, 774 F.2d at 1108-10.[4]

---

4. With regard to scientific presentations, it is important to note than an entirely oral presentation at a scientific conference that includes neither slides nor copies of the presentation is without question not a "printed publication" for the purposes of 35 U.S.C. §102(b). Furthermore, a presentation that includes a transient display of slides is likewise not necessarily a "printed publication." *See, e.g., Regents of the Univ. of Cal. v. Howmedica, Inc.*, 530 F. Supp. 846, 860 (D.N.J.1981). While *Howmedica* is not binding on this court, it stands for the important proposition that the mere presentation of slides accompanying an oral presentation at a professional conference is not per se a "printed publication" for the purposes of §102(b).

Finally, the *Wyer* court determined that an Australian patent application kept on microfilm at the Australian Patent Office was "sufficiently accessible to the public and to persons skilled in the pertinent art to qualify as a 'printed publication.'" *In re Wyer*, 655 F.2d at 226. The court so found even though it did not determine whether or not there was "actual viewing or dissemination" of the patent application. *Id.* It was sufficient for the court's purposes that the records of the application were kept so that they could be accessible to the public. *Id.*[5] According to the *Wyer* court, the entire purpose of the "printed publication" bar was to "prevent withdrawal" of disclosures "already in the possession of the public" by the issuance of a patent. *Id.*

Thus, throughout our case law, public accessibility has been the criterion by which a prior art reference will be judged for the purposes of §102(b). Oftentimes courts have found it helpful to rely on distribution and indexing as proxies for public accessibility. But when they have done so, it has not been to the exclusion of all other measures of public accessibility. In other words, distribution and indexing are not the only factors to be considered in a §102(b) "printed publication" inquiry.

## C.

In this case, the Liu reference was displayed to the public approximately two years before the '950 application filing date. The reference was shown to a wide variety of viewers, a large subsection of whom possessed ordinary skill in the art of cereal chemistry and agriculture. Furthermore, the reference was prominently displayed for approximately three cumulative days at AACC and the AES at Kansas State University. The reference was shown with no stated expectation that the information would not be copied or reproduced by those viewing it. Finally, no copies of the Liu display were distributed to the public and the display was not later indexed in any database, catalog or library.

Given that the Liu reference was never distributed to the public and was never indexed, we must consider several factors relevant to the facts of this case before determining whether or not it was sufficiently publicly accessible in order to be considered a "printed publication" under §102(b). These factors aid in resolving whether or not a temporarily displayed reference that was neither distributed nor indexed was nonetheless made sufficiently publicly accessible to count as a "printed publication" under §102(b). The factors relevant to the facts of this case are: the length of time the display was exhibited, the expertise of the target audience, the existence (or lack thereof) of reasonable expectations that the material displayed would not be copied, and the simplicity or ease with which the material displayed could have been copied. Only after considering and balancing these factors can we determine whether or not the Liu reference was sufficiently publicly accessible to be a "printed publication" under §102(b).

The duration of the display is important in determining the opportunity of the public in capturing, processing and retaining the information conveyed by the reference. The more transient the display, the less likely it is

---

5. Unlike in *Cronyn*, it was the actual patent application—and not just an index card searchable by author name only—that was made publicly accessible.

to be considered a "printed publication." *See, e.g. Howmedica*, 530 F. Supp. at 860 (holding that a presentation of lecture slides that was of limited duration was insufficient to make the slides "printed publications" under §102(b)). Conversely, the longer a reference is displayed, the more likely it is to be considered a "printed publication." In this case, the Liu reference was displayed for a total of approximately three days. It was shown at the AACC meeting for approximately two and a half days and at the AES at Kansas State University for less than one day.

The expertise of the intended audience can help determine how easily those who viewed it could retain the displayed material. As Judge Learned Hand explained in *Jockmus v. Leviton*, 28 F.2d 812, 813-14 (2d Cir.1928), a reference, "however ephemeral its existence," may be a "printed publication" if it "goes direct to those whose interests make them likely to observe and remember whatever it may contain that is new and useful." In this case, the intended target audience at the AACC meeting was comprised of cereal chemists and others having ordinary skill in the art of the '950 patent application. The intended viewers at the AES most likely also possessed ordinary skill in the art.

Whether a party has a reasonable expectation that the information it displays to the public will not be copied aids our §102(b) inquiry. Where professional and behavioral norms entitle a party to a reasonable expectation that the information displayed will not be copied, we are more reluctant to find something a "printed publication." This reluctance helps preserve the incentive for inventors to participate in academic presentations or discussions. Where parties have taken steps to prevent the public from copying temporarily posted information, the opportunity for others to appropriate that information and assure its widespread public accessibility is reduced. These protective measures could include license agreements, non-disclosure agreements, anti-copying software or even a simple disclaimer informing members of the viewing public that no copying of the information will be allowed or countenanced. Protective measures are to be considered insofar as they create a reasonable expectation on the part of the inventor that the displayed information will not be copied. In this case, the appellants took no measures to protect the information they displayed—nor did the professional norms under which they were displaying their information entitle them to a reasonable expectation that their display would not be copied. There was no disclaimer discouraging copying, and any viewer was free to take notes from the Liu reference or even to photograph it outright.

Finally, the ease or simplicity with which a display could be copied gives further guidance to our §102(b) inquiry. The more complex a display, the more difficult it will be for members of the public to effectively capture its information. The simpler a display is, the more likely members of the public could learn it by rote or take notes adequate enough for later reproduction. The Liu reference was made up of 14 separate slides. One slide was a title slide; one was an acknowledgement slide; and four others represented graphs and charts of experiment results. The other eight slides contained information presented in bullet point format, with no more than three bullet points to a slide. Further, no bullet point was longer than two concise sentences. Finally, as noted earlier, the fact that extrusion lowers cholesterol levels was already known by those who worked with SCF. The discovery disclosed in the Liu reference was that double extrusion increases this effect. As a result, most of the eight substantive slides only recited what had already been known in the field, and only a few slides presented would have needed to have been copied by an observer to capture the novel information presented by the slides.

Upon reviewing the above factors, it becomes clear that the Liu reference was sufficiently publicly accessible to count as a "printed publication" for the purposes of 35 U.S.C. §102(b). The reference itself was shown for an extended period of time to members of the public having ordinary skill in the art of the invention behind the '950 patent application. Those members of the public were not precluded from taking notes or even photographs of the reference. And the reference itself was presented in such a way that copying of the information it contained would have been a relatively simple undertaking for those to whom it was exposed—particularly given the amount of time they had to copy the information and the lack of any restrictions on their copying of the information. For these reasons, we conclude that the Liu reference was made sufficiently publicly accessible to count as a "printed publication" under §102(b).

## Comment

1. *Public Accessibility.* Section 102(b) states that no patent shall issue if the invention was patented or described in a printed publication more than one year before the application was filed. Public accessibility is the key to determining whether a reference constitutes a printed publication. Importantly, accessibility focuses on the public interested in the art, so that by examining the reference, one could make the claimed invention without further research or experimentation. There is no requirement that particular members of the public actually received the printed publication or the information contained therein. The court in *Hall* held that a single doctoral thesis deposited and indexed in a German library was sufficiently accessible to invoke §102(b), but the "indexing" system in *Cronyn* was not sufficient. Of course, as *Klopfenstein* holds, indexing is not a requirement for a finding of public accessibility. A slide presentation continuously displayed at a conference over a period of two days is a printed publication under §102(b).

## C. NOVELTY

The novelty requirement, embodied in §102 of the patent code, precludes a patent from issuing on claimed subject matter that was not new at the time or date of invention. The reason for the novelty requirement is straightforward: It makes no sense to grant someone a patent on an invention that already exists. It follows that proving date of invention is potentially very important. Sections 1 and 3 explore how one determines date of invention. The date of invention is shown by proving *reduction to practice,* which can be either actual (when a prototype of the invention has been built that works for its intended purpose) or constructive (the date the patent application was filed). The materials also describe the notions of *conception* and *diligence*, which are sometimes relevant to proving date of invention.

Sections 102(a), (e) and (g)(2) embody the novelty requirement. Of particular importance with respect to §102(a) is that to be anticipated the "invention" must be *publicly* used or known by others before the date of invention. On the other hand, §102(e) and (g)(2), as discussed in the Comments following *Rosaire*, allow for so-called "secret" prior art, which may have a patent-defeating effect.

The novelty requirement concerns itself with when the applicant actually *invented* the claimed invention. Novelty simply asks: is the applicant's invention *new*. Think of novelty as focusing on just one applicant and asking whether some third person, who is not seeking a patent, previously disclosed or invented what the applicant is seeking to patent. If an invention isn't new, it is said to be *anticipated* by the prior art. The novelty provisions pertain to third-party activity prior to the date of invention because the applicant could not have known or used the invention or patented or published it before he invented it.

Contrast the novelty provisions with the statutory bar provision in §102(b). The latter focuses on activity of both the inventor and third parties; and the critical date is one year before the application was filed whereas novelty focuses on activity before the date of invention. Consider the following table, which compares §102(a) and (b).

*STATUTE:* **Conditions for Patentability; Novelty and Loss of Right to Patent**
35 U.S.C. §102(a), (e) & (g)(2)

# 1. Proving Date of Invention

The critical date for §102's novelty provisions is "before date of invention." Also, as discussed in Section C.3, the United States is a "first-to-invent" country, which means when two or more parties are vying for a patent on the same invention, the patent is awarded to the party who invented first, not the party who filed a patent application first. Thus, proving when "invention" occurred is very important. Proving date of invention can be a complex endeavor, and is relevant whether an inventor is trying to antedate a prior art reference to show novelty or trying to show he invented before a third party who is also seeking a patent on the same invention. The fundamentals of proving date of invention are as follows: (1) The first to reduce the invention to practice is the prima facie "first and true inventor." But where more than one party is seeking a patent on the same invention, a party who was second to reduce to practice will be considered the first and true inventor if he can show that he was the first to conceive and exercised reasonable diligence in reducing his invention to practice (more on diligence and abandonment in Section C.3, *infra*); (2) reduction to practice is shown if the inventor can prove that the invention works for its intended purpose; and (3) conception is proved through the presentation of corroborated evidence that the inventor formed in his mind "a definite and permanent idea of the complete and operative invention, as it is thereafter applied in practice."

There are two types of reduction to practice (RTP): (1) actual, and (2) constructive. *Actual* RTP occurs when the invention is shown to be suitable or work for its intended purpose; that is, when the invention is physically made and tested (e.g., a prototype). Actual working conditions may not be required for testing. Indeed, laboratory tests may be sufficient if they simulate actual working conditions. The amount and degree of testing depends on the complexity of the invention. Less complicated inventions and problems do not demand stringent testing. Lastly, neither perfection nor commercial viability are required to show actual reduction to practice.

*Constructive* RTP happens when the patent application is filed. Constructive RTP may occur even if the applicant never built or tested his invention as long as the applicant satisfies §112's disclosure requirements. The policy behind constructive RTP is to encourage early disclosure of the invention. Requiring actual testing may delay disclosure. The Federal Circuit has held that there can be no reduction to practice unless the inventor has a contemporaneous "recognition and appreciation" that the invention works for its intended purpose. In other words, an inventor will not be entitled to a prior date of invention if he only came to appreciate his discovery at a later time.

Prior to the implementation of NAFTA and the international agreement on the Trade-Related Aspects of Intellectual Property Rights (TRIPs) of GATT, inventive activity (i.e., conception and reduction to practice) outside of the United States could not be used to prove date of invention under 35 U.S.C. §104. For example, prior to these international treaties, an inventor who filed his application in the United States, but conceived and reduced the invention to practice in Germany would not be able to offer his conception and RTP as proof of date of invention because it occurred in Germany. But taking a step toward harmonization, §104 was amended to permit patent applicants to rely on inventive activity in any NAFTA or World Trade Organization (WTO) member country. The amendments to §104 became effective for NAFTA and WTO countries on December 8, 1993 and January 1, 1996, respectively. Inventive activity occurring before December 8, 1993 in NAFTA countries and before January 1, 1996 in WTO countries cannot be used to prove date of invention.

Like §104, §102(g) was also amended because it limited inventive activity to acts "*in this country.*" The American Inventors Protection Act of 1999 created §102(g)(1) to allow foreign-based inventive activity to be used in obtaining patent rights. For example, Inventor A conceives and reduces to practice in Spain on October 1, 2001. Inventor B does the same in the United States on November 1, 2001, but Inventor B files his application in the United States before Inventor A. Both inventors claim the same subject matter. As such the PTO is likely to declare an interference, which is an administrative proceeding to determine who invented first. Recall, in the United States the patent is awarded to the party who invented first. In the interference, Inventor A can use his conception and RTP in Spain to prove he invented before Inventor B.

# Problem

**10-3.** On January 4, 2002, Cosmo, Inc. scientists Esto and Lado conceived, during a thorough "brainstorming" session, of an idea for a composition for treating skin damaged by excessive exposure to the sun. On that same day, they quickly wrote the details of their discussion in a laboratory notebook. On February 11, Esto and Lado, after several weeks in the lab, developed a composition in accordance with their notes and sent the composition to a laboratory for testing, as was customary at Cosmo. The test results, which were transmitted to Esto and Lado on March 31, showed that the composition was "successful" or that it worked for its intended purpose. Cosmo subsequently filed for a patent on the composition on July 1, 2002. The PTO rejected the application under §102(a) citing a prior art publication dated March 25, 2002. Assume the publication discloses Cosmo's claimed composition. Does the publication anticipate the Cosmo invention? *See Estee Lauder Inc. v. L'Oreal S.A.*, 129 F.3d 588, 593 (Fed. Cir. 1997).

## 2. "Known or Used"

The words "known" and "used" in §102(a) are not as straightforward as one may initially think. The *Rosaire* case explores the nuances of this language in the context of patent law's policy objectives.

### ROSAIRE v. BAROID SALES DIVISION
#### 218 F.2d 72 (5th Cir. 1955)

TUTTLE, Circuit Judge.

In this suit for patent infringement there is presented to us for determination the correctness of the judgment of the trial court, based on findings of fact and conclusions of law, holding that the two patents involved in the litigation were invalid and void and that furthermore there had been no infringement by defendant.

The Rosaire and Horvitz patents relate to methods of prospecting for oil or other hydrocarbons. The inventions are based upon the assumption that gases have emanated from deposits of hydrocarbons which have been trapped in the earth and that these emanations have modified the surrounding rock. The methods claimed involve the steps of taking a number of samples of soil from formations which are not themselves productive of hydrocarbons, either over a horizontal area or vertically down a well bore, treating each sample, as by grinding and heating in a closed vessel, to cause entrained or absorbed hydrocarbons therein to evolve as a gas, quantitatively measuring the amount of hydrocarbon gas so evolved from each sample, and correlating the measurements with the locations from which the samples were taken.

Plaintiff claims that in 1936 he and Horvitz invented this new method of prospecting for oil. In due course the two patents in suit, Nos. 2,192,525 and 2,324,085, were issued thereon. Horvitz assigned his interest to Rosaire. Appellant alleged that appellee Baroid began infringing in 1947; that he learned of this in 1949 and asked Baroid to take a license, but no license agreement was worked out, and this suit followed, seeking an injunction and an accounting.

In view of the fact that the trial court's judgment that the patents were invalid, would of course dispose of the matter if correct, we turn our attention to this issue. Appellee's contention is that the judgment of the trial court in this respect should be supported on two principal grounds. The first is that the prior art, some of which was not before the patent office, anticipated the two patents; the second is that work carried on by one Teplitz for the Gulf Oil Corporation invalidated both patents by reason of the relevant provisions of the patent laws which state that an invention is not patentable if it "was known or used by others in this country" before the patentee's invention thereof, 35 U.S.C.A. §102(a). Appellee contends that Teplitz and his coworkers knew and extensively used in the field the same alleged inventions before any date asserted by Rosaire and Horvitz.

On this point appellant himself in his brief admits that "Teplitz conceived of the idea of extracting and quantitatively measuring entrained or absorbed gas from the samples of rock, rather than relying upon the free gas in the samples. We do not deny that Teplitz conceived of the methods of the patents in suit." And further appellant makes the following admission: "We admit that the Teplitz — Gulf work was done before Rosaire and Horvitz conceived of the inventions. We will show, however, that Gulf did not apply for patent until 1939, did not publish Teplitz's ideas, and did not otherwise give the public the benefit of the experimental work."

In support of their respective positions, both appellant and appellee stress the language in our opinion in the case of *Pennington v. National Supply Co.*, where, speaking through Judge Holmes, we said: "Appellant insists that the court erred in considering the prior use of the Texas machine, because that machine was abandoned by the Texas Company and was not successful until modified and rebuilt. As to this, it does not appear that the Texas machine was a failure, since it drilled three wells for the Texas Company, which was more than was usually accomplished by the rotary drilling machines then in use."

"An unsuccessful experiment which is later abandoned does not negative novelty in a new and successful device". *T. H. Symington Co. v. National Malleable Castings Co.*, 250 U.S. 383, 386; *Clark Thread Co. v. Willimantic Linen Co.*, 140 U.S. 481, 489. Nevertheless, the existence and operation of a machine, abandoned after its completion and sufficient use to demonstrate its practicability, is evidence that the same ideas incorporated in a later development along the same line do not amount to invention. *Corona Cord Tire Co. v. Dovan Chemical Corporation.* If the prior machine does not anticipate, it would not have done so if it had been neither unsuccessful nor abandoned. Novelty is ascribed to new things, without regard to the successful and continued use of old things. Correlatively, it is denied to old things, without regard to the circumstances which caused their earlier applications to be unsatisfactory or their use to be abandoned.

The question as to whether the work of Teplitz was "an unsuccessful experiment," as claimed by appellant, or was a successful trial of the method in question and a reduction of that method to actual practice, as contended by appellee, is, of course, a question of fact. On this point the trial court made the following finding of fact: "I find as a fact, by clear and substantial proof beyond a reasonable doubt, that Abraham J. Teplitz and his coworkers with Gulf Oil Corporation and its Research Department during 1935 and early 1936, before any date claimed by Rosaire, spent more than a year in the oil fields and adjacent territory around Palestine, Texas, taking and analyzing samples both over an area and down drill holes, exactly as called for in the claims of the patents which Rosaire and Horvitz subsequently applied for and which are here in suit. This Teplitz work was a successful and adequate field trial of the prospecting method involved and a reduction to practice of that method. The work was performed in the field under ordinary conditions without any deliberate attempt at concealment or effort to exclude the public and without any instructions of secrecy to the employees performing the work."

As we view it, if the court's findings of fact are correct then under the statute as construed by the courts, we must affirm the finding of the trial court that appellee's patents were invalid. As to the finding of fact we are to affirm unless we conclude that it is "clearly erroneous." Rule 52, Fed. Rules Civ. Proc., 28 U.S.C.A.

A close analysis of the evidence on which the parties rely to resolve this question clearly demonstrates that there was sufficient evidence to sustain the finding of the trial court that there was more here than an unsuccessful or incomplete experiment. It is clear that the work was not carried forward, but that appears to be a result of two things: (1) that the geographical area did not lend itself properly to the test, and (2) that the "entire gas prospecting program was therefore suspended in September of 1936, in order that the accumulated information might be thoroughly reviewed." It will be noted that the program was not suspended to test the worth of the method but to examine the data that was produced by use of the method involved. The above quotation came from one of the recommendations at the end of Teplitz's report, and was introduced on behalf of the appellant himself. Expert testimony presented by witnesses Rogers, Eckhardt and Weaver supported appellee's contention.

With respect to the argument advanced by appellant that the lack of publication of Teplitz's work deprived an alleged infringer of the defense of prior use, we find no case which constrains us to hold that where such work was done openly and in the ordinary course of the activities of the employer, a large producing company in the oil industry, the statute is to be so modified by construction as to require some affirmative act to bring the work to the attention of the public at large.

While there is authority for the proposition that one of the basic principles underlying the patent laws is the enrichment of the art, and that a patent is given to encourage disclosure of inventions, no case we have found requires a holding that, under the circumstances that attended the work of Teplitz, the fact of public knowledge must be shown before it can be urged to invalidate a subsequent patent. The case of *Corona Cord Tire Co. v. Dovan Chemical Corporation, supra,* is authority for the opposing view, that taken by the court below. In that case the Supreme Court said: "In 1916, while with the Norwalk Company, Kratz prepared D.P.G. and demonstrated its utility as a rubber accelerator by making test slabs of vulcanized or cured rubber with its use. Every time that he produced such a slab he recorded his test in cards which he left with the Norwalk Company and kept a duplicate of his own. . . . This work was known to, and was participated in, by his associate in the Norwalk Company, his immediate superior and the chief chemist of the company, Dr. Russell, who fully confirms Kratz's records and statement." *Corona Cord Tire*, 276 U.S. 358, 378, 379.

The court further states in the *Corona* case at page 382 of 276 U.S.: "But, even if we ignore this evidence of Kratz's actual use of D.P.G. in these rubber inner tubes which were sold, what he did at Norwalk, supported by the evidence of Dr. Russell, his chief, and by the indubitable records that are not challenged, leaves no doubt in our minds that he did discover in 1916 the strength of D.P.G. as an accelerator as compared with the then known accelerators, and that he then demonstrated it by a reduction of it to practice in production of cured or vulcanized rubber. This constitutes priority in this case."

Concluding, as we do, that the trial court correctly held that patents invalid, it is not necessary to consider the question of infringement. The judgment of the trial court is affirmed.

## Comments

1. *"A Manner Accessible to the Public."* When asking whether an invention was "known or used" under §102(a), we are really asking whether the invention was "known or used" by someone other than the inventor. As Justice Story explained in *Pennock v. Dialogue*, 27 U.S. (2 Pet.) 1, 18 (1829), known or used cannot mean knowledge or use by the inventor because that would "prohibit him from the only means to obtain a patent."

2. *How Accessible to the Public?* It does not take much to satisfy the publicity requirement of §102(a). Recall the work of Teplitz in *Rosaire*, from a practical standpoint, was inaccessible to the public, yet it served as prior art. So the publicity requirement of §102(a) must be understood as the absence of secrecy."

---

### COMPARATIVE PERSPECTIVE
### Defining Prior Art and Geographical Limitations

Section 102(a) says that an invention will be anticipated if it was "known or used *in this country.*" Recall that §104 was amended so that one may use foreign inventive activity to prove date of invention in the obtainment of patent rights, but foreign knowledge and use cannot act as prior art to defeat patent rights. This geographic disparity differs sharply with the European Patent Convention (Article 54(2)) and the Japan Patent Law (§29(1)), both of which treat public foreign knowledge and use as prior art.

Why is knowledge and use limited to the United States? This geographic limitation did not make its way into our patent law until 1836, but the Senate Report accompanying the 1836 Act offers little if any explanation. Common sense tells us that unpublished knowledge and use are less difficult for a U.S. inventor to discover in the United States as opposed to Europe or Japan. How does one search for unpublished knowledge in foreign lands without incurring a great deal of expense or "search costs." It is difficult enough to obtain such knowledge in the United States, let alone a foreign country. At least with many foreign publications and most foreign patents, there exist databases that one can search relatively cheaply today. Foreign patents and publications may be anticipatory under §102(a) and (b) (we will discuss patents and printed publications in detail in the next section). Furthermore, as a matter of policy, it is difficult for Americans to enjoy unpublished knowledge and uses if they are extant only in a foreign land. *Gayler v. Wilder*, 51 U.S. 477 (1850) addressed the geographic issue:

> If the foreign invention had been printed or patented, it was already given to the world and open to the people of this country, as well as of others, upon reasonable inquiry. They would therefore derive no advantage from the invention here. It would confer no benefit upon the community, and the inventor therefore is not considered to be entitled to the reward. But if the foreign discovery is not patented, nor described in any printed publication, it might be known and used in remote places for ages, and the people of this country be unable to profit by it. The means of obtaining knowledge would not be within their reach; and, as far as their interest is concerned, it would be the same thing as if the improvement had never been discovered.

But our world today is much smaller than it was in 1850. As such, does the geographic distinction still make sense? Consider the concern of developing nations and their inability to do much to prevent American patents from issuing (or from securing compensation from commercial exploitation of such patents) on inventions derived from indigenous flora and fauna, what is sometimes referred to as "biopiracy" or "bioprospecting." Indeed, §102(a) provides refuge for inventors who seek to patent inventions based on foreign knowledge. A prominent example is the neem tree controversy. The leaves and bark of the neem tree, which is indigenous to India, have been used as natural pesticides and fuel by the people of India for years. In the early 1990s, a multinational company, W.R. Grace, obtained U.S. and European patents on pesticide products derived from the neem tree. The patents were challenged by two Indian nongovernmental organizations, resulting in one of the European patents being invalidated for lacking novelty. But the validity of the American patents remained intact. The central reason for this difference in result is that unlike the European Patent Convention, namely Article 54(2), American patent law, specifically §102(a), distinguishes between domestic knowledge and use and foreign knowledge and use. Notably, §29 of the Japan Patent Law, like Article 54(2) of the EPC, does not distinguish between domestic and foreign knowledge in this regard.

## 3. Priority

The United States is a first-to-invent country. This means that between or among competing claims to obtain patent rights on the same invention, patent rights are awarded to the person who is able to prove that he was the first to invent. Recall from the discussion in Section C.1, the party who first reduced the invention to practice is ordinarily deemed the first inventor. But a party who was not the first to reduce to practice may be considered the first inventor (and obtain the patent) if he was the first to conceive the invention and exercised diligence in reducing it to practice. The *Fujikawa* case explores these complex concepts.

These priority disputes are resolved in what is known as an *interference*, which is an *inter partes*, administrative proceeding within the PTO. Section 102(g)(1) is the relevant statutory provision. As you can imagine, an interference can be quite convoluted and cumbersome given the potential for numerous dates and parties, different types of inventive activity, and potentially complex technology. A first-to-invent system is to be compared to a first-to-file regime, which has been adopted by every other industrialized nation in the world. As the name suggests, the party who first filed its patent application with a given patent office is awarded the patent.

In the *Fujikawa* case that follows, note that Fujikawa's earliest invention date is the date he filed his application in the United States. This is because that at the time the case was decided, U.S. patent law, namely §104, did not allow for foreign inventive activity such as conception and reduction to practice to be used to prove an earlier date of invention; conception and reduction to practice had to occur in the United States for it to be used as proof of date of invention. This law was amended when NAFTA and the international agreement on the Trade-Related Aspects of Intellectual Property Rights (TRIPs) of GATT were implemented on *December 8, 1993* and *January 1, 1996*, respectively. Now, inventive activity in any NAFTA or WTO member country can be used to prove date of invention. *See* Comment 4 following the *Mahurkar* case, *supra*.

## FUJIKAWA v. WATTANASIN

### 93 F.3d 1559 (Fed. Cir. 1996)

CLEVENGER, Circuit Judge.

Yoshihiro Fujikawa *et al.* (Fujikawa) appeal from two decisions of the Board of Patent Appeals and Interferences of the United States Patent & Trademark Office (Board) granting priority of invention in two related interferences to Sompong Wattanasin, and denying Fujikawa's motion to add an additional sub-genus count to the interferences. We affirm.

## I

These interferences pertain to a compound and method for inhibiting cholesterol biosynthesis in humans and other animals. The compound count recites a genus of novel mevalonolactones. The method count recites a method of inhibiting the biosynthesis of cholesterol by administering to a "patient in need of said treatment" an appropriate dosage of a compound falling within the scope of the compound count.

The real parties in interest are Sandoz Pharmaceuticals Corporation (Sandoz), assignee of Wattanasin, and Nissan Chemical Industries, Ltd. (Nissan), assignee of Fujikawa.

The inventive activity of Fujikawa, the senior party, occurred overseas. Fujikawa can thus rely only on his filing date, August 20, 1987, to establish priority. 35 U.S.C. §102(g) (1994). Whether Wattanasin is entitled to priority as against Fujikawa therefore turns on two discrete questions. First, whether Wattanasin has shown conception coupled with diligence from just prior to Fujikawa's effective filing date until reduction to practice. *Id.* Second, whether Wattanasin suppressed or concealed the invention between reduction to practice and filing. *Id.* With respect to the first question, Fujikawa does not directly challenge the Board's holdings on Wattanasin's conception or diligence, but rather contends that the Board incorrectly fixed the date of Wattanasin's reduction to practice. As for the second question, Fujikawa contends that the Board erred in concluding that Wattanasin had not suppressed or concealed the invention. Fujikawa seeks reversal, and thus to establish priority in its favor, on either ground.

## II

The Board divided Wattanasin's inventive activity into two phases. The first phase commenced in 1979 when Sandoz began searching for drugs which would inhibit the biosynthesis of cholesterol. Inventor Wattanasin was assigned to this project in 1982, and during 1984-1985 he synthesized three compounds falling within the scope of the compound count. When tested *in vitro*, each of these compounds exhibited some cholesterol-inhibiting activity, although not all the chemicals were equally effective. Still, according to one Sandoz researcher, Dr. Damon, these test results indicated that, to a high probability, the three compounds "would be active when administered *in vivo* to a patient to inhibit cholesterol biosynthesis, *i.e.* for the treatment of hypercholesteremia or atherosclerosis." Notwithstanding these seemingly positive results, Sandoz shelved Wattanasin's project for almost two years, apparently because the level of *in vitro* activity in two of the three compounds was disappointingly low.

By January 1987, however, interest in Wattanasin's invention had revived, and the second phase of activity began. Over the next several months, four more compounds falling within the scope of the compound count were synthesized. In October, these compounds were tested for *in vitro* activity, and each of the four compounds yielded positive results. Again, however, there were significant differences in the level of *in vitro* activity of the four compounds. Two of the compounds in particular, numbered 64-935 and 64-936, exhibited *in vitro* activity significantly higher than that of the other two compounds, numbered 64-933 and 64-934.

Soon after, in December 1987, the three most active compounds *in vitro* were subjected to additional *in vivo* testing. For Sandoz, one primary purpose of these tests was to determine the *in vivo* potency of the three compounds relative to that of Compactin, a prior art compound of known cholesterol-inhibiting potency. From the results of the *in vivo* tests, reproduced in the margin, Sandoz calculated an $ED_{50}$ for each of the compounds and compared it to the $ED_{50}$ of Compactin. Only one of the compounds, compound 64-935, manifested a better $ED_{50}$ than Compactin: an $ED_{50}$ of 0.49 as compared to Compactin's $ED_{50}$ of 3.5. All of the tests performed by Sandoz were conducted in accordance with established protocols.

During this period, Sandoz also began to consider whether, and when, a patent application should be filed for Wattanasin's invention. Several times during the second phase of activity, the Sandoz patent committee considered the question of Wattanasin's invention but decided that it was too early in the invention's development to file a patent application. Each time, however, the patent committee merely deferred decision on the matter and specified that it would be taken up again at subsequent meetings. Finally, in January 1988, with the *in vivo* testing completed, the Committee assigned Wattanasin's invention an "A" rating which meant that the invention was ripe for filing and that a patent application should be prepared. The case was assigned to a Ms. Geisser, a young patent attorney in the Sandoz patent department with little experience in the pharmaceutical field.

Over the next several months the Sandoz patent department collected additional data from the inventor which was needed to prepare the patent application. This data gathering took until approximately the end of May 1988. At that point, work on the case seems to have ceased for several months until Ms. Geisser began preparing a draft sometime in the latter half of 1988. The parties dispute when this preparation began. Fujikawa contends that it occurred as late as October, and that Ms. Geisser was spurred to begin preparing the draft application by the discovery that a patent to the same subject matter had been issued to a third party, Picard. Fujikawa, however, has no evidence to support that contention. In contrast, Sandoz contends that Ms. Geisser began the draft as early as August, and that she was already working on the draft when she first heard of Picard's patent. The evidence of record, and in particular the testimony of Ms. Geisser, supports that version of events. In any event, the draft was completed in November and, after several turn-arounds with the inventor, ultimately filed in March of 1989.

Both Wattanasin and Fujikawa requested an interference with Picard. The requests were granted and a three-party interference between Picard, Fujikawa, and Wattanasin was set up. Early in the proceedings, however, Picard filed a request for an adverse judgment presumably because he could not antedate Fujikawa's priority date. What remained was a two-party interference between Fujikawa and Wattanasin. Ultimately, for reasons not significant to this appeal, the interference was divided into two interferences: one relating to the method count and one relating to the compound count. The Board decided each of these interferences adverse to Fujikawa.

With respect to the compound count, the Board made two alternative findings regarding reduction to practice. First, it found that the *in vitro* results in October 1987 showed sufficient practical utility for the compound so as to constitute a reduction to practice as of the date of those tests.[3] In the alternative, the Board held, the *in vivo* tests which showed significant activity in the 64-935 compound at doses of 1.0 and 0.1 mg were sufficient to show practical utility. Consequently, Wattanasin had reduced the compound to practice, at the latest, as of December 1987. Since Fujikawa did not challenge Wattanasin's diligence for the period between Fujikawa's effective filing date of August 20, 1987 and Wattanasin's reduction to practice in either October or December 1987, the Board held that Wattanasin was de facto the first inventor of the compound count. Finally, the Board found that the seventeen month period (counting from the *in vitro* testing) or fifteen month period (counting from the *in vivo* testing) between Wattanasin's reduction to practice and filing was not sufficient to raise an inference of suppression or concealment given the complexity of the invention, and therefore awarded priority of the compound count to Wattanasin. In reaching this conclusion, the Board rejected Fujikawa's argument that Wattanasin was spurred to file by Picard because it held that spurring by Picard, a third party, had no legal effect in a priority dispute between Fujikawa and Wattanasin.

With respect to the method count, the Board determined that Wattanasin reduced to practice in December 1987 on the date that *in vivo* testing of the 64-935 compound was concluded. In reaching that conclusion, the Board first noted that a reduction to practice must include every limitation of the count. Consequently, Wattanasin's early *in vitro* testing could not constitute a reduction to practice of the method count, since that count recites administering the compound to a "patient." The *in vivo* testing, however, met the limitations of the count since the word "patient" was sufficiently broad to include the laboratory rats to whom the compounds were administered. The *in vivo* testing also proved that 64-935 had practical utility because the compound displayed significant cholesterol inhibiting activity at doses of 1.0 and 0.1 mg. Given this date of reduction to practice, the Board again held that Wattanasin was the de facto first inventor of the count and that the delay in filing of fifteen months was not sufficient to trigger an inference of suppression or concealment. The Board therefore awarded priority of the method count to Wattanasin.

### III.

\* \* \*

### B.

Turning to the method count, the Board found that Wattanasin reduced the method to practice in December 1987 when successful *in vivo* testing of the compound was completed. This finding, too, was based on testimony that the *in vivo* data for one of the compounds tested, 64-935, showed significant cholesterol inhibiting activity in the laboratory rats tested.

---

3. As explained more fully below, reduction to practice requires a showing of practical utility, which may be satisfied by an "adequate showing of any pharmacological activity." *Nelson v. Bowler*, 626 F.2d 853, 856 (CCPA 1980).

Fujikawa challenges the Board's holding by referring to an anomaly in the test data of the 64-935 compound which it contends undercuts the reliability of the *in vivo* tests. In particular, Fujikawa points to the fact that the compound's potency was less at a dosage of 0.3 mg than it was at a dosage of 0.1 mg. On the basis of this aberration, Fujikawa's expert, Dr. Holmlund, testified that this test data was unreliable and could not support a finding that the compound was pharmacologically active.

It is clear from the Board's opinion, however, that to the extent Dr. Holmlund was testifying that this aberration would lead one of ordinary skill to completely reject these test results, the Board did not accept his testimony. This decision of the Board was not clear error. Admittedly, the decreased potency at 0.3 mg is curious. The question remains, however, as to how much this glitch in the data would undercut the persuasiveness of the test results as a whole in the mind of one of ordinary skill. Each party presented evidence on this point and the Board resolved this disputed question of fact by finding that the test results as a whole were sufficient to establish pharmacological activity in the minds of those skilled in the art. In doing so, the Board properly exercised its duty as fact finder, and we therefore affirm its finding on this point.[7]

As noted above, Fujikawa does not challenge the Board's conclusions that Wattanasin conceived prior to Fujikawa's effective date or that Wattanasin pursued his invention with diligence prior to Fujikawa's date until his reductions to practice in October and December 1987. Consequently, we affirm the Board's finding that Wattanasin has shown conception coupled with diligence from just prior to Fujikawa's effective date of August 20, 1987 up to the date he reduced the invention to practice in October 1987, for the compound, or December 1987, for the method.

## IV

Having determined that Wattanasin was the de facto first inventor, the remaining question before the Board was whether Wattanasin had suppressed or concealed the invention between the time he reduced to practice and the time he filed his patent application. Suppression or concealment of the invention by Wattanasin would entitle Fujikawa to priority. 35 U.S.C. §102(g).

Suppression or concealment is a question of law which we review *de novo*. Our case law distinguishes between two types of suppression and conceal-

7. Before the Board, Fujikawa additionally argued that *in vivo* testing cannot establish reduction to practice of the method count because it does not fulfill every limitation of the count. In particular, Fujikawa argued that only human beings can be considered "patients in need of" cholesterol biosynthesis inhibition, as required by the count. As noted above, the Board rejected this argument and held that the term "patient" in the count is broad enough to encompass mammals, such as the laboratory rats tested *in vivo*.

In its brief to this court, Fujikawa renews this argument. In the process, however, Fujikawa seems to add an additional ground which it did not argue before the Board below. We are not absolutely certain, but it appears that Fujikawa is now contending that *in vivo* testing cannot constitute a reduction to practice because the rats tested were, from all that would appear, healthy animals, rather than animals in need of cholesterol biosynthesis inhibition. To the extent that Fujikawa's argument before this court is directed to this novel ground not raised below, we consider the argument waived and decline to address it. To the extent that Fujikawa is still arguing that the count requires administration of the compound to a human, we disagree, and affirm the Board's decision on this point.

ment: cases in which the inventor deliberately suppresses or conceals his invention, and cases in which a legal inference of suppression or concealment is drawn based on "too long" a delay in filing a patent application.

Fujikawa first argues that there is evidence of intentional suppression or concealment in this case. Intentional suppression refers to situations in which an inventor "designedly, and with the view of applying it indefinitely and exclusively for his own profit, withholds his invention from the public." *Id.* (*quoting Kendall v. Winsor*, 62 U.S. (21 How.) 322, 328 (1858)). Admittedly, Sandoz was not overly efficient in preparing a patent application, given the time which elapsed between its reduction to practice in late 1987 and its ultimate filing in March 1989. Intentional suppression, however, requires more than the passage of time. It requires evidence that the inventor intentionally delayed filing in order to prolong the period during which the invention is maintained in secret. Fujikawa presented no evidence that Wattanasin delayed filing for this purpose. On the contrary, all indications are that throughout the period between reduction to practice and filing, Sandoz moved slowly (one might even say fitfully), but inexorably, toward disclosure. We therefore hold that Wattanasin did not intentionally suppress or conceal the invention in this case.

Absent intentional suppression, the only question is whether the 17 month period between the reduction to practice of the compound, or the 15 month period between reduction to practice of the method, and Wattanasin's filing justify an inference of suppression or concealment. *See id.* The Board held that these facts do not support such an inference. As the Board explained: "In our view, this hiatus in time is not sufficiently long to raise the inference that Wattanasin suppressed or concealed the invention considering the nature and complexity of the invention here."

Fujikawa attacks this finding of the Board on two grounds. First, it contends that the Board should not have held that a 15 or 17 month delay is *per se* insufficient to raise an inference of suppression or concealment without examining the circumstances surrounding the delay and whether, in view of those circumstances, Wattanasin's delay was reasonable. Second, Fujikawa argues that the Board failed to consider evidence that Wattanasin was spurred to file by the issuance of a patent to a third party, Picard, directed to the same genus of compounds invented by Wattanasin. Evidence that a first inventor was spurred to disclose by the activities of a second inventor has always been an important factor in priority determinations because it creates an inference that, but for the efforts of the second inventor, "the public would never have gained knowledge of [the invention]." *Brokaw*, 429 F.2d at 480. Here, however, the Board expressly declined to consider the evidence of spurring because it held that spurring by a third party who is not a party to the interference is irrelevant to a determination of priority as between Wattanasin and Fujikawa. We first address Fujikawa's arguments concerning spurring.

### A

We are not certain that the Board is correct that third party spurring is irrelevant in determining priority. After all, "[w]hat is involved here is a policy question as to which of the two rival inventors has the greater right to a patent." *Brokaw*, 429 F.2d at 480. Resolution of this question could well be affected by the fact that one of the inventors chose to maintain his invention in secrecy until disclosure by another spurred him to file, even when the spurrer was a third party not involved in the interference. We need not resolve that question here, however, because we hold that no reasonable fact finder could have found spurring on the facts of this case. The only evidence in the record on the question of spurring is the testimony of Ms. Geisser who expressly testified that she had already begun work on the Wattanasin draft application before she learned of Picard's patent, in other words, that she had not been spurred by Picard. Consequently, we leave the question of the relevance of third-party spurring for another case.

B

Fujikawa's other argument also requires us to examine the evidence of record in this case. As Fujikawa correctly notes, this court has not set strict time limits regarding the minimum and maximum periods necessary to establish an inference of suppression or concealment. Rather, we have recognized that "it is not the time elapsed that is the controlling factor but the total conduct of the first inventor." *Young v. Dworkin*, 489 F.2d 1277, 1285 (CCPA 1974) (Rich, J., concurring). Thus, the circumstances surrounding the first inventor's delay and the reasonableness of that delay are important factors which must be considered in deciding questions of suppression or concealment.

Fujikawa again correctly notes that the Board's opinion gives short shrift to the question of whether this delay on the facts of this case was reasonable. In seeking reversal of the Board's decision, Fujikawa asks us to assess the factual record for ourselves to determine whether Wattanasin engaged in sufficient disclosure-related activity to justify his 17-month delay in filing.

The facts of record, however, do not support Fujikawa's position.

In our view, the circumstances in this case place it squarely within the class of cases in which an inference of suppression or concealment is not warranted. We acknowledge, of course, that each case of suppression or concealment must be decided on its own facts. Still, the rich and varied case law which this court has developed over many years provides some guidance as to the type of behavior which warrants an inference of suppression or concealment. In this case Wattanasin delayed approximately 17 months between reduction to practice and filing. During much of that period, however, Wattanasin and Sandoz engaged in significant steps towards perfecting the invention and preparing an application. For example, we do not believe any lack of diligence can be ascribed to Wattanasin for the period between October and December 1987 when *in vivo* testing of the invention was taking place. *See Young.* Similarly, at its first opportunity following the *in vivo* testing, the Sandoz patent committee approved Wattanasin's invention for filing. This takes us up to the end of January 1988.

Over the next several months, until May 1988, the Sandoz patent department engaged in the necessary collection of data from the inventor and others in order to prepare Wattanasin's patent application. We are satisfied from the record that this disclosure-related activity was sufficient to avoid any inference of suppression or concealment during this period.[8] Also, as noted above, the record indicates that by August 1988, Ms. Geisser was already at work preparing the application, and that work continued on various drafts until Wattanasin's filing date in March 1989. Thus, the only real period of unexplained delay in this case is the approximately three month period between May and August of 1988.

Given a total delay of 17 months, an unexplained delay of three months, the complexity of the subject matter at issue, and our sense from the record as a whole that throughout the delay Sandoz was moving, albeit slowly, towards filing an application, we conclude that this case does not warrant an inference of suppression or concealment. Consequently, we affirm the Board on this point.

### C

Finally, Fujikawa contends that assuming *in vitro* tests are sufficient to establish reduction to practice, Wattanasin reduced the compound count to practice in 1984 when he completed in vitro testing of his first three compounds falling within the scope of the count. If so, Fujikawa argues, the delay between reduction to practice and filing was greater than four years, and an inference of suppression or concealment is justified.[9]

We reject this argument in view of *Paulik v. Rizkalla*. In *Paulik*, we held that a suppression or concealment could be negated by renewed activity prior to an opposing party's effective date. There, inventor Paulik reduced his invention to practice and submitted an invention disclosure to his employer's patent department. For four years the patent department did nothing with the disclosure. Then, just two months before Rizkalla's effective date, the patent department allegedly picked up Paulik's disclosure and worked diligently to prepare a patent application which it ultimately filed. *See id.* We held that although Paulik could not rely on his original date of reduction to practice to establish priority, he could rely on the date of renewed activity in his priority contest with Rizkalla. In large measure, this decision was driven by the court's concern that denying an inventor the benefit of his renewed activity, might "discourage inventors and their supporters from working on projects that had been 'too long' set aside, because of the impossibility of relying, in a priority contest, on either their original work or their renewed work." *Id.* at 1275-76.

*Paulik's* reasoning, if not its holding, applies squarely to this case. A simple hypothetical illustrates why this is so. Imagine a situation similar to the one facing Sandoz in early 1987. A decisionmaker with limited funds must decide whether additional research funds should be committed to a project which has been neglected for over two years. In making this decision, the decisionmaker would certainly take into account

8. Our conclusion in this regard is based, in small part, on the testimony of Mr. Melvyn Kassenoff, a lawyer in Sandoz's patent department. Before the Board, Fujikawa challenged large parts of this testimony as inadmissible. In this opinion we therefore rely only on those portions of the testimony which even Fujikawa concedes are admissible, *i.e.*, testimony relating to Mr. Kassenoff's legal services rendered in connection with the prosecution of Wattanasin's application.

9. This argument, of course, relates only to the compound count, since, as explained above, the method count was not reduced to practice until the in vivo testing in December 1987.

the likelihood that the additional research might yield valuable patent rights. Furthermore, in evaluating the probability of securing those patent rights, an important consideration would be the earliest priority date to which the research would be entitled, especially in situations where the decisionmaker knows that he and his competitors are "racing" toward a common goal. Thus, the right to rely on renewed activity for purposes of priority would encourage the decisionmaker to fund the additional research. Conversely, denying an inventor the benefit of renewed activity would discourage the decisionmaker from funding the additional research.

Here, Wattanasin returned to his abandoned project well before Fujikawa's effective date and worked diligently towards reducing the invention to practice a second time. For the reasons explained above, we hold that, on these facts, Wattanasin's earlier reduction to practice in 1984 does not bar him from relying on his earliest date of renewed activity for purposes of priority.

## Comments

1. **Abandonment, Suppression, and Concealment (ASC).** As shown in *Mahurkar*, a party who is the first to reduce to practice is considered the first to invent. But, consistent with the patent policy favoring prompt disclosure, an inventor who was the first to reduce to practice may lose his right of priority if he abandons, suppresses, or conceals his invention.

There are two types of ASC: (1) explicit or active; and (2) inferential based on delay. With respect to inferential ASC, there are no set time limits on when an inventor must publicly disclose his invention having first made it. The Federal Circuit has stated that after first making the invention, an inventor's failure to file a patent application, describe the invention in a published document, or publicly use the invention within a "reasonable time" may result in ASC. But mere delay is not enough to show ASC. Although the statute uses three words, "abandon," "suppress," and "conceal," there is very little difference among them. They all reflect a single concept, which is the failure of the inventor to disclose his invention to the public in a timely manner.

2. **Diligence.** Diligence only comes into play when a party is the first to conceive, but the second to reduce to practice. There is no "race of diligence" between or among the parties vying for a patent. Diligence of the party who was the first to reduce to practice is irrelevant. And diligence never comes into play if a party is both the first to conceive and first to reduce to practice.

The diligence requirement is one way to ask what Party A, for example, was doing given the fact that another party (Party B) was the second to conceive, but the first to reduce to practice. In this scenario, Party A can only be deemed the first inventor if he can show continuous and reasonable diligence from just prior to Party B's entering the field (Party B's date of conception in Figure 10.3 and reduction to practice in Figure 10.4) to Party A's reduction to practice, either actual or constructive. The connection between Party A's conception and his reduction to practice must be "substantially one continuous act."

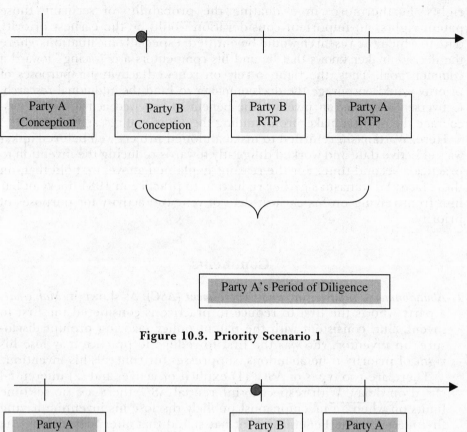

**Figure 10.3. Priority Scenario 1**

**Figure 10.4. Priority Scenario 2**

While a showing of constant effort is not required to prove diligence, the inventor must account for the entire critical period. There are a variety of ways to prove diligence, including ongoing laboratory experimentation. The question is whether the applicant was pursuing his goal in a reasonable manner. Thus, periods of inactivity may not be fatal to a showing of diligence if the inventor has an adequate excuse such as (1) poverty or illness of the inventor, (2) obligations of the inventor's regular employment, or (3) excessive workload of the inventor's patent attorney.

Proving date of invention for novelty purposes (as well as for determining who is entitled to a patent between two or more parties claiming the same invention) is unique to American patent law. Other industrialized nations are first-to-file countries, meaning that their focus is on the *priority date* (not the invention date), which is the earliest *filing* date of the patent application. For example, in determining novelty, Article 54(2) of the European Patent Convention looks to the "state of the art . . . before the *date of filing of the European patent application*" (emphasis added). And Article 29(1) of the Japanese Patent Law recites that one is entitled to a patent unless the invention was "publicly known in Japan or elsewhere *prior to the filing of the patent application*" (emphasis added). Recent patent reform efforts in the United States would make the United States a first-to-file country, but this provision is controversial and passage is uncertain. *See* H.R. 2795.

The pros and cons of the first to invent vis-à-vis a first-to-file system have been well mined. Those who advocate a first-to-invent approach frequently assert that it is a more equitable basis for given rewards and fear a first-to-file system would unfairly burden the independent and small inventor class, those individuals who do not have the resources to file as promptly as larger entities. Moreover, first-to-invent advocates assert that a first-to-file system would encourage the filing of sloppy or incomplete patent applications. The first-to-file devotees point out that a vast majority of the interferences (*i.e.*, procedural mechanism for determining priority of invention) are won by the party who was the first to file, and therefore, the United States already has a de facto first-to-file system. Moreover, they claim that a first-to-file system is cleaner in that one is not subjected to the burdens and arcana associated with proving date of invention.

# D. NON-OBVIOUSNESS

An invention must be non-obvious to be patentable. The non-obviousness requirement, embodied in §103 of the patent code, is fundamental to our patent system and, in many ways, is the most significant obstacle that a patent applicant faces. Although the novelty requirement of §102 casts a watchful eye over the public domain so as to prevent a patent applicant from obtaining protection on an invention that a person of ordinary skill in the art could retrieve from the technical literature or other available sources, the test for novelty is rather confining in that each and every limitation of the claimed invention must be present in a single prior art reference. The non-obviousness requirement, on the other hand, cast a broader net and recognizes that the limitations of a claimed invention may be scattered throughout more than one prior art reference, and it would be "obvious" to a person of ordinary skill in the art to assemble these elements in the form of the claimed invention. Note that the claimed invention must be significantly *different* from, not necessarily better than, the prior art to satisfy §103.

The non-obviousness requirement did not originate with the 1952 Patent Act, for it is considered to have been a common law principle since 1850. In that year, the Supreme Court decided *Hotchkiss v. Greenwood*, 52 (11 How.) 248 (1850) (the "doorknob case"). In *Hotchkiss*, the invention related to an old method of making doorknobs whereby the doorknob had a certain shaped hole for the fastening of a shank. The only difference was that the inventor substituted a clay or porcelain knob for a metallic knob. Although the invention was technically new, the Court denied the patent, stating that "there was an absence of that degree of skill and ingenuity, which constitute essential elements of every invention."

The *Hotchkiss* case is widely regarded as creating an additional patentability hurdle, above and beyond novelty and utility, which required an inventor to display "more ingenuity and skill" than that possessed by the "ordinary mechanic." But there was a great deal of ambiguity in the *Hotchkiss* test, which resulted in divergent applications of the non-obviousness requirement. In an attempt to foster consistency and stability, the drafters of the 1952 Patent Act, by constructing §103, sought to provide a judge with a clearly marked road map to follow and well-defined parameters to work within when deciding whether an invention is obvious.

But how do we know when an invention is obvious or non-obvious? This question, which is much more complex than meets the eye, is the focus of this section.

*STATUTE:* **Conditions for Patentability; Non-Obvious Subject Matter**
35 U.S.C. §103

## 1. The *Graham* Test

In 1965, the United States Supreme Court granted certiorari in *Graham v. John Deere* (as well as two companion cases) to consider the questions (1) "what effect the 1952 act had upon traditional statutory and judicial tests of patentability," and (2) "what definitive tests are now required."

### GRAHAM v. JOHN DEERE CO.
#### 383 U.S. 1 (1966)

Mr. Justice CLARK delivered the opinion of the Court.

After a lapse of 15 years, the Court again focuses its attention on the patentability of inventions under the standard of Art. I, §8, cl. 8, of the Constitution and under the conditions prescribed by the laws of the United

States. Since our last expression on patent validity, *A. & P. Tea Co. v. Supermarket Equipment Corp.*, the Congress has for the first time expressly added a third statutory dimension to the two requirements of novelty and utility that had been the sole statutory test since the Patent Act of 1793. This is the test of obviousness, *i.e.*, whether "the subject matter sought to be patented and the prior art are such that the subject matter as a whole would have been obvious at the time the invention was made to a person having ordinary skill in the art to which said subject matter pertains. Patentability shall not be negatived by the manner in which the invention was made." §103 of the Patent Act of 1952.

The questions, involved in each of the companion cases before us, are what effect the 1952 Act had upon traditional statutory and judicial tests of patentability and what definitive tests are now required. We have concluded that the 1952 Act was intended to codify judicial precedents embracing the principle long ago announced by this Court in *Hotchkiss v. Greenwood*, and that, while the clear language of §103 places emphasis on an inquiry into obviousness, the general level of innovation necessary to sustain patentability remains the same.

\* \* \*

### III.

The difficulty of formulating conditions for patentability was heightened by the generality of the constitutional grant and the statutes implementing it, together with the underlying policy of the patent system that "the things which are worth to the public the embarrassment of an exclusive patent," as Jefferson put it, must outweigh the restrictive effect of the limited patent monopoly. The inherent problem was to develop some means of weeding out those inventions which would not be disclosed or devised but for the inducement of a patent.

This Court formulated a general condition of patentability in 1851 in *Hotchkiss v. Greenwood.... Hotchkiss*, by positing the condition that a patentable invention evidence more ingenuity and skill than that possessed by an ordinary mechanic acquainted with the business, merely distinguished between new and useful innovations that were capable of sustaining a patent and those that were not. The *Hotchkiss* test laid the cornerstone of the judicial evolution suggested by Jefferson and left to the courts by Congress. The language in the case, and in those which followed, gave birth to "invention" as a word of legal art signifying patentable inventions. Yet, as this Court has observed, "[t]he truth is, the word ['invention'] cannot be defined in such manner as to afford any substantial aid in determining whether a particular device involves an exercise of the inventive faculty or not." *McClain v. Ortmayer*, 141 U.S. 419, 427 (1891). Its use as a label brought about a large variety of opinions as to its meaning both in the Patent Office, in the courts, and at the bar. The *Hotchkiss* formulation, however, lies not in any label, but in its functional approach to questions of patentability. In practice, *Hotchkiss* has required a comparison between the subject matter of the patent, or patent application, and the background skill of the calling. It has been from this comparison that patentability was in each case determined.

**IV.**

*The 1952 Patent Act.*

The pivotal section around which the present controversy centers is §103. It provides:

> **§103. Conditions for patentability; non-obvious subject matter**
>
> A patent may not be obtained though the invention is not identically disclosed or described as set forth in section 102 of this title, if the differences between the subject matter sought to be patented and the prior art are such that the subject matter as a whole would have been obvious at the time the invention was made to a person having ordinary skill in the art to which said subject matter pertains. Patentability shall not be negatived by the manner in which the invention was made.

The section is cast in relatively unambiguous terms. Patentability is to depend, in addition to novelty and utility, upon the "non-obvious" nature of the "subject matter sought to be patented" to a person having ordinary skill in the pertinent art.

The first sentence of this section is strongly reminiscent of the language in *Hotchkiss.* Both formulations place emphasis on the pertinent art existing at the time the invention was made and both are implicitly tied to advances in that art. The major distinction is that Congress has emphasized "nonobviousness" as the operative test of the section, rather than the less definite "invention" language of *Hotchkiss* that Congress thought had led to "a large variety" of expressions in decisions and writings. In the title itself the Congress used the phrase "Conditions for patentability; *non-obvious subject matter*" (italics added), thus focusing upon "nonobviousness" rather than "invention."

\* \* \*

It is undisputed that this section was, for the first time, a statutory expression of an additional requirement for patentability, originally expressed in *Hotchkiss.* It also seems apparent that Congress intended by the last sentence of §103 to abolish the test it believed this Court announced in the controversial phrase "flash of creative genius," used in *Cuno Engineering Corp. v. Automatic Devices Corp.*

**V.**

While the ultimate question of patent validity is one of law, *A. & P. Tea Co. v. Supermarket Equipment Corp.*, the §103 condition, which is but one of three conditions, each of which must be satisfied, lends itself to several basic factual inquiries. Under §103, the scope and content of the prior art are to be determined; differences between the prior art and the claims at issue are to be ascertained; and the level of ordinary skill in the pertinent art resolved. Against this background, the obviousness or nonobviousness of the subject matter is determined. Such secondary considerations as commercial success, long felt but unsolved needs, failure of others, etc., might be utilized to give light to the circumstances surrounding the origin of the subject matter sought to be patented. As indicia of obviousness or nonobviousness, these inquiries may have relevancy.

This is not to say, however, that there will not be difficulties in applying the nonobviousness test. What is obvious is not a question upon which there is likely to be uniformity of thought in every given factual context. The difficulties, however, are comparable to those encountered daily by the courts in such frames of reference as negligence and scienter, and should be amenable to a case-by-case development. We believe that strict observance of the requirements laid down here will result in that uniformity and definiteness which Congress called for in the 1952 Act.

Although we conclude here that the inquiry which the Patent Office and the courts must make as to patentability must be beamed with greater intensity on the requirements of §103, it bears repeating that we find no change in the general strictness with which the overall test is to be applied. We have been urged to find in §103 a relaxed standard, supposedly a congressional reaction to the "increased standard" applied by this Court in its decisions over the last 20 or 30 years. The standard has remained invariable in this Court. Technology, however, has advanced(and with remarkable rapidity in the last 50 years. Moreover, the ambit of applicable art in given fields of science has widened by disciplines unheard of a half century ago. It is but an evenhanded application to require that those persons granted the benefit of a patent monopoly be charged with an awareness of these changed conditions. The same is true of the less technical, but still useful arts. He who seeks to build a better mousetrap today has a long path to tread before reaching the Patent Office.

## VI.

*** *** ***

Graham v. John Deere Co., an infringement suit by petitioners, presents a conflict between two Circuits over the validity of a single patent on a 'Clamp for vibrating Shank Plows.' The invention, a combination of old mechanical elements, involves a device designed to absorb shock from plow shanks as they plow through rocky soil and thus to prevent damage to the plow....

This patent, No. 2,627,798 (hereinafter called the '798 patent) relates to a spring clamp which permits plow shanks to be pushed upward when they hit obstructions in the soil, and then springs the shanks back into normal position when the obstruction is passed over. The device, which we show diagrammatically in the accompanying sketches (See Fig. 1), is fixed to the plow frame as a unit. The mechanism around which the controversy center is basically a hinge. The top half of it, known as the upper plate (marked 1 in the sketches), is a heavy metal piece clamped to the plow frame (2) and is stationary relative to the plow frame. The lower half of the hinge, known as the hinge plate (3), is connected to the rear of the upper plate by a hinge pin (4) and rotates downward with respect to it. The shank (5), which is bolted to the forward end of the hinge plate (at 6), runs beneath the plate and parallel to it for about nine inches, passes through a stirrup (7), and then continues backward for several feet curving down toward the ground. The chisel (8), which does the actual plowing, is attached to the rear end of the shank. As the plow frame is pulled forward, the chisel rips through the soil, thereby plowing it. In the normal position, the hinge plate and the shank are kept tight against the upper plate by a spring (9), which is atop the upper plate. A rod (10) runs through the center of the spring, extending down through holes in both plates and the shank. Its upper end is bolted to the top of the spring while its lower end is hooked against the underside of the shank.

When the chisel hits a rock or other obstruction in the soil, the obstruction forces the chisel and the rear portion of the shank to move upward. The shank is pivoted (at 11) against the rear of the hinge plate and pries open the hinge against the closing tendency of the spring. (See sketch labeled 'Open Position,' Fig. 1.) This closing tendency is caused by the fact that, as the hinge is opened, the connecting rod is pulled downward and the spring is compressed. When the obstruction is passed over, the upward force on the chisel disappears and the spring pulls the shank and hinge plate back into their original position. The lower, rear portion of the hinge plate is constructed in the form of a stirrup (7) which brackets the shank, passing around and beneath it. The shank fits loosely into the stirrup (permitting a slight up and down play). The stirrup is designed to prevent the shank from recoiling away from the hinge plate, and thus prevents excessive strain on the shank near its bolted connection. The stirrup also girds the shank, preventing it from fishtailing from side to side.

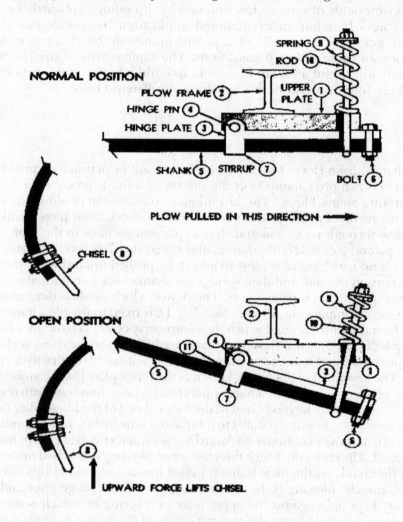

Figure 1

In practical use, a number of spring-hinge-shank combinations are clamped to a plow frame, forming a set of ground-working chisels capable of withstanding the shock of rocks and other obstructions in the soil without breaking the shanks. . . .

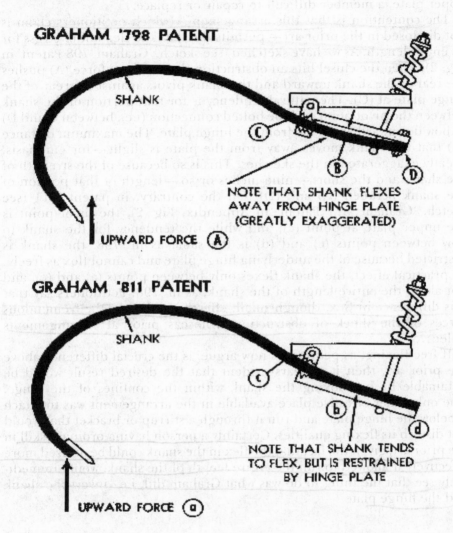

Figure 2

We confine our discussion to the prior patent of Graham, '811, and to the Glencoe clamp device, both among the references asserted by respondents. The Graham '811 and '798 patent devices are similar in all elements, save two: (1) the stirrup and the bolted connection of the shank to the hinge plate do not appear in '811; and (2) the position of the shank is reversed, being placed in patent '811 above the hinge plate, sandwiched between it and the upper plate. The shank is held in place by the spring rod which is hooked against the bottom of the hinge plate passing through a slot in the shank. Other differences are of no consequence to our examination. In practice the '811 patent arrangement permitted the shank to wobble or fishtail because it was not rigidly fixed to the hinge plate; moreover, as the hinge plate was below the shank, the latter caused wear on the upper plate, a member difficult to repair or replace....

The contention is that this arrangement—which petitioners claim is not disclosed in the prior art—permits the shank to flex under stress for its entire length. As we have sketched (see sketch, 'Graham '798 Patent' in Fig. 2), when the chisel hits an obstruction the resultant force (A) pushes the rear of the shank upward and the shank pivots against the rear of the hinge plate at (C). The natural tendency is for that portion of the shank between the pivot point and the bolted connection (i.e., between C and D) to bow downward and away from the hinge plate. The maximum distance (B) that the shank moves away from the plate is slight—for emphasis, greatly exaggerated in the sketches. This is so because of the strength of the shank and the short—nine inches or so—length of that portion of the shank between (C) and (D). On the contrary, in patent '811 (see sketch, 'Graham '811 Patent' in Appendix, Fig. 2), the pivot point is the upper plate at point (c); and while the tendency for the shank to bow between points (c) and (d) is the same as in '798, the shank is restricted because of the underlying hinge plate and cannot flex as freely. In practical effect, the shank flexes only between points (a) and (c), and not along the entire length of the shank, as in '798. Petitioners say that this difference in flex, though small, effectively absorbs the tremendous forces of the shock of obstructions whereas prior art arrangements failed....

If free-flexing, as petitioners now argue, is the crucial difference above the prior art, then it appears evident that the desired result would be obtainable by not boxing the shank within the confines of the hinge. The only other effective place available in the arrangement was to attach it below the hinge plate and run it through a stirrup or bracket that would not disturb its flexing qualities. Certainly a person having ordinary skill in the prior art, given the fact that the flex in the shank could be utilized more effectively if allowed to run the entire length of the shank, would immediately see that the thing to do was what Graham did, i.e., invert the shank and the hinge plate.

## Comments

1. **The Factual Inquiries.** The *Graham* court stated that although the question of patent validity is one of law, there are several underlying factual determinations. These include: (1) the scope and content of the prior art; (2) differences between the prior art and the claims at issue; (3) and the level of ordinary skill in the pertinent art. Once these facts are determined, the obviousness or non-obviousness of the subject matter is determined.

2. **Synergism, Combination Patents, and a Flash of Creative Genius.** It is now well-settled, just over 50 years after the enactment of the 1952 Patent Act, that a lack of synergism, a combination of known elements in a

patent, or the manner in which an invention was made will not preclude patentability under §103. With respect to the "flash of creative genius" issue, the last sentence of §103(a) explicitly states that "[p]atentability shall not be negatived by the manner in which the invention was made." Thus, it is irrelevant whether the invention was a product of accident or design; a flash of genius or extensive labor.

---

**COMPARATIVE PERSPECTIVE**
**Section 103's European Counterpart — "Inventive Step"**

The European Patent Convention (EPC) requires that an invention claim an "inventive step," which is comparable to the non-obviousness requirement embodied in §103. Specifically, Article 56 of the EPC states:

> An invention shall be considered as involving an inventive step if, having regard to the state of the art, it is not obvious to a person skilled in the art. If the state of the art also includes documents within the meaning of Article 54, paragraph 3. These documents are not to be considered in deciding whether there has been an inventive step.

While there are many parallels between the EPC's "inventive step" and Title 35's §103, there are also important differences. For instance, the EPC employs the "problem and solution approach" to the inventive step analysis. The basis is that an invention presumably provides a solution to a problem, and thus "inventive step" can be viewed as "a step from the technical problem to its solution." Lionel Bently & Brad Sherman, INTELLECTUAL PROPERTY LAW 440-441 (Oxford 2001). According to Professors Bently and Sherman:

> [R]ather than asking whether an invention is obvious, the European Patent Office asks whether the solution that an invention provides to the problem being addressed would have been obvious to the person skilled in the art. In more positive terms, this means that for an invention to be patentable, the solution must *not* have been obvious to the person skilled in the art at the priority date of the invention in question.

*Id.* at 441 (emphasis in original).

---

## 2. Combining References

Recall that under §102, an invention is anticipated if only a *single* prior art reference discloses each and every limitation of the claimed invention. That is, one cannot combine references under §102. There is no such restriction imposed upon §103. In fact, an overwhelming majority of obviousness decisions involve more than one prior art reference. But the Federal Circuit and its predecessor, the CCPA, have made it perfectly clear on numerous occasions that before prior art references can be combined under §103, the references must *suggest* to a person of ordinary skill in the art that he should make the invention and, once made, would have a *reasonable expectation of success*. Thus, although §103, unlike §102, permits one to combine prior art references, one must have a reason to do so. The *McGinley* case explores the combination requirement.

## MCGINLEY v. FRANKLIN SPORTS, INC.

### 262 F.3d 1339 (Fed. Cir. 2001)

CLEVENGER, Circuit Judge.

This is a patent infringement suit in which Michael L. McGinley charges Franklin Sports, Inc. ("FSI") with infringement of claims 1, 2, 6, and 7 of U.S. Patent No. 5,407,193 ("the '193 patent"). On summary judgment, the United States District Court for the District of Kansas ruled in favor of McGinley on the issue of infringement, and the case proceeded to trial on the issues of validity. The jury found that the asserted claims were not invalid. On a subsequent motion filed by FSI for judgment as a matter of law ("JMOL"), the trial court set aside the jury verdict on validity, holding that the asserted claims of the '193 patent are invalid as obvious pursuant to 35 U.S.C. §103(a).

McGinley appeals the district court's grant of JMOL of invalidity....

Because we conclude that the district court erred in finding that no reasonable jury could have reached a verdict of nonobviousness, we reverse the JMOL of invalidity....

### I
### BACKGROUND

The application for the '193 patent was filed on July 3, 1991, and the patent issued on April 18, 1995. In general terms, the '193 patent discloses and claims an instructional pitching device in the form of a regulation baseball with specific "finger placement indicia" for teaching students how to grasp a baseball for throwing different types of pitches. With the endorsement of a famous professional baseball pitcher, McGinley's invention was marketed and distributed as the Roger Clemens Instructional Baseball ("RCIB"). FSI also manufactured and sold a baseball designed to teach students to throw different types of pitches. The accused device in this case, the Franklin Pitch Ball Trainer 2705 ("FSI's 2705 baseball"), was sold in the United States from at least as early as April 1995 to March 1999.

In the preferred embodiment of the claimed invention, an aspect of which is illustrated in the following figure, three sets of finger placement indicia 11 are positioned on the cover 17 of a regulation baseball 10. Each set of indicia 11 is intended to illustrate the placement of a student pitcher's index and middle fingers so as to throw a particular type of pitch (*e.g.*, two-seam fast ball, slider, curve ball, etc.).

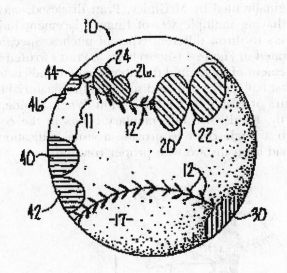

Indicia 11 are presented in two sizes, to allow the indicia intended for a left-handed student to be easily distinguished from the indicia intended for a right-handed student. The smaller indicia, exemplified by indicia 24 and 26, are intended for use by left-handed pitchers, while the larger indicia, as represented by indicia 20 and 22, are intended for use by right-handed pitchers. Moreover, indicia 11 are coded by coloring all indicia which are representative of a certain type of pitch in one color and indicia representative of another type of pitch in a different color. To further assist a student in learning how to throw a particular pitch, the indicia are shaped so as to indicate the relationship of the palm of the hand in grasping the ball. Specifically, the portion of each "egg-shaped" indicium to be situated closest to the palm is slightly tapered so as to indicate the correct orientation of the baseball in the palm. Although the preferred embodiment of the '193 patent makes no provisions for "thumb placement indicia," the written description of the '193 patent repeatedly states that the thumb is generally to be positioned on the baseball at a location opposite the corresponding set of finger placement indicia.

As originally filed in 1991, the claims of the '193 patent required that eight sets of finger placement indicia be provided on a single baseball pitching training device. Specifically, the four original claims all required the presence of indicia demarcating the placement of fingers for four specific types of pitches (*i.e.*, curve ball, two-seam fast ball, slider, and four-seam fast ball), for both left-handed and right-handed students. These claims were rejected on obviousness grounds in view of U.S. Patent No. 2,925,273 ("Pratt"), which had issued on February 16, 1960, more than thirty years before McGinley's filing date. Pratt was brought to the attention of the Patent and Trademark Office ("PTO") via an Information Disclosure Statement ("IDS") filed concurrently with McGinley's priority patent application by McGinley's counsel.

Like the claims originally filed by McGinley, Pratt disclosed, *inter alia*, a conventional baseball having multiple sets of finger placement indicia for teaching baseball players to throw different types of pitches. Specifically, in the embodiment illustrated in Figure 4 (shown below), Pratt's written description disclosed the placement of finger and thumb placement indicia for three types of pitches (*i.e.*, fast ball, curve ball, and screw ball). Equatorial band 17 was an important feature of Pratt's claimed invention. When a student threw Pratt's baseball correctly, bands of complementary colors in the equatorial band would blend into a single color to provide a visual indication to the student that the ball had been thrown with proper rotation.

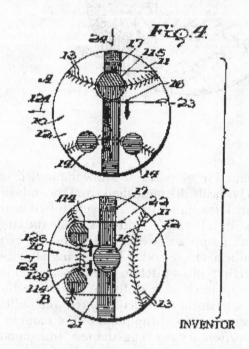

Although the similarities between Pratt's disclosure and McGinley's then-existing claims are striking, there are also a few differences between Pratt's teachings and McGinley's initially claimed invention. First, Pratt did not provide for different sets of indicia on a single ball for distinguishing between left-handed and right-handed students. Also, Pratt's finger placement indicia were described and illustrated as being circular, but "phantom lines" illustrating the placement of fingers 21, 22 and thumb 23 were included in the patent figures. These phantom lines, however, are not described in Pratt as actual markings on the baseball. In contrast, the finger placement indicia in the preferred embodiment of McGinley's invention are actually marked on the ball, and are "egg-shaped" and slightly tapered at one end to indicate the proper orientation of the ball with respect to the student's palm.

Another prior art reference which was brought to the attention of the PTO via McGinley's IDS was U.S. Patent No. 3,110,494 ("Morgan"), which issued on November 12, 1963. In contrast to Pratt and the '193 patent, which are based on using a conventional regulation baseball, Morgan describes a baseball training device using a lightweight and inexpensive baseball "replica" fabricated in the form of plastic or metallic hemispherical shells which occupy a minimum of space before use, but which can be easily assembled by gluing the two hemispherical halves together. In Figure 6 of Morgan (shown below) and the accompanying written description, a single set of finger-shaped marks D", E", and L" (for teaching proper placement of the forefinger, middle finger, and thumb, respectively) are provided on the baseball training device to teach a student how to throw a baseball with a particular curve or break.

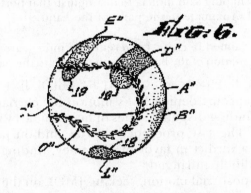

Throughout the prosecution history of the '193 patent, McGinley's claims at issue in this case were rejected in view of Pratt on anticipation grounds. With respect to Morgan, although this reference was before the PTO during the entire pendency of McGinley's patent application, it was never explicitly relied upon as a basis for a rejection based on a prima facie case of anticipation or obviousness.

Ultimately, in 1995, after a series of rejections, amendments, and responses (including a partially successful appeal to the Board of Patent Appeals and Interferences and the filing of a continuation application), the '193 patent issued with 14 claims. Ten of the issued claims (*i.e.*, claims 3-5 and 8-14) explicitly retain the original limitation requiring the inclusion of finger placement indicia on a single baseball pitching training device for both left-handed and right-handed students. These claims were not asserted in this case. Instead, McGinley asserted the remaining four claims (*i.e.*, independent claim 1 and dependent claims 2, 6, and 7) against FSI, alleging willful infringement by making and selling the 2705 baseball. The asserted claims read as follows in their entirety:

> 1. A baseball pitching training device for duplicating finger placement on a baseball by a student comprising:
> a baseball cover;
> a plurality of sets of finger placement indicia on said cover, said sets of indicia comprising:
> a first set of indicia demarcating the placement of finger [sic] for throwing a first pitch;
> a second set of indicia demarcating the placement of fingers for throwing, [sic] a second pitch;

a third set of indicia demarcating the placement of fingers for throwing a third pitch;
means for indicating the orientation of the baseball relative to the palm of the hand; and
means for coding said finger placement indicia sets for identification of each of said indicia associated with any one of said sets.

2. The device as claimed in claim 1 wherein said means for coding comprises a color for association with each indicia of a particular set.

6. The device as claimed in claim 1, wherein said means for indicating orientation comprises shaping said indicia to distinguish that portion of the baseball to be located proximate to the palm of the hand.

7. The device as claimed in claim 1 wherein said indicia are shaped to indicate a correct orientation of the baseball with respect to the palm of the hand.

'193 patent, col. 5, ll. 29-48; col. 5, ll. 61-64; col. 6, ll. 1-3.

....[T]he district court denied FSI's motion for partial summary judgment on validity, finding disputed issues of material fact with respect to the obviousness issue. The case proceeded to trial, and on January 19, 2000, the jury returned a verdict in favor of McGinley, finding the '193 patent not invalid and willfully infringed.

FSI then filed a post-trial motion, seeking JMOL on the issue of validity. In the alternative, FSI also moved for a new trial. On April 5, 2000, the district court set aside the jury's verdict and granted FSI's motion for JMOL on invalidity, concluding that "as a matter of law, plaintiff's patent is invalid as obvious in light of Pratt or the combination of Pratt and Morgan." Judgment was entered in favor of FSI, and this appeal followed, vesting us with jurisdiction pursuant to 28 U.S.C. §1295(a)(1).

\* \* \*

## IV

### OBVIOUSNESS

A patent is invalid for obviousness if "differences between the subject matter sought to be patented and the prior art are such that the subject matter as a whole would have been obvious at the time the invention was made to a person having ordinary skill in the art to which said subject matter pertains." 35 U.S.C. §103(a) (1994). "Throughout the obviousness determination, a patent retains its statutory presumption of validity, see 35 U.S.C. §282, and the movant retains the burden to show the invalidity of the claims by clear and convincing evidence as to underlying facts." *Rockwell Int'l. Corp. v. United States*, 147 F.3d 1358, 1364 (Fed. Cir. 1998).

Although it is well settled that the ultimate determination of obviousness is a question of law, it is also well understood that there are factual issues underlying the ultimate obviousness decision. *Richardson-Vicks Inc. v. Upjohn Co.* Specifically, the obviousness analysis is based on four underlying factual inquiries, the well-known *Graham* factors: (1) the scope and content of the prior art; (2) the differences between the claims and the prior art; (3) the level of ordinary skill in the pertinent art; and (4) secondary considerations, if any, of nonobviousness. *Graham v. John Deere Co.*

At trial, FSI argued, *inter alia*, that the asserted claims of the '193 patent were obvious in view of either Pratt alone, or in view of Pratt in combination with Morgan. FSI's obviousness theories are best summarized in its own words from its opening brief on appeal:

> The only element of the asserted claims that is not clearly anticipated by the Pratt patent is the finger shaped marks that orient the ball with respect to the palm of the user's hand. However, this feature is obvious in light of the lines indicating finger placement on the drawings of the Pratt patent. Moreover, the concept of a set of finger marks to orient the ball is clearly taught in the Morgan patent. It would have been obvious to one of ordinary skill in the art to substitute the finger marks of the Morgan patent for the marks of the Pratt patent. Or, stated another way, it would have been obvious to place three sets of marks on the Morgan ball in light of the teaching of Pratt.

In other words, FSI argued to the jury that the "missing element" in Pratt (*i.e.*, the "means for orientation") can be found either in the "phantom lines" of Pratt or in Figure 6 of Morgan. McGinley argued at trial that there was no motivation to combine the prior art as suggested by FSI....

The jury agreed with McGinley. Specifically, in the special verdict form used in this case, the jury answered three questions that are relevant to this appeal in favor of McGinley. First, the jury found that FSI had not proven by clear and convincing evidence that each of the elements of the invention defined in claims 1, 2, 6 and 7 of the '193 patent is disclosed in Pratt. This was a factual finding. *In re Beattie*, 974 F.2d 1309, 1311 (Fed. Cir. 1992) ("What a reference teaches is a question of fact.").

Second, the jury found that FSI had not proven by clear and convincing evidence that any of the asserted claims were invalid as being obvious in view of Pratt alone. Finally, the jury found that FSI had not proven by clear and convincing evidence that any of the asserted claims were invalid as being obvious in view of a combination of Pratt and Morgan. These latter two findings by the jury are directed to the ultimate legal issue of obviousness, and provide no insight as to the jury's findings with respect to the underlying factual underpinnings....

In its motion for JMOL, FSI argued that no reasonable jury could have concluded that the asserted claims were not obvious in view of either Pratt alone or in view of Pratt in combination with Morgan. The district court agreed, and granted FSI's motion for JMOL. Specifically, the court found that "no reasonable jury could conclude that the motivation to combine Pratt and Morgan did not exist."...

\* \* \*

Whether a patent claim is obvious under section 103 depends upon the answer to several factual questions and how the factual answers meld into the legal conclusion of obviousness *vel non*. In this case, we think that the central question is whether there is reason to combine the Pratt and Morgan references, because if the references are properly combined, it is certain that the claims are prima facie invalid for obviousness. If the jury was entitled to conclude that these two references should not be combined, then the asserted claims of the '193 patent cannot be invalid for obviousness in the light of the proposed combination. If those claims are not invalid under a combination of Pratt and Morgan, then, as a matter of logic, those claims cannot be invalid in the light of Pratt alone. We thus turn first to the issue of whether Pratt and Morgan must be combined.

The genius of invention is often a combination of known elements which in hindsight seems preordained. To prevent hindsight invalidation of patent claims, the law requires some "teaching, suggestion or reason" to combine cited references. *Gambro Lundia AB v. Baxter Healthcare Corp.* When the art in question is relatively simple, as is the case here, the opportunity to judge by hindsight is particularly tempting. Consequently, the tests of whether to combine references need to be applied rigorously.

Whether a motivation to combine prior art references has been demonstrated is a question of fact. *Winner Int'l Royalty Corp. v. Wang.* The assessment of whether to combine references in a given case has sometimes been viewed conceptually as a subset of the first *Graham* factor, the scope and content of the prior art. Although that view is not incorrect, accurate assessment of whether to combine references may require attention to other *Graham* factors. For example, the level of skill in the art may inform whether the artisan would find a suggestion to combine in the teachings of an exemplar of prior art. Where the level of skill is high, one may assume a keener appreciation of nuances taught by the prior art. Similarly, appreciation of the differences between the claims in suit and the scope of prior art references, a matter itself informed by the operative level of skill in the art, informs the question of whether to combine prior art references. At bottom, in each case the factual inquiry whether to combine references must be thorough and searching.

There is no question here that FSI presented sufficient evidence at trial from which a jury could have decided that one of ordinary skill in this case would have been motivated to combine Pratt and Morgan to produce a prima facie obvious invention. Specifically, FSI argued to the jury that the only elements of the asserted claims that are not clearly anticipated by Pratt are the finger-shaped marks that orient the ball with respect to the palm of the user's hand. Referring to the "phantom lines" in Pratt as suggestive of finger placement on the ball, FSI argued that one of ordinary skill would have been motivated to substitute the finger marks from the Morgan ball for the circular marks on Pratt, or alternatively to place three sets of marks on the Morgan ball in the light of Pratt's teachings. In addition, FSI argued that one of ordinary skill would have known to add the finger orientation means of the Morgan patent to Pratt by "filling in" the phantom lines in Pratt's drawings and treating them as finger orientation means.

But the jury did not hear a one-sided case on the issue of obviousness, generally and in particular on whether to combine Pratt and Morgan. As FSI conceded at oral argument, McGinley presented reasons to the jury to reject a combination of the references. McGinley argued many grounds to support his contention that the asserted claims are not obvious in the light of Pratt and Morgan. To counter FSI's claim that those references should be combined to render McGinley's "means for orientation" obvious, McGinley pointed to specific differences between the prior art and the asserted claims. For example, Morgan does not disclose the required markings for at least three different kinds of pitches, as do the asserted claims. And Morgan does not disclose markings on a real baseball, as do Pratt and the asserted claims. We recount the gist of this testimony below.

> The jury heard from Mr. Charles Quinn, FSI's vice president of marketing and corporate representative at trial. Quinn testified in detail as to the express teachings of Pratt and Morgan, and as to the differences between these references and the asserted claims. For example, he conceded that the markings on the baseball in Pratt's invention were circular, and therefore incapable of indicating orientation. He also acknowledged that the "phantom lines" in Pratt's drawings were not actually markings on a baseball. Quinn also pointed out that Morgan did not discuss implementing a baseball training device using a regulation baseball. Moreover, he acknowledged that Morgan taught only the provision of indicia for throwing a single type of pitch on each training device, instead of three sets of indicia as required in the asserted claims.

The jury also heard from Mr. Richard Stitt, the attorney who prosecuted the '193 patent. Stitt testified at length about the prosecution history of the '193 patent and the fact that Pratt and Morgan were considered by the PTO throughout the entire pendency of McGinley's application. He confirmed that the "phantom lines" in Pratt's drawings were not actually marked on a baseball. Stitt also pointed out that the PTO never rejected the asserted claims as obvious in view of Pratt, and that it was never suggested by the PTO that the phantom lines of Pratt could easily be transferred to the actual baseball to arrive at McGinley's claimed invention.

Stitt testified that the PTO never rejected McGinley's claims by saying that one could substitute the "elongate finger-shaped markings" shown in Figure 6 of Morgan in place of the "circular dots" in Pratt. He also pointed out that the PTO could have issued an obviousness rejection of the asserted claims based on a theory of transferring Pratt's phantom lines onto the baseball, but never did so. Similarly, he testified that the PTO could have issued an obviousness rejection of the asserted claims based on a theory of combining Pratt with Morgan, but never did so either.

Stitt also testified that he flew to the Patent Office in Washington, D.C., with McGinley for an interview with the Examiner to discuss the differences between Pratt and Morgan and the claimed invention. Finally, he explained in detail why neither Pratt nor Morgan alone or in combination with each other would provide the claimed "means for orientation."

In addition, McGinley relied heavily on the presumption of validity to which his patent is entitled by the terms of 35 U.S.C. §282, mainly in the context of Stitt's tutorial concerning how McGinley's patent was prosecuted, and in McGinley's opening statement and closing argument to the jury. As noted above, throughout the trial, McGinley pointed out that both the Pratt and Morgan references were before the examiner who tested McGinley's patent for validity. Indeed, those two references were discussed in an interview between the applicant and the examiner. The examiner rejected McGinley's claims as anticipated by Pratt, and made no mention of any concern as to obviousness in view of Pratt alone or of a combination of Pratt and Morgan. The Board of Patent Appeals and Interferences reversed the examiner's anticipation rejection, holding that Pratt failed to teach McGinley's means for orienting the baseball relative to the palm of the hand. In due course, McGinley's patent issued and became clothed with the statutory presumption of validity, with no obviousness challenge having been mounted against it, either on the basis of Pratt alone, or of Pratt in combination with Morgan.

The jury in this case was expressly charged that the patent in suit is entitled to the presumption of validity, and that FSI could only overcome that burden with clear and convincing evidence to the contrary. It is well established in our case law that FSI's burden in this case was especially heavy:

> When no prior art other than that which was considered by the PTO examiner is relied on by the attacker [FSI], he has the added burden of overcoming the deference that is due to a qualified government agency presumed to have properly done its job, which includes one or more examiners who are assumed to have some expertise in interpreting the references and to be familiar from their work with the level of skill in the art and whose duty it is to issue only valid patents. In some cases a PTO board of appeals may have approved the issuance of the patent.

*American Hoist & Derrick Co. v. Sowa & Sons, Inc.*, 725 F.2d 1350, 1359 (Fed. Cir. 1984).

Perhaps McGinley's best argument to save his claims from prima facie obviousness in the light of Pratt and Morgan is his contention that those references together teach away from their combination. We have noted elsewhere, as a "useful general rule," that references that teach away cannot serve to create a prima facie case of obviousness. *In re Gurley*, 27 F.3d 551, 553 (Fed. Cir. 1994). If references taken in combination would produce a "seemingly inoperative device," we have held that such references teach away from the combination and thus cannot serve as predicates for a prima facie case of obviousness. *In re Sponnoble*, 405 F.2d 578, 587 (1969) (references teach away from combination if combination produces seemingly inoperative device).

McGinley argues in his brief that Pratt itself teaches away from combining the finger orientation of Morgan, because Pratt, by teaching only the placement of finger tips on the baseball, leads away from placing a full finger orientation on the ball. Such may be the case, but we have no assurance that the jury heard that argument. At oral argument in this court, however, FSI confirmed that McGinley argued to the jury that adding the finger marks of Morgan to Pratt's baseball, by "filling in" the phantom marks to create structure that defines orientation as claimed, would require obliteration of the claimed rotation arrows, a feature that is necessary in order to permit the Pratt invention to operate properly. FSI also confirmed at oral argument that the jury heard McGinley's argument that to combine the finger placements of Morgan onto the Pratt ball would also render the Pratt ball inoperable, by eliminating the multi-colored equatorial band, a claimed feature of the Pratt patent also required for successful operation of Pratt's invention.

We are satisfied that McGinley presented sufficient evidence as well to counter FSI's alternative argument that it would have been obvious to place three sets of marks on the Morgan ball in light of the teaching of Pratt. First, a reasonable jury could have determined from examining the Morgan reference that the finger placement indicia on Morgan are too large to allow the inclusion of more than a single set of markings. This point is important, because Morgan expressly requires markings on the ball to accommodate the placement of two full fingers and a thumb to simulate throwing a single pitch. The jury could have certainly concluded that one of ordinary skill would not attempt to place markings for two additional pitches on Morgan's ball. Two more sets of markings as shown by Morgan itself would require markings for two additional sets of fingers and thumbs. On the other hand, two sets of markings as shown by Pratt would lead to confusion as to the correct means for orientation on Morgan's ball. Any such configurations, *i.e.*, Morgan's invention with markings for throwing three different pitches, would risk, if not achieve, obliteration of the clear and unmistakable markings shown on Morgan's ball to teach the throwing of a single curving pitch. Moreover, a reasonable jury could have considered that all of the embodiments described and illustrated in the Morgan reference are expressly limited to teaching a student pitcher to throw a baseball with a "particular curve or break," and that none of the embodiments discuss or suggest using a conventional baseball as opposed to a hollow shell comprising two metallic or plastic hemispheres glued or otherwise bonded together. The jury also could have concluded that Morgan — with its full finger and thumb imprint markings on the ball — teaches away from a means for orientation using the smaller tear-drop markings disclosed by McGinley or the small truncated finger-shaped markings used in FSI's accused baseballs.

Given the strength of the teaching away point, we think it remarkable that FSI makes no attempt whatsoever in its brief to counter McGinley's argument. The jury's verdict that the claims in suit are not obvious is supported by the evidence brought forward by McGinley to resist FSI's contrary evidence. Here we have the classic example of sufficient evidence to support each position argued to the jury. The key issue, namely what the references teach and whether they teach the necessity of combination or the requirement of separation, is a fact issue. When the jury is supplied with sufficient valid factual information to support the verdict it reaches, that is the end of the matter. In such an instance, the jury's factual conclusion may not be set aside by a JMOL order.

Given the multiple bases upon which the jury's verdict in favor of McGinley can be sustained over FSI's arguments for combining the references, we must conclude that FSI fares no better in arguing a combination of Pratt into Morgan than it does in arguing a combination of Morgan into Pratt. The jury was thus entitled to reach its verdict of nonobviousness on the ground that one of ordinary skill in the art would not deem the asserted claims of the '193 patent obvious in light of Pratt and Morgan in combination. That being the case, it is illogical to think that one of ordinary skill in the art would have deemed McGinley's claims obvious in the light of Pratt alone. If one of ordinary skill is not taught by Morgan to extend Pratt's circular markings into the phantom lines, that person would not be taught by the phantom lines alone to do so.

Nonetheless, we think the district court erred as well in its decision that McGinley's asserted claims were obvious as a matter of law in view of Pratt alone. According to the district court's reasoning, no reasonable jury could have failed to conclude that an ordinarily skilled artisan would have been motivated to transfer the finger-shaped "phantom lines" shown in the Pratt reference onto the actual Pratt baseball itself, thus providing the missing "means for orientation" that is admittedly otherwise missing in Pratt.

It should be noted that the "phantom lines" shown in Pratt are virtually identical to the finger-shaped markings on Fig. 6 of the Morgan reference, except that the Morgan markings are "filled-in" and actually marked on the ball. Therefore, many of the arguments mentioned above with respect to Morgan apply with equal force with respect to the Pratt phantom lines. Specifically, as FSI conceded at oral argument before this court, the jury heard McGinley's argument that transferring large finger-shaped markings (such as those illustrated in Fig. 6 of Morgan or in the phantom lines of Pratt) would render the Pratt invention inoperable by interfering with the multi-colored equatorial band. Thus, according to this evidence, one of ordinary skill in designing baseballs for use as pitching trainers would not be motivated to modify Pratt by filling in the phantom lines to express palm-oriented finger placement on the ball. As mentioned above, the jury also heard extensive testimony concerning the prosecution history of the '193 patent, including the critical facts that (1) Pratt was before the PTO during the entire pendency of the patent application, and (2) although the PTO continued to reject the asserted claims as anticipated by Pratt until McGinley won an appeal before the Board on that point, the PTO never rejected the asserted claims as obvious in view of Pratt alone. Surely, relying on the presumption of regularity that applies to all administrative agencies such as the PTO, the jury could have reasonably concluded that if the PTO believed that an obviousness rejection based on Pratt alone was warranted, such a rejection would have been promptly been made. Also, just as was the case with the Morgan markings, the jury could have reasonably concluded from an examination of the references that the Pratt phantom lines are so large that it would not be feasible to include three sets of them on a single baseball, as required by the asserted claims. Because substantial evidence supports the jury's implicit factual finding that no motivation to modify Pratt in that manner has been demonstrated in this case, the district court's ruling that Pratt alone renders the asserted claims obvious as a matter of law was erroneous.

Due to the "black box" nature of the jury's verdict, it is impossible to determine which of the above pieces of evidence, alone or in combination, carried the day in the jury room, and how much weight was assigned to each piece. All that can be said with certainty is that? as a whole? the evidence enumerated above (all of which was admittedly before the jury) constitutes substantial evidence to support the jury's verdict....

For the reasons set forth above, we conclude that the district court erred when it ruled on JMOL that no reasonable juror could have ruled that FSI failed to make out a case of obviousness by clear and convincing evidence.

# Comments

*1. **The Two-Part Test.*** An obviousness rejection requires both a suggestion in the art to combine the references and a reasonable expectation of success once combined.

  a. ***A Suggestion in the Art.*** A finding of obviousness requires that there be a suggestion, teaching, or motivation to combine the prior art references. The policy behind this requirement is to prevent the use of hindsight to invalidate patent claims. What is obvious today was not necessarily obvious yesterday. As such, the court must cast its mind back to the time of invention when determining obvious. The source of the suggestion may come from (1) the references themselves; (2) knowledge of those skilled in the art that certain references, or disclosures in the references, are known to be of special interest or importance in the particular field; and (3) the nature of a problem to be solved, leading inventors to look to references relating to possible solutions to that problem. Thus, the suggestion does not have to be explicit.

  An illustrative case is *Pro-Mold & Tool Company v. Great Lakes Plastics, Inc.* 75 F.3d 1568 (Fed. Cir. 1996). Neugebauer obtained a patent on a card holder for baseball cards that was slightly larger than a stored card so that the stored card would fit a conventional storage box. Neugebauer developed his invention after conversations with his son, who collected sports cards and was familiar with the card market. The son stored his more valuable cards in individual card holders, but these individual holders did not fit in the conventional storage box the son was using; prompting the son to tape the individual cards to the top of the storage box so that the entire set could be stored together. The son's experience led Neugebaurer to design the claimed invention, which had the advantage of allowing entire sets of cards to be stored together because cards that were held in an individual card holder could now be stored with cards that were not in such holders.

  The Federal Circuit held that the claimed invention was obvious in the light of two prior art references, the "Squeeze Tite" card holder and the "Classic Line Thick and Thin" card holder. The Squeeze Tite was a two-piece holder with a friction fit cover. The Classic Line Thin holder was only slightly larger than the stored card and was designed to hold one card. The Federal Circuit stated that the Squeeze Tite contained all of the claim limitations except for size, but the Classic Line Thin holder, because it was only slightly larger than the stored card, provided this missing limitation.

  Pro-Mold, Neugebauer's company and owner of the patent, argued that there was no reason to combine the two prior art references. The court disagreed, noting that the subject matter of the claimed invention provided the reason to combine. According to the court:

> The suggestion or motivation to combine these features of the prior art was . . . evident from the very size of the card itself. Card holders larger than the card had already been designed, as evidenced at least by the Squeeze Tite card holder. On the other hand, a card holder no

larger than necessary clearly was desirable in order to enable the card holders to fit in a set box....Accordingly, the size of the card provided the motivation to combine the features of the prior art card holders and hence modify the size of the Squeeze Tite card holder so that it was not larger or smaller than the card, but rather substantially the size of the card.

*Id.* at 1573.

b. *A Reasonable Expectation of Success and the Obvious-to-Try Standard.* In addition to proving that the prior art suggests to a person of ordinary skill in the art to make the claimed invention, one must also show that once the invention is made the person with ordinary skill in the art would have a reasonable expectation of success; absolute predictability is not required.

The word "reasonable" in the law is very elusive, but the Federal Circuit has provided some guidance, in the §103 context, by explaining what is *not* "reasonable." For instance, the court has held that an invention that is "obvious to try" is not necessarily obvious under §103. Thus, because the expectation of success must be reasonable (not slight or absolute), an invention can be *non*-obvious even though the prior art suggests that it was "obvious to try." According to the Federal Circuit, an obvious-to-try "situation exists when a general disclosure may pique the scientist's curiosity, such that further investigation might be done as a result of the disclosure, but the disclosure itself does not contain a sufficient teaching of how to obtain the desired result, or that the claimed result would be obtained if certain directions were pursued." *Gillette Co. v. S.C. Johnson & Son, Inc.*, 919 F.2d 720, 725 (Fed. Cir. 1990).

2. *References Must Be "Analogous."* Not just any reference can be used for §103 purposes. Throughout the years, courts have developed what is known as the doctrine of analogous and non-analogous art. Only prior art that is considered to be "analogous" to the subject matter sought to be patented can be used under §103. The Federal Circuit has held prior art is analogous (1) if it is from the same field of endeavor, regardless of the problem the prior art addresses, or (2) if the prior art is not within the same field of endeavor, the reference is reasonably pertinent to the problem the claimed invention seeks to address. *See In re Clay*, 966 F.2d 656, 658 (Fed. Cir. 1992); *In re Deminski*, 796 F.2d 436, 442 (Fed. Cir. 1986); *In re Wood*, 599 F.2d 1032, 1036 (CCPA 1979).

The analogous art requirement highlights a key distinction between a §102 novelty determination and a §103 obviousness inquiry. With respect to the former, a reference's analogous nature or lack thereof to the claimed subject matter is entirely irrelevant. To prove anticipation under §102, one could point to *any* single prior art reference so long as it discloses the same invention including each and every limitation of the claimed invention; not so for §103 purposes. Why do we require art to be analogous for §103 purposes, but not for §102? The answer to this question may be driven by a practical concern. To prove obviousness under §103, one can combine the teachings of several prior art references. In contrast, anticipation under §102 must reside in a *single* prior art reference. Therefore, while it is a difficult enough burden to presume that an inventor is knowledgeable of prior art in his own inventive field and fields related thereto, it is not only unfair but also unrealistic to require an inventor to be presumptively aware of non-analogous prior art.

An interesting analogous art case is *In re Bigio*, 381 F.3d 1320 (Fed. Cir. 2004). In *Bigio*, the Federal Circuit, in affirming a finding of obviousness, had to decide whether prior art patents disclosing a tooth brush were analogous art to Bigio's claimed hairbrush. The PTO and court focused on the structure and function of the claimed invention. The court first interpreted the claims of the hairbrush and found that the claim is not limited to the kind of hair to be groomed. The claimed invention, for instance, could be used for scalp or facial hair. The court then agreed with the PTO that the prior art "toothbrush was in Bigio's field of endeavor because 'the structural similarities between toothbrushes and small brushes for hair would have led one of ordinary skill in the art working in the specific field of hairbrushes to consider all similar brushes including toothbrushes.'" *Id.* at 1326. Moreover, the court agreed that it would be readily apparent to a person having ordinary skill in the art that, "in view of the size of the bristle segment and arrangement of the bristle bundles described in the" prior art, the toothbrushes could be used to brush facial hair. *Id.*

Another interesting case is *In re Paulsen*, 30 F.3d 1475 (Fed. Cir. 1994), which involved prior art that was not within the same field of endeavor of the claimed invention. In *Paulsen*, the patent related to a portable computer contained within a compact metal case. A salient feature of the claimed invention was the "clam shell" configuration, in which the computer's display housing is connected to the computer at its midsection by a hinge assembly that enables the display to swing from a closed, latched position for portability and protection to an open, erect position for viewing and operation. In other words, the patent claimed the design of a "laptop" computer. During a reexamination, the PTO rejected the claims under §103 in the light of references directed to hinges and latches as used in a desktop telephone directory, a piano lid, a kitchen cabinet, a washing machine cabinet, a wooden furniture cabinet, or a two-part housing for storing audiocassettes. The Federal Circuit, in affirming the PTO, rejected the applicant's argument that the prior art was non-analogous. The court agreed that the prior art was not in the same field of endeavor as computers, but the "problems encountered by the inventors of the '456 patent were problems that were not unique to portable computers." *Id.* at 1482.

> They concerned how to connect and secure the computer's display housing to the computer while meeting certain size constraints and functional requirements. The prior art cited by the examiner discloses various means of connecting a cover (or lid) to a device so that the cover is free to swing radially along the connection axis, as well as means of securing the cover in an open or closed position. We agree with the Board that given the nature of the problems confronted by the inventors, one of ordinary skill in the art "would have consulted the mechanical arts for housings, hinges, latches, springs, etc."

*Id.*

3. *The "Person Having Ordinary Skill in the Art."* A §103 obviousness determination is based on whether a person having ordinary skill in the art (sometimes referred to by the acronym PHOSITA), to which the claimed invention pertains, would have found the claimed invention obvious. Thus, constructing a PHOSITA is of crucial importance. It is well settled that a PHOSITA is not the inventor or any particular expert or handyman, but rather a *hypothetical* person, which renders immaterial the subjective motivations of inventors. The level of skill, of course, is "ordinary," a term that was placed in §103 to curb judges who had a penchant for permitting too high of a skill level (e.g., extra-ordinary skill). The Federal Circuit has set forth several factors that should be considered in determining "ordinary skill," including educational level of inventor and workers in the field, types of problems encountered in the art, prior art solutions to those problems, rapidity with which innovations are made, sophistication of the technology. Lastly, although the level of skill in the art is ordinary, the breadth of our hypothetical person is perfect. Complete knowledge of all pertinent art is presumed, despite that such a presumption is unrealistic. As Judge Learned Hand stated, "[w]e must suppose the inventor to be endowed, as in fact no inventor is endowed; we are to impute to him knowledge of all that is not only in his immediate field, but in all fields nearly akin to that field." *International Cellucotton Prod. Co. v. Sterilek* Co., 94 F.2d 10, 13 (2d Cir. 1938).

4. *Secondary Considerations.* Secondary considerations are relevant to, and sometimes determinative of, a §103 obviousness determination. The "real world" considerations, thought to be objective in nature, include *commercial success, long-felt need, failure of others,* and *licensing/acquiescence*. As the *Graham* court noted, these considerations "focus our attention on economic and motivational rather than technical issues and are, therefore more susceptible of judicial treatment than are the highly technical facts often present in patent litigation." *Graham*, 383 U.S. at 35-36.

   a. *Commercial Success.* Commercial success is the most important and most often asserted of the secondary considerations. Commercial success of an invention is relevant to non-obviousness because it assumes that if the invention were obvious, competitors of the inventor would have produced the invention given its significant consumer demand. Thus, competitors must have tried and failed to produce the invention, thus leading to the conclusion that the invention was non-obvious.

   Of course, commercial success may be due to, and consumer demand may be a result of, factors unrelated to the technical quality of the claimed invention (e.g., clever advertising, aggressive marketing, business acumen, or significant market share). Thus, raw sales data is insufficient to prove commercial success. For evidence of commercial success to be persuasive, the patentee must show comparative success with other products on the market *and* a nexus must be established between commercial success and the merits of the claimed invention.

   b. *Long-Felt Need and Failure of Others.* The fact that there is a long-felt need for an invention or a solution to a particular problem in an industry and others in the industry have tried and failed to satisfy that need may imply non-obviousness. As Judge Easterbrook wrote in *In re Mahurkar Patent Litigation*, "if people are clamoring for a solution, and the best minds do not find it for years, that is practical evidence — the kind that can't be bought from a hired expert, the kind that does not depend on fallible memories or doubtful inferences — of the state of knowledge." 831 F. Supp. 1354, 1377-1378 (N.D. Ill. 1993).

But the fact that there was a failure to achieve the patented solution may simply be the result of a company's complacency toward its existing technology even though such technology is not state of the art. Furthermore, certain firms may not be willing to commit the time and resources to solving identified problems within the industry. That is, economic and business decisions must be considered when one analyzes long-felt need and failure of others.

c. *Licensing and Acquiescence*. A patentee may assert that the acceptance of a license by the defendant or other competitors is an implicit recognition that the patent is non-obvious. The rationale is that firms would not pay royalties on a patent unless it thought the patent was valid.

But there are several factors unrelated to validity that a firm considers when entering into a license agreement. For example, taking a license may reflect a business judgment that it is less expensive to pay royalties than to defend an infringement suit. In other words, sometimes it just makes business sense not to contest the validity of a patent even though you may have strong evidence of obviousness. As a result, the patentee must show a nexus between the merits of the invention and the licenses of record.

# E. UTILITY

In order to be patentable, a claimed invention must be "useful." The utility requirement is found in the Constitution ("*useful* arts") and the patent code (35 U.S.C. §101). At first glance, the utility requirement in patent law appears to be somewhat superfluous. Why would anyone make or buy a useless invention? Indeed, it is a rare occasion that lack of utility is raised as an invalidating defense in a patent litigation context. But there is a purpose behind the utility requirement in that it secures a *quid pro quo* for society. The claimed invention is required to be operative; in other words, the invention must function for its intended purpose. Thus, before we grant to an inventor the right to exclude others from making, using, or selling her invention, she must provide society with an invention that operates in accordance with its intended purpose or a purpose discernible by a person of ordinary skill in the art. The utility requirement imposes a very low bar and is rarely a concern for patent applicants. Inventions that satisfy the utility requirement include a "propeller enhanced toy football" (U.S. Patent No. 6,669,587) and a "pizza box" (U.S. Patent No. 4,441,626), for instance. To the extent that the requirement remains an issue, it is in the biotechnology/genomics area as discussed in the Comments following *In re Swartz*, the principal case.

*STATUTE:* **Inventions Patentable**
35 U.S.C. §101

## IN RE SWARTZ
### 232 F.3d 862 (Fed. Cir. 2000)

PER CURIAM.

Mitchell R. Swartz appeals from the decision of the United States Patent and Trademark Office (PTO) Board of Patent Appeals and Interferences (Board), affirming the examiner's final rejection of claims 25-48 of application Serial No. 07/760,970 for lack of operability or utility under 35 U.S.C. §101....

* * *

The PTO has the initial burden of challenging a patent applicant's presumptively correct assertion of utility. If the PTO provides evidence showing that one of ordinary skill in the art would reasonably doubt the asserted utility, however, the burden shifts to the applicant to submit evidence sufficient to convince such a person of the invention's asserted utility. Here the PTO provided several references showing that results in the area of cold fusion were irreproducible. Thus the PTO provided substantial evidence that those skilled in the art would "reasonably doubt" the asserted utility and operability of cold fusion, *See In re Brana,* 51 F.3d 1560 (Fed. Cir. 1995). The examiner found that Mr. Swartz had not submitted evidence of operability that would be sufficient to overcome reasonable doubt. After its review of the evidence, the Board found that Mr. Swartz had "produced no persuasive objective evidence, in our view, that overcomes the examiner's position."

On this appeal, Mr. Swartz complains that the Board "ignored" evidence that he submitted and disregarded his arguments, and he invites this Court to examine voluminous record material that he urges supports his position on the issue of utility. Such conclusory allegations in an appeal brief are quite insufficient to establish that the Board's decision on the issue of utility is not supported by substantial evidence or to establish that the Board's ultimate conclusion of a lack of enablement is incorrect as a matter of law.

Finally, Mr. Swartz's attempt to show that his claims are directed to a process other than cold fusion must fail. In his written description and throughout prosecution of his application, Mr. Swartz continually represented his invention as relating to cold fusion.

For the reasons discussed above, the Board did not err in concluding that the utility of Mr. Swartz's claimed process had not been established and that his application did not satisfy the enablement requirement. Accordingly, the judgment of the Board is affirmed.

## Comments

1. *Utility's Modern Application.* The *Swartz* case represents the modern approach to utility that can be traced to *In re Brana.* In *Brana,* the Federal Circuit articulated a two-step test for determining whether the utility requirement has been met. First, the PTO "has the initial burden of challenging a *presumptively* correct assertion of utility in the disclosure." Second,

"[o]nly after the PTO provides evidence showing that one of ordinary skill in the art would reasonably doubt the asserted utility does the burden shift to the applicant" to prove utility. *Brana*, 51 F.3d at 1566 (Fed. Cir. 1995) (emphasis added). The *Swartz* case notwithstanding, the PTO, with the exception of biotechnology cases as discussed in Comment 2, rarely invokes the utility doctrine.

2. ***Utility Still an Issue in Biotechnology/Genomics.*** Over the past 10 years the PTO, although inconsistently, has turned to the utility requirement to cast doubt on the patentability of certain genomic-related inventions. For example, while patents on fully sequenced genes and proteins are regularly patented, the PTO has denied patents on so-called ESTs, or express sequence tags, as lacking utility. ESTs are partial gene sequences, and the PTO's position was that these partial sequences were insufficiently useful under §101, despite applicants' arguments that ESTs could be used as a probe to discover the entire gene of which it was a part.

The EST issue resurfaced recently in *Ex parte Fisher* (Bd. Pat. App. & Int., unpublished No. 2002-2046, April 1, 2004), a decision by the Board of Patent Appeals and Interferences, which is the PTO's adjudicative administrative body for patent law. The Federal Circuit affirmed the Board. *See In re Fisher*, 431 F.3d 1365 (Fed. Cir. 2005). In *Fisher*, the applicant claimed ESTs that encode for a maize protein or fragment thereof. The Examiner and the Board rejected these claims as lacking utility, namely that the specification simply listed nonspecific uses relevant only to nucleic acids generally, not those being claimed. Fisher argued on appeal that the claimed nucleic acids could be used as a probe to locate the presence or absence of polymorphisms. The Board, relying on *Brenner v. Manson*, 383 U.S. 519 (1966), was not persuaded. *Brenner* is a famous utility case, which, until *Fisher*, was of uncertain contemporary relevance. The invention at issue in *Brenner* was a process for making a chemical compound, namely a steroid. The Court held that the applicant failed to disclose sufficient utility for the compound made by the claimed process; therefore, the process itself lacked utility. The Court rejected the argument that utility is satisfied if the process "produces a compound whose potential usefulness is under investigation by serious scientific researchers." In other words, the invention was an intermediate step or research platform on the way to commercialization. The Court demanded the "substantial utility." According to the Court:

> The basic *quid pro quo* contemplated by the Constitution and the Congress for granting a patent monopoly is the benefit derived by the public from an invention with substantial utility. Unless and until a process is refined and developed to this point(where specific benefit exists in currently available form — there is insufficient justification for permitting an applicant to engross what may prove to be a broad field.

*Id.* at 534. Moreover, the Court was concerned with permitting overly broad, ambiguous claims:

> Until the process claim has been reduced to production of a product shown to be useful, the metes and bounds of that monopoly are not cap-

able of precise delineation. It may engross a vast, unknown, and perhaps unknowable area. Such a patent may confer power to block off whole areas of scientific development, without compensating benefit to the public.

*Id.*

Relying heavily on *Brenner*, the Board in *Fisher* stated that detecting the presence or absence of polymorphisms provides "the barest information in regard to genetic heritage." The *Brenner* decision and §101, according to the Board, require more than "de minimis" utility; they require "substantial utility."

# F. STATUTORY SUBJECT MATTER

The statutory subject matter requirement is similar to the utility requirement in two ways. First, they both find a home in §101 of Title 35, and second, neither of them present a significant obstacle to patentability. Yet they each have generated a great deal of academic discussion and remain conceptually important to our understanding of what types of inventions we want to allow in and be subject to the more rigorous requirements embodied in §§102, 103, and 112. The courts have taken an expansive view of the statutory subject matter requirement; indeed, Chief Justice Burger famously wrote that "Congress intended statutory subject matter to 'include anything under the sun that is made by man.'" *Diamond v. Chakrabarty*, discussed *infra*. As a result, genetic materials such as DNA sequences, proteins, software, and business methods are eligible subject matter under §101. It is important to note, however, that there are certain types of things that are not eligible for patent protection, namely laws of nature and abstract ideas such as $E=mc^2$.

## COMPARATIVE PERSPECTIVE
### Subject Matter Eligibility Under the European Patent Convention

It is interesting to compare the approach of §101 under U.S. law with the provisions of the European Patent Convention (EPC). Section 101 defines subject matter eligibility positively, and leaves the exclusions to the common law, whereas the EPC itself sets forth both a positive and negative definition of patentable subject matter. For example, Article 52 of the EPC provides generally that patents "shall be granted for any inventions which are susceptible of industrial application." Article 57 provides that "an invention shall be considered as susceptible of industrial application if it can be made or used in any kind of industry, including agriculture." But the EPC goes on to specify several exceptions. For example, Article 52(2) excludes from patent protection: "(a) discoveries, scientific theories and mathematical methods; (b) aesthetic creations; (c) schemes, rules and methods for performing mental acts, playing games or doing business, and programs for computers; and (d) presentations of information" *but only* insofar as the patent "relates to such subject-matter or activities as such." Moreover, Article 53(a) excludes from patent protection "inventions the publication or exploitation of which would be contrary to '*ordre public*' or morality . . ." and 53(b) excludes "plant or animal varieties or essentially biological processes for the production of plants or animals," but notes that "this provision does not apply to microbiological processes or the products thereof."

The most important (and interesting) subject matter questions relate to (1) biotechnology-related inventions; and (2) software and business methods. The principal cases are devoted to these technologies.

*STATUTE:* **Inventions Patentable**
35 U.S.C. §101

# 1. Biotechnology-Related Inventions

### DIAMOND v. CHAKRABARTY
**447 U.S. 303 (1980)**

Mr. Chief Justice BURGER delivered the opinion of the Court.

We granted certiorari to determine whether a live, human-made microorganism is patentable subject matter under 35 U.S.C. §101.

I

In 1972, respondent Chakrabarty, a microbiologist, filed a patent application, assigned to the General Electric Co. The application asserted 36 claims related to Chakrabarty's invention of "a bacterium". . . . This human-made, genetically engineered bacterium is capable of breaking down multiple components of crude oil. Because of this property, which is possessed by no naturally occurring bacteria, Chakrabarty's invention is believed to have significant value for the treatment of oil spills.[2]

Chakrabarty's patent claims were of three types: first, process claims for the method of producing the bacteria; second, claims for an inoculum comprised of a carrier material floating on water, such as straw, and the new bacteria; and third, claims to the bacteria themselves. The patent examiner allowed the claims falling into the first two categories, but rejected claims for the bacteria. His decision rested on two grounds: (1) that micro-organisms are "products of nature," and (2) that as living things they are not patentable subject matter under 35 U.S.C. §101.

Chakrabarty appealed the rejection of these claims to the Patent Office Board of Appeals, and the Board affirmed the Examiner on the second

---

2. At present, biological control of oil spills requires the use of a mixture of naturally occurring bacteria, each capable of degrading one component of the oil complex. In this way, oil is decomposed into simpler substances which can serve as food for aquatic life. However, for various reasons, only a portion of any such mixed culture survives to attack the oil spill. By breaking down multiple components of oil, Chakrabarty's micro-organism promises more efficient and rapid oil-spill control.

ground.[3] Relying on the legislative history of the 1930 Plant Patent Act, in which Congress extended patent protection to certain asexually reproduced plants, the Board concluded that §101 was not intended to cover living things such as these laboratory created micro-organisms.

The Court of Customs and Patent Appeals, by a divided vote, [in an opinion by Judge Rich,] reversed on the authority of its prior decision in *In re Bergy*, 563 F.2d 1031, 1038 (1977), which held that "the fact that microorganisms . . . are alive . . . [is] without legal significance" for purposes of the patent law. Subsequently, we granted the Acting Commissioner of Patents and Trademarks' petition for certiorari in *Bergy*, vacated the judgment, and remanded the case "for further consideration in light of *Parker v. Flook*." The Court of Customs and Patent Appeals then vacated its judgment in *Chakrabarty* and consolidated the case with *Bergy* for reconsideration. After re-examining both cases in the light of our holding in *Flook*, that court, with one dissent, [again through Judge Rich,] reaffirmed its earlier judgments.

The Commissioner of Patents and Trademarks again sought certiorari, and we granted the writ as to both *Bergy* and *Chakrabarty*. Since then, *Bergy* has been dismissed as moot, leaving only *Chakrabarty* for decision.

## II

The Constitution grants Congress broad power to legislate to "promote the Progress of Science and useful Arts, by securing for limited Times to Authors and Inventors the exclusive Right to their respective Writings and Discoveries." Art. I, §8, cl. 8. The patent laws promote this progress by offering inventors exclusive rights for a limited period as an incentive for their inventiveness and research efforts. *Kewanee Oil Co. v. Bicron Corp.*; *Universal Oil Co. v. Globe Co.* The authority of Congress is exercised in the hope that "[t]he productive effort thereby fostered will have a positive effect on society through the introduction of new products and processes of manufacture into the economy, and the emanations by way of increased employment and better lives for our citizens." *Kewanee*, 416 U.S. at 480.

The question before us in this case is a narrow one of statutory interpretation requiring us to construe 35 U.S.C. §101, which provides:

> Whoever invents or discovers any new and useful process, machine, manufacture, or composition of matter, or any new and useful improvement thereof, may obtain a patent therefor, subject to the conditions and requirements of this title.

Specifically, we must determine whether respondent's micro-organism constitutes a "manufacture" or "composition of matter" within the meaning of the statute.[5]

---

3. The Board concluded that the new bacteria were not "products of nature," because Pseudomonas bacteria containing two or more different energy-generating plasmids are not naturally occurring.

5. This case does not involve the other "conditions and requirements" of the patent laws, such as novelty and nonobviousness. 35 U.S.C. §§102, 103.

## III

In cases of statutory construction we begin, of course, with the language of the statute. *Southeastern Community College v. Davis*. And "unless otherwise defined, words will be interpreted as taking their ordinary, contemporary common meaning." *Perrin v. United States*, 444 U.S. 37, 42 (1979). We have also cautioned that courts "should not read into the patent laws limitations and conditions which the legislature has not expressed." *United States v. Dubilier Condenser Corp.*, 289 U.S. 178, 199 (1933).

Guided by these canons of construction, this Court has read the term "manufacture" in §101 in accordance with its dictionary definition to mean "the production of articles for use from raw or prepared materials by giving to these materials new forms, qualities, properties, or combinations, whether by hand-labor or by machinery." *American Fruit Growers, Inc. v. Brogdex Co.*, 283 U.S. 1, 11 (1931). Similarly, "composition of matter" has been construed consistent with its common usage to include "all compositions of two or more substances and . . . all composite articles, whether they be the results of chemical union, or of mechanical mixture, or whether they be gases, fluids, powders or solids." *Shell Development Co. v. Watson*, 149 F. Supp. 279, 280 (D.C.1957) (citing 1 A. Deller, Walker on Patents §14, p. 55 (1st ed. 1937)). In choosing such expansive terms as "manufacture" and "composition of matter," modified by the comprehensive "any," Congress plainly contemplated that the patent laws would be given wide scope.

The relevant legislative history also supports a broad construction. The Patent Act of 1793, authored by Thomas Jefferson, defined statutory subject matter as "any new and useful art, machine, manufacture, or composition of matter, or any new or useful improvement [thereof]." Act of Feb. 21, 1793, §1, 1 Stat. 319. The Act embodied Jefferson's philosophy that "ingenuity should receive a liberal encouragement." 5 Writings of Thomas Jefferson 75-76 (Washington ed. 1871). *See Graham v. John Deere Co.*, 383 U.S. 1, 7-10 (1966). Subsequent patent statutes in 1836, 1870, and 1874 employed this same broad language. In 1952, when the patent laws were recodified, Congress replaced the word "art" with "process," but otherwise left Jefferson's language intact. The Committee Reports accompanying the 1952 Act inform us that Congress intended statutory subject matter to "include anything under the sun that is made by man." S. Rep. No. 1979, 82d Cong., 2d Sess., 5 (1952); H.R. Rep. No. 1923, 82d Cong., 2d Sess., 6 (1952).[6]

This is not to suggest that §101 has no limits or that it embraces every discovery. The laws of nature, physical phenomena, and abstract ideas have been held not patentable. See *Parker v. Flook*; *Gottschalk v. Benson*; *Funk Brothers Seed Co. v. Kalo Inoculant Co.*; *O'Reilly v. Morse*; *Le Roy v. Tatham*. Thus, a new mineral discovered in the earth or a new plant found in the wild is not patentable subject matter. Likewise, Einstein could not patent his celebrated law that $E=mc^2$; nor could Newton have patented the law of

---

6. This same language was employed by P. J. Federico, a principal draftsman of the 1952 recodification, in his testimony regarding that legislation: "[U]nder section 101 a person may have invented a machine or a manufacture, which may include anything under the sun that is made by man. . . ." Hearings on H.R. 3760 before Subcommittee No. 3 of the House Committee on the Judiciary, 82d Cong., 1st Sess., 37 (1951).

gravity. Such discoveries are "manifestations of...nature, free to all men and reserved exclusively to none." *Funk Brothers*, *supra*, 333 U.S., at 130.

Judged in this light, respondent's micro-organism plainly qualifies as patentable subject matter. His claim is not to a hitherto unknown natural phenomenon, but to a nonnaturally occurring manufacture or composition of matter—a product of human ingenuity "having a distinctive name, character [and] use." *Hartranft v. Wiegmann*, 121 U.S. 609, 615 (1887). The point is underscored dramatically by comparison of the invention here with that in *Funk*. There, the patentee had discovered that there existed in nature certain species of root-nodule bacteria which did not exert a mutually inhibitive effect on each other. He used that discovery to produce a mixed culture capable of inoculating the seeds of leguminous plants. Concluding that the patentee had discovered "only some of the handiwork of nature," the Court ruled the product nonpatentable:

> Each of the species of root-nodule bacteria contained in the package infects the same group of leguminous plants which it always infected. No species acquires a different use. The combination of species produces no new bacteria, no change in the six species of bacteria, and no enlargement of the range of their utility. Each species has the same effect it always had. The bacteria perform in their natural way. Their use in combination does not improve in any way their natural functioning. They serve the ends nature originally provided and act quite independently of any effort of the patentee. 333 U.S., at 131.

Here, by contrast, the patentee has produced a new bacterium with markedly different characteristics from any found in nature and one having the potential for significant utility. His discovery is not nature's handiwork, but his own; accordingly it is patentable subject matter under §101.

## IV

Two contrary arguments are advanced, neither of which we find persuasive.

### A

The petitioner's first argument rests on the enactment of the 1930 Plant Patent Act, which afforded patent protection to certain asexually reproduced plants, and the 1970 Plant Variety Protection Act, which authorized protection for certain sexually reproduced plants but excluded bacteria from its protection. [Footnote omitted] In the petitioner's view, the passage of these Acts evidences congressional understanding that the terms "manufacture" or "composition of matter" do not include living things; if they did, the petitioner argues, neither Act would have been necessary.

We reject this argument. Prior to 1930, two factors were thought to remove plants from patent protection. The first was the belief that plants, even those artificially bred, were products of nature for purposes of the patent law. This position appears to have derived from the decision of the patent office in *Ex parte Latimer*, in which a patent claim for fiber found in the needle of the Pinus australis was rejected. The Commissioner reasoned that a contrary result would permit "patents [to] be obtained upon the trees of the forest and the plants of the earth, which of course would be unreasonable and impossible." *Id.*, at 126. The *Latimer* case, it seems, came to "se[t] forth the general stand taken in these matters" that plants were natural products not subject to patent protection. Thorne, Relation of Patent Law to Natural Products, 6 J. Pat. Off. Soc. 23, 24 (1923).[8] The second obstacle to patent protection for plants was the fact that plants were thought not amenable to the "written description" requirement of the patent law. *See* 35 U.S.C. §112. Because new plants may differ from old only in color or perfume, differentiation by written description was often impossible.

In enacting the Plant Patent Act, Congress addressed both of these concerns. It explained at length its belief that the work of the plant breeder "in aid of nature" was patentable invention. S. Rep. No. 315, 71st Cong., 2d Sess., 6-8 (1930); H. R. Rep. No. 1129, 71st Cong., 2d Sess., 7-9 (1930). And it relaxed the written description requirement in favor of "a description...as complete as is reasonably possible." 35 U.S.C. §162. No Committee or Member of Congress, however, expressed the broader view, now urged by the petitioner, that the terms "manufacture" or "composition of matter" exclude living things. The sole support for that position in the legislative history of the 1930 Act is found in the conclusory statement of Secretary of Agriculture Hyde, in a letter to the Chairmen of the House and Senate Committees considering the 1930 Act, that "the patent laws- ...at the present time are understood to cover only inventions or discoveries in the field of inanimate nature." *See* S. Rep. No. 315, *supra*, at Appendix A; H. R. Rep. No. 1129, *supra*, at Appendix A. Secretary Hyde's opinion, however, is not entitled to controlling weight. His views were solicited on the administration of the new law and not on the scope of patentable subject matter—an area beyond his competence. Moreover, there is language in the House and Senate Committee Reports suggesting that to the extent Congress considered the matter it found the Secretary's dichotomy unpersuasive. The Reports observe:

> There is a clear and logical distinction *between the discovery of a new variety of plant and of certain inanimate things*, such, for example, as a new and useful natural mineral. The mineral is created wholly by nature unassisted by man. ...On the other hand, a plant discovery resulting from cultivation is unique, isolated, and is not repeated by nature, nor can it be reproduced by nature unaided by man....(emphasis added).

Congress thus recognized that the relevant distinction was not between living and inanimate things, but between products of nature, whether living or not, and human-made inventions. Here, respondent's microorganism is the result of human ingenuity and research. Hence, the passage of the Plant Patent Act affords the Government no support.

Nor does the passage of the 1970 Plant Variety Protection Act support the Government's position. As the Government acknowledges, sexually

---

8. Writing three years after the passage of the 1930 Act, R. Cook, Editor of the Journal of Heredity, commented:

It is a little hard for plant men to understand why [Art. I, §8] of the Constitution should not have been earlier construed to include the promotion of the art of plant breeding. The reason for this is probably to be found in the principle that natural products are not patentable. Florists Exchange and Horticultural Trade World, July 15, 1933, p. 9.

reproduced plants were not included under the 1930 Act because new varieties could not be reproduced true-to-type through seedlings. Brief for Petitioner 27, n. 31. By 1970, however, it was generally recognized that true-to-type reproduction was possible and that plant patent protection was therefore appropriate. The 1970 Act extended that protection. There is nothing in its language or history to suggest that it was enacted because §101 did not include living things.

In particular, we find nothing in the exclusion of bacteria from plant variety protection to support the petitioner's position. The legislative history gives no reason for this exclusion. As the Court of Customs and Patent Appeals suggested, it may simply reflect congressional agreement with the result reached by that court in deciding *In re Arzberger*, which held that bacteria were not plants for the purposes of the 1930 Act. Or it may reflect the fact that prior to 1970 the Patent Office had issued patents for bacteria under §101.[9] In any event, absent some clear indication that Congress "focused on [the] issues . . . directly related to the one presently before the Court," *SEC v. Sloan*, 436 U.S. 103, 120-121 (1978), there is no basis for reading into its actions an intent to modify the plain meaning of the words found in §101.

## B

The petitioner's second argument is that micro-organisms cannot qualify as patentable subject matter until Congress expressly authorizes such protection. His position rests on the fact that genetic technology was unforeseen when Congress enacted §101. From this it is argued that resolution of the patentability of inventions such as respondent's should be left to Congress. The legislative process, the petitioner argues, is best equipped to weigh the competing economic, social, and scientific considerations involved, and to determine whether living organisms produced by genetic engineering should receive patent protection. In support of this position, the petitioner relies on our recent holding in *Parker v. Flook*, and the statement that the judiciary "must proceed cautiously when . . . asked to extend patent rights into areas wholly unforeseen by Congress." *Id.*, at 596.

It is, of course, correct that Congress, not the courts, must define the limits of patentability; but it is equally true that once Congress has spoken it is "the province and duty of the judicial department to say what the law is." *Marbury v. Madison*, 1 Cranch 137, 177 (1803). Congress has performed its constitutional role in defining patentable subject matter in §101; we perform ours in construing the language Congress has employed. In so doing, our obligation is to take statutes as we find them, guided, if ambiguity appears, by the legislative history and statutory purpose. Here, we perceive no ambiguity. The subject-matter provisions of the patent law have been cast in broad terms to fulfill the constitutional and statutory goal of promoting "the Progress of Science and the useful Arts" with all that means for the social and economic benefits envisioned by Jefferson.

---

9. In 1873, the Patent Office granted Louis Pasteur a patent on "yeast, free from organic germs of disease, as an article of manufacture." And in 1967 and 1968, immediately prior to the passage of the Plant Variety Protection Act, that Office granted two patents which, as the petitioner concedes, state claims for living micro-organisms. See Reply Brief for Petitioner 3, and n. 2.

Broad general language is not necessarily ambiguous when congressional objectives require broad terms.

Nothing in *Flook* is to the contrary. That case applied our prior precedents to determine that a "claim for an improved method of calculation, even when tied to a specific end use, is unpatentable subject matter under §101." 437 U.S., at 595, n. 18. The Court carefully scrutinized the claim at issue to determine whether it was precluded from patent protection under "the principles underlying the prohibition against patents for 'ideas' or phenomena of nature." *Id.*, at 593. We have done that here. *Flook* did not announce a new principle that inventions in areas not contemplated by Congress when the patent laws were enacted are unpatentable per se.

To read that concept into *Flook* would frustrate the purposes of the patent law. This Court frequently has observed that a statute is not to be confined to the "particular application[s]...contemplated by the legislators." *Barr v. United States*, 324 U.S. 83, 90 (1945). This is especially true in the field of patent law. A rule that unanticipated inventions are without protection would conflict with the core concept of the patent law that anticipation undermines patentability. *See Graham v. John Deere Co.*, 383 U.S., at 12-17. Mr. Justice Douglas reminded that the inventions most benefiting mankind are those that "push back the frontiers of chemistry, physics, and the like." *Great A. & P. Tea Co. v. Supermarket Corp.*, 340 U.S. 147, 154 (1950) (concurring opinion). Congress employed broad general language in drafting §101 precisely because such inventions are often unforeseeable.

To buttress his argument, the petitioner, with the support of *amicus*, points to grave risks that may be generated by research endeavors such as respondent's. The briefs present a gruesome parade of horribles. Scientists, among them Nobel laureates, are quoted suggesting that genetic research may pose a serious threat to the human race, or, at the very least, that the dangers are far too substantial to permit such research to proceed apace at this time. We are told that genetic research and related technological developments may spread pollution and disease, that it may result in a loss of genetic diversity, and that its practice may tend to depreciate the value of human life. These arguments are forcefully, even passionately, presented; they remind us that, at times, human ingenuity seems unable to control fully the forces it creates—that with Hamlet, it is sometimes better "to bear those ills we have than fly to others that we know not of."

It is argued that this Court should weigh these potential hazards in considering whether respondent's invention is patentable subject matter under §101. We disagree. The grant or denial of patents on micro-organisms is not likely to put an end to genetic research or to its attendant risks. The large amount of research that has already occurred when no researcher had sure knowledge that patent protection would be available suggests that legislative or judicial fiat as to patentability will not deter the scientific mind from probing into the unknown any more than Canute could command the tides. Whether respondent's claims are patentable may determine whether research efforts are accelerated by the hope of reward or slowed by want of incentives, but that is all.

What is more important is that we are without competence to entertain these arguments — either to brush them aside as fantasies generated by fear of the unknown, or to act on them. The choice we are urged to make is a matter of high policy for resolution within the legislative process after the kind of investigation, examination, and study that legislative bodies can provide and courts cannot. That process involves the balancing of competing values and interests, which in our democratic system is the business of elected representatives. Whatever their validity, the contentions now pressed on us should be addressed to the political branches of the Government, the Congress and the Executive, and not to the courts.

We have emphasized in the recent past that "[o]ur individual appraisal of the wisdom or unwisdom of a particular [legislative] course . . . is to be put aside in the process of interpreting a statute." *TVA v. Hill*, 437 U.S., at 194. Our task, rather, is the narrow one of determining what Congress meant by the words it used in the statute; once that is done our powers are exhausted. Congress is free to amend §101 so as to exclude from patent protection organisms produced by genetic engineering. Cf. 42 U.S.C. §2181(a), exempting from patent protection inventions "useful solely in the utilization of special nuclear material or atomic energy in an atomic weapon." Or it may choose to craft a statute specifically designed for such living things. But, until Congress takes such action, this Court must construe the language of §101 as it is. The language of that section fairly embraces respondent's invention.

Accordingly, the judgment of the Court of Customs and Patent Appeals is *AFFIRMED*.

Mr. Justice BRENNAN, with whom Mr. Justice WHITE, Mr. Justice MARSHALL, and Mr. Justice POWELL join, dissenting.

I agree with the Court that the question before us is a narrow one. Neither the future of scientific research, nor even, the ability of respondent Chakrabarty to reap some monopoly profits from his pioneering work, is at stake. Patents on the processes by which he has produced and employed the new living organism are not contested. The only question we need decide is whether Congress, exercising its authority under Art. I, §8, of the Constitution, intended that he be able to secure a monopoly on the living organism itself, no matter how produced or how used. Because I believe the Court has misread the applicable legislation, I dissent.

The patent laws attempt to reconcile this Nation's deep seated antipathy to monopolies with the need to encourage progress. *Deepsouth Packing Co. v. Laitram Corp.*, 406 U.S. 518, 530-531 (1972); *Graham v. John Deere Co.*, 383 U.S. 1, 7-10 (1966). Given the complexity and legislative nature of this delicate task, we must be careful to extend patent protection no further than Congress has provided. In particular, were there an absence of legislative direction, the courts should leave to Congress the decisions whether and how far to extend the patent privilege into areas where the common understanding has been that patents are not available.[1] Cf. *Deepsouth Packing Co. v. Laitram Corp.*, *supra*.

---

1. I read the Court to admit that the popular conception, even among advocates of agricultural patents, was that living organisms were unpatentable. See *ante*, n. 8 [and accompanying text].

In this case, however, we do not confront a complete legislative vacuum. The sweeping language of the Patent Act of 1793, as re-enacted in 1952, is not the last pronouncement Congress has made in this area. In 1930 Congress enacted the Plant Patent Act affording patent protection to developers of certain asexually reproduced plants. In 1970 Congress enacted the Plant Variety Protection Act to extend protection to certain new plant varieties capable of sexual reproduction. Thus, we are not dealing — as the Court would have it — with the routine problem of "unanticipated inventions." *Ante*. In these two Acts Congress has addressed the general problem of patenting animate inventions and has chosen carefully limited language granting protection to some kinds of discoveries, but specifically excluding others. These Acts strongly evidence a congressional limitation that excludes bacteria from patentability.[2]

First, the Acts evidence Congress' understanding, at least since 1930, that §101 does not include living organisms. If newly developed living organisms not naturally occurring had been patentable under §101, the plants included in the scope of the 1930 and 1970 Acts could have been patented without new legislation. Those plants, like the bacteria involved in this case, were new varieties not naturally occurring.[3] Although the Court, *ante*, rejects this line of argument, it does not explain why the Acts were necessary unless to correct a pre-existing situation.[4] I cannot share the Court's implicit assumption that Congress was engaged in either idle exercises or mere correction of the public record when it enacted the 1930 and 1970 Acts. And Congress certainly thought it was doing something significant. The Committee Reports contain expansive prose about the previously unavailable benefits to be derived from extending patent protection to plants.[5] H. R. Rep. No. 91-1605, pp. 1-3 (1970), U. S. Code Cong. & Admin. News 1970, p. 5082; S. Rep. No. 315, 71st Cong., 2d Sess., 1-3 (1930). Because Congress thought it had to legislate in order to make agricultural "human-made inventions" patentable and because the legisla-

2. But even if I agreed with the Court that the 1930 and 1970 Acts were not dispositive, I would dissent. This case presents even more cogent reasons than *Deepsouth Packing Co.* not to extend the patent monopoly in the face of uncertainty. At the very least, these Acts are signs of legislative attention to the problems of patenting living organisms, but they give no affirmative indication of congressional intent that bacteria be patentable. The caveat of *Parker v. Flook*, 437 U.S. 584, 596 (1978), an admonition to "proceed cautiously when we are asked to extend patent rights into areas wholly unforeseen by Congress," therefore becomes pertinent. I should think the necessity for caution is that much greater when we are asked to extend patent rights into areas Congress has foreseen and considered but has not resolved.

3. The Court refers to the logic employed by Congress in choosing not to perpetuate the "dichotomy" suggested by Secretary Hyde. Ante, at 2209. But by this logic the bacteria at issue here are distinguishable from a "mineral . . . created wholly by nature" in exactly the same way as were the new varieties of plants. If a new Act was needed to provide patent protection for the plants, it was equally necessary for bacteria. Yet Congress provided for patents on plants but not on these bacteria. In short, Congress decided to make only a subset of animate "human-made inventions," *ibid.*, patentable.

4. If the 1930 Act's only purpose were to solve the technical problem of description referred to by the Court, *ante*, at 2209, most of the Act, and in particular its limitation to asexually reproduced plants, would have been totally unnecessary.

5. Secretary Hyde's letter was not the only explicit indication in the legislative history of these Acts that Congress was acting on the assumption that legislation was necessary to make living organisms patentable. The Senate Judiciary Committee Report on the 1970

tion Congress enacted is limited, it follows that Congress never meant to make items outside the scope of the legislation patentable.

Second, the 1970 Act clearly indicates that Congress has included bacteria within the focus of its legislative concern, but not within the scope of patent protection. Congress specifically excluded bacteria from the coverage of the 1970 Act. 7 U.S.C. §2402(a). The Court's attempts to supply explanations for this explicit exclusion ring hollow. It is true that there is no mention in the legislative history of the exclusion, but that does not give us license to invent reasons. The fact is that Congress, assuming that animate objects as to which it had not specifically legislated could not be patented, excluded bacteria from the set of patentable organisms.

The Court protests that its holding today is dictated by the broad language of §101, which cannot "be confined to the 'particular application [s]...contemplated by the legislators.'" *Ante*, quoting *Barr v. United States*, 324 U.S. 83, 90 (1945). But as I have shown, the Court's decision does not follow the unavoidable implications of the statute. Rather, it extends the patent system to cover living material even though Congress plainly has legislated in the belief that §101 does not encompass living organisms. It is the role of Congress, not this Court, to broaden or narrow the reach of the patent laws. This is especially true where, as here, the composition sought to be patented uniquely implicates matters of public concern.

## Comments

1. **Chakrabarty *and the then Nascent Biotechnology Industry.*** In *Chakrabarty*, the Court held that a living, genetically altered microorganism constituted patentable subject matter. Such a modified microorganism, due to human intervention, was not a product of nature and fell within the broadly defined concepts of manufacture or composition of matter. This momentous decision was important for several reasons, namely it held that life can be patented and it gave a significant boost to the nascent biotechnology industry.

Despite *Chakrabarty's* significance, there were strong dissenting arguments that garnered four of the nine Justices. Perhaps the most persuasive argument from the dissent was essentially *expressio unius est exclusio alterius*, which is a canon of construction that holds "to express or include one thing implies the exclusion of the other." BLACK'S LAW

---

Act states the Committee's understanding that patent protection extended no further than the explicit provisions of these Acts:

> Under the patent law, patent protection is limited to those varieties of plants which reproduce asexually, that is, by such methods as grafting or budding. No protection is available to those varieties of plants which reproduce sexually, that is, generally by seeds. S. Rep. No. 91-1246, p. 3 (1970).

Similarly, Representative Poage, speaking for the 1970 Act, after noting the protection accorded asexually developed plants, stated that "for plants produced from seed, there has been no such protection." 116 Cong. Rec. 40295 (1970).

DICTIONARY (7th ed. 1999). The applicability of this doctrine to *Chakrabarty* was that living matter, namely plants in this instance, was not patentable until Congress enacted the 1930 and 1970 plant acts; and since Congress only spoke to plants, living matter other than plants, such as microorganisms, are not patentable. This argument was also made below, unsuccessfully.

According to recent empirical studies, the pharmaceutical and biotechnology industries rely heavily on the patent system. *See* Wesley M. Cohen et al., *Protecting Their Intellectual Assets: Appropriability Conditions and Why U.S. Manufacturing Firms Patent (or Not)*, (Nat'l Bureau of Econ. Research, Working Paper No. 7552, 2000). Research and development costs range from $100 to $500 million, depending on which study to read. Because of the high R&D costs, the issue for many commentators is not whether the patent system has a role to play in biotechnology, but where on the developmental continuum should patent law be inserted. That is, is patent policy best served by allowing patent protection on upstream biotech research (e.g., genes and proteins) or downstream research (e.g., marketable therapeutics).

2. ***Laws of Nature, Physical Phenomena, and Abstract Ideas Not Patentable.*** Despite noting that Congress, in enacting §101, "intended statutory subject matter to 'include anything under the sun that is made my man,'" the Court also stated there were limits on §101. For instance, §101 does not embrace "laws of nature, physical phenomena, and abstract ideas." Interestingly, unlike the European Patent Convention, which specifically sets out what is not available for patent protection, §101 is positive in its approach and leaves it to the common law to carve out exceptions.

So why is it that one may not patent a principle (e.g., $E=mc^2$), abstract ideas, or law or product of nature (e.g., law of gravity or a naturally occurring mineral or plant)? Public policy dictates that there are some things that are so fundamental to the advancement of technology that they must remain in the public domain. (Recall Samuel Morse's claim 8 in *O'Reilly v. Morse*, but also recall the Court struck it down based on lack of commensuration.) Also, laws or products of nature, for example, do not constitute a machine, composition of matter, or manufacture; that is, there is no invention or human intervention, only discovery. But isn't discovery a form of human intervention?

3. ***DNA, Proteins, and Notions of Purity and Isolation.*** If naturally occurring substances are not patentable, then how is it that firms obtain patents on DNA sequences (i.e., genes) and proteins? The answer is human intervention, which allows, for instance, one to claim a purified and isolated gene itself or claim the gene as part of a vector or transformed cell. In other words, a gene as it exists in the human body is not subject to patent protection, but a gene "isolated from its natural state and processed through purifying steps that separate the gene from other molecules naturally associated with it" is eligible for patent protection under §101.

But purified naturally occurring substances were not always patentable. *See, e.g., American Wood Paper Co. v. Fiber Disintegrating Co.*, 90 U.S. 566 (1874) (In response to the patentee's argument that the patented subject matter (i.e., cellulose) was purified, the Court stated, rather skeptically: "There are many things well known and valuable in medicine or in the arts which may be extracted from diverse substances. But extract is the same, no matter from what it has been taken....Whether a slight difference in the degree of purity of an article produced by several processes justifies denominating the products different manufactures, so that different patents may be obtained for each, may well be doubted, and it is not necessary to decide.").

As the chemical arts and the like progressed, however, the law began to evolve and became much more receptive to arguments based on human intervention and purification. Perhaps the most significant case in this regard, a case that has provided support for patenting purified DNA sequences and proteins, is *Parke-Davis & Co. v. H.K. Mulford & Co.*, 189 F.95 (S.D.N.Y. 1911). This case involved a patent on an adrenalin compound derived from the suprarenal glands of certain animals. It had been previously known that suprarenal glands in powdered form had "hemostatic, blood pressure raising and astringent properties," but could not be used for those purposes in its gross form. The patentee, Takamine, produced a substance possessing the desired characteristics in pure and stable form. Judge Learned Hand framed the issue as whether the new compound differed from the natural one in kind or merely in degree:

> [E]ven if it were merely an extracted product without change, there is no rule that such products are not patentable. Takamine was the first to make it available for any use by removing it from the other gland-tissue in which it was found, and, while it is of course possible logically to call this a purification of the principle, it became for every practical purpose a new thing commercially and therapeutically....Everyone, not already saturated with scholastic distinctions, would recognize that Takamine's crystals were not merely the old dried glands in a purer state, nor would his opinion change if he learned that the crystals were obtained from the glands by a process of eliminating the inactive organic substances. The line between different substances and degrees of the same substance is to be drawn rather from the common usages of men than from nice considerations of dialectic.

*Id.* at 103.

### COMPARATIVE PERSPECTIVE
### Patentable Subject Matter, Morality & Biotechnology in Europe

It is interesting to compare the approach of §101 under U.S. law with the provisions of the European Patent Convention (EPC). Section 101 defines subject matter eligibility positively, and leaves the exclusions to the common law, whereas the EPC itself sets forth both a positive and negative definition of patentable subject matter. For example, Article 52 of the EPC provides generally that patents "shall be granted for any inventions which are susceptible of industrial application." Article 57 provides that "an invention shall be considered as susceptible of industrial application if it can be made or used in any kind of industry, including agriculture." But the EPC goes on to specify several exceptions. For example, Article 52(2) excludes from patent protection: "(a) discoveries, scientific theories and mathematical methods; (b) aesthetic creations; (c) schemes, rules and methods for performing mental acts, playing games or doing business, and programs for computers; and (d) presentations of information" *but only* insofar as the patent "relates to such subject-matter or activities as such." Moreover, Article 53(a) excludes from patent protection "inventions the publication or exploitation of which would be contrary to '*ordre public*' or morality . . ." and 53(b) excludes "plant or animal varieties or essentially biological processes for the production of plants or animals," but notes that "this provision does not apply to microbiological processes or the products thereof."

In 1998, the European Parliament, concerned about the competitive threat of a robust American biotech industry, issued a biotechnology directive codifying patent protection for biotech-related inventions, including DNA sequences. *See* Directive 98/44/EC Legal Protection of Biotechnological Inventions. The directive was over 10 years in the making and has been, as of this writing, adopted by only a minority of European Community member states, despite a deadline of July 30, 2000. One of the principal points of contention among several countries (e.g., Netherlands) and political parties (e.g., the Green Party) in adopting the directive continues to be the patenting of DNA sequences, which is stridently opposed on grounds of public morality. In an attempt to address this concern, Article 6(1) of the directive states that inventions are "unpatentable where their commercial exploitation would be contrary to *ordre public* or morality." This section mirrors Article 53(a) of the European Patent Convention, which excludes from patent protection "inventions the publication or exploitation of which would be contrary to *ordre public* or morality."

The public morality argument is but a whisper in American patent law circles. But while this argument commands greater attention in Europe, it is interesting to note that prior to the biotech directive, the European Patent Office (EPO) issued (and continues to issue) patents on human DNA. For instance, in 1995, the EPO granted a patent on a DNA sequence encoding for a protein used during childbirth. Hormone Relaxin, 1995 O.J. E.P.O. 388 (Opp. Div.). The Opposition Division relied on the fact that the DNA sequence was "isolated from its surroundings." Perhaps the reason the biotech directive has been adamantly opposed is that directives are binding on member states in terms of results to be achieved.

Therefore, an EU directive would require every EC member state to recognize patents on DNA sequences. This controversy becomes clearer when the procedural mechanism of the EU and American patent systems are compared. Contrary to the American system, a patent granted by the EPO matures into individual national patents (as designated by the applicant), which are governed by their respective national laws. There is no such thing, in other words, as a European patent that is valid throughout the entire EU. Member states, which often have divergent interpretations of the EPC, retain jurisdiction over issues of infringement and scope of patent protection, thus increasing the likelihood of disparate enforcement. *See* EPC Articles 64 and 138. As such, a directive would lead to greater uniformity.

## 2. Software and Business Methods

### STATE STREET BANK AND TRUST CO. v. SIGNATURE FINANCIAL GROUP, INC.

149 F.3d 1368 (Fed. Cir. 1998).

RICH, Circuit Judge.

Signature Financial Group, Inc. (Signature) appeals from the decision of the United States District Court for the District of Massachusetts granting a motion for summary judgment in favor of State Street Bank & Trust Co. (State Street), finding U.S. Patent No. 5,193,056 (the '056 patent) invalid on the ground that the claimed subject matter is not encompassed by 35 U.S.C. §101 (1994). We reverse and remand because we conclude that the patent claims are directed to statutory subject matter.

#### BACKGROUND

Signature is the assignee of the '056 patent which is entitled "Data Processing System for Hub and Spoke Financial Services Configuration." The '056 patent issued to Signature on 9 March 1993, naming R. Todd Boes as the inventor. The '056 patent is generally directed to a data processing system (the system) for implementing an investment structure which was developed for use in Signature's business as an administrator and accounting agent for mutual funds. In essence, the system, identified by the proprietary name Hub and Spoke (R), facilitates a structure whereby mutual funds (Spokes) pool their assets in an investment portfolio (Hub) organized as a partnership. This investment configuration provides the administrator of a mutual fund with the advantageous combination of economies of scale in administering investments coupled with the tax advantages of a partnership.

State Street and Signature are both in the business of acting as custodians and accounting agents for multi-tiered partnership fund financial services. State Street negotiated with Signature for a license to use its patented data processing system described and claimed in the '056 patent. When negotiations broke down, State Street brought a declaratory judgment action asserting invalidity, unenforceability, and noninfringement in Massachusetts district court, and then filed a motion for partial summary judgment of patent invalidity for failure to claim statutory subject matter under §101. The motion was granted and this appeal followed.

#### DISCUSSION

On appeal, we are not bound to give deference to the district court's grant of summary judgment, but must make an independent determination that the standards for summary judgment have been met....

The following facts pertinent to the statutory subject matter issue are either undisputed or represent the version alleged by the nonmovant. *See Anderson v. Liberty Lobby, Inc.* The patented invention relates generally to a system that allows an administrator to monitor and record the financial information flow and make all calculations necessary for maintaining a partner fund financial services configuration. As previously mentioned, a partner fund financial services configuration essentially allows several mutual funds, or "Spokes," to pool their investment funds into a single portfolio, or "Hub," allowing for consolidation of, inter alia, the costs of administering the fund combined with the tax advantages of a partnership. In particular, this system provides means for a daily allocation of assets for two or more Spokes that are invested in the same Hub. The system determines the percentage share that each Spoke maintains in the Hub, while taking into consideration daily changes both in the value of the Hub's investment securities and in the concomitant amount of each Spoke's assets.

In determining daily changes, the system also allows for the allocation among the Spokes of the Hub's daily income, expenses, and net realized and unrealized gain or loss, calculating each day's total investments based on the concept of a book capital account. This enables the determination of a true asset value of each Spoke and accurate calculation of allocation ratios between or among the Spokes. The system additionally tracks all the relevant data determined on a daily basis for the Hub and each Spoke, so that aggregate year end income, expenses, and capital gain or loss can be determined for accounting and for tax purposes for the Hub and, as a result, for each publicly traded Spoke.

It is essential that these calculations are quickly and accurately performed. In large part this is required because each Spoke sells shares to the public and the price of those shares is substantially based on the Spoke's percentage interest in the portfolio. In some instances, a mutual fund administrator is required to calculate the value of the shares to the nearest penny within as little as an hour and a half after the market closes. Given the complexity of the calculations, a computer or equivalent device is a virtual necessity to perform the task.

The '056 patent application was filed 11 March 1991. It initially contained six "machine" claims, which incorporated means-plus-function clauses, and six method claims. According to Signature, during prosecution the examiner contemplated a §101 rejection for failure to claim statutory subject matter. However, upon cancellation of the six method claims, the examiner issued a notice of allowance for the remaining present six claims on appeal. Only claim 1 is an independent claim.

The district court began its analysis by construing the claims to be directed to a process, with each "means" clause merely representing a step in that process. However, "machine" claims having "means" clauses may only be reasonably viewed as process claims if there is no supporting structure in the written description that corresponds to the claimed "means" elements. *See In re Alappat.* This is not the case now before us.

When independent claim 1 is properly construed in accordance with §112, ¶6, it is directed to a machine, as demonstrated below, where representative claim 1 is set forth, the subject matter in brackets stating the structure the written description discloses as corresponding to the respective "means" recited in the claims.

  1. A data processing system for managing a financial services configuration of a portfolio established as a partnership, each partner being one of a plurality of funds, comprising:

  (a) computer processor means [a personal computer including a CPU] for processing data;

  (b) storage means [a data disk] for storing data on a storage medium;

  (c) first means [an arithmetic logic circuit configured to prepare the data disk to magnetically store selected data] for initializing the storage medium;

  (d) second means [an arithmetic logic circuit configured to retrieve information from a specific file, calculate incremental increases or decreases based on specific input, allocate the results on a percentage basis, and store the output in a separate file] for processing data regarding assets in the portfolio and each of the funds from a previous day and data regarding increases or decreases in each of the funds, [sic, funds'] assets and for allocating the percentage share that each fund holds in the portfolio;

  (e) third means [an arithmetic logic circuit configured to retrieve information from a specific file, calculate incremental increases and decreases based on specific input, allocate the results on a percentage basis and store the output in a separate file] for processing data regarding daily incremental income, expenses, and net realized gain or loss for the portfolio and for allocating such data among each fund;

  (f) fourth means [an arithmetic logic circuit configured to retrieve information from a specific file, calculate incremental increases and decreases based on specific input, allocate the results on a percentage basis and store the output in a separate file] for processing data regarding daily net unrealized gain or loss for the portfolio and for allocating such data among each fund; and

  (g) fifth means [an arithmetic logic circuit configured to retrieve information from specific files, calculate that information on an aggregate basis and store the output in a separate file] for processing data regarding aggregate year-end income, expenses, and capital gain or loss for the portfolio and each of the funds.

Each claim component, recited as a "means" plus its function, is to be read, of course, pursuant to §112, ¶6, as inclusive of the "equivalents" of the structures disclosed in the written description portion of the specification. Thus, claim 1, properly construed, claims a machine, namely, a data processing system for managing a financial services configuration of a portfolio established as a partnership, which machine is made up of, at the very least, the specific structures disclosed in the written description and corresponding to the means-plus-function elements (a)-(g) recited in the claim. A "machine" is proper statutory subject matter under §101. We note that, for the purposes of a §101 analysis, it is of little relevance whether claim 1 is directed to a "machine" or a "process," as long as it falls within at least one of the four enumerated categories of patentable subject matter, "machine" and "process" being such categories.

This does not end our analysis, however, because the court concluded that the claimed subject matter fell into one of two alternative judicially-created exceptions to statutory subject matter. The court refers to the first exception as the "mathematical algorithm" exception and the second exception as the "business method" exception. . . .

The plain and unambiguous meaning of §101 is that any invention falling within one of the four stated categories of statutory subject matter may be patented, provided it meets the other requirements for patentability set forth in Title 35, i.e., those found in §§102, 103, and 112, ¶2.

The repetitive use of the expansive term "any" in §101 shows Congress's intent not to place any restrictions on the subject matter for which a patent may be obtained beyond those specifically recited in §101. Indeed, the Supreme Court has acknowledged that Congress intended §101 to extend to "anything under the sun that is made by man." *Diamond v. Chakrabarty*, 447 U.S. 303, 309 (1980). Thus, it is improper to read limitations into §101 on the subject matter that may be patented where the legislative history indicates that Congress clearly did not intend such limitations. *See Chakrabarty*, 447 U.S. at 308 ("We have also cautioned that courts 'should not read into the patent laws limitations and conditions which the legislature has not expressed.'" (citations omitted)).

### The "Mathematical Algorithm" Exception

The Supreme Court has identified three categories of subject matter that are unpatentable, namely "laws of nature, natural phenomena, and abstract ideas." *Diamond v. Diehr*, 450 U.S. 175, 185 (1981). Of particular relevance to this case, the Court has held that mathematical algorithms are not patentable subject matter to the extent that they are merely abstract ideas. *See Diehr*; *Parker v. Flook*; *Gottschalk v. Benson*. In *Diehr*, the Court explained that certain types of mathematical subject matter, standing alone, represent nothing more than abstract ideas until reduced to some type of practical application, i.e., "a useful, concrete and tangible result." *In re Alappat*, 33 F.3d at 1544.

Unpatentable mathematical algorithms are identifiable by showing they are merely abstract ideas constituting disembodied concepts or truths that are not "useful." From a practical standpoint, this means that to be patentable an algorithm must be applied in a "useful" way. In *Alappat*, we held that data, transformed by a machine through a series of mathematical calculations to produce a smooth waveform display on a rasterizer monitor, constituted a practical application of an abstract idea (a mathematical algorithm, formula, or calculation), because it produced "a useful, concrete and tangible result" — the smooth waveform.

Similarly, in *Arrhythmia Research Technology Inc. v. Corazonix Corp.*, we held that the transformation of electrocardiograph signals from a patient's heartbeat by a machine through a series of mathematical calculations constituted a practical application of an abstract idea (a mathematical algorithm, formula, or calculation), because it corresponded to a useful, concrete or tangible thing — the condition of a patient's heart.

Today, we hold that the transformation of data, representing discrete dollar amounts, by a machine through a series of mathematical calculations into a final share price, constitutes a practical application of a mathematical algorithm, formula, or calculation, because it produces "a useful, con-

crete and tangible result"—a final share price momentarily fixed for recording and reporting purposes and even accepted and relied upon by regulatory authorities and in subsequent trades.

The district court erred by applying the *Freeman-Walter-Abele* test to determine whether the claimed subject matter was an unpatentable abstract idea. The *Freeman-Walter-Abele* test was designed by the Court of Customs and Patent Appeals, and subsequently adopted by this court, to extract and identify unpatentable mathematical algorithms in the aftermath of *Benson* and *Flook*. *See In re Freeman* as modified by *In re Walter*. The test has been thus articulated:

> First, the claim is analyzed to determine whether a mathematical algorithm is directly or indirectly recited. Next, if a mathematical algorithm is found, the claim as a whole is further analyzed to determine whether the algorithm is "applied in any manner to physical elements or process steps," and, if it is, it "passes muster under §101."

*In re Pardo*, 684 F.2d 912, 915 (CCPA 1982).

After *Diehr* and *Chakrabarty*, the *Freeman-Walter-Abele* test has little, if any, applicability to determining the presence of statutory subject matter. As we pointed out in *Alappat*, application of the test could be misleading, because a process, machine, manufacture, or composition of matter employing a law of nature, natural phenomenon, or abstract idea is patentable subject matter even though a law of nature, natural phenomenon, or abstract idea would not, by itself, be entitled to such protection. The test determines the presence of, for example, an algorithm. Under *Benson*, this may have been a sufficient indicium of nonstatutory subject matter. However, after *Diehr* and *Alappat*, the mere fact that a claimed invention involves inputting numbers, calculating numbers, outputting numbers, and storing numbers, in and of itself, would not render it nonstatutory subject matter, unless, of course, its operation does not produce a "useful, concrete and tangible result." *Alappat*, 33 F.3d at 1544. After all, as we have repeatedly stated,

> every step-by-step process, be it electronic or chemical or mechanical, involves an algorithm in the broad sense of the term. Since §101 expressly includes processes as a category of inventions which may be patented and §100(b) further defines the word "process" as meaning "process, art or method, and includes a new use of a known process, machine, manufacture, composition of matter, or material," it follows that it is no ground for holding a claim is directed to nonstatutory subject matter to say it includes or is directed to an algorithm. This is why the proscription against patenting has been limited to mathematical algorithms. . . .

*In re Iwahashi*, 888 F.2d 1370, 1374 (Fed. Cir. 1989).

The question of whether a claim encompasses statutory subject matter should not focus on which of the four categories of subject matter a claim is directed to[9]—process, machine, manufacture, or composition of matter—but rather on the essential characteristics of the subject matter, in parti-

---

9. Of course, the subject matter must fall into at least one category of statutory subject matter.

cular, its practical utility. Section 101 specifies that statutory subject matter must also satisfy the other "conditions and requirements" of Title 35, including novelty, nonobviousness, and adequacy of disclosure and notice. *See In re Warmerdam*. For purpose of our analysis, as noted above, claim 1 is directed to a machine programmed with the Hub and Spoke software and admittedly produces a "useful, concrete, and tangible result." This renders it statutory subject matter, even if the useful result is expressed in numbers, such as price, profit, percentage, cost, or loss.

### THE BUSINESS METHOD EXCEPTION

As an alternative ground for invalidating the '056 patent under §101, the court relied on the judicially-created, so-called "business method" exception to statutory subject matter. We take this opportunity to lay this ill-conceived exception to rest. Since its inception, the "business method" exception has merely represented the application of some general, but no longer applicable legal principle, perhaps arising out of the "requirement for invention" — which was eliminated by §103. Since the 1952 Patent Act, business methods have been, and should have been, subject to the same legal requirements for patentability as applied to any other process or method.

The business method exception has never been invoked by this court, or the CCPA, to deem an invention unpatentable. Application of this particular exception has always been preceded by a ruling based on some clearer concept of Title 35 or, more commonly, application of the abstract idea exception based on finding a mathematical algorithm. Illustrative is the CCPA's analysis in *In re Howard*, wherein the court affirmed the Board of Appeals' rejection of the claims for lack of novelty and found it unnecessary to reach the Board's section 101 ground that a method of doing business is "inherently unpatentable." 394 F.2d at 872.

Similarly, *In re Schrader*, while making reference to the business method exception, turned on the fact that the claims implicitly recited an abstract idea in the form of a mathematical algorithm and there was no "transformation or conversion of subject matter representative of or constituting physical activity or objects." 22 F.3d at 294.

State Street argues that we acknowledged the validity of the business method exception in *Alappat* when we discussed *Maucorps* and *Meyer*:

> *Maucorps* dealt with a business methodology for deciding how salesmen should best handle respective customers and *Meyer* involved a "system" for aiding a neurologist in diagnosing patients. Clearly, neither of the alleged "inventions" in those cases falls within any §101 category.

*Alappat*, 33 F.3d at 1541. However, closer scrutiny of these cases reveals that the claimed inventions in both *Maucorps* and *Meyer* were rejected as abstract ideas under the mathematical algorithm exception, not the business method exception.

Even the case frequently cited as establishing the business method exception to statutory subject matter, *Hotel Security Checking Co. v. Lorraine Co.*, did not rely on the exception to strike the patent. In that case, the patent was found invalid for lack of novelty and "invention," not because it was improper subject matter for a patent. The court stated "the fundamental principle of the system is as old as the art of bookkeeping, i.e., charging the goods of the employer to the agent who takes them." 160 F. at 469. "If at the time of [the patent] application, there had been no system of bookkeeping of any kind in restaurants, we would be confronted with the question whether a new and useful system of cash registering and account checking is such an art as is patentable under the statute." *Id.* at 472.

This case is no exception. The district court announced the precepts of the business method exception as set forth in several treatises, but noted as its primary reason for finding the patent invalid under the business method exception as follows:

> If Signature's invention were patentable, any financial institution desirous of implementing a multi-tiered funding complex modelled [sic] on a Hub and Spoke configuration would be required to seek Signature's permission before embarking on such a project. This is so because the '056 Patent is claimed [sic] sufficiently broadly to foreclose virtually any computer-implemented accounting method necessary to manage this type of financial structure.

927 F. Supp. 502, 516. Whether the patent's claims are too broad to be patentable is not to be judged under §101, but rather under §§102, 103 and 112. Assuming the above statement to be correct, it has nothing to do with whether what is claimed is statutory subject matter.

## Comments

1. ***Software as "Useful, Concrete, and Tangible."*** The *State Street Bank* decision noted that the *Freeman-Walter-Abele* test "has been the source of much confusion" and "has little, if any, applicability to determining the presence of statutory subject matter." According to the court, "the mere fact that a claimed invention involves inputting numbers, calculating numbers, outputting numbers, and storing numbers, in and of itself," would not render it nonstatutory subject matter, unless, of course, its operation does not produce a "useful, concrete and tangible result." 149 F.3d at 1374. Although software patents are firmly established in the United States, and have been for some time, some economists have cast doubt on the need for software patents or, worse, have suggested they are harmful to software innovation. *See, e.g,* James Bessen & Robert M. Hunt, *An Empirical Look at Software Patents* (Federal Reserve Bank of Philadelphia, Working Paper 03-17, 2003).

2. ***Business Method Patents.*** The *State Street Bank* court expressly endorsed the patentability of business methods, and did away with the so-called business exception, an "ill-conceived exception," according to the court. Since *State Street* the PTO has been inundated with business method patent applications, creating concern among some commentators that the PTO is ill-equipped to handle this increased work load. A high-profile example of a controversial business method patent is Amazon.com's patent on its "one-click" ordering method. *See* U.S. Patent No. 5,960,411. Amazon.com successfully obtained a preliminary injunction against Barnes & Noble just before the December holiday season. Although the district court's decision was subsequently vacated

by the Federal Circuit due to the patent's questionable validity, the injunction enabled Amazon.com to obtain a competitive advantage over a key competitor at a crucial time of the year. Other noteworthy business method patents are Priceline.com's "reverse auction" patent (U.S. Patent No. 5,794,207), and Doubleclick's patent on Internet advertisements (U.S. Patent No. 5,948,061).

Several scholars have argued that opening up patent protection to business methods will lead to inefficiencies in business operations and the issuance of more invalid patents. But other commentators have argued that the criticism of business method patents lacks empirical support, which has led to unwelcome results.

### COMPARATIVE PERSPECTIVE
### Software and Business Method Patents in Europe

Section 52(2)(c) of the European Patent Convention (EPC) expressly excludes from patent protection methods for "doing business and programs for computers." Article 52(3) states:

> The provisions of paragraph 2 shall exclude patentability of the subject-matter or activities referred to in that provision only to the extent to which a European patent application or European patent relates to such subject-matter or activities as such.

While the European Patent Office (EPO) has remained largely faithful to the business method exclusion, it has essentially disregarded the software exception. In fact, it is not uncommon for the EPO to issue software patents as long as the invention possesses a "technical character." *See* EPO Guidelines for Substantive Examination, Part 3, Chapter IV, §§2.1, 2.2. *See also* Computer Program Product/IBM, T 1173/97-3.5.1 (EPO Bd. of App. July 1, 1998). For instance, 6,856 applications in the "computing" field were filed in 2002, more than double the amount in 1998 (3,306), and more than the number of applications in the fields of biochemistry/genetic engineering, which had 4,427 applications in 2002. EPO 2002 ANNUAL REPORT, (Business Report, Figure 11).

---

While it is clear that the EPO issues patents on software-related inventions, despite Article 52's apparent prohibition, there remains a degree of uncertainty due to the lack of a European-wide patent. In other words, there is disparate treatment of software-related patents among the EU member states. Thus, much like the biotechnology industry, the software industry wants to enhance certainty for software patents throughout Europe. To this end, the European Parliament considered a directive on European software patents in 2005, but rejected it overwhelmingly. In a study commissioned by the Parliament, the authors wrote that "conclusive evidence supporting a liberalization of existing European patent law and practice in respect of software..., on the basis of U.S. experience, does not exist." BNA Patent, Trademark & Copyright Law Daily (September 26, 2003).

On the business method front, the EPO has been much more stingy with patents. *See, e.g.,* Pension Benefit Systems Partnership/T 0931/97 (Sept. 8, 2000), which involved a computer-implemented business method. The EPO held that "methods only involving economic concepts and practices of doing business are not inventions" because they lack a "technical contribution." Thus, the EPO refused to be influenced by *State Street Bank* and distinguished the present case from *Computer Program Product.*

## Note on Design Patents

A design patent protects the ornamental features (e.g., shape or configuration) as embodied in or applied to a utilitarian or functional article. The design must be new, original, and ornamental. *See* 35 U.S.C. §§171-173. A design patent application has only one claim, which refers to the drawings. Design patents differ from utility patents in that the latter protects the functional features of the claimed article, the way it is used and how it works whereas a design patent simply covers the way in which the article looks. A single article can be subject to both a utility and design patent. For instance, the PTO recently issued design patent No. 500,000 in December, 2004 on a design of an automobile body. (Certainly, the automobile itself has several features eligible for utility patent protection.) Note on the cover page shown below that the letter "D" precedes the patent number to indicate the patent is a design patent. The claim of the design patent reads: "An ornamental design for an automobile body, as shown and described."

There is a two-part test for determining design patent infringement: (1) construction of the patent claim, and (2) comparison of the construed claim to the accused product. Construing the scope of a design patent claim encompasses "its visual appearance as a whole," *Elmer v. ICC Fabricating, Inc.,* 67 F.3d 1571, 1577, (Fed. Cir. 1995). and in particular "the visual impression it creates." *See Durling v. Spectrum Furniture Co.,* 101 F.3d 100, 104-105, (Fed. Cir. 1996). The comparison of the construed claim to the accused product involves two separate tests that must both be satisfied. First is the "ordinary observer" test, and second, the "point of novelty" test. *See Unidynamics Corp. v. Automatic Prods. Int'l, Ltd.,* 157 F.3d 1311, 1323 (Fed. Cir. 1998). Regarding the "ordinary observer" test, the Supreme Court stated:

> if, in the eye of an ordinary observer, giving such attention as a purchaser usually gives, two designs are substantially the same, if the resemblance is such as to deceive such an observer, inducing him to purchase one supposing it to be the other, the first one patented is infringed by the other.

81 U.S. (14 Wall.) 511, 528 (1871). The "point of novelty" test demands proof that the "accused design appropriates the novelty which distinguishes the patented design from the prior art." *Litton Sys., Inc. v. Whirlpool Corp.,* 728 F.2d 1423, 1444 (Fed. Cir. 1984). The Federal Circuit stated that application of the "point of novelty" and "ordinary observer" tests "some-

(12) **United States Design Patent** (10) Patent No.: **US D500,000 S**
Dyson et al. (45) Date of Patent: ** **Dec. 21, 2004**

(54) **AUTOMOBILE BODY**

(75) Inventors: **Andrew P Dyson**, West Bloomfield, MI
(US); **Joseph S Dehner**, Bloomfield,
MI (US); **David C McKinnon**,
Bloomfield, MI (US); **Glenn W Abbott**,
West Bloomfield, MI (US)

(73) Assignee: **DaimlerChrysler Corporation**, Auburn
Hills, MI (US)

(**) Term: **14 Years**

(21) Appl. No.: **29/201,094**

(22) Filed: **Mar. 10, 2004**

(51) LOC (7) Cl. ........................... **12-08**
(52) U.S. Cl. ........................... **D12/92**
(58) Field of Search ............... D12/90–92, 86;
D21/424, 433; 296/185

(56) **References Cited**

U.S. PATENT DOCUMENTS

D406,328 S * 4/1999 Ayoub et al. ........... D12/92
D465,436 S * 11/2002 Dehner et al. .......... D12/92
D476,601 S * 7/2003 Stoddard et al. ......... D12/92
D477,253 S * 7/2003 Mizuni et al. .......... D12/92
D483,606 S * 12/2003 Howell et al. .......... D12/92

* cited by examiner

Primary Examiner—Melody N. Brown
(74) Attorney, Agent, or Firm—Ralph E. Smith

(57) **CLAIM**

The ornamental design for an automobile body, as shown
and described.

**DESCRIPTION**

FIG. 1 is a front perspective view of an automobile body
showing our new design;
FIG. 2 is a side view thereof;
FIG. 3 is a rear perspective view thereof;
FIG. 4 is a front view thereof;
FIG. 5 is a rear view thereof;
FIG. 6 is a front perspective view of an automobile body
showing a second embodiment of our new design;
FIG. 7 is a side view of FIG. 6;
FIG. 8 is a rear perspective view of FIG. 6;
FIG. 9 is a front view of FIG. 6; and,
FIG. 10 is a rear view of FIG. 6.
It will be understood that the dashed lines presented in the
drawings are for illustration only, and do not form a part of
the claimed design.

**1 Claim, 8 Drawing Sheets**

times lead to the same result." See *Shelcore, Inc. v. Durham Indus., Inc.*, 745
F.2d 621, 628 n. 16 (Fed. Cir. 1984).

Filings of design patents have increased substantially over the past 20 years.
In 1980, for instance, 7,830 applications were filed with 3,949 issuing. And in
2003, 22,602 were filed with 16,574 issuing. See *http://www.uspto.gov/*. This
increase reflects the commercial value of many designs. Indeed, the Federal
Circuit recently upheld a $813,000 verdict in favor of a design patent holder.
See *Junker v. Eddings*, 396 F.3d 1359 (Fed. Cir. 2005).

## Note on Plant Patents

Plant patents have become extremely important to the agricultural/bio-
tech industry. Proprietary protection for commercially valuable plants is
potentially available under three statutory schemes: (1) Plant Patent Act
(35 U.S.C. §§161-164); (2) Plant Variety Protection Act (7 U.S.C.
§§2321 *et seq.*); and (3) the utility patent statute (35 U.S.C. §101).

*The Plant Patent Act of 1930*

Recall in *Diamond v. Chakrabarty*, the Court noted that prior to 1930
patent protection was thought not to be available for plants because of

"the belief that plants, even those artificially bred, were products of nature" and that they "were not amenable to the 'written description' requirement" of §112. Opening up patent law to plants was, as early as the late nineteenth century, thought to be desirable. In fact, plant patent legislation was proposed in 1892, *see Imazio Nursey, Inc. v. Dania Greenhouses*, 69 F.3d 1560, 1562-1563 (Fed. Cir. 1995), and was supported by prominent inventors such as Thomas Edison, who had argued "[n]othing that Congress could do to help farming would be of greater value and permanence than to give the plant breeder the same status as the mechanical and chemical inventors now have through the law." S. Rep. No. 315, 71st Cong., 2d Sess. 3 (1930) (Senate Report).

It wasn't until 1930, however, that Congress addressed these obstacles to plant patent protection by enacting the Plant Patent Act, which allows patent protection to "[w]hoever invents or discovers and asexually reproduces any distinct and new variety of plant, including cultivated sports, mutants, hybrids, and newly found seedlings, other than a tuber propagated plant or a plant found in an uncultivated state...." 35 U.S.C. §161. Section 162 addresses the disclosure issue by providing that "[n]o plant patent shall be declared invalid for noncompliance with section 112 ...if the description is as complete as is reasonably possible." And §163 gives the patent owner the "right to exclude others from asexually reproducing the plant, and from using, offering for sale, or selling the plant so reproduced, or any of its parts, throughout the United States, or from importing the plant so reproduced, or any parts thereof, into the United States."

Section 161 is limited to "asexually" reproduced plant varieties. Asexual reproduction means that the reproduction is done in a manner other than from seeds, such as by budding or grafting. Importantly, §161 excludes from patent protection "a plant found in an uncultivated state," a plant found in nature so to speak. A variety is a subdivision of a species. For example, the grape varietals Cabernet Sauvignon or Chardonnay (for wine) and Emperor or Perlette (for table grapes) are subdivisions of the grape species *Vitis vinifera*, which in turn, is from the *Vitis* genus. Lastly, §161 excludes from patent protection uncultivated plants. The Senate and House Committee Reports on the 1930 Act stressed that the Act did not include within its scope "varieties of plants which exists in an uncultivated or wild state, but are newly found by plant explorers or others." S. Rep., *supra*; H.R. Rep. 1129, 71st Cong., 2d Sess. (1930).

### The Plant Variety Protection Act of 1970

The Plant Variety Protection Act (PVPA) was enacted by Congress in 1970 and recognizes the ability of plant breeders to produce seeds expressing stable genetic characteristics. In other words, it offers patent-like protection to *sexually* reproduced plants by authorizing the issuance of certificates of plant variety protection. The PVPA was thought to be necessary because it did not make economic sense to asexually reproduce major cash crops such as soybeans and cotton. *See* S. Rep. No. 91-1246 (Oct. 2, 1970) and H.R. No. 91-1605 (Oct. 13, 1970) ("[n]o protection is available to those varieties of plants which reproduce sexually, that is, generally, by seeds. Thus, patent protection is not available with respect to new varieties of most of the economically important agricultural crops such as cotton or soybeans."). Unlike the Plant Patent Act, which is administered by the PTO, the PVPA is administered by the Department of Agriculture. *See* 7 U.S.C. §§2321 *et seq.* Congress subsequently amended the PVPA in order to conform to international plant patent law and to facilitate U.S. entry into the International Union for the Protection of New Varieties of Plants (UPOV).

The certification standards of the PVPA are less rigorous than the standards for utility, design, and plant patents. The variety must merely be a "novel variety." There is no required standard of non-obviousness, and the disclosure requirements are not as demanding. But the PVPA contains a research exemption and a save-seed exemption (or "crop exemption"), which allows farmers to save seed from a previous crop for replanting on their own holdings or for noncommercial and private purposes. 7 U.S.C. §2543. But, since 1994, PVPA certificate holders can preclude the sale of seed for reproductive purposes (known as "brown bag sales"). Also, it is quite common for major PVPA certificate holders to ask farmers to contractually waive the statutory save-seed exemption. These contracts would usually state that the farmer/buyer could use the seed "only for a single season." This type of agreement has been upheld by the Federal Circuit. *See Monsanto v. McFarling*, 302 F.3d 1291, 1298-1299 (Fed. Cir. 2002) (holding that contract does not violate antitrust laws or patent exhaustion/first sale doctrines). The use of these types of contracts has irritated farmers. *See* N.Y. Times, A-14 (Nov. 2, 2003) (responding to patent owners' enforcement of its single-season contracts, one farmer stated: "It's a God-given right that farmers were given when they were born to save these seeds. All we are is farmers trying to scrape a living out of this dirt.").

As agriculture-biotechnology became increasingly lucrative, it became apparent that the PVPA did not offer adequate protection vis-à-vis the Patent Act. It also became apparent that a utility patent for plants was desirable because Title 35 does not have a save-seed exemption and there is no research exemption. *See, e.g., Ex parte Hibberd*, 227 U.S.P.Q. 443 (Bd. Pat. App. & Int'l. 1985) (holding utility patent protection available for plant tissue, cells, seeds, or whole plants). The Supreme Court, in what was a wholehearted endorsement of *Chakrabarty's* broad reading of §101, held that utility patents are available for plants, and that the Plant Patent Act and PVPA were not the only means for protecting plant varieties. *See J.E.M. AG Supply, Inc. v. Pioneer Hi-Bred Int'l, Inc.*, 534 U.S. 124 (2001). The percentage of issuances per filings has gone up considerably in the wake of *Pioneer Hi-Bred.* For instance, in 1999, there were 863 filings and 420 issuances (49 percent); in 2000, 797 filings and 548 issuances (69 percent); in 2001, 944 filings and 584 issuances (62 percent). But in 2002, there were 1,144 filings with 1,133 issuances (99 percent); and in 2003, 1,000 filings and 994 issuances (99 percent). *See http://www.uspto.gov/.* These high percentages reflect the generous subject matter requirements of §101.

# CHAPTER

# 11

# Enforcing Patent Rights

## INTRODUCTION

A patent is enforceable from the date it issues[1] and is presumed valid under 35 U.S.C. §282. A party challenging the validity of a patent, therefore, has the burden of proving invalidity by clear and convincing evidence. Patent law is exclusively federal; thus, a patentee may only enforce his patent rights by filing a patent infringement suit in federal district court. Patent litigation has become increasingly more costly. One survey showed that for litigation with less than $1 million at risk, litigation fees from initiation of the lawsuit through appeal were $500,000; with $1 to $25 million at risk, the fees rose to just over $2 million; and when more than $25 million was at stake, litigation expenses approached $4 million.[2] Moreover, recent scholarship has shown that patent litigation has risen dramatically over the past 20 years,[3] with patents in some industries much more likely to be litigated than in other industries.[4]

All appeals relating to patent law are heard by the United States Court of Appeals for the Federal Circuit. The Federal Circuit was created by Congress in 1982 as the thirteenth federal court of appeals.[5] (*See http:// www.fedcir.gov/.*) The creation of the court has been called "perhaps the

---

1. But for applications filed on or after November 29, 2000, the patent applicant enjoys provisional rights beginning on the date the application is published and ending on the date the patent issues. Recovering damages during the provisional period depends on the patent application ultimately issuing.

2. AIPLA Report of the Economic Survey 21-2 (2003).

3. *See* Jean O. Lanjouw & Mark Schankerman, *Protecting Intellectual Property Rights: Are Small Firms Handicapped?*, 47 J.L. & ECON. 45 (2004) (noting an "almost 10-fold" increase in patent litigation over the past two decades).

4. *See* John R. Allison, Mark A. Lemley, Kimberly A. Moore & R. Derek Trunkey, *Valuable Patents*, 92 GEO. L.J. 435, 471-475 (2004) (finding "patents on medical devices, computer-related inventions, software, electronics, and mechanics are significantly more likely to be litigated than the average of all patents. By contrast, chemistry, automotive, and semiconductor patents are significantly less likely to be litigated"). *See also* Josh Lerner, *Patenting in the Shadow of Competitors*, 38 J.L. & ECON. 463 (1995) (finding biotechnology patents more likely to be litigated).

5. *See* Federal Courts Improvement Act of 1982, P.l. 97-164, 96 Stat. 25 (April 2, 1982). This Act merged the Court of Claims, which had seven judges, and the Court of Customs and Patent Appeals, which had five judges. The Federal Circuit came into existence on October 1, 1982. For a discussion of the history of the court's creation, *see* THE UNITED STATES COURT OF APPEALS FOR THE FEDERAL CIRCUIT: A HISTORY (1991).

single most significant institutional innovation in the field of intellectual property in the last quarter-century."[6] Prior to the court's creation in 1982, patent appeals were heard by the regional circuit courts of appeal, much like they hear copyright and trademark cases today. The Federal Circuit court was created primarily in response to a lack of uniformity in the application of our patent laws and a high invalidity rate among litigated patents, particularly in certain circuits, which in turn led to excessive forum shopping. Unlike the regional circuit courts, the Federal Circuit, which is located in Washington, D.C., has unlimited geographic jurisdiction nationwide with limited subject matter jurisdiction. As such, the court enjoys exclusive jurisdiction over cases arising "under any Act of Congress relating to patents," as well as over cases involving several other areas of the law. *See* 28 U.S.C. §§1295, 1338.[7] The Federal Circuit has profoundly affected patent law. The court ushered in a new approach to subject matter eligibility, patent validity and defenses to infringement, and is widely viewed as the "supreme court" of patent law.

In a patent infringement suit, a patentee asserts that the patent *claims* are infringed, not the commercial embodiment of the claimed invention or what is set forth in the specification. Patent claims are the touchstone of patent protection, and it is the claims that set forth the patentee's proprietary boundaries. Thus, a crucial and oftentimes determinative aspect of patent litigation is determining what the claims mean. The process whereby the courts determine the precise meaning of patent claim language is called *claim construction* or *claim interpretation*. Construing the claims is always the first step in an infringement (and validity) analysis. The second step is determining whether the accused product infringes the patent claim(s) at issue. Of course, with the exception of preliminary injunctions, appropriate remedies are ascertained only upon a finding of infringement.

The causes of action for patent infringement can be divided into two broad categories: (1) *direct infringement*; and (2) *indirect infringement.* Under the theory of direct infringement, the patentee may bring an action against a defendant who himself is committing acts (e.g., making a product or practicing a process) that infringe one or more patent claims. Direct patent infringement comprises both (1) *literal* infringement; and (2) infringement under the *doctrine of equivalents* (or DOE). Literal infringement of a patent is straightforward and occurs when every limitation recited in the claim is found in the accused device. Recall the chair example in the introductory section to the previous chapter, but replace Inventor 2 with Competitor who instead of filing a patent application on an improvement, makes and uses a competing chair having a seat portion, a back portion, and four legs. Competitor literally infringes Inventor's patent claim because Competitor practices each and every limitation set forth in Inventor's claim. Sometimes patent professionals would say that Inventor's claim "reads on" Competitor's product.

---

6. William M. Landes & Richard A. Posner, THE ECONOMIC STRUCTURE OF INTELLECTUAL PROPERTY LAW 7 (2003).
7. The Federal Circuit has subject matter jurisdiction over appeals from the Court of International Trade, U.S. Court of Veterans Appeals, the Merit Systems Protection Board, the PTO, the Court of Federal Claims, Boards of Contract Appeal, and the International Trade Commission. But the driving force behind its creation was patent law, and the court devotes a majority of its time to patent law matters.

The doctrine of equivalents is a common law doctrine that comes into play when there is no literal infringement. The DOE allows for a finding of infringement when an accused infringing device (or process) is an "equivalent" to that claimed in the patent. Returning to the chair example, let's say Inventor still claims a chair having a seat portion, a back portion, and four legs. But now Competitor makes a chair having a seat portion, a back portion, and *three* legs. There is no literal infringement because Competitor's product does not have each and every limitation of Inventor's claim, but Competitor may still infringe under the DOE if it is determined that three legs are equivalent to four legs. How that determination is made and the analytical structure of the DOE are explored in Section B, below.

There are two important limitations on the DOE, namely *prosecution history estoppel* (PHE) and the *public dedication* rule. The PHE precludes a patent owner in an infringement proceeding from obtaining a claim scope that would in effect resurrect subject matter surrendered (through, for example, amendment or cancellation) during the prosecution of the patent application before the PTO. For instance, during prosecution Inventor initially claims three legs as part of his invention. The patent examiner rejects the application because there is prior art that discloses a chair having three legs. In response, Inventor amends the claim by deleting "three legs" and adding "four legs." The patent issues. When Inventor tries to enforce his patent, Competitor can invoke the doctrine of prosecution history estoppel and argue, correctly, that Inventor surrendered "three legs" to obtain a patent and, therefore, the DOE cannot extend the claim scope to capture three legs.

The public dedication rule holds that subject disclosed in the specification but not claimed is dedicated to the public domain. So, Inventor claims a chair having a seat portion, a back portion, and four legs, but the specification expressly refers both to a chair having three legs and a chair having four legs. The public dedication rule can be used by Competitor during litigation to argue that Inventor dedicated "three legs" to the public domain because Inventor, while expressly disclosing three legs in the specification, only claimed four legs.

The DOE is controversial because its application leads to less certainty, an important ingredient to any property-rights regime. The PHE and the public dedication rule, which are also controversial, impose constraints on the DOE's reach. A significant portion of this chapter is devoted to exploring these three doctrines.

### COMPARATIVE PERSPECTIVE
### Enforcing Patent Rights in Developing Countries

As discussed in the trademark and copyright chapters, the issue of counterfeit goods and enforcement of IP rights in developing countries are real concerns for high-end fashion designers and the entertainment and software industries. Patent law has its own concerns. One way to address enforcement issues in developing countries is to require them to provide a minimum level of protection for innovations and an enforcement structure. Indeed, these were the principal goals of TRIPs (Trade Related Aspects of Intellectual Property Rights), the international IP treaty that required signatory countries to enact minimum levels of IP protection. In return for offering minimum IP protection, developing countries were given the prospect of receptive developed markets for their domestically produced goods such as textiles and agricultural products. Whether this tradeoff has been beneficial for the developing world is a subject of debate. *See* Keith E. Maskus, INTELLECTUAL PROPERTY RIGHTS IN THE GLOBAL ECONOMY (2000) (economic analysis of TRIPs on various national countries).

Among developing countries, China is the one most frequently mentioned in the press as a violator of U.S. IP law. Yet Chinese companies have engaged in aggressive patenting over the past five years and venture capital is on the rise in China. Of course, protecting and enforcing IP is much more complex than simply enacting a law; there are multilayered cultural considerations that must also be addressed. And, as some commentators have pointed out, the United States has its own history of "piracy." *See* Doren Ben-Atar, TRADE SECRETS: INTELLECTUAL PROPERTY AND THE ORIGINS OF AMERICAN INDUSTRIAL POWER (2004).

## HOWARD FRENCH, WHOSE PATENT IS IT, ANYWAY?

### New York Times, Saturday March 5, 2005, p. B1 columns 1-3

For Western companies competing with China as well as those doing business here . . . [i]n one sector after another, companies warn that China's swift industrial rise is being greased by brazen and increasingly sophisticated theft of intellectual property. . . .

[T]he counterfeit activity has been moving relentlessly upscale, with General Motors, Sony and Pfizer, just to name the most high-profile companies, complaining that their designs or formulas for everything from cars and PlayStations to routers and Viagra, have been violated.

"Until recently, when China began putting intellectual property laws in place, for the past 40 years, all patents were owned by the government, and could be shared by any company that was willing to use them," said Paul Gao, a Shanghai-based expert on consumer electronics. . . . "The Chinese government actually encouraged this, and that has left a deep impression on companies that intellectual property is there fore anyone to use it."

\*\*\*

[M]any Chinese legal experts simply deny there is any special problem with theft of intellectual property in China. "It may look like it's a China problem, but it's a worldwide problem, just like piracy on the Internet, and it exists in America as well," said Zhang Ping, a law professor at Beijing University, and one of China's leading experts on intellectual property rights. "There are many problems with fake products, with low levels of technology. These can't be counted as intellectual property violations. They are just cheap fakes."

Like many people professionally involved with this issue here, Ms. Zhang denied that China was a leading violator of intellectual property rights, which she acknowledged was still a relatively new concept in China. She also said that the country's efforts at improving enforcement, though steady, would require more time to reach the standards of intellectual property rights in many advanced industrialized countries.

Lawyers who represent Western companies embroiled in intellectual property disputes in China, however, point to many loopholes in Chinese law.... Many Chinese patents, for example, are granted without any examination of their originality, making it easy for local companies to claim others' innovations as their own.

\*\*\*

One of the most problematic areas, experts say, are joint ventures between foreign and Chinese companies, which are legion. When the joint venture dissolves, or sometimes even while it remains active, the Chinese party makes use of the technology or manufacturing processes illegally. A perennially told war story in business circles here involves the foreign factory owner who makes a wrong turn while driving to his plant only to discover an exact copy of his factory on the other side of the mountain.

Although this story might be apocryphal, Mr. [Xiang] Wang, [a Chinese IP lawyer], said he saw cases all the time that are not so different in their details. "We have a client in the power business who found that one of his key employees had quit and joined a competitor, revealing confidential information to him straight away, and filing patents of these materials which were literal copies of the original technology," he said. "When our client warned he would sue over patent infringement, the Chinese company said it was also planning to sue. 'And by the way,' they asked, 'what patent are you talking about? This is our patent now.'"

*STATUTE:* **Contents and Term of Patent; Provisional Rights**
35 U.S.C. §154

*STATUTE:* **Infringement of Patent**
35 U.S.C. §271

## A. CLAIM INTERPRETATION

Two of the most important tenets of claim interpretation are: (1) there is a strong presumption that claim language is to be given its ordinary meaning as understood by persons having ordinary skill in the art at the time of invention; and (2) claims are *not* to be construed by reference to the accused device; rather, claims are to be interpreted in the context of the entire patent, namely the specification, prosecution history, and other claims. *See Phillips v. AWH Corp.*, 415 F.3d 1303 (Fed. Cir. 2005) (en banc). But this second tenet is restrained by two complimentary caveats, both of which flow from the fundamental principle that it is the function and purpose of claims, not the specification itself, to delimit the right to exclude.

The two caveats are: First, it is improper to import (i.e., "read in") into the claim a limitation from the specification's general discussion, embodiments, and examples. Second, it is improper to eliminate or ignore (i.e., "read out") a claim limitation in order to extend a patent to subject matter disclosed, but not claimed. In other words, all claim limitations are material. There is sometimes a fine line between reading a claim in light of the specification, and reading a limitation into the claim from the specification. For example, if Inventor claims a box comprising upper and lower members that open and close relative to each other. The specification discloses that the members could be made of corrugated cardboard or plastic. Although claims are to be read in view of the specification, it may be improper for a court to define "member" as being made of corrugated cardboard or plastic for purposes of validity and infringement.

In addition to these tenets, there are two fundamental process questions relating to claim interpretation: (1) who interprets the claim language; and (2) what are the "proper" tools of claim interpretation.

The Supreme Court has held that it is the responsibility of the court (i.e., the judge), as opposed to the jury, to interpret claim language. The rationale underlying this decision is twofold. First, judges are better able than juries at interpreting text. Second, having a judge interpret claim language facilitates uniformity based on the principle of *stare decisis* on issues not yet subject to the Federal Circuit's jurisdiction. *See Markman v. Westview Instruments, Inc.*, 517 U.S. 370, 388-389 (1996). This decision has prompted several district court judges to hold so-called *Markman* hearings, a minitrial to determine the meaning of the claim language at issue. Moreover, *Markman* has led several district courts, such as the Northern District of California, to adopt special local rules for patent cases and *Markman* hearings, which, in effect, impose more detailed pleading and disclosure rules than are generally mandated by the Federal Rules of Civil Procedure. Also worth noting is that claim interpretation is a question of law, reviewed de novo by the Federal Circuit.

The question of what interpretive aides a court may use to determine claim meaning has proven to be one of the more controversial in modern patent law. The oft-cited cases of *Vitronics Corp. v. Conceptronics, Inc.*, 90 F.3d 1576, 1581-1583 (Fed. Cir. 1996), and *Phillips v. AWH Corp.*, 415 F.3d 1303 (Fed. Cir. 2005) (en banc), distinguish between *intrinsic* and *extrinsic* evidence and set forth an interpretive road map. The intrinsic record is comprised of the claims, specification, and the prosecution history, which is a complete record of the proceedings before the PTO. The intrinsic record must be consulted first, beginning with the claims themselves, then the specification, which acts as a guide to the meaning of the claim language; and lastly, the prosecution history, which may have express representations regarding claim meaning. The extrinsic record, which primarily comprises expert testimony, should only be used if the intrinsic record is ambiguous. The rationale for this interpretive road map is that the intrinsic evidence is part of the public record, and therefore, serves the public notice function of the patent system. Competitors, for instance, who are thinking of designing around the claimed invention can review the intrinsic record and act accordingly. The extrinsic evidence, while it may be useful in helping the judge to understand the technology, should not be used to alter or change the public record because the extrinsic evidence used at trial was presumably not available to the defendant/competitor at the time of the alleged infringement.

Other types of interpretative evidence that are somewhere between traditional intrinsic and extrinsic evidence are dictionaries, encyclopedias, and technical treatises. The Federal Circuit views these sources as unbiased reflections of common understanding not influenced by expert testimony. The court went so far as to state these materials may be the most meaningful sources of information to aid judges in better understanding both the technology and the terminology used by those skilled in the art. But as with expert testimony, the dictionary cannot be used to contradict the clear meaning of the intrinsic record.

### POLICY PERSPECTIVE
### Claim Construction Methodology

One of the most important questions in patent law is what interpretive methodology should a court adopt in construing claims. On the one hand, a methodology that is wedded to the intrinsic evidence has several virtues. For instance, it relies on publicly available information, which may lend itself to more predictability and is consistent with the important notice function of the claim. Moreover, a strict textual approach forces patent attorneys and agents to be more careful in drafting patent applications. Lastly, *Vitronics'* concerns about expert testimony are certainly legitimate. The patentee's and defendant's well-trained, technical experts, who are not part of the public record, will almost invariably provide the court and jury with divergent testimony relating to identical claim language. On the other hand, an interpretive approach that is more receptive to context outside of the express text may more accurately reflect how a person having ordinary skill in the art would understand the claim language. Everyone agrees that claims are to be construed through the eyes of the skilled artisan. Such an approach is also more sensitive to technological custom and linguistic meaning — so-called "facts on the ground." This tenet makes sense because patents are technical documents written largely to a technical audience. District court judges rarely have the requisite technical training or background to fully comprehend, for example, biotechnological or computer-related principles. As such, there may be a concern about judicial presumptions regarding the meaning of technological descriptions without the aid of technical experts, particularly when words of degree (e.g., "substantial" or "about") are used. This approach would also most likely lead to greater deference to district court judges, and therefore, instill greater certainty earlier in the litigation process.

# B. LITERAL INFRINGEMENT

Literal infringement of a patent is straightforward and occurs when every limitation recited in the claim is found in the accused device. There are far fewer literal infringement cases than DOE cases because the former usually has greater certainty of outcome resulting in more settlement/licensing opportunities.

## TRANSMATIC, INC. v. GULTON INDUSTRIES, INC.

### 53 F.3d 1270 (Fed. Cir. 1995)

Gulton Industries, Inc. appeals from the court's April 8, 1994 order holding Gulton liable for infringement of claim 1 of the '415 patent under the doctrine of equivalents. Transmatic cross-appeals from the court's March 31, 1993 order granting partial summary judgment of no literal infringement. We reverse the finding of no literal infringement. . . .

### BACKGROUND

Transmatic owns the '415 patent directed to a cornice lighting fixture for public transit vehicles, such as buses. This type of lighting fixture is capable of supporting and illuminating an advertising card, while also illuminating the interior of the transit vehicle.

Claim 1, the sole claim at issue, reads as follows:

1. A cornice lighting fixture for public transit vehicles, the lighting fixture comprising: a unitary member made as a pultrusion from resin and glass fibers so as to have an elongated shape with a uniform cross section along the length thereof, said unitary member including *a light housing that defines one longitudinal margin of the fixture* and a trim panel that extends vertically and horizontally from the light housing to define another longitudinal margin of the fixture. . . .

(emphasis added). Transmatic's device was the first cornice lighting fixture to be made by "pultrusion," a technique for making glass-reinforced plastics whereby continuous bundles of glass fibers are impregnated with a liquid resin, then passed through a high temperature oven. The invention achieved considerable success, garnering a 90% share of the front-lighted bus fixture market before Gulton introduced its competing device.

[The cover page of the patent with abstract and drawing are shown in Figure 1]:

## Figure 1. Sample U.S. patent cover page.

**United States Patent** [19]

Domas

[11]   **4,387,415**

[45]   **Jun. 7, 1983**

[54]   **CORNICE LIGHTING FIXTURE**

[75]   Inventor:   **Ben V. Domas, Lake Orion, Mich.**

[73]   Assignee:   **Transmatic, Inc., Waterford, Mich.**

[21]   Appl. No.:   **209,448**

[22]   Filed:   **Nov. 24, 1980**

**Related U.S. Application Data**

[63]   Continuation of Ser. No. 34,301, Apr. 30, 1979, abandoned.

[51]   Int. Cl.³ ............................................. **B60Q 1/00**
[52]   U.S. Cl. ..................................... **362/74; 362/151**
[58]   Field of Search ..................... 362/74, 147, 151;
427/389.8, 407.3; 428/268

[56]   **References Cited**

**U.S. PATENT DOCUMENTS**

| | | | |
|---|---|---|---|
| 2,650,184 | 8/1953 | Biefeld | 427/407.3 |
| 2,948,950 | 8/1960 | Finger | 428/268 |
| 3,210,875 | 10/1965 | Schwenkler | 362/74 |
| 4,157,584 | 6/1979 | Bhatt | 362/74 |

*Primary Examiner*—Donald P. Walsh
*Attorney, Agent, or Firm*—Reising, Ethington, Barnard, Perry, Brooks & Milton

[57]   **ABSTRACT**

A cornice lighting fixture (10) disclosed is designed for use on public transit vehicles (12) and includes a unitary member (20) defining a light housing (22) and a trim panel (24) that extends horizontally and vertically from the light housing. A light cover (28) encloses a fluorescent tube (26) mounted within the housing by an electrical connector support (84). The unitary member defining the housing and trim panel is preferably made as a pultrusion from resin and glass fibers so as to have an elongated shape of a uniform cross-section with the light housing defining an upper and inward longitudinal margin of the fixture and with an outer mounting flange (70) of the trim panel defining a lower and outward longitudinal margin of the fixture. Upon mounting of the fixture, the housing and the trim panel cooperate to partially define an air duct (30) for carrying heated or cooled air. A horizontal wall (44) of the housing has an inward securement formation (50, 52) that receives an upper edge (54) of the light cover while a vertical wall (60) of the housing extends downwardly from the horizontal wall thereof for connection to the trim panel at which connection a cover mounting flange (62) extends inwardly to secure a lower edge (64) of the light cover. The trim panel has a curved shape that is concave with respect to the interior of the vehicle and also has upper and lower tabs (32, 34) for mounting an advertising sign thereon so that light shining through the cover illuminates the sign from its front side.

**6 Claims, 3 Drawing Figures**

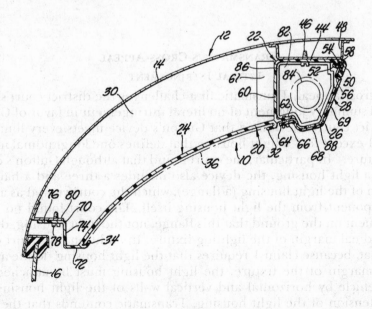

Gulton's product is also a single-piece (unitary) cornice lighting fixture made as a pultrusion from resin and glass fibers. Structurally, it is essentially the same as the preferred embodiment of Transmatic's device disclosed in the '415 patent, except that the light housing in Gulton's device includes an approximately three and a half inch extension or flange [see Figure 2 and arrow pointing to flange]. The flange extends the light housing to a point beyond a light cover associated with the light housing. Although Gulton's own design drawings had labeled the flange as part of the light housing, Gulton characterized the flange during litigation as a component separate and distinct from the light housing itself. This distinction is the basis for the infringement decisions. A cross-sectional view of the accused product is shown below, with the key portion [the flange] of the device indicated by an arrow:

**Figure 2. Gultons Accused Product.**

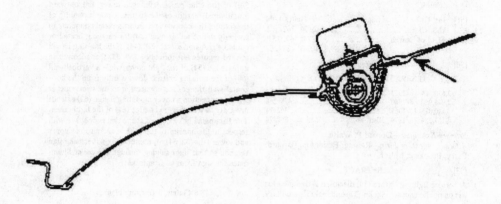

**TRANSMATIC'S CROSS-APPEAL**

**LITERAL INFRINGEMENT**

In its cross-appeal, Transmatic first challenges the district court's grant of partial summary judgment of no literal infringement in favor of Gulton. The district court determined that Gulton's device meets every limitation of claim 1 except for "a light housing that defines one longitudinal margin of the fixture." In particular, the court found that although Gulton's device includes a light housing, the device also includes a three and a half inch extension of the light housing (a flange), which the court viewed as a separate component from the light housing itself. The court found no literal infringement on the ground that this flange, not the light housing, defines a longitudinal margin of the lighting fixture. In addition, the court determined that, because claim 1 requires that the light housing define a longitudinal margin of the fixture, the light housing must be attached to a transit vehicle by horizontal and vertical walls of the light housing, not by an extension of the light housing. Transmatic contends that the court erred in its claim interpretation and thus improperly granted summary judgment for Gulton. Had the court properly construed claim 1, Transmatic argues, it would have determined that the claim literally covers the accused device. We agree.

Determining whether a patent claim is infringed requires a two-step analysis: "First, the claim must be properly construed to determine its scope and meaning. Second, the claim as properly construed must be compared to the accused device or process." *Carroll Touch, Inc. v. Electro Mechanical Sys.*, 15 F.3d 1573, 1576 (Fed. Cir. 1993). Literal infringement requires that the accused device include every limitation of the patent claim. *Mannesmann Demag Corp. v. Engineered Metal Prod. Co.*, 793 F.2d 1279, 1282 (Fed. Cir. 1986).

We find two basic errors in the court's infringement analysis. First, the court erred in interpreting the claim term "light housing" as limited to a structure having an upper, horizontal wall that does not extend beyond a light cover associated with the light housing. While the preferred embodiment disclosed in the patent has this configuration, a patent claim is not necessarily limited to a preferred embodiment disclosed in the patent.

Here, the patentee clearly did not intend to limit the definition of "light housing" in claim 1 in the manner suggested by the district court. The record does not support the court's claim interpretation. Although claim 3 requires that the light housing have "a horizontal wall with an inward securement formation and also having a vertical wall extending downwardly from the outward extremity of the horizontal wall," claim 1 contains no such structural limitations. Consistent with the claim differentiation doctrine, the term "light housing" in claim 1 is broader in scope than in claim 3 and the other dependent claims. *See D.M.I., Inc. v. Deere & Co.*, 755 F.2d 1570, 1574 (Fed. Cir. 1985) ("Where some claims are broad and others narrow, the narrow claim limitations cannot be read into the broad...."). Thus, the court erred by reading unnecessary structural limitations into claim 1.

Second, the district court erred by importing unnecessary functional limitations into the claim. The court limited claim 1 to a lighting fixture configured to be attached to a vehicle by horizontal and vertical walls; however, the claim contains no limitations concerning how the device may be attached to a vehicle. The court also considered significant the apparently different air flow characteristics of the patented and accused devices. Again, this consideration was irrelevant because the claim contains no limitations regarding air flow. While differences in the way the patented invention and accused device function certainly are relevant to a doctrine of equivalents analysis, these considerations are not legally relevant to whether Gulton's device falls within the *literal* language of the asserted claim.

Without these extraneous structural and functional limitations, claim 1 reads directly on Gulton's device. We are persuaded that the flange in Gulton's device is simply an extension of the light housing and thus part of it. Gulton's own design drawings labeled the flange as part of the light housing. Gulton's recharacterization of its light housing as being comprised of two separate components, light housing and flange, appears to be a litigation-induced interpretation to avoid infringement. Further, the light housing (with flange) clearly defines a longitudinal margin of the lighting fixture. Gulton's device therefore includes "a light housing that defines one longitudinal margin of the fixture." As this is the only claim limitation in dispute, we conclude that no reasonable fact-finder could conclude that Gulton's product does not meet each and every limitation of claim 1 of the '415 patent. . . . We therefore reverse the court's finding of no literal infringement.

[The court, ruling in favor of Gulton on the DOE issue, vacated the district court's finding of infringement under the DOE.]

## Comments

1. *That Which Infringes if Later Will Anticipate if Earlier.* Literal infringement is analogous to anticipation. Recall from Chapter 10, that to anticipate a patent, a prior art reference must disclose each and every claim limitation. In an infringement context, however, it is the accused device, not a prior art reference, that must embody each and every claim limitation. Thus, the fundamental patent law maxim: "that which infringes, if later, would anticipate, if earlier."

Importantly, an accused product that has each and every limitation of the claim in question will still infringe even if the accused product has additional elements associated with it. For example, patentee claims A, B, and C. Competitor infringes if his accused device has A, B, C, and D. The presence of D does not allow Competitor to escape literal infringement because the accused product has A, B, and C.

2. *Claim Differentiation Doctrine.* The doctrine of claim differentiation states that limitations of one claim cannot be read into another claim. For example, the limitations stated in dependent claims should not be read into an independent claim from which they depend. In other words, words used in separate claims are presumed to indicate that the claims have different meanings and scope. *See Karlin Tech., Inc. v. Surgical Dynamics, Inc.*, 177 F.3d 968, 971-972 (Fed. Cir. 1999).

## C. DOCTRINE OF EQUIVALENTS

The introductory text to this chapter discussed the two types of direct infringement: literal infringement and infringement under the doctrine of equivalents (DOE). This section is devoted to the latter. Unlike literal infringement, the DOE is controversial and thorny, and thus deserving of more attention. What makes the DOE controversial is its inherent tension with patent law's clear claiming requirement (*see* §112, ¶2) and the importance of certainty in a property rights regime. Indeed, on the one hand, it is frequently quite difficult to discern *ex ante* what is or is not an "equivalent." As such, a degree of uncertainty hangs over the patentee's competitors and their decision-making process regarding investment in the manufacture or sale of competing products. On the other hand, strict and literal adherence to the written claim in determining the scope of protection can invite unfair subversion of a valuable right, which would substantially diminish the economic value of patents.

In recent years, the Federal Circuit has erred on the side of certainty and clear claiming, which has invited numerous challenges to the DOE, two of which made their way to the United States Supreme Court. The DOE survived these challenges, although, as explored in Section D, *infra*, the reach of the doctrine has been curtailed. The following two cases nicely capture the arguments for and against the DOE.

## GRAVER TANK v. LINDE AIR PRODS. CO.
### 339 U.S. 605 (1950)

Mr. Justice JACKSON delivered the opinion of the Court.

[Linde Air Products Co. owned a patent for certain electric welding compositions known as fluxes, which facilitated the fusing of metals. Two sets of claims were involved. One set of claims described a major element as any "silicate." The other set of claims, which were narrower, described the element as any "alkaline earth metal silicate." The Supreme Court held the first set of claims invalid for undue breadth. The narrower claims were held not invalid and the question became whether these claims were infringed.]

\*\*\*

At the outset it should be noted that the single issue before us is whether the trial court's holding that the four flux claims have been infringed will be sustained. Any issue as to the validity of these claims was unanimously determined by the previous decision in this Court and attack on their validity cannot be renewed now by reason of limitation on grant of rehearing. The disclosure, the claims, and the prior art have been adequately described in our former opinion and in the opinions of the courts below.

In determining whether an accused device or composition infringes a valid patent, resort must be had in the first instance to the words of the claim. If accused matter falls clearly within the claim, infringement is made out and that is the end of it.

But courts have also recognized that to permit imitation of a patented invention which does not copy every literal detail would be to convert the protection of the patent grant into a hollow and useless thing. Such a limitation would leave room for — indeed encourage — the unscrupulous copyist to make unimportant and insubstantial changes and substitutions in the patent which, though adding nothing, would be enough to take the copied matter outside the claim, and hence outside the reach of law. One who seeks to pirate an invention, like one who seeks to pirate a copyrighted book or play, may be expected to introduce minor variations to conceal and shelter the piracy. Outright and forthright duplication is a dull and very rare type of infringement. To prohibit no other would place the inventor at the mercy of verbalism and would be subordinating substance to form. It would deprive him of the benefit of his invention and would foster concealment rather than disclosure of inventions, which is one of the primary purposes of the patent system.

The doctrine of equivalents evolved in response to this experience. The essence of the doctrine is that one may not practice a fraud on a patent. Originating almost a century ago in the case of *Winans v. Denmead*, it has been consistently applied by this Court and the lower federal courts, and continues today ready and available for utilization when the proper circumstances for its application arise. "To temper unsparing logic and prevent an infringer from stealing the benefit of the invention" a patentee may invoke this doctrine to proceed against the producer of a device "if it performs substantially the same function in substantially the same way to obtain the same result." *Sanitary Refrigerator Co. v. Winters*, 280 U.S. 30, 42. The theory on which it is founded is that "if two devices do the same work in substantially the same way, and accomplish substantially the same result, they are the same, even though they differ in name, form or shape." *Union Paper — Bag Machine Co. v. Murphy*, 97 U.S. 120, 125. The doctrine operates not only in favor of the patentee of a pioneer or primary invention, but also for the patentee of a secondary invention consisting of a combination of old ingredients which produce new and useful results, although the area of equivalence may vary under the circumstances. *See Continental Paper Bag Co. v. Eastern Paper Bag Co.*, and cases cited; *Seymour v. Osborne*; *Gould v. Rees*. The wholesome realism of this doctrine is not always applied in favor of a patentee but is sometimes used against him. Thus, where a device is so far changed in principle from a patented article that it performs the same or a similar function in a substantially different way, but nevertheless falls within the literal words of the claim, the doctrine of equivalents may be used to restrict the claim and defeat the patentee's action for infringement. *Westinghouse v. Boyden Power — Brake Co.* In its early development, the doctrine was usually applied in cases involving devices where there was equivalence in mechanical components. Subsequently, however, the same principles were also applied to compositions, where there was equivalence between chemical ingredients. Today the doctrine is applied to mechanical or chemical equivalents in compositions or devices.

What constitutes equivalency must be determined against the context of the patent, the prior art, and the particular circumstances of the case. Equivalence, in the patent law, is not the prisoner of a formula and is not an absolute to be considered in a vacuum. It does not require complete identity for every purpose and in every respect. In determining equivalents, things equal to the same thing may not be equal to each other and, by the same token, things for most purposes different may sometimes be equivalents. Consideration must be given to the purpose for which an ingredient is used in a patent, the qualities it has when combined with the other ingredients, and the function which it is intended to perform. An important factor is whether persons reasonably skilled in the art would have known of the interchangeability of an ingredient not contained in the patent with one that was.

A finding of equivalence is a determination of fact. Proof can be made in any form: through testimony of experts or others versed in the technology; by documents, including texts and treatises; and, of course, by the disclosures of the prior art. Like any other issue of fact, final determination requires a balancing of credibility, persuasiveness and weight of evidence. It is to be decided by the trial court and that court's decision, under general principles of appellate review, should not be disturbed unless clearly erroneous. Particularly is this so in a field where so much depends upon familiarity with specific scientific problems and principles not usually contained in the general storehouse of knowledge and experience.

In the case before us, we have two electric welding compositions or fluxes: the patented composition, Unionmelt Grade 20, and the accused composition, Lincolnweld 660. The patent under which Unionmelt is made claims essentially a combination of alkaline earth metal silicate and calcium fluoride; Unionmelt actually contains, however, silicates of calcium and magnesium, two alkaline earth metal silicates. Lincolnweld's composition is similar to Unionmelt's, except that it substitutes silicates of calcium and manganese — the latter not an alkaline earth metal — for silicates of calcium and magnesium. In all other respects, the two compositions are alike. The mechanical methods in which these compositions are employed are similar. They are identical in operation and produce the same kind and quality of weld.

The question which thus emerges is whether the substitution of the manganese which is not an alkaline earth metal for the magnesium which is, under the circumstances of this case, and in view of the technology and the prior art, is a change of such substance as to make the doctrine of equivalents inapplicable; or conversely, whether under the circumstances the change was so insubstantial that the trial court's invocation of the doctrine of equivalents was justified.

Without attempting to be all-inclusive, we note the following evidence in the record: Chemists familiar with the two fluxes testified that manganese and magnesium were similar in many of their reactions (R. 287, 669). There is testimony by a metallurgist that alkaline earth metals are often found in manganese ores in their natural state and that they serve the same purpose in the fluxes (R. 831-832); and a chemist testified that "in the sense of the patent" manganese could be included as an alkaline earth metal (R. 297). Much of this testimony was corroborated by reference to recognized texts on inorganic chemistry (R. 332). Particularly important, in addition, were the disclosures of the prior art, also contained in the record. The Miller patent, No. 1,754,566, which preceded the patent in suit, taught the use of manganese silicate in welding fluxes (R. 969, 971). Manganese was similarly disclosed in the Armor patent, No. 1,467,825, which also described a welding composition (R. 1346). And the record contains no evidence of any kind to show that Lincolnweld was developed as the result of independent research or experiments.

It is not for this Court to even essay an independent evaluation of this evidence. This is the function of the trial court. And, as we have heretofore observed, "To no type of case is this . . . more appropriately applicable than to the one before us, where the evidence is largely the testimony of experts as to which a trial court may be enlightened by scientific demonstrations. This trial occupied some three weeks, during which, as the record shows, the trial judge visited laboratories with counsel and experts to observe actual demonstrations of welding as taught by the patent and of the welding accused of infringing it, and of various stages of the prior art. He viewed motion pictures of various welding operations and tests and heard many experts and other witnesses."

The trial judge found on the evidence before him that the Lincolnweld flux and the composition of the patent in suit are substantially identical in operation and in result. He found also that Lincolnweld is in all respects equivalent to Unionmelt for welding purposes. And he concluded that "for all practical purposes, manganese silicate can be efficiently and effectively substituted for calcium and magnesium silicates as the major constituent of the welding composition." These conclusions are adequately supported by the record; certainly they are not clearly erroneous.

It is difficult to conceive of a case more appropriate for application of the doctrine of equivalents. The disclosures of the prior art made clear that manganese silicate was a useful ingredient in welding compositions. Specialists familiar with the problems of welding compositions understood that manganese was equivalent to and could be substituted for magnesium in the composition of the patented flux and their observations were confirmed by the literature of chemistry. Without some explanation or indication that Lincolnweld was developed by independent research, the trial court could properly infer that the accused flux is the result of imitation rather than experimentation or invention. Though infringement was not literal, the changes which avoid literal infringement are colorable only. We conclude that the trial court's judgment of infringement respecting the four flux claims was proper, and we adhere to our prior decision on this aspect of the case.

Mr. Justice BLACK, with whom Mr. Justice DOUGLAS concurs, dissenting.

I heartily agree with the Court that "fraud" is bad, "piracy" is evil, and "stealing" is reprehensible. But in this case, where petitioners are not charged with any such malevolence, these lofty principles do not justify the Court's sterilization of Acts of Congress and prior decisions, none of which are even mentioned in today's opinion.

R.S. §4888 [now 35 U.S.C. §112, ¶2] provides that an applicant "shall particularly point out and distinctly claim the part, improvement, or combination which he claims as his invention or discovery." We have held in this very case that this statute precludes invoking the specifications to alter a claim free from ambiguous language, since "it is the claim which measures the grant to the patentee." *Graver Mfg. Co. v. Linde Co.*, 336 U.S. 271, 277. What is not specifically claimed is dedicated to the public. *See, e.g., Miller v. Brass Co.* For the function of claims under R.S. §4888, as we have frequently reiterated, is to exclude from the patent monopoly field all that is not specifically claimed, whatever may appear in the specifications. *See, e.g., Marconi Wireless Co. v. United States*, and cases there cited. Today the Court tacitly rejects those cases. It departs from the underlying principle which, as the Court pointed out in *White v. Dunbar*, forbids treating a patent claim "like a nose of wax, which may be turned and twisted in any direction, by merely referring to the specification, so as to make it include something more than, or something different from, what its words express. . . . The claim is a statutory requirement, prescribed for the very purpose of making the patentee define precisely what his invention is; and it is unjust to the public, as well as an evasion of the law, to construe it in a manner different from the plain import of its terms." Giving this patentee the benefit of a grant that it did not precisely claim is no less "unjust to the public" and no less an evasion of R.S. §4888 merely because done in the name of the "doctrine of equivalents."

In seeking to justify its emasculation of R.S. §4888 by parading potential hardships which literal enforcement might conceivably impose on patentees who had for some reason failed to claim complete protection for their discoveries, the Court fails even to mention the program for alleviation of such hardships which Congress itself has provided. 35 U.S.C. §64 [now 35 U.S.C. §251] authorizes reissue of patents. . . . * It also entrusted the Patent Office, not the courts, with initial authority to determine whether expansion of a claim was justified,[3] and barred suits for retroactive infringement based on such expansion. Like the Court's opinion, this congressional plan adequately protects patentees from "fraud," "piracy," and "stealing." Unlike the Court's opinion, it also protects business men from retroactive infringement suits and judicial expansion of a monopoly sphere beyond that which a patent expressly authorizes. The plan is just, fair, and reasonable. In effect it is nullified by this decision undercutting what the Court has heretofore recognized as wise safeguards. One need not be a prophet to suggest that today's rhapsody on the virtue of the "doctrine of equivalents" will, in direct contravention of the *Miller* case *supra*, make enlargement of patent claims the "rule" rather than the "exception."

## COMPARATIVE PERSPECTIVE
### Non-Literal Infringement in Europe

The tensions and issues engendered by the DOE were confronted by European patent scholars, lawyers, and judges in the 1970s during the process of harmonizing the patent laws of the European nations. Traditionally, the United Kingdom focused heavily on claim language while Germany emphasized the nature of the underlying invention. Reconciling these views was a considerable problem in the drafting of the European Patent Convention. Article 69 of the convention provides that the "extent of the protection conferred by a European

---

* [§251 allows for a patentee to return to the PTO and broaden claim language of an existing patent within two years of issuance if "through error and without any deceptive intention" he "claimed less than he had a right to claim" when he originally prosecuted the patent in question. — EDS.]

3. This provision was inserted in the law for the purpose of relieving the courts from the duty of ascertaining the exact invention of the patentee by inference and conjecture, derived from a laborious examination of previous inventions, and a comparison thereof with that claimed by him. This duty is now cast upon the Patent Office. There his claim is, or is supposed to be, examined, scrutinized, limited, and made to conform to what he is entitled to. If the office refuses to allow him all that he asks, he has an appeal. But the courts have no right to enlarge a patent beyond the scope of its claim as allowed by the Patent Office, or the appellate tribunal to which contested applications are referred. When the terms of a claim in a patent are clear and distinct (as they always should be), the patentee, in a suit brought upon the patent, is bound by it. *Merrill v. Yeomans*, 94 U.S. 568, 24 L. Ed. 235." *Keystone Bridge Co. v. Phoenix Iron Co.*, 95 U.S. 274, 278.

patent...shall be determined by the terms of the claims" and that "nevertheless the description and drawings shall be used to interpret the claims." The parties adopted a "Protocol on the Interpretation of Article 69 of the Convention," which reads:

> Article 69 should not be interpreted in the sense that the extent of the protection conferred by a European patent is to be understood as that defined by the strict literal meaning of the wording used in the claim, the description and drawings being employed only for the purpose of resolving an ambiguity found in the claims. Neither should it be interpreted in the sense that the claims serve only as a guideline and that the actual protection conferred may extend to what from a consideration of the description and drawings by a person skilled in the art, the patentee has contemplated. On the contrary, it is to be interpreted as defining a position between these extremes which combines a fair protection for the patentee with a reasonable degree of certainty for third parties.

For a nice discussion of Article 69's Protocol, see the House of Lords' opinion of *Kirin-Amgen. Inc. v. Hoechst Marion Roussel Ltd.*, [2004] UKHL 46. In this opinion, Lord Hoffmann nicely traces the history of Article 69 and lays out a methodology for interpreting claim language as well as the House of Lords' view of the DOE and its understanding of the American approach to DOE.

## WARNER-JENKINSON COMPANY, INC. v. HILTON DAVIS CHEMICAL, INC.

### 520 U.S. 17 (1997)

Justice THOMAS delivered the opinion of the Court.

Nearly 50 years ago, this Court in *Graver Tank & Mfg. Co. v. Linde Air Products Co.*, set out the modern contours of what is known in patent law as the "doctrine of equivalents." Under this doctrine, a product or process that does not literally infringe upon the express terms of a patent claim may nonetheless be found to infringe if there is "equivalence" between the elements of the accused product or process and the claimed elements of the patented invention.... Petitioner, which was found to have infringed upon respondent's patent under the doctrine of equivalents, invites us to speak the death of that doctrine. We decline that invitation. The significant disagreement within the Court of Appeals for the Federal Circuit concerning the application of *Graver Tank* suggests, however, that the doctrine is not free from confusion. We therefore will endeavor to clarify the proper scope of the doctrine.

### I

The essential facts of this case are few. Petitioner Warner-Jenkinson Co. and respondent Hilton Davis Chemical Co. manufacture dyes. Impurities in those dyes must be removed. Hilton Davis holds United States

Patent No. 4,560,746 ('746 patent), which discloses an improved purification process involving "ultrafiltration." The '746 process filters impure dye through a porous membrane at certain pressures and pH levels,[1] resulting in a high purity dye product.

The '746 patent issued in 1985. As relevant to this case, the patent claims as its invention an improvement in the ultrafiltration process as follows:

> In a process for the purification of a dye...the improvement which comprises: subjecting an aqueous solution...to ultrafiltration through a membrane having a nominal pore diameter of 5-15 Angstroms under a hydrostatic pressure of approximately 200 to 400 p.s.i.g., at a pH from approximately 6.0 to 9.0, to thereby cause separation of said impurities from said dye.... App. 36-37.

The inventors added the phrase "at a pH from approximately 6.0 to 9.0" during patent prosecution. At a minimum, this phrase was added to distinguish a previous patent (the "Booth" patent) that disclosed an ultrafiltration process operating at a pH above 9.0. The parties disagree as to why the low-end pH limit of 6.0 was included as part of the claim.[2]

In 1986, Warner-Jenkinson developed an ultrafiltration process that operated with membrane pore diameters assumed to be 5-15 Angstroms, at pressures of 200 to nearly 500 p.s.i.g., and at a pH of 5.0. Warner-Jenkinson did not learn of the '746 patent until after it had begun commercial use of its ultrafiltration process. Hilton Davis eventually learned of Warner-Jenkinson's use of ultrafiltration and, in 1991, sued Warner-Jenkinson for patent infringement.

The jury found that the '746 patent was not invalid and that Warner-Jenkinson infringed upon the patent under the doctrine of equivalents. A fractured *en banc* Court of Appeals for the Federal Circuit affirmed.

The majority below held that the doctrine of equivalents continues to exist and that its touchstone is whether substantial differences exist between the accused process and the patented process. The court also held that the question of equivalence is for the jury to decide and that the jury in this case had substantial evidence from which it could conclude that the Warner-Jenkinson process was not substantially different from the ultrafiltration process disclosed in the '746 patent.

We granted *certiorari*, and now reverse and remand.

---

1. The pH, or power (exponent) of Hydrogen, of a solution is a measure of its acidity or alkalinity. A pH of 7.0 is neutral; a pH below 7.0 is acidic; and a pH above 7.0 is alkaline. Although measurement of pH is on a logarithmic scale, with each whole number difference representing a ten-fold difference in acidity, the practical significance of any such difference will often depend on the context. Pure water, for example, has a neutral pH of 7.0, whereas carbonated water has an acidic pH of 3.0, and concentrated hydrochloric acid has a pH approaching 0.0. On the other end of the scale, milk of magnesia has a pH of 10.0, whereas household ammonia has a pH of 11.9. 21 Encyclopedia Americana 844 (Int'l ed. 1990).

2. Petitioner contends that the lower limit was added because below a pH of 6.0 the patented process created "foaming" problems in the plant and because the process was not shown to work below that pH level. Brief for Petitioner 4, n. 5, 37, n. 28. Respondent counters that the process was successfully tested to pH levels as low as 2.2 with no effect on the process because of foaming, but offers no particular explanation as to why the lower level of 6.0 pH was selected. Brief for Respondent 34, n. 34.

## II

***

### A

Petitioner's primary argument in this Court is that the doctrine of equivalents, as set out in *Graver Tank* in 1950, did not survive the 1952 revision of the Patent Act, 35 U.S.C. §100 *et seq.*, because it is inconsistent with several aspects of that Act. In particular, petitioner argues: (1) the doctrine of equivalents is inconsistent with the statutory requirement that a patentee specifically "claim" the invention covered by a patent, 35 U.S.C. §112; (2) the doctrine circumvents the patent reissue process — designed to correct mistakes in drafting or the like — and avoids the express limitations on that process, 35 U.S.C. §§251–252; (3) the doctrine is inconsistent with the primacy of the Patent and Trademark Office (PTO) in setting the scope of a patent through the patent prosecution process; and (4) the doctrine was implicitly rejected as a general matter by Congress' specific and limited inclusion of the doctrine in one section regarding "means" claiming, 35 U.S.C. §112, ¶6. All but one of these arguments were made in *Graver Tank* in the context of the 1870 Patent Act, and failed to command a majority.[3]

[The Court rejected all four of Petitioner's arguments.]

### B

We do, however, share the concern of the dissenters below that the doctrine of equivalents, as it has come to be applied since *Graver Tank*, has taken on a life of its own, unbounded by the patent claims. There can be no denying that the doctrine of equivalents, when applied broadly, conflicts with the definitional and public-notice functions of the statutory claiming requirement....

## III

Understandably reluctant to assume this Court would overrule *Graver Tank*, petitioner has offered alternative arguments in favor of a more

---

3. *Graver Tank* was decided over a vigorous dissent. In that dissent, Justice Black raised the first three of petitioner's four arguments against the doctrine of equivalents. *See* 339 U.S., at 613-614, 70 S. Ct., at 858-859 (doctrine inconsistent with statutory requirement to "distinctly claim" the invention); *id.*, at 614-615, 70 S. Ct., at 859-860 (patent reissue process available to correct mistakes); *id.*, at 615, n. 3, 70 S. Ct., at 859 n. 3 (duty lies with the Patent Office to examine claims and to conform them to the scope of the invention; inventors may appeal Patent Office determinations if they disagree with result).

Indeed, petitioner's first argument was not new even in 1950. Nearly 100 years before *Graver Tank*, this Court approved of the doctrine of equivalents in *Winans v. Denmead*. The dissent in *Winans* unsuccessfully argued that the majority result was inconsistent with the requirement in the 1836 Patent Act that the applicant "particularly 'specify and point' out what he claims as his invention," and that the patent protected nothing more. Id., 15 How. at 347 (Campbell, J., dissenting).

restricted doctrine of equivalents than it feels was applied in this case. We address each in turn.

## A

Petitioner first argues that *Graver Tank* never purported to supersede a well-established limit on non-literal infringement, known variously as "prosecution history estoppel" and "file wrapper estoppel." *See Bayer Aktiengesellschaft v. Duphar Int'l Research B.V.* According to petitioner, any surrender of subject matter during patent prosecution, regardless of the reason for such surrender, precludes recapturing any part of that subject matter, even if it is equivalent to the matter expressly claimed. Because, during patent prosecution, respondent limited the pH element of its claim to pH levels between 6.0 and 9.0, petitioner would have those limits form bright lines beyond which no equivalents may be claimed. Any inquiry into the reasons for a surrender, petitioner claims, would undermine the public's right to clear notice of the scope of the patent as embodied in the patent file.

We can readily agree with petitioner that *Graver Tank* did not dispose of prosecution history estoppel as a legal limitation on the doctrine of equivalents. But petitioner reaches too far in arguing that the reason for an amendment during patent prosecution is irrelevant to any subsequent estoppel. In each of our cases cited by petitioner and by the dissent below, prosecution history estoppel was tied to amendments made to avoid the prior art, or otherwise to address a specific concern—such as obviousness—that arguably would have rendered the claimed subject matter unpatentable. Thus, in *Exhibit Supply Co. v. Ace Patents Corp.*, Chief Justice Stone distinguished inclusion of a limiting phrase in an original patent claim from the "very different" situation in which "the applicant, in order to meet objections in the Patent Office, based on references to the prior art, adopted the phrase as a substitute for the broader one" previously used. 315 U.S. 126, 136 (1942). Similarly, in *Keystone Driller Co. v. Northwest Engineering Corp.*, estoppel was applied where the initial claims were "rejected on the prior art," and where the allegedly infringing equivalent element was outside of the revised claims and within the prior art that formed the basis for the rejection of the earlier claims.

It is telling that in each case this Court probed the reasoning behind the Patent Office's insistence upon a change in the claims. In each instance, a change was demanded because the claim as otherwise written was viewed as not describing a patentable invention at all—typically because what it described was encompassed within the prior art. But, as the United States informs us, there are a variety of other reasons why the PTO may request a change in claim language. Brief for United States as Amicus Curiae 22-23 (counsel for the PTO also appearing on the brief). And if the PTO has been requesting changes in claim language without the intent to limit equivalents or, indeed, with the expectation that language it required would in many cases allow for a range of equivalents, we should be extremely reluctant to upset the basic assumptions of the PTO without substantial reason for doing so. Our prior cases have consistently applied prosecution history estoppel only where claims have been amended for a limited set of reasons, and we see no substantial cause for requiring a more rigid rule invoking an estoppel regardless of the reasons for a change.[6]

In this case, the patent examiner objected to the patent claim due to a perceived overlap with the Booth patent, which revealed an ultrafiltration process operating at a pH above 9.0. In response to this objection, the phrase "at a pH from approximately 6.0 to 9.0" was added to the claim. While it is undisputed that the upper limit of 9.0 was added in order to distinguish the Booth patent, the reason for adding the lower limit of 6.0 is unclear. The lower limit certainly did not serve to distinguish the Booth patent, which said nothing about pH levels below 6.0. Thus, while a lower limit of 6.0, by its mere inclusion, became a material element of the claim, that did not necessarily preclude the application of the doctrine of equivalents as to that element. *See Hubbell v. United States*, 179 U.S. 77, 82 (1900) ("'[A]ll [specified elements] must be regarded as material,'" though it remains an open "'question whether an omitted part is supplied by an equivalent device or instrumentality'"). Where the reason for the change was not related to avoiding the prior art, the change may introduce a new element, but it does not necessarily preclude infringement by equivalents of that element.[7]

We are left with the problem, however, of what to do in a case like the one at bar, where the record seems not to reveal the reason for including the lower pH limit of 6.0. In our view, holding that certain reasons for a claim amendment may avoid the application of prosecution history estoppel is not tantamount to holding that the absence of a reason for an amendment may similarly avoid such an estoppel. Mindful that claims do indeed serve both a definitional and a notice function, we think the better rule is to place the burden on the patent-holder to establish the reason for an amendment required during patent prosecution. The court then would decide whether that reason is sufficient to overcome prosecution history estoppel as a bar to application of the doctrine of equivalents to the element added by that amendment. Where no explanation is established, however, the court should presume that the PTO had a substantial reason related to patentability for including the limiting element added by amendment. In those circumstances, prosecution history estoppel would

6. That petitioner's rule might provide a brighter line for determining whether a patentee is estopped under certain circumstances is not a sufficient reason for adopting such a rule. This is especially true where, as here, the PTO may have relied upon a flexible rule of estoppel when deciding whether to ask for a change in the first place. To change so substantially the rules of the game now could very well subvert the various balances the PTO sought to strike when issuing the numerous patents which have not yet expired and which would be affected by our decision.

7. We do not suggest that, where a change is made to overcome an objection based on the prior art, a court is free to review the correctness of that objection when deciding whether to apply prosecution history estoppel. As petitioner rightly notes, such concerns are properly addressed on direct appeal from the denial of a patent, and will not be revisited in an infringement action. *Smith v. Magic City Kennel Club, Inc., supra*, 282 U.S. at 789-790, 51 S. Ct., at 293-294. What is permissible for a court to explore is the reason (right or wrong) for the objection and the manner in which the amendment addressed and avoided the objection.

bar the application of the doctrine equivalents as to that element. The presumption we have described, one subject to rebuttal if an appropriate reason for a required amendment is established, gives proper deference to the role of claims in defining an invention and providing public notice, and to the primacy of the PTO in ensuring that the claims allowed cover only subject matter that is properly patentable in a proffered patent application. Applied in this fashion, prosecution history estoppel places reasonable limits on the doctrine of equivalents, and further insulates the doctrine from any feared conflict with the Patent Act.

Because respondent has not proffered in this Court a reason for the addition of a lower pH limit, it is impossible to tell whether the reason for that addition could properly avoid an estoppel. Whether a reason in fact exists, but simply was not adequately developed, we cannot say. On remand, the Federal Circuit can consider whether reasons for that portion of the amendment were offered or not and whether further opportunity to establish such reasons would be proper.

*** *

C

Finally, petitioner proposes that in order to minimize conflict with the notice function of patent claims, the doctrine of equivalents should be limited to equivalents that are disclosed within the patent itself. A milder version of this argument, which found favor with the dissenters below, is that the doctrine should be limited to equivalents that were known at the time the patent was issued, and should not extend to after-arising equivalents.

As we have noted . . . with regard to the objective nature of the doctrine, a skilled practitioner's knowledge of the interchangeability between claimed and accused elements is not relevant for its own sake, but rather for what it tells the fact-finder about the similarities or differences between those elements. Much as the perspective of the hypothetical "reasonable person" gives content to concepts such as "negligent" behavior, the perspective of a skilled practitioner provides content to, and limits on, the concept of "equivalence." Insofar as the question under the doctrine of equivalents is whether an accused element is equivalent to a claimed element, the proper time for evaluating equivalency—and thus knowledge of interchangeability between elements—is at the time of infringement, not at the time the patent was issued. And rejecting the milder version of petitioner's argument necessarily rejects the more severe proposition that equivalents must not only be known, but must also be actually disclosed in the patent in order for such equivalents to infringe upon the patent.

IV

The various opinions below, respondents, and amici devote considerable attention to whether application of the doctrine of equivalents is a task for the judge or for the jury. However, despite petitioner's argument below that the doctrine should be applied by the judge, in this Court petitioner makes only passing reference to this issue.

Petitioner's comments go more to the alleged inconsistency between the doctrine of equivalents and the claiming requirement than to the role of the jury in applying the doctrine as properly understood. Because resolution of whether, or how much of, the application of the doctrine of equivalents can be resolved by the court is not necessary for us to answer the question presented, we decline to take it up. The Federal Circuit held that it was for the jury to decide whether the accused process was equivalent to the claimed process. There was ample support in our prior cases for that holding. *See, e.g., Union Paper-Bag Machine Co. v. Murphy,* 97 U.S., at 125 ("in determining the question of infringement, the court or jury, as the case may be,....are to look at the machines or their several devices or elements in the light of what they do, or what office or function they perform, and how they perform it, and to find that one thing is substantially the same as another, if it performs substantially the same function in substantially the same way to obtain the same result"); *Winans v. Denmead,* 15 How., at 344 ("[It] is a question for the jury" whether the accused device was "the same in kind, and effected by the employment of [the patentee's] mode of operation in substance"). Nothing in our recent *Markman* decision necessitates a different result than that reached by the Federal Circuit. Indeed, *Markman* cites with considerable favor, when discussing the role of judge and jury, the seminal *Winans* decision. Whether, if the issue were squarely presented to us, we would reach a different conclusion than did the Federal Circuit is not a question we need decide today.[8]

## V

All that remains is to address the debate regarding the linguistic framework under which "equivalence" is determined. Both the parties and the Federal Circuit spend considerable time arguing whether the so-called "triple identity" test—focusing on the function served by a particular claim element, the way that element serves that function, and the result thus obtained by that element—is a suitable method for determining equivalence, or whether an "insubstantial differences" approach is better. There seems to be substantial agreement that, while the triple identity test

8. With regard to the concern over unreviewability due to black-box jury verdicts, we offer only guidance, not a specific mandate. Where the evidence is such that no reasonable jury could determine two elements to be equivalent, district courts are obliged to grant partial or complete summary judgment. *See* Fed. Rule Civ. Proc. 56; *Celotex Corp. v. Catrett,* 477 U.S. 317, 322-323, 106 S. Ct. 2548, 2552-2553, 91 L. Ed. 2d 265 (1986). If there has been a reluctance to do so by some courts due to unfamiliarity with the subject matter, we are confident that the Federal Circuit can remedy the problem. Of course, the various legal limitations on the application of the doctrine of equivalents are to be determined by the court, either on a pretrial motion for partial summary judgment or on a motion for judgment as a matter of law at the close of the evidence and after the jury verdict. Fed. Rule Civ. Proc. 56; Fed. Rule Civ. Proc. 50. Thus, under the particular facts of a case, if prosecution history estoppel would apply or if a theory of equivalence would entirely vitiate a particular claim element, partial or complete judgment should be rendered by the court, as there would be no further material issue for the jury to resolve. Finally, in cases that reach the jury, a special verdict and/or interrogatories on each claim element could be very useful in facilitating review, uniformity, and possibly postverdict judgments as a matter of law. *See* Fed. Rule Civ. Proc. 49; Fed. Rule Civ. Proc. 50. We leave it to the Federal Circuit how best to implement procedural improvements to promote certainty, consistency, and reviewability to this area of the law.

may be suitable for analyzing mechanical devices, it often provides a poor framework for analyzing other products or processes. On the other hand, the insubstantial differences test offers little additional guidance as to what might render any given difference "insubstantial."

In our view, the particular linguistic framework used is less important than whether the test is probative of the essential inquiry: Does the accused product or process contain elements identical or equivalent to each claimed element of the patented invention? Different linguistic frameworks may be more suitable to different cases, depending on their particular facts. A focus on individual elements and a special vigilance against allowing the concept of equivalence to eliminate completely any such elements should reduce considerably the imprecision of whatever language is used. An analysis of the role played by each element in the context of the specific patent claim will thus inform the inquiry as to whether a substitute element matches the function, way, and result of the claimed element, or whether the substitute element plays a role substantially different from the claimed element. With these limiting principles as a backdrop, we see no purpose in going further and micro-managing the Federal Circuit's particular word-choice for analyzing equivalence. We expect that the Federal Circuit will refine the formulation of the test for equivalence in the orderly course of case-by-case determinations, and we leave such refinement to that court's sound judgment in this area of its special expertise.

\* \* \*

## Comments

1. *The Objective Standard for Equivalency.* The linguistic test for equivalency is either the triple identity test set forth in *Graver* or the "insubstantial differences" test. The Court stated that "the particular linguistic framework used is less important than whether the test is probative of the essential inquiry: Does the accused product or process contain elements identical or equivalent to each claimed element of the patented invention?"

2. *The All-Limitations Rule.* The Court adopted an "all-limitations" rule as a means of reducing uncertainty engendered by the DOE. Under this rule, each limitation of a patent claim is material to defining the scope of the patented invention and must not be vitiated or rendered meaningless. Thus, for there to be infringement under the DOE an equivalent of each claim limitation must be found in the accused device. In other words, the DOE is applied to each limitation, not to the invention as a whole. *See* Section D.3, *infra*, for a discussion of this rule.

3. *Time of Infringement and After-Arising Technology.* According to the Supreme Court, infringement for DOE purposes is measured at the "time of infringement," rejecting arguments that equivalency should be limited to either "equivalents that are disclosed within the patent itself" or to "equivalents that were known at the time the patent was issued." 520 U.S. at 41. The infringement inquiry is an objective one: Does the accused product or process conform to the language of the claim, literally or in substance? Other subjective or time-variable issues,

such as when or how the accused infringer developed the accused product or process, are not determinative.

Why focus on "time of infringement" as opposed to time of issuance? The Federal Circuit has noted that the DOE is applied at the time of infringement because of the cumulative and unforeseeable nature of complex and ramified technologies, whereby one inventor opens a door for a subsequent inventor, a door which was perhaps not foreseeable at the time the first inventor filed for a patent, yet was eventually made possible because of the first inventor's patent disclosure. An example can be found in *Hughes Aircraft Co. v. United States*, 717 F.2d 1351 (Fed. Cir. 1983). An employee of Hughes, Williams, invented a means of controlling the attitude of a synchronous communications satellite. The claim specified that the satellite have means for receiving and directly executing control signals from a ground control station on earth. After the patent issued, satellites were developed that did not respond directly to control signals, as required by the claim, because they utilized on-board microprocessors that received control signals and then executed them after processing. Such microprocessors were unknown at the time the patent application was filed. The court found there was infringement, noting that "partial variation in technique, an embellishment made possible by post-Williams technology, does not allow the accused spacecraft to escape the web of infringement." *Id.* at 1365. In other words, the inventor is not required to predict all future developments that enable the practice of his invention in substantially the same way.

## Note on Contributory Infringement

Section 271(c) pertains to contributory infringement, a type of indirect infringement. Contributory infringement concerns itself with the third-party sale of a component of a patented device or the sale of a component for use in practicing a patented process. The component must be a nonstaple item that is not "suitable for substantial noninfringing use." Also, a seller under §271(c) must have knowledge that the component is "especially made or especially adapted for use in an infringement of" a patent. Contributory infringement can only be found if there is direct infringement. Assuming there is direct infringement and the nonstaple and knowledge requirements are met, contributory infringement acts to prevent a third party from successfully arguing that he is not infringing the patent because he is merely making or selling only a part of what is claimed. The rationale for contributory infringement was recognized as early as the late nineteenth century in *Wallace v. Holmes*, 29 F. Cas. 74, 80 (C.C.D. 1871), wherein the court stated: "It cannot be, that, where a useful machine is patented as a combination of parts, two or more can engage in its construction and sale, and protect themselves by showing that, though united in an effort to produce the same machine, and sell it, and bring it into extensive use, each makes and sells one part only, which is useless without the others, and still another person, in precise conformity with the purpose in view, puts them together for use."

The substantial noninfringing use requirement was at play in *C.R. Bard, Inc. v. Advanced Cardiovascular Systems, Inc.,* 911 F.3d 670 (Fed. Cir. 1990). In *Bard*, the claimed invention related to a method for using a catheter in coronary angioplasty. The accused infringer, ACS, was marketing and selling a catheter for use in coronary angioplasty. The ACS catheter had a series of ten openings. Bard asserted that ACS was a contributory infringer because ACS sold catheters to surgeons, who would then use the catheter in a way that directly infringed Bard's method patent. (Note that Bard could also sue the surgeons for direct infringement.) ACS argued that the catheters it sells have substantial noninfringing uses, and therefore, ACS cannot be a contributory infringer under §271(c).

The court noted that there are three possible ways to use the catheter. The first way to use the ACS catheter would be to locate all of the catheter openings within the coronary artery. This method is claimed by Bard's patent. But the two other methods of using the ACS catheter qualified, stated the court, as substantial noninfringing uses. For instance, one method was to position the catheter such that all of its side openings were located only in the aorta. This method of using the ACS catheter was disclosed in the prior art, and thus, constituted a substantial noninfringing use.

In addition to the nonstaple requirement, §271(c) has a knowledge requirement. Under §271(c), the alleged contributory infringer must sell his component "knowing the same adapted for use in an infringement of such patent." Prior to 1952, it was unclear whether the knowledge element meant knowledge of the use to which the component would be put or knowledge of both the character of the use and the existence of a patent and a claim of infringement. The legislative history of (271(c) is equally unclear as to the intended meaning of "knowing." But in *Aro Mfg. Co. v. Convertible Top Replacement Co. (Aro II)*, 377 U.S. 476, 488-490 (1964), the Supreme Court stated that "§271(c) does require a showing that the alleged contributory infringer knew that the combination for which his component was especially designed was both patented and infringing." The Federal Circuit has followed suit. *See, e.g., Preemption Devices, Inc. v. Minn. Mining & Mfg. Co.,* 803 F.2d 1170, 1174 (Fed. Cir. 1986) (stating patentee must show that alleged contributory infringer "knew that the combination for which its components were especially made was both patented and infringing").

# D. LIMITATIONS ON THE DOCTRINE OF EQUIVALENTS AND CLAIM SCOPE

## 1. Prosecution History Estoppel

The doctrine of *prosecution history estoppel* (PHE) is the most significant and important limitation on the DOE. The PHE precludes a patent owner in an infringement proceeding from obtaining a claim scope that would in effect resurrect subject matter surrendered (through, for example, amendment or cancellation) during the prosecution of the patent application before the PTO; thus the name *prosecution* history estoppel. PHE, when applicable, supersedes the doctrine of equivalents. PHE's rationale is based on the notice function of the claim and on third-party detrimental reliance. As the Supreme Court noted in *Warner-Jenkinson,* PHE is linked to both "the role of claims in defining an invention and providing public notice" and to the "primacy of the PTO in ensuring that the claims allowed cover only subject matter that is properly patentable in a proffered patent application." *Warner-Jenkinson,* 520 U.S. at 33-34.

PHE has evolved in recent years to become a powerful defensive tool of alleged infringers. As will become evident from the following case, patent applicants must exercise caution during the prosecution of their applications lest they fall prey to PHE.

## FESTO CORPORATION v. SHOKETSU KINZOKU KOGYO KABUSHIKI CO., LTD.

### 535 U.S. 722 (2002)

Justice KENNEDY delivered the opinion of the Court.

This case requires us to address once again the relation between two patent law concepts, the doctrine of equivalents and the rule of prosecution history estoppel. The Court considered the same concepts in *Warner-Jenkinson Co. v. Hilton Davis Chemical Co.,* and reaffirmed that a patent protects its holder against efforts of copyists to evade liability for infringement by making only insubstantial changes to a patented invention. At the same time, we appreciated that by extending protection beyond the literal terms in a patent the doctrine of equivalents can create substantial uncertainty about where the patent monopoly ends. If the range of equivalents is unclear, competitors may be unable to determine what is a permitted alternative to a patented invention and what is an infringing equivalent.

To reduce the uncertainty, *Warner-Jenkinson* acknowledged that competitors may rely on the prosecution history, the public record of the patent proceedings. In some cases the Patent and Trademark Office (PTO) may have rejected an earlier version of the patent application on the ground that a claim does not meet a statutory requirement for patentability. 35 U.S.C. §132 (1994 ed., Supp. V). When the patentee responds to the rejection by narrowing his claims, this prosecution history estops him from later arguing that the subject matter covered by the original, broader claim was nothing more than an equivalent. Competitors may rely on the estoppel to ensure that their own devices will not be found to infringe by equivalence.

In the decision now under review the Court of Appeals for the Federal Circuit held that by narrowing a claim to obtain a patent, the patentee surrenders all equivalents to the amended claim element. Petitioner asserts this holding departs from past precedent in two respects. First, it applies estoppel to every amendment made to satisfy the requirements of the Patent Act and not just to amendments made to avoid pre-emption by an earlier invention, *i.e.,* the prior art. Second, it holds that when estoppel arises, it bars suit against every equivalent to the amended claim element.

The Court of Appeals acknowledged that this holding departed from its own cases, which applied a flexible bar when considering what claims of equivalence were estopped by the prosecution history. Petitioner argues that by replacing the flexible bar with a complete bar the Court of Appeals cast doubt on many existing patents that were amended during the application process when the law, as it then stood, did not apply so rigorous a standard.

We granted certiorari to consider these questions.

## I

Petitioner Festo Corporation owns two patents for an improved magnetic rodless cylinder, a piston-driven device that relies on magnets to move objects in a conveying system. The device has many industrial uses and has been employed in machinery as diverse as sewing equipment and the Thunder Mountain ride at Disney World. Although the precise details of the cylinder's operation are not essential here, the prosecution history must be considered.

Petitioner's patent applications, as often occurs, were amended during the prosecution proceedings. The application for the first patent, the Stoll Patent (U.S. Patent No. 4,354,125), was amended after the patent examiner rejected the initial application because the exact method of operation was unclear and some claims were made in an impermissible way. The inventor, Dr. Stoll, submitted a new application designed to meet the examiner's objections and also added certain references to prior art. The second patent, the Carroll Patent (U.S. Patent No. 3,779,401), was also amended during a reexamination proceeding. The prior art references were added to this amended application as well. Both amended patents added a new limitation—that the inventions contain a pair of sealing rings, each having a lip on one side, which would prevent impurities from getting on the piston assembly. The amended Stoll Patent added the further limitation that the outer shell of the device, the sleeve, be made of a magnetizable material.

After Festo began selling its rodless cylinder, respondents (whom we refer to as SMC) entered the market with a device similar, but not identical, to the ones disclosed by Festo's patents. SMC's cylinder, rather than using two one-way sealing rings, employs a single sealing ring with a two-way lip. Furthermore, SMC's sleeve is made of a nonmagnetizable alloy. SMC's device does not fall within the literal claims of either patent, but petitioner contends that it is so similar that it infringes under the doctrine of equivalents.

SMC contends that Festo is estopped from making this argument because of the prosecution history of its patents. The sealing rings and the magnetized alloy in the Festo product were both disclosed for the first time in the amended applications. In SMC's view, these amendments narrowed the earlier applications, surrendering alternatives that are the very points of difference in the competing devices—the sealing rings and the type of alloy used to make the sleeve. As Festo narrowed its claims in these ways in order to obtain the patents, says SMC, Festo is now estopped from saying that these features are immaterial and that SMC's device is an equivalent of its own.

The United States District Court for the District of Massachusetts disagreed. It held that Festo's amendments were not made to avoid prior art, and therefore the amendments were not the kind that give rise to estoppel. A panel of the Court of Appeals for the Federal Circuit affirmed. We granted certiorari, vacated, and remanded in light of our intervening decision in *Warner-Jenkinson v. Hilton Davis Chemical Co*. After a decision by the original panel on remand, the Court of Appeals ordered rehearing en banc to address questions that had divided its judges since our decision in *Warner-Jenkinson*.

The en banc court reversed, holding that prosecution history estoppel barred Festo from asserting that the accused device infringed its patents under the doctrine of equivalents. The court held, with only one judge dissenting, that estoppel arises from any amendment that narrows a claim to comply with the Patent Act, not only from amendments made to avoid prior art. More controversial in the Court of Appeals was its further holding: When estoppel applies, it stands as a complete bar against any claim of equivalence for the element that was amended. The court acknowledged that its own prior case law did not go so far. Previous decisions had held that prosecution history estoppel constituted a flexible bar, foreclosing some, but not all, claims of equivalence, depending on the purpose of the amendment and the alterations in the text. The court concluded, however, that its precedents applying the flexible-bar rule should be overruled because this case-by-case approach has proved unworkable. In the court's view a complete-bar rule, under which estoppel bars all claims of equivalence to the narrowed element, would promote certainty in the determination of infringement cases.

Four judges dissented from the decision to adopt a complete bar. In four separate opinions, the dissenters argued that the majority's decision to overrule precedent was contrary to *Warner-Jenkinson* and would unsettle the expectations of many existing patentees. Judge Michel, in his dissent, described in detail how the complete bar required the Court of Appeals to disregard 8 older decisions of this Court, as well as more than 50 of its own cases.

We granted certiorari.

\*\*\*

### III

Prosecution history estoppel requires that the claims of a patent be interpreted in light of the proceedings in the PTO during the application process. Estoppel is a "rule of patent construction" that ensures that claims are interpreted by reference to those "that have been cancelled or rejected." *Schriber-Schroth Co. v. Cleveland Trust Co.*, 311 U.S. 211, 220-221 (1940). The doctrine of equivalents allows the patentee to claim those insubstantial alterations that were not captured in drafting the original patent claim but which could be created through trivial changes. When, however, the patentee originally claimed the subject matter alleged to infringe but then narrowed the claim in response to a rejection, he may not argue that the surrendered territory comprised unforeseen subject matter that should be deemed equivalent to the literal claims of the issued patent. On the contrary, "[b]y the amendment [the patentee] recognized and emphasized the difference between the two phrases[,]...and [t]he difference which [the patentee] thus disclaimed must be regarded as material." *Exhibit Supply Co. v. Ace Patents Corp.*, 315 U.S. 126, 136-137 (1942).

A rejection indicates that the patent examiner does not believe the original claim could be patented. While the patentee has the right to appeal, his decision to forgo an appeal and submit an amended claim is taken as a concession that the invention as patented does not reach as far as the original claim. *See Goodyear Dental Vulcanite Co. v. Davis,* 102 U.S. 222, 228 (1880) ("In view of [the amendment] there can be no doubt of what [the patentee] understood he had patented, and that both he and the commissioner regarded the patent to be for a manufacture made exclusively of vulcanites by the detailed process"). Were it otherwise, the inventor might avoid the PTO's gatekeeping role and seek to recapture in an infringement action the very subject matter surrendered as a condition of receiving the patent.

Prosecution history estoppel ensures that the doctrine of equivalents remains tied to its underlying purpose. Where the original application once embraced the purported equivalent but the patentee narrowed his claims to obtain the patent or to protect its validity, the patentee cannot assert that he lacked the words to describe the subject matter in question. The doctrine of equivalents is premised on language's inability to capture the essence of innovation, but a prior application describing the precise element at issue undercuts that premise. In that instance the prosecution history has established that the inventor turned his attention to the subject matter in question, knew the words for both the broader and narrower claim, and affirmatively chose the latter.

### A

The first question in this case concerns the kinds of amendments that may give rise to estoppel. Petitioner argues that estoppel should arise when amendments are intended to narrow the subject matter of the patented invention, for instance, amendments to avoid prior art, but not when the amendments are made to comply with requirements concerning the form of the patent application. In *Warner-Jenkinson* we recognized that prosecution history estoppel does not arise in every instance when a patent application is amended. Our "prior cases have consistently applied prosecution history estoppel only where claims have been amended for a limited set of reasons," such as "to avoid the prior art, or otherwise to address a specific concern — such as obviousness — that arguably would have rendered the claimed subject matter unpatentable." 520 U.S., at 30-32. While we made clear that estoppel applies to amendments made for a "substantial reason related to patentability," *id.,* at 33, we did not purport to define that term or to catalog every reason that might raise an estoppel. Indeed, we stated that even if the amendment's purpose were unrelated to patentability, the court might consider whether it was the kind of reason that nonetheless might require resort to the estoppel doctrine. *Id.,* at 40-41.

Petitioner is correct that estoppel has been discussed most often in the context of amendments made to avoid the prior art. Amendment to accommodate prior art was the emphasis, too, of our decision in *Warner-Jenkinson*. It does not follow, however, that amendments for other purposes will not give rise to estoppel. Prosecution history may rebut the inference that a thing not described was indescribable. That rationale does not cease simply because the narrowing amendment, submitted to secure a patent, was for some purpose other than avoiding prior art.

We agree with the Court of Appeals that a narrowing amendment made to satisfy any requirement of the Patent Act may give rise to an estoppel. As that court explained, a number of statutory requirements must be satisfied before a patent can issue. The claimed subject matter must be useful, novel, and not obvious. 35 U.S.C. §§101-103 (1994 ed. and Supp. V). In addition, the patent application must describe, enable, and set forth the best mode of carrying out the invention. §112 (1994 ed.). These latter requirements must be satisfied before issuance of the patent, for exclusive patent rights are given in exchange for disclosing the invention to the public. *See Bonito Boats*. What is claimed by the patent application must be the same as what is disclosed in the specification; otherwise the patent should not issue. The patent also should not issue if the other requirements of §112 are not satisfied, and an applicant's failure to meet these requirements could lead to the issued patent being held invalid in later litigation.

Petitioner contends that amendments made to comply with §112 concern the form of the application and not the subject matter of the invention. The PTO might require the applicant to clarify an ambiguous term, to improve the translation of a foreign word, or to rewrite a dependent claim as an independent one. In these cases, petitioner argues, the applicant has no intention of surrendering subject matter and should not be estopped from challenging equivalent devices. While this may be true in some cases, petitioner's argument conflates the patentee's reason for making the amendment with the impact the amendment has on the subject matter.

Estoppel arises when an amendment is made to secure the patent and the amendment narrows the patent's scope. If a §112 amendment is truly cosmetic, then it would not narrow the patent's scope or raise an estoppel. On the other hand, if a §112 amendment is necessary and narrows the patent's scope — even if only for the purpose of better description — estoppel may apply. A patentee who narrows a claim as a condition for obtaining a patent disavows his claim to the broader subject matter, whether the amendment was made to avoid the prior art or to comply with §112. We must regard the patentee as having conceded an inability to claim the broader subject matter or at least as having abandoned his right to appeal a rejection. In either case estoppel may apply.

**B**

Petitioner concedes that the limitations at issue — the sealing rings and the composition of the sleeve — were made for reasons related to §112, if not also to avoid the prior art. Our conclusion that prosecution history estoppel arises when a claim is narrowed to comply with §112 gives rise to the second question presented: Does the estoppel bar the inventor from asserting infringement against any equivalent to the narrowed element or might some equivalents still infringe? The Court of Appeals held that prosecution history estoppel is a complete bar, and so the narrowed element must be limited to its strict literal terms. Based upon its experience the Court of Appeals decided that the flexible-bar rule is unworkable because it leads to excessive uncertainty and burdens legitimate innovation. For the reasons that follow, we disagree with the decision to adopt the complete bar.

Though prosecution history estoppel can bar challenges to a wide range of equivalents, its reach requires an examination of the subject matter surrendered by the narrowing amendment. The complete bar avoids this inquiry by establishing a *per se* rule; but that approach is inconsistent with the purpose of applying the estoppel in the first place — to hold the inventor to the representations made during the application process and to the inferences that may reasonably be drawn from the amendment. By amending the application, the inventor is deemed to concede that the patent does not extend as far as the original claim. It does not follow, however, that the amended claim becomes so perfect in its description that no one could devise an equivalent. After amendment, as before, language remains an imperfect fit for invention. The narrowing amendment may demonstrate what the claim is not; but it may still fail to capture precisely what the claim is. There is no reason why a narrowing amendment should be deemed to relinquish equivalents unforeseeable at the time of the amendment and beyond a fair interpretation of what was surrendered. Nor is there any call to foreclose claims of equivalence for aspects of the invention that have only a peripheral relation to the reason the amendment was submitted. The amendment does not show that the inventor suddenly had more foresight in the drafting of claims than an inventor whose application was granted without amendments having been submitted. It shows only that he was familiar with the broader text and with the difference between the two. As a result, there is no more reason for holding the patentee to the literal terms of an amended claim than there is for abolishing the doctrine of equivalents altogether and holding every patentee to the literal terms of the patent.

This view of prosecution history estoppel is consistent with our precedents and respectful of the real practice before the PTO. While this Court has not weighed the merits of the complete bar against the flexible bar in its prior cases, we have consistently applied the doctrine in a flexible way, not a rigid one. We have considered what equivalents were surrendered during the prosecution of the patent, rather than imposing a complete bar that resorts to the very literalism the equivalents rule is designed to overcome.

The Court of Appeals ignored the guidance of *Warner-Jenkinson*, which instructed that courts must be cautious before adopting changes that disrupt the settled expectations of the inventing community. In that case we made it clear that the doctrine of equivalents and the rule of prosecution history estoppel are settled law. The responsibility for changing them rests with Congress. *Ibid.* Fundamental alterations in these rules risk destroying the legitimate expectations of inventors in their property. The petitioner in *Warner-Jenkinson* requested another bright-line rule that would have provided more certainty in determining when estoppel applies but at the cost of disrupting the expectations of countless existing patent holders. We rejected that approach: "To change so substantially the rules of the game now could very well subvert the various balances the PTO sought to strike when issuing the numerous patents which have not yet expired and which would be affected by our decision." *Id.*, at 32, n. 6. As *Warner-Jenkinson* recognized, patent prosecution occurs in the light of our case law. Inventors who amended their claims under the previous regime had no reason to believe they were conceding all equivalents. If they had known, they might have appealed the rejection instead. There is no justification for applying a new and more robust estoppel to those who relied on prior doctrine.

In *Warner-Jenkinson* we struck the appropriate balance by placing the burden on the patentee to show that an amendment was not for purposes of patentability:

> Where no explanation is established, however, the court should presume that the patent application had a substantial reason related to patentability for including the limiting element added by amendment. In those circumstances, prosecution history estoppel would bar the application of the doctrine of equivalents as to that element. *Id.* at 33.

When the patentee is unable to explain the reason for amendment, estoppel not only applies but also "bar[s] the application of the doctrine of equivalents as to that element." *Ibid.* These words do not mandate a complete bar; they are limited to the circumstance where "no explanation is established." They do provide, however, that when the court is unable to determine the purpose underlying a narrowing amendment — and hence a rationale for limiting the estoppel to the surrender of particular equivalents — the court should presume that the patentee surrendered all subject matter between the broader and the narrower language.

Just as *Warner-Jenkinson* held that the patentee bears the burden of proving that an amendment was not made for a reason that would give rise to estoppel, we hold here that the patentee should bear the burden of showing that the amendment does not surrender the particular equivalent in question. This is the approach advocated by the United States, see Brief for United States as *Amicus Curiae* 22-28, and we regard it to be sound. The patentee, as the author of the claim language, may be expected to draft claims encompassing readily known equivalents. A patentee's decision to narrow his claims through amendment may be presumed to be a general disclaimer of the territory between the original claim and the amended claim. *Exhibit Supply*, 315 U.S., at 136-137 ("By the amendment [the patentee] recognized and emphasized the difference between the two phrases and proclaimed his abandonment of all that is embraced in that difference"). There are some cases, however, where the amendment cannot reasonably be viewed as surrendering a particular equivalent. The equivalent may have been unforeseeable at the time of the application; the rationale underlying the amendment may bear no more than a tangential relation to the equivalent in question; or there may be some other reason suggesting that the patentee could not reasonably be expected to have described the insubstantial substitute in question. In those cases the patentee can overcome the presumption that prosecution history estoppel bars a finding of equivalence.

This presumption is not, then, just the complete bar by another name. Rather, it reflects the fact that the interpretation of the patent must begin with its literal claims, and the prosecution history is relevant to construing those claims. When the patentee has chosen to narrow a claim, courts may presume the amended text was composed with awareness of this rule and that the territory surrendered is not an equivalent of the territory claimed. In those instances, however, the patentee still might rebut the presumption that estoppel bars a claim of equivalence. The patentee must show that at the time of the amendment one skilled in the art could not reasonably be expected to have drafted a claim that would have literally encompassed the alleged equivalent.

## IV

On the record before us, we cannot say petitioner has rebutted the presumptions that estoppel applies and that the equivalents at issue have been surrendered. Petitioner concedes that the limitations at issue — the sealing rings and the composition of the sleeve — were made in response to a rejection for reasons under §112, if not also because of the prior art references. As the amendments were made for a reason relating to patentability, the question is not whether estoppel applies but what territory the amendments surrendered. While estoppel does not effect a complete bar, the question remains whether petitioner can demonstrate that the narrowing amendments did not surrender the particular equivalents at issue. On these questions, respondents may well prevail, for the sealing rings and the composition of the sleeve both were noted expressly in the prosecution history. These matters, however, should be determined in the first instance by further proceedings in the Court of Appeals or the District Court.

The judgment of the Federal Circuit is vacated, and the case is remanded for further proceedings consistent with this opinion.

## Comments

1. *Rigid Flexibility.* Perhaps the most significant portion of the Federal Circuit's *Festo* decision was the court's adoption of the "complete bar" rule. In discussing this rule, the court held "that prosecution history estoppel acts as a complete bar to the application of the doctrine of equivalents when an amendment has narrowed the scope of a claim for a reason related to patentability." Although the Supreme Court in *Festo* acknowledged the importance of certainty in a property rights-based system such as patent law, the Court, based on the inherent descriptive limitations of language and a recognition that literalism would "greatly diminish[ ]" the value of patents, rejected the "complete bar" rule and adopted a modified version of the "flexible bar" rule. The Court candidly noted that the patent system must tolerate some "uncertainty as the price of ensuring the appropriate incentives for innovation." But the Court did infuse a good amount of rigidity into the "flexible bar." *See* Comment 2, *infra*.

2. *Presumptions and Burdens.* Most significantly, the Court reaffirmed and expanded upon the presumption it established in *Warner-Jenkinson* that "[w]hen the patentee is unable to explain the reason for amendment,

estoppel not only applies but also 'bar[s] the application of the doctrine of equivalents as to that element.'" In *Festo*, the Supreme Court broadened this presumption, holding that the decision of the patentee to file a narrowing amendment "may be presumed to be a general disclaimer of the territory between the original and the amended claim"; that is, "the territory surrendered is not an equivalent of the territory claimed." This presumption led the Court to impose a burden on the patentee "of showing that the amendment does not surrender the particular equivalent in question." In particular,

> The patentee must show that at the time of the amendment one skilled in the art could not reasonably be expected to have drafted a claim that would have literally encompassed the alleged equivalent.

To rebut the presumption, the patentee must show (1) equivalent was unforeseeable at the time of amendment; (2) the rationale underlying the amendment was tangentially related to the equivalent; or (3) some other reason suggesting that the patentee could not reasonably be expected to have described the insubstantial substitute in question.

**3. Rebutting Festo's Presumption.** The Federal Circuit has had several opportunities to decide whether *Festo*'s presumption applies and whether it has been rebutted. For example, in *SmithKline Beecham Corp. v. Excel Pharmaceuticals, Inc.*, 356 F.3d 1357 (Fed. Cir. 2004), the patent related to an antidepressant, particularly "controlled sustained release tablets" containing bupropion hydrochloride, which were developed to avoid multiple dosages. The key ingredient for obtaining sustained release was hydroxypropyl methylcellulose (HPMC). But the claims in question did not originally recite HPMC. Rather, HPMC was added through a narrowing amendment in response to a §112 enablement rejection. The accused product, made by Excel, did not literally infringe the patent because the accused product used polyvinyl alcohol or PVA (not HPMC) as its release agent. And Excel argued that the patentee is precluded from arguing that PVA is equivalent to HPMC because the patentee narrowed its claim to add HPMC. The patentee argued that it could not have claimed PVA because its patent disclosure only recited HPMC, and therefore, asserted (correctly) that there was no support in the specification as required by §112 for PVA. The Federal Circuit rejected this argument because it did not fit into one of the three *Festo* exceptions. PVA was not an unforeseeable equivalent at the time of amendment, and the rationale underlying the amendment was germane to the equivalent in question — in other words, not tangentially related. As the court stated, "the Supreme Court in *Festo* neither excuses an applicant from failing to claim 'readily known equivalents' at the time of application nor allows a patentee to rebut the *Festo* presumption by invoking its own failure to include a known equivalent in its original disclosure."

But in another opinion, the Federal Circuit held that the patentee successfully rebutted the *Festo* presumption. In *Insituform Technologies, Inc. v. CAT Contracting, Inc.*, 385 F.3d 1360 (Fed. Cir. 2004), the patent related to a process for repairing cracks and structural defects of

## The *Festo* Flowchart

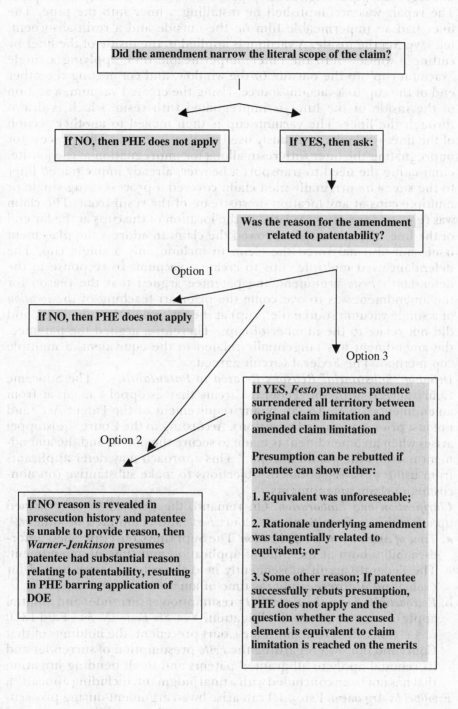

**Did the amendment narrow the literal scope of the claim?**

**If NO, then PHE does not apply**

**If YES, then ask:**

**Was the reason for the amendment related to patentability?**

Option 1

**If NO, then PHE does not apply**

Option 3

Option 2

**If NO reason is revealed in prosecution history and patentee is unable to provide reason, then *Warner-Jenkinson* presumes patentee had substantial reason relating to patentability, resulting in PHE barring application of DOE**

**If YES, *Festo* presumes patentee surrendered all territory between original claim limitation and amended claim limitation**

**Presumption can be rebutted if patentee can show either:**

**1. Equivalent was unforeseeable;**

**2. Rationale underlying amendment was tangentially related to equivalent; or**

**3. Some other reason; If patentee successfully rebuts presumption, PHE does not apply and the question whether the accused element is equivalent to claim limitation is reached on the merits**

underground pipes (e.g., sewer pipes) without having to dig up the pipe. The repair was accomplished by installing a liner into the pipe. The liner had an impermeable film on the outside and a resin-absorbent, felt layer on the inside. A vacuum is applied to the inside of the liner by cutting a window into the outer, impermeable film, applying a single "vacuum cup" to the outside of the window, and connecting the other end of the cup to a vacuum source. Using the created vacuum, a section of the inside of the liner is impregnated with resin, which is drawn through the liner. The vacuum cup is then moved to another section of the liner while the previously used window is sealed. This process for impregnating the liner with resin allows for impregnation at the jobsite, eliminating the need to transport a heavier, already impregnated liner to the site. The originally filed claim covered a process using single or multiple cups at any location downstream of the resin front. The claim was rejected for reasons related to the location of the cups at the far end of the line. The patentee narrowed the claim to address the placement issue, but also narrowed the claim to include only a single cup. The defendant used multiple cups to create a vacuum. In response to the defendant's *Festo* argument, the patentee argued that the reason for the amendment was to overcome the prior art teaching of the *location* of a single vacuum source (i.e., cup) at the far end of the tube liner, and did not relate to the number of cups. Therefore, argued the patentee, the amendment was tangentially related to the equivalent, a multiple cup method. The Federal Circuit agreed.

4. *Defining "Substantial Reasons Related to Patentability."* The Supreme Court agreed with the Federal Circuit that estoppel can arise from amendments "made to satisfy any requirement of the Patent Act" and not just prior art — based rejections. According to the Court, "[e]stoppel arises when an amendment is made to secure the patent and the amendment narrows the patent's scope." This approach may deter applicants from using §112 rejections or objections to make substantive (on non-cosmetic) claim amendments.

5. *Clarification and Elaboration.* On remand, the Federal Circuit cleaned up a few things from Supreme Court *Festo* and elaborated on others.

   a. *Time of Amendment or Application.* The Supreme Court discussed unforeseeability both at the time of application and time of amendment. The Federal Circuit subsequently held the relevant time period for evaluating unforeseeability is time of amendment.

   b. *Retroactivity.* Does the *Festo VIII* presumption of surrender and rebuttal apply to extant patents and litigation? Yes. See *Festo IX*, 344 F.3d 1370 n. 4 ("Consistent with Supreme Court precedent, the holdings of that Court and our own regarding the *Festo* presumption of surrender and its rebuttal apply to all granted patents and to all pending litigation that has not been concluded with a final judgment, including appeals").

6. *Estoppel by Argument.* Estoppel can arise by an argument during prosecution even when the claims are not amended. The possibility of estoppel by argument may become more critical in the future if applicants, aware of the estoppel effect of any narrowing amendment under *Festo*, elect not to amend claims in response to rejections but, instead, to dispute the basis for an examiner's rejection of the claims.

## 2. Public Dedication Rule

A significant limitation on claim scope is the "Public Dedication Rule" or "Disclosure-Dedication Rule," which has its basis in the nineteenth-century Supreme Court case of *Miller v. Bridgeport Brass Co.*, cited by the *Graver* dissent. The *Miller* Court held that subject matter disclosed in the patent specification, but not claimed, is dedicated to the public. The public dedication rule played out in *Maxwell v. J. Baker, Inc.* and *YBX Magnex, Inc. v. Int'l Trade Comm'n*, two cases that offered conflicting approaches to the rule. In the following case, the Federal Circuit sat en banc to decide the rule's fate.

### JOHNSON & JOHNSTON ASSOCIATES, INC. v. R.E. SERVICE CO., INC.

**285 F.3d 1046 (Fed. Cir. 2002) (en banc)**

PER CURIAM.

Johnson and Johnston Associates (Johnston) asserted United States Patent No. 5,153,050 (the '050 patent) against R.E. Service Co. and Mark Frater (collectively RES). A jury found that RES willfully infringed claims 1 and 2 of the patent under the doctrine of equivalents and awarded Johnston $1,138,764 in damages. After a hearing before a three-judge panel on December 7, 1999, this court ordered *en banc* rehearing of the doctrine of equivalents issue. Because this court concludes that RES, as a matter of law, could not have infringed the '050 patent under the doctrine of equivalents, this court reverses the district court's judgment of infringement under the doctrine of equivalents, willfulness, damages, attorneys fees, and expenses.

### I.

The '050 patent, which issued October 6, 1992, relates to the manufacture of printed circuit boards. Printed circuit boards are composed of extremely thin sheets of conductive copper foil joined to sheets of a dielectric (nonconductive) resin-impregnated material called "prepreg." The process for making multi-layered printed circuit boards stacks sheets of copper foil and prepreg in a press, heats them to melt the resin in the prepreg, and thereby bonds the layers.

In creating these circuit boards, workers manually handle the thin sheets of copper foil during the layering process. Without the invention claimed in the '050 patent, stacking by hand can damage or contaminate the fragile foil, causing discontinuities in the etched copper circuits. The '050 patent claims an assembly that prevents most damage during manual handling. The invention adheres the fragile copper foil to a stiffer substrate sheet of aluminum. With the aluminum substrate for protection, workers can handle the assembly without damaging the fragile copper foil. After the pressing and heating steps, workers can remove and even recycle the aluminum substrate. Figure 5 of the '050 patent shows the foil-substrate combination, with the foil layer peeled back at one corner for illustration:

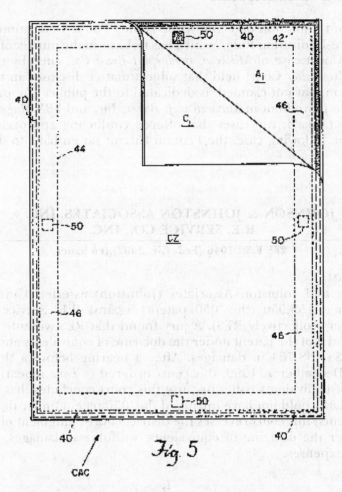

*Fig. 5*

Surface $C_1$ is the protected inner surface of the copper foil; $C_2$ is the inner surface of the aluminum substrate. A band of flexible adhesive 40 joins the substrate and the foil at the edges, creating a protected central zone CZ. The specification explains:

> Because the frail, thin copper foil C was adhesively secured to its aluminum substrate A, the [laminate] is stiffer and more readily handled resulting in far fewer spoils due to damaged copper foil. The use of the adhered substrate A, regardless of what material it is made of, makes the consumer's (manufacturer's) objective of using thinner and thinner foils and ultimately automating the procedure more realistic since the foil, by use of the invention, is no longer without the much needed physical support.

'050 patent, col. 8, ll. 21-30.

The specification further describes the composition of the substrate sheet:

> While aluminum is currently the preferred material for the substrate, other metals, such as stainless steel or nickel alloys, may be used. In some instances...polypropelene [sic] can be used.

'050 patent, col. 5, ll. 5-8.

As noted, the jury found infringement of claims 1 and 2:

Claim 1. A component for use in manufacturing articles such as printed circuit boards comprising:

a laminate constructed of a sheet of copper foil which, in a finished printed circuit board, constitutes a functional element and a sheet of *aluminum* which constitutes a discardable element;

one surface of each of the copper sheet and the *aluminum* sheet being essentially uncontaminated and engageable with each other at an interface;

a band of flexible adhesive joining the uncontaminated surfaces of the sheets together at their borders and defining a substantially uncontaminated central zone inwardly of the edges of the sheets and unjoined at the interface.

'050 patent, Claim 1, col. 8, ll. 47-60 (emphasis supplied). Claim 2 defines a similar laminate having sheets of copper foil adhered to both sides of the aluminum sheet.

\*\*\*

In 1997, RES began making new laminates for manufacture of printed circuit boards. The RES products, designated "SC2" and "SC3," joined copper foil to a sheet of steel as the substrate instead of a sheet of aluminum. Johnston filed a suit for infringement. In this case, the district court granted RES's motion for summary judgment of no literal infringement. With respect to the doctrine of equivalents, RES argued, citing *Maxwell v. J. Baker, Inc.*, that the '050 specification, which disclosed a steel substrate but did not claim it, constituted a dedication of the steel substrate to the public. Johnston argued that the steel substrate was not dedicated to the public, citing *YBM Magnex, Inc. v. Int'l Trade Comm'n*. On cross-motions for summary judgment, the district court ruled that the '050 patent did not dedicate the steel substrate to the public, and set the question of infringement by equivalents for trial, along with the issues of damages and willful infringement.

\*\*\*

## II.

On appeal, RES does not challenge the jury's factual finding of equivalency between the copper-steel and copper-aluminum laminates. Instead, citing *Maxwell*, RES argues that Johnston did not claim steel substrates, but limited its patent scope to aluminum substrates, thus dedicating to the public this unclaimed subject matter. On this ground, RES challenges the district court's denial of its motion for summary judgment that RES's copper-steel laminates are not equivalent, as a matter of law, to the claimed copper-aluminum laminates. Johnston responds that the steel substrates are not dedicated to the public, citing *YBM Magnex*. In other words, the two parties dispute whether *Maxwell* or *YBM Magnex* applies in this case with regard to infringement under the doctrine of equivalents.

In *Maxwell*, the patent claimed a system for attaching together a mated pair of shoes. Maxwell claimed fastening tabs between the inner and outer soles of the attached shoes. Maxwell disclosed in the specification, but did not claim, fastening tabs that could be "stitched into a lining seam of the shoes." Based on the "well-established rule that 'subject matter disclosed but not claimed in a patent application is dedicated to the public,'" this court held that Baker could not, as a matter of law, infringe under the doctrine of equivalents by using the disclosed but unclaimed shoe attachment system. *Maxwell*, 86 F.3d at 1106 (quoting *Unique Concepts, Inc. v. Brown*, 939 F.2d 1558, 1562-63 (Fed. Cir. 1991)). This court stated further:

> By [Maxwell's failure] to claim these alternatives, the Patent and Trademark Office was deprived of the opportunity to consider whether these alternatives were patentable. A person of ordinary skill in the shoe industry, reading the specification and prosecution history, and interpreting the claims, would conclude that Maxwell, by failing to claim the alternate shoe attachment systems in which the tabs were attached to the inside shoe lining, dedicated the use of such systems to the public.

*Maxwell*, 86 F.3d at 1108.

In *YBM Magnex*, the patent claimed a permanent magnet alloy comprising certain elements, including "6,000 to 35,000 ppm oxygen." The accused infringer used similar magnet alloys with an oxygen content between 5,450 and 6,000 ppm (parts per million), which was allegedly disclosed but not claimed in the '439 patent. In *YBM Magnex*, this court stated that *Maxwell* did not create a new rule of law that doctrine of equivalents could never encompass subject matter disclosed in the specification but not claimed. Distinguishing *Maxwell*, this court noted:

> Maxwell avoided examination of the unclaimed alternative, which was distinct from the claimed alternative. In view of the distinctness of the two embodiments, both of which were fully described in the specification, the Federal Circuit denied Maxwell the opportunity to enforce the unclaimed embodiment as an equivalent of the one that was claimed.

145 F.3d at 1320. In other words, this court in *YBM Magnex* purported to limit *Maxwell* to situations where a patent discloses an unclaimed alternative distinct from the claimed invention. Thus, this court must decide whether a patentee can apply the doctrine of equivalents to cover unclaimed subject matter disclosed in the specification.

### III.

Both the Supreme Court and this court have adhered to the fundamental principle that claims define the scope of patent protection. *See, e.g., Aro Mfg. v. Convertible Top Replacement Co.*, 365 U.S. 336, 339 (1961) ("[T]he claims made in the patent are the sole measure of the grant. . . ."); *Atl. Thermoplastics Co. v. Faytex Corp.*, 974 F.2d 1299, 1300 (Fed. Cir. 1992) ("The claims alone define the patent right"). The claims give notice both to the examiner at the U.S. Patent and Trademark Office during prosecution, and to the public at large, including potential competitors, after the patent has issued. Consistent with its scope definition and notice functions, the claim requirement presupposes that a patent applicant defines his invention in the claims, not in the specification. After all, the claims, not the specification, provide the measure of the patentee's right to exclude. Moreover, the law of infringement compares the accused product with the claims as construed by the court. Infringement, either literally or under the doctrine of equivalents, does not arise by comparing the accused product "with a preferred embodiment described in the specification, or with a commercialized embodiment of the patentee." *SRI Int'l*, 775 F.2d at 1121.

Even as early as the 1880s, the Supreme Court emphasized the predominant role of claims. For example, in *Miller v. Bridgeport Brass Co.*, a case addressing a reissue patent filed fifteen years after the original patent, the Supreme Court broadly stated: "[T]he claim of a specific device or combination, and an omission to claim other devices or combinations apparent on the face of the patent, are, in law, a dedication to the public of that which is not claimed." 104 U.S. 350, 352 (1881). Just a few years later, the Court repeated that sentiment in another reissue patent case: "[T]he claim actually made operates in law as a disclaimer of what is not claimed; and of all this the law charges the patentee with the fullest notice." *Mahn*, 112 U.S. at 361. The Court explained further:

> Of course, what is not claimed is public property. The presumption is, and such is generally the fact, that what is not claimed was not invented by the patentee, but was known and used before he made his invention. But, whether so or not, his own act has made it public property if it was not so before. The patent itself, as soon as it is issued, is the evidence of this. The public has the undoubted right to use, and it is to be presumed does use, what is not specifically claimed in the patent.

*Id.* at 361.

The doctrine of equivalents extends the right to exclude beyond the literal scope of the claims. The Supreme Court first applied the modern doctrine of equivalents in *Graver Tank & Mfg. Co. v. Linde Air Prods. Co.* (*Graver Tank II*). In that case, the Court explained: "equivalency must be determined against the context of the patent, the prior art, and the particular circumstances of the case." 339 U.S. 605, 609 (1950). In *Graver I*, a predecessor case addressing the validity of the claims at issue, the Court held invalid composition claims 24 and 26 comprising "silicates" and "metallic silicates." *Graver Tank & Mfg. v. Linde Air Prods. Co.*, 336 U.S. 271, 276-77 (1949) (*Graver I*). Specifically, the Court found those claims too broad because they encompassed some inoperative silicates along with the nine operative metallic silicates in the specification. The Court did not hold invalid narrower claims comprising "alkaline earth metals."

Thus, in the infringement action of *Graver II*, the Supreme Court addressed only the narrower claims comprising "alkaline earth metals." The alleged infringing compositions in *Graver II* are similar to the compositions of the narrower claims, except that they substitute silicate of manganese — a metallic silicate such as in the earlier invalidated claims — for silicates of "alkaline earth metals" (*e.g.*, magnesium or calcium) claimed in the narrower claims. Because the Court determined that "under the circumstances the change was so insubstantial," and because the accused compositions "perform[ed] substantially the same function in substantially the same way to obtain the same result," the Court upheld the finding of infringement under the doctrine of equivalents. *Graver II*. The Court's holding and the history of *Graver II* show that the patentee had not dedicated unclaimed subject matter to the public. In fact, the patentee had claimed the "equivalent" subject matter, even if the Court eventually held the relevant claims too broad.

In 1997, less than a year after this court decided *Maxwell*, the Supreme Court addressed the doctrine of equivalents again in *Warner-Jenkinson v. Hilton Davis*. In that case, Warner-Jenkinson invited the Court "to speak the death" of the doctrine of equivalents. 520 U.S. at 21. The Court declined that invitation. In *Warner-Jenkinson*, the patentee added the phrase "at a pH from approximately 6.0 to 9.0" to claim 1 during prosecution. The alleged infringer operated its ultrafiltration process at a pH of 5.0. The Supreme Court stated that "while a lower limit of [pH] 6.0, by its mere inclusion, became a material element of the claim, that did not necessarily preclude the application of the doctrine of equivalents as to that element." *Id.* at 32. On remand, the Supreme Court instructed this court to determine the patentee's reason, if any, for adding the lower pH limit of 6.0 during prosecution.

The patent at issue in *Warner-Jenkinson* did not disclose or suggest an ultrafiltration process where the pH of the reaction mixture was 5.0. In fact, the specification practically repeated the claim language: "it is preferred to adjust the *pH to approximately 6.0 to 8.0* before passage through the ultrafiltration membrane." U.S. Patent No. 4,560,746, col. 7, ll. 59-61 (emphasis added). Thus, *Warner-Jenkinson* did not present an instance of the patentee dedicating subject matter to the public in its specification. In 1998, less than a year later, this court decided *YBM Magnex*.

## IV.

As stated in *Maxwell*, when a patent drafter discloses but declines to claim subject matter, as in this case, this action dedicates that unclaimed subject matter to the public. Application of the doctrine of equivalents to recapture subject matter deliberately left unclaimed would "conflict with the primacy of the claims in defining the scope of the patentee's exclusive right." *Sage Prods. Inc. v. Devon Indus., Inc.*, 126 F.3d 1420, 1424 (Fed. Cir. 1997) (citing *Warner-Jenkinson*, 520 U.S. at 29, 117 S. Ct. 1040).

Moreover, a patentee cannot narrowly claim an invention to avoid prosecution scrutiny by the PTO, and then, after patent issuance, use the doctrine of equivalents to establish infringement because the specification discloses equivalents. "Such a result would merely encourage a patent applicant to present a broad disclosure in the specification of the application and file narrow claims, avoiding examination of broader claims that the applicant could have filed consistent with the specification." *Maxwell*, 86 F.3d at 1107 (citing *Genentech, Inc. v. Wellcome Found. Ltd.*, 29 F.3d 1555, 1564 (Fed. Cir. 1994)). By enforcing the *Maxwell* rule, the courts avoid the problem of extending the coverage of an exclusive right to encompass more than that properly examined by the PTO. *Keystone Bridge Co. v. Phoenix Iron Co.* 95 U.S. 274, 278 (1877) ("[T]he courts have no right to enlarge a patent beyond the scope of its claim as allowed by the Patent Office, or the appellate tribunal to which contested applications are referred.").

## V.

In this case, Johnston's '050 patent specifically limited the claims to "a sheet of aluminum" and "the aluminum sheet." The specification of the '050 patent, however, reads: "While aluminum is currently the preferred material for the substrate, other metals, such as stainless steel or nickel alloys may be used." Col. 5, ll. 5-10. Having disclosed without claiming the steel substrates, Johnston cannot now invoke the doctrine of equivalents to extend its aluminum limitation to encompass steel. Thus, Johnston cannot assert the doctrine of equivalents to cover the disclosed but unclaimed steel substrate. To the extent that *YBM Magnex* conflicts with this holding, this *en banc* court now overrules that case.

A patentee who inadvertently fails to claim disclosed subject matter, however, is not left without remedy. Within two years from the grant of the original patent, a patentee may file a reissue application and attempt to enlarge the scope of the original claims to include the disclosed but previously unclaimed subject matter. 35 U.S.C. §251 (2000).[*] In addition, a patentee can file a separate application claiming the disclosed subject matter under 35 U.S.C. §120 (2000) (allowing filing as a continuation application if filed before all applications in the chain issue). Notably, Johnston took advantage of the latter of the two options by filing two continuation applications that literally claim the relevant subject matter.

PAULINE NEWMAN, Circuit Judge, Dissenting.

Patentees often must draw lines in order to claim their invention with specificity. *See* 35 U.S.C. §112 (the claims must "particularly point [ ] out and distinctly claim[ ] the subject matter which the applicant regards as his invention.") The establishment of a *per se* rule so heavily weighted against disclosure is not only inappropriately simplistic, but is contrary to the policy of the patent law.

\*\*\*

The public interest in fostering innovation and technological advance is not served by a judicial decision that imposes legal obstacles to the disclosure of scientific and technologic information. Information dissemination is a critical purpose of the patent system. By penalizing the inclusion of information in the specification the patent becomes less useful as a source of knowledge, and more a guarded legal contract.

No patentee deliberately chooses the doctrine of equivalents to protect commercial investment. Yet every patentee must guard against infringement at the edges of the invention. After today, whenever a patentee draws a line in a disclosed continuum, the copier who simply crosses the line can avoid even the charge of equivalency; a safe and cheap way to garner the successes of another. Each new pitfall for inventors simply diminishes the value of the patent incentive, and ultimately inhibits technological innovation. Concern for the effectiveness of the patent system has always been a factor in innovation activity. A study by Wesley M. Cohen *et al.*, *Protecting Their Intellectual Assets: Appropriability Conditions and Why U.S. Manufacturing Firms Patent (Or Not)*, Nat'l Bureau of Econ. Research Working Paper 7552, at 14 (2000), reported that in a 1994 survey of R & D managers 65% of the respondents cited the ease of avoiding patent claims as the main deterrent to patent-based investment in technology, and 47%

---

[*] [Recall this point was made by Justice Black in his *Graver* dissent. — EDS.]

also cited concern for disclosing technical information without adequate protection.

Discovery of and commercialization of new things is notoriously risk-laden, yet it is the inventor and the innovator, those whose ingenuity and ambition create new things while taking the risk of loss, who provide the basis of industrial advance and economic growth.

*\*\**

A judicial change in the balance between innovator and imitator should not be made in disregard of the consequences. The neatness of a *per se* rule is not necessarily sound legal or economic policy. Nor is it sound judicial policy, for in addition to issues of commerce and technology-based industry, this case raises questions of fundamental fairness as to disputes that will now be excluded from judicial review. Fairness is the foundation of due process; it is superior to, not subordinate to, *per se* rules.

## Comments

1. *Sufficiency of the Disclosure?* How specific must the disclosure be to dedicate subject matter to the public? Does the disclosure have to be enabling or simply mention the equivalent? The Federal Circuit addressed this issue in *PSC Computer Products, Inc. v. Foxconn Intern., Inc.*, 355 F.3d 1353 (Fed. Cir. 2004). According to the court, a mere "generic reference in a written specification" does not "necessarily dedicate[ ] all members of that particular genus to the public." *Id.* at 1360. Rather, for subject matter to be deemed dedicated to the public, a PHOSITA must be able to "understand the unclaimed disclosed teaching upon reading the written description." But the court then stated, arguably inconsistently, the "disclosure must be of such specificity that one of ordinary skill in the art could identify the subject matter that had been disclosed and not claimed." *Id.* What is the difference, if any, between the terms "understand the unclaimed disclosed teaching" and "identify" the disclosed subject matter? Although the word "teaching," unlike "identify," suggest an enablement-like standard, the Federal Circuit held in *Toro Co. v. White Consolidated Industries, Inc.*, 383 F.3d 1326 (Fed. Cir. 2004), that the public dedication rule "does not impose a §112 requirement on the disclosed but unclaimed subject matter." *Id.* at 1334.

2. *Judge Newman's Dissent.* Judge Newman asserts or implies that patent applicants will be more reluctant to disclose technical information in their specification in the light of *Johnson & Johnston*. And that the public dedication rule is inconsistent with patent policy. Can one also argue that the public dedication rule may make patent applicants and their attorneys more careful during the drafting and prosecution process.

## 3. All-Limitations Rule

In *Warner-Jenkinson* the Court, relying on the late Judge Nies' dissent below, adopted an all-limitations rule (or all-elements rule)[8] when applying the DOE. According to the Court, this rule "reconcile[s] the prohibition against enlarging the scope of claims and the doctrine of equivalents by applying the doctrine to each element of a claim, rather than to the accused product or process 'overall.'"[9] Under this rule, each limitation of a patent claim is material to defining the scope of the patented invention and must not be vitiated or rendered meaningless.[10] Thus, for there to be infringement under the DOE an equivalent of each claim limitation must be found in the accused device. In other words, the DOE is applied to each limitation, not to the invention as a whole.

The all-limitations approach to equivalency was part of the Federal Circuit's DOE jurisprudence prior to *Warner-Jenkinson*.[11] But identifying what exactly constitutes a limitation, and when is a claim limitation vitiated are questions that are sometimes difficult to answer. For example, in *Corning Glass Works v. Sumitomo Electric U.S.A.*,[12] the court recognized that the all-limitations rule has led to "confusion . . . because of misunderstanding or misleading uses of the term 'element' in discussing claims." According to the court, " '[e]lement' may be used to mean a single limitation, but it has also been used to mean a series of limitations which, taken together, make up a component of the claimed invention."[13] The court continued, stating that under the all-limitations rule, "[a]n equivalent must be found for every limitation of the claim somewhere in an accused device, but not necessarily in a corresponding component, although that is generally the case."[14] This language suggests the all-limitations rule is more flexible than a one-to-one correspondence that demands each claim limitation to have a corresponding equivalent in the accused device.

---

8. The Federal Circuit has expressed a preference for the word "limitation" (instead of "element") when referring to claim language, and "element" when referring to the accused device. *See Festo Corp. v. Shoketsu Kinzoku Kogyo Kabushiki Co., Inc.*, 234 F.3d 558, 563 n.1 (Fed. Cir. 2000) (*en banc*) ("In our prior cases, we have used both the term 'element' and the term 'limitation' to refer to words in a claim. It is preferable to use the term 'limitation' when referring to claim language and the term 'element' when referring to the accused device"). To this end, the court has also noted that the "All Elements rule might better be called the All-Limitations rule." *Ethicon Endo-Surgery, Inc. v. U.S. Surgical Corp.*, 149 F.3d 1309, 1317 n.* (Fed. Cir. 1998).

9. *Warner-Jenkinson*, 517 U.S. at 25.

10. *See Bell Atlantic Network Services, Inc. v. Covad Communications Group, Inc.*, 262 F.3d 1258, 1279-1280 (Fed. Cir. 2001) (stating "if a court determines that a finding of infringement under the doctrine of equivalents 'would entirely vitiate a particular claim element,' then the court should rule that there is no infringement under the doctrine of equivalents.") (citing *Warner-Jenkinson Co., Inc. v. Hilton Davis Chemical Co.*, 520 U.S. 17, 39 n.8 (1997)).

11. *See Pennwalt Corp. v. Durand-Wayland*, 833 F.2d 931 (Fed. Cir. 1987) (en banc). Judge Nies concurred with the majority, but filed "additional views," which provides a wonderful discussion of nineteenth- and twentieth-century precedent relating to infringement under the DOE. *See Pennwalt*, 833 F.2d at 949-955.

12. 868 F.2d 1251 (Fed. Cir. 1989).

13. *Id.* at 1259.

14. *Id.*

But subsequent decisions sought to clarify *Corning Glass*. In *Dolly, Inc. v. Spalding & Evenflo Companies, Inc.*,[15] for instance, the Federal Circuit, referring to the *Corning Glass* language noted above, stated the "language in *Corning Glass* did not substitute a broader limitation-by-limitation comparison for the doctrine of equivalents than the element-by-element comparison in *Pennwalt*. Rather, *Corning Glass* reaffirmed that the rule requires an equivalent for every limitation of the claim, even though the equivalent may not be present in the corresponding component of the accused device."[16] Thus, the court remarked that equivalency will result "when two components of the accused device perform a single function of the patented invention" or "when separate claim limitations are combined into a single component of the accused device."[17] A recent example of the latter can be found in *Eagle Comtronics, Inc. v. Arrow Communication Laboratories, Inc.*[18] In *Eagle*, the invention related to an improved cable filter structure used to decode or unscramble protected television signals. Claim 1, the only independent claim, recited several limitations, three of which included a (1) front cap, (2) a rear insert body including a rear end portion, and (3) a seal located between the front cap and the rear insert body. The accused products did not have separate elements corresponding to the front cap and rear insert body limitations, but did have a seal located along the periphery of the accused products. The patentee conceded there was no literal infringement, but argued infringement under the DOE. The accused infringer asserted because the accused devices do not possess a corresponding element to the aforementioned claim limitations, therefore, applying of the DOE would impermissibly vitiate these limitations. The Federal Circuit disagreed, stating:

> While a claim limitation cannot be totally missing from an accused device, whether or not a limitation is deemed to be vitiated must take into account that when two elements of the accused device perform a single function of the patented invention, or when separate claim limitations are combined into a single element of the accused device, a claim limitation is not necessarily vitiated, and the doctrine of equivalents may still apply if the differences are insubstantial.[19]

In *Sage Prods. v. Devon Indus.*,[20] however, vitiation was a concern and led to a finding of no infringement under the DOE. In *Sage*, the invention was a container for disposing of hazardous medical waste. The relevant claim language stated the invention comprised a container body with "an elongated slot at the top of the container body...."[21] The defendant made a similar container, but the slot for disposing the waste was within

15. 16 F.3d 394 (Fed. Cir. 1994).
16. *Id.* at 399. *See also Forest Labs v. Abbott Labs*, 239 F.3d 1305, 1313 (Fed. Cir. 2001) (noting *Corning Glass* "did not dispense with the need for one-to-one correspondence of limitations and elements").
17. *Dolly*, 16 F.3d at 398. *See also Eagle Comtronics, Inc. v. Arrow Communication Laboratories, Inc.*, 305 F.3d 1303, 1317 (Fed. Cir. 2002) (same).
18. 305 F.3d 1303 (Fed. Cir. 2002).
19. *Id.* at 1317.
20. 126 F.3d 1420 (Fed. Cir. 1997).
21. *Id.* at 1422.

the container body.[22] Both containers featured two constrictions that kept the waste securely within the container. The plaintiff argued "having two constrictions below the top of the container is the same, for purposes of infringement, as having one constriction above and one constriction below."[23] The court found no literal infringement and ruled the all-limitations rule would be violated if the patentee were allowed to show the slot within the container was equivalent to a slot at the top of the container.

---

22. *Id.* at 1423.
23. *Id.* at 1424.

# CHAPTER
# 12

# Defenses to Patent Infringement

## INTRODUCTION

The most common defenses to a patent infringement suit are noninfringement and patent invalidity. The former asserts that the accused product does not literally or equivalently fall within the patent's claim scope, while the latter provides that the patent should never have issued because of the patentee's failure to satisfy one or more of the patentability requirements, which were discussed in Chapter 10.

In addition to noninfringement and invalidity, there are numerous other defenses. This chapter is devoted to four of them, namely (1) inequitable conduct; (2) repair/reconstruction; (3) limitations on use of contracts; and (4) antitrust.

## A. INEQUITABLE CONDUCT

The defense of inequitable conduct relates to the patentee's behavior during the prosecution of his patent application. While there is no duty to conduct a prior art search, every patent applicant and others associated with filing a patent application (e.g., the patent attorney) owe a duty of candor and good faith to the PTO, which includes a duty to disclose all information known to be material to patentability. *See* 37 C.F.R. §1.56(a). Thus, there are two elements to inequitable conduct: (1) intent, and (2) materiality. The rationale underlying the duty of candor is that a patent is affected with a public interest, and that interest is best served when the patent examiner has the most relevant information before him when examining the application.

REGULATION: **Duty to Disclose Information Material to Patentability**
37 C.F.R. §1.56

## PURDUE PHARMA L.P. v. ENDO PHARMACEUTICALS INC.

— F.3d — , 2006 WL 231480 (Fed. Cir. 2006)

This is a patent case. It arose when Purdue Pharma L.P., The Purdue Frederick Company, The P.F. Laboratories, Inc., and The Purdue Pharma Company (collectively, "Purdue") filed an infringement suit against Endo Pharmaceuticals Inc. and Endo Pharmaceuticals Holdings Inc. (collectively, "Endo") in the United States District Court for the Southern District of New York. Plaintiffs alleged that Endo's proposed generic versions of OxyContin ®, Purdue's controlled release oxycodone product, would infringe three Purdue patents.

After a bench trial, the trial court found that Endo would infringe Purdue's patents, but determined that the patents were unenforceable due to inequitable conduct that occurred during prosecution before the United States Patent and Trademark Office ("PTO"). Purdue appealed the inequitable conduct judgment; Endo cross-appealed the infringement judgment. On appeal, we initially affirmed the trial court's judgment that the patents were unenforceable due to the inequitable conduct by Purdue. The cross-appeal was deemed moot.

On petition for rehearing, we have further examined the issues in the case. The trial judge had provided us with a thorough and complete opinion, explaining the case and his view of it. Our further examination suggested, nevertheless, that there were some issues that needed more development. In addition to fact-finding regarding materiality and intent, inequitable conduct requires a special kind of balancing, weighing the level of materiality against the weight of the evidence of intent.

Our further review has persuaded us that the trial judge may have erred in how he viewed certain of the evidence, and that this may have caused an error in the balancing step. Accordingly, we have withdrawn the earlier opinion and replaced it with this one. The judgment of inequitable conduct is now vacated, and the matter is remanded to the trial court for further proceedings in accordance with this opinion.

### BACKGROUND

The three patents asserted by Purdue against Endo are directed to controlled release oxycodone medications for the treatment of moderate to severe pain. The patents are related: U.S. Patents No. 5,656,295 (the " '295 patent") and No. 5,508,042 (the " '042 patent") are, respectively, a continuation-in-part and a divisional of U.S. Patent No. 5,549,912 (the " '912 patent"). The '912 patent itself is a continuation-in-part of U.S. Patent No. 5,266,331 (the " '331 patent"), which Purdue has not asserted against Endo. The '331 patent is the parent patent, and for ease of reference will be identified as such from time to time.

The written descriptions of the '912, '295 and '042 patents are virtually identical. The asserted claims include composition claims (claims 1-4 of the

'912 patent and claims 1-4 and 6-7 of the '295 patent) and method claims (claims 8-10 of the '295 patent and claims 1 and 2 of the '042 patent). Claim 1 of the '912 patent is representative of the composition claims and reads:

> A controlled release oxycodone formulation for oral administration to human patients, comprising from about 10 to about 40 mg oxycodone or a salt thereof, said formulation providing a mean maximum plasma concentration of oxycodone from about 6 to about 60 ng/ml from a mean of about 2 to about 4.5 hours after administration, and a mean minimum plasma concentration from about 3 to about 30 ng/ml from a mean of about 10 to about 14 hours after repeated administration every 12 hours through steady-state conditions.

Claim 1 of the '042 patent is representative of the method claims and reads:

> A method for reducing the range in daily dosages required to control pain in human patients, comprising administering an oral controlled release dosage formulation comprising from about 10 to about 40 mg oxycodone or a salt thereof which provides a mean maximum plasma concentration of oxycodone from about 6 to about 60 ng/ml from a mean of about 2 to about 4.5 hours after administration, and a mean minimum plasma concentration from about 3 to about 30 ng/ml from a mean of about 10 to about 14 hours after repeated administration every 12 hours through steady-state conditions.

The "Detailed Description" section of the written description in each asserted patent opens with the following statement, which played a prominent role in the trial court's inequitable conduct determination:

> It has now been *surprisingly discovered* that the presently claimed controlled release oxycodone formulations acceptably control pain over a substantially narrower, approximately four — fold [range] (10 to 40 mg every 12 hours — around-the-clock dosing) in approximately 90% of patients. This is in sharp contrast to the approximately eight-fold range required for approximately 90% of patients for opioid analgesics in general.

'912 patent, col. 3, ll. 34-41 (emphasis added).

The thrust of this language is that the invented oxycodone formulation using a four-fold range of dosages (e.g., between 10 mg and 40 mg) achieves the same clinical results as the prior art opioid formulations using an eight-fold range of dosages (e.g., between 10 mg and 80 mg). The written description later explains that the "clinical significance" of the four-fold dosage range of the oxycodone formulations of the present invention, as compared to other opioid analgesics, such as morphine, requiring twice the dosage range, is a more efficient titration process, which is the process of adjusting a patient's dosage to provide acceptable pain relief without unacceptable side effects. *Id.*, col. 4, ll. 51-63.

In December 1995, after obtaining FDA approval, Purdue introduced its controlled release oxycodone product under the name OxyContin ®. In September 2000, pursuant to the procedures of the Hatch-Waxman Act, 21 U.S.C. § 355(j), Endo filed an Abbreviated New Drug Application ("ANDA") with the FDA seeking approval to make and sell a generic version of Purdue's OxyContin ® formulation. Endo notified Purdue it had filed a paragraph IV certification asserting that Purdue's patents either would not be infringed by Endo's generic drug or were invalid. In October 2000 Purdue initiated a patent infringement suit under 35 U.S.C. § 271(e)(2) on the basis of Endo's ANDA filing, alleging that Endo's generic drug would infringe the '912, '295, and '042 patents. Endo subsequently twice amended its ANDA to seek approval for additional dosage strengths. Purdue filed two additional infringement suits, which the trial court consolidated with the original action.

Endo filed counterclaims seeking a declaratory judgment that Purdue's patents were invalid, unenforceable, and not infringed.... The trial court also concluded that Endo had shown by clear and convincing evidence that Purdue's patents were unenforceable due to Purdue's inequitable conduct during prosecution of the patents before the PTO. The court based its inequitable conduct determination on underlying findings of materiality and intent. First, the court found that in view of Purdue's repeated statements to the PTO that it had discovered an oxycodone formulation for controlling pain over a four-fold range of dosages for 90% of patients, compared to an eight-fold range for other opioids, Purdue failed to disclose material information because it did not inform the PTO that the "discovery" was based on "insight" without "scientific proof." Second, the trial court found the record as a whole reflected a "clear pattern of intentional misrepresentation."

As a result of its inequitable conduct determination, the trial court enjoined Purdue from enforcing the '912, '295, and '042 patents, *id.*, and entered final judgment pursuant to Fed. R. Civ. P. 54(b). Purdue took a timely appeal from the trial court's inequitable conduct judgment; Endo filed a cross-appeal from the trial court's infringement judgment. We have jurisdiction pursuant to 28 U.S.C. § 1295(a)(1).

## DISCUSSION

### A. INEQUITABLE CONDUCT

Applicants for patents have a duty to prosecute patents in the PTO with candor and good faith, including a duty to disclose information known to the applicants to be material to patentability. 37 C.F.R. § 1.56(a) (2004); *see also Molins PLC v. Textron, Inc.*, 48 F.3d 1172, 1178 (Fed. Cir. 1995). A breach of this duty may constitute inequitable conduct, which can arise from an affirmative misrepresentation of a material fact, failure to disclose material information, or submission of false material information, coupled with an intent to deceive or mislead the PTO. A party asserting that a patent is unenforceable due to inequitable conduct must prove materiality and intent by clear and convincing evidence. Once threshold findings of materiality and intent are established, the trial court must weigh them to determine whether the equities warrant a conclusion that inequitable conduct occurred. This requires a careful balancing: when the misrepresentation or withheld information is highly material, a lesser quantum of proof is needed to establish the requisite intent. In contrast, the less material the information, the greater the proof must be. See *id.*

We review the trial court's rulings on inequitable conduct deferentially. The court's factual findings regarding materiality and intent are reviewed for clear error, and thus will not be disturbed on appeal unless this court has a "definite and firm conviction" that a mistake has been made. *Kingsdown*, 863 F.2d at 872. The trial court's ultimate conclusion that inequitable conduct has occurred is reviewed for an abuse of discretion. *Id.*

### 1. MATERIALITY

In evaluating materiality, this court has consistently referred to the standard set forth in PTO Rule 56. Because all of the patent applications at issue in this case were pending on or filed after March 16, 1992, we look to the current version of Rule 56, rather than the pre-1992 version of the rule. Under the current rule, information is material to patentability when:

> [I]t is not cumulative to information already of record or being made of record in the application, and
> (1) It establishes, by itself or in combination with other information, a prima facie case of unpatentability of a claim; or (2) It refutes, or is inconsistent with, a position the applicant takes in:
> (i) Opposing an argument of unpatentability relied on by the Office, or
> (ii) Asserting an argument of patentability.

37 C.F.R. §1.56(b) (2004).[6] In applying this version of the rule, "we give deference to the PTO's formulation at the time an application is being prosecuted before an examiner of the standard of conduct it expects to be followed in proceedings in the Office." *Bruno*, 394 F.3d at 1353. The trial court in this case based its materiality finding on Purdue's repeated and convincing representations to the PTO that it had discovered its controlled release oxycodone formulations controlled pain over a four-fold range of dosages for 90% of patients, compared to an eight-fold range for other opioids. Purdue had no clinical evidence supporting its claim at the time it was made or at any time before the patents issued. During prosecution of the patents, the examiner repeatedly rejected the applications on the grounds that the invention was obvious in light of prior art. Eventually, however, in response to the applicants' further explanations, the examiner allowed the claims.

The trial court found that the lack of scientific proof of a four-fold dosage range for oxycodone was a material fact inconsistent with statements made by Purdue to obtain allowance of the patent claims over the examiner's rejections. (The phrase "four-fold dosage range" is sometimes used herein as shorthand for the fact that the claimed controlled release oxycodone formulation acceptably controls pain over a four-fold range of dosages in approximately 90% of patients.) In the trial court's view, by representing to the PTO that it had "discovered" that oxycodone acceptably controlled pain over a four-fold dosage range, while withholding from the PTO the fact that the discovery was based on insight without scientific proof, Purdue failed to disclose material information.

---

6. This new standard was not intended to constitute a significant substantive break with the pre-1992 standard. *Hoffman-La Roche, Inc. v. Promega Corp.*, 323 F.3d 1354, 1368 n. 2 (Fed. Cir. 2003).

Purdue does not dispute the absence of clinical evidence during the relevant timeframe to support its claim of a four-fold dosage range for oxycodone. Indeed, Dr. Kaiko testified at trial that it was "insight" that led to discovery of the reduced range. He asserted that, based on his knowledge of the pharmacological properties of opioids and the differences between oxycodone and other opioids such as morphine, he "envisioned" a controlled release oxycodone product that would control pain over a four-fold dosage range in 90% of patients.

Purdue, however, contends it is irrelevant that it lacked scientific proof of the four-fold dosage range for oxycodone because the inventors never stated during prosecution of the patents that the discovery had been clinically tested, and thus did not expressly misrepresent a material fact. But that was not the basis for the trial court's materiality finding. The trial court found Purdue had relied on its discovery of a four-fold dosage range throughout prosecution of the '331 parent patent and the related patents-in-suit as "a prominent, and at times, the only, argument in favor of patentability before the PTO, resulting in allowance of the claims." *Purdue Pharma*, 2004 WL 26523, at *24. In the trial court's view, by failing to explain to the PTO that Dr. Kaiko's "insight" provided the only support for its "discovery," Purdue failed to disclose material information that was inconsistent with its arguments for patentability..

Purdue first told the PTO it had "surprisingly discovered" the four-fold dosage range for controlled release oxycodone, compared to the eight-fold range for other opioids, during prosecution of the '331 parent patent in October 1992, prior to the filing date of the '912 patent. In response to an obviousness rejection, under headings containing the phrases "Surprisingly Improved Results" and "Results Obtained," Purdue distinguished its oxycodone formulations from other opioids based on the "surprising result" of the four-fold dosage range and its "clinical significance" — a more efficient titration process. Purdue presented this argument even though neither the written description nor the pending claims of the '331 patent application made reference to the four-fold dosage range. Purdue's response contained language identical to that which was soon to appear in the written description of the '912 patent application.

Purdue continued to rely on oxycodone's four-fold dosage range and more efficient titration process to support its patentability arguments throughout prosecution of the '331 patent. After another obviousness rejection and an interview between the examiner and Purdue's attorney, Purdue submitted a response accompanied by the declaration of Dr. Robert Kaiko (named as an inventor on the '912, '295, and '042 patents, but not on the '331 patent). The Kaiko declaration emphasized the difficulty of predicting the pharmacological characteristics of opioids and cautioned that "the most meaningful therapeutic conclusions" should be based on "the results of the most adequate and well-controlled therapeutic evaluations."

Dr. Kaiko's declaration referenced an attachment, which appears to be an invention disclosure prepared by Dr. Kaiko. In that attachment, under the heading "INVENTION," Dr. Kaiko asserted that controlled release oxycodone acceptably controls pain over a four-fold dosage range for 90% of patients. Dr. Kaiko then discussed clinical studies that compared

the resulting in vivo plasma concentrations of controlled release oxycodone with those of immediate release oxycodone. The Kaiko attachment
concluded by stating that the "CLINICAL SIGNIFICANCE" of the four-
fold dosage range compared to other opioids requiring twice the dosage
range was "the most efficient and humane method of managing pain requiring repeated dosing", i.e., an improved titration process. This explanation
of the clinical significance of the four-fold dosage range, placed after a
discussion of clinical studies, suggests that Dr. Kaiko's discovery was supported by clinical results. By the time Purdue submitted the Kaiko declaration and attachment to the PTO, the application that resulted in the '912
patent had been filed as a continuation-in-part of the '331 patent. The
written description of the '912 patent contains several paragraphs of
text not in the written description of the '331 patent, including the statements that the four-fold dosage range had been "surprisingly discovered"
and that the clinical significance of the discovery was a more efficient titration process. During prosecution of the '912 patent, Purdue again found it
necessary to distinguish its controlled release oxycodone formulations over
prior art directed to a different opioid analgesic by emphasizing its "surprising discovery" of oxycodone's four-fold dosage range and more efficient titration process. Purdue further stated that the in vivo parameters set
forth in the claims "are specifically related to the surprising results
obtained by the invention," thereby directly linking the features of the
claimed invention to the newly discovered four-fold dosage range.

In light of Purdue's consistent representations of the four-fold dosage
range for controlled release oxycodone as a "surprising discovery" and the
context in which that statement was repeatedly made, we cannot say the
trial court's finding that Purdue failed to disclose material information was
clearly erroneous. While Purdue never expressly stated that the discovery
of the four-fold dosage range was based on the results of clinical studies,
that conclusion was clearly to be inferred from the language used by Purdue in both the patents and prosecution history.

For example, Purdue a number of times during prosecution referred to
the four-fold dosage range as a "result," implying that clinical results had
been obtained. Purdue also frequently emphasized the "clinical significance" of its discovery. As noted, the discussion regarding clinical significance in the Kaiko attachment in particular suggests that discovery of the
four-fold dosage range was based on clinical studies. In addition, Purdue
continually compared the dosage range of controlled release oxycodone to
that of other opioid analgesics in concise, quantitative terms (e.g., four-fold vs.
eight-fold for approximately 90% of patients). In the absence of any statements indicating the true origin of its "surprising discovery," Purdue's
arguments to the PTO provide enough of a suggestion that clinical trials
had been performed that failure to tell the PTO the discovery was based on
Dr. Kaiko's insight and not scientific proof was a failure to disclose material
information.

Purdue contends it did not make material misrepresentations or fail to
disclose material information to the PTO because the examiner did not
rely on its assertion of a four-fold dosage range for oxycodone. According
to Purdue, the examiner could have allowed the claims based on other
arguments it made to distinguish the oxycodone claims over the prior

art. Even assuming the examiner did not necessarily rely on Purdue's discovery of a four-fold dosage range, however, that would not be inconsistent with a finding of materiality. A review of the prosecution history of the patents-in-suit and the parent '331 patent leaves no doubt that Purdue disclosed its "surprising discovery" of oxycodone's four-fold dosage range to support one of its central patentability arguments and to oppose the examiner's argument that Purdue's claims were unpatentable in view of the prior art. Information that Purdue's assertion of a four-fold dosage range was based only on Dr. Kaiko's insight and not on experimental results was material because it was inconsistent with Purdue's statements suggesting otherwise.

Purdue also argues that the trial court's materiality finding was unduly influenced by the court's allegedly erroneous conclusion that the claims of the patents-in-suit must be construed to include the four-fold dosage range as a limitation. Purdue's argument is without merit for two reasons. First, the trial court stated it would have reached the same result even if the claims were not so limited. Second, materiality "is not limited to matters reflected in the claims of a patent." *Hoffmann-La Roche,* 323 F.3d at 1367.

We are also unpersuaded by Purdue's argument that the four-fold dosage range is simply a benefit of the claimed invention and therefore not material because the examiner would have given it little weight. Purdue relies on this court's decision in *CFMT, Inc. v. Yieldup International Corp.,* 349 F.3d 1333 (Fed. Cir. 2003), which reversed the trial court's materiality finding based on a list of advantages of the claimed invention identified by the applicants during prosecution. In that case, however, this court found that the applicants' "advantages advocacy recited only the natural, expected results of a closed system [for cleaning semiconductor wafers]." *Id.* at 1342. At most the applicants had overemphasized the benefits of the invention. *Id.* Purdue's assertion of a four-fold dosage range for oxycodone and more efficient titration process compared to other opioids was much more than "advantages advocacy;" it was one of the key arguments Purdue made consistently and repeatedly during prosecution to overcome prior art cited by the examiner in an obviousness rejection. Purdue did not present the four-fold dosage range as a general benefit of the claimed oxycodone formulations, but instead relied on the four-fold dosage range to distinguish its invention over other opioid analgesics in precise, quantitative terms.

Finally, Purdue and the supporting *amicus curiae* brief of Guilford Pharmaceuticals argue that the trial court erred by requiring that a patent application for a pharmaceutical discovery be supported by clinical results. Purdue and Guilford are correct that the manner in which an invention is discovered, whether by insight or experiment, does not by itself affect patentability. But the trial court's materiality finding was not based only on the fact that Purdue described the four-fold dosage range in its patents as a "surprising discovery" without providing any scientific proof. Rather, the trial court examined the entire record and found materiality because Purdue repeatedly argued to the PTO that the four-fold dosage range distinguished the invention over prior art and, while using language that implied, if not suggested, experimental results had been obtained, failed to tell the PTO its discovery was based only on Dr. Kaiko's insight.

In this respect the case is similar to *Hoffmann-La Roche*. In that case, the patentees had erroneously stated in the written description that a procedure had been performed and presented "results" of that procedure. *Hoffmann-La Roche*, 323 F.3d at 1363. This court affirmed the trial court's finding of materiality, not on the ground that experimental results were required for patentability, but on the ground that the patentees misrepresented the results and made reference to them during prosecution in responding to a PTO office action. Similarly, the trial court's finding in this case was not based on Purdue's failure to provide scientific proof of its "surprising discovery," but on its failure to tell the PTO that the discovery was based only on the inventor's insight after suggesting during prosecution that the discovery was based on the results of clinical studies.

We emphasize that this case is an unusual one. A failure to inform the PTO whether a "surprising discovery" was based on insight or experimental data does not in itself amount to a material omission. In this case, however, Purdue did much more than characterize the four-fold dosage range of the claimed oxycodone formulation as a surprising discovery. Purdue repeatedly relied on that discovery to distinguish its invention from other prior art opioids while using language that suggested the existence of clinical results supporting the reduced dosage range. Presented with these unique facts, we cannot say the trial court erred in finding that Purdue failed to disclose material information to the PTO.

While we affirm the trial court's finding that Purdue's actions met a threshold level of materiality, we stress that the level of materiality is not especially high. Purdue did not expressly misrepresent to the PTO that it had obtained experimental results establishing a four-fold dosage range for oxycodone, an act that likely would have been highly material. Instead, Purdue made statements implying that an empirical basis existed for its discovery and then failed to disclose that the discovery was based only on insight. This omission of information was material, but not as material as an affirmative misrepresentation would have been. See *Hoffmann-La Roche*, 323 F.3d at 1367 (holding that affirmative misrepresentations, in contrast to misleading omissions, are more likely to be regarded as material). The trial court did not make an explicit finding regarding the level of materiality. Some language in its opinion, however, indicates the trial court considered Purdue's failure to tell the PTO the basis for its discovery to be highly material. As discussed below, the trial court may have erred to the extent it relied on a high level of materiality in determining whether Purdue intended to deceive the PTO and whether Purdue ultimately committed inequitable conduct.

### 2. INTENT

Direct evidence of intent to deceive or mislead the PTO is "'rarely available but may be inferred from clear and convincing evidence of the surrounding circumstances.'" *Baxter Int'l, Inc. v. McGaw, Inc.*, 149 F.3d 1321, 1329 (Fed. Cir. 1998) (quoting *LaBounty Mfg., Inc. v. USITC*, 958 F.2d 1066, 1076 (Fed. Cir. 1992)). Intent to deceive, however, cannot be "inferred solely from the fact that information was not disclosed; there must be a factual basis for a finding of deceptive intent." *Hebert v. Lisle*

*Corp.*, 99 F.3d 1109, 1116 (Fed. Cir. 1996). When determining whether intent has been shown, a court must weigh all evidence, including evidence of good faith. This court has held that "a patentee facing a high level of materiality and clear proof that it knew or should have known of that materiality, can expect to find it difficult to establish 'subjective good faith' sufficient to prevent the drawing of an inference of intent to mislead." *Critikon, Inc. v. Becton Dickinson Vascular Access, Inc.*, 120 F.3d 1253, 1257 (Fed. Cir. 1997). Nevertheless, it is important to remember that "'materiality does not presume intent, which is a separate and essential component of inequitable conduct.'" *Allen Eng'g Corp. v. Bartell Indus., Inc.*, 299 F.3d 1336, 1352 (Fed. Cir. 2002) (quoting *Allen Organ Co. v. Kimball Int'l, Inc.*, 839 F.2d 1556, 1567 (Fed. Cir. 1988)).

There are two problems with the trial court's analysis of the intent prong. First, in discounting any evidence of good faith put forth by Purdue, the trial court relied heavily on internal memoranda and trial testimony regarding Purdue's admitted inability to prove with experimental results that OxyContin ® was the most efficiently titratable analgesic. This evidence, however, relates primarily to Purdue's attempt to gain FDA approval for a proposed labeling claim rather than its attempt to obtain allowance of its patent claims.

We agree with Purdue that evidence regarding the difficulty in proving the titration claim is not inconsistent with Purdue's asserted belief that it had discovered its oxycodone formulations were effective over a four-fold dosage range, compared to an eight-fold dosage range for other opioids. While Purdue alleged during prosecution that ease of titration would result from a reduced dosage range, the two concepts are different. Furthermore, the quantum of proof necessary for FDA approval is significantly higher than that required by the PTO. Therefore, evidence that Purdue personnel believed it would be difficult to satisfy FDA requirements is at best marginally related to whether they intended to deceive the PTO. For these reasons, the trial court erred in giving the weight it did to this evidence when determining that Purdue acted with deceptive intent during prosecution of its patents. The trial court's second problem was its failure to properly consider the level of materiality. It appears the trial court perceived the level of materiality to be high and inferred deceptive intent from that high materiality, combined with the court's erroneous finding that any good faith on the part of Purdue was undercut by its admitted inability to prove the ease of titration claim. It is true that in some cases this court has inferred the requisite intent to deceive when a patentee has withheld highly material information such as a key prior art reference and knew or should have known of its materiality. As discussed previously, however, Purdue's failure to disclose to the PTO that the asserted four-fold dosage range of the claimed oxycodone formulation was based on insight rather than experimental data does not rise to such a high level of materiality. In a case such as this, when the materiality of the undisclosed information is relatively low, there is less basis for inferring intent from materiality alone.

Because of these errors in the trial court's intent analysis, we are unable to uphold the court's finding that Purdue intended to deceive the PTO when it failed to disclose that its "surprising discovery" of the reduced dosage range was based only on insight. However, since the trial court is in a better position than we are to evaluate the evidence of record, we think the prudent course is to vacate the inequitable conduct judgment and remand the case to give the trial court an opportunity to reconsider its intent finding. In doing so, the trial court should rethink the relevance of the evidence relating to whether Purdue could prove that OxyContin ® was the most easily titratable analgesic. If the trial court still finds that a threshold level of intent to deceive has been established, the court should reweigh its materiality and intent findings to determine whether the sanction of unenforceability due to inequitable conduct is warranted. In making this determination, the trial court should keep in mind that when the level of materiality is relatively low, the showing of intent must be proportionately higher.

# Comments

1. *Unenforceability versus Invalidity.* A finding of inequitable conduct renders the entire patent unenforceable, a very heavy sanction. A patent may be unenforceable even though the claimed invention satisfies the patentability requirements of §§101 through 103, and 112. This high price is the result of intentionally deceiving the PTO. Thus, patent applicants should take heed of the Federal Circuit's admonition that in close cases, the question of materiality should be resolved by disclosure.

2. *Materiality.* The standard for materiality is stated in 37 C.F.R. Rule 1.56(a) of the Patent and Trademark Office (PTO), which the Federal Circuit has said "is an appropriate starting point for any discussion of materiality, for it appears to be the broadest . . . and because that materiality boundary most closely aligns with how one ought to conduct business with the PTO." *American Hoist & Derrick Co. v. Sowa & Sons*, 725 F.2d 1350, 1363 (Fed. Cir. 1984). As the Federal Circuit has cautioned, in "[c]lose cases, the question of materiality should be resolved by disclosure." *LaBounty Mfg., Inc. v. United States Int'l Trade Comm'n*, 958 F.2d 1066, 1076 (Fed. Cir. 1992). To this end, note undisclosed prior art may be material even though it did not pose a threat to the claimed invention under §102 or 103. *See Critikon, Inc. v. Becton Dickinson Vascular Access, Inc.*, 120 F.3d 1253 (Fed. Cir. 1997).

   Prior to March 16th, 1992, §1.56 provided that information would be deemed material if a reasonable examiner would have considered the information important in deciding whether to allow the application to issue as a patent. The scope of materiality was made considerably more precise in 1992 with the revision of §1.56. After March 1992, as per 37 C.F.R. §1.56, information is deemed material "when it is not cumulative to information already of record or being made of record," and

   (1) It establishes, by itself or in combination with other information, a prima facie case of unpatentability of a claim; or
   (2) It refutes, or is inconsistent with, a position the applicant takes in:
   (i) Opposing an argument of unpatentability relied on by the Office, or
   (ii) Asserting an argument of patentability.

37 C.F.R. §1.56(b) (1999). This new rule 56 was applied by the *Purdue* court because all of the patents in suit were pending on or already filed after March 16th, 1992. Patent applications that were filed and issued prior to that date are subject to old rule 56.

**3. Intent.** As stated by the court in *Purdue*, direct proof of an intent to mislead or deceive the PTO is rarely available. In simple terms, a "smoking gun" is almost never found in the files of a patent attorney. What considerations might tempt a patent applicant or his attorney to withhold a damaging reference from the PTO? Is there a reasonable expectation that another party would not find the damaging reference in litigation? What advantages could be gained from owning a patent which could easily be invalidated by a damaging reference?

Though direct evidence of intent to deceive is rare, such an intent may be inferred from circumstantial evidence. *See Hewlett-Packard Co. v. Bausch & Lomb, Inc.*, 882 F.2d 1556, 1562 (Fed. Cir. 1989). Nevertheless, as the *Kingsdown* court held, circumstantial evidence consisting solely of conduct amounting to gross negligence does not, by itself, justify drawing an inference of intent to deceive. *See Kingsdown Med. Consultants, Ltd. v. Hollister Inc.*, 863 F.2d 867, 876 (Fed. Cir. 1988). This holding overruled *J.P. Stevens'* holding that gross negligence was sufficient to draw an inference of an intent to deceive. The Federal Circuit in *Molins PLC v. Textron, Inc.* 48 F.3d 1172, 1181 n. 11 (Fed. Cir. 1995), followed the ruling in *Kingsdown* that gross negligence was insufficient to establish the intent prong of inequitable conduct. But "[w]here an applicant knows of information the materiality of which may so readily be determined, he or she cannot intentionally avoid learning of its materiality, even through gross negligence; in such cases the district court may find that the applicant should have known of the materiality of the information." *Brasseler, U.S.A. I, L.P. v. Stryker Sales Corp.*, 267 F.3d 1370, 1380 (Fed. Cir. 2001).

The court in *Kingsdown* also stated that when making a finding regarding intent to deceive the PTO, all circumstances, including those indicating good faith, must be considered. *See Kingsdown Med. Consultants*, 863 F.2d at 876. Generally, regarding drawing the inference of intent to mislead and good faith of the patentee, the Federal Circuit has stated:

> No single factor or combination of factors can be said always to *require* an inference of intent to mislead; yet a patentee facing a high level of materiality and clear proof that it knew or should have known of that materiality, can expect to find it difficult to establish "subjective good faith" sufficient to prevent the drawing of an inference of intent to mislead. A mere denial of intent to mislead (which would defeat every effort to establish inequitable conduct) will not suffice in such circumstances.

*FMC Corp. v. Manitowoc Co., Inc.*, 835 F.2d 1411, 1416 (Fed. Cir. 1987).

In *Semiconductor Energy Laboratory Co., Ltd. v. Samsung Electronics Co., Ltd.*, 204 F.3d 1368 (Fed. Cir. 2000), the Federal Circuit further explored the metes and bounds of the intent prong of inequitable conduct. In this case, the inventor, Dr. Yamazaki, was well aware of the requirements of disclosure set forth in §1.56. When Dr. Yamazaki provided a 29-page Japanese-language reference to the PTO, he also composed a concise English-language summary (Dr. Yamazaki was fluent in Japanese and English) of the reference which he included in his disclosure to the PTO. But in his summary, he omitted a portion of the reference that was material to the patent application. The Federal Circuit affirmed the District Court's finding of intent on the part of Dr. Yamazaki because he fully understood (a) the reference, (b) his duty of disclosure, and (c) the concise summary provided to the PTO. The effect of this case is to raise the bar for patent applicants who place foreign language references before the Patent and Trademark Office and have the ability to easily translate the references but neglect to do so.

4. *Inequitable Conduct and Patent Reform.* It is thought among some judges and commentators that inequitable conduct is a claim that is made too frequently and without significant support. Thus, recent patent reform efforts would allow the PTO to impose a "duty of candor and good faith" on patent applicants and those who are "adverse to a patent or application." The proposed legislation, if enacted, would authorize the PTO to investigate alleged violations of the "duty of candor and good faith." To this end, during litigation federal courts could ask the PTO to investigate misconduct and issue sanctions. The PTO would be required to create a new office charged with investigating violations of the duty. The test for inequitable conduct would change, too. An inequitable conduct finding would result only if it is found that the patent in question would not have issued.

## B. REPAIR/RECONSTRUCTION AND THE DOCTRINE OF FIRST SALE

A patentee loses a certain amount of legal control over any patented product he sells. Under the doctrine of first sale, a purchaser of a patented product can re-sell or use the product without obtaining permission from the patent owner. (It is permissible, however, for the patentee to restrict or prevent certain uses through contract, as discussed in Section C.) And the related doctrine of repair/reconstruction allows the purchaser to repair the patented product. But the purchaser cannot reconstruct the product because that is deemed tantamount to making or manufacturing, something expressly prohibited by §154 of the patent code. How one determines what is permissible repair and impermissible reconstruction is the subject of the principal case.

### HUSKY INJECTION MOLDING SYS. LTD. v. R & D TOOL & ENGINEERING CO.

**291 F.3d 780 (Fed. Cir. 2002)**

Dyk, Circuit Judge.

Husky Injection Molding Systems Ltd. ("Husky") appeals from the decision of the United States District Court for the Western District of Missouri,

granting the motion of R & D Tool & Engineering Co. ("R & D") for
summary judgment of non-infringement of U.S. Patent No. Re. 33,237
(the "'237 patent"). Because we find that there were no genuine issues
of material fact regarding infringement of the '237 patent and that the
district court correctly concluded that R & D's replacement of the mold
and carrier plate of the injection molding system was more akin to repair
than reconstruction, we affirm.

## BACKGROUND

Husky manufactures and sells injection molding systems (the "X-series
systems") that produce hollow plastic articles known as preforms. These
preforms are subsequently reheated and blow molded into hollow plastic
containers.

Husky is the assignee of the '237 patent, entitled "Apparatus for Producing Hollow Plastic Articles," which is directed to an injection molding
machine that includes a carrier plate containing at least two sets of cavities
for cooling the hollow plastic articles. The molds and carrier plates are not
separately patented.

Generally preforms are made by injecting molten plastic into molds.
One half of the mold contains at least one cavity [Fig. 2, 11]; the other
half [Fig. 1, 12] contains a number of cores [Fig. 1, 14] corresponding to
the number of cavities. '237 patent at col. 3, l. 65, col. 4, l. 4. The cores
engage with their respective cavities [Fig. 2, 13] to form a closed mold and
produce the shape of the hollow plastic articles. *Id.* at col. 4, ll. 4-7. To
prevent damage to the preforms, each article must be adequately cooled
before it is handled. *Id.* at col. 3, ll. 26-30. Traditionally the preforms were
cooled in the molding machine, which was a time-consuming process. Having a lengthy cooling time in the molding machine was the limiting step in
the production process of the articles and was at odds with the "high rate of
production [that] is important in commercial operations...." *Id.* at col. 1,
ll. 20-24. Other injection molding systems have increased the speed of the
molding cycle, although there have been corresponding increases in costs
or risks of damage to the articles. *Id.* at col. 1, ll. 66-68, col. 2, ll. 21-23.
According to the summary of the invention of the patent, the present
invention economically allows a high rate of production while permitting
the preforms to cool for an extended period of time inside the cavities of
the carrier plate, rather than in the injection molds of the molding
machine. *Id.* at col. 3, ll. 20-26.

When a customer wishes to make a change in the preform design, it
generally must buy a substitute mold and corresponding carrier plate in
order to operate the Husky injection molding system as it was designed.
Customers change the preform design on average after three to five years.
When a system owner wants to make a different type of plastic article, it
may purchase a replacement mold and carrier plate combination from
Husky.

The alleged contributory infringer, R & D, makes molds and carrier
plates, which substitute for components of Husky's injection molding system. To make the substitute molds and carrier plates, R & D purchased
Husky's X-series system in 1997 without the mold or the carrier plate. At

the time of the sale, R & D informed Husky's salesman of its intent to use the Husky system to make substitute molds. Moreover, all sales of X-series systems were without contractual restriction on the future purchase of molds or carrier plates.

In the summer of 2000, R & D shipped to Grafco, the owner of a Husky system, a new mold and carrier plate to allow Grafco to produce a different preform design. On June 9, 2000, Husky sued R & D for infringement of the '237 patent, urging that R & D had contributed to the infringement of the '237 patent. Husky concedes that the sale of the molds alone did not constitute contributory infringement because the molds were staple items. But Husky urged that R & D's sales to Husky's customers of a mold and carrier plate combination constituted contributory infringement because the substitution of a new carrier plate amounted to reconstruction of Husky's patented invention. R & D did not argue that the products it sold were outside the scope of the claims, but instead defended on the ground that its sales were akin to repair, and alternatively that Husky granted R & D an implied license to make and sell molds and carrier plates.

On September 8, 2000, R & D filed a motion for summary judgment of non-infringement, which the district court granted on March 30, 2001. Based on Husky's own admission that "no reconstruction occurs if the customer replaces the combination for repair purposes," the Court focused on whether substitution of a new mold and carrier plate combination for an unspent combination constituted reconstruction. In light of *Wilbur-Ellis Co. v. Kuther,* the district court held that "the use of R & D's retrofit mold/carrier plate assembly to substitute for an unspent original mold/carrier plate assembly does not rise to the level of impermissible reconstruction set out by the Supreme Court in [*Aro Manufacturing Co. v. Convertible Top Replacement Co.* (*'Aro I'*)]." The court noted that *Wilbur-Ellis* supports the holding that changing the shape of components to produce a different preform design is more akin to repair than reconstruction. *Id.* at 7. The district court further held that "the use of a substitution mold/carrier plate assembly offered by R & D is within the rights of purchasers of a Husky X-series due to the Plaintiff's admission of its awareness of a replacement mold market...." *Id.* at 8. Alternatively, the court concluded that Husky's customers had an implied license to substitute the mold/carrier plate assembly in order to produce different preform designs because Husky had sold its system without restriction. *Id.* at 11.

### DISCUSSION

### II.

Here Husky alleges that R & D is a contributory infringer. The law of contributory infringement is well settled. Section 271 of title 35 provides in pertinent part:

(a) Except as otherwise provided in this title, whoever *without authority makes, uses, offers to sell, or sells any patented invention,* within the United States or imports into the United States any patented invention during the term of the patent therefor, *infringes the patent.*

* * *

(c) Whoever offers to sell or sells within the United States or imports into the United States a component of a patented machine, manufacture, combination or composition, or a material or apparatus for use in practicing a patented process, constituting a *material part of the invention, knowing the same to be especially made or especially adapted for use in an infringement of such patent,* and *not a staple article* or commodity of commerce suitable for substantial noninfringing use, shall be liable as a contributory infringer.

35 U.S.C. §271 (1994) (emphases added).

Thus, a seller of a "material part" of a patented item may be a contributory infringer if he makes a non-staple article that he knows was "especially made or especially adapted for use in an infringement of such patent." *Id.; Dawson Chem. Co. v. Rohm & Haas Co.* For R & D to be liable as a contributory infringer, Husky's customers who purchased the replacement parts from R & D must be liable for direct infringement. 35 U.S.C. §271(c) (1994); *Aro I.* Both an alleged direct infringer and an alleged contributory infringer benefit from the permissible repair exception.

### III.

The Supreme Court and this court have struggled for years to appropriately distinguish between repair of a patented machine and reconstruction. Based on those decisions, we can identify at least three primary repair and reconstruction situations.

First, there is the situation in which the entire patented item is spent, and the alleged infringer reconstructs it to make it useable again. This situation was first considered by the Supreme Court in *American Cotton-Tie Co. v. Simmons. Cotton-Tie* involved a metallic cotton-bale tie consisting of a band and a buckle. *Id.* at 91. After the cotton-bale tie was cut, it became scrap iron. *Id.* The defendants subsequently purchased the scrap iron, riveted the pieces together, and recreated the bands. *Id.* Although the defendants reused the original buckle, the Court found that the defendants "reconstructed [the band]," *id.* at 94, and thereby infringed the patent, *id.* at 95. Moreover, in *Morgan Envelope Co. v. Albany Perforated Wrapping Paper Co.*, the Court explained its decision in *Cotton-Tie.* Specifically, the Court noted that "the use of the tie was intended to be as complete a destruction of it as would be the explosion of a patented torpedo. In either case, the repair of the band or the refilling of the shell would be a practical reconstruction of the device." *Morgan Envelope,* 152 U.S. at 434.

Second, there is the situation in which a spent part is replaced. The Supreme Court first addressed this situation in *Wilson v. Simpson. Wilson* involved the replacement of cutter-knives in a wood-planing machine. In concluding that replacement of the cutter-knives was permissible repair, the Court stated that

repairing partial injuries, whether they occur from accident or wear and tear, is only refitting a machine for use. And it is no more than that, though it shall be a replacement of an essential part of a combination. It is the use of the whole of that which a purchaser buys, when the patentee sells to him a machine; and when he repairs the damages which may be done to it, it is no more than the exercise of that right of care which every one may use to give duration to that which he owns, or has a right to use as a whole.

*Id.* at 123. . . .

Subsequently, the Supreme Court set forth a definitive test in *Aro Manufacturing Co. v. Convertible Top Replacement Co.*, 365 U.S. 336 (1961) (*"Aro I"*). *Aro I* involved a combination patent on a convertible folding top of an automobile. *Id.* at 337. The fabric of the convertible top had a shorter useful life than the other parts of the patented combination. *Id.* at 337-38. In reaching the conclusion that replacement of the worn-out fabric of the convertible top was permissible repair, *id.* at 346, the Supreme Court adopted a bright-line test, *id.* at 345. Specifically, the Court concluded that replacement of a spent part of a combination patent, which is not separately patented, is not impermissible reconstruction no matter how "essential it may be to the patented combination and no matter how costly or difficult replacement may be." *Id.* In adopting this bright-line test, the majority rejected Justice Brennan's suggestion in his concurrence that a multi-factor fact intensive test was appropriate to distinguish repair from reconstruction. Even if the owner sequentially replaces all of the worn-out parts of a patented combination, this sequential replacement does not constitute reconstruction. *See FMC Corp. v. Up-Right, Inc.* Moreover, in *Sage Products, Inc. v. Devon Industries, Inc.*, where we held that replacement was not limited to worn out articles, but also included articles that were effectively spent.

Third, there is the situation in which a part is not spent but is replaced to enable the machine to perform a different function. This is a situation "a kin to repair." In *Wilbur-Ellis*, the Supreme Court addressed whether changing the size of cans in fish-canning machines constituted reconstruction when the fish-canning machines were not spent, although they needed cleaning and repair. 377 U.S. at 424. The Court concluded that the "[p]etitioners in adapting the old machine to a related use were doing more than repair in the customary sense; but what they did was kin to repair for it bore on the useful capacity of the old combination. . . ." *Id.* at 425. This form of adaptation was within the scope of the purchased patent rights because the size of the cans was not "part of the invention." *Id.* at 424.

This court has followed the holding of *Wilbur-Ellis* when addressing replacement of unpatented parts of a combination patent. For example, in *Surfco* we recently addressed a similar situation involving the modification of a surfboard. Surfco manufactured fins that had an additional safety feature and were interchangeable with the patentee's releasable fins on its surfboard. *Surfco*, 264 F.3d at 1064 (Fed. Cir. 2001). This safety feature created an incentive to replace the patentee's fins with Surfco's fins. Once again we reiterated that permissible repair encompasses the situation where parts are replaced. *Id.* at 1065.

## IV.

Despite the number of cases concerning repair and reconstruction, difficult questions remain. One of these arises from the necessity of determining what constitutes replacement of a part of the device, which is repair or akin to repair, and what constitutes reconstruction of the entire device, which would not be repair or akin to repair. Some few situations suggest an obvious answer. For example, if a patent is obtained on an automobile, the replacement of the spark plugs would constitute permissible repair, but few would argue that the retention of the spark plugs and the replacement of the remainder of the car at a single stroke was permissible activity akin to repair. Thus, there may be some concept of proportionality inherent in the distinction between repair and reconstruction.

Nonetheless, in *Aro I*, the Supreme Court explicitly rejected a "heart of the invention" standard, noting that no matter how essential an element of the combination is to the patent, "no element, separately viewed, is within the [patent] grant." *Aro I*, 365 U.S. at 344. Similarly, in *Dawson Chemical Co. v. Rohm & Haas Co.*, the Court noted that in *Aro I* it had "eschewed the suggestion that the legal distinction between 'reconstruction' and 'repair' should be affected by whether the element of the combination that has been replaced is an 'essential or 'distinguishing' part of the invention." 448 U.S. 176, 217 (1980).

However, *Aro I* itself was clearly dealing with "replaceable" parts, and we have interpreted *Aro I* as merely defining permissible repair in the context of "replaceable" parts, and as not foreclosing an inquiry into whether a particular part is replaceable. In *Sandvik Aktiebolag v. E.J. Co.*, the defendant offered a drill repair service that retipped the drill when it could no longer be resharpened. In that case, retipping did not involve "just attach[-ing] a new part for a worn part," but instead required "several steps to replace, configure and integrate the tip onto the shank." *Id*. at 673. We concluded that retipping the drill was impermissible reconstruction, applying the following test:

> There are a number of factors to consider in determining whether a defendant has made a new article, after the device has become spent, including the nature of the actions by the defendant, the nature of the device and how it is designed (namely, whether one of the components of the patented combination has a shorter useful life than the whole), whether a market has developed to manufacture or service the part at issue and objective evidence of the intent of the patentee.

*Id*. In reaching the conclusion that reconstruction occurred, we noted that "[t]he drill tip was not manufactured to be a replaceable part"; "[i]t was not intended or expected to have a life of temporary duration in comparison to the drill shank"; and "the tip was not attached to the shank in a manner to be easily detachable." *Id*. at 674. Difficult questions may exist as to the line between *Sandvik Aktiebolag* and *Wilbur-Ellis* where readily replaceable parts are not involved. We need not resolve those questions here. At a minimum, repair exists if the part being repaired is a readily replaceable part.

We conclude that the same safe harbor exists where activity "akin to repair" is involved as when repair is involved. In both cases, there is no infringement if the particular part is readily "replaceable." For example, in *Surfco*, the patents in suit were directed to a surfboard having releasable fins. *Surfco*, 264 F.3d at 1064. In describing *Aro I*, this court noted that "the concept of permissible 'repair' is directed primarily to the replacement of broken or worn parts. *However, permissible 'repair' also includes replacement of parts that are neither broken nor worn." Surfco*, 264 F.3d at 1065 (emphasis added). Accordingly, we held that "[t]he patented surf craft [was] not 'recreated' by the substitution of a different set of fins, even when the new fins [were] specifically adapted for use in the patented combination." *Id.* at 1066. Having determined that a part is readily replaceable, it is irrelevant whether the part was an essential element of the invention. We reject Husky's attempt to revive the heart of the invention standard in different words. *See, e.g., Aro I.*

Husky also urges that the owner of a patented combination has no right to voluntarily replace an unspent part, unless there is a valid public policy justification for the replacement such as increased safety. This argument is directly inconsistent with both *Wilbur-Ellis* and *Surfco.*

In *Wilbur-Ellis*, the replacement of the 1 pound cans with 5 ounce cans did not enhance safety. In *Surfco*, we addressed whether a part needed to be spent or broken before there was a right to replace or modify it. We concluded that it was not a reconstruction to substitute different fins, even if the original fins were not in need of repair or replacement. *Id.* Although the fins provided enhanced safety features, our holding in *Surfco* was not based on this policy justification, but instead on the right of a purchaser to modify a machine. *Id.* A purchaser is within its rights to modify a machine by substituting a readily replaceable part whether or not the replacement served some public policy purpose.

## V.

Here there is no question that the particular parts were readily "replaceable" parts. The design of the injection molding machine allowed replacement of the mold and carrier plates. Typically, after three to five years, a customer purchases a new mold and carrier plate in order to change the preform design. Moreover, Husky sold substitute molds and carrier plates, and provided separate quotations for the injection molding system and the mold/carrier plate assembly. We conclude that the carrier plates were readily replaceable.

In this case, the carrier plate is just one element of the patented combination and not separately patented, and selling replacement parts cannot constitute contributory infringement. We conclude that Husky's customers did not directly infringe the patent by replacing the molds and carrier plates; thus, R & D did not contributorily infringe the '237 patent.

## Comments

**1. The Repair/Reconstruction Factors.** The *Husky* court identified three repair/reconstruction scenarios. First, the entire patented item is spent, and the defendant reconstructs it to make it usable again. This scenario usually leads to a finding of reconstruction. Second, a spent part is replaced. The court, citing *Aro Manufacturing Co. v. Convertible Top Replacement Co.*, concluded that the replacement of a spent part, "which is not separately patented, is not impermissible reconstruction no matter how 'essential it may be to the patented combination and no matter how costly or difficult replacement may be.'"

Moreover, replacement is not limited to worn out components. (Of course, one way for the patentee to avoid the repair/reconstruction issue is to patent, if available, the various components of the device.) Third, there are the "akin to repair" cases, which involve a part that is not spent, but is replaced to enable the machine to perform a different function. The courts have found that this type of activity is permissible repair.

Therefore, there is an important distinction between replacement of a part of the device, no matter how essential or spent the part may be, and reconstruction of an entire device. The former is permissible if the part is "readily replaceable" (e.g., meant to be replaced), and the latter is impermissible. Where to draw the line between these two can be difficult. A properly drafted contract, however, can render this inquiry irrelevant. *See Kendall Co. v. Progressive Medical Tech., Inc.*, 85 F.3d 1570, 1575 (Fed. Cir. 1996) ("[A]s long as reconstruction does not occur or a contract is not violated, nothing in the law prevents a purchaser of a device from prematurely repairing it or replacing un unpatented component. Premature repair is the business of the purchaser of the product, who owns it, rather than the patentee, who sold it").

2. *Supreme Court Views on Repair/Reconstruction.* The germinal case on repair and reconstruction is *Wilson v. Simpson*, 50 U.S. (9 How.) 109 (1850). The defendant *Wilson* lawfully obtained a planing machine covered by the plaintiff's patent. Thereafter and without authority of the plaintiff, the defendant replaced cutting knives, which typically wore out after 60 to 90 days of use. The Court held that such a replacement was within the category of permissible repair rather than that of impermissible reconstruction.

More than 100 years later, the Court decided *Aro Mfg. Co. v. Convertible Top Replacement*, 365 U.S. 336 (1961). The plaintiff (Convertible Top Replacement Co.) was assignee of the Mackie-Duluk patent on a convertible top mechanism for automobiles consisting of a flexible top fabric, supporting structures, and a sealing mechanism, all mounted on the automobile body. The fabric element normally deteriorated in about three years from wear and tear. The rest of the elements normally lasted for the life of the automobile. The defendant (Aro Mfg.) manufactured and sold replacement fabrics designed for automobiles fitted with the Mackie-Duluk combination. The plaintiff sued the defendant for infringement and contributory infringement.

The Court, in an opinion written by Justice Whittaker, reversed a finding of infringement below. First, the Court noted that the defendant did not *directly* infringe because the fabrics were unpatented elements of a patented combination. Second, it noted that the defendant could not *contributorily* infringe unless its ultimate customers (owners of automobiles) directly infringed when they replaced the fabrics on their convertibles. This in turn depended on "whether such a replacement by the car owner is infringing 'reconstruction' or permissible 'repair.' "

The Court rejected a test suggested by the plaintiff that would consider the relative durability and expense of the replaced part and whether the part represented the "essential" or "distinguishing" element of the patented combination. In holding that "maintenance of the 'use of the whole' of the patented combination through replacement of a spent, unpatented element" does not constitute reconstruction, the Court cited Judge Learned Hand's statement of the "distilled essence" of *Wilson v. Simpson*:

> [R]econstruction of a patented entity, comprised of unpatented elements, is limited to such a true reconstruction of the entity as to "in fact make a new article," *United States v. Aluminum Co. of America* ..., after the entity, viewed as a whole, has become spent. In order to call the monopoly, conferred by the patent grant, into play for a second time, it must, indeed, be a second creation of the patented entity. Mere replacement of individual unpatented parts, one at a time, whether of the same part repeatedly or different parts successively, is no more than the lawful right of the owner to repair his property.

365 U.S. at 346. Justice Harlan wrote a dissenting opinion in which two other justices concurred. Justice Harlan concluded that "the issue of reconstruction *vel non* turns not upon any single factor, but depends instead upon a variety of circumstances." 365 U.S. at 376. He disagreed with the Court's view that reconstruction is limited to "where the patented combination has been rebuilt de novo from the ground up." *Id.*

# C. THE USE (AND MISUSE) OF CONTRACTS IN PATENT LAW

Under the first-sale doctrine, as discussed in the previous section, the patentee loses a certain degree of control of patented products once introduced into commerce. Purchasers on patented products, for example, can use or re-sell the product. But a patentee can turn to contract law to limit or prevent certain types of uses of the patented technology that may have been permissible without a contract. Another use of contract is to regulate activity (e.g., royalty payments) after the patent expires. The *Mallinckrodt* case explores the contours and limits of contractual restrictions on the use of patented technology — so-called "field-of-use" restrictions. The *Scheiber* case discusses the use of contracts that govern behavior after the patent expires.

## 1. Field-of-Use Restrictions

### MALLINCKRODT v. MEDIPART
#### 976 F.2d 700 (Fed. Cir. 1992)

NEWMAN, Circuit Judge.

This action for patent infringement and inducement to infringe relates to the use of a patented medical device in violation of a "single use only" notice that accompanied the sale of the device. Mallinckrodt sold its patented device to hospitals, which after initial use of the devices sent them to Medipart for servicing that enabled the hospitals to use the device again. Mallinckrodt claimed that Medipart thus induced infringement by the hospitals and itself infringed the patent.

The district court held that violation of the "single use only" notice can not be remedied by suit for patent infringement, and granted summary judgment of noninfringement.

\* \* \*

[T]he district court held that no restriction whatsoever could be imposed under the patent law, whether or not the restriction was enforceable under some other law, and whether or not this was a first sale to a purchaser with notice. This ruling is incorrect, for if Mallinckrodt's restriction was a valid condition of the sale, then in accordance with *General Talking Pictures Corp. v. Western Electric Co.*, it was not excluded from enforcement under the patent law.

\* \* \*

We conclude that the district court misapplied precedent in holding that there can be no restriction on use imposed as a matter of law, even on the first purchaser. The restriction here at issue does not per se violate the doctrine of patent misuse or the antitrust law. Use in violation of a valid restriction may be remedied under the patent law, provided that no other law prevents enforcement of the patent. The district court's misapplication of precedent also led to an incorrect application of the law of repair/reconstruction, for if reuse is established to have been validly restricted, then even repair may constitute patent infringement.

### BACKGROUND

The patented device is an apparatus for delivery of radioactive or therapeutic material in aerosol mist form to the lungs of a patient, for diagnosis and treatment of pulmonary disease. Radioactive material is delivered primarily for image scanning in diagnosis of lung conditions. Therapeutic agents may be administered to patients suffering various lung diseases.

The device is manufactured by Mallinckrodt, who sells it to hospitals as a unitary kit that consists of a "nebulizer" which generates a mist of the radioactive material or the prescribed drug, a "manifold" that directs the flow of oxygen or air and the active material, a filter, tubing, a mouthpiece, and a nose clip. In use, the radioactive material or drug is placed in the nebulizer, is atomized, and the patient inhales and exhales through the closed system. The device traps and retains any radioactive or other toxic material in the exhalate. The device fits into a lead-shielded container that is provided by Mallinckrodt to minimize exposure to radiation and for safe disposal after use.

The device is marked with the appropriate patent numbers, [footnote omitted] and bears the trademarks "Mallinckrodt" and "UltraVent" and the inscription "Single Use Only." The package insert provided with each unit states "For Single Patient Use Only" and instructs that the entire contaminated apparatus be disposed of in accordance with procedures for the disposal of biohazardous waste. The hospital is instructed to seal the used apparatus in the radiation-shielded container prior to proper disposal. The hospitals whose activities led to this action do not dispose of the UltraVent apparatus, or limit it to a single use.

Instead, the hospitals ship the used manifold/nebulizer assemblies to Medipart, Inc. Medipart in turn packages the assemblies and sends them to Radiation Sterilizers Inc., who exposes the packages to at least 2.5 megarads of gamma radiation, and returns them to Medipart. Medipart personnel then check each assembly for damage and leaks, and place the assembly in a plastic bag together with a new filter, tubing, mouthpiece, and nose clip. The "reconditioned" units, as Medipart calls them, are shipped back to the hospitals from whence they came. Neither Radiation Sterilizers nor Medipart tests the reconditioned units for any residual biological activity or for radioactivity. The assemblies still bear the inscription "Single Use Only" and the trademarks "Mallinckrodt" and "UltraVent."

Mallinckrodt filed suit against Medipart, asserting patent infringement and inducement to infringe. . . .

The district court granted Medipart's motion on the patent infringement counts, holding that the "Single Use Only" restriction could not be enforced by suit for patent infringement. The court also held that Medipart's activities were permissible repair, not impermissible reconstruction, of the patented apparatus. . . .

The district court also enjoined Mallinckrodt *pendente lite* from distributing a new notice to its hospital customers. The proposed new notice emphasized the "Single Use Only" restriction and stated that the purpose of this restriction is to protect the hospital and its patients from potential adverse consequences of reconditioning, such as infectious disease transmission, material instability, and/or decreased diagnostic performance; that the UltraVent device is covered by certain patents; that the hospital is licensed under these patents to use the device only once; and that reuse of the device would be deemed infringement of the patents.

Mallinckrodt appeals the grant of summary judgment on the infringement issue, and the grant of the preliminary injunction.

## I
### THE RESTRICTION ON REUSE

Mallinckrodt describes the restriction on reuse as a label license for a specified field of use, wherein the field is single (*i.e.*, disposable) use. On this motion for summary judgment, there was no issue of whether this form of license gave notice of the restriction. Notice was not disputed. Nor was it disputed that sale to the hospitals was the first sale of the patented device. The issue that the district court decided on summary judgment was the enforceability of the restriction by suit for patent infringement. The court's premise was that even if the notice was sufficient to constitute a valid condition of sale, violation of that condition can not be remedied under the patent law.

Mallinckrodt states that the restriction to single patient use is valid and enforceable under the patent law because the use is within the scope of the patent grant, and the restriction does not enlarge the patent grant. Mallinckrodt states that a license to less than all uses of a patented article is well recognized and a valid practice under patent law, and that such license does not violate the antitrust laws and is not patent misuse. Mallinckrodt also states that the restriction here imposed is reasonable because it is based on health, safety, efficacy, and liability considerations and violates no public policy. Thus Mallinckrodt argues that the restriction is valid and enforceable under the patent law. Mallinckrodt concludes that use in violation of the restriction is patent infringement, and that the district court erred in holding otherwise.

Medipart states that the restriction is unenforceable, for the reason that "the *Bauer* trilogy and *Motion Picture Patents* clearly established that *no* restriction is enforceable under patent law upon a purchaser of a sold article." (Medipart's emphasis). The district court so held. The district court also held that since the hospitals purchased the device from the patentee, not from a manufacturing licensee, no restraint on the use of the device could lawfully be imposed under the patent law.

* * *

The enforceability of restrictions on the use of patented goods derives from the patent grant, which is in classical terms of property: the right to exclude.

> 35 U.S.C. §154. Every patent shall contain . . . a grant . . . for the term of seventeen years . . . of the right to exclude others from making, using, or selling the invention throughout the United States. . . .

This right to exclude may be waived in whole or in part. The conditions of such waiver are subject to patent, contract, antitrust, and any other applicable law, as well as equitable considerations such as are reflected in the law of patent misuse. As in other areas of commerce, private parties may contract as they choose, provided that no law is violated thereby:

> [T]he rule is, with few exceptions, that any conditions which are not in their very nature illegal with regard to this kind of property, imposed by the patentee and agreed to by the licensee for the right to manufacture or use or sell the [patented] article, will be upheld by the courts.

*E. Bement & Sons v. National Harrow Co.*, 186 U.S. 70, 91 (1902).

The district court's ruling that Mallinckrodt's restriction on reuse was unenforceable was an application of the doctrine of patent misuse, although the court declined to use that designation. The concept of patent misuse arose to restrain practices that did not in themselves violate any law, but that drew anticompetitive strength from the patent right, and thus were deemed to be contrary to public policy. The policy purpose was to prevent a patentee from using the patent to obtain market benefit beyond that which inheres in the statutory patent right.

The district court's holding that Mallinckrodt's restriction to single patient use was unenforceable was, as we have remarked, based on "policy" considerations. The district court relied on a group of cases wherein resale price-fixing of patented goods was held illegal, viz. *Bauer & Cie. v. O'Donnell*; *Straus v. Victor Talking Machine Co.*; *Boston Store of Chicago v. American Graphophone Co.*, ("the *Bauer* trilogy"), and that barred patent-enforced tie-ins, viz. *Motion Picture Patents Co. v. Universal Film Mfg. Co.*

* * *

These cases established that price-fixing and tying restrictions accompanying the sale of patented goods were per se illegal. These cases did not hold, and it did not follow, that all restrictions accompanying the sale of patented goods were deemed illegal. In *General Talking Pictures* the Court, discussing restrictions on use, summarized the state of the law as follows:

> That a restrictive license is legal seems clear. *Mitchell v. Hawley* [83 U.S.], 16 Wall. 544 (1873). As was said in *United States v. General Electric Co.*, 272 U.S. 476, 489 (1926), the patentee may grant a license "upon any condition the performance of which is reasonably within the reward which the patentee by the grant of the patent is entitled to secure"....

The practice of granting licenses for restricted use is an old one, *see Rubber Company v. Goodyear*. So far as it appears, its legality has never been questioned. 305 U.S. at 127.

In *General Talking Pictures* the patentee had authorized the licensee to make and sell amplifiers embodying the patented invention for a specified use (home radios). The defendant had purchased the patented amplifier from the manufacturing licensee, with knowledge of the patentee's restriction on use. The Supreme Court stated the question as "whether the restriction in the license is to be given effect" against a purchaser who had notice of the restriction. The Court observed that a restrictive license to a particular use was permissible, and treated the purchaser's unauthorized use as infringement of the patent, deeming the goods to be unlicensed as purchased from the manufacturer.

The Court, in its opinion on rehearing, stated that it

> [did not] consider what the rights of the parties would have been if the amplifier had been manufactured under the patent and had passed into the hands of a purchaser in the ordinary channels of trade.

305 U.S. at 127. The district court interpreted this reservation as requiring that since the hospitals purchased the UltraVent device from the patentee Mallinckrodt, not from a manufacturing licensee, no restraint on the purchasers' use of the device could be imposed under the patent law. However, in *General Talking Pictures* the Court did not hold that there must be an intervening manufacturing licensee before the patent can be enforced against a purchaser with notice of the restriction. The Court did not decide the situation where the patentee was the manufacturer and the device reached a purchaser in ordinary channels of trade.

The UltraVent device was manufactured by the patentee; but the sale to the hospitals was the first sale and was with notice of the restriction. Medipart offers neither law, public policy, nor logic, for the proposition that the enforceability of a restriction to a particular use is determined by whether the purchaser acquired the device from a manufacturing licensee or from a manufacturing patentee. We decline to make a distinction for which there appears to be no foundation. Indeed, Mallinckrodt has pointed out how easily such a criterion could be circumvented. That the viability of a restriction should depend on how the transaction is structured was denigrated as "formalistic line drawing" in *Continental T.V., Inc. v. GTE Sylvania, Inc.*, 433 U.S. 36, 57-59 (1977), the Court explaining, in overruling *United States v. Arnold, Schwinn & Co.*, 388 U.S. 365 (1967), that the legality of attempts by a manufacturer to regulate resale does not turn on whether the reseller had purchased the merchandise or was merely acting as an agent of the manufacturer. The Court having disapproved reliance on formalistic distinctions of no economic consequence in anti-trust analysis, we discern no reason to preserve formalistic distinctions of no economic consequence, simply because the goods are patented.

The district court, holding Mallinckrodt's restriction unenforceable, described the holding of *General Talking Pictures* as in "some tension" with the earlier price-fixing and tie-in cases. The district court observed that the Supreme Court did not cite the *Bauer, Boston Store*, or *Motion Picture Patents* cases when it upheld the use restriction in *General Talking Pictures*. That observation is correct, but it should not be remarkable. By the time of *General Talking Pictures*, price-fixing and tie-ins were generally prohibited under the antitrust law as well as the misuse law, while other conditions were generally recognized as within the patent grant. The pro-hibitions against price-fixing and tying did not make all other restrictions per se invalid and unenforceable. [footnote omitted] Further, the Court could not have been unaware of the *Bauer* trilogy in deciding *General Talk-ing Pictures*, because Justice Black's dissent is built upon those cases.

Restrictions on use are judged in terms of their relation to the patentee's right to exclude from all or part of the patent grant, and, with rare excep-tions, now continues only with those devices"); and where an anticompe-titive effect is asserted, the rule of reason is the basis of determining the legality of the provision. In *Windsurfing International, Inc. v. AMF, Inc.*, this court stated:

> To sustain a misuse defense involving a licensing arrangement not held to have been per se anticompetitive by the Supreme Court, a factual determi-nation must reveal that the overall effect of the license tends to restrain competition unlawfully in an appropriately defined relevant market.

782 F.2d at 1001-1002. The district court, stating that it "refuse[s] to limit *Bauer* and *Motion Picture Patents* to tying and price-fixing not only because their language suggests broader application, but because there is a strong public interest in not stretching the patent laws to authorize restrictions on the use of purchased goods", *Mallinckrodt*, 15 U.S.P.Q.2d at 1119, has contravened this precedent.

In support of its ruling, the district court also cited a group of cases in which the Court considered and affirmed the basic principles that uncon-ditional sale of a patented device exhausts the patentee's right to control the purchaser's use of the device; and that the sale of patented goods, like other goods, can be conditioned. The principle of exhaustion of the patent right did not turn a conditional sale into an unconditional one.

\* \* \*

Viewing the entire group of these early cases, it appears that the Court simply applied, to a variety of factual situations, the rule of contract law that sale may be conditioned. *Adams v. Burke* and its kindred cases do not stand for the proposition that no restriction or condition may be placed upon the sale of a patented article. It was error for the district court to derive that proposition from the precedent. Unless the condition violates some other law or policy (in the patent field, notably the misuse or antitrust law, *e.g.*, *United States v. Univis Lens Co.*, private parties retain the freedom to contract concerning conditions of sale. As we have discussed, the district court cited the price-fixing and tying cases as reflecting what the court deemed to be the correct policy, viz., that no condition can be placed on the sale of patented goods, for any reason. However, this is not a price-fixing or tying case, and the per se antitrust and misuse violations found in the *Bauer* trilogy and *Motion Picture Patents* are not here present. The appropriate criterion is whether Mallinckrodt's restriction is reasonably within the patent grant, or whether the patentee has ventured beyond the patent grant and into behavior having an anticompetitive effect not justifiable under the rule of reason.

Should the restriction be found to be reasonably within the patent grant, *i.e.*, that it relates to subject matter within the scope of the patent claims, that ends the inquiry. However, should such inquiry lead to the conclusion that there are anticompetitive effects extending beyond the patentee's statutory right to exclude, these effects do not automatically impeach the restriction. Anticompetitive effects that are not per se violations of law are reviewed in accordance with the rule of reason. Patent owners should not be in a worse position, by virtue of the patent right to exclude, than owners of other property used in trade.

We conclude that the district court erred in holding that the restriction on reuse was, as a matter of law, unenforceable under the patent law. If the sale of the UltraVent was validly conditioned under the applicable law such as the law governing sales and licenses, and if the restriction on reuse was within the scope of the patent grant or otherwise justified, then violation of the restriction may be remedied by action for patent infringement. The grant of summary judgment is reversed, and the cause is remanded.

\* \* \*

## Comments

*1. Conditional Sales, Misuse, and First Sale/Exhaustion.* A well-known default rule in patent law and contract law states that the voluntary introduction of a patented product into the market significantly limits the patentee's ability to control the use of the product. But the court in *Mallinckrodt* noted that "the sale of patented goods, like other goods, can be conditioned." *Mallinckrodt*, 976 F.2d at 706. *See also B. Braun Med., Inc. v. Abbott Labs.*, 124 F.3d 1419, 1426 (Fed. Cir. 1997) (noting the exhaustion doctrine "does not apply to an expressly conditional sale or license"). This statement is a reminder that the first sale/exhaustion doctrine is indeed a default rule around which parties can otherwise agree — in this case for a so-called field-of-use restriction. *See Mallinckrodt*, 976 F.2d at 706 (stating that "[t]he principle of exhaustion of the patent right did not turn a conditional sale into an unconditional one"). The use of this restrictive contract term in that case was adjudicated to be both (1) enforceable, and (2) not misuse.

It is not clear whether all such efforts will be successful. That is, although "express conditions accompanying the sale or license of a patented product are generally upheld," *Braun*, 124 F.3d at 1426, "[s]uch express conditions...are contractual in nature and are subject to antitrust, patent, contract, and any other applicable law, as well as equitable considerations such as patent misuse." *Id. See also Braun*, 124 F.3d at 1426 ("The key inquiry under this fact-intensive doctrine is whether, by imposing the condition, the patentee has 'impermissibly broadened the "physical or temporal" scope of the patent grant with anticompetitive effect'"). Thus, the "basics matter" for each area of law — for example, antitrust law and contract law.

2. **The Absence of a Contract.** Recall in *Husky* the court noted that the "X-series systems were without contractual restriction on the future purchase of molds or carrier plates." What result if Husky contractually required the molds and carrier plates to be purchased from Husky? Would Grafco be a direct infringer and R & D a contributory infringer? Does *Mallinckrodt* help your analysis? In *Mallinckrodt*, the court noted that a breach of an enforceable contract of sale may result in a finding of infringement on the part of the breaching party. *Mallinckrodt*, 976 F.2d at 709. *See also Kendall Co. v. Progressive Medical Tech., Inc.*, 85 F.3d 1570 (Fed. Cir. 1996) (noting that in a "single use" contract case such as *Mallinckrodt*, there is "'no need to choose between repair and reconstruction' because 'even repair of an unlicensed device constitutes infringement'"). Some have asserted that the "repair-reconstruction distinction has nothing to do with patent policy"; rather, "[i]t is solely a matter of interpreting the license." William M. Landes & Richard A. Posner, THE ECONOMIC STRUCTURE OF INTELLECTUAL PROPERTY 381-382 (2003).

In *Kendall*, there was a contract with a "Single Patient Use Only" provision similar to *Mallinckrodt*, but unlike the patentee in *Mallinckrodt*, who required its customers to purchase the entire patented device from the patentee, the *Kendall* patentee (i.e., the Kendall Company) neither required its customers to purchase the entire device, nor the unpatented replacement parts. In this regard, the Kendall Company is like Husky. Perhaps patent protection was not available to Husky and the Kendall Company for the replacement parts, but one would think that a properly drafted contract would have helped both patentees.

## Problem

12-1. L'Mark makes and sells laser printers and toner (printer) cartridges. ACRID represents wholesalers that remanufacture emptied L'Mark printer cartridges for reuse. Before 1997, L'Mark did not compete against ACRID's members because it sold only new replacement printer cartridges. In 1997, however, L'Mark began to remanufacture its own cartridges and launched an aggressive new strategy to improve its position in the market for remanufacturing the used cartridges. Most notably, the company introduced its "Prebate" program — a play on the word "rebate" — which gives consumers an upfront discount on L'Mark's patented printer cartridges.

The Prebate cartridges cost consumers on average $30 (or 20 percent) less than a regular cartridge. In return, L'Mark requires the consumer to return the depleted cartridge to L'Mark or its agent. The Prebate cartridge package sets forth the following license agreement on the outside of the package:

> RETURN EMPTY CARTRIDGE TO L'MARK FOR REMANUFACTURING AND RECYCLING
>
> Please read before opening. Opening of this package or using the patented cartridge inside confirms your acceptance of the following license agreement. The patented cartridge is sold at a special price subject to a restriction that it may be used only once. Following this initial use, you agree to return the empty cartridge only to L'Mark for remanufacturing and recycling. If you don't accept these terms, return the unopened package to your point of purchase. A regular price cartridge without these terms is available.

Consumers can opt to buy L'Mark cartridges without the Prebate post-sale restriction, but at the higher price. According to L'Mark, its post-sale restriction on reusing the Prebate cartridges does not require consumers to return the cartridge at all; it only precludes giving the cartridge to another remanufacturer.

L'Mark asserts that it devised the Prebate program to boost its competitive position in the remanufacturing market, to preserve the quality of the product offered consumers and to be environmentally conscious by recycling used cartridges. L'Mark advertises the program in packaging, media, and on the company's Web site. It pays a fee to authorized resellers who collect and return empty cartridges.

The program has been successful. The company estimates that 50 percent of the cartridges sold are returned as empty cartridges to L'Mark, and cartridge returns have increased by 300 percent since the implementation of the Prebate program. Additionally, from 1997 to 2001, L'Mark's cartridge sales in the United States increased by nearly 100 percent and its sale of printers that use Prebate cartridges increased by 60 percent.

ACRID filed an action against L'Mark in federal district court alleging that L'Mark's Prebate program is inconsistent with *Malinckrodt* and patent law's first-sale doctrine. What result? *See Arizona Cartridge Remanufacturers Ass'n, Inc. v. Lexmark Intern., Inc.*, 421 F.3d 981 (9th Cir. 2005).

## 2. Post-Expiration Royalty Contracts

### SCHEIBER v. DOLBY LABORATORIES, INC.
#### 293 F.3d 1014 (7th Cir. 2002)

POSNER, Circuit Judge.

The plaintiff in a suit to enforce a patent licensing agreement appeals to us from the grant of summary judgment to the defendants, Dolby for short. Scheiber, the plaintiff, a musician turned inventor who held U.S. and Canadian patents on the audio system known as "surround sound," sued

Dolby in 1983 for infringement of his patents. The parties settled the suit by agreeing that Scheiber would license his patents to Dolby in exchange for royalties. The last U.S. patent covered by the agreement was scheduled to expire in May 1993, while the last Canadian patent was not scheduled to expire until September 1995. During the settlement negotiations Dolby suggested to Scheiber that in exchange for a lower royalty rate the license agreement provide that royalties on all the patents would continue until the Canadian patent expired, including, therefore, patents that had already expired. That way Dolby could, it hoped, pass on the entire royalty expense to its sublicensees without their balking at the rate. Scheiber acceded to the suggestion and the agreement was drafted accordingly, but Dolby later refused to pay royalties on any patent after it expired, precipitating this suit. Federal jurisdiction over the suit is based on diversity of citizenship, because a suit to enforce a patent licensing agreement does not arise under federal patent law.

Dolby argues that the duty to pay royalties on any patent covered by the agreement expired by the terms of the agreement itself as soon as the patent expired, because the royalties were to be based on Dolby's sales of equipment within the scope of the patents and once a patent expires, Dolby argues, there is no equipment within its scope. The argument would make meaningless the provision that Dolby itself proposed for continuing the payment of royalties until the last patent expired. Anyway the reference to equipment within the scope of the patent was clearly meant to *identify* the equipment on which royalties would be based (Dolby makes equipment that does not utilize Scheiber's patents as well as equipment that does) rather than to limit the duration of the obligation to pay royalties.

Dolby's principal argument is that the Supreme Court held in a decision that has never been overruled that a patent owner may not enforce a contract for the payment of patent royalties beyond the expiration date of the patent. The decision was *Brulotte v. Thys Co.*, 379 U.S. 29 (1964), dutifully followed by lower courts. *Brulotte* involved an agreement licensing patents that expired at different dates, just like this case; the two cases are indistinguishable. The decision has, it is true, been severely, and as it seems to us, with all due respect, justly, criticized, beginning with Justice Harlan's dissent, 379 U.S. at 34, and continuing with our opinion in *USM Corp. v. SPS Technologies, Inc.*, 694 F.2d 505, 510-11 (7th Cir.1982). The Supreme Court's majority opinion reasoned that by extracting a promise to continue paying royalties after expiration of the patent, the patentee extends the patent beyond the term fixed in the patent statute and therefore in violation of the law. That is not true. After the patent expires, anyone can make the patented process or product without being guilty of patent infringement. The patent can no longer be used to exclude anybody from such production. Expiration thus accomplishes what it is supposed to accomplish. For a licensee in accordance with a provision in the license agreement to go on paying royalties after the patent expires does not extend the duration of the patent either technically or practically, because, as this case demonstrates, if the licensee agrees to continue paying royalties after the patent expires the royalty rate will be lower. The duration of the patent fixes the limit of the patentee's power to extract royalties; it is a detail whether he extracts them at a higher rate over a shorter period of time or a lower rate over a longer period of time.

This insight is not original with us. "The *Brulotte* rule incorrectly assumes that a patent license has significance after the patent terminates. When the patent term ends, the exclusive right to make, use or sell the licensed invention also ends. Because the invention is available to the world, the license in fact ceases to have value. Presumably, licensees know this when they enter into a licensing agreement. If the licensing agreement calls for royalty payments beyond the patent term, the parties base those payments on the licensees' assessment of the value of the license during the patent period. These payments, therefore, do not represent an extension in time of the patent monopoly.... Courts do not remove the obligation of the consignee to pay because payment after receipt is an extension of market power — it is simply a division of the payment-for-delivery transaction. Royalties beyond the patent term are no different. If royalties are calculated on post-patent term sales, the calculation is simply a risk-shifting credit arrangement between patentee and licensee. The arrangement can be no more than that, because the patentee at that time has nothing else to sell." Harold See & Frank M. Caprio, *The Trouble with* Brulotte: *The Patent Royalty Term and Patent Monopoly Extension,* 1990 UTAH L. REV. 813, 814, 851.

These criticisms might be wide of the mark if *Brulotte* had been based on a interpretation of the patent clause of the Constitution, or of the patent statute or any other statute; but it seems rather to have been a free-floating product of a misplaced fear of monopoly ("a patentee's use of a royalty agreement that projects beyond the expiration date of the patent is unlawful *per se*. If that device were available to patentees, the free market visualized for the post-expiration period would be subject to monopoly influences that have no proper place there," 379 U.S. at 32-33) that was not even tied to one of the antitrust statutes. The doctrinal basis of the decision was the doctrine of patent misuse, of which more later.

A patent confers a monopoly, and the longer the term of the patent the greater the monopoly. The limitation of the term of a patent, besides being commanded by the Constitution, and necessary to avoid impossible tracing problems (imagine if some caveman had gotten a perpetual patent on the wheel), serves to limit the monopoly power conferred on the patentee. But as we have pointed out, charging royalties beyond the term of the patent does not lengthen the patentee's monopoly; it merely alters the timing of royalty payments. This would be obvious if the license agreement between Scheiber and Dolby had become effective a month before the last patent expired. The parties could have agreed that Dolby would pay royalties for the next 100 years, but obviously the royalty rate would be minuscule because of the imminence of the patent's expiration.

However, we have no authority to overrule a Supreme Court decision no matter how dubious its reasoning strikes us, or even how out of touch with the Supreme Court's current thinking the decision seems. In *Agostini v. Felton,* 521 U.S. 203, 237 (1997), the Supreme Court "reaffirm[ed] that '[i]f a precedent of this Court has direct application in a case, yet appears to rest on reasons rejected in some other line of decisions, the Court of Appeals should follow the case which directly controls, leaving to this Court the prerogative of overruling its own decisions,'" quoting *Rodriguez de Quijas v. Shearson/American Express, Inc.,* 490 U.S. 477, 484 (1989). In *Khan,* the lower court (namely us), pointing out that the Supreme Court decision that we refused to declare defunct was clearly out of touch with the Court's current antitrust thinking, invited the Court to reverse, see *Khan v. State Oil Co.,* 93 F.3d 1358, 1363 (7th Cir. 1996), vacated and remanded, and it did, but pointedly noted that we had been right to leave the execution and interment of the Court's discredited precedent to the Court.

Now it is true that in *Aronson v. Quick Point Pencil Co.,* 440 U.S. 257 (1979), a case decided some years after *Brulotte,* the Supreme Court upheld an agreement superficially similar to the one invalidated in *Brulotte* and at issue in the present case: a patent applicant granted a license for the invention it hoped to patent to a firm that agreed, if a patent were not granted, to pay the inventor-applicant royalties for as long as the firm sold products embodying the invention. The Court was careful to distinguish *Brulotte,* and not a single Justice suggested that any cloud had been cast over the earlier decision. Since no patent was granted, the doctrine of patent misuse could not be brought into play, and there was no other federal ground for invalidating the license. The Court emphasized that *Brulotte* had been based on the "leverage" that the patent had granted the patentee to extract royalties beyond the date of expiration, 440 U.S. at 265, and that leverage was of course missing in *Aronson.*

If *Aronson* and *Brulotte* were inconsistent with each other and the Court had not reaffirmed *Brulotte* in *Aronson,* then we would have to follow *Aronson,* the later opinion, since to follow *Brulotte* in those circumstances would be to overrule *Aronson.* But the reaffirmation of *Brulotte* in *Aronson* tells us that the Court did not deem the cases inconsistent, and so, whether we agree or not, we have no warrant for declaring *Brulotte* overruled.

Scheiber argues further, however, that *Brulotte* has been superseded by a 1988 amendment to the patent statute which provides, so far as bears on this case, that "no patent owner otherwise entitled to relief for infringement...shall be...deemed guilty of misuse or illegal extension of the patent right by reason of his having...conditioned the license of any rights to the patent or the sale of the patented product on the acquisition of a license to rights in another patent or purchase of a separate product" unless the patentee has market power in the market for the conditioning product (which is not argued here). 35 U.S.C. §271(d)(5). The statute is doubly inapplicable to this case. It merely limits defenses to infringement suits, and Scheiber isn't suing for infringement; he's suing to enforce a license agreement. He can't sue for infringement; his patents have expired. Scheiber argues that since the agreement was in settlement of his infringement suit, the only effect of limiting the statute to such suits would be to dissuade patentees from settling them. Not so. Had Scheiber pressed his 1983 infringement suit against Dolby to judgment, he would not have obtained royalties beyond the expiration date of his patents, because Dolby had not as yet agreed to pay any royalties; there was no license agreement before the case was settled. The significance of the statute is that if some subsequent infringer should point to the license agreement with Dolby as a misuse of Scheiber's patent by reason of the tying together of different patents, Scheiber could plead the statute as a bar to the infringer's defense of patent misuse.

In any event, the new statutory defense is explicitly limited to tying, *Lasercomb America, Inc. v. Reynolds*; normally of a nonpatented product to a patented product, as in a number of famous patent misuse cases, such as *Henry v. A.B. Dick Co.*, and antitrust tying cases, such as *International Business Machines Corp. v. United States*. The 1988 amendment limited the tying doctrine, in cases in which the tying product is a patent, to situations in which the patentee has real market power, not merely the technical monopoly (right to exclude) that every patent confers. *Virginia Panel Corp. v. MAC Panel Co.*, 133 F.3d at 869. There are multiple products here, and they are tied together in the sense of having been licensed as a package. The more exact term is bundling, because a single price is charged for the tied goods, rather than separate prices as in the canonical tying cases. *United States v. Microsoft Corp.*, 253 F.3d 34, 87, 96 (D. C. Cir. 2001) (en banc). We may assume that the statute encompasses bundling. We can't find a case on the point, but certainly the statutory language encompasses it and the objections to tying and bundling, such as they are, are the same. (The naive objection is that they extend monopoly; the sophisticated objection is that they facilitate price discrimination.) But it is not the bundling of the U.S. and Canadian patents on which Dolby pitches its refusal to pay royalties; it is the duration of the royalty obligation. The objection would be the same if there were a single patent and the agreement required the licensee to continue paying royalties after the patent expired.

There just is no evidence that Congress in the 1988 amendment wanted to go or did go beyond tying. Had it wanted to, it would have chosen different words. We are not literalists, but there must be *some* semantic handle on which to hang a proposed statutory interpretation, and there is none here, though we have found a district court case that did hold that the 1988 amendment had overruled *Brulotte*.

* * *

## Comments

*1. The Criticism of* **Brulotte**. As Judge Posner's *Scheiber* opinion makes clear, the *Brulotte* decision has not been immune from criticism. Consistent with *Scheiber* and building of Justice Harlan's dissent, Professor William Landes and Judge Richard Posner write:

> After the patent expires, anyone can make the patented process or product without being guilty of patent infringement. As the patent can no longer be used to exclude anybody from such production, expiration has accomplished what is was supposed to accomplish. If the licensee agrees to continue paying royalties after the patent expires, the royalty rate will be lower during the period before expiration. The duration of the patent fixes the limit of the patentee's power to extract royalties; it is a detail whether he extracts them at a higher rate over a shorter period of time or at a lower rate over a longer period of time.

William M. Landes & Richard A. Posner, THE ECONOMIC STRUCTURE OF INTELLECTUAL PROPERTY LAW 380 (2003). *See also* Rochelle Cooper Dreyfuss, *Dethroning Lear: Licensee Estoppel and the Incentive to Innovate*, 72 VA. L. REV. 677, 709 (1986) (noting that the *Brulotte* decision is "vulnerable on several grounds").

2. *Patents and Market Power.* A plaintiff under §2 of the Sherman Act must prove the patent owner has market power or is likely to obtain market power. The Supreme Court has defined market power as "the ability to raise prices above those that would be charged in a competitive market." *NCAA v. Board of Regents*, 468 U.S. 85, 108 n. 38 (1984). Other definitions include "the ability of a single seller to raise price and restrict output," *Eastman Kodak Co. v. Image Technical Services, Inc.*, 504 U.S. 451, 464 (1992), and "the power to control prices or exclude competition." *United States v. E.I. du Pont de Nemours & Co.*, 351 U.S. 377, 391 (1956). In a patent context specifically, the Court has stated that "a patent holder has no market power in any relevant sense if there are close substitutes for the patented product. Similarly, a high market share indicates market power only if the market is properly defined to include all reasonable substitutes for the product." *Jefferson Parish Hospital Dist. No. 2 v. Hyde*, 466 U.S. 2, 38 n. 7 (1984). Thus, a patent alone does not necessarily create market power and convert a patentee into a "prohibited monopolist." *Abbott Lab. v. Brennan*, 952 F.2d 1346, 1354 (Fed. Cir. 1991).

3. *Tying Arrangements and Market Power.* Section 271(d)(5) seems to embrace the notion that it is difficult to leverage through tying or bundling arrangements of market power from a patented product into a separate market, usually a market for the tied, unpatented good. For example, in *Scheiber*, Judge Posner writes "[t]he naive objection [to tying or bundling arrangements] is that they extend monopoly; the sophisticated objection is that they facilitate price discrimination." He continues:

> The traditional objection to tying is that by telling the buyer that he can't buy the tying product unless he agrees to buy a separate product from the seller as well, the seller is trying to "lever" or "extend" his monopoly to the market for that separate product. Yet if the seller tries to charge a monopoly price for that separate product, the buyer will not be willing to pay as much for the tying product as he would if the separate product, which he has to buy also, were priced at a lower rate. Acquiring monopoly power in the tied-product market comes at the expense of losing it in the tying-product market. Thus, as these cases and a tidal wave of legal and economic scholarship point out, the idea that you can use tying to lever your way to a second monopoly is economic nonsense, imputing systematic irrationality to businessmen. Congress seems to have recognized this in the 1988 amendment.

293 F.3d 1014, 1020 (7th Cir. 2002). *See also* Robert H. Bork, THE ANTITRUST PARADOX: A POLICY AT WAR WITH ITSELF 372-381 (1978) (discussing why tying arrangements do not injure competition). This approach, which is a relatively recent development, should be contrasted with the more traditional notion that tying is a means of leveraging to restrain competition, and therefore, should be deemed illegal

per se. *See also U.S. Philips Corp. v. International Trade Comm'n*, 424 F.3d 1179 (Fed. Cir. 2005) (finding no misuse on patent-to-patent tying arrangement).

4. *Patent Law and Antitrust.* Patent law and antitrust law are closely related. There are two instances, independent of each other, where the improper obtainment and exercise of patent rights can lead to a violation of the antitrust laws. These instances are known as *Walker Process* claims and *Handgards* claims. *See Walker Process Equipment, Inc. v. Food Machinery & Chemical Corp.*, 382 U.S. 172, 177 (1965); *Handgards, Inc. v. Ethicon, Inc.*, 601 F.2d 986 (9th Cir. 1979). While both claims possess different elements and seek to address different problems, a crucial element common to both is proof that the patent owner has market power or is likely to obtain market power. This finding is essential under §2 of the Sherman Act.

   a. **Walker Process *Claim.*** A *Walker Process* claim concerns the enforcement of a fraudulently obtained patent by a patent owner with market power. The fraud needed to prove a *Walker Process* violation is narrower and more serious than inequitable conduct fraud. The court in *Nobelpharma AB v. Implant Innovations, Inc.*, 141 F.3d 1059 (Fed. Cir. 1998), noted that *Walker Process* fraud "must evidence a clear intent to deceive the examiner and thereby cause the PTO to grant an invalid patent," whereas "a conclusion of inequitable conduct may be based on evidence of a lesser misrepresentation or omission, such as omission of a reference that would merely have been considered important to the patentability of a claim by a reasonable examiner." *Nobelpharma* 141 F.3d at 1070. Thus, *Walker Process* fraud is but-for causation.

   In addition to fraudulent conduct in obtaining the patent, a *Walker Process* plaintiff must prove enforcement of the patent or some other behavior that adversely affects the market (e.g., threatening to sue competitors) *and*, to satisfy §2 of the Sherman Act, evidence that the patent owner has market power or will likely obtain market power. *See* Comment 1 for a discussion of market power.

   b. **Handgards *Claim.*** A *Handgards* claim relates to the filing of an infringement suit that was "a mere sham to cover what is actually nothing more than an attempt to interfere directly with the business relationships of a competitor." The concern here is with the enforcement of a patent, though properly obtained (i.e., no inequitable conduct or fraud), is believed by the patent owner to be invalid or not infringed.

   To prove that an infringement suit is a "mere sham," an "antitrust plaintiff must show that the suit was both objectively baseless and subjectively motivated by a desire to impose collateral, anticompetitive injury rather than to obtain a justifiable legal remedy." *Nobelpharma*, 141 F.3d at 1071. *See Professional Real Estate Investors, Inc. v. Columbia Pictures Industries, Inc.*, 508 U.S. 49 (1993) (*PRE*). In *PRE*, the Supreme Court stated that "objectively baseless" means "that no reasonable litigant could realistically expect success on the merits." Regarding "subjective motivation," the focus is on "whether the baseless lawsuit conceals 'an attempt to interfere directly with the business relationships of a competitor,' through the 'use [of] the governmental *pro-*

*cess* — as opposed to the *outcome* of that process (as an anticompetitive weapon.'" *Id.* at 60-61 (emphasis in original).

5. **Settlement Agreements.** It is not uncommon for patent litigants to settle. Indeed, a vast majority of cases find resolution outside of the courtroom, a result that as a general matter should be encouraged. A settlement can take many forms, licensing (both exclusive and non-exclusive) being perhaps the most common. Usually, settlement activity does not invoke antitrust law, even though many settlements are horizontal — i.e., between competitors. But there are settlement agreements that may raise antitrust issues, particularly when the public welfare is diminished. The principal case provides a nice discussion of the issues at play at the intersection of patent law and antitrust law in the context of settlement activity.

6. **Refusals to Deal.** It is well settled that a patent owner has no duty to practice his invention, and he is within his rights to suppress the invention. *See Continental Paper Bag Co. v. Eastern Paper Bag Co.*, 210 U.S. 405 (1908); 35 U.S.C. §271(d)(4). And a patentee, perhaps with one caveat discussed in the next several paragraphs, may refuse to sell or license its patented product without violating the antitrust laws. *See In re Independent Service Organizations Antitrust Litigation v. Xerox*, 203 F.3d 1322, 1325 (Fed. Cir. 2000) (*ISO II*) ("[n]o patent owner otherwise entitled to relief...shall be denied relief or deemed guilty of misuse or illegal extension of the patent right by reason of his having...refused to license or use any rights to the patent...").

But the more controversial notion is the refusal to license patented products to gain a monopoly in a market beyond the scope of the patent. The facts and holding of *ISO II* are worth exploring here. In *ISO II*, Xerox adopted a policy of not selling patented parts (for its copiers) to independent service organizations. (Xerox wanted to protect its ability to price discriminate, thus it sought to prevent arbitrage by refusing to sell patented components.) One such organization, CSU, charged that Xerox had violated the antitrust laws by leveraging its market power acquired through patent rights into a separate market for the service of Xerox's copiers. CSU relied on a footnote in *Eastman Kodak Co. v. Image Technical Services, Inc.*, 504 U.S. 451, 480 n. 29 (1992) (*Kodak I*), wherein the footnote read: "[t]he Court has held many times that power gained through some natural and legal advantage such as a patent...can give rise to liability if 'a seller exploits his dominant position in one market to expand his empire into the next.'" 203 F.3d at 1326-1327. The Federal Circuit distinguished *Kodak I* by noting that it was a "tying case," and in the present case, there are no assertions "of illegally tying the sale of Xerox's patented parts to unpatented products." *Id.* at 1327. According to the Federal Circuit, the footnote in *Kodak I* "can be interpreted as restating the undisputed premise that the patent holder cannot use his statutory right to refuse to sell patented parts to gain a monopoly in a market beyond the scope of the patent." *Id.*

CSU also relied on the Ninth Circuit's holding in *Kodak II*, which was a decision from remand of *Kodak I*. Specifically, CSU relied on *Kodak II* for the proposition that the court must evaluate the patentee's subjective motivation for refusing to sell or license its patented products. The Federal Circuit "declined to follow" *Kodak II*, stating:

> We have held that "if a [patent infringement] suit is not objectively base-less, an antitrust defendant's subjective motivation is immaterial." [citing *Nobelpharma*]. We see no more reason to inquire into the subjective motivation of Xerox in refusing to sell or license its patented works than we found in evaluating the subjective motivation of a patentee in bringing suit to enforce that same right. In the absence of any indication of illegal tying, fraud in the [PTO], or sham litigation, the patent holder may enforce the statutory right to exclude others from making, using, or selling the claimed invention free from liability under the antitrust laws. We therefore will not inquire into his subjective motivation for exerting his statutory rights, even though his refusal to sell or license his patented invention may have an anticompetitive effect, so long as that anticompetitive effect is not illegally extended beyond the statutory patent grant.

203 F.3d at 1327-1328. The court's analysis focuses heavily on the patent right, which includes the right not to practice or license the patented product. But does the court give insufficient weight to anticompetitive effects resulting from the refusal to deal?

# CHAPTER

# 13

# Remedies for Patent Infringement

## INTRODUCTION

This chapter explores the types of remedies available to a patentee. A patent owner is entitled to both money damages and equitable relief. Damages must be "adequate to compensate for the infringement," 35 U.S.C. §284, and are measured based on either lost profits or a reasonable royalty. A court may also "grant injunctions...to prevent the violation of any" of the rights conferred by a patent. *See* 35 U.S.C. §283. The injunction is a remedy typically associated with a property right; and injunctive relief for patent infringement is conceptually similar to a real property owner enjoining a third party from trespassing on his land. A court has the power to issue preliminary and permanent injunctions.

> *STATUTE:* **Injunction**
> 35 U.S.C. §283
>
> *STATUTE:* **Damages**
> 35 U.S.C. §284

## A. MONEY DAMAGES

Money damages are usually measured by calculating the patent owner's *lost profits* or, if lost profits cannot be proved, by using a *reasonable royalty* method, which may be based on either an established or hypothetical royalty. The *Micro* case explores a lost profit analysis, and the *Trio Process* case discusses the framework for constructing a reasonable royalty.

## 1. Lost Profits

Lost profits are based on profits lost by the patentee, not the profits made by the infringer. The modern legal framework for determining lost profits can be found in *Panduit Corp.* v. *Stahlin Bros. Fibre Works*. In *Panduit*, the court stated:

> To obtain as damages the profits on sales he would have made absent the infringement, i.e., the sales made by the infringer, a patent owner must prove: (1) demand for the patented product, (2) the absence of acceptable noninfringing substitutes, (3) his manufacturing and marketing capability to exploit the demand, and (4) the amount of the profit he would have made.

575 F.2d 1152, 1156 (6th Cir. 1978). The Federal Circuit modified the *Panduit* test in *Grain Processing*, particularly the determination of available substitutes. *Grain Processing* seeks to discern market value in a hypothetical, constructed world. The following case discusses *Panduit*, *Grain Processing*, and the methodology of a lost profits determination.

## MICRO CHEMICAL, INC. v. LEXTRON, INC.

### 318 F.3d 1119 (Fed. Cir. 2003)

RADER, Circuit Judge.

This case, which spans a fourteen-year period, has been the subject of two previous appeals to this court. The present appeal involves only damages. The United States District Court for the District of Colorado granted summary judgment denying Micro Chemical, Inc. lost profits. The district court then conducted a bench trial to determine the proper reasonable royalty for Lextron, Inc.'s infringement of Micro's U.S. Patent No. 4,733,971 ('971 patent). Micro seeks review of the district court's judgment denying it lost profits and granting a reasonable royalty of only one percent....

### BACKGROUND

Animal feedlots generally add microingredients to livestock and poultry feed. Microingredients are feed additives, such as vitamins, antibiotics, hormones, medicines, and nutritional supplements, that provide a balanced diet, stimulate growth, and protect the animals from disease. One method of adding microingredients to livestock and poultry feed involves mixing dry supplements that contain microingredients into the feed. Alternatively, feedlots may spread dry microingredients directly on top of the feed in the trough (called "top dressing"). Both methods have some disadvantages in that they do not ensure uniform, accurate dosages, and they limit the feedlot's flexibility to alter dosages.

Microingredient dispensing machines overcame some of those problems. These machines measure and dispense microingredients by mixing them into a liquid carrier that is sprayed over livestock and poultry feed rations. One example of such a machine measures and dispenses microingredients by volume. Micro's '971 patent claims a machine that dispenses microingredients by weight. Weigh machines measure microingredients by weight before mixing them into the liquid carrier. This technology improved on the prior volume machine technology.

Micro and Lextron both produce microingredient weigh machines. They place their weigh machines in feedlots at no cost to the feedlots.

They recoup their expenses by selling microingredients to the feedlots at an eight- to ten-percent premium. Although not required by contract to do so, feedlots generally purchase their microingredients—at premium prices—from the company that placed its machine on the feedlot. In the liability phase of this case, this court held that Lextron's Type 2 weigh machine infringed the '971 patent. Lextron used primarily the infringing Type 2 machine during the infringement period, 1988 to 1997. After Micro sued Lextron in 1988, Lextron developed its Type 3 "no mix" weigh machine. The Type 3 machine had clumping problems that limited its commercial use. By 1997, there was only one Type 3 machine still in use. After this court's 1997 opinion issued, Lextron began modifying its existing Type 2 machines into a new Type 5 weigh machine.

During the damages phase, Micro sought recovery under both lost profits and reasonable royalty theories. On summary judgment, the district court held that Micro was not entitled to lost profits under either the two-supplier or the *Panduit* test. Trial proceeded on a reasonable royalty damage theory, and the court awarded Micro a royalty of one percent on Lextron's microingredient sales.

## DISCUSSION

### I.

To recover lost profits a patentee must show that "but for" infringement it reasonably would have made the additional profits enjoyed by the infringer. *King Instruments Corp. v. Perego*. This court has not restricted patentees to any one particular method of proving "but for" causation. *Id.; see also Rite-Hite Corp. v. Kelley Co., Inc*. A patentee may resort to any method showing, with reasonable probability, entitlement to lost profits "but for" the infringement. *King Instruments*, 65 F.3d at 952; *Rite-Hite*, 56 F.3d at 1545. Once the patentee establishes the reasonableness of this inference, the burden shifts to the infringer to show that the inference is unreasonable for some or all of the lost profits. *Rite-Hite*, 56 F.3d at 1545. The *Panduit* . . . test[ is a] recognized method[] of showing "but for" causation. *See Lam, Inc. v. Johns-Manville Corp*.

### A.

The district court found that Micro could not satisfy two of the four *Panduit* factors: demand for the patented product and absence of available, noninfringing substitutes. *See Panduit Corp. v. Stahlin Bros. Fibre Works*. Specifically, the court found that Lextron's Type 5 weigh machine was an available, noninfringing substitute, and that there was no demand for Micro's patented weigh machines.

The district court deemed the Type 5 machine available under *Grain Processing Corp. v. American Maize-Products Co*. In *Grain Processing*, this court reaffirmed its earlier precedent stating that a technology not on the market at the time of infringement can, in certain circumstances, constitute an available, noninfringing alternative. 185 F.3d at 1351-52. *Grain Processing* did not erect a rigid test for determining availability. Rather, it provided guidelines for when an alternative not actually "on sale" during the infringement period may have been readily "available" and thus part of the economic calculation of lost profits.

In *Grain Processing*, for example, the material and know-how for the alleged substitute were readily available at the time of infringement. *Id.* at 1354. According to the record in that case, the infringer "had all of the necessary equipment, know-how, and experience" to make the substitution at that time. *Id.* Therefore, the infringer was able to convert to the substitute manufacturing process in the remarkably short period of two weeks. *Id.* at 1346. In *Grain Processing*, even the ready availability of material and know-how alone did not make the substitute process "available" for the lost profits calculus. This court also weighed the fact that "the high cost of a necessary material can conceivably render a substitute 'unavailable.' " *Id.* Similarly, this court noted that the finding that an infringer had to design or invent around the patented technology to develop an alleged substitute weighs against a finding of availability. *Id.* In sum, this court in *Grain Processing* weighed the factors that would show the substitute's effect on the market.

In this case, the record evidence does not support the district court's grant of summary judgment on the availability of the Lextron Type 5 machine. The record shows that Lextron did not have the necessary equipment, know-how, and experience to make the Type 5 machine at the time of infringement. Lextron expended 984 hours to design the Type 5 machine and another 330 to test it. Charles Hoff, a Lextron engineer, worked full-time for several months on the design of the Type 5 machine. Thereafter, he continued to work part-time on the project, estimating that he tested and rejected five potential design changes. Lextron took over four months to convert all of its infringing Type 2 machines to Type 5 machines.

The effects of the changes also were not well known or readily available. Lextron hired consultants to help it consider the impact and effectiveness of the new designs. Lextron hired a firm to consider "alternative designs." Additionally, Lextron retained a Ph.D. nutritionist "to assure the effectiveness of the new designs in delivering the microingredients to the animal feed."

The summary judgment record also shows that the materials for the alleged substitutions were not readily available. Lextron requested a 120-day extension to delay the injunction on the use of its Type 2 machines because the "parts required for the conversion" were "difficult to obtain in bulk, particularly since some must be specially fabricated according to our specifications and most are not maintained in inventory." Thus, in Lextron's own words, the needed materials and equipment were "difficult to obtain in bulk," "specially fabricated," and "not maintained in inventory." This record shows that the Type 5 machine was not available at the time of infringement. To the contrary, the record shows that Lextron designed around the patented technology after Micro established infringement.

The district court also granted summary judgment on the *Panduit* demand factor, finding no demand for the patented technology. The record does not provide a basis for granting summary judgment on this point. Although the parties provided the patented weigh machines to feedlots at no cost, the record indicates that these machines had benefits over other methods. Indeed, the number of weigh machines in commercial use increased during the infringement period. Both Micro and Lextron made profits on placement of their machines. Lextron advertised its weigh machines as providing "accurate mixing and delivery" benefits. Drawing all reasonable factual inferences in Micro's favor, this record at least raises a genuine issue of material fact concerning demand. A reasonable jury could find demand for the patented features of Micro's weigh machines.

In sum, the district court erred in granting summary judgment that the Type 5 machine was an available substitute for the patented invention at the time of infringement. This court reverses the grant of summary judgment of availability. The district court should have granted summary judgment that the Type 5 machine was not available at the time of infringement. Because the Type 5 machine was not available during the infringement period, this court need not reach the question of whether the Type 5 machine infringes the '971 patent. On the question of demand, this court vacates the grant of summary judgment. Based on this record, Micro is entitled to an opportunity to prove lost profits under the *Panduit* test.

\* \* \*

## Comments

1. **The** *Panduit* *Foundation.* The *Panduit* test is the modern foundation for determining lost profits and usually the starting point for a damages analysis. *Panduit* sets forth a standard "but for" test for proving lost profits; that is, the patentee must show a reasonable probability that he would have made the lost sales "but for" the infringing activity. But the Federal Circuit has stated the *Panduit* test, while "accepted as useful," is a "non-exclusive way for a patentee to prove entitlement to lost profits damages." *Rite-Hite*, 56 F.3d at 1545. As a result, the Federal Circuit has moved beyond *Panduit* in certain instances as described in the following notes.

2. *Noninfringing Substitutes.* Of *Panduit*'s four factors, the "absence of acceptable non-infringing substitutes" is perhaps the most important and controversial. Under *Panduit*, a patentee cannot recover lost profits if acceptable noninfringing substitutes are available. In a two-supplier market, one can assume that consumers would have purchased the product from the patentee absent the infringing activity. *See State Indus., Inc. v. Mor-Flo, Inc.*, 883 F.2d 1573 (Fed. Cir. 1989) ("In the two-supplier market, it is reasonable to assume, provided the patent owner has the manufacturing and marketing capabilities, that it would have made the infringer's sales. In these instances, the *Panduit* test is usually straightforward and dispositive."). But for this assumption to hold, the patentee must prove that it and the infringer sell substantially similar products in the same market to the same customers.

   Moreover, the plausibility of the two-supplier assumption is greatly weakened in a multisupplier scenario because consumers have other options besides the patentee. The Federal Circuit addressed this problem in *State Indus., supra*, by adopting a "market share" approach, which is an alternative to and quite different from the approach taken in *Micro Chemical* and *Grain Processing*. This *State Indus.* approach allows the patentee to recover lost profits based on market share, even though there are available noninfringing substitutes. The patentee is permitted to substitute market share for absence of noninfringing products because it nevertheless can prove with reasonable probability sales it would have made "but for" the infringement. This approach assumes that the patentee, who, for example, has 30 percent of the market, would have made 30 percent of the sales absent infringing activity. Thus, *State Indus.* rendered neutral the "absence of acceptance non-infringing substitutes" factor. Importantly, as with the *Panduit* test, the market share approach requires proof that the patentee and the infringer compete in the same market. *Grain Processing* and *Micro Chemical* do not necessarily conflict with *State Indus.* because under *State Indus.* lost profits are available even though a court determines the existence of noninfringing substitutes.

3. *Foreseeability—Proximate Cause and Lost Profits.* It is a basic tenet of patent law that the patentee does not have to practice his invention. And the Federal Circuit, somewhat controversially, has held that a patentee may recover lost profit damages whether or not he makes, uses, or sells the patented invention as long as the damages were foreseeable. In *Rite-Hite Corp. v. Kelley Co.*, 56 F.3d 1538 (Fed. Cir. 1995) (en banc), Rite-Hite's (the patentee) '847 patent claimed a mechanism for restraining trucks during loading and unloading. The patentee sold two types of restraining devices, the MDL-55, which was covered by the '847 patent and the ADL-100, which was not covered by the '847 patent, but was claimed by other Rite-Hite patents not in suit. The defendant's product, which competed with both the MDL-55 and ADL-100, was found to infringe the '847 patent. But the Federal Circuit, in affirming the district court, held that it was permissible to include lost sales associated with the ADL-100 when calculating lost profits even though the ADL-100 was not covered by the '847 patent. According to the court:

> If a particular injury was or should have been reasonably foreseeable by an infringing competitor in the relevant market, broadly defined, that injury is generally compensable absent a persuasive reason to the contrary. Here, the court determined that Rite-Hite's lost sales of the ADL-100, a product that directly competed with the infringing product, were reasonably foreseeable. We agree with that conclusion. Being responsible for lost sales of a competitive product is surely foreseeable; such losses constitute the full compensation set forth by Congress, as interpreted by the Supreme Court, while staying well within the traditional meaning of proximate cause. Such lost sales should therefore clearly be compensable.

* * *

There is no requirement in this country that a patentee make, use, or sell its patented invention. If a patentee's failure to practice a patented invention frustrates an important public need for the invention, a court need not enjoin infringement of the patent. *See* 35 U.S.C. §283...Whether a patentee sells its patented invention is not crucial in determining lost profits damages. Normally, if the patentee is not selling a product, by definition there can be no lost profits. However, in this case, Rite-Hite did sell its own patented products, the MDL-55 and the ADL-100 restraints. Kelley next argues that to award lost profits damages on Rite-Hite's ADL-100s would be contrary to precedent. Citing *Panduit*, Kelley argues that case law regarding lost profits uniformly requires that "the intrinsic value of the patent in suit is the only proper basis for a lost profits award."...Generally, the *Panduit* test has been applied when a patentee is seeking lost profits for a device covered by the patent in suit. However, *Panduit* is not the *sine qua non* for proving "but for" causation. If there are other ways to show that the infringement in fact caused the patentee's lost profits, there is no reason why another test should not be acceptable.

*Rite-Hite*, 56 F.3d at 1546-48.

## 2. Reasonable Royalty

Damages are determined using the "reasonable royalty" method when it is too difficult to prove lost profits or if lost profits are simply not claimed. In discerning a reasonable royalty, usually courts will look to established (extant) royalties or, if none exist, a hypothetical negotiation between what courts refer to as a willing licensor and willing licensee. The time of the hypothetical negotiation is at the time the infringement began.

The common issues associated with the established royalty method are what constitutes an established royalty, how many licenses must exist before a royalty is "established," and how similar must the existing licensing agreements be to the relationship between the patentee and infringer.

### TRIO PROCESS CORP. v. GOLDSTEIN'S SONS, INC.
#### 612 F.2d 1353 (3rd Cir. 1980)

ROSENN, Circuit Judge.

The infringement has been established and is no longer at issue. We are, however, revisited with the troublesome issue of damages. When this case was last before us on appeal from the original determination of damages, we vacated the judgment and remanded to the district court with instructions to recalculate the damages. We are now asked to decide whether the district court's action is consistent with our holding in that earlier appeal. We hold that it is not and, therefore, again vacate the district court's judgment.

### I.

At the heart of this controversy is a patented process for removing insulation from copper wire in order to allow the copper to be salvaged. This process is covered by United States Patent No. 3,076,421, owned by Trio Process Corporation ("Trio"). In 1972 we upheld the validity of the patent and determined that it had been willfully infringed by L. Goldstein's Sons, Incorporated ("Goldstein"). The case was remanded to the district court for a determination of damages.

On remand the district court appointed a master to assist in the determination of damages. When we last reviewed the proceedings, we observed:

> The master approached the damage issue by comparing Goldstein's costs of operating the patented process with the costs of a similar, unpatented process. He found that use of the Trio process saved Goldstein $52,791 per furnace year in labor costs alone, and that other, smaller savings accrued to Goldstein from use of the patented method as well.
>
> In order to reach a "reasonable royalty" for use of the patent by the infringer, the master halved Goldstein's savings in labor costs, and concluded that $26,390 was a reasonable royalty for each furnace year. Multiplying this figure by the number of furnace years of infringement and making slight modifications, the master found damages of $1,564,804. The district court viewed the damage computation not with regard to the money saved by the defendant as a result of the infringement, as the master had, but in terms of what Trio had lost. It looked first to the initial sum of $2,600 per furnace year the amount actually charged by Trio for licenses in the 1960-1970 era. The district court then increased the $2,600 figure on the assumption that the open infringement had reduced the market price of the license, and proceeded to set damages at $7,800 per furnace year for the years prior to the decision by this Court on validity, a figure three times the rate charged by Trio during the 1960's. Damages were set at $15,000 per furnace year for the period following the 1972 adjudication. The employment of these two figures resulted in total primary damages of $653,839. The trial judge then proceeded to use a double multiplier in contrast to the master's trebling figure and denied attorneys' fees. With interest, the total damages computed by the district court were $1,726,525.

"*Trio Process III.*"

On appeal we affirmed in part and reversed in part. *Trio Process III, supra.* We held that there was "no error in the first step of the district court's damage calculation, namely, focusing upon the losses suffered by the patent holder rather than upon the profits illegally made by the patent infringer." *Id.* at 129. We also affirmed the district court in its finding "that the license rate established by Trio in the 1960's may have been artificially depressed by Goldstein's ongoing infringement, and that the reasonable royalty should therefore be set at a level above the actual license rate."[1]

We held, however, that the district court had erred in two respects. First, it had calculated not one royalty rate but two: one for the period before our decision upholding the patent's validity and the second for the period after.[2] We held that a single reasonable royalty rate should be calculated for the entire period of infringement. The district court has done that and the point is no longer at issue. Second, and most importantly for purposes

---

1. Contrary to Trio's assertion, however, we did not hold that the reasonable royalty rate was, as a matter of law, higher than the actual license rate. We held only that it might be higher if the actual license rate had, In fact, been artificially depressed by Goldstein's infringement. Thus, we held in *Trio Process* III that the reasonable royalty should be set at a level above the actual license rate if it was demonstrated, on the basis of the submitted evidence, that Goldstein's infringing activities had artificially depressed the actual license rate established by Trio.

2. The district court had set damages based on a reasonable royalty of $7,800 per furnace year for the period prior to our adjudication of the patent's validity and $15,000 per furnace year for the period thereafter.

of deciding this appeal, there was a failure to articulate the reasons underlying the determination of the royalty rate. Thus, the cause was remanded to the trial court for reconsideration of the damages issue. We noted specifically that

> on remand, the district court should give proper regard to the rule that the extent of the deviation of existing license fees from a reasonable royalty must be determined solely on the basis of the submitted evidence and upon an evaluation of the factors that could affect the reasonable royalty rate, not upon mere conjecture.

*Trio Process III*, 533 F.2d at 130. This has not been done, however, and we therefore vacate the determination of damages.

## II.

In calculating damages for patent infringement, a patent holder is entitled to receive compensation for the infringement but in no event less than a reasonable royalty. 35 U.S.C. §284. An exhaustive list of factors relevant to the determination of a reasonable royalty can be found in *Georgia-Pacific Corp. v. United States Plywood Corp.*, 318 F. Supp. 1116, 1120 (S.D.N.Y. 1970). The district court in this case found a number of those factors to be relevant in its own calculation of damages:

(1) (T)he existing value of the (patented) process to the licensor as a generator of sales of his non-patented items; and the extent of such derivative or convoyed sales.
(2) The duration of the patent and the term of the license.
(3) The established profitability of the product made under the patent; its commercial success; and its current popularity.
(4) The utility and advantages of the patent property over old modes or devices, if any, that had been used for working out similar results.
(5) The nature of the patent (process)...and the benefits to those who have used the (process).
(6) The extent to which the infringer has made use of the (patented process); and any evidence probative of the value of that use.
(7) The portion of the realizable profit that should be credited to the invention as distinguished from nonpatented elements, the manufacturing process, business risks, or significant features or improvements added by the infringer.
(8) The opinion testimony of qualified experts.

Applying the "willing buyer and willing seller" rule, the district court considered these factors in the context of hypothetical negotiations between the parties conducted in the absence of the infringing activity. The court found that the first two of the above factors would have had only a "minimal effect" in the determination of a reasonable royalty. As to the remaining factors, the court noted that "(they) all touch upon the benefits obtained by defendant through its infringing use of plaintiff's patented process." Thus, the court found that "the license fee the parties would have agreed upon absent defendant's infringement would to a large extent have been determined by the economic benefits that were obtained through the use of plaintiff's patented process."

The court found that Goldstein had obtained four distinct benefits from its use of the Trio process: (1) a reduction in labor costs; (2) an increased recovery of copper from the scrap wire; (3) lower fuel consumption per ton of processed material; and (4) the ability to attract more electrical scrap for processing by advertising the advantages of the Trio process. The court, however, was unable to assign a dollar value to each of these benefits but indicated that "the only dollar figure available is the value of the direct and indirect labor savings achieved by defendant."

The court began its calculation of the labor savings with expert testimony, credited by the master, which indicated that Goldstein had realized labor savings of $52,791 per furnace year by virtue of its infringing use of the Trio process.[3] Because Goldstein operated a number of infringing furnaces over an eight and one-half year period, the court reduced this figure to $41,652 per furnace year, reflecting the wages prevailing in 1969, the mid-point in the infringing period. The court then found that "(i)n voluntary royalty negotiations untainted by defendant's infringing practices, defendant might well have been willing to split this saving with plaintiff and paid plaintiff a royalty of approximately $20,000 for each furnace year." For two reasons, however, the court further reduced this to $15,000 per furnace year. First, the court held that, as a seller of furnaces, "(Trio) would have been willing to accept somewhat less than the maximum royalty negotiable in order to promote its sales." Second, prior to the lawsuit, "plaintiff was unaware . . . of the exact extent of the labor savings that were obtainable through the use of its process." After multiplying $15,000 by the number of infringing furnaces, the court then doubled the primary damages and added interest of 6% per annum. The total damage award was $2,901,336 plus costs.

Georgia-Pacific lists first among the factors relevant to the determination of a reasonable royalty "(t)he royalties received by the patentee for the licensing of the patent in suit, proving or tending to prove an established royalty." *Georgia-Pacific*, 318 F. Supp at 1120. In this case, the district court chose to disregard the license fees received by Trio because "they did not show that there was an established royalty and since the fees received were artificially depressed by defendant's ongoing infringement." The court noted its belief that "a royalty negotiated in the absence of defendant's infringement would have been several times higher than the license fees actually received by the plaintiff." We have not, however, been able to discover any evidence in this record to support this conclusion.

It is true that the actual license rate does not necessarily constitute a reasonable royalty. Thus, when the actual license rate is artificially low, a reasonable royalty may be set above that rate. *Trio Process III, supra*. Nevertheless, the actual license rate is an important factor in the determination of a reasonable royalty, at least when those royalties prove or tend to prove an established royalty. See *Georgia-Pacific*, 318 F. Supp at 1120.

We are mindful that the district court concluded that the royalties trio received under the license agreements did not constitute an established

---

3. This figure was arrived at by comparing the cost of operating a similar, noninfringing furnace. Goldstein disputes the basis for this comparison but we need not address this issue in view of our disposition of the case.

royalty. Nevertheless, the existing license rate does tend to show an established license rate. The evidence indicates little, if any, variation in the rate charged before or after the infringement. Further, the district court, in its first consideration of the damage issue, apparently found the actual license rate to be probative, although not conclusive, evidence of a reasonable royalty. Thus, the reasonable royalty rate determined by the district court in its first consideration of the damage issue was related to the actual license rate charged. That approach was correct. As we indicated in our earlier opinion, however, the district court erred in failing to demonstrate, on the basis of the evidence, the extent of the deviation of existing license fees from a reasonable royalty. That same void continues to exist in the district court's most recent damage calculation.

We are again unable to discover any support for the district court's conclusion that the existing license rate was depressed by Goldstein's infringement. Thus, its reliance on the rationale of *Tights, Inc. v. Kayser-Roth Corp.*, 442 F. Supp. 159 (M.D.N.C. 1977), is misplaced. In *Tights* the court disregarded the standard royalty rate, finding it had been artificially depressed "because it was established in an atmosphere of industry-wide infringement of and disrespect for the...patent." *Id.* at 165. The court thereupon calculated a reasonable royalty based on hypothetical negotiations between a "willing licensee" and a "willing licensor."[4] Unlike the instant case, the depressing effect in *Tights* was evident. There, the low license rate had been negotiated against a background of open industry-wide infringement. Further, there was evidence that the existing license rate had dramatically declined because of that infringement. Thus, there was a substantial factual basis which justified the court's decision to disregard the existing license rate. In the case before us, however, such factors are not present. The license rate agreed upon between Trio and Goldstein was arrived at in free and open negotiations conducted prior to any infringing activity by Goldstein.[5] Furthermore, there are no allegations in this case of industry-wide infringement. Unlike *Tights*, there is no indication that the license rates here declined after Goldstein's infringement. Indeed, even after Trio learned of the infringement, it offered Goldstein a license at the same rate as had been earlier agreed upon. Further, in the years following our decision upholding the validity of the patent, there were apparently no new licenses granted. Thus, the thrust of the evidence in this case indicates the absence of a depressing effect caused by Goldstein's infringement. Nor have we been referred to any permissible evidentiary basis to the contrary. Thus, we are compelled to vacate the court's assessment of damages.

* * *

4. In Georgia-Pacific, supra, the court also determined damages on the basis of the "willing buyer and willing seller" rule. This was used, however, only after the parties agreed there was no established royalty for the patented item. Indeed, the apparent policy of the patent holder was not to enter into licensing agreements but rather, to maintain its patent monopoly.

5. Goldstein and Trio entered into two license agreements in 1960. There is no indication in the record that Goldstein's infringing activities began any earlier than 1964 when it contracted with a metal fabricator for the construction of a copy of a furnace Goldstein had purchased from Trio.

**IV.**

We begin with the rule that we noted in our last opinion, that the extent of the deviation of the actual licensing rate from a reasonable royalty must be explained solely on the basis of the submitted evidence. In the absence of such an explanation, we must examine the record ourselves to determine whether it contains such evidence.

Trio itself did not utilize the patented process. Instead, its only use of the patent was to license it for use by others. The licenses sold were for five year periods. The first license was sold for $20,000. This amount covered the license and the furnace necessary to utilize the process; $7,000 represented the cost of the furnace and $13,000 the cost of the license, i.e., $2,600 per furnace year. In 1960, Goldstein purchased two sets of licenses and furnaces, one for $20,000 and the other for $15,000. Between 1962 and 1969 four more buyers purchased licenses and furnaces at the $20,000 rate. In 1967, another company bought the package with a modified furnace for $25,000. Later that year the package was purchased by another buyer for $19,500. After a decision by Trio to raise the price, two more were sold in 1972 to purchasers other than Goldstein, for a price of $25,000. Thus, throughout this period, the license rate of $2,600 per furnace year appears to have remained relatively constant.

Goldstein's infringing activities began in 1965. However, Trio and Goldstein had in free and open negotiations previously agreed to a license rate of $2,600 per furnace year. The license rate Trio charged other licensees did not decline after Goldstein's infringement began. Consequently, if the infringing activity did have a depressing effect on the license rate it could only have been in deterring Trio from charging the rate it otherwise would have negotiated in the open market. The district court, however, disregarded the license fees received by Trio, because it believed they did not reveal an established royalty, and they were artificially depressed by the ongoing infringement. The court found that Trio was a seller of furnaces and thus in negotiating a royalty rate (prior to the infringement) "would have been willing to accept somewhat less than the maximum royalty negotiable in order to promote its sales." It further observed that prior to this lawsuit, Trio was unaware of the exact extent of the labor savings effected by the patented process. But the record indicates that even after learning of the infringement, Trio offered Goldstein a license for the infringing furnace "Under the same terms and conditions as the previous two incinerators."

It is true that "(a) patentee who has attempted to avoid costly and time-consuming litigation by settling for less than a reasonable royalty should not be penalized when an infringer forces full litigation." *Tights*, 442 F. Supp at 165. Here, however, there is no reason to believe that the license rate negotiated by the parties was anything other than a balanced consideration by both Goldstein and Trio of those competing concerns that normally enter into the determination of price in an open marketplace economy. Trio consistently offered licenses at the rate of $2,600 per furnace year. Thus, the possibility that Trio, had it chosen to do so, might have obtained a higher license rate than that actually charged, is irrelevant. We believe the rate fixed by the parties prior to any infringement is pertinent and highly persuasive. Further, our examination of the record has not disclosed any reason to distrust the existing license rate as a measure of actual damages. Thus, we hold that the $2600 per furnace year rate negotiated between Trio and Goldstein prior to the infringement, constitutes a reasonable royalty.

* * *

## Comments

1. **Statutory Bases for Reasonable Royalty.** Section 284 of the patent code expressly provides a baseline amount of damages, stating that damages should be "in no event less than a reasonable royalty." It is up to the court, balancing several factors, to determine what is reasonable.

2. **Reasonable Royalty Factors.** The district court in *Georgia-Pacific Corp. v. United States Plywood Corp.*, 318 F. Supp. 1116, 1120 (S.D.N.Y. 1970), an oft-cited case, listed 15 factors relevant to the determination of the amount of a reasonable royalty. The *Trio Process* court relied on eight of these factors. Perhaps the most important factors are those relating to established conditions within the market or industry. For instance, *Trio Process* placed a great deal of emphasis on the existence of an established royalty as a guide to what rate a willing licensee–willing licensor would have agreed. If the patentee had licensed the patent to five competitors at a 5 percent rate, there is a greater likelihood the patentee and defendant would have agreed on the same rate. Of course, an established royalty rate may not reflect the assumptions of an arm's-length negotiation between a willing licensee–willing licensor because the parties to the prior license may not be competitors, the market was not fully developed at the time the license was negotiated, or the rate was artificially low due to industry-wide infringement and lack of respect for the patent. *See Tights, Inc. v. Kayser-Roth Corp.*, 442 F. Supp. 159 (M.D.N.C. 1977), discussed in *Trio Process*.

3. **Willing Licensor–Willing Licensee.** Courts oftentimes construct a hypothetical negotiation to arrive at a royalty rate. The time frame for this negotiation is at the time defendant began infringing and is based on the assumption that the patent is not invalid. But this fictional construct is not without criticism. In *Georgia-Pacific*, for example, the court warned against placing the negotiation in a "vacuum of pure logic," outside a marketplace context that includes relative bargaining strength, commercial preferences of the parties, and commercial past performance of the claimed invention. 318 F. Supp. at 1121. And the Federal Circuit in *Fromson v. Western Litho Plate & Supply Co.*, 853 F.2d 1568, 1574 (Fed. Cir. 1988), conceded that the hypothetical negotiation "must be used on occasion for want of a better" device.

## B. EQUITABLE RELIEF

Equitable relief can be broken down into two forms of injunctions: (1) preliminary; and (2) permanent. The latter is issued after a final ruling on the defendant's infringement liability. Naturally, the court will enjoin the continuation of infringing activity once the court or a jury finds the defendant is indeed engaging in infringing activity. The preliminary injunction is sought by the patentee before a final ruling on the defendant's infringement liability. In this instance, the patentee is asserting that he is likely to succeed on the merits regarding infringement and validity. Therefore, the court should enjoin the alleged infringing activity before a final ruling lest the patentee suffer irreparable harm. The following case explores the preliminary injunction.

## AMAZON.COM, INC. v. BARNESANDNOBLE.COM, INC.
### 239 F.3d 1343 (Fed. Cir. 2001)

CLEVENGER, Circuit Judge.

This is a patent infringement suit brought by Amazon.com, Inc. ("Amazon") against barnesandnoble.com, inc., and barnesandnoble.com llc (together, "BN"). Amazon moved for a preliminary injunction to prohibit BN's use of a feature of its web site called "Express Lane." BN resisted the preliminary injunction on several grounds, including that its Express Lane feature did not infringe the claims of Amazon's patent, and that substantial questions exist as to the validity of Amazon's patent. The United States District Court for the Western District of Washington rejected BN's contentions. Instead, the district court held that Amazon had presented a case showing a likelihood of infringement by BN, and that BN's challenges to the validity of the patent in suit lacked sufficient merit to avoid awarding extraordinary preliminary injunctive relief to Amazon. The district court granted Amazon's motion, and now BN brings its timely appeal from the order entering the preliminary injunction.

After careful review of the district court's opinion, the record, and the arguments advanced by the parties, we conclude that BN has mounted a substantial challenge to the validity of the patent in suit. Because Amazon is not entitled to preliminary injunctive relief under these circumstances, we vacate the order of the district court that set the preliminary injunction in place and remand the case for further proceedings.

### I

This case involves United States Patent No. 5,960,411 ("the '411 patent"), which issued on September 28, 1999, and is assigned to Amazon. On October 21, 1999, Amazon brought suit against BN alleging infringement of the patent and seeking a preliminary injunction.

\* \* \*

The '411 patent describes a method and system in which a consumer can complete a purchase order for an item via an electronic network using only a "single action," such as the click of a computer mouse button on the client computer system. Amazon developed the patent to cope with what it considered to be frustrations presented by what is known as the "shopping cart model" purchase system for electronic commerce purchasing events. In previous incarnations of the shopping cart model, a purchaser using a

client computer system (such as a personal computer executing a web browser program) could select an item from an electronic catalog, typically by
clicking on an "Add to Shopping Cart" icon, thereby placing the item in
the "virtual" shopping cart. Other items from the catalog could be added
to the shopping cart in the same manner. When the shopper completed the
selecting process, the electronic commercial event would move to the
check-out counter, so to speak. Then, information regarding the purchaser's identity, billing and shipping addresses, and credit payment method
would be inserted into the transactional information base by the soon-to-be
purchaser. Finally, the purchaser would "click" on a button displayed on
the screen or somehow issue a command to execute the completed order,
and the server computer system would verify and store the information
concerning the transaction.

. . . . The '411 patent sought to reduce the number of actions required from
a consumer to effect a placed order. . . . How, one may ask, is the number of
purchaser interactions reduced? The answer is that the number of purchaser
interactions is reduced because the purchaser has previously visited the seller's web site and has previously entered into the database of the seller all of
the required billing and shipping information that is needed to effect a sales
transaction. Thereafter, when the purchaser visits the seller's web site and
wishes to purchase a product from that site, the patent specifies that only a
single action is necessary to place the order for the item. . . .

## II

The '411 patent has 26 claims, 4 of which are independent. Independent
claims 1 and 11 are method claims directed to placing an order for an item,
while independent claim 6 is an apparatus claim directed to a client system
for ordering an item, and independent claim 9 is an apparatus claim directed to a server system for generating an order. Amazon asserted claims 1-3,
5-12, 14-17, and 21-24 against BN. Although there are significant differences among the various independent and dependent claims in issue, for
purposes of this appeal we may initially direct our primary focus on the
"single action" limitation that is included in each claim. This focus is
appropriate because BN's appeal attacks the injunction on the grounds
that either its accused method does not infringe the "single action" limitation present in all of the claims, that the "single action" feature of the
patent is invalid, or both.

\* \* \*

BN's Express Lane thus presents a product page that contains the
description of the item to be purchased and a "description" of the single
action to be taken to effect placement of the order. Because only a single
action need be taken to complete the purchase order once the product
page is displayed, the district court concluded that Amazon had made a
showing of likelihood of success on its allegation of patent infringement.

In response to BN's contention that substantial questions exist as to the
validity of the '411 patent, the district court reviewed the prior art references upon which BN's validity challenge rested. The district court concluded that none of the prior art references anticipated the claims of the

'411 patent under 35 U.S.C. §102 (1994) or rendered the claimed invention obvious under 35 U.S.C. §103 (1994).

## III

The grant or denial of a preliminary injunction under 35 U.S.C. §283 (1994) is within the sound discretion of the district court. *Novo Nordisk of N. Am., Inc. v. Genentech, Inc.* "An abuse of discretion may be established by showing that the court made a clear error of judgment in weighing relevant factors or exercised its discretion based upon an error of law or clearly erroneous factual findings." 77 F.3d at 1367.

As the moving party, Amazon is entitled to a preliminary injunction if it can succeed in showing: (1) a reasonable likelihood of success on the merits; (2) irreparable harm if an injunction is not granted; (3) a balance of hardships tipping in its favor; and (4) the injunction's favorable impact on the public interest. "These factors, taken individually, are not dispositive; rather, the district court must weigh and measure each factor against the other factors and against the form and magnitude of the relief requested." *Hybritech, Inc. v. Abbott Labs.*, 849 F.2d 1446, 1451 (Fed. Cir. 1988).

Irreparable harm is presumed when a clear showing of patent validity and infringement has been made. *Bell & Howell Document Mgmt. Prods. Co. v. Altek Sys.* "This presumption derives in part from the finite term of the patent grant, for patent expiration is not suspended during litigation, and the passage of time can work irremediable harm." 132 F.3d at 708.

Our case law and logic both require that a movant cannot be granted a preliminary injunction unless it establishes *both* of the first two factors, *i.e.*, likelihood of success on the merits and irreparable harm.

In order to demonstrate a likelihood of success on the merits, Amazon must show that, in light of the presumptions and burdens that will inhere at trial on the merits, (1) Amazon will likely prove that BN infringes the '411 patent, and (2) Amazon's infringement claim will likely withstand BN's challenges to the validity and enforceability of the '411 patent. If BN raises a substantial question concerning either infringement or validity, *i.e.*, asserts an infringement or invalidity defense that the patentee cannot prove "lacks substantial merit," the preliminary injunction should not issue.

Of course, whether performed at the preliminary injunction stage or at some later stage in the course of a particular case, infringement and validity analyses must be performed on a claim-by-claim basis. Therefore, in cases involving multiple patent claims, to demonstrate a likelihood of success on the merits, the patentee must demonstrate that it will likely prove infringement of one or more claims of the patents-in-suit, and that at least one of those same allegedly infringed claims will also likely withstand the validity challenges presented by the accused infringer.

Both infringement and validity are at issue in this appeal. It is well settled that an infringement analysis involves two steps: the claim scope is first determined, and then the properly construed claim is compared with the accused device to determine whether all of the claim limitations are present either literally or by a substantial equivalent. Conceptually, the first step of an invalidity analysis based on anticipation and/or obviousness in view of prior art references is no different from that of an infringement analysis. "It is elementary in patent law that, in determining whether a patent is valid and, if valid, infringed, the first step is to determine the meaning and scope of each claim in suit." *Lemelson v. Gen. Mills, Inc.*, 968 F.2d 1202, 1206 (Fed. Cir. 1992). Because the claims of a patent measure the invention at issue, the claims must be interpreted and given the same meaning for purposes of both validity and infringement analyses.

## IV

BN contends on appeal that the district court committed legal errors that undermine the legitimacy of the preliminary injunction. In particular, BN asserts that the district court construed key claim limitations one way for purposes of its infringement analysis, and another way when considering BN's validity challenges. BN asserts that under a consistent claim interpretation, its Express Lane feature either does not infringe the '411 patent, or that if the patent is interpreted so as to support the charge of infringement, then the claims of the patent are subject to a severe validity challenge. When the key claim limitations are properly interpreted, BN thus asserts, it will be clear that Amazon is not likely to succeed on the merits of its infringement claim, or that BN has succeeded in calling the validity of the '411 patent into serious question. In addition, BN asserts that the district court misunderstood the teaching of the prior art references, thereby committing clear error in the factual predicates it established for comprehension of the prior art references.

## V

It is clear from the district court's opinion that the meaning it ascribed to the "single action" limitation includes a temporal consideration. The "single action" to be taken to complete the purchase order, according to the district court, only occurs after other events have transpired. These preliminary events required pursuant to the district court's claim interpretation are the presentation of a description of the item to be purchased and the presentation of the single action the user must take to complete the purchase order for the item.

\* \* \*

[W]e ultimately agree with Amazon and construe all four independent claims (*i.e.*, claims 1, 6, 9, and 11) to call for the single action to be performed immediately after a display of information about an item and without any intervening action, but not necessarily immediately after the first display or every display.

\* \* \*

## VI

### A

When the correct meaning of the single action limitation is read on the accused BN system, it becomes apparent that the limitations of claim 1 are likely met by the accused system. The evidence on the record concerning the operation of BN's "Express Lane" feature is not in dispute. At the time that the '411 patent was issued, BN offered customers two purchasing options. One was called "Shopping Cart," and the other was called "Express Lane." The Shopping Cart option involved the steps of adding items to a "virtual" shopping cart and then "checking out" to complete the purchase. In contrast, the Express Lane option allowed customers who had registered for the feature to purchase items simply by "clicking" on the "Express Lane" button provided on the "detail page" or "product page" describing and identifying the book or other item to be purchased. The text beneath the Express Lane button invited users to "Buy it now with just 1 click!"

\* \* \*

We note that the district court concluded that "[b]arnesandnoble.com infringes claims 1, 2, 3, 5, 11, 12, 12, 14, 15, 16, 17, 21, 22, 23, [and] 24," and "also infringes claims 6-10 of the '411 patent." However, the relevant determination at the preliminary injunction stage is substantial likelihood of success by Amazon of its infringement claims, not a legal conclusion as to the ultimate issue of infringement. We therefore interpret the district court's conclusions as determining that Amazon had demonstrated a substantial likelihood of establishing literal infringement of the enumerated claims.

\* \* \*

### E

After full review of the record before us, we conclude that under a proper claim interpretation, Amazon has made the showing that it is likely to succeed at trial on its infringement case. Given that we conclude that Amazon has demonstrated likely literal infringement of at least the four independent claims in the '411 patent, we need not consider infringement under the doctrine of equivalents. The question remaining, however, is whether the district court correctly determined that BN failed to mount a substantial challenge to the validity of the claims in the '411 patent.

### VII

The district court considered, but ultimately rejected, the potentially invalidating impact of several prior art references cited by BN. Because the district court determined that BN likely infringed all of the asserted claims, it did not focus its analysis of the validity issue on any particular claim. Instead, in its validity analysis, the district court appears to have primarily directed its attention to determining whether the references cited by BN implemented the single action limitation.

\* \* \*

In this case, we find that the district court committed clear error by misreading the factual content of the prior art references cited by BN and by failing to recognize that BN had raised a substantial question of invalidity of the asserted claims in view of these prior art references.

Validity challenges during preliminary injunction proceedings can be successful, that is, they may raise substantial questions of invalidity, on evidence that would not suffice to support a judgment of invalidity at trial. The test for invalidity at trial is by evidence that is clear and convincing. To succeed with a summary judgment motion of invalidity, for example, the movant must demonstrate a lack of genuine dispute about material facts and show that the facts not in dispute are clear and convincing in demonstrating invalidity. In resisting a preliminary injunction, however, one need not make out a case of actual invalidity. Vulnerability is the issue at the preliminary injunction stage, while validity is the issue at trial. The showing of a substantial question as to invalidity thus requires less proof than the clear and convincing showing necessary to establish invalidity itself. That this is so is plain from our cases.

When moving for the extraordinary relief of a preliminary injunction, a patentee need not establish the validity of a patent beyond question. The patentee must, however, present a clear case supporting the validity of the patent in suit. Such a case might be supported, for example, by showing that the patent in suit had successfully withstood previous validity challenges in other proceedings. Further support for such a clear case might come from a long period of industry acquiescence in the patent's validity. Neither of those considerations benefit Amazon in this case, however, because the '411 patent has yet to be tested by trial, and it was issued only a few weeks before the start of this litigation.

In *Helifix*, we recently confronted the situation in which a district court had granted a motion of summary judgment of invalidity based on allegedly anticipatory prior art references, and shortly thereafter denied a motion for a preliminary injunction based on a validity challenge using the same prior art references. 208 F.3d at 1344-45. On appeal, the patentee sought reversal of the summary judgment and claimed entitlement to a preliminary injunction. We held that the summary judgment could not stand, because disputed issues of material fact on invalidity remained for resolution at trial. *Id.* at 208 F.3d 1352. Nonetheless, we expressly held that the quantum of evidence put forth — while falling short of demonstrating invalidity itself — was sufficient to prevent issuance of the preliminary injunction. *Id.* Particularly instructive for purposes of this case is the treatment of the anticipation issue in *Helifix*. A particular reference which did not on its face disclose all the limitations of the claim in suit was argued to be anticipatory, even though there was a conflict in the testimony as to whether the reference would have taught one of ordinary skill in the art the claim limitations not expressly stated on the face of the reference. Although insufficient to demonstrate invalidity for the purposes of the summary judgment motion, the reference *was* enough to prevent issuance of the preliminary injunction. *Id.* at 208 F.3d 1351-52.

The situation before us is similar. Here, we have several references that were urged upon the court as invalidating the asserted claims. The district court dismissed those references, for purposes of its invalidity analysis, because it did not perceive them to recite each and every limitation of the claims in suit. As we explain below in our review of the asserted prior art in this case, each of the asserted references clearly teaches key limitations of the claims of the patent in suit. BN argued to the district court that one of ordinary skill in the art could fill in the gaps in the asserted references, given the opportunity to do so at trial.

When the heft of the asserted prior art is assessed in light of the correct legal standards, we conclude that BN has mounted a serious challenge to the validity of Amazon's patent. We hasten to add, however, that this conclusion only undermines the prerequisite for entry of a preliminary injunction. Our decision today on the validity issue in no way resolves the ultimate question of invalidity. That is a matter for resolution at trial. It remains to be learned whether there are other references that may be cited against the patent, and it surely remains to be learned whether any shortcomings in BN's initial preliminary validity challenge will be magnified or dissipated at trial. All we hold, in the meantime, is that BN cast enough doubt on the validity of the '411 patent to avoid a preliminary injunction, and that the validity issue should be resolved finally at trial.

* * *

## Comments

1. *The Federal Circuit's Influence on Irreparable Harm.* A preliminary injunction has historically been extremely difficult to obtain, particularly if the alleged infringing party was financially solvent. But in 1983, the Federal Circuit dramatically altered the irreparable harm analysis, in turn making it easier to acquire a preliminary injunction. Once validity and continuing infringement are established, a presumption of irreparable harm is likely to follow. This change came soon after the Federal Circuit was created and is consistent with the court's early work in strengthening patent rights.

2. *Balance of Hardships.* The balancing focuses on the hardships of the patentee and the defendant. The Federal Circuit stated the hardship on a manufacturer, who is preliminarily enjoined, can be devastating because he must withdraw his produce from the market before trial. On the other hand, the hardship on a patentee denied an injunction after showing a strong likelihood of success on validity and infringement can also be quite harmful as his patent rights are of limited term.

# PATENT STATUTES

### §101. Inventions patentable

Whoever invents or discovers any new and useful process, machine, manufacture, or composition of matter, or any new and useful improvement thereof, may obtain a patent therefor, subject to the conditions and requirements of this title.

### §102. Conditions for patentability; novelty and loss of right to patent

A person shall be entitled to a patent unless —

(a) the invention was known or used by others in this country, or patented or described in a printed publication in this or a foreign country, before the invention thereof by the applicant for patent, or

(b) the invention was patented or described in a printed publication in this or a foreign country or in public use or on sale in this country, more than one year prior to the date of the application for patent in the United States; ...

(g)(1) during the course of an interference conducted under section 135 or section 291, another inventor involved therein establishes, to the extent permitted in section 104, that before such person's invention thereof the invention was made by such other inventor and not abandoned, suppressed, or concealed, or (2) before such person's invention thereof, the invention was made in this country by another inventor who had not abandoned, suppressed, or concealed it. In determining priority of invention under this subsection, there shall be considered not only the respective dates of conception and reduction to practice of the invention, but also the reasonable diligence of one who was first to conceive and last to reduce to practice, from a time prior to conception by the other.

### §103. Conditions for patentability; non-obvious subject matter

(a) A patent may not be obtained though the invention is not identically disclosed or described as set forth in section 102 of this title, if the differences between the subject matter sought to be patented and the prior art are such that the subject matter as a whole would have been obvious at the time the invention was made to a person having ordinary skill in the art to which said subject matter pertains. Patentability shall not be negatived by the manner in which the invention was made.

### §112. Specification

¶1 The specification shall contain a written description of the invention, and of the manner and process of making and using it, in such full, clear, concise, and exact terms as to enable any person skilled in the art to which it pertains, or with which it is most nearly connected, to make and use the same, and shall set forth the best mode contemplated by the inventor of carrying out his invention.

873

¶2 The specification shall conclude with one or more claims particularly pointing out and distinctly claiming the subject matter which the applicant regards as his invention.

### §154. Contents and term of patent; provisional rights

(a) In General. —

(1) Contents. — Every patent shall contain a short title of the invention and a grant to the patentee, his heirs or assigns, of the right to exclude others from making, using, offering for sale, or selling the invention throughout the United States or importing the invention into the United States, and, if the invention is a process, of the right to exclude others from using, offering for sale or selling throughout the United States, or importing into the United States, products made by that process, referring to the specification for the particulars thereof.

(2) Term. — Subject to the payment of fees under this title, such grant shall be for a term beginning on the date on which the patent issues and ending 20 years from the date on which the application for the patent was filed in the United States or, if the application contains a specific reference to an earlier filed application or applications under section 120, 121, or 365(c) of this title, from the date on which the earliest such application was filed.

### §271. Infringement of patent

(a) Except as otherwise provided in this title, whoever without authority makes, uses, offers to sell, or sells any patented invention, within the United States or imports into the United States any patented invention during the term of the patent therefor, infringes the patent.

(b) Whoever actively induces infringement of a patent shall be liable as an infringer.

(c) Whoever offers to sell or sells within the United States or imports into the United States a component of a patented machine, manufacture, combination or composition, or a material or apparatus for use in practicing a patented process, constituting a material part of the invention, knowing the same to be especially made or especially adapted for use in an infringement of such patent, and not a staple article or commodity of commerce suitable for substantial noninfringing use, shall be liable as a contributory infringer.

### §283. Injunction

The several courts having jurisdiction of cases under this title may grant injunctions in accordance with the principles of equity to prevent the violation of any right secured by patent, on such terms as the court deems reasonable.

### §284. Damages

Upon finding for the claimant the court shall award the claimant damages adequate to compensate for the infringement, but in no event less than a reasonable royalty for the use made of the invention by the infringer, together with interest and costs as fixed by the court.

When the damages are not found by a jury, the court shall assess them. In either event the court may increase the damages up to three times the amount found or assessed. Increased damages under this paragraph shall not apply to provisional rights under section 154(d) of this title.

The court may receive expert testimony as an aid to the determination of damages or of what royalty would be reasonable under the circumstances.

# CHAPTER
# 14

# Trade Secrets

## INTRODUCTION

Trade secret law offers an extremely important means of protecting a firm's commercial information. Indeed, many industries rely heavily on trade secrecy vis-à-vis patent law, particularly for process-related inventions. *See* Wesley M. Cohen, Richard R. Nelson & John P. Walsh, *Protecting Their Intellectual Assets: Appropriability Conditions and Why U.S. Manufacturing Firms Patent (Or Not)* (NBER Working Paper Series 7552, 2000). There are important distinctions between patent law and trade secret law. First, information eligible for trade secret protection may or may not be eligible for patent protection. Trade secrets include not only technological information, but also customer lists, business plans, and marketing strategies. Also, there is no novelty requirement for trade secret protection; only that the commercial information provide an economic advantage. Second, trade secret protection can last in perpetuity as long as the information remains secret and maintains its value whereas a patent expires 20 years from its filing date. Third, with the exception of the Economic Espionage Act, trade secret protection is a creature of state law and is recognized in one form or another by every jurisdiction. Patent law is a strictly federal regime.

Trade secret law is grounded in both property and tort law. Under the property theory, trade secret law takes on a utilitarian justification and seeks to incentivize the production of valuable commercial information — much like patent law. But the tort theory of trade secrets, first expressed in the 1939 Restatement of Torts, is more concerned with deterring unethical commercial behavior (e.g., theft). Thus, while trade secret law is considered a form of intellectual property, creating a protectable interest in valuable information, it is also concerned with ethical duties and behavior among commercial entities. As such, a cause of action for trade secret misappropriation will reside only if the trade secret is acquired by "improper means" or through a breach of a confidential relationship, usually in the form of an express or implied contract. Indeed, independent creation and reverse engineering are defenses to a trade secret misappropriation claim, but are unavailable to an alleged patent infringer.

Enforcing trade secrets can be a daunting task due to the secrecy associated with the protected information. Litigation can prove to be unsatisfactory because trade secret owners are reluctant to divulge the information to the court, even when a protective order is in place. As a result, it is common for firms to require their employees to sign a non-competition agreement, which temporally and geographically restricts employee mobility. It is much easier for a firm to monitor a former employee's future employment activity than it is to police the improper use of the firm's trade secret. But these agreements are viewed skeptically, with courts balancing the interest of the employer in maintaining the secrecy of its information against the interest of the employee of realizing his professional livelihood. The final part of this chapter is devoted to the employer/employee relationship.

# A. DEFINING A TRADE SECRET

## LEARNING CURVE TOYS, INC. v. PLAYWOOD TOYS, INC.
### 342 F.3d 714 (7th Cir. 2003)

RIPPLE, Circuit Judge.

PlayWood Toys, Inc. ("PlayWood") obtained a jury verdict against Learning Curve Toys, Inc. and its representatives, Roy Wilson, Harry Abraham and John Lee (collectively, "Learning Curve"), for misappropriation of a trade secret in a realistic looking and sounding toy railroad track under the Illinois Trade Secrets Act. Although there was substantial evidence of misappropriation before the jury, the district court did not enter judgment on the jury's verdict. Instead, it granted judgment as a matter of law in favor of Learning Curve, holding that PlayWood did not have a protectable trade secret in the toy railroad track. PlayWood appealed. For the reasons set forth in the following opinion, we reverse the judgment of the district court and reinstate the jury's verdict. We further remand the case to the district court for a jury trial on exemplary damages and for consideration of PlayWood's request for attorneys' fees.

## I
### BACKGROUND

In 1992, Robert Clausi and his brother-in-law, Scott Moore, began creating prototypes of wooden toys under the name PlayWood Toys, Inc., a Canadian corporation. Clausi was the sole toy designer and Moore was the sole officer and director of PlayWood. Neither Clausi nor Moore had prior experience in the toy industry, but Clausi had "always been a bit of a doodler and designer," and the two men desired to "create high-quality hard-wood maple toys for the independent toy market," As a newly formed corporation, PlayWood did not own a facility in which it could produce toys. Instead, it worked in conjunction with Mario Borsato, who owned a wood-working facility. Subject to a written confidentiality agreement with PlayWood, Borsato manufactured prototypes for PlayWood based on Clausi's design specifications.

PlayWood's first attempt to market publicly its toys was at the Toronto Toy Fair on January 31, 1992. PlayWood received favorable reviews from many of the toy retailers in attendance; PlayWood also learned that the best way to get recognition for its toys was to attend the New York Toy Fair ("Toy Fair") the following month. Based on this information, Clausi and Moore secured a position at the Toy Fair in order to display PlayWood's prototypes. It was during this Toy Fair that Clausi and Moore first encountered Learning Curve representatives Roy Wilson, Harry Abraham and John Lee.

On the morning of February 12, 1993, the first day of the Toy Fair, Roy Wilson stopped at PlayWood's booth and engaged Clausi and Moore in conversation. Wilson identified himself as Learning Curve's toy designer and explained that his company had a license from the Britt Allcroft Company to develop Thomas the Tank Engine & Friends TM (hereinafter "Thomas") trains and accessories. Wilson commented that he was impressed with the look and quality of PlayWood's prototypes and raised the possibility of working together under a custom manufacturing contract to produce Learning Curve's line of Thomas products. Clausi and Moore responded that such an arrangement would be of great interest to Play-Wood. Later that same day, Harry Abraham, Learning Curve's vice president, and John Lee, Learning Curve's president, also stopped by PlayWood's booth. They too commented on the quality of PlayWood's prototypes and indicated that PlayWood might be a good candidate for a manufacturing contract with Learning Curve.

Clausi and Moore continued to have discussions with Learning Curve's representatives over the remaining days of the Toy Fair, which ended on February 14. During these discussions, Lee indicated that he would like two of his people, Abraham and Wilson, to visit PlayWood in Toronto the day after the Toy Fair ended in order to determine whether the two parties could work out a manufacturing arrangement for some or all of Learning Curve's wooden toys. Clausi, feeling a little overwhelmed by the suggestion, requested that their visit be postponed a few days so that he could better acquaint himself with Learning Curve's products. The parties ultimately agreed that Abraham and Wilson would visit PlayWood at Borsato's facility on February 18, 1993, four days after the conclusion of the Toy Fair. Clausi spent the next several days after the Toy Fair researching Learning Curve's products and considering how PlayWood could produce Learning Curve's trains and track.

On February 18, 1993, Abraham and Wilson visited PlayWood in Toronto as planned. The meeting began with a tour of Borsato's woodworking facility, where the prototypes on display at the Toy Fair had been made. After the tour, the parties went to the conference room at Borsato's facility. At this point, according to Clausi and Moore, the parties agreed to make their ensuing discussion confidential. Clausi testified:

> After we sat down in the board room, Harry [Abraham of Learning Curve] immediately said: "Look, we're going to disclose confidential information to you guys, and we're going to disclose some designs that Roy [Wilson of Learning Curve] has that are pretty confidential. If Brio were to get their hands on them, then we wouldn't like that. And we're going to do it under the basis of a confidential understanding."

And I said: "I also have some things, some ideas on how to produce the track and produce the trains now that I've had a chance to look at them for the last couple of days, and I think they're confidential as well. So if we're both okay with that, we should continue." So we did.

Moore testified to the existence of a similar conversation: It was at this point that Harry Abraham told us that they were going to disclose some confidential documents, drawings, pricing, margins, and asked us if we would keep that information confidential.

***

I believe it was Robert [Clausi] who said that, you know, absolutely, we would keep it confidential. In fact, we had some ideas that we felt would be confidential we would be disclosing to them, and would they keep it, you know, confidential? Would they reciprocate? And Harry [Abraham] said: "Absolutely." And then we proceeded to go along with the meeting.

Immediately after the parties agreed to keep their discussion confidential, Wilson, at Abraham's direction, showed Clausi and Moore drawings of various Thomas characters and provided information on the projected volume of each of the products. Clausi testified that he considered the documents disclosed by Learning Curve during the meeting confidential because they included information on products not yet released to the public, as well as Learning Curve's projected volumes, costs and profit margins for various products. After viewing Wilson's various drawings, the parties discussed PlayWood's ideas on how to manufacture Learning Curve's trains. Clausi suggested that they might use a CNC machine, which he defined as a computer numerically controlled drill that carves in three dimensions, to create Learning Curve's trains out of a single piece of wood (as opposed to piecing together separate pieces of wood).

The parties' discussion eventually moved away from train production and focused on track design. Wilson showed Clausi and Moore drawings of Learning Curve's track and provided samples of their current product. At this point, Abraham confided to Clausi and Moore that track had posed "a bit of a problem for Learning Curve." Abraham explained that sales were terrific for Learning Curve's Thomas trains, but that sales were abysmal for its track. Abraham attributed the lack of sales to the fact that Learning Curve's track was virtually identical to that of its competitor, Brio, which had the lion's share of the track market. Because there was "no differentiation" between the two brands of track, Learning Curve's track was not even displayed in many of the toy stores that carried Learning Curve's products. Learning Curve had worked unsuccessfully for several months attempting to differentiate its track from that of Brio.

After detailing the problems with Learning Curve's existing track, Abraham inquired of Clausi whether "there was a way to differentiate" its track from Brio's track. Clausi immediately responded that he "had had a chance to look at the track and get a feel for it [over] the last few days" and that his "thoughts were that if the track were more realistic and more functional, that kids would enjoy playing with it more and it would give the retailer a reason to carry the product, especially if it looked different than the Brio track." Clausi further explained that, if the track "made noise and [ ] looked like real train tracks, that the stores wouldn't have any problem, and the Thomas the Tank line, product line would have [ ] its own different track" and could "effectively compete with Brio." Abraham and Wilson indicated that they were "intrigued" by Clausi's idea and asked him what he meant by "making noise."

Clausi decided to show Abraham and Wilson exactly what he meant. Clausi took a piece of Learning Curve's existing track from the table, drew some lines across the track (about every three-quarters of an inch), and stated: "We can go ahead and machine grooves right across the upper section . . ., which would look like railway tracks, and down below machine little indentations as well so that it would look more like or sound more like real track. You would roll along and bumpity-bumpity as you go along." Clausi then called Borsato into the conference room and asked him to cut grooves into the wood "about a quarter of an inch deep from the top surface." Borsato left the room, complied with Clausi's request, and returned with the cut track three or four minutes later. Clausi ran a train back and forth over the cut piece of track. The track looked more realistic than before, but it did not make noise because the grooves were not deep enough. Accordingly, Clausi instructed Borsato to cut the grooves "just a little bit deeper so that they go through the rails." Borsato complied with Clausi's request once again and returned a few minutes later with the cut piece of track. Clausi proceeded to run a train back and forth over the track. This time the track made a "clickety-clack" sound, but the train did not run smoothly over the track because the grooves were cut "a little bit too deep." Based on the sound produced by the track, Clausi told Abraham and Moore that if PlayWood procured a contract with Learning Curve to produce the track, they could call it "Clickety-Clack Track."

Both Abraham and Wilson indicated that Clausi's concept of cutting grooves into the track to produce a clacking sound was a novel concept. Thereafter, Wilson and Clausi began to discuss how they could improve the idea to make the train run more smoothly on the track, but Abraham interrupted them and stated: "No, focus. You guys have to get the contract for the basic product first, and then we can talk about new products, because . . . it takes [our licensor] a long time to approve new products and new designs."

The meeting ended shortly thereafter without further discussion about Clausi's concept for the noise-producing track. Before he left, Wilson asked Clausi if he could take the piece of track that Borsato had cut with him while the parties continued their discussions. Clausi gave Wilson the piece of track without hesitation. The piece of track was the only item that Abraham and Wilson took from the meeting. Clausi and Moore did not ask Wilson for a receipt for the cut track, nor did they seek a written confidentiality agreement to protect PlayWood's alleged trade secret. After the meeting, Clausi amended PlayWood's confidentiality agreement with Borsato to ensure that materials discussed during the meeting would remain confidential. Clausi also stamped many of the documents that he received from Learning Curve during the meeting as confidential because they included information on products not yet released to the public. PlayWood never disclosed the contents of Learning Curve's documents to anyone.

During March of 1993, PlayWood and Learning Curve met on three separate occasions to discuss further the possibility of PlayWood manufacturing Learning Curve's Thomas products. At one of the meetings, and at Learning Curve's request, PlayWood submitted a manufacturing proposal for the Thomas products. Learning Curve rejected PlayWood's proposal. Learning Curve told Clausi that its licensor wanted the Thomas products to be made in the United States.

Thereafter, PlayWood had no contact with Learning Curve until late October of 1993, when Abraham contacted Clausi to discuss another possible manufacturing contract because Learning Curve's secondary supplier was not providing enough product. Again, PlayWood submitted a manufacturing proposal at Learning Curve's request, but it too was rejected. Learning Curve later stated that its new business partner had decided to manufacture the product in China.

Clausi and Moore continued to work on PlayWood's toy concepts. After the 1994 New York Toy Fair, which was not particularly successful for PlayWood, Clausi and Moore began to focus their efforts on refining PlayWood's concept for the noise-producing track. During this time, Clausi and Moore made no attempt to license or sell the concept to other toy companies because they believed that PlayWood still had "an opportunity to get in the door" with Learning Curve if they could perfect the concept and also because they believed that they were bound by a confidentiality agreement.

In December of 1994, while shopping for additional track with which to experiment, Moore discovered that Learning Curve was selling noise-producing track under the name "Clickety-Clack Track." Like the piece of track that Clausi had Borsato cut during PlayWood's February 18, 1993, meeting with Learning Curve, Clickety-Clack Track TM has parallel grooves cut into the wood, which cause a "clacking" sound as train wheels roll over the grooves. Learning Curve was promoting the new track as

> the first significant innovation in track design since the inception of wooden train systems. . . . It is quite simply the newest and most exciting development to come along recently in the wooden train industry, and it's sure to cause a sensation in the marketplace. . . . [I]t brings that sound and feel of the real thing to a child's world of make-believe without bells, whistles, electronic sound chips or moving parts.

Moore was "stunned" when he saw the track because he believed that Learning Curve had stolen PlayWood's concept. He testified: "This was our idea. This is what we've been working on even up to that day to go back to [Learning Curve] as an opportunity to get in the door, and there it is on the shelf." Moore purchased a package of Clickety-Clack Track TM and showed it to Clausi. Clausi testified that he was disappointed when he saw the track because he believed that Learning Curve had taken PlayWood's name and design concept "almost exactly as per [their] conversation" on February 18, 1993.

PlayWood promptly wrote a cease and desist letter to Learning Curve. The letter accused Learning Curve of stealing PlayWood's concept for the noise-producing track that it disclosed to Learning Curve "in confidence in the context of a manufacturing proposal." Learning Curve responded by seeking a declaratory judgment that it owned the concept.

Previously, on March 16, 1994, Learning Curve had applied for a patent on the noise-producing track. The patent, which was obtained on October 3, 1995, claims the addition of parallel impressions or grooves in the rails, which cause a "clacking" sound to be emitted as train wheels roll over them. The patent identifies Roy Wilson of Learning Curve as the inventor.

Clickety-Clack Track TM provided an enormous boost to Learning Curve's sales. Learning Curve had $20 million in track sales by the first quarter of 2000, and $40 million for combined track and accessory sales.

\*\*\*

## II

### DISCUSSION

### A. TRADE SECRET STATUS

\*\*\*

The parties agree that their dispute is governed by the Illinois Trade Secrets Act ("Act"). The issue currently before us is whether there was legally sufficient evidence for the jury to find that PlayWood had a trade secret in its concept for the noise-producing toy railroad track that it revealed to Learning Curve on February 18, 1993.

The Act defines a trade secret as:

> [I]nformation, including but not limited to, technical or non-technical data, a formula, pattern, compilation, program, device, method, technique, drawing, process, financial data, or list of actual or potential customers or suppliers, that:
>
> (1) is sufficiently secret to derive economic value, actual or potential, from not being generally known to other persons who can obtain economic value from its disclosure or use; and
> (2) is the subject of efforts that are reasonable under the circumstances to maintain its secrecy or confidentiality.

Both of the Act's statutory requirements focus fundamentally on the secrecy of the information sought to be protected. However, the requirements emphasize different aspects of secrecy. The first requirement, that the information be sufficiently secret to impart economic value because of its relative secrecy, "precludes trade secret protection for information generally known or understood within an industry even if not to the public at large." *Pope*, 694 N.E.2d at 617. The second requirement, that the plaintiff take reasonable efforts to maintain the secrecy of the information, prevents a plaintiff who takes no affirmative measures to prevent others from using its proprietary information from obtaining trade secret protection.

Although the Act explicitly defines a trade secret in terms of these two requirements, Illinois courts frequently refer to six common law factors (which are derived from §757 of the Restatement (First) of Torts) in determining whether a trade secret exists: (1) the extent to which the information is known outside of the plaintiff's business; (2) the extent to which the information is known by employees and others involved in the plaintiff's business; (3) the extent of measures taken by the plaintiff to guard the secrecy of the information; (4) the value of the information to the plaintiff's business and to its competitors; (5) the amount of time, effort and money expended by the plaintiff in developing the information; and (6) the ease or difficulty with which the information could be properly acquired or duplicated by others.

Contrary to Learning Curve's contention, we do not construe the foregoing factors as a six-part test, in which the absence of evidence on any single factor necessarily precludes a finding of trade secret protection. Instead, we interpret the common law factors as instructive guidelines for ascertaining whether a trade secret exists under the Act. The language of the Act itself makes no reference to these factors as independent requirements for trade secret status, and Illinois case law imposes no such requirement that each factor weigh in favor of the plaintiff. In this respect, Illinois law is compatible with the approach in other states. Courts from other jurisdictions, as well as legal scholars, have noted that the Restatement factors are not to be applied as a list of requisite elements.

The existence of a trade secret ordinarily is a question of fact. As aptly observed by our colleagues on the Fifth Circuit, a trade secret "is one of the most elusive and difficult concepts in the law to define." *Lear Siegler, Inc. v. Ark-Ell Springs, Inc.*, 569 F.2d 286, 288 (5th Cir. 1978). In many cases, the existence of a trade secret is not obvious; it requires an ad hoc evaluation of all the surrounding circumstances. For this reason, the question of whether certain information constitutes a trade secret ordinarily is best "resolved by a fact finder after full presentation of evidence from each side." *Id.* at 289. . . . PlayWood presented sufficient evidence for the jury reasonably to conclude that the Restatement factors weighed in PlayWood's favor.

### 1. Extent to which PlayWood's concept for noise-producing toy railroad track was known outside of PlayWood's business

PlayWood presented substantial evidence from which the jury could have determined that PlayWood's concept for noise-producing toy railroad track was not generally known outside of Playwood's business. It was undisputed at trial that no similar track was on the market until Learning Curve launched Clickety-Clack Track TM in late 1994, more than a year after PlayWood first conceived of the concept. Of course, as Learning Curve correctly points out, "[m]erely being the first or only one to use particular information does not in and of itself transform otherwise general knowledge into a trade secret." *George S. May Int'l*, 195 Ill. Dec. 183, 628 N.E.2d at 654. "If it did, the first person to use the information, no matter how ordinary or well known, would be able to appropriate it to his own use under the guise of a trade secret." *Serv. Ctrs.*, 129 Ill. Dec. 367, 535 N.E.2d at 1137. However, in this case, there was additional evidence from which the jury could have determined that PlayWood's concept was not generally known within the industry.

First, there was substantial testimony that Learning Curve had attempted to differentiate its track from that of its competitors for several months, but that it had been unable to do so successfully.

Furthermore, PlayWood's expert witness, Michael Kennedy, testified that PlayWood's concept, as embodied in Clickety-Clack Track TM, was unique and permitted "its seller to differentiate itself from a host of competitors who [were] making a generic product." Kennedy explained that the look, sound and feel of the track made it distinct from other toy railroad track: "[W]hen a child runs a train across this track, he can feel it hitting those little impressions. And when you're talking about young children[,] having the idea that they can see something that they couldn't see before, feel something that they couldn't feel before, hear something that they couldn't hear before, that is what differentiates this toy from its other competitors."

Finally, PlayWood presented evidence that Learning Curve sought and obtained a patent on the noise-producing track. It goes without saying that the requirements for patent and trade secret protection are not synonymous. Unlike "a patentable invention, a trade secret need not be novel or unobvious." 2 Rudolf Callmann, *The Law of Unfair Competition, Trademarks and Monopolies* §14.15, at 14-124 (4th ed. 2003). "The idea need not be complicated; it may be intrinsically simple and nevertheless qualify as a secret, unless it is common knowledge and, therefore, within the public domain." *Forest Labs., Inc. v. Pillsbury Co.*, 452 F.2d 621, 624 (7th Cir. 1971). However, it is commonly understood that "[i]f an invention has sufficient novelty to be entitled to patent protection, it may be said *a fortiori* to be entitled to protection as a trade secret." 1 Roger M. Milgrim, *Milgrim on Trade Secrets* §1.08[1], at 1-353 (2002). In light of this evidence, we cannot accept Learning Curve's argument that no rational jury could have found that PlayWood's concept was unknown outside of its business.

### 2. Extent to which PlayWood's concept was known to employees and others involved in PlayWood's business

The district court did not address the extent to which PlayWood's concept was known to employees and others involved in PlayWood's business. However, we agree with PlayWood that the evidence was sufficient to establish that its concept for noise-producing track was known only by key individuals in its business.

At the outset, we note briefly that PlayWood was a small business, consisting only of Clausi and Moore. Illinois courts have recognized on several occasions that the expectations for ensuring secrecy are different for small companies than for large companies. Apart from Clausi (PlayWood's sole toy designer and the person who conceived of the concept for noise-producing track) and Moore (PlayWood's sole officer and director), the only person who knew about the concept was Borsato, the person who physically produced PlayWood's prototype at Clausi's direction. The concept was disclosed to Borsato in order for PlayWood to develop fully its trade secret. *See* 1 Roger M. Milgrim, *Milgrim on Trade Secrets* §1.04, at 1-173 (2002) ("A trade secret does not lose its character by being confidentially disclosed to agents or servants, without whose assistance it could not be made of any value."). Moreover, Borsato's actions were governed by a written confidentiality agreement with PlayWood. Indeed, as an extra precaution, Clausi

even amended PlayWood's confidentiality agreement with Borsato immediately after the February 18, 1993, meeting to ensure that materials discussed during the meeting would remain confidential. From this evidence,
the jury reasonably could have determined that this factor also weighed in
favor of PlayWood.

### 3. Measures taken by PlayWood to guard the secrecy of its concept

There also was sufficient evidence for the jury to determine that PlayWood
took reasonable precautions to guard the secrecy of its concept. The Act
requires the trade secret owner to take actions that are "reasonable under
the circumstances to maintain [the] secrecy or confidentiality" of its trade
secret; it does not require perfection.... Here, the jury was instructed that
it must find "by a preponderance of the evidence that PlayWood's trade
secrets were given to Learning Curve as a result of a confidential relationship between the parties." By returning a verdict in favor of PlayWood, the
jury necessarily found that Learning Curve was bound to PlayWood by a
pledge of confidentiality. The jury's determination is amply supported by
the evidence. Both Clausi and Moore testified that they entered into an
oral confidentiality agreement with Abraham and Wilson before beginning
their discussion on February 18, 1993. In particular, Clausi testified that he
told Abraham and Wilson: "I also have some things, some ideas on how to
produce the track and produce the trains now that I've had a chance to look
at them for the last couple of days, and I think they're confidential as well.
So if we're both okay with that, we should continue." In addition to this
testimony, the jury heard that Learning Curve had disclosed substantial
information to PlayWood during the February 18th meeting, including
projected volumes, costs and profit margins for various products, as well
as drawings for toys not yet released to the public. The jury could have
inferred that Learning Curve would not have disclosed such information in
the absence of a confidentiality agreement. Finally, the jury also heard
(from several of Learning Curve's former business associates) that Learning Curve routinely entered into oral confidentiality agreements like the
one with PlayWood.

PlayWood might have done more to protect its secret. As Learning Curve
points out, PlayWood gave its only prototype of the noise-producing track
to Wilson without first obtaining a receipt or written confidentiality agreement from Learning Curve — a decision that proved unwise in hindsight.
Nevertheless, we believe that the jury was entitled to conclude that Play-
Wood's reliance on the oral confidentiality agreement was reasonable
under the circumstances of this case. First, it is well established that
"[t]he formation of a confidential relationship imposes upon the disclosee
the duty to maintain the information received in the utmost secrecy" and
that "the unprivileged use or disclosure of another's trade secret becomes
the basis for an action in tort." *Burten v. Milton Bradley Co.*, 763 F.2d 461,
463 (1st Cir. 1985). Second, both Clausi and Moore testified that they
believed PlayWood had a realistic chance to "get in the door" with Learning Curve and to produce the concept as part of Learning Curve's line
of Thomas products. Clausi and Moore did not anticipate that Learning Curve would violate the oral confidentiality agreement and utilize

PlayWood's concept without permission; rather, they believed in good faith that they "were going to do business one day again with Learning Curve with respect to the design concept." Finally, we believe that, as part of the reasonableness inquiry, the jury could have considered the size and sophistication of the parties, as well as the relevant industry. Both PlayWood and Learning Curve were small toy companies, and PlayWood was the smaller and less experienced of the two. Viewing the evidence in the light most favorable to PlayWood, as we must, we conclude that there was sufficient evidence for the jury to determine that PlayWood took reasonable measures to protect the secrecy of its concept.

### 4. Value of the concept to PlayWood and to its competitors

There was substantial evidence from which the jury could have determined that PlayWood's concept had value both to PlayWood and to its competitors. It was undisputed at trial that Learning Curve's sales skyrocketed after it began to sell Clickety-Clack Track TM. In addition, PlayWood's expert witness, Michael Kennedy, testified that PlayWood's concept for noise-producing track had tremendous value. Kennedy testified that the "cross-cuts and changes in the [track's] surface" imparted value to its seller by causing the track to "look different, feel different and sound different than generic track." Kennedy further testified that, in his opinion, the track would have commanded a premium royalty under a negotiated license agreement because the "invention allows its seller to differentiate itself from a host of competitors who are making a generic product with whom it is competing in a way that is proprietary and exclusive, and it gives [the seller] a significant edge over [its] competition."

Despite this evidence, the district court concluded that PlayWood's concept had no economic value. The court's conclusion was based, in part, on the fact that PlayWood's prototype did not work perfectly; as noted by the court, the first set of cuts were too shallow to produce sound and the second set of cuts were too deep to permit the train to roll smoothly across the track. In the district court's view, even if the concept of cutting grooves into the wooden track in order to produce noise originated with Clausi, the concept lacked value until it was refined, developed and manufactured by Learning Curve.

We cannot accept the district court's conclusion because it is belied by the evidence. At trial, Kennedy was asked whether, in his opinion, the fact that PlayWood's prototype did not work perfectly affected the value of PlayWood's concept, and he testified that it did not. Kennedy testified that he would assign the same value to PlayWood's concept as it was conceived on February 18, 1993, as he would the finished product that became known as Clickety-Clack Track because, at that time, he would have known "that most of the design [had] already been done and that [he] just need[ed] to go a little bit further to make it really lovely." Kennedy further testified that it was standard practice in the industry for a license to be negotiated based on a prototype (much like the one PlayWood disclosed to Learning Curve) rather than a finished product and that the license generally would cover the prototypical design, as well as any enhancements or improvements of that design.[5] Based on this testimony, we cannot accept the district court's conclusion that PlayWood's concept possessed no economic value.

It is irrelevant under Illinois law that PlayWood did not actually use the concept in its business. "[T]he proper criterion is not 'actual use' but whether the trade secret is 'of value' to the company." *Syntex Ophthalmics, Inc. v. Tsuetaki*, 701 F.2d 677, 683 (7th Cir. 1983).[6] Kennedy's testimony was more than sufficient to permit the jury to conclude that the concept was "of value" to PlayWood. It is equally irrelevant that PlayWood did not seek to patent its concept. So long as the concept remains a secret, *i.e.*, outside of the public domain, there is no need for patent protection. It was up to PlayWood, not the district court, to determine when and how the concept should have been disclosed to the public.

**5.  *Amount of time, effort and money expended by PlayWood in developing its concept***

PlayWood expended very little time and money developing its concept; by Clausi's own account, the cost to PlayWood was less than one dollar and the time spent was less than one-half hour. The district court determined that "[s]uch an insignificant investment is...insufficient as a matter of Illinois law to establish the status of a 'trade secret.'" We believe that the district court gave too much weight to the time, effort and expense of developing the track.

5. Specifically, Kennedy testified:

Q: Now, when you were at Tyco, you were in the toy business and people were bringing you inventions, did people bring you inventions or trade secrets that were in the kind of form that we find Defendants' Exhibit 9 [Clickety-Clack Track], fully polished and finished and so on?
A: I've seen some pretty rough-looking toys in meeting with inventors. I've seen toys that were obviously made by hand. I've seen toys that had cracks, seams and joints that you don't expect to see when they're manufactured. Certainly that's true....So the answer is: You don't see a final product when you meet with an inventor. You see a preliminary product or a prototype kind of product.
Q: Now, when a prototype is brought to you as a disclosure, as a secret, as an invention that somebody wants to license to you, does it make a difference to you whether it's a prototype or a finished product?
A: Not necessarily, because it depends on who is going to make it, which is uncertain at the time. It depends on how difficult it is to make, which could be uncertain at that time. It's helpful if we know that it's easy to make. It's helpful if we know how much it costs to make. But you don't always know that.
Q: When you go to license that kind of invention that's brought to you, is it your intent to license only the prototype that's brought to you?
A: No. I think every license agreement that I negotiate in the toy industry includes the prototypical design. It includes enhancements and improvements on that design, regardless of whether they're made by the inventor or whether they're made by the manufacturer. It includes something called line extensions, which is the transfer of this invention to a toy which maybe wasn't first thought of for its application. It includes all of those things.

6. Both the Uniform Trade Secrets Act and the Restatement (Third) of Unfair Competition expressly reject prior use by the person asserting rights in the information as a prerequisite to trade secret protection. *See* Unif. Trade Secrets Act §1 cmt. (1990) ("The broader definition in the proposed Act extends protection to a plaintiff who has not yet had an opportunity or acquired the means to put a trade secret to use."); Restatement (Third) of Unfair Competition §39 cmt. e (1995) ("Use by the person asserting rights in the information is not a prerequisite to protection under the rule stated in this Section," in part, because such a "requirement can deny protection during periods of research and development and is particularly burdensome for innovators who do not possess the capability to exploit their innovations.").

Although Illinois courts commonly look to the Restatement factors for guidance in determining whether a trade secret exists, as we have noted earlier, the requisite statutory inquiries under Illinois law are (1) whether the information "is sufficiently secret to derive economic value, actual or potential, from not being generally known to other persons who can obtain economic value from its disclosure or use"; and (2) whether the information "is the subject of efforts that are reasonable under the circumstances to maintain its secrecy or confidentiality." 765 ILCS 1065/2(d). A significant expenditure of time and/or money in the production of information may provide evidence of value, which is relevant to the first inquiry above. However, we do not understand Illinois law to require such an expenditure in all cases.

As pointed out by the district court, several Illinois cases have emphasized the importance of developmental costs. However, notably, none of those cases concerned the sort of innovative and creative concept that we have in this case. Indeed, several of the cases in Illinois that emphasize developmental costs concern compilations of data, such as customer lists. In that context, it makes sense to require the expenditure of significant time and money because there is nothing original or creative about the alleged trade secret. Given enough time and money, we presume that the plaintiff's competitors could compile a similar list.

Here, by contrast, we are dealing with a new toy design that has been promoted as "the first significant innovation in track design since the inception of wooden train systems." Toy designers, like many artistic individuals, have intuitive flashes of creativity. Often, that intuitive flash is, in reality, the product of earlier thought and practice in an artistic craft. We fail to see how the value of PlayWood's concept would differ in any respect had Clausi spent several months and several thousand dollars creating the noise-producing track. Accordingly, we conclude that PlayWood's lack of proof on this factor does not preclude the existence of a trade secret.

### 6. Ease or difficulty with which PlayWood's concept could have been properly acquired or duplicated by others

Finally, we also believe that there was sufficient evidence for the jury to determine that PlayWood's concept could not have been easily acquired or duplicated through proper means. PlayWood's expert witness, Michael Kennedy, testified: "This is a fairly simple product if you look at it. But the truth is that because it delivers feeling and sound as well as appearance, it isn't so simple as it first appears. It's a little more elegant, actually, than you might think." In addition to Kennedy's testimony, the jury heard that Learning Curve had spent months attempting to differentiate its track from Brio's before Clausi disclosed PlayWood's concept of noise-producing track. From this evidence, the jury could have inferred that, if PlayWood's concept really was obvious, Learning Curve would have thought of it earlier.

Despite this evidence, the district court concluded that PlayWood's concept was not a trade secret because it could have been easily duplicated, stating that "[h]ad PlayWood succeeded in producing and marketing [the] notched track, the appearance of the track product itself would have fully revealed the concept PlayWood now claims as a secret." Of course, the district court was correct in one sense; PlayWood's own expert recognized that, in the absence of patent or copyright protection, the track could have been reverse engineered just by looking at it. However, the district court failed to appreciate the fact that PlayWood's concept was not publicly available. As Professor Milgrim states: "A potent distinction exists between a trade secret which *will be* disclosed if and when the product in which it is embodied is placed on sale, and a 'trade secret' embodied in a product which has been placed on sale, which product admits of discovery of the 'secret' upon inspection, analysis, or reverse engineering." 1 Roger M. Milgrim, *Milgrim on Trade Secrets* §1.05[4], at 1-228 (2002). "Until disclosed by sale the trade secret should be entitled to protection." *Id.* Reverse engineering can defeat a trade secret claim, but only if the product could have been properly acquired by others, as is the case when the product is publicly sold. Here, PlayWood disclosed its concept to Learning Curve (and Learning Curve alone) in the context of a confidential relationship; Learning Curve had no legal authority to reverse engineer the prototype that it received in confidence. Accordingly, we must conclude that the jury was entitled to determine that PlayWood's concept could not easily have been acquired or duplicated through proper means.

## Comments

1. *Sources of Trade Secret Law.* While trade secrets have their origin in state common law, over 40 states have adopted the Uniform Trade Secrets Act (UTSA) in its original form or a version thereof. To qualify as a trade secret under the UTSA, the information sought to be protected must provide its owner with economic value and not be readily discoverable through proper means. Thus, the owner must take reasonable measures for securing the subject matter's secrecy. The *Learning Curve* court also relied on the First Restatement of Torts drafted in 1939. Even with the UTSA on the books in numerous states, this Restatement continues to be very influential both in its definition of a trade secret and what constitutes misappropriation. Yet another source is the Restatement (Third) of Unfair Competition §39, which defines a trade secret as "any information that can be used in the operation of a business or other enterprise and that is sufficiently valuable and secret to afford an actual or potential economic advantage over others."

2. *Maintaining Secrecy.* The UTSA states that information, to be subject to trade secret protection, cannot be "generally known" and reasonable efforts must be made to maintain the information's secrecy. The obvious question is what constitutes "reasonable efforts." The courts tend to weigh the costs and benefits of secrecy measures. Consider the following discussion by Judge Posner:

> On the one hand, the more the owner of the trade secret spends on preventing the secret from leaking out, the more he demonstrates that the secret has real value deserving of legal protection, that he really was hurt as a result of the misappropriation of it, and that there really *was* misappropriation. On the other hand, the more he spends, the higher his

costs. The costs can be indirect as well as direct. The more Rockwell restricts access to its drawings, either by its engineers or by the vendors, the harder it will be for either group to do the work expected of it. Suppose Rockwell forbids *any* copying of its drawings. Then a team of engineers would have to share a single drawing, perhaps by passing it around or by working in the same room, huddled over the drawing. . . . [T]herefore perfect security is not optimum security.

*Rockwell Graphic Systems, Inc. v. DEV Industries, Inc.*, 925 F.2d 174, 177-180 (7th Cir. 1991). In this regard, the *DuPont* court held that DuPont took reasonable measures to maintain secrecy, and while the court appreciated the need for healthy competition, it would not require a trade secret owner to take costly protective action that would dampen the "spirit of inventiveness." As the court aptly stated, "[t]o require DuPont to put a roof over the unfinished plant to guard its secret would impose an enormous expense to prevent nothing more than a school boy's trick." In *Learning Curve*, the court, in finding that an oral confidentiality agreement was a reasonable measure toward maintaining secrecy, considered the small size and corresponding sophistication level of the parties.

Protecting secrets during litigation is also difficult. The Coca-Cola Company has defied court orders to turn over its Coca-Cola formula in some cases, risking being held in contempt and having a default judgment ordered against it. A variety of procedural mechanisms are available for protecting trade secrets in court, including granting protective orders in connection with discovery proceedings, holding in-camera hearings, sealing the records of the action, closing courtrooms, and ordering people involved in the litigation not to disclose trade secrets without prior court approval.

## Problem

**14-1.** Plaintiff asserts that defendant misappropriated the former's customer lists, which included customer phone numbers, addresses, and email addresses. These lists were kept on plaintiff's password-protected server. Only high-level sales representatives were given passwords. Plaintiff did not require its sales reps to sign a confidentiality agreement, nor did it restrict access to paper copies of the customer lists, however, sales reps were discouraged from printing customer lists. Has plaintiff done enough to protect the secrecy of its customer lists? *See Liebert Corp. v. Mazur* (Ill. App. Ct., Second Division, No. 1-04-2794, April 5, 2005).

## B. MISAPPROPRIATION OF TRADE SECRETS: "IMPROPER MEANS"

A trade secret misappropriation cause of action must be based on either an assertion that the defendant acquired the trade secret through "improper means" or by a breach of a duty of confidentiality, based on an express or implied contract. As noted in the introduction to this chapter, independent creation and reverse engineering are deemed proper means, and therefore, serve as defenses to a trade secret misappropriation claim. Thus, as the *DuPont* court discusses, trade secret law is concerned with encouraging ethical commercial behavior.

## E.I. DUPONT DE NEMOURS & COMPANY v. CHRISTOPHER
### 431 F.2d 1012 (5th Cir. 1970)

GOLDBERG, Circuit Judge.

This is a case of industrial espionage in which an airplane is the cloak and a camera the dagger. The defendants-appellants, Rolfe and Gary Christopher, are photographers in Beaumont, Texas. The Christophers were hired by an unknown third party to take aerial photographs of new construction at the Beaumont plant of E. I. duPont deNemours & Company, Inc. Sixteen photographs of the DuPont facility were taken from the air on March 19, 1969, and these photographs were later developed and delivered to the third party.

DuPont employees apparently noticed the airplane on March 19 and immediately began an investigation to determine why the craft was circling over the plant. By that afternoon the investigation had disclosed that the craft was involved in a photographic expedition and that the Christophers were the photographers. DuPont contacted the Christophers that same afternoon and asked them to reveal the name of the person or corporation requesting the photographs. The Christophers refused to disclose this information, giving as their reason the client's desire to remain anonymous.

Having reached a dead end in the investigation, DuPont subsequently filed suit against the Christophers, alleging that the Christophers had wrongfully obtained photographs revealing DuPont's trade secrets which they then sold to the undisclosed third party. DuPont contended that it had developed a highly secret but unpatented process for producing methanol, a process which gave DuPont a competitive advantage over other producers. This process, DuPont alleged, was a trade secret developed after much expensive and time-consuming research, and a secret which the company had taken special precautions to safeguard. The area photographed by the Christophers was the plant designed to produce methanol by this secret process, and because the plant was still under construction parts of the process were exposed to view from directly above the construction area. Photographs of that area, DuPont alleged, would enable a skilled person to deduce the secret process for making methanol. DuPont thus contended that the Christophers had wrongfully appropriated DuPont trade secrets by taking the photographs and delivering them to the undisclosed third party. In its suit DuPont asked for damages to cover the loss it had already sustained as a result of the wrongful disclosure of the trade secret and sought temporary and permanent injunctions prohibiting any further circulation of the photographs already taken and prohibiting any additional photographing of the methanol plant.

***

The only question involved in this interlocutory appeal is whether DuPont has asserted a claim upon which relief can be granted. The Christophers argued both at trial and before this court that they committed no "actionable wrong" in photographing the DuPont facility and passing these photographs on to their client because they conducted all of their activities in public airspace, violated no government aviation standard, did not breach any confidential relation, and did not engage in any fraudulent or illegal conduct. In short, the Christophers argue that for an appropriation of trade secrets to be wrongful there must be a trespass, other illegal conduct, or breach of a confidential relationship. We disagree.

It is true, as the Christophers assert, that the previous trade secret cases have contained one or more of these elements. However, we do not think that the Texas courts would limit the trade secret protection exclusively to these elements. On the contrary, in *Hyde Corporation v. Huffines,* 1958, 158 Tex. 566, the Texas Supreme Court specifically adopted the rule found in the Restatement of Torts which provides:

> One who discloses or uses another's trade secret, without a privilege to do so, is liable to the other if (a) he discovered the secret by improper means, or (b) his disclosure or use constitutes a breach of confidence reposed in him by the other in disclosing the secret to him. . . .

Restatement of Torts §757 (1939).

Thus, although the previous cases have dealt with a breach of a confidential relationship, a trespass, or other illegal conduct, the rule is much broader than the cases heretofore encountered. Not limiting itself to specific wrongs, Texas adopted subsection (a) of the Restatement which recognizes a cause of action for the discovery of a trade secret by any "improper" means.

\*\*\*

The question remaining, therefore, is whether aerial photography of plant construction is an improper means of obtaining another's trade secret. We conclude that it is and that the Texas courts would so hold. The Supreme Court of that state has declared that "the undoubted tendency of the law has been to recognize and enforce higher standards of commercial morality in the business world." *Hyde Corporation v. Huffines, supra,* 314 S.W.2d at 773. That court has quoted with approval articles indicating that the proper means of gaining possession of a competitor's secret process is "through inspection and analysis" of the product in order to create a duplicate. *K & G Tool & Service Co. v. G & G Fishing Tool Service,* 1958, 158 Tex. 594. Later another Texas court explained:

> The means by which the discovery is made may be obvious, and the experimentation leading from known factors to presently unknown results may be simple and lying in the public domain. But these facts do not destroy the value of the discovery and will not advantage a competitor who by unfair means obtains the knowledge without paying the price expended by the discoverer.

Brown v. Fowler, Tex. Civ. App. 1958, 316 S.W.2d 111, 114.

We think, therefore, that the Texas rule is clear. One may use his competitor's secret process if he discovers the process by reverse engineering applied to the finished product; one may use a competitor's process if he discovers it by his own independent research; but one may not avoid these labors by taking the process from the discoverer without his permission at a time when he is taking reasonable precautions to maintain its secrecy. To obtain knowledge of a process without spending the time and money to discover it independently is improper unless the holder voluntarily discloses it or fails to take reasonable precautions to ensure its secrecy.

In the instant case the Christophers deliberately flew over the DuPont plant to get pictures of a process which DuPont had attempted to keep secret. The Christophers delivered their pictures to a third party who was certainly aware of the means by which they had been acquired and who may be planning to use the information contained therein to manufacture methanol by the DuPont process. The third party has a right to use this process only if he obtains this knowledge through his own research efforts, but thus far all information indicates that the third party has gained this knowledge solely by taking it from DuPont at a time when DuPont was making reasonable efforts to preserve its secrecy. In such a situation DuPont has a valid cause of action to prohibit the Christophers from improperly discovering its trade secret and to prohibit the undisclosed third party from using the improperly obtained information.

We note that this view is in perfect accord with the position taken by the authors of the Restatement. In commenting on improper means of discovery the savants of the Restatement said:

> f. Improper means of discovery. The discovery of another's trade secret by improper means subjects the actor to liability independently of the harm to the interest in the secret. Thus, if one uses physical force to take a secret formula from another's pocket, or breaks into another's office to steal the formula, his conduct is wrongful and subjects him to liability apart from the rule stated in this Section. Such conduct is also an improper means of procuring the secret under this rule. But means may be improper under this rule even though they do not cause any other harm than that to the interest in the trade secret. Examples of such means are fraudulent misrepresentations to induce disclosure, tapping of telephone wires, eavesdropping or other espionage. A complete catalogue of improper means is not possible. In general they are means which fall below the generally accepted standards of commercial morality and reasonable conduct.

Restatement of Torts §757, comment f at 10 (1939).

In taking this position we realize that industrial espionage of the sort here perpetrated has become a popular sport in some segments of our industrial community. However, our devotion to free wheeling industrial competition must not force us into accepting the law of the jungle as the standard of morality expected in our commercial relations. Our tolerance of the espionage game must cease when the protections required to prevent another's spying cost so much that the spirit of inventiveness is dampened. Commercial privacy must be protected from espionage which could not have been reasonably anticipated or prevented. We do not mean to imply, however, that everything not in plain view is within the protected vale, nor that all information obtained through every extra optical extension is forbidden. Indeed, for our industrial competition to remain healthy there must be breathing room for observing a competing industrialist.

A competitor can and must shop his competition for pricing and examine his products for quality, components, and methods of manufacture. Perhaps ordinary fences and roofs must be built to shut out incursive eyes, but we need not require the discoverer of a trade secret to guard against the unanticipated, the undetectable, or the unpreventable methods of espionage now available.

In the instant case DuPont was in the midst of constructing a plant. Although after construction the finished plant would have protected much of the process from view, during the period of construction the trade secret was exposed to view from the air. To require DuPont to put a roof over the unfinished plant to guard its secret would impose an enormous expense to prevent nothing more than a school boy's trick. We introduce here no new or radical ethic since our ethos has never given moral sanction to piracy. The market place must not deviate far from our mores. We should not require a person or corporation to take unreasonable precautions to prevent another from doing that which he ought not do in the first place. Reasonable precautions against predatory eyes we may require, but an impenetrable fortress is an unreasonable requirement, and we are not disposed to burden industrial inventors with such a duty in order to protect the fruits of their efforts. "Improper" will always be a word of many nuances, determined by time, place, and circumstances. We therefore need not proclaim a catalogue of commercial improprieties. Clearly, however, one of its commandments does say "thou shall not appropriate a trade secret through deviousness under circumstances in which countervailing defenses are not reasonably available."

\*\*\*

## Comments

1. *Improper Means and Readily Ascertainable by Proper Means.* Section 1 of the UTSA defines "improper means" as "theft, bribery, misrepresentation, breach or inducement of a breach of duty to maintain secrecy, or espionage through electronic or other means." *See also* Restatement (Third) of Unfair Competition, §43 (1995). The existence of "improper means," implies there are "proper means" to acquire a trade secret. The *Christopher* court mentioned two of them: reverse engineering and independent research. The former is simply the taking of something apart to figure out how it works or how it is built. Why should trade secret law treat reverse engineering as a proper method of acquisition? Judge Posner suggests that "reverse engineering involves the use of technical skills that we want to encourage, and that anyone should have the right to take apart and to study a product that he has bought." *Rockwell Graphic*, 925 F.2d at 178. To the extent that trade secret law is concerned with commercial behavior, does reverse engineering have an unseemly side? Is it significantly different than Christopher's behavior in *DuPont*?

The UTSA precludes trade secret protection if the information could be "readily ascertainable by proper means." As noted above, reverse engineering and independent creation are two such means. Trade secrets can also be properly obtained through traditional forms of research, including patent and literature searches or an Internet search. Thus, trade secret protection is unavailable if a competitor independently obtained the "trade secret" by performing a Google search. But what if instead of searching the Internet, the competitor decides to "crack" the trade secret owner's safe or, like Christopher, fly over his facility? Should the information nonetheless be deemed protected as a trade secret even though the competitor *could have* obtained the information through proper means? In *Rohm & Haas Co. v. Adco Chemical Co.,* 689 F.2d 424 (3rd Cir. 1982), the defendant memorized plaintiff's trade secret and delivered it to a competitor. The defendant argued that there was no trade secret because the information was already published and, therefore, publicly available. The court held for the plaintiff because the defendant did not obtain the information from publicly available sources. This holding reflects the position of the Restatement (First) of Torts §757 set forth in comment 1, and highlights trade secret law's concern with regulating commercial behavior. Section 757 states that information is subject to trade secret protection as long as "competitors . . . do not know or use" the information. This approach, which offers a broad view of trade secret law, requires actual knowledge on the part of the competitor and is more concerned with commercial behavior. On the other hand, the UTSA states that trade secret protection is not available if the information is "readily ascertainable by proper means." Thus, if the information is knowable from a public source, it does not matter under the UTSA if the competitor learns of the information from that source or from the party claiming trade secret protection. The UTSA approach is more protective of the public domain.

*Learning Curve* seems to follow the Restatement approach. The district held that PlayWood's concept was not a trade secret because it could have been easily duplicated, stating that "the appearance of the track product itself would have fully revealed the concept PlayWood now claims as a secret." In other words, the track could have been reverse engineered, something PlayWood's own expert conceded. But the Seventh Circuit emphasized the fact that PlayWood's concept was not publicly available, thus making the distinction between a trade secret that will be disclosed if and when the product in which it is embodied is placed on sale, and a trade secret embodied in a product that has already been placed on sale, which allows for reverse engineering. According to the court, PlayWood's concept was entitled to protection until it was placed on sale because reverse engineering can defeat a trade secret claim only if the product could have been properly acquired by others, such as legal purchase.

2. **Breach of a Confidential Relationship.** Contractual relationships, express and implied, are common when dealing with trade secrets, how they can be used, and to whom they may (or may not) be disclosed. Section 7(b) of the UTSA recognizes the importance of contracts by stating the Act "does not affect contractual remedies, whether or not based upon misappropriation of a trade secret." The Restatement (Third) of Unfair Competition §41, defines a confidential relationship as follows:

A person to whom a trade secret has been disclosed owes a duty of confidence to the owner of the trade secret for purposes of the rule stated in §40 if:

(a) the person made an express promise of confidentiality prior to the disclosure of the trade secret; or

(b) the trade secret was disclosed to the person under circumstances in which the relationship between the parties to the disclosure or the other facts surrounding the disclosure justify the conclusions that, at the time of the disclosure, (1) the person knew or had reason to know that the disclosure was intended to be in confidence, and (2) the other party to the disclosure was reasonable in inferring that the person consented to an obligation of confidentiality.

## C. THE EMPLOYER-EMPLOYEE RELATIONSHIP

### PROCTER & GAMBLE CO. v. STONEHAM
#### 747 N.E.2d 268 (2000)

HILDEBRANDT, Presiding Judge.

Plaintiff-appellant, the Procter & Gamble Company ("P&G"), appeals from the judgment of the trial court dismissing its claims against defendant-appellee, Paul Stoneham, for breach of contract and misappropriation of trade secrets. P&G sought damages and injunctive relief against Stoneham, claiming that he had violated a non-compete agreement that he had signed while employed at P&G and that he had misappropriated trade secrets when he began working for a company called Alberto-Culver.

Upon Stoneham's motion, the trial court dismissed P&G's claims. Because we hold that the court's decision was erroneous as a matter of law and contrary to the manifest weight of the evidence, we reverse the judgment and remand the cause for further proceedings.

#### SUMMARY OF FACTS

Paul Stoneham worked for P&G for thirteen years. He had a master's degree in marketing. During the latter part of his employment, he worked in the haircare division, focusing primarily on hair-conditioning products. As a senior-level manager, he had responsibility for international marketing. As a member of several teams of managers formulating P&G's global business goals and strategies related to haircare, Stoneham was required to know and use information such as market research results, financial data related to the costs and profits of the products, and the technological developments in existing and new products.

As part of its drive to substantially expand its global haircare business, P&G obtained raw market research data from a market research firm. The marketing division compiled the information for use in developing consumer models, determining the product areas in which P&G would expand or reduce its business, assessing the types of advertising that were most successful for different products, and creating a line of products that would optimize P&G's profits. Stoneham's expertise was the foreign markets, that is, the markets other than the United States, and the needs of the foreign consumers, the products that sold best in the foreign markets, the areas in which P&G should concentrate its resources to increase sales in haircare products, and the types of claims and advertising that would be most successful in foreign markets.

As part of his job, Stoneham was also privy to the development of new haircare products by P&G. He knew, among other things, which products were closest to market, when and where they would be launched, the target consumers, the type of advertising to be used, the strengths and weaknesses of the products, the strengths and weaknesses of the company's scientific backup for its claims about the products, the price for the new products, and the targeted profits. He was also involved in the "relaunch" or revitalization of existing products, and knew, among other things, which products were going to be relaunched, the perceived weaknesses of the products, the changes made or to be made in the products, the changes in the advertising and marketing focus, and the anticipated costs of the relaunch.

As a member of worldwide multi-functional teams at P&G, Stoneham developed a confidential ten-year marketing plan for one of P&G's hair-conditioning products, participated in the development of new products, and helped develop a ten-year plan for P&G's best-selling brand, Pantene. No one was more knowledgeable about the foreign marketing of P&G's haircare products, and no one was more knowledgeable about P&G's hair-conditioning products, both existing and potential, than Stoneham.

When he reached a certain management level at P&G, Stoneham, like other employees at that level, was given the opportunity to obtain P&G stock options. Only about ten percent of P&G's employees, the highest levels of management, were eligible for these options. To receive the stock options, Stoneham was required to sign an agreement not to compete with P&G for three years after the termination of his employment. Agreeing to the covenant not to compete was entirely voluntary, but failure to agree would have required Stoneham to forgo the stock options. Stoneham signed the non-compete agreement. Like all other employees at P&G, Stoneham had signed a confidentiality agreement when he was hired, in which he had agreed not to disclose any of P&G's confidential information or trade secrets.

In 1998, Stoneham decided to take a job with Alberto-Culver, a company whose haircare products, including its conditioners, competed with P&G products to some extent. Alberto-Culver's VO5 brand of hair conditioner was the best-selling leave-in conditioner on the market at the time. Stoneham's position was to be President of Alberto-Culver International, the complement to the company's President of Alberto-Culver U.S.

Shortly after he accepted the position, P&G filed suit, alleging that Stoneham had breached the covenant not to compete and that his employment with Alberto-Culver posed an immediate threat that P&G's trade secrets would be disclosed. Following a hearing on P&G's requests for a preliminary and a permanent injunction, the trial court held that P&G had not established an entitlement to relief.

P&G's complaint alleged that Stoneham had breached the non-compete agreement when he began working for Alberto-Culver. The complaint also alleged that Stoneham had misappropriated trade secrets in violation of R.C. 1333.62. P&G requested monetary damages, as well as a preliminary injunction and a permanent injunction.

***

The issue on appeal is the propriety of the trial court's denial of the permanent injunction. P&G contends that the trial court failed to use the appropriate standards for determining the validity of the non-compete agreement. P&G also claims that the trial court erroneously held that P&G had failed to prove that Stoneham was exposed to trade secrets and confidential information while employed at P&G.

In Ohio, non-compete agreements that are reasonable are enforced, and those that are unreasonable are "enforced to the extent necessary to protect an employer's legitimate interest." The Supreme Court of Ohio has stated, "A covenant restraining an employee from competing with his former employer upon termination of employment is reasonable if the restraint is no greater than is required for the protection of the employer, does not impose undue hardship on the employee, and is not injurious to the public."

To determine whether a particular non-compete agreement is reasonable, the court must consider whether the agreement contains time and space limitations, whether the employee is the sole contact with the customer, whether the employee has confidential information and trade secrets, whether the agreement seeks to limit only unfair competition or is designed more broadly to eliminate ordinary competition, whether the agreement seeks to stifle the employee's inherent skill and experience, whether the benefit to the employer is disproportional to the detriment to the employee, whether the agreement bars the employee's sole means of support, whether the skills that the agreement seeks to restrain were actually developed during the employment, and whether the forbidden employment is merely incidental to the main employment. *See Raimonde v. Van Vlerah*, 42 Ohio St. 2d 21, 325 N.E.2d 544 (1975).

The trial court in this case did not cite or refer to the *Raimonde* factors explicitly. Our review of the trial court's decision convinces us that the trial court also failed to implicitly use any of these factors in determining the agreement's validity, with the possible exception of Stoneham's receipt of confidential information or trade secrets. The court noted only that P&G had "waive[d] the non-compete provision as to some executives who [had] the same exposure to confidential information," that "[t]he non-compete agreement [was not] a condition of receipt of information," and that P&G had failed to show "that [Stoneham] was taken into Procter & Gamble's confidence to any greater extent because he signed the agreement." The court also stated that the non-competition covenant was "not being used to protect confidential information, but it is used as a measure to retain valued employees."

None of these factors is relevant, pursuant to *Raimonde*, to the enforceability of the covenant. Although they might be relevant to a determination of whether the contract was supported by consideration, such an inquiry was unnecessary because the undisputed evidence showed that Stoneham received valuable stock options in consideration for his agreement not to compete. Therefore, we hold that the trial court erred as a matter of law in failing to judge the enforceability of the agreement by the factors set forth in *Raimonde*.

The court's error was not harmless because P&G presented clear and convincing evidence to show that the non-compete agreement was reasonable under *Raimonde*. The record demonstrates that Stoneham had access to confidential information and trade secrets, that the agreement sought to limit only unfair competition by prohibiting Stoneham's employment in the international haircare industry with a direct competitor, that the enforcement of the agreement would not stifle Stoneham's inherent skills in marketing or destroy Stoneham's sole means of support, that Stoneham could work at Alberto-Culver in areas other than haircare for the term of the non-compete agreement, and that Stoneham's talents and knowledge in the area of haircare marketing were actually developed during his employment with P&G. The three-year limitation on competition was shown to be reasonable by evidence that the confidential information to which Stoneham had access had a useful life of three to five years.

As stated above, the trial court's decision indicated that it might have considered whether Stoneham was exposed to confidential information and trade secrets. It is not clear from the decision, however, whether the court credited or discounted all of the evidence presented regarding Stoneham's receipt of confidential and trade-secret information. The court at one point stated that "[m]arket research [was] available to competitors," and "documents claimed to be confidential...were not so marked pursuant to company security requirements, and this Court will not infer confidential status when the company itself has not done so where the same information is possessed by employees not subject to non-compete contracts,...and where [P&G] waives the non-compete provision as to some executives who have the same exposure to confidential information."

To the extent that the trial court held that Stoneham was not exposed to confidential information and trade secrets, the court's decision is contrary to the manifest weight of the evidence. "Confidential information," as that term was used in *Raimonde* in the context of enforcement of covenants not to compete, is not defined under Ohio law. "Confidential" can mean "known only to a limited few; not publicly disseminated." *See* Webster's Third New International Dictionary, Unabridged (1981) 476. "Trade secrets" is defined by R.C. 1333.61(D), which states,

> Trade secret means information, including the whole or any portion or phase of any scientific or technical information, design, process, procedure, formula, pattern, compilation, program, device, method, technique, or improvement, or any business information or plans, financial information, or listing of names, addresses, or telephone numbers, that satisfies both of the following:
>
> (1) It derives independent economic value, actual or potential, from not being generally known to, and not being readily ascertainable by proper means by, other persons who can obtain economic value from its disclosure or use.

(2) It is the subject of efforts that are reasonable under the circumstances to maintain its secrecy.

In determining the existence of a trade secret, a trial court must consider (1) the extent to which the information is known outside the business; (2) the extent to which it is known to those inside the business, *i.e.*, by the employees; (3) the precautions taken by the holder of the trade secret to guard the secrecy of the information; (4) the savings effected and the value to the holder in having the information withheld from competitors; (5) the amount of effort or money expended in obtaining and developing the information; and (6) the amount of time and expense it would take for others to acquire and duplicate the information.

The court in this case incorrectly focused on only one of the factors identified above: the precautions taken to guard the secrecy of the information. The overwhelming weight of the evidence presented at the hearing demonstrates that Stoneham was privy to massive amounts of information that constituted trade secrets.

Although the court correctly noted that the raw data that P&G received from the marketing firm was available to any other company that could pay for it, P&G presented evidence that the data was compiled and used in a way unique to P&G, and that it could have been duplicated only by the expenditure of vast amounts of time, money, and other resources. P&G used the material to create a consumer model to guide all of the marketing for particular products. The information was, for lack of a better term, cross-indexed so that P&G could study subsets of the information, such as the consumer behavior in a certain country related to a certain product. It was not the raw data but the analysis and interpretation of the data that P&G considered confidential. The court's conclusion that the marketing data known to Stoneham was not a trade secret or confidential information was contrary to the manifest weight of the evidence.

Even if some of the written information to which Stoneham had access was not marked as confidential in accordance with company procedure, P&G presented substantial evidence that numerous documents that contained confidential information and that bore the stamp of confidentiality were in Stoneham's possession and used by him during his employment. These documents contained information about new products and their costs, advertising and marketing; about changes in marketing strategy for existing products; about consumer research analysis performed by P&G at great expense and effort, and the consumer research models that resulted from its analysis; and about P&G's future plans for its haircare business on an international level. All of this information was of a confidential nature and constituted trades secrets. To the extent that the trial court held that this information was not confidential, the court's decision was contrary to the manifest weight of the evidence.

P&G demonstrated that the non-compete agreement was reasonable when analyzed in accordance with the standards that were enumerated in *Raimonde,* and the trial court's contrary decision was erroneous as a matter of law. We also hold that the trial court erred to the extent that it held that Stoneham was not privy to confidential information and trade secrets. The overwhelming weight of the evidence demonstrated that substantially all of Stoneham's work, particularly in the last two years of his employment, required the use of confidential information and trade secrets.

## PEPSICO, INC. v. REDMOND
### 54 F.3d 1262 (7th Cir. 1995)

FLAUM, Circuit Judge.

Plaintiff PepsiCo, Inc., sought a preliminary injunction against defendants William Redmond and the Quaker Oats Company to prevent Redmond, a former PepsiCo employee, from divulging PepsiCo trade secrets and confidential information in his new job with Quaker and from assuming any duties with Quaker relating to beverage pricing, marketing, and distribution. The district court agreed with PepsiCo and granted the injunction. We now affirm that decision.

### I.

The facts of this case lay against a backdrop of fierce beverage-industry competition between Quaker and PepsiCo, especially in "sports drinks" and "new age drinks." Quaker's sports drink, "Gatorade," is the dominant brand in its market niche. PepsiCo introduced its Gatorade rival, "All Sport," in March and April of 1994, but sales of All Sport lag far behind those of Gatorade. Quaker also has the lead in the new-age-drink category. Although PepsiCo has entered the market through joint ventures with the Thomas J. Lipton Company and Ocean Spray Cranberries, Inc., Quaker purchased Snapple Beverage Corp., a large new-age-drink maker, in late 1994. PepsiCo's products have about half of Snapple's market share. Both companies see 1995 as an important year for their products: PepsiCo has developed extensive plans to increase its market presence, while Quaker is trying to solidify its lead by integrating Gatorade and Snapple distribution. Meanwhile, PepsiCo and Quaker each face strong competition from Coca Cola Co., which has its own sports drink, "PowerAde," and which introduced its own Snapple-rival, "Fruitopia," in 1994, as well as from independent beverage producers.

William Redmond, Jr., worked for PepsiCo in its Pepsi-Cola North America division ("PCNA") from 1984 to 1994. Redmond became the General Manager of the Northern California Business Unit in June, 1993, and was promoted one year later to General Manager of the business unit covering all of California, a unit having annual revenues of more than 500 million dollars and representing twenty percent of PCNA's profit for all of the United States.

Redmond's relatively high-level position at PCNA gave him access to inside information and trade secrets. Redmond, like other PepsiCo management employees, had signed a confidentiality agreement with PepsiCo. That agreement stated in relevant part that he

> w[ould] not disclose at any time, to anyone other than officers or employees of [PepsiCo], or make use of, confidential information relating to the business of [PepsiCo]...obtained while in the employ of [PepsiCo], which shall

not be generally known or available to the public or recognized as standard practices.

Donald Uzzi, who had left PepsiCo in the beginning of 1994 to become the head of Quaker's Gatorade division, began courting Redmond for Quaker in May, 1994. Redmond met in Chicago with Quaker officers in August, 1994, and on October 20, 1994, Quaker, through Uzzi, offered Redmond the position of Vice President–On Premise Sales for Gatorade. Redmond did not then accept the offer but continued to negotiate for more money. Throughout this time, Redmond kept his dealings with Quaker secret from his employers at PCNA.

On November 8, 1994, Uzzi extended Redmond a written offer for the position of Vice President–Field Operations for Gatorade and Redmond accepted. Later that same day, Redmond called William Bensyl, the Senior Vice President of Human Resources for PCNA, and told him that he had an offer from Quaker to become the Chief Operating Officer of the combined Gatorade and Snapple company but had not yet accepted it. Redmond also asked whether he should, in light of the offer, carry out his plans to make calls upon certain PCNA customers. Bensyl told Redmond to make the visits.

Redmond also misstated his situation to a number of his PCNA colleagues, including Craig Weatherup, PCNA's President and Chief Executive Officer, and Brenda Barnes, PCNA's Chief Operating Officer and Redmond's immediate superior. As with Bensyl, Redmond told them that he had been offered the position of Chief Operating Officer at Gatorade and that he was leaning "60/40" in favor of accepting the new position.

On November 10, 1994, Redmond met with Barnes and told her that he had decided to accept the Quaker offer and was resigning from PCNA. Barnes immediately took Redmond to Bensyl, who told Redmond that PepsiCo was considering legal action against him.

True to its word, PepsiCo filed this diversity suit on November 16, 1994, seeking a temporary restraining order to enjoin Redmond from assuming his duties at Quaker and to prevent him from disclosing trade secrets or confidential information to his new employer. The district court granted PepsiCo's request that same day but dissolved the order *sua sponte* two days later, after determining that PepsiCo had failed to meet its burden of establishing that it would suffer irreparable harm. The court found that PepsiCo's fears about Redmond were based upon a mistaken understanding of his new position at Quaker and that the likelihood that Redmond would improperly reveal any confidential information did not "rise above mere speculation."

From November 23, 1994, to December 1, 1994, the district court conducted a preliminary injunction hearing on the same matter. At the hearing, PepsiCo offered evidence of a number of trade secrets and confidential information it desired protected and to which Redmond was privy. First, it identified PCNA's "Strategic Plan," an annually revised document that contains PCNA's plans to compete, its financial goals, and its strategies for manufacturing, production, marketing, packaging, and distribution for the coming three years. Strategic Plans are developed by Weatherup and his staff with input from PCNA's general managers, including

Redmond, and are considered highly confidential. The Strategic Plan derives much of its value from the fact that it is secret and competitors cannot anticipate PCNA's next moves. PCNA managers received the most recent Strategic Plan at a meeting in July, 1994, a meeting Redmond attended. PCNA also presented information at the meeting regarding its plans for Lipton ready-to-drink teas and for All Sport for 1995 and beyond, including new flavors and package sizes.

Second, PepsiCo pointed to PCNA's Annual Operating Plan ("AOP") as a trade secret. The AOP is a national plan for a given year and guides PCNA's financial goals, marketing plans, promotional event calendars, growth expectations, and operational changes in that year. The AOP, which is implemented by PCNA unit General Managers, including Redmond, contains specific information regarding all PCNA initiatives for the forthcoming year. The AOP bears a label that reads "Private and Confidential — Do Not Reproduce" and is considered highly confidential by PCNA managers.

In particular, the AOP contains important and sensitive information about "pricing architecture" — how PCNA prices its products in the marketplace. Pricing architecture covers both a national pricing approach and specific price points for given areas. Pricing architecture also encompasses PCNA's objectives for All Sport and its new age drinks with reference to trade channels, package sizes and other characteristics of both the products and the customers at which the products are aimed. Additionally, PCNA's pricing architecture outlines PCNA's customer development agreements. These agreements between PCNA and retailers provide for the retailer's participation in certain merchandising activities for PCNA products. As with other information contained in the AOP, pricing architecture is highly confidential and would be extremely valuable to a competitor. Knowing PCNA's pricing architecture would allow a competitor to anticipate PCNA's pricing moves and underbid PCNA strategically whenever and wherever the competitor so desired. PepsiCo introduced evidence that Redmond had detailed knowledge of PCNA's pricing architecture and that he was aware of and had been involved in preparing PCNA's customer development agreements with PCNA's California and California-based national customers. Indeed, PepsiCo showed that Redmond, as the General Manager for California, would have been responsible for implementing the pricing architecture guidelines for his business unit.

PepsiCo also showed that Redmond had intimate knowledge of PCNA "attack plans" for specific markets. Pursuant to these plans, PCNA dedicates extra funds to supporting its brands against other brands in selected markets. To use a hypothetical example, PCNA might budget an additional $500,000 to spend in Chicago at a particular time to help All Sport close its market gap with Gatorade. Testimony and documents demonstrated Redmond's awareness of these plans and his participation in drafting some of them.

Finally, PepsiCo offered evidence of PCNA trade secrets regarding innovations in its selling and delivery systems. Under this plan, PCNA is testing a new delivery system that could give PCNA an advantage over its competitors in negotiations with retailers over shelf space and merchandising. Redmond has knowledge of this secret because PCNA, which has invested over a million dollars in developing the system during the past two years, is testing the pilot program in California.

Having shown Redmond's intimate knowledge of PCNA's plans for 1995, PepsiCo argued that Redmond would inevitably disclose that information to Quaker in his new position, at which he would have substantial input as to Gatorade and Snapple pricing, costs, margins, distribution systems, products, packaging and marketing, and could give Quaker an unfair advantage in its upcoming skirmishes with PepsiCo. Redmond and Quaker countered that Redmond's primary initial duties at Quaker as Vice President — Field Operations would be to integrate Gatorade and Snapple distribution and then to manage that distribution as well as the promotion, marketing and sales of these products. Redmond asserted that the integration would be conducted according to a pre-existing plan and that his special knowledge of PCNA strategies would be irrelevant. This irrelevance would derive not only from the fact that Redmond would be implementing pre-existing plans but also from the fact that PCNA and Quaker distribute their products in entirely different ways: PCNA's distribution system is vertically integrated (i.e., PCNA owns the system) and delivers its product directly to retailers, while Quaker ships its product to wholesalers and customer warehouses and relies on independent distributors. The defendants also pointed out that Redmond had signed a confidentiality agreement with Quaker preventing him from disclosing "any confidential information belonging to others," as well as the Quaker Code of Ethics, which prohibits employees from engaging in "illegal or improper acts to acquire a competitor's trade secrets." Redmond additionally promised at the hearing that should he be faced with a situation at Quaker that might involve the use or disclosure of PCNA information, he would seek advice from Quaker's in-house counsel and would refrain from making the decision.

PepsiCo responded to the defendants' representations by pointing out that the evidence did not show that Redmond would simply be implementing a business plan already in place. On the contrary, as of November, 1994, the plan to integrate Gatorade and Snapple distribution consisted of a single distributorship agreement and a two-page "contract terms summary." Such a basic plan would not lend itself to widespread application among the over 300 independent Snapple distributors. Since the integration process would likely face resistance from Snapple distributors and Quaker had no scheme to deal with this probability, Redmond, as the person in charge of the integration, would likely have a great deal of influence on the process. PepsiCo further argued that Snapple's 1995 marketing and promotion plans had not necessarily been completed prior to Redmond's joining Quaker, that Uzzi disagreed with portions of the Snapple plans, and that the plans were open to re-evaluation. Uzzi testified that the plan for integrating Gatorade and Snapple distribution is something that would happen in the future. Redmond would therefore likely have input in remaking these plans, and if he did, he would inevitably be making decisions with PCNA's strategic plans and 1995 AOP in mind. Moreover, PepsiCo continued, diverging testimony made it difficult to know exactly what Redmond would be doing at Quaker. Redmond described his job as "managing the entire sales effort of Gatorade at the field level, possibly including strategic planning," and at least at one point considered his job to be equivalent to that of a Chief Operating Officer. Uzzi, on the other hand, characterized Redmond's position as "primarily and initially to restructure and integrate our — the distribution systems for Snapple and for Gatorade, as per our distribution plan" and then to "execute marketing, promotion and sales plans in the marketplace." Uzzi also denied having given Redmond detailed information about any business plans, while Redmond described such a plan in depth in an affidavit and said that he received the information from Uzzi. Thus, PepsiCo asserted, Redmond would have a high position in the Gatorade hierarchy, and PCNA trade secrets and confidential information would necessarily influence his decisions. Even if Redmond could somehow refrain from relying on this information, as he promised he would, his actions in leaving PCNA, Uzzi's actions in hiring Redmond, and the varying testimony regarding Redmond's new responsibilities, made Redmond's assurances to PepsiCo less than comforting.

On December 15, 1994, the district court issued an order enjoining Redmond from assuming his position at Quaker through May, 1995, and permanently from using or disclosing any PCNA trade secrets or confidential information. The court, which completely adopted PepsiCo's position, found that Redmond's new job posed a clear threat of misappropriation of trade secrets and confidential information that could be enjoined under Illinois statutory and common law. The court also emphasized Redmond's lack of forthrightness both in his activities before accepting his job with Quaker and in his testimony as factors leading the court to believe the threat of misappropriation was real. This appeal followed.

## II.

Both parties agree that the primary issue on appeal is whether the district court correctly concluded that PepsiCo had a reasonable likelihood of success on its various claims for trade secret misappropriation and breach of a confidentiality agreement.

## A.

[The court affirmed that PepsiCo's marketing and distribution plans were trade secrets.]

The question of threatened or inevitable misappropriation in this case lies at the heart of a basic tension in trade secret law. Trade secret law serves to protect "standards of commercial morality" and "encourage [ ] invention and innovation" while maintaining "the public interest in having free and open competition in the manufacture and sale of unpatented goods." §IL.03 at IL-12. Yet that same law should not prevent workers from pursuing their livelihoods when they leave their current positions. It has been said that federal age discrimination law does not guarantee tenure for older employees. Similarly, trade secret law does not provide a reserve clause for solicitous employers.

This tension is particularly exacerbated when a plaintiff sues to prevent not the actual misappropriation of trade secrets but the mere threat that it will occur. While the [Illinois Trade Secret Act or ITSA] plainly permits a court to enjoin the threat of misappropriation of trade secrets, there is little law in Illinois or in this circuit establishing what constitutes threatened or inevitable misappropriation.[7] Indeed, there are only two cases in this circuit that address the issue: *Teradyne, Inc. v. Clear Communications Corp.*, 707 F. Supp. 353 (N.D. Ill 1989), and *AMP Inc. v. Fleischhacker*, 823 F.2d 1199 (7th Cir. 1987).

In *Teradyne*, Teradyne alleged that a competitor, Clear Communications, had lured employees away from Teradyne and intended to employ them in the same field. In an insightful opinion, Judge Zagel observed that "[t]hreatened misappropriation can be enjoined under Illinois law" where there is a "high degree of probability of inevitable and immediate . . . use of . . . trade secrets." *Teradyne*, 707 F. Supp. at 356. Judge Zagel held, however, that Teradyne's complaint failed to state a claim because Teradyne did not allege "that defendants have in fact threatened to use Teradyne's secrets or that they will inevitably do so." Teradyne's claims would have passed Rule 12(b)(6) muster had they properly alleged inevitable disclosure, including a statement that Clear intended to use Teradyne's trade secrets or that the former Teradyne employees had disavowed their confidentiality agreements with Teradyne, or an allegation that Clear could not operate without Teradyne's secrets. However,

> [t]he defendants' claimed acts, working for Teradyne, knowing its business, leaving its business, hiring employees from Teradyne and entering the same field (though in a market not yet serviced by Teradyne) do not state a claim of threatened misappropriation. All that is alleged, at bottom, is that defendants could misuse plaintiff's secrets, and plaintiffs fear they will. This is not enough. It may be that little more is needed, but falling a little short is still falling short.

*Id.* at 357.

In *AMP*, we affirmed the denial of a preliminary injunction on the grounds that the plaintiff AMP had failed to show either the existence of any trade secrets or the likelihood that defendant Fleischhacker, a former AMP employee, would compromise those secrets or any other confidential business information. AMP, which produced electrical and electronic connection devices, argued that Fleischhacker's new position at AMP's competitor would inevitably lead him to compromise AMP's trade secrets regarding the manufacture of connectors. *AMP*, 823 F.2d at 1207. In rejecting that argument, we emphasized that the mere fact that a person assumed a similar position at a competitor does not, without more, make it "inevitable that he will use or disclose . . . trade secret information" so as to "demonstrate irreparable injury." *Id.*

It should be noted that *AMP*, which we decided in 1987, predates the ITSA, which took effect in 1988. The ITSA abolishes any common law remedies or authority contrary to its own terms. 765 ILCS 1065/8. The ITSA does not, however, represent a major deviation from the Illinois

---

7. The ITSA definition of misappropriation relevant to this discussion is "the disclosure or use of a trade secret of a person without express or implied consent by another person who . . . at the time of disclosure or use, knew or had reason to know that the knowledge of the trade secret was . . . acquired under circumstances giving rise to a duty to maintain its secrecy. . . ." 765 ILCS 1065/2(b).

common law of unfair trade practices. The ITSA mostly codifies rather than modifies the common law doctrine that preceded it. Thus, we believe that *AMP* continues to reflect the proper standard under Illinois's current statutory scheme.

The ITSA, *Teradyne*, and *AMP* lead to the same conclusion: a plaintiff may prove a claim of trade secret misappropriation by demonstrating that defendant's new employment will inevitably lead him to rely on the plaintiff's trade secrets. The defendants are incorrect that Illinois law does not allow a court to enjoin the "inevitable" disclosure of trade secrets. Questions remain, however, as to what constitutes inevitable misappropriation and whether PepsiCo's submissions rise above those of the *Teradyne* and *AMP* plaintiffs and meet that standard. We hold that they do.

PepsiCo presented substantial evidence at the preliminary injunction hearing that Redmond possessed extensive and intimate knowledge about PCNA's strategic goals for 1995 in sports drinks and new age drinks. The district court concluded on the basis of that presentation that unless Redmond possessed an uncanny ability to compartmentalize information, he would necessarily be making decisions about Gatorade and Snapple by relying on his knowledge of PCNA trade secrets. It is not the "general skills and knowledge acquired during his tenure with" PepsiCo that PepsiCo seeks to keep from falling into Quaker's hands, but rather "the particularized plans or processes developed by [PCNA] and disclosed to him while the employer-employee relationship existed, which are unknown to others in the industry and which give the employer an advantage over his competitors." *AMP*, 823 F.2d at 1202. The *Teradyne* and *AMP* plaintiffs could do nothing more than assert that skilled employees were taking their skills elsewhere; PepsiCo has done much more.

Admittedly, PepsiCo has not brought a traditional trade secret case, in which a former employee has knowledge of a special manufacturing process or customer list and can give a competitor an unfair advantage by transferring the technology or customers to that competitor. PepsiCo has not contended that Quaker has stolen the All Sport formula or its list of distributors. Rather PepsiCo has asserted that Redmond cannot help but rely on PCNA trade secrets as he helps plot Gatorade and Snapple's new course, and that these secrets will enable Quaker to achieve a substantial advantage by knowing exactly how PCNA will price, distribute, and market its sports drinks and new age drinks and being able to respond strategically. This type of trade secret problem may arise less often, but it nevertheless falls within the realm of trade secret protection under the present circumstances.[8]

Quaker and Redmond assert that they have not and do not intend to use whatever confidential information Redmond has by virtue of his former employment. They point out that Redmond has already signed an agreement with Quaker not to disclose any trade secrets or confidential information gleaned from his earlier employment. They also note with regard to

---

8. PepsiCo does contend that Quaker may well misappropriate its new, trade-secret distribution system because Snapple has a similar system and Quaker is not familiar with it. This argument approaches the sort of speculation we rejected in *AMP* and Judge Zagel rejected in *Teradyne*. We need not pass on its validity, however, because it is not central to PepsiCo's case.

distribution systems that even if Quaker wanted to steal information about PCNA's distribution plans, they would be completely useless in attempting to integrate the Gatorade and Snapple beverage lines.

The defendants' arguments fall somewhat short of the mark. Again, the danger of misappropriation in the present case is not that Quaker threatens to use PCNA's secrets to create distribution systems or co-opt PCNA's advertising and marketing ideas. Rather, PepsiCo believes that Quaker, unfairly armed with knowledge of PCNA's plans, will be able to anticipate its distribution, packaging, pricing, and marketing moves. Redmond and Quaker even concede that Redmond might be faced with a decision that could be influenced by certain confidential information that he obtained while at PepsiCo. In other words, PepsiCo finds itself in the position of a coach, one of whose players has left, playbook in hand, to join the opposing team before the big game. Quaker and Redmond's protestations that their distribution systems and plans are entirely different from PCNA's are thus not really responsive.

The district court also concluded from the evidence that Uzzi's actions in hiring Redmond and Redmond's actions in pursuing and accepting his new job demonstrated a lack of candor on their part and proof of their willingness to misuse PCNA trade secrets, findings Quaker and Redmond vigorously challenge. The court expressly found that:

> Redmond's lack of forthrightness on some occasions, and out and out lies on others, in the period between the time he accepted the position with defendant Quaker and when he informed plaintiff that he had accepted that position leads the court to conclude that defendant Redmond could not be trusted to act with the necessary sensitivity and good faith under the circumstances in which the only practical verification that he was not using plaintiff's secrets would be defendant Redmond's word to that effect.

The facts of the case do not ineluctably dictate the district court's conclusion. Redmond's ambiguous behavior toward his PepsiCo superiors might have been nothing more than an attempt to gain leverage in employment negotiations. The discrepancy between Redmond's and Uzzi's comprehension of what Redmond's job would entail may well have been a simple misunderstanding. The court also pointed out that Quaker, through Uzzi, seemed to express an unnatural interest in hiring PCNA employees: all three of the people interviewed for the position Redmond ultimately accepted worked at PCNA. Uzzi may well have focused on recruiting PCNA employees because he knew they were good and not because of their confidential knowledge. Nonetheless, the district court, after listening to the witnesses, determined otherwise. That conclusion was not an abuse of discretion.

Thus, when we couple the demonstrated inevitability that Redmond would rely on PCNA trade secrets in his new job at Quaker with the district court's reluctance to believe that Redmond would refrain from disclosing these secrets in his new position (or that Quaker would ensure Redmond did not disclose them), we conclude that the district court correctly decided that PepsiCo demonstrated a likelihood of success on its statutory claim of trade secret misappropriation.

# Comments

1. *Trade Secrets and Employer-Employee Relationships.* It is not uncommon for an employee to leave his current position and go to work for a competitor or to start his own company. Occupational mobility is natural and something to be encouraged. But matters can turn controversial when trade secrets are involved. On the one hand, the former employer's incentive to innovate will suffer if his erstwhile employee is permitted to take the employer's trade secrets and use them in competition with the employer. And from an efficiency perspective, an employer should be encouraged to disclose his trade secrets to certain employees and foster communication among employees, rather than overly compartmentalize his trade secrets. On the other hand, the employee has an interest in fulfilling his livelihood and pursuing his occupation of choice. The mobile employee is more likely to be exposed to and work with other similarly skilled workers, leading to the development of a higher skill set, synergies, and informational spillovers that result in more innovations and greater social welfare.

To address this potential problem, employers frequently require their employees to sign an employment agreement that requires the employee to maintain the trade secrets in confidence and to use them only in a manner consistent with his employment. An employer can certainly prevent a former employee from disclosing the employer's trade secrets to a third party, but the employee is free to use his general knowledge or skill for his own benefit or the benefit of others. Where to draw the line between trade secret and general knowledge is difficult and controversial.

In addition, employees are often required to sign a noncompete agreement, which, as the name suggests, seeks to prevent the employee from entering into competition with the employer for a period of time and within a particular geographic area. These clauses, as *Procter & Gamble* held, are enforceable, but they must be, among other things, reasonable in temporal and geographic scope. Several states subject noncompete agreements to significant scrutiny. For example, California does not enforce noncompete agreements unless they narrowly constrain competition or only seek to preclude former employees from disclosing trade secrets. The noncompete agreement in *Procter & Gamble* will likely not be recognized in California. *See Walia v. Aetna*, 113 Cal. Rptr. 2d 737 (2001) and Cal. Bus. & Prof. Code, §16600.

2. *Doctrine of Inevitable Disclosure.* A former employee is likely to seek a job that is similar (or requires the same or similar skill set) or in the same industry to the one from which he departed. This means that there may be a high probability that the employee will go to work for his former employer's competitor. As such, the employee may inevitably disclose his former employer's trade secrets even though that is not his intention. Should the former employee be enjoined from working for his new employer or from working in a particular capacity for his new employer? Some trade secret owners have made this argument with mixed success. *PepsiCo* provided one result, and has led to an increase in inevitable disclosure claims. Several jurisdictions allow for application of the inevi-

table disclosure doctrine. *See Maxxim Medical, Inc. v. Michelson*, 51 F. Supp. 2d 773, 776 (S.D. Tex. 1999) (noting that "*Redmond* has been widely followed"). Some jurisdictions have established a list of factors that must be considered when applying inevitable disclosure. *See Merck & Co., Inc. v. Lyon*, 941 F. Supp. 1443, 1459-1460 (M.D.N.C. 1996) ("(1) The circumstances surrounding the termination of employment, (2) the importance of the employee's job or position, (3) the type of work performed by the employee, and (4) the kind of information sought to be protected and the value of the information or the need of the competitor for it"). *But see Bayer Corp. v. Roche Molecular Systems, Inc.*, 72 F. Supp. 2d 1111, 1120 (N.D. Cal. 1999) ("the Court holds that California trade-secrets law does not recognize the theory of inevitable disclosure; indeed, such a rule would run counter to the strong public policy in California favoring employee mobility. A trade-secrets plaintiff must show an actual use or an actual threat.").

# UNIFORM TRADE SECRETS ACT

## §1. Definitions

As used in this Act, unless the context requires otherwise:

(1) "Improper means" includes theft, bribery, misrepresentation, breach or inducement of a breach of duty to maintain secrecy, or espionage through electronic or other means.

(2) "Misappropriation" means: (i) acquisition of a trade secret of another by a person who knows or has reason to know that the trade secret was acquired by improper means; or (ii) disclosure or use of a trade secret of another without express or implied consent by a person who (A) used improper means to acquire knowledge of the trade secret; or (B) at the time of disclosure or use knew or had reason to know that his knowledge of the trade secret was (I) derived from or through a person who has utilized improper means to acquire it; (II) acquired under circumstances giving rise to a duty to maintain its secrecy or limit its use; or (III) derived from or through a person who owed a duty to the person seeking relief to maintain its secrecy or limit its use; or (C) before a material change of his position, knew or had reason to know that it was a trade secret and that knowledge of it had been acquired by accident or mistake.

(3) "Person" means a natural person, corporation, business trust, estate, trust, partnership, association, joint venture, government, governmental subdivision or agency, or any other legal or commercial entity.

(4) "Trade secret" means information, including a formula, pattern, compilation, program device, method, technique, or process, that: (i) derives independent economic value, actual or potential, from not being generally known to, and not being readily ascertainable by proper means by, other persons who can obtain economic value from its disclosure or use, and (ii) is the subject of efforts that are reasonable under the circumstances to maintain its secrecy.

# CHAPTER
# 15

# Rights in Ideas

## INTRODUCTION

In most rights in ideas cases, one person submits an unsolicited idea to another person or firm that subsequently uses the idea without payment. The submitter usually seeks damages under a contract theory and sometimes includes a property or torts theory. Contract theories may include breach of an express or implied-in-fact contract or quasi-contract, which is also referred to as an unjust enrichment theory. The property and torts theories are related and classified interchangeably as either misappropriation or conversion claims. All of these legal theories have their roots in the common law and thus state law governs rights in ideas.

Federal IP regimes do not apply to the protection of ideas because copyright law protects only the expression of ideas, not ideas themselves; and patent law only protects ideas that have gone through the extensive scrutiny required by the patentability requirements. The law of ideas does have a concreteness requirement, which demands that the idea in question be fairly well developed, certainly beyond mere abstraction. This requirement, while somewhat analogous to patent law's reduction to practice, is different in that reduction to practice requires the invention to be built and work for its intended purpose or set forth on paper in much greater detail than concreteness requires.

The general rule is that novelty and concreteness are required for all idea law claims, though some states have created significant exceptions to this rule. The general rule and its exceptions are illustrated and discussed in this chapter. This chapter begins, however, with a discussion of the contract theories on which most idea law suits are brought.

## A. CONTRACT LAW BASIS FOR IDEA LAW SUITS

The principal case of *Reeves v. Alyeska Pipeline Service Co.* provides a nice discussion of the various contractual theories of recovery related to rights in ideas, including express contract, contract implied-in-law (quasi-contract) and implied-in-fact, and promissory estoppel. Each has different requirements derived from contract law. The court briefly discusses the relationship between the novelty requirement and contract law protection of ideas, though details of that relationship are left to the next section.

## REEVES v. ALYESKA PIPELINE SERVICE CO.

### 926 P.2d 1130 (Alaska 1996)

PER CURIAM.

## I. INTRODUCTION

This case raises issues concerning the protection of ideas. It arises out of John Reeves' claims that in 1991 Alyeska Pipeline Service Company (Alyeska) appropriated his idea for a visitor center at a popular turnout overlooking the Trans-Alaska Pipeline....

## II. FACTS AND PROCEEDINGS

In 1985 Alyeska created a visitor turnout at Mile 9 of the Steese Highway between Fox and Fairbanks. The turnout had informational signs and provided visitors a view of the Trans-Alaska Pipeline. Before Alyeska constructed the turnout, visitors gained access to the pipeline by a nearby road and trespassed on the Trans-Alaska Pipeline right-of-way.

John Reeves, owner of Gold Dredge No. 8, a tourist attraction outside Fairbanks and near the turnout, contacted Alyeska in January 1991 to discuss a tourism idea he had. He spoke with Keith Burke, Alyeska's Fairbanks Manager. After receiving Burke's assurance that the tourism idea was "between us," Reeves orally disclosed his idea to build a visitor center at the turnout. He proposed that Alyeska lease him the land and he build the center, sell Alyeska merchandise, and display a "pig"[2] and a cross-section of pipe.

Burke told him the idea "look[ed] good" and asked Reeves to submit a written proposal, which Reeves did two days later. The proposal explained Reeves' idea of operating a visitor center on land leased to him by Alyeska. The proposal included plans to provide small tours, display a "pig," pipe valve, and section of pipe, sell refreshments and pipeline memorabilia, and plant corn and cabbage.

After submitting the proposal, Reeves met with Burke once again. At this meeting Burke told Reeves the proposal looked good and was exactly what he wanted. In Reeves' words, Burke told him, "We're going to do this deal, and I'm going to have my Anchorage lawyers draw it." Reeves claimed he and Burke envisioned that the visitor center would be operating by the 1991 summer tourist season.

Reeves alleges that Alyeska agreed during this meeting (1) to grant access to the turnout for twenty years; (2) to allow Reeves to construct

---

2. A "pig" is a device which passes through the pipeline to clean interior pipe walls, survey interior pipe shape and detect corrosion.

and operate an information center; and (3) to allow Reeves to sell merchandise and charge a $2.00 admission fee. Reeves stated that, in exchange, he agreed to pay Alyeska ten percent of gross receipts.

Over the next several months, Burke allegedly told Reeves that the deal was "looking good" and not to worry because it takes time for a large corporation to move. However, in spring 1991, Burke told Reeves that the visitor center was such a good idea that Alyeska was going to implement it without Reeves. By August 1991 Alyeska had installed a portable building at the turnout to serve as a visitor center; it built a permanent log cabin structure in 1992.

The members of the Alyeska Pipeline Club North (APCN) operated the visitor center and sold T-shirts, hats, and other items.[3] APCN does not charge admission. A section of pipeline and a "pig" are on display. APCN employees provide information and answer visitors' questions. Members of APCN had suggested in 1987 that Alyeska create a visitor center at the turnout. However, Alyeska had rejected the idea at that time. Before meeting with Reeves, Burke did not know that APCN's visitor center idea had been raised and rejected by Alyeska in 1987.

Approximately 100,000 people visited the visitor center each summer in 1992 and 1993. It grossed over $50,000 in sales each year. The net profit for 1993 was calculated to be $5,000-$15,000. APCN received all the profit.

Reeves filed suit in May 1993. By amended complaint, he [brought claims of breach of oral contract, promissory estoppel, breach of implied contract, and quasi contract (unjust enrichment and quantum meruit)]. Judge Charles R. Pengilly granted Alyeska's motion for summary judgment on all claims; Reeves appeals.

### III. DISCUSSION

#### A. PROTECTION OF IDEAS

The law pertaining to the protection of ideas must reconcile the public's interest in access to new ideas with the perceived injustice of permitting some to exploit commercially the ideas of others. Federal law addresses the protection of new inventions and the expression of ideas. Federal patent law protects inventors of novel, nonobvious, and useful inventions by excluding others from "making, using, or selling the invention" for a period of seventeen years. Federal copyright law protects an individual's tangible *expression* of an idea, but not the intangible idea itself. Copyright law creates a monopoly for the author that allows him or her to benefit economically from the author's creative efforts. It does not create a monopoly on the idea from which the expression originates; the idea remains available for all to use. Reeves' claims do not fall under these federal protections because his idea is not a new invention, nor is it expressed in a copyrighted work. Nevertheless, federal law is not the only protection available to individuals and their ideas.

Creating a middle ground between no protection and the legal monopolies created by patent and copyright law, courts have protected ideas

---

3. Alyeska Pipeline Club North is a non-profit corporation run by Alyeska employees. It raises money to fund activities such as picnics and Christmas parties for Alyeska employees.

under a variety of contract and contract-like theories. These theories protect individuals who spend their time and energy developing ideas that may benefit others. It would be inequitable to prevent these individuals from obtaining legally enforceable compensation from those who voluntarily choose to benefit from the services of the "idea-person."...*Desny v. Wilder,* 299 P.2d 257, 265 (1956). The scope of idea protection, although primarily raised in the entertainment field, is not limited to that industry; it may also apply to business and scientific ideas.

We have not had occasion to address these theories in the context of the protection of ideas. In addressing each of Reeves' claims we must determine whether the special nature of ideas affects the application of traditional contract and contract-like claims. In making these determinations we are mindful of the competing policies of retaining the free exchange of ideas and compensating those who develop and market their ideas. On the one hand, protecting ideas by providing compensation to the author for their use or appropriation rewards the idea person and encourages the development of creative and intellectual ideas which will benefit humankind. On the other hand, protecting ideas also inevitably restricts their free use, potentially delaying or restricting the benefit any given idea might confer on society.

Reeves argues that requiring novelty and originality, as did the trial court, erroneously imports property theories into contract-based claims. He contends that so long as the parties bargained for the disclosure of the idea, the disclosure serves as consideration and the idea itself need not have the qualities of property. Alyeska argues that novelty and originality should be employed as limiting factors in idea cases because these cases are based on a theory of idea as intellectual property. Alyeska contends that in order to be protected, an idea must have "not been suggested to or known by the public at any prior time."

We find that the manner in which requirements such as novelty or originality are applied depends largely on which theory of recovery is pursued. Thus, we will address the parties' arguments concerning novelty as they apply to each of Reeves' theories of recovery.

### B. EXPRESS CONTRACT CLAIMS

Reeves argues that he and Alyeska entered into three different oral contracts: (1) a confidentiality or disclosure agreement by which Alyeska promised not to use Reeves' idea without his participation, if Reeves disclosed the idea; (2) a lease agreement by which Alyeska promised to lease the turnout to Reeves in exchange for a percentage of the center's profits; and (3) a memorialization agreement by which Alyeska promised to commit the agreement to writing.

#### 1. The Disclosure Agreement

Reeves alleges that in exchange for the disclosure of his idea, Alyeska promised to keep the idea confidential and not to use the idea without entering into a contract with Reeves to implement the idea. Reeves' deposition testimony, when all inferences are taken in his favor, supports the existence of a disclosure agreement. Reeves testified that in his early conversations with Burke, he told Burke that he was in the tourism industry and had an idea that would help Alyeska. Reeves stated that Burke told him the idea "was between us." Reeves testified that he "didn't offer anything to Keith Burke until [Reeves] was told by [Burke] that we had a deal. This was between me and him, and this was going no place else." Reeves also testified that Burke had promised confidentiality and that Reeves believed that he and Burke had a "done deal."

Alyeska . . . argues that the statute of frauds applies because the alleged agreement concerns a lease for a period longer than one year and because performance would not be completed within one year.[8]

We conclude that the statute of frauds does not apply to the alleged disclosure agreement. That alleged agreement was to be completed within one year. If Alyeska chose to implement the idea, it was to enter into a lease agreement with Reeves by the summer tourist season. Moreover, Reeves' disclosure to Alyeska constituted full performance of his side of the contract for disclosure. The statute of frauds consequently does not apply. [The court held that the statute of frauds did apply to the oral lease and the oral memorialization agreements, making them unenforceable.]

### C. Implied-in-Fact Contract

The trial court's opinion did not address whether Reeves established a contract implied-in-fact. Reeves argues that he "submitted uncontroverted evidence sufficient to find as a matter of law that Alyeska's actions established a contract implied in fact." We conclude that Alyeska failed to carry its burden of showing that it is entitled to judgment as a matter of law on this claim.

Reeves has made out a prima facie case for an implied contract. We have held that an implied-in-fact contract, like an express contract, is based on the intentions of the parties. "It arises where the court finds from the surrounding facts and circumstances that the parties intended to make a contract but failed to articulate their promises and the court merely implies what it feels the parties really intended." *Martens v. Metzgar*, 524 P.2d 666, 672 (Alaska 1974).

In *Aliotti v. R. Dakin & Co.*, 831 F.2d 898, 902 (9th Cir. 1987), the court listed the requirements for demonstrating an implied-in-fact contract under California law:

> [O]ne must show: that he or she prepared the work; that he or she disclosed the work to the offeree for sale; under all circumstances attending disclosure it can be concluded that the offeree voluntarily accepted the disclosure

---

8. AS 09.25.010, the statute of frauds, provides in pertinent part:

(a) In the following cases and under the following conditions an agreement, promise, or undertaking is unenforceable unless it or some note or memorandum of it is in writing and subscribed by the party charged or by an agent of that party:

(1) an agreement that by its terms is not to be performed within a year from the making of it;

. . . .

(6) an agreement for leasing for a longer period than one year, or for the sale of real property. . . .

knowing the conditions on which it was tendered (i.e., the offeree must have the opportunity to reject the attempted disclosure if the conditions were unacceptable); and the reasonable value of the work.

There are three primary factual scenarios under which ideas may be submitted to another. The first involves an unsolicited submission that is involuntarily received. The idea is submitted without warning; it is transmitted before the recipient has taken any action which would indicate a promise to pay for the submission. Under this scenario, a contract will not be implied.

The second involves an unsolicited submission that is voluntarily received. In this situation, the idea person typically gives the recipient advance warning that an idea is to be disclosed; the recipient has an opportunity to stop the disclosure, but through inaction allows the idea to be disclosed. Under California law, if the recipient at the time of disclosure understands that the idea person expects to be paid for the disclosure of the idea, and does not attempt to stop the disclosure, inaction may be seen as consent to a contract.

This view has been criticized as unfairly placing a duty on the recipient to take active measures to stop the submission. The critics argue that inaction generally should not be considered an expression of consent to a contract.

We believe that a contract should not be implied under this scenario. An implied-in-fact contract is based on circumstances that demonstrate that the parties intended to form a contract but failed to articulate their promises. Only under exceptional circumstances would inaction demonstrate an intent to enter a contract.

The third scenario involves a solicited submission. Here, a request by the recipient for disclosure of the idea usually implies a promise to pay for the idea if the recipient uses it. Nimmer, *supra* §16.05[D] at 16-40. Nimmer states,

> The element of solicitation of plaintiff's idea by defendant is therefore of great importance in establishing an implied contract. If defendant makes such a request, even if he attempts to frame the request in ambiguous or exculpatory language, most courts will nevertheless imply a promise to pay if the idea is used.

*Id.* at 16-40 to 16-41.

Reeves argues that Alyeska solicited his idea. He alleges that Burke asked him what the idea was, and later requested a written proposal. He contends that the request and Alyeska's later use of the idea created an implied contract for payment. These allegations are sufficient to survive summary judgment. A reasonable fact-finder could determine that Burke's actions implied a promise to pay for the disclosure of Reeves' idea. A fact-finder could also determine that Reeves volunteered the idea before Burke took any affirmative action that would indicate an agreement to pay for the disclosure. These possible conclusions present genuine issues of material fact.

Relying largely on cases from New York, Alyeska argues that novelty and originality should be required in an implied-in-fact claim. Reeves responds that we should follow California's example and not require novelty as an essential element of this sort of claim.

Idea-based claims arise most frequently in the entertainment centers of New York and California, but New York requires novelty, whereas California does not. We prefer the California approach. An idea may be valuable to the recipient merely because of its timing or the manner in which it is presented. In *Chandler v. Roach*, 319 P.2d 776 (1957), the court stated that "the fact that the [recipient of the idea] may later determine, with a little thinking, that he could have had the same ideas and could thereby have saved considerable money for himself, is no defense against the claim of the [idea person]. This is so even though the material to be purchased is abstract and unprotected material." *Id.* 319 P.2d at 781.

Implied-in-fact contracts are closely related to express contracts. Each requires the parties to form an intent to enter into a contract. It is ordinarily not the court's role to evaluate the adequacy of the consideration agreed upon by the parties. The bargain should be left in the hands of the parties. If parties voluntarily choose to bargain for an individual's services in disclosing or developing a non-novel or unoriginal idea, they have the power to do so. The *Desny* court analogized the services of a writer to the services of a doctor or lawyer and determined there was little difference; each may provide a product that is not novel or original. *Desny*, 299 P.2d at 266. It held that it would not impose an additional requirement of novelty on the work. Although Reeves is not a writer, his ideas are entitled to no less protection than those of writers, doctors, or lawyers. Therefore, Reeves should be given the opportunity to prove the existence of an implied-in-fact contract for disclosure of his idea.

### D. PROMISSORY ESTOPPEL

Reeves claims that the trial court erred in granting summary judgment to Alyeska on his promissory estoppel claim. He argues that there were genuine fact questions. Alyeska argues that Reeves presented no evidence of detrimental reliance.

Under Alaska law, a promissory estoppel claim has four requirements:

1) The action induced amounts to a substantial change of position;
2) it was either actually foreseen or reasonably foreseeable by the promisor;
3) an actual promise was made and itself induced the action or forbearance in reliance thereon; and
4) enforcement is necessary in the interest of justice.

*Zeman*, 699 P.2d at 1284. Reference to a set formula does not determine whether particular promises and actions satisfy the requirements of promissory estoppel; all circumstances are to be considered.

Reeves contends that in reliance on promises made by Alyeska in context of separate disclosure, lease, and memorialization agreements, he took two actions that changed his position: he disclosed the idea, and he failed to hire an attorney to draft the contract. Although forbearance may sometimes be considered an action that changes one's position, Reeves' failure to hire an attorney did not amount to a substantial change of position. As noted above, even if Reeves had presented a written contract to Alyeska, no evidence permits an inference Alyeska would have executed it.

By disclosing his idea, however, Reeves substantially changed his position. Once he disclosed the idea, Reeves' ability to bargain for terms was significantly reduced. It was reasonably foreseeable that a promise of confidentiality and a promise to allow Reeves to participate in any use of the idea would induce disclosure. There was evidence permitting an inference Alyeska's alleged promises induced the disclosure. Consequently, genuine fact disputes exist regarding the first three requirements for promissory estoppel.

The fourth requirement, that enforcement is necessary in the interest of justice, presents fact questions that ordinarily should not be decided on summary judgment. The record demonstrates that this issue presents fact questions. It is therefore necessary to remand Reeves' promissory estoppel claim based on his disclosure of the idea in reliance on promises of confidentiality and participation.[16]

### E. QUASI-CONTRACT CLAIM

Reeves argues that Alyeska was unjustly enriched because it solicited and received Reeves' services, ideas, and opinions without compensating Reeves. He argues that the trial court erred in granting summary judgment to Alyeska on his quasi-contract cause of action.[17]

We have required the following three elements for a quasi-contract claim:

1) a benefit conferred upon the defendant by the plaintiff;
2) appreciation by the defendant of such benefit; and
3) acceptance and retention by the defendant of such benefit under such circumstances that it would be inequitable for him to retain it without paying the value thereof.

*Alaska Sales and Serv., Inc. v. Millet*, 735 P.2d 743, 746 (Alaska 1987). Quasi-contracts are "judicially-created obligations to do justice." *Id.* "Consequently, the obligation to make restitution that arises in quasi-contract is not based upon any agreement between the parties, objective or subjective." *Id.*

The trial court understood Reeves to be arguing that his idea was a property right that was stolen by Alyeska. Reeves, however, argues that "Alyeska took Reeves' concept, proposal *and services* without any payment to Reeves." (Emphasis added.) Reeves' quasi-contract claims must be divided into two categories. His claim that Alyeska appropriated his idea for a visitor center is necessarily a property-based claim that seeks recovery for the value of the idea itself; Reeves seeks a recovery based on "his" idea. His claims that Alyeska benefitted from his proposal and services, however,

---

16. Alyeska argues that a promissory estoppel claim based on an idea requires a showing of novelty. However, Alyeska does not explain why novelty is required for a promissory estoppel claim and none of the cases it cites addresses promissory estoppel claims. We therefore treat this argument as abandoned. . . .

17. The concepts of quasi-contract, unjust enrichment, contract implied in law, and quantum meruit are very similar and interrelated. *Alaska Sales & Service, Inc. v. Millet*, 735 P.2d 743, 746 n. 6 (Alaska 1987). Unjust enrichment is not itself a theory of recovery. "Rather, it is a prerequisite for the enforcement of the doctrine of restitution; that is, if there is no unjust enrichment, there is no basis for restitution." *Id.* at 746. Restitution also is not a cause of action; it is a remedy for various causes of action. Quasi-contract is one of the causes of action Reeves has pursued.

do not necessarily rely on the visitor center idea being property; these claims are based on his services of disclosing and drafting the proposal. The property and non-property claims are treated differently.

An idea is usually not regarded as property because our concept of property implies something that can be owned and possessed to the exclusion of others. To protect an idea under a property theory requires that the idea possess property-like traits. Courts consider the elements of novelty or originality necessary for a claim of "ownership" in an idea or concept. These elements distinguish protectable ideas from ordinary ideas that are freely available for others to use. It is the element of originality or novelty that lends value to the idea itself.

If the idea is not distinguished in this manner, its use cannot satisfy the requirements of a quasi-contract claim. The idea, even if beneficial to the defendant, cannot be conferred if the plaintiff has no right of possession. With no right of possession, the idea cannot be said to have been conferred by the plaintiff.[18] Despite Reeves' protestations, the idea of establishing a visitor center near the pipeline is neither original nor novel.[19]

Nevertheless, not all of Reeves' quasi-contract claims require that his idea be considered property and consequently novel or original. Reeves argues that Alyeska was unjustly enriched "by Reeves' efforts on its behalf, not merely on the 'concept that [Reeves'] idea was intellectual property.'" Therefore, we must analyze whether the parties' transactions give rise to a quasi-contract.

The facts alleged by Reeves demonstrate that Burke specifically asked Reeves to draw up a proposal and that Alyeska was going to "do this deal." There is also evidence Reeves was familiar with the Fairbanks summer tourist industry and had special expertise in that area. These facts present a genuine issue of fact as to whether Alyeska benefited from Reeves' experience or his written plan. Thus, there is a question of fact whether Reeves' idea had value to Alyeska in its timing or in how it was presented, rather than in its novelty or originality. Reeves' endorsement of the idea, in combination with his experience in the Fairbanks tourism industry, may have also been valuable to Alyeska. The fact that Alyeska rejected a similar idea in 1987 may indicate that some feature of Reeves' plan or presentation caused Alyeska to go forward with a visitor center. If Reeves' services unjustly enriched Alyeska, he should be compensated for the value of those services....

## IV.  CONCLUSION

For the reasons stated above, we REVERSE that part of the summary judgment entered for Alyeska on Reeves' express contract [relating to disclosure], implied contract, promissory estoppel, [and] quasi-contract

18.  The court correctly granted summary judgment on Reeves' conversion claim for the same reason. If an idea is not considered property, it cannot be converted.

19.  There may be some question about whether the idea was novel to Burke because he had not heard that in 1987 Alyeska Pipeline Club North had suggested the same idea. Reeves argues that the idea was novel as to Alyeska because Burke did not know of the rejected 1987 proposal until after he contracted with Reeves. The visitor center idea was not novel to Alyeska. It was aware of the 1987 visitor center proposal, and it already operated a visitor center in Valdez. Burke's ignorance of the specific 1987 proposal does not make the visitor center idea novel.

...and remand to the trial court for further proceedings consistent with this opinion.

## Comments

1. ***Implied-in-Fact Contracts.*** When there is no express contract, a court may nonetheless find a contractual relationship or treat the parties "as if" they had formed a contract under either an implied-in-fact or implied-in-law contract theory. An implied-in-fact contract exists when the parties manifest an intention to be bound, but their intention is conveyed through conduct, circumstances, or ordinary course of dealing rather than words or language. According to the Restatement (Second) of Contracts §4, cmt a, there is no difference in legal effect between express and implied-in-fact contracts. The difference rather "lies merely in the mode of manifesting assent. Just as assent may be manifested by words or other conduct, sometimes including silence, so intention to make a promise may be manifested in language or by implication from other circumstances, including course of dealing or usage of trade or course of performance." Contracts students may recall the well-known case of *Wood v. Duff-Gordon,* 118 N.E. 214 (N.Y. 1917), in which Justice Cardozo found that Wood had an implied obligation to market Lady Duff Gordon's endorsement and designs because "[u]nless he gave his efforts, she could never get anything." The implied-in-fact obligation was not based on equitable principles, but on the idea that, even though the contract did not say that this obligation existed, the parties must have meant for it to exist or the contract would be meaningless.

2. ***Implied-in-Law Contracts.*** Implied-in-law contracts are sometimes referred to as quasi-contracts. A quasi-contract is not based on the intention of the parties to exchange performances. Rather, according to the Restatement (Second) of Contracts §4 cmt. b, quasi-contracts "are obligations created by law for reasons of justice." In other words, quasi- or implied-in-law contracts arise from principles of equity. Accordingly, an idea submitter may not officiously thrust an idea upon a recipient and expect payment. Nor may an idea submitter expect payment if the recipient did not use the idea.

   An example of the distinction between legal and equitable claims can be seen in the *Alyeska* court's treatment of Reeves' claims. The court interpreted Reeves' claims as having both a legal and an equitable component. Express and implied-in-fact contract claims and property and tort law claims are legal claims. Many states require that the disclosed ideas forming the bases of these claims be novel and original. Their reasoning is that well-known ideas are in the public domain and cannot be owned by the plaintiff. If the plaintiff gives up nothing he owns, there is no consideration for the contract. California is widely known as a state that does not have these requirements. Its reasoning is that courts do not customarily question the adequacy of consideration and also that, under the circumstances, the plaintiff may have given up something of value. In *Reeves* the Alaska court followed the California approach. These issues are explored in some of the following cases.

The equitable component of Reeves' claim was for giving property (the idea) and services (preparation of proposal and sharing of expertise) to Alyeska without getting paid. Under that quasi-contract theory, Alyeska may have been unjustly enriched by benefiting from Reeves' efforts and disclosure. If so, Reeves should receive payment even if there was neither an express nor an implied-in-fact contract. The Alaska court found that the property part of this claim required novelty and originality because ideas cannot generally be owned or possessed, and it is novelty and originality that give value to an idea. If Reeves cannot be said to have possessed the idea, he cannot be said to have conferred the idea on Alyeska, as is required for a quasi-contract claim. Thus the property part fails. The court did not explain why there is no conferring of a benefit in the property part of the quasi-contract claim but there is consideration for an express or implied-in-fact contract claim. Concluding that the conferring of services could not logically require novelty or originality (as distinct from the idea disclosure claim), the court found there was a basis for an equitable claim for services rendered.

3. *Property and Tort Theories.* Conversion and misappropriation theories of liability are based in both property and tort and are analogous to theft of property. A misappropriation claim typically has three component parts: (a) the plaintiff has developed something at some expense to the plaintiff, (b) the defendant has taken and used that thing (the idea in these cases) without compensation and thus been a free rider on the efforts of the plaintiff, and (c) as a policy matter it is appropriate to give the plaintiff exclusive rights to the thing. Whether, as a policy matter, there should be exclusive rights to the idea depends on, among other considerations, whether the idea is novel and concrete or sufficiently well-developed. If not, the idea will not be considered a type of property deserving protection.

The analogy between theft and conversion is easy to see. A conversion involves one person exercising dominion or control over the property of another in a way that seriously interferes with the other person's legal rights. *See* Restatement (Second) of Torts §222A. In a conversion action, the owner of the property is entitled to recover the full value of the property. As for a misappropriation claim, it is necessary to establish that the claimant has legal rights in the idea.

4. *Overlapping Claims and Remedies.* The same facts may support recovery under a contract theory (express or implied-in-fact) and a misappropriation or conversion theory. It is consistent to find liability under all of these theories. In contract law, it is typically inconsistent, and unnecessary, to find both a breach of contract and unjust enrichment under an implied-in-law theory. The reasoning is that if a remedy can be given based on contract breach, there is no equitable foundation for finding an injustice. Similarly, it would be inconsistent, and unnecessary, to find both an express and an implied contract.

Finding liability on multiple theories presents no particular difficulty for remedies. Just because there are multiple theories of recovery does not mean there will be multiple damage awards. Under contract, property, or tort theories, the plaintiff is entitled to be restored to the position he would have enjoyed but for the defendant's conduct. For idea law, this might be measured by the market value of the idea or the service performed in conveying the idea. It might be based on what payments are typical in the industry. Keep in mind that the value of the idea for a toy or a TV show or an advertising campaign is likely to be considerably less than the revenues derived from the associated sales. Other creative and real resources contributed to the end product and the underlying idea is only one component.

Under an implied-in-law theory, the plaintiff is entitled to the value of the benefit conferred on the recipient. This measures the extent to which the recipient has been unjustly enriched by the disclosure. Unjust enrichment damages are discussed in other parts of this book where provisions of intellectual property statutes authorize an accounting for the defendant's profits. See Chapter 5, Trademark Remedies; Chapter 9, Copyright Remedies; and Chapter 12, Patent Remedies.

## B. THE NOVELTY REQUIREMENT

The California Supreme Court recognized the fundamental dilemma involved in enforcing rights to ideas in a 1956 case, *Desny v. Wilder*, 299 P.2d 257, 266:

> Generally speaking, ideas are as free as the air and as speech and the senses, and as potent or weak, interesting or drab, as the experiences, philosophies, vocabularies, and other variables of speaker and listener may combine to produce, to portray, or to comprehend. But there can be circumstances when neither air nor ideas may be acquired without cost. The diver who goes deep in the sea, even as the pilot who ascends high in the troposphere, knows full well that for life itself he, or someone on his behalf, must arrange for air (or its respiration essential element, oxygen) to be specially provided at the time and place of need. The theatrical producer likewise may be dependent for his business life on the procurement of ideas from other persons as well as the dressing up and portrayal of his self-conceptions; he may not find his own sufficient for survival. As counsel for the Writers Guild aptly say, ideas "are not freely usable by the entertainment media until the latter are made aware of them." The producer may think up the idea himself, dress it and portray it; or he may purchase either the conveyance of the idea alone or a manuscript embodying the idea in the author's concept of a literary vehicle giving it form, adaptation and expression. It cannot be doubted that some ideas are of value to a producer.

Thus, the question of when the law ought to give a remedy for use of an idea that another has disclosed arises. The novelty requirement is one limit on enforcement of contract and property rights in ideas.

*Murray v. National Broadcasting Co., Inc.* considers whether ideas can be protected under *any* legal theory if it is not novel. The opinion explicitly considers whether an idea can be property. But observe that its holding

applies to contract, property, and torts claims. Like the originality requirement in copyright law and the non-obviousness and novelty requirements
in patent law, the novelty requirement in idea law ensures that ideas
already in the public domain remain in the public domain.

After the *Murray* decision, the New York Court of Appeals adopted a
rule distinguishing between contract claims and other legal theories. This
approach is described in *Nadel v. Play-By-Play Toys & Novelties, Inc.* States
have split on whether novelty is required for contract law claims, with
some states insisting that there can be no consideration in a promise to
exchange property one does not own and others concluding that it is not
the province of courts to determine the adequacy of consideration for a
contract.

## MURRAY v. NATIONAL BROADCASTING CO., INC.
### 844 F.2d 988 (2nd Cir. 1988)

Altimari, Circuit Judge.

It was almost a generation ago that a young comedian named Bill Cosby
became the first black entertainer to star in a dramatic network television
series. That program, *I Spy*, earned Cosby national recognition as an actor,
including three Emmy Awards (1966, 1967 and 1968) for best performance
in a dramatic series, and critical acclaim for the portrayal of a character without regard to the actor's race. Although keenly aware of the significance of his
achievement in breaking the color line on network television, Cosby set his
sights then on "accomplish[ing] something more significant for the Negro
on TV." In an interview in 1965, he envisioned a different approach to the
situation comedy genre made popular by *The Dick Van Dyke Show*. The *Daily
News* described Cosby's "dream" series as not unlike other situation come-
dies. There'll be the usual humorous exchanges between husband and
wife. . . . Warmth and domestic cheerfulness will pervade the entire program.

Nearly twenty years later, on September 20, 1984, Cosby's dream for a
"color-blind" family series materialized with the premier of *The Cosby
Show* — a situation comedy about a family known as the Huxtables. Bill
Cosby stars in the leading role as Heathcliff ("Cliff") Huxtable together
with his TV wife Clair and their five children.

Plaintiff-appellant Hwesu Murray, an employee of defendant-appellee
("NBC"), claims in the instant case that in 1980, four years prior to the
premier of *The Cosby Show* on NBC's television network, he proposed to
NBC a "new" idea for a half-hour situation comedy starring Bill Cosby. In a
written proposal submitted to NBC, Murray described his series called
"Father's Day" as "wholesome . . . entertainment" which will focus upon
the family life of a Black American family. . . . The leading character will
be the father, . . . a devoted family man and a compassionate, proud,
authority figure. . . . The program may well resemble "Father Knows
Best" and "The Dick Van Dyke Show." It will be radically different from
"The Jeffersons," "Good Times," "Different Strokes," and "That's My
Mama." The father will not be a buffoon, a supermasculine menial, or a
phantom. . . . The program will show how a Black father can respond with
love . . . , and will present . . . a closely-knit family. . . .

On this appeal from an order of the United States District Court for the Southern District of New York (Cedarbaum, J.) granting defendants-appellees' motion for summary judgment, we are asked to determine whether, under New York law, plaintiff has a legally protectible interest in his idea which he maintains was used by NBC in developing *The Cosby Show*. Because we agree with the district court's conclusion that, under New York law, lack of novelty in an idea precludes plaintiff from maintaining a cause of action to prevent its unauthorized use, we affirm the district court's order granting summary judgment and dismissing the complaint.

## BACKGROUND

Plaintiff Hwesu S. Murray has been employed in the television industry for the past ten years. Murray holds a Bachelor of Arts degree in English and graduate degrees in broadcast journalism and law. In 1979, defendant-appellee NBC hired Murray as a Unit Manager and financial analyst in its sports division. A year later, plaintiff contacted an NBC official outside of NBC Sports about some "extracurricular" ideas he had for future television programs, and the official apparently instructed him to submit his proposals in writing. Soon thereafter, in June 1980, plaintiff submitted five written proposals, one of which was entitled "Father's Day." Murray allegedly informed NBC that if it were interested in any of the proposals, he expected to be named executive producer and to receive appropriate credit and compensation as the creator of the eventual program. Plaintiff also allegedly told NBC that his ideas were being submitted in confidence.

Murray's proposal for "Father's Day" is the subject matter of this action. The NBC official who originally had requested it encouraged Murray to "flesh out" his proposal and submit it to Josh Kane, then an NBC vice-president and a top official with NBC Entertainment, the division of NBC responsible for network television programming. Plaintiff thereupon submitted to Kane an expanded proposal for "Father's Day." In a two-page memorandum dated November 1, 1980, Murray first suggested that Bill Cosby play the part of the father. At that time, plaintiff also made several other casting suggestions, including roles for a working spouse and five children, and again indicated that the proposed series would "combine humor with serious situations in a manner similar to that of the old *Dick Van Dyke Show*" but "with a Black perspective." Murray's expanded proposal concluded with the observation that, "[l]ike *Roots*, the show will attempt to depict life in a [closely-knit] Black family, with the addition of a contemporary, urban setting."

NBC apparently decided not to pursue Murray's proposal. On November 21, 1980, Kane returned the "Father's Day" submission to plaintiff and informed him that "we are not interested in pursuing [its] development at this time."

Four years later, in the fall of 1984, *The Cosby Show* premiered on NBC. *The Cosby Show* is a half-hour weekly situation comedy series about everyday life in an upper middle-class black family in New York City. The father, played by Bill Cosby, is a physician, and the mother is a lawyer. In its first season, *The Cosby Show* soared to the top of the Nielsen ratings and has become one of the most popular programs in television history. The show is highly regarded by critics and is also a huge commercial success.

Less than a month after viewing the premier, plaintiff wrote to NBC to advise it that *The Cosby Show* had been derived from his idea for "Father's Day." In January 1985, NBC responded through its Law Department, stating its position that " 'Father's Day' played absolutely no role in the development of 'The Cosby Show' . . . [since m]uch of the substance and style of 'The Cosby Show' is an outgrowth of the humor and style developed by Bill Cosby throughout his career." NBC further maintained that *The Cosby Show* was developed and produced by The Carsey-Werner Company ("Carsey-Werner"), an independent production company and the executive producers of the series.

In his complaint, plaintiff claimed that *The Cosby Show*'s portrayal of a strong black family in a nonstereotypical manner is the essence of "Father's Day," and "[i]t is that portrayal of Black middle-class life that originated with plaintiff." Murray also alleged that Josh Kane showed plaintiff's "Father's Day" proposal to his superiors at NBC, including defendant-appellee Brandon Tartikoff, President of NBC Entertainment. Tartikoff, together with Cosby and Carsey-Werner, have been credited with the creation and development of *The Cosby Show*. Plaintiff maintains that NBC and Tartikoff deliberately deceived plaintiff into believing that NBC had no interest in "Father's Day" and then proceeded to develop and eventually produce plaintiff's idea as *The Cosby Show*.

Plaintiff sought, *inter alia*, damages and declaratory and injunctive relief as the "sole owner of all rights in and to the idea, proposal and property [known as] 'Father's Day.' "

In a decision dated July 15, 1987, the district court considered whether plaintiff's idea was "property" that could be subject to legal protection. In *Downey*, the New York court established the general proposition that "[l]ack of novelty in an idea is fatal to *any* cause of action for its unlawful use." 334 N.Y.S.2d at 877. The district court, therefore, determined that the "sole issue" before it was the novelty of plaintiff's "Father's Day" proposal, and accordingly assumed, for purposes of defendants' motion, that defendants in fact used plaintiff's idea in the development of *The Cosby Show*.

In focusing on the novelty of plaintiff's proposal, the district court determined that Murray's idea was not subject to legal protection from unauthorized use because "Father's Day"

> merely combined two ideas which had been circulating in the industry for a number of years — namely, the family situation comedy, which was a standard formula, and the casting of black actors in non-stereotypical roles.

The district court found that, to the extent "Father's Day," in Murray's words, "may well resemble 'Father Knows Best' and 'The Dick Van Dyke Show,' " it could not be considered novel. In addition, the portrayal of a black family in nonstereotypical roles, according to the court, precluded a finding of novelty because 1) the television networks already had cast some black actors, including Bill Cosby himself, e.g., *I Spy* (1965-68), *The Bill Cosby Show* (1969-71), and *Fat Albert and the Cosby Kids* (1972-79), in such roles, and 2) the idea of combining the family situation comedy theme with an all-black cast already had been suggested publicly by Bill Cosby some twenty years before the creation of *The Cosby Show*. The district court also determined that Murray's casting of Bill Cosby in the lead role in "Father's Day" was no mere coincidence. Rather, it was "further evidence that Cosby is connected—even in plaintiff's mind—with the concept that plaintiff seeks to monopolize."

In view of the foregoing, the district court granted defendants' motion for summary judgment and dismissed the various claims presented in the complaint, concluding that the lack of novelty in plaintiff's proposal was fatal to any cause of action for unauthorized use of that idea.

## DISCUSSION

### I

As the district court recognized, the dispositive issue in this case is whether plaintiff's idea is entitled to legal protection. Plaintiff points to "unique"—"even revolutionary"—aspects of his "Father's Day" proposal that he claims demonstrate "genuine novelty and invention." Specifically, plaintiff contends that his idea suggesting the nonstereotypical portrayal of black Americans on television is legally protectible because it represents a real breakthrough. As he stated in his affidavit in opposition to defendants' motion,

> [w]hen I created "Father's Day", I had in mind . . . a show that . . . would portray a Black family as it had never been shown before on television. . . . I also . . . desire[d] to produce a show with strong and positive role models for the Black community, and to make a statement regarding the love and integrity of the Black family to the world. I think every Black person in this country knows there has been a need for this, and that never before on television had there been a portrayal of a Black family as I created it for "Father's Day."

Murray claims that the novelty of his idea subsequently was confirmed by the media and the viewing public which instantly recognized the "unique" and "revolutionary" portrayal of a black family on *The Cosby Show*.

We certainly do not dispute the fact that the portrayal of a nonstereotypical black family on television was indeed a breakthrough. Nevertheless, that breakthrough represents the achievement of what many black Americans, including Bill Cosby and plaintiff himself, have recognized for many years—namely, the need for a more positive, fair and realistic portrayal of blacks on television. While NBC's decision to broadcast *The Cosby Show* unquestionably was innovative in the sense that an intact, nonstereotypical black family had never been portrayed on television before, the mere fact that such a decision had not been made before does not necessarily mean that the idea for the program is itself novel.

Consequently, we do not agree with appellant's contention that the nonstereotypical portrayal of a black middle-class family in a situation comedy is novel because

> [t]o argue otherwise would be the equivalent of arguing that since there had always been baseball, and blacks in baseball, there was nothing new about Jackie Robinson playing in the major leagues—or that since there had

always been schools in Little Rock, Arkansas, and blacks in schools, there was nothing new about integrating schools in Little Rock.

As appellees persuasively point out in response to this analogy, Murray has "confuse[d] the 'idea' with its execution.... Indeed, the idea of integration ... had been discussed for decades prior to the actual events taking place." Similarly, we believe, as a matter of law, that plaintiff's idea embodied in his "Father's Day" proposal was not novel because it merely represented an "adaptation of existing knowledge" and of "known ingredients" and therefore lacked "genuine novelty and invention." *Educational Sales Programs,* 317 N.Y.S.2d at 844.

We recognize of course that even novel and original ideas to a greater or lesser extent combine elements that are themselves not novel. Originality does not exist in a vacuum. Nevertheless, where, as here, an idea consists in essence of nothing more than a variation on a basic theme — in this case, the family situation comedy — novelty cannot be found to exist. *Id.* The addition to this basic theme of the portrayal of blacks in nonstereotypical roles does not alter our conclusion, especially in view of the fact that Bill Cosby previously had expressed a desire to do a situation comedy about a black family and that, as the district court found, Cosby's entire career has been a reflection of the positive portrayal of blacks and the black family on television.

Appellant would have us believe that by interpreting New York law as we do, we are in effect condoning the theft of ideas. On the contrary, ideas that reflect "genuine novelty and invention" are fully protected against unauthorized use. *Educational Sales Programs,* 317 N.Y.S.2d at 844. But those ideas that are not novel "are in the public domain and may freely be used by anyone with impunity." *Ed Graham Productions,* 347 N.Y.S.2d at 769. Since such non-novel ideas are not protectible as property, they cannot be stolen.

In assessing whether an idea is in the public domain, the central issue is the uniqueness of the creation. Murray insists that there is at least a question of fact as to the novelty of "Father's Day" because *The Cosby Show* is indisputably unique. In support of this contention, plaintiff points to the fact that NBC contracted with Carsey-Werner for the right of NBC to broadcast *The Cosby Show.* The contract apparently was executed by the parties before there had been any written development of the proposed series. The "program idea" for *The Cosby Show,* however, was described in the contract as "unique, intellectual property." According to plaintiff, the inescapable conclusion is that the idea — whether it be "Father's Day" or *The Cosby Show* — could not possibly have been in the public domain if NBC expressly contracted to purchase it from Carsey-Werner.

We disagree. The Carsey-Werner contract contemplates a fully-produced television series. The contract refers to, *inter alia,* the program format, titles, set designs, theme music, stories, scripts, and art work as well as to the "program idea." Taken together, these elements no doubt would be considered original and therefore protectible as property. On the other hand, we think it equally apparent that the mere idea for a situation comedy about a nonstereotypical black family — whether that idea is in the hands of Murray, Carsey-Werner, NBC, or anyone else — is not novel and thus may be used with impunity.

Finally, as an alternative attack on the propriety of the district court's order granting summary judgment, plaintiff posits that even if his idea was not novel as a matter of law, summary judgment still was inappropriate because his proposal was solicited by defendants and submitted to them in confidence. In this regard, Murray relies on *Cole v. Phillips H. Lord, Inc.*, 28 N.Y.S.2d 404 (1st Dep't 1941). Murray contends that *Cole* stands for the proposition that when an idea is protected by an agreement or a confidential relationship, a cause of action arises for unauthorized use of that idea irrespective of the novelty of the subject matter of the contract. Plaintiff's reliance on *Cole* is misplaced in light of subsequent cases, particularly the New York Court of Appeals decision in *Downey v. General Foods Corp.*, 334 N.Y.S.2d 874 (1972). *See also Ferber v. Sterndent Corp.*, 51 N.Y.2d 782, 433 N.Y.S.2d 85, 86, 412 N.E.2d 1311 (1980) ("[a]bsent a showing of novelty, plaintiff's action to recover damages for illegal use of 'confidentially disclosed ideas' must fail as a matter of law"); *Educational Sales Programs*, 317 N.Y.S.2d at 844 ("[o]ne cannot be forever barred from using a worthwhile but unoriginal idea merely because it was once asked to be treated in confidence").

Consequently, we find that New York law requires that an idea be original or novel in order for it to be protected as property. Since, as has already been shown, plaintiff's proposal for "Father's Day" was lacking in novelty and originality, we conclude that the district court correctly granted defendants' motion for summary judgment.

## II.

Having determined that plaintiff's idea is not property under New York law, we turn now to a consideration of the district court's dismissal of the various claims in the complaint.

### A.  STATE LAW CLAIMS

"[W]hen one submits an idea to another, no promise to pay for its use may be implied, and no asserted agreement enforced, if the elements of novelty and originality are absent. . . ." *Downey*, 334 N.Y.S.2d at 877. As the district court recognized, non-novel ideas do not constitute property. As a result, there can be no cause of action for unauthorized use of Murray's proposal since it was not unlawful for defendants to use a non-novel idea. We conclude therefore that the district court properly dismissed plaintiff's state law claims for breach of implied contract, misappropriation, conversion, and unjust enrichment.

\*\*\*

### CONCLUSION

Our review of New York intellectual property law leads us to the inescapable conclusion that the district court did not err in deciding that there was no material issue of fact as to the novelty of plaintiff's proposal. In our judgment, the basic premise underlying the concept of novelty under New

York law is that special protection is afforded only to truly innovative ideas while allowing the free use of ideas that are "merely clever or useful adaptation[s] of existing knowledge." *Educational Sales Programs*, 317 N.Y.S.2d at 844. In this case, the record indicates that plaintiff's idea for a situation comedy featuring the nonstereotypical portrayal of a black family simply was not uniquely plaintiff's creation. Accordingly, we affirm the district court's order granting summary judgment and dismissing the complaint.

## NADEL v. PLAY-BY-PLAY TOYS & NOVELTIES, INC.

### 208 F.3d 368 (2d Cir. 2000)

SOTOMAYOR, Circuit Judge.

Plaintiff-appellant Craig P. Nadel ("Nadel") brought this action against defendant-appellee Play-By-Play Toys & Novelties, Inc. ("Play-By-Play") for breach of contract, quasi contract, and unfair competition. The thrust of Nadel's complaint was that Play-By-Play took his idea for an upright, sound-emitting, spinning plush toy and that, contrary to industry custom, Play-By-Play used the idea in its "Tornado Taz" product without paying him compensation.

\*\*\*

[The District Court granted summary judgment to the manufacturer on the plaintiff's claims and the plaintiff appeals.]

Nadel is a toy idea man. Toy companies regularly do business with independent inventors such as Nadel in order to develop and market new toy concepts as quickly as possible. To facilitate the exchange of ideas, the standard custom and practice in the toy industry calls for companies to treat the submission of an idea as confidential. If the company subsequently uses the disclosed idea, industry custom provides that the company shall compensate the inventor, unless, of course, the disclosed idea was already known to the company.

Our analysis begins with the New York Court of Appeals' most recent discussion of the law governing idea submission cases, *Apfel v. Prudential-Bache Securities, Inc.*, 81 N.Y.2d 470, 616 N.E.2d 1095 (1993). In *Apfel,* the Court of Appeals discussed the type of novelty an idea must have in order to sustain a contract-based or property-based claim for its uncompensated use. Specifically, *Apfel* clarified an important distinction between the requirement of "novelty to the buyer" for contract claims, on the one hand, and "originality" (or novelty generally) for misappropriation claims, on the other hand.

Under the facts of *Apfel,* the plaintiff disclosed his idea to the defendant pursuant to a confidentiality agreement and, subsequent to disclosure, entered into another agreement wherein the defendant agreed to pay a stipulated price for the idea's use. *See id.* at 474. The defendant used the idea but refused to pay plaintiff pursuant to the post-disclosure agreement on the asserted ground that "no contract existed between the parties because the sale agreement lacked consideration." *Id.* at 475. The defendant argued that an idea could not constitute legally sufficient consideration unless it was original or novel generally and that, because plaintiff's idea was not original or novel generally (it had been in the public domain at the time of the post-disclosure agreement), the idea provided insufficient consideration to support the parties' post-disclosure contract.

In rejecting defendant's argument, the Court of Appeals held that there was sufficient consideration to support plaintiff's contract claim because the idea at issue had value to the defendant at the time the parties concluded their post-disclosure agreement. *See id.* at 476. The *Apfel* court noted that "traditional principles of contract law" provide that parties "are free to make their bargain, even if the consideration exchanged is grossly unequal or of dubious value," *id.* at 475, and that, so long as the "defendant received something of value" under the contract, the contract would not be void for lack of consideration, *id.* at 476. *See also id.* at 478 ("[T]he buyer knows what he or she is buying and has agreed that the idea has value, and the Court will not ordinarily go behind that determination.").

The *Apfel* court explicitly rejected defendant's contention that the court should carve out "an exception to traditional principles of contract law" for submission-of-idea cases by requiring that an idea must also be original or novel generally in order to constitute valid consideration. *Id.* at 477. In essence, the defendant sought to impose a requirement that an idea be novel in absolute terms, as opposed to only the defendant buyer, in order to constitute valid consideration for the bargain. In rejecting this argument, the *Apfel* court clarified the standards for both contract-based and property-based claims in submission-of-idea cases. That analysis guides our decision here....

We note, moreover, that the "novelty to the buyer" standard comports with traditional principles of contract law. While an idea may be unoriginal or non-novel in a general sense, it may have substantial value to a particular buyer who is unaware of it and therefore willing to enter into contract to acquire and exploit it. *See* Robert Unikel, *Bridging the "Trade Secret" Gap: Protecting "Confidential Information" Not Rising to the Level of Trade Secrets,* 29 Loy. U. Chi. L.J. 841, 877 n. 151 (1998) (noting that, if a valuable idea is already known to an industry but has not yet been acquired by a prospective buyer, one of two circumstances may exist: "(1) the person[ ] ha[s] not identified the potential value of the easily acquired information; or (2) the person[ ] ha[s] not identified the means, however easy or proper, for obtaining the valuable information"). As the *Apfel* court emphasized, "the buyer may reap benefits from such a contract in a number of ways — for instance, by not having to expend resources pursuing the idea through other channels or by having a profit-making idea implemented sooner rather than later." *Apfel,* 81 N.Y.2d at 478....

In contrast to contract-based claims, a misappropriation claim can only arise from the taking of an idea that is original or novel in absolute terms, because the law of property does not protect against the misappropriation or theft of that which is free and available to all....

In sum, we find that New York law in submission-of-idea cases is governed by the following principles: Contract-based claims require only a showing that the disclosed idea was novel to the buyer in order to find consideration.[10]...

10. Of course, the mere formation of a contract in a submission-of-idea case does not necessarily mean that the contract has been breached by the defendant upon his use of the idea. In order to recover for breach of contract, a plaintiff must demonstrate some nexus or

[The court remanded for the trial court to determine whether there existed sufficient general novelty to support the misappropriation claim and sufficient novelty to the buyer to support the contract claims.]

# Comments

1. *The Novelty Requirement.* In some states, a novelty requirement applies to all idea law claims. After *Apfel*, the novelty requirement applies differently to property and contract theories of recovery in New York. To recover under a property theory, the idea must be novel in an absolute or general sense whereas under contract law, the idea only has to be novel to the buyer. The California Supreme Court takes an approach that is more generous to idea submitters, having held that even if an idea is "widely known and generally understood" recovery may be had for breach of either express or implied-in-fact contracts. In *Desny v. Wilder*, 299 P.2d 257, 266 (1956), the court analogized to doctors and lawyers who apply specialized knowledge and give advice for a fee even though they have no property rights in their ideas and could not distinguish freelance writers merely on the basis that they were not necessarily members of a learned profession and bound to the exalted standards to which doctors and lawyers are dedicated. The court recognized the hazards faced by producers and publishers who are confronted with a deluge of unsolicited scripts, but also that the law is dedicated to assisting those who have been wronged: "The law, however, is dedicated to the proposition that for every wrong there is a remedy and for the sake of protecting one party it must not close the forum to the other. It will hear both and seek to judge the cause by standards fair to both."

2. *General Novelty and Novelty to the Buyer.* Even with New York's relaxation of the novelty requirement for contracts, there may still be New York cases where the idea is so well known that, as a matter of law, the idea was not novel to the buyer. In *Downey v. General Foods Corp.*, 286 N.E.2d 257 (N.Y. Ct. App. 1972), the plaintiff submitted to the manufacturer of JELLO the idea that they use the words "Mr. Wiggle" in their commercials. Because "wiggle" is such an obvious characteristic of gelatin, the suggestion could not have been novelty, even to the defendant and no idea claim could survive. Similarly, in *Bram v. Dannon Milk Products, Inc.*, 307 N.Y.S.2d 571 (Sup. Ct. App. Div. 1970), the concept of depicting a baby in a highchair enjoying yogurt in a Dannon Yogurt advertisement was deemed too well-known as a matter of law for any idea claim to survive. In *Ed Graham Productions, Inc. v. National Broadcasting Company Co.*, 347 N.Y.S.2d 766 (N.Y. Sup. Ct. 1973), the court said, "The idea of

---

causal connection between his or her disclosure and the defendant's use of the idea, *i.e.*, where there is an independent source for the idea used by the defendant, there may be no breach of contract, and the plaintiff's claim for recovery may not lie. *See, e.g., Ferber,* 51 N.Y.2d at 784, 433 N.Y.S.2d 85, 412 N.E.2d 1311 (noting that, even if plaintiff's idea were novel to the defendant at the time of disclosure, his claim would have been extinguished when the idea subsequently fell into the public domain through the issuance of patents disclosing the idea).

larger-than-life heroes with juvenile helpers fighting evil-doers and
embarking on all sorts of fantastic adventures probably goes back
beyond 'Jack and the Beanstalk' and even further back beyond Hercules.
Such characters have been the staple of comic strip adventure books and
radio and television juvenile dramas for almost all children who came of
age in twentieth-century America. Ideas such as those presented by the
plaintiff are in the public domain and may freely be used by anyone with
impunity."

## Problem

**15-1.** Ms. Ring conceived of a way to promote sales of cosmetics by videotaping what is commonly known as a "makeover," which entails a representative from a cosmetic company applying make-up to a would-be
customer in a store while explaining the benefits and purpose of the
make-up as applied and answering questions the customer may have.
Based on Ring's idea the customer would keep the videotape for future
reference. Ring presented this idea to Estee Lauder. Although interested
in the idea, Estee Lauder declined to hire Ring to organize a one-week in-
store promotion, citing Ring's $10,000 fee. Two years later, Estee Lauder
began employing Ring's idea and Ring sued. It was agreed that makeovers
were common and videos (although not "makeover" videos) were commonly used in a number of contexts where customers or patrons are paying
to learn self-improvement techniques. Using the approach applied in *Murray*, would there be an enforceable contract in this case? *See Ring v. Estee
Lauder, Inc.*, 702 F. Supp. 76 (S.D.N.Y. 1988).

## C. CONCRETENESS

Courts have held that submitted ideas that are abstract or vague will preclude a viable cause of action. The idea as submitted must be well developed or "concrete." The concreteness requirement is discussed in *Tate*.

## TATE v. SCANLAN INTERNATIONAL, INC.
### 403 N.W.2d 666 (Ct. App. Minn. 1987)

FORSBERG, Judge.

This case arises from respondent Karen Tate's action against Scanlan
International for damages as a result of Scanlan's use of Tate's unpatented
idea for a surgical supply product. Tate's claims were for breach of express
or implied contract, unjust enrichment, conversion and breach of confidence. A jury trial resulted in a verdict for Tate in the amount of
$520,313....

Respondent has been an operating room nurse at the University of
Minnesota for the past 19 years. In 1978 she came up with an idea to
solve a common problem experienced by operating room nurses working

with Prolene suture which, although possessing great tensile strength, was extremely delicate and often broke when clamped in place during surgery. Nurses had developed a practice of cutting pieces of catheter tubing to fit over the ends of the clamps to allow for a firm grip while protecting the suture from damage. Yet, this method was time consuming, the pieces of tubing were uneven and were not radiopaque (capable of being seen under x-ray), and it was difficult to keep track of the number of pieces cut, making mandatory accounting of operating room supplies difficult. Respondent's idea was to have available pre-cut uniform shods or tips to put on the ends of the clamps. The tips would be accessible, easily accountable, radiopaque, sterile, and able to hold the suture.

In September of 1979, respondent contacted Timothy Scanlan, president of appellant Scanlan International, a designer and marketer of surgical supplies. Respondent set up a meeting with Scanlan to present her idea, with the understanding that he would keep her idea confidential and that if he used her idea, she would be compensated. At the meeting, respondent explained the problem of working with the Prolene suture. She brought a "Kittner" sponge holder to illustrate a possible method for achieving some of the characteristics of the product she envisioned. The Kittner holder is a foam block with holes which secures the sponges until use, but allows them to be extracted with only one hand holding a clamp. With Kittners, nurses can determine from the number of empty holes in the block how many sponges are still in a patient's body.

Scanlan later wrote respondent that he liked her idea and that the company was going to look into it, including a package of "Tip-Guards" as an example after which they might model the proposed product. Tip-Guards, manufactured by appellant, were unsterilized, uniform plastic tips sold in bulk, and used to protect the ends of surgical instruments.

After their initial meeting, and over the course of the next two years, respondent was kept apprised of developments of the product by Scanlan, who consulted with her on various aspects of the design of the prototype such as color, number per package, and serrated vs. non-serrated surface ridges. Respondent gave Scanlan a list of potential customers.

In April of 1980, respondent and Scanlan met again, at which time respondent inquired as to her compensation. Scanlan told respondent that she would make money when the company made money, but no definite terms were discussed.

In February of 1981, respondent and Scanlan met to examine prototypes prepared by appellant. Respondent approved of the design of the prototype, and Scanlan told her that his company planned to sell a box of the products called "Suture Boots" for about $6.00 and that she would receive about $.35 per box, which would have been slightly less than six percent of gross sales.

When Suture Boots hit the market in May of 1981, each package contained one foam block which held ten plastic tips. The block had an adhesive strip on the bottom, and its entire contents were sterile. On June 22, 1981, appellant sent respondent two contract proposals. The first contract proposed payment of a royalty of 5% of appellant's net profit on Suture Boots for five years. Net profit was $2.00 per box. The alternative proposal was the immediate and final payment of $3,000. These proposals were revoked by letter dated July 7, 1981, before respondent had an opportunity to respond to either of them.

Appellant revoked the offers after learning from its patent attorney that the foam holder from the Kittner sponges that respondent had brought to the first meeting with Scanlan, and which had been incorporated into Suture Boots, had been previously patented (the Chapel patent). Appellant consequently revoked its contract proposals to respondent, and by letter dated September 2, 1981, presented her with a new proposal. The new proposal offered respondent $1,000 for her time and help plus a commission on any sales by her to customers. Respondent did not respond to this offer, and instead instituted this action against Scanlan International.

Appellant subsequently entered into a licensing agreement with the patent holder, Surgicott, to permit the use of the block in Suture Boots. This agreement required appellant to pay Surgicott a royalty of slightly more than 2% of gross sales.

At trial, testimony from patent attorneys was conflicting on the issue of whether Suture Boots actually infringed on the Chapel patent. Testimony revealed that appellant had previously investigated the idea of using plastic tips over the ends of clamps to aid in grasping suture. In the 1970's, Timothy Scanlan and Dr. Jose Ernesto Molina had unsuccessfully experimented with permanently affixing plastic to clamp jaws. Dr. Molina and Dr. Walton Lillehei testified that prior to May of 1981, there was no product on the market designed to handle the suture without damage or slippage.

The case was submitted to the jury by special verdict. The jury found respondent's idea was novel and concrete; that her idea was not covered by a patent; that respondent communicated her idea to appellant with the understanding that the idea would be kept confidential were it not used; that appellant expressly or impliedly agreed to compensate respondent if it profitably marketed a product using her idea; and that appellant breached its agreement with respondent. The jury awarded Tate $245,033 for the use of her idea up to the time of trial, and $275,280 in future damages.

Appellant moved for judgment notwithstanding the verdict and for a new trial, and sought an order reducing the amount of prejudgment interest as claimed in respondent's notice of taxation of costs and disbursements. The trial court denied appellant's motions. . . . Appellant appeals from the trial court's denial of its motions.

Generally, abstract ideas are not protectable property interests. In order for an abstract idea to be the subject of an express or implied contract or to be otherwise protected by the law, it must be novel and concrete. Appellant argues that respondent's idea was neither novel nor concrete, and that the evidence was insufficient to support these findings by the jury.

### A. NOVELTY

[The court affirmed the jury's finding that respondent's idea was novel.]

### B. CONCRETENESS

Concreteness of an idea pertains to the requisite developmental stage of the idea when it is presented. An idea is a protectable property interest, if it is sufficiently developed to be ready for immediate use without additional embellishment. If an idea requires extensive investigation, research, and planning before it is ripe for implementation, it is not concrete.

Appellant argues that since the key to Suture Boots as a new product was the foam block, and respondent admitted she provided only an example, expecting appellant to develop a suitable holder, the idea was not sufficiently developed so as to be usable, and was therefore not concrete.

The evidence here showed that respondent developed an idea for a system of elements, using something like the Kittner foam block to hold plastic, radiopaque, sterile tips to fit on the ends of clamps and provide strength and sensitivity in a convenient, efficient way. Respondent orally presented her specific idea to Scanlan, demonstrating the elements of the product and its goal. Respondent expected Scanlan to develop the idea further — by producing the parts of the product as she had specified. With respondent's help, Scanlan researched the idea and produced just what respondent had ordered in Suture Boots.

Oral presentations and demonstrations of ideas and written proposals of ideas have been held to be sufficiently developed to be "usable," and thus satisfy the concreteness requirement. *See Bergman v. Electrolux Corp.*, 558 F. Supp. 1351 (D. Nev. 1983) (salesman's oral presentation of idea was sufficiently concrete to create a jury question); *Galanis v. Procter and Gamble Corp.*, 153 F. Supp. 34 (S.D.N.Y. 1957) (plaintiff's letter describing idea about a new detergent combining two other products and called "Blue" was sufficiently concrete to create a jury question).

The undisputed testimony of Mr. McGoldrick was that "concrete" in the field of medical marketing meant that the concept was very well defined, with reasonable access to all parts necessary to develop it. He also testified that in this field a working model of an idea was rarely presented. A review of the evidence adduced at trial shows that there was more than adequate support for the jury's determination that respondent's idea was usable and was concrete.

# Comments

1. **The Concreteness Requirement.** This requirement demands that the submitted idea be "sufficiently developed to be ready for immediate use without additional embellishment." An idea is not concrete if it requires extensive experimentation, research, or planning before implementation. Thus, mere abstract or vague ideas will not give rise to a contract between the submitter and recipient. For example, in *Alberts v. Remington Rand*, 23 N.Y.S.2d 892 (1940), the plaintiff submitted a written suggestion that the recipient make a chart or graph of the directions in which the hairs on each individual's face grow and issue the resulting graphs to its customers and prospective customers as an aid in the sale and use of the defendant's razors. The court held the idea was too abstract and not reduced to concrete form. Another court held that a submission merely outlining a "system" for soliciting life insurance was insufficiently concrete. *See Bristol v. Equitable Life Assur. Society of New York*. And in *Williamson v. New York Central R. R. Co.*, the court held as too

vague a plan for the promotion of a miniature railroad exhibit. On the other hand, plaintiff's idea consisting of a color chart with a written description and set of directions accompanied by a complete color map was held to be adequately concrete. *Ketcham v. New York World's Fair 1939, Inc.*, D.C., 34 F. Supp. 657.

2. *Use of Idea.* Courts often say that, in addition to proving the basic elements of a contract, property, or tort claim, there are three elements peculiar to an idea case: the plaintiff's idea must be novel, concrete, and used by the defendant. Even if a defendant has used the same idea as was revealed by the plaintiff, that does not mean the defendant got the idea from the plaintiff. In the JELLO case, the defendant had previously used phrases such as "wiggles" and "wigglewam" in its advertisement. In the yogurt case, the defendant had previously depicted a baby in a highchair.

To avoid claims that it has used an idea another had submitted to it, developers of ideas (potential defendants) often create a corporate wall between their submissions departments and their development departments. No information passes between the departments until an express agreement between the parties has been formalized. By this method, the developer reduces the risk of receiving a submission of an idea it is already developing. There can be no recovery for submission of a novel and concrete idea if the defendant's subsequent work is not based on that particular submission. Some developers protect themselves by refusing to consider ideas submitted by unknown people.

3. *How to Protect Submitted Ideas.* It should be clear that it is ideal for both parties to have an express contract related to an idea. The obvious difficulty is that the receiver of the idea does not want to agree to pay without seeing the idea while the submitter does not want to disclose the idea without payment. In the absence of an express contract, whether there is adequate protection depends heavily on the facts of the particular case, but courts have provided some general guidance. For instance, a contract will not be found if based on only the submission itself. As the California Supreme Court noted in *Desny v. Wilder*, 46 Cal. 2d 715, 739 (1956), the "idea man who blurts out his idea without having first made his bargain has no one but himself to blame for the loss of his bargaining power.... The law will not imply a promise to pay for an idea from the mere facts that the idea has been conveyed, is valuable, and has been used for profit; this is true even though the conveyance has been made with the hope or expectation that some obligation will ensue." In *Keane v. Fox Television Stations, Inc.*, 297 F. Supp. 2d 921 (S.D. Tex. 2004), the court denied an idea submitter's claim that defendant misappropriated his idea for "American Idol" television show, stating that "[n]either the act of mass-mailing a 'sales packet' to a stranger, wherein an idea is described, nor the act of advertising an unprotected idea for sale on the Internet is an act likely to create an implied contract between the idea man and those who read of his idea as a result." By analogy to contract law, past performance is not ordinarily the basis for a contract because there is no consideration for the contract.

On the other hand, a contract may exist if at the time of disclosure, the submitter made it clear that the disclosure was conditioned on payment if used by the recipient, and the recipient knew of the condition before accepting the disclosure. The court in *Flemming v. Ronson Corp.*, 107 N.J. Super. 311, 317 (1969), stated that, "It has been held that where a person communicates a novel idea to another with the intention that the latter may use the idea and compensate him for such use, the other party is liable for such use and must pay compensation if he actually appropriates the idea and employs it in connection with his own activities." Recall that the court in *Reeves* stated that inaction on the part of the recipient should not be the basis for an implied contract, but noted that under California law inaction may be seen as consent. Often these cases involve the question of whether a confidential relationship has arisen between the submitter and developer of the idea.

Thus, the idea submitter will be in a better position if he has a contract with the developer, even if it is a conditional one based on future use. Failing that, the submitter should not disclose the idea unless the recipient agreed to pay if the idea is used. Knowledge by the recipient of the expectation of payment is crucial. Whether a submission is accompanied only by a representation, written or verbal, that payment is expected for use will be sufficient for a contract depends on state law and the precise circumstances surrounding the submission. A prudent submitter will, of course, seek some acknowledgement that payment is expected. And it is more likely that a contract will be found to exist if the recipient solicited the idea.

## Problem

**15-2.** Plaintiff submitted to Macy an idea for a slogan for a Christmas advertising campaign, which Macy used. The slogan was "A Macy Christmas Means a Happy New Year." Is this idea "concrete"? If not, what would you advise Plaintiff to submit to satisfy the concreteness requirement? A complete advertising plan in writing? Drawings and sketches? *See Healey v. R. H. Macy & Co.*, 14 N.E.2d 388, 277 N.Y. 681 (1938).

# TABLE OF CASES

*Principal cases indicated by italics.*

# TABLE OF STATUTES

*Extracts from statutes indicated by italics.*

# INDEX